Lecture Notes in Computer Science 8586

Commenced Publication in 1973
Founding and Former Series Editors:
Gerhard Goos, Juris Hartmanis, and Jan van Leeuwen

Advanced Research in Computing and Software Science
Subline of Lectures Notes in Computer Science

T0215756

Richard Jones (Ed.)

ECOOP 2014 – Object-Oriented Programming

28th European Conference
Uppsala, Sweden, July 28 – August 1, 2014
Proceedings

 Springer

no doubt that reviewers usually overcome these anchors to make a sound judgements. But often this is at the cost of additional reviewing time. Before I conclude that Alan's paper is actually poor, I will probably have spent much longer than normal to ensure that I really have understood it. Equally, because I fear that I might be prejudiced against the unknown author, I am likely to spend extra time bending over backwards to ensure that I am really being fair.

ECOOP 2014 used light double-blind reviewing, whereby authors' names were withheld from a reviewer until they have submitted their initial review. At that point, the authors' identities were revealed and the reviewer was free to investigate their work further, update their review, etc. The prime aim of LDBR is to remove the initial anchor point; it is not to strive for perfection. But why not use fully blind reviewing, whereby authors identities are not revealed at all during the review process? In his report [SIGPLAN Notices 47(4a), 2012] as Programme Chair of POPL 2012, Mike Hicks argues that LDBR helps with mistaken judgements based on identity, and avoids potential abuses such as arguing for a friend's paper. It also helps to check that any author-supplied conflicts are valid.

ECOOP 2014 received 101 submissions, with authors from 29 countries; 11% of authors were women. Each paper was reviewed by at least 4 reviewers; where necessary, further reviews were solicited from PC, ERC or external reviewers. 411 reviews were produced. Authors were given an opportunity to respond to reviews, after which there was an intensive period of discussion through CyberChairPRO. The ERC met online to determine the fate of PC submissions shortly before the PC meeting in Canterbury. The 27 papers accepted (only 1 PC submission) were written by authors from 13 countries. 30% of accepted papers included at least one female author (matching the 31% of submissions). The PC made two distinguished paper awards to *Safely Composable Type-Specific Languages* by Cyrus Omar, Darya Kurilova, Ligia Nistor, Benjamin Chung, Alex Potanin and Jonathan Aldrich; and *Stream Processing with a Spreadsheet* by Mandana Vaziri, Olivier Tardieu, Rodric Rabbah, Philippe Suter and Martin Hirzel.

The final programme included four keynote talks: two from the winners of the 2014 Dahl-Nygaard Senior Award, Robert France and William Cook; one from the winner of the 2014 Dahl-Nygaard Junior Award, Tudor Gîrba; and the fourth from Luca Cardelli, who was invited by the PC.

Every conference depends on the quality of the research it presents. I would like to thank all the authors who submitted their work to ECOOP 2014 (well, all except the 'author' who submitted a paper generated by SCIgen). I would also like to pay tribute to members of the PC and the ERC. I was truly impressed with the care and time they put into producing reviews of very high quality, and doing so on time. It was a honour to work with all of you. I would also like to thank the ECOOP 2014 Organising Chair, Tobias Wrigstad; the Artifact Evaluation Co-Chairs, Camil Demetrescu and Erik Ernst; and Richard van de Stadt for his excellent support through CyberChairPRO.

May 2014   Richard Jones

Artifacts

This is the second year where Artifact Evaluation (AE) was part of the ECOOP publication process, and similar processes are being adopted at several other top conferences. AE is a process where artifacts associated with the published papers — software, data, proofs, videos, etc. — are submitted, reviewed, and accepted or rejected by an Artifact Evaluation Committee (AEC). The long-term goal is to foster a culture of reproducibility of experimental results by considering software artifacts as first-class citizens, a perspective that has long been missing at software conferences. Following the AE tradition, the ECOOP 2014 AEC was entirely formed by junior outstanding researchers.

The ECOOP 2014 AE process introduced two novelties. First, authors were invited to include in their papers a one-page appendix describing the artifact, its goals, and the requirements for installing and running it. Second, accepted artifacts were collected as supplementary material on the publisher's digital library for permanent and durable storage.

The aim of artifact evaluation is to enhance and deepen the information provided to the community about the research results described in the associated papers, thus improving the perspectives for confirming those research results under similar or different conditions, and for creating derived results. Artifacts are reviewed and accepted even if they cannot be made available to the public, e.g., because of confidentiality requirements or intellectual property difficulties, but it is certainly the intention that they should be made available if possible.

The Artifact Evaluation process was similar in complexity to the paper reviewing process, but not identical. Each artifact was independently evaluated by three AEC members. First, each reviewer would 'kick the tires' of the artifact in order to check that it could be reviewed at all; this ruled out corrupt artifact archive files and similar low-level problems that ought not cause a bad review for the artifact and could easily be resolved. The approach used was to go through the 'Getting Started Guide' for the artifact, which was a mandatory part of the submission, and then get feedback from the artifact submitters to eliminate any low-level problems.

In the second phase, the reviewers evaluated the artifact and wrote the reviews. Each reviewer read the paper and wrote a summary providing a brief characterization of the context for the artifact. In the artifact evaluation, reviewers focused on four key questions: (1) *Is the artifact consistent with the paper?* (2) *Is the artifact complete?* (3) *Is the artifact well documented?* and (4) *Is the artifact easy to reuse?* The AEC members decided on acceptance or rejection, and provided the review text itself, containing characterizations of strong and weak sides of the artifact as well as advice about potential improvements. Many updates were applied to the reviews, reflecting that the discussions gave rise to new insights and changed evaluations. During the discussions, all AEC members not conflicted with each artifact could see all reviews and discussions, thus allowing for a calibration of the reviews across different artifacts.

Among the 27 papers accepted at ECOOP 2014, we received 13 artifacts for evaluation. Of those, the AEC accepted 11 and rejected 2. It should be noted that a high acceptance rate is natural for the AE process, because it only included artifacts related to papers that had already been accepted for publication at the conference. The reason for having a firewall between paper acceptance and artifact evaluation was that the latter was not supposed to influence the former. As the AE process evolves, it is possible that this will change in the future, but currently a strict separation is intended, and it was enforced by postponing the entire AE process until decisions about paper acceptance had been reached.

The papers with accepted artifacts in this proceedings are marked with a rosette representing the seal of approval by the AEC, and the table of contents contains a similar but smaller mark on these papers. We were glad to note that this year all accepted artifacts were collected on SpringerLink.

The AE process is currently under development, and we learned a lot from former AE organizers. In particular, we relied on the guidelines by Shriram Krishnamurthi, Matthias Hauswirth, Steve Blackburn, and Jan Vitek published in the foundational on-line article *Artifact Evaluation for Software Conferences* available at http://www.artifact-eval.org. The *Artifact Evaluation Artifact* effort by Steve Blackburn and Matthias Hauswirth, available at the address http://evaluate.inf.usi.ch/artifacts/aea, was also of inspiration. A warm acknowledgement goes to Jan Vitek and to Shriram Krishnamurthi for many useful suggestions and comments. We wish to thank the Programme Committee Chair Richard Jones and the Organizing Chair Tobias Wrigstad for a fruitful cooperation. We acknowledge Anna Kramer from Springer for endorsing the idea of making artifacts available free of charge on the SpringerLink digital library and Stephan Brandauer for efficiently handling the AE pages of the ECOOP 2014 Website. We are also indebted to Richard van de Stadt for his help with the CyberChair conference management system, which was tailored to support this year's AE process. We warmly acknowledge the impressive effort of AEC members: they did the hardest part of the job with dedication and enthusiasm. Finally, we deeply thank all authors for packaging and documenting their artifacts for ECOOP 2014 and for making them publicly available on SpringerLink; we believe that this is an invaluable service to the community that deserves to be commended.

We hope that readers will enjoy the published artifacts and will find them useful for their future work.

May 2014   Camil Demetrescu

Erik Ernst

Organization

ECOOP 2014 was organized by Uppsala Universitet and the University of Kent, under the auspices of AITO (Association Internationale pour les Technologies Objets) and in cooperation with ACM SIGPLAN and ACM SIGSOFT.

**UPPSALA
UNIVERSITET**

Organising Chair

Tobias Wrigstad   Uppsala Universitet, Sweden

Programme Chair

Richard Jones   University of Kent, UK

Workshop Chair

Nate Nystrom   University of Lugano, Switzerland

Poster and Demo Chair

Wolfgang Ahrendt   Chalmers University of Technology, Sweden

Artifact Evaluation Chairs

Camil Demetrescu   Sapienza University of Rome, Italy
Erik Ernst   Aarhus University, Denmark

Publicity Chair

Werner Dietl   University of Waterloo, Canada

Student Volunteer Chair

Jürgen Börstler   Blekinge Institute of Technology, Sweden

Summer School Chairs

James Noble   Victoria University of Wellington, New Zealand
Jan Vitek   Purdue University, USA

Sponsor Chairs

Einar Broch Johnsen   University of Oslo, Norway
Erik Ernst   Aarhus University, Denmark

Local Organising Chairs

Johannes Borgström   Uppsala University, Sweden
Kostis Sagonas   Uppsala University, Sweden
Lars-Henrik Eriksson   Uppsala University, Sweden

Professional Conference Organiser

Karin Hornay   Akademikonferens, Sweden

Local Student Aid

Johan Östlund   Uppsala University, Sweden
Stephan Brandauer   Uppsala University, Sweden
Elias Castegren   Uppsala University, Sweden

Webmaster

Stephan Brandauer   Uppsala University, Sweden

Programme Committee

Davide Ancona   DIBRIS, Università di Genova, Italy
Sven Apel   University of Passau, Germany
Walter Binder   University of Lugano, Switzerland
Steve Blackburn   Australian National University, Australia

Ana Cavalcanti	University of York, UK
Satish Chandra	Samsung Electronics, USA
Dave Clarke	KU Leuven, Belgium; Uppsala University, Sweden
Wolfgang De Meuter	Vrije Universiteit Brussel, Belgium
Isil Dillig	University of Texas, USA
Amer Diwan	Google, USA
Lieven Eeckhout	Ghent University, Belgium
Robby Findler	Northwestern University, USA
Irene Finocchi	Sapienza University of Rome, Italy
Christian Hammer	Saarland University, Germany
Laurie Hendren	McGill University, Canada
Atsushi Igarashi	Kyoto University, Japan
Tomas Kalibera	Purdue University, USA
Doug Lea	SUNY Oswego, USA
Yu David Liu	SUNY Binghamton, USA
Cristina Lopes	University of California, Irvine, USA
Ana Milanova	Rensselaer Polytechnic Institute, USA
Nick Mitchell	IBM Research, USA
Eliot Moss	University of Massachusetts Amherst, USA
Jens Palsberg	UCLA, USA
Matthew Parkinson	Microsoft Research, UK
Arnd Poetzsch-Heffter	University of Kaiserslautern, Germany
Dirk Riehle	Friedrich-Alexander-Universität Erlangen-Nürnberg, Germany
Yannis Smaragdakis	University of Athens, Greece
Arie van Deursen	Delft University of Technology, The Netherlands
Hongseok Yang	University of Oxford, UK

External Review Committee

Vikram Adve	University of Illinois at Urbana-Champaign, USA
Jonathan Aldrich	Carnegie Mellon University, USA
Ioana Baldini	IBM Research, USA
Eric Bodden	Fraunhofer SIT and TU Darmstadt, Germany
Sebastian Burckhardt	Microsoft Research, USA
Shigeru Chiba	University of Tokyo, Japan
Ferruccio Damiani	Università di Torino, Italy
Werner Dietl	University of Waterloo, Canada
Sophia Drossopolou	Imperial College London, UK
Erik Ernst	Aarhus Universitet, Denmark
Matthew Flatt	University of Utah, USA
Michael Franz	University of California, Irvine, USA

Kathryn E. Gray	University of Cambridge, UK
Sam Guyer	Tufts University, USA
Matthias Hauswirth	University of Lugano, Switzerland
Einar Broch Johnsen	University of Oslo, Norway
Christian Kästner	Carnegie Mellon University, USA
Jörg Kienzle	McGill University, Canada
Ondřej Lhoták	University of Waterloo, Canada
Hidehiko Masuhara	Tokyo Institute of Technology, Japan
Romain Robbes	University of Chile, Chile
Sukyoung Ryu	KAIST, South Korea
Mooly Sagiv	Tel Aviv University, Israel
Ina Schaefer	TU Braunschweig, Germany
Friedrich Steimann	Fernuniversität in Hagen, Germany
Alexander J. Summers	ETH Zurich, Switzerland
Frank Tip	University of Waterloo, Canada
Laurence Tratt	King's College London, UK
Greta Yorsh	Queen Mary University of London, UK

External Reviewers

George Balatsouras	Will Harwood	Tillmann Rendel
Thomas Bartenstein	Jaakko Järvi	Haris Ribic
Abhishek Bichhawat	George Kastrinis	Jeremy Siek
Stefan Brunthaler	Christoph Kerschbaumer	Suriya Subramaniam
Lubomir Bulej	Giovanni Lagorio	Viktor Vafeiadis
Emilio Coppa	Per Larsen	Alex Villazon
Andrea Corradi	Klaus Ostermann	Haitao Steve Zhu
Mariangola Dezani	Gustavo Pinto	Elena Zucca
Mike Dodds	David Pfaff	
Paolo Giarrusso	Andrej Podzimek	

Artifact Evaluation Committee

Adriana E. Chis	University College Dublin, Ireland
Alberto Bacchelli	Delft University of Technology, The Netherlands
Carl Ritson	University of Kent, UK
Dominic Orchard	University of Cambridge, UK
Dominique Devriese	KU Leuven, Belgium
Emilio Coppa	Sapienza University of Rome, Italy
George Kastrinis	University of Athens, Greece
Georgios Gousios	Delft University of Technology, The Netherlands
Ilya Sergey	IMDEA Software Institute, Spain
Karim Ali	University of Waterloo, Canada

Mahdi Eslamimehr	Viewpoints Research Institute, USA
Mike Rainey	INRIA-Rocquencourt, France
Oscar E.A. Callaú	PLEIAD, University of Chile, Chile
Valentin Wüstholz	ETH Zurich, Switzerland
Valerio Panzica La Manna	Politecnico di Milano, Italy
Veselin Raychev	ETH Zurich, Switzerland
Wei Huang	Rensselaer Polytechnic Institute, USA

Sponsors

Gold

Silver

Bronze

IBM Research

Abstracts of Keynote Lectures

Molecular Programming

Luca Cardelli

Microsoft Research Cambridge, UK
University of Oxford, UK

Abstract. Nucleic acids (DNA/RNA) encode information digitally, and are currently the only truly 'user-programmable' entities at the molecular scale. They can be used to manufacture nano-scale structures, to produce physical forces, to act as sensors and actuators, and to do computation in between. Eventually we will be able to use them to produce nanomaterials at the bottom end of Moore's Law, and to interface them with biological machinery to detect and cure diseases at the cellular level under program control. Recently, computational schemes have been developed that are autonomous (run on their own power) and involve only short, easily producible, DNA strands with no other complex molecules. While simple in mechanism, these schemes are highly combinatorial and concurrent.

Understanding and programming systems of this new kind requires new software technologies. Computer science has developed a large body of techniques for analyzing (modeling) and developing (engineering) complex programmable systems. Many of those techniques have a degree of mathematical generality that makes them suitable for applications to new domains. This is where we can make critical contributions: in developing and applying programming techniques (in a broad sense) that are unique to computing to other areas of science and engineering, and in particular at the interface between biology and nanotechnology.

A View on the Past, Present and Future of Objects

William R. Cook

University of Texas at Austin, USA

Abstract. Object-oriented programming has always been somewhat mysterious. It has been realized in a fairly pure form in several ways, in Smalltalk, Beta, COM, and SELF. There are several theories (three in Pierce's Types and Programming Languages, and more given by Abadi & Cardelli, Bruce and others). Many partial and failed theories have been published. Most programming languages today are hybrids of objects with other styles of programming. Yet many programming language researchers believe that objects are somehow evil. And still we are experimenting with different forms and inventing new ideas on top of objects. Objects have 'won' as far as I am concerned, or at least objects have won a place at the table. So where do we go from here? While there are many low-level improvements that can be made, it is a reasonable time to consider the big picture. One of the original views of objects was as a form of modeling. Modeling has taken on a life of its own, but has not been as successful as objects were. In this talk I will sketch out a path forward for objects and modeling to work together.

How Do You Like Your Software Models? Towards Empathetic Design of Software Modeling Methods and Tools

Robert B. France

Colorado State University, USA
INRIA, France

Abstract. The terms Model Driven Development/Engineering (MDD/E) are typically used to describe software development approaches in which models of software systems play a pivotal role. In the past I have argued that good support for software modeling is essential to bringing software development closer to an engineering endeavor. As in other engineering disciplines, modeling should be an integral part of software processes that tackle the very challenging problems associated with the creation and evolution of complex software-based systems. While MDD/E research targets important software development problems, the results have not yet led to widespread effective use of software modeling practices. While the wicked problems associated with the development of complex systems is a factor, another is a lack of attention to the issue of fitness-for-purpose with respect to modeling methods and tools. The state-of-the-art leaves some practitioners with the impression that modeling techniques add significant accidental complexity to the software development process.

In this talk, I argue that there is a need to take a more empathetic approach to the design of tools and methods. In *empathetic design*, methodologists and tool developers actively consider and evaluate how their tools and methods fit with how modeling practitioners across a wide skill spectrum (expert, average, novice modelers) work. This should lead to methods and tools that are fit-for-purpose, and open the door for more widespread use of software modeling techniques.

Software Environmentalism

Tudor Gîrba

CompuGroup Medical Schweiz AG
tudor@tudorgirba.com

Abstract. Software systems get larger and larger, and they are being created at an ever increasing rate. While this might appear to be great, we are facing a significant long run problem as we need to assess and recycle them.

In fact, the problem is already here: Engineers spend as much as half of the effort on understanding software systems to figure out how to approach subsequent evolutions and the percentage grows with the size and age of the system. In essence, software engineering is more about dealing with existing systems as it is about building systems.

Reverse engineering and program comprehension are established areas that deal with the problem of approaching existing systems. However, in spite of several decades of research and many proposed approaches, the state of practice still shows that, to a large extent, engineers rely on manual code reading as the preferred means to understand the system. The main reason for it is that most existing approaches tend to be generic and ignore the context of systems. This situation does not scale and it should not perpetuate given the large costs associated with it.

We cannot continue to let systems loose in the wild without any concern for how we will deal with them at a later time. Two decades ago, Richard Gabriel coined the idea of software habitability. Indeed, given that engineers spend a significant part of their active life inside software systems, it is desirable for that system to be suitable for humans to live there.

We go further and introduce the concept of software environmentalism as a systematic discipline to pursue and achieve habitability.

Engineers have the right to build upon assessable systems and have the responsibility of producing assessable systems. For example, even if code has often a text shape, it is not text. The same applies to logs and anything else related to a software system. It's all data, and data is best dealt with through tools. No system should get away without dedicated tools that help us take it apart and recycle it effectively. For example, every significant object in a system should be allowed to have dedicated inspectors to reveal its various facets and interactions, and every significant library should come with dedicated debugging possibilities.

Who should build those tools? Engineers. This implies that they have to be empowered to do it, and that the cost of building those tools is manageable.

We need to go back to the drawing board to (1) construct moldable development environments that help us drill into the context of systems effectively, (2) reinvent our underlying languages and technologies so that we can build assessable systems all the way down, and (3) reeducate our perception of what software engineering is.

Table of Contents

Types

Implementation

Refactoring

JavaScript, PHP and Frameworks

Parallelism

State-Sensitive Points-to Analysis for the Dynamic Behavior of JavaScript Objects

Shiyi Wei and Barbara G. Ryder

Department of Computer Science,
Virginia Tech, Blacksburg, VA, USA
{wei,ryder}@cs.vt.edu

Abstract. JavaScript object behavior is dynamic and adheres to prototype-based inheritance. The behavior of a JavaScript object can be changed by adding and removing properties at runtime. Points-to analysis calculates the set of values a reference property or variable may have during execution. We present a novel, partially flow-sensitive, context-sensitive points-to algorithm that accurately models dynamic changes in object behavior. The algorithm represents objects by their creation sites and local property names; it tracks property updates via a new control-flow graph representation. The calling context comprises the receiver object, its local properties and prototype chain. We compare the new points-to algorithm with an existing JavaScript points-to algorithm in terms of their respective performance and accuracy on a client application. The experimental results on real JavaScript websites show that the new points-to analysis significantly improves precision, uniquely resolving on average 11% more property lookup statements.

Keywords: JavaScript, program analysis, points-to analysis.

1 Introduction

Dynamic programming languages, including JavaScript, Ruby and PHP, are widely used in developing sophisticated software systems, especially Web applications. These languages share several dynamic features, including dynamic code generation and dynamic typing, used in real-world programs [20]. For example, JavaScript code can be generated at runtime using *eval* and JavaScript functions can be variadic (i.e., functions can be called with different numbers of arguments). Despite the popularity of these dynamic languages, there is insufficient tool support for developing and testing programs because their dynamic features render many traditional analyses, and tools which depend on them, ineffective.

In addition, instead of class-based inheritance JavaScript supports prototype-based inheritance [16,27] that results in a JavaScript object inheriting properties from a chain of (at least one) prototype objects. The model also allows the properties of a JavaScript object to be added, updated, or deleted at runtime. This means that JavaScript objects can exhibit different behaviors at different

R. Jones (Ed.): ECOOP 2014, LNCS 8586, pp. 1–26, 2014.
© Springer-Verlag Berlin Heidelberg 2014

times during execution. Moreover, object constructors may be polymorphic so that objects created by the same constructor may have distinct properties. These aspects of JavaScript further complicate tool building.

Some tools have been developed to support JavaScript software development (e.g., [19,22]). Points-to analysis is the enabling analysis for such tools. Researchers have proposed several points-to analyses that handle different features of JavaScript (e.g., [8,17,26]). Nevertheless, there are opportunities to significantly improve the precision of points-to analysis through better modeling of object property set changes.

In this paper, we present a novel points-to algorithm that can accurately model JavaScript objects. Changes to object properties are tracked more accurately to reflect object run-time behavior at different program points. A new graph decomposition for control-flow graphs is used to better track object property changes. Prototype-based inheritance is more accurately modeled to locate delegated properties. The analysis identifies objects by their creation site as well as their local property names upon construction, more accurately than the per-creation-site representation. To distinguish polymorphic constructors, this analysis can incorporate dynamic information collected at runtime (see Section 3.6). Technically, the analysis is *partially flow-sensitive* (on our new control-flow graph structure) and *context-sensitive*, using a new form of object sensitivity [18].[1] Rather than using the receiver object creation site as a calling context in the analysis, we use an approximation of the receiver object and its properties at the call site (i.e., *obj-ref state*).

In order to compare this algorithm with previous techniques, we instantiated our new points-to analysis as the static component of the JavaScript Blended Analysis Framework (*JSBAF*) [28]. Blended analysis collects run-time information through instrumentation to define the calling structure used by a subsequent static analysis, and to capture dynamically generated code. It has been demonstrated that blended analysis is practical and effective on JavaScript programs [28]. We measured the performance and accuracy of our new analysis on a statement-level points-to client (*REF* analysis) that calculates how many objects are returned by a property lookup (e.g., a read of $x.p$).

The major contributions of this work are:

- We have designed a novel *state-sensitive points-to analysis that accurately and safely handles dynamic changes in the behavior of JavaScript objects.* This algorithm presents a new program representation that enables partially flow-sensitive analysis, a more accurate object representation, and an expanded points-to graph that facilitates strong updates for the statements changing object properties.

---

[1] Informally, a flow-sensitive analysis follows the execution order of statements in a program; a flow-sensitive analysis can perform strong updates, but a flow-insensitive one cannot. A context-sensitive analysis distinguishes between different calling contexts of a method, producing different analysis results for each context [21,24]. A context-insensitive analysis calculates one solution per method.

– Experimental results from our new analysis compared to a recent points-to analysis [26], both implemented in *JSBAF*, showed that *state-sensitive analysis significantly improved precision*. On average over all the benchmarks (i.e., 12 popular websites), 48% of the property lookup statements were resolved to a single object by our new analysis, while the existing analysis [26] uniquely resolved only 37% of these statements. Although our analysis incurred a 127% time overhead on average to achieve the increased precision, it was able to analyze each of the programs in the benchmarks in under 5 minutes, attesting to its scalability in practice.

Overview. Section 2 defines the notion of *obj-ref state* and then uses an example to illustrate the sources of imprecision in JavaScript points-to analysis. Section 3 describes our new points-to analysis algorithm and implementation. Section 4 presents the *REF* analysis and the experimental results. Section 5 discusses related work, and Section 6 offers conclusions and future work.

2 Definitions and Motivating Example

In this section we define key concepts and use an example to illustrate the sources of imprecision in current points-to analyses for JavaScript.

2.1 JavaScript Object-Reference State

JavaScript is a dynamically typed programming language whose object behavior can change as object properties are added or deleted at runtime. In strongly typed programming languages, the notion of *type* is used to abstract the possible behavior of an object (e.g., the class of an object in Java) [23]; however, in dynamically typed languages, the type of an object can change during execution. In order to avoid confusion, we call the type of a JavaScript object its *obj-ref state*.[2]

Definition 1. The *obj-ref state* at a program point denotes all of its accessible properties and their non-primitive values.

The accessible properties of an object conform to the property lookup mechanism implemented in JavaScript. Every JavaScript object includes an internal reference to its prototype object from which it inherits non-local properties. A JavaScript object may have a sequence of prototype objects (i.e., a prototype chain) whose properties it can inherit. When reading a property p of an object o, the JavaScript runtime checks the local properties of o to see if o has a property named p. If not, the JavaScript runtime checks to see if the prototype object of o has a property named p, continuing to check along the prototype chain from object to object until the property is found (or not) [7].

---

[2] This general notion can be used for other dynamic languages and is related to structured typing for strongly typed languages [23].

Definition 2. *State-update statements* are: (1) property write statement (i.e., $x.p = y$ or $x['p'] = y$), (2) property delete statement (i.e., *delete x.p* or *delete x['p']*), and (3) an invocation that directly or indirectly results in execution of (1) and/or (2).

The *state-update statements* are the set of statements in JavaScript that may affect the *obj-ref states*. In Figure 1, we illustrate the *obj-ref state* with an example that shows the objects connected to O_1 at a program point. The local properties of object O_1 are named p_1 and p_2 and O_4 is its prototype object. O_7 is visible from O_1 by accessing $O_1.p_4$ while O_6 is not visible from O_1 by accessing $O_1.p_2$ because a local property named p_2 exists for O_1. To sum up, the shaded nodes (i.e., O_6 and O_9) are not accessible from O_1 and the unshaded nodes constitute O_1's reference state.

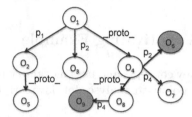

Fig. 1. *obj-ref state* for O_1. (Unshaded nodes only)

2.2   Imprecision of Points-to Analysis

A flow-insensitive analysis may produce imprecise results when *obj-ref state* changes, because it must safely approximate points-to relations and it cannot do strong updates. Existing context-sensitive analyses may produce imprecise results because they lack the power to distinguish between different *obj-ref states* for the same JavaScript object. In Figure 2, we present a JavaScript example to illustrate the sources of imprecision of a flow-insensitive, context-insensitive points-to analysis resulting from several dynamic features of JavaScript. We also demonstrate that an existing context-sensitive analysis using the same object representation as [18] is ineffective at distinguishing the function calls in the example.

Lines 2-6 show a constructor function $X()$. Objects created by $X()$ may or may not have the local property named p or q (lines 4 and 5) depending on the value of its argument. The statement in line 12 updates the value of local property p of an object pointed to by x if p exists; otherwise, the statement adds the local property named p to the object. Figures 3(a) and 3(b) show the points-to graphs that reflect the run-time behavior of this code. We use the line number to represent the object created (e.g., the object created at line 7 (*new X*) is O_7). We focus on two program points in the execution, lines 10 and 15. The nodes O_7, O_4, and O_3 and O_9 constitute the *obj-ref state* of O_7 at line 10 and the nodes O_7, O_{12}, O_3 and O_{14} constitute the *obj-ref state* of O_7 at line 15.

```
1   function P(){ this.p = new Y1(); }
2   function X(b){
3       this.__proto__ = new P();
4       if(b) { this.p = new Y2(); }
5       else this.q = new Y3();
6   }
7   var x = new X(true);
8   x.bar = function(v, z){ v.f = z; }
9   var z1 = new Z();
10  x.bar(x.p, z1);
11  ...
12  x.p = new A();
13  ...
14  var z2 = new Z();
15  x.bar(x.p,z2);
```

Fig. 2. JavaScript example

Note that O_1 is not visible from O_7 at lines 10 or 15 because of the existence of the local property named p. The *obj-ref state* of object O_7 is different at these two program points.

Constructor polymorphism (lines 2-6), object property change (line 12) and function invocations (lines 10 and 15) in the example make precise static points-to analysis hard to achieve with current techniques. Figure 3(c) shows a points-to graph for the example built by a flow- and context-insensitive points-to analysis. Dashed nodes and edges are imprecise points-to relations that cannot exist at runtime.

There are several sources of imprecision. Line 7 creates an object pointed to by variable x by invoking the polymorphic constructor $X()$. Not knowing the value of b, static analysis conservatively builds all the points-to relations possible from execution of $X()$.[3] When reading the property p of x (line 10), static analysis returns objects O_4 and O_1 because a conservative analysis cannot distinguish whether or not O_4 actually exists. Furthermore, because of the imprecise result of the read of $x.p$, invoking the $bar()$ function results in imprecise property reference from O_1 to O_9. Flow-insensitive points-to analysis simply adds O_{12} to $O_7.p$ (line 12) because it cannot perform strong updates. Because the analysis does not distinguish which objects v and z point to on different calls of $bar()$, line 15 results in additional imprecision with respect to $O_4.f$ and $O_{12}.f$.

Flow-sensitive analysis is not sufficient to resolve the imprecision in the example without an appropriate context for call sites. First, indirect assignment statements cannot be strongly updated in general. Second, assuming $x.p$ is strongly updated to point to O_{12} at line 12, a context-insensitive analysis does not remove the imprecise edges $(< O_4, f >, O_{14})$ and $(< O_{12}, f >, O_9)$ because calls to $bar()$ (lines 10 and 15) are not distinguished by calling contexts. Object sensitivity [18]

---

[3] In this short example, constant propagation of parameters would help static analysis precision but clearly this is not always possible.

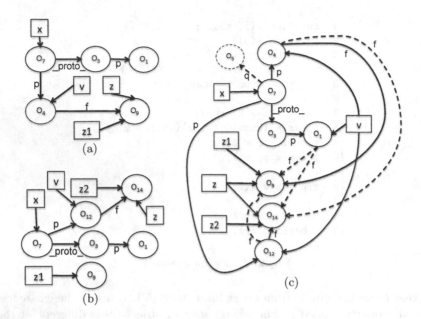

Fig. 3. Imprecision of static points-to analysis. (a) Run-time points-to graph at line 10. (b) Run-time points-to graph at line 15. (c) Flow- and context-insensitive points-to graph.

has been shown to perform better than call-string context sensitivity [24] for the idioms used in object-oriented languages [15]. However, object-sensitive analysis is not able to differentiate these two call sites because they have the same receiver object O_7, which has two different *obj-ref states* at these call sites. Our new points-to analysis is designed to handle these constructs more accurately and to address the challenges raised by *obj-ref state* updating and prototype-based inheritance.

3   State-Sensitive Points-to Analysis

In this section we will present our *state-sensitive points-to analysis* for JavaScript. We will explain key ideas used in the analysis, including the intra-procedural program representation (i.e., the block-sensitive decomposition of control-flow graphs), the solution space (i.e., the annotated points-to graph with access path edges and in-construction nodes), the transfer functions of the state-update statements as well as the state-preserving statements, state sensitivity (i.e., a form of context sensitivity based on object sensitivity that captures changes in object behavior during execution) and block sensitivity (i.e., a partial flow sensitivity performed on the transformed CFG). Finally, we will discuss the implementation details of our algorithm.

3.1 State-Preserving Block Graph

A flow-insensitive analysis ignores the control flow of a program while a flow-sensitive analysis typically uses an intra-procedural control-flow graph (CFG). Our analysis aims to provide a better model of a JavaScript object whose reference state exhibits flow-sensitive characteristics (e.g., allowing addition and deletion of object properties at any program point). Cognizant of the possible overhead introduced by a fully flow-sensitive analysis, we designed a partially flow-sensitive analysis that only performs strong updates when possible on state-update statements using a transformed CFG, called the *State-Preserving Block Graph (SPBG)*. Recall that the state-update statements, including the property write (i.e., add or update a property) and delete (i.e., remove a property), directly change the *obj-ref state* in JavaScript; all other statements (e.g., property read) are state-preserving statements.

Figure 4 shows an example *SPBG* (Figure 4(b)) compared to its original CFG (Figure 4(a)). An *SPBG* is a transformed control-flow graph whose basic blocks are aggregated into region nodes according to whether or not they contain a state-update statement. The *SPBG* also contains state-update statements as special singleton statement nodes (i.e., *state-update* nodes). An example of a region node (i.e., *state-preserving* node) is 2-4-5-7 in Figure 4(b) whereas node x = *new A()* is an example of a *state-update* node. Note that in creating singleton nodes the algorithm breaks apart former basic blocks (e.g., $1 \rightarrow \{1', x = new A(), 1''\}$).

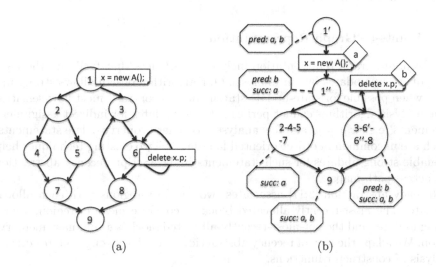

(a)   (b)

Fig. 4. *SPBG* generation. (a) CFG. (b) *SPBG*.

We first split any basic blocks in the CFG that contain at least one state-update statement (see Definition 2 in Section 2), obtaining a *split-CFG*. State-update statements (1) and (2) can be detected syntactically and invocations that may result in an *obj-ref state* change (i.e., category (3)) are found by a linear call graph traversal.[4] We then use a variant of the standard CFG construction algorithm [1] to build the split-CFG. The header nodes used include the standard headers [1] plus (i) any state-update statement is a region header of a state-update node containing only that statement, and (ii) any state-preserving statement that immediately follows a state-update statement is a region header of a state-preserving node.

In an *SPBG*, state-preserving region nodes are formed based on grouping nodes in the split-CFG that share the same control-flow relations with respect to state-update nodes. The possible control-flow relations of node n_1 and n_2 in a split-CFG include: (1) n_1 is a successor of n_2, (2) n_1 is a predecessor of n_2, (3) n_1 is both a successor and a predecessor of n_2 (i.e., n_1 and n_2 exist in a loop) and (4) n_1 and n_2 have no control-flow relation (e.g., n_1 and n_2 are present in different branches). We label each node in a split-CFG with its relations to each state-update node via depth-first searches. The set of labels form a signature for that node. If nodes share the same signature it means that they have the same control-flow relationship(s) to a (set of) state-update statement(s) so that they can be collapsed to a state-preserving node in the *SPBG*. Figure 4(b) shows the signatures of the state-preserving regions in the generated *SPBG*; a and b represent the state-update statements *x=new A()* and *delete x.p*, respectively. Basic blocks 2, 4, 5 and 7 are aggregated because they only appear as successors of *x=new A()* and have no control-flow relation to *delete x.p*. The region node 2-4-5-7 is not further aggregated with basic block 9 because 9 is a successor of *delete x.p* but 2-4-5-7 is not.

3.2   Points-to Graph Representation

Our points-to graph representation includes constructs that facilitate the handling of strong updates by our analysis. Our algorithm design allows strong updates when possible for state-update statements. In contrast, most flow-sensitive Java analysis algorithms cannot perform strong updates for indirect assignment statements (e.g., $x.p = y$) and few analyses consider property delete statements, which are uncommon in object-oriented languages. Two existing techniques help to enable strong updates for such statements in JavaScript: recency abstraction and access path maps.

Recency abstraction [2,11] associates two memory-regions with each allocation site. The most-recently-allocated block, a concrete memory-region, allows strong updates and the not-most-recently-allocated block is a summary memory-region. We adapt the idea of recency abstraction to enable strong updates during analysis of constructor functions.

De *et al.* [6] performed strong updates at indirect assignments by computing the map from access paths (i.e., a variable followed a sequence of property accesses) to sets of abstract objects. This work demonstrated the validity of using access path maps to perform strong updates for indirect write statements in

---

[4] Our analysis requires a pre-computed call graph as input. See Section 3.6 for details.

Table 1. Expanded points-to graph with annotations

points-to graph G	node N	variable v	v
		abstract object o	o
		in-construction object $@o$	@o
	edge E	variable reference $(v, \phi o)$	v → o
		property reference $(< \phi o_i, p >, \phi o_j)$	o_i →p→ o_j
		access path $(< v, p >, \phi o)$	v →p→ o
	annotation A	d annotation p^d	v →p^d→
		$*$ annotation p^*	o_i →p^*→ o_j

Java. We adapt this approach to points-to analysis for JavaScript by expanding the points-to graph representation instead of using separate maps.

Table 1 lists the nodes, edges and annotations in our points-to graph. In addition to variable nodes v and abstract object nodes o, our points-to graph contains *in-construction object nodes* $@o$.[5] Details of the in-construction objects will be discussed in Section 3.3. For sake of simplicity, we use ϕo to represent either kind of object node (i.e., o or $@o$).

There are three kinds of edges. Variable reference and property reference edges exist in a traditional points-to graph. An *access path edge*, $(< v, p >, \phi o)$, denotes that the property p of variable v refers to object ϕo. $< v, p >$ represents an access path with length of 2 (i.e., a variable followed by one field access $v.p$).[6]

Our analysis calculates *may* pointer information, meaning that a points-to edge in the graph may or may not exist at runtime. To better approximate the *obj-ref states* of JavaScript objects, we introduce annotations on property reference edges as well as access path edges. The annotations help to calculate *must exist* information for object property names. In our analysis, the d annotation on a property name p (i.e., p^d) denotes that the local property named p must not exist. This annotation only applies to access path edges in our points-to graph. The other annotation, $*$, applies to both property reference edges and

---

[5] Similar to the recency abstraction, an in-construction object always describes exactly one concrete object. In our analysis, it exists only during analysis of a constructor.

[6] The length of an access path is one more than the number of field accesses [6].

access path edges. p^* denotes that the local property named p may not exist. Property reference edges without annotation or access path edges without annotation represent *must exist* information for the property names. We use p^ϕ to represent any kind of p^d, p^* or p edge. These annotated edges help us perform a more accurate property lookup (see Section 3.3).

$Pt(x)$ denotes the points-to set of x and $Pt(< \phi o, p >)$ denotes the points-to set of the property p of ϕo. $Pt(< v, p >)$ denotes the points-to set of access path $v.p$. We also define the operation $Alias(v)$ which returns the set of variables W such that v and $w \in W$ point to the same object. $apset(v)$ denotes the set of all access path edges of v (i.e., $apset(v) = \forall q : \{(< v, q^\phi >, \phi o)\})$.

In addition to the points-to graph, we use a mapping data structure to store intermediate information in the analysis. The map M is used to record the list of property names when an object is constructed. An abstract object (e.g., o) is the key in M whose value is the set of local property names that exist when the constructor function of the abstract object returns (e.g., {p1, p2, p3}).

3.3   Points-to Analysis Transfer Functions

In this section we describe the data-flow transfer functions for the statements shown in Table 2.

Object creation ($x = new\ X(a_1, a_2, ..., a_n)$). In our analysis, an object creation statement (i.e., *new* statement) is modeled in three steps. $x = new\ X$ creates an in-construction object $@o_i$. Then the invocation of the constructor $new\ X((a_1, a_2, ..., a_n))$ is modeled as a function call on $@o_i$. Upon the return of the constructor (i.e., ret_X), the analysis removes the in-construction object from the points-to graph and redirects all points-to relations from $@o_i$ to an abstract object (i.e., $remove(G,\ @o_i)$). If the local property set of the in-construction object matches that of an existing abstract object with the same allocation site, the in-construction object is merged into the abstract object; otherwise, a new abstract object is created to replace the in-construction object. There is at most one in-construction object for each creation site.[7]

The transfer function of the object creation statement ensures that abstract objects are based on their allocation site as well as their constructed local properties (i.e., an approximation of actual *obj-ref state*); in other words, the objects created at the same allocation site that contain the same set of local property names share the same abstract object in our analysis. This object representation is more precise than using one abstract object per creation site.

Property write ($x.p = y$). In general, strong updates cannot be performed on the property write statement because an abstract object may summarize multiple

---

[7] Recursive constructor calls involve the creation of an in-construction object when the in-construction object for the same allocation site already exists (before it resolves into an abstract object). In our analysis, the existing in-construction object is resolved into a *special abstract object* whose set of properties upon construction is *unknown*. A fixed point calculation is done using the special abstract object.

Table 2. Transfer functions of program statements

Statement	Transfer function
$s_i : x = new\ X(a_1, a_2, ..., a_n)$	(1) $x = new\ X : (G - apset(x))\bigcup(x, @o_i)$ (2) $new\ X((a_1, a_2, ..., a_n)) : G\bigcup\{invoke(G, X, @o_i, a_1, a_2, ..., a_n)\}$ (3) $ret_X : remove(G, @o_i)$
$x.p = y$	(1) $if\ |Pt(x)| = 1\ and\ \{\phi o_i \in @O|\phi o_i \in Pt(x)\}$: $G - \{(<@o_i, p^\phi>, \phi o_j)|@o_i \in Pt(x) \wedge \phi o_j \in Pt(<@o_i, p^\phi>)\}\bigcup\{(<@o_i, p>, \phi o_j)|@o_i \in Pt(x) \wedge \phi o_j \in Pt(y)\}$ (2) $otherwise$: (2.1) $(G - \{(<x, p^\phi>, \phi o_i)|\phi o_i \in Pt(<x, p^\phi>)\})\bigcup\{(<x, p>, \phi o_j)|\phi o_j \in Pt(y)\}$ (2.2) $G\bigcup\{(<\phi o_i, p^*>, \phi o_j)|\phi o_i \in Pt(x) \wedge \phi o_j \in Pt(y)\}$ (2.3) $G\bigcup\{(<z, p^*>, \phi o_i)|z \in Alias(x) \wedge Pt(z, p^\phi) \neq \emptyset \wedge \phi o_i \in Pt(y)\}$
$delete\ x.p$	(1) $if\ |Pt(x)| = 1\ and\ \{\phi o_i \in @O|\phi o_i \in Pt(x)\}$: $G - \{(<@o_i, p^\phi>, \phi o_j)|@o_i \in Pt(x) \wedge \phi o_j \in Pt(<@o_i, p^\phi>)\}$ (2) $otherwise$: (2.1) $(G - \{(<x, p^\phi>, \phi o_i)|\phi o_i \in Pt(<x, p^\phi>)\})\bigcup\{(<x, p^d>, null)\}$ (2.2) $G\bigcup\{(<\phi o_i, p^*>, \phi o_j)|\phi o_i \in Pt(x) \wedge \phi o_j \in Pt(<\phi o_i, p>, \phi o_j)\} - \{(<\phi o_i, p>, \phi o_j)|\phi o_i \in Pt(x) \wedge \phi o_j \in Pt(<\phi o_i, p>)\}$ (2.3) $G\bigcup\{(<z, p^*>, \phi o_i)|z \in Alias(x) \wedge Pt(z, p) \neq \emptyset \wedge \phi o_i \in Pt(<z, p>)\} - \{(<z, p>, \phi o_i)|z \in Alias(x) \wedge Pt(z, p) \neq \emptyset \wedge \phi o_i \in Pt(<z, p>)\}$
$x = y$	$(G - apset(x))\bigcup\{(x, \phi o_i)|\phi o_i \in Pt(y)\}$
$x = y.p$	$(G - apset(x))\bigcup\{(<x, \phi o_i>)|o_i \in lookup(y, p)\}$
$x = y.m(a_1, a_2, ..., a_n)$	$(G - apset(x))\bigcup\{invoke(G, M, \phi o_i, a_1, a_2, ..., a_n)|\phi o_i \in Pt(y) \wedge M \in lookup(y, m)\}$

run-time objects; however, use of in-construction objects and access path edges enable strong updates in our analysis. In the points-to graph G, if x only refers to one object and the object is an in-construction object, we know that x refers to a specific concrete object. The analysis then performs strong updates on the property reference edges by removing the points-to edges in G denoting @$o_i.p$ (if they exist) and adding the new edges implied by $Pt(y)$. In other cases (i.e., the cardinality of $Pt(x)$ is more than 1 or x refers to an abstract object), we use access path edges to enable strong updates on property write statements. First, the access path of $x.p$ can be strongly updated by removing the access path edges in G denoting $x.p$ (if they exist) and adding the new edges (e.g., $(< x, p >, o_j)$ where o_j is referred to by y). Second, the object(s) x points to are weakly updated (e.g., the edge $(< o_i, p^* >, o_j)$ is inserted if x points to o_i and y points to o_j). The property reference edges are inserted with the $*$ annotation because the property write statement may not affect all variables pointing to the updated object. Last, the access path edges of the variables that have a may alias relation to x need to be weakly updated. For example, $(< z, p^* >, o_i)$ is inserted to G if z may be an alias of x, and there exists at least an edge denoting $z.p$ (with or without annotation).

In Figure 5, we show an example of the effects of a property write statement on the points-to graph. Figure 5(a) illustrates the input points-to graph for the property write statement $x.p = y$. In Figure 5(b), our analysis performs a strong update on the access path $x.p$ (i.e., delete $(< x, p >, O_4)$ and add $(< x, p >, O_2)$, $(< x, p >, O_3)$) and inserts the edges $(< O_1, p^* >, O_2)$, $(< O_1, p^* >, O_3)$ (i.e., weak updates). The updated points-graph shows that the property p *must* exist on x, while either $(< x, p >, O_2)$ or $(< x, p >, O_3)$ *may* exist.

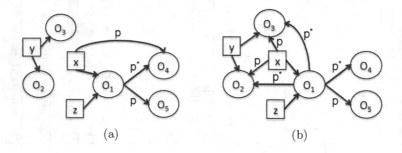

(a)   (b)

Fig. 5. Property write example. (a) Input points-to graph. (b) Updated points-to graph.

Property delete (*delete x.p*). The transfer function of the delete statement is similar to the property write statement. Our analysis strongly updates the access path edges by removing the existing edges and adding a new edge (i.e., $(< x, p^d >, null)$) that denotes x must not have a local access path $x.p$. When performing weak updates on the property reference edges of an object o_i that is referred to by x, all existing edges denoting $o_i.p$ should be annotated by $*$ because the property named p may not exist locally for o_i. The same rule applies when updating the access path edges of the aliases of x.

Direct write $(x = y)$. The effects of direct variable assignment on the points-to graph are relatively straightforward. $x = y$ creates points-to edges from x to all objects pointed to by y. Note that we perform weak updates on direct assignments. Although the analysis removes all the access path edges of x from the points-to graph (i.e., $G - apset(x)$), soundness is ensured because lookups through the abstract objects reflect *less precise, yet safe approximations* (see Procedure 1). Also, the access path edges of y cannot be copied to x because access path edges can only be added via strong updates.

Property read $(x = y.p)$. JavaScript enforces an asymmetry between reading and writing property values. When writing the value of a property or deleting a property, JavaScript always uses the local property, ignoring the prototype object. When reading a property of a variable (e.g., $x = y.p$), recall that JavaScript supports prototype-based inheritance. In some existing points-to analyses for JavaScript, when reading property p of an object, the property lookup mechanism is modeled by reporting *all* properties named p in the prototype chain of the object to ensure analysis safety.

Procedure 1. Optimized object property lookup: $lookup(v, p)$

Output: accessible objects $v.p$: P

1: **if** $Pt(< v, p >) \neq \emptyset$ **then**
2:     $P \cup Pt(< v, p >) \cup Pt(< v, p^* >)$
3:     **return**
4: **else if** $Pt(< v, p^* >) \neq \emptyset$ **or** $Pt(< v, p^d >) \neq \emptyset$ **then**
5:     $P \cup Pt(< v, p^* >)$
6:     **for** each object ϕo in $lookup(v, \_proto\_)$ **do**
7:         $S.push(\phi o)$
8:     **end for**
9: **else**
10:     **for** each object ϕo in $Pt(v)$ **do**
11:         $S.push(\phi o)$
12:     **end for**
13: **end if**
14: **while** S is not empty **do**
15:     $\phi o_i \leftarrow S.pop()$
16:     $P \cup Pt(< \phi o_i, p >) \cup Pt(< \phi o_i, p^* >)$
17:     **if** $|Pt(< \phi o_i, p >)| = 0$ **and** $(Pt(< \phi o_i, \_proto\_ >) \neq null$ **or** $Pt(< \phi o_i, \_proto\_^* >) \neq null)$ **then**
18:         **for** each object ϕo_j in $Pt(< \phi o_i, \_proto\_ >) \cup Pt(< \phi o_i, \_proto\_^* >)$ **do**
19:             $S.push(\phi o_j)$
20:         **end for**
21:     **end if**
22: **end while**

Procedure 1 illustrates our potentially more precise property lookup procedure enabled by our edge types and their annotations. This worklist algorithm iterates through all the accessible objects in the points-to graph when property p of variable v is read. Intuitively, it favors the use of access path edges in property lookup because they reflect the results of strong updates, before examining property reference edges. Lines 1 to 12 initialize the algorithm upon three conditions. (1) If there exist access path edges for $v.p$ without annotation (i.e., property p must exist locally), the objects in the $Pt(< v, p >)$ and $Pt(< v, p^* >)$ are considered to be accessible properties (line 2) and the algorithm returns (line 3). (2) If there exist access path edges for $v.p$ with either annotation, the algorithm needs to lookup objects in the prototype chain. In this case, the objects in the $Pt(< v, p^* >)$ (if $v.p^*$ exists) are considered to be accessible properties (line 5) and the algorithm pushes all the immediate prototype objects of v onto the worklist (lines 6 to 8). (3) Otherwise (i.e., no access path edge for $v.p$ exists), only the abstract objects are used for looking up so that all the objects in the $Pt(v)$ are pushed onto the worklist (lines 10 to 12). Lines 14 to 22 iterate the worklist. All the objects in $Pt(< \phi o, p >)$ and $Pt(< \phi o, p^* >)$ are considered to be accessible properties by our analysis (Line 16). Since an edge annotated with $*$ means that the property may not exist locally, the algorithm will continue looking up the prototype chain, until it reaches at least one points-to edge named p without annotation or the end of the prototype chain (Line 17 to 21). Thus, instead of finding *all* the properties named p in the prototype chain (i.e., *lookup_all(v, p)*), our algorithm can stop when it finds an *existing* property p (i.e., a property named p without annotation).

This new property lookup algorithm *lookup(v, p)* mimics the run-time property lookup mechanism of JavaScript while still assuring the safety of our analysis. For the example in Figure 5(b), *lookup(z, p)* results in O_2 and O_3 through the access path while *lookup(x, p)* results in O_2, O_3, O_4 and O_5 through the abstract object O_1. In Table 2, the transfer function of the property read statements refers to this optimized object property lookup algorithm. Because we perform weak updates on the property read statements, similar to direct writes, the analysis removes all the access path edges of x from the points-to graph to ensure safety.

Method invocation $(x = y.m(a_1, a_2, ..., a_n))$. The method invocation (e.g., $x = y.m(a_1, a_2, ..., a_n)$) resolves for every receiver object pointed to by y. The invoked methods are determined by reading the property $y.m$ through our optimized lookup algorithm. Upon the return of method invocation, x is weakly updated by removing all its access path edges from G.

3.4   State Sensitivity

State sensitivity for JavaScript is a new form of context sensitivity derived from the notion of object sensitivity for languages such as Java [18]. In object sensitivity, each method is analyzed separately for each object on which it may be invoked. For strongly typed languages like Java, often object sensitivity identifies objects in the analysis by their creation sites. Calls of a method using two different receiver objects (i.e., created at different sites) will result in two separate analyses of the method, even if the calls originated from the same call site. However, this is insufficient for JavaScript analysis, because object behavior may change dynamically at any program point during execution.

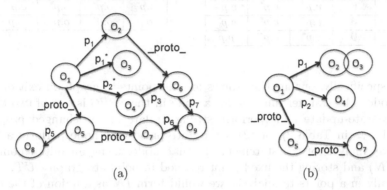

(a)   (b)

Fig. 6. Approximate *obj-ref state* as a context. (a) *obj-ref state* of O_1. (b) Approximate *obj-ref state* of O_1.

Ideally, state sensitivity would analyze each method separately for each *obj-ref state* on which it may be invoked. However, the graph representation of *obj-ref state* may contain many edges and nodes both locally and along prototype chains (e.g., *obj-ref state* of O_1 in Figure 6(a)), which would be prohibitively expensive to use as a context. Therefore, we use an *approximation* of the *obj-ref state* of the receiver object to differentiate calls that will be analyzed separately. Our approximation consists of the object, its local properties and their object values plus its chain of prototype objects. In Figure 6(b) we show the approximation corresponding to the *obj-ref state* of object O_1 in Figure 6(a). Note that the edges with the same local property name (annotated and not annotated) in the points-to graph are merged in the approximate *obj-ref state* (e.g., $(< O_1, p_1 >, O_2)$ and $(< O_1, p_1^* >, O_3)$ in Figure 6(a)). An object-sensitive analysis groups the calls using a receiver object created at the same allocation site and our state-sensitive analysis more accurately groups the calls where receiver objects have the same approximate *obj-ref state*. We intend to study the effects of using different *obj-ref state* approximations as calling contexts in future work.

3.5   Block-Sensitive Analysis

Our new points-to analysis algorithm is a fixed point calculation on the call graph, initialized with an empty points-to graph on entry to the JavaScript program, in which every constitutent *SPBG* is traversed in a flow-sensitive manner. Essentially, we have designed the points-to algorithm to emphasize precision for the *obj-ref state* information in the points-to graph and the *SPBG* to hide control flow not relevant to reference state updates.

Table 3. Union rules. (a) Access path edges union rules. (b) Property reference edges union rules.

(a)

$\cup$	$\emptyset$	$v.p^d$	$v.p^*$	$v.p$
$\emptyset$	$\emptyset$	$\emptyset$	$\emptyset$	$\emptyset$
$v.p^d$	$\emptyset$	$v.p^d$	$v.p^*$	$v.p^*$
$v.p^*$	$\emptyset$	$v.p^*$	$v.p^*$	$v.p^*$
$v.p$	$\emptyset$	$v.p^*$	$v.p^*$	$v.p$

(b)

$\cup$	$\emptyset$	$o.p^*$	$o.p$
$\emptyset$	$\emptyset$	$o.p^*$	$o.p$
$o.p^*$	$o.p^*$	$o.p^*$	$o.p^*$
$o.p$	$o.p^*$	$o.p^*$	$o.p$

More specifically, our analysis solves for the points-to graph on exit of each $SPBG$ node. The transfer function for a node in the $SPBG$ is one of two kinds: (1) for a state-update node perform strong update of the changed property, if possible (as in Table 2), or (2) for a state-preserving node perform a flow-insensitive analysis of the statements in that node, using an initial points-to graph (IN) and storing the fixed point reached in points-to graph OUT.

Normally in a points-to analysis, we would form IN as a union of the OUT points-to graphs of predecessors of a node. In our algorithm, we need to maintain the invariant of our annotated property edges, namely that a property name without an annotation means that property exists and a property name with the d annotation means that property must not exist.

Table 3 shows the union rules for the access path edges and property reference edges when two points-to graphs are unioned. For the access path edges: (1) if access path $v.p^\phi$ does not exist in at least one predecessor, then $v.p^\phi$ does not exist after union; (2) if $v.p^d$ or $v.p$ exists in both predecessors, then $v.p^d$ or $v.p$ respectively exists after union; (3) otherwise, $v.p^*$ exists after union. For the property reference edges: (1) if $o.p$ exists in both predecessors, then $o.p$ exists after union; (2) otherwise, if $o.p$ or $o.p^*$ exists in at least one predecessor, then $o.p^*$ exists after union. These rules ensure analysis safety when property lookup is performed.

3.6 Implementation of State-Sensitive Analysis in *JSBAF*

Our new points-to analysis was implemented with a client as the static component of the *JavaScript Blended Analysis Framework* (*JSBAF*), a general-purpose analysis framework for JavaScript [28]. This framework was designed to strongly couple dynamic and static analyses to account for the effects of the dynamic features of JavaScript. We chose this implementation platform because blended analysis has been demonstrated to be more efficient and effective in analyzing real JavaScript programs.[8]

JSBAF can be applied to analyze a JavaScript program (i.e., JavaScript code on a webpage) automatically in the presence of a good test suite. The dynamic phase gathers run-time information by executing tests. A trace of each test

---

[8] A static analysis was not able to finish analyzing most webpages in [28].

is collected, including call statements, object creations, variadic function calls with parameters, and dynamically created code. The implementation separates each trace into its constituent page traces. Each subtrace on a page is analyzed separately in the static phase. Data-flow solutions from different page subtraces are combined into a entire solution for that page.

Blended analysis uses only the observed calling structure as a basis to model the JavaScript program. Knowledge of unexecuted calls or object creations can be used to prune other unexecuted code sharing the same control dependence. For example, knowing $Y3()$ is not called at line 5 in Figure 2, blended analysis prunes this unexecuted statement so that the imprecise node O_5 and its connected edges will not be created. Thus, blended analysis is unsafe because not all executions are explored, but sound on the observed executions.

Our points-to algorithm was implemented on the *IBM T.J. Watson Libraries for Analysis (WALA)* open-source static analysis framework[9] which contains several existing static points-to analysis algorithms. *WALA* has been extended to enable blended analysis by providing dynamic information (i.e., a run-time collected call graph, dynamically generated code, object creation sites) [28].

Our algorithm takes as inputs the run-time collected calling structure (i.e., call graph[10]) and source code including dynamically generated code. Code pruning was performed on function bodies so that the code in polymorphic constructors and variadic functions was specialized. Hence, constructor polymorphism was handled by our improved object representation combined with dynamic information (i.e., objects created at the same allocation site with different sets of property names are represented as separate abstract objects).

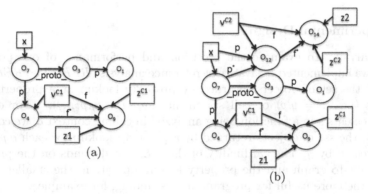

(a)

(b)

Fig. 7. Blended state-sensitive points-to analysis. (a) points-to graph at line 10. (b) points-to graph at line 15.

Example. In comparison to the inaccurate points-to solution of a flow- and context-insensitive analysis for the JavaScript code in Figure 2, we now

---

[9] http://wala.sourceforge.net/

[10] Each node in the call graph is associated with the object creations observed during its execution.

demonstrate the results of our state-sensitive points-to analysis in the context of blended analysis. Figures 7(a) and 7(b) show the points-to graphs obtained at lines 10 and 15, respectively. Because blended analysis executes the program and does not observe an object created by the constructor $Y3$, the code at line 5 is pruned so that our analysis does not generate the inaccurate node O_5 nor the edge $(< O_7, q >, O_5)$. For the call statement at line 10, our points-to analysis calculates the *obj-ref state* approximation of O_7, namely $C1$: $\{O_7, p{:}O_4, \_proto\_{:} O_3\}$. Also, when looking up $x.p$ at line 10, our algorithm returns O_4 because there is no annotation on the property reference edge so that further lookup through the prototype chain is not necessary. Note that the points-to graph in Figure 7(a) is as precise as the run-time points-to graph (Figure 3(a)).

At line 12, $x.p$ is strongly updated via the access path edge $(< x, p >, O_{12})$. For the call statement at line 15, our points-to analysis calculates the *obj-ref state* approximation of O_7, $C2$: $\{O_7, p{:}[O_4, O_{12}], \_proto\_{:} O_3\}$. Our points-to algorithm distinguishes this call site from line 10 because O_7 has a different *obj-ref state* here. The lookup of $x.p$ at line 15 follows the access path edge so that the node O_{12} is returned. Thus, in this example our analysis results in none of the inaccurate edges in the flow- and context-insensitive analysis (Figure 3(c)) and reflects the actual run-time behavior of JavaScript objects (Figure 3(b)).

4 Evaluation

In this section, we present experiments using *JSBAF* with our state-sensitive points-to analysis compared to an existing points-to analysis [26], evaluating both with a *REF* client.

4.1 Experimental Design

REF **Analysis.** To evaluate the precision and performance of our points-to analysis, we implemented a JavaScript reference analysis (*REF*). The *REF* client calculates the set of objects returned by property lookup at a property read statement (i.e., $x = y.p$) or call statement (i.e., $x = y.p(...)$).[11] For each of these statements s in a function being analyzed in calling context c, we compute $REF(s, c)$, the set of objects returned by a property lookup for each $o.p$ where o is pointed to by y. The cardinality of the *REF* set depends on the precision of the points-to graph and the property lookup operation; the smaller the set returned, the more useful for program understanding, for example.

In Figure 2, assume we add the function property

$$x.foo = function()\{var\ a = this.p;\ return\ a;\}$$

Effectively, $foo()$ returns the property lookup result for $this.p$. If $x.foo()$ is called at line 11 before the property update statement $x.p = new\ A()$, it will return O_4.

---

[11] All source code instances of property lookups (e.g., *return y.p*) occur as one of these two statements in the *WALA* intermediate code.

If $x.foo()$ is called at line 13 after $x.p=new\ A()$, it will return O_{12}. For an analysis that is flow-insensitive or that cannot distinguish these call sites by calling context, the return value of each of these function calls will contain at least two objects (i.e., O_4 and O_{12}).

Comparison with Points-to Analysis in [26]. We use the term *Corr* to refer to a blended version of correlation-tracking points-to analysis [26] (see Section 5 for more details) and its *REF* client. To demonstrate the additional precision of our analysis over *Corr*, we applied the correlation extraction transformation to our JavaScript benchmarks before performing our points-to analysis. We use the term *CorrBSSS* to refer to a blended version of this augmented new points-to analysis and its *REF* client. For each algorithm, an object property lookup returns a *REF* set whose cardinality $|REF(s,c)|$ is calculated. For *Corr*, the *lookup_all()* approximate algorithm described in Section 3.3 is used. For *CorrBSSS*, we use our optimized lookup algorithm *lookup()* in Procedure 1.

Benchmarks. We conducted the experiments with the benchmarks collected from 12 websites among the top 25 most popular sites on *alexa*, reusing website traces originally used in [28]. The results in [28] showed that the collected traces covered a large portion of the executable JavaScript code in those websites, including dynamically generated code. Although the benchmarks we used cover the most popular websites, it will require further investigation to determine how representative these benchmarks are of other websites. The experimental results were obtained on a 2.53GHz Intel Core 2 Duo MacBook Pro with 4GB memory running the Mac OS X 10.5 operating system.

4.2   Experimental Results

Improved *REF* Precision. Table 4 shows the *REF* client results for the 12 websites. Columns 2-4 present the results for *Corr* and columns 5-7 present the results for *CorrBSSS*. For each website, columns 2 & 5, 3 & 6, and 4 & 7 in Table 4 correspond to the percentage of property lookup statements that return 1 object, 2-4 objects, and more than 4 objects, respectively. The result shown for each website is averaged over the corresponding percentage numbers for all the webpages in that domain; for example, the 38% entry for *facebook.com* in column 2 is the average for *Corr* over the 27 webpages analyzed of the percentage of property lookup statements returning only 1 object.

Comparing columns 2-4 with 5-7 in Table 4 for each website, we see the relative precision improvement of *CorrBSSS* over *Corr*. For *REF* analysis, the best result is that the lookup returns only one object and the property lookup is more precise if the number of objects returned is smaller. On average over all the websites, *Corr* reported **37%** of the property lookup statements were resolved to a single object, while *CorrBSSS* improved this metric to **48%**, *a significant improvement*. In addition, *REF* analysis results may become too approximate to be useful if too many objects are returned. Although **15%** of the statements on average returned more than 4 objects for *Corr*, *CorrBSSS* reduced that number to **7%**.

Table 4. *REF* analysis precision

Website	Corr			CorrBSSS		
	1	2-4	≥ 5	1	2-4	≥5
facebook.com	38%	52%	10%	50%	47%	3%
google.com	32%	51%	17%	53%	42%	5%
youtube.com	41%	47%	12%	54%	41%	5%
yahoo.com	48%	46%	6%	52%	45%	3%
wikipedia.org	29%	45%	26%	43%	39%	18%
amazon.com	45%	52%	3%	46%	51%	3%
twitter.com	32%	53%	15%	39%	49%	12%
blogspot.com	35%	34%	31%	53%	36%	11%
linkedin.com	34%	49%	17%	44%	50%	6%
msn.com	40%	36%	24%	48%	37%	15%
ebay.com	30%	40%	30%	46%	40%	14%
bing.com	41%	34%	25%	54%	37%	9%
Geom. Mean	**37%**	**44%**	**15%**	**48%**	**43%**	**7%**

Table 5. *REF* analysis cost (in seconds) on average per webpage

Website	Corr	CorrBSSS	overhead
facebook	17.4	45.9	163%
google	13.0	30.4	134%
youtube	31.2	75.3	141%
yahoo	28.5	54.1	90%
wiki	16.0	40.1	151%
amazon	15.1	24.2	61%
twitter	38.1	94.5	148%
blog	15.9	42.4	137%
linkedin	27.8	62.0	167%
msn	34.4	57.9	68%
ebay	8.3	27.2	227%
bing	22.1	50.4	128%
Geom. Mean	**20.4**	**46.7**	**127%**

These improved precision results indicate the potential for greater practical use of state-sensitive points-to information by client analyses.

We also investigated the average number of objects returned by a property lookup statement. For each website, we calculated the number of objects per statement on average over all its webpages. Over all the benchmarks, *Corr* produced on average **2.8** objects and *CorrBSSS* only reported on average **2.3** objects. Intuitively, this means that on average fewer objects at each property lookup statement must be examined to gain better understanding of the code.

REF **Performance.** An analysis approach is practical if it scales to real-world programs, such as JavaScript code from actual websites. Because *CorrBSSS* is partially flow-sensitive and context-sensitive, it is important to demonstrate that this analysis is scalable. Table 5 shows the time performance of *Corr* versus *CorrBSSS*.[12] Columns 2 and 3 present the average webpage analysis time for each website, averaging over all of its webpages. Both *Corr* and *CorrBSSS* completely analyzed all the benchmark programs. On average over all the websites, *Corr* completely analyzed a webpage in **20.4** seconds, while *CorrBSSS* did so in **46.7** seconds, incurring an 127% average time overhead per webpage, acceptable for a research prototype implementation which has not been optimized.

Discussion. We collected data characterizing benchmark program structure and complexity to relate these characteristics to observed analysis precision and performance. The entries in Table 6 all represent averages per webpage that are averaged over an entire website. Column 2 shows the average number of functions in a JavaScript program. Column 3 shows the percentage of functions containing at least one state-update statement. Column 4 shows the percentage of statements that are state-update statements. Column 5 shows the number of contexts produced by *CorrBSSS* as a multiplier for column 2. On average over all the websites, **9%** of the functions contained local state-update statement(s); these averages ranged from **4%** for *yahoo.com* to **18%** for *msn.com*. This suggests that *the state-update statements are localized in a relatively small portion of the JavaScript program (e.g., in constructor functions)*. Manual inspection of several websites (i.e., *facebook, google* and *youtube*) revealed there were significant object behavior changes in JavaScript code outside of constructors. On average over all the websites, **8%** of the statements were identified as state-update statements. The relatively small number of state-update statements means that our *SPBG* contained many fewer nodes than the corresponding CFGs; therefore the flow-sensitive analysis was more practical in cost on the *SPBGs*.

Now we compare the analysis precision observed in Table 4 with the number of contexts generated on average per function per page (column 5 in Table 6) to observe the effect of state sensitivity. *google, blog,* and *ebay* were the websites for which *CorrBSSS* improved precision the most, whereas *amazon, yahoo, twitter,* and *msn* were the websites for which *CorrBSSS* produced similar results to *Corr*. For the former websites, *CorrBSSS* generated the greatest number of contexts per function per webpage. For the latter websites, *CorrBSSS* generated the fewest. We observe strong correlation between the precision gain and the number of contexts generated by *CorrBSSS*, demonstrating that *state sensitivity significantly increased analysis precision on these benchmarks*, and suggesting that state sensitivity will be an effective form of context sensitivity for JavaScript analysis.

---

[12] The time cost in Table 5 reflects the performance of the static phase of blended analysis. In the experiments, the dynamic phase of *Corr* and *CorrBSSS* is the same for both analyses. The work in [28] has demonstrated that the static phase dominates the blended analysis cost.

Table 6. Benchmark and context statistics. (Total contexts per website is approximately column 2 times column 5.)

Website	No. of functions	% of functions w/ update(s)	% of state-update stmt	No. of contexts
facebook	2123	9%	8%	4.0
google	1002	17%	6%	6.7
youtube	1329	7%	6%	3.9
yahoo	3810	4%	4%	2.4
wiki	270	10%	19%	4.8
amazon	729	6%	6%	1.9
twitter	618	15%	5%	3.4
blog	583	14%	14%	6.1
linkedin	920	8%	11%	3.6
msn	1537	8%	8%	2.8
ebay	581	18%	13%	7.5
bing	1131	7%	11%	4.9
Geom. Mean	**972**	**9%**	**8%**	**4.0**

As shown in Table 5, the *CorrBSSS* time overhead differed significantly for different websites, from 61% (*amazon.com*) to 227%(*ebay.com*). We investigate several program characteristics to reason about such differences. First, the *SPBG*s created by *CorrBSSS* determine the efficiency of the flow-sensitive analysis. On average over all the websites, an *SPBG* was comprised of about **6** nodes, explaining why *CorrBSSS* scaled on real websites. Functions with large numbers of nodes in their *SPBG* usually contained multiple state-update statements and complex control flow. The largest number of nodes for an *SPBG* was **23** in *linkedin*. Second, the websites with the least performance overhead from *CorrBSSS* were *amazon, msn* and *yahoo*. These websites contained a relatively small percentage of update statements (i.e., all below average) and *CorrBSSS* generated the lowest number of contexts for them. The website that incurred the most overhead (i.e., *ebay*) contained **13%** update statements, (i.e., the third highest percentage in our benchmarks), and the greatest number of contexts per function (i.e., **7.5**) generated by *CorrBSSS*. These results support the reasoning that more complex block structure and more context comparisons contribute to the higher overhead for *CorrBSSS*.

5   Related Work

Due to space limitations, we present only the work most closely related to our state-sensitive points-to algorithm.

Related Analyses of JavaScript. Several approaches were proposed to analyze JavaScript programs. Sridharan *et al.* presented a points-to analysis for JavaScript that focused on handling correlated dynamic property accesses [26].

Correlated property accesses were identified and then extracted into a function. Using the property name as the calling context, points-to analysis tracking correlation was shown to be more precise and efficient than a field-sensitive Andersen's points-to analysis. In our experiments, *CorrBSSS* was augmented by correlation analysis (i.e., *Corr*) demonstrating a significant improvement in the analysis precision.

Jensen *et al.* presented a static analysis that can precisely model prototype chains [12]. In their analysis, the *absent* set indicated potentially missing properties. The property edges annotated with * play a similar role in our analysis. Jensen's analysis is context-sensitive similar to 1-object-sensitivity used in Java [18]. The static flow-sensitive analysis presented in [12] was not scalable on large JavaScript programs, whereas our experiments showed the *CorrBSSS* was practical for blended analysis of real-world websites.

Several points-to analyses were proposed to handle other important challenges introduced by JavaScript. Guarnieri and Livshits designed a points-to analysis to detect security and reliability issues in JavaScript widgets [8]. They used a subset of JavaScript language, $JavaScript_{SAFE}$, that can be statically approximated. Guarnieri *et al.* presented a static taint analysis based on a points-to analysis finding security vulnerabilities in real-world websites [10]. The points-to algorithm focused on addressing features of JavaScript including object creations and accesses through constructed property names. In these analyses, prototyping was modeled as *lookup_all* rather than our more accurate property lookup algorithm *lookup*. The points-to analysis in [10] and our algorithm are both implemented in *WALA*.

A hybrid analysis (i.e., a combination of static and dynamic analyses) is attractive when analyzing JavaScript programs. Chugh *et al.* presented a staged information flow analysis for JavaScript [4]. The approach analyzed the static code and incrementally analyzed the dynamically generated code. A similar approach was proposed by Guarnieri and Livshits [9]; their experiments studied the performance of the incremental analysis. In addition to collecting the dynamically generated/loaded code, blended analysis uses run-time information to make the analysis more precise (e.g., polymorphic constructors are distinguished via object initialization and some unexecuted code is pruned).

Several type-based points-to techniques have been proposed for JavaScript that support dynamic features such as prototype-based inheritance (e.g., [3,5,14]). It is difficult to compare our analysis with them as to practicality, because no empirical evidence on large JavaScript programs was presented.

Software tools supporting large JavaScript software including libraries are desirable. Schafer *et al.* provided an IDE support for JavaScript programming [22]. Points-to analysis was used to calculate code completion suggestions. Points-to analysis precision is crucial to determine the effectiveness of the tool. Madsen *et al.* presented a static analysis of JavaScript focusing on frameworks and libraries [17]. A novel use analysis was proposed to analyze libraries precisely and a points-to analysis was used to find aliases in the program. Our work is complementary to these techniques, in that more precise points-to results would make them more practical.

Context-Sensitive Analysis. Our state-sensitive analysis is inspired by object sensitivity. Milanova *et al.* first introduced object sensitivity and implemented an object-sensitive points-to analysis for Java using a receiver object represented by its creation site as the calling context [18]. The experiments in [15] showed object sensitivity is the better choice as a calling context when analyzing an object-oriented language. Changes to object properties in JavaScript render object creation sites insufficient to represent object behavior, whereas state sensitivity captures object behavior changes better.

Smaragdakis *et al.* formalized object sensitivity, summarizing its variations [25]. They introduced type sensitivity where object type was used as the calling context. For dynamically-typed languages like JavaScript, type is a runtime notion, encapsulated in the idea of *obj-ref state* used as a calling context. Kastrinis *et al.* presented a hybrid context-sensitive analysis that combined object-sensitivity and call-site-sensitivity [13]. Hybrid context-sensitive analysis for JavaScript is planned for our future work.

6   Conclusion

JavaScript object behavior is difficult to analyze well because of prototype-based inheritance and allowed changes to object properties during execution. In this paper, we introduced a state-sensitive points-to analysis that models object behavior changes accurately by using a hierarchical program representation emphasizing state-update statements, by defining state sensitivity, a better context sensitivity mechanism for a dynamic language, and by enhancing the points-to graph representation for improving object property lookups. We implemented our new points-to algorithm as the static phase of a blended analysis in *JSBAF*. Experimental results on a *REF* client showed our analysis, *CorrBSSS*, significantly improved the precision of a previous good JavaScript points-to analysis *Corr* [26]. For example, 48% of property lookups were resolved to a single object by our analysis versus 37% by *Corr*. Although our research prototype implementation incurred on average 127% overhead versus *Corr* on the popular website benchmarks used, further optimization will improve the performance, which is in the practical range.

In future work, we intend to investigate variations of state sensitivity, to study the effects of different *obj-ref state* approximations on analyzing JavaScript programs. We are interested in exploring the capability of state-sensitive analysis to support program understanding. We also plan to generalize the proposed techniques to other dynamic programming languages.

References

1. Aho, A.V., Sethi, R., Ullman, J.D.: Compilers: Principles, Techniques and Tools. Addison Wesley (1986)

2. Balakrishnan, G., Reps, T.: Recency-abstraction for heap-allocated storage. In: Yi, K. (ed.) SAS 2006. LNCS, vol. 4134, pp. 221–239. Springer, Heidelberg (2006)
3. Chugh, R., Herman, D., Jhala, R.: Dependent types for JavaScript. In: Proceedings of the ACM International Conference on Object Oriented Programming Systems Languages and Applications, pp. 587–606 (2012)
4. Chugh, R., Meister, J.A., Jhala, R., Lerner, S.: Staged information flow for JavaScript. In: Proceedings of the 2009 ACM SIGPLAN Conference on Programming Language Design and Implementation, pp. 50–62 (2009)
5. Chugh, R., Rondon, P.M., Jhala, R.: Nested refinements: a logic for duck typing. In: Proceedings of the 39th Annual ACM SIGPLAN-SIGACT Symposium on Principles of Programming Languages, pp. 231–244 (2012)
6. De, A., D'Souza, D.: Scalable flow-sensitive pointer analysis for Java with strong updates. In: Noble, J. (ed.) ECOOP 2012. LNCS, vol. 7313, pp. 665–687. Springer, Heidelberg (2012)
7. Flanagan, D.: JavaScript: The Definitive Guide. O'Reilly Media, Inc. (2006)
8. Guarnieri, S., Livshits, B.: Gatekeeper: mostly static enforcement of security and reliability policies for JavaScript code. In: Proceedings of the 18th Conference on USENIX Security Symposium, pp. 151–168 (2009)
9. Guarnieri, S., Livshits, B.: Gulfstream: staged static analysis for streaming JavaScript applications. In: Proceedings of the 2010 USENIX Conference on Web Application Development, p. 6 (2010)
10. Guarnieri, S., Pistoia, M., Tripp, O., Dolby, J., Teilhet, S., Berg, R.: Saving the world wide web from vulnerable JavaScript. In: Proceedings of the 2011 International Symposium on Software Testing and Analysis, pp. 177–187 (2011)
11. Heidegger, P., Thiemann, P.: Recency types for analyzing scripting languages. In: D'Hondt, T. (ed.) ECOOP 2010. LNCS, vol. 6183, pp. 200–224. Springer, Heidelberg (2010)
12. Jensen, S.H., Møller, A., Thiemann, P.: Type analysis for javaScript. In: Palsberg, J., Su, Z. (eds.) SAS 2009. LNCS, vol. 5673, pp. 238–255. Springer, Heidelberg (2009)
13. Kastrinis, G., Smaragdakis, Y.: Hybrid context-sensitivity for points-to analysis. In: Proceedings of the 34th ACM SIGPLAN Conference on Programming Language Design and Implementation, pp. 423–434 (2013)
14. Lerner, B.S., Joe Gibbs, P., Guha, A., Shriram, K.: TeJaS: Retrofitting type systems for JavaScript. In: Proceedings of the 9th Symposium on Dynamic Languages (2013)
15. Lhoták, O., Hendren, L.: Context-sensitive points-to analysis: Is it worth it? In: Mycroft, A., Zeller, A. (eds.) CC 2006. LNCS, vol. 3923, pp. 47–64. Springer, Heidelberg (2006)
16. Lieberman, H.: Using prototypical objects to implement shared behavior in object-oriented systems. In: Conference proceedings on Object-Oriented Programming Systems, Languages and Applications, pp. 214–223 (1986)
17. Madsen, M., Livshits, B., Fanning, M.: Practical static analysis of JavaScript applications in the presence of frameworks and libraries. In: Proceedings of the 2013 9th Joint Meeting on Foundations of Software Engineering, pp. 499–509 (2013)
18. Milanova, A., Rountev, A., Ryder, B.G.: Parameterized object sensitivity for points-to analysis for Java. ACM TOSEM 14(1), 1–41 (2005)
19. Orion, http://www.eclipse.org/orion/
20. Richards, G., Lebresne, S., Burg, B., Vitek, J.: An analysis of the dynamic behavior of JavaScript programs. In: Proceedings of the 2010 ACM SIGPLAN Conference on Programming Language Design and Implementation, pp. 1–12 (2010)

21. Ryder, B.G.: Dimensions of precision in reference analysis of object-oriented programming languages. In: Hedin, G. (ed.) CC 2003. LNCS, vol. 2622, pp. 126–137. Springer, Heidelberg (2003)
22. Schafer, M., Sridharan, M., Dolby, J., Tip, F.: Effective smart completion for JavaScript. Technical Report RC25359, IBM (2013)
23. Sethi, R.: Programming Languages, Concepts & Constructs, 2nd edn. Addison Wesley (1996)
24. Sharir, M., Pnueli, A.: Two approaches to interprocedural data flow analysis. In: Program Flow Analysis: Theory and Applications, pp. 189–234 (1981)
25. Smaragdakis, Y., Bravenboer, M., Lhoták, O.: Pick your contexts well: understanding object-sensitivity. In: Proceedings of the 38th Annual ACM SIGPLAN-SIGACT Symposium on Principles of Programming Languages, pp. 17–30 (2011)
26. Sridharan, M., Dolby, J., Chandra, S., Schäfer, M., Tip, F.: Correlation tracking for points-to analysis of JavaScript. In: Noble, J. (ed.) ECOOP 2012. LNCS, vol. 7313, pp. 435–458. Springer, Heidelberg (2012)
27. Wegner, P.: Dimensions of object-based language design. In: Conference Proceedings on Object-Oriented Programming Systems, Languages and Applications, pp. 168–182 (1987)
28. Wei, S., Ryder, B.G.: Practical blended taint analysis for JavaScript. In: Proceedings of the 2013 International Symposium on Software Testing and Analysis, pp. 336–346 (2013)

Self-inferencing Reflection Resolution for Java

Yue Li, Tian Tan, Yulei Sui, and Jingling Xue

School of Computer Science and Engineering, UNSW Australia
{yueli,tiantan,ysui,jingling}@cse.unsw.edu.au

Abstract. Reflection has always been an obstacle both for sound and for effective under-approximate pointer analysis for Java applications. In pointer analysis tools, reflection is either ignored or handled partially, resulting in missed, important behaviors. In this paper, we present our findings on reflection usage in Java benchmarks and applications. Guided by these findings, we introduce a static reflection analysis, called ELF, by exploiting a *self-inferencing property* inherent in many reflective calls. Given a reflective call, the basic idea behind ELF is to automatically infer its targets (methods or fields) based on the dynamic types of the arguments of its target calls and the downcasts (if any) on their returned values, if its targets cannot be already obtained from the Class, Method or Field objects on which the reflective call is made. We evaluate ELF against DOOP's state-of-the-art reflection analysis performed in the same context-sensitive Andersen's pointer analysis using all 11 DaCapo benchmarks and two applications. ELF can make a disciplined tradeoff among soundness, precision and scalability while also discovering usually more reflective targets. ELF is useful for any pointer analysis, particularly under-approximate techniques deployed for such clients as bug detection, program understanding and speculative compiler optimization.

1 Introduction

Pointer analysis is an important enabling technology since it can improve the precision and performance of many program analyses. However, reflection poses a major obstacle to pointer analysis. Despite the large literature on whole-program [1, 6, 7, 11, 15, 21] and demand-driven [10, 13, 14, 17] pointer analysis for Java, almost all the analyses reported are unsound in the presence of reflection since it is either ignored or handled partially. As a result, under-approximate or unsound techniques represent an attractive alternative in cases where sound analysis is not required [18] (e.g., for supporting bug detection, program understanding and speculative compiler optimization). Even so, ignoring reflection often leads to missed, important behaviors [18]. This explains why modern pointer analysis tools for Java [4, 19–21] provide some forms of reflection handling.

As reflection is increasingly used in Java programs, the cost of imprecise reflection handling has increased dramatically. To improve the effectiveness of a pointer analysis tool for Java, automatic techniques for handling reflection by balancing soundness, precision and scalability are needed. Despite its importance, this problem has received little attention. Some solutions include

R. Jones (Ed.): ECOOP 2014, LNCS 8586, pp. 27–53, 2014.

```
1   A a = new A();
2   String cName, mName, fName = ...;
3   Class clz = Class.forName(cName);
4   Object obj = clz.newInstance();
5   B b = (B)obj;
6   Method mtd = clz.getDeclaredMethod(mName,{A.class});
7   Object l = mtd.invoke(b, {a});
8   Field fld = clz.getField(fName);
9   X r = (X)fld.get(a);
10  fld.set(NULL, a);
```

Fig. 1. An example of reflection usage in Java

(1) dynamic analysis [2] for recording reflective (call) targets discovered during input-dependent program runs and passing these annotations to a subsequent pointer analysis, (2) online analysis [5] for discovering reflective targets at run time and performing a pointer analysis to support JIT optimizations, and (3) static analysis [4, 8, 20] for resolving reflective targets together with a pointer analysis.

In this paper, we present a new static reflection analysis, called ELF, which is integrated into DOOP, a state-of-the-art Datalog-based pointer analysis tool [4] for analyzing Java programs. ELF draws its inspirations from the two earlier reflection analyses [4, 8] and benefits greatly from the open-source reflection analysis implemented in DOOP [4]. Livshits et al. [8] suggested resolving reflective calls by tracking the flow of class/method/field names in the program. In the code from Figure 1, this involves tracking the flow of cName into clz in line 3, mName into mtd in line 6, and fName into fld in line 8, if cName, mName and fName are string constants. If cName is, say, read from a configuration file, they suggested narrowing the types of reflectively-created objects, e.g., obj in line 4, optimistically by using the downcast (B) available in line 5. Later, DOOP [4] handles reflection analogously, but context-sensitively, to obtain the full benefit from the mutual increase in precision of both component analyses.

However, ELF goes beyond [4, 8] by taking advantage of a *self-inferencing property* inherent in reflective code to strike a disciplined tradeoff among soundness, precision and scalability. Our key observation (made from a reflection-usage study described in Section 2) is that many reflective calls are *self-inferenceable*. Consider r = (X)fld.get(a) in Figure 1. Its target fields accessed can often be approximated based on the dynamic types (i.e., A) of argument a and the downcast that post-dominates its return values, if fld represents a statically unknown field named fName. In this case, the reflective call is resolved to all possible field reads r = a.f. Here, f is a field of type T (where T is X or a supertype or subtype of X), declared in a class C (where C is A or a supertype of A). To the best of our knowledge, ELF is the first static reflection analysis that exploits such self-inferencing property to resolve reflective calls.

Due to the intricacies and complexities of the Java reflection API, we will postpone a detailed comparison between ELF and the two state-of-the-art reflection analyses [4, 8] later in Section 3 after we have introduced ELF in full.

In summary, this paper makes the following main contributions:

- We report findings on a reflection-usage study using 14 representative Java benchmarks and applications (Section 2). We expect these findings to be useful in guiding the design and implementation of reflection analysis.
- We introduce a static reflection analysis, ELF, to improve the effectiveness of pointer analysis tools for Java (Section 3). ELF adopts a new *self-inferencing* mechanism for reflection resolution and handles a significant part of the Java reflection API that was previously ignored or handled partially.
- We formulate ELF in Datalog consisting of 207 rules, covering the majority of reflection methods frequently used in Java programs (Section 4).
- We have evaluated ELF against a state-of-the-art reflection analysis in DOOP (version r160113) under the same context-sensitive Andersen's pointer analysis framework, using all 11 DaCapo benchmarks and two Java applications, Eclipse4 and Javac (Section 5). Our results show that ELF can make a disciplined tradeoff among soundness, precision and scalability while resolving usually more reflective call targets than DOOP.

2   Understanding Reflection Usage

Section 2.1 provides a brief introduction to the Java reflection API. Section 2.2 reports our findings on reflection usage in Java benchmarks and applications.

2.1   Background

The Java reflection API provides metaobjects to allow programs to examine themselves and make changes to their structure and behavior at run time. In Figure 1, the metaobjects clz, mtd and fld are instances of the metaobject classes Class, Method and Field, respectively. Constructor can be seen as Method except that the method name "<init>" is implicit. Class provides accessor methods such as getDeclaredMethod() in line 6 and getField in line 8 to allow the other metaobjects (e.g., of Method and Field) related to a Class object to be introspected. With dynamic invocation, a Method object can be commanded to invoke the method that it represents (line 7) and a Field object can be commanded to access the field that it represents (lines 9 and 10).

As far as pointer analysis is concerned, we can divide the pointer-affecting methods in the Java reflection API into three categories: (1) *entry methods*, e.g., forName() in line 3, for creating Class objects, (2) *member-introspecting methods*, e.g., getDeclaredMethod() in line 6 and getField() in line 8, for retrieving Method (Constructor) and Field objects from a Class object, and (3) *side-effect methods*, e.g., newInstance(), invoke(), get() and set() in lines 4, 7, 9 and 10, that affect the pointer information in the program reflectively.

Class provides a number of accessor methods for introspecting methods, constructors and fields in a target class. Unlike [4, 8], ELF is the first to handle all such accessor methods in reflection analysis. Let us recall the four on returning Method objects. getDeclaredMethod(String, Class[]) returns a Method object that represents a declared method of the target Class object with the name (formal parameter types) specified by the first (second) parameter (line 6 in Figure 1). getMethod(String, Class[]) is similar except that the returned Method object is public (either declared or inherited). If the target Class does not have a matching method, then its superclasses are searched first recursively (bottom-up) before its interfaces (implemented). getDeclaredMethods() returns an array of Method objects representing all the methods declared in the target Class object. getMethods() is similar except that all the public methods (either declared or inherited) in the target Class object are returned. Given a Method object mtd, its target method can be called as shown in line 7 in Figure 1.

2.2 Empirical Study

The Java reflection API is rich and complex in details. We conduct an empirical study to understand reflection usage in practice in order to guide the design and implementation of a sophisticated reflection analysis.

We select 14 representative Java programs, including nine DaCapo benchmarks (2006-10-MR2), three latest versions of popular desktop applications, javac-1.7.0, jEdit-5.1.0 and Eclipse-4.2.2 (denoted Eclipse4), and two latest versions of popular server applications, Jetty-9.0.5 and Tomcat-7.0.42. Note that DaCapo consists of 11 benchmarks, including an older version of Eclipse (version 3.1.2). We exclude bloat since its application code is reflection-free. We consider lucene instead of luindex and lusearch separately since these two benchmarks are derived from lucene with the same reflection usage.

We consider a total of 191 methods in the Java reflection API (version 1.5), including the ones in java.lang.reflect and java.lang.Class, loadClass() in java.lang.ClassLoader, and getClass() in java.lang.Object. We have also considered A.class, which represents the Class object of a class A.

We use Soot [19] to pinpoint the calls to reflection methods in the bytecode of a program. To understand reflection usage, we consider only the reflective calls found in the application classes and their dependent libraries but exclude the standard Java libraries. To increase the code coverage for the five applications considered, we include the jar files whose names contain the names of these applications (e.g., *jetty*.jar for Jetty) and make them available under the *process-dir* option supported by Soot. For Eclipse4, we use org.eclipse.core.runtime.adaptor.EclipseStarter to enable Soot to locate all the other jar files used. We manually inspect the reflection usage in a program in a demand-driven manner, starting from its side-effect methods, assisted by *Open Call Hierarchy* in Eclipse, by following their backward slices. For a total of 609 side-effect callsites examined, 510 callsites for calling entry methods and 304 callsites for calling member-introspecting methods are tracked and analyzed.

Below we describe our five findings on reflection usage in our empirical study.

Side-Effect Methods. Table 1 lists a total of nine side-effect methods that can possibly modify or use (as their side effects) the pointer information in a program.

Table 1. Nine side-effect methods and their side effects, assuming that the target class of *clz* and *ctor* is A and the target method (field) of *mtd* (*fld*) is m (*f*)

Simplified Method	Calling Scenario	Side Effect
Class::newInstance	o = *clz*.newInstance()	o = new A()
Constructor::newInstance	o = *ctor*.newInstance({arg$_1$, ...})	o = new A(arg$_1$, ...)
Method::invoke	a = *mtd*.invoke(o, {arg$_1$, ...})	a = o.m(arg$_1$, ...)
Field::get	a = *fld*.get(o)	a = o.f
Field::set	*fld*.set(o, a)	o.f = a
Array::newInstance	o = *Array*.newInstance(*clz*, size)	o = new A[size]
Array::get	a = *Array*.get(o, i)	a = o[i]
Array::set	*Array*.set(o, i, a)	o[i] = a
Proxy::newProxyInstance	o = *Proxy*.newProxyInstance(...)	o = new Proxy\$*(...)

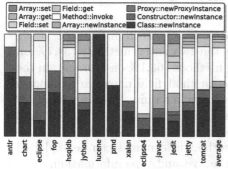

Fig. 2. Side-effect methods

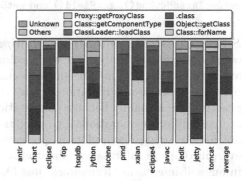

Fig. 3. Entry methods

Figure 2 depicts their percentage frequency distribution in the 14 programs studied. We can see that `invoke()` and `Class::newInstance()` are the two most frequently used (32.7% and 35.3%, respectively, on average), which are handled by prior pointer analysis tools [4, 20, 21]. However, `Array`-related side-effect methods, which are also used in many programs, are previously ignored but handled by ELF. Note that `newProxyInstance()` is used in `jEdit` only.

Entry Reflection Methods. Figure 3 shows the percentage frequency distribution of different types of entry methods used. The six as shown are the only ones found in the first 12 programs. In the last two (`Jetty` and `Tomcat`), "*Others*" stands for `defineClass()` in `ClassLoader` and `getParameterTypes()` in `Method` only. "*Unknown*" is included since we failed to find the entry methods for some side-effect calls such as `invoke()` even by using `Eclipse`'s *Open Call Hierarchy* tool. Finally, `getComponentType()` is usually used in the form of `getClass().getComponentType()` for creating a `Class` object argument for `Array.newInstance()`. On average, `Class.forName()` and `.class` are the top two most frequently used entry methods (48.1% and 18.0%, respectively).

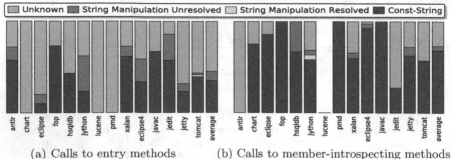

(a) Calls to entry methods   (b) Calls to member-introspecting methods

Fig. 4. Classification of the `String` arguments of two entry methods, `forName()` and `loadClass()`, and four member-introspecting methods, `getMethod()`, `getDeclaredMethod()`, `getField()` and `getDeclaredField()`

String Constants and String Manipulation. As shown in Figure 4, string constants are commonly used when calling the two entry methods (34.7% on average) and the four member-introspecting methods (63.1% on average). In the presence of string manipulations, many class/method/field names are unknown exactly. This is mainly because their static resolution requires *precisely* handling of many different operations e.g., `subString()` and `append()`. Thus, ELF does not handle string manipulations presently. As suggested in Section 5.3.2, however, incomplete information about class/method/field names can be exploited in our self-inferencing framework, just like the cast and type information.

We also found that many string arguments are *Unknown* (55.3% for calling entry methods and 25.1% for calling member-introspecting methods, on average). These are the strings that may be read from, say, configuration files or command lines. Finally, string constants are found to be more frequently used for calling the four member-introspecting methods than the two entry methods: 146 calls to `getDeclaredMethod()` and `getMethod()`, 27 calls to `getDeclaredField()` and `getField()` in contrast with 98 calls to `forName()` and `loadClass()`. This suggests that the analyses [4, 20] that ignore string constants flowing into some of these member-introspecting methods may be imprecise (Table 2).

Self-inferenceable Reflective Calls. In real applications, many reflective calls are self-inferenceable, as illustrated in Figures 8 – 10. Therefore, we should try to find their targets by aggressively tracking the flow of constant class/method/field names in the program. However, there are also many input-dependent strings. For many input-dependent reflective calls, such as `factoryField.get(null)` in Figure 8, `field.set(null, value)` in Figure 9 and `method.invoke(target, parameters)` in Figure 10, we can approximate their targets reasonably accurately based on the dynamic types of the arguments of their target calls and the downcasts (if any) on their returned values. ELF will exploit such self-inferencing property inherent in reflective code during its reflection analysis.

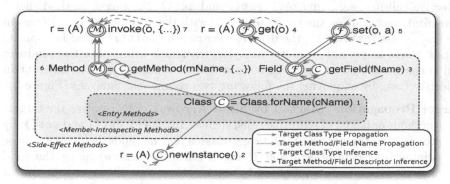

Fig. 5. Self-inferencing reflection analysis in ELF

Retrieving an Array of `Method/Field/Constructor` ***Objects.*** `Class` contains a number of accessor methods for returning an array of such metaobjects for the target `Class` object. In the two `Eclipse` programs, there are four `invoke` callsites called on an array of `Method` objects returned from `getMethods` and 15 `fld.get()` and `fld.set()` callsites called on an array of `Field` objects returned by `getDeclaredFields()`. Ignoring such methods as in prior work [4, 8, 21] may lead to many missed methods in the call graph of a program.

3   Methodology

We start with a set of assumptions made. We then describe our self-inferencing approach adopted by ELF. Finally, we compare ELF with the two prior reflection analyses [4, 8] by summarizing their similarities and differences.

3.1   Assumptions

We adopt all the assumptions from [8]: (1) *Closed World*: only the classes reachable from the class path at analysis time can be used by the program at run time, (2) *Well-behaved Class Loaders*: the name of the class returned by a call to `forName(cName)` equals `cName`, and (3) *Correct Casts*: the downcasts operating on the result of a call to `newInstance()` are correct. Due to (1), we will not consider the side-effect method `Proxy::newProxyInstance` in Table 1 and the entry method `loadClass` in Figure 3 as both may use custom class loaders. Finally, we broaden *Correct Casts* by also including `fld.get()` and `mtd.invoke()`.

3.2   Self-inferencing Reflection Resolution

Figure 5 depicts a typical reflection scenario and illustrates how ELF works. In this scenario, a `Class` object $\mathcal{C}$ is first created for the target class named `cName`. Then a `Method` (`Field`) object $\mathcal{M}$ ($\mathcal{F}$) representing the target method (field) named `mName` (`fName`) in the target class of $\mathcal{C}$ is created. Finally, at some reflective callsites, e.g., `invoke()`, `get()` and `set()`, the target method (field) is invoked (accessed) on the target object o, with the arguments, {...} or a. In the case of `newInstance()`, the default constructor "init()" called is implicit.

ELF works as part of a pointer analysis, with each being both the producer and consumer of the other. It exploits a self-inferencing property inherent in reflective code, by employing the following two component analyses (Figure 5):

Target Propagation (Marked by Solid Arrows). ELF resolves the targets (methods or fields) of reflective calls, such as `invoke()`, `get()` and `set()`, by propagating the names of the target classes and methods/fields (e.g., those pointed by `cName`, `mName` and `fName` if statically known) along the solid lines into the points symbolized by circles. Note that the second argument of `getMethod()` is an array of type `Class[]`. It may not be beneficial to analyze it to disambiguate overloaded methods, because (1) its size may be statically unknown, (2) its components are collapsed by the pointer analysis, and (3) its components may be `Class` objects with unknown class names.

Target Inference (Marked by Dashed Arrows). By using *Target Propagation* alone, a target method/field name (blue circle) or its target class type (red circle) at a reflective callsite may be missing, i.e., unknown, due to the presence of input-dependent strings (Figure 4). If the target class type (red circle) is missing, ELF will infer it from the dynamic type of the target object o (obtained by pointer analysis) at `invoke()`, `get()` or `set()` (when o != null) or the downcast (if any), such as (A), that post-dominantly operates on the result of a call to `newInstance()`. If the target method/field name (blue circle) is missing, ELF will infer it from (1) the dynamic types of the arguments of the target call, e.g., {...} of `invoke()` and a of `set()`, and/or (2) the downcast on the result of the call, such as (A) at `invoke()` and `get()`. Just like `getMethod`, the second argument of `invoke()` is also an array, which is also similarly hard to analyze statically. To improve precision, we disambiguate overloaded target methods with a simple intraprocedural analysis only when the array argument can be analyzed exactly element-wise.

To balance soundness, precision and scalability in a disciplined manner, ELF adopts the following inference principle: *a target method or field is resolved at a reflective callsite if both its target class type (red circle) and its target method/field name (blue circle) can be resolved (i.e., statically discovered) during either Target Propagation or Target Inference.* As a result, the number of spurious targets introduced when analyzing a reflective call, `invoke()`, `get()` or `set()`, is minimized due to the existence of two simultaneous constraints (the red and blue circles). How to relax ELF in the presence of just one such a constraint will be investigated in future work. Note that the cast operations on `newInstance()` will still have to be handled heuristically as only one of the two constraints exists. As ELF is unsound, so is the underlying pointer analysis. Therefore, a reflective callsite is said to be *resolved* if at least one of its targets is resolved.

Let us illustrate *Target Inference* by considering r = (A) $\mathcal{F}$.`get(o)` in Figure 5. If a target field name is known but its target class type (i.e., red circle) is missing, we infer it by looking at the types of all pointed-to objects o' by o.

Table 2. Comparing ELF with the two closely-related reflection analyses [4, 8]

Side-Effect Methods	Member-Introspecting Methods	[8] → → --→	DOOP [4] → →	ELF → → --→ --→
invoke	getMethod	√		√ √ √ √
	getDeclaredMethod	√	√	√ √ √ √
	getMethods	n/a	n/a	√ n/a √ √
	getDeclaredMethods	n/a	n/a	√ n/a √ √
get set	getField	√		√ √ √ √
	getDeclaredField	√	√	√ √ √ √
	getFields	n/a	n/a	√ n/a √ √
	getDeclaredFields	n/a	n/a	√ n/a √ √
newInstance		√ n/a √	√ n/a	√ n/a √ n/a

If B is the type of o', then a potential target class of o is B or any of its super-types. If the target class type of $\mathcal{F}$ is B but a potential target field name (i.e., blue circle) is missing, we can deduce it from the downcast (A) to resolve the call to r = o.f, where f is a member field in B whose type is A or a supertype or subtype of A. A supertype is possible because a field of this supertype may initially point to an object of type, say, A and then downcast to A.

In Figure 5, if `getMethods()` (`getFields()`) is called at Label 6 (Label 3) instead, then an array of Method (Field) objects will be returned so that *Target Propagation* from them is implicitly performed. All the other methods available in Class for introspecting methods/fields/constructors are handled similarly.

3.3 ELF vs. Livshits et al.'s Analysis and DOOP

Table 2 compares ELF with Livshits et al.'s and DOOP's analyses [4, 8] in terms of how four representative side-effect reflective calls are resolved.

Target Propagation. ELF resolves a target method/field at a reflective callsite by requiring both its target class type (red circle) and its target name (blue circle) to be known. However, this is not the case in the other two analyses. In the case of Livshits et al.'s analysis, the target class type is always ignored. Therefore, the target methods/fields with a given name in all the classes in the program are conservatively included. DOOP suffers the opposite problem by ignoring the target method/field names. As a result, all methods/fields in the target class are included. Finally, of the three analyses, ELF is the only one that can handle all the member-introspecting methods listed.

Target Inference. Of the three analyses, ELF is the only one to adopt a self-inferencing principle to find the target classes and methods/fields at a reflective callsite. Livshits et al.'s analysis narrows the type of reflectively-created objects at `newInstance()` in Figure 5, but DOOP does not do this. However, DOOP is more sophisticated than Livshits et al.'s analysis in distinguishing virtual, static and special calls and considering the modifiers of fields for loads and stores. These are all handled by the ELF reflection analysis.

4   Reflection Resolution

We specify the reflection resolution in ELF as a set of Datalog rules, i.e., monotonic logical inferences (with no negation in a recursion cycle), following the style of [6]. The main advantage is that the specification is close to the actual implementation. Datalog has been the basis of several pointer analysis tools [4, 6, 8, 21]. Our rules are declarative: the order of evaluation of rules or examination of their clauses do not affect the final results. Given a program to be analyzed, these rules are repeatedly applied to infer more facts until a fixed point is reached.

ELF works as part of a flow-insensitive Andersen's pointer analysis context-sensitively. However, all the Datalog rules are given here context-insensitively.

There are 207 Datalog rules. One set of rules handles all the 98 possible scenarios (i.e., combinations) involving the methods listed in Table 2 (illustrated in Figure 5), where $98 = 4$ (four member-introspecting methods) $\times$ 3 (three side-effect methods, `invoke()`, `get()` and `set()`) $\times$ 4 (four possible arrows in Figure 5) $\times$ 2 (two types of side-effect methods each, instance or static) $+$ 2 (`newInstance()` with a statically known or unknown type). This set of rules is further divided into those for performing target propagation (involving $4 \times 3 \times 1 \times 2 + 1 = 25$ scenarios) and those for performing target inference. The remaining set of rules handles `Constructor` and arrays and performs bookkeeping duties.

Section 4.1 gives a set of domains and input/output relations used. Section 4.2 describes the seven target propagation scenarios corresponding to Labels $1 - 7$ in Figure 5. Section 4.3 describes four representative target inference scenarios. All the other rules (available as an open-source tool) can be understood analogously. Section 4.4 discusses briefly some properties about our analysis.

T: set of class types	V: set of program variables
M: set of methods	F: set of fields
H: set of heap abstractions	I: set of invocation sites
N: set of natural numbers	S: set of strings
SCALL($invo{:}I$, $mtd{:}M$)	VCALL($invo{:}I$, $base{:}V$, $mtd{:}M$)
ACTUALARG($invo{:}I$, $i{:}N$, $arg{:}V$)	ACTUALRETURN($invo{:}I$, $var{:}V$)
HEAPTYPE($heap{:}H$, $type{:}T$)	ASSIGNABLE($toType{:}T$, $fromType{:}T$)
THISVAR($mtd{:}M$, $this{:}V$)	LOOKUPMTD($type{:}T$, $mName{:}H$, $dp{:}S$, $mtd{:}M$)
MTDSTRING($mtd{:}M$, $str{:}S$)	STRINGTOCLASS($strConst{:}H$, $type{:}T$)
MTDDECL($type{:}T$, $mName{:}H$, $dp{:}S$, $mtd{:}M$)	FLDDECL($type{:}T$, $fName{:}H$, $fType{:}T$, $fld{:}F$)
PUBLICMTD($type{:}T$, $mName{:}H$, $mtd{:}M$)	PUBLICFLD($type{:}T$, $fName{:}H$, $fld{:}F$)
NEWINSTANCEHEAP($type{:}T$, $heap{:}H$)	TYPE-CLASSHEAP($type{:}T$, $clzHeap{:}H$)
MTD-MTDHEAP($mtd{:}M$, $mtdHeap{:}H$)	FLD-FLDHEAP($fld{:}F$, $fldHeap{:}H$)
VARPOINTSTO($var{:}V$, $heap{:}H$)	CALLGRAPH($invo{:}I$, $mtd{:}M$)
FLDPOINTSTO($base{:}H$, $fld{:}F$, $heap{:}H$)	REFCALLGRAPH($invo{:}I$, $mtd{:}M$)

Fig. 6. Domains and input/output relations

4.1   Domains and Input/Output Relations

Figure 6 shows the eight domains used, 18 input relations and four output relations. Given a method mtd called at an invocation site I, as a static call (SCALL) or a virtual call (VCALL), its i-th argument arg is identified by ACTUALARG and its returned value is assigned to var as identified by ACTUALRETURN.

HEAPTYPE describes the types of heap objects. ASSIGNABLE is the usual subtyping relation. THISVAR correlates $this$ to each method where it is declared. MTDSTRING specifies the signatures (in the form of strings) for all the methods, including also their containing class types and return types. STRINGTO-CLASS records the class type information for all compile-time string names. LOOKUPMTD matches a method mtd named $mName$ with descriptor dp to its definition in a class, $type$. For simplicity, $mName$ is modeled as a heap object in domain H rather than a string in S. We have done the same for method/field names in MTDDECL, FLDDECL, PUBLICMTD and PUBLICFLD.

MTDDECL records all methods and their declaring classes and FLDDECL records all fields and their declaring classes. To find the metaobjects returned by getMethod() and getField(), PUBLICMTD matches a public target method m named $mName$ in a class of type $type$, its superclasses or its interfaces searched in that order (as discussed in Section 2.1) and PUBLICFLD does the same for fields except that $type$'s interfaces are searched before $type$'s superclasses.

The last four input relations record four different types of heap objects created. NEWINSTANCEHEAP relates the heap objects created at newInstance() calls with their class types. TYPE-CLASSHEAP, MTD-MTDHEAP and FLD-FLDHEAP relate all the classes, methods and fields in the (closed-world) program to their metaobjects (i.e., Class, Method and Field objects), respectively.

When working with a pointer analysis, ELF both uses and modifies the four output relations recording the results of the pointer analysis. VARPOINTSTO and FLDPOINTSTO maintain the points-to relations and CALLGRAPH encodes the call graph of the program. As in [4], REFCALLGRAPH is used to record the potential callees resolved from a call to invoke(). The second argument of invoke() is an array containing the arguments of its target calls; special handling is needed to assign these arguments to the corresponding parameters of its target methods.

4.2 Target Propagation

We give seven target propagation scenarios corresponding to Labels 1 – 7 in Figure 5 when both a target method/field name and its target class type are known. These rules (used later in Section 4.3) are standard except for getField() and getMethod(). These two methods are ignored by DOOP [4] but handled conservatively in [8], as shown in Table 2, with the target class of a target method/field ignored, causing the targets in all the classes in the program to be included.

The syntax of a rule is easy to understand: "←" separates the inferred fact (i.e., the $head$ of the rule) from the preciously established facts (i.e., the $body$ of the rule). In Scenario P1, the rule for FORNAME says that among all static invocation sites, record the calls to forName() in the FORNAME relation. The rule for RESOLVEDCLASSTYPE records the fact that all such invocation sites with constant names are resolved. Note that $const$ is a heap object representing "string constant". Meanwhile, the points-to and call-graph relations are updated. For each resolved class, its static initialiser "<clinit>()", at the callsite is discovered in case the class has never been referenced in the program.

In Scenario P2, a `newInstance()` call is analyzed for each statically known class type pointed by *clz*. For such a type, a call to its default constructor "<init> ()" is noted. In Scenario P3 for handling a `getField()` call, both the statically known field and all the known target classes pointed by *clz*, i.e., *fld-Name* (a heap object representing "string constant") and *type* are considered. Similarly, a `getMethod()` call is handled in Scenario P6. Note that its second argument is ignored as discussed in Section 3.2. In Scenarios P4 and P5, calls to `get()` and `set()` are analyzed, respectively. Finally, in Scenario P7, an `invoke()` call is handled, identically as in DOOP [4] but differently from [8], which approximates its target methods by disregarding the target object *obj*, on which the target methods are called.

Scenario P1: *Class clz = Class.forName("string constant");*

FORNAME(*invo*) ←
  SCALL(*invo*, *mtd*), MTDSTRING(*mtd*,
  "java.lang.Class: java.lang.Class forName(java.lang.String)").
RESOLVEDCLASSTYPE(*invo*, *type*) ←
  FORNAME(*invo*), ACTUALARG(*invo*, 1, *arg*),
  VARPOINTSTO(*arg*, *const*), STRINGTOCLASS(*const*, *type*).
CALLGRAPH(*invo*, *clinit*), **VARPOINTSTO**(*clz*, *clzHeap*) ←
  RESOLVEDCLASSTYPE(*invo*, *type*), TYPE-CLASSHEAP(*type*, *clzHeap*),
  MTDSTRING(*clinit*, *type.toString()*+*".<clinit>()"*), ACTUALRETURN(*invo*, *clz*).

Scenario P2: *Object obj = clz.newInstance();*

NEWINSTANCE(*invo*, *clz*) ←
  VCALL(*invo*, *clz*, *mtd*), MTDSTRING(*mtd*, *"java.lang.Class: java.lang.Object newInstance()"*).
CALLGRAPH(*invo*, *init*), **HEAPTYPE**(*heap*, *type*),
VARPOINTSTO(*this*, *heap*), **VARPOINTSTO**(*obj*, *heap*) ←
  NEWINSTANCE(*invo*, *clz*), VARPOINTSTO(*clz*, *clzHeap*), TYPE-CLASSHEAP(*type*, *clzHeap*),
  NEWINSTANCEHEAP(*type*, *heap*), MTDSTRING(*init*, *type.toString()*+*".<init>()"*),
  THISVAR(*init*, *this*), ACTUALRETURN(*invo*, *obj*).

Scenario P3: *Field f = clz.getField("string constant");*

GETFIELD(*invo*, *clz*) ←
  VCALL(*invo*, *clz*, *mtd*), MTDSTRING(*mtd*,
  "java.lang.Class: java.lang.reflect.Field getField(java.lang.String)").
RESOLVEDFIELD(*invo*, *fld*) ←
  GETFIELD(*invo*, *clz*), VARPOINTSTO(*clz*, *clzHeap*),
  TYPE-CLASSHEAP(*type*, *clzHeap*), ACTUALARG(*invo*, 1, *arg*),
  VARPOINTSTO(*arg*, *fldName*), PUBLICFLD(*type*, *fldName*, *fld*).
VARPOINTSTO(*f*, *fldHeap*) ←
  RESOLVEDFIELD(*invo*, *fld*), FLD-FLDHEAP(*fld*, *fldHeap*), ACTUALRETURN(*invo*, *f*).

Scenario P4: *Object to = f.get(obj);*

GET(*invo*, *f*) ←
  VCALL(*invo*, *f*, *mtd*), MTDSTRING(*mtd*,
  "java.lang.reflect.Field: java.lang.Object get(java.lang.Object)").
VARPOINTSTO(*to*, *valHeap*) ←
  GET(*invo*, *f*), VARPOINTSTO(*f*, *fldHeap*), FLD-FLDHEAP(*fld*, *fldHeap*),
  ACTUALARG(*invo*, 1, *obj*), VARPOINTSTO(*obj*, *baseHeap*),
  FLDPOINTSTO(*baseHeap*, *fld*, *valHeap*), ACTUALRETURN(*invo*, *to*).

Scenario P5: *f.set(obj, val);*

SET(*invo*, *f*) ←
   VCALL(*invo*, *f*, *mtd*), MTDSTRING(*mtd*,
   "java.lang.reflect.Field: void set(java.lang.Object, java.lang.Object)").

FLDPOINTSTO(*baseHeap*, *fld*, *valHeap*) ←
   SET(*invo*, *f*), VARPOINTSTO(*f*, *fldHeap*), FLD-FLDHEAP(*fld*, *fldHeap*),
   ACTUALARG(*invo*, 1, *obj*), VARPOINTSTO(*obj*, *baseHeap*),
   ACTUALARG(*invo*, 2, *val*), VARPOINTSTO(*val*, *valHeap*).

Scenario P6: *Method m = clz.getMethod("string const", {...});*

GETMETHOD(*invo*, *clz*) ←
   VCALL(*invo*, *clz*, *mtd*), MTDSTRING(*mtd*,
   "java.lang.Class: java.lang.reflect.Method getMethod(java.lang.String, java.lang.Class[])").

RESOLVEDMETHOD(*invo*, *mtd*) ←
   GETMETHOD(*invo*, *clz*), VARPOINTSTO(*clz*, *clzHeap*),
   TYPE-CLASSHEAP(*type*, *clzHeap*), ACTUALARG(*invo*, 1, *arg*),
   VARPOINTSTO(*arg*, *mtdName*), PUBLICMTD(*type*, *mtdName*, *mtd*).

VARPOINTSTO(*m*, *mtdHeap*) ←
   RESOLVEDMETHOD(*invo*, *mtd*), MTD-MTDHEAP(*mtd*, *mtdHeap*), ACTUALRETURN(*invo*, *m*).

Scenario P7: *Object to = m.invoke(obj, {...});*

INVOKE(*invo*, *m*) ←
   VCALL(*invo*, *m*, *mtd*), MTDSIGSTRING(*mtd*, *"java.lang.reflect.Method:*
   java.lang.Object invoke(java.lang.Object, java.lang.Object[])").

REFCALLGRAPH(*invo*, *virtualMtd*), VARPOINTSTO(*this*, *heap*) ←
   INVOKE(*invo*, *m*), VARPOINTSTO(*m*, *mtdHeap*), MTD-MTDHEAP(*mtd*, *mtdHeap*),
   ACTUALARG(*invo*, 1, *obj*), VARPOINTSTO(*obj*, *heap*), HEAPTYPE(*heap*, *type*),
   MTDDECL(_ , *mtdName*, *mtdDescriptor*, *mtd*), THISVAR(*virtualMtd*, *this*),
   LOOKUPMETHOD(*type*, *mtdName*, *mtdDescriptor*, *virtualMtd*).

4.3 Target Inference

When a target method/field name or a target class type is unknown, ELF will infer the missing information, symbolized by red and blue circles along the dashed arrows in Figure 5. Below we give the Datalog rules for four representative scenarios (out of a total of 73 scenarios mentioned earlier for target inference).

Scenario I1: *Class clz1 = Class.forName(?); A a = (A) clz2.newInstance().*
The post-dominating cast *(A)* is used to infer the target class types of the objects reflectively created and pointed to by *a*, where *clz2* points to a Class object of an unknown type that is initially pointed to by *clz1*.

Scenario I2: *Field[] fs1=clz.getDeclaredFields();f2=fs2[i]; a=(A)f1.get(obj).*
The post-dominating type *(A)* is used to infer the target fields reflectively accessed at `get()` on the Field objects that are initially stored into *fs1* and later pointed to by *f1*. Note that *clz* is known in this case.

Scenario I3: *Field[] fs1 = clz.getDeclaredFields(); f2 = fs2[i]; f1.set(obj, val).*
The dynamic types of *val* are used to infer the target fields modified.

Scenario I4: *Method m1 = clz.getMethod(?, params); a = m2.invoke(obj, args).*
The dynamic types of *args* will be used to infer the target methods called on the Method objects that are pointed to by *m2* but initially created at a call to *m1=clz.getMethod()*, where *clz* is known.

Figure 7 gives a few new relations used for handling these four scenarios. The first three are used to identify metaobjects with non-constant names (called *placeholder objects*). CLASSPH identifies all the invocation sites, e.g., `Class.forName(?)`, where `Class` objects with unknown class names are created. MEMBERPH identifies the invocation sites, e.g., calls to *clz.*getMethod(?, ...) (*clz.*getField(?)), where `Method` (`Field`) objects are created to represent unknown method (field) names '?' in a known class *clz* of type *type*. If *clz* is also unknown, a different relation (not used here) is called for. Furthermore, MEMBERPHARRAY identifies which placeholder objects represent arrays. For example, a call to *clz.*getDeclaredFields() returns an array of `Field` objects.

CLASSPH(*invo:I, heap:H*)	MEMBERPH(*invo:I, type:T, heap:H*)
MEMBERPHARRAY(*invo:I, array:H*)	NEWINSTANCECAST(*invo:I, castType:T*)
GETCAST(*invo:I, castType:T*)	HIERARCHYTYPE(*castType:T, type:T*)
ARRAYPOINTSTO(*arr:H, heap:H*)	

Fig. 7. Input and output relations for handling target inference

We leverage the type cast information in target inference. The NEWINSTANCE-CAST and GETCAST relations correlate each downcast with their post-dominated invocation sites `newInstance()` and `get()`, respectively. HIERARCHYTYPE(*type, castType*) records all the types such that either ASSIGNABLE(*castType, type*) or ASSIGNABLE(*type, castType*) holds. Finally, the output relation ARRAYPOINTSTO records the heap objects stored in an array heap object *arr*.

Below we describe the target inference rules for the four scenarios above. Note that once a missing target name or a target class or both are inferred, some target propagation rules that could not be applied earlier may be fired.

Scenario I1: Class clz1 = `Class.forName(?)`; A a = (A) clz2.newInstance(). If the string argument *strHeap* marked by '?' in `Class.forName(?)` is not constant (i.e., if STRINGTOCLASS does not hold), then *clz1* points to a placeholder object *phHeap*, indicating a `Class` object of an unknown type. Such pointer information is computed together with the pointer analysis used. If *clz2* points to a placeholder object, then *a* can be inferred to have a type *type* that is assignable to the post-dominating cast *castType*, i.e., *A*. As *type* may not be initialized elsewhere, a call to its "<clinit>()" is conservatively assumed. After this, the second rule in Scenario P2 can be applied to the *clz2.newInstance()* call.

Scenario I1: *Class clz1 = Class.forName(?); A a = (A) clz2.newInstance();*
VARPOINTSTO(*clz1, phHeap*) ←
FORNAME(*invo*), ACTUALARG(*invo, 1, arg*), VARPOINTSTO(*arg, strHeap*),
¬STRINGTOCLASS(*strHeap, _*), CLASSPH(*invo, phHeap*), ACTUALRETURN(*invo, clz1*).
CALLGRAPH(*invo, clinit*), **VARPOINTSTO**(*clz2, clzHeap*) ←
NEWINSTANCE(*invo, clz2*), VARPOINTSTO(*clz2, phHeap*), CLASSPH(*_, phHeap*),
NEWINSTANCECAST(*invo, castType*), ASSIGNABLE(*castType, type*),
TYPE-CLASSHEAP(*type, clzHeap*), MTDSTRING(*clinit, type.toString()+".<clinit>()"*).

Unlike [8], ELF does not use the cast *(A)* to further constrain the `Class` objects that are created for *clz1* and later passed to *clz2*, because the cast operation may not necessarily post-dominate the corresponding `forName()` call.

Scenario   I2: Field[]   fs1=clz.getDeclaredFields();   f2=fs2[i];   a=(A)
f1.get(obj). Let us first consider a real case in Figure 8. In line 1683,
factoryField is obtained as a Field object from an array of Field objects
created in line 1653 for all the fields in URLConnection. In line 1687, the object
returned from get() is cast to java.net.ContentHandlerFactory. By using
the cast information, we know that the call to get() may only access the static
fields of URLConnection with the type java.net.ContentHandlerFactory, its
supertypes or its subtypes. Otherwise, all the static fields in URLConnection
must be assumed. The reason why both the supertypes and subtypes must be
considered was explained in Section 3.2. These type relations are captured by
HIERARCHYTYPE.

```
Application:Eclipse(v4.2.2):
Class:org.eclipse.osgi.framework.internal.core.Framework
1652 public static Field getField(Class clazz, ...) {
1653   Field[] fields = clazz.getDeclaredFields(); ...
1654   for(int i=0; i<fields.length; i++) { ...
1658     return fields[i]; }}
1682 private static void forceContentHandlerFactory(...) {
1683   Field factoryField = getField(URLConnection.class, ...);
1687   java.net.ContentHandlerFactory factory =
            (java.net.ContentHandlerFactory) factoryField.get(null);...}
```

Fig. 8. Target field inference based on the type cast at get()

The same code pattern in Figure 8 also appears in five other places in
Eclipse4. The prior analyses [4, 8, 20] cannot resolve the call get() above since
getDeclaredFields() is ignored. ELF has succeeded in deducing that only two
out of a total of 13 static fields in URLConnection are accessed at the callsite.

Scenario I2: *Field[] fs1 = clz.getDeclaredFields(); f2 = fs2[i]; a = (A) f1.get(obj);*

GETDECLAREDFIELDS(*invo, clz*) ←
   VCALL(*invo, clz, mtd*), MTDSTRING(*mtd,*
   "java.lang.Class: java.lang.reflect.Field[] getDeclaredFields()").
ARRAYPOINTSTO(*phArray, phHeap*), VARPOINTSTO(*fs1, phArray*) ←
   GETDECLAREDFIELDS(*invo, clz*), VARPOINTSTO(*clz, clzHeap*), TYPE-CLASSTYPE(*type, clzHeap*)
   MEMBERPHARRAY(*invo, phArray*), MEMBERPH(*invo, type, phHeap*), ACTUALRETURN(*invo, fs1*).
VARPOINTSTO(*f1, fldHeap*) ←
   GET(*invo, f1*), VARPOINTSTO(*f1, phHeap*),
   MEMBERPH(*getDecInvo, type, phHeap*), GETDECLAREDFIELDS(*getDecInvo, _*),
   GETCAST(*invo, castType*), HIERARCHYTYPE(*castType, fldType*),
   FLDDECL(*type, _, fldType, fld*), FLD-FLDHEAP(*fld, fldHeap*).

It is now easy to understand Scenario I2. The second rule processes each
call to getDeclaredFields(). For each class *clz* of a known type, *type, fs1* is
made to point to *phArray* (a placeholder representing an array), which points to
phHeap (a placeholder representing implicitly all the fields obtained in the call
to getDeclaredFields()). When *f2 = fs2[i]* is analyzed by the pointer analysis
engine, *f1* will point to whatever *fs1* contains if the values of *fs1* flow into *fs2*
and the values of *f2* flow into *f1*. The last rule leverages the type cast information
to resolve *f1* at a get() call to its potential target Field objects, *fldHeap*. As a
result, the second rule in Scenario P4 has now been enabled.

Scenario I3: Field[] fs1=clz.getDeclaredFields(); f2=fs2[i]; f1.set(obj, val). This is similar to Scenario I2, except that the dynamic types of *val* (e.g., the dynamic type of value in line 290 in Figure 9 is java.lang.String) are used to infer the target fields modified. Thus, the second rule in Scenario P5 is enabled.

```
Application:Eclipse(v4.2.2):
Class:org.eclipse.osgi.util.NLS
300 static void load(final String bundleName, Class<?> clazz) {
302    final Field[] fieldArray = clazz.getDeclaredFields();
336    computeMissingMessages(..., fieldArray, ...);...}
267 private static void computeMissingMessages(..., Field[] fieldArray, ...) {
272    for (int i = 0; i < numFields; i++) {
273    Field field = fieldArray[i];
284    String value = "NLS missing message: " + ...;
290    field.set(null, value);...}}
```

Fig. 9. Target field inference based on the dynamic type of value in set()

Note that the set() call that appears in line 290 in Figure 9 cannot be handled by the prior analyses [4, 8, 20] since getDeclaredFields() is ignored. This code pattern appears one more time in line 432 in the same class, i.e., org.eclipse.osgi.util.NLS. These two set() calls are used to initialize all non-final static fields in four classes (by writing a total of 276 fields each time). Based on target inference, ELF has found all the target fields accessed precisely.

Scenario I3: *Field[] fs1 = clz.getDeclaredFields(); f2 = fs2[i]; f1.set(obj, val);*
VARPOINTSTO(*f1, fldHeap*) ←
　SET(*invo, f1*), VARPOINTSTO(*f1, phHeap*), MEMBERPH(*getDecInvo, clzType, phHeap*),
　GETDECLAREDFIELDS(*getDecInvo, _*), ACTUALARG(*invo, 2, val*), VARPOINTSTO(*val, valHeap*),
　HEAPTYPE(*valHeap, type*), ASSIGNABLE(*fldType, type*),
　FLDDECL(*clzType, _, fldType, fld*), FLD-FLDHEAP(*fld, fldHeap*).

Scenario I4: Method m1=clz.getMethod(?, params); a=m2.invoke(obj, args). Let us consider a real case from Eclipse4 in Figure 10. In line 174, the Class objects on which getMethod() is invoked can be deduced from the types of the objects pointed to by target but cmd is read from input. Thus, in line 174, method is unknown even though its target class is known. Note that parameters is explicitly initialized to {this} in line 155. As the type FrameworkCommandInterpreter has not subtypes, we conclude that the corresponding parameter of each potential target method must have this type or one of its supertypes.

```
Application:Eclipse(v4.2.2):
Class:org.eclipse.osgi.framework.internal.core.FrameworkCommandInterpreter
123 public Object execute(String cmd){...
155    Object[] parameters = new Object[]{this}; ...
167    for(int i=0; i<size; i++) {
174    method = target.getClass().getMethod("_"+cmd, parameterTypes);
175    retval = method.invoke(target, parameters); ...}}
```

Fig. 10. Target inference based on the dynamic types of parameters in invoke()

As explained in Section 3.2, we have relied on an intraprocedural analysis to perform the inference when *args* can be analyzed exactly element-wise as is the

case in Figure 10. The MATCHARGS(*args, mtd*) relation over $V \times M$ maintains
target methods *mtd* found from *args* this way.

Scenario I4: *Method m1 = clz.getMethod(?, params); a = m2.invoke(obj, args);*

VARPOINTSTO(*m1, phHeap*) ←
    GETMETHOD(*getInvo, clz*), ACTUALARG(*getInvo, 1, arg*), VARPOINTSTO(*arg, strHeap*),
    ¬MTDDECL(_, *strHeap*, _, _), VARPOINTSTO(*clz, clzHeap*), TYPE-CLASSHEAP(*type, clzHeap*),
    MEMBERPH(*getInvo, type, phHeap*), ACTUALRETURN(*getInvo, m1*).

VARPOINTSTO(*m2, mtdHeap*) ←
    INVOKE(*invo, m2*), VARPOINTSTO(*m2, phHeap*), MEMBERPH(*getInvo, type, phHeap*),
    GETMETHOD(*getInvo, _*), PUBLICMTD(*type, _, mtd*), ACTUALARG(*invo, 2, args*),
    MATCHARGS(*args, mtd*), MTD-MTDHEAP(*mtd, mtdHeap*).

Let us now look at the rules given in Scenario I4 where *clz* points to statically
known class, *type*, but the target methods at `invoke()` are unknown, just like
the the the case illustrated in Figure 10. In the first rule applied to `getMethod()`,
MTHDECL(_, *strHeap*, _, _) does not hold, since *strHeap* is not a constant. As
a result, *m1* points to a placeholder `Method` object (indicating that its method
name is unknown). In the second rule, if *m2* at the `invoke()` callsite points to a
placeholder object, PUBLICMTD will be used to find all the target methods from
the class *type* based on the ones inferred from *args* and stored in MATCHARGS.

Once the `Method` objects at an `invoke` callsite are resolved, the second rule
in Scenario P7 can be applied to resolve the target methods.

Note that the `invoke()` call in Figure 10 cannot be resolved by the prior
analyses [4, 8] since `getMethod()` is either ignored [4] or cannot be handled due
to unknown method name [8]. Based on target inference, ELF has found 50 target
methods at this callsite, out of which 48 are real targets by manual inspection.

4.4 Properties

Like the prior reflection analyses [4, 8, 20], ELF is unsound. Firstly, ELF ignores
the part of the Java reflection API related to dynamic class loading. Second, ELF
infers a target at a reflective callsite if and only if both its target name and its
target class are known to strike a good tradeoff between soundness and precision.
However, ELF's rules can soundly analyze a reflective callsite if all its targets
are known (by its target propagation) or inferred (by its target inference). These
properties follow directly from the Datalog rules formulated in this section.

5 Evaluation

The goal of this research is to produce an open-source reflection analysis to improve the effectiveness of modern pointer analysis tools for Java applications.
We evaluate ELF against a state-of-the-art reflection analysis implemented in
DOOP [4]. Being unsound, both analyses make different tradeoffs among soundness, precision and scalability. Our evaluation has validated the following hypotheses about our self-inferencing approach in handling reflective code.

Soundness and Precision Tradeoffs. ELF can usually resolve more reflective call targets than DOOP while avoiding many of its spurious targets.

Target Propagation vs. Target Inference. ELF can resolve more reflective
call targets when target propagation fails, by inferring the missing target
information with target inference. This can be particularly effective for some
reflection idioms used in practice (as highlighted in Figures 8 – 10).

Effectiveness. When used as part of an under-approximate pointer analysis,
ELF is effective measured in terms of a few popular metrics used.

Scalability. Compared to DOOP, ELF achieves the above results at small analysis time increases for a set of Java programs evaluated.

5.1   Implementation

We have implemented ELF with context sensitivity in DOOP (r160113) [4], a
modern pointer analysis tool for Java. On top of DOOP's 64 Datalog rules for
reflection handling, we have added 207 rules. ELF is comprehensive in handling
the Java reflection API, by tackling significantly more methods than prior work
[4, 8, 9, 20]. Specifically, ELF handles the first eight side-effect methods listed
in Table 1, all *member-introspecting* methods in the reflection API, and four
out of the six *entry* methods, forName(), getClass(), getComponentType()
and .class, shown in Figure 3. For the three side-effect methods on Array,
Array::newInstance is handled similarly as Class::newInstance. We have
ignored Proxy::newProxyInstance(...) in Table 1 and loadClass() and
getProxyClass() in Figure 3 due to the closed-world assumption (Section 3.1).

We have modified the fact generator in DOOP by using an intraprocedural
post-dominance algorithm in SOOT [19] to generate the post-dominance facts,
e.g., NEWINSTANCECAST and GETCAST in Figure 7 (and INVOKECAST not given).

5.2   Experimental Setup

Our setting uses the LogicBlox Datalog engine (v3.9.0), on a Xeon E5-2650 2GHz
machine with 64GB of RAM. We use all the 11 DaCapo benchmarks (v.2006-
10-MR2) and two real-world applications from our reflection-usage study,
Eclipse-4.2.2 and javac-1.7.0. We have excluded Tomcat, Jetty and jEdit,
since neither DOOP nor ELF handles the custom class loaders used in the first
two applications and neither can terminate in three hours for the last one. We
have used recent (large) standard libraries: JDK 1.7.0_25 for Eclipse v4.2.2
and javac v1.7.0 and JDK 1.6.0_45 for the remaining programs. For the *fop*
benchmark from DaCapo, we added org.w3c.dom and org.w3c.css to enable it
to be analyzed. Since java.util.CurrencyData is only used reflectively, we have
made it available in the class path of the fact generator to make it analyzable.

We compare ELF with DOOP's reflection analysis, when both are performed
in the DOOP's pointer analysis framework. Both analyses for a program are
performed in the SSA form of the program generated by Soot, under 1-callsite
context sensitivity implemented in DOOP. An array is treated as a whole.

5.3 Results and Analysis

For each program analyzed, the results presented are obtained from all the analyzed code, in both the application itself and the libraries used.

5.3.1 Soundness and Precision Tradeoffs

ELF and DOOP are unsound in different ways. So either reflection analysis, when working with the same pointer analysis, may resolve some *true* targets that are missed by the other, in general. ELF handles a significant part of the Java reflection API that is ignored by DOOP (Table 2). To eliminate the impact of this aspect of ELF on its analysis results, we have designed a configuration of ELF, called ELF^d, that is restricted to the part of the reflection API handled by DOOP. These include three entry methods, forName(), getClass() and .class, two member-introspecting methods, getDeclaredMethod() and getDeclaredField(), as well as four side-effect methods, invoke(), set(), get() and newInstance() without using the cast inference. ELF^d behaves identically as DOOP except for the following three differences. First, ELF^d applies target propagation since this is more precise than DOOP's analysis in cases when both target method/field names and their target class names are known. Second, ELF^d uses target inference wherever target propagation fails. Finally, ELF^d handles $m=clz$.getDeclaredMethod(mName, ...) ($m=clz$.getDeclaredField(fName)) identically as DOOP for each known Class object C pointed to by clz only when mName (fName) points to a target name that cannot be resolved by either target propagation or target inference. In this case, m is resolved to be the set of all declared targets in the target class C.

There are two caveats. First, a call to getDeclaredMethod("str-const") or getDeclaredField("str-const") is ignored if str-const is absent in the closed-world. Second, in its current release (r160113), DOOP resolves mtd.invoke(o,args) to calls to potential target methods unsoundly by using B from the dynamic types $B[]$ of the array objects obj pointed by args to help filter out many objects passed from args to the corresponding parameters in the target methods.[1] We have modified two rules, LOADHEAPARRAYINDEX in reflective.logic and VARPOINTSTO in context-sensitive.logic, to make this handling sound by using the dynamic types of the objects pointed to by obj instead. Both ELF^d and DOOP handle all such interprocedural assignments exactly this way.

Table 3 compares ELF^d and DOOP in terms of their soundness and precision tradeoffs made when resolving invoke(), get() and set() calls. Both analyses happen to resolve the same number of reflective callsites. For a program, ELF^d usually discovers the same target methods/fields while avoiding many spurious ones introduced by DOOP. We have carried out a recall experiment for all the 11 DaCapo benchmarks by using Tamiflex [2] under its three inputs (small, default and large). We have excluded Eclipse4 and Javac since the former cannot be

---

[1] DOOP has recently fixed this unsound handling in its latest beta version (r5459247), which also includes analyzing some reflective calls not handled in Table 2.

Table 3. Comparing ELF^d and DOOP on reflection resolution. According to this particular configuration of ELF, C denotes the same number of resolved side-effect callsites in both analyses and T denotes the number of target methods/fields resolved by either.

		antlr	bloat	chart	eclipse	fop	hsqldb	jython	luindex	lusearch	pmd	xalan	eclipse4	javac
invoke	C	2	2	5	2	5	-	3	2	2	2	2	6	0
	T DOOP	77	77	1523	77	1730	-	897	77	77	77	77	78	0
	ELF^d	3	3	11	3	11	-	15	3	3	3	3	8	0
set	C	0	0	0	0	0	-	0	0	0	0	0	2	0
	T DOOP	0	0	0	0	0	-	0	0	0	0	0	31	0
	ELF^d	0	0	0	0	0	-	0	0	0	0	0	2	0
get	C	9	9	9	9	9	-	10	9	9	9	9	2	2
	T DOOP	194	194	194	194	194	-	1292	194	194	194	194	132	3401
	ELF^d	28	28	28	28	28	-	1094	28	28	28	28	21	23

analyzed by Tamiflex and the latter has no standard inputs. We found that the set of true targets resolved by ELF^d is always the same as the set of true targets resolved by DOOP for all the benchmarks except jython (analyzed below).

In jython, there is a call m=clz.getDeclaredMethod("typeSetup", ...) in method PyType::addFromClass(), where clz points to a spurious Class object representing the class _builtin_ during the analysis. ELF^d ignores _builtin_ since typeSetup is not one of its members. However, DOOP resolves m to be any of the declared methods in the class, including classDictInit(), opportunistically. As a result, a spurious call edge to _builtin_:: classDictInit() is added from an invoke() site in PyType::fillFromClass(). However, this target method turns out to be called from the (only) invoke site contained in PyJavaClass ::initialize() on a Method object created at the (only) getMethod call, which is also contained in initialize(). By analyzing this target method, DOOP eventually resolves five true target methods named typeSetup at m=clz.getDeclaredMethod ("typeSetup", ...) and seven true target fields at clz.getDeclareField ("exposed_" + name).get(null) in PyType::exposed_decl_get_object(). These 12 targets are missed by ELF^d.

In ELF^d, the primary contributor for ELF's precision improvement (over DOOP) is its target propagation component. It is significantly more beneficial to track both constant class names and constant method/field names simultaneously rather than either alone, as suggested earlier in Figure 4.

5.3.2   Target Propagation vs. Target Inference

To evaluate their individual contributions to the soundness and precision tradeoff made, we have included a version of ELF, named ELF^p, in which only target propagation is used. Table 4 is an analogue of Table 3 except that ELF and ELF^p are compared. By examining their results for a side-effect method across the 13 programs, we find that both component analyses have their respective roles to play. For most programs, ELF has added zero or a moderate number of additional targets on top of ELF^p. This has two implications. First, target propagation can be quite effective for some programs if they exhibit many constant class/method/field names (Figure 4). Second, target inference does not introduce many spurious targets since ELF resolves a reflective target only when

Table 4. Comparing ELF and ELF^p, where C and T are as defined in Table 3

			antlr	bloat	chart	eclipse	fop	hsqldb	jython	luindex	lusearch	pmd	xalan	eclipse4	javac
invoke	ELF^p	C	2	2	9	5	9	6	7	2	2	2	15	15	4
		T	3	3	30	20	30	53	58	3	3	3	31	91	25
	ELF	C	2	2	10	8	10	8	7	2	2	2	16	26	4
		T	3	3	37	94	37	228	58	3	3	3	36	227	25
set	ELF^p	C	0	0	0	0	0	0	0	0	0	0	0	2	0
		T	0	0	0	0	0	0	0	0	0	0	0	2	0
	ELF	C	0	0	0	2	0	0	0	0	0	0	0	4	0
		T	0	0	0	580	0	0	0	0	0	0	0	555	0
get	ELF^p	C	9	9	9	9	9	11	9	9	9	9	9	2	2
		T	28	28	28	28	28	32	28	28	28	28	28	21	23
	ELF	C	9	9	9	9	9	11	11	9	9	9	9	8	2
		T	28	28	28	28	28	41	34	28	28	28	28	35	23

both its name and its target class are known (symbolized by the simultaneous presence of two circles in Figure 5).

From the same recall experiment described earlier, ELF is found to resolve no fewer true targets across the 11 DaCapo benchmarks except jython than DOOP. In jython, ELF has resolved all the true target methods resolved by DOOP by analyzing all member-introspecting methods. In the case of this afore-mentioned call to clz.getDeclareField("exposed_" + name).get(null), ELF fails to discover any target fields due to the absence of cast information. In contrast, DOOP has resolved 1098 target fields declared in all Class objects pointed to by clz, with only 22 sharing exposed_ as the prefix in their names. In our recall experiment, 21 of these 22 targets are accessed. ELF can be easily generalized to infer the target fields accessed (the blue circle shown in Figure 5) at this get() callsite in a disciplined manner. By also exploiting the partially known information about target names (such as the common prefix exposed_), ELF will only need to resolve the 22 target names starting with exposed_ at this callsite.

Target inference can often succeed where target propagation fails, by resolving more reflective targets at some programs. Let us consider Eclipse4. The situation for Eclipse in DaCapo is similar. In Eclipse4, there are two set() callsites with their usage pattern illustrated in Figure 9. ELF^p discovers one target from each callsite. However, ELF has discovered 553 more, one from one of the two callsites and 552 true targets at the two callsites as discussed in Section 4.3. As for get(), ELF has found 14 more targets than ELF^p, with 12 true targets found from the six code fragments (with their usage pattern given in Figure 8), contributing two each, as explained in Section 4.3. Finally, there are two invoke() callsites similar to the one illustrated in Figure 10. ELF has discovered a total of $2 \times 48 = 96$ true target methods invoked at the two callsites. How to resolve one such invoke() call is also discussed in Section 4.3.

When analyzing Java programs, a reflection analysis works together with a pointer analysis. Each benefits from precision improvements from the other. If the pointer analysis used from DOOP is 2-callsite-sensitive+heap, then $C = 5$ and $T = 22$ for ELF^p and $C = 8$ and $T = 83$ for ELF for hsqldb in Table 4.

Table 5. Comparing ELF and DOOP in terms of five pointer analysis precision metrics (*smaller is better*): the average size of points-to sets, the number of edges in the computed call-graph (including regular and reflective call graph edges), the number of virtual calls whose targets cannot be disambiguated, the number of casts that cannot be statically shown safe, and the total points-to set size. The benchmarks for which ELF produced larger numbers than DOOP are highlighted in **bold**.

		average objects per var	call graph edges ~ reachable methods	poly v-calls / reachable v-calls	may-fail casts / reachable casts	size of var points-to (M)
antlr	DOOP^b	29.26	61107~8.9K	2000/33K	1040/1.8K	16.1
	DOOP	29.43	61701~9.1K	2002/33K	1060/1.8K	16.3
	ELF	29.02	61521~9.0K	2001/33K	1051/1.8K	16.1
bloat	DOOP^b	42.36	70661~10.1K	2144/31K	1998/2.8K	32.7
	DOOP	42.29	71202~10.3K	2146/31K	2016/2.8K	32.9
	ELF	42.01	71075~10.3K	2145/31K	2009/2.8K	32.7
chart	DOOP^b	43.06	82148~15.7K	2820/39K	2414/3.7K	47
	DOOP	43.55	85878~16.3K	2928/40K	2534/3.9K	48.8
	ELF	42.99	83872~16.1K	2845/40K	2454/3.8K	48.1
eclipse	DOOP^b	21.11	53738~9.4K	1520/23K	1149/2.0K	12.3
	DOOP	21.31	54357~9.6K	1521/23K	1169/2.0K	12.5
	ELF	**21.41**	**55885~9.9K**	**1582/25K**	**1297/2.2K**	**12.8**
fop	DOOP^b	36.72	77052~15.4K	2751/34K	2082/3.3K	39.7
	DOOP	37.3	80958~16.1K	2871/35K	2177/3.5K	41.5
	ELF	36.7	78758~15.8K	2775/35K	2119/3.4K	40.7
hsqldb	DOOP^b	23.79	73950~13.2K	1888/36K	1765/2.8K	17.8
	DOOP	—	—	—	—	—
	ELF	34.4	78290~13.7K	1939/37K	1825/2.9K	27.5
jython	DOOP^b	28.31	57127~9.8K	1652/24K	1305/2.2K	17.4
	DOOP	107.29	96200~13.4K	2534/29K	2252/3.2K	89
	ELF	**112.09**	93503~12.9K	2478/28K	**2291/3.2K**	88.5
luindex	DOOP^b	16.65	42130~7.9K	1189/18K	829/1.5K	7.7
	DOOP	16.92	42724~8.1K	1191/18K	849/1.5K	7.8
	ELF	16.52	42544~8.0K	1190/18K	840/1.5K	7.7
lusearch	DOOP^b	17.57	45399~8.5K	1368/19K	930/1.6K	8.6
	DOOP	17.82	45992~8.7K	1370/20K	950/1.7K	8.7
	ELF	17.43	45812~8.7K	1369/19K	941/1.6K	8.6
pmd	DOOP^b	18.9	49230~9.3K	1258/21K	1265/2.0K	11.2
	DOOP	19.12	49825~9.5K	1260/21K	1285/2.0K	11.4
	ELF	18.76	49644~9.5K	1259/21K	1276/2.0K	11.2
xalan	DOOP^b	25.84	58356~10.6K	1977/26K	1202/2.1K	15.5
	DOOP	25.95	58896~10.8K	1979/26K	1220/2.1K	15.7
	ELF	**27.25**	**60260~10.9K**	**2085/26K**	**1263/2.1K**	**16.7**
eclipse4	DOOP^b	30.48	57141~10.1K	1634/25K	1223/2.2K	20.3
	DOOP	30.4	58060~10.4K	1671/25K	1335/2.3K	20.4
	ELF	**33.01**	**61129~10.8K**	**1733/27K**	**1410/2.4K**	**23.1**
javac	DOOP^b	48.99	84084~13.1K	4102/35K	2925/4.0K	43.6
	DOOP	54.62	84425~13.3K	4103/36K	2930/4.0K	45
	ELF	**55.56**	**84747~13.4K**	**4105/36K**	**2934/4.0K**	**47.9**

5.3.3   Effectiveness

Table 5 shows the effectiveness of ELF when it is used in an under-approximate pointer analysis, which is usually regarded as being sound in the literature. In addition to DOOP, DOOP^b is its baseline version with reflection ignored except that only calls to newInstance() are analyzed (precisely). As in [6], the same five precision metrics are used, including two clients, poly v-calls and may-fail casts (smaller is better). ELF distinguishes different constant class/method/field names. As mentioned in an afore-mentioned caveat, DOOP has been modified to behave identically. However, DOOP^b distinguishes only different constant class

Table 6. Comparing ELF and DOOP in term of analysis times (secs)

	antlr	bloat	chart	eclipse	fop	hsqldb	jython	luindex	lusearch	pmd	xalan	eclipse4	javac
DOOP	171	299	503	151	442	-	730	103	112	167	215	262	563
ELF	211	309	538	193	804	475	3561	115	122	550	733	445	755

names as it ignores the first `String` parameter in calls to `getDeclaredMethod()` or `getDeclaredField()`. As a result, DOOP^b represents all other string constants (the ones which do not represent class names) with a single string object. To ensure a fair comparison (and follow [6, 15]), we have post-processed the analysis results from both DOOP and ELF using the same string abstraction as in DOOP^b. As DOOP does not exploit the type cast for `newInstance()`, ELF does not do it either. In addition, ELF's capability for handling reflective code on `Array` is turned off as DOOP ignores it.

As all the three analyses are unsound, the results in Table 5 must be interpreted with caution. Having compared ELF^d and DOOP earlier, we expect these results to provide a rough indication about the effectiveness of ELF (relative to DOOP) in reflection resolution. Despite the fact that ELF usually resolves more true targets as explained earlier (Tables 3 and 4), ELF exhibits smaller numbers in eight programs in terms of all the five metrics and slightly larger ones in the remaining five programs (highlighted in bold font). Thus, these results suggest that ELF appears to strike a good tradeoff between soundness and precision.

For `jython`, both DOOP and ELF have significantly increased the code coverage of the underlying pointer analysis used. For the `invoke()` site in `PyType::fillFromClass()`, both DOOP and ELF have resolved 17 methods named `typeSetup` residing in 17 classes, with five being resolved differently as explained earlier. When each of these methods is executed (during our recall experiment), 1 to 47 inner classes are exercised. So this benchmark demonstrates once again the importance of reflection analysis, in practice.

5.3.4 Scalability

Table 6 compares ELF with DOOP in terms of analysis time consumed. In the case of `hsqldb`, DOOP cannot run to completion in three hours. In prior work [6, 15], `jython` and `hsqldb` are often analyzed with reflection disabled and `hsqldb` has its entry point set manually in a special harness. Note that if only target method/field names are tracked as described in [8, 9], the resulting version of ELF cannot terminate in three hours for these two benchmarks. As ELF handles more reflection methods than DOOP, by performing target propagation as well as more elaborate and more time-consuming target inference, ELF exhibits a slowdown of 1.9X on average with `hsqldb` disregarded.

6   Related Work

Static Analysis. In Section 3.3, we have compared ELF in great detail with the two most-closely related static analyses [4, 8]. Briefly, Livshits et al. [8] introduced the first static reflection analysis for Java, which has influenced the design and implementation of several pointer analysis tools [4, 20, 21]. They suggested tracking the flow of string constants and leveraging the cast information to narrow the types of objects created at newInstance(), and implemented their analysis in bddbddb [21], a tool for specifying and querying program analyses. However, ELF is the first to leverage the cast information to resolve targets at other reflective calls, such as invoke(), get() and set().

DOOP [4] includes a few pointer analyses for Java programs using the Datalog language. Its reflection handling can be seen as analogous to adding a sophisticated analysis similar as [8] but in conjunction with a context-sensitive pointer analysis. In addition, DOOP considers more Java features (such as distinguishing instance from static field operations) when handling reflection.

Wala [20] is a tool from IBM Research designed for static analysis. Its reflection handling is similar to DOOP's (i.e., by considering only class types to resolve reflective calls), but without handling Field-related methods.

In summary, existing solutions focus on target propagation by tracking the flow of string constants representing either method/field names [8, 21] or class names [4, 20] in a program. ELF takes a disciplined approach to balance soundness, precision and scalability by exploiting a self-inferencing property inherent in reflective code. As illustrated in Figure 5, ELF resolves a reflective target when both its target class (red circle) and its target method/field name (blue circle) are known, by performing target propagation (through tracking string constants) and target inference (through type inference). In future work, we will improve ELF to infer missing target method/field names based on some partial information obtained from string manipulation operations and to handle the situations when either a target method/field name or a target class type is missing.

Dynamic Analysis. Hirzel et al. [5] proposed an online pointer analysis for handling various dynamic features of Java at run time. To tackle reflection, their analysis instruments a program so that constraints are generated dynamically when the injected code is triggered during program execution. Thus, pointer information is incrementally updated when new constraints are gradually introduced by reflection. This technique on reflection handling can be used in JIT optimizations but may not be suitable for whole-program pointer analysis.

To facilitate (static) pointer analysis, Bodden et al. [2] suggested leveraging the runtime information gathered for reflective calls. Their tool, TAMIFLEX, records usage information of reflective calls in the program at run time, interprets the logging information, and finally, transforms these reflective calls into regular Java method calls. In addition, TAMIFLEX inserts runtime checks to warn the user in cases that the program encounters reflective calls that diverge from the recorded information of previous runs. ELF is complementary to TAMIFLEX by resolving reflective calls statically rather than dynamically.

Soot [19] is a static analysis and optimization framework for Java. For reflective callsites found in the standard libraries, the Soot developers have discovered a list of their possible targets manually. Soot has now a special built-in support for TAMIFLEX [2], allowing some reflective call targets to be found dynamically.

Others. Braux and Noyé [3] provided offline partial evaluation support for reflection in order to perform aggressive compiler optimizations for Java applications. It transforms a program by compiling away the reflection code into regular operations on objects according to their concrete types that are constrained manually. ELF can be viewed as a tool for inferring such constraints automatically.

To increase code coverage, some static analysis tools [4, 21] allow the user to provide ad hoc manual specifications about reflection usage in a program. However, due to the diversity and complexity of applications, it is not yet clear how to do so in a systematic manner. For framework-based web applications, Sridharan et al. [16] introduced a framework that exploits domain knowledge to automatically generate a specification of framework-related behaviours (e.g., reflection usage) by processing both application code and configuration files. ELF may also utilize domain knowledge to analyze some particular configuration files, but only for those reflective call sites that cannot be resolved effectively.

Finally, the dynamic analyses [2, 5] work in the presence of both dynamic class loading and reflection. Nguyen, Potter and Xue [12, 22, 23] introduced an interprocedural side-effect analysis for open-world Java programs (by allowing dynamic class loading but disallowing reflection). Like other static reflection analyses [4, 8, 20, 21], ELF can presently analyze closed-world Java programs only.

7   Conclusion

Reflection analysis is difficult but increasingly important both for sound and for under-approximate pointer analysis for Java applications, especially framework-based applications. This paper advances the state-of-the art in reflection analysis for Java, by (1) presenting some useful findings on reflection usage in Java benchmarks and applications, (2) introducing a self-inferencing resolution approach, (3) contributing an open-source implementation consisting of 207 Datalog rules, and (4) demonstrating the effectiveness of our new reflection analysis.

Acknowledgements. The authors wish to thank the anonymous reviewers for their valuable comments, the DOOP team for making DOOP available, and LogicBlox Inc. for providing us its Datalog engine. This work is supported by an ARC grant, DP130101970.

References

1. Berndl, M., Lhoták, O., Qian, F., Hendren, L.J., Umanee, N.: Points-to analysis using BDDs. In: PLDI 2003, pp. 103–114 (2003)
2. Bodden, E., Sewe, A., Sinschek, J., Oueslati, H., Mezini, M.: Taming reflection: Aiding static analysis in the presence of reflection and custom class loaders. In: ICSE 2011, pp. 241–250 (2011)
3. Braux, M., Noyé, J.: Towards partially evaluating reflection in Java. In: PEPM 2000, pp. 2–11 (2000)

4. Bravenboer, M., Smaragdakis, Y.: Strictly declarative specification of sophisticated points-to analyses. In: OOPSLA 2009, pp. 243–262 (2009)
5. Hirzel, M., Dincklage, D.V., Diwan, A., Hind, M.: Fast online pointer analysis. ACM Trans. Program. Lang. Syst. 29(2) (2007)
6. Kastrinis, G., Smaragdakis, Y.: Hybrid context-sensitivity for points-to analysis. In: PLDI 2013, pp. 423–434 (2013)
7. Lhoták, O., Hendren, L.: Scaling Java points-to analysis using Spark. In: Hedin, G. (ed.) CC 2003. LNCS, vol. 2622, pp. 153–169. Springer, Heidelberg (2003)
8. Livshits, B., Whaley, J., Lam, M.S.: Reflection analysis for Java. In: Yi, K. (ed.) APLAS 2005. LNCS, vol. 3780, pp. 139–160. Springer, Heidelberg (2005)
9. Livshits, B., Whaley, J., Lam, M.S.: Reflection analysis for Java. Technical report, Stanford University (2005)
10. Lu, Y., Shang, L., Xie, X., Xue, J.: An incremental points-to analysis with CFL-reachability. In: Jhala, R., De Bosschere, K. (eds.) Compiler Construction. LNCS, vol. 7791, pp. 61–81. Springer, Heidelberg (2013)
11. Milanova, A., Rountev, A., Ryder, B.G.: Parameterized object sensitivity for points-to analysis for Java. ACM Trans. Softw. Eng. Methodol. 14(1) (2005)
12. Nguyen, P.H., Xue, J.: Interprocedural side-effect analysis and optimisation in the presence of dynamic class loading. In: ACSC 2005, pp. 9–18 (2005)
13. Shang, L., Lu, Y., Xue, J.: Fast and precise points-to analysis with incremental CFL-reachability summarisation. In: ASE 2012, pp. 270–273 (2012)
14. Shang, L., Xie, X., Xue, J.: On-demand dynamic summary-based points-to analysis. In: CGO 2012, pp. 264–274 (2012)
15. Smaragdakis, Y., Bravenboer, M., Lhoták, O.: Pick your contexts well: understanding object-sensitivity. In: POPL 2011, pp. 17–30 (2011)
16. Sridharan, M., Artzi, S., Pistoia, M., Guarnieri, S., Tripp, O., Berg, R.: F4F: Taint analysis of framework-based web applications. In: OOPSLA 2011, pp. 1053–1068 (2011)
17. Sridharan, M., Bodík, R.: Refinement-based context-sensitive points-to analysis for Java. In: PLDI 2006, pp. 387–400 (2006)
18. Sridharan, M., Chandra, S., Dolby, J., Fink, S.J., Yahav, E.: Alias Analysis for Object-Oriented Programs. In: Clarke, D., Noble, J., Wrigstad, T. (eds.) Aliasing in Object-Oriented Programming. LNCS, vol. 7850, pp. 196–232. Springer, Heidelberg (2013)
19. Vallée-Rai, R., Co, P., Gagnon, E., Hendren, L., Lam, P., Sundaresan, V.: Soot - a Java bytecode optimization framework. In: CASCON 1999 (1999)
20. WALA. T.J. Watson Libraries for Analysis, http://wala.sf.net.
21. Whaley, J., Lam, M.S.: Cloning-based context-sensitive pointer alias analysis using binary decision diagrams. In: PLDI 2004, pp. 131–144 (2004)
22. Xue, J., Nguyen, P.H.: Completeness analysis for incomplete object-oriented programs. In: Bodik, R. (ed.) CC 2005. LNCS, vol. 3443, pp. 271–286. Springer, Heidelberg (2005)
23. Xue, J., Nguyen, P.H., Potter, J.: Interprocedural side-effect analysis for incomplete object-oriented software modules. Journal of Systems and Software 80(1), 92–105 (2007)

A   Artifact Description

Authors of the Artifact. Design: Yue Li, Tian Tan and Jingling Xue. Developers: Tian Tan and Yue Li.

Summary. The artifact includes all the four analyses evaluated in the paper, namely Doop, Elf and two variations of Elf, Elf^d and Elf^p.

Content. The artifact package includes:

- an index.html file containing the detailed instructions for using the artifact and for reproducing the experimental results in the paper;
- the four analysis tools, Doop, Elf, Elf^d and Elf^p;
- a modified version of the fact generator provided by Doop;
- a *Python* script exec.py (and some auxiliary scripts) for driving all the provided analyses and formatting the output results;
- all the necessary JREs, applications and benchmarks analyzed.

Elf and its two variations, Elf^d and Elf^p, are all built on top of Doop (version r160113). Elf presently consists of 207 rules (with about 1800 LOC). To simplify repeatability of our experiments, we have provided these analysis configurations directly instead of Doop patches.

Getting the Artifact. The artifact endorsed by the Artifact Evaluation Committee is available free of charge as supplementary material of this paper on SpringerLink. The latest version of our code is available at http://www.cse.unsw.edu.au/~jingling/elf.

Tested Platforms. The artifact works on 64-bit Linux (Ubuntu 13.10 LTS in our case) machine with at least 8 GB of RAM.

License. MIT license (http://opensource.org/license/MIT)

MD5 sum of the Artifact. 024b6fccc7c7bb2edc7dac443f457761

Size of the Artifact. 358M

Constructing Call Graphs of Scala Programs

Karim Ali[1], Marianna Rapoport[1], Ondřej Lhoták[1],
Julian Dolby[2], and Frank Tip[1]

[1] University of Waterloo, Canada
{karim,mrapoport,olhotak,ftip}@uwaterloo.ca
[2] IBM T.J. Watson Research Center, USA
dolby@us.ibm.com

Abstract. As Scala gains popularity, there is growing interest in programming tools for it. Such tools often require call graphs. However, call graph construction algorithms in the literature do not handle Scala features, such as traits and abstract type members. Applying existing call graph construction algorithms to the JVM bytecodes generated by the Scala compiler produces very imprecise results due to type information being lost during compilation. We adapt existing call graph construction algorithms, Name-Based Resolution (RA) and Rapid Type Analysis (RTA), for Scala, and present a formalization based on Featherweight Scala. We evaluate our algorithms on a collection of Scala programs. Our results show that careful handling of complex Scala constructs greatly helps precision and that our most precise analysis generates call graphs with 1.1-3.7 times fewer nodes and 1.5-18.7 times fewer edges than a bytecode-based RTA analysis.

1 Introduction

As Scala [20] gains popularity, the need grows for program analysis tools for it that automate tasks such as refactoring, bug-finding, verification, security analysis, and whole-program optimization. Such tools typically need call graphs to approximate the behavior of method calls. Call graph construction has been studied extensively [11,21]; algorithms vary primarily in how they handle indirect function calls. Several Scala features such as traits, abstract type members, and closures affect method call behavior. However, to our knowledge, no call graph construction algorithms for Scala have yet been proposed or evaluated.

One could construct call graphs of Scala programs by compiling them to JVM bytecode, and then using existing bytecode-based program analysis frameworks such as WALA [15] or SOOT [29] on those generated bytecodes. However, as we shall demonstrate, this approach is not viable because significant type information is lost during the compilation of Scala programs, causing the resulting call graphs to become extremely imprecise. Furthermore, the Scala compiler translates certain language features using hard-to-analyze reflection. While solutions exist for analyzing programs that use reflection, such approaches tend to be computationally expensive or they make very conservative assumptions that result in a loss of precision.

R. Jones (Ed.): ECOOP 2014, LNCS 8586, pp. 54–79, 2014.

Therefore, we explore how to adapt existing call graph construction algorithms for Scala, and we evaluate the effectiveness of such algorithms in practice. Our focus is on adapting low-cost algorithms to Scala, in particular Name-Based Resolution (RA) [26], Class Hierarchy Analysis (CHA) [9], and Rapid Type Analysis (RTA) [6]. We consider how key Scala features such as traits, abstract type members, and closures can be accommodated, and present a family of successively more precise algorithms. In a separate technical report [4], we formally define our most precise algorithm for FS_{alg}, the "Featherweight Scala" subset of Scala that was previously defined by Cremet et al. [8], and prove its correctness by demonstrating that for each execution of a method call in the operational semantics, a corresponding edge exists in the constructed call graph.

Our new algorithms differ primarily in how they handle the two key challenges of analyzing Scala: *traits*, which encapsulate a group of method and field definitions so that they can be mixed into classes, and *abstract type members*, which provide a flexible mechanism for declaring abstract types that are bound during trait composition. We implement our algorithms in the Scala compiler, and compare the number of nodes and edges in the call graphs computed for a collection of publicly available Scala programs. In addition, we evaluate the effectiveness of applying the RTA algorithm to the JVM bytecodes generated by the Scala compiler. For each comparison, we investigate which Scala programming idioms result in differences in cost and precision of the algorithms.

Our experimental results indicate that careful handling of complex Scala features greatly improves call graph precision. We also found that call graphs constructed from the JVM bytecodes using the RTA algorithm are much less precise than those constructed using our source-based algorithms, because significant type information is lost due to the transformations and optimizations performed by the Scala compiler.

In summary, this paper makes the following contributions:

1. We present variations on the RA [26] and RTA [6] algorithms for Scala. To our knowledge, these are the first call graph construction algorithms designed for Scala.
2. We evaluate these algorithms, comparing their relative cost and precision on a set of publicly available Scala programs.
3. We evaluate the application of the RTA algorithm to the JVM bytecodes produced by the Scala compiler, and show that such an approach is not viable because it produces highly imprecise call graphs.

In addition, we have formalized our most precise algorithm and proven its correctness in a separate technical report [4].

The remainder of this paper is organized as follows. Section 2 reviews existing call graph construction algorithms that serve as the inspiration for our work. Section 3 presents a number of motivating examples that illustrate the challenges associated with constructing call graphs of Scala programs. Section 4 presents our algorithms. Section 5 presents the implementation in the context of the Scala compiler. An evaluation of our algorithms is presented in Section 6. Lastly, Section 7 concludes and briefly discusses directions for future work.

2   Background

Algorithms for call graph construction [11] have been studied extensively in the context of object-oriented programming languages such as Java [10, 17], C++ [6] and Self [1], of functional programming languages such as Scheme [24] and ML [12], and of scripting languages such as JavaScript [25]. Roughly speaking, most call graph construction algorithms can be classified as being either *type-based* or *flow-based* [7, 13, 14, 17, 18]. The former class of algorithms uses only local information given by static types to determine possible call targets, whereas the latter analyzes the program's data flow.

We focus on type-based algorithms, so we will briefly review some important type-based call graph construction algorithms for object-oriented languages upon which our work is based. In the exposition of these algorithms, we use a constraint notation that is equivalent to that of [27], but that explicitly represents call graph edges using a relation '$\mapsto$' between call sites and methods.

Name-Based Resolution (RA). The main challenge in constructing call graphs of object-oriented programs is in approximating the behavior of dynamically dispatched (virtual) method calls. Early work (see, e.g., [26]) simply assumed that a virtual call $e.m(\cdots)$ can invoke any method with the same name m. This approach can be captured using the following constraints:

$$\frac{}{main \in R} \text{ RA}_{\text{MAIN}} \qquad \begin{array}{c} \text{call } c : e.m(\ldots) \text{ occurs in method } M \\ \text{method } M' \text{ has name } m \\ \hline M \in R \end{array}$$

$$\frac{c \mapsto M}{M \in R} \text{ RA}_{\text{REACHABLE}} \qquad \frac{\begin{array}{c} \text{call } c : e.m(\ldots) \text{ occurs in method } M \\ \text{method } M' \text{ has name } m \\ M \in R \end{array}}{c \mapsto M'} \text{ RA}_{\text{CALL}}$$

Intuitively, rule RA$_{\text{MAIN}}$ reads "the main method is reachable" by including it in the set R of reachable methods. Rule RA$_{\text{CALL}}$ states that "if a method is reachable, and a call site $c : e.m(\ldots)$ occurs in its body, then every method with name m is reachable from c." Finally, rule RA$_{\text{REACHABLE}}$ states that any method M reachable from a call site c is contained in the set R of reachable methods.

Class Hierarchy Analysis (CHA). Obviously, Name-Based Resolution can become very imprecise if a class hierarchy contains unrelated methods that happen to have the same name. Class Hierarchy Analysis [9] improves upon name-based resolution by using the static type of the receiver expression of a method call in combination with class hierarchy information to determine what methods may be invoked from a call site. Following the notation of [27], we use $StaticType(e)$ to denote the static type of an expression e, and $StaticLookup(C, m)$ to denote the method definition that is invoked when method m is invoked on an object with run-time type C. Using these definitions, CHA is defined as follows:

$$\frac{}{main \in R} \text{ CHA}_{\text{MAIN}} \qquad \begin{array}{c} \text{call } c : e.m(\ldots) \text{ occurs in method } M \\ C \in SubTypes(StaticType(e)) \\ StaticLookup(C, m) = M' \\ \hline M \in R \end{array}$$

$$\frac{c \mapsto M}{M \in R} \text{ CHA}_{\text{REACHABLE}} \qquad \frac{\begin{array}{c} \text{call } c : e.m(\ldots) \text{ occurs in method } M \\ C \in SubTypes(StaticType(e)) \\ StaticLookup(C, m) = M' \\ M \in R \end{array}}{c \mapsto M'} \text{ CHA}_{\text{CALL}}$$

Rules CHA_{MAIN} and $\text{CHA}_{\text{REACHABLE}}$ are the same as their counterparts for RA. Intuitively, rule CHA_{CALL} now reads: "if a method is reachable, and a call site $c : e.m(\ldots)$ occurs in the body of that method, then every method with name m that is inherited by a subtype of the static type of e is reachable from c."

Rapid Type Analysis (RTA). Bacon and Sweeney [5,6] observed that CHA produces very imprecise results when only a subset of the classes in an application is instantiated. In such cases, CHA loses precision because, effectively, it assumes for a method call $e.m(\cdots)$ that all subtypes of the static type of e may arise at run time. In order to mitigate this loss of precision, RTA maintains a set of types $\hat{\Sigma}$ that have been instantiated in reachable methods. This set is used to approximate the types that a receiver expression may assume at run time. The constraint formulation of RTA is as follows:

$$\frac{}{main \in R} \text{ RTA}_{\text{MAIN}}$$

$$\frac{\begin{array}{c}\text{"new } C() \text{" occurs in } M \\ M \in R\end{array}}{C \in \hat{\Sigma}} \text{ RTA}_{\text{NEW}}$$

$$\frac{\begin{array}{c}\text{call } e.m(\ldots) \text{ occurs in method } M \\ C \in SubTypes(StaticType(e)) \\ StaticLookup(C, m) = M' \\ M \in R \\ C \in \hat{\Sigma}\end{array}}{c \mapsto M'} \text{ RTA}_{\text{CALL}}$$

$$\frac{c \mapsto M}{M \in R} \text{ RTA}_{\text{REACHABLE}}$$

Rules RTA_{MAIN} and $\text{RTA}_{\text{REACHABLE}}$ are again the same as before. Intuitively, RTA_{CALL} refines CHA_{CALL} by requiring that $C \in \hat{\Sigma}$, and rule RTA_{NEW} reads: "$\hat{\Sigma}$ contains the classes that are instantiated in a reachable method."

Sallenave and Ducourneau [22] recently presented an extension of RTA for the C# language that determines the types with which parameterized classes are instantiated by maintaining sets of type tuples for parameterized classes and methods. They use their analysis to generate efficient CLI code for embedded applications that avoids expensive boxing/unboxing operations on primitive types, while permitting a space-efficient shared representation for reference types.

3 Motivating Examples

Before presenting our algorithms in Section 4, we briefly review the Scala features that pose the most significant challenges for call graph construction.

3.1 Traits

Traits are one of the cornerstone features of Scala. They provide a flexible mechanism for distributing the functionality of an object over multiple reusable components. Traits are similar to Java's abstract classes in the sense that they may provide definitions of methods, and in that they cannot be instantiated by themselves. However, they resemble Java interfaces in the sense that a trait may extend ("mix-in") multiple super-traits.

```
1  object Traits {                        10    trait C {
2    trait A {                            11      def foo = println ("C.foo")
3      def foo = println ("A.foo")        12    }
4      def bar                            13
5    }                                    14    def main(args: Array[String]) =
6    trait B {                            15      { (new A with B).bar }
7      def foo                            16  }
8      def bar = this.foo
9    }
```

Fig. 1. A Scala program illustrating the use of traits

Figure 1 shows an example program that declares a trait A in which a concrete method foo and an abstract method bar are defined. The program also declares a trait B that defines a concrete method bar and an abstract method foo. Lastly, trait C defines a concrete method foo. The program contains a main method that creates an object by composing A and B, and then calls bar on that object.

Before turning our attention to call graph construction, we need to consider how method calls are resolved in Scala. In Scala, the behavior of method calls depends on the class linearization order of the receiver object [19, Section 5.1.2]. The *linearization* of a class C with parents C_1 with $\cdots$ with C_n is defined as:

$$\mathcal{L}(C) = C, \mathcal{L}(C_n) \vec{+} \cdots \vec{+} \mathcal{L}(C_1)$$

where $\vec{+}$ denotes concatenation where elements of the right operand replace identical elements of the left one[1]. Scala defines the set of *members* of a class in terms of its linearization. Ignoring a number of complicating factors detailed in the Scala specification [19, §5.1.3 and §5.1.4], the members of a class C include all members m declared in classes in $\mathcal{L}(C)$, except for those overridden in classes that precede C in the linearization order. Given this notion of class membership, the resolution of method calls is straightforward: a call $x.m(\cdots)$ where x has type C at run time dispatches to the unique member named m in C.

For the example of Figure 1, the linearization order of type new A with B on line 15 is: X, B, A (here, we use X to denote the anonymous class that is implicitly declared by the allocation expression new A with B). Following the definitions above, the set of members of X is: { B.bar, A.foo }. Hence, the call to bar on line 15 resolves to B.bar. Using a similar argument, the call to foo on line 8 resolves to A.foo. Therefore, executing the program will print "A.foo".

Implications for call graph construction. The presence of traits complicates the construction of call graphs because method calls that occur in a trait typically cannot be resolved by consulting the class hierarchy alone. In the example of Figure 1, B.bar contains a call this.foo on line 8. How should a call graph construction algorithm approximate the behavior of this call, given that there is no inheritance relation between A, B, and C?

---

[1] The presence of an allocation expression such as new C with D is equivalent to a declaration of a new empty class with parents C with D.

To reason about the behavior of method calls in traits, a call graph construction algorithm needs to make certain assumptions about how traits are combined. One very conservative approach would be to assume that a program may combine each trait with any set of other traits in the program in any order[2], such that the resulting combination is syntactically correct[3]. Then, for each of these combinations, one could compute the members contained in the resulting type, and approximate the behavior of calls by determining the method that is selected in each case. For the program of Figure 1, this approach would assume that B is composed with either A or with C. In the former case, the call on line 8 is assumed to be invoked on an object of type A with B (or B with A), and would dispatch to A.foo. In the latter, the call is assumed to be invoked on an object of type C with B (or B with C), and would dispatch to C.foo. Hence, a call graph would result in which both A.foo and C.foo are reachable from the call on line 8.

The conservative approach discussed above is likely to be imprecise and inefficient in cases where a program contains many traits that can be composed with each other. For practical purposes, a better approach is to determine the set of combinations of traits that actually occur in the program, and to use that set of combinations of traits to resolve method calls. Returning to our example program, we observe that the only combination of traits is A with B, on line 15. If the call on line 8 is dispatched on an object of this type, it will dispatch to A.foo, as previously discussed. Hence, this approach would create a smaller call graph in which there is only one outgoing edge for the call on line 8.

This more precise approach requires that the set of all combinations of traits in the program can be determined. The conservative approach could still have merit in cases where this information is not available (e.g., libraries intended to be extended with code that instantiates additional trait combinations).

3.2   Abstract Type Members

Scala supports a flexible mechanism for declaring *abstract type members* in traits and classes. A *type declaration* [19, §4.3] defines a name for an abstract type, along with upper and lower bounds that impose constraints on the concrete types that it could be bound to. An abstract type is bound to a concrete type when its declaring trait is composed with (or extended by) another trait that provides a concrete definition in one of two ways: either it contains a class or trait with the same name as the abstract type, or it declares a *type alias* [19, §4.3] that explicitly binds the abstract type to some specified concrete type.

Figure 2 shows a program that declares traits X, Y, Z, and HasFoo. Traits X and Y each declare a member class A that is a subclass of HasFoo. Traits Y and Z each declare an abstract type member B and a field o, which is assigned a new

---

[2] Note that an X with Y object may behave differently from a Y with X object in certain situations because these objects have different linearization orders.

[3] If multiple traits that provide concrete definitions of the same method are composed, all but the last of these definitions in the linearization order must have the override modifier in order for the composition to be syntactically correct [19, Section 5.1.4].

```
17  object AbstractTypeMembers {        31      ...
18    trait HasFoo {                    32      type B = A
19      def foo: Unit                   33      val o = new A
20    }                                 34    }
21    trait X {                         35    trait Z {
22      class A extends HasFoo {        36      type B <: HasFoo
23        def foo = println("X.A.foo")  37      val o: B
24      }                               38      def bar = o.foo
25    }                                 39    }
26    trait Y {                         40
27      class A extends HasFoo {        41    def main(args: Array[String]) =
28        def foo = println("Y.A.foo")  42      { (new Y with Z {}).bar }
29      }                               43  }
30      ...
```

Fig. 2. A Scala program illustrating the use of abstract type members

A object in Y. Note that Y defines its B to be the same as Y.A. Observe that the abstract member type B of Z has a bound HasFoo, and that o is declared to be of type B. The presence of this bound means that we can call foo on o on line 38.

On line 42, the program creates an object by composing Y with Z, and calls bar on it. Following Scala's semantics for method calls, this call will dispatch to Z.bar. To understand how the call o.foo on line 38 is resolved, we must understand how abstract type members are bound to concrete types as a result of trait composition. In this case, the composition of Y with Z means that the types Y.B and Z.B are unified. Since Y.B was defined to be the same as Y.A, it follows that the abstract type member Z.B is bound to the concrete type Y.A. Thus, executing the call on line 38 dispatches to Y.A.foo, so the program prints "Y.A.foo".

Implications for call graph construction. How could a call graph construction algorithm approximate the behavior of calls such as o.foo in Figure 2, where the receiver expression's type is abstract? A conservative solution relies on the bound of the abstract type as follows: For a call $o.f(\cdots)$ where o is of an abstract type T with bound B, one could assume the call to dispatch to definitions of $f(\cdots)$ in any subtype of B. This approach is implemented in our TCA^{bounds} algorithm and identifies both X.A.foo and Y.A.foo as possible targets of the call on line 38.

However, the above approach may be imprecise if certain subtypes of the bound are not instantiated. Our TCA^{expand} algorithm implements a more precise approach that considers how abstract type members are bound to concrete types in observed combinations of traits, in the same spirit of the more precise treatment of trait composition discussed above. In Figure 2, the program only creates an object of type Y with Z, and Z.B is bound to Y.A in this particular combination of traits. Therefore, the call on line 38 must dispatch to Y.A.foo.

Scala's parameterized types [19, §3.2.4] resemble abstract type members and are handled similarly. Similar issues arise in other languages with generics [22].

```
44  object Closures {
45      def bar1(y:  () => A) = { y() }
46      def bar2(z:  () => B) = { z() }
47
48      class A
49      class B
```

```
50      def main(args: Array[String]) = {
51          val foo1 = () => { new A }
52          val foo2 = () => { new B }
53          this.bar1(foo1)
54          this.bar2(foo2)
55      }
56  }
```

Fig. 3. A Scala program illustrating the use of closures

3.3   Closures

Scala allows functions to be bound to variables and passed as arguments to other functions. Figure 3 illustrates this feature, commonly known as "closures". On line 51, the program creates a function and assigns it to a variable foo1. The function's declared type is () => A, indicating that it takes no parameters and returns an object of type A. Likewise, line 52 assigns to foo2 a function that takes no arguments and returns a B object.

Next, on line 53, bar1 is called with foo1 as an argument. Method bar1 (line 45) binds this closure to its parameter y, which has declared type () => A, and then calls the function bound to y. Similarly, on line 54 bar2 is called with foo2 as an argument. On line 46, this closure is bound to a parameter z and then invoked. From the simple data flow in this example, it is easy to see that the call y() on line 45 always calls the function that was bound to foo1 on line 51, and that the call z() on line 46 always calls the function that was bound to foo2 on line 52.

Implications for call graph construction. In principle, one could use the declared types of function-valued expressions and the types of the closures that have been created to determine if a given call site could invoke a given function. For example, the type of y is () => A, and line 53 creates a closure that can be bound to a variable of this type. Therefore, a call graph edge needs to be constructed from the call site y() to the closure on line 53. By the same reasoning, a call graph edge should be constructed from the call site z() to the closure on line 54.

Our implementation takes a different approach to handle closures. Rather than performing the analysis at the source level, we apply it after the Scala compiler has "desugared" the code by transforming closures into anonymous classes that extend the appropriate scala.runtime.AbstractFunctionN. Each such class has an apply() method containing the closure's original code. Figure 4 shows a desugared version of the program of Figure 3. After this transformation, closures can be treated as ordinary parameterized Scala classes without loss of precision. This has the advantage of keeping our implementation simple and uniform.

3.4   Calls on the Variable this

Figure 5 shows a program that declares a trait A with subclasses B and C. Trait A declares an abstract method foo, which is overridden in B and C, and a concrete

```
57  object Closures {                          72    val foo2: () => B = {
58    def bar1(y: () => A) = { y.apply() }    73    class $anonfun extends
59    def bar2(z: () => B) = { z.apply() }    74      scala.runtime.
60                                             75        AbstractFunction0[B] {
61    class A                                  76        def apply(): B = {
62    class B                                  77          new B()
63                                             78        }
64    def main(args: Array[String]) = {       79    };
65      val foo1: () => A = {                  80      new $anonfun()
66      class $anonfun extends                 81    };
67        scala.runtime.AbstractFunction0[A] { 82    this.bar1(foo1)
68        def apply(): A = { new A() }         83    this.bar2(foo2)
69      };                                     84  }
70      new $anonfun()                         85 }
71    };
```

Fig. 4. Desugared version of the program of Figure 3 (slightly simplified)

```
86  object This {                   96   class C extends A {
87    trait A {                     97     def foo = println("C.foo")
88      def foo                     98     override def bar = println("C.bar")
89      // can only call B.foo      99   }
90      def bar = this.foo         100
91    }                            101   def main(args: Array[String]) = {
92                                 102     (new B).bar
93    class B extends A {          103     (new C).bar
94      def foo = println("B.foo") 104   }
95    }                            105 }
```

Fig. 5. A Scala program illustrating a call on this

method bar, which is overridden in C (but not in B). The program declares a main method that calls bar on objects of type B and C (lines 102–103). Executing the call to bar on line 102 dispatches to A.bar(). Executing the call this.foo() in that method will then dispatch to B.foo(). Finally, executing the call to bar on line 103 dispatches to C.bar, so the program prints "B.foo", then "C.bar".

Consider how a call graph construction algorithm would approximate the behavior of the call this.foo() at line 90. The receiver expression's type is A, so CHA concludes that either B.foo or C.foo could be invoked, since B and C are subtypes of A. However, note that this cannot have type C in A.bar because C provides an overriding definition of bar. Stated informally, this cannot have type C inside A.bar because then execution would not have arrived in A.bar in the first place. The TCA$^{expand\text{-}this}$ algorithm, presented in Section 4, exploits such knowledge. Care must be taken in the presence of super-calls, as we will discuss.

3.5   Bytecode-Based Analysis

The above examples show that Scala's traits and abstract type members pose new challenges for call graph construction. Several other Scala features, such as path-dependent types and structural types, introduce further complications, and will be discussed in Section 5. At this point, the reader may wonder if all these complications could be avoided by simply analyzing the JVM bytecodes produced by the Scala compiler.

We experimentally determined that such an approach is not viable for two reasons. First, the translation of Scala source code to JVM bytecode involves significant code transformations that result in the loss of type information, causing the computed call graphs to become imprecise. Second, the Scala compiler generates code containing hard-to analyze reflection for certain Scala idioms.

Loss of Precision. Consider Figure 6, which shows JVM bytecode produced by the Scala compiler for the program of Figure 3. As can be seen in the figure, the closures that were defined on lines 51 and 52 in Figure 3 have been translated into classes Closures$$anonfun$1 (lines 128–138 in Figure 6) and Closures$$anonfun$2 (lines 140–150). These classes extend scala.runtime.AbstractFunction0<T>, which is used for representing closures with no parameters at the bytecode level. Additionally, these classes provide overriding definitions for the apply method inherited by scala.runtime.AbstractFunction0<T> from its super-class scala.Function0<T>. This apply method returns an object of type T. The issue to note here is that Closures$$anonfun$1 and Closures$$anonfun$2 each instantiate the type parameter T with different types, Closures$A and Closures$B, respectively. Therefore, their apply methods return objects of type Closures$A and Closures$B. However, at the bytecode level, all type parameters are erased, so that we have a situation where:

- scala.Function0.apply has return type Object
- Closures$$anonfun$1.apply   and   Closures$$anonfun$2.apply   each   override scala.Function0.apply and also have return type Object
- there are two calls to scala.Function0.apply on lines 118 and 123

Given   this   situation,   the   RTA   algorithm   creates   edges   to   Closures$$anonfun$1.apply   and   Closures$$anonfun$2.apply   from   each   of   the   calls on lines 118 and 123. In other words, a bytecode-based RTA analysis creates 4 call graph edges for the closure-related calls, whereas the analysis of Section 3.3 only created 2 edges. In Section 6, we show that this scenario commonly arises in practice, causing bytecode-based call graphs to become extremely imprecise.

Reflection in Generated Code. We detected several cases where the Scala compiler generates code that invokes methods using java.lang.reflect.Method.invoke(). In general, the use of reflection creates significant problems for static analysis, because it must either make very conservative assumptions that have a detrimental effect on precision (e.g., assuming that calls to java.lang.reflect.Method.invoke() may invoke any method in the application) or the analysis will become unsound.

Figure 7 shows a small example (taken from the ENSIME program, see Section 6) for which the Scala compiler generates code containing reflection.

```
106  public final class Closures$ {
107    public void main(java.lang.String []);
108       0: new Closures$$anonfun$1
109       ...
110       8: new Closures$$anonfun$2
111       ...
112      18: invokevirtual Closures$.bar1(scala.Function0) : void
113       ...
114      23: invokevirtual Closures$.bar2(scala.Function0) : void
115      26: return
116    public void bar1(scala.Function0);
117       0: aload_1
118       1: invokeinterface scala.Function0.apply() : java.lang.Object
119       6: pop
120       7: return
121    public void bar2(scala.Function0);
122       0: aload_1
123       1: invokeinterface scala.Function0.apply() : java.lang.Object
124       6: pop
125       7: return
126  }
127
128  public final class Closures$$anonfun$1 extends scala.runtime.AbstractFunction0 {
129    public final Closures$A apply();
130       0: new Closures$A
131       3: dup
132       4: invokespecial Closures$A()
133       7: areturn
134    public final java.lang.Object apply();
135       0: aload_0
136       1: invokevirtual Closures$$anonfun$1.apply() : Closures$A
137       4: areturn
138  }
139
140  public final class Closures$$anonfun$2 extends scala.runtime.AbstractFunction0 {
141    public final Closures$B apply();
142       0: new Closures$B
143       3: dup
144       4: invokespecial Closures$B()
145       7: areturn
146    public final java.lang.Object apply();
147       0: aload_0
148       1: invokevirtual Closures$$anonfun$2.apply() : Closures$B
149       4: areturn
150  }
```

Fig. 6. JVM bytecode produced by the Scala compiler for the program of Figure 3

```
151  trait ClassHandler
152
153  object LuceneIndex {
154    def buildStaticIndex (): Int = {
155      val handler = new ClassHandler {
156        var classCount = 0
157        var methodCount = 0
158      }
159      handler.classCount + handler.methodCount
160    }
161  }
```

Fig. 7. A Scala program for which the compiler generates code containing reflective method calls (taken from the ENSIME program, see Section 6)

4   Algorithms

We present a family of call graph construction algorithms using generic inference rules, in the same style that we used in Section 2. The algorithms presented here are: TCA^{names}, a variant of RA that considers only types instantiated in reachable code, TCA^{bounds}, a variant of RTA adapted to deal with Scala's trait composition and abstract type members, TCA^{expand}, which handles abstract type members more precisely, and TCA$^{expand\text{-}this}$, which is more precise for call sites where the receiver is this.

We use Figure 8 to illustrate differences between the algorithms. When executed, the call site on line 172 calls method B.foo; our different algorithms resolve this call site to various subsets of the foo methods in classes A, B, C, and D.

```
162  class A { def foo = "A.foo" }
163  class B extends A { override def foo = "B.foo" }
164  class C { def foo = "C.foo" }
165  class D { def foo = "D.foo" }
166  class CallSiteClass [T <: A](val receiver : T) {
167    def callsite = {
168      /* resolves to:
169       *   TCA^expand: { B.foo }, TCA^bounds: { B.foo, A.foo }
170       *   TCA^names: { B.foo, A.foo, C.foo } ,  RA: { B.foo, A.foo, C.foo, D.foo }
171       */
172      receiver .foo
173    }
174  }
175  def main(args: Array[String ]): Unit = {
176    new A
177    val receiver = new B
178    new C
179    val callSiteClass = new CallSiteClass[B]( receiver );
180    callSiteClass . callsite
181  }
```

Fig. 8. A Scala program illustrating the varying precision of the analyses

4.1   TCA^{names}

The RA algorithm of Section 2 is sound for Scala because it resolves calls based only on method names, and makes no use of types. However, it is imprecise because it considers as possible call targets all methods that have the appropriate name, even those in unreachable code. For Figure 8, RA resolves the call site as possibly calling all four foo methods, even though D is never instantiated in code reachable from main. Since RA already computes a set R of reachable methods, we extend it to consider only classes and traits instantiated in reachable methods.

We add rule RTA_{NEW} from RTA, which computes a set $\hat{\Sigma}$ of types instantiated in reachable methods. The CALL rule[4] is adapted as follows to make use of $\hat{\Sigma}$:

$$\frac{\begin{array}{c} \text{call } c : e.m(\ldots) \text{ occurs in method } M \\ \text{method } M' \text{ has name } m \\ \boxed{\text{method } M' \text{ is a member of type } C} \\ M \in R \qquad \boxed{C \in \hat{\Sigma}} \end{array}}{c \mapsto M'} \quad TCA_{CALL}^{names}$$

The resulting TCA^{names} analysis consists of the rule RTA_{NEW} and the rules of RA, except that RA_{CALL} is replaced with TCA_{CALL}^{names}. In TCA_{CALL}^{names}, a method is considered as a possible call target only if it is a member of some type C that has been instantiated in a reachable method in R[5].

For the program of Figure 8, TCA^{names} resolves the call site to A.foo, B.foo, and C.foo, but not D.foo because D is never instantiated in reachable code.

4.2 TCA^{bounds}

To improve precision, analyses such as RTA and CHA use the static type of the receiver e to restrict its possible runtime types. Specifically, the runtime type C of the receiver of the call must be a subtype of the static type of e.

A key difficulty when analyzing a language with traits is enumerating all subtypes of a type, as both CHA and RTA do in the condition $C \in SubTypes(StaticType(e))$ in rules CHA_{CALL} and RTA_{CALL} of Section 2. Given a trait T, any composition of traits containing T is a subtype of T. Therefore, enumerating possible subtypes of T requires enumerating all compositions of traits. Since a trait composition is an ordered list of traits, the number of possible compositions is exponential in the number of traits[6].

In principle, an analysis could make the conservative assumption that all compositions of traits are possible, and therefore that any method defined in any trait can override any other method of the same name and signature in any other trait (a concrete method overrides another method with the same name and signature occurring later in the linearization of a trait composition). The resulting analysis would have the same precision as the name-based algorithms RA and TCA^{names}, though it would obviously be much less efficient.

Therefore, we consider only combinations of traits occurring in reachable methods of the program. This set of combinations is used to approximate the

---

[4] When we present an inference rule in this section, we use shading to highlight which parts of the rule are modified relative to similar preceding rules.

[5] Calls on super require special handling, as will be discussed in Section 5.

[6] Although some trait compositions violate the well-formedness rules of Scala, such violations are unlikely to substantially reduce the exponential number of possible compositions. Moreover, the well-formedness rules are defined in terms of the members of a specific composition, so it would be difficult to enumerate only well-formed compositions without first examining all of them.

behavior of method calls. In essence, this is similar to the closed-world assumption of RTA. Specifically, the TCA^{bounds} analysis includes the rule RTA_{NEW} to collect the set $\hat{\Sigma}$ of trait combinations occurring at reachable allocation sites. The resulting set is used in the following call resolution rule:

$$\frac{\begin{array}{c} \text{call } e.m(\ldots) \text{ occurs in method } M \\ \boxed{C \in SubTypes(StaticType(e))} \\ \text{method } M' \text{ has name } m \\ \text{method } M' \text{ is a member of type } C \\ M \in R \qquad C \in \hat{\Sigma} \end{array}}{c \mapsto M'} \; \text{TCA}^{bounds}_{\text{CALL}}$$

The added check $C \in SubTypes(StaticType(e))$ relies on the subtyping relation defined in the Scala language specification, which correctly handles complexities of the Scala type system such as path-dependent types.

According to Scala's definition of subtyping, abstract types do not have subtypes, so $\text{TCA}^{bounds}_{\text{CALL}}$ does not apply. Such a definition of subtyping is necessary because it cannot be determined locally, just from the abstract type, which actual types will be bound to it elsewhere in the program. However, every abstract type in Scala has an upper bound (if it is not specified explicitly, scala.Any is assumed), so an abstract type T can be approximated using its upper bound B:

$$\frac{\begin{array}{c} \text{call } e.m(\ldots) \text{ occurs in method } M \\ \boxed{StaticType(e) \text{ is an abstract type with upper bound } B} \\ C \in SubTypes(\boxed{B}) \\ \text{method } M' \text{ has name } m \\ \text{method } M' \text{ is a member of type } C \\ M \in R \qquad C \in \hat{\Sigma} \end{array}}{c \mapsto M'} \; \text{TCA}^{bounds}_{\text{ABSTRACT-CALL}}$$

For the program of Figure 8, TCA^{bounds} resolves the call site to A.foo and B.foo, but not D.foo because D is never instantiated, and not C.foo, because C is not a subtype of A, the upper bound of the static type T of the receiver.

4.3 TCA^{expand}

The TCA^{bounds} analysis is particularly imprecise for abstract types that do not have a declared upper bound, since using the default upper bound of scala.Any makes the bound-based analysis as imprecise as the name-based analysis.

It is more precise to consider only concrete types with which each abstract type is instantiated, similar to the approach of [22]. To this end, we introduce a mapping $expand()$, which maps each abstract type[7] T to those concrete types with which it has been instantiated:

---

[7] Similar rules (not shown) are needed to handle the type parameters of generic types and type-parametric methods. Our implementation fully supports these cases.

$$\frac{\begin{array}{c} C \in \hat{\Sigma} \\ \text{``type } A = B\text{'' is a member of } C \\ D \text{ is a supertype of } C \\ \text{``type } A\text{'' is a member of } D \end{array}}{B \in expand(D.A)} \; \text{TCA}^{expand}_{\text{EXPAND-TYPE}}$$

$$\frac{\begin{array}{c} R \in expand(S) \\ S \in expand(T) \end{array}}{R \in expand(T)} \; \text{TCA}^{expand}_{\text{EXPAND-TRANS}}$$

$$\frac{\begin{array}{c} C \in \hat{\Sigma} \\ \text{``trait } A \; \{ \, \ldots \}\text{'' is a member of } C \\ D \text{ is a supertype of } C \\ \text{``type } A\text{'' is a member of } D \end{array}}{C.A \in expand(D.A)} \; \text{TCA}^{expand}_{\text{EXPAND-TRAIT}}$$

The $\text{TCA}^{bounds}_{\text{CALL}}$ rule is then updated to use the $expand()$ mapping to determine the concrete types bound to the abstract type of a receiver:

$$\frac{\begin{array}{c} \text{call } e.m(\ldots) \text{ occurs in method } M \\ StaticType(e) \text{ is an abstract type } T \\ C \in SubTypes(\; expand(T) \;) \\ \text{method } M' \text{ has name } m \\ \text{method } M' \text{ is a member of type } C \\ M \in R \qquad C \in \hat{\Sigma} \end{array}}{c \mapsto M'} \; \text{TCA}^{expand}_{\text{ABSTRACT-CALL}}$$

Rule $\text{TCA}^{expand}_{\text{EXPAND-TYPE}}$ handles situations such as the one where a type assignment type A = B is a member of some instantiated trait composition C. Now, if a supertype D of C declares an abstract type A, then B is a possible concrete instantiation of the abstract type D.A, and this fact is recorded in the $expand()$ mapping by $\text{TCA}^{expand}_{\text{EXPAND-TYPE}}$. Rule $\text{TCA}^{expand}_{\text{EXPAND-TRAIT}}$ handles a similar case where an abstract type is instantiated by defining a member trait with the same name. The right-hand-side of a type assignment might be abstract, so it is necessary to compute the transitive closure of the $expand()$ mapping (rule $\text{TCA}^{expand}_{\text{EXPAND-TRANS}}$).

Cycles among type assignments may exist. In Scala, cyclic references between abstract type members are a compile-time error. However, recursion in generic types is allowed. For example, the parameter B in a generic type A[B] could be instantiated with A[B] itself, leading to B representing an unbounded sequence of types A[B], A[A[B]], ... This kind of recursion can be detected either by limiting the size of $expand(T)$ for each abstract type to some fixed bound, or by checking for occurrences of T in the expansion $expand(T)$. The current version of our implementation limits the size of $expand(T)$ to 1000 types. This bound was never exceeded in our experimental evaluation, implying that recursive types did not occur in the benchmark programs. The same issue also occurs in Java and C#, and was previously noted by Sallenave and Ducourneau [22]. Their implementation issues a warning when it detects the situation. Our algorithm resolves the issue soundly: when a recursive type T is detected, the algorithm falls back to using the upper bound of T to resolve calls on receivers of type T.

4.4   TCA$^{expand\text{-}this}$

In both Java and Scala, calls on the this reference are common. In some cases, it is possible to resolve such calls more precisely by exploiting the knowledge that the caller and the callee must be members of the same object. Care must be taken in the presence of super-calls, as will be discussed in Section 5.1.

For example, at the call this.foo() on line 90 of Figure 5, the static type of the receiver this is A, which has both B and C as subtypes. Since B and C are both instantiated, all of the analyses described so far would resolve the call to both B.foo (line 94) and C.foo (line 97). However, any object that has C.foo as a member also has C.bar as a member, which overrides the method A.bar containing the call site. Therefore, the call site at line 90 can never resolve to method C.foo.

This pattern is handled precisely by the following rule:

$$
\frac{
\begin{array}{c}
\text{call}\ \ \boxed{D.this.m(\ldots)}\ \ \text{occurs in method}\ M \\
\boxed{D\ \text{is the declaring trait of}\ M} \\
C \in SubTypes(D) \\
\text{method}\ M'\ \text{has name}\ m \\
\text{method}\ M'\ \text{is a member of type}\ C \\
\boxed{\text{method}\ M\ \text{is a member of type}\ C} \\
M \in R \qquad C \in \hat{\Sigma}
\end{array}
}{
c \mapsto M'
}\ \ \text{TCA}^{expand\text{-}this}_{\text{THIS-CALL}}
$$

The rule requires not only the callee M', but also the caller M to be members of the same instantiated type C. The rule applies only when the receiver is the special variable this. Because nested classes and traits are common in Scala, it is possible that a particular occurrence of the special variable this is qualified to refer to the enclosing object of some outer trait. Since it would be unsound to apply TCA$^{expand\text{-}this}_{\text{THIS-CALL}}$ in this case, we require that the receiver be the special variable this of the innermost trait D that declares the caller method M.

After adding rule TCA$^{expand\text{-}this}_{\text{THIS-CALL}}$, we add a precondition to rule TCA$^{expand\text{-}this}_{\text{CALL}}$ so that it does not apply when TCA$^{expand\text{-}this}_{\text{THIS-CALL}}$ should, i.e., when the receiver is the special variable this of the declaring trait D of the caller method M.

4.5   Correctness

In a separate technical report [4], we provide a formalization of the inference rules for TCA$^{expand\text{-}this}$ based on the FS_{alg} ("Featherweight Scala") representation of Cremet et al. [8]. We also prove the TCA$^{expand\text{-}this}$ analysis correct with respect to the operational semantics of FS_{alg} by demonstrating that:

1. For any FS_{alg} program P, the set of methods called in an execution trace of P is a subset of the set R of reachable methods computed for P by TCA$^{expand\text{-}this}$.
2. For any FS_{alg} program P, if the execution trace of P contains a call from call site c to a target method M, then TCA$^{expand\text{-}this}$ applied to P derives $c \mapsto M$.

5   Implementation

We implemented RA, TCA^{names}, TCA^{bounds}, TCA^{expand}, and $\text{TCA}^{expand\text{-}this}$ as a plugin for version 2.10.2 of the Scala compiler, and tested the implementation on a suite of programs exhibiting a wide range of Scala features. To the best of our knowledge, our analyses soundly handle the entire Scala language, but we assume that all code to be analyzed is available and we ignore reflection and dynamic code generation. We also used the implementation of RTA in the WALA framework to construct call graphs from JVM bytecode.

The analysis runs after the uncurry phase, which is the 12th of 30 compiler phases. At this stage, most of the convenience features in Scala that are specified as syntactic sugar have been desugared. However, the compiler has not yet transformed the program to be closer to JVM bytecode, and has not yet erased any significant type information. In particular, closures have been turned into function objects with apply methods, pattern matching has been desugared into explicit tests and comparisons, and implicit calls and parameters have been made explicit, so our analysis does not have to deal with these features explicitly.

Some Scala idioms, e.g., path-dependent types, structural types, singletons, and generics, make the subtype testing in Scala complicated [19, §3.5]. Fortunately, we can rely on the Scala compiler infrastructure to answer subtype queries. Two issues, however, require special handling in the implementation: super calls and incomplete programs.

5.1   Super Calls

Normally, when a method is called on some receiver object, the method is a member of that object. Super calls violate this general rule: a call on super invokes a method in a supertype of the receiver's type. This method is generally not a member of the receiver object, because some other method overrides it.

At a call on super, the analysis must determine the method actually invoked. When the call site is in a class (not a trait), the call is resolved statically as in Java. When the call site is in a trait, however, the target method is selected using a dynamic dispatch mechanism depending on the runtime type of the receiver [19, §6.5]. Our analysis resolves such calls using a similar procedure as for ordinary dynamically dispatched calls. For each possible run-time type of the receiver, the specified procedure is followed to find the actual call target.

The $\text{TCA}^{expand\text{-}this}$ analysis requires that within any method M, the this variable refers to an object of which M is a member. This premise is violated when M is invoked using a super call. To restore soundness, we blacklist the signatures of the targets of all reachable super calls. Within a method whose signature is blacklisted, we fall back to the TCA^{expand} analysis instead of $\text{TCA}^{expand\text{-}this}$.

5.2   Incomplete Programs

Our analyses are defined for complete programs, but a practical implementation must deal with incomplete programs. A typical example of an incomplete program is a situation where user code calls unanalyzed libraries.

Our implementation analyzes Scala source files presented to the compiler, but not referenced classes provided only as bytecode such as the Scala and Java standard libraries. The analysis soundly analyzes call sites occurring in the provided Scala source files using a Scala analogue of the Separate Compilation Assumption [2,3], which asserts that unanalyzed "library" classes do not directly reference analyzed "application" classes. If application code passes the name of one of its classes to the library and the library instantiates it by reflection, then our analysis faces the same challenges as any Java analysis, and the same solutions would apply.

If the declaring class of the static target of a call site is available for analysis, then so are all its subtypes. In such cases, the analysis can soundly determine all possible actual call targets. On the other hand, if the declaring class of the static target of a call is in an unanalyzed class, it is impossible to determine all possible actual target methods, because some targets may be in unanalyzed code or in trait compositions that are only created in unanalyzed code. The implementation records the existence of such call sites, but does not attempt to resolve them soundly. However, such call sites, as well as those in unanalyzed code, may call methods in analyzed code via call-backs. For soundness, the analysis must treat such target methods as reachable. This is achieved by considering a method reachable if it occurs in an instantiated type and if it overrides a method declared in unanalyzed code. This is sound because in both cases (a call whose static target is in unanalyzed code, or a call in unanalyzed code), the actual runtime target method must override the static target of the call.

Determining the method overriding relationship is more difficult than in Java. Two methods declared in two independent traits do not override each other unless these traits are composed in the instantiation of some object. Therefore, the overriding relation must be updated as new trait compositions are discovered.

6   Evaluation

We evaluated our implementation on publicly available Scala programs covering a range of different application areas and programming styles.[8] Table 1 shows, for each program, the number of lines of Scala source code (excluding library code), classes, objects, traits, trait compositions, methods, closures, call sites, call sites on abstract types, and call sites on the variable this. ARGOT is a command-line argument parser for Scala. ENSIME is an Emacs plugin that provides an enhanced Scala interactive mode, including a read-eval-print loop (REPL) and many features commonly found in IDEs such as live error-checking, package/-type browsing, and basic refactorings. FIMPP is an interpreter for an imperative,

---

[8] The benchmark source code is available from http://github.com/bmc/argot, http://github.com/aemoncannon/ensime, http://github.com/KarolS/fimpp, http://code.google.com/p/kiama, http://github.com/colder/phantm, http://github.com/eed3si9n/scalaxb, http://github.com/Mononofu/Scalisp, http://scee.sourceforge.net, http://github.com/max-l/Squeryl, and http://github.com/nickknw/arbitrarily-sized-tic-tac-toe

Table 1. Various characteristics of our benchmark programs

	LOC	# classes	# objects	# traits	# trait compositions	# methods	# closures	# call sites	# call sites on abstract types	# call sites on this
ARGOT	1,074	18	4	6	185	485	168	2,543	2	276
ENSIME	7,832	223	172	36	984	4,878	532	19,555	23	3,195
FIMPP	1,089	42	53	5	685	2,060	549	5,880	4	1,159
KIAMA	17,914	801	664	162	5,324	19,172	3,963	69,352	401	16,256
PHANTM	9,319	317	358	13	1,498	7,208	561	36,276	15	6,643
SCALAXB	10,290	324	259	222	3,024	10,503	2,204	47,382	35	7,305
SCALISP	795	20	14	0	125	428	115	2,313	23	293
SEE	4,311	130	151	17	415	2,280	262	9,566	11	1,449
SQUERYL	7,432	255	55	110	1,040	3,793	826	13,585	173	2,540
TICTACTOE	247	2	7	0	32	112	24	603	0	41

dynamically-typed language that supports integer arithmetic, console output, dynamically growing arrays, and subroutines. KIAMA is a library for language processing used to compile and execute several small languages. PHANTM is a tool that uses a flow-sensitive static analysis to detect type errors in PHP code [16]. SCALAXB is an XML data-binding tool for Scala. SCALISP is a LISP interpreter written in Scala. SEE is a simple engine for evaluating arithmetic expressions. SQUERYL is a Scala library that provides Object-Relational mapping for SQL databases. TICTACTOE is an implementation of the classic "tic-tac-toe" game with a text-based user-interface. Both KIAMA and SCALAXB are part of the Da-Capo Scala Benchmarking project [23]. We did not use the other DaCapo Scala benchmarks as they are not compatible with the latest version of Scala.

We ran all of our experiments on a machine with eight dual-core AMD Opteron 1.4 GHz CPUs (running in 64-bit mode) and capped the available memory for the experiments to 16 GB of RAM.

6.1 Research Questions

Our evaluation aims to answer the following Research Questions:

RQ1. How precise are call graphs constructed for the JVM bytecode produced by the Scala compiler compared to analyzing Scala source code?

RQ2. What is the impact on call graph precision of adopting subtype-based call resolution instead of name-based call resolution?

RQ3. What is the impact on call graph precision of determining the set of concrete types that may be bound to abstract type members instead of using a bounds-based approximation?

RQ4. What is the impact of the special treatment of calls on this?

Table 2. Number of nodes and edges in the summarized version of call graphs computed using the RA, TCA^{names}, TCA^{bounds}, TCA^{expand}, TCA$^{expand-this}$, and RTA^{wala}

		RA	TCA^{names}	TCA^{bounds}	TCA^{expand}	TCA$^{expand-this}$	RTA^{wala}
ARGOT	nodes	265	184	161	161	161	236
	edges	3,516	1,538	442	442	440	648
ENSIME	nodes	3,491	3,018	2,967	2,966	2,965	4,525
	edges	191,435	150,974	8,025	8,023	8,017	61,803
FIMPP	nodes	870	773	771	771	771	1,381
	edges	12,716	10,900	2,404	2,404	2,404	8,327
KIAMA	nodes	11,959	8,684	7,609	7,600	7,200	13,597
	edges	1,555,533	845,120	35,288	34,062	32,494	609,255
PHANTM	nodes	5,945	5,207	4,798	4,587	4,587	5,157
	edges	376,065	296,252	14,727	13,899	13,870	213,264
SCALAXB	nodes	6,795	2,263	1,196	1,196	1,196	3,866
	edges	1,832,473	322,499	5,819	5,819	5,818	48,966
SCALISP	nodes	283	196	186	186	186	307
	edges	3,807	2,380	526	526	526	908
SEE	nodes	1,869	1,711	1,645	1,572	1,572	2,016
	edges	77,303	63,706	8,349	7,466	7,418	14,520
SQUERYL	nodes	2,484	1,488	408	408	408	1,507
	edges	91,342	46,160	1,677	1,677	1,676	8,669
TICTACTOE	nodes	79	78	78	78	78	112
	edges	524	523	170	170	170	327

RQ5. How does the running time of the analyses compare?

RQ6. For how many call sites can the algorithms find a single outgoing edge?

6.2 Results

Table 2 summarizes the precision of the call graphs computed by our analyses. For each benchmark and analysis combination, the table shows the number of reachable methods and call edges in the call graph. All call graphs presented in this section include only the analyzed code of the benchmark itself, excluding any library code. For RTA^{wala}, such "summarized call graphs" were obtained by collapsing the parts of the call graph in the library into a single node.

RQ1. To answer this question, we compare the call graphs from the TCA^{bounds} and RTA^{wala} analyses. The call graphs constructed from bytecode have on average 1.7x as many reachable methods and 4.4x as many call edges as the call graphs constructed by analyzing Scala source. In other words, analyzing generated bytecode incurs a very large loss in precision.

Investigating further, we found that the most significant cause of precision loss is due to apply methods, which are generated from closures. These account for, on average, 25% of the spurious call edges computed by RTA^{wala} but not by TCA^{bounds}. The second-most significant cause of precision loss are toString methods, which account for, on average, 13% of the spurious call edges.

The ENSIME program is an interesting special case because it uses Scala constructs that are translated into code that uses reflection (see Section 3.5). As a result, the RTA^{wala} analysis makes conservative approximations that cause the call graph to become extremely large and imprecise[9]. This further reaffirms that a bytecode-based approach to call graph construction is highly problematic.

RQ2. To answer this question, we compare TCA^{names} and TCA^{bounds} and find that name-based analysis incurs a very significant precision loss: The call graphs generated by TCA^{names} have, on average, 10.9x as many call edges as those generated by TCA^{bounds}. Investigating further, we found that, on average, 66% of the spurious call edges computed by the name-based analysis were to apply methods, which implement closures.

RQ3. To answer this question, we compare TCA^{bounds} and TCA^{expand}. On the smaller benchmark programs that make little use of abstract types, the two produce identical results. Since KIAMA, PHANTM, and SEE contain some call sites on receivers with abstract types, TCA^{expand} computes more precise call graphs for them. For SCALAXB, SCALISP, and SQUERYL, call graph precision is not improved despite the presence of abstract types because the call sites on abstract receivers occur in unreachable code.

RQ4. To answer the fourth research question, we compare the TCA^{expand} and $\text{TCA}^{expand-this}$ analyses. In general, we found that the precision benefit of the special handling of this calls is small and limited to specific programs. In particular, we found that the number of call edges is reduced by 5% on KIAMA and by 1% on SEE, but that there is no significant difference on the other benchmarks. The situation for KIAMA is interesting in that TCA^{expand} finds 3.7% more instantiated types than $\text{TCA}^{expand-this}$. Those types are instantiated in methods found unreachable by $\text{TCA}^{expand-this}$.

The two most common reasons why the more precise rule $\text{TCA}^{expand-this}_{\text{THIS-CALL}}$ may fail to rule out a given call graph edge are that the caller M actually is inherited

---

[9] The summarized call graph computed by RTA^{wala} shown in Table 2 has 4,525 nodes and 61,803 edges. However, the size of the call graph originally computed by RTA^{wala} (before summarizing the library code) has 78,901 nodes and 7,835,170 edges. We experimentally confirmed that nearly half of these edges are in parts of the libraries related to the reflection API.

Table 3. The time (in seconds) taken by RA, TCA^{names}, TCA^{bounds}, TCA^{expand}, TCA$^{expand\text{-}this}$, and RTA^{wala} to compute the call graphs

	RA	TCA^{names}	TCA^{bounds}	TCA^{expand}	TCA$^{expand\text{-}this}$	RTA^{wala}	scalac
ARGOT	4	3.4	3.2	3.5	3.5	11.3	25.3
ENSIME	32.1	24.8	25	29	27.5	510.2	60.6
FIMPP	5.5	4.9	7.4	7.5	8	14.3	36.1
KIAMA	286	83	125.6	132.9	115.3	66.9	104.1
PHANTM	55.4	43.2	51.1	54.3	52.5	26.8	70.2
SCALAXB	113.4	16.3	10.9	11.5	12.7	21.1	85.9
SCALISP	3	2.9	3	3.1	3.2	12.6	25.6
SEE	6.9	6.3	8.2	8.1	8.8	13.9	40
SQUERYL	21	11.5	5.6	6.3	6.8	20.9	61.6
TICTACTOE	1.7	1.7	1.9	2	2	9.9	16.3

into the run-time receiver type C, so the call can occur, or that the caller M can be called through super, so using the rule would be unsound, as explained in Section 5.1. Across all the benchmark programs, the rule failed to eliminate a call edge at 80% of call sites on this due to the caller M being inherited into C, and at 15% of call sites on this due to the caller M being called through super.

RQ5. The running times of the analyses are presented in Table 3. For comparison, the last column of the table also shows the time required to compile each benchmark using the unmodified Scala compiler. Although our implementation has not been heavily tuned for performance, the analysis times are reasonable compared to scalac compilation times. The high imprecision of the RA analysis generally makes it significantly slower than the other, more complicated but more precise analyses. The TCA^{names} analysis is sometimes significantly faster and sometimes significantly slower than the TCA^{bounds} analysis, since it avoids the many expensive subtype tests, but is significantly less precise. The TCA^{expand} and TCA$^{expand\text{-}this}$ analyses have generally similar execution times as the TCA^{bounds} analysis because abstract types and this calls are a relatively small fraction of all call sites in the benchmark programs.

The long running time of nearly 500 seconds of RTA^{wala} on ENSIME is because the computed call graph becomes extremely large (see discussion of RQ1).

RQ6. Certain applications of call graphs require call sites to have a unique outgoing edge. For example, whole-program optimization tools [28] may inline such "monomorphic" call sites. It is therefore interesting to measure the ability of the different algorithms to resolve call sites to a unique target method. Table 4 shows, for each benchmark program, the number of monomorphic and

Table 4. Number of monomorphic and polymorphic reachable call sites in the summarized version of call graphs computed using RA, and how many of them became unreachable, monomorphic, or polymorphic in TCA$^{expand\text{-}this}$

		RA	Unreachable	Mono	Poly
			TCA$^{expand\text{-}this}$		
ARGOT	Mono	1,200	459	741	-
	Poly	1,296	575	687	34
ENSIME	Mono	10,901	398	10,503	-
	Poly	8,433	430	7,545	458
FIMPP	Mono	4,058	56	4,002	-
	Poly	1,636	7	1,478	151
KIAMA	Mono	40,974	15,103	25,871	-
	Poly	27,869	11,586	15,337	946
PHANTM	Mono	17,500	1,023	16,477	-
	Poly	18,611	631	16,387	1,593
SCALAXB	Mono	22,170	12,206	9,964	-
	Poly	24,809	17,181	7,083	545
SCALISP	Mono	1,163	143	1,020	-
	Poly	1,106	154	890	62
SEE	Mono	5,327	258	5,069	-
	Poly	4,126	321	2,998	807
SQUERYL	Mono	6,453	4,092	2,361	-
	Poly	6,369	4,794	1,498	77
TICTACTOE	Mono	330	1	329	-
	Poly	204	0	187	17

polymorphic call sites, as determined by the RA analysis. The table also shows how these calls are resolved by the TCA$^{expand\text{-}this}$ analysis. For example, for EN-SIME, the RA analysis finds 10,901 monomorphic calls and 8,433 polymorphic calls. Of the 10,901 calls that are identified as monomorphic by RA, 398 are identified as unreachable by the more precise TCA$^{expand\text{-}this}$ analysis and the remaining 10,503 remain as monomorphic calls. More interestingly, of the 8,433 calls that RA identifies as polymorphic, 430 become unreachable, 7,545 become monomorphic, and only 458 remain polymorphic according to TCA$^{expand\text{-}this}$.

7 Conclusions

We presented a family of low-cost algorithms for constructing call graphs of Scala programs, in the spirit of Name-Based Resolution (RA) [26], Class Hierarchy Analysis (CHA) [9] and Rapid Type Analysis (RTA) [6]. Our algorithms consider how traits are combined in a Scala program to improve precision and handle the full Scala language, including features such as abstract type members, closures, and path-dependent types. Furthermore, we proposed a mechanism for resolving calls on the this reference more precisely, by considering overriding definitions of the method containing the call site.

We implemented the algorithms in the context of the Scala compiler, and compared their precision and cost on a collection of Scala programs. We found that TCA^{names} is significantly more precise than RA, indicating that maintaining a set of instantiated trait combinations greatly improves precision. Furthermore, TCA^{bounds} is significantly more precise than TCA^{names}, indicating that subtyping-based call resolution is superior to name-based call resolution. The improvements of TCA^{expand} over TCA^{bounds} occur on a few larger subjects that make nontrivial use of abstract type members and type parameters. Similarly, $TCA^{expand-this}$ only did significantly better than TCA^{expand} on programs that make nontrivial use of subtyping and method overriding.

Prior to our work, if one needed a call graph for a Scala program, the only available method was to analyze the JVM bytecodes produced by the Scala compiler. Since significant type information is lost during the compilation process, RTA call graphs constructed from the JVM bytecodes can be expected to be much less precise than the call graphs constructed using our new algorithms, as is confirmed by our experimental results.

While our research has focused on Scala, several aspects of the work are broadly applicable to other statically typed object-oriented languages. In particular, the special handling of calls on this can be integrated with existing algorithms such as CHA and RTA for languages such as Java, C#, and C++.

Acknowledgments. We are grateful to Max Schäfer and the anonymous ECOOP reviewers for many invaluable comments and suggestions, and to Rob Schluntz for assistance with testing. This research was supported by the Natural Sciences and Engineering Research Council of Canada and the Ontario Ministry of Research and Innovation.

References

1. Agesen, O.: Constraint-based Type Inference and Parametric Polymorphism. In: LeCharlier, B. (ed.) SAS 1994. LNCS, vol. 864, pp. 78–100. Springer, Heidelberg (1994)
2. Ali, K., Lhoták, O.: Application-only Call Graph Construction. In: Noble, J. (ed.) ECOOP 2012. LNCS, vol. 7313, pp. 688–712. Springer, Heidelberg (2012)
3. Ali, K., Lhoták, O.: AVERROES: Whole-program analysis without the whole program. In: Castagna, G. (ed.) ECOOP 2013. LNCS, vol. 7920, pp. 378–400. Springer, Heidelberg (2013)
4. Ali, K., Rapoport, M., Lhoták, O., Dolby, J., Tip, F.: Constructing call graphs of Scala programs. Tech. Rep. CS-2014-09, U. of Waterloo (2014)
5. Bacon, D.F.: Fast and Effective Optimization of Statically Typed Object-Oriented Languages. PhD thesis, University of California, Berkeley (1997)
6. Bacon, D.F., Sweeney, P.F.: Fast static analysis of C++ virtual function calls. In: OOPSLA, pp. 324–341 (1996)

7. Bravenboer, M., Smaragdakis, Y.: Strictly Declarative Specification of Sophisticated Points-to Analyses. In: OOPSLA, pp. 243–262 (2009)
8. Cremet, V., Garillot, F., Lenglet, S., Odersky, M.: A core calculus for Scala type checking. In: Královič, R., Urzyczyn, P. (eds.) MFCS 2006. LNCS, vol. 4162, pp. 1–23. Springer, Heidelberg (2006)
9. Dean, J., Grove, D., Chambers, C.: Optimization of object-oriented programs using static class hierarchy analysis. In: Olthoff, W. (ed.) ECOOP 1995. LNCS, vol. 952, pp. 77–101. Springer, Heidelberg (1995)
10. DeFouw, G., Grove, D., Chambers, C.: Fast Interprocedural Class Analysis. In: POPL, pp. 222–236 (1998)
11. Grove, D., Chambers, C.: A framework for call graph construction algorithms. ACM Trans. Program. Lang. Syst. 23(6), 685–746 (2001)
12. Heintze, N.: Set-Based Analysis of ML Programs. In: LISP and Functional Programming, pp. 306–317 (1994)
13. Heintze, N., Tardieu, O.: Ultra-fast Aliasing Analysis using CLA: A Million Lines of C Code in a Second. In: PLDI, pp. 254–263 (2001)
14. Henglein, F.: Dynamic Typing. In: Krieg-Brückner, B. (ed.) ESOP 1992. LNCS, vol. 582, pp. 233–253. Springer, Heidelberg (1992)
15. IBM. T.J. Watson Libraries for Analysis WALA (April 2013), http://wala.sourceforge.net/
16. Kneuss, E., Suter, P., Kuncak, V.: Phantm: PHP analyzer for type mismatch. In: SIGSOFT FSE, pp. 373–374 (2010)
17. Lhoták, O., Hendren, L.: Scaling Java Points-to Analysis Using SPARK. In: Hedin, G. (ed.) CC 2003. LNCS, vol. 2622, pp. 153–169. Springer, Heidelberg (2003)
18. Lhoták, O., Hendren, L.: Context-Sensitive Points-to Analysis: Is It Worth It? In: Mycroft, A., Zeller, A. (eds.) CC 2006. LNCS, vol. 3923, pp. 47–64. Springer, Heidelberg (2006)
19. Odersky, M.: The Scala Language Specification version 2.9. Tech. rep., EPFL, DRAFT (May 2011)
20. Odersky, M., Spoon, L., Venners, B.: Programming in Scala, 2nd edn. Artima Press (2012)
21. Ryder, B.: Constructing the call graph of a program. IEEE Transactions on Software Engineering 5(3), 216–226 (1979)
22. Sallenave, O., Ducourneau, R.: Lightweight generics in embedded systems through static analysis. In: LCTES, pp. 11–20 (2012)
23. Sewe, A., Mezini, M., Sarimbekov, A., Binder, W.: Da capo con scala: design and analysis of a Scala benchmark suite for the Java virtual machine. In: OOPSLA, pp. 657–676 (2011)
24. Shivers, O.: Control-Flow Analysis of Higher-Order Languages. PhD thesis, CMU (May 1991)
25. Sridharan, M., Dolby, J., Chandra, S., Schäfer, M., Tip, F.: Correlation Tracking for Points-To Analysis of JavaScript. In: Noble, J. (ed.) ECOOP 2012. LNCS, vol. 7313, pp. 435–458. Springer, Heidelberg (2012)
26. Srivastava, A.: Unreachable procedures in object oriented programming. ACM Letters on Programming Languages and Systems 1(4), 355–364 (1992)
27. Tip, F., Palsberg, J.: OOPSLA, pp. 281–293 (2000)
28. Tip, F., Sweeney, P.F., Laffra, C., Eisma, A., Streeter, D.: Practical extraction techniques for Java. ACM Trans. Program. Lang. Syst. 24(6), 625–666 (2002)
29. Vallée-Rai, R., Gagnon, E.M., Hendren, L., Lam, P., Pominville, P., Sundaresan, V.: Optimizing Java Bytecode Using the Soot Framework: Is It Feasible? In: Watt, D.A. (ed.) CC 2000. LNCS, vol. 1781, pp. 18–34. Springer, Heidelberg (2000)

A   Artifact Description

Authors of the Artifact. Karim Ali, Marianna Rapoport, Ondřej Lhoták, Julian Dolby, and Frank Tip

Summary. The artifact is based on the implementation of the Scala source-level call graph construction algorithms we have discussed in this paper, RA, TCA^{names}, TCA^{bounds}, TCA^{expand}, and TCA$^{expand-this}$. Additionally, the artifact includes the implementation of the bytecode-based call graph construction algorithm, RTA^{wala}. The source-level algorithms are implemented as a Scala compiler plugin. On the other hand, RTA^{wala} is the state-of-the-art implementation of the RTA algorithm provided by the WALA framework. The provided artifact package is designed to support the repeatability of the experiments of the paper. In particular, it allows users to generate the call graphs for a variety of benchmarks using one or more of the six algorithms. Instructions for the general use of our Scala compiler call graph plugin "scalacg" with any Scala source code are also provided.

Content. The artifact package includes:

- `scalabench.tar.gz`: all the necessary scripts, runnable JARs, required to replicate our experiments.
- `scalacg.tar.gz`: the source code of our Scala compiler plugin.
- `callgraph-plugin.jar`: our Scala compiler plugin. Additionally, it contains the ProBe tool to compare and visualize call graphs.
- `walacg.jar`: a runnable JAR for the implementation of RTA^{wala}.
- `index.html`: detailed instructions for using the artifact.

We provide a VirtualBox appliance containing Ubuntu 13.10 (Saucy Salamander), fully configured to simplify repeatability of our experiments. The image includes the file `scalabench.tar.gz` on the desktop.

Getting the Artifact. The artifact endorsed by the Artifact Evaluation Committee is available free of charge as supplementary material of this paper on SpringerLink. The latest version of our code and runnable JAR files are available at: `http://plg.uwaterloo.ca/~karim/projects/scalacg`.

Tested Platforms. The artifact is known to work on any platform running Oracle VirtualBox version 4 (`https://www.virtualbox.org/`) with at least 8 GB of free space on disk and at least 16 GB of free space in RAM. However, the Scala compiler call graph plugin itself is known to work on any platform running Scala 2.10.2, though it has been only tested on Linux and Mac OS X environments.

License. EPL-1.0 (`http://www.eclipse.org/legal/epl-v10.html`), except for any external packages, tools, sources (including benchmark sources) used in the artifact, those respect their original licenses.

MD5 Sum of the Artifact. b92d617c9636a0022eac665595982386

Size of the Artifact. 5.3 GB

Finding Reference-Counting Errors in Python/C Programs with Affine Analysis

Siliang Li and Gang Tan

Lehigh University, Bethlehem PA 18015, USA

Abstract. Python is a popular programming language that uses reference counting to manage heap objects. Python also has a Foreign Function Interface (FFI) that allows Python extension modules to be written in native code such as C and C++. Native code, however, is outside Python's system of memory management; therefore extension programmers are responsible for making sure these objects are reference counted correctly. This is an error prone process when code becomes complex. In this paper, we propose Pungi, a system that statically checks whether Python objects' reference counts are adjusted correctly in Python/C interface code. Pungi transforms Python/C interface code into affine programs with respect to our proposed abstractions of reference counts. Our system performs static analysis on transformed affine programs and reports possible reference counting errors. Our prototype implementation found over 150 errors in a set of Python/C programs.

Keywords: Python/C, reference counting, affine programs, static analysis.

1 Introduction

The Python programming language has become widely adopted in the software development community over the years because of many appealing features of the language itself and a robust ecosystem [1]. Similar to many other languages, Python provides a Foreign Function Interface (FFI), called the Python/C interface. The interface allows Python programs to interoperate with native modules written in C/C++. Through the interface, Python programs can reuse legacy native libraries written in C/C++ or use native code to speed up their performance-critical parts. Python provides a comprehensive set of Python/C API functions. Through these functions, native modules can create Python objects, manipulate objects, raise and handle Python exceptions, and perform other actions [2].

Another important feature of Python is its memory management. Python allocates objects on its heap. When objects are no longer in use, Python's memory manager garbage collects these objects from the heap. The standard implementation of Python uses the reference-counting algorithm. The representation of every Python object has a reference-count field. When Python code is running, the Python runtime automatically adjusts the reference counts during program execution and maintains the invariant that an object's reference count be the

R. Jones (Ed.): ECOOP 2014, LNCS 8586, pp. 80–104, 2014.

same as the number of references to the object. Specifically, the reference count of an object is incremented when there is a new reference to the object or decremented when a reference disappears. When an object's reference count becomes zero, its space is reclaimed from the heap by the garbage collector.

Native modules incorporated in a Python program, on the other hand, are outside the control of Python's garbage collector. When those native modules manipulate Python objects through the Python/C interface, reference counts are not adjusted automatically by the Python runtime and it is the native code's responsibility to adjust reference counts in a correct way (through Py_INCREF and Py_DECREF, discussed later). This is an error-prone process. Incorrect adjustments of reference counts result in classic memory errors such as memory leaks and use of dangling references.

In this paper, we describe a system called Pungi, which performs static analysis to identify reference-counting errors in native C modules of Python programs. Pungi abstracts a native module to an affine program, which models how reference counts are changed in the native module. In an affine program, the right-hand side of an assignment can only be an affine expression of the form $a_0 + \Sigma_{i=1}^n a_i x_i$, where a_i are constants and x_i are program variables. A previous theoretical study [3] has shown that an affine program is sufficient to model reference-count changes in the case of *shallow aliasing* (which assumes multi-level references to be non-aliases). That study, however, is mainly concerned with computational complexity and does not consider many practical issues, including function calls with parameter passing and references that escape objects' scopes. Furthermore, its proposed affine-abstraction step has not been implemented and tested for effectiveness. In fact, its affine-abstraction step is non-intuitive by requiring reversing the control flow of programs. Moreover, it does not describe how to analyze the resulting affine program to identify reference-counting errors. More detailed discussion of that work and its comparison with Pungi will be presented when we discuss the design of Pungi.

Major contributions of Pungi are described as follows:

- We propose a set of ideas that make the affine-abstraction step more complete and practical. In particular, we show how to perform affine abstraction interprocedurally and how to accommodate escaping references. We further show that the affine-abstraction step can be simplified by first performing a Static-Single Assignment (SSA) transform on the input program.
- We propose to use path-sensitive, interprocedural static analysis on the resulting affine programs to report possible reference-counting errors. We show this step is precise and efficient.
- We have built a practical reference-count analysis system that analyzes Python/C extension modules. Our system over 150 errors in 13 benchmark programs, with a modest false-positive rate of 22%.

The main limitation of Pungi is the assumption of shallow aliasing, which allows direct references to be aliases but multi-level references are assumed to reference distinct objects. For instance, if a Python program has a reference to

```
1 static PyObject* create_ntuple(PyObject *self, PyObject *args) {
2   int n, i, err;
3   PyObject *tup = NULL;
4   PyObject *item = NULL;
5   // parse args to get input number n
6   if (!PyArg_Parse(args, "(i)", &n)) return NULL;
7   tup = PyTuple_New(n);
8   if (tup == NULL) return NULL;
9   for (i=0; i<n; i++) {
10    item = PyInt_FromLong(i);
11    if (item == NULL) {Py_DECREF(tup); return NULL;}
12
13    err = PyTuple_SetItem(tup, i, item);
14    if (err) { // no need to dec-ref item
15      Py_DECREF(tup); return NULL;}
16  }
17  return tup;
18 }
```

Fig. 1. An example Python/C extension module called `ntuple` (its registration table and module initializer code are omitted)

a list object, then all objects within the list are assumed to be distinct objects. Pungi's assumption of shallow aliasing and its other assumptions may cause it to have false positives and false negatives. However, our experience shows that Pungi remains an effective tool given that it can find many reference-counting errors and its false-positive rate is moderate.

The rest of the paper is structured as follows. Sec. 2 includes the background information about the Python/C interface and reference counting. Related work is discussed in Section 3. In Sec. 4, we provide an overview of Pungi. The detailed design of Pungi is presented in Sec. 5 and 6. Pungi's implementation and a summary of its limitations are in Sec. 7. Experimental results are discussed in Sec. 8. We conclude in Sec. 9.

2   Background: The Python/C Interface and Reference Counting

The Python/C interface allows a Python program to incorporate a native library by developing a native extension module. The extension module provides a set of *native functions*. Some of the native functions are registered to be *entry native functions*, which can be imported and directly called by Python code; the rest are helper functions. An entry native function takes Python objects as input, uses Python/C API functions to create/manipulate objects, and possibly returns a Python object as the result.

Fig. 1 presents a simple C extension module called `ntuple`. It implements one function **create_ntuple**, which takes an integer **n** and constructs a tuple

$(0, 1, \ldots, n-1)$. In more detail, references to Python objects have type "PyObject *".[1] Parameter args at line 1 is a list object, which contains the list of objects passed from Python. The call to the API function PyArg_Parse at line 6 decodes args and puts the result into integer n; format string "(i)" specifies that there should be exactly one argument, which must be an integer object. API function PyTuple_New creates a tuple with size n. The loop from line 9 to line 16 first creates an integer object using PyInt_FromLong and updates the tuple with the integer object at the appropriate index. For brevity, we have omitted the extension module's code for registering entry native functions and for initialization.

After the ntuple extension module is compiled to a dynamically linked library, it can be imported and used in Python, as shown below.

```
>>> import ntuple
>>> ntuple.create_ntuple(5)
(0, 1, 2, 3, 4)
```

2.1 Python/C Reference Counting and Its Complexities

As mentioned, native extension modules are outside the reach of Python's garbage collector. Native code must explicitly increment and decrement reference counts (we abbreviate reference counts as refcounts hereafter). Specifically,

- Py_INCREF(p) increments the refcount of the object referenced by p.
- Py_DECREF(p) decrements the refcount of the object referenced by p. When the refcount becomes zero, the object's space is reclaimed and the refcounts of all objects whose references are in object p get decremented.

Correct accounting of refcounts of objects, however, is a complex task. We next discuss the major complexities.

Control flow. Correct reference counting must be performed in all control flow paths, including those paths resulting from error conditions or interprocedural control flows. Take code in Fig. 1 as an example. At line 10, an integer object is allocated, but the allocation may fail. In the failure case, the code returns immediately, but it is also important to perform Py_DECREF on the previously allocated tup object; forgetting it would cause a memory leak. Similarly, at line 15, a Py_DECREF(tup) is necessary. Clearly, taking care of reference counts of all objects in all control-flow paths is a daunting task for programmers.

Borrowed and stolen references. It is common in native code to use the concept of *borrowed references* to save some reference-counting work. According to the Python/C manual [2], when creating a new reference to an object in a variable, "if we know that there is at least one other references to the object that lives at

---

[1] The Python/C interface defines type PyObject and a set of subtypes that can be used by extension code, such as PyIntObject and PyStringObject. Pungi does not distinguish these types in its analysis and treats them as synonyms. Therefore, we will just use PyObject in the rest of the paper.

least as long as our variable, there is no need to increment the reference count temporarily".

For instance, if function `foo` calls `bar` and passes `bar` a reference to an object:

```
void foo () {
   PyObject *p = PyInt_FromLong (...);
   bar (p); }
void bar (PyObject *q) { ... }
```

Within the scope of `bar`, there is one more reference (namely, `q`) to the object allocated in `foo`. However, it is safe not to increment the refcount of the object inside `bar`. The reason is that, when the control is within `bar`, we know there is at least one more reference in the caller and that reference outlives local reference `q`. Therefore, it is safe to allow more references than the refcount of the object. In this situation, the callee "borrows" the reference from the caller, meaning that the callee creates a new reference without incrementing the refcount.

Moreover, certain Python/C API functions allow callers of those functions to borrow references. For instance, `PyList_GetItem` returns a reference to an item in a list. Even though it returns a new reference to the list item, `PyList_GetItem` does not increment the refcount of the list item. This is safe when the list is not mutated before the new reference is out of scope; in this case, the reference stored in the list will outlive the new reference.[2] The Python/C reference manual lists the set of API functions with this behavior.

Dual to the situation that callers may borrow references from some API functions, certain API functions can "steal" references from the callers. For instance, in a call `PyTuple_SetItem(tuple,i,item)`, if `tuple[i]` contains an object, the object's refcount is decremented; then `tuple[i]` is set to `item`. Critically, `item`'s refcount is not incremented even though a new reference is created in the tuple. This practice is safe if we assume the `item` reference is never used after the set-item operation, which is often the case. Another behavior is that `PyTuple_SetItem(tuple,i,item)` may fail, in which case `Py_DECREF(item)` is automatically performed by the API function. This is why at line 15 in Fig. 1 there is no need to decrement the refcount on `item`.

API reference-count semantics. We have already alluded to the fact that Python/C API functions may have different effects on the refcounts of involved objects. Certain functions borrow references and certain functions steal references. Certain functions allocate objects. For instance, the calls to the API functions `PyTuple_New` and `PyInt_FromLong` in Fig. 1 allocate objects and set the refcounts of those objects to be one when allocation succeeds. And certain functions do not affect the refcounts of objects. When programmers use those API functions, they can often be confused by their effects on refcounts and make mistakes.

---

[2] If the list may be mutated, then the caller should increment the refcount of the retrieved object after calling `PyList_GetItem`.

All of the above factors make correct reference counting in native code extremely difficult. As a result, reference-counting errors are common in Python/C native extensions.

3   Related Work

Emmi *et al.* have used software model checking to find reference-counting errors in an OS kernel and a file system [4]. Their system's focus, assumptions, and techniques are quite different from Pungi's. The focus of their system is to find reference-counting errors in the presence of multiple threads. It assumes there is an array of reference-counted resources and assumes each resource in the array is used uniformly by a thread. Therefore, their system can use a technique called temporal case splitting to reduce the reference-counting verification of multiple resources and multiple threads to the verification of a single resource and a single thread. In the context of Python/C, however, objects passed from Python are not used uniformly by native code: an object's refcount may be adjusted differently from how other objects' refcounts are adjusted. Pungi uses an affine program to capture the effects of reference counts on objects. Another note is that the system by Emmi *et al.* assumes simple code for adjusting refcounts and has not dealt with any aliasing situation (including shallow aliasing).

Malcom has constructed a practical tool called CPyChecker [5], which is a gcc plug-in that can find a variety of errors in Python's native extension modules, including reference-counting errors. CPyChecker traverses a finite number of paths in a function and reports errors on those paths. It does not perform inter-procedural analysis and ignores loops, while Pungi covers both. CPyChecker also produces wrong results when a variable is statically assigned multiple times, while Pungi uses SSA to make variables assigned only once. Experimental comparison between Pungi and CPyChecker is presented in the evaluation section.

Python/C interface code can also be generated by tools such as SWIG [6] and Cython [7]. They would reduce the number of reference-counting errors as most of the interface code is automatically generated. However, these tools do not cover all possible cases of code generation; in particular, they do not handle every feature of C/C++. As a result, a lot of interface code is still written manually in practice.

This work is an example of finding errors in Foreign Function Interface (FFI) code. Errors occur often in FFI code [8–11] because writing interface code requires resolving language differences such as memory management between two languages. Past work on improving FFIs' safety can be put into several categories. First, some systems use dynamic checking to catch errors (e.g., [12]), to enforce atomicity [13], or to isolate errors in native code so that they do not affect the host language's safety and security [14, 15]. Second, some researchers have designed new interface languages to help programmers write safer interface code (e.g.,[16]). Finally, static analysis has been used to identify specific classes of errors in FFI code, including type errors [8, 17] and exception-handling errors [11, 18]. Pungi belongs to this category and finds reference-counting errors in Python/C interface code.

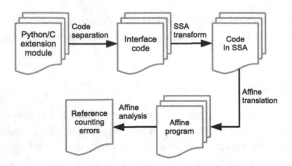

Fig. 2. An overview of Pungi

Pungi uses affine programs to abstract the reference-counting aspect of Python/C programs and performs analysis on the resulting affine programs. Affine analysis has been used in program verification in the past (e.g., [19–23]).

4 Pungi Overview

Fig. 2 shows the main steps in Pungi. It takes a Python/C extension module as input and reports reference-counting errors. Pungi analyzes only C code, but does not analyze Python code that invokes the C code.

The first step performed by Pungi is to separate *interface code* from *library code* in the extension module. As observed by a previous static-analysis system on the Java Native Interface [18], code in an FFI package can be divided into interface and library code. The library code is part of the package that belongs to a common native library. The interface code glues the host language such as Python with the native library. A native function is part of the interface code if 1) it invokes a Python/C API function, or 2) it invokes another native function that is part of the interface code. For example, the PyCrypto package has a thin layer of interface code that links Python with the underlying cryptography library. Typically, the size of interface code is much smaller than the size of library code. Therefore, Pungi performs a static analysis to separate interface code and library code so that the following steps can ignore the library code. Pungi implements a simple worklist algorithm to find functions in the interface code. If a native function does not belong to the interface code, then its execution should not have any effect on Python objects' refcounts.

After separation, *affine abstraction* converts the interface code to an affine program. The conversion is performed in two steps: Static Single Assignment (SSA) transform and affine translation. First, the SSA transform is applied on the interface code. The SSA transform makes the following affine-translation step easier to formulate; each variable is assigned only once, making it easy to track the association between variables and Python objects. In affine translation, the interface code in the SSA form is translated into an affine program. In the affine program, variables are used to track properties of Python objects, such as their refcounts. Statements are affine operations that model how properties such as refcounts are changed in the interface code. Assertions about refcounts are also inserted into affine programs; assertion failures suggest reference-counting errors. Details of the process of affine abstraction are presented in Sec. 5.

After affine abstraction, Pungi performs an interprocedural and path-sensitive analysis that analyzes the affine program and statically checks whether assertions in the affine program hold. If an assertion might fail, a warning about a possible reference-counting error is reported. Details of affine analysis are presented in Sec. 6.

5   Affine Abstraction

For better understanding, we describe Pungi's affine abstraction in two stages. We will first present its design with the assumption that object references do not escape their scopes. We will then relax this assumption and generalize the design to allow escaping object references (*e.g.*, via return values or via a memory write to a heap data structure).

5.1   Bug Definition with Non-escaping References

One natural definition of a reference-counting error is as follows: at a program location, there is an error if the refcount of an object is not the same as the number of references to the object. However, this bug definition is too precise and an analysis based on the definition would generate too many false positives in real Python/C extension modules. This is due to the presence of borrowed and stolen references we discussed. In both cases, it is safe to make the refcount be different from the number of actual references.

Pungi's reference-counting bug definition is based on a notion of object scopes and the intuition that the expected *refcount change* of an object should be zero at the end of the object's scope (when references to the object do not escape its scope). To define an object's scope, we distinguish two kinds of objects:

- An object is a *Natively Created (NC) object* if it is created in a Python/C extension module. In Fig. 1, objects referenced by tup and item are NC objects. An NC object's scope is defined to be the immediate scope surrounding the object's creation site. For instance, the scope of the object referenced by tup is the function scope of create_ntuple.
- An object is a *Python Created (PC) object* when its reference is passed from Python to an entry native function through parameter passing. Note that we call objects whose references are passed to a native function *parameter objects*, but those parameter objects are PC objects only if that native function is an entry function. In Fig. 1, the self and args objects are PC objects. We define the scope of a PC object to be the function scope of the entry native function that receives the reference to the PC object because Pungi analyzes only native code,

```
1 void buggy_foo () {
2   PyObject * pyo = PyInt_FromLong(10);
3   if (pyo == NULL) return;
4   return;
5 }
```

Fig. 3. A contrived example of a buggy Python/C function

Definition 1. *In the case of non-escaping object references, there is a reference-counting error if, at the end of the scope of an NC or PC object, its refcount change is non-zero. If the change is greater than zero, we call it an error of reference over-counting. If the change is less than zero, we call it an error of reference under-counting.*

We next justify the bug definition. In the discussion, we use rc to stand for the refcount change of an object. Suppose the object is an NC object. If $rc > 0$, it results in a memory leak at the end of the scope because (1) the refcount remains positive and (2) the number of references to the object becomes zero (as object references do not escape the scope). Take the contrived code in Fig. 3 as an example. The object creation at line 2 may result in two cases. In the failure case, the object is not created and PyInt_FromLong returns NULL. In the successful case, the object is created with refcount one; in this case, the net refcount change to the object is one before returning, signaling a reference over-counting error. The correct code should have Py_DECREF(pyo) before line 4.

If $rc < 0$ for an NC object, then there is a use of a dangling reference because at some point of the native function execution, the refcount of the object becomes zero and the object is deallocated as a result; the next Py_DECREF dereferences the dangling reference.

Suppose the object is a PC object of an entry native function. We can safely assume at the beginning of the function the object's refcount is the same as the number of references to the object because the object is passed from Python, whose runtime manages refcounts automatically. If $rc > 0$ at the end of the entry native function, then after the execution of the function the object's refcount must be greater than the number of references to the object (because object references do not escape). This leads to a potential memory leak. If $rc < 0$, this leads to a dangling reference when the native function is invoked with an object whose refcount is one. Since Pungi analyzes only native code, not Python code; it has to be conservative.

One limitation of the bug definition is that it misses some dangling-reference errors that happen in the middle of native functions. For example, a native function can first decrement the refcount of a PC object and then increment the refcount. Although at the end the refcount change is zero, the object gets deallocated after the decrement if the object's original refcount is one; the following increment would use a dangling reference. This is a limitation of Pungi and we leave it to future work.

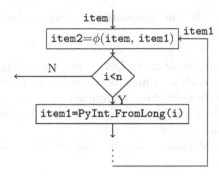

Fig. 4. Part of the control-flow graph for the code in Fig. 1 after SSA

5.2   SSA Transform

Inspired by a previous theoretical study, Pungi uses an affine program to model how refcounts are changed in the interface code of a Python/C extension module. The previous study, however, requires reversing the control-flow graph: the changes at a program location are computed based on changes that follow the location in the control-flow graph (meaning that changes for program locations later in the control-flow graph have to be computed first). The resulting affine program's control flow reverses the control flow of the original program. This process is non-intuitive and it is also unclear how to generalize it to cover function calls with parameter passing.

We observe that the fundamental reason why reversing the control-flow graph is necessary is that variables may be assigned multiple times to reference different objects. Based on this observation, Pungi simplifies the affine abstraction step by first applying the Static Single Assignment (SSA) transform to the interface code. The SSA transform inserts ϕ nodes into the program at control-flow join points and renames variables so that they are statically assigned only once. As we will show, the benefit is that Pungi does not need to reverse the control-flow graph when performing the affine-translation step; further, we can also generalize the affine translation to cover function calls with parameter passing.

Pungi's SSA transform performs transformation on only variables of type "PyObject *" because only Python objects are of interests to Pungi. Variables of other types are not SSA transformed. For the example in Fig. 1, variable i is not SSA transformed even though it is statically assigned twice. On the other hand, the item variable is initialized at the beginning of the code and assigned in the loop. Therefore, one ϕ node is inserted before the conditional test $i < n$ and the item variable is split to multiple ones. The critical parts of the control-flow graph after the SSA transform are visualized in Fig. 4

5.3   Affine Translation

The affine-translation step translates C interface code in the SSA form to an affine program that models the refcount changes of Python objects. We next explain the intuition behind the translation, before presenting the translation algorithm.

Intuition about the affine translation. Let us assume a function takes n input references: $p_1, p_2, ..., p_n$, each of which is a reference to some Python object. Shallow aliasing allows some of these references to be aliases. For instance, p_1 and p_2 may reference the same object, in which case the refcount of the object can be changed via either p_1 or p_2.

With the assumption of shallow aliasing, Lal and Ramalingam [3] proved the following key properties:

(i) the refcount change to an object is the sum of the amount of changes made via references in $p_1, p_2, ..., p_n$ that point to the object.
(ii) the refcount change to an object via a reference is independent from the initial aliasing situation and therefore can be computed assuming an initial aliasing situation in which $p_1, p_2, ..., p_n$ are non-aliases.

We next illustrate via an example as follows:

```
p3 = p1;
Py_INCREF(p1);
Py_DECREF(p3);
Py_INCREF(p1);
Py_DECREF(p2);
```

Let us first assume p1, p2, and p3 reference distinct objects initially. Let rc_i be the refcount change made by the program to the object that pi initially points to. Since it is a simple program, we can easily see that $rc_1 = 1, rc_2 = -1, rc_3 = 0$. The reason why rc_3 is zero is because p3 is updated to be p1 in the first statement; so there is no refcount change to the object that p3 initially references.

Now suppose the program is actually run in an initial aliasing situation where p1 and p2 are aliases referencing object a and p3 references a different object b. In this case, according to the stated properties (i) and (ii), we can compute that the refcount change to object a is $rc_1 + rc_2$, which is zero, and the refcount change to object b is rc_3, which is also zero.

The follow-up question is how to compute rc_i for an arbitrary program. The computation is modeled by an affine program, which is discussed next.

Affine program syntax. The syntax of our affine programs is presented in Fig. 5. In the syntax, we use meta-symbol x for variables and i for integer constants. An affine program consists of a set of mutually recursive functions; we assume the first function is the main function. A function declaration contains a name and a body. The body contains the declaration of a list of local variables and a block, which is a list of statements.

A statement in an affine program contains various forms of assignments, of which the right-hand sides are affine expressions. The condition c in an if-statement or a while-statement can be either a predicate, which compares a

$$
\begin{array}{rll}
(Program) & Prog ::= & f_1; f_2; ...; f_n \\
(Function) & f ::= & \text{fname}()\{\text{locals } x_1, ..., x_k; \; b\} \\
(Block) & b ::= & s_1; ...; s_n \\
(Statement) & s ::= & x = i \mid x = x + i \mid x = x + y \\
& & \mid \text{if } c \text{ then } \{b_1\} \text{ else } \{b_2\} \mid \text{while } c \text{ do } \{b\} \mid \text{assert } p \\
& & \mid (x_1, ..., x_n) = \text{fname}() \mid \text{return } (x_1, ..., x_n) \\
(Condition) & c ::= & p \mid ? \\
(Predicate) & p ::= & x == i \mid x \neq i \mid x > i \mid x < i \mid x \geq i \mid x \leq i
\end{array}
$$

Fig. 5. Syntax of affine programs

variable to a constant, or a question mark. The question mark introduces non-determinism into an affine program and is used when translating an if-statement or a while-statement with complex conditions in C code. The statement "assert p" makes an assertion about predicate p. During affine translation, the translator inserts assertions about objects' refcount changes into the affine program.

There are also function-call and function-return statements. An affine function takes zero parameters and returns a tuple. As we will discuss, a native C function with n object-reference parameters is translated to an affine function that has zero parameters and returns a tuple with n components, which are the refcount changes of the n parameter objects.

Intraprocedural affine translation. The translation from C interface code into an affine program is syntax directed, translating one function at a time. We next explain how Pungi translates a C function.

Suppose the C function takes n parameters $p_1, ..., p_n$, each of which is a reference to a Python object. We assume unique numeric labels have been given to parameter objects and object creation sites in the C function. Assume there are m labels in total, ranging from 1 to m. Among those labels, the first n labels are given to the n parameter objects and the rest to objects created in the function.

There are two important aspects about the affine translation. First, the translation maintains a *variable-object map* that maps from C variables to object labels; it tracks which object a C variable references at a program location. Second, for a Python object with label i, the affine program after translation uses a set of affine variables to track properties of the object. The most important one is the rc_i variable, which tracks the refcount change to the object. (Other affine variables will be described later.)

Fig. 6 presents the translation rules for typical C constructs. The first column of the table presents a C construct, the second column presents the updates to the variable-object map, and the last column contains the translation result.

At the function entry, the variable-object map is initialized to map from parameters to labels of parameter objects. Recall that with shallow aliasing the refcount change to an object is independent from the initial aliasing situation; this is why initially parameters are mapped to unique labels, essentially assuming they are non-aliases. In terms of translation for the function entry, refcount changes for all objects are initialized to be zero.

C construct	map updates	affine translation
function entry	forall $i \in [1..n]$ $\text{map}(p_i) = i$	forall $i \in [1..m]$ $rc_i = 0$
$x = y$	$\text{map}(x) = \text{map}(y)$	none
Py_INCREF(x)		$rc_{\text{map}(x)} + +$
Py_DECREF(x)		$rc_{\text{map}(x)} - -$
$x = \text{PyInt\_FromLong}_l(\ldots)$	$\text{map}(x) = l$	if ? then { $rc_l = 1$; $on_l = 1$ } else { $rc_l = 0$; $on_l = 0$ }
if ($x == \text{NULL}$) then $s1$ else $s2$		if $on_{\text{map}(x)} == 0$ then { $\mathcal{T}(s1)$ } else { $\mathcal{T}(s2)$ }
return		forall $i \in \text{OutScope}([1..m])$ assert ($rc_i == 0$) return ($rc_1, \ldots, rc_n$)
$\text{f}(x_1, \ldots, x_k)$		$(tmp_1, \ldots, tmp_k) = \text{f}()$; $rc_{\text{map}(x_1)} += tmp_1$; $\ldots$; $rc_{\text{map}(x_k)} += tmp_k$;

Fig. 6. Affine translation $\mathcal{T}(-)$ for typical C constructs

Reference assignment $x = y$ results in an update to the variable-object map: afterwards, x references the same object as y. Py_INCREF(x) is translated to an affine statement that increments the rc variable of the object that x currently references. We use "$rc_i + +$" as an abbreviation for $rc_i = rc_i + 1$. Similarly, Py_DECREF(x) is translated to a decrement on the corresponding rc variable.

The translation also translates Python/C API function calls. Such a translation required us to carefully read the Python/C reference manual about the refcount effects of API functions (and sometimes even required us to read the source code of the Python interpreter when the manual is unclear). One complication when translating API functions is the need to deal with error conditions, which are common in the Python/C interface. In the example in Fig. 3 on page 88, PyInt_FromLong is supposed to allocate an integer object, but the allocation may fail. The subsequent code tests whether the object is null and proceeds with two cases. Error conditions are typically signaled in the Python/C interface by returning a null reference. To deal with error conditions, Pungi introduces another affine variable for an object during translation: an object non-null variable, called the on variable. It is one when the object is non-null and zero when the object is null. Fig. 6 presents the translation of PyInt_FromLong with object label l. It is translated into a non-deterministic if-statement. In the case of an allocation success, the rc variable is set to be one and the on variable is also one (meaning it is non-null); in the failure case, both variables are set to be zero.

Pungi translates an if-statement in C code in a heuristic way. It recognizes a set of boolean conditions (testing for null, testing for nonnull, etc.) in the if-statement and translates those conditions accurately. Fig. 6 presents one such case when the condition is to test whether an object reference is null; the translated code tests the corresponding object's on variable. For complex boolean conditions, Pungi just translates them to question marks.

```
buggy_foo () {
  locals rc1, on1;
  rc1 = 0;
  if (?) {rc1 = 1; on1 = 1} else {rc1 = 0; on1 = 0};
  if (on1 == 0) { assert (rc1 == 0); return ();}
  assert (rc1 == 0); return ();
}
```

Fig. 7. Translation of the example in Fig. 3

A return statement is translated to assertions about object refcount changes followed by the returning of a tuple of refcount changes of the parameter objects. We delay the discussion why the tuple of refcount changes is returned when we discuss the interprocedural translation. An assertion is inserted for every object that is about to go outside its scope. This is according to the bug definition we discussed in Sec. 5.1. The auxiliary OutScope function returns a set of labels whose corresponding objects are about to go outside their scopes. NC (Natively Created) objects created in the function being translated belong to this set. Parameter objects are also in this set if the function is an entry native function; that is, when they are PC (Python Created) objects.

We present in Fig. 7 the translation result for the function in Fig. 3. Since the original function takes no parameters, the resulting affine function returns an empty tuple. From the affine function, we can see that the last assertion fails, which implies a reference-counting error in the original function.

We note that the SSA transform makes the presented affine-translation possible. Without the SSA, the variable-object map would possibly be updated differently in two different branches of a control-flow graph; then the translation would face the issue of how to merge two maps at a control-flow join point. After the SSA transform, an object-reference variable is statically assigned once and conflicts in variable-object maps never arise. The previous study [3] addressed the issue of variables being assigned multiple times by reversing the control flow during the affine translation. By performing the SSA transform first, Pungi simplifies the affine translation in the intraprocedural case and allows function calls that pass parameters.

Interprocedural translation. As we have seen, the affine function translated from a native function returns the refcount changes of parameter objects by assuming those parameter objects are distinct. This assumption, however, may not be true as the native function may be called with aliases and different call sites may have different aliasing situations. Fortunately, because of property (ii) in Sec. 5.3 (on page 89), it is possible to make *post-function-call refcount adjustments* according to the aliasing situation of a specific call site. The last entry in Fig. 6 describes how a function call is translated. First, the corresponding function is invoked and it returns the refcount changes of the parameter objects assuming they are distinct. After the function call, the *rc* variables of the parameter objects are adjusted according to the variable-object map of the caller.

```
void foo (PyObject *x1,              void foo () {
          PyObject *x2) {               locals rc1,on1,rc2,on2,tmp1,tmp2;
  if (...) bar(x1,x1)                   rc1=0; rc2=0;
  else bar(x2,x2);                      if (?) {
                                          (tmp1,tmp2)=bar();
  return;                                 rc1+=tmp1; rc1+=tmp2;
}                                       } else {
                                          (tmp1,tmp2)=bar();
void bar (PyObject *p1,                    rc2+=tmp1; rc2+=tmp2;
          PyObject *p2) {               }
  Py_IncRef(p1); Py_DecRef(p2);         assert (rc1==0); assert (rc2==0);
}                                       return ();
                                      }

                                      bar () {
                                        locals rc1,on1,rc2,on2;
                                        rc1=0; rc2=0;
                                        rc1++; rc2--;
                                        return (rc1,rc2);
                                      }
```

Fig. 8. An example of interprocedural affine translation

Fig. 8 presents an example. On the left is some Python/C interface code, which has two functions. Function foo is assumed to be a native entry function. It invokes bar at two places. On the right of Fig. 8 is the translated affine program. Note that the post-function refcount adjustments are different for the two call sites. For the first call f(x1,x1), the two refcounts are both added to rc1; for the second call f(x2,x2), the two refcounts are both added to rc2.

Another note about the interprocedural translation is that, if the SSA form of a native function has ϕ nodes, then the native function is translated to multiple affine functions with one affine function created for one ϕ node. In particular, for a ϕ node, the translation finds the set of nodes in the control-flow graph that are dominated by the ϕ node and are reachable from the ϕ node without going through other ϕ nodes. This set of nodes is then translated to become the body of the affine function created for the ϕ node. Afterwards, the affine function is lifted to be a function at the global scope (that is, lambda-lifting [24]). As an example, Pungi translates the following function to exactly the same affine program on the right-hand side of Fig. 8. This is because after the SSA transform, there is a ϕ node inserted before line 4 and an additional affine function is created for that ϕ node.

```
1 void foo (PyObject *x1, PyObject *x2) {
2   PyObject *p1, *p2;
3   if (...) {p1=x1; p2=x1} else {p1=x2; p2=x2};
4   Py_IncRef(p1); Py_DecRef(p2);
5   return;
6 }
```

For the `ntuple` program in Fig. 1, since a ϕ node is inserted before the testing for loop condition (see Fig. 4), an affine function is created for the loop body; it makes a recursive call to itself because there is a control-flow edge back to the ϕ node because of the loop.

5.4   Escaping References

References to an object may escape the object's scope. In this case, the expected refcount change to the object is greater than zero. Object references may escape in several ways. A reference may escape via the return value of a function. The left-hand side of Fig. 9 presents such an example. When the integer object is successfully created, the function returns the `pyo` reference. In this case, the refcount change to the integer object is one. A reference may also escape to the heap. The code in Fig. 1 on page 82 contains such an example. At line 13, The `item` reference escapes to the heap in the tuple object when the set-item operation succeeds. In that case, the refcount change to the object created at line 10 is also one.

To deal with escaping references, we revise the bug definition as follows:

Definition 2. *There is a reference-counting error if, at the end of the scope of an NC or PC object, its refcount change is not the same as the number of times references to the object escape. If the refcount change is greater than the number of escapes, we call it an error of reference over-counting. If the change is less than the number of escapes, we call it an error of reference under-counting.*

The previous bug definition with non-escaping references is a specialization of the new definition when the number of escapes is zero. The new definition essentially uses the number of escapes to approximate the number of new references created outside the object's scope. One limitation is that an object reference may escape to the same heap location multiple times and a later escape may overwrite the references created in earlier escapes. This would result in missed errors, although this happens rarely in practice as suggested by our experience with real Python/C extension modules.

Given the new bug definition, the affine-translation step is adjusted in the following ways. First, an *escape variable, ev*, is introduced for each Python object and records the number of escapes. It is initialized to be zero at the beginning of a function. Second, the translator recognizes places where an object's references escape and increments the object's escape variable in the affine program by one. Third, assertions are changed to assert an objects' refcount change be the same as the number of escapes. Finally, a function not only returns the refcount changes of its parameter objects, but also returns the numbers of escapes of the parameter objects. The post-function-call adjustments adjust both the refcount changes and the numbers of escapes of the arguments.

The right-hand side of Fig. 9 presents the translated result of the code on the left. Variable `ev1` is introduced to record the number of escapes for the integer object created. This example also illustrates that the number of escapes may be different on different control-flow paths.

```
PyObject* foo () {                  foo () {
  PyObject *pyo=PyInt_FromLong(10);   locals rc1,ev1,on1;
  if (pyo==NULL) {                    rc1=0; ev1=0;
    return NULL;                      if (?) {rc1=1; on1=1}
  }                                   else {rc1=0; on1=0};
  return pyo;                         if (on1==0) {
}                                       assert (rc1==ev1);
                                        return;
                                      }
                                      if (on1==1) ev1++;
                                      assert (rc1==ev1);
                                      return (rc1,ev1);
                                    }
```

Fig. 9. An example of escaping references

One final note is that in Pungi, with the assumption of shallow aliasing, callers of functions that return a reference are assumed to get a reference to a new object. That is, a function call that returns a reference is treated as an object-creation site.

6   Affine Analysis and Bug Reporting

The final step of Pungi is to perform analysis on the generated affine program and reports possible reference-counting errors. There are several possible analysis algorithms on affine programs, such as random interpretation [19]. Pungi adapts the ESP algorithm [25] to perform affine analysis. The major reason for choosing ESP is that it is both path-sensitive and interprocedural. The analysis has to be path sensitive to rule out impossible paths. The affine program in Fig. 9 shows a typical example. In the statement "if (on1==0) ...", the analysis must be able to remember the path condition on1==0 to rule out the impossible case where rc1==1 and on1==1. Without that capability, the analysis would not be able to see that the first assertion always holds. The analysis also must be interprocedural as the affine program in Fig. 8 illustrates.

ESP symbolically evaluates the program being analyzed, tracks and updates symbolic states. At every program location, it infers a set of possible symbolic states of the following form:

$$\{ \langle ps_1, es_1 \rangle, \ldots, \langle ps_n, es_n \rangle \}$$

In ESP, a symbolic state consists of a property state ps and an execution state es. The important thing about the split between property and execution states is that ESP is designed so that it is path- and context-sensitive only to the property states. Specifically, at a control-flow join point, symbolic states merge based on the property state; the execution states of all states that have the same property

```
foo () {
  locals rc1,ev1,on1;
  rc1=0; ev1=0;
  // {<[rc1=0,ev1=0], []>}
  if (?) {
    rc1=1; on1=1
    // {<[rc1=1,ev1=0], [on1=1]>}
  } else {
    rc1=0; on1=0
    // {<[rc1=0,ev1=0], [on1=0]>}
  };
  // {<[rc1=1,ev1=0], [on1=1]>, <[rc1=0,ev1=0], [on1=0]>}
  if (on1==0) {
    // {<[rc1=0,ev1=0], [on1=0]>}
    assert (rc1==ev1);
    return;
  }
  // {<[rc1=1,ev1=0], [on1=1]>}
  if (on1==1) ev1++;
  // {<[rc1=1,ev1=1], [on1=1]>}
  assert (rc1==ev1);
  return (rc1,ev1);
}
```

Fig. 10. An example of affine analysis

state are merged. By splitting property and execution states in different ways, we can control the tradeoff between efficiency and precision of the algorithm.

A particular analysis needs to decide how to split between property and execution states in ESP. We next discuss how they are defined in Pungi but leave the detailed algorithm to the ESP paper. When analyzing an affine program, Pungi's property state is the values of refcount-change variables and escape variables. The execution state is the values of all other variables.

Fig. 10 presents the analysis result at key program locations for the affine program in Fig. 9. As we can see, after the first if-statement, there are two symbolic states, representing the two branches of the if-statement. Then path sensitivity allows the analysis to eliminate impossible symbolic states after the testing of on1==0 in the second if-statement.

We note that ESP was originally designed with a finite number of property states, while values of refcount changes and escapes can be arbitrarily large. In our implementation, we simply put a limit on those values (10 in our implementation) and used a top value when they go out of the limit.

7   Implementation and Limitations

We have built a prototype implementation of Pungi. The implementation is written in OCaml within the framework of CIL [26], which is a tool that allows analysis and transformation of C source code. Pungi's prototype implementation cannot analyze C++ code because CIL can parse only C code. Passes are inserted into CIL to perform the separation of interface code from library code, the SSA transform, the affine translation, and the affine analysis. Our implementation of the SSA transform follows the elegant algorithm by Aycock and Horspool [27]. The total size of the implementation is around 5,000 lines of OCaml code.

Pungi also needs to identify entry native functions because assertions about parameter objects are inserted only to entry functions. Native extensions typically have a registration table to register entry functions to Python statically. Pungi searches for the table and extracts information from the table to identify entry functions. Since Python is a dynamically typed language, a native extension module can also dynamically register entry functions. Therefore, Pungi also uses some heuristics to recognize entry functions. In particular, if a function uses PyArg_Parse (or several other similar functions) to decode arguments, then it is treated as an entry function.

Limitations. Before we present the evaluation results of Pungi, we list its major limitations. We will discuss our plan to address some of these limitations when discussing future work. Some of these limitations have been discussed before, but we include them below for completeness.

First, Pungi assumes shallow aliasing. Whenever an object reference is retrieved from a collection object such as a list, read from a field in a struct, or returned from a function call, the reference is assumed to point to a distinct object; such a site is treated as an object-creation site.

Second, Pungi reports errors assuming Python invokes entry native functions with distinct objects. This is reflected by the fact that an assertion of the form $rc = ev$ is inserted for every parameter object of an entry native function. This assumption can be relaxed straightforwardly and please see discussion in future work.

Third, Pungi's bug definition may cause it to miss some dangling reference errors in the middle of functions, because assertions are inserted only at the end of functions.

Finally, a native extension module can call back Python functions through the Python/C API, resulting in a Ping-Pong behavior between Python and native code. An accurate analysis of such situations would require analyzing both Python and C code. On the other hand, we have not encountered such code in our experiments.

8 Evaluation

We selected 13 Python/C programs for our evaluation. These programs are common Python packages in Fedora OS and they use the Python/C interface to invoke the underlying C libraries. For instance, PyCrypto is a Python cryptography toolkit, which provides Python secure hash functions and various encryption algorithms including AES and RSA. One major reason we selected those

Table 1. Statistics about selected benchmark programs

Benchmark	Total (KLOC)	Interface code (KLOC)	Time (s)
krbV	7.0	3.7	0.78
pycrypto	16.6	7.0	1.32
pyxattr	1.0	1.0	0.09
rrdtool	31.4	0.6	0.01
dbus	93.1	7.0	0.66
gst	2.7	1.8	0.03
canto	0.3	0.2	0.001
duplicity	0.5	0.4	0.001
netifaces	1.1	1.0	0.09
pyaudio	2.9	2.7	0.03
pyOpenSSL	9.6	9.3	1.27
ldap	3.8	3.4	0.23
yum	3.0	2.4	0.20
TOTAL	173	40.5	4.7

programs for evaluation is that a previous tool, CPyChecker [5], has reported its results on those programs and we wanted to compare Pungi's results with CPy-Checker's. All evaluation was run on a Ubuntu 9.10 box with 512MB memory and 2.8GHz CPU.

Table 1 lists the selected benchmarks, their sizes in terms of thousands of lines of code (KLOC), sizes of their interface code (recall that the first step Pungi performs is to separate interface from library code), and the amount of time Pungi spent on analyzing their code for reference-counting errors. The time is an average of ten runs. As we can see, Pungi is able to analyze a total of 173K lines of code in a few seconds, partly thanks to the separation between interface and library code.

The main objective in our evaluation is to know how effective our tool is in identifying the reference-counting errors as defined. This includes the number of bugs Pungi reports, the false positive rate, and the accuracy of our tool compared to CPyChecker.

Errors Found. For a benchmark program, Table 2 shows the number of warnings issued by Pungi, the numbers of true reference over- and under-counting errors, and the number of false positives. For the 13 benchmark programs, Pungi issued a total of 210 warnings, among which there are 142 true reference over-counting errors and a total of 22 true reference under-counting errors. We manually checked all true errors to the best of our ability via a two-person team. Common errors reported by both CPyChecker and Pungi have been reported to the developers by the CPyChecker author and some of those errors have been fixed in later versions of the tested benchmarks. Most of the additional true errors found by Pungi were easy to confirm manually.

Table 2. All warnings reported by Pungi, which include true reference over- and under-counting errors and false positives

Benchmark	All Warnings	Reference Over-counting	Reference Under-counting	False Positives (%)
krbV	85	74	0	11 (13%)
pycrypto	10	6	1	3 (30%)
pyxattr	4	2	0	2 (50%)
rrdtool	0	0	0	0 (0%)
dbus	3	1	0	2 (67%)
gst	30	12	13	5 (17%)
canto	6	0	4	2 (33%)
duplicity	4	2	0	2 (50%)
netifaces	8	2	1	5 (63%)
pyaudio	35	28	2	5 (14%)
pyOpenSSL	9	3	1	5 (56%)
ldap	15	11	0	4 (27%)
yum	1	1	0	0 (0%)
TOTAL	210	142	22	46 (22%)

There are 46 false positives and the overall false-positive rate is moderate, about 22%. We investigated those false positives and found most false positives are because of the following reasons:

– Object references in structs. With the assumption of shallow aliasing, Pungi treats the assignment of an object reference to a field in a struct as an escape of the reference, and treats the reading an object reference from a field of a struct as returning a reference to a new object. For example, in the following code p and q would reference two distinct objects in Pungi's analysis.

```
f->d = p;
q = f->d;
```

As a result, Pungi loses precision when tracking refcounts in such cases. This may cause both false positives and false negatives and it contributes to the majority (22 in total) of all the false positives seen in packages such as pycrypto and ldap.

– Type casting. Pungi treats references of PyObject type (and its subtytpes such as PyLongObject, PyIntObject, and PyStringObeject) as references to Python objects. In some package code, a Python object reference is cast into another type such as an integer and then escapes to the heap. Pungi's affine translation cannot model this casting and would incorrectly issue a reference over-counting warning. 20 false positives in packages such as gst and pyOpenSSL were caused by this reason.

Table 3. Comparison of errors found between Pungi and CPyChecker

Benchmark	Pungi Common	MA	Proc	Loop	CPyChecker Errors found
krbV	39	33	1	1	39
pycrypto	6	0	1	0	6
pyxattr	2	0	0	0	2
rrdtool	0	0	0	0	0
dbus	1	0	0	0	1
gst	21	2	0	2	21
canto	4	0	0	0	4
duplicity	2	0	0	0	2
netifaces	3	0	0	0	3
pyaudio	25	3	1	1	25
pyOpenSSL	1	3	0	0	1
ldap	8	3	0	0	8
yum	1	0	0	0	1
TOTAL	112	43	3	4	112

Comparison with CPyChecker. Table 3 shows the comparison of errors found between Pungi and CPyChecker. We looked into the differences and found that Pungi found all errors reported by CPyChecker. In addition, Pungi found 50 more errors than CPyChecker. The reason is because Pungi employs more precise analysis that applies the SSA and analyzes loops as well as function calls. CPyChecker's analysis is intraprocedural and ignores loops. We categorize the causes in the table. In the column Common, we put the number of errors that are reported by both Pungi and CPyChecker. Column MA (Multiple Assignments) shows the number of errors that Pungi found but missed by CPyChecker because CPyChecker's implementation cannot deal with the case when variables are statically assigned multiple times with different object references; Pungi can deal with this by the SSA transform. Column Proc shows the number of errors Pungi found but missed by CPyChecker because it cannot perform interprocedural analysis. Column Loop shows the number of errors Pungi found but missed by CPyChecker because it cannot analyze loops. The comparison shows that Pungi compares favorably to CPyChecker.

9   Conclusions and Future Work

We have described Pungi, a static-analysis tool that identifies reference-counting errors in Python/C extension modules. It translates extension code to an affine program, which is analyzed for errors of reference counting. Pungi's affine abstraction is novel in that it applies the SSA transform to simplify affine translation and in that it can deal with the interprocedural case and escaping references. The prototype implementation found over 150 bugs in over 170K lines. We believe that Pungi makes a solid step toward statically analyzing code that uses reference counting to manage resources.

As future work, we plan to generalize Pungi to relax some of its assumptions. Pungi assumes shallow aliasing and assumes parameter objects to entry native functions are distinct objects. One possibility is to report errors for any possible aliasing situation, by adding nondeterminism into native functions. As one example, suppose an entry native function takes two parameter objects referenced by p1 and p2, respectively. Suppose the function can be called either with p1 and p2 referencing two distinct objects or with p1 and p2 referencing the same object. We can insert the following code at the beginning of the native function before translation: "if (?) {p1=p2}", which nondeterministically initializes p1 and p2 for the two aliasing situations. As another example, after an object is retrieved from a list, we can nondeterministically assume the object can be a new object, or any existing object. This approach can be further improved if Python and C code are analyzed together and some alias analysis is used to eliminate impossible aliasing situations. Another possible approach to relax the shallow aliasing assumption is to keep and maintain a set of finite access paths to each Python object, as suggested by Shaham *et al.* [28].

Acknowledgement. We thank the anonymous reviewers whose comments and suggestions have helped improve the paper. This research is supported by NSF grants CCF-0915157 and CCF-1149211.

References

1. Meyerovich, L.A., Rabkin, A.S.: Empirical analysis of programming language adoption. In: ACM Conference on Object-Oriented Programming, Systems, Languages, and Applications (OOPSLA), pp. 1–18 (2013)
2. Python/C API reference manual (2013),
   http://docs.python.org/3.3/c-api/index.html
3. Lal, A., Ramalingam, G.: Reference count analysis with shallow aliasing. Information Processing Letters 111(2), 57–63 (2010)
4. Emmi, M., Jhala, R., Kohler, E., Majumdar, R.: Verifying reference counting implementations. In: Kowalewski, S., Philippou, A. (eds.) TACAS 2009. LNCS, vol. 5505, pp. 352–367. Springer, Heidelberg (2009)
5. Malcom, D.: Cpychecker,
   https://gcc-python-plugin.readthedocs.org/en/latest/cpychecker.html
6. Beazley, D.M.: SWIG Users Manual: Version 1.1 (June 1997)
7. Cython, http://cython.org/
8. Furr, M., Foster, J.S.: Polymorphic type inference for the JNI. In: Sestoft, P. (ed.) ESOP 2006. LNCS, vol. 3924, pp. 309–324. Springer, Heidelberg (2006)

9. Tan, G., Morrisett, G.: ILEA: Inter-language analysis across Java and C. In: ACM Conference on Object-Oriented Programming, Systems, Languages, and Applications (OOPSLA), pp. 39–56 (2007)

10. Kondoh, G., Onodera, T.: Finding bugs in Java Native Interface programs. In: ISSTA 2008: Proceedings of the 2008 International Symposium on Software Testing and Analysis, pp. 109–118. ACM, New York (2008)

11. Li, S., Tan, G.: Finding bugs in exceptional situations of JNI programs. In: 16th ACM Conference on Computer and Communications Security (CCS), pp. 442–452 (2009)

12. Lee, B., Hirzel, M., Grimm, R., Wiedermann, B., McKinley, K.S.: Jinn: Synthesizing a dynamic bug detector for foreign language interfaces. In: ACM Conference on Programming Language Design and Implementation (PLDI), pp. 36–49 (2010)

13. Li, S., Liu, Y.D., Tan, G.: Native code atomicity for Java. In: Jhala, R., Igarashi, A. (eds.) APLAS 2012. LNCS, vol. 7705, pp. 2–17. Springer, Heidelberg (2012)

14. Siefers, J., Tan, G., Morrisett, G.: Robusta: Taming the native beast of the JVM. In: 17th ACM Conference on Computer and Communications Security (CCS), pp. 201–211 (2010)

15. Tan, G., Appel, A., Chakradhar, S., Raghunathan, A., Ravi, S., Wang, D.: Safe Java Native Interface. In: Proceedings of IEEE International Symposium on Secure Software Engineering, pp. 97–106 (2006)

16. Hirzel, M., Grimm, R.: Jeannie: Granting Java Native Interface developers their wishes. In: ACM Conference on Object-Oriented Programming, Systems, Languages, and Applications (OOPSLA), pp. 19–38 (2007)

17. Furr, M., Foster, J.: Checking type safety of foreign function calls. In: ACM Conference on Programming Language Design and Implementation (PLDI), pp. 62–72 (2005)

18. Li, S., Tan, G.: JET: Exception checking in the Java Native Interface. In: ACM Conference on Object-Oriented Programming, Systems, Languages, and Applications (OOPSLA), pp. 345–358 (2011)

19. Gulwani, S., Necula, G.C.: Discovering affine equalities using random interpretation. In: 30th ACM Symposium on Principles of Programming Languages (POPL), pp. 74–84 (2003)

20. Müller-Olm, M., Seidl, H.: Precise interprocedural analysis through linear algebra. In: 31st ACM Symposium on Principles of Programming Languages (POPL), pp. 330–341 (2004)

21. Karr, M.: Affine relationships among variables of a program. Acta Informatica 6, 133–151 (1976)

22. Müller-Olm, M., Rüthing, O.: On the complexity of constant propagation. In: Sands, D. (ed.) ESOP 2001. LNCS, vol. 2028, pp. 190–205. Springer, Heidelberg (2001)

23. Elder, M., Lim, J., Sharma, T., Andersen, T., Reps, T.: Abstract domains of affine relations. In: Yahav, E. (ed.) Static Analysis. LNCS, vol. 6887, pp. 198–215. Springer, Heidelberg (2011)

24. Johnsson, T.: Lambda lifting: Transforming programs to recursive equations. In: Jouannaud, J.-P. (ed.) FPCA 1985. LNCS, vol. 201, pp. 190–203. Springer, Heidelberg (1985)

25. Das, M., Lerner, S., Seigle, M.: ESP: path-sensitive program verification in polynomial time. In: ACM Conference on Programming Language Design and Implementation (PLDI), pp. 57–68 (2002)
26. Necula, G.C., McPeak, S., Rahul, S.P., Weimer, W.: CIL: Intermediate language and tools for analysis and transformation of C programs. In: Nigel Horspool, R. (ed.) CC 2002. LNCS, vol. 2304, pp. 213–228. Springer, Heidelberg (2002)
27. Aycock, J.: Simple generation of static single-assignment form. In: Watt, D.A. (ed.) CC 2000. LNCS, vol. 1781, pp. 110–124. Springer, Heidelberg (2000)
28. Shaham, R., Yahav, E., Kolodner, E.K., Sagiv, M.: Establishing local temporal heap safety properties with applications to compile-time memory management. In: Cousot, R. (ed.) SAS 2003. LNCS, vol. 2694, pp. 483–503. Springer, Heidelberg (2003)

Safely Composable Type-Specific Languages

Cyrus Omar[1], Darya Kurilova[1], Ligia Nistor[1], Benjamin Chung[1],
Alex Potanin[2], and Jonathan Aldrich[1]

[1] Carnegie Mellon University, Pittsburgh, USA
[2] Victoria University of Wellington, Wellington, New Zealand
{comar,darya,lnistor,bwchung,aldrich}@cs.cmu.edu,
alex@ecs.vuw.ac.nz

Abstract. Programming languages often include specialized syntax for common datatypes (e.g. lists) and some also build in support for specific specialized datatypes (e.g. regular expressions), but user-defined types must use general-purpose syntax. Frustration with this causes developers to use strings, rather than structured data, with alarming frequency, leading to correctness, performance, security, and usability issues. Allowing library providers to modularly extend a language with new syntax could help address these issues. Unfortunately, prior mechanisms either limit expressiveness or are not safely composable: individually unambiguous extensions can still cause ambiguities when used together. We introduce *type-specific languages* (TSLs): logic associated with a type that determines how the bodies of *generic literals*, able to contain arbitrary syntax, are parsed and elaborated, hygienically. The TSL for a type is invoked only when a literal appears where a term of that type is expected, guaranteeing non-interference. We give evidence supporting the applicability of this approach and formally specify it with a bidirectionally typed elaboration semantics for the Wyvern programming language.

Keywords: extensible languages, parsing, bidirectional typechecking, hygiene.

1 Motivation

Many data types can be seen, semantically, as modes of use of general purpose product and sum types. For example, lists can be seen as recursive sums by observing that a list can either be empty, or be broken down into a product of the *head* element and the *tail*, another list. In an ML-like functional language, sums are exposed as datatypes and products as tuples and records, so list types can be defined as follows:

```
datatype 'a list = Nil | Cons of 'a * 'a list
```

In class-based object-oriented language, objects can be seen as products of their instance data and classes as the cases of a sum type [9]. In low-level languages, like C, structs and unions expose products and sums, respectively.

By defining user-defined types in terms of these general purpose constructs, we immediately benefit from powerful reasoning principles (e.g. induction), language support (e.g. pattern matching) and compiler optimizations. But these semantic benefits often come at a syntactic cost. For example, few would claim that writing a list of numbers as a sequence of Cons cells is convenient:

R. Jones (Ed.): ECOOP 2014, LNCS 8586, pp. 105–130, 2014.
© Springer-Verlag Berlin Heidelberg 2014

```
Cons(1, Cons(2, Cons(3, Cons(4, Nil))))
```

Lists are a common data structure, so many languages include *literal syntax* for introducing them, e.g. [1, 2, 3, 4]. This syntax is semantically equivalent to the general-purpose syntax shown above, but brings cognitive benefits both when writing and reading code by focusing on the content of the list, rather than the nature of the encoding. Using terminology from Green's cognitive dimensions of notations [8], it is more *terse*, *visible* and *maps more closely* to the intuitive notion of a list. Stoy, in discussing the value of good notation, writes [31]:

> A good notation thus conceals much of the inner workings behind suitable abbreviations, while allowing us to consider it in more detail if we require: matrix and tensor notations provide further good examples of this. It may be summed up in the saying: "A notation is important for what it leaves out."

Although list, number and string literals are nearly ubiquitous features of modern languages, some languages provide specialized literal syntax for other common collections (like maps, sets, vectors and matrices), external data formats (like XML and JSON), query languages (like regular expressions and SQL), markup languages (like HTML and Markdown) and many other types of data. For example, a language with built-in notation for HTML and SQL, supporting type safe *splicing* via curly braces, might define:

```
1  let webpage : HTML = <html><body><h1>Results for {keyword}</h1>
2    <ul id="results">{to_list_items(query(db,
3      SELECT title, snippet FROM products WHERE {keyword} in title))}
4    </ul></body></html>
```

as shorthand for:

```
1  let webpage : HTML = HTMLElement(Dict.empty(), [BodyElement(Dict.empty(),
2    [H1Element(Dict.empty(), [TextNode("Results for " + keyword)]),
3    ULElement((Dict.add Dict.empty() ("id","results")), to_list_items(query(db,
4      SelectStmt(["title", "snippet"], "products",
5      [WhereClause(InPredicate(StringLit(keyword), "title"))])))))])])
```

When general-purpose notation like this is too cognitively demanding for comfort, but a specialized notation as above is not available, developers turn to run-time mechanisms to make constructing data structures more convenient. Among the most common strategies in these situations, no matter the language paradigm, is to simply use a string representation, parsing it at run-time:

```
1  let webpage : HTML = parse_html("<html><body><h1>Results for "+keyword+"</h1>
2    <ul id=\"results\">" + to_string(to_list_items(query(db, parse_sql(
3      "SELECT title, snippet FROM products WHERE '"+keyword+"' in title")))) +
4    "</ul></body></html>")
```

Though recovering some of the notational convenience of the literal version, it is still more awkward to write, requiring explicit conversions to and from structured representations (parse_html and to_string, respectively) and escaping when the syntax of the data language interferes with the syntax of string literals (line 2). Such code also causes a number of problems that go beyond cognitive load. Because parsing occurs at run-time, syntax errors will not be discovered statically, causing potential run-time errors in production scenarios. Run-time parsing also incurs performance overhead, particularly relevant when code like this is executed often (as on a heavily-trafficked website).

But the most serious issue with this code is that it is highly insecure: it is vulnerable to cross-site scripting attacks (line 1) and SQL injection attacks (line 3). For example, if a user entered the keyword '; DROP TABLE products --, the entire product database could be erased. These attack vectors are considered to be two of the most serious security threats on the web today [26]. Although developers are cautioned to sanitize their input, it can be difficult to verify that this was done correctly throughout a codebase. The best way to avoid these problems today is to avoid strings and other similar conveniences and insist on structured representations. Unfortunately, situations like this, where maintaining strong correctness, performance and security guarantees entails significant syntactic overhead, causing developers to turn to less structured solutions that are more convenient, are quite common (as we will discuss in Sec. 5).

Adding new literal syntax into a language is generally considered to be the responsibility of the language's designers. This is largely for technical reasons: not all syntactic forms can unambiguously coexist in the same grammar, so a designer is needed to decide which syntactic forms are available, and what their semantics should be. For example, conventional notations for sets and maps are both delimited by curly braces. When Python introduced set literals, it chose to distinguish them based on whether the literal contained only values (e.g. {3}), or key-value pairs ({"x": 3}). But this causes an ambiguity with the syntactic form { } – should it mean an empty set or an empty map (called a dictionary in Python)? The designers of Python avoided the ambiguity by choosing the latter interpretation (in this case, for backwards compatibility reasons).

Were this power given to library providers in a decentralized, unconstrained manner, the burden of resolving ambiguities would instead fall on developers who happened to import conflicting extensions. Indeed, this is precisely the situation with SugarJ [6] and other extensible languages generated by Sugar* [7], which allow library providers to extend the base syntax of the host language with new forms in a relatively unconstrained manner. These new forms are imported transitively throughout a program. To resolve syntactic ambiguities that arise, clients must manually augment the composed grammar with new rules that allow them to choose the correct interpretation explicitly. This is both difficult to do, requiring a reasonably thorough understanding of the underlying parser technology (in Sugar*, generalized LR parsing) and increases the cognitive load of using the conflicting notations (e.g. both sets and maps) together because disambiguation tokens must be used. These kinds of conflicts occur in a variety of circumstances: HTML and XML, different variants of SQL, JSON literals and maps, or differing implementations ("desugarings") of the same syntax (e.g. two regular expression engines). Code that uses these common abstractions together is very common in practice [13].

In this work, we will describe an alternative parsing strategy that sidesteps these problems by building into the language only a delimitation strategy, which ensures that ambiguities do not occur. The parsing and elaboration of literal bodies occurs during typechecking, rather than in the initial parsing phase. In particular, the typechecker defers responsibility to library providers, by treating the body of the literal as a term of the *type-specific language (TSL)* associated with the type it is being checked against. The TSL definition is responsible for elaborating this term using only general-purpose syntax. This strategy permits significant semantic flexibility – the meaning of a form like { } can differ depending on its type, so it is safe to use it for empty sets, maps and JSON literals. This frees these common forms from being tied to the variant of a data structure built into a language's standard library, which may not provide the precise semantics that a programmer needs (for example, Python dictionaries do not preserve key insertion order).

We present our work as a variant of an emerging programming language called Wyvern [22]. To allow us to focus on the essence of our proposal and provide the community with a minimal foundation for future work, the variant of Wyvern we develop here is simpler than the variant we previously described: it is purely functional (there are no effects other than non-termination) and it does not enforce a uniform access principle for objects (fields can be accessed directly), so objects are essentially just recursive labeled products with simple methods. It also adds recursive sum types, which we call *case types*, similar to those found in ML. One can refer to our version of the language as *TSL Wyvern* when the variant being discussed is not clear. Our work substantially extends and makes concrete a mechanism we sketched in a short workshop paper [23].

The paper is organized as a language design for TSL Wyvern:

- In Sec. 2, we introduce TSL Wyvern with a practical example. We introduce both inline and forward referenced literal forms, splicing, case and object types and an example of a TSL definition.
- In Sec. 3, we specify the layout-sensitive concrete syntax of TSL Wyvern with an Adams grammar and introduce the abstract syntax of TSL Wyvern.
- In Sec. 4, we specify the static semantics of TSL Wyvern as a *bidirectionally typed elaboration semantics*, which combines two key technical mechanisms:

  1. **Bidirectional Typechecking:** By distinguishing locations where an expression must synthesize a type from locations where an expression is being analyzed against a known type, we precisely specify where generic literals can appear and how dispatch to a TSL definition (an object with a parse method serving as metadata of a type) occurs.
  2. **Hygienic Elaboration:** Elaboration of literals must not cause the inadvertent capture or shadowing of variables in the context where the literal appears. It must, however, remain possible for the client to do so in those portions of the literal body treated as spliced expressions. The language cannot know *a priori* where these spliced portions will be. We give a clean type-theoretic formulation that achieves of this notion of hygiene.

- In Sec. 5, we gather initial data on how broadly applicable our technique may be by conducting a corpus analysis, finding that existing code often uses strings where specialized syntax might be more appropriate.
- In Sec. 6, we briefly report on the current implementation status of our work.
- We discuss related work in Sec. 7 and conclude in Sec. 8 with a discussion of present limitations and future research directions.

```
1   let imageBase : URL = <images.example.com>
2   let bgImage : URL = <%imageBase%/background.png>
3   new : SearchServer
4     def resultsFor(searchQuery, page)
5       serve(~) (* serve : HTML -> Unit *)
6          >html
7            >head
8              >title Search Results
9              >style ~
10                 body { background-image: url(%bgImage%) }
11                 #search { background-color: %darken('#aabbcc', 10pct)% }
12             >body
13               >h1 Results for <{HTML.Text(searchQuery)}:
14               >div[id="search"]
15                 Search again: < SearchBox("Go!")
16             < (* fmt_results : DB * SQLQuery * Nat * Nat -> HTML *)
17               fmt_results(db, ~, 10, page)
18                 SELECT * FROM products WHERE {searchQuery} in title
```

Fig. 1. Wyvern Example with Multiple TSLs

```
<literal body here, <inner angle brackets> must be balanced>
{literal body here, {inner braces} must be balanced}
[literal body here, [inner brackets] must be balanced]
'literal body here, ''inner backticks'' must be doubled'
'literal body here, ''inner single quotes'' must be doubled'
"literal body here, ""inner double quotes"" must be doubled"
12xyz (* no delimiters necessary for number literals; suffix optional *)
```

Fig. 2. Inline Generic Literal Forms

2   Type-Specific Languages in Wyvern

We begin with an example in Fig. 1 showing several different TSLs being used in a fragment of a web application showing search results from a database. We will review this example below to develop intuitions about TSLs in Wyvern; a formal and more detailed description will follow. For clarity of presentation, we color each character by the TSL it is governed by. Black is the base language and comments are in italics.

2.1   Inline Literals

Our first TSL appears on the right-hand side of the variable binding on line 1. The variable imageBase is annotated with its type, URL. This is a named object type declaring several fields representing the components of a URL: its protocol, domain name, port, path and so on (below). We could have created a value of type URL using the general-purpose introductory form new, which *forward references* an indented block of field and method definitions beginning on the line after it appears:

```
1   objtype URL                    1   let imageBase : URL = new
2     val protocol : String        2     val protocol = "http"
3     val subdomain : String       3     val subdomain = "images"
4     (* ... *)                    4     (* ... *)
```

This is tedious. By associating a TSL with the URL type (we will show how later), we can instead introduce precisely this value using conventional notation for URLs by placing it in the *body* of a *generic literal*, <images.example.com>. Any other delimited form in Fig. 2 can equivalently be used when the constraints indicated can be obeyed. The type annotation on `imageBase` (or equivalently, ascribed directly to the literal) implies that this literal's *expected type* is `URL`, so the body of the literal (the characters between the angle brackets, in blue) will be governed by the `URL` TSL during the type-checking phase. This TSL will parse the body (at compile-time) and produce an *elaboration*: a Wyvern abstract syntax tree (AST) that explicitly instantiates a new object of type `URL` using general-purpose forms only, as if the above had been written directly.

2.2   Splicing

In addition to supporting conventional notation for URLs, this TSL supports *splicing* another Wyvern expression of type `URL` to form a larger URL. The spliced term is here delimited by percent signs, as seen on line 2 of Fig. 1. The TSL chooses to parse code between percent signs as a Wyvern expression, using its abstract syntax tree (AST) to construct the overall elaboration. A string-based representation of the URL is never constructed at run-time. Note that the delimiters used to go from Wyvern to a TSL are controlled by Wyvern while the TSL controls how to return to Wyvern.

2.3   Layout-Delimited Literals

On line 5 of Fig. 1, we see a call to a function `serve` (not shown) which has type `HTML -> Unit`. Here, `HTML` is a user-defined *case type*, having cases for each HTML tag as well as some other structures, such as text nodes and sequencing. Declarations of some of these cases can be seen on lines 2-6 of Fig. 3 (note that TSL Wyvern also includes simple product types for convenience, written `T1 * T2`). We could again use Wyvern's general-purpose introductory form for case types, e.g. `BodyElement((attrs, child))`. But, as discussed in the introduction, this can be cognitively demanding. Thus, we have associated a TSL with `HTML` that provides a simplified notation for writing HTML, shown being used on lines 6-18 of Fig. 1. This literal body is layout-delimited, rather than delimited by explicit tokens as in Fig. 2, and introduced by a form of *forward reference*, written ~ ("tilde"), on the previous line. Because the forward reference occurs in a position where the expected type is `HTML`, the literal body is governed by that type's TSL. The forward reference will be replaced by the general-purpose term, of type `HTML`, generated by the TSL during typechecking. Because layout was used as a delimiter, there are no syntactic constraints on the body, unlike with inline forms (Fig. 2). For HTML, this is quite useful, as all of the inline forms impose constraints that would cause conflict with some valid HTML, requiring awkward and error-prone escaping. It also avoids issues with leading indentation in multi-line literals, as the parser strips these automatically for layout-delimited literal bodies.

2.4   Implementing a TSL

Portions of the implementation of the TSL for `HTML` are shown on lines 8-15 of Fig. 3. A TSL is associated with a named type using a general mechanism for associating a statically-known value with a named type, called its *metadata*. Type metadata, in this

```
1   casetype HTML
2     Empty
3     Seq of HTML * HTML
4     Text of String
5     BodyElement of Attributes * HTML
6     StyleElement of Attributes * CSS
7     (* ... *)
8     metadata = new : HasTSL
9       val parser = ~
10        start <- '>body'= attributes start>
11          fn (attrs, child) => Inj('BodyElement', Pair(attrs, child))
12        start <- '>style'= attributes EXP>
13          fn (attrs, e) => 'StyleElement((%attrs%, %e%))'
14        start <- '<'= EXP>
15          fn (e) => '%e% : HTML'
```

Fig. 3. A Wyvern case type with an associated TSL

```
1   objtype HasTSL                              10   casetype Exp
2     val parser : Parser                       11     Var of ID
3   objtype Parser                              12     Lam of ID * Type * Exp
4     def parse(ps : ParseStream) : Result      13     Ap of Exp * Exp
5     metadata : HasTSL = new                   14     Inj of Id * Exp
6       val parser = (*parser generator*)       15     ...
7   casetype Result                             16     Spliced of ParseStream
8     OK of Exp * ParseStream                   17     metadata : HasTSL = new
9     Error of String * Location                18       val parser = (*quasiquotes*)
```

Fig. 4. Some of the types included in the Wyvern prelude

context, is comparable to class annotations in Java or class/type attributes in C#/F# and internalizes the practice of writing metadata using comments, so that it can be checked by the language and accessed programmatically more easily. This can be used for a variety of purposes – to associate documentation with a type, to mark types as being deprecated, and so on. Note that we allow programs to extract the metadata value of a named type T programmatically using the form **metadata[T]**.

For the purposes of this work, metadata values will always be of type HasTSL, an object type that declares a single field, parser, of type Parser. The Parser type is an object type declaring a single method, parse, that transforms a ParseStream extracted from a literal body to a Wyvern AST. An AST is a value of type Exp, a case type that encodes the abstract syntax of Wyvern expressions. Fig. 4 shows portions of the declarations of these types, which live in the Wyvern *prelude* (a collection of types that are automatically loaded before any other).

Notice, however, that the TSL for HTML is not provided as an explicit parse method but instead as a declarative grammar. A grammar is specialized notation for defining a parser, so we can implement a grammar-based parser generator as a TSL atop the lower-level interface exposed by Parser. We do so using a layout-sensitive grammar formalism developed by Adams [1]. Wyvern is itself layout-sensitive and has a grammar that can be written down using this formalism, as we will discuss, so it is sensible to expose it to TSL providers as well. Most aspects of this formalism are conventional. Each non-terminal (e.g. the designated start non-terminal) is defined by a number of disjunctive rules, each introduced using <-. Each rule defines a sequence of terminals (e.g. '>body') and non-terminals (e.g. start, or one of the built-in non-terminals ID, EXP or TYPE, representing Wyvern identifiers, expressions and types, respectively). Unique to Adams grammars is that each terminal and non-terminal in a rule can also have an optional *layout constraint* associated with it. The layout constraints available are = (meaning that the leftmost column of the annotated term must be aligned with that of the parent term), > (the leftmost column must be indented further) and >= (the leftmost column *may* be indented further). Note that the leftmost column is not simply the first character, in the case of terms that span multiple lines. For example, the production rule of the form A → B= C≥ D> approximately reads as: "Term B must be at the same indentation level as term A, term C may be at the same or a greater indentation level as term A, and term D must be at an indentation level greater than term A's." In particular, if D contains a NEWLINE character, the next line must be indented past the position of the left-most character of A (typically, though not always, constructed so that it must appear at the beginning of a line). There are no constraints relating D to B or C other than the standard sequencing constraint: the first character of D must be further along in the file than the others. Using Adams grammars, the syntax of real-world languages like Python and Haskell can be written declaratively.

Each rule is followed, in an indented block, by a spliced function that generates an elaboration given the elaborations recursively generated by each of the n non-terminals in the rule, ordered left-to-right. Elaborations are of type Exp, which is a case type containing each form in the abstract syntax of Wyvern (as well as an additional case, Spliced, that is used internally), which we will describe later. Here, we show how to generate an elaboration using the general-purpose introductory form for case types (line 11, Inj corresponds to the introductory form for case types) as well as using *quasiquotes* (line 13). Quasiquotes are expressions written in concrete syntax that are not evaluated for their value, but rather evaluate to their corresponding syntax trees. We observe that quasiquotes too fall into the pattern of "specialized notation associated with a type": quasiquotes for expressions, types and identifiers are simply TSLs associated with Exp, Type and ID (Fig. 4). They support the Wyvern concrete syntax as well as an additional delimited form, written with %s, that supports "unquoting": splicing another AST into the one being generated. Again, splicing is safe and structural, not string-based.

We can see how HTML splicing works on lines 12-15: we simply include the Wyvern expression non-terminal EXP in our rule and insert it into our quoted result where appropriate. The type that the spliced Wyvern expression will be expected to have is determined by where it is placed. On line 13 it is known to be CSS by the declaration of HTML, and on line 15, it is known to be HTML by the use of an explicit ascription.

3 Syntax

3.1 Concrete Syntax

We will begin our formal treatment by specifying the concrete syntax of Wyvern declaratively, using the same layout-sensitive formalism that we have introduced for TSL grammars, developed recently by Adams [1]. Adams grammars are useful because they allow us to implement layout-sensitive syntax, like that we've been describing, without relying on context-sensitive lexers or parsers. Most existing layout-sensitive languages (e.g. Python and Haskell) use hand-rolled context-sensitive lexers or parsers (keeping

```
1   (* programs *)
2   p → 'objtype'= ID> NEWLINE> objdecls> metadatadecl> NEWLINE> p=
3   p → 'casetype'= ID> NEWLINE> casedecls> metadatadecl> NEWLINE> p=
4   p → e=
5   metadatadecl → ε | 'metadata'= '='> e>
6   objdecls → ε
7   objdecls → 'val'= ID> ':'> type NEWLINE> objdecls>
8   objdecls → 'def'= ID> '('> typelist> ')'> ':'> type> NEWLINE> objdecls>
9   casedecls → ε
10  casedecls → ID= (ε | 'of'> type>) NEWLINE> casedecls>
11
12  type → ID= | type= '->'> type> | type= '*'> type>
13
14  e → ē=
15  e → ē['~']= NEWLINE> chars>
16  e → ē['new']= NEWLINE> m>
17  e → ē['case(' ē ')']= NEWLINE> r>
18
19  (* object definitions *)
20  m → ε
21  m → 'val'= ID> '='> e> NEWLINE> m=
22  m → 'def'= ID> '('> idlist> ')'> '='> e> NEWLINE> d=
23
24  (* rules for case analysis (case types and products) *)
25  r → rc | rp
26  rc → ID= '('> ID> ')'> '=>'> e>
27  rc → ID= '('> ID> ')'> '=>'> e> NEWLINE> rc=
28  rp → '('= idlist> ')'> '=>'> e>
29
30  (* expressions containing zero forward references *)
31  ē → ID=
32  ē → ē= ':'> type>
33  ē → 'let'= ID> (ε | ':'> type>) '='> e> NEWLINE> ē=
34  ē → 'fn'= '('> idlist> ')'> (ε | ':'> type>) '=>'> ē>
35  ē → ē= '('> āl> ')'>
36  ē → '('> āl> ')'>
37  ē → ē= '.'> ID>
38  ē → 'toast'= '('> ē> ')'>
39  ē → 'metadata'= '['> ID> ']'>
40  ē → inlinelit=
41  āl → ε | āl_nonempty=
42  āl_nonempty → ē= | ē= ','> āl_nonempty>
43  inlinelit → samedelims= | matcheddelims= | numlit=
44
45  (* expressions containing exactly one forward reference *)
46  ẽ[fwd] → fwd=
47  ẽ[fwd] → ẽ[fwd]= ':'> type>
48  ẽ[fwd] → 'let'= ID> (ε | ':'> type>) '='> e> NEWLINE> ẽ[fwd]=
49  ẽ[fwd] → 'let'= ID> (ε | ':'> type>) '='> ẽ[fwd]> NEWLINE> ē=
50  ẽ[fwd] → 'fn'= idlist> (ε | ':'> type>) '=>'> ẽ[fwd]>
51  ẽ[fwd] → ẽ[fwd]= '('> āl> ')'>
52  ẽ[fwd] → ē= '('> ãl[fwd]> ')'>
53  ẽ[fwd] → '('> ãl[fwd]> ')'>
54  ẽ[fwd] → ẽ[fwd]= '.'> ID>
55  ẽ[fwd] → 'toast'= '('> ẽ[fwd]> ')'>
56  ãl[fwd] → ẽ[fwd] | ẽ[fwd]= ','> āl_nonempty> | ē= ','> ãl[fwd]>
```

Fig. 5. Concrete syntax of TSL Wyvern specified as an Adams grammar. Some standard productions and precedence handling rules have been omitted for concision.

```
1   objtype T
2     val y : HTML
3   let page : HTML->HTML = (fn(x) => ~)
4     >html
5       >body
6         <{x}
7   page(case(5 : Nat))
8     Z(_) => (new : T).y
9       val y = ~
10        >h1 Zero!
11    S(x) => ~
12      >h1 Successor!
```

objtype$[T, (y[\textbf{named}[HTML]], \emptyset), ()]; \emptyset;$
elet(easc[arrow[**named**$[HTML]$,
    named$[HTML]$]](**elam**$(x$.lit$[>html$
    $>body$
     $<\{x\}])), page.$
eap$(page; \textbf{ecase}(\textbf{easc}[\textbf{named}[Nat]](\textbf{lit}[5]))$ {
  erule$[Z](\_.\textbf{eprj}[y](\textbf{easc}[\textbf{named}[T]](\textbf{enew}$ {
    eval$[y](\textbf{lit}[>h1\ Zero!]); \emptyset$})));
  erule$[S](x.\textbf{lit}[>h1\ Sucessor!]); \emptyset$
})}

Fig. 6. An example Wyvern program demonstrating all three forward referenced forms. The corresponding abstract syntax is on the right.

track of, for example, the indentation level using special INDENT and DEDENT tokens), but these are more problematic because they could not be used to generate editor modes, syntax highlighters and other tools automatically. In particular, we will show how the forward references we have described can be correctly encoded without requiring a context-sensitive parser or lexer using this formalism. It is also useful that the TSL for Parser, above, uses the same parser technology as the host language, so that it can be used to generate the quasiquote TSL for Exp more easily.

3.2   Program Structure

The concrete syntax of TSL Wyvern is shown in Fig 5. An example Wyvern program showing several unique syntactic features of TSL Wyvern is shown in Fig. 6 (left).

The top level of a program (the p non-terminal) consists of a series of named type declarations – object types using **objtype** or case types using **casetype** – followed by an expression, e. Each named type declaration can also include a metadata declaration. Metadata is simply an expression associated with the type, used to store TSL logic (and in future work, other metadata). In the grammar, sequences of top-level declarations use the form p$^=$ to signify that all the succeeding p terms must begin at the same indentation. We do not specify separate compilation here, as this is an orthogonal issue.

3.3   Forward Referenced Blocks

Wyvern makes extensive use of forward referenced blocks to make its syntax clean. In particular, layout-delimited TSLs, **new** expressions for introducing objects, and **case** expressions for eliminating case types and tuples all make use of forward referenced blocks. Fig. 6 shows these in use (assuming suitable definitions of Nat and HTML).

Each line in the concrete syntax can contain either zero or one forward references. We distinguish these in the grammar by defining separate non-terminals $\bar{e}$ and $\tilde{e}$[fwd], where the parameter fwd is the particular forward reference form that occurs. Note particularly the rule for **let** (which permits an expression to span multiple lines and so can be used to support multiple forward references in a single expression).

$$\rho ::= \theta; e \qquad\qquad \tau ::= \mathbf{named}[T] \mid \mathbf{arrow}[\tau, \tau]$$

$$\theta ::= \emptyset$$
$$\mid \mathbf{objtype}[T, \omega, e]; \theta \qquad \omega ::= \emptyset \mid \ell[\tau]; \omega$$
$$\mid \mathbf{casetype}[T, \chi, e]; \theta \qquad \chi ::= \emptyset \mid C[\tau]; \chi$$

$e ::= x$	$\hat{e} ::= x$	$i ::= x$
$\mid \mathbf{easc}[\tau](e)$	$\mid \mathbf{hasc}[\tau](\hat{e})$	$\mid \mathbf{iasc}[\tau](i)$
$\mid \mathbf{elet}(e; x.e)$	$\mid \mathbf{hlet}(\hat{e}; x.\hat{e})$	$\mid \mathbf{ilet}(i; x.i)$
$\mid \mathbf{elam}(x.e)$	$\mid \mathbf{hlam}(x.\hat{e})$	$\mid \mathbf{ilam}(x.i)$
$\mid \mathbf{eap}(e; e)$	$\mid \mathbf{hap}(\hat{e}; \hat{e})$	$\mid \mathbf{iap}(i; i)$
$\mid \mathbf{enew}\,\{m\}$	$\mid \mathbf{hnew}\,\{\hat{m}\}$	$\mid \mathbf{inew}\,\{\dot{m}\}$
$\mid \mathbf{eprj}[\ell](e)$	$\mid \mathbf{hprj}[\ell](\hat{e})$	$\mid \mathbf{iprj}[\ell](i)$
$\mid \mathbf{einj}[C](e)$	$\mid \mathbf{hinj}[C](\hat{e})$	$\mid \mathbf{iinj}[C](i)$
$\mid \mathbf{ecase}(e)\,\{r\}$	$\mid \mathbf{hcase}(\hat{e})\,\{\hat{r}\}$	$\mid \mathbf{icase}(i)\,\{\dot{r}\}$
$\mid \mathbf{etoast}(e)$	$\mid \mathbf{htoast}(\hat{e})$	$\mid \mathbf{itoast}(i)$
$\mid \mathbf{emetadata}[T]$	$\mid \mathbf{hmetadata}[T]$	
$\mid \mathbf{lit}[body]$	$\mid \mathbf{spliced}[e]$	

$m ::= \emptyset$	$\hat{m} ::= \emptyset$	$\dot{m} ::= \emptyset$
$\mid \mathbf{eval}[\ell](e); m$	$\mid \mathbf{hval}[\ell](\hat{e}); \hat{m}$	$\mid \mathbf{ival}[\ell](i); \dot{m}$
$\mid \mathbf{edef}[\ell](x.e); m$	$\mid \mathbf{hdef}[\ell](x.\hat{e}); \hat{m}$	$\mid \mathbf{idef}[\ell](x.i); \dot{m}$

$r ::= \emptyset$	$\hat{r} ::= \emptyset$	$\dot{r} ::= \emptyset$
$\mid \mathbf{erule}[C](x.e); r$	$\mid \mathbf{hrule}[C](x.\hat{e}); \hat{r}$	$\mid \mathbf{irule}[C](x.i); \dot{r}$

Fig. 7. Abstract Syntax of TSL Wyvern programs (ρ), type declarations (θ), types (τ), external terms (e), translational terms ($\hat{e}$) and internal terms (i) and auxiliary forms. Metavariable T ranges over type names, ℓ over object member (field and method) labels, C over case labels, x over variables and $body$ over literal bodies. Tuple types are a mode of use of object types, so they are not included in the abstract syntax. For concision, we continue to write unit as () and pairs as (i_1, i_2) in abstract syntax as needed.

3.4 Abstract Syntax

The concrete syntax of a Wyvern program, p, is parsed to a program in the abstract syntax, ρ, shown in Fig. 7. Forward references are internalized. Note that all literal forms are unified into the abstract literal form $\mathbf{lit}[body]$, including the layout-delimited form and number literals. The body remains completely unparsed at this stage. The abstract syntax for the example in Fig. 6 is shown to its right and demonstrates the key rewriting done at this stage. Simple product types can be rewritten as object types in this phase. We assume that this occurs so that we can avoid specifying them separately in the remainder of the paper, though we continue to use tuple notation for concision.

4   Bidirectional Typechecking and Elaboration

We will now specify a type system for the abstract syntax in Fig. 7. Conventional type systems are specified using a typing judgement written like $\Gamma \vdash_\Theta e : \tau$, where the typing context, Γ, maps bound variables to types, and the named type context, Θ, maps type names to their declarations. Such typing judgements do not fully specify whether, when writing a typechecker, the type should be considered an input or an output. In some situations, a type propagates in from the surrounding syntactic context (e.g. when the term appears as a function argument, or an explicit ascription has been provided), so that we simply need to *analyze e* against it. In others, we need to *synthesize* a type for *e* (e.g. when the term appears at the top-level). Here, this distinction is crucial: a literal can only appear in an analytic context. *Bidirectional type systems* [28] make this distinction explicit by specifying the type system instead using two simultaneously defined typechecking judgements corresponding to these two situations.

To support TSLs, we need to also, simultaneously with this process, perform an elaboration from external terms, which contain literals, to *internal terms*, i, the syntax for which is shown on the right side of Fig. 7. Internal terms contain neither literals nor the form for accessing the metadata of a named type explicitly (the elaboration process inserts the statically known metadata value, tracked by the named type context, directly). This manner of specifying a type-directed mapping from external terms to a smaller collection of internal terms, which are the only terms that are given a dynamic semantics, is related to the Harper-Stone elaboration semantics for Standard ML [10]. Note that both terms share a type system.

Our static semantics are thus formulated by combining these two ideas, forming a *bidirectionally typed elaboration semantics*. The judgement $\Gamma \vdash_\Theta e \rightsquigarrow i \Rightarrow \tau$ means that under typing context Γ and named type context Θ, external term e elaborates to internal term i and synthesizes type τ. The judgement $\Gamma \vdash_\Theta e \rightsquigarrow i \Leftarrow \tau$ is analagous but for situations where we are analyzing e against type τ.

4.1   Programs and Type Declarations

Before considering these judgements in detail, let us briefly discuss the steps leading up to typechecking and elaboration of the top-level term, specified by the compilation judgement, $\rho \sim \Theta \rightsquigarrow i : \tau$, defined in Fig. 8. We first load the prelude, Θ_0 (see Fig. 4), then validate the provided user-defined type declarations, θ, to produce a corresponding named typed context, Θ. During this process, we synthesize a type for the associated metadata terms (under the empty typing context) and store their elaborations in the type context Θ (we do not evaluate the elaboration to a value immediately here, though in a language with effects, the choice of when to evaluate the term is important). Note that type names must be unique (we plan to use a URI-based mechanism in practice). Finally, the top-level external term must synthesize a type τ and produce an elaboration i under an empty typing context and a named type context combining the prelude with the named type context induced by the user-defined types, written $\Theta_0\Theta$.

4.2   External Terms

The bidirectional typechecking and elaboration rules for external terms are specified beginning in Fig. 9. Most of the rules are standard for a simply typed lambda calculus with labeled sums and labeled products, and the elaborations are direct to a corresponding internal form. We refer the reader to standard texts on type systems (e.g. [9]) to understand the basic constructs, and to course material[1] on bidirectional typechecking

---

[1] http://www.cs.cmu.edu/~fp/courses/15312-f04/
handouts/15-bidirectional.pdf

$$\boxed{\rho \sim \Theta \rightsquigarrow i : \tau} \qquad \Theta ::= \emptyset \mid \Theta, T[\delta, \mu] \quad \delta ::= \; ? \mid \mathbf{ot}[\omega] \mid \mathbf{ct}[\chi] \qquad \mu ::= \; ? \mid i : \tau$$

$$\boxed{\vdash_\Theta \theta \sim \Theta} \qquad \dfrac{\vdash_{\Theta_0} \theta \sim \Theta \quad \emptyset \vdash_{\Theta_0 \Theta} e \rightsquigarrow i \Rightarrow \tau}{\theta; e \sim \Theta \rightsquigarrow i : \tau} \; \textit{Compile}$$

$$\dfrac{T \notin \mathrm{dom}(\Theta) \quad \vdash_{\Theta, T[?, ?]} \omega \quad \emptyset \vdash_{\Theta, T[\mathbf{ot}[\omega], ?]} e_m \rightsquigarrow i_m \Rightarrow \tau_m \quad \vdash_{\Theta, T[\mathbf{ot}[\omega], i_m : \tau_m]} \theta \sim \Theta'}{\vdash_\Theta \mathbf{objtype}[T, \omega, e_m]; \theta \sim T[\mathbf{ot}[\omega], i_m : \tau_m]; \Theta'} \; \textit{OT}$$

$$\dfrac{T \notin \mathrm{dom}(\Theta) \quad \vdash_{\Theta, T[?, ?]} \chi \quad \emptyset \vdash_{\Theta, T[\mathbf{ct}[\chi], ?]} e_m \rightsquigarrow i_m \Rightarrow \tau_m \quad \vdash_{\Theta, T[\mathbf{ct}[\chi], i_m : \tau_m]} \theta \sim \Theta'}{\vdash_\Theta \mathbf{casetype}[T, \chi, e_m]; \theta \sim T[\mathbf{ct}[\chi], i_m : \tau_m]; \Theta'} \; \textit{CT}$$

$$\boxed{\vdash_\Theta \omega} \quad \dfrac{\ell \notin \mathrm{dom}(\omega) \quad \vdash_\Theta \tau \quad \vdash_\Theta \omega}{\vdash_\Theta \ell[\tau]; \omega} \; \textit{M-decl} \qquad \boxed{\vdash_\Theta \chi} \quad \dfrac{C \notin \mathrm{dom}(\chi) \quad \vdash_\Theta \tau \quad \vdash_\Theta \chi}{\vdash_\Theta C[\tau]; \chi} \; \textit{C-decl}$$

$$\boxed{\vdash_\Theta \tau} \quad \dfrac{T[\delta, \mu] \in \Theta}{\vdash_\Theta \mathbf{named}[T]} \; \textit{Ty-named} \qquad \dfrac{\vdash_\Theta \tau_1 \quad \vdash_\Theta \tau_2}{\vdash_\Theta \mathbf{arrow}[\tau_1, \tau_2]} \; \textit{Ty-arrow}$$

Fig. 8. Typechecking and elaboration of programs, ρ. Note that type declarations can only be recursive, not mutually recursive, with these rules. The prelude Θ_0 (see Fig. 4) defines mutually recursive types, so we cannot write a θ_0 corresponding to Θ_0 given the rules above. For concision, the rules to support mutual recursion as well as omitted rules for empty declarations are available in a technical report [24].

for background. In our presentation, as in many simple formulations, all introductory forms are analytic and all elimination forms are synthetic, though this can be relaxed in practice to support some additional idioms.

The introductory form for object types, **enew** $\{m\}$, prevents the manual introduction of parse streams (only the semantics can introduce parse streams, to permit us to enforce hygiene, as we will discuss below). The auxiliary judgement $\Gamma \vdash_\Theta^T m \rightsquigarrow \dot{m} \Leftarrow \omega$ analyzes the member definitions m against the member declarations ω while rewriting them to the internal member definitions, $\dot{m}$. Method definitions involve a self-reference, so the judgement keeps track of the type name, T. We implicitly assume that member definitions and declarations are congruent up to reordering.

The introduction form for case types is written **einj**$[C](e)$, where C is the case name and e is the associated data. The type of the data associated with each case is stored in the case type's declaration, χ. Because the introductory form is analytic, multiple case types can use the same case names (unlike in, for example, ML). The elimination form, **ecase**(e) $\{r\}$, performs simple exhaustive case analysis (we leave support for nested pattern matching as future work) using the auxiliary judgement $\Gamma \vdash_\Theta r \rightsquigarrow \dot{r} \Leftarrow \chi \Rightarrow \tau$, which checks that each case in χ appears in a rule in the rule sequence r, elaborating it to the internal rule sequence $\dot{r}$. Every rule must synthesize the same type, τ.

The rule *T-metadata* shows how the appropriate metadata is extracted from the named type context and inserted directly in the elaboration. We will return to the rule *T-toast* when discussing hygiene.

$$\boxed{\Gamma \vdash_\Theta e \rightsquigarrow i \Rightarrow \tau} \quad \boxed{\Gamma \vdash_\Theta e \rightsquigarrow i \Leftarrow \tau} \quad \Gamma ::= \emptyset \mid \Gamma, x : \tau$$

$$\frac{\Gamma \vdash_\Theta e \rightsquigarrow i \Rightarrow \tau}{\Gamma \vdash_\Theta e \rightsquigarrow i \Leftarrow \tau} \; \textit{T-syn-to-ana} \qquad \frac{\vdash_\Theta \tau \quad \Gamma \vdash_\Theta e \rightsquigarrow i \Leftarrow \tau}{\Gamma \vdash_\Theta \mathbf{easc}[\tau](e) \rightsquigarrow \mathbf{iasc}[\tau](i) \Rightarrow \tau} \; \textit{T-asc}$$

$$\frac{x : \tau \in \Gamma}{\Gamma \vdash_\Theta x \rightsquigarrow x \Rightarrow \tau} \; \textit{T-var} \qquad \frac{\Gamma \vdash_\Theta e_1 \rightsquigarrow i_1 \Rightarrow \tau_1 \quad \Gamma, x : \tau_1 \vdash_\Theta e_2 \rightsquigarrow i_2 \Rightarrow \tau}{\Gamma \vdash_\Theta \mathbf{elet}(e_1; x.e_2) \rightsquigarrow \mathbf{ilet}(i_1; x.i_2) \Rightarrow \tau} \; \textit{T-let}$$

$$\frac{\Gamma, x : \tau_1 \vdash_\Theta e \rightsquigarrow i \Leftarrow \tau_2}{\Gamma \vdash_\Theta \mathbf{elam}(x.e) \rightsquigarrow \mathbf{ilam}(x.i) \Leftarrow \mathbf{arrow}[\tau_1, \tau_2]} \; \textit{T-abs}$$

$$\frac{\Gamma \vdash_\Theta e_1 \rightsquigarrow i_1 \Rightarrow \tau_1 \rightarrow \tau_2 \quad \Gamma \vdash_\Theta e_2 \rightsquigarrow i_2 \Leftarrow \tau_1}{\Gamma \vdash_\Theta \mathbf{eap}(e_1; e_2) \rightsquigarrow \mathbf{iap}(i_1; i_2) \Rightarrow \tau_2} \; \textit{T-ap}$$

$$\frac{T \neq ParseStream \quad T[\mathbf{ot}[\omega], \mu] \in \Theta \quad \Gamma \vdash_\Theta^T m \rightsquigarrow \dot{m} \Leftarrow \omega}{\Gamma \vdash_\Theta \mathbf{enew}\{m\} \rightsquigarrow \mathbf{inew}\{\dot{m}\} \Leftarrow \mathbf{named}[T]} \; \textit{T-new}$$

$$\frac{\Gamma \vdash_\Theta e \rightsquigarrow i \Rightarrow \mathbf{named}[T] \quad T[\mathbf{ot}[\omega], \mu] \in \Theta \quad \ell[\tau] \in \omega}{\Gamma \vdash_\Theta \mathbf{eprj}[\ell](e) \rightsquigarrow \mathbf{iprj}[\ell](i) \Rightarrow \tau} \; \textit{T-prj}$$

$$\frac{T[\mathbf{ct}[\chi], \mu] \in \Theta \quad C[\tau] \in \chi \quad \Gamma \vdash_\Theta e \rightsquigarrow i \Leftarrow \tau}{\Gamma \vdash_\Theta \mathbf{einj}[C](e) \rightsquigarrow \mathbf{iinj}[C](i) \Leftarrow \mathbf{named}[T]} \; \textit{T-inj}$$

$$\frac{\Gamma \vdash_\Theta e \rightsquigarrow i \Rightarrow \mathbf{named}[T] \quad T[\mathbf{ct}[\chi], \mu] \in \Theta \quad \Gamma \vdash_\Theta r \rightsquigarrow \dot{r} \Leftarrow \chi \Rightarrow \tau}{\Gamma \vdash_\Theta \mathbf{ecase}(e)\{r\} \rightsquigarrow \mathbf{icase}(i)\{\dot{r}\} \Rightarrow \tau} \; \textit{T-case}$$

$$\frac{\Theta_0 \subset \Theta \quad \Gamma \vdash_\Theta e \rightsquigarrow i \Rightarrow \tau}{\Gamma \vdash_\Theta \mathbf{etoast}(e) \rightsquigarrow \mathbf{itoast}(i) \Rightarrow \mathbf{named}[Exp]} \; \textit{T-toast}$$

$$\frac{T[\delta, i : \tau] \in \Theta}{\Gamma \vdash_\Theta \mathbf{emetadata}[T] \rightsquigarrow i \Rightarrow \tau} \; \textit{T-metadata}$$

$$\boxed{\Gamma \vdash_\Theta^T m \rightsquigarrow \dot{m} \Leftarrow \omega}$$

$$\frac{}{\Gamma \vdash_\Theta^T \emptyset \rightsquigarrow \emptyset \Leftarrow \emptyset} \; \textit{T-unit}$$

$$\frac{\Gamma \vdash_\Theta e \rightsquigarrow i \Leftarrow \tau \quad \Gamma \vdash_\Theta^T m \rightsquigarrow \dot{m} \Leftarrow \omega}{\Gamma \vdash_\Theta^T \mathbf{eval}[\ell](e); m \rightsquigarrow \mathbf{ival}[\ell](i); \dot{m} \Leftarrow \ell[\tau]; \omega} \; \textit{T-val}$$

$$\frac{\Gamma, x : \mathbf{named}[T] \vdash_\Theta e \rightsquigarrow i \Leftarrow \tau \quad \Gamma \vdash_\Theta^T m \rightsquigarrow \dot{m} \Leftarrow \omega}{\Gamma \vdash_\Theta^T \mathbf{edef}[\ell](x.e); m \rightsquigarrow \mathbf{idef}[\ell](x.i); \dot{m} \Leftarrow \ell[\tau]; \omega} \; \textit{T-def}$$

$$\boxed{\Gamma \vdash_\Theta r \rightsquigarrow \dot{r} \Leftarrow \chi \Rightarrow \tau}$$

$$\frac{}{\Gamma \vdash_\Theta \emptyset \rightsquigarrow \emptyset \Leftarrow \emptyset \Rightarrow \tau} \; \textit{T-void}$$

$$\frac{\Gamma, x : \tau_1 \vdash_\Theta e \rightsquigarrow i \Rightarrow \tau_2 \quad \Gamma \vdash_\Theta r \rightsquigarrow \dot{r} \Leftarrow \chi \Rightarrow \tau_2}{\Gamma \vdash_\Theta \mathbf{erule}[C](x.e); r \rightsquigarrow \mathbf{irule}[C](x.i); \dot{r} \Leftarrow C[\tau_1]; \chi \Rightarrow \tau_2} \; \textit{T-rule}$$

Fig. 9. Statics for external terms, e. The rule for literals is shown in Fig. 10.

$$\Theta_0 \subset \Theta \quad T[\delta, i_m : HasTSL] \in \Theta \quad \mathbf{parsestream}(body) = i_{ps}$$
$$\mathbf{iap}(\mathbf{iprj}[parse](\mathbf{iprj}[parser](i_m)); i_{ps}) \Downarrow \mathbf{iinj}[OK]((i_{ast}, i'_{ps}))$$
$$\dfrac{i_{ast} \uparrow \hat{e} \quad \Gamma; \emptyset \vdash_\Theta \hat{e} \rightsquigarrow i \Leftarrow \mathbf{named}[T]}{\Gamma \vdash_\Theta \mathbf{lit}[body] \rightsquigarrow i \Leftarrow \mathbf{named}[T]} \textit{T-lit}$$

Fig. 10. Statics for external terms, e, continued. This is the key rule (described below).

4.3   Literals

In the example in Fig. 3, we showed a TSL being defined using a parser generator based an Adams grammars. As we noted, a parser generator can itself be seen as a TSL for a parser, and a parser is the fundamental construct that becomes associated with a type to form a TSL. The declaration for the prelude type Parser, shown in Fig. 4, shows that it is an object type with a parse function taking in a ParseStream and producing a Result, which is a case type that indicates either that parsing succeeded, in which case an elaboration of type Exp is paired with the remaining parse stream (to allow one parser to call another), or that parsing failed, in which case an error message and location is provided. This function is called by the typechecker when analyzing the literal form, as specified by the key rule of our system, *T-lit*, shown in Fig. 10. Note that we do not explicitly handle failure in the specification, but in practice we would use the data provided in the failure case to report the error to the user.

The rule *T-lit* operates as follows:

1. This rule requires that the prelude is available. For technical reasons, we include a check that the prelude was actually included in the named type context.
2. The metadata of the type the literal is being checked against, which must be of type *HasTSL*, is extracted from the named type context. Note that in a language with subtyping or richer forms of type equality, which would be necessary for situations where the metadata might serve other roles, the check that i_m defines a TSL would perform this check explicitly (as an additional premise).
3. A parse stream, i_{ps}, which is an internal term of type $\mathbf{named}[ParseStream]$, is generated from the body of the literal. This is an object that allows the TSL to read the body and supports some additional conveniences, discussed further below.
4. The parse method is called with this parse stream. If it produces the appropriate case containing a *reified elaboration*, i_{ast} (of type Exp) and the remaining parse stream, i'_{ps}, then parsing was successful. Note that we use shorthand for pairs in the rule for concision, and the relation $i \Downarrow i'$ defines evaluation to a value (the maximal transitive closure, if it exists, of the small-step evaluation relation in Fig. 14).
5. The reified elaboration is *dereified* into a corresponding *translational term*, $\hat{e}$, as specified in Fig. 11. The syntax for translational terms mirrors that of external terms, but does not include literal forms. It adds the form $\mathbf{spliced}[e]$, representing an external term spliced into a literal body.

The key rule is *U-Spl*. The only way to generate a translational term of this form is by asking for (a portion of) a parse stream to be parsed as a Wyvern expression. The reified form, unlike the translational form it corresponds to, does not contain

$$\boxed{i \uparrow \hat{e}}$$

$$\frac{i_{id} \uparrow x}{\mathbf{iinj}[Var](i_{id}) \uparrow x} \; U\text{-}Var$$

$$\frac{i_1 \uparrow \tau \quad i_2 \uparrow \hat{e}}{\mathbf{iinj}[Asc]((i_1, i_2)) \uparrow \mathbf{hasc}[\tau](\hat{e})} \; U\text{-}Asc$$

$$\frac{i_{id} \uparrow x \quad i \uparrow \hat{e}}{\mathbf{iinj}[Lam]((i_{id}, i)) \uparrow \mathbf{hlam}(x.\hat{e})} \; U\text{-}Lam$$

$$\frac{i_1 \uparrow \hat{e}_1 \quad i_2 \uparrow \hat{e}_2}{\mathbf{iinj}[Ap]((i_1, i_2)) \uparrow \mathbf{hap}(\hat{e}_1, \hat{e}_2)} \; U\text{-}Ap$$

$$\cdots$$

$$\frac{\mathsf{body}(i_{ps}) = body \quad \mathsf{eparse}(body) = e}{\mathbf{iinj}[Spliced](i_{ps}) \uparrow \mathbf{spliced}[e]} \; U\text{-}Spl$$

$$\boxed{i \uparrow \tau}$$

$$\frac{i_{id} \uparrow T}{\mathbf{iinj}[Named](i_{id}) \uparrow \mathbf{named}[T]} \; U\text{-}N$$

$$\frac{i_1 \uparrow \tau_1 \quad i_2 \uparrow \tau_2}{\mathbf{iinj}[Arrow]((i_1, i_2)) \uparrow \mathbf{arrow}[\tau_1, \tau_2]} \; U\text{-}A$$

Fig. 11. Dereification rules, used by rule *T-lit* (above) to determine the translational term encoded by the internal term of type **named**[Exp]. We assume a bijection between internal terms of type **named**[ID] (written i_{id}) and variables, type names and case and member labels.

$$\boxed{i \downarrow i}$$

$$\frac{x \downarrow i_{id}}{x \downarrow \mathbf{iinj}[Var](i_{id})} \; R\text{-}Var$$

$$\frac{\tau \downarrow i_1 \quad i \downarrow i_2}{\mathbf{iasc}[\tau](i) \downarrow \mathbf{iinj}[Asc]((i_1, i_2))} \; R\text{-}Asc$$

$$\frac{x \downarrow i_{id} \quad i \downarrow i'}{\mathbf{ilam}(x.i) \downarrow \mathbf{iinj}[Lam]((i_{id}, i'))} \; R\text{-}Lam$$

$$\frac{i_1 \downarrow i_1' \quad i_2 \downarrow i_2'}{\mathbf{iap}(i_1; i_2) \downarrow \mathbf{iinj}[Ap]((i_1', i_2))} \; R\text{-}Ap$$

$$\cdots$$

$$\boxed{\tau \downarrow i}$$

$$\frac{T \downarrow i_{id}}{\mathbf{named}[T] \downarrow \mathbf{iinj}[Named](i_{id})} \; R\text{-}N$$

$$\frac{\tau_1 \downarrow i_1 \quad \tau_2 \downarrow i_2}{\mathbf{arrow}[\tau_1, \tau_2] \downarrow \mathbf{iinj}[Arrow]((i_1, i_2))} \; R\text{-}A$$

Fig. 12. Reification rules, used by the **itoast** ("to AST") operator (Fig. 14) to permit generating an internal term of type **named**[Exp] corresponding to the value of the argument (a form of serialization).

the expression itself, but rather just the portion of the parse stream that should be treated as spliced. Because parse streams (and thus portions thereof) can originate only metatheoretically (i.e. from the compiler), we know that e must be an external term written concretely by the TSL client in the body of the literal being analyzed. This is key to guaranteeing hygiene in the final step, below.

The convenience methods `parse_exp` and `parse_id` return a value having this reified form corresponding to the first external term found in the parse stream (but, as just described, not necessarily the term itself) paired with the remainder of the parse stream. These methods themselves are not treated specially by the compiler but, for convenience, are associated with `ParseStream`.

6. The final step is to typecheck and elaborate this translational term. This involves the bidirectional typing judgements shown in Fig. 13. This judgement has a form similar to that for external terms, but with the addition of an "outer typing context", written Γ_{out} in the rules. This holds the context that the literal appeared in, so that the "main" typing context can be emptied to ensure that elaborations is hygienic, as we will describe next. Each rule in Fig. 9 should be thought of as having a corresponding rule in Fig. 13. Two examples are shown for concision.

$$\boxed{\Gamma;\Gamma \vdash_{\Theta} \hat{e} \rightsquigarrow i \Rightarrow \tau} \quad \boxed{\Gamma;\Gamma \vdash_{\Theta} \hat{e} \rightsquigarrow i \Leftarrow \tau}$$

$$\frac{x : \tau \in \Gamma}{\Gamma_{\text{out}};\Gamma \vdash_{\Theta} x \rightsquigarrow x \Rightarrow \tau}\ H\text{-}var \qquad \frac{\Gamma_{\text{out}};\Gamma, x : \tau_1 \vdash_{\Theta} \hat{e} \rightsquigarrow i \Leftarrow \tau_2}{\Gamma_{\text{out}};\Gamma \vdash_{\Theta} \mathbf{hlam}(x.\hat{e}) \rightsquigarrow \mathbf{ilam}(x.i) \Leftarrow \mathbf{arrow}[\tau_1, \tau_2]}\ H\text{-}abs$$

$$\cdots$$

$$\frac{\Gamma_{\text{out}} \vdash_{\Theta} e \rightsquigarrow i \Leftarrow \tau}{\Gamma_{\text{out}};\Gamma \vdash_{\Theta} \mathbf{spliced}[e] \rightsquigarrow i \Leftarrow \tau}\ H\text{-}spl\text{-}A \qquad \frac{\Gamma_{\text{out}} \vdash_{\Theta} e \rightsquigarrow i \Rightarrow \tau}{\Gamma_{\text{out}};\Gamma \vdash_{\Theta} \mathbf{spliced}[e] \rightsquigarrow i \Rightarrow \tau}\ H\text{-}spl\text{-}S$$

Fig. 13. Statics for translational terms, $\hat{e}$. Each rule in Fig. 9 corresponds to an analogous rule here by threading the outer context through opaquely (e.g. the rules for variables and functions, shown here). The outer context is only used by the rules for **spliced**[e], representing external terms that were spliced into TSL bodies. Note that elaboration is implicitly capture-avoiding here (see Sec. 6).

$$\boxed{i \mapsto i} \quad \cdots \quad \frac{i \mapsto i'}{\mathbf{itoast}(i) \mapsto \mathbf{itoast}(i')}\ D\text{-}Toast\text{-}1 \qquad \frac{i\,\mathbf{val} \quad i \downarrow i'}{\mathbf{itoast}(i) \mapsto i'}\ D\text{-}Toast\text{-}2$$

Fig. 14. Dynamics for internal terms, i. Only internal terms have a dynamic semantics. Most constructs in TSL Wyvern are standard and omitted, as our focus in this paper is on the statics. The only novel internal form, **itoast**(i), extracts an AST (of type **named**[Exp]) from the value of i, shown.

4.4 Hygiene

A concern with any term rewriting system is *hygiene* – how should variables in the elaboration be bound? In particular, if the rewriting system generates an *open term*, then it is making assumptions about the names of variables in scope at the site where the TSL is being used, which is incorrect. Those variables should only be identifiable up to alpha renaming. Only the *user* of a TSL knows which variables are in scope. The strictest rule would simply reject all open terms, but this would then, given our setting, prevent even spliced terms from referring to local variables. These are written by the TSL client, who is aware of variable bindings at the use site, so this should be permitted.

Furthermore, the variables in spliced terms should be bound as the client expects. The elaboration should not be able to surreptitiously or accidentally shadow variables in spliced terms that may be otherwise bound at the use site (e.g. by introducing a variable tmp outside a spliced term that "leaks" into the spliced term).

The solution to both of these issues, given what we have outlined above, is now quite simple: we have constructed the system so that we know which sub-terms originate from the TSL client, marking them as **spliced**[e]. These terms are permitted to refer only to variables in the client's context, Γ_{out}, as seen in the premises of the two rules pertaining to this form (one for analysis, one for synthesis). The portions of the elaboration that aren't marked in this way were generated by the TSL provider, so they can refer only to variables introduced earlier in the elaboration, tracked by the context Γ, initially empty. The two are kept separate. If the TSL wishes to introduce values into spliced terms, it must do so by via a function application (as in the TSL for Parser discussed earlier), ensuring that the client has full control over variable binding.

$$\boxed{\Gamma \vdash_\Theta i \Rightarrow \tau} \quad \boxed{\Gamma \vdash_\Theta i \Leftarrow \tau} \quad \cdots \quad \frac{T[\mathbf{ot}[\omega], \mu] \in \Theta \quad \Gamma \vdash_\Theta^T \dot{m} \Leftarrow \omega}{\Gamma \vdash_\Theta \mathbf{inew}\,\{\dot{m}\} \Leftarrow \mathbf{named}[T]}\ IT\text{-}new$$

Fig. 15. Statics for internal terms, i. Each rule in Fig. 9 except *T-metadata* corresponds to an analogous rule here by removing the elaboration portion. Only the rule for object introduction differs, in that we no longer restrict the introduction of parse streams (internal terms are never written directly by users of the language).

4.5 From Values to ASTs

By this formulation, elaborations containing free variables are always erroneous. In some rewriting systems, a free variable is not an error, but are instead replaced with the AST corresponding to the value of the variable at the generation site. We permit this explicitly by including the form **toast**(e). This simply takes the value of e and reifies it, producing a term of type Exp, as specified in Figs. 14 and Fig. 12. The rules for reification, used here, and dereification, used in the literal rule above, are dual.

The TSL associated with Exp, implementing quasiquotes, can perform free variable analysis and insert this form automatically, so they need not be inserted manually in most cases. That is, Var('x') : Exp elaborates to x which is ill-typed in an empty context, 'x' : Exp produces the translational term **htoast**(**spliced**$[x]$), which will elaborate to **itoast**(x) in the context where the quotation appears (i.e. in the TSL definition), thus behaving as described without requiring that quotations are entirely implemented by the language. This can be seen as a form of serialization and could be implemented as a library using reflection or compile-time metaprogramming techniques (e.g. [20]).

4.6 Metatheory

The semantics we have defined constitute a type safe language. We will outline the key theorems and lemmas here, referring the reader to an accompanying technical report for fuller details [24]. The two key theorems are: internal type safety, and type preservation of the elaboration process.

To prove internal type safety, we must define a bidirectional typing judgement for the internal language, shown and described in Fig. 15 (by the external type preservation theorem, we should never need to explicitly implement this, however). We must also define a well-formedness judgement for named type contexts (not shown).

Theorem 1 (Internal Type Safety). *If* $\vdash \Theta$ *and* $\emptyset \vdash_\Theta i \Leftarrow \tau$ *or* $\emptyset \vdash_\Theta i \Rightarrow \tau$, *then either* i val *or* $i \mapsto i'$ *such that* $\emptyset \vdash_\Theta i' \Leftarrow \tau$.

Proof. The dynamics, which we omit for concision, are standard, so the proof is by a standard preservation and progress argument. The only interesting case of the proof involves **etoast**(e), for which we need the following lemma.

Lemma 1 (Reification). *If* $\Theta_0 \subset \Theta$ *and* $\emptyset \vdash_\Theta i \Leftarrow \tau$ *then* $i \downarrow i'$ *and* $\emptyset \vdash_\Theta i' \Leftarrow$ *named*$[Exp]$.

Proof. The proof is by a straightforward induction. Analogous lemmas about reification of identifiers and types are similarly straightforward.   □

If the elaboration of a closed, well-typed external term generates an internal term of the same type, then internal type safety implies that evaluation will not go wrong, achieving type safety. We generalize this argument to open terms by defining a well-formedness judgement for contexts (not shown). The relevant theorem is below:

Theorem 2 (External Type Preservation). *If* $\vdash \Theta$ *and* $\vdash_\Theta \Gamma$ *and* $\Gamma \vdash_\Theta e \rightsquigarrow i \Leftarrow \tau$ *or* $\Gamma \vdash_\Theta e \rightsquigarrow i \Rightarrow \tau$ *then* $\Gamma \vdash_\Theta i \Leftarrow \tau$.

Proof. We proceed by inducting over the the typing derivation. Nearly all the elaborations are direct, so the proof is by straightforward applications of induction hypotheses and lemmas about well-formed contexts. The only cases of note are:

- $e = \textbf{enew}\,\{m\}$. Here the corresponding rule for the elaboration is identical but more permissive, so the induction hypothesis applies.
- $e = \textbf{emetadata}[T]$. Here, the elaboration generates the metadata value directly. Well-formedness of Θ implies that the metadata term is of the type assigned.
- $e = \textbf{lit}[body]$. Here, we need to apply internal type safety as well as a mutually defined type preservation lemma about translational terms, below.

Lemma 2 (Translational Type Preservation). *If* $\vdash \Theta$ *and* $\vdash_\Theta \Gamma_{out}$ *and* $\vdash_\Theta \Gamma$ *and* $dom(\Gamma_{out}) \cap dom(\Gamma) = \emptyset$ *(which we can assume implicitly due to alpha renaming) and* $\Gamma_{out}; \Gamma \vdash_\Theta \hat{e} \rightsquigarrow i \Leftarrow \tau$ *or* $\Gamma_{out}; \Gamma \vdash_\Theta \hat{e} \rightsquigarrow i \Rightarrow \tau$ *then* $\Gamma_{out}\Gamma \vdash_\Theta i \Leftarrow \tau$.

Proof. The proof by induction over the typing derivation follows the same outline as above for all the shared cases. The outer context is threaded through opaquely when applying the inductive hypothesis. The only rules of note are the two for the spliced external terms, which require applying the external type preservation theorem recursively. This is well-founded by a metric measuring the size of the spliced external term, written in concrete syntax, since we know it was derived from a portion of the literal body.   □

Moving up to the level of programs, we can prove the correctness of compilation theorem below. Together, this implies that derivation of the compilation judgement produces an internal term that does not go wrong.

Theorem 3 (Compilation). *If* $\rho \sim \Theta \rightsquigarrow i : \tau$ *then* $\vdash \Theta$ *and* $\emptyset \vdash_\Theta i \Leftarrow \tau$.

Proof. We simply need a lemma about checking type declarations and the result follows straightforwardly.

Lemma 3 (Type Declaration). *If* $\vdash_{\Theta_0} \theta \sim \Theta$ *then* $\vdash \Theta_0\Theta$.

Proof. The proof is a simple induction using the definition of $\vdash \Theta$ (not shown).

4.7 Decidability

Because we are executing user-defined parsers during typechecking, we do not have a straightforward statement of decidability (i.e. termination) of typechecking: the parser might not terminate, because TSL Wyvern is not a total language (due to self-reference in methods). Indecidability of typechecking is strictly for this reason. Typechecking of terms not containing literals is guaranteed to terminate. Termination of parsers and parser generators has previously been studied (e.g. [15]) and the techniques can be applied to user-defined parsing code to increase confidence in termination. Few compilers, even those with high demands for correctness (e.g. CompCert [17]), have made it a priority to fully verify and prove termination of the parser, because it is perceived that most bugs in compilers arise due to incorrect optimization passes, not initial parsing.

5 Corpus Analysis

We performed a corpus analysis on existing Java code to assess how frequently there are opportunities to use TSLs. As a lower bound for this metric, we examined String arguments passed into Java constructors, for two reasons:

1. The String type may be used to represent a large variety of notations, many of which may be expressed using TSLs.
2. We hypothesized that opportunities to use TSLs would often come when instantiating an object.

Methodology. We ran our analysis on a recent version (20130901r) of the Qualitas Corpus [33], consisting of 107 Java projects, and searched for constructors that used Strings that could be substituted with TSLs. To perform the search, we used command line tools, such as grep and sed, and a text editor features such as search and substitution. After we found the constructors, we chose those that took at least one String as an argument. Via a visual scan of the names of the constructors and their String arguments, we inferred how the constructors and the arguments were intended to be used. Some additional details are provided in the technical report [24].

Results. We found 124,873 constructors and that 19,288 (15%) of them could use TSLs. Table 1 gives more details on types of String arguments we found that could be substituted with TSLs. The "Identifier" category comprises process IDs, user IDs, column or row IDs, etc. that usually must be unique; the "Pattern" category includes regular expressions, prefixes and suffixes, delimiters, format templates, etc.; the "Other" category contains Strings used for ZIP codes, passwords, queries, IP addresses, versions, HTML and XML code, etc.; and the "Directory path" and "URL/URI" categories are self-explanatory.

Limitations. There are three limitations to our corpus analysis. First, the proxy that we chose for finding how often TSLs could be used in existing Java code is imprecise. Our corpus analysis focused exclusively on Java constructors and thus did not consider other programming constructs, such as method calls, assignments, etc., that could possibly use TSLs. We did not count types that themselves could have a TSL associated with them (e.g. URL), only uses of Strings that we hypothesized might not have been Strings had better syntax been available. Our search for constructors with the use of command line tools and text editor features may not have identified every Java constructors present in the corpus. Finally, the inference of the intended functionality of the constructor and

Table 1. Types of `String` arguments in Java constructors that could use TSLs

Type of String	Number	Percentage
Identifier	15,642	81%
Directory path	823	4%
Pattern	495	3%
URL/URI	396	2%
Other (ZIP code, password, query, HTML/XML, IP address, version, etc.)	1,932	10%
Total:	**19,288**	**100%**

the passed in `String` argument was based on the authors' programming experience and was thus subjective.

Despite the limitations of our corpus analysis, it shows that there are many potential use cases where type-specific languages could be considered, given that numerous `String` arguments appeared to specify a parseable format.

6   Implementation

Because Wyvern itself is an evolving language and we believe that the techniques herein are broadly applicable, we have implemented the abstract syntax, typechecking and elaboration rules precisely as specified in this paper, including the hygiene mechanism, in Scala as a stable resource. We have also included a simple compiler from our representation of internal terms, which includes explicit type information at each node, to Scala source code. We represent both external terms and translational terms using the same case classes, using traits to distinguish them when necessary. This code can be used to better understand the implementation overhead of our mechanisms. The key "trick" is to make sure that the typing context also maps each source variable to a unique internal variable, so that elaboration of spliced terms is capture-avoiding. This code can be found at http://github.com/wyvernlang/tslwyvern.

Wyvern itself also supports a variant of this mechanism. The Wyvern language is an evolving effort involving a number of techniques other than TSLs, so the implementation does not precisely coincide with the specification presented herein. In particular, Wyvern's object types and case types have substantially different semantics. Moreover, Adams grammars do not presently have a robust implementation, so their presentation here is merely expository. The top-level parser for Wyvern is instead produced by the Copper parser generator [36] which uses stateful LALR parsing to handle whitespace. Forward references, such as the TSL tilde, the new keyword, and case expressions, are handled by inserting a special "signal" token into the parse stream at the end of an expression containing a forward reference. When the parser subsequently reads this signal token, it enters the appropriate state depending on the type of forward reference encountered. TSL blocks are handled as if they were strings, preserving all non-leading whitespace, and new and case expression bodies are parsed using their respective grammars. Wyvern performs literal parsing during typechecking essentially as described, using a standard bidirectional type system. It does not enforce the constraints on parse streams and the hygiene mechanisms as of this writing. Some of the API is implemented using a Java interoperability layer rather than directly in Wyvern. This implementation does support some simpler examples fully, however (unlike the implementation above, which does not have a concrete syntax at all). The code can be found at http://github.com/wyvernlang/wyvern.

7 Related Work

Closely related to our approach of type-driven parsing is a concurrent paper by Ichikawa et al. [11] that presents *protean operators*. The paper describes the *ProteaJ* language, based on Java, which allows a programmer to define flexible operators annotated with named types. Syntactic conflict is resolved by looking at the expected type. Conflicts may still arise when the expected type matches two protean operators; in this case ProteaJ allows the programmer to explicitly disambiguate, as in other systems. In contrast, by associating parsers with types, our approach avoids all conflicts, achieving a stricter notion of modularity at the cost of some expressiveness (we only consider delimited literals – these may define operators inside, but we cannot support custom operator syntax directly at the top level). We also give a type theoretic foundation for our approach.

Another way to approach language extensibility is to go a level of abstraction above parsing, as is done via metaprogramming and macro facilities, with Scheme and other Lisp-style languages' hygienic macros being the 'gold standard' for hygiene. In those languages, macros are written in the language itself and use its simple syntax – parentheses universally serve as expression delimiters (although proposals for whitespace as a substitute for parentheses have been made [21]). Our work is inspired by this flexibility, but aims to support richer syntax as well as maintain a static type discipline. Wyvern's use of types to trigger parsing avoids the overhead of invoking macros explicitly by name, and makes it easier to compose TSLs declaratively. Static macro systems also exist. For instance, OJ (previously, OpenJava) [32] provides a macro system based on a meta-object protocol, and Backstage Java [27], Template Haskell [30] and Converge [34] also employ compile-time meta-programming, the latter with some support for whitespace delimited blocks. Each of these systems provide macro-style rewriting of source code, but they provide at most limited extension of language parsing. String literals can be reinterpreted, but splicing is not hygienic if this is done.

Other systems aim at providing forms of syntax extension that change the host language, as opposed to our whitespace-delimited approach. For example, Camlp4 [4] is a preprocessor for OCaml that can be used to extend the concrete syntax of the language with parsers and extensible grammars. SugarJ [6] supports syntactic extension of the Java language by adding libraries. Wyvern differs from these approach in that the core language is not extended directly, so conflicts cannot arise at link-time.

Scoping TSLs to expressions of a single type comes at the expense of some flexibility, but we believe that many uses of domain-specific languages are of this form already. A previous approach has considered type-based disambiguation of parse forests for supporting quotation and anti-quotation of arbitrary object languages [2]. Our work is similar in spirit, but does not rely on generation of parse forests and associates grammars with types, rather than types with grammar productions. This provides stronger modularity guarantees and is arguably simpler. C# expression trees [19] are similar in that, when the type of a term is, e.g., Expression<T->T'>, it is parsed as a quotation. However, like the work just mentioned, this is *specifically* to support quotations. Our work supports quotations as one use case amongst many.

Many approaches to syntax extension, such as XJ [3] are keyword-delimited in some form. We believe that a type-directed approach is more seamless and natural, coinciding with how one would build in language support directly. These approaches also differ in that they either do not support hygienic expansion, or have not specified it in the simple manner that we have.

In terms of work on safe language composition, Schwerdfeger and van Wyk [29] proposed a solution that make strong safety guarantees provided that the languages comply with certain grammar restrictions, concerning first and follow sets of the host language and the added new languages. It also relied on strongly named entry tokens, as with keyword delimited approaches. Our approach does not impose any such restrictions while still making safety guarantees.

Domain-specific language frameworks and language workbenches, such as Spoofax [14], Ensō [18] and others [35], also provide a possible solution for the language extension task. They provide support for generating new programming languages and tooling in a modular manner. The Marco language [16] similarly provides macro definition at a level of abstraction that is largely independent of the target language. In these approaches, each TSL is *external* relative to the host language; in contrast, Wyvern focuses on *internal* extensibility, improving interoperability and composability.

Ongoing work on projectional editors (e.g., [12,5]) uses a special graphical user interface to allow the developer to implicitly mark where the extensions are placed in the code, essentially directly specifying the underlying ASTs. This solution to the language extension problem is of considerable interest to us, but remains relatively understudied formally. It is likely that a type-oriented approach to projectional editing, inspired by that described herein, could be fruitful.

We were informed by our previous work on Active Code Completion (ACC), which associates code completion palettes with types [25], much as we associate parsers with types. ACC palettes could be used for defining a TSL syntax for types in a complementary manner. In ACC that syntax is immediately translated to Java syntax at edit time, while this work integrates with the language, so the syntax is retained with the code. ACC supports more general interaction modes than just textual syntax, situated between our approach and projectional editors.

8   Discussion

We have presented a minimal but complete language design that we believe is particularly elegant, practical and theoretically well-motivated. The key to this is our organization of language extensions around types, rather than around grammar fragments.

There are several directions that remain to be explored:

- TSL Wyvern does not support polymorphic types, like 'a list in our first example. Were we to add support for them, we would expect that the type constructor (list) would determine the syntax, not the particular type. Thus, we may fundamentally be proposing *type constructor specific languages*.
- Similarly, TSL Wyvern does not support abstract types. It may be useful to include the ability to associate metadata with an abstract type, much in the same way that we associate metadata with a named type here.
- TSLs as described here allow one to give an alternative syntax for introductory term forms, but elimination forms cannot be defined directly. There are two directions we may wish to go to support this:
  1. Pattern matching is a powerful feature supported by an increasing number of languages. Pattern syntax is similar to term syntax. It may be possible for a TSL definition to include parse functions for "literal-like" forms appearing in patterns, elaborating them to pattern terms rather than expression terms.
  2. Keywords are more useful when defining custom elimination forms (e.g. if based on case). It may be possible to support "typed syntax macros" using the same hygiene mechanisms we described here.
- We do not provide TSLs with the ability to diverge based on the type of a spliced expression. This might be useful if, for example, our HTML TSL wanted to treat spliced strings differently from other spliced HTML terms. For polymorphic types, we might also wish to diverge based on the type index.
- We may wish to design less restrictive shadowing constraints, so that TSLs can introduce variables directly into the scope of a spliced expression if they explicitly wish to (bypassing the need for the client to provide a function for the TSL to call). The community may wish to discuss whether this is worth the cost in terms of difficulty of determining where a variable has been bound.
- We need to provide further empirical validation. This may benefit from the integration of TSLs into existing languages other than Wyvern.
- We need to consider broader IDE support – custom syntax benefits from custom editor support, and it may be possible to design IDEs that dispatch to type metadata in much the way the typechecker does in this paper. Our informal considerations of existing IDE extension mechanisms suggests that this may be non-trivial.

Acknowledgements. We thank the anonymous reviewers, Joshua Sunshine, Filipe Militão and Eric Van Wyk for helpful comments and discussions, and acknowledge the support of the United States Air Force Research Laboratory and the National Security Agency lablet contract #H98230-14-C-0140, as well as the Royal Society of New Zealand Marsden Fund. Cyrus Omar was supported by an NSF Graduate Research Fellowship.

References

1. Adams, M.D.: Principled parsing for indentation-sensitive languages: Revisiting Landin's offside rule. In: Principles of Programming Languages (2013)

2. Bravenboer, M., Vermaas, R., Vinju, J.J., Visser, E.: Generalized type-based disambiguation of meta programs with concrete object syntax. In: Glück, R., Lowry, M. (eds.) GPCE 2005. LNCS, vol. 3676, pp. 157–172. Springer, Heidelberg (2005)

3. Clark, T., Sammut, P., Willans, J.S.: Beyond annotations: A proposal for extensible Java (XJ). In: Source Code Analysis and Manipulation (2008)

4. de Rauglaudre, D.: Camlp4 - Reference Manual (2003),
   http://caml.inria.fr/pub/docs/manual-camlp4/

5. Diekmann, L., Tratt, L.: Parsing composed grammars with language boxes. In: Workshop on Scalable Language Specification (2013)

6. Erdweg, S., Rendel, T., Kästner, C., Ostermann, K.: SugarJ: library-based language extensibility. In: Object-Oriented Programming Systems, Languages, and Applications (2011)

7. Erdweg, S., Rieger, F.: A framework for extensible languages. In: Generative Programming: Concepts & Experiences (2013)

8. Green, T., Petre, M.: Usability analysis of visual programming environments: A 'cognitive dimensions' framework. Journal of Visual Languages and Computing 7(2), 131–174 (1996)

9. Harper, R.: Practical Foundations for Programming Languages. Cambridge University Press (2012)

10. Harper, R., Stone, C.: A Type-Theoretic Interpretation of Standard ML. In: Proof, Language and Interaction: Essays in Honour of Robin Milner. MIT Press (2000)

11. Ichikawa, K., Chiba, S.: Composable user-defined operators that can express user-defined literals. In: Modularity (2014)

12. JetBrains. JetBrains MPS – Meta Programming System,
    http://www.jetbrains.com/mps/

13. Karakoidas, V.: On domain-specific languages usage (why DSLs really matter). Crossroads 20(3), 16–17 (2014)

14. Kats, L.C.L., Visser, E.: The Spoofax language workbench: Rules for declarative specification of languages and IDEs. In: Object-Oriented Programming Systems, Languages, and Applications (2010)

15. Krishnan, L., Van Wyk, E.: Termination analysis for higher-order attribute grammars. In: Czarnecki, K., Hedin, G. (eds.) SLE 2012. LNCS, vol. 7745, pp. 44–63. Springer, Heidelberg (2013)

16. Lee, B., Grimm, R., Hirzel, M., McKinley, K.S.: Marco: Safe, expressive macros for any language. In: Noble, J. (ed.) ECOOP 2012. LNCS, vol. 7313, pp. 589–613. Springer, Heidelberg (2012)

17. Leroy, X.: Formal verification of a realistic compiler. Communications of the ACM (2009)

18. Loh, A., van der Storm, T., Cook, W.R.: Managed data: Modular strategies for data abstraction. In: Onward! (2012)

19. Microsoft Corporation. Expression Trees (C# and Visual Basic),
    http://msdn.microsoft.com/en-us/library/bb397951.aspx

20. Miller, H., Haller, P., Burmako, E., Odersky, M.: Instant pickles: Generating object-oriented pickler combinators for fast and extensible serialization. In: Object Oriented Programming Systems, Languages & Applications (2013)

21. Möller, E.: SRFI-49: Indentation-sensitive syntax (2005),
    http://srfi.schemers.org/srfi-49/srfi-49.html

22. Nistor, L., Kurilova, D., Balzer, S., Chung, B., Potanin, A., Aldrich, J.: Wyvern: A simple, typed, and pure object-oriented language. In: MechAnisms for SPEcialization, Generalization and Inheritance (2013)

23. Omar, C., Chung, B., Kurilova, D., Potanin, A., Aldrich, J.: Type-directed, whitespace-delimited parsing for embedded DSLs. In: Globalization of Domain Specific Languages (2013)

24. Omar, C., Kurilova, D., Nistor, L., Chung, B., Potanin, A., Aldrich, J.: Safely Composable Type-Specific Languages. Technical Report CMU-ISR-14-106, Carnegie Mellon University (2014)
25. Omar, C., Yoon, Y., LaToza, T.D., Myers, B.A.: Active code completion. In: International Conference on Software Engineering (2012)
26. OWASP. OWASP Top 10 2013 (2013),
    https://www.owasp.org/index.php/Top_10_2013-Top_10
27. Palmer, Z., Smith, S.F.: Backstage Java: Making a Difference in Metaprogramming. In: Object-Oriented Programming Systems, Languages, and Applications (2011)
28. Pierce, B.C., Turner, D.N.: Local type inference. ACM Trans. Program. Lang. Syst. 22(1), 1–44 (2000)
29. Schwerdfeger, A.C., Van Wyk, E.R.: Verifiable composition of deterministic grammars. In: Programming Language Design and Implementation (2009)
30. Sheard, T., Jones, S.: Template meta-programming for Haskell. ACM SIGPLAN Notices 37(12), 60–75 (2002)
31. Stoy, J.E.: Denotational Semantics: The Scott-Strachey Approach to Programming Language Theory. MIT Press, Cambridge (1977)
32. Tatsubori, M., Chiba, S., Killijian, M.-O., Itano, K.: OpenJava: A Class-based Macro System for Java. In: Cazzola, W., Houmb, S.H., Tisato, F. (eds.) Reflection and Software Engineering. LNCS, vol. 1826, pp. 117–133. Springer, Heidelberg (2000)
33. Tempero, E., Anslow, C., Dietrich, J., Han, T., Li, J., Lumpe, M., Melton, H., Noble, J.: Qualitas corpus: A curated collection of Java code for empirical studies. In: Asia Pacific Software Engineering Conference (2010)
34. Tratt, L.: Domain specific language implementation via compile-time meta-programming. ACM Trans. Program. Lang. Syst. 30(6) (October 2008)
35. van den Brand, M.G.J.: Pregmatic: A Generator for Incremental Programming Environments. PhD thesis, Katholieke Universiteit Nijmegen (1992)
36. Van Wyk, E.R., Schwerdfeger, A.C.: Context-aware scanning for parsing extensible languages. In: Generative Programming and Component Engineering (2007)

Graceful Dialects

Michael Homer[1], Timothy Jones[1],
James Noble[1], Kim B. Bruce[2], and Andrew P. Black[3]

[1] Victoria University of Wellington, Wellington, New Zealand
{mwh,tim,kjx}@ecs.vuw.ac.nz
[2] Pomona College, Claremont, California, USA
kim@cs.pomona.edu
[3] Portland State University, Portland, Oregon, USA
black@cs.pdx.edu

Abstract. Programming languages are enormously diverse, both in their essential concepts and in their accidental aspects. This creates a problem when teaching programming. To let students experience the diversity of essential concepts, the students must also be exposed to an overwhelming variety of accidental and irrelevant detail: the accidental differences between the languages are likely to obscure the teaching point.

The dialect system of the Grace programming language allows instructors to tailor and vary the language to suit their courses, while staying within the same stylistic, syntactic and semantic framework, as well as permitting authors to define advanced internal domain-specific languages. The dialect system achieves this power though a combination of well-known language features: lexical nesting, lambda expressions, multi-part method names, optional typing, and pluggable checkers. Grace's approach to dialects is validated by a series of case studies, including both extensions and restrictions of the base language.

Keywords: Grace, language variants, domain-specific languages, pluggable checkers, graphical microworlds, error reporting, object-oriented programming.

1 Introduction

Grace is an imperative, gradually typed, object-oriented language designed for use in education, particularly for introductory programming courses [3,4]. The goals of Grace are similar to those of Pascal, of which Wirth wrote (in 1971!)

> The development of the language ... is based on two principal aims. The first is to make available a language suitable to teach programming as a systematic discipline based on certain fundamental concepts clearly and naturally reflected by the language [27].

In the intervening forty-plus years, object-orientation has evolved into the dominant style of programming, and thus *one* of the styles to which students should be exposed if they are to receive a well-rounded education in computing. The design of Grace was intended to take advantage of recent research in programming language design

R. Jones (Ed.): ECOOP 2014, LNCS 8586, pp. 131–156, 2014.

to create a syntactically and conceptually simple language that could be used to teach the fundamental concepts of object-oriented programming. The focus of the language design was on consolidation of known features, rather than on innovation.

Grace supports a variety of approaches to teaching programming, including objects-early, objects-late, graphics-early, and functional-first. Grace makes it possible to teach courses using dynamic types or static types, to start with dynamic typing and then gradually move to static typing, or to do the reverse, without having to change to another language with a different syntax, semantics, IDE, and libraries.

This paper describes Grace's dialect system, which we introduced to support this variety. A *dialects* is package of extensions to and restrictions on the core Grace language that can be used for all or part of a program. A dialect can restrict access to some language features, replace existing functionality, and create new constructs and control structures. We show how we have built this system for dialects entirely out of existing well-known features, found both in Grace and in other languages; both the semantics of a dialect and the code that implements it are defined in core Grace.

In adding dialects to Grace, we intend to allow an instructor to use a succession of language variants tailored to the students' stage of learning and to the instructor's course design. The idea of a succession of teaching languages was introduced in SP/k [12], and revived in DrScheme [8] (now Racket) as "language levels". Language levels demonstrated the benefits of limiting the student programming language to the concepts that they have already learned, and excluding the features that they don't yet know about.

Because we expect different courses using Grace to use different approaches to teaching programming, we do not want to provide only a single sequence of dialects, as in Racket. Rather, we envisage a directed graph of such dialects — indeed, we hope that instructors, tutors, and course designers will be able to create custom dialects to suit their individual approaches to teaching. To make this hope realistic, we took care to ensure that defining a dialect requires nothing more than programming with ordinary Grace constructs. Instructors do not have to learn a new macro language, or generate code, or engage with the whole panoply of "professional" language building tools, like lexers, parsers, typecheckers, interpreters, and compilers. To keep the Grace language itself small and simple, we also tried to minimise both the number and the complexity of the features that we added to support dialects. As a consequence, Grace's dialect mechanism is limited in power: Grace dialects cannot implement a language with a completely different syntax or underlying semantic model. For our intended audience, we see this as an advantage.

The contributions of this paper are a description (in Sect. 3) of Grace's dialect mechanism: a system that extends (through libraries) and restricts (using pluggable checkers) the language available to a program module. The dialect system is made possible by some key features of Grace — lexical nesting, lambda-expressions, multi-part method names, and optional typing, which are described in Sect. 2. We demonstrate the power of this approach to dialects by presenting a range of case studies: dialects that define a graphical micro-world inspired by Logo (§ 4.1), implement assertions and design by contract (§ 4.2), require explicit type annotations (§ 4.4), suggest fixes to students who make simple errors (§ 4.6), support the writing of other dialects (§ 4.3), and perform static type-checking (§ 4.5). Section 5 discusses alternatives and extensions to our design; Section 6 compares Graceful dialects to a range of related work.

2   Grace in a Nutshell

This section introduces the core of the Grace programming language; it provided a basis for Sect. 3, which describes the elements that we added to support dialects.

Objects. A Grace object is created using an object constructor expression; each time the object constructor is executed, it creates a new object. Here is an example

```
object {
  def name = "Fido"
  var age := 2
  method say(phrase : String) {
    print "{name} says: {phrase}"
  }
  print "{name} has been born."
}
```

This object contains a method (say) and two fields; def name defines a constant (using "="), while var age declares a variable, whose initial value is assigned with :=. Variables can be re-assigned, also with :=. When an object constructor is executed, any code inside its body is also executed, so the above object constructor will have the side effect of printing "Fido has been born." when the object is created. This example also shows that strings can include expressions enclosed in braces: the expression is evaluated, converted to a string, and inserted in place of the brace expression.

Of course, to be useful, the object created by executing an object constructor typically needs to be bound to an identifier, or returned from an enclosing method. For example,

```
def fido = object {
  ... code from above example ...
}
fido.say "Hello"
```

will create an object and bind it to the name fido, and then *request* the say method on that object. This will print "Fido was born." and then "Fido says: Hello". Grace uses the term "method request" in preference to "message send", because "sending a message" might easily be misinterpreted as referring to a network message. We prefer "request" over "call" to recognise that the receiver must cooperate in responding to the request.

Program Structure. Every file containing a Grace program is considered to be surrounded by object { ... }. This means that top-level declarations actually declare fields and methods in an anonymous object, which we call the *module object*. When a file is run, it is the constructor of this module object that is executed; this has the effect of running any code written at the top level of the file. Module objects have access to Grace's standard prelude, which defines the language's basic objects (numbers, strings, booleans, etc.), control structures, and methods.

Object constructors can be nested inside other objects or methods. Method requests without an explicit receiver are resolved in the lexical scope, finding a valid receiver in one of the surrounding objects. In the case of ambiguity, the programmer must resolve the receiver explicitly to **self** or **outer**. Classes in Grace are syntactic sugar for methods that return the result of an object constructor; classes do not serve as types. We do not use classes in this paper, and so we omit further details.

Visibility. By default, methods are publicly accessible. This default can be changed using an *annotation*: a name attached to a declaration using the keyword **is**. If a method is annotated **confidential**, it can be requested inside the object itself, and by any object that inherits from it, but not from outside objects. In contrast, fields are confidential[1] by default; they can be made **public** by an annotation. Regardless of visibility, code can access names defined in any of the surrounding scopes. This includes not just requests of methods and fields, but also parameters and temporaries. The implementation creates closures when necessary.

When visible, a variable or constant can be requested using *exactly* the same syntax as a parameterless method, as demanded by Ross's Uniform Referent Principle [24]. A variable can be assigned in a similar way, using a special request syntax that is syntactically identical to an assignment. Thus, the clients of an object need not know whether an attribute is implemented as a constant, as a variable, or as a method.

Types. Variables, definitions, method parameters and method return values can optionally be annotated with types. Grace supports a special annotation syntax for types, using : for variables, definitions and parameters, and $->$ for method results, for example:

```
method square(n : Number) -> Number { n * n }
```

A type annotation is an assertion on the part of the programmer that no attempt will be made to bind a value with a non-conforming type to the annotated program element — in this case, the programmer is asserting that arguments and the return value of the method **square** will conform to **Number**. The implementation will emit a warning or error if a type assertion does not hold; sometimes the warning will be produced at run time, and sometimes at compile time, depending on how the erroneous value is generated and on how many type annotations are present.

Types in Grace are structural. A type is a set of methods, where each method is decorated with the types of its parameters and the type of its result. Type a conforms to type b if it obeys the usual contravariant rule: a must support all of the methods of b, and for each common method m, the result type of m in a must conform to the result type of m in b, and the arguments types of m in b must conform to the argument types of m in a. Types can be given names for convenience, but the name of the type plays no role in checking type conformance. Types and objects can have attributes that define names for types.

---

[1] Grace uses the term *confidential* rather than *private* or *protected* because Grace's *confidential* is incomparable with the meaning of private and protected in Java and C++.

Grace supports gradual typing. Identifiers without type annotations are considered to have type Unknown, which is compatible with all types, but which may allow type errors at runtime.

Blocks. Grace *blocks* provide a concise syntax for lambda expressions (first-class functions). Grace's blocks are written between braces; if the block has parameters, the names of the parameters are written after the opening brace, separated from the body of the block by an arrow, so { x -> x + 1} defines the successor function. A block creates an object with an apply method with the same number of parameters as the block; requesting that a block apply itself evaluates the body of the block, and returns the value of the final expression in the body. Thus, { x -> x + 1}.apply(3) returns 4.

Patterns. Grace supports an object-oriented form of pattern matching [15]. A unary block with a type annotation on its parameter can be interpreted as a partial function — the block will execute if the argument matches the type annotation, otherwise the block will fail to match. The following code will add one to obj if it is a numeric object, suffix " one " to obj if it is a string object, and otherwise raise an error:

```
match (obj)
    case { x : Number -> x + 1 }
    case { s : String -> s ++ "one" }
    case { _ -> Error.raise "no match: {o} is neither a Number nor a
        String" }
```

In this example, the type acts as a pattern, but types are not the only patterns. In general, any object that responds to a match request with a MatchResult can be used as a pattern. For example, pattern.match(datum) tests if datum is matched by pattern. Type patterns match when the argument object has the methods of the type, but user-defined patterns can define their own criteria for matching. Primitive objects like numbers and strings match when they are equal to their argument.

Exceptions. Grace supports exception handling through an extension of the pattern system. Exceptions are raised using the raise method and caught by a special construct, using the exception as a pattern.

```
try { IndexOutOfBounds.raise "index {i} exceeds upper bound {u}" }
    catch { e : IndexOutOfBounds -> ... }
    catch { e : RuntimeError -> ... }
    finally { ... }
```

When an exception is raised, it is handled by the first block that matches the exception object. The raiseWith method permits the user to attach additional data to the exception packet.

Multi-part Method Names. Grace method names may contain multiple parts, making Grace method requests similar to Smalltalk message sends. For example, we can write

$2 < x < 5$ as x.isBetween (2) and (5). The combination of blocks and multi-part names allows control structures to be defined as methods:[2]

```
method if (cond : Boolean) then (body : Block) {
   cond.ifTrue(body)
}
method while (cond : Block) do (body : Block) {
   if (cond.apply) then {
      body.apply
      while (cond) do (body)
   }
}
while { x > 0 } do {
   print "{x} bottles of beer on the wall"
   x := x − 1
}
```

Because "control structures" are method requests, the placement of braces and parentheses is not arbitrary. The condition of an if statement is parenthesised, because the if's condition is a boolean expression that is evaluated exactly once. In contrast, the condition in a while may be re-evaluated many times, and must therefore be a block, which means that it is surrounded by braces. This is a departure from most other curly-brace languages, but represents semantic consistency. Of course, these two condition arguments have different types, so errors can be detected statically or dynamically.

Multi-part names do not cause a syntactic ambiguity like Algol 60's "dangling else" problem. This is because method arguments must always be delimited — either with parentheses, or, in the case of string and block literals, by the literals' own delimiters. A Grace program's layout must be consistent with its parse: a method request terminates at the end of the line, unless the next line is indented to indicate a continuation.

We included multi-part method names, along with blocks, to allow objects that represent data structures to provide methods that implement internal iterators and other control structures to look much as they do in other "curly bracket" languages. Combined with implicit receivers, multi-part names also make it easy to provide the "statements" of a dialect, as we show in this paper.

Modules. Any file containing Grace code can be treated as a module [14]. To access another module, the programmer uses an import statement, such as

```
import "examples/greeter" as doorman
```

The string that follows the import keyword must be a string literal (not an expression) that identifies (in an implementation-dependent fashion) the module to be imported. The effect of the import statement is to bind the name that follows as to the imported module object.

As mentioned earlier, the code in every file is treated as the body of an object constructor. The *module object* — the object generated by this constructor — behaves like

---

[2] Implementations may make these structures primitive for efficiency, as does our current prototype. The code shown here illustrates how they could be defined in Grace.

any other object. In particular, a module object may have types and methods as attributes, and can have state. Here is a complete, if simple, module:

```
def person = "reader"
type Greeter = { greet(name : String)->Done }
method greet(name) {
  print "Hello, {name}!"
}
greet(person)
```

Executing this module will print "Hello, reader!" and construct a module object containing the type Greeter and the method greet.

If we assume that "examples/greeter" refers to the module shown above, then import "examples/greeter" as doorman introduces the name doorman into the local scope, bound to the module object. Every import of the same string within a program will access the *same* module object, although each import may bind it to a different name.

Implementation. We added the dialect functionality to Minigrace, our prototype Grace compiler. Minigrace is available from http://www.gracelang.org/ and includes the case studies described in this paper along with others. Minigrace is expected to function on POSIX-compatible systems with GCC. A web-based version of the compiler, running in JavaScript in the client's browser, is available at http://ecs.vuw.ac.nz/~mwh/minigrace/js/. This version includes all of the case studies described in this paper as loadable samples.

3   Dialects

Dialects are modules that can both extend and restrict the standard Grace language. Dialects can not only make extra definitions available to their users; they can also restrict the language by defining and reporting new kinds of errors, and can change the way in which existing errors are reported. Dialects support the definition of language subsets to aid novice programmers, and of domain-specific languages.

3.1   Structure

A module declares the dialect in which it is written with a dialect declaration, like dialect "beginner", which loads the module named by the string, just as if it were imported. However, unlike an import statement, the dialect declaration does not bind the imported object to a name: instead, the dialect object is installed as the lexically-surrounding scope of the module that uses it, as shown in Fig. 1. Any request in the client module for a method defined in that outer scope — most often a receiverless request — will access a method of the dialect. This resolution rule is the same rule used for any other receiverless request in a lexically nested scope. Thus, if diaMeth is a method defined in the dialect, then, in a module (such as ModuleC) that is written in the dialect and does not contain a new definition of diaMeth, a receiverless request for diaMeth will invoke the method defined in the dialect.

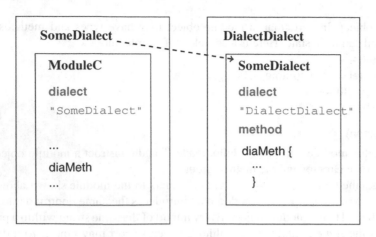

Fig. 1. Object nesting with dialects. The declaration **dialect** "d" logically nests the current module inside the module d. Notice that dialect use is not transitive: ModuleC is inside SomeDialect, and SomeDialect is inside DialectDialect, but ModuleC is not in DialectDialect.

When no dialect is specified, the module is assumed to be written in the standard Grace language, which uses the standard prelude as its dialect. The dialect mechanism thus provides a coherent explanation of how Grace's standard prelude works: a program in standard Grace generates a module object nested inside the standard prelude object. Because a dialect *replaces* this nesting, the author of a dialect can choose whether or not to expose the standard prelude's methods to their clients. If they wish, they can write

    inherits StandardPrelude.methods

at the top of their dialect, and expose all of the methods of standard Grace.

A module that defines a dialect may itself be written in a dialect. This reveals a difference between dialectical nesting and other kinds of lexical nesting: the dialect is the *outermost* lexical scope, so dialectical nesting is not transitive, as shown in Fig. 1. The reason for this design decision is that special-purpose dialects, particularly those defining educational subsets, will commonly be less powerful than the language as a whole. These dialects will thus typically be written in a dialect — such as standard Grace — that provides the dialect writer with features that should not be exposed to clients.

3.2 Pluggable Checkers

As well as providing new definitions, dialects may restrict access to particular features of the language, or offer additional and more specific error and warning messages. The latter are useful because novice students can benefit from error messages that are tailored to the more restricted things that they are trying to do, compared to more advanced programmers.

Restrictions and new error messages are implemented by the dialect module defining a *checker method*, which is executed when modules written in the dialect are compiled.

The checker method is passed as argument the abstract syntax tree of the module, and typically traverses that tree using one or more visitors. The visitors cannot change the tree, but can implement any checks the dialect needs, and can also indicate to the compiler whether it should proceed, or terminate with an error.

Checkers have the same ability to find and report errors as the compiler itself. They can perform any analysis they require: for example, a dialect may wish to perform a flow analysis to ensure that method parameters are used. If an error is found, the checker can report that error to the user, including whatever information the dialect author thinks is relevant, and either carry on to find more errors or stop at that point. Several modules that provide varied degrees of checking can be used within the same program, so a student's code can be subjected to strict constraints, while still being able to use a module provided by their instructor written in a more powerful dialect.

While a checker can examine the code of its client module using any technique the programmer wishes, we provide two mechanisms to make dialect-creation easier. One is support for the Visitor pattern [10] on the AST nodes, which we illustrate in Sect. 4.4; the other is a dialect to support largely-declarative definitions of checkers, which is presented in Sect. 4.3.

3.3 Run-Time Protocol

A dialect may wish to run code immediately before or after a module using it, perhaps for logging, initialising data structures, or launching a user interface. To enable this, the dialect protocol includes two further methods the dialect can define: atModuleStart and atModuleEnd. The method atModuleStart is requested, if it exists, immediately before the module written in the dialect is executed, and receives a single argument: a string containing the name of the module using the dialect. In Fig. 1, the string `"ModuleC"` would be provided to SomeDialect.atModuleStart(...). At this point in execution, the module object does not yet exist, so it cannot be passed to the dialect. The method atModuleEnd is requested immediately after the code of the module completes, and is passed a reference to the module object itself. The dialect can use this reference in the same way as any other object, including storing it for future use, requesting methods on it, and passing it to other methods.

4 Case Studies of Dialects

To illustrate the power of our design, this section presents six case studies of dialects and their implementations. Further case studies are reported in the first author's thesis [13]. Sample code for the case studies is included in the downloadable implementation and artifact, and is also accessible (and runnable) in the web-browser-based implementation.

4.1 Logo-Like Turtle Graphics

Our first case study is a simple dialect that supports procedural turtle graphics, inspired by Logo. This dialect is designed to be used by beginning students to learn geometry and basic control structures with as little overhead as possible — in particular, without

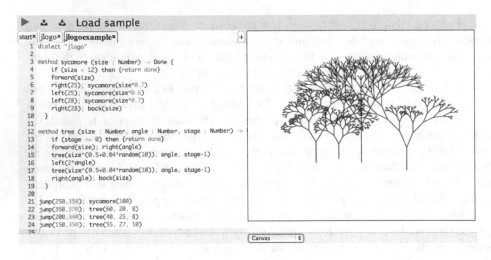

Fig. 2. A simple program in our Logo-like dialect and its output

the syntactic and semantic overhead of a more object-oriented style. We define a dialect giving access to simple movement primitives and presenting what amounts to a procedural language. Figure 2 shows a simple program in this dialect, and its output, in the web implementation.

This dialect is straightforward to implement. First, variables to hold the turtle's state can be declared at the top level of the dialect module:

```
var x : Number := 250
var y : Number := 250
var heading : Number := 270
var nib : Boolean := true
```

Then, the commands to move the turtle and draw can be written straightforwardly as Grace methods, e.g:

```
import "simplegraphics" as sg
...
method left(deg : Number) −> Done { heading := (heading − deg) % 360 }
method right(deg : Number) −> Done { heading := (heading + deg) % 360 }
method forward(n : Number) {
  def nx = x + math.cos(heading / 180 * π) * n
  def ny = y + math.sin(heading / 180 * π) * n
  if (nib) then {sg.drawLineFrom (x,y) to (nx,ny) in (ink)}
  x := nx; y := ny
}
```

This is basically the same way turtle graphics would be implemented in any procedural or scripting language. Note that the drawLineFrom()to()in() method is requested on the sg object — this delegates drawing to Grace's "simple graphics" library.

Grace's support for blocks also allows us to implement new control structures as methods that take blocks as arguments. For example, the dialect can provide a Logo-style repeat loop as a method that declares a counter variable and delegates to Grace's while ()do() loop.

```
method repeat (n : Number) times (b : Block) –> Done {
  var counter := 1
  while {counter <= n} do {
    b.apply
    counter := counter + 1 } }
```

4.2 Design by Contract

Courses taking a formal approach to software engineering may wish to teach programming disciplines such as Design by Contract, using pre- and post-conditions, and loop variants and invariants, as in Eiffel [19]. A dialect can provide these facilities in Grace. Our approach here is reminiscent of Scala, but based on dialects rather than traits [20].

The simplest support is for assertions — for example, asserting that the arrays used to store keys and values in a hash table have the same size:

```
assert {hashTable.keyArray.size == hashTable.valueArray.size}
```

This assert "statement" is defined in a dialect as a method that accepts a Predicate (a parameterless block that returns a Boolean when evaluated). If the value of the predicate is false, the assertion has failed, so we raise an appropriate exception:

```
method assert( condition : Predicate ) {
  if ( ! condition.apply) then { InvariantFailure.raise }
}
```

We can extend this technique to support pre- and post-conditions on methods, inspired by Eiffel's "require", "do", and "ensure" clauses:

```
method setHours ( hours' : Number ) {
  require { (0 <= hours') && (hours' <= 23) }
    do { hours := hours'; hours }
      ensure { result –> (result == hours') && (hours == hours') }
}
```

The identifier result in the ensure clause refers to the value returned by the method.

This construct can be defined straightforwardly in a dialect, using multi-part method names for the syntax. As in Eiffel, pre- and post-conditions are checked dynamically.

```
method require( precondition : Predicate )
    do ( body : Block )
      ensure ( postcondition : Predicate ) {
  if ( ! precondition.apply )
    then { InvariantFailure.raise "Precondition Failure" }
  var result
  try { result := body.apply }
    catch { _ –> InvariantFailure.raise "Unexpected Exception" }
    finally {
      if ( ! postcondition.apply(result) )
        then { InvariantFailure.raise "Postcondition Failure" }
    }
  return result
}
```

Going still further towards Eiffel, we can add support to the dialect for specifying and checking loop variants and invariants:

```
loop {
    print(letters[i])
    i := i+1
}
invariant { i <= (letters.size + 1) }
until { i > letters.size }
variant { letters.size − i + 1 }
```

Once again, expressions defining variants and invariants, as well as the code for the loop body and the termination condition, are supplied as blocks, which are evaluated as required by the implementation of the loop()invariant()... method.

4.3 Dialect for Writing Dialects

Programmers writing different dialects tend to have similar needs. In particular, writing a checker requires inspecting the user's code and determining whether or not it is acceptable; the *form* of this inspection will be the same in many dialects. We have abstracted these repeated tasks into a dialect of their own. Our dialect dialect makes it easy to declare rules to test different parts of the source code and to report errors; these rules are used in the static dialect described in Sect. 4.4. The dialect dialect can also maintain state; we demonstrate how this is used for type checking in Sect. 4.5. The dialect dialect hides the details of the checking process and allows programmers to write dialect definitions that are largely declarative.

Fundamentally, Grace checkers are methods that examine the nodes of the program's abstract syntax tree at compile time. A checker either accepts a node, or raises an exception to report an error. The AST nodes support the Visitor Pattern to assist in this examination. Although quite efficient, this kind of code is too low-level to be written by most instructors, who may nevertheless need to write dialects for use in their teaching.

The dialect for writing dialects simplifies the process of writing a checker by implementing a generic visitor that applies *rules* defined by the dialect-writer. The dialect maintains a list of rules to apply in a module-level object rules. The rule method takes an ASTBlock (a block that accepts an AST node) as an argument, and adds it to the list of rules.

```
method rule(block : ASTBlock) −> Done {
    rules.push(block)
}
```

More complex kinds of rule, such as when()error() rules, are defined in terms of the basic rule method:

```
method when(pred : UnaryPredicate) error(msg : String) {
    rule { node −>
        def matches = pred.match(node)
        if (matches.andAlso {matches.result}) then { fail(msg) }
    }
}
```

The first argument to when()error() is a UnaryPredicate, that is, a block that takes a single argument and returns a Boolean. The body of the method declares a primitive rule that accepts an AST node, and then applies pred as a partial function to that node. If the function is applicable, *and* the result of invoking the the predicate is true, then an error is raised using fail.

The dialect dialect defines a single visitor over the AST, which runs all the rules over every node:

```
method visitDefDec(node) -> Boolean {
  runRules(node)
}

method visitVarDec(node) -> Boolean {
  runRules(node)
}
```

It is sometimes useful to examine a node from a perspective that is different from the way that the AST is defined. For example, parameters appear within method, block, and class definition nodes, but the dialect-writer may wish to treat them all in the same way. To simplify the matching of all parameters, regardless of their location in the AST, the dialect constructs special parameter nodes against which to run the rules:

```
method visitMethod(node) -> Boolean {
  runRules(node)

  for(node.signature) do { part ->
    for(part.params) do { param ->
      runRules(aParameter.fromNode(param))
    }
  }

  for(node.body) do { stmt ->
    stmt.accept(self)
  }

  return false
}
```

The dialect also defines a pattern Parameter to match these nodes; this allows the dialect author to write a rule against all parameters, rather than having to write separate rules to deal with each place in which a parameter may appear. The static dialect in Sect. 4.4 uses this pattern to ensure that all parameters are annotated with types. Similarly, specialised patterns While and For match while and for loops, common cases that a dialect may want to examine. A dialect author can easily create similar patterns for their own constructs using the aRequestPattern.forName(...) method provided by the dialect dialect.

The pattern-matching approach trades off some efficiency for ease of programming, but efficiency is not a primary goal of Grace. Moreover, we expect most programs, especially in beginner dialects (which are likely to have the most additional checks) to be quite small. A declarative approach allows checkers to be expressed concisely, and to be understood without a deep understanding of the whole of the implementation.

```
import "ast" as ast
def CheckerFailure = Exception.refine "CheckerFailure"
def staticVisitor = object {
  inherits ast.baseVisitor
  method visitDefDec(v) {
    if (v.decType.value == "Unknown") then {
      CheckerFailure.raiseWith("no type on '{v.name.value}'", v.name)
  } }
  method visitMethod(v) {
    for (v.signature) do {s->
      for (s.params) do {p->
        if (p.decType.value == "Unknown") then {
          CheckerFailure.raiseWith("no type on '{p.value}'", p)
  } } }
    if (v.returnType.value == "Unknown") then {
      CheckerFailure.raiseWith("no return type on '{v.value.value}'", v.
        value)
  } }
  }
  method checker(code : List<ASTNode>) {
    for (code) do {n -> n.accept(staticVisitor) }
  }
```

Fig. 3. Requiring static types implemented as a Visitor. Similar code for **var** declarations and blocks is omitted for space.

4.4   Requiring Explicit Type Annotations

An instructor can require that, for all or part of a course, all student code is fully annotated with types, so that no dynamically-typed code is permitted. The static dialect allows access to all of the ordinary language features, while reporting compile-time errors to students who omit the types on their declarations. The definition of this dialect is relatively straightforward. We can use a visitor, as shown in Fig. 3, or the dialect-writing dialect to express it more concisely:

```
dialect "dialect"
inherits StandardPrelude.methods
when { d : Def | Var -> d.decType.value == "Unknown" }
  error "declarations must have a static type"
when { m : Method -> m.returnType.value == "Unknown" }
  error "methods must have a static return type"
when { p : Parameter -> p.decType.value == "Unknown" }
  error "parameters must have a static type"
method checker(code : Code) {
  check(code)
}
```

The first two rules provide a particular error message to display, specify what kind of node they care about—**var**, **def**, and **method** declarations— and what should trigger the error message. Here, the error appears when the declaration type is Unknown (which is the type of an un-annotated declaration). The last when()error() clause matches against the Parameter pattern from the dialect dialect, which was described in Sect. 4.3 The checker method in the static dialect delegates to check from the dialect dialect; check applies all of the declarative rules we have given.

4.5 Type Checking

Because dialects can perform checks over the whole of a module, various static checks that would typically be built into the compiler can be moved into a dialect. The Minigrace compiler does not perform any compile-time type checking, instead deferring type checks until runtime. However, if a module is written in the structural dialect, the dialect will perform structural subtyping checks before the compiler generates code for the module.

```
dialect "structural"
type Foo = { bar −> String }
method takesFoo(foo : Foo) {
   print(foo.bar)
}
takesFoo("foo") // Fails: argument does not satisfy parameter type
```

Type checking is implemented by extending the dialect dialect with the typeOf method, which takes an AST node and executes the rule defined for it, returning the type of the execution. Rules written in the structural dialect ensure that the typing of a node is correct, and return the static type information of nodes that represent expressions.

The dialect mechanisms are entirely agnostic to the nature of the type information used, allowing different forms of type checking to be implemented in the same dialect. The structural dialect includes several classes for describing types, providing a basis for building and testing type information in the rules that follow. The anObjectType class provides the isSubtypeOf method, which determines if one type is a subtype of another. For instance, the type error generated above comes from the request typing rule, given in Fig. 4, that ensures that the method exists in the receiver and the parameters

```
rule { req : Request −>
 match(typeOf(req.in).getMethod(req.name))
  case { _ : NoSuchMethod −> fail "no such method" }
  case { mt : MethodType −>
   for (mt.signature) and(req.with) do { s, w −>
    for (s.params) and(w.args) do { p, a −>
     if (!typeOf(a).isSubtypeOf(p.decType)) then {
       fail "argument does not satify parameter type" }
   }}
      mt.returnType  // A request for typeOf(req) will receive this value
 }}
```

Fig. 4. Request typing rule in the structural dialect

are correctly typed before producing a type for the result of the request. The nested
requests to the method for(aCollection)and(anotherCollection) do(aBinaryBlock) iterate
through the signature parts and parameters, testing that each argument is a subtype of
its corresponding parameter.

The extension to the **dialect** dialect also supplies tools for managing information
about what variables, methods and types are available in the current scope. Rules can
enter into new scopes, introduce new values, and retrieve them again with identifiers.
The two rules below ensure that a block like { x : Number —> x } produces the appropriate type.

```
rule { blk : BlockLiteral —>
  scope.enter {
    for(blk.params) do { param —>
      def pType = anObjectType.fromDecType(param.decType)
      scope.variables.at(param.name) put(pType)
    }
    typeOf(blk.body.last) } }
rule { idnt : Identifier —> scope.variables.find(idnt.value) }
```

Although variables, methods, and types all inhabit the same namespace in Grace,
keeping them separated in the scope management makes it easier to distinguish between run-time and compile-time information. Essentially, every type declaration introduces new type information *and* a new runtime object into the local scope bound to that
information.

Structural type checking is compatible with other checkers. To complete the implementation of a fully static variant of Grace, the **structural** and **static** dialects can be
combined.

```
import "static" as static
import "structural" as structural
inherits StandardPrelude.methods
method checker(code : Code) {
  static.checker(code)
  structural.checker(code)
}
```

Because two imports of the same module access the same module object, multiple
checkers written in the **dialect** dialect are able to share type information with one another. This allows a checker to extend the typing of another by providing extra type
information, and type checking rules that operate in tandem with the existing rules. The
following dialect adds basic type inference to definitions. It uses the type information
provided by **structural**, and adds extra information into the type environments of the
shared **scope** object.

```
dialect "dialect"
import "structural" as structural
inherits StandardPrelude.methods
rule { d : Def —>
  if (d.decType.value == "Unknown") then {
    scope.at(d.name) put(typeOf(d.value))
  } }
method checker(code : Code) { structural.checker(code) }
```

4.6   Literal Blocks

Because control structures in Grace are simply methods with the same semantics as other parts of the language, a programmer (particularly one familiar with other languages) may make mistakes that are not syntactically invalid, but lead to errors they find difficult to understand. In particular, the condition of a while loop is a block, as it may be executed repeatedly, and so is written in braces. If the programmer writes the condition in parentheses instead, or writes some other expression in place of the condition, they will receive a type error they may find difficult to understand.

This dialect ensures that the condition of a while loop is written in braces, as a literal block, and will not permit passing a reference to a block defined elsewhere. The dialect dialect provides checking rules and a special While pattern that allows us to write the body of the dialect very briefly:

```
rule { req : While(cond, _) ->
    if (cond.kind != "block") then {
        reportWhile(req)
    }
}
method reportWhile(req) {
    // Report an explicit error to the user and suggest what they may have intended.
}
```

The reportWhile method uses the dialect dialect's error-reporting and the compiler's suggestions infrastructure to tell the user what they did wrong, and what they might have intended to write. In a simple case like the following, the error is reported as ranging from the first parenthesis to the last, and the user will be prompted as follows:

```
literal_test.grace[4:7-14]: Syntax error: The condition of
a while loop must be written in {}.
  3: var x := 0
  4: while (x < 10) do {
-----------^^^^^^^^
  5:     print "Counted to {x}."

Did you mean:
  4: while {x < 10} do {
```

A user interface can present this suggestion as an action to be taken, as the web-based IDE does.

5   Discussion

We considered three major alternative approaches to dialects: inheritance, delegation, and special-purpose macros. We rejected all of these in favour of the approach described here, each for a different reason.

5.1   Inheritance

With an inheritance-based approach, the module using a dialect inherits from the dialect, and dialectical methods can be invoked using a receiverless request, since they
would be available on **self** in the module scope, and through **outer** in any nested scopes.
The dialect's methods could also be defined as confidential if required.

This approach was inspired by SIMULA, and envisaged in the early descriptions of
Grace. As the language developed, several problems with this approach revealed themselves. Most of these problems arise because inheritance in Grace (as in most other
languages) is transitive, so dialects implemented via inheritance would also be transitive. What this means is that a module that inherits from a dialect will have all of the
dialect's methods available on the module object itself. For example, if a dialect were
itself defined by a dialect (as in Sect. 4.3) then all the features of the dialect-defining
dialect would also be included in any module that uses that dialect. For these reasons
we discounted the inheritance approach.

5.2   Delegation

We also considered supporting dialects by delegation. In particular, we considered
translating a dialect statement into an import statement for the dialect module, along
with a set of local (re)declarations of methods, one for each of the public methods of
the dialect. Each of these local methods would forward to the corresponding method of
the dialect. In this way, encapsulation of the dialect module is preserved; the effect is
similar to unqualified imports in other languages. For example, given a dialect module
containing:

```
method for(i)do(b) is public { ... }
method helper is confidential { ... }
```

and a module using it, the **dialect** keyword would be translated into:

```
import "someDialect" as secret
method for(a1)do(a2) is confidential {
   secret.for(a1) do(a2)
}
```

Only public dialect methods would get local forwarding methods, so local definitions of
the dialect would be hidden. The local forwarding methods would be marked
confidential, so that they would not be available to clients of the module. This approach
would again make the dialect methods available as requests on **self** in the module scope.

Many of the issues with the inheritance approach do not arise here. The dialect object
is used compositionally, but new methods are defined in the client module. The concept
of exposing only public methods seemed attractive, but did not allow for a method to be
exposed to a client written in the dialect without also exposing that method to all other
code.

There were two reasons why we rejected this design. The first is that it added another
mechanism — delegation — into the language. Grace already has three relationships between objects: simple references, inheritance, and lexical nesting: delegation would add
a fourth. The second reason is that the proposed semantics for delegation were very

similar to the existing semantics for lexical nesting. Nesting makes outer objects' methods available to the objects nested inside them, but not to those objects' clients; those methods can be involved via implicit requests, or explicitly via **outer** (rather than **self**); self-requests in the outer object go to that object, not back to the original **self**. Given these similarities, it seemed simpler overall to extend nesting to encompass dialects, rather than introduce another separate mechanism.

5.3 Macros

The third option was to add macros, an additional language mechanism, allowing a dialect to define their own syntax and semantics from scratch. This is the approach taken in Racket [25], discussed in more detail in section 6.1 below. Macros provide vastly more power than Grace's dialects: they may reorder or prevent the evaluation of arguments, introduce new bindings not mentioned in the source code, or transform the program in arbitrary ways.

For example, an SQL-style **select** macro in Racket could share an iteration variable across several expressions:

```
(for n (numbers)
  (where (< n 5))
  (select (* 3 n)))
```

In contrast, an equivalent form in Grace would make the sub-expressions (arguments to where and select clauses) blocks, with the value of the current number being provided as an argument to each block in turn:

```
for (numbers)
  where { n -> n < 5 }
  select { n -> n * 3 }
```

(C#'s lambdas have the same limitations as Grace's blocks, which is why C# has a built-in "macro" that re-writes its select statement into expression using multiple lambdas. [2]).

There are a number of reasons why we chose not to use macros to implement dialects in Grace. The first is that, without macros, dialects can't introduce new syntactic forms; this means that code written in a dialect remains readable without knowledge of the dialect it is using. Thus, the parse of a Grace program does not depend on dialects, types, or operator definitions: syntactically, there are only method requests. A novice can understand that control passes to a given method on a given receiver, with the arguments written in the source, without needing to understand what that method does or how it does it.

The second reason is that, without macros, Grace code that *implements* a dialect uses essentially the same language features as code that *uses* a dialect. Instructors do not have to learn a powerful new feature (macros) to write dialects, and don't have to understand a new feature to be able to debug code using dialects.

The final reason is that macros are an additional feature that have not (so far) been required in Grace. Because we want to keep Grace minimal, and hopefully easy to learn and easy to use, we didn't want to add complex and powerful additional features unless we could not find any simpler alternatives.

5.4 Local Dialects

In the current design, dialects are chosen for the whole of a module. Because dialects rely on lexical scope, an obvious extension is to permit dialects to be applied to smaller "local" lexical scopes, perhaps for the extent of a block, an object constructor, or a class. For example, we could shift into the turtle graphics dialect in the middle of a for loop to draw the bars of a histogram.

```
...
def histogram = source.getData
for (histogram) do { datum ->
 dialect "turtle" do {
   forward(datum * 10)
   right(90); forward(10); right(90)
   forward(datum * 10)
   left(90); forward(10); left(90)
 }
}
```

We have not pursued this extension for several reasons. Local dialects do not seem to be necessary to support teaching—the primary purpose of Grace dialects. Local lexically scoped dialects may indeed be useful for domain specific languages used to support modelling, such as the relationship and finite state machine dialects described in the thesis [13], but for pedagogical purposes, students will typically write a single module in a single dialect.

The interaction of dialect scoping and ordinary lexical scoping needs careful thought. In many cases, code in the new dialect may well want to access identifiers from elsewhere in the module, but not from the outer dialect, while in other cases programmers may want to augment the existing dialect on a temporary basis.

Pragmatically, we can generally do without lexical dialects at the cost of extra modules. The above code example could be refactored so that the body of the for loop becomes a method in a separate module that is written in the turtle dialect; the loop would then request that method from the other module.

6 Related Work

6.1 Racket

Tobin-Hochstadt *et al.* [25] describe languages as libraries in Racket, a Scheme-based language with an accompanying IDE designed for teaching. Racket supports multiple language definitions through the use of avowedly *"Advanced Macrology"* [6] to translate the input source text down to core Racket, adding new functionality, or even replacing the language syntax and semantics along the way.

Racket (then DrScheme) reintroduced the concept of using multiple "language levels" for teaching [8], originally from SP/k [12]: Grace's dialects were inspired by Racket's language levels. Racket's levels are intended to be moved through in sequence with gradually increasing power: earlier levels restrict functionality that novices will not need to use, and provide more informative error messages and suggestions based on their knowledge of what the programmer can write.

Racket languages are strictly more powerful than our dialects, because Racket macros are full Scheme procedures that manipulate syntax trees. This is particularly useful when creating new defining forms, allowing their arguments to span multiple scopes.

A Racket language also has the ability to provide information to the Racket integrated development environment. This information can aid syntax highlighting and error reporting when the language has been modified. Because Grace dialects do not make such modifications, this tight coupling with the editing environment is not required: all programs are in standard Grace syntax. The dialect's checker can provide error reporting to whatever level of detail is required.

Racket also offers significant support for defining new languages from scratch. A Racket language definition can entirely replace the Racket "reader", and parse the source text itself, allowing arbitrary input. A Racket implementation of Algol-60 is included in the Racket distribution, and programs need only declare `#lang algol60` in order for the rest of the source to be treated as Algol. Our system does not support this; while a dialect may, by the combination of multi-part methods, operators, and predefined objects, present a language with a similar feel to another, programs written in that dialect must still conform to the overarching Grace syntax. This limitation is both a blessing and a curse. A programmer who already knows the other language may not be immediately at home, but working within a single consistent syntax allows integrating code from different paradigms and gradually moving from one to another.

Compared with Racket, the author of a Grace dialect does not need to embark upon full-scale metaprogramming (nor do they have the opportunity). To define a dialect without a checker, programmers define the methods, classes, variables, and types they want to have available to users exactly as they would in any other program. To provide dialect checkers, programmers need to understand the visitor pattern, or use the "dialect" dialect to write a largely declarative specification of a visitor, within Grace's standard syntax and semantics.

All Grace dialects have the same semantics as any other Grace program — method requests with arguments passed by value. Grace's parse depends only upon syntax, not on types or other implicit operations, so programmers can always determine the flow of execution from a program's surface syntax. By avoiding macros we avoid code that does not do what it appears to do: arguments are always evaluated before methods are requested, new bindings are never introduced implicitly, and parse or type errors can stem only from what was actually written in the input source code. A macro-based system cannot guarantee any of these points.

6.2   Scala

Scala [21,23] includes several features supporting domain-specific languages. The language syntax permits methods acting like built-in structures and operators with many levels of precedence and associativity. Scala implicit parameters allow an argument to be passed without naming it, determined by the type. In combination these allow domain-specific languages that are aware of the context in which they are used. Scala's treatment of syntax and semantics is determined by the static type information it has available. By contrast, Grace programs have the same semantics with or without type definitions, and Grace's syntax, while flexible, does not admit ambiguities that need to be resolved by static types.

Scala also includes powerful macro features [7,5] integrating the compiler and runtime. There is no formal "dialect" system in Scala, although similar functionality can be built using other constructs of the language. Scala mirrors have the ability to perform both run-time and compile-time reflection, and these can be used to implement domain-specific languages with similar ability to those in Racket, including the ability to defer some processing until run time, although with the same fundamental syntax. Compile-time execution in Grace dialects is limited to reading and proscribing: they cannot modify or specialise code, and the run-time behaviour of dialects is exactly Grace method execution.

6.3 Ruby

In Ruby internal domain-specific languages (DSLs) are common, supported by particular language features [9]. Two common strategies for Ruby DSLs involve using the language's open classes, and using per-instance dynamically-bound evaluation.

Open classes permit modifying third-party classes — including built-in objects — to add new methods, enabling users of the DSL to write, for example, 3.years.ago to represent a time. These modifications are globally visible, and work only so long as they don't conflict with other modifications.

The second strategy depends on dynamically-bound block evaluation using the method instance_eval. This method allows one to execute a block of code inside the context of another object L as though the block were written inside L's definition, and thus with access to methods defined in L. The language syntax permits reasonably fluid code to be written in this way. Moreover, different DSLs may be used at different points by evaluating code inside different objects.

Grace's dialects are more static than Ruby's. Whereas Ruby uses dynamic metaprogramming to modify existing classes or modules, Grace uses nesting to make definitions available where they are needed; in Grace, the bindings seen by a block depend on where it is defined, and not on where it is evaluated.

6.4 Haskell

Haskell is also used to define domain specific languages [1,16]. Haskell DSLs typically use the language's type classes to embed themselves in the language. Existing functions and operators become part of the language by defining type-class instances for the language representation — whether that representation is the data the DSL consumes, or a reflexive representation of the program itself. Static type information directs which functions are actually executed for a particular expression, often based upon the calling context (i.e. the expected return type). A programmer can temporarily enter the domain of a DSL simply by declaring the return type of their function.

Static type information is crucial to the semantics of Haskell DSLs (as it is in Haskell programs generally). A semantics relying on static types is undesirable for a gradually-typed language like Grace. Haskell's available syntax is more constrained than Grace's dialects, and the scope for extension is more constrained by what already exists in the language. A Haskell DSL will have difficulty relying on some subset of the functions or operators from a Haskell type class, while Grace dialects may define exactly the methods and operators they need.

6.5   Cedalion

Cedalion [17] is a language for defining domain-specific languages. Cedalion aims to promote "language-oriented programming", a programming style in which many DSLs are used in combination, with a new language defined for each subdomain spanned by the program. Lorenz and Rosenan, Cedalion's designers, define four kinds of language-oriented programming system: internal DSLs, where a DSL is implemented within a host language (as in a Grace dialect), external DSLs, where the DSL is a separate language with its own compiler or interpreter, language workbenches, which combine tools and an IDE to present external DSLs as though they were internal, and language-oriented programming languages, like Cedalion.

All Cedalion languages are interoperable because they share the same host language. In this respect they resemble Grace dialects: within the same fundamental semantics, many different variants may coexist simultaneously. On the other hand, Cedalion uses a special "projectional editor" [26] to edit code: the abstract syntax tree is edited, rather than textual source. A Cedalion language defines a display grammar for that syntax tree, rather than a parsing grammar for text. This approach contrasts with Grace, where the same surface syntax persists in every dialect, but where the syntax itself is quite flexible. A reader of one Cedalion language has no more benefit in understanding another than an outsider, while an author in the language needs not conform to any other overriding syntax. In both cases, Cedalion takes the opposite position to Grace.

6.6   Pluggable Checkers

JavaCOP [18] is a framework for implementing pluggable type systems in Java. This framework provides a declarative language for specifying new type rules and a system for enforcing those rules during compilation. JavaCOP rules may enforce, for example, that a parameter must not be null, or that a field is transitively read-only. A dialect can enforce these rules as well, but is also able to enforce broader constraints by extending or limiting the constructs available to the user of the dialect.

The Checker Framework [22] is a mature library that provides similar functionality to JavaCOP, with better support for overloading and some other Java language features in part by using an only-partially-declarative syntax. Imperative rules provide more power to the Checker Framework than JavaCOP at the expense of concision. Our system allows combining the two by building dialects specifically for the purpose of writing other dialects and checkers, which may provide declarative syntax as well as allowing flexible imperative tests.

7   Conclusion

The language designer should be familiar with many alternative features
designed by others, and should have excellent judgment in choosing the best
— Tony Hoare,
Hints on Programming Language Design [11].

We have described how a novel combination of language features — lexically nested objects, syntax for blocks and multi-part method names, optional typing, and pluggable checkers — supports dialects in Grace. Because Grace's dialects are based on these standard language features, programmers can write dialects much as they write any other Grace program — by defining objects and methods — without having to learn additional macro systems, define lexers, parsers, and semantic rules, or use metaprogramming to modify class definitions on the fly. To illustrate the power of Grace's dialect mechanism, we have presented a number of case studies of dialects of varying complexity. These range from a Logo-style turtle graphics microworld, through an Eiffel-style design by contract dialect, to a dialect that ensures that programs are statically typed, and a dialect that helps instructors to write dialects.

A more mature implementation (compiler and IDE) will enable us to begin empirical evaluations of Grace in use in teaching. We hope to begin these evaluations in October 2014, and expect to refine Grace's design based on this experience. Much work remains to be completed with Grace in general and dialects in particular. Grace's implementation, although sufficient to host the compiler, and to support small assignments in programming-language classes, is still a proof-of-concept prototype.

Acknowledgements. We thank Matthias Felleisen and the other (anonymous) reviewers for their comments on a previous versions of this paper.

References

1. Augustsson, L., Mansell, H., Sittampalam, G.: Paradise: a two-stage DSL embedded in Haskell. In: ICFP 2008, pp. 225–228. ACM, New York (2008)
2. Bierman, G.M., Meijer, E., Torgersen, M.: Lost in translation: formalizing proposed extensions to C#. In: OOPSLA (2007)
3. Black, A.P., Bruce, K.B., Homer, M., Noble, J.: Grace: the absence of (inessential) difficulty. In: Onward!, pp. 85–98. ACM, New York (2012)
4. Black, A.P., Bruce, K.B., Homer, M., Noble, J., Ruskin, A., Yannow, R.: Seeking Grace: a new object-oriented language for novices. In: SIGCSE (2013)
5. Burmako, E., Odersky, M., Vogt, C., Zeiger, S., Moors, A.: Scala macros (April 2012), http://scalamacros.org
6. Culpepper, R., Tobin-Hochstadt, S., Flatt, M.: Advanced macrology and the implementation of Typed Scheme. In: ICFP Workshop on Scheme and Functional Programming (2007)
7. EPFL: Environment, universes, and mirrors - Scala documentation (2013), http://docs.scala-lang.org/overviews/reflection/environment-universes-mirrors.html

8. Findler, R.B., Clements, J., Flanagan, C., Flatt, M., Krishnamurthi, S., Steckler, P., Felleisen, M.: DrScheme: a programming environment for Scheme. J. Funct. Program. 12(2), 159–182 (2002)
9. Fowler, M.: Domain Specific Languages. AW (2011)
10. Gamma, E., Helm, R., Johnson, R.E., Vlissides, J.: Design Patterns. AW (1994)
11. Hoare, C.: Hints on programming language design. Tech. Rep. AIM-224, Stanford Artificial Intelligence Laboratory (1973)
12. Holt, R.C., Wortman, D.B.: A sequence of structured subsets of PL/I. SIGCSE Bull. 6(1), 129–132 (1974), http://doi.acm.org/10.1145/953057.810456
13. Homer, M.: Graceful Language Features and Interfaces. Ph.D. thesis, Victoria University of Wellington (2014)
14. Homer, M., Bruce, K.B., Noble, J., Black, A.P.: Modules as gradually-typed objects. In: Proceedings of the 7th Workshop on Dynamic Languages and Applications, DYLA 2013, pp. 1:1–1:8. ACM, New York (2013), http://doi.acm.org/10.1145/2489798.2489799
15. Homer, M., Noble, J., Bruce, K.B., Black, A.P., Pearce, D.J.: Patterns as objects in Grace. In: Dynamic Language Symposium. ACM, New York (2012)
16. Jones, M.P.: Experience report: playing the DSL card. In: ICFP (2008)
17. Lorenz, D.H., Rosenan, B.: Cedalion: a language for language oriented programming. In: OOPSLA, vol. 46 (October 2011)
18. Markstrum, S., Marino, D., Esquivel, M., Millstein, T.D., Andreae, C., Noble, J.: JavaCOP: Declarative pluggable types for Java. ACM Trans. Program. Lang. Syst. 32(2) (2010)
19. Meyer, B.: Eiffel: The Language. Prentice Hall (1992)
20. Odersky, M.: Contracts for scala. In: Barringer, H., Falcone, Y., Finkbeiner, B., Havelund, K., Lee, I., Pace, G., Roşu, G., Sokolsky, O., Tillmann, N. (eds.) RV 2010. LNCS, vol. 6418, pp. 51–57. Springer, Heidelberg (2010)
21. Odersky, M.: The Scala language specification. Tech. rep., Programming Methods Laboratory, EPFL (2011)
22. Papi, M.M., Ali, M., Correa, J. T.L., Perkins, J.H., Ernst, M.D.: Practical pluggable types for Java. In: ISSTA (2008)
23. Rompf, T., Odersky, M.: Lightweight modular staging: a pragmatic approach to runtime code generation and compiled DSLs. In: GPCE, New York, NY, USA, pp. 127–136 (2010)
24. Ross, D.T.: Uniform referents: An essential property for a software engineering language. In: Tou, J.T. (ed.) Software Engineering, vol. 1, pp. 91–101. Academic Press (1970)
25. Tobin-Hochstadt, S., St-Amour, V., Culpepper, R., Flatt, M., Felleisen, M.: Languages as libraries. In: PLDI (2011)
26. Voelter, M.: Embedded software development with projectional language workbenches. In: Petriu, D.C., Rouquette, N., Haugen, Ø. (eds.) MODELS 2010, Part II. LNCS, vol. 6395, pp. 32–46. Springer, Heidelberg (2010)
27. Wirth, N.: The programming language PASCAL. Acta Informatica 1(1) (1971)

A Artifact Description

Authors of the Artifact. Core developer: Michael Homer. Dialect case studies: Michael Homer, Timothy Jones, James Noble.

Summary. The artifact is based on Minigrace, a prototype compiler for Grace implemented by the first author. Minigrace has been extended to include dialects, language variants that extend or restrict the language available to the programmer. The artifact includes several case studies exploring different areas of the dialect space, including both extensional and restrictive dialects.

Content. The artifact package includes:

- a version of Minigrace including the dialect system described in the paper;
- twelve case study dialects: the six described in the paper (turtle graphics, design-by-contract, dialect dialect, mandatory type annotations, structural subtyping, and requiring literal blocks) and six others;
- detailed instructions for using the artifact, for rebuilding it from scratch, and for obtaining the newest source code, provided as an `index.html` file.

To simplify experimenting with our case studies, we provide a VirtualBox disk image containing our prototype fully installed and with all case study dialects immediately available. The image contains Ubuntu 13.10, logs the user in by default, and includes the `minigrace` tool in the path with all case studies in the initial directory. All dependencies are preinstalled and the tool is ready to run.

We also include a tarball of the complete source code of the newest version of Minigrace, which includes our dialect changes. Minigrace compiles to both C and JavaScript, and some dialects function only on one backend or the other; to that end, we include a fully set-up version of the JavaScript backend including all case studies and instructions for accessing it.

Getting the Artifact. The artifact endorsed by the Artifact Evaluation Committee is available free of charge as supplementary material of this paper on SpringerLink. The latest version of our code is available from the Grace language website, http://gracelang.org.

Tested Platforms. The virtual machine is known to work on any platform running VirtualBox version 4 with at least 8 GB or free space on disk and at least 1 GB of free space in RAM. Minigrace is known to work on most POSIX-compatible systems, including Linux and Mac OS X. Installation instructions are included in the source tarballs. The JavaScript interface of Minigrace is known to work on all current major desktop browsers, including Firefox, Chrome, Safari, and Internet Explorer.

License. GPL 3 or later (https://www.gnu.org/licenses/gpl-3.0.html)

MD5 Sum of the artifact. 1995f3ef018c83de31dfe445c9cafd4b

Size of the Artifact. 1489950046 bytes (1.4 GB)

Structuring Documentation to Support State Search: A Laboratory Experiment about Protocol Programming

Joshua Sunshine, James D. Herbsleb, and Jonathan Aldrich

Institute for Software Research, School of Computer Science
Carnegie Mellon University
{sunshine,jdh,aldrich}@cs.cmu.edu

Abstract. Application Programming Interfaces (APIs) often define object protocols. Objects with protocols have a finite number of states and in each state a different set of method calls is valid. Many researchers have developed protocol verification tools because protocols are notoriously difficult to follow correctly. However, recent research suggests that a major challenge for API protocol programmers is effectively searching the state space. Verification is an ineffective guide for this kind of search. In this paper we instead propose Plaiddoc, which is like Javadoc except it organizes methods by state instead of by class and it includes explicit state transitions, state-based type specifications, and rich state relationships. We compare Plaiddoc to a Javadoc control in a between-subjects laboratory experiment. We find that Plaiddoc participants complete state search tasks in significantly less time and with significantly fewer errors than Javadoc participants.

1 Introduction

Many Application Programming Interfaces (APIs) define object protocols, which restrict the order of client calls to API methods. Objects with protocols have a finite number of states and in each state a different set of method calls is valid. Protocols also specify transitions between states that occur as part of some method calls. A client of such a library must be aware of the protocol in order to use it correctly. For example, a file may be in the open or closed state. In the open state, one may read or write to a file, or one may close it, which causes a state transition to the closed state. In the closed state, the only permitted operation is to (re-)open the file.

Files provide a simple example of states, but there are many more examples. Streams may be open or closed, iterators may have elements available or not, collections may be empty or not, and even lowly exceptions can have their cause set, or not. More than 8% of Java Standard Library classes and interfaces define protocols, which is more than three times as many as define type parameters [1].

Protocols are implemented in mainstream languages like Java with low-level constructs: the state of an object is tracked with boolean, integer, or enum fields; violations are checked explicitly and cause runtime exceptions like IllegalStateException; and constraints are specified in prose documentation. It is perhaps

R. Jones (Ed.): ECOOP 2014, LNCS 8586, pp. 157–181, 2014.

unsurprising, therefore, that APIs with protocols are difficult to use. In a study of problems developers experienced when using a portion of the ASP.NET framework, three quarters of the issues identified involved temporal constraints [19]. Three recent security papers have identified serious vulnerabilities in widely used security applications resulting from API protocol violations [14,4,28].

Many researchers have developed protocol checkers which are designed to make it easier for programmers to correctly use APIs with protocols (e.g. [3,10,13]). These tools require programmers to specify protocols using alias and typestate annotations that are separate from code. To automate the annotation process, several tools mine protocol specifications using dynamic analysis [8] or static analysis [2,36]. A recent survey of automated API property inference techniques described 35 inference techniques for ordering specifications [24].

However, the qualitative studies described in [31, ch.3] found that programmers using API protocols spend their time primarily on four types of searches of the protocol state space. Protocol checker output is unlikely to help programmers perform many of these searches.

Instead, in this paper we introduce a novel documentation generator called Plaiddoc, which is like Javadoc except it organizes methods by state instead of by class and it includes explicit state transitions, state-based type specifications, and rich state relationships. Plaiddoc is extracted automatically from the standard Javadoc annotations plus new Plaiddoc specifications. Plaiddoc is named for the Plaid programming language [32], which embeds similar state-oriented features, and from which Plaiddoc could, in principle, be automatically generated. We evaluate Plaiddoc against a Javadoc control in a 20-participant between-subjects laboratory experiment.

The experiment attempts to answer the following five research questions:

RQ1. Can programmers answer state search questions more efficiently using Plaiddoc than Javadoc?

RQ2. Are programmers as effective answering non-state questions using Plaiddoc as they are with Javadoc?

RQ3. Will programmers who use Plaiddoc answer state search questions more correctly than programmers who use Javadoc?

RQ4. Will programmers get better at answering state search questions as they get more practice?

RQ5. Are programmers who use Plaiddoc better than programmers who use Javadoc at mapping general state concepts to API details?

All of the tasks performed by participants asked participants to answer a question. We therefore use the words task and question interchangeably in the rest of this paper. Most of these questions were instances of four state search categories discovered in two earlier, qualitative studies [31]. Some of the questions were not state related and were chosen to benefit Javadoc. Task ordering was alternated to measure learning effects, and a post-study quiz was administered to gauge concept understanding.

Participants using Plaiddoc completed state tasks in 46% of the time it took Javadoc participants, but were approximately equally fast on non-state tasks.

Plaiddoc participants were also 7.6x less likely to answer questions incorrectly than Javadoc participants. Finally, Plaiddoc and Javadoc participants were approximately equally able to map state concepts to API details. Nevertheless, our overall results suggest that Plaiddoc can provide a lightweight mechanism for improving programmer performance on state-related tasks without negatively impacting traditional tasks.

More broadly, the results of this study also provide indirect support for several programming language design choices. This study provides quantitative evidence for the productivity benefits of type annotations as documentation and state-oriented language features.

2   Background and Related Work

The seminal paper entitled "Why a diagram is (sometimes) worth ten thousand words," [21] introduces a computational model of human cognition to compare informationally equivalent diagrams and text. They demonstrate in this model that solving math and physics problems with text-based information can require many more steps than solving the same problems with diagrams. The most important difference between the diagram steps and text steps is that much more effort in text is spent searching for needed details. One particularly noteworthy reason for the search difference is that diagrams often collocate details that are needed together.

Larkin and Simon's theory has been effectively applied to many other (non-diagramatic) information contexts. For example, Chandler shows in a series of experiments that integrated instructional material and the removal of non-essential material can facilitate learning in a variety of educational settings [5] . There are many more closely related examples: Green [15] develops cognitive dimensions to evaluate visual programming languages, the GOMS [20] model has proven effective at predicting user response to graphical user interfaces (GUIs), and MCRpd [34] models physical representations of digital objects.

The results of two studies of API design choices are best understood through Larkin and Simon's search lens. It is easier for programmers to use constructors to create instances than factory methods, because constructors are the default and are therefore the start of any search [11]. Methods that are located in the class a programmer starts with are easier to find than methods in related classes [30]. The impact of small design changes shown in these papers emphasizes the importance of information seeking on API usability, and suggests that a similar impact may be possible with other small interventions.

All of this research suggests that there is an opportunity to modify an API artifact to create an informationally equivalent alternative that will improve programmer performance with protocol search. Which artifact? Which changes will be most effective? To answer these questions it is useful to look at the interventions that have proven effective with other complex APIs.

One effective way to learn to use an API is to find a related example. A study of programmers using reusable Smalltalk GUI components and found that participants "relied heavily on code in example applications that provided an implicit specification for reuse of the target class." The significance of examples encouraged researchers to develop example repositories to enable programmers to find examples easily [23,37]. Unfortunately, the effectiveness of these repositories was limited by the retrieval mechanism which required too much (and too complex) input from programmers.

More recently, MAPO [38] and Strathcona [18] automatically retrieve examples from the structure of the program the programmer is writing. In a controlled experiment, participants using MAPO produced code with fewer bugs than participants in other conditions. This result is notable because it shows that API interventions can produce higher quality responses, not just more rapid responses.

The eMoose IDE plugin has proven similarly useful to developers using complex API specifications [9].The eMoose tool pushes directives—rules required to use a method correctly—to the method invocation site. The concrete rules that make up a protocol (e.g. one cannot call setDoInput on a connected URLConnection) are examples of directives. Dekel's evaluation of eMoose demonstrated significant programmer performance improvements during library-usage tasks (including one library with a protocol).

Unfortunately, examples and directives are labor intensive for API designers to produce. In large complex APIs it is often impossible to generate examples for every possible use case. Even after they are produced, it is hard to keep them in sync with the API as it changes, because there is no mechanism to enforce conformance. Examples can also serve as a crutch toward learning, and the most effective students learn to generate their own examples [6].

The design of Plaiddoc is inspired by all of the research discussed in this section. We modify Javadoc to produce an informationally equivalent documentation format aimed at facilitating speedier state search. Plaiddoc is generated from specifications whose conformance with code can be checked automatically. Plaiddoc specifications, like eMoose directives, are co-located with each method. The specifications themselves contain just the right state details so programmers can generate their own examples of correct API usage. The details of the Plaiddoc design are discussed in the next section.

3   Plaiddoc

To follow the rest of this paper, it is important to understand the design of Plaiddoc. To do so, it is necessary to first explain Javadoc. Javadoc is a tool for generating HTML documentation for Java programs. The documentation is generated from Java source code annotated with "doc comments" which contain both prose description and descriptive tags which tie the prose to specific program features. For example, a doc comment on a method will describe the method in general and then provide tags and associated comments for the parameters, the return value, and/or any exception the method throws.

The webpage generated by Javadoc for a class has six parts. The top and bottom contain navigation elements which allow the reader to quickly browse to related documentation. The class description appears below the navigation elements at the top of the page. It states the name of the class and links to superclasses and known subclasses. It then follows with an often long description which can include: the purpose of the class, how it is used, examples of use, class-level invariants, relationships to other classes, etc.

After the class description, the page includes four related elements: the field summary, method summary, field details, and method details. The field summary is a table containing the modifier, type, name, and short description of each public field sorted in alphabetical order. The method summary is extremely similar: it shows the modifier, return type, method name, type and name of all parameters, and short method description in alphabetical order. The field and method details show each field (or method) in the order they appear in the source file with the full description including historical information and any tags.

The Plaiddoc generated webpage maintains all of the look and feel of the Javadoc page. The fonts, colors, and visual layout are identical. However, the method summary section is restructured and extra information is added to the method details section. The full ResultSet page is available on the web.[1] The screenshot shows the method summary for the top-level Result state and the Open state.

As in Plaid, methods in the summary are organized by abstract state. In Javadoc, there is one table containing all of the methods of a class, while in Plaiddoc there is one table per abstract state. For example, the Disconnected state of URLConnection has a table containing all of the methods available in it, including setDoInput and connect.

One important rule we followed when designing Plaiddoc is that there is exactly one Plaiddoc page per Javadoc page. This rule ensures that the any observed differences between participants using Plaiddoc and Javadoc is a consequence of Plaiddoc's extra features and not the result of differences in page switching. There are two consequences of this rule: 1) All of the possible states of single Java class appear in the same Plaiddoc page.[2] 2) Multi-object protocols appear in multiple Plaiddoc pages. Six of the tasks in this study involve the Timer and TimerTask classes which impose a multi-object protocol. In these tasks, Javadoc participants were given two pages and Plaiddoc participants were given two pages.

An automatically generated diagram which shows all of the states of the class and where the particular state fits in, appears above each state table. The current state is bolded and italicized, while other states are displayed in the standard font. This diagram is *primitive*; it does not contain extensive capabilities like hyperlinks from state names to state tables, collapsing/expanding children, transition arrows, or even a nice graphical look. The diagram is primitive for three reasons: 1) Plaiddoc was designed for this experiment, and was therefore not polished for use outside the laboratory. 2) More capabilities gives

---

[1] http://www.cs.cmu.edu/~jssunshi/pubs/thesis-extras/
PlaiddocResultSet.html
[2] e.g. The "Open" and "Closed" states of ResultSet appear on a single page.

participants more potential paths to solve tasks and thus introduces variation into the study. 3) If one adds features it is harder to understand which particular features are important or unimportant. Plaiddoc was designed with the minimum set of features we believed would be an effective group.

The Plaiddoc page also contains two new columns in the method details table. These columns are state preconditions and postconditions. The only valid predicates are state names, state names with a parameter, or combination of the two separated by the AND or OR logical operators. For example, "Disconnected," "Scheduled task," and "Updatable AND Scrollable" are valid preconditions or postconditions but "value > 0" is not. The same information is added to the method summary. The state to which a method belongs is an implicit precondition for that method. For example, the close method lists no preconditions, but since it belongs to the Open state, the ResultSet must be in the Open state to call the close method.

To generate a Plaiddoc class page, the Plaiddoc tool requires three inputs: the class's Javadoc page, a JSON file specifying the state relationships of the class, and a JSON file containing preconditions and postconditions for each method and mapping methods to states. Sample JSON files are available on the web.[3]

The JSON files are very simple. The state file must contain a single object whose fields are states, each of which must contain either an "or-children" or "and-children" field. These "children" fields are arrays containing state names, which in turn must be defined in the same file. The methods file must contain an array of method objects which contain four fields: "name" (including parameter types to distinguish statically overloaded methods), "state" (which must map to a state defined in the state file), "pre" for preconditions, and "post" for postconditions.

It is important to map the features of Plaiddoc just described to concepts, in order to understand the implications of the experiment described here on other research (e.g. the Plaid language itself). Plaiddoc organizes methods by state instead of by class, by separating the method summary table by state. Plaiddoc makes state transitions explicit when state postconditions differ from preconditions. The Plaiddoc preconditions and postconditions make use of state-based type specifications. Finally, rich state relationships are displayed to programmers at the top of each method table. See e.g. the "State relationships" box.

4   State Search Categories

As we mentioned in Section 1, an earlier two-part qualitative study of the barriers programmers face when using APIs with protocols feeds directly into the methodology of the study in this paper [31, ch. 3]. In the first part of that study, we mined the popular developer forum StackOverflow for problems developers have using APIs with protocols. In the second part, they performed a think-aloud observational study of professional programmers in which the programers worked through exactly the problems uncovered in the first part.

---

[3] http://www.cs.cmu.edu/~jssunshi/pubs/thesis-extras/Car_States.json   and
http://www.cs.cmu.edu/~jssunshi/pubs/thesis-extras/Car_Methods.json

In this second part, they analyzed each task, by assigning task time to participant questions or comments and performing open coding on the transcript. This analysis showed that programmers in spent 71% of their total time answering instances of four question categories. We list here each general category followed by two specific instances of that category drawn from the study transcripts:

A What abstract state is an object in?
- "Is the TimerTask scheduled?"
- "Is [the ResultSet] x scannable?"

B What are the capabilities of an object in state X?
- "Can I schedule a scheduled TimerTask?"
- "What can I do on the insert row?"

C In what state(s) can I do operation Z?
- "When can I call doInput?"
- "Which ResultSets can I update?"

D How do I transition from state X to state Y?
- "How do I get off the insert row to the current row?"
- "Which method schedules the TimerTask?'

These search problems are all specific to protocols, and therefore the protocol tasks are dominated by state search. Most of the tasks performed by participants in this study are instances of these general categories.

5 Methodology

The experimental evaluation of Plaiddoc uses a standard two by two between-subjects design, with five participants in each of the four conditions. The experiment compares Plaiddoc to a Javadoc control and presents two task orderings to measure learning effects. The recruitment, training, experimental design, tasks, and post-experiment interview are presented in the following sections. All of the study materials can be found in Appendix C [31].

5.1 Recruitment

All 20 participants were recruited on the Carnegie Mellon campus. Half of the participants responded to posters displayed in the engineering and computer science buildings. The other half were solicited in-person in a hallway outside classrooms which typically contain technical classes. Participants were screened for Java or C# knowledge and experience with standard API documentation. Participants were paid $10 for 30-60 minutes of their time. The 20 participants that made it past the screening all completed the study.

Twelve of the participants were undergraduate students, all of whom were majoring in computer science, electrical and computer engineering, or information systems. The other eight were masters students in information systems or computer engineering programs. Eleven students had no professional programming experience outside summer internships, five students had one year of full-time professional experience, and four had more than one year of experience.

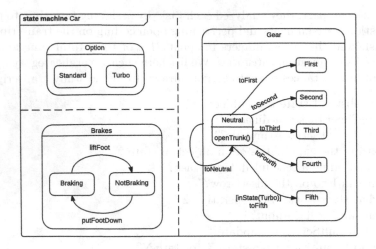

Fig. 1. Car state machine used for participant training

5.2   Training

After signing consent forms, participants were given approximately 10 minutes of training. Every participant, regardless of experimental condition, received exactly the same training. The training was read from a script to help ensure uniformity.

All participants were familiar with Javadoc, but the training included an explanation of both Javadoc and Plaiddoc to ensure baseline knowledge in both formats. The goal of this study is to compare the impact of the documentation formats on state search tasks, not the impact of training. Therefore, we kept training consistent to avoid a confounding factor. All of the state concepts are first taught via UML state machines, then Javadoc, then Plaiddoc.

The training materials introduce participants to the basic concepts of object protocols and to the documentation formats used in the study. The training makes concepts concrete using a Car API we constructed for the purpose. Regarding protocols, participants learn:

- that methods are available in some states and not others
- that some methods transition objects between states
- that states can be hierarchical
- that child states can be either or-children or and-children

These concepts were reinforced by asking participants simple, scripted questions about the Car API. The questions were designed to be answerable very quickly by participants. We created a UML state machine (shown in Figure 1), Javadoc documentation, and Plaiddoc documentation for the Car API and these were printed and handed to participants.

The top-level state for Car objects (named "Car") has three and-children, each of which has two or more or-children: *gear* to represent the car's manual transmission, *brakes* to represent whether the car is braking or not, and *option* to represent whether the car has the "turbo" option or not. We used these states to introduce state hierarchy, or-states, and and-states. We introduced transitions via brakes. One can transition to the "Braking" state from the "NotBraking" state by calling the "putFootDown" method. The `openTrunk` method, which does not change the gear state, introduces state-dependent methods. In the example, like in many real-world cars, one can only open the trunk when the car is in the neutral gear.

Like all and-children, the car's three substates are independent, in the sense that changing the gear state has no effect on the braking or option states. However, one unique wrinkle in the example is that the turbo state enables a fifth gear substate of gear that is not available otherwise. The `toFifth` method has two preconditions — the car must be in the neutral gear and it must have the turbo option. In the study tasks discussed later, some of the ResultSet methods also have multiple preconditions.

5.3 Experimental Setup

Participants were asked 21 questions about three Java APIs: 1) Six questions about `java.util.Timer` and `java.util.TimerTask`. We refer to these questions as the Timer questions throughout the rest of this paper. 2) Ten questions about `java.sql.ResultSet`. 3) Five questions about `java.net.URLConnection`. The experimenter read each question aloud and handed the participant a piece of paper with the same question written on it.

Participants were seated in front of a computer, and asked to answer the question by looking at documentation on the computer screen. The experimenter opened the documentation for the participant in a browser window. Both the Javadoc and Plaiddoc documentation were opened from the local file system to present a consistent URL and to prevent network-related problems. The computer screen and audio (speech) were recorded with Camtasia.

Half of the participants were shown standard Javadoc documentation for all questions and half Plaiddoc documentation. Participants were allowed to make use of the browser's text search (i.e. Control-F). However, they were not allowed to use internet resources (e.g. Google, StackOverflow).

We chose a between-subjects design to control for cross-task contamination. Many software engineering studies use within-subjects designs to reduce the noise from individual variability. We guessed based on pilot data that individual variability in our study would be relatively low and we therefore opted for the cleaner between-subjects design. As we will see in §6, the study was sufficiently sensitive to distinguish between conditions so our guess turned out to be accurate.

Questions were asked in batches — all of the questions related to a particular API were asked without interruption from questions about another API. Within each batch, each question was asked in the same order to every participant. However, half of the participants were asked the Timer batch first and half were asked the UrlConnection batch first. The ResultSet batch always appeared second and the remaining batch appeared third. We wanted the Timer and URLConnection batches to each appear last so we could measure the learning effects on those batches. All other ordering was uniform across conditions to avoid unnecessary confounding factors.

The study had a total of four between-subjects conditions: Plaiddoc with Timer first (condition #1), Plaiddoc with URLConnection first (condition #2), Javadoc with Timer first (condition #3), and Javadoc with URLConnection first (condition #4). Participants were assigned to conditions based on the order they appeared in the study. The nth participant was assigned to condition #n modulo 4. Using commonly accepted practice, participants were assigned to conditions pseudorandomly, in the order they arrived. Therefore, there were exactly five participants in each condition.

5.4 Tasks

The 21 questions asked of the participants are shown in Table 1. Sixteen of the questions were instances of the four categories of state search enumerated in §4. Since these questions are state specific, we refer to them as the state questions. The remaining five questions were non-state questions, which were designed to be just as easy or easier with Javadoc than Plaiddoc. These questions were not about states or protocols, and we therefore refer to them as the non-state questions.

We selected the state questions with a three-phase process. First, we generated all of the instances of the general categories we could think of for each API. Second, since we did not want the answer or the process of answering one question to affect others, we removed questions which were not independent. Some additional non-independent questions were removed during piloting. Third, we pruned the ResultSet questions to include two instances of each question category by random selection. The study was too long with the full set of ResultSet questions.

The final question set includes three instances of A) "What abstract state is an object in?", five instances of B) "What are the capabilities of an object in state X?", four instances of C)"In what state(s) can I do operation Z?'," and four instances of D) "How do I transition from state X to state Y?" Participants in all conditions were given a glossary listing all of the states of the API in question with a short description of each. Participants were instructed to answer questions in categories A and C with the name of a state from the glossary. In other words, these questions were multiple choice.

The names of states in the glossary matched those in Plaiddoc. The names themselves were taken from the Javadoc as much as possible. We did not want to disadvantage Javadoc unnecessarily, so we tried to make it as easy as possible for participants to perform the mapping from the prose description in the Javadoc to the state names in the glossary. In two cases there was no obvious name to give the state from the Javadoc. First, we called a URLConnection that has not yet connected "Disconnected," which is a word that appears neither in the Javadoc nor the Java source code. Second, we called a TimerTask that is

Table 1. Category, identifier and question text for all of the questions asked of participants in the main part of the study. Questions with identifiers beginning with T involved `java.util.Timer` and `java.util.TimerTask`, R involved `java.sql.ResultSet`, and U involved `java.net.URLConnection`.

Cat.	ID	Question text
T	T-1	How do I transition a Timer Task from the Virgin state to the Scheduled state?
N	T-2	What is the effect of calling the purge method on the behavior of the Timer?
C	T-3	What methods can I call on a Scheduled TimerTask?
N	T-4	What is the difference between schedule(TimerTask task, long delay, long period) and scheduleAtFixedRate(TimerTask task, long delay, long period)?
O	T-5	What state does a TimerTask need to be in to call scheduledExecution-Time?
C	T-6	Can I schedule a TimerTask that has already been scheduled?
N	R-1	How is a ResultSet instance created?
C	R-2	Can I call the getArray method when the cursor is on the insert row?
O	R-3	What state does the ResultSet need to be in to call the wasNull method?
T	R-4	How do I transition a ResultSet object from the ForwardOnly to the Scrollable State?
O	R-5	Which states does the ResultSet need to be in to call the updateInt method?
A	R-6	What state is the ResultSet object if a call to the next method returns false?
T	R-7	How do I transition a ResultSet object from the CurrentRow to the InsertRow state?
N	R-8	Why does getMetadata take no arguments and getArray take a int columnIndex or String columnLabel as an argument?
C	R-9	Can I call the isLast method on a forward only ResultSet?
A	R-10	What states could the ResultSet object in when a call to the next method throws a java.sql.SQLException because it is in the ResultSet is in the wrong state?
A	U-1	What state is the URLConnection in after successfully calling the getContent method?
C	U-2	If the URLConnection is in the connected state can I call the setDoInput method?
N	U-3	How do I create a URLConnection instance?
O	U-4	What state does the URLConnection need to be in to call the getInputStream method?
T	U-5	What method transitions the URLConnection from the Connected to the Disconnected state?

Category definitions

A Instance of the "What abstract state is an object in?" question category.

C Instance of the "What are the capabilities of an object in state X?" question category.

N Instance of the non-state question category.

T Instance of the "How do I transition from state X to state Y?" question category.

O Instance of the "In what state(s) can I do operation Z?" question category.

unscheduled, "Virgin" even though this word never appears in the Javadoc. In this case we borrowed the word from the implementation code—the state of a TimerTask is encoded with an integer, and the integer constant used for an unscheduled TimerTask is called VIRGIN. Finally, we wrote all of the descriptions to succinctly explain the meaning of the state name.

All of the non-state questions require understanding a non-state detail of the API or comparing two details. Since the Plaiddoc API documentation is larger than the Javadoc documentation one might expect that it would be slightly easier to answer these questions with Javadoc. Two of the non-state question are instances of "how do I create an instance of class X?", two ask participants to compare two methods (in one case the methods were in different states), and one asks participants to understand non-state details of the behavior of an individual method.

Participants were instructed to "find the answer to each question in the documentation and tell the experimenter the answer as soon as you have found it." Whenever a participant answered a question for the first time, the experimenter asked, "is that your final answer?" Participants were limited to ten minutes per task. The experiment proceeded to the next task whenever a participant answered a question and confirmed it or the time limit was reached. Participants were not told whether their answer was correct and the experiment proceeded regardless of answer correctness.

5.5   Post-experiment Interview

After completing the experiment participants were asked four questions to see how well they could map the state concepts we trained them about before the study (e.g. and-states, or-states, state hierarchy, impact of transitions on and-states) to the particular APIs they saw in the study. For example, we asked "What is an example of two ResultSet and-states?" Participants were also asked to rate their affinity to the documentation they used, and if they used Plaiddoc to compare Plaiddoc to Javadoc on a five point Likert scale. Then they were asked "Which documentation format that you learned about before the study—Javadoc, Plaiddoc, or UML state diagram—do you think would have been most helpful to complete this study?" Finally, some individuals were also asked additional questions about their task performance at the experimenter's discretion.

6   Results

In this section, we discuss the study results and try to give the best evidence to answer the research questions presented in the introduction. We first compare the task completion performance of Plaiddoc and Javadoc participants. Then we compare the correctness of these responses provided by those same groups. We follow with an evaluation of the learning effects of performing study tasks. Finally we discuss the post-study interview and pilot results. Raw timing and correctness data is available on the web.[4]

---

[4] http://www.cs.cmu.edu/~jssunshi/pubs/thesis-extras/
RawPlaiddocStudyData.pdf

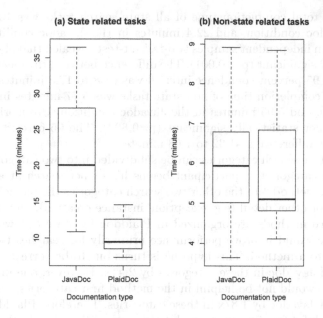

Fig. 2. Box plot comparing the completion time of Javadoc and Plaiddoc participants

6.1   Task Completion Time

In this subsection we discuss the results related to the task completion time output variable. This output variable addresses RQ1 and RQ2 (Can programmers answer state search questions more efficiently using Plaiddoc than Javadoc? and Are programmers as effective answering non-state questions using Plaiddoc as they are with Javadoc?) by comparing task completion times across conditions.

To determine completion time we analyzed the video and marked when we finished reading the task question and when the participant confirmed his or her "final answer." The difference between these two marks was noted in the task completion time.

The ten-minute task time limit was reached by many participants on question R-4, but never on any other question. In fact, only two participants exceeded five minutes while answering any other question, and they did so for only one question each. Timeouts are not directly comparable to other timing data, and therefore we evaluate question R-4 separately, and in detail, in §6.2. This subsection does not include data from question R-4.

The total completion time for each of the Plaiddoc and Javadoc participants on state questions is visualized by the box plot in Figure 2(a), and for non-state question in Figure 2(b). A two-factor fixed-effects ANOVA revealed no significant interaction between documentation type and task ordering (p=0.25) on total task completion time. Therefore, we compare all 10 Plaiddoc participants against their 10 Javadoc counterparts.

The mean total completion time of all state search tasks was 10.3 minutes in the Plaiddoc condition, and 22.4 minutes in the Javadoc condition (2.17x difference). An independent samples two-tailed t-test revealed that the difference is statistically significant ($p < 0.001$). The difference between the means was 12.1 minutes, and 95-percent confidence interval was 6.38 to 17.8 minutes.

The mean completion time of non-state tasks was 5.77 minutes in the Plaiddoc condition, and 5.95 minutes in the Javadoc condition. Unsurprisingly, this difference is not statistically significant (p=0.802). The 95-percent confidence interval of the difference is -1.32 to 1.68 minutes.

The four state search categories can be subdivided into two categories. In two of the search categories, a participant begins his or her search at a state and tries to find a method.[5] In the other two search categories the participant starts at a method or other detail (e.g. exception, instance creation), and tries to find a state.[6] Since methods are organized in Plaiddoc by state one would expect that Plaiddoc would improve performance primarily for searches that proceed from a state to a method. This hypothesis turns out to be correct — Plaiddoc outperformed Javadoc in these categories by 2.41x. However, one might expect that Plaiddoc would not be helpful in the method first categories, but Plaiddoc outperformed Javadoc by 1.87x in these categories. Therefore, Plaiddoc appears to be more helpful for state-first search than method-first search. We performed two factor, fixed-effects ANOVA in which the two factors are documentation type and search type and the output variable is time. The interaction term between documentation type and search type is only marginally significant (p=0.089).

Demographics. We did not balance participants in conditions by any demographic factor. By random chance, six of nine students with experience and three of four with more than one year of experience were assigned to the Javadoc conditions. However, experience had no significant impact on the timing results. A two-factor ANOVA where the two factors were experience and documentation type showed no significant effects from experience ($F=.058$, $df=1$, $p=.813$) or the experience by documentation type interaction term ($F=1.34$, $df=1$, $p=.719$).

Feature Comparison Discussion. Every participant used text-search (i.e. CTRL-F in the browser window) to find method names. They then used the location in a state box, pre-conditions, post-conditions, and state relationship diagrams to answer the question efficiently. Plaiddoc is like Javadoc except it organizes methods by state instead of by class and it includes explicit state transitions, state-based type specifications, and rich state relationships. The difference in relative performance between the state categories allows us to (very roughly) compare the benefits of state organization to the other three features. Since the method based search does not benefit from the state-based organization, all of the performance differences observed in the method based search tasks

---

[5] What are the capabilities of an object in state X? How do I transition from state X to state Y?

[6] What abstract state is an object in? In what state(s) can I do operation Z?

Table 2. Correctness results for each participant on the 16 state search questions

	Paricipant #																				Total	
	1	2	3	4	5	6	7	8	9	10	11	12	13	14	15	16	17	18	19	20	Pdoc	Jdoc
DocType	P	P	J	J	P	P	J	J	P	P	J	J	P	P	J	J	P	P	J	J	P	J
Correct	15	15	14	16	15	16	15	14	15	15	14	14	15	15	16	16	15	15	11	13	151	143
Incorrect	1	0	2	0	0	0	1	1	0	0	2	2	1	0	0	0	0	0	5	2	2	15
Timed-out	0	1	0	0	1	0	0	1	1	1	0	0	0	1	0	0	1	1	0	1	7	2

are likely to derive from explicit state transitions, state-based type specifications, and rich state relationships. The extra performance of the state based search is likely to derive from the state-based organization. We do not think it's possible to separate the benefits of the embedded state diagram from the preconditions and postconditions. In one early pilot we did not include the state diagram and the participant struggled to answer questions that required knowledge of state relationships. Similarly, a state diagram without detailed information about the requirements and impact of method calls would likely not be effective.

6.2   Correctness

Almost half of the participants provided at least one wrong "final" answer to a state-search question. Among the 320 total answers provided to the 16 state search questions 294 were correct, 17 incorrect, and nine were not provided because the question timed out. In this subsection, we compare the correctness of Plaiddoc answers to Javadoc answers (RQ3). The number of right, wrong, and timed-out answers for each participant are shown in Table 2.

Only two of the 17 wrong answers were provided by Plaiddoc participants. Plaiddoc participants answered 98.75% of the questions correctly, and Javadoc participants answered 90.5% correctly. The odds ratio in the sample is 7.92.[7] We analyzed the contingency table of Javadoc vs. Plaiddoc and Correct vs. Incorrect using a two-tailed Fisher's exact test. The contingency table is shown in Table 2 in the rows labeled "Correct" and "Incorrect" and the columns labeled "Pdoc" and "Jdoc". The test revealed that the difference is very significant (p=0.002). The 95-percent confidence interval of the odds ratio is 1.78 to 72.1.

Incorrect Responses. All of the wrong answers and time-outs were provided to just five of the 16 state questions. No wrong answers were provided to any of the non-state questions. It is worth discussing the content of the wrong answers to provide insight into the types of problems programmers face when answering state-related questions.

In response to question T-3, a Plaiddoc participant (#19) incorrectly suggested that none of the TimerTask methods could be called on a scheduled

---

[7] The odds ratio is a standard metric for quantifying association between two properties. In our example, it is the ratio of the odds of being correct when using Plaiddoc to the odds of being correct when using Javadoc.

TimerTask because "the methods are called by the Timer." This participant correctly noted the main mode of usage, but incorrectly assumed this was the exclusive mode of usage.

In response to question T-5, three[8] Javadoc participants incorrectly suggested that TimerTask scheduledExecutionTime can be called in any state when in fact it can only be called in the executed state. Three of these wrong participants noted correctly that scheduledExecutionTime does not throw an exception. Unfortunately, not every protocol violation results in an exception, a fact that was noted in pre-test training.[9] In this case, the protocol is documented in the description of the return value, which is described as "undefined if the task has yet to commence its first execution." In the post-experiment interview all three incorrect participants said that they did not notice this return value description.

In response to T-6, two Javadoc participants incorrectly replied that one can schedule an already-scheduled TimerTask. Participant #19 answered very quickly (15 seconds) without thoroughly examining the documentation. Participant #8 read aloud from the documentation, noting that the method throws an IllegalStateException "if task was already scheduled or cancelled, timer was cancelled, or timer thread terminated." However, #8 somehow skipped "scheduled or" while reading.

Three Javadoc participants and one Plaiddoc participant incorrectly answered U-5. The question asks, "What method transitions the URLConnection from the Connected to the Disconnected state?" There is no such method, as 16 participants correctly noted. The three incorrect Javadoc participants suggested one could transition the URLConnection to the Disconnected state by calling its setConnectionTimeout method with 0 as the timeout value argument. This method "sets a timeout value, to be used when opening a communications link to the resource referenced by this URLConnection. If the timeout expires before the connection can be established, a java.net.SocketTimeOutException is raised." Therefore, setConnectionTimeout has no impact at all on a URLConnection instance that has already connected. Participant #1, a Plaiddoc participant, incorrectly answered that the non-existent "disconnect" method could be used to transition the URLConnection. This was the last question that participant #1 answered, so perhaps #1 was ready to leave and so didn't investigate this question thoroughly.

Finally, R-4 produced the most varied responses. The question asks the participant to transition a ResultSet object from the ForwardOnly to the Scrollable state. However, no transition is possible since ForwardOnly and Scrollable are *type qualifiers* and therefore are permanent after instance creation. Seven Plaiddoc and two Javadoc participants never answered this question because they timed out. One Plaiddoc and five Javadoc participants answered the question

---

[8] Participant #19 also answered T-5 incorrectly because, as in question T-3, #19 thought all TimerTask "methods are called by the Timer" including scheduledAtFixedRate.

[9] The openTrunk method's protocol is documented by its description of the return value Javadoc training materials.

incorrectly. Many of the timed-out Plaiddoc participants considered but then ultimately rejected the incorrect answers provided by the Javadoc respondents. This suggests that the specifications provided by Plaiddoc participants can provide confidence that an answer is *incorrect*. The Plaiddoc participants likely traded no-answers for incorrect answers.

Four Javadoc participants incorrectly answered that the setFetchDirection method will transition a ResultSet object from the ForwardOnly to the Scrollable state. Unfortunately, this method does no such thing, instead it "gives a hint as to the direction in which the rows in this ResultSet object will be processed." These four participants did skim the description, but it seems that they relied primarily on the method name to make their determination.

One Javadoc and one Plaiddoc participant noticed the following sentences in the class description: "A default ResultSet object is not updatable and has a cursor that moves forward only ... It is possible to produce ResultSet objects that are scrollable." which is immediately followed by a code example in which the createStatement method is called on TYPE_SCROLL_INSENSITIVE as an argument on a *connection* instance. Upon reading this, both participants immediately answered that the createStatement method should be called on a *ResultSet* instance. The Plaiddoc participant even suggested that the createStatement was missing from the method details list because "Plaiddoc is just a prototype."

Questions U-5 and R-4 both ask participants to find a method that does not exist. These questions, like all state-search questions in the study, are derived from the questions participants asked in the observational study discussed in Sunshine [31, ch.3]. However, participants in empirical studies are well-known to be compliant to experimenter demands. Therefore, some may therefore consider them to be "trick" questions. If these questions are excluded, then Plaiddoc participants answered 140 state-search questions correctly (100%) and 0 incorrectly while Javadoc participants answered 133 correctly (95%) and 7 incorrectly. A two-tailed Fisher's exact test of this contingency table is statistically significant (p=0.014). Since Plaiddoc participants in this sample answered every question correctly, the odds ratio is infinite. The 95-percent confidence interval of the odds ratio is 1.48 (the corresponding value is 1.78 when including every state-search question) to infinity (7.92 when including state-search question). Therefore, Plaiddoc participants were significantly more likely to respond correctly than Javadoc participants even when excluding "trick" questions.

Discussion. Three themes emerge from the incorrect and timed-out answers provided by participants. First, all of the time-outs occurred in question R-4 when participants were asked to find a non-existent method to transition between two states. Therefore, to answer this question correctly, participants needed to prove the absence of something to themselves.[10] Some participants felt the need to perform a brute force search of the method documentation to ensure that

---

[10] In [31, ch.3] many forum questioners had similar problems with missing state transitions.

no methods were available that perfumed the transition. Of particular note, Plaiddoc participants didn't seem to trust that the ForwardOnly section of the Plaiddoc contained all of the potential methods.

It is also worth noting that question U-5 is in the same category but resulted in no time-outs. One possible explanation is that the ResultSet interface is much larger than the the URLConnection class,so it is easier to be confident that no such method exists. In addition, participants seemed to intuit that the URL-Connection transition is missing, but not intuit that the ResultSet transition is missing.

Second, the questions required the participants to digest a lot of text. Participants commonly relied on heuristics and skimming to answer questions quickly. For example, the five Javadoc participants who answered R-4 with setFetchDirection matched the method name to the task and quickly confirmed the match in the description, but did not fully digest the description text. The participant who missed the word "scheduled" in the exception details was being similarly hasty. This phenomenon may partially explain why Plaiddoc participants were so much quicker than Javadoc participants, as we saw in §6.1. Plaiddoc presents a natural heuristic to participants — when examining a method, look first at the state it is defined in, then at its preconditions and postconditions.

Third, participants were tripped up by non-normal modes of use. We saw that participant #19 thought only the Timer could call TimerTask methods because that is the normal mode of use. Similarly, most protocol violations throw exceptions and are documented in the method or exception descriptions. However, scheduledExecutionTime somewhat abnormally documents the protocols in the return value description which confused three participants. Finally, abstract states normally map well to the primitive state of object instances. However, a URLConnection that has been disconnected from the remote resource is not in the Disconnected abstract state, as expected by three participants.

6.3   Learning

To answer RQ4, which asks whether state search performance improves with practice, we alternated the order that question batches were asked of participants. As we describe in §5.3, half of the participants first received URLConnection questions and half first received Timer questions. The output variable we discuss in this section is the ratio of total Timer batch completion time to total URLConnection batch completion time (the "T/U ratio"). If learning occurs, then the T/U ratio should be larger for participants who performed the Timer batch first than for those who performed the URLConnection batch first.

In the Javadoc condition, the mean T/U ratio of the Timer first sub-condition is 1.07 and .948 in the UrlConnection first sub-condition. This difference is not statistically significant ($p=0.695$). On the other hand, in the Plaiddoc condition the mean T/U ratio of the Timer first sub-condition is 1.50 and 0.743 in the Url-Connection first sub-condition. An independent samples two-tailed t-test shows that this difference is statistically significant ($p=0.003$).

Table 3. Analysis of observed variance of T/U Ratio. The fixed-effects sources of variation considered are documentation type and batch order.

	Df	Sum Sq	Mean Sq	F value	Pr(>F)
DocType	1	0.06695	0.06695	0.4560	0.50914
BatchOrder	1	0.96519	0.96519	6.5737	0.02081
DocType:BatchOrder	1	0.51496	0.51496	3.5073	0.07949

We performed a two factor, fixed-effects ANOVA in which the two factors are documentation type and batch order and the output variable is the T/U ratio. The results are show in Table 3. This ANOVA reveals that there is a marginally significant interaction between documentation type and batch ordering ($p=0.079$). This should be interpreted as weak evidence that task-completion speed improved more for Plaiddoc participants than for Javadoc participants. However, more data is needed to know for sure.

Discussion. The Plaiddoc participants performance improved significantly during the study, which is perhaps unsurprising since Plaiddoc was new to all of the participants. We would like to say with confidence that state-search performance of programmers using Plaiddoc would improve over time relative to programmers using Javadoc. However, the learning observed in the Plaiddoc condition was not significantly stronger than the learning observed in the Javadoc condition.

6.4   State Concept Mapping

To investigate RQ5, we asked four questions to map the concepts they learned about in training to the Timer, TimerTask, ResultSet, and URLConnection. Plaiddoc participants responded correctly 23 of 40 times, while Javadoc participants answered correctly 25 times. This difference is not statistically significant.

Discussion. We hypothesized that Plaiddoc participant would be better at mapping API specifics to general state concepts. We thought this because Plaiddoc makes many state concepts more salient. There is no evidence for this hypothesis in the data. Javadoc participants spent much more total time with the documentation and they read much more of the detailed prose contained inside the documentation. Perhaps this extra time and detail compensated for the state salience of Plaiddoc.

We told all of the participants that timed out while trying to find a method to transition the ResultSet from ForwardOnly to the Scrollable state, that the method did not exist. We asked if they had any ideas about how to better represent missing state transitions. Most didn't give any suggestion, but one suggested that methods that perform state transitions should be separated from other methods so they're easier to find. This suggestion is worthy of further investigation.

6.5   Participant Preference

In the post-experiment interview we also gauged participant preferences. Nine of ten Plaiddoc participants said that a different documentation format would have been more helpful in performing the study. Seven selected UML state diagrams and two selected Javadoc. The Javadoc participants also primarily selected UML State diagrams (five of ten), followed by Javadoc (3), and Plaiddoc (2).

Discussion. The results in this study show that Plaiddoc participants outperformed Javadoc participants. Therefore participant preferences does not match the measured outcome. Why do so many Plaiddoc participants prefer another documentation format? The simplest explanation is that Plaiddoc is unfamiliar, while Javadoc is familiar. In addition, one participant in the Plaiddoc condition who preferred Javadoc explained that he "felt lost" while using Plaiddoc. A Plaiddoc page is divided into many more subsections (one for each state) than a Javadoc page. Improved visual cues indicating the which state is being viewed might alleviate this problem. Another possible reason, is that the Plaiddoc state diagram is produced in ASCII and therefore looks old and amateurish. The state diagram does not match well with the modern look of the rest of the page. Regardless of the reason for the preference, this study's results are a cautionary tale for researchers who rely only on user preferences to evaluate tools.

7   Threats to Validity

In this section we discuss threats to validity of our causal claims. We divide this section using the canonical categories of validity: construct validity, internal validity, and external validity.

7.1   Construct Validity

We trained all participants equally, including training of Javadoc participants to use Plaiddoc. There is some risk in this design that Javadoc participants will be disappointed that they did not get to use Plaiddoc. They were familiar with Javadoc so they may have preferred to try something new. Therefore, Javadoc participants may have performed worse because they experienced what Shadish [27, p. 80] calls "resentful demoralization." Two facts suggest that demoralization had at most a small effect on the results: First, only two of 10 Javadoc participants said they would have preferred to use Plaiddoc in the post-experiment interview. Second, both Javadoc and Plaiddoc are documentation formats and neither is particularly exciting. The classic examples in which "resentful demoralization" was measurable include much more severe differences between the control group and the experimental group. Fetterman [12] describes an experiment evaluating a job-training program in which the control group includes participants who were denied access to the training program. Walther [35] compared an experimental group that is paid a substantially higher participation reward to a control group paid much less. We would not expect to see anywhere near as much demoralization in our study as in these studies, even for participants who would have preferred to use Plaiddoc.

Although participants were never told explicitly, it is likely participants realized that Plaiddoc was our design. Therefore, Plaiddoc participants may have performed better and Javadoc participants worse because of "experimenter expectancies" [25, p. 224]. In other words, the very fact that we expected Plaiddoc to outperform Javadoc *and* the participants could possibly infer this expectation, may have impacted in the result in the direction we expected.

7.2   Internal Validity

The focus of this study's design is internal validity. Participants were randomly assigned, participants were isolated from outside events in equivalent settings, we used a between-subjects design, and there was no attrition during the study. All that being said, one threat to internal validity is worth mentioning. Participants were assigned to conditions randomly, but it could be that the participants in the Plaiddoc group were better equipped to answer the questions in the study. We discussed the distribution of programming experience in §6.1 and showed that it did not seem to have an effect on outcomes. However, it could be the groups differ along another dimension—for example, programming skill, experience with protocols, intelligence—that we did not measure and this impacted the results.

7.3   External Validity

Our earlier qualitative studies and the experiment discussed here have opposing strengths and weaknesses. The qualitative studies emphasize external validity with realistic tasks and professional participants, but cannot be used to draw conclusions about causal relationships. The experiment in this paper focuses on internal validity with a carefully controlled experimental design that allows strong causal conclusions. However, the external validity of the experiment is enhanced because participants performed tasks in which they were required to tackle protocol programming barriers observed in the qualitative studies. Therefore, the experimental results are likely to translate to real-world problems and the processes that programmers use to solve them. All that being said, the threats to external validity in those earlier studies extend into this study [31, §3.4].

The state search tasks are connected to our qualitative results—they use the same APIs that were problematic for Stack Overflow questioners and they are instances of the state search categories that were observed repeatedly in the observational study. However, the non-state search tasks did not come from developer forums or any other real-world programming resource. Instead they were designed to simply *not* make use of Plaiddoc's novel state features. In our results, Plaiddoc participants did not perform worse on these tasks than Javadoc participants. However, it could be that there are other important categories of tasks for which Javadoc is better than Plaiddoc.

Another noteworthy external validity concern in the experiment here has to do with the student population studied. None of the participants seem to have struggled with the concept of preconditions and postconditions which are used heavily by Plaiddoc. This may be because the concept as used in the study is simple, but it may also be that the Carnegie Mellon student population we studied is especially exposed to formal methods. The very first course in the Carnegie Mellon undergraduate computer science sequence teaches students to verify imperative programs with Hoare-style contracts.

8   Type Annotations as Documentation

Many research groups have developed specialized type-based annotation systems for particular domains. Prominent examples include information flow [26], thread usage policies [33], and application partitioning [7]. In the vast majority of these systems, including all of the examples just cited, the primary benefit of the annotation systems touted by their creators is either verification or automated code generation. The preconditions and postconditions that appear next to methods in Plaiddoc are essentially state-based type annotations. Therefore, this study provides indirect evidence that type based annotations can have benefits as documentation.

In the last few years, there have been a flurry of studies comparing the benefits of static and dynamic types [16,29,17]. This research suggests that dynamic types have an advantage for small, greenfield tasks, while static types have an advantage for larger, maintenance tasks.

The most closely related study [22], evaluated the benefits of type annotations in undocumented software. The results were mixed—types were significantly helpful in some tasks, and significantly harmful in others. One possible interpretation of the results is that types were helpful in tasks that were more complex (involved more classes) and harmful otherwise. Our results provide a clearer picture — Plaiddoc provided benefits in every state-search category. In their study, programmers performed programming tasks using two "structurally identical," synthetic, undocumented APIs. In our study, programmers answered search questions with well-documented real-world APIs. One important consequence of these differences, is that our study evaluates types *only* for their documentation purpose, while theirs evaluates the collective value of both static-checking and types as documentation.

9   Conclusion

In this study we demonstrate the effectiveness of Plaiddoc documentation relative to Javadoc documentation in answering state-related questions. The barrier to entry for using the Plaiddoc tool are minimal—only 1-3 annotations are required per method. We annotated all three APIs in less than one day of work. The main barrier to using Plaiddoc in production is training programmers to consume the documentation effectively. Untrained participants in pilot studies were not able to use Plaiddoc effectively. Even basic protocol concepts were foreign to our participants before training. That said, the training we provided was very quick and required no specialized knowledge. Regardless, it seems clear that any mainstream language that adopts first-class state constructs should also adopt a Plaiddoc like documentation structure. More generally, our study shows that state-based type annotations provide documentation-related benefits even for well-documented code. Thus, our results open the door to future work investigating the documentation-related productivity benefits of type-like annotations in a broad range of domains.

Acknowledgements. This work was supported by supported by the U.S. National Science Foundation under grants #CCF-1116907 and #IIS-1111750. National Security Agency lablet contract #H98230-14-C-0140, and the Air Force Research Laboratory.

References

1. Beckman, N.E., Kim, D., Aldrich, J.: An empirical study of object protocols in the wild. In: Mezini, M. (ed.) ECOOP 2011. LNCS, vol. 6813, pp. 2–26. Springer, Heidelberg (2011)
2. Beckman, N.E., Nori, A.V.: Probabilistic, modular and scalable inference of typestate specifications. In: Proceedings of the 32nd ACM SIGPLAN Conference on Programming Language Design and Implementation, PLDI 2011, pp. 211–221. ACM, New York (2011)
3. Bierhoff, K., Beckman, N.E., Aldrich, J.: Practical API protocol checking with access permissions. In: Drossopoulou, S. (ed.) ECOOP 2009. LNCS, vol. 5653, pp. 195–219. Springer, Heidelberg (2009)
4. Bortolozzo, M., Centenaro, M., Focardi, R., Steel, G.: Attacking and fixing PKCS#11 security tokens. In: Proceedings of the 17th ACM Conference on Computer and Communications Security, CCS 2010, pp. 260–269. ACM, New York (2010)
5. Chandler, P., Sweller, J.: Cognitive load theory and the format of instruction. Cognition and Instruction 8(4), 293–332 (1991)
6. Chi, M.T., Bassok, M., Lewis, M.W., Reimann, P., Glaser, R.: Self-explanations: How students study and use examples in learning to solve problems. Cognitive Science 13(2), 145–182 (1989)
7. Chong, S., Liu, J., Myers, A.C., Qi, X., Vikram, K., Zheng, L., Zheng, X.: Secure web applications via automatic partitioning. In: Proceedings of Twenty-first ACM SIGOPS Symposium on Operating Systems Principles, SOSP 2007, pp. 31–44. ACM, New York (2007)
8. de Caso, G., Braberman, V., Garbervetsky, D., Uchitel, S.: Program abstractions for behaviour validation. In: Proceedings of the 33rd International Conference on Software Engineering, ICSE 2011, pp. 381–390. ACM, New York (2011)
9. Dekel, U., Herbsleb, J.D.: Improving API documentation usability with knowledge pushing. In: Proceedings of the 31st International Conference on Software Engineering, ICSE 2009, pp. 320–330 (2009)
10. Dwyer, M.B., Kinneer, A., Elbaum, S.: Adaptive online program analysis. In: Proceedings of the 29th international conference on Software Engineering, ICSE 2007, pp. 220–229. IEEE Computer Society, Washington, DC (2007)

11. Ellis, B., Stylos, J., Myers, B.: The factory pattern in API design: A usability evaluation. In: Proceedings of the 29th international conference on Software Engineering, ICSE 2007, pp. 302–312 (2007)

12. Fetterman, D.M.: Ibsen's baths: Reactivity and insensitivity (a misapplication of the treatment-control design in a national evaluation). Educational Evaluation and Policy Analysis 4(3), 261–279 (1982)

13. Foster, J.S., Terauchi, T., Aiken, A.: Flow-sensitive type qualifiers. In: Proceedings of the ACM SIGPLAN 2002 Conference on Programming language design and implementation, PLDI 2002, pp. 1–12. ACM, New York (2002)

14. Georgiev, M., Iyengar, S., Jana, S., Anubhai, R., Boneh, D., Shmatikov, V.: The most dangerous code in the world: Validating SSL certificates in non-browser software. In: Proceedings of the 2012 ACM Conference on Computer and Communications Security, CCS 2012, pp. 38–49. ACM, New York (2012)

15. Green, T.R.G., Petre, M.: Usability analysis of visual programming environments: a 'cognitive dimensions' framework. Journal of Visual Languages & Computing 7(2), 131–174 (1996)

16. Hanenberg, S.: An experiment about static and dynamic type systems: Doubts about the positive impact of static type systems on development time. In: Proceedings of the ACM International Conference on Object Oriented Programming Systems Languages and Applications, OOPSLA 2010, pp. 22–35. ACM, New York (2010)

17. Hanenberg, S., Kleinschmager, S., Robbes, R., Tanter, É., Stefik, A.: An empirical study on the impact of static typing on software maintainability. Empirical Software Engineering, 1–48 (2013)

18. Holmes, R., Walker, R.J., Murphy, G.C.: Strathcona example recommendation tool. In: Proceedings of the 10th European Software Engineering Conference Held Jointly with 13th ACM SIGSOFT International Symposium on Foundations of Software Engineering, ESEC/FSE-13, pp. 237–240. ACM, New York (2005)

19. Jaspan, C.N.: Proper Plugin Protocols. PhD thesis, Carnegie Mellon University. Technical Report: CMU-ISR-11-116 (December 2011)

20. John, B.E., Kieras, D.E.: The GOMS family of user interface analysis techniques: Comparison and contrast. ACM Trans. Comput.-Hum. Interact. 3(4), 320–351 (1996)

21. Larkin, J.H., Simon, H.A.: Why a diagram is (sometimes) worth ten thousand words. Cognitive Science 11(1), 65–100 (1987)

22. Mayer, C., Hanenberg, S., Robbes, R., Tanter, É., Stefik, A.: An empirical study of the influence of static type systems on the usability of undocumented software. In: Proceedings of the ACM International Conference on Object Oriented Programming Systems Languages and Applications, pp. 683–702. ACM (2012)

23. Neal, L.R.: A system for example-based programming. In: Proceedings of the SIGCHI Conference on Human Factors in Computing Systems, CHI 1989, pp. 63–68. ACM, New York (1989)

24. Robillard, M.P., Bodden, E., Kawrykow, D., Mezini, M., Ratchford, T.: Automated api property inference techniques. IEEE Transactions on Software Engineering 39(5), 613–637 (2013)

25. Rosenthal, R., Rosnow, R.L.: Essential of Behavioiural Research: Methods and Data Analysis, 3rd edn. McGraw-Hill Higher Education, New York (2008)

26. Sabelfeld, A., Myers, A.: Language-based information-flow security. IEEE Journal on Selected Areas in Communications 21(1), 5–19 (2003)

27. Shadish, W.R., Cook, T.D., Campbell, D.T.: Experimental and Quasi-Experimental Designs for Generalized Causal Inference. Wadsworth Cengage Learning (2002)
28. Somorovsky, J., Mayer, A., Schwenk, J., Kampmann, M., Jensen, M.: On breaking SAML: Be whoever you want to be. In: Proceedings of the 21st USENIX Conference on Security Symposium, Security, vol. 12, p. 21 (2012)
29. Stuchlik, A., Hanenberg, S.: Static vs. dynamic type systems: An empirical study about the relationship between type casts and development time. In: Proceedings of the 7th Symposium on Dynamic Languages, DLS 2011, pp. 97–106. ACM, New York (2011)
30. Stylos, J., Myers, B.A.: The implications of method placement on API learnability. In: Proceedings of the 16th ACM SIGSOFT International Symposium on Foundations of Software Engineering, SIGSOFT 2008/FSE-16, pp. 105–112. ACM, New York (2008)
31. Sunshine, J.: Protocol Programmability. PhD thesis, Carnegie Mellon University (December 2013)
32. Sunshine, J., Naden, K., Stork, S., Aldrich, J., Tanter, E.: First-class state change in plaid. In: Proceedings of the 2011 ACM International Conference on Object Oriented Programming Systems Languages and Applications, OOPSLA 2011, pp. 713–732. ACM, New York (2011)
33. Sutherland, D.F., Scherlis, W.L.: Composable thread coloring. In: Proceedings of the 15th ACM SIGPLAN Symposium on Principles and Practice of Parallel Programming, PPoPP 2010, pp. 233–244. ACM, New York (2010)
34. Ullmer, B., Ishii, H.: Emerging frameworks for tangible user interfaces. IBM Systems Journal 39(3.4), 915–931 (2000)
35. Walther, B.J., Ross, A.S.: The effect on behavior of being in a control group. Basic and Applied Social Psychology 3(4), 259–266 (1982)
36. Whaley, J., Martin, M.C., Lam, M.S.: Automatic extraction of object-oriented component interfaces. In: Proceedings of the 2002 ACM SIGSOFT International Symposium on Software Testing and Analysis, ISSTA 2002, pp. 218–228. ACM, New York (2002)
37. Ye, Y., Fischer, G., Reeves, B.: Integrating active information delivery and reuse repository systems. In: Proceedings of the 8th ACM SIGSOFT International Symposium on Foundations of Software Engineering: Twenty-first Century Applications, SIGSOFT 2000/FSE-8, pp. 60–68. ACM, New York (2000)
38. Zhong, H., Xie, T., Zhang, L., Pei, J., Mei, H.: MAPO: Mining and recommending API usage patterns. In: Drossopoulou, S. (ed.) ECOOP 2009. LNCS, vol. 5653, pp. 318–343. Springer, Heidelberg (2009)

Reusable Concurrent Data Types

Vincent Gramoli[1] and Rachid Guerraoui[2]

[1] NICTA and University of Sydney
vincent.gramoli@sydney.edu.au
[2] EPFL
rachid.guerraoui@epfl.ch

Abstract. This paper contributes to address the fundamental challenge of building Concurrent Data Types (CDT) that are reusable and scalable at the same time. We do so by proposing the abstraction of Polymorphic Transactions (PT): a new programming abstraction that offers different compatible transactions that can run concurrently in the same application.

We outline the commonality of the problem in various object-oriented languages and implement PT and a reusable package in Java. With PT, annotating sequential ADTs guarantee novice programmers to obtain an atomic and deadlock-free CDT and let an advanced programmer leverage the application semantics to get higher performance.

We compare our polymorphic synchronization against transaction-based, lock-based and lock-free synchronizations on SPARC and x86-64 architectures and we integrate our methodology to a travel reservation benchmark. Although our reusable CDTs are sometimes less efficient than non-composable handcrafted CDTs from the JDK, they outperform all reusable Java CDTs.

1 Introduction

Abstract data types (ADTs) have shown to be instrumental in making sequential programs reusable [1]. ADTs promote (a) *extensibility* when an ADT is specialized through, for example, inheritance by overriding or adding new methods, and (b) *composability* when two ADTs are combined into another ADT whose methods invoke the original ones. Key to this reusability is that there is no need to know the internals of an ADT to reuse it: its interface suffices. With the latest technology development of multi-core architectures many programs are expected to scale with a large number of cores: ADTs need thus to be shared by many threads.

Unfortunately, most ADTs that export shared methods, often called *Concurrent Data Types (CDTs)*, are not reusable: the programmer can hardly build upon them. For example, programmers cannot reuse the popular concurrent data types of C++, Java and C# libraries. CDTs typically export a set of methods, guaranteeing that, even if invoked concurrently, each of these methods always appears as if it was executed in sequence. This property, known as *atomicity* (or linearizability [2]), lets the programmer reason in terms of sequential accesses. However, atomicity is generally not preserved under extension or composition, hence annihilating reusability.

Basically, CDTs are synchronized using either lock-based (i.e., mutual exclusion) or lock-free primitives (e.g., compare-and-swap). On the one hand, CDTs that rely

R. Jones (Ed.): ECOOP 2014, LNCS 8586, pp. 182–206, 2014.
© Springer-Verlag Berlin Heidelberg 2014

on locks have limited composability as a user could accidentally write two composite methods that deadlock when calling in different order two existing methods that require distinct locks. The same CDTs might not be extensible either as adding a new method may require to know the lock granularity used by existing methods. On the other hand, lock-free CDTs relying on hardware primitives can generally modify only one or two memory words atomically, requiring the user to precisely identify these words before obtaining a scalable and atomic composite method. Knowing these internals may, however, not even help extending lock-free CDTs as we will describe in Section 2.

Some synchronization schemes do enable reusability, yet their performance does not scale with concurrency. Typically, *Transactional Memory (TM)* systems ensure that within a sequence of shared memory reads/writes, all execute atomically (the transaction *commits*) or none of them execute (the transaction *aborts*) [3,4]. One can exploit TM to write an atomic CDT easily: it suffices to (a) write the bare sequential code of the ADT and then (b) to encapsulate each of the methods of the resulting ADT into a transaction. Transactional methods commit only if their execution is equivalent to a serial one. TMs typically provide composability [5] as a new composite operation encapsulated in a transaction can invoke multiple existing methods from a (transactional) CDT. Also, specific transactions facilitate extensibility by preventing anomalies when inheriting from an existing CDT [6]. Nevertheless, classic transactions are overly conservative and clearly hamper scalability simply because they cannot exploit the application semantics [7,8,9,10,11,12].

In light of this lack of scalability, expert programmers would implement handcrafted libraries whose semantics is difficult to understand to say the least: instead of being simply equivalent to a sequential execution (or atomic), an iteration over a CDT would typically return different results depending on the current status of concurrent updates of the same CDT. This strategy clearly promotes scalability while preventing a programmer, who ignores the underlying implementation details, from reusing the abstraction. Built-in C++ thread building block library, java.util.concurrent package and C# System libraries all adopt this strategy, hence limiting the ability for novices to write concurrent code in main object-oriented languages.

In this paper, we propose the *Polymorphic Transaction* (PT) methodology, which helps write concurrent programs that are both scalable and reusable. Its main novelty is not in providing a novel transaction semantics but in combining multiple of them to

Table 1. The use-cases in which we applied the PT methodology

Use-cases of the PT methodology	Data structure	Type	Annotated methods	Non-protected methods	Total
ReusableLinkedQueue	Linked list	Queue	13	2	15
ReusableVector	Vector	Collection	37	11	48
ReusableLinkedListSortedSet	Linked list	Set	11	4	15
ReusableHashMap	Hash table	Map	11	3	14
ReusableSkipListSet	Skip list	Set	11	4	15
Vacation	Red-black trees	Database	3	88	91
Total			86	112	198

scale to high levels of parallelism as they let advanced programmers exploit the application semantics. The PT methodology achieves better scalability than classic TM systems because it ensures the atomicity of the CDT operations but not of their read/write sequences. It also retains the appealing simplicity of TM systems as novice programmers obtain a safe (but less efficient) concurrent program if they ignore these semantics. In summary, it gives a framework for all programmers to write software pieces that combine with one another. To illustrate the performance potential of the PT methodology, we implemented (a) the *polymorphic* software transactional memory (PSTM), (b) on top of which we built a Java package of reusable CDTs that we use as a new TM benchmark suite on x86-64 and SPARC architectures, (c) we compared this library to the JDK (incuding java.util.concurrent) and (d) we integrated our solution to the STAMP travel reservation application, called vacation [13].

In contrast with lock-based and lock-free libraries, our library is reusable, thereby simplifying the life of concurrent programmers. In fact, we prove that our semantics combine with each other which translates into the composability and extensibility of our library as opposed to mainstream Java, C++ and C# concurrent libraries. To write an atomic (linearizable) CDT, the programmer writes a semantically equivalent bare sequential ADT and annotates each of its methods with one of the existing transaction forms without the need of altering the sequential code. To reuse existing CDTs, the programmer can either (a) compose these CDTs by invoking their methods in a method annotated with one existing transaction form or (b) extend these CDTs by inheriting from them and adding new methods annotated with one of the transaction forms. If the form of the annotation is omitted then the default form guarantees atomicity regardless of the application semantics. The four forms of PSTM, detailed in Section 3, are as follows:

- **Hand-over-hand:** A form of transaction that allows update methods to run concurrently. It builds upon a locking technique where each accessed location remains protected until the next location(s) within the same sequence gets protected. This technique is known as chain-locking, lock-coupling, or hand-over-hand locking [14]. As opposed to hand-over-hand locking, a hand-over-hand transaction may abort and release all its locks rather than blocking, thus being deadlock-free. (Hand-over-hand transactions guarantee elastic-opacity [9].)

- **Snapshot:** A form of transaction that allows read-only methods to run concurrently with updates. This form exploits multiversion concurrency control [15] to provide *snapshot isolation*, a property of production database systems that allows reads to execute at a different time from writes. Snapshot isolated transactions are prone to the write-skew problem when they concurrently read a set of data and later update disjoint subsets of these data, however, our form applies exclusively to read-only methods and guarantees atomicity.

- **Opacity:** the default form of transaction. Similar to strict-serializability targeted by database systems, opacity guarantees that transactions execute as if all their accesses were executed at some indivisible point in time (serializability) between the time they are invoked and the time they return (strictness). In contrast with database transactions, opaque transactions are guaranteed to never observe an inconsistent state of the system (even transiently) be they doomed to abort or still pending [16].

– **Irrevocability:** The form of a transaction that never aborts [17]. This form can be used to enforce that an atomic series of accesses executes exactly once. It is typically useful for executing I/O operations or invoking legacy code that cannot be rolled back, however, this form should be avoided when possible as it prevents transactions from executing concurrently.

A novel aspect of this work is to allow several transactional forms in the same application hence raising a new interesting *compatibility* challenge: guaranteeing that methods synchronized with different semantics do not affect the semantics of each other when accessing the same mutable data concurrently. For example, consider a hand-over-hand transaction, t_h, reading x before a concurrent opaque transaction, t_o, writes x. This write-after-read (WAR) conflict would typically be detected by t_o but ignored by t_h. Upon writing and detecting the conflict, if t_o resolves the conflict by aborting or delaying one of the two transactions, then concurrency would be suboptimal. Conversely, if t_o ignores the conflict, it may violate its semantics by committing: if say a later conflict on y requires that t_o be serialized before t_h. To cope with this, we prevent a WAR conflict from being resolved eagerly by the transaction that conflicts by writing, instead it is always resolved by the transaction that conflicts by reading (regardless of its form). This is described in Section 4 along with the resolution of write-after-write (WAW) and read-after-write (RAW) conflicts.

To integrate our methodology in the Java programming language, we extended the Deuce [18] bytecode instrumentation framework, so that synchronizing a bare sequential method simply consists of annotating it with either a hand-over-hand, a snapshot, an opaque or an irrevocable transaction. As detailed in Section 5, the produced bytecode is automatically instrumented so that shared reads/writes get redirected to the transactional reads/writes of the appropriate form featured by PSTM. We only annotated few methods in our benchmarks (cf. Table 1): all methods they call are automatically instrumented. We compared our reusable package to the JDK packages. First, we devised reusable CDTs using specific but restrictive techniques from the JDK like java.util.Collections.synchronizedSet or java.util.concurrent.copyOnWriteArraySet. Note that we could have also used our own implementation of a universal construction [19] to achieve similar results. Second, we tested mainstream non-reusable CDTs like the lock-based java.util.Vector or the lock-free java.util.concurrent.ConcurrentLinkedQueue [20].

While our implementation could benefit from recent speculative hardware instructions, even in its software form, the PT methodology helps improving significantly the performance of existing reusable techniques from the JDK ($2.4\times$ speedup). We also tested as a baseline the performance of non-reusable but well-engineered JDK CDTs and we observed great differences: while our CDTs could, in some executions, speedup the performance of the non-reusable JDK CDTs by $4\times$, our experiments also outline circumstances where reusability comes at a cost. All these experimental results are reported in Section 6.

Finally, we discuss the related work in Section 7 and conclude in Section 8.

2 Overview

Most concurrent object-oriented libraries trade reusability off for efficiency. We distinguish their two reusability limitations, namely extensibility and composability issues, and describe how the PT methodology addresses them.

2.1 Extensibility

Illustrating the issue. In Java, the ConcurrentLinkedQueue type of the JDK 7 exports an inconsistent size method. The problem comes from the fact that this CDT aims at implementing the lock-free algorithm from Michael and Scott designed to provide efficient offer (i.e., push) and poll (i.e., pop) [20] but aims also at implementing the Collection interface including a size method for a neat integration in the Java API. On the one hand, a size method is useful to count the number of elements comprised in this collection: although size remains optional, various Collection CDTs do provide it. On the other hand, the algorithm of Michael and Scott was optimized to export deadlock-free offer and poll without aiming at supporting a size method or allowing extensibility.

The problem of extending the Michael and Scott's algorithm with a size, which could access concurrently the same data as offer and poll, is far from being trivial, precisely due to the way the algorithm was originally proposed. In short, the algorithm was made deadlock-free by relying exclusively on compare-and-swap for synchronization. Comparing-and-swapping versions of the data structure to compute the size would annihilate effective concurrency while using locks to protect the data structure would not prevent the offer and poll from concurrently updating the structure. This lack of extensibility, which is inherent to the synchronization used, led expert programmers to implement a non-atomic size method.

Specifically, this size consists of traversing the underlying linked list from the head to the tail while elements are pushed at the head and popped at the tail. Assume that some elements are moved from the tail to the head, one after the other, so that the size s changes by ± 1. As the size method does not protect the head and the tail of the queue, it simply ignores any of these moved elements and returns an incorrect value way smaller than $s - 1$. Precisely because predicting the outcomes of this size requires to understand the implementation internals, the resulting CDT is not reusable.

We reported this ConcurrentLinkedQueue issue to the JSR166 expert group. Following up our report, this unexpected behavior has been warned in the documentation of the class ConcurrentLinkedQueue on the JSR166 site since revision 1.54 and the issue is still present in the JDK 7. Since then other researchers unaware of this warning observed the same problem [21]. This size problem simply illustrates the more general lack of extensibility. One may think of using ArrayBlockingQueue to obtain a correct size that returns the current value of a counter, however, such a size implementation requires to modify all insertion and removal methods to make them adjust the counter. Apart from the size example, a programmer would have similar problems as soon as she tries to extend these CDTs with, for example, a sum method.

The PT solution. Figure 1 illustrates how to exploit the PT methodology to cope with the ConcurrentLinkedQueue issue. It requires that the methods pop and push accessing

```
class ReusableLinkedQueue {
  ...
  @Transactional(form = SNAPSHOT)
  public int size() {
    int count = 0;
    for (Node<E> p=first(); p!=null;
            p=p.getNext()) {
      if (p.getItem() != null) {
        if (++count == Integer.MAX_VALUE)
          break;
      }
    }
    return count;
  }
```

Fig. 1. PT fixes the ConcurrentLinkedQueue.size() problem and allows extensibility

mutable shared variables use no explicit synchronizations besides annotations. In this particular example, the size is added as a sequential size method annotated with a form called *snapshot* denoted by @Transactional(form = SNAPSHOT).

The resulting implementation is inherently extensible. The snapshot transaction form guarantees that all shared read accesses of the size method, including the one to p.getNext(), return values present at a common point in time between the invocation and the response of size. To this end, the implementation (detailed in Section 3) associates a version to each value written by any transaction, a snapshot transaction records the highest version upon start and identifies the correct value to return upon reading based on the associated version. In particular, all updates to mutable shared variables are tracked using metadata so that size can detect that a field of ReusableLinkedQueue is being or has been overridden by a concurrent method (e.g., offer or poll) and choose to return a preceding version of the field to bypass the conflict or to abort.

Note that one could have safely omitted the form parameter here (@Transactional) hence adopting the default opaque semantics instead, however, it would limit concurrency by often aborting the size or its potential conflicting updates.

Related issues. Similarly, C# concurrent libraries trade reusability for efficiency. Consider the System.Collections.ConcurrentDictionary CDT as another example. This CDT cannot be easily extended with a correct size() or sum() method, in particular one should not use the existing GetEnumerator() to count or sum-up the elements as the resulting method would not be atomic.

Note that a subset of these problems arise upon inheritance and are thus referred to as *inheritance anomalies* [22].

2.2 Composability

Illustrating the issue. In most languages, there is no clear way of ensuring that atomicity gets preserved under composition of methods into another (the new one invoking the existing ones). This difficulty made it hard to identify bugs in basic Java CDTs, like java.util.Vector. Similar bugs have been unveiled thanks to automated frameworks helping researchers detect atomicity violations [23,24,25,26,27]. As noted earlier [24,26], the version 1.4.2 of the JDK suffered from a critical issue related to one

```
public ReusableOldVector(Collection c) {
  init(c);
}

@Transactional(form = OPAQUE)
public void init(Collection c) {
  elementCount = c.size();
  elementData = new Object[(int)Math.min(
    (elementCount*110L)/100,Integer.MAX_VALUE)];
  c.toArray(elementData);
}
```

Fig. 2. PT fixes the Vector constructor problem and allows composability

of the constructors of java.util.Vector, a widely used abstraction that is supposed to be thread-safe. Upon constructing a new Vector based on an existing Collection c of objects, an ArrayOutOfBoundsException could be raised. The reason is that between the time the size of the collection c is computed and the time c gets converted into an array, a concurrent update may modify the size of the collection c.

The PT solution. The java.util.Vector issue can be easily fixed using our PT methodology that instruments all transactional shared accesses (including to the Collection). The obtained ReusableOldVector simply consists of the original constructor placed into the init method that is annotated with a keyword @Transactional(form = OPAQUE) as depicted in Figure 2. We actually copy-pasted the constructor into a transactional init method simply because the instrumentation is automated for methods but not constructors. Note that we use the opaque form in this example as we motivate later in Section 3.1.

We implemented a ReusableVector CDT by converting all the synchronized methods of the java.util.Vector of the JDK 7 (hence the name ReusableOldVector for the fix of the version 1.4.2) into sequential methods annotated using the opaque transactional wrapper. An advantage of our transaction annotations is that each method, be it private (e.g., ensureCapacityHelper) or public (e.g., ensureCapacity) can be annotated as a transaction. In contrast, nesting of locks may be problematic leading to deadlocks when a programmer encapsulates in a synchronized block a call to an external method already using synchronized.

Related issues. In C#, the aforementioned ConcurrentDictionary CDT exposes GetOrAdd(k, v) and AddOrUpdate(k, v') that are not the (atomic) composition of getting, adding and updating actions. Actually, we observed a lost update problem when GetOrAdd(k, v) and AddOrUpdate(k, v') run concurrently. Intuitively, any concurrent execution of these two methods should always end up in a final state where k is present and its associated value is v': either GetOrAdd fails in adding if AddOrUpdate is linearized first, or v is updated to v' if AddOrUpdate is linearized second. The lost update may lead, however, to an inconsistent final state in which k is present with value v. Precisely because its behavior is incorrect, such subtlety is not visible at the level of the interface of this CDT.

Within the last two years, more than 300 bugs due to this lack of composability were identified in real-world applications [28,27].

Table 2. Domain and states of the algorithm

Domain of the algorithm	
X	the set of references
V	the set of values
$T \subseteq \mathbb{N}$	the set of versions
State of transaction t	
$form \in \{opaque, hand\text{-}over\text{-}hand, snapshot, irrevocable\}$	transaction form (initially opaque)
$wset \subset X \times V$	the write set (initially $\emptyset$)
$rset \subset X \times T$	the read set (initially $\emptyset$)
$bkp \subset X \times V \times T$	backup of value-version (init. $\emptyset$)
$lb \in \mathbb{N}$	versions lower bound (initially 0)
$ub \in \mathbb{N}$	versions higher bound (initially 0)

3   Polymorphic Transactional Memory

We present a polymorphic software transactional memory (PSTM) that underlies our PT methodology. The PSTM implementation has four distinct forms of transactions, opaque, hand-over-hand, snapshot, and irrevocable, hence the name. A bytecode instrumentation phase automatically redirects all shared memory accesses of annotated methods, including the accesses within their nested methods, to the proper transaction form. (Details about nesting semantics are given in Section 5.3.) At run-time the method starts by calling the tx-start passing the optional form as a parameter, invokes tx-read/tx-write instead of directly accessing the shared memory and calls tx-commit right before returning. If the corresponding transaction aborts it restarts and the method returns after the transaction successfully commits.

The domain and transaction states of PSTM are depicted in Table 2, the revocable transactions code is depicted in Algorithm 1. Conflicts are detected at the level of accesses to an object field to enable higher concurrency than object-based detection, thus we say that PSTM is *field-based*. Each field reference is associated with a *versioned lock* that stores the version of the associated reference if unlocked, or its owner if locked ($\ell.owner = \perp$ indicates that the lock is not held). Each transaction consults a global counter, *clock* (Line 2), and maintains version lower and upper bounds, resp. *lb* and *ub*, that help checking whether an access is consistent. Like most time-based software transactional memories (STMs) [29], all transactions update the memory lazily by buffering writes into a write-set, *wset*, until it commits, and have *invisible reads*: none of the read accesses from any transaction is visible from other transactions.

Our solution is deadlock-free because a transaction that cannot acquire a lock simply releases all the previous locks it acquired (and aborts). Adapting more elaborate contention managers [30] to obtain stronger progress guarantees, e.g., to avoid starvation, is left to future work. For the sake of efficiency, only writes lock and reads do not lock, however, the values read must be validated each time a read or a write occurs to make sure that they have not been overridden by concurrent transactions.

We omitted the pseudocode of several helper functions. The function vervalver (Lines 6) is a three-read process spinning until the value and versioned lock returned are guaranteed to be consistent (as if they were both read atomically). The truncate function (Line 20) discards the oldest entries from the read-set *rset* to keep the two most recent ones. Finally, lock acquires a lock on a given reference and returns the previous lock state or raises an exception if the lock is taken while unlock releases the lock on the given reference, store reports changes in memory, set-ver associates a new version with some value, get-ver/get-val return the versioned lock and the value of the reference, respectively, and *bkp*.version/value returns the old (backup) version/value of the given reference.

3.1 Opaque Transactions

The opaque semantics captures the intuitive single-global-lock semantics provided by common monomorphic (i.e., non-polymorphic) STMs. It has the strongest semantics, hence, it can be used to guarantee atomicity of any method. It clearly benefits the novice programmers who ignore other forms, but in general it limits scalability when applied to long methods. In our package, we used opaque transactions for the short methods with few accesses, like head, first, firstEntry, firstKey and most of the ReusableVector methods because their exploitable concurrency is limited.

Our implementation of opaque transactions follows the LSA algorithm [31]: it acquires locations eagerly, upon write at Line 28. Upon reading a location with a lower version than *ub*, the opaque transaction knows that this value has not been concurrently overridden so it can safely read it and record the corresponding read entry for further validation (Line 11). If the read location has a higher version than *ub*, then the opaque transaction tries to increase its *ub* (Line 15): if the validation is successful then it upgrades *ub* to the value the clock had at the time right before the validate was invoked. This upgrade allows an opaque transaction that observes a value committed after it started to be serialized after the conflicting transaction.

Upon writing, the transaction tries to lock the reference and aborts if it read the *ref* before it got overridden (Line 30). Upon commit, the read set is revalidated (Line 46), the value-version pair is copied (Line 48), the *wset* is reported to memory (Line 49) with a higher version (Lines 44), and locks are released (Line 51).

3.2 Hand-over-Hand Transactions

Hand-over-hand transactions relax the opaque semantics to one that resembles hand-over-hand locking [14]. More precisely, they guarantee elastic-opacity but their implementation differ from $\mathscr{E}$-STM elastic transactions [9] to be made compatible with other transactions (e.g., hand-over-hand transactions record backup versions). Hand-over-hand transactions are well-suited for ensuring atomicity of search structures that are traversed in a specific order. These transactions speed up traversals looking for a single location and possibly updating multiple ones. If used in other circumstances, like for computing the size of a structure, the size method may return a semantically incorrect result (like most concurrent libraries do), hence the need for complementary forms. In our package we used it for wrapping the methods contains, get, insert, insertAll, put, remove, replace, removeAll, putIfAbsent and the like.

Algorithm 1. PSTM algorithm for revocable transaction t

 1: **tx-start**$(tx\text{-}form)_t$:   ▷ *the form parameter*
 2:   $lb \leftarrow ub \leftarrow clock$ ▷ *versions lower-/upper-bound*
 3:   **if** $tx\text{-}form \neq \bot$ **then** $form \leftarrow tx\text{-}form$ ▷ *initialize tx form*
 4:   **else** $form \leftarrow$ opaque   ▷ *opaque by default*

 5: **tx-read**$(ref)_t$:   ▷ *transactional read*
 6:   $\langle \ell, v \rangle \leftarrow$ vervalver(ref) ▷ *get lock and value copies atomically*
 7:   **if** $\ell.owner \notin \{t, \bot\}$ **then** abort()   ▷ *locked by other, conflict*
 8:   **if** $\ell.owner = t$ **then**   ▷ *if locked by me*
 9:     $v \leftarrow w.val : w \in wset \wedge w.ref = ref$ ▷ *return my written value*
10:   **if** $\ell.owner = \bot \wedge \ell.version \leq ub$ **then**   ▷ *if no conflict*
11:     $rset \leftarrow rset \cup \{\langle ref, \ell.version \rangle\}$ ▷ *record read entry*
12:   **if** $\ell.owner = \bot \wedge \ell.version > ub$ **then**   ▷ *ref's been written, conflict*
13:     **if** $form =$ opaque **then**   ▷ *if opaque tx*
14:       $now \leftarrow clock$ ▷ *record clock locally*
15:       **if** validate() **then** $ub \leftarrow now$ **else** abort()   ▷ *upgrade upper bound*
16:       $rset \leftarrow rset \cup \{\langle ref, \ell.version \rangle\}$ ▷ *record read entry*
17:     **else if** $form =$ hand-over-hand **then**   ▷ *if hand-over-hand tx*
18:       **if** $\neg$validate() **then** abort()   ▷ *validate (potentially truncated) read-set*
19:       $rset \leftarrow rset \cup \{\langle ref, \ell.version \rangle\}$ ▷ *record read entry*
20:       **if** $wset = \emptyset$ **then** truncate$(rset, 2)$ ▷ *keep only last two entries*
21:     **else if** $form =$ snapshot **then**   ▷ *if snapshot tx*
22:       **if** $(old = bkp.version(ref)) \leq ub$ **then**   ▷ *sufficiently old version*
23:         $v \leftarrow bkp.value(ref)$ ▷ *return old version*
24:         $rset \leftarrow rset \cup \{\langle ref, old \rangle\}$ ▷ *record read entry*
25:       **else** abort()   ▷ *old version is too recent*
26:   **return** v

27: **tx-write**$(ref, value)_t$:   ▷ *transactional write*
28:   **try** $\ell =$ lock(ref) **catch-e** abort()   ▷ *acquire the lock and copy old lock state*
29:   **if** $\ell.owner = \bot \wedge \ell.version > ub$ **then**   ▷ *ref's been written, WAW conflict*
30:     **if** $ref \in rset$ **then** abort()   ▷ *cycle in precedence graph*
31:     **if** $\neg$validate() **then** abort()   ▷ *validation of some of the conflicts*
32:   $wset \leftarrow wset \cup \{\langle ref, value \rangle\}$ ▷ *buffer write entry*
33:   **return** ok

34: **validate**$()_t$:   ▷ *make sure read set has not changed*
35:   **for all** $\langle r, ver \rangle \in rset$ **do**   ▷ *for any read entry...*
36:     $\ell \leftarrow$ get-ver(r) ▷ *reread its versioned lock*
37:     **if** $ver \neq \ell.version \vee \ell.owner \notin \{t, \bot\}$ **then** ▷ *if has been overriden/locked*
38:       **return** false   ▷ *validation fails (simplified)*
39:   **return** true

40: **abort**$()_t$:   ▷ *rollback before automatic restart*
41:   **for all** $w \in wset$ **do** unlock$(w.ref)$ ▷ *release all locks*

42: **tx-commit**$()_t$:   ▷ *try to commit*
43:   **if** $wset \neq \emptyset$ **then**   ▷ *if something to redo*
44:     $ts \leftarrow clock$++   ▷ *fetch-and-increment global counter*
45:     **if** $ts > lb + 1$ **then**   ▷ *if concurrent update...*
46:       **if** $\neg$validate() **then** abort()   ▷ *validate read set, check WAR conflicts*
47:     **for all** $w \in wset$ **do**   ▷ *apply writes and release locks*
48:       $bkp \leftarrow bkp \cup \{\langle w.ref, \text{get-val}(w.ref), \text{get-ver}(w.ref) \rangle\}$ ▷ *backup*
49:       store$(w.val, w.ref)$ ▷ *write in memory*
50:       set-ver$(w.ref, ts)$ ▷ *upgrade version*
51:       unlock$(w.ref)$ ▷ *release lock*

A hand-over-hand transaction automatically ignores the old values read during its read-only prefix (i.e., as long as $wset = \emptyset$). When a hand-over-hand transaction still in its read-only prefix reads a location, it creates a new read entry in its *rset* and discards all but the two last entries by truncation (Line 20). By contrast, the $\mathscr{E}$-STM elastic transactions [9] used to keep only one extra entry to ensure the atomicity of the list-based set. This was made possible thanks to a marking trick used before re-allocating the memory in unmanaged language. As we do not control memory reclamation in Java, we could not use the same trick, which explains why a hand-over-hand transaction needs to maintain up to two read entries to guarantee correctness of pointer-based structures. Although keeping two entries is actually sufficient for multiple search structures (e.g., linked lists, skip lists, hash tables), more entries could be thought for other application semantics. If the read location has a higher version than ub, the entries of its (potentially truncated) read set get revalidated (Line 18) to make sure its read values are still up-to-date. By exploiting the semantics of search structures, hand-over-hand transactions enable higher concurrency than traditional transactions. In particular, a hand-over-hand transaction that has traversed an ordered structure and that is updating its end would not conflict with a concurrent transaction updating the beginning of the structure.

When a hand-over-hand transaction writes for the first time, it has to revalidate the two entries of its *rset*. When a hand-over-hand transaction has already written (i.e., it is no longer executing its read-only prefix) it behaves like an opaque transaction: it stops truncating the *rset*. A hand-over-hand transaction commits as an opaque transaction except that its validation may occur on a truncated read set (Line 46).

3.3   Snapshot Transactions

In contrast with opaque transactions, snapshot transactions are read-only and tolerate concurrent updates by potentially returning values that can be slightly out-of-date at the time it commits. Note that atomicity is ensured because all its read values are guaranteed to be up-to-date at a common point of the execution between the invocation and the response of the transaction. In our package, snapshot transactions are used for methods iterating over a collection of elements: descendingSet, headMap, headSet, size, subMap, subSet, tailMap, toArray, toString and the like.

To exploit concurrency between updates and snapshots the implementation of a snapshot transaction builds upon multi-version concurrency control. Multi-version concurrency control has proved useful in software transactional memories, like JVSTM [32], to guarantee either opacity or snapshot isolation but not to combine both. Maintaining the minimum of versions per object that maximizes the variety of output histories comes at a cost [33]: the proposed useless-prefix multi-version (UP MV) STM guarantees this property but, as a drawback, does not support invisible reads. To avoid such constraints, we chose to maintain two versions at each location. All update transactions create a backup value-version pair before overriding them (Line 48). The snapshot transaction has simply to detect that the location it aims to access has a higher version than its upper bound ub (Line 12) to try getting an older version (Line 22). The transaction has to abort if the old version is too recent at Line 25 as there are no older versions.

3.4   Irrevocable Transactions

We provide irrevocable transactions that never abort. They are used to execute atomically a series of statements in a pessimistic manner without speculation, similar to critical sections, and are particularly useful for executing external actions like I/O. One can delimit an irrevocable transaction using a dedicated Irrevocable annotation. We omitted the pseudocode of irrevocable transactions, as they simply consist of (implicit) mutual exclusion [34]. All regions annotated as irrevocable are identified by the underlying Java agent, Deuce [18], and automatically wrapped in a critical section. In contrast with other forms, an irrevocable transaction starts by trying to acquire a reader-writer lock in exclusive mode that is held until the commit of the irrevocable transaction is called. This strategy prevents an irrevocable transaction from running concurrently with any other transaction but lets revocable transactions run concurrently. A revocable transaction actually acquires a shared reader-writer lock to guarantee this. Hence, any transaction trying to execute while an irrevocable transaction is running is blocked until the irrevocable transaction commits.

4 Correctness

In this section, we discuss the correctness of PSTM. First, it is crucial that all transaction forms be pairwise *compatible*, meaning that the semantics of each transaction form be preserved despite concurrency. In particular, the semantics of some writing transaction should not impact the semantics of another transaction accessing the written elements. Second, a concurrent library should always be linearizable and *reusable*.

4.1 Invariants

The model is a concurrent environment where a set of threads execute transactional methods on shared data types. The synchronization semantics of each method is given by its transaction form that can be of the type *opaque*, *hand-over-hand* or *snapshot* but we ignore the *irrevocable* form as it cannot run concurrently with others. A *transaction* is the execution sequence of a method read and write accesses to the shared memory. It *completes* either by committing, meaning that the corresponding method returns and all its changes are visible from other transactions, or by aborting, meaning that no changes are visible. Note that the system implicitly starts a new transaction executing the same method if the preceding one aborted. A *well-formed* execution of this model is an execution where each transaction executed by one thread completes before the same thread starts another: the nesting discussion is deferred to Section 5.3.

For the sake of compatibility our three revocable forms defer conflict resolution to the same conflicting transaction and never ignore WAW conflicts.

Invariant 1. *Let t_1 and t_2 be two transactions involved in a WAW conflict. At least one of these two aborts.*

For the sake of high concurrency, we adjust the conflict resolution strategy depending on the transaction form. We differentiate the semantics of our forms in the way they handle RAW and WAR conflicts. Reads are *idempotent*, as they do not affect the system state; hence the decision taken by the reading transaction detecting a RAW conflict, which depends on the semantics of this transaction, never affects the semantics of other transactions. Specifically, reads can interchangeably return committed values or abort, this result is invisible from the standpoint of concurrent transactions.

Invariant 2. *Let two transactions t_r and t_w be involved in a RAW conflict where t_r executes the conflicting read whereas t_w executes the conflicting write. Transaction t_r either ignores the conflict by resuming or resolves it by aborting itself.*

The problem of enhancing concurrency is more subtle upon WAR conflicts. If a transaction tries to solve a WAR conflict upon detecting it by writing, then it could either conservatively limit concurrency (e.g., by aborting while its semantics is hand-over-hand) or it could violate the semantics of other transactions (e.g., committing while the conflicting transaction is opaque and this conflict would induce a cycle in the precedence graph observed by this transaction). This issue is addressed by forcing the reading transaction to solve all WAR conflicts, which requires all reading transactions to (re-)validate either at some later read, write or commit.

Invariant 3. *Let two transactions t_r and t_w be involved in a WAR conflict where t_r executes the conflicting read whereas t_w executes the conflicting write. Transaction t_r either ignores the conflict by resuming or resolves it by aborting itself.*

4.2 Semantics Preservation

Opacity requires committed transactions to be strictly serializable and non-committed ones to observe consistent states [16]. The semantics of opaque transactions is preserved due to Invariant 1 and the fact that all transactions write values at commit time so that the read operations cannot return transient values (Line 15). As opposed to other forms of optimistic transactions [35,36], a snapshot transaction is not necessarily serialized at its commit time as it only returns values that were present at its start time (Lines 10 and 22) to exploit multi-versioning while ensuring strict serializability. Finally, hand-over-hand transactions prevent some read/write from being interleaved with conflicting writes to ensure elastic opacity [9]. As they are not necessarily strictly serializable, they allow to implement efficient linearizable CDTs.

4.3 Linearizability of the Data Type

One can easily deduce a linearization point for each operation of a transaction form, at which the transaction of the corresponding form appears to execute instantaneously. The opaque transaction always keep the locks until commit hence a valid linearization point is the point at which it starts releasing its first lock (Line 51); a read-only opaque transaction linearization point is at Line 6 of its last read. The snapshot transaction may return values that have been overridden, hence its linearization point cannot be taken from its commit phase, however, since it makes sure that all versions it observes falls in its range upper bound, ub, a valid linearization point is the point where it sets its timestamp to the global clock (Line 2). The hand-over-hand transaction is well-suited for some data types but not all, and this is the responsibility of the expert to use it appropriately. For example, one cannot implement a data type exporting a putIfAbsent(x, y) method synchronized with hand-over-hand transaction. The hand-over-hand transaction may ignore conflicting writes, hence acting as if it was linearized after them: a valid linearization point for an appropriate data type is when it grabs the lock of its first write (Line 28) or at Line 6 of its last read (if read-only). Recall that linearizability is ensured precisely because it is defined for arbitrary objects (or types) without requiring that all low-level reads and writes of a method appear as if they were all executed instantaneously [2].

4.4 Reusability

Extensibility is ensured by the fact that our transaction forms are compatible as discussed previously, hence adding a new method annotated with one of the proposed forms guarantees that the semantics of existing methods will not be affected.

Composability is guaranteed by the fact that whatever forms protect original methods, the programmer always has the possibility to derive a composite annotated method that will execute atomically. By default the semantics of the composite method would be opaque which guarantees the atomicity of any method. In particular, while two traversals may be originally annotated as hand-over-hand ignoring some conflicts for the sake of concurrency, a new composite method annotated as opaque that reuses them switches their semantics to opaque. The simplicity stems from the fact that the source code of the original methods does not need to be available as the switch is transparently done at the bytecode level. The nesting of different forms is discussed in Section 5. Note that in addition to concurrent methods annotated with transactions, bare sequential methods (without annotation) can be composed into a composite concurrent method that is annotated. This allows programmers to reuse existing sequential ADTs (in addition to transactional CDTs) to produce CDTs that are themselves reusable.

5   Language Integration

We integrated the PT methodology to Java to simplify the development and reuse of concurrent objects using annotations. We detail below how the bytecode gets automatically instrumented, how exceptions are handled, how transactions nest within each other and to which extend one can use legacy code.

5.1   Bytecode Instrumentation

Our implementation of the PT methodology extends the Deuce [18] bytecode instrumentation framework to support multiple forms of transactions. Figure 3 depicts the process of the PT methodology: (1) The programmer first compiles the data types whose methods accessing mutable shared variables are annotated with transaction forms— these annotations persist in the bytecode. Then (2) the Java agent automatically produces a transactional version of all objects used to redirect all their shared accesses invoked within a transaction to the tx-read/tx-write of the corresponding transaction form of PSTM. (3) This outputs the bytecode of the corresponding reusable CDT that can be run by any JVM.

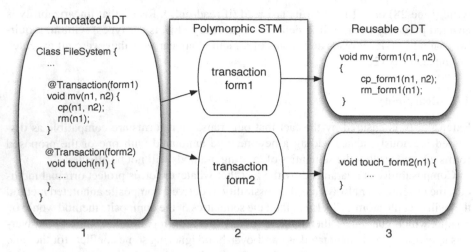

Fig. 3. Our PT methodology relies on annotating manually a sequential (or transactional) type, and producing a reusable CDT by automatically instrumenting methods using the transactional wrappers of the underlying polymorphic transactional memory system (e.g., PSTM)

5.2 Exception Handling

Our framework supports exception handling within transactions. An exception raised within a transaction provokes the transaction to commit and the exception gets propagated outside the scope of the transaction similarly to synchronized blocks and as implemented in Deuce. The advantage of this semantics is to guarantee that the cause of the exception remains visible if the exception itself is visible. An alternative interesting semantics is *failure atomicity* where an exception is considered a failure from which the system recovers by rolling back to the most recent checkpoint. For a failure-atomic exception handler in Java using STMs we refer the reader to the CXH compiler [37].

5.3 Nesting Semantics

For the sake of safety, we adopt a conservative flat nesting approach by imposing the most restrictive (when comparable) form of the inner/outer transaction to always prevail. In our form examples, opaque prevails over snapshot and hand-over-hand. To motivate our choice take the following non-trivial example where Alice would like to reuse Bob's package. For efficiency purpose Bob's package provides a hand-over-hand contains(y) and a hand-over-hand put(x) methods. Alice would like to derive a new data type by nesting these two methods into an opaque putIfAbsent(x, y) that inserts x in a data structure only if y is absent. It is crucial that the contains(y) and put(x) inherit the opaque semantics of its parent putIfAbsent(x, y) transaction to avoid a write-skew problem if a putIfAbsent(y, x) happens to run concurrently. If the opaque semantics is not inherited, then there exists an execution in which both contains(x) and contains(y) executing concurrently return false and then both x and y get successfully inserted, leading to an inconsistent state where both x and y are present. Note that Alice has to be an expert who understands the semantics of a transaction to use it. This is particularly important for her to be aware that putIfAbsent cannot be executed as a hand-over-hand transactions in her new data type.

5.4 Legacy Code

The PT methodology recommend not to use other forms of synchronization besides transaction forms, however, legacy code can be invoked through irrevocable transactions. In particular, the PT methodology does not guarantee compatibility between the transaction forms and the explicit use of compare-and-swap and mutual exclusion as it there is no clear semantics on conflicting accesses using these different synchronization techniques. A potential risk is that non-transactional accesses would typically observe transient states if they could access transactional CDTs as we do not provide strong atomicity [38]. Note that requiring CDTs to be accessed transactionally can be enforced in Java through the use of pre-existing setters and getters as, for example, when accessing ThreadLocal variables. Finally, the PT methodology can still be used to turn most sequential ADTs into equivalent atomic CDT.

6 Evaluation

In this section, we evaluate our methodology in Java. We compare our reusable library to lock-based and lock-free libraries from the JDK and STM-based libraries, on SPARC and x86-64 architectures using Synchrobench and the Vacation application.

6.1 Settings

We used two 64-way machines with different architectures: an UltraSPARC T2 (Niagara 2) 1.165GHz with 32GB of memory and a 2U server with 4 AMD Opteron 6378 2.4GHz 16-core processors with 128GB of memory. (All graphs except the last ones report the results from SPARC.) Each data point of the graphs corresponds to the throughput averaged over 3 runs of 13 seconds executed in separate JVM instances and where the 10 first seconds of each run are used to warmup each JVM. (Each point of the graph thus takes nearly 40 seconds to be computed and we carefully checked that the variance was negligible enough for the results to be meaningful.) The JVM runs in server mode with 2G of initial/maximum Java heap size.

6.2 PT Methodology vs JDK

First, we evaluate two techniques from the JDK 6 to construct reusable set CDTs: (1) the copy-on-write wraps a set ADT into a java.util.concurrent.copyOnWriteArraySet to obtain an array whose methods are guaranteed to be atomic and whose read-only methods are wait-free (JDKCopyOnWrite), and (2) a lock-based one consisting of wrapping a set ADT into a synchronizedSet (JDKLocks) to transparently make its methods atomic. Second, we evaluate the PT methodology when based on PSTM and when using four implementations of state-of-the-art (monomorphic) STMs:

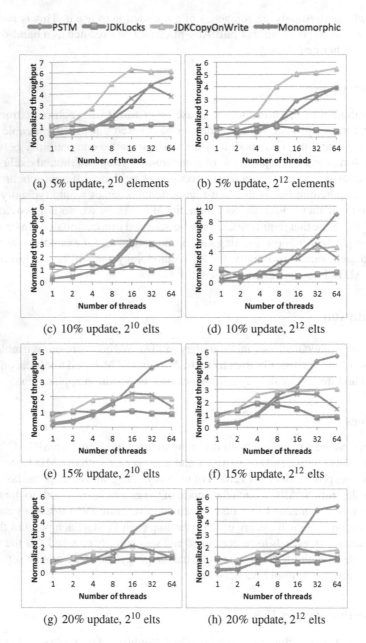

Fig. 4. Throughput (normalized over sequential) obtained when using polymorphic transactions (PSTM), the lock-based synchronizedSet from the JDK, the copyOnWriteArraySet from the JDK and the highest throughput we obtained from our four monomorphic STMs (LSA, TL2, SwissTM, NOrec). Workloads include 10% of size, from 5% to 20% of updates (add or remove with the same probability) and from 70% to 85% of contains.

LSA [31], TL2 [39], SwissTM [40] and NOrec [41]. For evaluating them on the same ground, all these implementations are field-based and match the interface of Deuce [18] (in particular, LSA, TL2, and NOrec are the standard versions provided with Deuce). We tested all STMs including PSTM and observed that PSTM was more efficient than other STMs on ReusableLinkedQueue, ReusableLinkedListSortedSet, ReusableHashMap and the ReusableSkipListSet thus we only report the data from the ReusableLinkedListSortedSet. This benchmark comprises add/remove (5–20%), contains (70–85%) and size (10%) methods on a sorted linked list data structure, methods that are all provided by Java CDTs.

Figure 4 depicts the throughput of our PT methology (PSTM), of existing monomorphic STMs, and of existing copy-on-write and pessimistic lock-based solutions, all normalized over the throughput of bare sequential code, on SPARC. About the monomorphic STMs curve, we have chosen, for each single point, the maximum throughput we obtained from LSA, TL2, SwissTM, and NOrec. The detailed speedup of PSTM over each of these STMs is presented in Section 6.5. The overall performance of PSTM is better than the synchronization alternatives. At low levels of contention, when update ratio is 5% or at low number of threads, PSTM executes slower than a copy-on-write and pessimistic lock-based alternatives. The reason is that PSTM suffers from the overhead (due to wrapping each individual access) that is common to STM implementations including monomorphic ones. This overhead is however rapidly compensated as PSTM scales well with contention whereas the copy-on-write solution scales badly and the lock-based solution does not even scale. More precisely, PSTM speeds up the existing copy-on-write solution by 2.4× on average, and the existing pessimistic lock-based solution by 4.7× on average at the highest level of parallelism we have at our disposal (64 hardware threads).

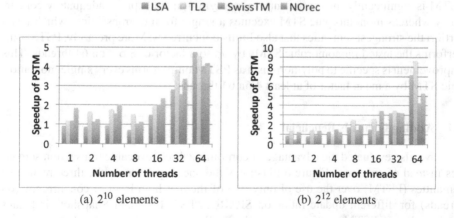

(a) 2^{10} elements   (b) 2^{12} elements

Fig. 5. Speedup of PSTM over each monomorphic STM: LSA, TL2, SwissTM and NOrec, from 1 to 64 threads (the throughput is identical when speedup has value 1)

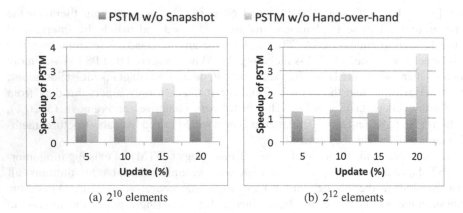

(a) 2^{10} elements   (b) 2^{12} elements

Fig. 6. Speedup of PSTM over the variant that does not use snapshot transactions and the one that does not use hand-over-hand transactions

6.3 Polymorphism vs Monomorphism

Figure 5 depicts the speedup of PSTM over monomorphic STMs, LSA, TL2, SwissTM, NOrec, as the throughput of PSTM divided by the throughput of the corresponding monomorphic STM (with 20% update) on SPARC.

These results show that PSTM scales better than other STMs. More precisely, PSTM presents a slight overhead at low levels of parallelism, typically when running a single thread but rapidly compensates this slight overhead in concurrent executions. This overhead is caused by the fact that polymorphism adds some necessary checks at each access to determine the type of the current transaction and that it records one version at each write for multi-version concurrency control. At large levels of parallelism, PSTM is significantly more efficient as its polymorphism exploits adequately concurrency whereas monomorphic STM executes a single form of transaction, which has a fortiori the strongest semantics that also limits concurrency. More precisely, PSTM outperforms the tested monomorphic STMs by up to a factor of $8.6\times$ on 64 threads. This improvement is specific to polymorphism as PSTM outperforms every single monomorphic STM by a mean factor of at least 4 on 64 threads.

6.4 Adding Forms Is Beneficial

We have also evaluated the advantage of combining three revocable transaction semantics instead of only two. Figure 6 illustrates the speedup of using the three revocable semantics (PSTM) over the use of only two of them at high level of concurrency (64 threads) for different update ratios on SPARC. "PSTM without Snapshot" indicates the speedup of PSTM over a variant where all snapshot transactions have been replaced by opaque transactions. (All transactions of this variant are either opaque or hand-over-hand.) "PSTM without Hand-over-hand" indicates the speedup of PSTM over another variant where all hand-over-hand transactions have been replaced by opaque transactions. (All transactions of this variant are either opaque or snapshot.)

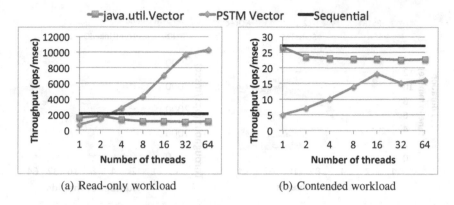

(a) Read-only workload   (b) Contended workload

Fig. 7. Comparison of our ReusableVector (PSTM Vector) against the java.util.Vector from the JDK and the bare sequential Vector

The overall result is that exploiting the three revocable forms of PSTM is always beneficial as the speedup is never below 1. In particular the speedup of PSTM over "PSTM without hand-over-hand" speedup tends to grow with the update ratio. This result is not surprising as we expected the combination of the three revocable semantics to be especially suited to limit the number of aborts, thus, it is natural for its gain to increase with the contention. An interesting observation is that the speedup of PSTM over "PSTM without snapshot" is generally low. This is explained in part by the implementation of the latter being particularly lightweight: "PSTM without snapshot" has less overhead because it does not backup values upon write as multiple versions are not needed. By contrast, both PSTM and "PSTM without hand-over-hand" have snapshot transactions and require one backup per write.

6.5   java.util.Vector vs ReusableVector

The vector benchmark comprises add, remove and contains and compare the performance obtained with our ReusableVector against the lock-based java.util.Vector from the JDK and against a bare sequential code version that is taken from the java.util.Vector from which we removed all locks.

Figure 7 depicts the throughput for a read-only workload and a contended workload (with 10% updates) on the java.util.Vector from the JDK 7 and on our ReusableVector (on SPARC). Interestingly, the PT methodology does a better job in outperforming sequential code when concurrency can be exploited. The reason is that our approach differentiates automatically read and write accesses to object fields and enables read sharing. By contrast, the java.util.Vector relies essentially on synchronized methods that act as mutual exclusion independently from their access mode. Consequently, our solution performs better than the java.util.Vector on the read-only workload by up to $4\times$ (Figure 7(a)). However, we can observe the high overhead due to the bookkeeping of TM wrappers at low levels of parallelism. When almost no concurrency can be exploited (Figure 7(b)), our approach executes significantly slower.

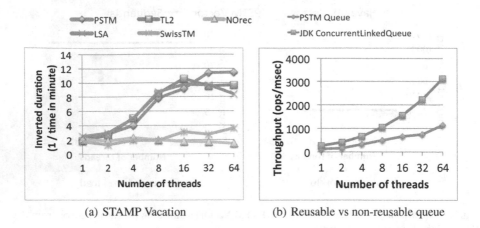

(a) STAMP Vacation   (b) Reusable vs non-reusable queue

Fig. 8. STAMP Vacation results and comparison of our ReusableLinkedQueue (PSTM Queue) against the j.u.c.ConcurrentLinkedQueue from the JDK

6.6 The Vacation Application

We evaluate our methodology with a Java version of STAMP vacation [13]. This application is a typical transactional application in that it uses a travel reservation database engine that organizes cars, rooms, flights and customers tables into four red-black trees. Tables are accessed through three transactions to (a) check prices and reserve few items, (b) delete customers and (c) add or remove items of a reservation. To evaluate the PT methodology, we made the first transaction read-only by simply returning prices and annotated it as snapshot, we annotated the two others as opaque (all transactions are opaque when running the monomorphic STMs). We set the initial and maximum Java heap size to 4G and use the recommended low contention parameters of vacation.

Figure 8(a) depicts the vacation performance as the inverted duration time on x86-64. The performance of PSTM keeps scaling up to 64 threads at which point it becomes 19% faster than monomorphic alternatives. Although monomorphic STMs stop scaling at 32 threads, they are more efficient than PSTM at lower levels of parallelism confirming our observations on micro-benchmarks. In particular, TL2 achieves good performance at 16 threads, which may be due to TL2's code being optimized through the use of metadata pools to reduce memory reclamation. This feature seems appealing in more realistic benchmarks, like vacation, that tend to use more memory for longer than our micro-benchmarks.

6.7 j.u.c.ConcurrentLinkedQueue vs ReusableQueue

We also evaluated the cost of reusability by comparing the performance of one of our reusable CDT against a similar but non-reusable lock-free CDT on the x86-64 architecture (our SPARC results were similar). We compare the queue CDT of the JDK 7 as described in Section 2.1 to the ReusableLinkedQueue as they both rely on a linked list implementation where elements are added to the head and the remove operation searches for the given value by traversing the list. Figure 8 shows the performance of our ReusableLinkedQueue against the ConcurrentLinkedQueue running 30% of size, 1% of updates (add/remove), 69% of contains on a 128-element queue. The performance difference is quite substantial as the non-reusable queue speeds up the reusable queue by up to 3×. We see two reasons: (a) some overhead is induced by the extra book-keeping of our synchronizations that triggers the Java garbage collector more often, (b) the atomicity of the reusable size and updates precludes a lot of non-atomic executions allowed by the non-reusable skip list. Even though we may reduce the overhead using hardware transactional memory opcodes, making sure that someone can reuse a concurrent library comes with a substantial cost. As opposed to transactional memories that tend to scale badly [12], PSTM performance scales.

7 Related Work

There is a large body of work on concurrent object-oriented programming languages. Some approaches rely on monitors, like Guava [42], that may restrict inter-method concurrency. SCOOP allows to specify an object accessed by a different process as *separate* [43]. A client object must acquire an exclusive lock on a separate object before invoking it through a routine. SCOOP was ported to Java [44] but is not inherently deadlock-free [45]. Some recent lock-inference techniques are deadlock-free, yet they require the programmer to provide a semantic description of methods [46].

One of the original motivations for transactional memory (TM) is to alleviate lock-related problems like deadlocks [3]. Without deadlocks the program is guaranteed to execute, and a simple exponential backoff strategy can manage contention so that the program progresses. The first TM to handle concurrency in a dynamic control flow redirects speculative accesses to Java object copies [47]. The back-end interface of this TM implementation was later improved in a Java library supporting interchangeable transactional factory [48]. Lightweight transactions were suggested to avoid copying entire objects by using a mapping of addresses to word-sized ownership records [49] before field-based instrumentation was proposed [18].

Exploiting highly concurrent transactions was extensively explored [7,50,51,52,8,35,53,54]. The aim of Galois [52], JANUS [53] and CSpec [54] was not to simplify concurrent programming but to enhance optimistic concurrency in complex scenarios; Galois requires explicit commutativity specifications, Janus exploits an offline learning phase of commutative relations and CSpec converts already concurrent code with annotations and locks.

Note that the PT methodology could potentially achieve similar concurrency results as open nesting [7] and transactional boosting [8] as they all exploit the application-level semantics. In contrast with our solution, both techniques acquire abstract locks eagerly and need explicit abort handlers to compensate their actions upon roll-back. Existing implementations of open nesting require to order transactions and to guarantee that transactions are nested in this specific order to prevent an abort handler from deadlocking [55]. Transactional boosting suggests to add timeouts to avoid deadlocks when two transactions acquire abstract locks in different order [8]. Note that our current implementation of the PT methodology needs annotated sequential code but does not use compensating actions. As it keeps all the locks it acquires until commit or abort time, it is inherently deadlock-free.

8 Concluding Remarks

Concurrent programming would greatly be simplified if concurrent libraries were made reusable: a programmer could build upon any CDT without having to understand its synchronization internals. The PT methodology helps reaching this goal by allowing collaborative development of scalable libraries any programmer can compose and extend, hence confirming our recent observation [11]. This new methodology promotes a clear separation of the implementation of synchronization semantics, which requires advanced programming skills, from the raw sequential code that describes the expected behavior of an abstract data type.

The ease of use of this methodology is demonstrated using automatic instrumentation of method bytecode. We confirmed using a novel Java library that reusability of CDTs comes at a cost. However, we also observe that this cost can be rapidly compensated by exploiting the high level of concurrency of existing multicore architectures. Actually, one does not even have to sacrifice scalability for reusability.

Future work includes (a) formalizing a framework to derive incompatibilities of synchronization semantics and (b) optimizing our current implementation through concurrent irrevocable transactions [56] or transactional instruction extensions with Java opcodes to reduce overhead.

Acknowledgments. The Java port of SwissTM is from Mihai Letia. NICTA is funded by the Australian Government through the Department of Communications and the Australian Research Council through the ICT Centre of Excellence Program.

References

1. Meyer, B.: Reusability: The case for object-oriented design. IEEE Software 4(2), 50–64 (1987)
2. Herlihy, M., Wing, J.: Linearizability: a correctness condition for concurrent objects. ACM Trans. Program. Lang. Syst. 12(3), 463–492 (1990)
3. Herlihy, M., Moss, J.E.B.: Transactional memory: architectural support for lock-free data structures. SIGARCH Comput. Archit. News 21(2), 289–300 (1993)
4. Shavit, N., Touitou, D.: Software transactional memory. In: PODC, pp. 204–213 (1995)
5. Harris, T., Marlow, S., Peyton-Jones, S., Herlihy, M.: Composable memory transactions. In: PPoPP, pp. 48–60 (2005)
6. Wakita, K., Yonezawa, A.: Linguistic supports for development of distributed organizational information systems in object-oriented concurrent computation frameworks. SIGOIS Bull. 12, 185–198 (1991)
7. Moss, J.E.B.: Open nested transactions: Semantics and support. In: Workshop on Memory Performance Issues (February 2006)
8. Herlihy, M., Koskinen, E.: Transactional boosting: A methodology for highly-concurrent transactional objects. In: PPoPP, pp. 207–216 (2008)

9. Felber, P., Gramoli, V., Guerraoui, R.: Elastic transactions. In: Keidar, I. (ed.) DISC 2009. LNCS, vol. 5805, pp. 93–107. Springer, Heidelberg (2009)

10. Kulkarni, M., Nguyen, D., Prountzos, D., Sui, X., Pingali, K.: Exploiting the commutativity lattice. In: PLDI, pp. 542–555 (2011)

11. Gramoli, V., Guerraoui, R.: Democratizing transactional programming. In: Kon, F., Kermarrec, A.-M. (eds.) Middleware 2011. LNCS, vol. 7049, pp. 1–19. Springer, Heidelberg (2011)

12. Turon, A.: Reagents: expressing and composing fine-grained concurrency. In: PLDI, pp. 157–168 (2012)

13. Minh, C.C., Chung, J., Kozyrakis, C., Olukotun, K.: Stamp: Stanford transactional applications for multi-processing. In: IISWC (2008)

14. Bayer, R., Schkolnick, M.: Concurrency of operations on b-trees. In: Readings in Database Systems, pp. 129–139 (1988)

15. Bernstein, P., Hadzilacos, V., Goodman, N.: Concurrency Control and Recovery in Database Systems. Addison-Wesley (1987)

16. Guerraoui, R., Kapalka, M.: On the correctness of transactional memory. In: PPoPP, pp. 175–184 (2008)

17. Welc, A., Saha, B., Adl-Tabatabai, A.R.: Irrevocable transactions and their applications. In: SPAA, pp. 285–296 (2008)

18. Korland, G., Shavit, N., Felber, P.: Deuce: Noninvasive software transactional memory. Transactions on HiPEAC 5(2) (2010)

19. Herlihy, M., Shavit, N.: The Art of Multiprocessor Programming. Morgan Kaufmann Publishers Inc., San Francisco (2008)

20. Michael, M.M., Scott, M.L.: Simple, fast, and practical non-blocking and blocking concurrent queue algorithms. In: PODC (1996)

21. Burnim, J., Necula, G., Sen, K.: Specifying and checking semantic atomicity for multithreaded programs. In: ASPLOS, pp. 79–90 (2011)

22. Matsuoka, S., Yonezawa, A.: Analysis of inheritance anomaly in object-oriented concurrent programming languages. In: Research Directions in Concurrent Object-Oriented Programming, pp. 107–150. MIT Press, Cambridge (1993)

23. Flanagan, C., Qadeer, S.: A type and effect system for atomicity. In: PLDI, pp. 338–349 (2003)

24. Wang, L., Stoller, S.D.: Runtime analysis of atomicity for multithreaded programs. IEEE Trans. Softw. Eng. 32(2), 93–110 (2006)

25. Burckhardt, S., Alur, R., Martin, M.M.K.: Checkfence: checking consistency of concurrent data types on relaxed memory models. In: PLDI, pp. 12–21 (2007)

26. Flanagan, C., Freund, S.N., Lifshin, M., Qadeer, S.: Types for atomicity: Static checking and inference for Java. ACM Trans. Program. Lang. Syst. 30 (2008)

27. Lin, Y., Dig, D.: Check-then-act misuse of java concurrent collections. In: ICST, pp. 164–173 (2013)

28. Shacham, O., Bronson, N., Aiken, A., Sagiv, M., Vechev, M., Yahav, E.: Testing atomicity of composed concurrent operations. In: OOPSLA, pp. 51–64 (2011)

29. Felber, P., Fetzer, C., Marlier, P., Riegel, T.: Time-based software transactional memory. IEEE Trans. Parallel and Distributed Systems 21(12), 1793–1807 (2010)

30. Scherer, I.W.N., Scott, M.L.: Advanced contention management for dynamic software transactional memory. In: PODC, pp. 240–248 (2005)

31. Riegel, T., Felber, P., Fetzer, C.: A lazy snapshot algorithm with eager validation. In: Dolev, S. (ed.) DISC 2006. LNCS, vol. 4167, pp. 284–298. Springer, Heidelberg (2006)

32. Cachopo, J.A., Rito-Silva, A.: Versioned boxes as the basis for memory transactions. Sci. Comput. Program. 63(2), 172–185 (2006)

33. Perelman, D., Fan, R., Keidar, I.: On maintaining multiple versions in STM. In: PODC, pp. 16–25 (2010)

34. Carlstrom, B.D., Chung, J., Chafi, H., McDonald, A., Cao Minh, C., Hammond, L., Kozyrakis, C., Olukotun, K.: Transactional execution of Java programs. In: SCOOL (2005)
35. Koskinen, E., Parkinson, M., Herlihy, M.: Coarse-grained transactions. In: POPL, pp. 19–30 (2010)
36. Hassan, A., Palmieri, R., Ravindran, B.: Optimistic transactional boosting. In: PPoPP, pp. 387–388 (2014)
37. Harmanci, D., Gramoli, V., Felber, P.: Atomic boxes: Coordinated exception handling with transactional memory. In: Mezini, M. (ed.) ECOOP 2011. LNCS, vol. 6813, pp. 634–657. Springer, Heidelberg (2011)
38. Martin, M., Blundell, C., Lewis, E.: Subtleties of transactional memory atomicity semantics. IEEE Comput. Archit. Lett. 5 (2006)
39. Dice, D., Shalev, O., Shavit, N.N.: Transactional locking II. In: Dolev, S. (ed.) DISC 2006. LNCS, vol. 4167, pp. 194–208. Springer, Heidelberg (2006)
40. Dragojević, A., Guerraoui, R., Kapałka, M.: Stretching transactional memory. In: PLDI, pp. 155–165 (2009)
41. Dalessandro, L., Spear, M.F., Scott, M.L.: NOrec: streamlining STM by abolishing ownership records. In: PPoPP, pp. 67–78 (2010)
42. Bacon, D.F., Strom, R.E., Tarafdar, A.: Guava: a dialect of Java without data races. In: OOPSLA, pp. 382–400 (2000)
43. Meyer, B.: Systematic concurrent object-oriented programming. Commun. ACM 36(9), 56–80 (1993)
44. Torshizi, F.A., Ostroff, J.S., Paige, R.F., Chechik, M.: The SCOOP concurrency model in Java-like languages. In: CPA, pp. 7–24 (2009)
45. West, S., Nanz, S., Meyer, B.: A modular scheme for deadlock prevention in an object-oriented programming model. In: Dong, J.S., Zhu, H. (eds.) ICFEM 2010. LNCS, vol. 6447, pp. 597–612. Springer, Heidelberg (2010)
46. Gueta, G.G., Ramalingam, G., Sagiv, M., Yahav, E.: Concurrent libraries with foresight. In: PLDI, pp. 263–274 (2013)
47. Herlihy, M., Luchangco, V., Moir, M., Scherer, I.W.N.: Software transactional memory for dynamic-sized data structures. In: PODC, pp. 92–101 (2003)
48. Herlihy, M., Luchangco, V., Moir, M.: A flexible framework for implementing software transactional memory. In: OOPSLA, pp. 253–262 (2006)
49. Harris, T., Fraser, K.: Language support for lightweight transactions. In: OOPSLA, pp. 388–402 (2003)
50. Carlstrom, B.D., McDonald, A., Chafi, H., Chung, J., Minh, C.C., Kozyrakis, C., Olukotun, K.: The atomos transactional programming language. In: PLDI, pp. 1–13 (2006)
51. Carlstrom, B.D., McDonald, A., Carbin, M., Kozyrakis, C., Olukotun, K.: Transactional collection classes. In: PPoPP, pp. 56–67 (2007)
52. Kulkarni, M., Pingali, K., Walter, B., Ramanarayanan, G., Bala, K., Chew, L.P.: Optimistic parallelism requires abstractions. In: PLDI, pp. 211–222 (2007)
53. Tripp, O., Manevich, R., Field, J., Sagiv, M.: JANUS: exploiting parallelism via hindsight. In: PLDI, pp. 145–156 (2012)
54. Xiang, L., Scott, M.L.: Compiler aided manual speculation for high performance concurrent data structures. In: PPoPP, pp. 47–56 (2013)
55. Ni, Y., Menon, V., Abd-Tabatabai, A.R., Hosking, A.L., Hudson, R.L., Moss, J.E.B., Saha, B., Shpeisman, T.: Open nesting in software transactional memory. In: PPoPP, pp. 68–78 (2007)
56. Spear, M.F., Silverman, M., Dalessandro, L., Michael, M.M., Scott, M.L.: Implementing and exploiting inevitability in software transactional memory. In: ICPP, pp. 59–66 (2008)

TaDA: A Logic for Time and Data Abstraction

Pedro da Rocha Pinto[1], Thomas Dinsdale-Young[2], and Philippa Gardner[1]

[1] Imperial College London
{pmd09,pg}@doc.ic.ac.uk
[2] Aarhus University
tyoung@cs.au.dk

Abstract. To avoid data races, concurrent operations should either be
at distinct times or on distinct data. *Atomicity* is the abstraction that
an operation takes effect at a single, discrete instant in time, with linearisability being a well-known correctness condition which asserts that
concurrent operations appear to behave atomically. *Disjointness* is the
abstraction that operations act on distinct data resource, with concurrent separation logics enabling reasoning about threads that appear to
operate independently on disjoint resources.

We present TaDA, a program logic that combines the benefits of abstract atomicity and abstract disjointness. Our key contribution is the
introduction of *atomic triples*, which offer an expressive approach to specifying program modules. By building up examples, we show that TaDA
supports elegant modular reasoning in a way that was not previously
possible.

1 Introduction

The specification and verification of concurrent program modules is a difficult
problem. When concurrent threads work with shared data, the resulting behaviour can be complex. Two abstractions provide useful simplifications: that
operations effectively act at distinct times; and that operations effectively act
on disjoint resources. Programmers work with sophisticated combinations of the
time and data abstractions. In constrast, existing reasoning techniques tend to
be limited to one or the other abstraction.

Atomicity is the abstraction that an operation takes effect at a single, discrete
instant in time. The concurrent behaviour of atomic operations is equivalent to
some sequential interleaving of the operations. *Linearisability* [9] is a correctness condition, which specifies that the operations of a concurrent module appear to behave atomically. For example, a set module might use a sophisticated
lock-free data structure to implement insert, remove and contains operations.
Linearisability allows a client to use these as if they were simple atomic operations, abstracting the implementation details. Various proof techniques have
been introduced and used to prove linearisability for concurrent modules such
as queues [9] and lists with fine-grained synchronisation [21].

With linearisability, each operation is given a sequential specification, and
the operations are asserted to behave atomically *with respect to each other*. Linearisability is therefore a whole-module property: if we extend the set module

R. Jones (Ed.): ECOOP 2014, LNCS 8586, pp. 207–231, 2014.
© Springer-Verlag Berlin Heidelberg 2014

with an atomic `insertBoth` operation, we would have to redo the linearisability proof to check that this new operation respects the atomicity of the others, and vice versa. Moreover, all operations are required to be atomic, so we could not specify a non-atomic `insertBoth` behaving like two consecutive atomic inserts. It is also possible to add operations to a module that break the abstraction of atomicity for existing operations. For example, if the set module were to expose the low-level heap operations used in its implementation, a client could use them to observe intermediate states in the underlying data structure. Consequently, the fiction of atomicity is fragile.

The sequential specifications used for linearisability can be inadequate for expressing concurrent behaviours. In particular, we might wish to constrain which operations a client can perform concurrently. For instance, a module might provide alternative update operations that only appear atomic if all other concurrent operations are reads. Constraining the client in this way reduces the burden on the implementation, which can be more efficient. However, a sequential specification cannot express the distinction between the alternative and regular updates.

Disjointness is the abstraction that operations act on specific resources. When threads operate on disjoint resources, they do not interfere with each other, and so their overall effect is the combined effects of each. *Concurrent separation logics* [12,3,17,16] embody this principle, by providing modular reasoning about disjoint resource. *Concurrent abstract predicates* (CAP) [3], in particular, support reasoning about *abstract* disjoint resource, which can be used to specify program modules. In the case of a set module, for instance, values may be seen as resources, which may be independently in or out of the set. If concurrent threads use disjoint values, reasoning about them is simple. CAP also supports reasoning about *shared regions*, which can be used to implement abstract disjoint resources with shared resources. In this way, sophisticated concurrent implementations can be verified against simple specifications. Such reasoning has been applied to, for example, locks [3], sets [3] and concurrent indexes [14].

The CAP approach is, however, limited. With CAP, it is only possible to access shared regions using *primitive atomic* operations. Yet operations provided by concurrent modules are rarely primitive atomic. Consequently, the abstract resources provided by a module are not easily shared and the nesting of modules is difficult. For example, the CAP specification of a set module [3] constrains concurrent threads to operate on disjoint values. Two threads cannot remove the same value: since `remove` is not primitive atomic, it cannot operate on shared resources. It is possible to give a specification that has a finer resource granularity [14], which can support some form of shared concurrent removal. Such specifications are complex and ad hoc, as they do not support general sharing.

Linearisability and CAP have complementary virtues and weaknesses. Linearisability gives strong, whole-module specifications based on abstract atomicity; CAP gives weaker, independent specifications based on abstract disjointness. Linearisability supports nested modules, but whole-module specifications make it difficult to extend modules; CAP supports the extension of modules, but the weak specifications make building up nested modules more difficult. Linearisability does not constrain the client, thus placing significant burden on the implementation; CAP constrains the client to use specific disjoint resource, enabling more flexibility in the implementation.

We propose a solution that combines the virtues of both approaches. Specifically, we introduce a new *atomic triple* judgement for specifying abstract atomicity in a program logic. The simplest form of atomic triple judgement is

$$\vdash \langle p \rangle \; \mathbb{C} \; \langle q \rangle$$

where p and q are assertions in the style of separation logic and $\mathbb{C}$ is a program. This judgement is read as "$\mathbb{C}$ atomically updates p to q". The program may actually take multiple steps, but each step before the atomic update from p to q must preserve the assertion p. Before the atomic update occurs, the concurrent environment may also update the state, provided that the assertion p is preserved. As soon as the atomic update has happened, the environment can do what it likes; it is not constrained to preserve q. Meanwhile, the program $\mathbb{C}$ may no longer have access to the resources in q.

The atomicity of $\mathbb{C}$ is *only* expressed with respect to the abstraction defined by p. If the environment makes an observation at a lower level of abstraction, it may perceive multiple updates rather than this single atomic update. For example, suppose that a set module, which provides an atomic remove operation, is implemented using a linked list. The implementation might first mark a node as deleted, before removing it from the list. The environment can observe the change from "marked" to "removed". This low-level step does not change the abstract set; the change already occurred when the node was marked.

Atomic triples are our key contribution, as they allow us to overcome limitations of the linearisability and CAP approaches. Atomic triples can be used to access shared resources concurrently, rather than relying on primitive atomic operations to do so. This makes it easier to build modules on top of each other. Atomic triples specify operations with respect to an abstraction, so they can be proved independently. This makes it possible to extend modules at a later date, and mix atomic and non-atomic operations as well as operations working at different levels of abstraction. Atomic triples can specify clear constraints on how a client can use them. For instance, they can enforce that the unlock operation on a lock should not be called by two threads at the same time (§2.1). Furthermore, atomic triples can specify the transfer of resources between a client and a module. For instance, they can specify an operation that non-atomically stores the result of an atomic read into a buffer provided by a client (§2.3).

Our other main contribution is TaDA, a program logic for Time and Data Abstraction, which extends CAP with rules for deriving and using atomic triples. Using TaDA, we first specify an atomic lock module (§2.1). From this specification, we then derive a resource-transferring CAP-style lock specification, which illustrates the weakening of the atomic specification to a specific use case. We also prove that a spin lock implementation satisfies the atomic lock specification. We show how the logic supports vertical reasoning about modules, by verifying an implementation of multiple-compare-and-swap (MCAS) using the lock specification (§2.2), and an implementation of a concurrent double-ended queue (deque) using the MCAS specification (§4). We present the details of TaDA's proof rules in §3, and briefly describe their semantics and soundness in §5. We thus demonstrate that TaDA combines the benefits of abstract atomicity and abstract disjointness within a single program logic.

2   Motivating Examples

We introduce TaDA by showing how two simple concurrent interfaces can be specified, implemented, and used: lock and multiple compare-and-swap.

2.1   Lock

We define a lock module with the operations lock(x) and unlock(x) and a constructor makeLock().

Atomic Lock Specification. The lock operations are specified in terms of abstract predicates [13] that represent the state of a lock: $L(x)$ and $U(x)$ assert the existence of a lock, addressed by x, that is in the locked and unlocked state, respectively. These predicates confer ownership of the lock: it is not possible to have more than one $L(x)$ or $U(x)$ for the same value of x. This contrasts with the style of specification given with CAP [3], but we shall see how the CAP specification can be derived using the atomic specification given here.

The specification for the makeLock() operation is a simple Hoare triple:

$$\vdash \{\texttt{emp}\} \; \texttt{x := makeLock()} \; \{U(x)\}$$

The operation allocates a new lock, which is initially unlocked, and returns its address. The specification says nothing about the granularity of the operation. In fact, the granularity is hardly relevant, since no concurrent environment can meaningfully observe the effects of makeLock until its return value is known — that is, once the operation has completed.

The specification for the unlock(x) operation uses an *atomic* triple:

$$\vdash \langle L(x) \rangle \; \texttt{unlock(x)} \; \langle U(x) \rangle$$

Intuitively, this specification means that unlock(x) will *atomically* take the lock x from the locked to unlocked state. This atomicity means that the resources in the specification may be *shared* — that is, concurrently accessible by multiple threads. Sharing in this way is not possible with ordinary Hoare triples, since they make no guarantee that intermediate steps preserve invariants on the resources. The atomic triple, by contrast, makes a strong guarantee: as long as the concurrent environment guarantees that the (possibly) shared resource $L(x)$ is available, the unlock(x) operation will preserve $L(x)$ until it transforms it into $U(x)$; after the transformation, the operation no longer requires $U(x)$, and is consequently oblivious to subsequent transformations by the environment (such as another thread acquiring the lock).

It is significant that the notion of atomicity is tied to the abstraction in the specification. The predicate $L(x)$ could abstract multiple underlying states in the implementation. If we were to observe the underlying state, the operation might no longer appear to be atomic.

Specifying $lock(x)$ is more subtle. It can be called whether the lock is in the locked or unlocked state, and always results in setting it to the locked state (if it ever terminates). A first attempt at a specification might therefore be:

$$\vdash \langle L(x) \vee U(x) \rangle \; lock(x) \; \langle L(x) \rangle$$

This specification has two significant flaws. Firstly, it allows $lock(x)$ to do nothing at all when the lock is already locked. This is contrary to what it should do, which is wait for it to become unlocked and then (atomically) lock it. Secondly, as the level of abstraction given by the precondition is $L(x) \vee U(x)$, an implementation could change the state of the lock arbitrarily *without appearing to have done anything*. In particular, an implementation could transition between the two states any number of times, so long as it is in the $L(x)$ state when it finishes.

A second attempt to overcome these issues might be:

$$\vdash \langle L(x) \rangle \; lock(x) \; \langle false \rangle \qquad \vdash \langle U(x) \rangle \; lock(x) \; \langle L(x) \rangle$$

In the left-hand triple, the lock is initially locked; the implementation may not terminate, nor change the state of the lock. In the right-hand triple, the lock is initially unlocked; the implementation may only make one atomic transformation from unlocked to locked. These specifications also have a subtle flaw: they assume that the environment will not change the state of the lock. This would prevent us from having multiple threads competing to acquire the lock, which is the essential purpose of a lock.

An equivalent specification makes use of a boolean logical variable:

$$\forall l \in \mathbb{B}. \vdash \langle (L(x) \wedge \neg l) \vee (U(x) \wedge l) \rangle \; lock(x) \; \langle L(x) \wedge l \rangle$$

The variable l records the state of the lock when the atomic operation takes effect. In particular, it cannot take effect unless the lock is already unlocked.

These specifications do not express the subtlety that the interference permitted before the atomic update is different for the environment and the operation. The environment should be allowed to change the value of l (i.e. acquire and release the lock) but the $lock$ operation should not. The correct specification expresses this by binding the variable l in a new way:

$$\vdash \mathbb{V}l \in \mathbb{B}. \langle (L(x) \wedge \neg l) \vee (U(x) \wedge l) \rangle \; lock(x) \; \langle L(x) \wedge l \rangle$$

The special role of l (indicated by the pseudo-quantifier $\mathbb{V}$) is in distinguishing the constraints on the environment and on the thread before the atomic operation takes effect. Specifically, the environment is at liberty to change the value of l for which the precondition holds (that is, lock and unlock the lock), but the thread executing the operation must preserve the value of l (that is, it cannot lock or unlock the lock except by performing the atomic operation).

CAP Lock Specification. The atomic specification of the lock captures its essence as a synchronisation primitive. In practice, a lock is often used to protect some resource. We demonstrate how a CAP-style lock specification [3], which views the lock as a mechanism for protecting a resource invariant, can be derived from the atomic specification. This illustrates a typical use of a TaDA specification: first prove a strong abstract-atomic specification, then specialise to whatever is required by the client.

The CAP specification is parametrised by an abstract predicate Inv, representing the resource invariant to be protected by the lock. The client can choose how to instantiate this predicate.[1] The specification provides two abstract predicates itself: $\mathsf{isLock}(x)$, which is a non-exclusive resource that allows a thread to compete for the lock; and $\mathsf{Locked}(x)$, which is an exclusive resource that represents that the thread has acquired the lock, and allows it to release the lock. The lock is specified as follows (we omit `makeLock` for brevity):

$$\vdash \{\mathsf{Locked}(x) * \mathsf{Inv}\} \; \mathtt{unlock(x)} \; \{\mathsf{emp}\}$$

$$\vdash \{\mathsf{isLock}(x)\} \; \mathtt{lock(x)} \; \{\mathsf{isLock}(x) * \mathsf{Locked}(x) * \mathsf{Inv}\}$$

$$\mathsf{isLock}(x) \iff \mathsf{isLock}(x) * \mathsf{isLock}(x)$$

$$\mathsf{Locked}(x) * \mathsf{Locked}(x) \implies \mathsf{false}$$

To implement this specification, we must provide an interpretation for the abstract predicates isLock and Locked. For this, we need to introduce a shared region. As in CAP, a shared region encapsulates some resource that is available to multiple threads. In our example, this resource will be the predicates $\mathsf{L}(x)$, $\mathsf{U}(x)$ and Inv, plus some additional guard resource (described below). A shared region is associated with a protocol, which determines how its contents change over time. Following iCAP [16], the state of a shared region is abstracted, and protocols are expressed as transition systems over these abstract states. A thread may only change the abstract state of a region when it has the *guard* resource associated with the transition to be performed. An interpretation function associates each abstract state of a region with a concrete assertion. In summary, to specify a region we must supply the guards for the region, an abstract state transition system that is labelled by these guards, and a function interpreting abstract states as assertions.

In CAP, guards consist of (parametrised) names, associated with fractional permissions. In TaDA, we are more general, effectively allowing guards to be taken from any separation algebra. This gives us more flexibility in specifying complex usage patterns for regions. For the CAP lock, we need only a very simple guard separation algebra: there is a single, indivisible guard named K (for 'key'), as well as the empty guard **0**. As a separation algebra, guard resources must have a partial composition operator that is associative and commutative. In this case, $\mathbf{0} \bullet x = x = x \bullet \mathbf{0}$ for all $x \in \{\mathbf{0}, \mathrm{K}\}$, and $\mathrm{K} \bullet \mathrm{K}$ is undefined.

---

[1] The restriction is that the predicate must be *stable* — i.e. invariant under interference from the environment.

The transition system for the region will have two states: 0 and 1, corresponding to unlocked and locked states respectively. Intuitively, any thread should be allowed to lock the lock, if it is unlocked, but only the thread holding the 'key' should be able to unlock it. This is specified by the labelled transition system:

$$0 \ : \ 0 \rightsquigarrow 1 \qquad\qquad K \ : \ 1 \rightsquigarrow 0$$

It remains to give an interpretation for the abstract states of the transition system. To do so, we must have a name for the type of region we are defining; we shall use **CAPLock**. It is possible for there to be multiple regions associated with the same region type name. To distinguish them, each region has a unique region identifier, which is typically annotated as a subscript. A region specification may take some parameters that are used in the interpretation. With **CAPLock**, for instance, the address of the lock is such a parameter. We thus specify the type name, region identifier, parameters and state of a region in the form $\textbf{CAPLock}_r(x, s)$.

The region interpretation for **CAPLock** is given by:

$$I(\textbf{CAPLock}_r(x, 0)) \triangleq \mathsf{U}(x) * [\mathrm{K}]_r * \mathsf{Inv}$$
$$I(\textbf{CAPLock}_r(x, 1)) \triangleq \mathsf{L}(x)$$

With this interpretation, the guard K and invariant Inv are in the region when it is in the unlocked state. This means that, when a thread acquires the lock, it takes ownership of the guard and the lock invariant by removing them from the region. Having the guard K allows the thread to subsequently release the lock, returning the guard and invariant to the region.

We can now give an interpretation to the predicates $\mathsf{isLock}(x)$ and $\mathsf{Locked}(x)$:

$$\mathsf{isLock}(x) \quad\triangleq\quad \exists r. \, \exists s \in \{0, 1\}. \, \textbf{CAPLock}_r(x, s)$$
$$\mathsf{Locked}(x) \quad\triangleq\quad \exists r. \, \textbf{CAPLock}_r(x, 1) * [\mathrm{K}]_r$$

It remains to prove the specifications for the procedures and the axioms. The key proof rule is "use atomic". A simplified version of the rule is as follows:

$$\frac{\forall x \in X. \, (x, f(x)) \in \mathcal{T}_t(\mathrm{G})^* \\ \vdash \mathbb{\forall} x \in X. \, \langle I(\mathsf{t}_a(x)) * [\mathrm{G}]_a \rangle \, \mathbb{C} \, \langle I(\mathsf{t}_a(f(x))) * q \rangle}{\vdash \{\exists x \in X. \, \mathsf{t}_a(x) * [\mathrm{G}]_a\} \, \mathbb{C} \, \{\exists x \in X. \, \mathsf{t}_a(f(x)) * q\}}$$

This rule allows a region a, with region type t, to be opened so that it may be updated by $\mathbb{C}$, from some state $x \in X$ to state $f(x)$. In order to do so, the precondition must include a guard G that is sufficient to perform the update to the region, in accordance with the labelled transition system — this is established by the first premiss.

The proofs of the `unlock` and `lock` operations are given in Fig. 1. In the `unlock` proof, note that the immediate postcondition of the "use atomic" is not stable, since it is possible for the environment to acquire the lock. For illustrative

$$
\begin{array}{l}
\{\,\mathsf{isLock}(\mathbf{x})\,\} \\
\{\,\exists s \in \{0,1\}.\,\mathbf{CAPLock}_r(\mathbf{x},s)\,\}
\end{array}
$$

The figure shows two side-by-side proof derivations:

Left derivation (abstract; quantify r):

$$
\{\,\mathsf{Locked}(\mathbf{x}) * \mathsf{Inv}\,\}
$$
$$
\{\,\mathbf{CAPLock}_r(\mathbf{x},1) * [\mathrm{K}]_r * \mathsf{Inv}\,\}
$$
$$
\langle\, \mathsf{L}(\mathbf{x}) * [\mathrm{K}]_r * \mathsf{Inv}\,\rangle
$$

(use atomic; frame: $[\mathrm{K}]_r * \mathsf{Inv}$)
$$
\langle\, \mathsf{L}(\mathbf{x})\,\rangle
$$
$$
\mathtt{unlock(x)}
$$
$$
\langle\, \mathsf{U}(\mathbf{x})\,\rangle
$$

$$
\langle\, \mathsf{U}(\mathbf{x}) * [\mathrm{K}]_r * \mathsf{Inv}\,\rangle
$$
$$
\{\,\mathbf{CAPLock}_r(\mathbf{x},0)\,\}
$$

// weaken to stabilise
$$
\{\,\exists s \in \{0,1\}.\,\mathbf{CAPLock}_r(\mathbf{x},s)\,\}
$$
$$
\{\,\mathsf{emp}\,\}
$$

Right derivation (abstract; quantify r):

$$
\{\,\exists s \in \{0,1\}.\,\mathbf{CAPLock}_r(\mathbf{x},s)\,\}
$$

(use atomic)
$$
\mathbb{W} s \in \{0,1\}.
$$
$$
\left\langle\,
\begin{array}{l}
(\mathsf{L}(\mathbf{x}) \wedge s = 1)\ \vee \\
(\mathsf{U}(\mathbf{x}) * [\mathrm{K}]_r * \mathsf{Inv} \wedge s = 0)
\end{array}
\,\right\rangle
$$
$$
\langle\, (\mathsf{L}(\mathbf{x}) \wedge s = 1) \vee (\mathsf{U}(\mathbf{x}) \wedge s = 0)\,\rangle
$$

(frame: $s = 0 \to [\mathrm{K}]_r * \mathsf{Inv}$, $1 :!: (s = 0)$)
$$
\mathbb{W} l \in \mathbb{B}.
$$
$$
\langle\, (\mathsf{L}(\mathbf{x}) \wedge \neg l) \vee (\mathsf{U}(\mathbf{x}) \wedge l)\,\rangle
$$
$$
\mathtt{lock(x)}
$$
$$
\langle\, \mathsf{L}(\mathbf{x}) \wedge l\,\rangle
$$

$$
\langle\, \mathsf{L}(\mathbf{x}) \wedge s = 0\,\rangle
$$

$$
\langle\, \mathsf{L}(\mathbf{x}) * [\mathrm{K}]_r * \mathsf{Inv}\,\rangle
$$
$$
\{\,\mathbf{CAPLock}_r(\mathbf{x},1) * [\mathrm{K}]_r * \mathsf{Inv}\,\}
$$
$$
\{\,\mathsf{isLock}(\mathbf{x}) * \mathsf{Locked}(\mathbf{x})\,\}
$$

Fig. 1. Derivation of CAP lock specifications

purposes, we weaken it minimally to a stable assertion, although it could be weakened to emp directly.

The lock proof uses the $\mathbb{W}$ quantifier in the premiss of the "use atomic" to account for the fact that, in the precondition, the lock could be in either state. The proof uses the frame rule, with a frame that is conditional on the state of the lock. It also uses the *substitution rule* to replace the boolean variable l, recording the state of the lock when the atomic operation happens, with the variable s, representing the state of **CAPLock** region. To derive the final postcondition, we use the fact that region assertions, since they refer to shared resource, are freely duplicable: *i.e.* $\mathbf{CAPLock}_r(\mathbf{x},1) \equiv \mathbf{CAPLock}_r(\mathbf{x},1) * \mathbf{CAPLock}_r(\mathbf{x},1)$. The axiom $\mathsf{isLock}(x) \Longleftrightarrow \mathsf{isLock}(x) * \mathsf{isLock}(x)$ similarly follows from the duplicability of region assertions. Finally, the axiom $\mathsf{Locked}(x) * \mathsf{Locked}(x) \Longrightarrow \mathsf{false}$ follows from the fact that $K \bullet K$ is undefined.

Note that neither of the bad specifications for $\mathtt{lock(x)}$ could be used in this derivation: the first because there would be no way to express that the frame $[\mathrm{K}]_r * \mathsf{Inv}$ is conditional on the state of the lock; and the second because we could not combine both cases in a single derivation.

Spin Lock Implementation. We consider a spin lock implementation of the atomic lock specification. The code is given in Fig. 2. We make use of three atomic operations that manipulate the heap. The operation $x := [y]$ reads the value of the heap position y to the variable x. The operation $[x] := y$ stores the value y in the heap position x. Finally, $\mathtt{CAS}(x, v, w)$ checks if the value at heap position x is v: if so, it replaces it with w and returns 1; if not, it returns 0.

```
function makeLock() {        function unlock(x) {        function lock(x) {
    v := alloc(1);               [x] := 0;                    do {
    [v] := 0;                }                                   b := CAS(x, 0, 1);
    return v;                                                 } while (b = 0);
}                                                         }
```

Fig. 2. Lock operations

To verify this implementation against the atomic specification, we must give a concrete interpretation of the abstract predicates. To do this, we introduce a new region type, **Lock**. There is only one non-empty guard for a **Lock** region, named G (for 'guard'), much as for **CAPLock**. There are also two states for a **Lock** region: 0 and 1, representing unlocked and locked respectively. A key difference from **CAPLock** is that transitions in both directions are guarded by G. The labelled transition system is as follows:

$$G \; : \; 0 \rightsquigarrow 1 \qquad\qquad G \; : \; 1 \rightsquigarrow 0$$

We also give an interpretation to each abstract state as follows:

$$I(\textbf{Lock}_a(x, 1)) \; \triangleq \; x \mapsto 1 \qquad\qquad I(\textbf{Lock}_a(x, 0)) \; \triangleq \; x \mapsto 0$$

We now define the interpretation of the predicates as follows:

$$\mathsf{L}(x) \quad \triangleq \quad \exists a.\, \textbf{Lock}_a(x, 1) * [G]_a$$
$$\mathsf{U}(x) \quad \triangleq \quad \exists a.\, \textbf{Lock}_a(x, 0) * [G]_a$$

The abstract predicate $\mathsf{L}(x)$ asserts there is a region with identifier a and the region is in state 1. It also states that there is a guard $[G]_a$ which will be used to update the region. $\mathsf{U}(x)$ analogously states that the region is in state 0.

To prove the implementations against our atomic specifications, we use TaDA's "make atomic" rule. A slightly simplified version of the rule is as follows:

$$\frac{\{(x, y) \mid x \in X, y \in Q(x)\} \subseteq \mathcal{T}_t(G)^* \qquad a : x \in X \rightsquigarrow Q(x) \vdash \left\{ \begin{array}{c} \exists x \in X.\, \mathsf{t}_a(x) \\ * a \mapsto \blacklozenge \end{array} \right\} \; \mathbb{C} \; \left\{ \begin{array}{c} \exists x \in X, y \in Q(x). \\ a \mapsto (x, y) \end{array} \right\}}{\vdash \forall x \in X.\, \langle \mathsf{t}_a(x) * [G]_a \rangle \; \mathbb{C} \; \langle \mathsf{t}_a(Q(x)) * [G]_a \rangle}$$

This rule establishes that $\mathbb{C}$ atomically updates region a, from some state $x \in X$ to some state $y \in Q(x)$. To do so, it requires the guard G for the region, which must permit the update according to the transition system — this is established by the first premiss.

The second premiss introduces two new notations. The first, $a : x \in X \rightsquigarrow Q(x)$, is called the *atomicity context*. The atomicity context records the abstract atomic action that is to be performed. The second, $a \mapsto -$, is the atomic tracking resource. The atomic tracking resource indicates whether the atomic update has occurred (the $a \mapsto \blacklozenge$ indicates it has not) and, if so, the state of the shared

$$\forall l \in \mathbb{B}.$$
$$\langle\, (\mathsf{L}(\mathbf{x}) \wedge \neg l) \vee (\mathsf{U}(\mathbf{x}) \wedge l)\,\rangle$$
$$\Big|\, \langle\, (\mathbf{Lock}_a(\mathbf{x},1) * [\mathsf{G}]_a \wedge \neg l) \vee (\mathbf{Lock}_a(\mathbf{x},0) * [\mathsf{G}]_a \wedge l)\,\rangle$$

abstract; quantity a | $y :=$ if l then 0 else 1 | make atomic | update region

$$\forall y \in \{0,1\}.$$
$$\langle\, \mathbf{Lock}_a(\mathbf{x},y) * [\mathsf{G}]_a\,\rangle$$
$$a : y \in \{0,1\} \rightsquigarrow 1 \wedge y = 0 \vdash$$
$$\{\, \exists y \in \{0,1\}.\mathbf{Lock}_a(\mathbf{x},y) * a \Mapsto \blacklozenge \,\}$$
$$\texttt{do}\ \{$$
$$\{\, \exists y \in \{0,1\}.\mathbf{Lock}_a(\mathbf{x},y) * a \Mapsto \blacklozenge \,\}$$
$$\forall n \in \{0,1\}.$$
$$\langle\, \mathbf{x} \mapsto n\,\rangle$$
$$\texttt{b} := \texttt{CAS}(\mathbf{x},0,1);$$
$$\left\langle\, \begin{array}{l} (\mathbf{x} \mapsto 1 \wedge n = 0 \wedge \texttt{b} = 1) \vee \\ (\mathbf{x} \mapsto n \wedge n \neq 0 \wedge \texttt{b} = 0) \end{array}\,\right\rangle$$
$$\left\{\, \begin{array}{l} \exists y \in \{0,1\}.\mathbf{Lock}_a(\mathbf{x},y) * \\ (a \Mapsto (0,1) \wedge \texttt{b} = 1 \vee a \Mapsto \blacklozenge \wedge \texttt{b} = 0) \end{array}\,\right\}$$
$$\}\ \texttt{while}\ (\texttt{b} = 0);$$
$$\{\, a \Mapsto (0,1) \wedge \texttt{b} = 1 \,\}$$
$$\langle\, \mathbf{Lock}_a(\mathbf{x},1) * [\mathsf{G}]_a \wedge y = 0\,\rangle$$
$$\langle\, \mathbf{Lock}_a(\mathbf{x},1) * [\mathsf{G}]_a \wedge l\,\rangle$$
$$\langle\, \mathsf{L}(\mathbf{x}) \wedge l\,\rangle$$

Fig. 3. Proof of the `lock(x)` operation

region immediately before and after (the $a \Mapsto (x,y)$). The resource $a \Mapsto \blacklozenge$ also plays two special roles that are normally filled by guards. Firstly, it limits the interference on region a: the environment may only update the state so long as it remains in the set X, as specified by the atomicity context. Secondly, it confers permission for the thread to update the region from state $x \in X$ to any state $y \in Q(x)$; in doing so, the thread also updates $a \Mapsto \blacklozenge$ to $a \Mapsto (x,y)$. This permission is expressed by the "update region" rule, and ensures that the atomic update only happens once.

In essence, the second premiss is capturing the notion of atomicity (with respect to the abstraction in the conclusion) and expressing it as a proof obligation. Specifically, the region must be in state x for some $x \in X$, which may be changed by the environment, until at some point the thread updates it to some $y \in Q(x)$. The atomic tracking resource bears witness to this.

The proof of the `lock(x)` implementation is given in Fig. 3. The proof first massages the specification into a form where we can apply the "make atomic" rule. The atomicity context allows the region a to be in either state, but insists that it must have been in the unlocked state when the atomic operation takes effect ($Q(1) = \emptyset$ while $Q(0) = \{1\}$). The "update region" rule conditionally performs the atomic action — transitioning the region from state 0 to 1, and recording this in the atomic tracking resource — if the atomic compare-and-swap operation succeeds. The proofs for `makeLock` and `unlock` are simpler, and may be found in the technical report [15].

Remark 1. It is possible to prove the following alternative implementation of
unlock(x) with the same atomic specification:

$$\vdash \langle \mathsf{L(x)} \rangle \ [\mathsf{x}] := 1; [\mathsf{x}] := 0 \ \langle \mathsf{U(x)} \rangle$$

The first write to x has no effect, since the specification asserts that the lock
must be locked initially. This code would clearly not be atomic in a different
context; it would not satisfy the specification $\vdash \langle \mathsf{L(x)} \vee \mathsf{U(x)} \rangle$ unlock(x) $\langle \mathsf{U(x)} \rangle$,
for example. Since the specification constrains the client, it allows flexibility in
the implementation.

2.2   Multiple Compare-And-Swap (MCAS)

Abstract Specification. We look at an interface over the heap which provides
atomic double-compare-and-swap (dcas) and triple-compare-and-swap (3cas)
operations, in addition to the basic read, write and compare-and-swap operations. It makes use of two abstract predicates: $\mathsf{MCL}(l)$ to represent an instance
of the MCAS library with address l; and $\mathsf{MCP}(l, x, v)$ to represent the "MCAS
heap cell" at address x with value v, protected by instance l. There is an abstract disjointness, as we can view each heap cell as disjoint from the others at
the abstract level, even if that is not the case with the implementation itself. The
specification for creating the interface, transferring memory cells to and from it
as well as manipulating it is given in Fig. 4.

Implementation. We give a straightforward coarse-grained implementation of
the MCAS specification. The operation makeMCL creates a lock which protects
updates to pointers under the control of the library. The other operations simply
acquire the lock, perform the appropriate reads and writes, and then release the
lock.

We interpret the abstract predicates using a single shared region, with type
name **MCAS**. The abstract states of the region are *partial heaps*, which represent
the part of the heap that is protected by the module. For instance, the abstract
state $x \mapsto v \bullet y \mapsto w$ indicates that heap cells x and y are under the protection
of the module, with logical values v and w respectively. Note that the physical
values at x and y need not be the same as their logical values, specifically when
the lock has been acquired and they are being modified.

For the **MCAS** region, there are five kinds of guard. The $\mathrm{OWN}(x)$ guard
confers ownership of the heap cell at address x under the control of the region.
This guard is used by all operations of the library that access the heap cell x. The
following implication ensures that there can only be one instance of $\mathrm{OWN}(x)$:

$$[\mathrm{OWN}(x)]_m * [\mathrm{OWN}(x)]_m \implies \mathsf{false}$$

We amalgamate the OWN guards for heap cells that are not currently under the
protection of the module into $\mathrm{OWNED}(X)$, where X is the set of all cells that
are protected. We have the following equivalence:

$$[\mathrm{OWNED}(X)]_m \iff [\mathrm{OWNED}(X \uplus \{x\})]_m * [\mathrm{OWN}(x)]_m$$

$$\vdash \{\text{emp}\}\ 1 := \texttt{makeMCL}()\ \{\text{MCL}(1)\}$$

$$\vdash \{\text{x} \mapsto v * \text{MCL}(1)\}\ \texttt{makeMCP}(1,\text{x})\ \{\text{MCP}(1,\text{x},v) * \text{MCL}(1)\}$$

$$\vdash \{\text{MCP}(1,\text{x},v)\}\ \texttt{unmakeMCP}(1,\text{x})\ \{\text{x} \mapsto v\}$$

$$\vdash \mathbb{V}v.\ \langle\text{MCP}(1,\text{x},v)\rangle\ \text{y} := \texttt{read}(1,\text{x})\ \langle\text{y} = v \wedge \text{MCP}(1,\text{x},v)\rangle$$

$$\vdash \mathbb{V}v.\ \langle\text{MCP}(1,\text{x},v)\rangle\ \texttt{write}(1,\text{x},\text{w})\ \langle\text{MCP}(1,\text{x},\text{w})\rangle$$

$$\vdash \mathbb{V}v.\ \left\langle\text{MCP}(1,\text{x},v)\right\rangle\ \text{b} := \texttt{cas}(1,\text{x},\text{v1},\text{v2})\ \left\langle\begin{matrix}\underline{\textbf{if}}\ v = \text{v1}\ \underline{\textbf{then}}\ \text{b} = 1 \wedge \text{MCP}(1,\text{x},v2) \\ \underline{\textbf{else}}\ \text{b} = 0 \wedge \text{MCP}(1,\text{x},v)\end{matrix}\right\rangle$$

$$\vdash \mathbb{V}v,w.\qquad \begin{matrix}\langle\text{MCP}(1,\text{x},v) * \text{MCP}(1,\text{y},w)\rangle \\ \text{b} := \texttt{dcas}(1,\text{x},\text{y},\text{v1},\text{w1},\text{v2},\text{w2}) \\ \underline{\textbf{if}}\ v = \text{v1} \wedge w = \text{w1} \\ \left\langle\begin{matrix}\underline{\textbf{then}}\ \text{b} = 1 \wedge \text{MCP}(1,\text{x},v2) * \text{MCP}(1,\text{y},w2) \\ \underline{\textbf{else}}\ \text{b} = 0 \wedge \text{MCP}(1,\text{x},v) * \text{MCP}(1,\text{y},w)\end{matrix}\right\rangle\end{matrix}$$

$$\vdash \mathbb{V}v,w,u.\qquad \begin{matrix}\langle\text{MCP}(1,\text{x},v) * \text{MCP}(1,\text{y},w) * \text{MCP}(1,\text{z},u)\rangle \\ \text{b} := \texttt{3cas}(1,\text{x},\text{y},\text{z},\text{v1},\text{w1},\text{u1},\text{v2},\text{w2},\text{u2}) \\ \underline{\textbf{if}}\ v = \text{v1} \wedge w = \text{w1} \wedge u = \text{u1} \\ \left\langle\begin{matrix}\underline{\textbf{then}}\ \text{b} = 1 \wedge \text{MCP}(1,\text{x},v2) * \text{MCP}(1,\text{y},w2) * \text{MCP}(1,\text{z},u2) \\ \underline{\textbf{else}}\ \text{b} = 0 \wedge \text{MCP}(1,\text{x},v) * \text{MCP}(1,\text{y},w) * \text{MCP}(1,\text{z},u)\end{matrix}\right\rangle\end{matrix}$$

$$\text{MCL}(l) \iff \text{MCL}(l) * \text{MCL}(l)$$

$$\text{MCP}(l,x,v) * \text{MCP}(l,x,w) \implies \textsf{false}$$

Fig. 4. The abstract specification for the MCAS module

Initially the set X will be empty. When we add an element $x \mapsto v$ to the region, we get a guard $\textsc{Own}(x)$ that allows us to manipulate the abstract state for that particular x. There can be only one $\textsc{Owned}$ guard:

$$[\textsc{Owned}(X)]_m * [\textsc{Owned}(Y)]_m \implies \textsf{false}$$

The remaining guards are effectively used as auxiliary state. When a thread acquires the lock, it removes some heap cells from the shared region in order to access them. The $\textsc{Locked}(h)$ guard will be used to record that the heap cells in h have been removed in this way. The thread that acquired the lock will have a corresponding $\textsc{Key}(h)$ guard. When it releases the lock, the two guards will be reunited inside the region to form the $\textsc{Unlocked}$ guard. This is expressed by the following equivalence:

$$[\textsc{Unlocked}]_m \iff [\textsc{Locked}(h)]_m * [\textsc{Key}(h)]_m$$

The transition system for the region is parametric in each heap cell. It allows anyone to add the resource $x \mapsto v$ to the region. (There is no need to guard this action, as the resource is unique and as such only one thread can do it for a particular value of x.) It allows the value of x to be updated using the guard $\text{OWN}(x)$. Finally, given the guard $\text{OWN}(x)$, $x \mapsto v$ can be removed from the region. We formally define the transition system as follows:

$$
\begin{aligned}
\mathbf{0} \quad &: \quad \forall h, x, v.\, h \rightsquigarrow x \mapsto v \bullet h \\
\text{OWN}(x) \quad &: \quad \forall h, v, w.\, x \mapsto v \bullet h \rightsquigarrow x \mapsto w \bullet h \\
\text{OWN}(x) \quad &: \quad \forall h, x, v.\, x \mapsto v \bullet h \rightsquigarrow h
\end{aligned}
$$

We define the interpretation of abstract states for the **MCAS** region:

$$
I(\mathbf{MCAS}_m(l, h)) \triangleq [\text{OWNED}(\text{dom}(h))]_m * (\mathsf{U}(l) * h * [\text{UNLOCKED}]_m \vee \\
\exists h_1, h_2.\, \mathsf{L}(l) * h_1 * [\text{LOCKED}(h_2)]_m \wedge h = h_1 \bullet h_2)
$$

Internally, the region may be in one of two states, indicated by the disjunction. Either the lock l is unlocked, and the heap cells corresponding to the abstract state of the region are actually in the region, as well as the UNLOCKED guard. Or the lock l is locked, and some portion h_1 of the abstract heap is in the region, while the remainder h_2 has been removed, together with the $\text{KEY}(h_2)$ guard, leaving behind the $\text{LOCKED}(h_2)$ guard. In both cases, the $\text{OWNED}(\text{dom}(h))$ guard belongs to the region, encapsulating the OWN guards for heap addresses that are not protected.

We now give an interpretation to the predicates as follows:

$$
\begin{aligned}
\text{MCL}(l) &\triangleq \exists m, h.\, \mathbf{MCAS}_m(l, h) \\
\text{MCP}(l, x, v) &\triangleq \exists m, h.\, \mathbf{MCAS}_m(l, x \mapsto v \bullet h) * [\text{OWN}(x)]_m
\end{aligned}
$$

The predicate $\text{MCL}(l)$ states the existence of the shared region, but makes no assumptions about its state. The predicate $\text{MCP}(l, x, v)$ states that there is x with value v, which it owns, and possibly other heap cells in the region.

We can now prove that the specification is satisfied by the implementation. For brevity, we only show the `dcas` command in Fig. 5. The other commands have similar proofs.

2.3 Resource Transfer

Consider an addition to the MCAS library: the `readTo` operation takes an MCAS heap cell and an ordinary heap cell and copies the value of the former into the latter. Such an operation could be implemented as follows:

```
function readTo(l, x, y) {  v := read(l, x);  [y] := v;  }
```

This implementation atomically reads the MCAS cell at x, then writes the value to the cell at y. The overall effect is non-atomic in the sense that a concurrent environment could update x and then witness y being updated to the old value

In the following, let $h_{v,w} = \mathtt{x} \mapsto v \bullet \mathtt{y} \mapsto w$ and $h_{\mathtt{v2},\mathtt{w2}} = \mathtt{x} \mapsto \mathtt{v2} \bullet \mathtt{y} \mapsto \mathtt{w2}$.

$\mathbb{A}v, w.$

$\langle\, \mathrm{MCP}(1, \mathtt{x}, v) * \mathrm{MCP}(1, \mathtt{y}, w) \,\rangle$

$\quad \Big\langle\, \exists h.\, \mathbf{MCAS}_m(1, h_{v,w} \bullet h) * [\mathrm{OWN}(\mathtt{x})]_m * [\mathrm{OWN}(\mathtt{y})]_m \,\Big\rangle$

$\quad\quad m : h_{v,w} \bullet h \leadsto \mathbf{if}\ v = \mathtt{v1} \wedge w = \mathtt{w1}\ \mathbf{then}\ h_{\mathtt{v2},\mathtt{w2}} \bullet h\ \mathbf{else}\ h_{v,w} \bullet h \vdash$

$\quad\quad \big\{\, \exists h, v, w.\, \mathbf{MCAS}_m(1, h_{v,w} \bullet h) * m \Rightarrow \blacklozenge \,\big\}$

$\quad\quad\quad \mathbb{A}h.$

$\quad\quad\quad \left\langle\, \left(\begin{array}{l} \mathrm{U}(1) * h * [\mathrm{UNLOCKED}]_m\ \vee \\ \mathrm{L}(1) * \exists h_1, h_2.\, h = (h_1 \bullet h_2) \wedge h_1 \\ \quad * [\mathrm{LOCKED}(h_2)]_m \end{array}\right) * [\mathrm{OWNED}(\mathrm{dom}(h))]_m * m \Rightarrow \blacklozenge \,\right\rangle$

$\quad\quad\quad \mathtt{lock(1);}$ // remove from the shared region the two heap cells

$\quad\quad\quad \left\langle\begin{array}{l} \exists h_1.\, \mathrm{L}(l) * h_1 * [\mathrm{LOCKED}(h_{v,w})]_m \wedge h = (h_1 \bullet h_{v,w}) * \\ {[\mathrm{OWNED}(\mathrm{dom}(h))]_m * m \Rightarrow \blacklozenge * [\mathrm{KEY}(h_{v,w})]_m * h_{v,w}} \end{array}\right\rangle$

$\quad\quad\quad \big\{\, \exists h.\, \mathbf{MCAS}_m(l, h_{v,w} \bullet h) * m \Rightarrow \blacklozenge * [\mathrm{KEY}(h_{v,w})]_m * h_{v,w} \,\big\}$

$\quad\quad\quad \mathtt{v := [x];}\quad \mathtt{w := [y];}$ // the environment cannot access either cell

$\quad\quad\quad \big\{\, \exists h.\, \mathbf{MCAS}_m(l, h_{v,w} \bullet h) * m \Rightarrow \blacklozenge * [\mathrm{KEY}(h_{v,w})]_m * h_{v,w} \wedge \mathtt{v} = v \wedge \mathtt{w} = w \,\big\}$

$\quad\quad\quad \mathtt{if\ (v = v1\ and\ w = w1)\ \{}$ // perform conditional update on the heap cells

$\quad\quad\quad\quad \mathtt{[x] := v2;}\quad \mathtt{[y] := w2;}\quad \mathtt{r := 1;}$

$\quad\quad\quad \mathtt{\}\ else\ \{}\quad \mathtt{r := 0;}\quad \mathtt{\}}$

$\quad\quad\quad \left\{\begin{array}{l} \exists h.\, \mathbf{MCAS}_m(l, h_{v,w} \bullet h) * m \Rightarrow \blacklozenge * [\mathrm{KEY}(h_{v,w})]_m \wedge \mathtt{v} = v \wedge \mathtt{w} = w * \\ \mathbf{if}\ v = \mathtt{v1} \wedge w = \mathtt{w1}\ \mathbf{then}\ \mathtt{r} = 1 \wedge h_{\mathtt{v2},\mathtt{w2}}\ \mathbf{else}\ \mathtt{r} = 0 \wedge h_{v,w} \end{array}\right\}$

$\quad\quad\quad \mathbb{A}h.$

$\quad\quad\quad \left\langle\begin{array}{l} \exists h_1.\, h = (h_1 \bullet h_{v,w}) \wedge \mathrm{L}(l) * [\mathrm{OWNED}(\mathrm{dom}(h))]_m * \\ {[\mathrm{LOCKED}(h_{v,w})]_m * [\mathrm{KEY}(h_{v,w})]_m * h_1 *} \\ \mathbf{if}\ v = \mathtt{v1} \wedge w = \mathtt{w1}\ \mathbf{then}\ \mathtt{r} = 1 \wedge h_{\mathtt{v2},\mathtt{w2}}\ \mathbf{else}\ \mathtt{r} = 0 \wedge h_{v,w} \end{array}\right\rangle$

$\quad\quad\quad \mathtt{unlock(1);}$ // put the heap cells in the shared region and update
$\quad\quad\quad\quad\quad\quad\quad$ // its abstract state if the heap cells were modified

$\quad\quad\quad \left\langle\begin{array}{l} \mathrm{U}(l) * [\mathrm{OWNED}(\mathrm{dom}(h))]_m * [\mathrm{UNLOCKED}]_m * \\ \mathbf{if}\ v = \mathtt{v1} \wedge w = \mathtt{w1}\ \mathbf{then}\ h[\mathtt{x} \mapsto \mathtt{v2}, \mathtt{y} \mapsto \mathtt{w2}]\ \mathbf{else}\ h \end{array}\right\rangle$

$\quad\quad\quad \left\{\begin{array}{l} \exists h.\, \mathbf{if}\ v = \mathtt{v1} \wedge w = \mathtt{w1}\ \mathbf{then}\ m \Rightarrow (h_{v,w} \bullet h, h_{\mathtt{v2},\mathtt{w2}} \bullet h) * \mathtt{r} = 1 \\ \mathbf{else}\ m \Rightarrow (h_{v,w} \bullet h, h_{v,w} \bullet h) * \mathtt{r} = 0 \end{array}\right\}$

$\quad\quad\quad \mathtt{return\ r;}$

$\quad\quad \left\langle\begin{array}{l} (\mathbf{if}\ v = \mathtt{v1} \wedge w = \mathtt{w1}\ \mathbf{then}\ \mathtt{ret} = 1 \wedge \exists h.\, \mathbf{MCAS}_m(l, h_{\mathtt{v2},\mathtt{w2}} \bullet h) \\ \mathbf{else}\ \mathtt{ret} = 0 \wedge \exists h.\, \mathbf{MCAS}_m(l, h_{v,w} \bullet h)) * [\mathrm{OWN}(\mathtt{x})]_m * [\mathrm{OWN}(\mathtt{y})]_m \end{array}\right\rangle$

$\left\langle\begin{array}{l} \mathbf{if}\ v = \mathtt{v1} \wedge w = \mathtt{w1}\ \mathbf{then}\ \mathtt{ret} = 1 \wedge \mathrm{MCP}(1, \mathtt{x}, \mathtt{v2}) * \mathrm{MCP}(1, \mathtt{y}, \mathtt{w2}) \\ \mathbf{else}\ \mathtt{ret} = 0 \wedge \mathrm{MCP}(1, \mathtt{x}, v) * \mathrm{MCP}(1, \mathtt{y}, w) \end{array}\right\rangle$

The left-margin labels read, from outer to inner: *abstract; quantify m*, *make atomic*, *open region*, *update region*.

Fig. 5. Proof of the `dcas` implementation

of x. However, if the environment's interaction is confined to the MCAS cell, the effect *is* atomic.

TaDA allows us to specify this kind of partial atomicity by splitting the pre- and postcondition of an atomic judgement into a *private* and a *public* part. The private part will contain resources that are particular to the thread — in this example, the heap cell at y. When the atomic triple is used to update a region (*e.g.* with the "use atomic" rule), these private resources cannot form part of the region's invariant. The public part will contain resources that can form part of a region's invariant — in this example, the MCAS cell at x.

The generalised form of our atomic judgements is:

$$\vdash \forall \mathbf{x} \in X. \langle p_p \,|\, p(\mathbf{x}) \rangle \; \mathbb{C} \;\; \exists \mathbf{y} \in Y. \langle q_p(\mathbf{x}, \mathbf{y}) \,|\, q(\mathbf{x}, \mathbf{y}) \rangle$$

Here, p_p is the private precondition, $p(\mathbf{x})$ is the public precondition, $q_p(\mathbf{x}, \mathbf{y})$ is the private postcondition, and $q(\mathbf{x}, \mathbf{y})$ is the public postcondition. The private precondition is independent of $\mathbf{x}$, since the environment can change $\mathbf{x}$. The two parts of the postcondition are linked by $\mathbf{y}$, which is chosen arbitrarily by the implementation when the atomic operation appears to take effect.

The `readTo` operation can be specified as follows:

$$\vdash \forall v, w. \langle \mathbf{y} \mapsto w \,|\, \mathsf{MCP}(1, \mathbf{x}, v) \rangle \;\; \mathtt{readTo}(1, \mathbf{x}, \mathbf{y}) \;\; \langle \mathbf{y} \mapsto v \,|\, \mathsf{MCP}(1, \mathbf{x}, v) \rangle$$

One way of understanding such specifications is in terms of ownership transfer between a client and a module, as in [8]: ownership of the private precondition is transferred from the client; ownership of the private postcondition is transferred to the client. In this example, the same resources (albeit modified) are transferred in and out, but this need not be the case in general. For instance, an operation could allocate a fresh location in which to store the retrieved value, which is then transferred to the client.

While it should be clear that this judgement generalises our original atomic judgement, it is revealing that it also generalises the non-atomic judgement. Indeed, $\vdash \{p\} \; \mathbb{C} \; \{q\}$ is equivalent to $\vdash \langle p \,|\, \mathsf{true} \rangle \; \mathbb{C} \; \langle q \,|\, \mathsf{true} \rangle$.

3   Logic

We give an overview of the key TaDA proof rules that deal with atomicity in Fig. 6. Here, we do not formally define the syntax and semantics of our assertions, although we describe how they are modelled in §5. These details are given in the technical report [15].

We implicitly require the pre- and postcondition assertions in our judgements to be *stable*: that is, they must account for any updates other threads could have sufficient resources to perform.

Until now, we have elided a detail of the proof system: region levels. Each judgement of TaDA includes a region level λ in the context. This level is simply a number that indicates that only regions below level λ may be opened in the derivation of the judgement. For this to be meaningful, each region is associated with a level (indicated as a superscript) and rules that open regions require that the level of the judgement is higher than the level of the region being opened. The purpose of the levels is to ensure that a region can never be opened twice in a single branch of the proof tree, which could unsoundly duplicate resources. The rules that open regions enforce this by requiring the level of the conclusion $(\lambda + 1)$ to be above the level of the region (λ), which is also the level of the premiss. For our examples, the level of each module's regions just needs to be greater than the levels of modules that it uses.

In all of our examples, the atomicity context describes an update to a single region. In the logic, there is no need to restrict in this way, and an atomicity

Frame rule

$$\frac{\lambda; \mathcal{A} \vdash \mathbb{W}x \in X. \langle p_p \,|\, p(x) \rangle \; \mathbb{C} \; \exists y \in Y. \langle q_p(x,y) \,|\, q(x,y) \rangle}{\lambda; \mathcal{A} \vdash \mathbb{W}x \in X. \langle r' * p_p \,|\, r(x) * p(x) \rangle \; \mathbb{C} \; \exists y \in Y. \langle r' * q_p(x,y) \,|\, r(x) * q(x,y) \rangle}$$

Substitution rule

$$\frac{\lambda; \mathcal{A} \vdash \mathbb{W}x \in X. \langle p_p \,|\, p(x) \rangle \; \mathbb{C} \; \exists y \in Y. \langle q_p(x,y) \,|\, q(x,y) \rangle \quad f : X' \to X}{\lambda; \mathcal{A} \vdash \mathbb{W}x' \in X'. \langle p_p \,|\, p(f(x')) \rangle \; \mathbb{C} \; \exists y \in Y. \langle q_p(f(x'),y) \,|\, q(f(x'),y) \rangle}$$

Atomicity weakening rule

$$\frac{\lambda; \mathcal{A} \vdash \mathbb{W}x \in X. \langle p_p \,|\, p' * p(x) \rangle \; \mathbb{C} \; \exists y \in Y. \langle q_p(x,y) \,|\, q'(x,y) * q(x,y) \rangle}{\lambda; \mathcal{A} \vdash \mathbb{W}x \in X. \langle p_p * p' \,|\, p(x) \rangle \; \mathbb{C} \; \exists y \in Y. \langle q_p(x,y) * q'(x,y) \,|\, q(x,y) \rangle}$$

Open region rule

$$\frac{\lambda; \mathcal{A} \vdash \mathbb{W}x \in X. \langle p_p \,|\, I(\mathbf{t}_a^\lambda(x)) * p(x) \rangle \; \mathbb{C} \; \exists y \in Y. \langle q_p(x,y) \,|\, I(\mathbf{t}_a^\lambda(x)) * q(x,y) \rangle}{\lambda + 1; \mathcal{A} \vdash \mathbb{W}x \in X. \langle p_p \,|\, \mathbf{t}_a^\lambda(x) * p(x) \rangle \; \mathbb{C} \; \exists y \in Y. \langle q_p(x,y) \,|\, \mathbf{t}_a^\lambda(x) * q(x,y) \rangle}$$

Use atomic rule

$$\frac{a \notin \mathcal{A} \quad \forall x \in X. (x, f(x)) \in \mathcal{T}_t(\mathsf{G})^* }{\lambda; \mathcal{A} \vdash \mathbb{W}x \in X. \langle p_p \,|\, I(\mathbf{t}_a^\lambda(x)) * p(x) * [\mathsf{G}]_a \rangle \; \mathbb{C} \; \exists y \in Y. \langle q_p(x,y) \,|\, I(\mathbf{t}_a^\lambda(f(x))) * q(x,y) \rangle}{\lambda + 1; \mathcal{A} \vdash \mathbb{W}x \in X. \langle p_p \,|\, \mathbf{t}_a^\lambda(x) * p(x) * [\mathsf{G}]_a \rangle \; \mathbb{C} \; \exists y \in Y. \langle q_p(x,y) \,|\, \mathbf{t}_a^\lambda(f(x)) * q(x,y) \rangle}$$

Update region rule

$$\lambda; \mathcal{A} \vdash \mathbb{W}x \in X. \left\langle p_p \,\middle|\, I(\mathbf{t}_a^\lambda(x)) * p(x) \right\rangle \; \mathbb{C} \; \exists y \in Y. \left\langle q_p(x,y) \,\middle|\, \begin{array}{c} I(\mathbf{t}_a^\lambda(Q(x))) * q_1(x,y) \\ \vee\, I(\mathbf{t}_a^\lambda(x)) * q_2(x,y) \end{array} \right\rangle$$

$$\overline{\lambda+1; a : x \in X \rightsquigarrow Q(x), \mathcal{A} \vdash \begin{array}{c} \mathbb{W}x \in X. \langle p_p \,|\, \mathbf{t}_a^\lambda(x) * p(x) * a \mapsto \blacklozenge \rangle \\ \mathbb{C} \\ \exists y \in Y. \left\langle q_p(x,y) \,\middle|\, \begin{array}{c} \exists z \in Q(x). \mathbf{t}_a^\lambda(z) * q_1(x,y) * a \mapsto (x,z) \\ \vee\, \mathbf{t}_a^\lambda(x) * q_2(x,y) * a \mapsto \blacklozenge \end{array} \right\rangle \end{array}}$$

Make atomic rule

$$\frac{a \notin \mathcal{A} \quad \{(x,y) \mid x \in X, y \in Q(x)\} \subseteq \mathcal{T}_t(\mathsf{G})^*}{\lambda'; a : x \in X \rightsquigarrow Q(x), \mathcal{A} \vdash \begin{array}{c} \{p_p * \exists x \in X. \mathbf{t}_a^\lambda(x) * a \mapsto \blacklozenge\} \\ \mathbb{C} \\ \{\exists x \in X, y \in Q(x). q_p(x,y) * a \mapsto (x,y)\} \end{array}}{\lambda'; \mathcal{A} \vdash \mathbb{W}x \in X. \langle p_p \,|\, \mathbf{t}_a^\lambda(x) * [\mathsf{G}]_a \rangle \; \mathbb{C} \; \exists y \in Q(x). \langle q_p(x,y) \,|\, \mathbf{t}_a^\lambda(y) * [\mathsf{G}]_a \rangle}$$

Fig. 6. Selected proof rules of TaDA

context $\mathcal{A}$ may describe updates to multiple regions (although only one update to each). Both atomic and non-atomic judgements may have atomicity contexts.

The *frame rule*, as in separation logic, allows us to add the same resources to the pre- and postcondition, which are untouched by the command. Our frame rule separately adds to both the private and public parts. Note that the frame for the public part may be parametrised by the $\mathbb{W}$-bound variable x. (We exploited this fact in deriving the CAP lock specification.)

The *substitution rule* allows us to change the domain of W-bound variables. A consequence of this rule is that we can instantiate W-variables much like universally quantified variables, simply by choosing X' to be a single-element set.

The *atomicity weakening rule* allows us to convert private state from the conclusion into public state in the premiss.

The next three rules allow us to access the content of a shared region by using an atomic command. With all of the rules, the update to the shared region must be atomic, so its interpretation is in the public part in the premiss. (The region is in the public part in the conclusion also, but may be moved by applying atomicity weakening.)

The *open region* rule allows us to access the contents of a shared region without updating its abstract state. The command may change the concrete state of the region, so long as the abstract state is preserved. This is exemplified by its use in the DCAS proof in Fig. 5, where concretely the lock becomes locked, but the abstract state of the **MCAS** region is not affected.

The *use atomic* rule allows us to update the abstract state of a shared region. To do so, it is necessary to have a guard for the region being updated, such that the change in state is permitted by this guard according to the transition system associated with the region. This rule takes a $\mathbb{C}$ which (abstractly) atomically updates the region a from some state $x \in X$ to the state $f(x)$. It requires the guard G for the region, which allows the update according to the transition system, as established by one of the premisses. Another premiss states that the command $\mathbb{C}$ performs the update described by the transition system of region a in an atomic way. This allows us to conclude that the region a is updated atomically by the command $\mathbb{C}$. Note that the command is not operating at the same level of abstraction as the region a. Instead it is working at a lower level of abstraction, which means that if it is atomic at that level it will also be atomic at the region a level.

The *update region* rule similarly allows us to update the abstract state of a shared region, but this time the authority comes from the atomicity context instead of a guard. In order to perform such an update, the atomic update to the region must not already have happened, indicated by $a \Mapsto \blacklozenge$ in the precondition of the conclusion. In the postcondition, there are two cases: either the appropriate update happened, or no update happened. If it did happen, the new state of the region is some $z \in Q(x)$, and both x and z are recorded in the atomicity tracking resource. If it did not, then both the region's abstract state and the atomicity tracking resource are unchanged. The premiss requires the command to make a corresponding update to the concrete state of the region. The atomicity context and tracking resource are not present in the premiss; their purpose is rather to record information about the atomic update that is performed for use further down the proof tree.

It is necessary for the update region rule to account for both the case where the update occurs and where it does not. One might expect that the case with no update could be dealt with by the open region rule, and the results combined using a disjunction rule. However, a general disjunction rule is not sound for atomic triples. (If we have $\langle p_1 \rangle \mathbb{C} \langle q \rangle$ and $\langle p_2 \rangle \mathbb{C} \langle q \rangle$, we may not have $\langle p_1 \vee p_2 \rangle \mathbb{C} \langle q \rangle$ since $\mathbb{C}$ might rely on the environment not changing between p_1 and p_2.) The proof of the atomic specification for the spin lock uses the conditional nature of the update region rule.

Finally, we revisit the *make atomic* rule, which elaborates on the version presented in §2.1. As before, a guard in the conclusion must permit the update in accordance with the transition system for the region. This is replaced in the premiss by the atomicity context and atomicity tracking resource, which tracks the occurrence of the update. One difference is the inclusion of the private state, which is effectively preserved between the premiss and the conclusion. A second difference is the ∃l-binding of the resulting state of the atomic update. This allows the private state to reflect the result of the update.

4   Case Study: Concurrent Deque

We show how to use TaDA to specify a double-ended queue (deque) and verify a fine-grained implementation. A deque has operations that allow elements to be inserted and removed from both ends of a list.

This example shows that TaDA can scale to multiple levels of abstraction: the deque uses MCAS, which uses the lock, which is based on primitive atomic heap operations. This proof development would not be possible with CAP, since atomicity is central to the abstractions at each level. It would also not be possible using traditional approaches to linearisability, since separation of resources between and within abstraction layers is also crucial.

4.1   Abstract Specification

We represent the deque state by the abstract predicate $\mathsf{Deque}(d, vs)$. It asserts that there is a deque at address d with list of elements vs. The $\mathtt{makeDeque}()$ operation creates an empty deque and returns its address. It has the following specification:

$$\lambda \vdash \{\mathsf{emp}\} \; \mathtt{d} := \mathtt{makeDeque}() \; \{\mathsf{Deque}(\mathtt{d}, [])\}$$

The operations $\mathtt{pushLeft}(\mathtt{d}, \mathtt{v})$ and $\mathtt{popLeft}(\mathtt{d})$ are specified to update the state of the deque atomically:

$$\lambda \vdash \mathbb{\forall} vs. \; \langle \mathsf{Deque}(\mathtt{d}, vs) \rangle \; \mathtt{pushLeft}(\mathtt{d}, \mathtt{v}) \; \langle \mathsf{Deque}(\mathtt{d}, \mathtt{v} : vs) \rangle$$

$$\lambda \vdash \mathbb{\forall} vs. \qquad\qquad \langle \mathsf{Deque}(\mathtt{d}, vs) \rangle$$
$$\mathtt{v} := \mathtt{popLeft}(\mathtt{d})$$
$$\left\langle \begin{array}{l} \underline{\text{if }} vs = [] \; \underline{\text{then }} \mathtt{v} = 0 \wedge \mathsf{Deque}(\mathtt{d}, vs) \\ \underline{\text{else }} vs = v : vs' \wedge \mathtt{v} = v \wedge \mathsf{Deque}(\mathtt{d}, vs') \end{array} \right\rangle$$

The $\mathtt{pushLeft}(\mathtt{d}, \mathtt{v})$ operation adds the value $\mathtt{v}$ to the left of the deque. The $\mathtt{popLeft}(\mathtt{d})$ operation tries to remove an element from the left end of the deque. However, if the deque is empty, then it returns 0 and does not change its state.

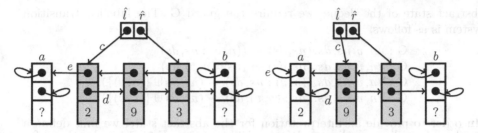

Fig. 7. Examples of a deque before and after performing `popLeft`, which uses `3cas` to updated pointers c, d and e

Otherwise, it removes the element at the left, updating the state of the deque, and returns the removed valued. The `pushRight` and `popRight` operations have analogous specifications, operating on the right end of the deque.

4.2 The "Snark" Linked-List Deque Implementation

We consider an implementation that represents the deque as a doubly-linked list of nodes, based on *Snark* [5]. An example of the shape of the data structure is shown in Fig. 7. Each node consists of a left-link pointer, a right-link pointer, and a value. There are two anchor variables, *left hat* and *right hat* ($\hat{l}$ and $\hat{r}$ in the figure), that generally point to the leftmost node and the rightmost node in the list, except when the deque is empty. When the deque is not empty, its leftmost node's left-link points to a so-called *dead* node — a node whose left- and right-links point to itself (e.g. node a in the figure). Symmetrically, the rightmost node's right-link points to a dead node. When the deque is empty, then the left hat and the right hat point to dead nodes.

We focus on the `popLeft` implementation. This implementation first reads the left hat value to a local variable. It then reads the left-link of the node referenced by that variable. If both values are the same, it means that the node is dead and the list might be empty. It is necessary to recheck the left hat to confirm, since the node might have died since the left hat was first read. If the deque is indeed empty, the operation returns 0; otherwise it is restarted. If the left node is not dead, it tries to atomically update the left hat to point to the node to its right, and, at the same time, update the left node to be dead. (This could fail, in which case the operation restarts.) An example of such update is shown in Fig. 7. In order to update three pointers atomically, the implementation makes use of the `3cas` command described in §2.2.

To verify the `popLeft`, we introduce a new region type, **Deque**. The region has two parameters, d standing for the deque address and L for the MCAS address. There is only one non-empty guard for the region, named G. We represent the abstract state by a tuple (ns, ds) where: ns is a list of pairs of node addresses and values, the values representing the elements stored in the deque; and ds is a set of pairs of nodes addresses and values that were part of the deque, but are now dead. We maintain the set of dead nodes to guarantee that after a node is removed from the deque, its value can still be read. In order to change the abstract state of the deque, we require the guard G. The labelled transition system is as follows:

$$G : \forall n, v, ns, ds. (ns, ds) \rightsquigarrow ((n, v) : ns, ds)$$
$$G : \forall n, v, ns, ds. (ns, ds) \rightsquigarrow (ns : (n, v), ds)$$
$$G : \forall n, v, ns, ds. ((n, v) : ns, ds) \rightsquigarrow (ns, ds \uplus \{(n, v)\})$$
$$G : \forall n, v, ns, ds. (ns : (n, v), ds) \rightsquigarrow (ns, ds \uplus \{(n, v)\})$$

In order to provide an interpretation for the abstract state, we first define a number of auxiliary predicates. We use field notation: $E.\texttt{field}$ is shorthand for $E + \texttt{offset}(\texttt{field})$. Here, $\texttt{offset}(\texttt{left}) = 0$, $\texttt{offset}(\texttt{right}) = 1$, and $\texttt{offset}(\texttt{value}) = \texttt{offset}(\texttt{mcl}) = 2$.

A node at address n in the deque will make use of the MCAS cells:

$$\mathsf{node}(L, n, l, r, v) \equiv \mathsf{MCP}(L, n.\texttt{left}, l) * \mathsf{MCP}(L, n.\texttt{right}, r) * n.\texttt{value} \mapsto v$$

Here l and r are the left- and right-link addresses. The L parameter is the address of the MCAS lock. A dead node is defined as:

$$\mathsf{dead}(L, n, v) \equiv \mathsf{node}(L, n, n, n, v)$$

We also define a predicate to stand for the doubly-linked list that contains all the elements in the list, (i.e. the shaded nodes in the figure).

$$\mathsf{dlseg}(L, l, r, n, m, ns) \equiv ns = [] \wedge l = m \wedge r = n \vee$$
$$\exists v, ns', p. \, ns = (l, v) : ns' \wedge \mathsf{node}(L, l, n, p, v) * \mathsf{dlseg}(L, p, r, l, m, ns')$$

We define a predicate to include the dead nodes (ds) as well as the doubly-linked list:

$$\mathsf{dls}(L, l, r, ns, ds) \equiv$$
$$\exists a, b. \, (a, -), (b, -) \in ds \wedge \mathsf{dlseg}(L, l, r, a, b, ns) * \underset{(n,v) \in ds}{\circledast} \mathsf{dead}(L, n, v)$$

Note that there must be at least one dead node in ds.

Our last auxiliary predicate to represent the whole deque: the double linked list; the anchors left hat and right hat; and the reference to the MCAS interface.

$$\mathsf{deque}(d, L, ns, ds) \equiv \exists l, r. \, \mathsf{dls}(L, l, r, ns, ds) *$$
$$\mathsf{MCP}(L, d.\texttt{left}, l) * \mathsf{MCP}(L, d.\texttt{right}, r) * d.\texttt{mcl} \mapsto L * \mathsf{MCL}(L)$$

We now define the interpretation of abstract states as follows:

$$I(\mathbf{Deque}_a(d, L, ns, ds)) \triangleq \mathsf{deque}(d, L, ns, ds)$$

We define the interpretation of the Deque predicate as follows:

$$\mathsf{Deque}(d, vs) \triangleq \exists a, L, ns, ds. \, \mathbf{Deque}_a(d, L, ns, ds) * [G]_a \wedge vs = \mathsf{snds}(ns)$$

where $\mathsf{snds}(ns)$ maps the second projection over the list of pairs ns.

To prove the implementation against our atomic specifications, we use the "make atomic" rule again. We show the proof of the popLeft operation in Fig. 8. The remaining proofs are given in the technical report [15].

$\forall vs.$
$\langle\, \mathsf{Deque}(\mathsf{d}, vs)\,\rangle$

$\Big|\quad \langle\, \mathbf{Deque}_a(\mathsf{d}, L, ns, ds) * [G]_a \wedge vs = \mathsf{snds}(ns)\,\rangle$

$\qquad a : (ns, ds) \rightsquigarrow \underline{\text{if }} ns = [] \underline{\text{ then }} (ns, ds) \underline{\text{ else }} (ns', (n,v) : ds) \wedge ns = (n,v) : ns' \vdash$

$\qquad \big\{\, \exists ns, ds.\, \mathbf{Deque}_a(\mathsf{d}, L, ns, ds) * a \mapsto \blacklozenge \,\big\}$

$\qquad \mathtt{L} := [\mathtt{d.mcl}];$

$\qquad \mathtt{while\ (true)\ \{}$

$\qquad\quad \big\{\, \exists ns, ds.\, \mathbf{Deque}_a(\mathsf{d}, L, ns, ds) * a \mapsto \blacklozenge \wedge \mathtt{L} = L\,\big\}$

$\qquad\quad \mathtt{lh} := \mathtt{read(L, l.left)}; \mathtt{lhR} := \mathtt{read(L, lh.right)}; \mathtt{lhL} := \mathtt{read(L, lh.left)};$

$\qquad\quad \left\{\begin{array}{l} \exists ns, ds.\, \mathbf{Deque}_a(\mathsf{d}, L, ns, ds) * a \mapsto \blacklozenge \wedge \mathtt{L} = L \wedge \\ \underline{\text{if }} \mathtt{lh} = \mathtt{lhL} \underline{\text{ then }} (\mathtt{lh}, -) \in ds \\ \quad \underline{\text{else }} \{(\mathtt{lh}, -), (\mathtt{lhL}, -), (\mathtt{lhR}, -)\} \in ns \,+\!\!+\, ds \end{array}\right\}$

$\qquad\quad \mathtt{if\ (lhL = lh)\ \{} \;\; // \text{ left hat seems dead}$

$\qquad\qquad \big\{\, \exists ns, ds.\, \mathbf{Deque}_a(\mathsf{d}, L, ns, ds) * a \mapsto \blacklozenge \wedge \mathtt{L} = L \wedge (\mathtt{lhL}, -) \in ds\,\big\}$

$\qquad\qquad \begin{array}{l} \forall ns, ds. \\ \langle\, \mathsf{deque}(\mathsf{d}, L, ns, ds) \wedge \mathtt{L} = L \wedge (\mathtt{lhL}, -) \in ds\,\rangle \\ \mathtt{lh2} := \mathtt{read(L, d.left)}; \\ \left\langle\, \begin{array}{l} \mathsf{deque}(\mathsf{d}, L, ns, ds) \wedge \mathtt{L} = L \wedge \\ (\mathtt{lh2} = \mathtt{lhL} \to ns = []) \end{array}\,\right\rangle \end{array}$

$\qquad\qquad \left\{\begin{array}{l} \exists ns, ds.\, \mathbf{Deque}_a(\mathsf{d}, L, ns, ds) \wedge \mathtt{L} = L \wedge \\ \underline{\text{if }} \mathtt{lh2} = \mathtt{lhL} \underline{\text{ then }} a \mapsto ([], ds), ([], ds) \underline{\text{ else }} a \mapsto \blacklozenge \end{array}\right\}$

$\qquad\qquad \mathtt{if\ (lh2 = lhL)\ \{} \;\; // \text{ left hat confirmed dead}$

$\qquad\qquad\quad \mathtt{return\ 0;}$

$\qquad\qquad\quad \big\{\, \exists ds.\, \mathtt{ret} = 0 * a \mapsto ([], ds), ([], ds)\,\big\}$

$\qquad\qquad \mathtt{\}} \;\; // \text{ left hat not dead --- try again}$

$\qquad\quad \mathtt{\}\ else\ \{}$

$\qquad\qquad \left\{\begin{array}{l} \exists ns, ds.\, \mathbf{Deque}_a(\mathsf{d}, L, ns, ds) * a \mapsto \blacklozenge \wedge \mathtt{L} = L \wedge \\ \{(\mathtt{lh}, -), (\mathtt{lhL}, -), (\mathtt{lhR}, -)\} \in ns \,+\!\!+\, ds \end{array}\right\}$

$\qquad\qquad \begin{array}{l} \forall ns, ds. \\ \left\langle\, \begin{array}{l} \mathsf{deque}(\mathsf{d}, L, ns, ds) \wedge \mathtt{L} = L \wedge \\ \{(\mathtt{lh}, -), (\mathtt{lhL}, -), (\mathtt{lhR}, -)\} \in ns \,+\!\!+\, ds \end{array}\,\right\rangle \\ \mathtt{b} := \mathtt{3cas(L, d.left, lh.right, lh.left, lh, lhR, lhL, lhR, lh, lh)}; \\ \left\langle\, \begin{array}{l} \exists ns', v.\, \underline{\text{if }} \mathtt{b} = 1 \underline{\text{ then }} \left(\begin{array}{l} \mathsf{deque}(\mathsf{d}, L, ns', (\mathtt{lh}, v) : ds) \wedge \\ \mathtt{L} = L \wedge (\mathtt{lh}, v) \in ds \wedge ns = (\mathtt{lh}, v) : ns' \end{array}\right) \\ \quad \underline{\text{else }} \mathsf{deque}(\mathsf{d}, L, ns, ds) \wedge \mathtt{L} = L \end{array}\,\right\rangle \end{array}$

$\qquad\qquad \left\{\begin{array}{l} \exists ns, ds, v.\, \underline{\text{if }} \mathtt{b} = 1 \underline{\text{ then }} \left(\begin{array}{l} a \mapsto ((\mathtt{lh}, v) : ns, ds), (ns, (\mathtt{lh}, v) : ds)) \\ \quad \wedge \mathtt{L} = L \wedge (\mathtt{lh}, v) \in ds \end{array}\right) \\ \quad \underline{\text{else }} \mathbf{Deque}_a(\mathsf{d}, L, ns, ds) * a \mapsto \blacklozenge \wedge \mathtt{L} = L \end{array}\right\}$

$\qquad\qquad \mathtt{if\ (b = 1)\ \{}$

$\qquad\qquad\quad \mathtt{v} := [\mathtt{lh.value}]; \mathtt{return\ v;}$

$\qquad\qquad\quad \big\{\, \exists ns, ds.\, \mathtt{ret} = \mathtt{v} * a \mapsto ((\mathtt{lh}, v) : ns, ds), (ns, (\mathtt{lh}, v) : ds)\,\big\}$

$\qquad\quad \mathtt{\}\ \}\ \}}$

$\quad \left\langle\, \begin{array}{l} \underline{\text{if }} vs = [] \underline{\text{ then }} \mathtt{ret} = 0 * \mathbf{Deque}_a(\mathsf{d}, L, ns, ds) * [G]_a \\ \quad \underline{\text{else }} \left(\begin{array}{l} \exists ns', v.\, ns = (n, v) : ns' \wedge \mathtt{ret} = v * \\ \mathbf{Deque}_a(\mathsf{d}, L, ns', (n,v) : ds) * [G]_a \wedge vs' = \mathsf{snds}(ns') \end{array}\right) \end{array}\,\right\rangle$

$\langle\, \begin{array}{l} \underline{\text{if }} vs = [] \underline{\text{ then }} \mathtt{ret} = 0 * \mathsf{Deque}(\mathsf{d}, vs) \\ \quad \underline{\text{else }} \exists vs', v.\, vs = v : vs' \wedge \mathtt{ret} = v * \mathsf{Deque}(\mathsf{d}, vs') \end{array}\,\rangle$

Fig. 8. Proof of the popLeft implementation

(left margin annotations:) abstract; quantify a, L, ns, ds — make atomic — update region — update region

5   Semantics

We briefly describe the model for TaDA and the intuition behind the soundness proof. Details can be found in the technical report [15].

Assertions are modelled as sets of *worlds*. A world includes (partial) information about the concrete heap state, as well as the instrumentation used by the proof system. This instrumentation consists of the type and state of each shared region, abstract predicate resources, and guard resources for each region. Depending on the atomicity context, it may also include atomicity tracking resources. Composition between worlds (which is lifted to sets to interpret $*$ in assertions) requires that they agree on the type and state of all regions, and that their resources (including heap resources) must be disjoint. Worlds are subject to interference, which is represented by a relation. This interference relation expresses the conditions under which the environment may modify the shared regions, which is dependent on guards and atomicity tracking resources. Assertions must be stable — closed under the interference relation — and are consequently *views* in the sense of the Views Framework [2], which we use as the basis for our soundness proof.

The judgements of TaDA are interpreted with a semantic judgement:

$$\lambda; \mathcal{A} \vDash \mathbb{\forall}\mathbf{x} \in X. \langle p_p | p(\mathbf{x}) \rangle \; \mathbb{C} \; \mathbb{\exists}\mathbf{y} \in Y. \langle q_p(\mathbf{x}, \mathbf{y}) | q(\mathbf{x}, \mathbf{y}) \rangle$$

The meaning of this judgement is expressed in terms of the steps that $\mathbb{C}$ may take in the operational semantics. Each step may either leave $p(\mathbf{x})$ intact, or update it to $q(\mathbf{x}, \mathbf{y})$ for some value of $\mathbf{y}$. Simultaneously, it may update its private state p_p arbitrarily, so long as any changes to shared regions are permitted by guards that it owns, or atomic tracking resources. Once the update from $p(\mathbf{x})$ to $q(\mathbf{x}, \mathbf{y})$ occurs, the thread gives up access to $q(\mathbf{x}, \mathbf{y})$. From then, it can only update the private state, and must ensure that $q_p(\mathbf{x}, \mathbf{y})$ holds when it terminates.

The key result for establishing soundness is the following:

Theorem 1. *If* $\lambda; \mathcal{A} \vdash \mathbb{\forall}\mathbf{x} \in X. \langle p_p | p(\mathbf{x}) \rangle \; \mathbb{C} \; \mathbb{\exists}\mathbf{y} \in Y. \langle q_p(\mathbf{x}, \mathbf{y}) | q(\mathbf{x}, \mathbf{y}) \rangle$ *is provable in the logic, then* $\lambda; \mathcal{A} \vDash \mathbb{\forall}\mathbf{x} \in X. \langle p_p | p(\mathbf{x}) \rangle \; \mathbb{C} \; \mathbb{\exists}\mathbf{y} \in Y. \langle q_p(\mathbf{x}, \mathbf{y}) | q(\mathbf{x}, \mathbf{y}) \rangle$ *holds semantically.*

The proof of soundness demonstrates that the semantic judgement obeys all of the syntactic proof rules. For the novel proof rules, such as "make atomic", the proof essentially establishes a simulation. Each step of the judgement in the conclusion of the rule is shown to correspond to a step in the judgement of the premiss. The technical report [15] gives the details.

6   Related Work

TaDA inherits from a family of logics deriving from concurrent separation logic [12]: RGSep [20], Deny-Guarantee [4], CAP [3], Higher-Order CAP (HO-CAP) [17] and Impredicative CAP (iCAP) [16]. In particular, it makes use of dynamic *shared regions* with capability resources (called *guards* in TaDA) that determine how the regions may be updated. Following iCAP, TaDA eschews the use of boxed assertions to describe the state of shared regions and instead represents regions by *abstract states*. The protocol for updating the region is specified as a transition system on these abstract states, labelled by guards. This use of transition systems to describe protocols derives from previous work by Dreyer *et al.* [6], and also appears in Turon *et al.* [19] as "local life stories".

By treating the abstract state-space of a region as a separation algebra, it is possible to localise updates on it, as in the MCAS example (§2.2). Such locality is in the spirit of local life stories [19], and can be seen as an instance of Ley-Wild and Nanevski's "subjective auxiliary state" [11].

While HOCAP and iCAP do not support abstract atomic specifications, they support an approach to atomicity introduced by Jacobs and Piessens [10] that achieves similar effects. In their work, operations may be parametrised by an update to auxiliary state that is performed when the abstract atomic operation appears to take effect. This update is performed atomically by the implementation, and can therefore involve shared regions. This approach is inherently higher-order, which has the disadvantage of leading to complex specifications. TaDA takes a first-order approach, leading to simpler specifications.

There has been extensive work understanding and generalising linearisability, especially in light of work on separation logic. Vafeiadis [20] has combined the ownership given by his RGSep reasoning with linearisability. Gotsman and Yang [8] have generalised linearisability to include ownership transfer of memory between a client and a module, which is also supported by our approach. Filipovic *et al.* [7] have demonstrated that linearisability can be viewed as a particular proof technique for contextual refinement. Turon *et al.* [18] have introduced CaReSL, a logic that combines contextual refinement and Hoare-style reasoning to prove higher-order concurrent programs. Like linearisability, contextual refinement requires a whole-module approach.

7   Conclusions

We have introduced a program logic, TaDA, which includes novel *atomic triples* for specifying abstract atomicity, as well as separation-style Hoare triples for specifying abstract disjointness. We have specified and verified several example modules: an atomic lock module, which cannot be fully specified using linearisability; an atomic MCAS module implemented using our lock module, a classic linearisability example which cannot be done using concurrency abstract predicates; and a double-ended queue module implemented using MCAS. With the combination of abstract atomicity and abstract disjointness that TaDA provides, we can specify and verify modules with atomic and non-atomic operations, posisbly at different levels of abstraction. Moreover, we can easily extend modules with new operations, and build new modules on top of existing ones.

7.1   Future Work

Helping. In some concurrent modules, one thread's abstract atomic action may actually be effected by another thread — a phenomenon termed *helping*. As presented, TaDA does not support helping, since each abstract atomic operation of a thread can be traced down to a concrete atomic action of that thread at which it takes effect. By transforming the atomic tracking component into a transferrable resource, it should be possible to support helping. However, this will require a different semantic model.

Higher-order. iCAP [16] makes use of impredicative protocols for shared regions — protocols that can reference arbitary protocols. This gives it the expressive power to handle higher-order programs and reentrancy. It would be interesting to combine TaDA with iCAP, which may be possible by proving the rules of TaDA in the metatheory of iCAP. Iterators on concurrent collections, which can have subtle specifications, could benefit from the expressive power of such a logic.

Weak Memory. Burkhardt *et al.* [1] have extended the concept of linearisability to the total store order (TSO) memory model. TaDA already has some potential to specify weak behaviours. For instance, the following three specifications for a read operation are increasingly weak:

$$\vdash \mathbb{A}v.\, \langle \mathbf{x} \mapsto v \rangle \; \mathbf{y} := [\mathbf{x}] \; \langle \mathbf{x} \mapsto v \wedge \mathbf{y} = v \rangle$$
$$\vdash \langle \mathbf{x} \mapsto v \rangle \; \mathbf{y} := [\mathbf{x}] \; \langle \mathbf{x} \mapsto v \wedge \mathbf{y} = v \rangle$$
$$\vdash \{ \mathbf{x} \mapsto v \} \; \mathbf{y} := [\mathbf{x}] \; \{ \mathbf{x} \mapsto v \wedge \mathbf{y} = v \}$$

The first of these specifications gives the usual atomic semantics; the second prohibits concurrent updates; the third prohibits any concurrent access. An interesting research direction would be to investigate extensions of TaDA that can specify and verify programs that make use of weak memory models such as TSO.

Acknowledgements. We thank Lars Birkedal, Daiva Naudžiūnienė, Matthew Parkinson, Julian Sutherland, Kasper Svendsen, Aaron Turon, Adam Wright, and the anonymous referees for discussions and useful feedback. This research was supported by an EPSRC Programme Grants EP/H008373/1 (all authors) and EP/K008528/1 (Dinsdale-Young, Gardner), and the ModuRes Sapere Aude Advanced Grant from The Danish Council for Independent Research for the Natural Sciences (Dinsdale-Young).

References

1. Burckhardt, S., Gotsman, A., Musuvathi, M., Yang, H.: Concurrent Library Correctness on the TSO Memory Model. In: Seidl, H. (ed.) Programming Languages and Systems. LNCS, vol. 7211, pp. 87–107. Springer, Heidelberg (2012)

2. Dinsdale-Young, T., Birkedal, L., Gardner, P., Parkinson, M., Yang, H.: Views: compositional reasoning for concurrent programs. In: POPL, pp. 287–300 (2013)
3. Dinsdale-Young, T., Dodds, M., Gardner, P., Parkinson, M.J., Vafeiadis, V.: Concurrent abstract predicates. In: D'Hondt, T. (ed.) ECOOP 2010. LNCS, vol. 6183, pp. 504–528. Springer, Heidelberg (2010)
4. Dodds, M., Feng, X., Parkinson, M., Vafeiadis, V.: Deny-Guarantee Reasoning. In: Castagna, G. (ed.) ESOP 2009. LNCS, vol. 5502, pp. 363–377. Springer, Heidelberg (2009)
5. Doherty, S., Detlefs, D.L., Groves, L., Flood, C.H., Luchangco, V., Martin, P.A., Moir, M., Shavit, N., Steele, J. G.L.: DCAS is Not a Silver Bullet for Nonblocking Algorithm Design. In: SPAA, pp. 216–224 (2004)
6. Dreyer, D., Neis, G., Birkedal, L.: The impact of higher-order state and control effects on local relational reasoning. In: ICFP, pp. 143–156 (2010)
7. Filipović, I., O'Hearn, P., Rinetzky, N., Yang, H.: Abstraction for Concurrent Objects. In: Castagna, G. (ed.) ESOP 2009. LNCS, vol. 5502, pp. 252–266. Springer, Heidelberg (2009)
8. Gotsman, A., Yang, H.: Linearizability with ownership transfer. In: Koutny, M., Ulidowski, I. (eds.) CONCUR 2012. LNCS, vol. 7454, pp. 256–271. Springer, Heidelberg (2012)
9. Herlihy, M.P., Wing, J.M.: Linearizability: a correctness condition for concurrent objects. ACM Trans. Program. Lang. Syst. 12(3), 463–492 (1990)
10. Jacobs, B., Piessens, F.: Expressive modular fine-grained concurrency specification. In: POPL, pp. 271–282 (2011)
11. Ley-Wild, R., Nanevski, A.: Subjective auxiliary state for coarse-grained concurrency. In: POPL, pp. 561–574 (2013)
12. O'Hearn, P.W.: Resources, concurrency, and local reasoning. Theor. Comput. Sci. 375(1-3), 271–307 (2007)
13. Parkinson, M., Bierman, G.: Separation logic and abstraction. In: POPL, pp. 247–258 (2005)
14. da Rocha Pinto, P., Dinsdale-Young, T., Dodds, M., Gardner, P., Wheelhouse, M.: A simple abstraction for complex concurrent indexes. In: OOPSLA, pp. 845–864 (2011)
15. da Rocha Pinto, P., Dinsdale-Young, T., Gardner, P.: TaDA: A Logic for Time and Data Abstraction. Tech. rep., Imperial College London (2014)
16. Svendsen, K., Birkedal, L.: Impredicative Concurrent Abstract Predicates. In: Shao, Z. (ed.) ESOP 2014 (ETAPS). LNCS, vol. 8410, pp. 149–168. Springer, Heidelberg (2014)
17. Svendsen, K., Birkedal, L., Parkinson, M.: Modular reasoning about separation of concurrent data structures. In: Felleisen, M., Gardner, P. (eds.) Programming Languages and Systems. LNCS, vol. 7792, pp. 169–188. Springer, Heidelberg (2013)
18. Turon, A., Dreyer, D., Birkedal, L.: Unifying refinement and hoare-style reasoning in a logic for higher-order concurrency. In: ICFP, pp. 377–390 (2013)
19. Turon, A.J., Thamsborg, J., Ahmed, A., Birkedal, L., Dreyer, D.: Logical relations for fine-grained concurrency. In: POPL, pp. 343–356 (2013)
20. Vafeiadis, V.: Modular fine-grained concurrency verification. Ph.D. thesis, University of Cambridge, Computer Laboratory (2008)
21. Vafeiadis, V., Herlihy, M., Hoare, T., Shapiro, M.: Proving Correctness of Highly-concurrent Linearisable Objects. In: PPoPP, pp. 129–136 (2006)

Infrastructure-Free Logging and Replay of Concurrent Execution on Multiple Cores

Kyu Hyung Lee, Dohyeong Kim, and Xiangyu Zhang

Department of Computer Science, Purdue University, West Lafayette, IN, 47907, USA
{kyuhlee,kim1051,xyzhang}@cs.purdue.edu

Abstract. We develop a logging and replay technique for real concurrent execution on multiple cores. Our technique directly works on binaries and does not require any hardware or complex software infrastructure support. We focus on minimizing logging overhead as it only logs a subset of system calls and thread spawns. Replay is on a single core. During replay, our technique first tries to follow only the event order in the log. However, due to schedule differences, replay may fail. An exploration process is then triggered to search for a schedule that allows the replay to make progress. Exploration is performed within a window preceding the point of replay failure. During exploration, our technique first tries to reorder synchronized blocks. If that does not lead to progress, it further reorders shared variable accesses. The exploration is facilitated by a sophisticated caching mechanism. Our experiments on real world programs and real workload show that the proposed technique has very low logging overhead (2.6% on average) and fast schedule reconstruction.

Keywords: Software reliability, Debugging, Recording and Replay.

1 Introduction

Logging and replay of concurrent execution in multi-core environment is very meaningful for debugging runtime failures and also very challenging. Much of the complexity stems from non-determinism that arises from the true parallel evaluation; the non-deterministic fine-grained interleavings are often difficult to precisely reproduce when replaying an erroneous execution. The challenge is exacerbated in the context of non-trivial production runs, in which a program may run for a while before a non-deterministic failure occurs and complex hardware/software infrastructure support for logging and replay is often not available.

Even though there have been a lot of recent efforts in testing, reproducing, diagnosing, and repairing concurrency bugs, existing techniques fall short in logging and replay of real concurrent production execution. Concurrency testing techniques [20,24,28] perform various guided searches of possible thread interleavings. They often assume that the failure inducing inputs are provided so that they can repetitively execute the program on these inputs. They do not log or replay the I/O interactions of the original failing execution. However, for production runs, inputs are often very complex, involving network packets, signals, and relying on specific file system state, which requires logging.

R. Jones (Ed.): ECOOP 2014, LNCS 8586, pp. 232–256, 2014.

Another line of work is to record the order of instructions that access shared state, when they are executed in parallel on different cores. However the entailed instruction-level monitoring [5,8,31,21,19,33,11] is expensive and often requires hardware or complex software infrastructure support, limiting its applicability.

PRES [25] is a technique that uses dynamic binary instrumentation framework called PIN [18] to log different levels of runtime information of a failing run, such as system calls, synchronizations, and even basic blocks. It then tries to reproduce the failure on top of PIN using such information. If it fails, it switches to performing bounded search of shared memory access schedule, supported by the log. However, the need of infrastructure support such as PIN makes it difficult to be used for production runs and causes high logging overhead. We have also found that the bounded search of shared memory access schedule could be very expensive for long runs due to the large search space.

In this paper, we aim to develop a logging and replay technique for execution on multiple cores, serving both software users and developers. It does not require any extended hardware or complex software infrastructure, but rather operates directly on compiled binaries. It features a very low logging overhead as it does not try to log the precise non-deterministic access level interleavings. Replay is a cost-effective search process that produces a deterministic schedule leading to the failure. The produced schedule is for a single core, to allow easy application of follow-up heavy-weight analysis (e.g. slicing [1]) to the failing execution, as most such analysis are for single core execution. *Users* can easily apply our logging component to production runs of deployed software. Logs can be submitted to *developers* for remote reproduction, saving the trouble of manually crafting the failure inducing inputs. *Users* can also choose to reproduce the schedule on their side before submitting a bug report, which would substantially lower the burden of developers. It is very helpful during software development as well since it can be used for in-house testing due to its low system requirement and low overhead.

In our technique, we log minimal information to replay an execution such as non-deterministic system calls, signals and thread spawns in the multi-core logging phase. In the replay phase, we combine I/O replay with schedule exploration to replay concurrency failures on a single core. We leverage the observation by PRES [25] that a lot of non-determinism in a concurrent execution is intentional and thus harmless. It is hence not necessary to faithfully reproduce such non-determinism. Instead,we use the I/O replay log as the validation of an *acceptable* schedule that may be different from the original schedule and yet induces the same failure. The intuition is that if the schedule becomes so different from the original schedule, the program state would differ as well so that variables may have different values and different control flows may be taken. As a result, the replay log becomes invalid, e.g., an event is expected by the replay but not present in the log or an event has different arguments from those recorded in the log. If the replay fails to make progress, we start a process that explores different sub-schedules *within a window* close to the point where the replay fails. We have two layers of exploration, one at the synchronized block level and the other at the fine-grained memory access level. Any new sub-schedule leading to some progress in replay is admitted to the final schedule. If both explorations cannot find a valid schedule in the current window, we continue to explore preceding windows until we make progress in the replay. We also observe that for long production runs, replay often fails to make progress at similar situations. We hence use caching to speedup exploration. The process is iterative and terminates when the whole log, including the original failure, is successfully replayed.

Our contributions are highlighted as follows.

- We develop a logging and replay technique that does not require infrastructure/kernel/compiler support. This makes it more applicable than existing techniques. We also precisely formulate the technique.
- Our logging techinique focuses on minimizing overhead. We only log a subset of system calls, signals and thread spawns. They constitute the minimal necessary set of events to replay an execution. The logging overhead is negligible, 2.6% on average and 3.84% on the worst case.
- We study the characteristics of replaying real concurrent executions of two large subjects with different levels of thread contention and reveal insights about the various reasons why replay fails, which provide critical guidance for our design.
- We propose the notion of window based on the happens-before relation of events. When replay fails to make progress, we perform two layers of schedule exploration only within the window. This strategy allows us substantially reduce the search space.
- We have developed a caching mechanism that can avoid redundant schedule exploration, which is very common in practice.
- We perform thorough evaluation of the technique on a set of real world benchmark programs. The results show that our schedule reconstruction algorithm is very effective and efficient. It is 10.55 times faster than the PRES replay algorithm. We have also demonstrated scalability using a 7-days long real workload.

2   Motivation

In this section, we present the overview of our technique through an example and observations from replaying two large scale multi-threaded applications.

2.1   Motivating Example

Consider the example in Fig. 1. The code snippet is executed by two threads. The example simulates a real bug in the logging module of the *Apache* webserver. Apache logs remote requests for administration purpose. We extend the buggy logic to better explain our technique. Upon a request, the program increases the global request count at line 4. The access is protected by a lock. For every 16 requests (as suggested by line 6), an administrative message is generated and supposed to be put in the log eventually. The message is first stored in a thread local buffer and later copied to a global log buffer; the length of the local buffer *len* is hence updated at line 8. Lines 11-14 copy the local buffer to the global buffer. In particular, it first tests if appending the local buffer would overflow the global buffer (with size 1024) at line 11. Variable *buf_len* is the current length of the global buffer. If not, it copies the message and increases the global counter.

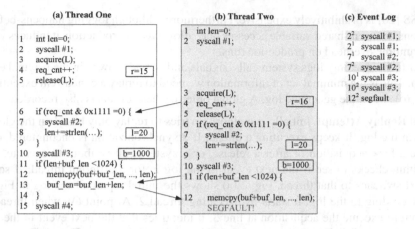

Fig. 1. A segfault caused by concurrent execution on two cores. Different background colors denote different threads. Important variable values are shown on the right of the threads with r, l, b denoting *req_cnt*, *len*, and *buf_len* respectively. Symbol 3^2 denotes line 3 in thread 2.

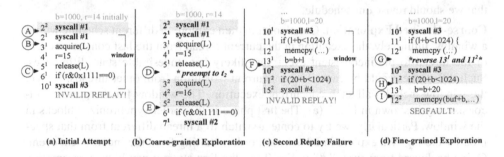

Fig. 2. The different phases of our single core replay scheme

Fig. 1 shows a concurrent execution on two cores. The vertical direction is the time line. Observe that statements may be executed at the same time to simulate real concurrency. A few important happens-before are explicitly noted by arrows. We also show the important variable values on the right. Note that both threads observe *req_cnt* to be 16 at line 6. Hence, both threads have a local message of size 20 generated. The local buffer size *len* is 20 in both threads. Because the current global buffer size is 1000, the test at line 11 passes in both threads, allowing copying the messages to the global buffer. However, the global buffer size is increased in thread one before the memory copy in thread two, resulting in copying 20 bytes at the location of 1020 and thus a segfault.

Observe that the failure cannot be easily replayed as it requires two data races, one is about variable *req_cnt* at lines 4 and 6 and the other is about *buf_len* at 11 and 13. If we simply re-execute the program on a single core and assumes thread one executes before thread 2, the message is not even generated in thread one as *req_cnt=15*. As a result, the execution terminates normally. Two preemptions are needed to mutate it to the failing run. However, in production runs, a program usually operates for a long time before a failure. Performing a 2-preemption schedule exploration using techniques like

CHESS [20] is prohibitively expensive. Furthermore, although logging happens-before relations between shared variable accesses may allow easy reproduction, it induces very high runtime overhead on production runs.

Our technique only logs system calls, signals and thread spawns in the original execution. This is the minimal set of information we need to replay a concurrent execution. Fig. 1 (c) shows the generated log. A global order of these events is also recorded.

Initial Replay Attempt. Initially, our algorithm tries to replay only based on the global order in the log. It keeps executing a thread. If a synchronization is encountered, e.g. before a lock acquisition or after a release, or a system call is about to execute, the algorithm checks to see if the next event in the log is for a different thread. If so, it context switches to that thread. Fig. 2 (a) shows the initial replay of the log in Fig. 1 (c). According to the log, it starts by executing thread 2. At point Ⓐ, when thread 2 is about to execute the acquisition at line 3, it identifies that the next event in the log belongs to thread 1. Hence, it context switches to thread 1. Points Ⓑ and Ⓒ are also synchronization points, but no switches are needed. At the end, the replay encounters *syscall #3* in thread one while the log has *syscall #2* as the next event. The root cause is that schedule differences cause a different control flow path. The inconsistency indicates that we should revise our schedule.

Coarse-Grained Exploration. Our algorithm then explores a different schedule within a window. Intuitively, the execution in the current thread from the last consistent event of the thread to the inconsistent event very likely has undesirable state differences. Such differences could be caused by concurrent execution from other threads. Hence, the window includes all such concurrent execution. The window for the previous inconsistency is shown in Fig. 2 (a). The first phase is to reorder synchronized blocks in the window. Particularly, we try to context-switch to a thread different from that specified by the log. We explore in a backward order, starting from the inconsistent event. Going backward from *syscall #3* in Fig. 2 (a), the first attempt would be a preemption at point Ⓒ. It results in an execution shown in (b). Note that although the execution is preempted to thread 2 at Ⓓ, it goes back to thread 1 at Ⓔ to respect the event order. As a result, *syscall #2* is correctly encountered. Hence, the preemption is admitted as part of the final schedule.

However, the replay later fails another validity check at the segfault event, as shown by Fig. 2 (c). That is, thread 2 is about to execute *syscall #4* at line 15 but the log indicates a *segfault* event. The root cause is that following the default replay strategy, thread 1 is able to execute lines 10-13 without being interleaved. As a result, the second data race critical to the failure does not occur such that line 11 in thread 2 takes the false branch. The window is determined as shown in the figure (more details about window identification will be disclosed in Section 4). Observe that there are no synchronizations in the window. We hence resort to the fine-grained access level schedule exploration.

Fine-Grained Exploration. In this phase, we detect all data races only within the window, and try to reverse the order of the two accesses in a race. The search is also backward. In the window in (c), the race closest to the inconsistent event is the write of buf_len at 13^1 (i.e. line 13 in thread 1) and the read at 11^2. Hence, our schedule is enhanced to reverse the order of these two accesses, leading to the execution in (d). Observe that right before the write, at Ⓖ, the algorithm switches to thread 2. Right after the read, at Ⓗ, it switches back to thread 1. At Ⓘ, when thread 1 is about to execute *syscall #4*, it observes that the next event is in thread 2. It switches to thread 2. The segfault occurs at the memory copy statement. The highlighted events and the preemptions in (b) and (d) constitute the final schedule that allows a valid replay and generates the original failure. Note that if both coarse-grained and fine-grained explorations cannot find a schedule to make progress in the current window, we continue to explore preceding windows until we find a valid schedule.

2.2 Observations

In order to motivate the idea, we perform a study on two large scale multi-threaded applications, namely `Apache` and `MySQL`, to understand the characteristics of replaying real concurrency. We execute them on a quad core machine and log the system calls. For `MySQL`, we use the input generated by the work-load emulation client, `mysqlslap`, which is provided with the program. For `Apache`, we use `httperf` to generate 1,000 concurrent requests. We create 4 worker threads for both subjects. Although these are benign executions, replaying them only with the system call logs is nonetheless challenging. Each time when replay fails to make progress due to deadlocks or unmatched events, called a replay failure, we manually study its root cause, leveraging our implementation of CHESS [20] in an interactive way. In particular, the implementation allows us to search backward from the execution point where replay fails to look for a number of preemptions at synchronizations or shared memory accesses that allow us to get through the failure point. For each replay failure, we manually try different configurations of the search (e.g. the distance to search backward and the number of preemptions) until we succeed. We also simulate different levels of thread contention by executing a configurable CPU-intensive threaded program in the background. We have studied three setups: (1) no contention – the subject program owns 100% of the CPU; (2) low – 66%; and (3) high – 50%.

Table 1. Replay failures

Applications	Observed replay failures	Root Cause	CPU contention			Need Fine-grained?	Within Window?	Distance (root cause→fail)	
			None	Low	High			# of instructions	# of calls
Apache-1	Unmatch(write,poll)	Control flow	2	3	9	No	Yes	4884	185
Apache-2	Unmatch(poll,write)	Control flow	8	6	17	No	Yes	94	8
Apache-3	Unmatch(argument)	Value	0	1	2	Yes	Yes	1044	15
Apache-4	Unmatch(gettimeofday, read)	Control flow	4	5	14	No	Yes	720	8
Apache-5	Unmatch(read,gettimeofday)	Control flow	1	8	6	No	Yes	834	10
Apache-6	Deadlock	User lock	1	1	2	No	Yes	21	3
Apache-7	Deadlock	Sync order	2	7	11	No	Yes	106	6
Apache-8	Unmatch(segfault,write)	Value	0	0	1	Yes	Yes	631	8
MySQL-1	Unmatch(sigtimedwait,alarm)	Control flow	21	39	47	No	Yes	2032	52
MySQL-2	Unmatch(sigtimedwait,time)	Control flow	2	7	11	No	Yes	33	3
MySQL-3	Unmatch(time,sigtimedwait)	Control flow	12	28	34	No	Yes	84	2
MySQL-4	Unmatch(time,open)	Control flow	4	10	9	No	Yes	952	31
MySQL-5	Unmatch(open,time)	Control flow	9	36	24	No	Yes	15	4
MySQL-6	Unmatch(select,time)	Control flow	13	17	15	No	Yes	412	19
MySQL-7	Deadlock	Control flow	3	3	3	No	Yes	102	11
MySQL-8	Deadlock	User lock	31	45	42	No	Yes	39	3
MySQL-9	Deadlock	Sync order	4	3	5	No	Yes	56	2
MySQL-10	Deadlock	Control flow	0	0	4	No	Yes	36	3

238   K.H. Lee, D. Kim, and X. Zhang

Table 1 presents our observations. Column 2 presents the unique replay failures we have observed and column 3 shows the root cause of each failure. Columns 4-6 present the number of occurrences of each replay failure at different contention levels. Column 7 shows if we need fine-grained exploration to get through the failure. Column 8 shows if we could find a correct schedule in the exploration window (defined in Section 4). Columns 9 and 10 present the distance from the root cause (i.e. the farthest preemption needed) to the replay failure point, measured by the number of instructions and function invocations.

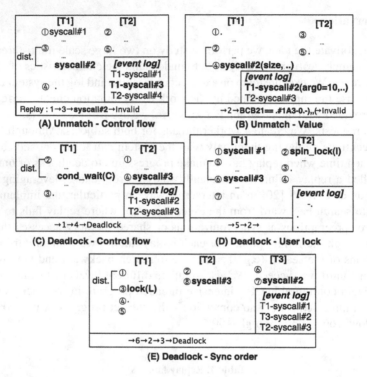

Fig. 3. The root causes of the observed replay failures

First of all, we observe much fewer replay failures than expected, even with the highest contention level. It seems to indicate that the non-determinism caused by real concurrency does not substantially affect system level behavior. We observe two kinds of replay failure symptoms: *unmatch* and *deadlock*. The former means that replay can not make progress because the event in the log does not match the expectation. In the table, we also present the mismatched events observed. These symptoms are caused by five possible reasons as demonstrated by the samples in Fig. 3. Circled numbers show the order of execution. The replay order is presented on the bottom of each example. Note that the replay is guided by the system call log in these examples. Upon each pthread synchronization or system call, the replay tries to switch to the thread indicated by the next event in the log. In (A), the replay fails at syscall#2 due to control flow difference. This is the most common type. In (B), the system call arguments do not match between the log and the replayed execution at ④. In (C), T1 is waiting for a conditional variable *cond_wait*, which did not happen in the original run. The replay then switches to T2, which cannot replay syscall#3 at ④ without T1 replaying syscall#2, and hence deadlock. In (D), the *spin_lock* function is a program specific lock invisible to our analysis. When T1 is about to execute ⑥, the replay context switches to T2 to respect the log order, but T2 cannot acquire the lock at ②, and hence deadlock. In (E), T1 is waiting for the conditional variable at ①, and then the replay context switches to T3 (hinted by the log order). T3 acquires lock L at ⑥ then it context switches to T2 before ⑦ because T2 is the only available thread at this point, again instructed by the log. Now T2 sends signal to T1 and it context switches to T1 at ⑧. However the mutex is already held by T3 and thus deadlock.

We also observe the following:

- Replay often fails during *normal* execution before it reaches the faulty point.
- Replay fails more often with higher contention.
- Replay tends to fail at the same failure repeatedly.
- Fine-grained exploration is rarely needed.
- Searching within the exploration window is sufficient for all cases we have seen.
- The distance between the root cause of replay failure and the symptom tends to be short.
- We have further observed that the repetition of replay failure is not caused by the re-occurrences of the same input. They are due to nondeterminism of low level shared data structures (e.g. *table* structures in MySQL, *buffered_log* in Apache) that have little to do with input values. In other words, we believe the repetitive behavior will always manifest, regardless of the input. This is supported by our experiment in Section 7.

3 Language and Semantics

To facilitate discussion, we introduce a kernel language. The syntax of the language is presented in Fig. 4. A method can be spawned as a thread. We model devices and I/O with **read**() and **write**(). Failures are modeled as assertion violations. Variables may be accessed by multiple threads.

KERNEL-LANGUAGE $\mathcal{L}$

Program $P ::= \overline{m()\{s\}};$	
Dev $d ::=$ **stdin** $\mid$ **stdout** $\mid f$	
Expr $e ::= x^\ell \mid c \mid e_1$ **binop** $e_2 \mid$ **read**$^\ell(d)$	
Stmt $s ::= x :=^\ell e \mid$ **write**$^\ell(d,e) \mid s_1;s_2 \mid$ **spawn**$^\ell m() \mid$	
acquire$^\ell(k) \mid$ **release**$^\ell(k) \mid$ **skip** $\mid$ **assert**$^\ell(e) \mid$ **fail**	

Method m, Var x, File f, Lock k $\in$ *Identifier   Constant c* $\in Z$

Fig. 4. Language Syntax

$$
\begin{array}{lll}
Store & \sigma: & Var \to Z \\
IOStore & \iota: & Dev \to \overline{Z} \\
LockState\ \mathcal{K}: & & Lock \to Z^+ \cup \{\bot\} \\
Log & \mathcal{L} ::= \overline{\alpha} \\
LogEntry & \alpha ::= & READ\langle i,t,d,\ell,c\rangle \mid WRITE\langle i,t,d,\ell,c\rangle \mid \\
& & SPAWN\langle i,t,\ell\rangle \mid FAIL\langle i,t,\ell\rangle \\
LogEntryId\ i \in Z^+ & & ThreadId\ t \in Z^+
\end{array}
$$

Fig. 5. Definitions

3.1 Logging Semantics

Compared to other execution artifacts, logging I/O interactions with the environment is necessary as they cannot be constructed by post-mortem analysis. Hence, we log system calls with global timestamps.

Fig. 5 presents definitions for the logging semantics. The device store ι denotes the state of device, which is a mapping from a device to a sequence of constant values. The lock state $\mathcal{K}$ is a mapping from a lock to a thread id or a special value $\bot$, denoting the owner of the lock, or its availability for acquisition, respectively. The evaluation generates a log $\mathcal{L}$, which is a sequence of events. In the semantics, we model the read, write, thread spawn, and assertion failure events. In our real implementation, we log most system calls, thread spawns, and all exceptions such as segfaults. Note that synchronizations or shared variable accesses are not logged in order to achieve the lowest possible logging overhead.

Each log entry consists of a global id i serving as a timestamp, the thread id t, and a label ℓ indicating the program point at which the event happened. For reads and writes, the value being read or written is also logged. Logging read values is to avoid accessing the device during replay. Logging write values is to validate a replay.

The logging semantics are presented in Fig. 6. Expression evaluation is of the form $\boxed{\sigma,\iota,\mathcal{L}: e \xrightarrow{e}_t \iota',\mathcal{L}',e'}$, with σ the store, ι the device store, $\mathcal{L}$ the log, and e the expression. The evaluation is carried out in thread t. Devices are modeled as streams. In particular, one value is read at a time from the head of a stream; and a value can be written to the tail of the stream. More I/O complexity is omitted to simplify the formal discussion. Our implementation supports most system calls and signals. In the evaluation of a read expression, a constant value c is removed from the head of the stream; a read event is appended to the log. Local statement evaluation evaluates program statements in a thread, with the form $\boxed{\sigma,\iota,\mathcal{K},\mathcal{L}: s \xrightarrow{s}_t \sigma',\iota',\mathcal{K}',\mathcal{L}',s'}$ with $\mathcal{K}$ the lock state and s the statement. For a write statement, it appends the value c to the end of the stream and a write event to the log. For a lock acquisition, if the lock is available or being held by the current thread, it updates the lock state and allows evaluation to proceed. Note that the lack of an evaluation rule when the lock is held by other threads means that the evaluation of the current thread cannot proceed. The global evaluation will pick another thread to continue. For a lock release, the state of the lock becomes available, which may allow some previously blocked thread to proceed. For an assertion statement, if the assertion fails, a log entry is appended and the whole evaluation terminates (through the **fail** statement). Otherwise, it allows the evaluation to proceed, without adding a log entry.

$$E ::= E;s \mid [\cdot]_s \mid x := [\cdot]_e \mid \mathbf{write}(d, [\cdot]_e) \mid \mathbf{assert}([\cdot]_e) \mid [\cdot]_e \text{ } \mathbf{binop} \text{ } e \mid c \text{ } \mathbf{binop} \text{ } [\cdot]_e$$

EXPRESSION RULES $\boxed{\sigma, \iota, \mathcal{L} : e \xrightarrow{e}_t \iota', \mathcal{L}', e'}$ parameterized on the current thread id t

$$\sigma, \iota, \mathcal{L} : x \xrightarrow{e}_t \iota, \mathcal{L}, \sigma(x) \qquad \sigma, \iota, \mathcal{L} : c_1 \text{ } \mathbf{binop} \text{ } c_2 \xrightarrow{e}_t \iota, \mathcal{L}, c_3 \quad \text{where } c_3 = c_1 \text{ } \mathbf{binop} \text{ } c_2$$

$$\sigma, \iota, \mathcal{L} : \mathbf{read}^\ell(d) \xrightarrow{e}_t \iota[d \mapsto \chi], \mathcal{L} \cdot READ \langle |\mathcal{L}|, t, d, \ell, c \rangle, c \quad \text{where } \iota(d) = c \cdot \chi$$

LOCAL STATEMENT RULES $\boxed{\sigma, \iota, \mathcal{K}, \mathcal{L} : s \xrightarrow{s}_t \sigma', \iota', \mathcal{K}', \mathcal{L}', s'}$ parameterized on thread id t.

$$\sigma, \iota, \mathcal{K}, \mathcal{L} : x := ^\ell c \xrightarrow{s}_t \sigma[x \mapsto c], \iota, \mathcal{K}, \mathcal{L}, \mathbf{skip}$$

$$\sigma, \iota, \mathcal{K}, \mathcal{L} : \mathbf{write}^\ell(d, c) \xrightarrow{s}_t \sigma, \iota[d \mapsto \iota(d) \cdot c], \mathcal{K}, \mathcal{L} \cdot WRITE \langle |\mathcal{L}|, t, d, \ell, c \rangle, \mathbf{skip}$$

$$\sigma, \iota, \mathcal{K}, \mathcal{L} : \mathbf{skip}; s \xrightarrow{s}_t \sigma, \iota, \mathcal{K}, \mathcal{L}, s$$

$$\sigma, \iota, \mathcal{K}, \mathcal{L} : \mathbf{acquire}^\ell(k) \xrightarrow{s}_t \sigma, \iota, \mathcal{K}[k \mapsto t], \mathcal{L}, \mathbf{skip} \quad \text{if } \mathcal{K}(k) = \bot \lor \mathcal{K}(k) = t$$

$$\sigma, \iota, \mathcal{K}, \mathcal{L} : \mathbf{release}^\ell(k) \xrightarrow{s}_t \sigma, \iota, \mathcal{K}[k \mapsto \bot], \mathcal{L}, \mathbf{skip}$$

$$\sigma, \iota, \mathcal{K}, \mathcal{L} : \mathbf{assert}^\ell(c) \xrightarrow{s}_t \sigma, \iota, \mathcal{K}, \mathcal{L} \cdot FAIL \langle |\mathcal{L}|, t, \ell \rangle, \mathbf{fail} \quad \text{if } c = 0$$

$$\sigma, \iota, \mathcal{K}, \mathcal{L} : \mathbf{assert}^\ell(c) \xrightarrow{s}_t \sigma, \iota, \mathcal{K}, \mathcal{L}, \mathbf{skip} \quad \text{if } c \neq 0$$

GLOBAL RULES $\boxed{\sigma, \iota, \mathcal{K}, \mathcal{L}, (s_1, ..., s_n) \longrightarrow \sigma', \iota', \mathcal{K}', \mathcal{L}', (s'_1, ..., s'_n)}$

$$\frac{\sigma, \iota, \mathcal{K}, \mathcal{L} : s \xrightarrow{s}_t \sigma', \iota', \mathcal{K}', \mathcal{L}', s'}{\sigma, \iota, \mathcal{K}, \mathcal{L}, (s_1, ..., s_{(t-1)}, E[s]_s, s_{(t+1)}, ..., s_n) \longrightarrow \sigma', \iota', \mathcal{K}', \mathcal{L}', (s_1, ..., s_{(t-1)}, E[s']_s, s_{(t+1)}, ..., s_n)}$$
[STMT-ANY-THRD]

$$\frac{\mathcal{L}' = \mathcal{L} \cdot SPAWN \langle |\mathcal{L}|, t, \ell \rangle \qquad m()\{s_\Delta\} \in P}{\sigma, \iota, \mathcal{K}, \mathcal{L}, (s_1, ..., s_{(t-1)}, E[\mathbf{spawn}^\ell m()]_s, s_{(t+1)}, ..., s_n) \longrightarrow \sigma, \iota, \mathcal{K}, \mathcal{L}', (s_1, ..., s_{(t-1)}, E[\mathbf{skip}]_s, s_{(t+1)}, ..., s_n, s_\Delta)}$$
[SPAWN]

$$\frac{\sigma, \iota, \mathcal{L} : e \xrightarrow{e}_t \iota', \mathcal{L}', c}{\sigma, \iota, \mathcal{K}, \mathcal{L}, (s_1, ..., s_{(t-1)}, E[e]_e, s_{(t+1)}, ..., s_n) \longrightarrow \sigma, \iota', \mathcal{K}, \mathcal{L}', (s_1, ..., s_{(t-1)}, E[c]_e, s_{(t+1)}, ..., s_n)}$$
[EXPR-ANY-THRD]

Fig. 6. Logging Semantics

Global rules $\boxed{\sigma, \iota, \mathcal{K}, \mathcal{L}, (s_1, ..., s_n) \longrightarrow \sigma', \iota', \mathcal{K}', \mathcal{L}', (s'_1, ..., s'_n)}$, denote the evaluation of n threads with each thread i executing statement s_i. Each step corresponds to a change in a single thread i, so $\forall j \neq i, s_j = s'_j$. The choice of which thread advances at any given point is *non-deterministic*, modeling concurrent execution on multiple cores. Terminated threads are left in the list with the **skip** statement. The whole evaluation terminates normally if all threads terminate normally. Rule [SPAWN] spawns a method as a thread, by expanding the list of threads.

In our implementation, each thread has its own log file to avoid contentions on a single log file. The log entry id remains global.

3.2 Replay Semantics

Replay is driven by a log and a schedule. It is deterministic, modeling execution on a single core. Our replay strategy is to evaluate the same thread as much as possible, unless it is indicated by the replay log or the schedule that a context switch should be performed. Initially, the schedule is empty. Replay is carried out following only the replay log. If such basic replay does not succeed, an exploration process is triggered to generate a schedule that can advance more during replay, until eventually all the events in the replay log, including the failure event, are correctly replayed.

The replay log serves the following three purposes. (1) The global timestamps specify a global order. Replay must follow the same order. (2) The values stored in the read events are used as inputs to drive the replay execution, avoiding accessing the devices. (3) The log is also used as a validation of the replayed execution.

Replay is facilitated by a schedule generated by the schedule exploration process to provide an additional harness. It specifies a set of preemptions that are at synchronization primitives. We will extend it to include preemptions at shared variable accesses in Section 4.3. The syntax of a schedule is presented in Fig. 7. It is a sequence of synchronization points. An entry $sync\langle n,t \rangle$ denotes that switching to thread t upon the nth synchronization operation.

ADDITIONAL LANGUAGE SYNTAX

$Preempt \quad \pi ::= pevnt \mid psync$

$DynChk \quad \omega ::= chkEvnt(\ell) \mid chkWrt(\ell,e) \mid chkAssrt(\ell,e)$

$Expr \quad e ::= ... \mid pevnt?\ \mathbf{read}^\ell(d)\ \mathbf{req.}\ chkEvnt(\ell)$

$Stmt \quad s ::= ... \mid \mathbf{invalid\_replay} \mid$

$\qquad\qquad pevnt?\ \mathbf{write}^\ell(d,e)\ \mathbf{req.}\ chkWrt(\ell,e) \mid$

$\qquad\qquad pevnt?\ \mathbf{spawn}^\ell\ m()\ \mathbf{req.}\ chkEvnt(\ell) \mid$

$\qquad\qquad psync?\ \mathbf{acquire}^\ell(k) \mid \mathbf{release}^\ell(k)\ psync? \mid$

$\qquad\qquad pevnt?\ \mathbf{assert}^\ell(e)\ \mathbf{req.}\ chkAssrt(\ell,e)$

ADDITIONAL DEFINITIONS FOR EVALUATION

$Schedule \quad S ::= sync\langle n,t \rangle$

$InstCnt \quad n \in \ Z^+$

Fig. 7. Definitions for Replay Semantics

New definitions relevant to the replay semantics are presented in Fig. 7. Preemption π denotes a preemption test, which determines whether a preemption should be performed, following the schedule or the log order. There are two kinds of preemption tests for syscalls (*pevnt*) and synchronizations (*psync*), respectively. Dynamic check ω denotes the runtime checks performed to validate a replay. There are three kinds of dynamic checks: checking a write event (*chkWrt*), an assertion failure (*chkAssrt*), and other events (*chkEvnt*).

The syntax of kernel language is extended. Statements and expressions that could produce events in the logging phase are preceded with preemption tests and followed by checks. Additionally, a preemption test precedes each lock acquisition and follows each lock release. Given a program in the original language in Fig.4, one can consider the corresponding program in the extended language is automatically generated.

We also introduce a special counter variable *sync_cnt* to record the number of synchronizations that have been evaluated. We use $\sigma[sync\_cnt \uparrow_c]$ to denote increasing the counter.

The replay rules are presented in Fig. 8. The evaluation order is given on the top. Observe that a preemption preceding an expression/statement is evaluated before the expression/statement, suggesting that the evaluation may switch to a different thread before evaluating the expression/statement. A check following an expression/statement

---

$E ::= \ldots \mid [\cdot]_\pi\, e \mid e\,[\cdot]_\omega \mid [\cdot]_\pi\, s \mid s\,[\cdot]_\omega \mid [\cdot]_s\, \pi? \mid \mathbf{skip}\,[\cdot]_\pi \mid chkWrt(\ell,[\cdot]_e) \mid chkAssrt(\ell,[\cdot]_e)$

PREEMPTION RULES $\boxed{\sigma,S,L,t:\ \pi \xrightarrow{\pi} \sigma',S',t'}$ $\alpha.t$ denotes the t field of a relation α.

$\sigma,\ S,\ \alpha\cdot L,\ t:\ pevnt? \xrightarrow{\pi} \sigma,S,\alpha.t$ $\sigma,\ sync\langle\sigma(sync\_cnt),t_0\rangle\cdot S,\ L,\ t:\ psync? \xrightarrow{\pi} \sigma,S,t_0$ [P-SYNC-PRMPT]

$\sigma,\ sync\langle n_0,t_0\rangle\cdot S,\ \alpha\cdot L,\ t:\ psync? \xrightarrow{\pi} \sigma[sync\_cnt \uparrow],\ S,\alpha.t\ \ \mathbf{if}\ n_0 \neq \sigma(sync\_cnt)$ [P-SYNC-NOPRMPT]

DYNAMIC CHECK RULES $\boxed{L,t:\ \omega \xrightarrow{\omega} b}$ $type(\alpha)$: return the type of a log entry α.

$\alpha\cdot L,\ t:\ chkEvnt(\ell) \xrightarrow{\omega} \alpha.t = t \wedge \alpha.\ell = \ell$

$\alpha\cdot L,\ t:\ chkWrt(\ell,c) \xrightarrow{\omega} type(\alpha) = WRITE \wedge \alpha.t = t \wedge \alpha.c = c \wedge \alpha.\ell = \ell$

$\alpha\cdot L,\ t:\ chkAssrt(\ell,c) \xrightarrow{\omega} (type(\alpha) \neq FAIL \wedge c \neq 0) \vee (type(\alpha) = FAIL \wedge \alpha.t = t \wedge \alpha.\ell = \ell \wedge c = 0)$

EXPRESSION RULES $\boxed{\sigma,L:\ e \xrightarrow{e} L',e'}$ $\sigma,\ READ\langle i,t,d,\ell,c\rangle\cdot L:\ \mathbf{read}^\ell(d) \xrightarrow{e} L,c$

LOCAL STATEMENT RULES $\boxed{\sigma,\mathcal{K},L:\ s \xrightarrow{s} \sigma',\mathcal{K}',L',s'}$

$\sigma,\ \mathcal{K},\ WRITE\langle i,t,d,\ell,c\rangle\cdot L:\ x := \mathbf{write}^\ell(d,c) \xrightarrow{s} \sigma,\ \mathcal{K},\ L,\ \mathbf{skip}$

$\sigma,\ \mathcal{K},\ FAIL\langle i,t,\ell\rangle\cdot L:\ \mathbf{assert}^\ell(0) \xrightarrow{s} \sigma,\ \mathcal{K},\ L,\ \mathbf{fail}$

$\sigma,\mathcal{K},L:\ \mathbf{assert}^\ell(c) \xrightarrow{s} \sigma,\ \mathcal{K},\ L,\ \mathbf{skip}\ \ \mathbf{if}\ c \neq 0$

GLOBAL RULES $\boxed{\sigma,\ \mathcal{K},\ L,\ S,\ t,\ (s_1,...,s_n) \longrightarrow \sigma',\ \mathcal{K}',\ L',\ S',\ t',\ (s'_1,...,s'_n)}$

$deterministic\_next\_thread(t,L)$: deterministically selects the next thread given the current thread t and the log.

$$\frac{\sigma,\mathcal{K},L:\ s \xrightarrow{s} \sigma',\mathcal{K}',L',s'}{\sigma,\ \mathcal{K},\ L,\ S,\ t,\ (s_1,...,s_{(t-1)},\ E[s]_s,\ s_{(t+1)},...,s_n) \longrightarrow \sigma',\ \mathcal{K}',\ L',S,\ t,\ (s_1,...,s_{(t-1)},\ E[s']_s,\ s_{(t+1)},...,s_n)}$$

[R-SAME-THRD]

$$\frac{\mathcal{K}(k) \neq \bot \quad \mathcal{K}(k) \neq t \quad t' = deterministic\_next\_thread(t,L)}{\sigma,\ \mathcal{K},\ L,\ S,\ t,\ (s_1,...,s_{(t-1)},\ E[\mathbf{acquire}^\ell(k)]_s,\ s_{(t+1)},...,s_n) \longrightarrow \sigma,\ \mathcal{K},\ L,S,\ t',(s_1,...,s_{(t-1)},\ E[\mathbf{acquire}^\ell(k)]_s,\ s_{(t+1)},...,s_n)}$$

[R-LOCKFAIL]

$$\frac{\sigma,S,L,t:\ \pi \xrightarrow{\pi} \sigma',S',t'}{\sigma,\ \mathcal{K},\ L,\ S,\ t,\ (s_1,...,s_{(t-1)},\ E[\pi]_\pi,\ s_{(t+1)},...,s_n) \longrightarrow \sigma',\ \mathcal{K},\ L,S',\ t',(s_1,...,s_{(t-1)},\ E[]_\pi,\ s_{(t+1)},...,s_n)}$$

[R-PREEMPT]

$$\frac{L,t:\ \omega \xrightarrow{\omega} \mathbf{true}}{\sigma,\ \mathcal{K},\ L,\ S,\ t,\ (s_1,...,s_{(t-1)},\ E[\omega]_\omega,\ s_{(t+1)},...,s_n) \longrightarrow \sigma,\ \mathcal{K},\ L,S,\ t,(s_1,...,s_{(t-1)},\ E[]_\omega,\ s_{(t+1)},...,s_n)}$$

[R-CHK-PASS]

$$\frac{L,t:\ \omega \xrightarrow{\omega} \mathbf{false}}{\sigma,\ \mathcal{K},\ L,\ S,\ t,\ (s_1,...,s_{(t-1)},\ E[\omega]_\omega,\ s_{(t+1)},...,s_n) \longrightarrow \sigma,\ \mathcal{K},\ L,S,\ t,(s_1,...,s_{(t-1)},\ \mathbf{invalid\_replay},\ s_{(t+1)},...,s_n)}$$

[R-CHK-FAIL]

Fig. 8. Replay Semantics. The subscripts in evaluation contexts denote the evaluation kind.

is also evaluated *before* the expression/statement. We have to perform the check first as an expression/statement cannot be properly evaluated if there is any inconsistency. If a preemption test follows a statement (as for the release statement), it is evaluated after the statement evaluation.

Preemption Rules. They have the form $\boxed{\sigma, S, L, t : \pi \xrightarrow{\pi} \sigma', S', t'}$. Given store σ, schedule S, replay log L and the current thread id t, a preemption test evaluates to a new thread id t', together with the new store and schedule. A preemption is indicated by $t' \neq t$. For a preemption test regarding a log event (i.e. *pevnt*), the resulting thread id is the one indicated by the next log event. For a synchronization (i.e. *psync*), if the value of the synchronization counter, acquired by $\sigma[sync\_cnt]$, equals to that specified in the next preemption in the schedule S, it yields the thread id specified in S ([P-SYNC-PRMPT]). Otherwise, it increases the synchronization count and continues evaluation with the thread specified by the log (P-SYNC-NOPRMPT).

 Checking Rules. The second set of rules is to validate a replay. They are of the form

$\boxed{L, t : \omega \xrightarrow{\omega} b}$. A check ω evaluates to a boolean value b. We define replay validity as follows.

Definition 1 (Replay Validity). *Given a log L, a replay execution is valid if the execution must encounter the exact sequence of events as specified in L.*

It dictates observable equivalence between the original and the replayed runs. Observe that a valid replay must successfully reproduce the same failure as the failure event is part of the log. According to the rules, checking events other than writes and assertions (i.e. *chkEvnt*) is to test whether the program point of the syscall and the current thread id are those specified in the log. To validate a write event (i.e. *chkWrt*), we additionally check the equivalence of the parameter computed in the replay and that in the log. To validate an assertion (i.e. *chkAssrt*), we ensure that if the assertion passes, there is not a *FAIL* event in the log; and if the assertion fails, the appropriate failure event must be present in the log.

Expression and Local Statement Rules. The configurations of expression and local rules are similar to those in the logging semantics. The difference is that the device state ι is not part of the configurations as devices are not accessed during replay. Inputs are loaded from the log instead. The rules in Fig. 8 are not complete, showing only those different from the logging semantics. In particular, a read expression reads the value from the first entry in the log. Note that its preceding check ensures progress of the evaluation. Statement rules are mainly removing the first log entry.

Global Rules. These rules model deterministic execution on a single core. In the configuration, we introduce a thread id t to explicitly constrain the thread where the evaluation happens; the resulting thread t' may be different, indicating a context switch. Rule [R-STMT-SAME-THRD] dictates that evaluation remains within the same thread as much as possible, ensured by the same thread id before and after the evaluation. Rule [R-LOCKFAIL] deterministically selects the next thread when it fails to acquire a lock. In our implementation, we select the next available thread following the log order. Rule [R-PREEMPT] switches to the thread t' indicated by the evaluation of a preemption test. It is a no-op if $t = t'$. Rules [R-CHK-FAIL] specifies that the evaluation terminates with **invalid_replay** if a check fails.

Example. Lets revisit the example in Section 2. In the initial replay in Fig. 2 (a), schedule $S = $ **nil** and the log is shown in Fig. 1 (c). It ends with an **invalid_replay**. In Fig. 2 (b), schedule $S = sync\langle 2,2 \rangle$, representing the preemption at ⒟, that is, switching to thread 2 upon the 2nd synchronization.

4   Incremental Schedule Exploration

When replay fails to make progress, our technique starts to explore different sub-schedules within a window close to the inconsistent event. The part of the schedule that happens before the window is considered finalized. The goal of exploration is to advance the replay, that is, to be able to replay at least one more event. The sub-schedule leading to advance is then admitted to the final schedule. The process is incremental and demand-driven. Exploration could be at two levels: the *coarse-grained* level that explores different orders of code blocks protected by synchronizations, and the *fine-grained* level that explores different orders of memory accesses. The algorithm first explores coarse-grained schedules, if it succeeds in advancing the replay, it will skip the fine-grained exploration.

4.1   Exploration Window

An important concept in our technique is the *exploration window*, which defines the scope of sub-schedule exploration. This allows us to avoid logging and reordering memory accesses for the whole execution as in PRES [25]. Intuitively, we consider that an inconsistent event α_x by state differences (compared with the original run) that occur in between the preceding event α_p *in the same thread* and α_x. Note that we consider the validity of the program state of the thread up to α_p is endorsed by the valid replay up to that event. The state between α_p and α_x could be affected by any parallel execution in other threads. Hence, *the exploration window includes the execution durations of all threads that could happen in parallel with the duration from α_p to α_x*. We consider two durations could happen in parallel if the happens-before relation between the two cannot be inferred from the event log order. Next, we formally define the window computation.

$$immPrec(\alpha_x^{tt},t) = \alpha^t \ \ s.t. \alpha^t \prec \alpha_x^{tt} \wedge \not\exists \alpha_0^t \ \ \alpha^t \prec \alpha_0^t \prec \alpha_x^t$$
$$immSucc(\alpha_x^{tt},t) = \alpha^t \ \ s.t. \alpha_x^{tt} \prec \alpha^t \wedge \not\exists \alpha_0^t \ \ \alpha_x^t \prec \alpha_0^t \prec \alpha^t$$

We first define two auxiliary functions. Function $immPrec(\alpha_x^{tt},t)$ computes the immediate preceding event in thread t regarding the given event α_x^{tt} in thread tt. We use the superscript to describe the thread where an event happens. We use operator $\prec$ to denote precedence in the log order. Similarly, function $immSucc()$ computes the immediate succeeding event. Given the two functions, the exploration window of a thread t regarding a given inconsistent event α_x^{tt} is computed as follows.

$$window(\alpha_x^{tt},t) = \langle immPrec(\alpha_p^{tt}, t), \ immSucc(\alpha_x^{tt}, t) \rangle$$
$$\textbf{where } \alpha_p^{tt} = immPrec(\alpha_x^{tt},tt)$$

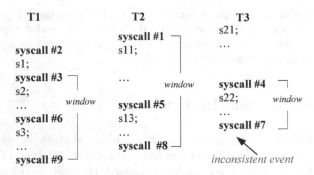

Fig. 9. Example for exploration window

In particular, α_p^{tt} denotes the immediate preceding event of the inconsistent event in the same thread tt. Hence, the window is delimited by an event in t that immediately precedes α_p^{tt} and an event in t that immediately succeeds α_x^{tt}.

Example. Consider the example in Fig. 9. The syscall numbers represent their global order. The inconsistent event is *syscall #7* in thread 3, denoted as α_7^3 for short.

$$immPrec(\alpha_7^3, 3) = \alpha_4^3$$
$$window(\alpha_7^3, 2) = \langle immPrec(\alpha_4^3, 2), immSucc(\alpha_7^3, 2)\rangle = \langle \alpha_1^2, \alpha_8^2\rangle$$

That is to say the window for thread **T2** is from *syscall #1* to *syscall #8*. Observe that

from the event order, we cannot tell the happens-before of statement *s11* in **T2** and *s22* in **T3**. The window for thread **T1** is similarly computed. Note that although α_2^1 happens after α_1^2, it is not in the window while α_1^2 is. In other words, an exploration window is not a consecutive sequence of global evaluation steps, but rather the aggregation of durations from all threads.

4.2 Coarse-Grained Exploration

The coarse-grained exploration aims to reorder the synchronized blocks within the window. Given a bound m, it tries to perform up to m preemptions. At each preemption, the algorithm tries to switch to a thread selected based on the order of the threads' first events in the remaining log. The intuition is that a thread that appears later is less likely to be part of the target interleaving. The exploration is backward: priority is given to preemptions close to the end of the window. The intuition is that perturbing schedules close to the inconsistent event is more likely to affect the event. Our implemetation supports multiple preemptions, but we observe that $m = 1$ is sufficient in this work.

Algorithm 1 presents the backward search algorithm of one preemption. It takes the inconsistent event as input and returns a new inconsistent event. It first collects the synchronization trace within the window. The main loop in lines 2-10 enumerates each synchronization in a backward fashion, and preempts at that point. For each preemption point, lines 3 and 4 sort the threads based on their first events that happen after the

Algorithm 1. One preemption coarse-grained exploration.

In: α_x: the inconsistent event;
Out: α': the new inconsistent event;
Def: R: ordered list of all threads;
    SyncTrace $T ::= \overline{\langle n, \ell, \alpha \rangle}$ with n the sync. counter, ℓ the program point of the sync., and α the first logged event that happens after the sync.;
    syncTraceInWindow(α_x): replay the execution and produce the sync trace within the exploration window of α_x;
    replay (L,S): replay and return the inconsistent event;
    sortThreadByLog (L): sort all threads by the first event in L

CoarsegrainedExplore (α_x)
1:    $T \leftarrow syncTraceInWindow\ (\alpha_x)$
2:    **foreach** $\langle n, \ell, \alpha \rangle \in T$ **in the backward order do**
3:       **let** $\mathcal{L}_p \cdot \alpha \cdot \mathcal{L}_s = \mathcal{L}$
4:       $R \leftarrow sortThreadByLog(\mathcal{L}_s)$
5:       **foreach** $t \in R$ **in the ascendent order do:**
6:          $S' \leftarrow sync\langle n, t \rangle$
7:          $\alpha' \leftarrow replay(L, S \cdot S')$;
8:          **if** $\alpha_x \prec \alpha'$ **then**
9:             $S \leftarrow S \cdot S'$
10:          **return** α'
11: **return** α_x

synchronization precluding the first such event α, as the default replay order has already followed the schedule inidicated by α. The loop in lines 5-10 tries the different target threads of the preemption based on the sorted order. In lines 8-9, if the new schedule leads to progress, it is appended to the final schedule to allow future replay.

Example. Consider the example in Fig. 9. Assume statement $s22$ in **T3** is a selected synchronization for preemption. Lines 3-4 sorts the threads to $R_1 = \{t_1, t_2\}$, suggested by *syscall#6* and #8. Hence, the algorithm first preempts to t_1. Note that the original replay switches to **T2** at $s22$ by default. □

For $m > 1$, we cannot simply enumerate an m subsequence of the synchronization trace as a preemption may change the control flow such that the following synchronization sequence is different. Hence, the implemented algorithm is a recursive version of Algorithm 1. Essentially, it first tries the different options of the first preemption and tentatively admits it to the final schedule and then recursively calls itself to look for the second preemption, and so on. Details are elided as $m = 1$ is sufficient in our experience.

4.3 Fine-Grained Exploration

If the coarse-grained exploration fails to make progress, the algorithm resorts to reordering shared variable accesses within the window. The idea is to first detect data races within the window. Then the algorithm selects a subset of races and reverses the order of the accesses in each race[1]. The size of the subset is limited by the preemption

---

[1] Here, a race is defined as a pair of accesses in the window on the same shared variable from different threads, with at least one being a write.

bound m. Reversing the order of a racy access pair is achieved by disabling the thread right before the first access, and then enabling it right after the second access (in a different thread). We call the set of races to be reversed the *memory schedule*. The search of memory schedule is also backward, giving priority to accesses close to the end of the window.

Our technique can continue to explore the preceding window if we cannot find a valid solution in the current window, although we haven't experienced such cases.

5   Caching Replay Failures

According to our study in Section 2, the same replay failure tends to happen repetitively. To avoid redundant schedule exploration, we develop a caching mechanism. We have two caches, corresponding to the two possible replay failures, *unmatched events* and *deadlocks*, respectively.

An unmatched event replay failure means that we expect to see an event α_c during replay but the next event α_x in the log is different. *Ideally*, the unmatched event cache C_{event} should have the following signature.

$$C_{event} : LogEntry \times LogEntry \rightarrow ThreadId \times InstCnt \times ThreadId$$

$C_{event}(\alpha_c, \alpha_x) = \langle t_0, n, t_1 \rangle$ means that upon a replay failure denoted by $\langle \alpha_c, \alpha_x \rangle$, the preemption should be performed in thread t_0 at the nth synchronization within the window when counting backward[2]. Note that we cannot use the global count as it is unique for each synchronization instance. The execution should switch to thread t_1. However in practice, it is not desirable to hard-code the thread id in the cache because it is very common that the different occurrences of the same replay failure may involve different sets of threads. For example, worker threads tend to execute the same piece of code, such as in `Apache` and `MySQL`. It is very likely that a replay failure such as (A) in Fig. 3 happens between worker threads T1 and T2 this time but T2 and T4 next time. Hence, we use the label of the next statement to execute in a thread to denote the thread. Therefore, in our design, $C_{event}(\alpha_c, \alpha_x) = \langle \ell_0, n, \ell_1 \rangle$ means that the preemption should occur in a thread that is about to execute statement ℓ_0 and the target thread is a thread that is about to execute ℓ_1.

For example, after the coarse-grained search succeeds in the example in Fig. 2 (a)-(b). A cache entry $C_{event}(\text{syscall\#3}, \text{syscall\#2}) = \langle 10, 1, 3 \rangle$ is added. Number 10 means that we should preempt a thread that is about to execute statement 10, which is thread one; 1 means the preemption point is the last synchronization in the window, i.e. ©; 3 means that the target thread is about to execute statement 3, i.e. thread two.

Note that our discussion limits to one preemption, extending the cache design to support multiple preemptions is omitted.

A deadlock may involve multiple threads. A complex design is needed if we use all the involved threads as the cache key. We have developed a much simpler design that is very effective in practice. We use the label of the replay failure statement of the thread of the next event in the log as the hash key. For example, in Fig. 3 (C), *syscall\#2* is the next event to replay and its thread fails to make progress at the conditional wait. We use the label of the wait as the key.

---

[2] Our discussion is limited to coarse-grained schedule for brevity.

6   Implementation

In the following, we highlight some of our engineering efforts.

System Call Recording. Minimizing logging overhead is one of our design goals. Therefore, we only log a subset of system calls which are necessary for replay. We currently intercept 84 out of 326 Linux system calls. Most of them are related to input, such as file and socket inputs, `select` and `gettimeofday`. We do not intercept/record output system calls.

Minimal Binary Rewriting. One of the important features of our technique is that it is hardware/software infrastructure-free. It works directly on binaries. Therefore, our technique intercepts syscalls by binary rewriting. In particular, it intercepts the dynamic linker interface. When an executable or a library is loaded, it scans the binary image and replaces all the syscall instructions with calls to our functions that realize the logging/replay functionalities. The binary rewriting component is adapted from that in Jockey [27], a logging/replay tool that does not support concurrent execution. Note that the rewriting is dynamic and very simple. It directly overwrites a small number of instructions in the code segment.

Intercepting Shared Variable Accesses. Without compiler support, it requires non-trivial efforts to intercept shared variable accesses, which is only needed during replay. It is not optimal to use dynamic instrumentation infrastructures such as Pin or Valgrind, due to their high cost. Our solution is to use memory protection to intercept memory accesses. In fine-grained exploration, we start protecting all global and heap pages *at the beginning of the window*. Upon a page fault (i.e. an access), we unprotect the page, and set the trap register to trap the next instruction. The execution is thus trapped after the access. We then log the access and re-protect the page. Observe that tracing is a one-time cost and it happens only within a window. Once the trace is acquired, the algorithm iteratively replays, reversing a set of races each time. In these replayed executions, only the pages specified by the memory schedule are protected, causing very few page faults. The majority of a replayed execution has no overhead.

Other Challenges. In the formal semantics, we use labels of syscall statements, which can be considered as the program counters (PCs). However, syscalls are mostly within libraries. We use stack-walk to identify the corresponding invocation in the user space and use its PC as the label. Threads in real-world programs tend to use *pipe* and *epoll* syscalls to communicate. They may send pointers through these syscalls. We cannot simply log the content of these syscalls and restore it during replay. We choose not to restore from the log but rather re-execute the relevant syscalls.

7   Evaluation

In this section, we evaluate the performance and the practicality of our technique. All experiments in this section were conducted on a quad-core Intel Xeon 2.40GHz with 4GB of RAM running Linux-2.6.35.

In the first experiment, we evaluate the performance of our technique over a set of real world bugs from 6 applications. Table 2 presents the programs and bugs.

Table 2. Application and Bug description.

Applications	LOC	Threads	Bug description
Apache-2.0.48	157K	7	#1: Unprotected buffer #2: Automicity violation (21287)
Apache-2.2.6	198K	7	#3: Automicity violation (45605)
MySQL-5.0.11	934K	14	#1: Atomicity violation (47761) #2: Atomicity violation (12845)
Cherokee-0.9.4	43K	4	Automicity violation (326)
Transmission-1.4.2	59K	2	Null pointer access (1818)
PBZip2-0.9.4	1.5K	6	Lock destroyed before it is accesses
Gftp-2.0.19	38K	5	Crash (546035)

Table 3. Recording and replay performance. CG denotes coarse-grained schedule exploration. FG denotes fine-grained schedule exploration.

	Original time(s)	Recording overhead (%)	PRES-like		Two-layer Exploration				Two-layer Exploration with caching					Replay time(s)
			FG Rep.	Time (sec)	CG Rep.	Log Mem	FG Rep.	Time (sec)	Cache Hit	CG Rep.	Log Mem	FG Rep.	Time (sec)	
Apache #1	12.43	3.22	28	301.21	24	1	1	40.21	10	14	1	1	29.85	1.64
Apache #2	7.14	3.78	22	615.42	32	1	1	281.42	8	10	1	1	92.59	6.12
Apache #3	10.89	2.94	16	196.73	27	1	1	43.85	9	14	1	1	31.23	1.28
MySQL #1	5.21	3.84	62	1342.6	46	1	2	137.1	17	24	1	2	81.47	2.47
MySQL #2	4.27	3.51	59	1429.1	39	1	1	151.82	15	22	1	1	92.5	3.71
Cherokee	120.42	2.11	15	684.29	12	1	3	61.51	2	7	1	3	42.11	4.15
Transmission	1.58	0.63	2	4.61	3	-	-	1.32	0	3	-	-	1.32	0.43
PBZip2	9.87	1.11	8	1615.78	6	-	-	201.42	0	6	-	-	201.42	35.42
Gftp	131.12	2.61	2	115	2	-	-	24.68	0	2	-	-	24.68	13.41

Cherokee is a web server. Transmission is a BitTorrent client. PBZip2 is a parallel implementation of the bzip2 file compressor. Gftp is a multithreaded file transfer client. We use test inputs provided with the programs if available or randomly generated inputs otherwise and we weave these inputs with the failure inducing inputs to trigger the bugs. For the UI program Gftp, the failures are induced by a sequence of user actions.

In the experiment, we also compare our technique with PRES. Note that it is difficult to compare the logging overhead of PRES with our technique as PRES was implemented on PIN and it logs a lot more events than our technique. The comparison hence focuses on the replay/schedule-reconstruction cost. We implemented PRES's replay algorithm according to the published paper [25]. We call it the PRES-like algorithm. Since PRES has multiple strategies, leveraging various kinds of information with some of them expensive to collect, we only adapted one of the strategies such that it operates on our log, which mainly consists of system calls, signals and thread spawns. Upon replay failures, the PRES-like algorithm identifies and logs all shared memory accesses, and then tries to reverse the order of the racy pairs.

Table 3 presents the results. Column 2 presents the original execution time without our logging tool for each application and column 3 shows recording overhead.

Columns 4-5 show the number of schedule exploration attempts and the accumulated time for the PRES-like approach. Columns 6-9 show the cost of two-layer exploration without caching. Column 6 presents the number of tries for coarse-grained schedules, column 7 shows the number of times of collecting shared-memory access trace within the window. Column 8 shows the number of tries for fine-grained schedules and column 9 presents the accumulated time. Columns 10-14 show the cost of two-layer exploration with caching. Column 10 shows the number of cache hits.

From the data, we make the following observations : (1) The logging overhead is very low, with the maximum 3.84% and average 2.6%. (2) Replay does not fail often compared to the total number of events in the log (see Column 2 in Table 4), showing the effectiveness of the default replay strategy. (3) Fine-grained exploration is rarely needed. (4) The caching mechanism is very effective in avoiding redundant exploration. (5) Our technique is more efficient than the PRES-like algorithm. Our schedule exploration with caching is an order of magnitude faster in most cases. This is mainly because we have two layers of exploration, limit schedule exploration within a window, and use caching.

Once we find a schedule to trigger a bug, we can replay the bug as many times as we want. The last column shows the replay time when we have the correct schedule. It is significantly less than the original run except for Apache#2 and PBZip2. This results from the time saved by emulating all syscalls during replay - no waiting time is incurred when replaying syscalls.

Table 4 presents the statistics about windows. Column 3 shows the average number of coarse-grained schedules which we can explore within an event's window. Column 4 shows the average number of data race pairs. For PBZip2, Transmission and Gftp, the correct schedules can be found with coarse-grained exploration and hence we do not need to detect data-races.

Table 4. Average window size

Bugs	# of logs	Window size	
		Coarse-grained	Fine-grained
Apache #1	32,578	50.32	13.03
Apache #2	128,589	40.32	3.46
Apache #3	33,261	48.27	10.15
MySQL #1	95,974	20.24	2.01
MySQL #2	87,425	25.19	2.42
PBZip2	3,426	31.77	-
Transmission	36	0.25	-
Cherokee	36,841	30.17	0.15
Gftp	22,332	28.15	-

Practicality Study with Real Workload. In order to evaluate the practicality of our technique, we acquired the high level web request log for our institution's web-site for one week. We wrote a script to regenerate the workloads for 1-7 days and fed them to the Apache and Cherokee server programs. At the end of each workload, we supplied the failure inducing requests to trigger the failure. The average logging overhead and aggregated space overhead are presented in Fig. 10. Observe that the logging overhead

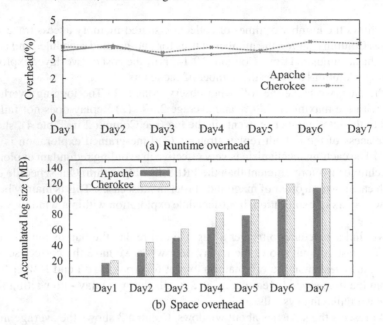

Fig. 10. Runtime and space overhead with real-world workload

Table 5. Performance with one day log. Number in braces indicates the number of times a memory access trace is collected.

Apps.	Exploration w/o caching			Exploration with caching			
	CG	FG	Time(s)	Hit	CG	FG	Time(s)
Apache	181	3(2)	13184.72	61	72	3(2)	5270.41
Cherokee	89	1(1)	6269.34	39	50	1(1)	3612.3

is more or less consistent and the space overhead is reasonable for a few day's execution. These results show the practicality of our logging technique.

Table 5 presents the replay cost with the real-world workload. Here we replay the last day's log only. The schedule exploration cost is high (2-4 hours without caching, 1-2 hours with caching), because we have to pay the cost of re-executing from the beginning for each exploration. We expect checkpointing would help a lot in this case, but we will leave it for our future work. The number of schedule explorations is not that high compared to the long duration of the workload. Caching substantially improves the performance. Note that a cache hit might save multiple exploration tries.

Synchronization Order Recording. If we have the global order of synchronization operations in the log, we can narrow down the search space. However the logging overhead increases. We measured the recording overhead including the global order of synchronization functions. It shows that the logging overhead becomes 7.6% for `Apache` and is increased by a factor of 2-3 for other benchmarks.

8 Related Work

The prior work most relevant to ours is PRES [25], which first tries to replay with syscall, synchronization, or even basic block log. If none of these succeeds, it tries to reverse shared memory access order. In comparison, PRES logs more information and it relies on PIN [18], entailing higher logging overhead. Moreover, we introduce exploration window, two-layer exploration, and caching, which are critical for reducing search space and improving replay performance. Our results show that our schedule exploration/reconstruction algorithm is 10.55 times faster on average. We have also formalized the technique and revealed in-depth observations about replaying real concurrent execution in general.

CLAP [12] presents a search-based deterministic replay system, which uses SMT solver and thread-local profiling to achieve replay determinism and to reduce the recording overhead. Compared to our technique, CLAP records more information such as control-flow paths, causing higher recording overhead (up to 296%).

There are also software based replay systems that record individual memory accesses and their happens-before relations [5,8]. Such systems entail substantial runtime overhead. In [2], a constraint solver is used to reproduce concurrent failures from incomplete log. There has been substantial work on software-based recording and replay for applications such as parallel and distributed system debugging [23,27,26,9,3,15,22,13]. These systems only perform coarse-grained logging at the level of system calls or control flow and hence are not sufficient for reproducing concurrency failures. We consider these techniques complementary to ours.

Recently, it has been shown that with architectural support, concurrent execution can be faithfully replayed [10,19,21,31,29]. While such techniques are highly effective, they demand deployment of special hardware, which limits their applicability.

Lee *et al.* [16] propose an execution reduction technique that aims to faithfully replay a failure with a reduced log. A key technique of their work is the unit-based loop analysis that reduces unnecessary iterations from the replay log. We consider this technique complementary to ours.

In recent years, significant progress has been made in testing concurrent programs. CHESS [20] is a stateless bounded model checker that performs systematic stress testing to expose bugs in concurrent programs. It can be adopted to reproduce Heisenbugs. CTrigger [24], PENELOPE [30] and PACER [6] are other concurrency testing techniques that search for schedule perturbations to break usual patterns of shared variable accesses to expose faults. Random schedule perturbations are also shown to be effective in debugging races and deadlocks [28,14]. These techniques do not log the original runs. They usually assume the (simplified) failure inducing inputs are provided.

DoublePlay [32] proposes a time-slicing technique of execution that runs multiple time intervals of a program on spare cores. Dthreads [17], PEREGRINE [7] and Coredet [4] propose deterministic execution system for multi-threaded applications.

9 Conclusion

We have developed a logging and replay technique for real concurrent execution. The technique is self-contained, does not require any infrastructure support. It features very low logging overhead as it does not log any synchronization operations or shared memory accesses. Replay is an incremental and demand-driven process. The technique always tries to replay by the log, but it may fail due to schedule differences. Upon a replay failure, an exploration process is triggered to search within a window for a schedule that allows progress. We have developed two kinds of explorations: one is at the synchronized block level and the other is at the shared memory access level. A sophisticated caching mechanism is developed to leverage the reoccurrences of replay failures. Our results show that the technique is effective and practical, and substantially improves the state of the art.

Acknowledgment. We would like to thank the anonymous reviewers for their insightful comments. This research is supported in part by the National Science Foundation (NSF) under grants 0917007 and 0845870. Any opinions, findings, and conclusions or recommendations in this paper are those of the authors and do not necessarily reflect the views of NSF.

References

1. Agrawal, H., Horgan, J.R.: Dynamic program slicing. In: Proceedings of the ACM SIGPLAN conference on Programming language design and implementation, PLDI 1990 (1990)
2. Altekar, G., Stoica, I.: Odr: output-deterministic replay for multicore debugging. In: Proceedings of the ACM SIGOPS Symposium on Operating Systems Principles, SOSP 2009 (2009)
3. Ayers, A., Schooler, R., Metcalf, C., Agarwal, A., Rhee, J., Witchel, E.: Traceback: first fault diagnosis by reconstruction of distributed control flow. In: Proceedings of the 2005 ACM SIGPLAN Conference on Programming Language Design and Implementation, PLDI 2005 (2005)
4. Bergan, T., Anderson, O., Devietti, J., Ceze, L., Grossman, D.: Coredet: a compiler and runtime system for deterministic multithreaded execution. In: Proceedings of the Fifteenth International Conference on Architectural Support for Programming Languages and Operating Systems, ASPLOS 2010 (2010)
5. Bhansali, S., Chen, W.-K., de Jong, S., Edwards, A., Murray, R., Drinic, M., Mihocka, D., Chau, J.: Framework for instruction-level tracing and analysis of program executions. In: Proceedings of the Second ACM SIGPLAN/SIGOPS International Conference on Virtual Execution Environments, VEE 2006 (2006)
6. Bond, M.D., Coons, K.E., McKinley, K.S.: Pacer: proportional detection of data races. In: Proceedings of the 2010 ACM SIGPLAN Conference on Programming Language Design and Implementation, PLDI 2010 (2010)
7. Cui, H., Wu, J., Gallagher, J., Guo, H., Yang, J.: Efficient deterministic multithreading through schedule relaxation. In: Proceedings of the Twenty-Third ACM Symposium on Operating Systems Principles, SOSP 2011 (2011)
8. Dunlap, G.W., Lucchetti, D.G., Fetterman, M.A., Chen, P.M.: Execution replay of multiprocessor virtual machines. In: Proceedings of the Fourth ACM SIGPLAN/SIGOPS International Conference on Virtual Execution Environments, VEE 2008 (2008)
9. Guo, Z., Wang, X., Tang, J., Liu, X., Xu, Z., Wu, M., Kaashoek, M.F., Zhang, Z.: R2: an application-level kernel for record and replay. In: Proceedings of the 8th USENIX Conference on Operating Systems Design and Implementation, OSDI 2008 (2008)

10. Hower, D.R., Hill, M.D.: Rerun: Exploiting episodes for lightweight memory race recording. In: Proceedings of the 35th International Symposium on Computer Architecture, ISCA 2008 (2008)

11. Huang, J., Liu, P., Zhang, C.: Leap: lightweight deterministic multi-processor replay of concurrent java programs. In: Proceedings of the Eighteenth ACM SIGSOFT International Symposium on Foundations of Software Engineering, FSE 2010 (2010)

12. Huang, J., Zhang, C., Dolby, J.: Clap: Recording local executions to reproduce concurrency failures. In: Proceedings of the 34th ACM SIGPLAN Conference on Programming Language Design and Implementation, PLDI 2013 (2013)

13. Hunt, N., Bergan, T., Ceze, L., Gribble, S.D.: Ddos: taming nondeterminism in distributed systems. In: Proceedings of the Eighteenth International Conference on Architectural Support for Programming Languages and Operating Systems, ASPLOS 2013 (2013)

14. Joshi, P., Park, C.-S., Sen, K., Naik, M.: A randomized dynamic program analysis technique for detecting real deadlocks. In: Proceedings of the 2009 ACM SIGPLAN Conference on Programming Language Design and Implementation, PLDI 2009 (2009)

15. King, S.T., Dunlap, G.W., Chen, P.M.: Debugging operating systems with time-traveling virtual machines. In: Proceedings of the Annual Conference on USENIX Annual Technical Conference, ATEC 2005 (2005)

16. Lee, K.H., Zheng, Y., Sumner, N., Zhang, X.: Toward generating reducible replay logs. In: Proceedings of the 32nd ACM SIGPLAN Conference on Programming Language Design and Implementation, PLDI 2011 (2011)

17. Liu, T., Curtsinger, C., Berger, E.D.: Dthreads: efficient deterministic multithreading. In: Proceedings of the Twenty-Third ACM Symposium on Operating Systems Principles, SOSP 2011 (2011)

18. Luk, C., Cohn, R., Muth, R., Patil, H., Klauser, A., Lowney, G., Wallace, S., Reddi, V., Hazelwood, K.: Pin: building customized program analysis tools with dynamic instrumentation. In: Proceedings of the 26rd ACM SIGPLAN Conference on Programming Language Design and Implementation, PLDI 2005 (2005)

19. Montesinos, P., Hicks, M., King, S.T., Torrellas, J.: Capo: a software-hardware interface for practical deterministic multiprocessor replay. In: Proceedings of the 14th International Conference on Architectural Support for Programming Languages and Operating Systems, ASPLOS 2009 (2009)

20. Musuvathi, M., Qadeer, S.: Iterative context bounding for systematic testing of multithreaded programs. In: Proceedings of the 2007 ACM SIGPLAN Conference on Programming Language Design and Implementation, PLDI 2007 (2007)

21. Narayanasamy, S., Pereira, C., Calder, B.: Recording shared memory dependencies using strata. In: 12th International Conference on Architectural Support for Programming Languages and Operating Systems, ASPLOS 2006 (2006)

22. Netzer, R.H.B., Weaver, M.H.: Optimal tracing and incremental reexecution for debugging long-running programs. In: Proceedings of the ACM SIGPLAN 2002 Conference on Programming Language Design and Implementation, PLDI 1994 (1994)

23. Pan, D.Z., Linton, M.A.: Supporting reverse execution for parallel programs. In: Proceedings of the 1988 ACM SIGPLAN and SIGOPS Workshop on Parallel and Distributed Debugging, PADD 1988 (1988)

24. Park, S., Lu, S., Zhou, Y.: Ctrigger: exposing atomicity violation bugs from their hiding places. In: Proceeding of the 14th International Conference on Architectural Support for Programming Languages and Operating Systems, ASPLOS 2009 (2009)

25. Park, S., Zhou, Y., Xiong, W., Yin, Z., Kaushik, R., Lee, K.H., Pres, S.L.: probabilistic replay with execution sketching on multiprocessors. In: Proceedings of the ACM SIGOPS Symposium on Operating Systems Principles, SOSP 2009 (2009)

26. Ronsse, M., De Bosschere, K., Christiaens, M., de Kergommeaux, J.C., Kranzlmüller, D.:
    Record/replay for nondeterministic program executions. Communcation of the ACM (2003)
27. Saito, Y.: Jockey: a user-space library for record-replay debugging. In: Proceedings of the
    Automated and Algorithmic Debugging, AADEBUG 2005 (2005)
28. Sen, K.: Race directed random testing of concurrent programs. In: Proceedings of the ACM
    SIGPLAN Conference on Programming Language Design and Implementation, PLDI 2008
    (2008)
29. Sheng, T., Vachharajani, N., Eranian, S., Hundt, R., Chen, W., Zheng, W.: Racez: a
    lightweight and non-invasive race detection tool for production applications. In: Proceeding
    of the 33rd International Conference on Software Engineering, ICSE 2011 (2011)
30. Sorrentino, F., Farzan, A., Madhusudan, P.: Penelope: weaving threads to expose atomicity
    violations. In: Proceedings of the Eighteenth ACM SIGSOFT International Symposium on
    Foundations of Software Engineering, FSE 2010 (2010)
31. Srinivasan, S.M., Kandula, S., Andrews, C.R., Zhou, Y.: Flashback: a lightweight extension
    for rollback and deterministic replay for software debugging. In: Proceedings of the USENIX
    Annual Technical Conference 2004 on USENIX Annual Technical Conference, ATEC 2004
    (2004)
32. Veeraraghavan, K., Lee, D., Wester, B., Ouyang, J., Chen, P.M., Flinn, J., Narayanasamy, S.:
    Doubleplay: parallelizing sequential logging and replay. In: Proceedings of the Sixteenth In-
    ternational Conference on Architectural Support for Programming Languages and Operating
    Systems, ASPLOS 2011 (2011)
33. Zhang, W., Lim, J., Olichandran, R., Scherpelz, J., Jin, G., Lu, S., Reps, T.: Conseq: detecting
    concurrency bugs through sequential errors. In: Proceedings of the Sixteenth International
    Conference on Architectural Support for Programming Languages and Operating Systems,
    ASPLOS 2011 (2011)

Understanding TypeScript

Gavin Bierman[1,*], Martín Abadi[2], and Mads Torgersen[2]

[1] Oracle
Gavin.Bierman@oracle.com
[2] Microsoft
{abadi,madst}@microsoft.com

Abstract. TypeScript is an extension of JavaScript intended to enable easier development of large-scale JavaScript applications. While every JavaScript program is a TypeScript program, TypeScript offers a module system, classes, interfaces, and a rich gradual type system. The intention is that TypeScript provides a smooth transition for JavaScript programmers—well-established JavaScript programming idioms are supported without any major rewriting or annotations. One interesting consequence is that the TypeScript type system is not statically sound by design. The goal of this paper is to capture the essence of TypeScript by giving a precise definition of this type system on a core set of constructs of the language. Our main contribution, beyond the familiar advantages of a robust, mathematical formalization, is a refactoring into a safe inner fragment and an additional layer of unsafe rules.

1 Introduction

Despite its success, JavaScript remains a poor language for developing and maintaining large applications. TypeScript is an extension of JavaScript intended to address this deficiency. Syntactically, TypeScript is a superset of EcmaScript 5, so every JavaScript program is a TypeScript program. TypeScript enriches JavaScript with a module system, classes, interfaces, and a static type system. As TypeScript aims to provide lightweight assistance to programmers, the module system and the type system are flexible and easy to use. In particular, they support many common JavaScript programming practices. They also enable tooling and IDE experiences previously associated with languages such as C[♯] and Java. For instance, the types help catch mistakes statically, and enable other support for program development (for example, suggesting what methods might be called on an object). The support for classes is aligned with proposals currently being standardized for EcmaScript 6.

The TypeScript compiler checks TypeScript programs and emits JavaScript, so the programs can immediately run in a huge range of execution environments. The compiler is used extensively in Microsoft to author significant JavaScript applications. For example, recently[1] Microsoft gave details of two substantial TypeScript

---

[*] This work was done at Microsoft Research, Cambridge.
[1] http://blogs.msdn.com/b/typescript/

R. Jones (Ed.): ECOOP 2014, LNCS 8586, pp. 257–281, 2014.
© Springer-Verlag Berlin Heidelberg 2014

projects: Monaco, an online code editor, which is around 225kloc, and XBox Music, a music service, which is around 160kloc. Since its announcement in late 2012, the compiler has also been used outside Microsoft, and it is open-source.

The TypeScript type system comprises a number of advanced constructs and concepts. These include structural type equivalence (rather than by-name type equivalence), types for object-based programming (as in object calculi), gradual typing (in the style of Siek and Taha [14]), subtyping of recursive types, and type operators. Collectively, these features should contribute greatly to a harmonious programming experience. One may wonder, still, how they can be made to fit with common JavaScript idioms and codebases. We regard the resolution of this question as one of the main themes in the design of TypeScript.

Interestingly, the designers of TypeScript made a conscious decision not to insist on static soundness. In other words, it is possible for a program, even one with abundant type annotations, to pass the TypeScript typechecker but to fail at run-time with a dynamic type error—generally a trapped error in ordinary JavaScript execution environments. This decision stems from the widespread usage of TypeScript to ascribe types to existing JavaScript libraries and codebases, not just code written from scratch in TypeScript. It is crucial to the usability of the language that it allows for common patterns in popular APIs, even if that means embracing unsoundness in specific places.

The TypeScript language is defined in a careful, clear, but informal document [11]. Naturally, this document contains certain ambiguities. For example, the language permits subtyping recursive types; the literature contains several rules for subtyping recursive types, not all sound, and the document does not say exactly which is employed. Therefore, it may be difficult to know exactly what is the type system, and in what ways it is sound or unsound.

Nevertheless, the world of unsoundness is not a shapeless, unintelligible mess, and unsound languages are not all equally bad (nor all equally good). In classical logic, any two inconsistent theories are equivalent. In programming, on the other hand, unsoundness can arise from a great variety of sins (and virtues). At a minimum, we may wish to distinguish blunders from thoughtful compromises—many language designers and compiler writers are capable of both.

The goal of this paper is to describe the essence of TypeScript by giving a precise definition of its type system on a core set of constructs of the language. This definition clarifies ambiguities of the informal language documentation. It has led to the discovery of a number of unintended inconsistencies and mistakes both in the language specification and in the compiler, which we have reported to the TypeScript team; fortunately, these have been relatively minor and easy to correct. It also helps distinguish sound and unsound aspects of the type system: it provides a basis for partial soundness theorems, and it isolates and explains the sources of unsoundness.

Specifically, in this paper, we identify various core calculi, define precisely their typing rules and, where possible, prove properties of these rules, or discuss why we cannot. The calculi correspond precisely to TypeScript in that every valid program in a given calculus is literally an executable TypeScript program. Since our work took place before the release of TypeScript 1.0, we based it on earlier versions, in particular TypeScript 0.9.5, which is almost identical to TypeScript 1.0 in most respects; the main differences concern generics. As the design of generics evolved until quite recently, in this paper we restrict attention to the non-generic fragment. Fortunately, for the most part, generics are an orthogonal extension.

The rest of the paper is organized as follows: In §2 we give an informal overview of the design goals of TypeScript. In §3 we give the syntax for a core, featherweight calculus, FTS. In §4 we define safeFTS, a safe, featherweight fragment of TypeScript, by giving details of a type system. In §5 we give an operational semantics for FTS and show how safeFTS satisfies a type soundness property. In §6 we extend the type system of safeFTS obtaining a calculus we refer to as 'production' FTS, or prodFTS for short. This calculus should be thought of as the featherweight fragment of the full TypeScript language, so it is not statically type sound, by design. We characterize the unsound extensions to help understand why the language designers added them. In §7 we give an alternative formulation of the assignment compatibility relation for prodFTS that is analogous to the consistent-subtyping relation of Siek and Taha [14]. We are able to prove that this relation is equal to our original assignment compatibility relation. We briefly review related work in §8 and conclude in §9.

2   The Design of TypeScript

The primary goal of TypeScript is to give a statically typed experience to JavaScript development. A syntactic superset of JavaScript, it adds syntax for declaring and expressing types, for annotating properties, variables, parameters and return values with types, and for asserting the type of an expression. This paper's main aim is to formalize these type-system extensions.

TypeScript also adds a number of new language constructs, such as classes, modules, and lambda expressions. The TypeScript compiler implements these constructs by translation to JavaScript (EcmaScript 5). However, these constructs are essentially back-ports of upcoming (EcmaScript 6) JavaScript features and, although they interact meaningfully with the type system, they do not affect its fundamental characteristics.

The intention of TypeScript is not to be a new programming language in its own right, but to enhance and support JavaScript development. Accordingly, a key design goal of the type system is to support current JavaScript styles and idioms, and to be applicable to the vast majority of the many existing—and very popular—JavaScript libraries. This goal leads to a number of distinctive properties of the type system:

Full erasure: The types of a TypeScript program leave no trace in the JavaScript emitted by the compiler. There are no run-time representations of types, and hence no run-time type checking. Current dynamic techniques for "type checking" in JavaScript programs, such as checking for the presence of certain properties, or the values of certain strings, may not be perfect, but good enough.

Structural types: The TypeScript type system is structural rather than nominal. Whilst structural type systems are common in formal descriptions of object-oriented languages [1], most industrial mainstream languages, such as Java and C$^\sharp$, are nominal. However, structural typing may be the only reasonable fit for JavaScript programming, where objects are often built from scratch (not from classes), and used purely based on their expected shape.

Unified object types: In JavaScript, objects, functions, constructors, and arrays are not separate kinds of values: a given object can simultaneously play several of these roles. Therefore, object types in TypeScript can not only describe members but also contain call, constructor, and indexing signatures, describing the different ways the object can be used. In Featherweight TypeScript, for simplicity, we include only call signatures; constructor and index signatures are broadly similar.

Type inference: TypeScript relies on type inference in order to minimize the number of type annotations that programmers need to provide explicitly. JavaScript is a pretty terse language, and the logic shouldn't be obscured by excessive new syntax. In practice, often only a small number of type annotations need to be given to allow the compiler to infer meaningful type signatures.

Gradual typing: TypeScript is an example of a gradual type system [14], where parts of a program are statically typed, and others dynamically typed through the use of a distinguished dynamic type, written `any`. Gradual typing is typically implemented using run-time casts, but that is not practical in TypeScript, because of type erasure. As a result, typing errors not identified statically may remain undetected at run-time.

The last point is particularly interesting: it follows from the view that an unsound type system can still be extremely useful. The significant initial uptake of TypeScript certainly suggests that this is the case. While the type system can be wrong about the shape of run-time structures, the experience thus far indicates that it usually won't be. The type system may not be good enough for applications that require precise guarantees (e.g., as a basis for performance optimizations, or for security), but it is more than adequate for finding and preventing many bugs, and, as importantly, for powering a comprehensive and reliable tooling experience of auto-completion, hover tips, navigation, exploration, and refactoring.

In addition to gradual typing, a few other design decisions deliberately lead to type holes and contribute to the unsoundness of the TypeScript type system.

Downcasting: The ability to explicitly downcast expressions is common in most typed object-oriented languages. However, in these languages, a downcast is compiled to a dynamic check. In TypeScript, this is not the case, as no trace of the type system is left in the emitted code. So incorrect downcasts are not detected, and may lead to (trapped) run-time errors.

Covariance: TypeScript allows unsafe covariance of property types (despite their mutability) and parameter types (in addition to the contravariance that is the safe choice). Given the ridicule that other languages have endured for this decision, it may seem like an odd choice, but there are significant and sensible JavaScript patterns that just cannot be typed without covariance.

Indexing: A peculiar fact of JavaScript is that member access through dot notation is just syntactic sugar for indexing with the member name as a string. Full TypeScript permits specifying indexing signatures, but (in their absence) allows indexing with any string. If the string is a literal that corresponds to a property known to the type system, then the result will have the type of that member (as usual with the dot notation). On the other hand, if the string is not a literal, or does not correspond to a known member, then the access is still allowed, and typed as `any`. Again, this aspect of TypeScript corresponds to common JavaScript usage, and results in another hole in the type system.

One further source of unsoundness may be the treatment of recursive definitions of generic type operators. Deciding type equivalence and subtyping in a structural type system with such definitions is notoriously difficult. Some versions of these problems are equivalent to the equivalence problem for deterministic pushdown automata [16], which was proved decidable relatively recently [13], and which remains a challenging research subject. We do not discuss these points further because we focus on the non-generic fragment of TypeScript, as explained above.

3 Featherweight TypeScript

In this section we define the syntax of a core calculus, Featherweight TypeScript (FTS). As mentioned in the introduction, this core calculus covers the non-generic part of TypeScript. To elucidate the design of TypeScript we will refactor the type system into two parts, which we then add to FTS and consider the results as two separate calculi: a 'safe' calculus containing none of the type holes, safeFTS and a complete, 'production' calculus, prodFTS.

Analogously to Featherweight Java [10], our calculi are small and there is a direct correspondence between our calculi and TypeScript: every safeFTS and prodFTS program is literally an executable TypeScript program. (We also make extensive use of the Featherweight Java 'overbar' notation.) However, our calculi are considerably more expressive than Featherweight Java as we retain many impure features that we view as essential to TypeScript programming, such as assignments, variables, and statements.

In this section we define the syntax of our core calculus. The safeFTS type system is defined in §4 and the prodFTS type system is defined in §6.

FTS expressions:

e, f ::=	Expressions
x	Identifier
l	Literal
{ ā }	Object literal
e=f	Assignment operator

e ⊕ f	Binary operator
e.n	Property access
e[f]	Computed property access
e(f̄)	Function call
<T>e	Type assertion
function c { s̄ }	Function expression
a ::= n: e	Property assignment
c ::=	Call signature
(p̄)	Parameter list
(p̄): T	Parameter list with return type
p ::=	Parameter
x	Identifier
x:T	Typed identifier

As TypeScript includes JavaScript as a sublanguage, thus Featherweight Type-Script contains what can be thought of as Featherweight JavaScript. We highlight in grey the constructs that are new to TypeScript and not part of JavaScript.

FTS expressions include literals, l, which can be a number n, a string s, or one of the constants **true**, **false**, **null**, or **undefined**.[2] We assume a number of built-in binary operators, such as ===, >, <, and +. In the grammar we use ⊕ to range over all the binary operators, and do not specify them further as their meaning is clear. We assume that x, y, and z range over valid identifiers and n ranges over property names. We also assume that the set of identifiers includes the distinguished identifier **this** which cannot be used as a formal parameter or declared as a local.

FTS supports both property access and computed property access. Function expressions extend those of JavaScript by optionally including parameter and return type annotations on call signatures. (TypeScript also features a more compact 'arrow' form for function expressions; for example one can write (x) => x+1 instead of the more verbose **function** (x) { **return** x + 1; }.)

FTS statements:

s, t ::=	Statement
e;	Expression statement
if (e) {s̄} else {t̄}	If statement
return;	Return statement
return e;	Return value statement
v;	Variable statement
u, v ::=	Variable declaration
var x:T	Uninitialized typed variable declaration
var x:T = e	Initialized typed variable declaration
var x	Uninitialized variable declaration
var x = e	Initialized variable declaration

---

[2] JavaScript somewhat confusingly supports two primitive values: **null** (an object) and **undefined** which, for example, is returned when accessing a non-existent property.

For the sake of compactness, we support conditional statements but not conditional expressions. Variable declarations are extended from JavaScript to include optional type annotations.

FTS types:

R, S, T ::=	Type
any	Any type
P	Primitive type
O	Object type
P ::=	Primitive type
number	Number
string	String
boolean	Boolean type
void	Void type
Null	Null type
Undefined	Undefined type
O ::=	Object type
I	Interface type
L	Literal type
L ::= { $\bar{M}$ }	Object type literal
M, N ::=	Type member
n : T	Property
$(\bar{x}: \bar{S})$: T	Call signature

FTS types fall into three categories: primitive types, object types, and a distinguished type, written any.

The primitive types include the run-time primitive types of JavaScript: number for 64 bit IEEE 754 floating point numbers, string for Unicode UTF-16 strings, and boolean to denote the boolean values. The void type denotes an absence of a value, which arises from running a function that simply returns without giving a result. There are no values of this type. There are two further types, *Null* and *Undefined*, that are expressible but not denotable; we write them in italics to further emphasize their special status. In other words, these two types cannot be referenced in valid TypeScript programs, but they arise within the typing process.

FTS object types consist of interface types and literal types. For compactness, we do not support classes in FTS. At the level of the type system, classes are secondary, and do not add any significant new issues, but complicate the formalization of the language and the operational semantics. For that reason we omit them, but do keep interfaces. Similarly we drop array, function, and constructor type literals. FTS supports object type literals, whose type members can include properties and call signatures. The inclusion of call signature properties enable us to encode function literal types; for example the type (x:S) => T can be encoded as the type {(x:S): T}. We refer to an object type literal that contains a call signature as a *callable* type, and we assume a predicate *callable* that returns

true if the type contains a call signature.[3] It is important to note that the type
{ } (i.e., the empty object type literal) is a valid type. In addition, TypeScript
has a number of predefined interfaces that are always in scope in TypeScript
programs. For the purposes of this paper, these interfaces are `Object`, `Function`,
`String`, `Number`, and `Boolean`.

FTS declaration:

D ::=	Interface declaration
`interface I { M̄ }`	
`interface I extends Ī { M̄ }`	(Ī non-empty)

FTS supports only one form of declaration: an interface. An interface allows a
name to be associated with an object type. Thus, a declaration `interface I { M̄ }`
associates with the name `I` the object type literal `{ M̄ }`. However, a couple
of subtleties arise. First, interfaces can be recursive; and indeed a collection of
interface declarations can be mutually recursive. Also, interfaces can inherit from
zero or more base types (which, in the case of FTS must be interfaces). In this
case an interface has all the members defined in its immediate declaration and
furthermore all the members of the base types.

In TypeScript this process of inheritance is further complicated by the notion
of an interface hiding members of its base types, but for FTS we shall make the
simplifying assumption that no hiding is possible. We do not model the notion
of private members; in FTS all members are public.

An interface table Σ is a map from an interface name `I` to an interface declaration `D`. A program is then a pair $(\Sigma, \bar{s})$ of an interface table and a sequence of
statements. In order to reduce notational overload, we assume a single fixed interface table Σ. The interface table induces relationships between types (subtyping
and assignment compatibility); these relations are defined in later sections.

The given interface table must satisfy some familiar sanity conditions:

1. $\Sigma(\text{I}) = \text{interface I} \ldots$ for every $\text{I} \in dom(\Sigma)$;
2. for every interface name `I` appearing anywhere in Σ, it is the case that
   $\text{I} \in dom(\Sigma)$; and
3. there are no cycles in the dependency graph induced by the `extends` clauses
   of the interface declarations defined in Σ.

This last point rules out declarations such as the following:

```
// Error: Self-cyclic extends clause
interface I extends I { ... }
```

```
// Error: Cyclic extends clauses
interface J extends K { ... }
interface K extends J { ... }
```

---

[3] In FTS we do not support functions with multiple call signatures and thus we ignore
the process of overloading resolution in TypeScript.

Throughout the rest of the paper, we write Γ to denote a type environment, which is a function from identifiers to types. We write $\Gamma, \mathtt{x} \colon \mathtt{T}$ to denote the extension of the type environment Γ with the mapping of identifier $\mathtt{x}$ to type $\mathtt{T}$. This extension is defined only if $\mathtt{x} \notin dom(\Gamma)$. In some cases we need to override a function mapping; we write $\Gamma \uplus \mathtt{x} \colon \mathtt{T}$ to denote the function that maps $\mathtt{x}$ to $\mathtt{T}$, and otherwise maps an identifier $\mathtt{y} \neq \mathtt{x}$ to $\Gamma(\mathtt{y})$.

4   Safe Featherweight TypeScript (safeFTS)

In this section we define the safeFTS calculus which adds a type system to the FTS calculus defined in the previous section. As suggested by its name, this type system, although a subsystem of the full TypeScript type system, has familiar safety properties. (These properties are treated in §5.)

Our first step is to define an important type relation in TypeScript: assignment compatibility [11, §3.8.3]. This relation is written $\mathtt{S} \leq \mathtt{T}$ and captures the intuition that a value of type $\mathtt{S}$ can be assigned to a value of type $\mathtt{T}$. However, the presence of interfaces immediately makes this relation a little tricky to define. For example, consider the following interface declaration.

```
interface I {
    a : number,
    (x: string): I
}
```

As TypeScript has a structural type system, this actually defines a type $\mathtt{I}$ which is described by the following *equation*.

$\mathtt{I = \{\ a\ :\ number,\ (x:\ string):\ I\ \}}$

A value of type $\mathtt{I}$ is an object with a property $\mathtt{a}$ of type $\mathtt{number}$, and a function that maps strings to values of type $\mathtt{I}$. Clearly this is equivalent to an object with a property $\mathtt{a}$ of type $\mathtt{number}$, and a function that maps strings to objects with a property $\mathtt{a}$ of type $\mathtt{number}$, and a function that maps strings to values of type $\mathtt{I}$, and so on, *ad infinitum*. The language specification notes this potential infinite expansion [11, §3.8.1] but gives few details about how it is to be dealt with. (Indeed, the discussion of types excludes any mention of interface names, which are assumed to have been replaced by their definitions.)

Fortunately, this equi-recursive treatment of recursive types has a pleasant, but slightly less well-known formalization that views types as (finite or infinite) trees, uses greatest fixed points to define type relationships, and coinduction as a proof technique. We give only the basic definitions but the excellent survey article [6] offers further details.

We represent types as possibly infinite trees, with nodes labelled by a symbol from the set $O = \{\mathtt{any}, \mathtt{null}, \mathtt{undefined}, \mathtt{boolean}, \mathtt{number}, \mathtt{string}, \{\}, \rightarrow\}$. The branches are labelled with a name taken from the set $B = \mathtt{X} \cup \mathtt{N} \cup \{\mathtt{ret}, \mathtt{cs}\}$, where $\mathtt{X}$ is the set of FTS identifiers, $\mathtt{N}$ is the set of FTS property names, and $\mathtt{ret} \notin \mathtt{X}$ and $\mathtt{cs} \notin \mathtt{N}$ are distinguished names (used to signify a return type and a call signature). We write $B^\star$ for the set of sequences of elements $b \in B$. The empty sequence is written $\bullet$, and if π and π' are sequences, then we write $\pi \cdot \pi'$ for the concatenation of π and π'.

Definition 1. *A* tree type *is a partial function* $T : B^* \rightharpoonup O$ *such that:*

- $T(\bullet)$ *is defined.*
- *If* $T(\pi \cdot \sigma)$ *is defined then* $T(\pi)$ *is defined.*
- *If* $T(\pi) = \{\}$ *then* $\exists P \subseteq (\mathbb{N} \cup \{cs\}).P = \{n_1, \dots, n_p\}$ *such that* $T(\pi \cdot n_1), \dots, T(\pi \cdot n_p)$ *are defined and* $\forall b \in B.b \notin P$ *implies* $T(\pi \cdot b)$ *is undefined.*
- *If* $T(\pi) = \rightarrow$ *then* $\exists X \subseteq X.X = \{x_1, \dots, x_p\}$ *such that* $T(\pi \cdot x_1), \dots, T(\pi \cdot x_p)$ *and* $T(\pi \cdot ret)$ *are defined and* $\forall b \in B.b \notin X$ *implies* $T(\pi \cdot b)$ *is undefined.*
- *If* $T(\pi) \in \{any, \text{Null}, \text{Undefined}, boolean, number, string\}$ *then* $\forall b \in B.T(\pi \cdot b)$ *is undefined.*

The set of all tree types is written $\mathcal{T}$. For notational convenience, we write any for the tree T with $T(\bullet) = any$, and likewise for the other nullary type constructors. If T_1 and T_2 are types, then we write $\{n_1:T_1, n_2:T_2\}$ for the tree type T such that $T(\bullet) = \{\}$, $T(n_1) = T_1$, and $T(n_2) = T_2$. Similarly, if T_1 and T_2 are types, then we write $\{(x:T_1): T_2\}$ for the tree type T such that $T(\bullet) = \{\}$, $T(cs) = \rightarrow$, $T(cs \cdot x) = T_1$ and $T(cs \cdot ret) = T_2$. We restrict our attention to finitely branching trees, but trees may well still be infinite.

Definition 2. *Two tree types* S *and* T *are* assignment compatible *if the pair* (S, T) *is in the greatest fixed point of the following function* $\mathcal{A} : \mathcal{P}(\mathcal{T} \times \mathcal{T}) \to \mathcal{P}(\mathcal{T} \times \mathcal{T})$.

$$
\begin{aligned}
\mathcal{A}(R) = {}& \{(S, S) \mid S \vdash \diamond\} \cup \{(S, any) \mid S \vdash \diamond\} \cup \{(\text{Undefined}, T) \mid T \vdash \diamond\} \\
& \cup \{(\text{Null}, T) \mid T \vdash \diamond \text{ and } T \neq \text{Undefined}\} \cup \{(P, T) \mid (\mathcal{I}(P), T) \in R\} \\
& \cup \{(\{\bar{M}_0, \bar{M}_1\}, \{\bar{M}_2\}) \mid \{\bar{M}_0, \bar{M}_1\} \vdash \diamond \text{ and } \bar{M}_1 \sim \bar{M}_2\} \\
& \text{where } n_1 : T_1 \sim n_2 : T_2 \text{ if } n_1 \equiv n_2 \text{ and } T_1 \equiv T_2 \\
& \qquad (\bar{x}:\bar{S}):R_0 \sim (\bar{y}:\bar{T}):R_1 \text{ if } (\bar{T}, \bar{S}) \in R, R_1 \neq void \text{ and } (R_0, R_1) \in R \\
& \qquad (\bar{x}:\bar{S}):R \sim (\bar{y}:\bar{T}):void \text{ if } (\bar{T}, \bar{S}) \in R
\end{aligned}
$$

In this definition we make use of a wellformedness predicate on types, written $S \vdash \diamond$, whose simple definition we omit for lack of space. We also make use of a helper function, $\mathcal{I}$, to replace a primitive type (boolean, number, string) with its associated interface type (Boolean, Number, String, respectively).

We can also define assignment compatibility using a familiar collection of inference rules, but it should be noted this is a *coinductively* defined relation. We use double horizontal lines to emphasize this distinction.

safeFTS assignment compatibility: $S \leqq T$ and $M_0 \leqq M_1$

$$\frac{S \vdash \diamond}{S \leqq S} \text{ [A-Refl]} \qquad \frac{S \vdash \diamond}{S \leqq any} \text{ [A-AnyR]} \qquad \frac{T \vdash \diamond}{\text{Undefined} \leqq T} \text{ [A-Undef]}$$

$$\frac{T \vdash \diamond \qquad T \neq \text{Undefined}}{\text{Null} \leqq T} \text{ [A-Null]} \qquad \frac{\mathcal{I}(P) \leqq T}{P \leqq T} \text{ [A-Prim]}$$

$$\frac{\{\ \bar{M}_0,\bar{M}_1\ \}\vdash\diamond \qquad \bar{M}_1\leqq\bar{M}_2}{\{\ \bar{M}_0,\bar{M}_1\ \}\leqq\{\ \bar{M}_2\ \}}\ \text{[A-Object]} \qquad\qquad n\!:\!T\leqq n\!:\!T\ \text{[A-Prop]}$$

$$\frac{\bar{T}\leqq\bar{S}\qquad R_1\neq\text{void}\qquad R_0\leqq R_1}{(\bar{x}\!:\!\bar{S})\!:\!R_0\leqq(\bar{y}\!:\!\bar{T})\!:\!R_1}\ \text{[A-CS]} \qquad \frac{\bar{T}\leqq\bar{S}\qquad R\vdash\diamond}{(\bar{x}\!:\!\bar{S})\!:\!R\leqq(\bar{y}\!:\!\bar{T})\!:\!\text{void}}\ \text{[A-CS-Void]}$$

Rule [A-Refl] states that any type can be assigned to itself, and rule [A-AnyR] that any type can be assigned to any. In rule [A-Undef] the type *Undefined* can be assigned to any type; and in rule [A-Null] the type *Null* can be assigned to any type except *Undefined*. The effect of these rules is that, when viewing assignment compatibility as an order, *Undefined* is the least type, *Null* is below any user-defined type, and that all types are below any, which is the top type. Rule [A-Prop] states that assignment compatibility is *invariant* on property members, and rules [A-CS] and [A-CS-Void] capture the fact that assignment compatibility is contra-/co-variant on call signatures.

Note that there is no explicit transitivity rule for assignment compatibility, but for safeFTS it is derivable.

Lemma 1 (Transitivity derived rule)

1. *If* $S\leq T$ *and* $T\leq U$ *then* $S\leq U$
2. *If* $M_0\leqq M_1$ *and* $M_1\leqq M_2$ *then* $M_0\leqq M_2$

The proof of this lemma is analogous to that of Gapeyev et al.'s Theorem 4.7 [6].

The type system for TypeScript, and hence safeFTS, consists of two inter-defined typing relations: one where type information is inferred and one where some type context is taken into account when a type is inferred. In this respect, TypeScript is reminiscent of local type inference systems [12], but the detail is different. The first relation is written $\Gamma\vdash e\!:\!T$ and is read "given type environment Γ, the expression e has type T." The second relation, written $\Gamma\vdash e\downarrow S\!:\!T$, is read "given type environment Γ, the expression e *in the context of type S* has type T." This relation is called 'contextual typing' in the language specification [11, §4.18].

Expression typing: $\Gamma\vdash e\!:\!T$

$$\text{[I-Id]}\frac{}{\Gamma,x\!:\!T\vdash x\!:\!T} \qquad\qquad \text{[I-Number]}\frac{}{\Gamma\vdash n\!:\!\text{number}}$$

$$\text{[I-String]}\frac{}{\Gamma\vdash s\!:\!\text{string}} \qquad\qquad \text{[I-Bool]}\frac{}{\Gamma\vdash\text{true},\text{false}\!:\!\text{boolean}}$$

$$\text{[I-Null]}\frac{}{\Gamma\vdash\text{null}\!:\!\textit{Null}} \qquad\qquad \text{[I-Undefined]}\frac{}{\Gamma\vdash\text{undefined}\!:\!\textit{Undefined}}$$

$$\text{[I-ObLit]}\frac{\Gamma\vdash\bar{e}\!:\!\bar{T}}{\Gamma\vdash\{\ \bar{n}\!:\bar{e}\ \}\!:\!\{\ \bar{n}\!:\bar{T}\ \}} \qquad \text{[I-Assign]}\frac{\Gamma\vdash e\!:\!S\qquad\Gamma\vdash f\downarrow S\!:\!T\qquad T\leqq S}{\Gamma\vdash e=f\!:\!T}$$

$$\text{[I-Op]}\frac{\Gamma\vdash e\!:\!S_0\qquad\Gamma\vdash f\!:\!S_1\qquad S_0\oplus S_1=T}{\Gamma\vdash e\oplus f\!:\!T}$$

$$[\text{I-Prop}] \; \frac{\Gamma \vdash \texttt{e}: \texttt{S} \quad lookup(\texttt{S}, \texttt{n}) = \texttt{T}}{\Gamma \vdash \texttt{e.n}: \texttt{T}}$$

$$[\text{I-CompProp}] \; \frac{\Gamma \vdash \texttt{e}: \texttt{S} \quad \texttt{S} \leq \texttt{Object} \quad \Gamma \vdash \texttt{f}: \texttt{string}}{\Gamma \vdash \texttt{e[f]}: \texttt{any}}$$

$$[\text{I-Call}] \; \frac{\Gamma \vdash \texttt{e}: \{\; (\bar{\texttt{x}}: \bar{\texttt{S}}): \texttt{R} \;\} \quad \Gamma \vdash \bar{\texttt{f}} \downarrow \bar{\texttt{S}}: \bar{\texttt{T}} \quad \bar{\texttt{T}} \leq \bar{\texttt{S}}}{\Gamma \vdash \texttt{e}(\bar{\texttt{f}}): \texttt{R}}$$

$$[\text{I-Assert}] \; \frac{\Gamma \vdash \texttt{e}: \texttt{S} \quad \texttt{S} \leq \texttt{T}}{\Gamma \vdash \texttt{<T>e}: \texttt{T}}$$

$$[\text{I-Func1}] \; \frac{\Gamma_1, \texttt{this}: \texttt{any}, |\bar{\texttt{p}}| \vdash getVars(\bar{\texttt{s}}) \rightsquigarrow \Gamma_2 \quad \Gamma_2 \vdash \bar{\texttt{s}} \downarrow \texttt{T}: \bar{\texttt{R}}}{\Gamma_1 \vdash \texttt{function } (\bar{\texttt{p}}): \texttt{T} \; \{\; \bar{\texttt{s}} \;\}: \{\; (|\bar{\texttt{p}}|): return(\bar{\texttt{R}}) \;\}}$$

$$[\text{I-Func2}] \; \frac{\Gamma_1, \texttt{this}: \texttt{any}, |\bar{\texttt{p}}| \vdash getVars(\bar{\texttt{s}}) \rightsquigarrow \Gamma_2 \quad \Gamma_2 \vdash \bar{\texttt{s}}: \bar{\texttt{R}}}{\Gamma_1 \vdash \texttt{function } (\bar{\texttt{p}}) \; \{\; \bar{\texttt{s}} \;\}: \{\; (|\bar{\texttt{p}}|): return(\bar{\texttt{R}}) \;\}}$$

On the whole, these rules are routine. In rule [I-Assign], the expression $\texttt{e = f}$ has type $\texttt{T}$, if the subexpression $\texttt{e}$ has some type $\texttt{S}$ and the subexpression $\texttt{f}$ *in the context of $\texttt{S}$* has type $\texttt{T}$. We also check that type $\texttt{T}$ is assignment compatible with type $\texttt{S}$(for reasons that should become clearer once contextual typing is defined).

In rule [I-Op], when typing the use of a built-in binary operator $\oplus$, we overload notation and use a binary (partial) function $\oplus$ to calculate the return type given the types of the two arguments. Interestingly, the current language specification states that certain combinations of types should be considered both an error *and* yield the return type $\texttt{any}$. The exact details of these type functions [11, §4.15] are omitted from this paper as they are somewhat orthogonal to our main concerns.

Rule [I-Prop] details typing for property access. It makes use of an auxiliary, partial function $lookup(\texttt{S}, \texttt{n})$ that returns the type of property $\texttt{n}$, if it exists, of a type $\texttt{S}$. This process is a little subtle as TypeScript allows primitive types to have properties, and all object types inherit properties from the $\texttt{Object}$ interface. The auxiliary function is defined for safeFTS as follows:[4]

$$lookup(\texttt{S}, \texttt{n}) = \begin{cases} lookup(\texttt{Number}, \texttt{n}) & \text{if } \texttt{S} = \texttt{number} \\ lookup(\texttt{Boolean}, \texttt{n}) & \text{if } \texttt{S} = \texttt{boolean} \\ lookup(\texttt{String}, \texttt{n}) & \text{if } \texttt{S} = \texttt{string} \\ \texttt{T} & \text{if } \texttt{S} = \{\; \bar{\texttt{M}}_0, \texttt{n}:\texttt{T}, \bar{\texttt{M}}_1 \;\} \\ lookup(\texttt{Object}, \texttt{n}) & \text{if } \texttt{S} = \{\; \bar{\texttt{M}} \;\} \text{ and } \texttt{n} \notin \bar{\texttt{M}} \end{cases}$$

In rule [I-CompProp] a computed property expression $\texttt{e[f]}$ has type $\texttt{any}$ if subexpression $\texttt{e}$ has type $\texttt{S}$ (which must be assignable to the type $\texttt{Object}$) and subexpression $\texttt{f}$ has type $\texttt{string}$.

In rule [I-Call] a function call $\texttt{e}(\bar{\texttt{f}})$ has type $\texttt{R}$ if the subexpression $\texttt{e}$ has the call signature type $\{\; (\bar{\texttt{x}}: \bar{\texttt{S}}): \texttt{R} \;\}$. We also check that the arguments $\bar{\texttt{f}}$ in the context

---

[4] TypeScript also allows all callable object types to inherit properties from the **Function** interface.

of types $\bar{S}$ have types $\bar{T}$, and that types $\bar{T}$ are assignment compatible with types $\bar{S}$.

In rule [I-Assert] a type assertion `<T>e` has type T if subexpression e has type S where type S is assignable to T. In safeFTS the only asserts permitted are those that are known to be correct.

Rules [I-Func1] and [I-Func2] address typing a function expression. Both rules assume that the type of `this` in a function expression is `any`. Both rules also make use of an auxiliary function $|\cdot|$ to extract types from the parameters in a call signature. If a parameter does not have a type annotation, then TypeScript assumes that it is of type `any`. One consequence of this design is that TypeScript does not try to infer types for the parameters of a function expression.

```
var fact = function (x) {
   if (x == 0) { return 1; }
   else { return x * fact(x - 1); }
};          // infers type { (x:any): number }
```

Both rules run into an "awful" feature (using the terminology of Crockford [5]) inherited from JavaScript: all variables declared in a function body are in scope regardless of nesting levels, order, or even how many times they are declared. The whole function body (except for functions nested inside it) is treated as a flat declaration space. In other words, JavaScript does not have block scoping. Thus the following (buggy) JavaScript code:

```
var scope = function (p) {
   var y = 1;
   var a = [y, x, z];
   var x = 2;
   if (test(p)) { var z = 3; }
   else { var z = 4; var w = 5; }
   return w + a[2];
};
```

is treated as if it had instead been written as follows.

```
var scope = function (p) {
   var y = 1;
   var x; var z; var w;          // implicit
   var a = [y, x, z];
   var x = 2;
   if (test(p)) { var z = 3; }
   else { var z = 4; var w = 5; }
   return w + a[2];
};
```

At the level of typing this means that when typing a function expression, we need two phases: first, we find the types of all the local variables declared in the function body; and second, we then type the function body using the type environment extended with the types determined from the first phase.

There is a further complication as TypeScript also infers types of local variables with initializers. Furthermore, TypeScript, again following JavaScript, supports mutually recursive variable declarations. We assume a function $getVars(\bar{s})$

that returns the variable declarations in the scope of the sequence of statements $\bar{s}$. This function needs to deal with the problem of a collection of untyped initialized variable declarations that depend on each other. In the case where such a collection is cyclic, the language specification states that they should all be treated as if they were explicitly typed as any. A non-cyclic collection of untyped variable declarations are reordered in reverse dependency order.

Given this sequence of variable declarations, we define a judgement written $\Gamma_1 \vdash \bar{v} \rightsquigarrow \Gamma_2$ to extend a given type environment Γ_1 with the type information contained in the variable declarations $\bar{v}$ yielding a new type environment Γ_2. The chief concern is dealing with repeated variable declarations. Such repetition is permitted in TypeScript provided that the multiple declarations associate the same type with the variable [11, §5.1].

Environment extension: $\Gamma_1 \vdash \bar{v} \rightsquigarrow \Gamma_2$

$$\frac{}{\Gamma \vdash \bullet \rightsquigarrow \Gamma} \qquad \frac{dupOK(\Gamma_1, x\colon T) \quad \Gamma_1 \uplus (x\colon T) \vdash \bar{v} \rightsquigarrow \Gamma_2}{\Gamma_1 \vdash \mathbf{var}\ x\colon T;\ \bar{v} \rightsquigarrow \Gamma_2}$$

$$\frac{dupOK(\Gamma_1, x\colon \mathbf{any}) \quad \Gamma_1 \uplus (x\colon \mathbf{any}) \vdash \bar{v} \rightsquigarrow \Gamma_2}{\Gamma_1 \vdash \mathbf{var}\ x;\ \bar{v} \rightsquigarrow \Gamma_2}$$

$$\frac{dupOK(\Gamma_1, x\colon T) \quad \Gamma_1 \uplus (x\colon T) \vdash \bar{v} \rightsquigarrow \Gamma_2}{\Gamma_1 \vdash \mathbf{var}\ x\colon T = e;\ \bar{v} \rightsquigarrow \Gamma_2}$$

$$\frac{\Gamma_1 \vdash e\colon T \quad dupOK(\Gamma_1, x\colon T) \quad \Gamma_1 \uplus (x\colon T) \vdash \bar{v} \rightsquigarrow \Gamma_2}{\Gamma_1 \vdash \mathbf{var}\ x = e;\ \bar{v} \rightsquigarrow \Gamma_2}$$

We use the following predicate to detect duplicates:

$$dupOK(\Gamma, x\colon T) = \begin{cases} true & \text{if } x \notin dom(\Gamma) \text{ or } \Gamma(x) = T \\ false & \text{otherwise} \end{cases}$$

Returning to the typing rules [I-Func1] and [I-Func2] we use an auxiliary function $return(\bar{R})$ to calculate the overall return type given the types $\bar{R}$ inferred from the return statements in the body of the function. This function is defined as follows.

$$return(\bar{R}) = \begin{cases} \mathbf{void} & \text{if } \bar{R} = \bullet \\ widen(S) & \text{if } S = bct(\bar{R}) \end{cases}$$

In calculating the return type we make use of two important functions on types. The first function, $widen(T)$, calculates the widened form [11, §3.9] of a type T. This is the type T with all occurrences of the expressible but not denotable types, $Null$ and $Undefined$, replaced by the type any.

The second function $bct(\bar{s})$ calculates the best common type [11, §3.10] of a sequence of types $\bar{s}$ and is defined to be a type taken from the sequence $\bar{s}$ such that all the other types in the sequence can be assigned to it. For example, the best common type of the primitive type number and the empty object type { } is the empty object type; whereas the types number and string have no best common type.

In a small number of situations, more precision can be gained by using explicit type information when typing expressions. For example, in TypeScript the expression `function(s) { return s.length; }` has type `{(s: any): any}`. But, in the context of the explicitly typed declaration

`var f: (s:string) => number;`

within the assignment expression `f = function(s) { return s.length; }` we should type the function knowing that the parameter `s` has the type `string`. Moreover, the information flow can be more than one-way. Thus given the declaration

`var g: (s:string) => any;`

the assignment expression `g = function(s) { return s.length; }` actually has the type `(s:string) => number`.

As mentioned earlier, the contextual typing relation is written $\Gamma \vdash e \downarrow S\colon T$, and defined as follows.

Expression contextual typing $\Gamma \vdash e \downarrow S\colon T$ and $\Gamma \vdash a \downarrow L\colon M$

$$[\text{C-ObLit}] \frac{\Gamma \vdash \bar{a} \downarrow L\colon \bar{M}}{\Gamma \vdash \{\,\bar{a}\,\} \downarrow L\colon \{\,\bar{M}\,\}}$$

$$[\text{C-PA1}] \frac{(x\colon S) \in \bar{M} \quad \Gamma \vdash e \downarrow S\colon T}{\Gamma \vdash (x\colon e) \downarrow \{\,\bar{M}\,\}\colon (x\colon T)} \qquad [\text{C-PA2}] \frac{(x\colon S) \notin \bar{M} \quad \Gamma \vdash e\colon T}{\Gamma \vdash (x\colon e) \downarrow \{\,\bar{M}\,\}\colon (x\colon T)}$$

$$[\text{C-Func}] \frac{\Gamma, \bar{x}\colon \bar{S}, \text{this}\colon \text{any} \vdash \bar{s} \downarrow T\colon \bar{R} \quad R = \mathit{return}(\bar{R})}{\Gamma \vdash \text{function } (\bar{x}) \,\{\bar{s}\} \downarrow \{\,(\bar{y}\colon \bar{S})\colon T\,\}\colon \{\,(\bar{y}\colon \bar{S})\colon R\,\}}$$

$$[\text{C-Inf}] \frac{\Gamma \vdash e\colon T}{\Gamma \vdash e \downarrow S\colon T}$$

In rule [C-ObLit], in order to contextually type the the object literal { $\bar{a}$ }, we contextually type the property assignments $\bar{a}$. In rule [C-PA1] the property assignment `x: e` in the context of the object type literal { $\bar{M}$ } (which supports property `x` at type `S`) has type `x: T` where the subexpression `e` has type `T` in the context of type `S`. Rule [C-PA2] covers the case where the contextual type does not support the property `x`. In this case the type is inferred from the subexpression `e`.

In rule [C-Func] the function expression `function (x̄) {s̄}` in the context of the type { ($\bar{y}$: $\bar{S}$): T } (where the length of the sequences $\bar{x}, \bar{y}$ and $\bar{S}$ are equal) has the type { ($\bar{y}$: $\bar{S}$): R } if the function body $\bar{s}$ has the types $\bar{R}$ in the context of type $\bar{T}$ and R is the result of the calculating the return type from the sequence of types $\bar{R}$. Rule [C-Inf] applies only if the expression `e` is not a function expression or an object literal, and asserts that expression `e` in the context of type `S` has type `T` simply if `e` has type `T`; the contextual type is ignored.

Thus contextual typing is highly (and to the authors' minds, uncomfortably) syntax dependent. For example, a misplaced pair of brackets can affect the contextual typing of a TypeScript expression [11, §4.18].

```
var t1: (s: string) => any;
var t2 = (t1 = function (s) { return s.length; });
           // Contextual typing! Infers { (s: string): number }
var t3 = (t1 = (function (s) { return s.length; }));
           // No contextual typing. Infers { (s: any): any }
```

The typing judgements for safeFTS have the pleasant property of unicity of typing; in other words, they define functions not relations.

Lemma 2 (Unicity of typing)

1. If $\Gamma \vdash e: T_1$ and $\Gamma \vdash e: T_2$ then $T_1 = T_2$.
2. If $\Gamma \vdash e \downarrow S: T_1$ and $\Gamma \vdash e \downarrow S: T_2$ then $T_1 = T_2$.

The proof of this lemma is by induction on typing derivations.

In safeFTS there are two typing relations for statements. We find it convenient to treat sequences of statements rather than single statements. The first typing relation, written $\Gamma \vdash \bar{s}: \bar{R}$, is read "given type environment Γ, the sequence of statements $\bar{s}$ has (return) types $\bar{R}$." The intention is that this judgement asserts both that the statements $\bar{s}$ are well-typed and that the types $\bar{R}$ are the types inferred for any **return** statements in the sequence (so the length of the type sequence $\bar{R}$ is always less than or equal to the length of the statement sequence $\bar{s}$). In line with the earlier discussion of scoping in JavaScript, it is assumed that when typing a sequence of statements $\bar{s}$ the type environment contains types for all the identifiers declared in $\bar{s}$.

Statement sequence typing: $\Gamma \vdash \bar{s}: \bar{R}$

$$[\text{I-EmpSeq}] \frac{}{\Gamma \vdash \bullet: \bullet} \qquad [\text{I-ExpSt}] \frac{\Gamma \vdash e: S \quad \Gamma \vdash \bar{s}: \bar{R}}{\Gamma \vdash e; \bar{s}: \bar{R}}$$

$$[\text{I-If}] \frac{\Gamma \vdash e: S \quad \Gamma \vdash \bar{t}_1: \bar{T}_1 \quad \Gamma \vdash \bar{t}_2: \bar{T}_2 \quad \Gamma \vdash \bar{s}: \bar{R}}{\Gamma \vdash \text{if (e) } \{\bar{t}_1\} \text{ else } \{\bar{t}_2\} \bar{s}: \bar{T}_1, \bar{T}_2, \bar{R}}$$

$$[\text{I-Return}] \frac{\Gamma \vdash \bar{s}: \bar{R}}{\Gamma \vdash \text{return}; \bar{s}: \text{void}, \bar{R}} \qquad [\text{I-ReturnVal}] \frac{\Gamma \vdash e: T \quad \Gamma \vdash \bar{s}: \bar{R}}{\Gamma \vdash \text{return e}; \bar{s}: T, \bar{R}}$$

$$[\text{I-UTVarDec}] \frac{\Gamma(x) = S \quad \Gamma \vdash \bar{s}: \bar{R}}{\Gamma \vdash \text{var x}:S; \bar{s}: \bar{R}}$$

$$[\text{I-ITVarDec}] \frac{\Gamma(x) = S \quad \Gamma \vdash e \downarrow S: T \quad T \leq S \quad \Gamma \vdash \bar{s}: \bar{R}}{\Gamma \vdash \text{var x}:S = e; \bar{s}: \bar{R}}$$

$$[\text{I-UVarDec}] \frac{\Gamma(x) = \text{any} \quad \Gamma \vdash \bar{s}: \bar{R}}{\Gamma \vdash \text{var x}; \bar{s}: \bar{R}}$$

$$[\text{I-IVarDec}] \frac{x \in dom(\Gamma) \quad \Gamma \vdash e: S \quad \Gamma \uplus x: widen(S) \vdash \bar{s}: \bar{R}}{\Gamma \vdash \text{var x} = e; \bar{s}: \bar{R}}$$

Rule [I-EmpSeq] asserts that the empty sequence is well typed. The rest of the rules are defined by the form of the first statement in the statement sequence; they are routine, so we just describe the typing of return statements.

In rule [I-Return] a `return` statement with no expression is well typed and has return type `void`. In rule [I-ReturnVal] a return statement `return e` is well typed and has the return type `T` if the expression `e` is of type `T`.

The second type relation for statement sequences is the analogue of contextual typing for expressions. It is written $\Gamma \vdash \bar{s} \downarrow T : \bar{R}$ and is read "given type environment Γ, the sequence of statements $\bar{s}$ in the context of type `T` has (return) types $\bar{R}$." The intention is that this judgement captures both that the statements $\bar{s}$ are well typed and that the types $\bar{R}$ are the types inferred *in the context* of type `T` for any return statements in the sequence.

Statement sequence contextual typing: $\Gamma \vdash \bar{s} \downarrow T : \bar{R}$

$$[\text{C-EmpSeq}]\frac{}{\Gamma \vdash \bullet \downarrow T : \bullet} \qquad [\text{C-ExpSt}]\frac{\Gamma \vdash e : S \quad \Gamma \vdash \bar{s} \downarrow T : \bar{R}}{\Gamma \vdash e; \bar{s} \downarrow T : \bar{R}}$$

$$[\text{C-If}]\frac{\Gamma \vdash e : S \quad \Gamma \vdash \bar{t}_1 \downarrow T : \bar{R}_1 \quad \Gamma \vdash \bar{t}_2 \downarrow T : \bar{R}_2 \quad \Gamma \vdash \bar{s} \downarrow T : \bar{R}_3}{\Gamma \vdash \text{if (e) } \{\bar{t}_1\} \text{ else } \{\bar{t}_2\} \ \bar{s} \downarrow T : \bar{R}_1, \bar{R}_2, \bar{R}_3}$$

$$[\text{C-Ret}]\frac{\Gamma \vdash \bar{s} \downarrow T : \bar{R}}{\Gamma \vdash \text{return}; \bar{s} \downarrow T : \bar{R}} \qquad [\text{C-RetVal}]\frac{\Gamma \vdash e \downarrow T : S \quad S \leqq T \quad \Gamma \vdash \bar{s} \downarrow T : \bar{R}}{\Gamma \vdash \text{return e}; \bar{s} \downarrow T : S, \bar{R}}$$

$$[\text{C-UTVarDec}]\frac{\Gamma(x) = S \quad \Gamma \vdash \bar{s} \downarrow T : \bar{R}}{\Gamma \vdash \text{var } x : S; \ \bar{s} \downarrow T : \bar{R}}$$

$$[\text{C-ITVarDec}]\frac{\Gamma(x) = S \quad \Gamma \vdash e \downarrow S : S_1 \quad S_1 \leqq S \quad \Gamma \vdash \bar{s} \downarrow T : \bar{R}}{\Gamma \vdash \text{var } x : S = e; \ \bar{s} \downarrow T : \bar{R}}$$

$$[\text{C-UVarDec}]\frac{\Gamma(x) = \text{any} \quad \Gamma \vdash \bar{s} \downarrow T : \bar{R}}{\Gamma \vdash \text{var } x; \ \bar{s} \downarrow T : \bar{R}}$$

$$[\text{C-IVarDec}]\frac{\Gamma(x) = \text{any} \quad \Gamma \vdash e : S \quad \Gamma \uplus x : widen(S) \vdash \bar{s} \downarrow T : \bar{R}}{\Gamma \vdash \text{var } x = e; \ \bar{s} \downarrow T : \bar{R}}$$

Most of these rules are routine; the two important rules involve `return` statements. In rule [C-Ret] we capture the fact that JavaScript permits functions that return values to also contain return statements with no expressions. In rule [C-RetVal] a return statement `return e` is well typed and has return type `S` in the context of type `T` if the expression `e` in the context of type `T` has type `S` and that type `S` is assignable to type `T`.

5 Operational Semantics

As explained in the introduction, the TypeScript compiler emits JavaScript code with no trace of the type system in the emitted code. So, the operational behaviour of TypeScript is just the behaviour of the underlying JavaScript implementation. However, in order to show that the safeFTS type system has the desired safety properties we will give an operational semantics for TypeScript directly. We take as our starting point the operational semantics of Gardner et al. [7], although we make a number of simplifications.

A heap, H, is a partial function that maps a location l to a heap object o. We assume a distinguished location `null`, which is not permitted to be in the domain of a heap. A heap object o is either an object map (a partial function from variables to values, representing an object literal) or a closure. A variable x is either a program variable x, a property name n or the internal property name @this. A value v is either a location l or a literal 1. A closure is a pair consisting of a lambda expression (where we abbreviate `function (x̄) { s̄ }` as $\lambda \bar{x}.\{ \bar{s} \}$) and a scope chain L (defined below).

We denote the empty heap by `emp`, a heap cell by $l \mapsto o$, the union of two disjoint heaps by $H_1 * H_2$, and a heap lookup by $H(l, x)$. We write heap update as $H[l \mapsto o]$, and where o is an object map, we use the shorthand $H[(l, x) \mapsto v]$ to denote an update/extension to the x element of the object map o.

JavaScript's dynamic semantics is complicated by the treatment of variables, which are not stored in an environment, but instead are resolved dynamically against an implicit scope object. A scope chain, L, is a list of locations of the scope objects, where we write $l: L$ for the list resulting from concatenating l to the scope chain L. As safeFTS does not support `new` expressions, for simplicity, we do not model prototype lists. Function calls cause fresh local scope objects to be placed at the beginning of a scope chain and removed when the function body has been evaluated. All programs are evaluated with respect to a default scope chain $[l_g]$ where l_g is the location of the global JavaScript object.

The lookup function σ returns the location of the first scope object in the scope chain to define a given variable:

$$\sigma(H, l : L, x) \stackrel{\text{def}}{=} \begin{cases} l & \text{if } H(l, x) \downarrow \\ \sigma(H, L, x) & \text{otherwise} \end{cases}$$

A result r can be either a value or a reference, which is a pair of a location and a variable; we make use of a function γ where $\gamma(H, r)$ returns r if r is a value, and if it is a reference (l, x) then it returns $H(l, x)$ if defined, or `undefined` if not.

The evaluation relation for FTS is written $\langle H_1, L, e \rangle \Downarrow \langle H_2, r \rangle$, which can be read "given initial heap H_1 and scope chain L, the expression e evaluates to a modified heap H_2 and a result r." We sometimes wish to dereference the result of evaluation, so we use the following shorthand $\langle H_1, L, e \rangle \Downarrow_v \langle H_2, v \rangle$ to mean that there exists a reference r such that $\langle H_1, L, e \rangle \Downarrow \langle H_2, r \rangle$ and $\gamma(H_2, r) = v$.

Expression evaluation: $\langle H_1, L, e \rangle \Downarrow \langle H_2, r \rangle$

$$[\text{E-Id}] \frac{\sigma(H, L, \mathsf{x}) = l}{\langle H, L, \mathsf{x} \rangle \Downarrow \langle H, (l, \mathsf{x}) \rangle} \qquad [\text{E-Lit}] \frac{}{\langle H, L, 1 \rangle \Downarrow \langle H, 1 \rangle}$$

$$[\text{E-this}] \frac{\sigma(H, L, \texttt{@this}) = l_1 \quad H(l_1, \texttt{@this}) = l}{\langle H, L, \texttt{this} \rangle \Downarrow \langle H, l \rangle}$$

$$[\text{E-ObLit}] \frac{\begin{array}{c} H_1 = H_0 * [l \mapsto new()] \\ \langle H_1, L, \texttt{e}_1 \rangle \Downarrow_{\text{v}} \langle H_1', v_1 \rangle \qquad H_2 = H_1'[(l, \mathbf{n}_1) \mapsto v_1] \\ \cdots \quad \langle H_m, L, \texttt{e}_m \rangle \Downarrow_{\text{v}} \langle H_m', v_m \rangle \qquad H = H_m'[(l, \mathbf{n}_m) \mapsto v_m] \end{array}}{\langle H_0, L, \{ \mathbf{n}_1\!:\!\texttt{e}_1, \ldots, \mathbf{n}_m\!:\!\texttt{e}_m \} \rangle \Downarrow \langle H, l \rangle}$$

$$[\text{E-AssignExp}] \frac{\langle H_0, L, \texttt{e}_1 \rangle \Downarrow \langle H_1, (l, x) \rangle \quad \langle H_1, L, \texttt{e}_2 \rangle \Downarrow_{\text{v}} \langle H_2, v \rangle}{\langle H_0, L, \texttt{e}_1 = \texttt{e}_2 \rangle \Downarrow \langle H_2[(l, x) \mapsto v], v \rangle}$$

$$[\text{E-Op}] \frac{\langle H_0, L, \texttt{e}_1 \rangle \Downarrow_{\text{v}} \langle H_1, \mathbf{l}_1 \rangle \quad \langle H_1, L, \texttt{e}_2 \rangle \Downarrow_{\text{v}} \langle H_2, \mathbf{l}_2 \rangle}{\langle H_0, L, \texttt{e}_1 \oplus \texttt{e}_2 \rangle \Downarrow \langle H_2, \mathbf{l}_1 \oplus \mathbf{l}_2 \rangle}$$

$$[\text{E-Prop}] \frac{\langle H_0, L, \texttt{e} \rangle \Downarrow_{\text{v}} \langle H_1, l \rangle \quad l \neq \texttt{null}}{\langle H_0, L, \texttt{e.n} \rangle \Downarrow \langle H_1, (l, \mathbf{n}) \rangle}$$

$$[\text{E-Prop'}] \frac{\langle H_0, L, \texttt{e} \rangle \Downarrow_{\text{v}} \langle H_1, \mathbf{l} \rangle \quad H_2 = H_1 * [l \mapsto box(\mathbf{l})]}{\langle H_0, L, \texttt{e.n} \rangle \Downarrow \langle H_2, (l, \mathbf{n}) \rangle}$$

$$[\text{E-CompProp}] \frac{\langle H_0, L, \texttt{e} \rangle \Downarrow_{\text{v}} \langle H_1, l \rangle \quad l \neq \texttt{null} \quad \langle H_1, L, \texttt{f} \rangle \Downarrow_{\text{v}} \langle H_2, \ulcorner \mathbf{n} \urcorner \rangle}{\langle H_0, L, \texttt{e[f]} \rangle \Downarrow \langle H_2, (l, \mathbf{n}) \rangle}$$

$$[\text{E-CompProp'}] \frac{\begin{array}{c} \langle H_0, L, \texttt{e} \rangle \Downarrow_{\text{v}} \langle H_1, \mathbf{l} \rangle \quad H_2 = H_1 * [l \mapsto box(\mathbf{l})] \\ \langle H_2, L, \texttt{f} \rangle \Downarrow_{\text{v}} \langle H_3, \ulcorner \mathbf{n} \urcorner \rangle \end{array}}{\langle H_0, L, \texttt{e[f]} \rangle \Downarrow \langle H_3, (l, \mathbf{n}) \rangle}$$

$$[\text{E-Call}] \frac{\begin{array}{cc} \langle H_0, L_0, \texttt{e} \rangle \Downarrow \langle H_1, r \rangle & \gamma(H_1, r) = l_1 \\ H(l_1) = \langle \lambda \bar{\mathbf{x}}.\{\bar{\mathbf{s}}\}, L_1 \rangle & \text{This}(H_1, r) = l_2 \\ \langle H_1, L_0, \texttt{e}_1 \rangle \Downarrow_{\text{v}} \langle H_2, v_1 \rangle \quad \cdots \quad & \langle H_n, L_0, \texttt{e}_n \rangle \Downarrow_{\text{v}} \langle H_{n+1}, v_n \rangle \\ H' = H_{n+1} * act(l, \bar{\mathbf{x}}, \bar{v}, \{\bar{\mathbf{s}}\}, l_2) & \langle H', l : L_1, \bar{\mathbf{s}} \rangle \Downarrow \langle H'', \texttt{return } v; \rangle \end{array}}{\langle H_0, L_0, \texttt{e}(\texttt{e}_1, \ldots, \texttt{e}_n) \rangle \Downarrow \langle H'', v \rangle}$$

$$[\text{E-CallUndef}] \frac{\begin{array}{cc} \langle H_0, L_0, \texttt{e} \rangle \Downarrow \langle H_1, r \rangle & \gamma(H_1, r) = l_1 \\ H(l_1) = \langle \lambda \bar{\mathbf{x}}.\{\bar{\mathbf{s}}\}, L_1 \rangle & \text{This}(H_1, r) = l_2 \\ \langle H_1, L_0, \texttt{e}_1 \rangle \Downarrow_{\text{v}} \langle H_2, v_1 \rangle \quad \cdots \quad & \langle H_n, L_0, \texttt{e}_n \rangle \Downarrow_{\text{v}} \langle H_{n+1}, v_n \rangle \\ H' = H_{n+1} * act(l, \bar{\mathbf{x}}, \bar{v}, \{\bar{\mathbf{s}}\}, l_2) & \langle H', l : L_1, \bar{\mathbf{s}} \rangle \Downarrow \langle H'', \texttt{return}; \rangle \end{array}}{\langle H_0, L_0, \texttt{e}(\texttt{e}_1, \ldots, \texttt{e}_n) \rangle \Downarrow \langle H'', \texttt{undefined} \rangle}$$

$$[\text{E-Func}] \frac{H_1 = H_0 * [l \mapsto \langle \lambda \bar{\mathbf{x}}.\{ \bar{\mathbf{s}} \}, L \rangle]}{\langle H_0, L, \texttt{function } (\bar{\mathbf{x}}) \{ \bar{\mathbf{s}} \} \rangle \Downarrow \langle H_1, l \rangle}$$

$$[\text{E-TypeAssert}] \frac{\langle H_0, L, \texttt{e} \rangle \Downarrow \langle H_1, r_1 \rangle}{\langle H_0, L, \texttt{<T>e} \rangle \Downarrow \langle H_1, r_1 \rangle}$$

Most of these rules are routine; Gardner et al. [7] give extensive details. We restrict our attention to just a few of the more important rules. In rule [E-ObLit] we create at fresh location l a new object map (using an auxiliary function new) and update its elements in order. In rule [E-CompProp] we require that the property subexpression f evaluates to a string that denotes a name n; this string we write as $\ulcorner n \urcorner$. In rules [E-Prop'] and [E-CompProp'] we cover the case where properties are accessed on primitive values (which are implicitly boxed, using an auxiliary function *box*). In rule [E-Call] the important step is that we create a fresh local scope object (stored at location l') with which we evaluate the body of the function. We make use of an auxiliary function This (taken from [7, §3.3]) that captures the behaviour of the this keyword, and an auxiliary function *act* that builds the new scope object.

$$\mathsf{This}(H, (l, x)) \overset{\text{def}}{=} l \text{ if } H(l, @\texttt{this}) \downarrow; \text{ and } \mathsf{This}(H, v) \overset{\text{def}}{=} l_g \text{ otherwise}$$
$$act(l, \bar{x}, \bar{v}, \bar{s}, l') \overset{\text{def}}{=} l \mapsto (\{\bar{x} \mapsto \bar{v}, @\texttt{this} \mapsto l'\} * defs(\bar{x}, l, \bar{s}))$$

The auxiliary function *defs* searches the statements $\bar{s}$ for all the declared variables and makes them in scope in the current local scope object; this is the operational counterpart to the "awful" feature of JavaScript scoping described in §4. Rule [E-CallUndef] reflects the JavaScript semantics that functions that do not specify a return value actually return the undefined value.

The evaluation relation for statement sequences is of the form $\langle H_0, L, \bar{s}_0 \rangle \Downarrow \langle H_1, s \rangle$ where s is a statement result, which is a statement of the form return;, return v;, or ;. The rules for evaluating statements are routine and omitted.

In order to prove type soundness, we need to extend the notion of typing to the operational semantics (in the style of [1,3]). A heap type Σ is a partial function from locations to types (which are either function types or object literal types). The statement of subject reduction then relies on a number of new judgements. First, we need a well-formedness relation for a heap H, written $H \models \diamond$. We also need a judgement that a heap H and scope chain L are compatible, written $H, L \models \diamond$, which essentially means that all the scope objects in the scope chain exist in the heap. We use a judgement written $\Sigma \models H$ that captures that a heap H is compatible with a heap type Σ. We also make use of a function $context(\Sigma, L)$ that builds a typing judgement corresponding to the variables in the scope chain L, using their types stored in Σ. Using these judgements, we can then write $\Sigma \models \langle H, L, \mathsf{e} \rangle : \mathsf{T}$ to mean $\Sigma \models H$, $H, L \models \diamond$ and $context(\Sigma, L) \vdash \mathsf{e} : \mathsf{T}$. Similarly we can define judgements $\Sigma \models \langle H, L, \mathsf{e} \rangle \downarrow \mathsf{S} : \mathsf{T}$, $\Sigma \models \langle H, L, \bar{s} \rangle : \bar{\mathsf{T}}$ and $\Sigma \models \langle H, L, \bar{s} \rangle \downarrow \mathsf{S} : \bar{\mathsf{T}}$. Finally, we can define two judgements on results of evaluation, written $\Sigma \models \langle H, r \rangle : \mathsf{T}$ and $\Sigma \models \langle H, r \rangle \downarrow \mathsf{S} : \mathsf{T}$ (along with variants for statement results). We write $\Sigma \subseteq \Sigma'$ to mean that Σ' is an extension of Σ in the usual sense.

Theorem 1 (Subject reduction)

1. If $\Sigma \models \langle H, L, \mathsf{e} \rangle : \mathsf{T}$ and $\langle H, L, \mathsf{e} \rangle \Downarrow \langle H', r \rangle$ then $\exists \Sigma', \mathsf{T}'$ such that $\Sigma \subseteq \Sigma'$, $\Sigma' \models \langle H', r \rangle : \mathsf{T}'$ and $\mathsf{T}' \leq \mathsf{T}$.
2. If $\Sigma \models \langle H, L, \mathsf{e} \rangle \downarrow \mathsf{S} : \mathsf{T}$ and $\langle H, L, \mathsf{e} \rangle \Downarrow \langle H', r \rangle$ then $\exists \Sigma', \mathsf{T}'$ such that $\Sigma \subseteq \Sigma'$, $\Sigma' \models \langle H', r \rangle \downarrow \mathsf{S} : \mathsf{T}'$ and $\mathsf{T}' \leq \mathsf{T}$.
3. If $\Sigma \models \langle H, L, \bar{s} \rangle : \bar{\mathsf{T}}$ and $\langle H, L, \bar{s} \rangle \Downarrow \langle H', s \rangle$ then $\exists \Sigma', \mathsf{T}'$ such that $\Sigma \subseteq \Sigma'$, $\Sigma' \models \langle H', s \rangle : \mathsf{T}'$ and $\mathsf{T}' \leq return(\bar{\mathsf{T}})$.
4. If $\Sigma \models \langle H, L, \bar{s} \rangle \downarrow \mathsf{S} : \bar{\mathsf{T}}$ and $\langle H, L, \bar{s} \rangle \Downarrow \langle H', s \rangle$ then $\exists \Sigma', \mathsf{T}'$ such that $\Sigma \subseteq \Sigma'$, $\Sigma' \models \langle H', s \rangle \downarrow \mathsf{S} : \mathsf{T}'$ and $\mathsf{T}' \leq return(\bar{\mathsf{T}})$.

6   Production Featherweight TypeScript (prodFTS)

In this section we define prodFTS which can be viewed as the core calculus of the full TypeScript language. We define it as a series of extensions to the type system of safeFTS. Each of these extensions is unsound. We organize them according to the source of unsoundness, along the lines suggested in §2.

6.1   Unchecked Downcasts

In addition to the upcasts allowed in safeFTS, prodFTS also supports downcasts.

$$\frac{\Gamma \vdash e : S \quad T \leqq S}{\Gamma \vdash \texttt{<T>}e : T}$$

Unlike in languages such as Java and C$^\sharp$, these downcasts are not automatically checked at runtime, because all type information is erased by the compiler. The following example illustrates this issue:

```
interface Shape { ... }
interface Circle extends Shape { ... }
interface Triangle extends Shape { ... }
function createShape(kind: string): Shape {
    if (kind === "circle") return buildCircle();
    if (kind === "triangle") return buildTriangle();
    ... }
var circle = <Circle> createShape("circle");
```

Here, the TypeScript type system will rely on the fact that, after the type assertion, `circle` is of type `Circle`. The responsibility of guarding against erroneous creation of, for example a `Triangle`, remains with the programmer. Should runtime checks be needed, the TypeScript programmer would have to simulate them using JavaScript's introspection capabilities.

6.2   Unchecked Gradual Typing (and Unchecked Indexing)

TypeScript has a gradual type system in the style of Siek and Taha [14]. However, unlike most languages with gradual type systems, dynamic checks are not made to ensure safety (again, because types are removed by the compiler).

The key to gradual type systems is that the `any` type is treated specially. This type serves as the boundary between the statically typed world (code typed without reference to `any`) and the dynamically typed world. The fundamental feature of `any` is that any type can be implicitly converted to `any` and `any` can be implicitly converted to any other type. The former of these conversions is allowed in safeFTS via the rule [A-AnyR]. prodFTS includes the following additional rule in order to support conversions in the opposite direction:

$$\frac{T \vdash \diamond}{\texttt{any} \leqq T}$$

This extension to assignment compatibility is quite drastic. In particular, assignment compatibility is no longer transitive! For example, we now have that string $\leq$ any and any $\leq$ boolean but not that string $\leq$ boolean. Moreover, this extension implies that assignment compatibility is not a good basis for determining best common types or for overloading resolution. Therefore, TypeScript introduces a new type relation, called subtyping. In contrast to the definition of assignment compatibility, it is not the case that any is a subtype of any other type. In all other respects, however, subtyping is defined identically to assignment compatibility [11, §3.8.2]. Accordingly, in prodFTS, subtyping replaces assignment compatibility in the definitions of best common types and for overloading resolution.

Furthermore, TypeScript allows the liberal use of subexpressions of type any. (Such use is how gradual type systems permit the mixing of dynamic and statically-typed code.) In particular, those subexpressions may be used for potentially unsafe indexing. We capture this aspect of TypeScript by including the following extra typing rules in prodFTS:

$$\frac{\Gamma \vdash \texttt{e: any}}{\Gamma \vdash \texttt{e.n: any}} \qquad\qquad \frac{\Gamma \vdash \texttt{e: any} \quad \Gamma \vdash \bar{\texttt{f}}\texttt{:}\,\bar{\texttt{S}}}{\Gamma \vdash \texttt{e(}\bar{\texttt{f}}\texttt{): any}}$$

$$\frac{\Gamma \vdash \texttt{e: any} \quad \Gamma \vdash \texttt{f: string}}{\Gamma \vdash \texttt{e[f]: any}} \qquad\qquad \frac{\Gamma \vdash \texttt{e: T} \quad \Gamma \vdash \texttt{f: any}}{\Gamma \vdash \texttt{e[f]: any}}$$

Siek and Taha employ occurrences of these rules in order to inject runtime checks into code, with the goal of ensuring that the code satisfies type contracts. Once more, as TypeScript removes all type information, analogous checks are not made in TypeScript, so runtime type errors are possible.

6.3   Unchecked Covariance

As mentioned in the introduction, TypeScript was designed as a language to which existing JavaScript programmers could migrate in a seamless way. In particular, existing libraries and codebases can be given type signatures without disturbing the source code. (An alternative approach would be to require programmers to restructure their code so particular features of some new type system could be used to greater effect.) Therefore, common programming idioms must be supported directly at the type level. One such idiom that occurs extensively in JavaScript codebases and thus is supported directly is covariance of property and parameter types in function signatures. Although this idiom is not in general safe, dynamic programmers frequently make safe use of it. For instance (much as in [1]), consider a program that uses the types Person and Vegetarian. In Person, a member eat takes arguments of type any; in Vegetarian, it takes arguments of a type Vegetables, which is also the type of another member myLunch. Covariance allows Vegetarian to be assignable to Person, and errors won't arise as long as objects of type Vegetarian are fed the contents of myLunch.

In prodFTS, we capture covariance via a revised notion of assignment compatibility of members, with the following rules:

$$\frac{S \leqq T}{n:S \leqq n:T} \qquad \frac{\bar{S} \cong \bar{T} \quad R_1 \neq \text{void} \quad R_0 \leqq R_1}{(\bar{x}:\bar{S}):R_0 \leqq (\bar{y}:\bar{T}):R_1} \qquad \frac{\bar{S} \cong \bar{T} \quad R \vdash \diamond}{(\bar{x}:\bar{S}):R \leqq (\bar{y}:\bar{T}):\text{void}}$$

The first rule permits covariance on member typing. The others permit call signatures to be bivariant (either covariant or contravariant) in their argument types and covariant in their result types (where $S \cong T \overset{\text{def}}{=} S \leqq T$ or $T \leqq S$).

7   Connection to Gradual Typing

In this section, we aim to give precise substance to our claim that TypeScript is a gradual type system in the style of Siek and Taha [14]. Specifically, we define a notion of consistent-subtyping for TypeScript types, and prove that it is equivalent to the notion of assignment compatibility in prodFTS, defined in the previous section.

Our first step is to define a restriction operator on types and members. Basically, $S|_T$ masks off the parts of S that are unknown (i.e., any) in T.

$$S|_T \overset{\text{def}}{=} \begin{cases} \text{any} & \text{if } T \equiv \text{any} \\ \{\, \bar{M}_0|_{\bar{M}_1} \,\} & \text{if } S \equiv \{\, \bar{M}_0 \,\} \text{ and } T \equiv \{\, \bar{M}_1, \bar{M}_2 \,\} \\ \{\, \bar{M}_0|_{\bar{M}_2}, \bar{M}_1 \,\} & \text{if } S \equiv \{\, \bar{M}_0, \bar{M}_1 \,\} \text{ and } T \equiv \{\, \bar{M}_2 \,\} \\ S & \text{otherwise} \end{cases}$$

$$M_0|_{M_1} \overset{\text{def}}{=} \begin{cases} n: S|_T & \text{if } M_0 \equiv n:S \text{ and } M_1 \equiv n:T \\ (\bar{x}:\bar{S}_0|_{\bar{S}_1}):T_0|_{T_1} & \text{if } M_0 \equiv (\bar{x}:\bar{S}_0):T_0 \text{ and } M_1 \equiv (\bar{x}:\bar{S}_1):T_1 \end{cases}$$

Next we introduce a simple subtyping relation. This relation, written $S <: T$ (and $M_0 <: M_1$ on members), gives no special status to the type **any**. It is covariant in members and, for call signatures, bivariant in argument types and covariant in return types. (We write $S <:> T$ to mean either $S <: T$ or $T <: S$.)

$$\frac{S \vdash \diamond}{S <: S} \qquad \frac{T \vdash \diamond}{\textit{Undefined} <: T} \qquad \frac{T \vdash \diamond \quad T \neq \textit{Undefined}}{\textit{Null} <: T}$$

$$\frac{\mathcal{I}(P) <: T}{P <: T} \qquad \frac{\{\, \bar{M}_0, \bar{M}_1 \,\} \vdash \diamond \quad \bar{M}_1 <: \bar{M}_2}{\{\, \bar{M}_0, \bar{M}_1 \,\} <: \{\, \bar{M}_2 \,\}} \qquad \frac{S <: T}{n:S <: n:T}$$

$$\frac{\bar{S} <:> \bar{T} \quad R_1 \neq \text{void} \quad R_0 <: R_1}{(\bar{x}:\bar{S}):R_0 <: (\bar{y}:\bar{T}):R_1} \qquad \frac{\bar{S} <:> \bar{T} \quad R \vdash \diamond}{(\bar{x}:\bar{S}):R <: (\bar{y}:\bar{T}):\text{void}}$$

Then, following Siek and Taha, we define consistent-subtyping, written $S \lesssim T$, as $S|_T <: T|_S$. The following theorem expresses the equivalence of consistent-subtyping and assignment compatibility. Its proof, which we omit, relies on coinduction.

Theorem 2. $S \lesssim T$ if and only if $S \leqq T$.

8   Related Work

Since JavaScript's recent rise to prominence, there has been considerable work on providing a suitable type system for the language. Here we can only mention a subset of that work. Various research efforts have explored sound approaches to this problem. Thiemann [17] proposed an early type system that uses singleton types and first-class record labels, and in the same year Anderson et al. [2] proposed another type system with a focus on type inference. A number of others have proposed systems of increasing complexity to deal with the complicated programming patterns found in JavaScript; for example, Chugh et al. [4] employed nested refinements and heap types in DJS, and Guha et al. [9] proposed a combination of a type system and a flow analysis.

Others have emphasized support for development at scale. In particular, like TypeScript, the Dart language [8] relaxes soundness in order to support dynamic programming. Dart is closely related to JavaScript, and can also compile directly to JavaScript in such a way that all traces of the type system are removed. However, unlike TypeScript, Dart is an entirely new language.

Whilst TypeScript favours convenience over soundness, our work can be used as the basis for defining safe variants of TypeScript. Bhargavan et al. [15] extend a similar safe fragment with a new type to denote values from untrusted JavaScript code and employ runtime type information instead of type erasure, focusing on using type-driven wrappers to ensure important security properties.

Further afield, various dynamic languages have been extended with type systems. For instance, Typed Scheme [18] adds a type system to Scheme. It introduces a notion of occurrence typing and combines a number of type system features such as recursive types, union types, and polymorphism.

9   Conclusion

This paper describes and analyses the core of the TypeScript language, and in particular its type system. The work that it represents has been useful in resolving ambiguities in the language definition, and in identifying minor unintended inconsistencies and mistakes in the language implementation. It provides a basis for partial soundness theorems, and it isolates and accounts for sources of unsoundness in the type system.

Beyond the details of this work (which are specific to TypeScript, and which may perhaps change, as TypeScript develops further), we hope that our results will contribute to the principled study of deliberate unsoundness. In this direction, we believe that there are various opportunities for intriguing further research. In particular, to the extent that any type system expresses programmer intent, we would expect that it could be useful in debugging, despite its unsoundness. Research on blame, e.g., [19], might be helpful in this respect. It may also be worthwhile to codify programmer guidance that would, over time, reduce the reliance on dangerous typing rules. Static analysis tools may support this guidance and complement a type system. These and related projects would aim to look beyond sound language fragments: the principles of programming languages may also help us understand and live with unsoundness.

References

1. Abadi, M., Cardelli, L.: A theory of objects. Springer (1996)
2. Anderson, C., Giannini, P., Drossopoulou, S.: Towards type inference for javaScript. In: Gao, X.-X. (ed.) ECOOP 2005. LNCS, vol. 3586, pp. 428–452. Springer, Heidelberg (2005)
3. Bierman, G., Parkinson, M., Pitts, A.: MJ: An imperative core calculus for Java and Java with effects. Technical Report 563, University of Cambridge Computer Laboratory (2003)
4. Chugh, R., Herman, D., Jhala, R.: Dependent types for JavaScript. In: Proceedings of OOSLA (2012)
5. Crockford, D.: JavaScript: The good parts. O'Reilly (2008)
6. Gapeyev, V., Levin, M., Pierce, B.: Recursive subtyping revealed. JFP 12(6), 511–548 (2002)
7. Gardner, P., Maffeis, S., Smith, G.: Towards a program logic for JavaScript. In: Proceedings of POPL (2013)
8. Google. Dart programming language, http://www.dartlang.org
9. Guha, A., Saftoiu, C., Krishnamurthi, S.: Typing local control and state using flow analysis. In: Barthe, G. (ed.) ESOP 2011. LNCS, vol. 6602, pp. 256–275. Springer, Heidelberg (2011)
10. Igarashi, A., Pierce, B., Wadler, P.: Featherweight Java: A minimal core calculus for Java and GJ. ACM TOPLAS 23(3), 396–450 (2001)
11. Microsoft Corporation. TypeScript Language Specification, 0.9.5 edn. (2014), http://typescriptlang.org
12. Pierce, B., Turner, D.: Local type inference. In: Proceedings of POPL (1998)
13. Sénizergues, G.: The equivalence problem for deterministic pushdown automata is decidable. In: Degano, P., Gorrieri, R., Marchetti-Spaccamela, A. (eds.) ICALP 1997. LNCS, vol. 1256, pp. 671–681. Springer, Heidelberg (1997)
14. Siek, J.G., Taha, W.: Gradual typing for objects. In: Ernst, E. (ed.) ECOOP 2007. LNCS, vol. 4609, pp. 2–27. Springer, Heidelberg (2007)
15. Swamy, N., Fournet, C., Rastogi, A., Bhargavan, K., Chen, J., Strub, P.-Y., Bierman, G.: Gradual typing embedded securely in JavaScript. In: Proceedings of POPL (2014)
16. Solomon, M.H.: Type definitions with parameters. In: Proceedings of POPL (1978)
17. Thiemann, P.: Towards a type system for analyzing javaScript programs. In: Sagiv, M. (ed.) ESOP 2005. LNCS, vol. 3444, pp. 408–422. Springer, Heidelberg (2005)
18. Tobin-Hochstadt, S., Felleisen, M.: The design and implementation of Typed Scheme. In: Proceedings of POPL (2008)
19. Wadler, P., Findler, R.B.: Well-typed programs can't be blamed. In: Castagna, G. (ed.) ESOP 2009. LNCS, vol. 5502, pp. 1–16. Springer, Heidelberg (2009)

Sound and Complete Subtyping between Coinductive Types for Object-Oriented Languages*

Davide Ancona and Andrea Corradi

DIBRIS, Università di Genova, Italy
`davide.ancona@unige.it`, `andrea.corradi@dibris.unige.it`

Abstract. Structural subtyping is an important notion for effective static type analysis; it can be defined either axiomatically by a collection of subtyping rules, or by means of set inclusion between type interpretations, following the more intuitive approach of semantic subtyping, which allows simpler proofs of the expected properties of the subtyping relation.

In object-oriented programming, recursive types are typically interpreted inductively; however, cyclic objects can be represented more precisely by coinductive types.

We study semantic subtyping between coinductive types with records and unions, which are particularly interesting for object-oriented programming, and develop and implement a sound and complete top-down direct and effective algorithm for deciding it. To our knowledge, this is the first proposal for a sound and complete top-down direct algorithm for semantic subtyping between coinductive types.

1 Introduction

Subtyping between structural types is an essential notion for effective static type analysis of object-oriented languages, and, in particular, of dynamically typed languages like JavaScript and Python.

In most cases the subtyping relation is defined axiomatically, then algorithms have to be defined and proved to be (at least) sound and complete (if the relation is decidable) w.r.t. the given axioms. Such approaches have some drawbacks: since the relation is specified in an axiomatic way, it may fail to convey the right intuition behind it, or it may not be completely clear whether the definition fully captures such an intuition (that is, if the axiomatization is sound and complete w.r.t. some intended model); furthermore, proving even simple properties, like transitivity, may be quite hard.

Semantic subtyping has been proposed as a possible solution to these problems for XDuce [13] and ℂDuce [12], two statically typed domain specific languages expressly designed for type safe manipulation of XML documents. In semantic

---

* Partly funded by the project MIUR CINA - Compositionality, Interaction, Negotiation, Autonomicity for the future ICT society.

R. Jones (Ed.): ECOOP 2014, LNCS 8586, pp. 282–307, 2014.

subtyping types are interpreted as sets of values, following the intuition that a type specifies all possible values that an expression of that type may denote; consequently, subtyping corresponds to set inclusion between type interpretations. In this way, the definition of subtyping is more intuitive, and several properties can be easily deduced (for instance, transitivity always holds trivially). Semantic subtyping is particularly suited to naturally supports Boolean type constructors; for instance, in terms of type interpretation Boolean disjunction and conjunction correspond to union and intersection on sets of values. Boolean type constructors (in particular union types) allow types and type analysis to be more precise, but their expressive power makes the definition of a sound and complete decision procedure for subtyping more challenging.

Another feature that complicates subtyping (but that is also indispensable) is type recursion; syntactically, a recursive type corresponds to a *regular* (a.k.a. rational) tree defined by a finite set of guarded syntactic equations. In the semantic subtyping approach, semantic interpretation of recursive types requires to consider the syntactic equations defining a type as semantics equations specifying sets of values; such equations can be interpreted either inductively or coinductively. Let us consider, for instance, the recursive type τ defined by

$$\tau = null \vee \langle el{:}int, nx{:}\tau \rangle.$$

The type is the union of *null*, denoting the null reference, and $\langle el{:}int, nx{:}\tau \rangle$, denoting all records equipped at least with the two fields el and nx having type int and τ, respectively (that is, τ corresponds to a simple implementation of linked lists of integer values). When we turn to consider the semantic interpretation of τ, denoted by $[\![\tau]\!]$, because the Boolean type constructor $\vee$ corresponds to union of values, we get the following recursive equation:

$$[\![\tau]\!] = \{\text{null}\} \cup [\![\langle el{:}int, nx{:}\tau \rangle]\!]$$

which is equivalent to the equation

$$[\![\tau]\!] = \{\text{null}\} \cup \{\langle el \mapsto v_{el}, nx \mapsto v_{nx}, \ldots \rangle \mid v_{el} \in [\![int]\!], v_{nx} \in [\![\tau]\!]\}$$

where $\langle el \mapsto v_{el}, nx \mapsto v_{nx}, \ldots \rangle$ denotes a record value with fields el and nx associated with values v_{el} and v_{nx}, and with possibly other fields. If such an equation is interpreted inductively (hence, τ is the least solution), then all values v in $[\![\tau]\!]$ are inductive, and the operation $v.nx.nx.\ldots.nx$ is defined only for a finite number of consecutive selections of field nx. If the equation is interpreted coinductively (hence, τ is the greatest solution), then $[\![\tau]\!]$ contains also coinductive values v for which the operation $v.nx.nx.\ldots.nx$ is defined also for an infinite number of consecutive selections of field nx; in other words, $[\![\tau]\!]$ contains also cyclic values.

To better outline the difference between the inductive and coinductive interpretation of recursive types, let us consider the recursive type τ' defined by

$$\tau' = \langle el{:}int, nx{:}\tau' \rangle.$$

In this case we get the equation

$$[\![\tau]\!] = \{\langle el \mapsto v_{el}, nx \mapsto v_{nx}, \ldots\rangle \mid v_{el} \in [\![int]\!], v_{nx} \in [\![\tau]\!]\}.$$

In this case the least solution of the equation is $[\![\tau]\!] = \emptyset$ (inductive interpretation), whereas the greatest solution is $[\![\tau]\!] = V$, with $V \neq \emptyset$; more precisely, V is the set of all integer lists for which the operation $v.nx.nx\ldots.nx$ is always correct for an infinite number of consecutive selections of field nx. Therefore, whereas τ' is not very useful if interpreted inductively, when interpreted coinductively it specifies an interesting property that is verified by all cyclic lists.

As explained in the next section, the ability of representing cyclic values (hence, to interpret recursive types coinductively) allow more precise type analysis in all those situations where type correctness depends on the fact that objects (or, more in generally, values) are cyclic. Furthermore, since termination cannot be usually guaranteed through type analysis, and coinductive interpretations of types contain both inductive and coinductive values, coinductive interpretation of types leads to more expressive type systems.

Subtyping on coinductive types has been initially proposed by Amadio and Cardelli [1] in the context of functional programming; subsequently, an equivalent but more concise definition has been proposed by Brandt and Henglein [10]. In both approaches the subtyping relation is defined axiomatically (no semantic subtyping) and Boolean type constructors are not considered.

Semantic subtyping has been extensively studied in the context of the languages XDuce and ℂDuce [13,12], but recursive types are interpreted inductively, because values in those languages correspond to XML documents, hence they cannot be cyclic. For XDuce the decision problem for the subtype relation reduces to the inclusion problem between tree automata, which is known to be EXPTIME-complete [14]. Despite this negative result, it is still possible to define practical top-down algorithms which work directly on types, and are not based on determinization of tree automata [14].

More recently, sound but not complete subtyping rules have been proposed for coinductive types with records and unions [4,5] in the context of abstract compilation. Subsequently, the problem of semantic subtyping has been proved to reduce to the inclusion problem between tree automata also for the coinductive case [9]; such a result has been generalized in the framework of coalgebras. However, to our knowledge, no practical sound and complete algorithm has been proposed for deciding semantic subtyping of coinductive types with Boolean type constructors.

The main contribution of this paper is the definition of a practical top-down algorithm for deciding semantic subtyping for coinductively interpreted types in the presence of record and union types. Such an algorithm is derived by a set of subtyping rules that is proved to be sound and complete w.r.t. semantic subtyping. To do that we propose and use a new proof technique that can be fruitfully used for proving soundness results for coinductively defined judgments (or, dually, for proving completeness results for inductively defined judgments). A prototype implementation of the algorithm has been developed and has been made available.

The rest of the paper is structured in the following way. Section 2 shows how coinductive types allow more precise type analysis in the presence of cyclic objects. Section 3 introduces basic definitions and results that are used in the rest of the paper. Section 4 defines semantic subtyping for coinductive record and union types, whereas subtyping rules and proofs of soundness and completeness can be found in Section 5. Finally, Section 6 presents the algorithm derived from the subtyping rules, and its prototype implementation, while Section 7 draws conclusion and proposes directions for future work.

2 A Motivating Example

In this section we present an example which shows how coinductive types allow more precise type analysis in the presence of cyclic objects. Let us consider the Python code in Figure 1 implementing circular linked lists (with dummy header).

Let us focus on the definition of the private method getNode of class Node, and try to find which type could be assigned to self for correctly type checking the body of the method (in Python the first argument of a method, conventionally called self, corresponds to this in Java).

Let us consider first the following possible candidate types:

$$\tau_1 = null \vee \langle elem{:}\tau_e, next{:}\tau_1\rangle$$
$$\tau_2 = \langle\ \rangle \vee \langle elem{:}\tau_e, next{:}\tau_2\rangle$$
$$\tau_3 = \langle elem{:}\tau_e\rangle \vee \langle elem{:}\tau_e, next{:}\tau_3\rangle$$

Since for this example we are not particularly interested in the specific type of the elements of the lists, we assume that field *elem* has a certain unspecified type τ_e.

Types τ_1, τ_2 and τ_3 only differ for the base case: in τ_1 and τ_2 a sequence of nodes is terminated by null, and by the empty record, respectively, whereas in τ_3 terminal nodes are represented by the record type $\langle elem{:}\tau_e\rangle$.

Independently of their interpretation (either inductive, or coinductive), all types do not allow correct typechecking of the body of getNode, because if we assume that self, and, hence, the local variable n, has one of the tree types defined above, then the statement n = n.next is not type correct, because access of field next is not defined for the types *null*, $\langle\ \rangle$, and $\langle elem{:}\tau_e\rangle$.

Note that if we consider the analogous code for languages with nominal types like Java, then the body of the method is correctly typechecked since this has type Node, but in fact the code is not type safe, because in Java reference types always include the null reference, and the type system does not check access to the null reference (hence, well-typed code can throw the NullPointerException exception).

Let us now consider the following type τ:

$$\tau = \langle elem{:}\tau_e, next{:}\tau\rangle$$

If self (and, hence, n) has type τ, then the body of getNode typechecks, because now the statement n = n.next is type safe.

```
class Node:
        def __init__(self,elem):
                self.elem = elem
                self.next = self

        def getNode(self,index):
                n = self
                for i in range(0,index):
                        n = n.next
                return n

class CircularList:
        def __init__(self):
                self.head = Node(None)
                self.size = 0

        def __checkBounds(self,index,limit):
                if index < 0 or index >= limit:
                        raise IndexError("list index out of range")

        def add(self,index,elem):
                self.__checkBounds(index,self.size+1)
                n = self.head.getNode(index)
                tmp = Node(elem)
                tmp.next = n.next
                n.next = tmp;
                self.size+=1

        def get(self,index):
                self.__checkBounds(index,self.size)
                return self.head.getNode(index+1).elem
```

Fig. 1. Implementation of circular linked lists in Python

This result is independent of the interpretation of τ; however, as already observed in the introduction, if τ is interpreted inductively, then we get $[\![\tau]\!] = \emptyset$; but if the type of self is empty, then method getNode is useless, since no value can be passed to it. Indeed, since $[\![\tau]\!] = \emptyset$, by semantic subtyping we have that τ is subtype of any type, therefore any well-typed expression that can possibly return a value, cannot have type τ, otherwise the type system would be unsound.

For instance, the return type of method __init__ of class Node (this is similar to a Java constructor) cannot be τ, because, otherwise the expression Node(elem) in method add would have the empty type τ, and this would not be sound. As a consequence, class Node and CircularList could not be typed if τ is interpreted inductively. On the contrary, if τ is interpreted coinductively, then $[\![\tau]\!] \neq \emptyset$, and both classes can be successfully typechecked.

We conclude this section by observing that if self has type τ_1, τ_2 or τ_3 as defined above, then method getNode can typecheck successfully if both the following items are verified:

1. the statement n = n.next is guarded by a suitable test; for instance, if self has type τ_1, then n = n.next should be replaced by the statement if(n != None): n = n.next (None is the equivalent of Java null);
2. type analysis has to be flow sensitive, and the type of n has to be narrowed in the then branch of the if statement we introduced.

Item 1 makes the code less efficient by adding a superfluous check that can be avoided if we know that class `Node` is only used by class `CircularList`. Item 2 requires a more sophisticated type analysis; flow sensitive typing and type narrowing are challenging tasks, especially in the presence of aliasing.

If `self` is assigned type τ (interpreted coinductively), then neither of the items above are required.

3 Background

In this section we define record and union coinductive types and present definitions and general results that will be used in the rest of the paper.

3.1 Types and Tree

In the rest of the paper we will deal with finitely branching trees which are allowed to contain infinite paths. A formalization of such infinite trees has been given by Courcelle [11]. In the rest of the paper by term we mean a finitely branching trees which are allowed to contain infinite paths, where nodes correspond to constructors, and the number of children of a node correspond to its arity.

These trees will represent, either types, or proof trees.

The following proposition states a well-known property of regular terms [11,16].

A system of guarded equations is a finite set of syntactic equations of shape $X = e$, where X is a variable, and e may contains variables, such that there exist no subsets of equations having shape $X_0 = X_1, \ldots, X_n = X_0$.

A solution to a set of guarded equations is a substitution to all variables contained in the equations that satisfies all syntactic equations.

Definition 1. *A regular tree is a possibly infinite tree containing a finite set of subtrees. A type is regular if it is a term that corresponds to a regular tree, that is, it has a finite set of subterms.*

Proposition 1. *Every regular tree t can be represented by a system of guarded equations.*

We define types as all regular terms coinductively defined as follows:

$$\tau ::= \mathbf{0} \mid int \mid null \mid \langle f_1{:}\tau_1, \ldots, f_n{:}\tau_n \rangle \mid \tau_1 \vee \tau_2$$

A record type $\langle f_1{:} \tau_1 \ldots f_n{:}\tau_n \rangle$ is a finite map from field names to types, therefore we implicitly assume that field names are distinct and their order is immaterial. If τ is a record type, then $dom(\tau)$ denotes the set of its fields, $\tau(f)$ the type associated with f (if $f \in dom(\tau)$), and $\tau[f{:}\tau']$ the update of record τ with the association of field f to type τ'.

Union type $\tau_1 \vee \tau_2$ intuitively represents the union of the value of τ_1 and τ_2 [8,15]. Type $\mathbf{0}$ is the empty type, and int represents the set $\mathbb{Z}$, and $null$ denotes the singleton set containing the null reference.

Example 1. The type of all cyclic or non-cyclic integer lists can be defined by the following guarded equation:

$$T = \langle elm{:}int, next{:}T \rangle \vee null$$

The type is regular and has only the following four subterms:

$$T \;\langle elm{:}int, next{:}T \rangle \;\; int \;\; null$$

Example 2. Let us consider the terms T_i for all natural numbers i, defined by the following system of infinite guarded equations:

$$
\begin{aligned}
T_0 \;\; &= null \\
T_{i+1} &= \langle pred{:}\,T_i \rangle \text{ (for all } i \geq 0)
\end{aligned}
$$

The type $T_0 \vee T_1 \vee \ldots \vee T_n \vee T_{n+1} \ldots$ is not a regular type.

We now introduce the notion of *contractive* type, which allows us to reject all those types whose interpretation is not well-defined (see the example at the end of Section 4 for the details).

Definition 2. *A type is contractive if it does not contain infinite paths whose nodes are all labeled by union types.*

Example 3. The type $T = T \vee int$ is not contractive, because there exists an infinite path whose nodes are all labeled by the union type $T \vee int$.

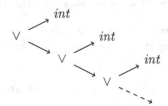

Example 4. The type $T = \langle f{:}\,T \vee int \rangle$ is contractive because all infinite paths have nodes that are alternatively labeled by a record and a union type.

$$\langle f{:}\,\_\rangle \rightarrow \vee \;\; int \quad \langle f{:}\,\_\rangle \rightarrow \vee \;\; int \quad \langle f{:}\,\_\rangle \dashrightarrow$$

In the rest of the paper all types are restricted to be regular and contractive.

3.2   Principle of Induction and Coinduction

Let $\mathcal{U}$ denotes a set universe, and $\mathcal{P}(\mathcal{U})$ the powerset of $\mathcal{U}$. Given a set of rules defining a subset of $\mathcal{U}$, the *immediate consequence* operator F is the endofunction on the parts of $\mathcal{U}$, that given a set of premises X, returns the set of consequences immediately derivable from the rules.

Definition 3. *Let X be a set in $\mathcal{P}(\mathcal{U})$. X is F-closed if $F(X) \subseteq X$; X is F-consistent if $X \subseteq F(X)$; X is a fixed point of F if $X = F(X)$.*

Theorem 1 (Tarski-Knaster)
Let $F:\mathcal{P}(\mathcal{U}) \to \mathcal{P}(\mathcal{U})$ be monotone.

- *The least fixed point (lfp) of F is the intersection of all F-closed sets.*
- *The greatest fixed point (gfp) of F is the union of all F-consistent sets.*

We denote as lfp(F) the least fixed point of F and as gfp(F) the greatest fixed point of F.

From the previous theorem the following induction and coinduction principles can be derived.

Induction principle. Let p and q be two predicates over $\mathcal{P}(\mathcal{U})$, and let p be inductively defined by a set of rules whose immediate consequence is F. If the rules for p are closed w.r.t. predicate q, then $\forall x \in \mathcal{U} \; p(x) \Rightarrow q(x)$ holds. This comes from the fact that by definition a rule is closed w.r.t. q iff the following implication holds: if the premises satisfy q, then the conclusion satisfies q. Indeed, this is equivalent to $F(\{x \mid q(x)\}) \subseteq \{x \mid q(x)\}$, which implies $\{x \mid p(x)\} \subseteq \{x \mid q(x)\}$ for the previous theorem.

Coinduction principle. Let p and q be two predicates over $\mathcal{P}(\mathcal{U})$, and let q be coinductively defined by a set of rules whose immediate consequence is F. Let us assume that the following property holds:
for all $x \in \mathcal{U}$, if $p(x)$ holds, then there exists a rule for q that can be applied to a set of premises satisfying p to derive the consequence x. Then $\forall x \in \mathcal{U} \; p(x) \Rightarrow q(x)$ holds. This comes from the fact that the condition above is equivalent to $\{x \mid p(x)\} \subseteq F(\{x \mid p(x)\})$, which implies $\{x \mid p(x)\} \subseteq \{x \mid q(x)\}$ for the previous theorem.

In the rest of the paper we will use the following convention: rules that have to be interpreted inductively use thin lines, while rules that have to be interpreted coinductively use thick lines.

4   Semantic Subtyping between Coinductive Types

We interpret types as sets of values. Values are all finite and infinite (but regular) terms coinductively defined as follows (where $i \in \mathbb{Z}$):

$$v ::= i \mid \text{null} \mid \langle f_1 \mapsto v_1, \ldots, f_n \mapsto v_n \rangle$$

Analogously to record types, record values are finite maps from field names to values, therefore we implicitly assume that field names are distinct and their order is immaterial. The interpretation of types is coinductively defined by the rules in Figure 2.

Thicker lines indicate that rules are interpreted coinductively, that is, also infinite proof trees are considered; this is equivalent to considering the greatest fixed-point of the function induced by the rules and corresponding to one step of inference [16].

Note that a record value can belong to a record type with fewer fields, the right-hand-side ellipsis in the record value indicates that the value is allowed to contain more fields.

$$(\text{null} \in) \frac{}{null \in null} \quad (\text{int} \in) \frac{}{i \in int} \ i{\in}\mathbf{Z} \quad (\text{l-or} \in) \frac{v \in \tau_1}{v \in \tau_1 \vee \tau_2} \quad (\text{r-or} \in) \frac{v \in \tau_2}{v \in \tau_1 \vee \tau_2}$$

$$(\text{rec} \in) \frac{v_1 \in \tau_1, \ldots, v_n \in \tau_n}{\langle f_1 \mapsto v_1, \ldots, f_n \mapsto v_n, \ldots \rangle \in \langle f_1{:}\tau_1, \ldots, f_n{:}\tau_n \rangle}$$

Fig. 2. Value membership

For instance, the following tree is a proof for $\langle f \mapsto 1 \rangle \in int \vee \langle f{:}int \rangle$.

$$(\text{r-or} \in) \frac{(\text{rec} \in) \dfrac{(\text{int} \in) \dfrac{}{1 \in int}}{\langle f \mapsto 1 \rangle \in \langle f{:}int \rangle}}{\langle f \mapsto 1 \rangle \in int \vee \langle f{:}int \rangle}$$

The following derivation for a non-contractive type motivates the definition of contractivity introduced in the previous section (see Def. 2); consider the regular type τ s.t. $\tau = \tau \vee int$, and the following infinite proof containing just applications of rules (l-or $\in$):

$$(\text{l-or} \in) \frac{(\text{l-or} \in) \dfrac{\vdots}{null \in \tau}}{null \in \tau}$$

Here we have a non-sound derivation as $null \in \tau$ derived above: τ corresponds to an infinite union of int, and therefore its interpretation cannot contain the $null$ type. Non-contractive types can be correctly handled by introducing the notion of contractive proof tree [4]. Since from contractive types only contractive proofs can be derived, and non contractive types do not extend the expressive power[1] of types, it is more convenient to restrict types to contractive ones.

---

[1] Indeed, for any non contractive type there exists an equivalent contractive one.

Definition 4. *The interpretation of τ, is defined by $[\![\tau]\!] = \{v \mid v \in \tau \ holds\}$.*

Lemma 1. *If $\tau = \mathbf{0}$ then $[\![\tau]\!] = \emptyset$, that is, $v \notin \mathbf{0}$.*

Proof. By definitions of membership rules we can not create a derivation for $v \in \mathbf{0}$ then by Def. 4 $[\![\tau]\!] = \emptyset$.

Lemma 2. *If $\tau = \tau_1 \vee \tau_2$ then $[\![\tau]\!] = \emptyset$ iff $[\![\tau_i]\!] = \emptyset$ $\forall i \in 1..2$, that is, $v \notin \tau_i$ $\forall i \in 1..2$.*

Proof.
$\Rightarrow$ By Def. 4 and by definitions of membership rules ($\nexists v.v \in \tau_i$ holds) $\forall \tau_i \in 1..n$, that is, by Def. 4 $[\![\tau_i]\!] = \emptyset$ $\forall t_i \in \tau$.
$\Leftarrow$ By Def. 4 we have ($\nexists v.v \in \tau_i$ holds) $\forall \tau_i \in \tau$, that is, by definitions of membership rules we can not create a derivation for $v \in \tau$ then by Def. 4 $[\![\tau]\!] = \emptyset$.

Lemma 3. *If $\tau = \langle f_1{:}\tau_1, \ldots, f_n{:}\tau_n \rangle$ then $[\![\tau]\!] = \emptyset$ iff $\exists i \in 1..n$ $[\![\tau_i]\!] = \emptyset$, that is, $\exists i \in 1..n$ $v_i \notin \tau_i$.*

Proof.
$\Rightarrow$ By Def. 4 and by definitions of membership rules $\exists i \in 1..n.$ ($\nexists v.v \in \tau_i$ holds), that is, by Def. 4 $\exists i \in 1..n$ $[\![\tau_i]\!] = \emptyset$.
$\Leftarrow$ By Def. 4 we have $\exists i \in 1..n.$ ($\nexists v.v \in \tau_i$ holds), that is, by definitions of membership rules we can not create a derivation for $v \in \tau$ then by Def. 4 $[\![\tau]\!] = \emptyset$.

Given a type τ, and a set of types Ξ, the restriction of τ w.r.t. Ξ, denoted by $\tau_{|\Xi}$, is coinductively defined as follows:

- $\tau_{|\Xi} = \tau$, if $\tau \in \{\mathbf{0}, null, int\}$;
- $(\tau_1 \vee \tau_2)_{|\Xi} = \tau_{1|\Xi} \vee \tau_{2|\Xi}$, if $\tau_1, \tau_2 \notin \Xi$;
- $(\tau_1 \vee \tau_2)_{|\Xi} = null$, if $\tau_1 \in \Xi$ or $\tau_2 \in \Xi$;
- $\langle f_1{:}\tau_1, \ldots, f_n{:}\tau_n \rangle_{|\Xi} = \langle f_i{:}\tau_{i|\Xi} \mid 1 \le i \le n, \tau_i \notin \Xi \rangle$.

The restriction $\tau_{|\Xi}$ removes from τ all types contained in Ξ; intuitively, if $\tau_{|\Xi}$ returns a type whose interpretation is empty, then it means that the emptiness of τ can be proved without assuming any assumption on the types in Ξ (that is, those types no longer need to be inspected; see Lemma 6). For this reason, if either τ_1 or τ_2 are contained in Ξ, then $\tau_1 \vee \tau_2$ cannot be proved empty, and, therefore, the restriction $(\tau_1 \vee \tau_2)_{|\Xi}$ returns a non empty type (for simplicity, the *null* type is returned, but any other non empty type could be returned as well). A similar reasoning applies to the case of record types.

In the following we show some examples of application of the restriction operator.

For all types τ, $\tau_{|\emptyset} = \tau$.

If τ_1 is the type s.t. $\tau_1 = \langle f{:}\tau_2 \rangle$, $\tau_2 = \langle g{:}\tau_1, h{:}\mathbf{0} \rangle$, then $\tau_{1|\{\tau_1\}} = \langle f{:}\langle h{:}\mathbf{0} \rangle \rangle$, $\tau_{2|\{\tau_1\}} = \langle h{:}\mathbf{0} \rangle$, and $\tau_{1|\{\tau_2\}} = \langle \rangle$.

If τ_3 is the type s.t. $\tau_3 = \tau_4 \vee \mathbf{0}, \tau_4 = \langle f{:}\tau_3 \rangle$, then $\tau_{3|\{\tau_3\}} = \langle \rangle \vee \mathbf{0}$, and $\tau_{4|\{\tau_3\}} = \langle \rangle$.

Lemma 4. *If* $[\![\tau_{|\Xi}]\!] = \emptyset$, *then* $[\![\tau_{|\Xi\cup\{\tau\}}]\!] = \emptyset$.

Proof. It is sufficient to prove that if $v \in \tau_{|\Xi\cup\{\tau\}}$, then there exists $v' \in \tau_{|\Xi}$. The value v' corresponds to $ext(v, \tau, \Xi, \tau, v)$, where $ext(v, \tau, \Xi, \tau', v')$ is coinductively defined as follows:

- $ext(v, \tau, \Xi, \tau', v') = v$, if $\tau \in \{null, int\}$;
- $ext(v, \tau_1 \vee \tau_2, \Xi, \tau, v') = ext(v, \tau_1, \Xi, \tau, v')$, if $\tau_1, \tau_2 \notin \Xi, v \in \tau_{1|\Xi\cup\{\tau\}}$
- $ext(v, \tau_1 \vee \tau_2, \Xi, \tau, v') = ext(v, \tau_2, \Xi, \tau, v')$, if $\tau_1, \tau_2 \notin \Xi$, not $v \in \tau_{1|\Xi\cup\{\tau\}}$, and $v \in \tau_{2|\Xi\cup\{\tau\}}$
- $ext(v, \tau_1 \vee \tau_2, \Xi, \tau, v') = null$ if $\tau_1 \in \Xi$ or $\tau_2 \in \Xi$
- $ext(v, \langle f_1{:}\tau_1, \ldots, f_n{:}\tau_n \rangle, \Xi, \tau, v') =$
  $\langle f_i \mapsto ext(v.f_i, \tau_i, \Xi, \tau, v') \mid 1 \leq i \leq n, \tau_i \notin \Xi \cup \{\tau\}\rangle \cup$
  $\langle f_i \mapsto ext(v', \tau, \Xi, \tau, v') \mid 1 \leq i \leq n, \tau_i = \tau\rangle$

The proof can be concluded by proving by coinduction on the definition of value membership that if $v \in \tau_{|\Xi\cup\tau'}$ and $v' \in \tau'_{|\Xi\cup\tau'}$, then $ext(v, \tau, \Xi, \tau', v') \in \tau_{|\Xi}$.

5   A Sound and Complete Inference System

In this section we define a system of coinductive subtyping rules and prove that it is sound and complete with respect to the definition of semantic subtyping given in Section 4.

Remark : Unless explicitly stated, in the rest of the section we only consider regular and contractive types.

5.1   Type Normalization

The problem of defining a decision procedure for subtyping becomes simpler if types are first normalized; such a normalization simplifies empty types, and is driven by the following laws:

$$\tau \vee \mathbf{0} = \mathbf{0} \vee \tau = \tau \qquad \langle \ldots f{:}\mathbf{0} \ldots \rangle = \mathbf{0}$$

This normalization needs to be performed only once, before deciding subtyping; the subtyping rules, and the derived subtyping algorithm preserve this type normalization, hence no further normalization steps are required.

We use the notation $\tau_1 \triangleright \tau_2$ to indicate that type τ_1 is normalized to type τ_2; for instance, the judgment $(int \vee \mathbf{0}) \vee (\mathbf{0} \vee int) \triangleright int \vee int$ holds. To see a more involved example, let us consider the regular type defined by $\tau = \mathbf{0} \vee \langle f{:}\tau, g{:}\mathbf{0} \vee \mathbf{0} \rangle$; then, $\tau \triangleright \mathbf{0}$ holds.

Normalization requires a decision procedure for testing emptiness of types; non-emptiness is naturally specified by the coinductive rules in Figure 3.

Clearly, the primitive types int and $null$ are not empty. A union type $\tau_1 \vee \tau_2$ is not empty if at least one between τ_1 and τ_2 is not empty. A record type is

$$\frac{}{int \not\cong \emptyset} \qquad \frac{}{null \not\cong \emptyset} \qquad \frac{\tau_i \not\cong \emptyset}{\tau_1 \vee \tau_2 \not\cong \emptyset}\, i \in 1..2 \qquad \frac{\tau_1 \not\cong \emptyset, \ldots, \tau_n \not\cong \emptyset}{\langle f{:}\tau_1, \ldots, f_n{:}\tau_n \rangle \not\cong \emptyset}$$

Fig. 3. Non-emptiness of types

not empty if all types of its fields are not empty. Note that the rules must be interpreted coinductively because in some cases infinite proof trees are required. Consider for instance the type defined by $\tau = \langle f{:}\tau \rangle$; if $v = \langle f \mapsto v \rangle$, then $v \in \tau$, therefore $\tau \not\cong \emptyset$ must hold. This can be proved by an infinite proof tree obtained by repeatedly applying the rule for records.

Soundness and Completeness of the Judgment $\tau \not\cong \emptyset$. Before proving that the judgment $\tau \not\cong \emptyset$ is sound and complete w.r.t. the predicate $[\![\tau]\!] \neq \emptyset$, we illustrate the new proof technique we propose and use; this is the same technique that will be adopted for proving soundness and completeness of the subtyping rules.

Soundness and completeness are expressed by the implications $\tau \not\cong \emptyset \Rightarrow [\![\tau]\!] \neq \emptyset$, and $[\![\tau]\!] \neq \emptyset \Rightarrow \tau \not\cong \emptyset$, respectively.

Since $\tau \not\cong \emptyset$ is defined coinductively, completeness can be proved in a standard way by coinduction on the rules defining $\tau \not\cong \emptyset$, as explained in Section 3. Unfortunately, the same technique cannot be adopted for proving soundness (hence, for coinductive systems the difficult direction to prove is soundness, whereas for inductive systems is completeness).

To prove soundness we first consider the equivalent implication ($[\![\tau]\!] = \emptyset \Rightarrow \tau \not\cong \emptyset$ does not hold) corresponding to a proof by contradiction; then we observe that this implication can be proved if we split the implication in the following two:

$$[\![\tau]\!] = \emptyset \Rightarrow \tau \cong \emptyset \Rightarrow (\tau \not\cong \emptyset \text{ does not hold}) \tag{1}$$

where $\tau \cong \emptyset$ is the complement judgment of $\tau \not\cong \emptyset$ corresponding to testing type emptiness. Now it seems we get stuck because if $\tau \cong \emptyset$ is defined inductively, then the implication on the left hand side cannot be proved easily, whereas if $\tau \cong \emptyset$ is defined coinductively, the same consideration applies for the implication on the right hand side.

However, we still can have the cake and eat it too if we are able to define the judgment $\tau \not\cong \emptyset$ with an inference system whose inductive and coinductive interpretation coincide (hence, there exists a unique fixed point which is both the least and the greatest). A sufficient condition for this is that all proof trees of the inference system are finite.

The complement judgment we are looking for is defined in Figure 4. We use thin lines in the rules because it is sufficient to interpret the system inductively to define the judgment, however if we interpret the rules coinductively we get the same definition of emptiness for regular and contractive types.

Note that the only role of the set of types $\varXi$ is to force the inductive and coinductive interpretation of the rules in Figure 4 to coincide, as proved in Lemma 5.

$$\frac{}{\varXi \vdash \mathbf{0} \cong \emptyset} \qquad \frac{\varXi \vdash \tau_1 \cong \emptyset \quad \varXi \vdash \tau_2 \cong \emptyset}{\varXi \vdash \tau_1 \vee \tau_2 \cong \emptyset} \qquad \frac{\varXi \cup \{\tau\} \vdash \tau_i \cong \emptyset}{\varXi \vdash \tau \cong \emptyset} \quad \begin{array}{l} \tau = \langle f{:}\tau_1, \ldots, f_n{:}\tau_n \rangle \\ \tau \notin \varXi \\ i \in \{1, \ldots, n\} \end{array}$$

Fig. 4. Emptiness of types

To distinguish between the two interpretations we use the notations $\varXi \vdash \tau \cong \emptyset$ and $\varXi \Vdash \tau \cong \emptyset$ to indicate judgments corresponding to the inductive and coinductive interpretation of the rules, respectively.

Lemma 5. $\varXi \Vdash \tau \cong \emptyset$ *implies* $\varXi \vdash \tau \cong \emptyset$.

Proof. A direct consequence of the fact that τ is regular (hence $\varXi$ cannot grow indefinitely) and contractive (hence the rule for union can be applied consecutively only a finite number of times).

We can now prove the two implications in (1) on the left and right side, respectively. The following two lemmas with Lemma 5 prove the soundness of $\tau \not\cong \emptyset$.

In Lemma 6 two different hypotheses are needed to ensure that the claim holds. For instance, $[\![\langle f{:}\mathbf{0}\rangle]\!] = \emptyset$, but $\{\langle f{:}\mathbf{0}\rangle\} \Vdash \langle f{:}\mathbf{0}\rangle \cong \emptyset$ does not hold because of the side condition of the rule for record types; in this case the hypothesis $\tau \notin \varXi$ is not verified, but $[\![\eta_\varXi]\!] = \emptyset$ holds. As another example, if τ is s.t. $\tau = \langle f{:}\langle g{:}\tau, h{:}\mathbf{0}\rangle\rangle$, then $[\![\tau]\!] = \emptyset$, but $\{\langle g{:}\tau, h{:}\mathbf{0}\rangle\} \Vdash \tau \cong \emptyset$ does not hold (again, because of the side condition of the rule for record types). In this case the hypothesis $\tau \notin \varXi$ is verified, but $[\![\eta_\varXi]\!] = \emptyset$ does not hold.

Lemma 6. *If* $\tau \notin \varXi$, *and* $[\![\eta_\varXi]\!] = \emptyset$, *then* $\varXi \Vdash \tau \cong \emptyset$.

Proof. By coinduction on the rules for $\varXi \Vdash \tau \cong \emptyset$. We only show the interesting case for $\tau = \langle f_1{:}\tau_1, \ldots, f_n{:}\tau_n \rangle$. By Lemma 4 $[\![\eta_\varXi]\!] = \emptyset$ implies $[\![\eta_{\varXi \cup \{\tau\}}]\!] = \emptyset$.

Furthermore, if $[\![\eta_{\varXi \cup \{\tau\}}]\!] = \emptyset$, then by *Lemma 3* and definition of $\eta_{\varXi \cup \{\tau\}}$ when τ is a record type, there exists $i \in \{1, \ldots, n\}$ s.t. $[\![\tau_{i \mid \varXi \cup \{\tau\}}]\!] = \emptyset$, and $\tau_i \notin \varXi \cup \{\tau\}$. Since $\tau \notin \varXi$ by hypothesis, we can conclude by coinduction and by using rule for record types.

Lemma 7. *If* $\varXi \vdash \tau \cong \emptyset$, *then* $\tau \not\cong \emptyset$ *does not hold.*

Proof. Easy induction on the rules defining $\varXi \vdash \tau \cong \emptyset$.

Completeness of $\tau \not\cong \emptyset$ can be easily proved by coinduction, as expected.

Lemma 8. $[\![\tau]\!] \neq \emptyset$ *implies* $\tau \not\cong \emptyset$.

Proof. By coinduction on the rules for $\tau \not\cong \emptyset$.

The following corollary simply derives the equivalence of $[\![\tau]\!] \neq \emptyset$ and $\tau \not\cong \emptyset$ from the lemmas above; as a byproduct, we also get the equivalence of $[\![\tau]\!] = \emptyset$ and $\tau \cong \emptyset$.

Corollary 1

1. $\tau \not\cong \emptyset$ if and only if $[\![\tau]\!] \neq \emptyset$.
2. $\emptyset \vdash \tau \cong \emptyset$ if and only if $[\![\tau]\!] = \emptyset$.

Proof

1. soundness: Lemma 6 + Lemma 5 + Lemma 7; completeness: Lemma 8.
2. soundness: Lemma 8 + Lemma 7; completeness: Lemma 6 + Lemma 5 .

We are now ready to define type normalization. This is defined by the coinductive rules in Figure 5.

$$(\text{prim} \triangleright) \frac{}{\tau \triangleright \tau} \ \tau \in \{0, null, int\} \qquad (\text{or} \triangleright) \frac{\tau_1 \triangleright \tau_1' \quad \tau_2 \triangleright \tau_2'}{\tau_1 \vee \tau_2 \triangleright \tau_1' \vee \tau_2'} \ \begin{array}{c} \tau_1 \not\cong \emptyset \\ \tau_2 \not\cong \emptyset \end{array}$$

$$(\text{r-or} \triangleright) \frac{\tau_1 \triangleright \tau_1'}{\tau_1 \vee \tau_2 \triangleright \tau_1'} \ \emptyset \vdash \tau_2 \cong \emptyset \qquad (\text{l-or} \triangleright) \frac{\tau_2 \triangleright \tau_2'}{\tau_1 \vee \tau_2 \triangleright \tau_2'} \ \emptyset \vdash \tau_1 \cong \emptyset$$

$$(\text{rec} \triangleright) \frac{\tau_1 \triangleright \tau_1', \dots, \tau_n \triangleright \tau_n'}{\langle f_1{:}\tau_1, \dots, f_n{:}\tau_n \rangle \triangleright \langle f_1{:}\tau_1', \dots, f_n{:}\tau_n' \rangle} \ \langle f_1{:}\tau_1, \dots, f_n{:}\tau_n \rangle \not\cong \emptyset$$

$$(\text{e-rec} \triangleright) \frac{}{\langle f_1{:}\tau_1, \dots, f_n{:}\tau_n \rangle \triangleright \mathbf{0}} \ \emptyset \vdash \langle f_1{:}\tau_1, \dots, f_n{:}\tau_n \rangle \cong \emptyset$$

Fig. 5. Type normalization

The empty and primitive types normalize to themselves, whereas normalizing a union type corresponds to coinductively normalizing its two subtypes, if they are both non-empty, or just one in case the other is empty. For record types two cases have to be distinguished: if $\langle f_1{:}\tau_1, \dots, f_n{:}\tau_n \rangle \not\cong \emptyset$ holds (that is, $\tau_i \not\cong \emptyset$ holds for all $i \in \{1, \dots, n\}$), then each subtype can be coinductively normalized to get the final type $\langle f_1{:}\tau_1', \dots, f_n{:}\tau_n' \rangle$. Otherwise the type normalizes to the empty set.

The following claims show that the normalization relation $\triangleright$ is actually a total function, and that it preserves type interpretation.

Lemma 9. *If $\tau \not\cong \emptyset$ does not hold, then $\tau \triangleright \mathbf{0}$.*

Proof. See the extended version [2].

Theorem 2. *For all τ there exists a unique type τ' such that $\tau \triangleright \tau'$.*

Proof. The proof uses Lemma 9 and Proposition 1. See the extended version [2].

Lemma 10. *If $\tau \triangleright \tau'$, and $\tau' \in \{\mathbf{0}, null, int\}$, then $[\![\tau]\!] = [\![\tau']\!]$.*

Proof. The proof uses Corollary 1. See the extended version [2].

Lemma 11. *If $\tau \rhd \tau_1' \vee \tau_2'$, and $v \in \tau$, then there exist τ_1, τ_2 s.t. $\tau = \tau_1 \vee \tau_2$, and ($\tau_1 \rhd \tau_1'$, and $v \in \tau_1$, or $\tau_2 \rhd \tau_2'$, and $v \in \tau_2$).*

Proof. The proof uses Corollary 1. See the extended version [2].

Theorem 3. *For all τ, τ', if $\tau \rhd \tau'$, then $[\![\tau]\!] = [\![\tau']\!]$.*

Proof. The proof uses Lemma 10 and Lemma 11. See the extended version [2].

Corollary 2. $\tau \rhd \mathbf{0}$ *if and only if* $[\![\tau]\!] = \emptyset$.

Proof. $\tau \rhd \mathbf{0} \Rightarrow [\![\tau]\!] = \emptyset$ can be derived directly from Theorem 3. For the other direction, if $[\![\tau]\!] = \emptyset$, then $\tau \not\gtrsim \emptyset$ does not hold by Corollary 1, therefore we can derive $\tau \rhd \mathbf{0}$ directly from Lemma 9.

5.2   Subtyping Rules

In this section we define the rules for subtyping. In the rest of the paper we assume that all types are normalized (besides being regular and contractive). Subtyping rules are based on the identity between sets $A \subseteq B \cup C \Leftrightarrow A \setminus B \subseteq C$.

For instance, if one would like to prove that

$$\langle f\!:\!null \vee int \rangle \leq \langle f\!:\!null \rangle \vee \langle f\!:\!int \rangle \vee int$$

holds, then one can prove that $\langle f\!:\!null \vee int \rangle \setminus \langle f\!:\!null \rangle \leq \langle f\!:\!int \rangle \vee int$ holds, which in turn holds if $(\langle f\!:\!null \vee int \rangle \setminus \langle f\!:\!null \rangle) \setminus \langle f\!:\!int \rangle \leq int$ holds.

Now $\langle f\!:\!null \vee int \rangle \setminus \langle f\!:\!null \rangle = \langle f\!:\!(null \vee int) \setminus null \rangle = \langle f\!:\!int \rangle$, and $\langle f\!:\!int \rangle \setminus \langle f\!:\!int \rangle = \mathbf{0}$, hence we can conclude the proof because trivially $\mathbf{0} \leq int$ holds.

Unfortunately, types are not closed w.r.t. complement. Even though this could be formally proved[2], for space reasons we only provides an informal argumentation.

Let us consider the two types τ and τ' introduced in Section 1:

$$\tau = null \vee \langle el\!:\!int, nx\!:\!\tau \rangle \qquad \tau' = \langle el\!:\!int, nx\!:\!\tau' \rangle$$

Since $[\![\tau]\!]$ contains all values corresponding to either finite or infinite lists, while $[\![\tau']\!]$ contains all values corresponding just to infinite lists, we deduce that $[\![\tau]\!] \setminus [\![\tau']\!]$ is the set of all values corresponding just to finite lists. If we assume that types are closed w.r.t. complement, then there must exist a regular and contractive type τ'' s.t. $[\![\tau'']\!] = [\![\tau]\!] \setminus [\![\tau']\!]$, but no regular contractive type can have a coinductive interpretation corresponding to the set of all values corresponding to finite lists, because such a set is not a complete metric space for the standard metric on infinite trees.

---

[2] The proof relies on the property that for all regular and contractive types τ, $[\![\tau]\!]$ is a complete metric space for the standard metric on infinite trees.

Given this negative result, we have to compute complement lazily, and extend the syntax of types to introduce the complement[3] type constructor, denoted by $-$. Note that while $-$ is a type constructor, $\setminus$ denotes an operation that given two types τ_1 and τ_2, returns a new type.

For instance $int \setminus int = \mathbf{0}$, and $int \setminus \langle f{:}int \rangle = int$. However, when both types are records the type returned by the complement is in general a extended type containing the type constructor $-$. For instance, if we assume that fields f, g, and h are all distinct, then $\langle f{:}\tau_1, g{:}\tau_2 \rangle \setminus \langle f{:}\tau_3, h{:}\tau_4 \rangle$ returns the extended type

$$\langle f{:}\tau_1 - \tau_3, g{:}\tau_2 \rangle \vee \langle f{:}\tau_1, g{:}\tau_2, h?{:}-\tau_4 \rangle$$

where $h?$ denotes an optional field: record type $\langle h?{:}-\tau_4 \rangle$ contains record values which either do not have field h, or have field h with a value v s.t. $v \notin [\![\tau_4]\!]$.

The reader can verify that

$$[\![\langle f{:}\tau_1, g{:}\tau_2 \rangle]\!] \setminus [\![\langle f{:}\tau_3, h{:}\tau_4 \rangle]\!] = [\![\langle f{:}\tau_1 - \tau_3, g{:}\tau_2 \rangle \vee \langle f{:}\tau_1, g{:}\tau_2, h?{:}-\tau_4 \rangle]\!].$$

Indeed $v \in [\![\langle f{:}\tau_1, g{:}\tau_2 \rangle]\!]$ and $v \notin [\![\langle f{:}\tau_3, h{:}\tau_4 \rangle]\!]$ if and only if v has the two fields f and g, where g is always associated with a value in $[\![\tau_2]\!]$, whereas f is associated either with a value in $[\![\tau_1]\!]$, but not in $[\![\tau_3]\!]$, or with a value in $[\![\tau_1]\!]$, but then either v does not have field h, or it has field h associated with a value not in $[\![\tau_4]\!]$. The definition of $\setminus$ for record types is the generalization of the following identity between sets:

$$(A_1 \times \ldots \times A_n) \setminus (B_1 \times \ldots \times B_n) =$$
$$(A_1 \setminus B_1) \times A_2 \times \ldots \times A_n \cup \ldots \cup A_1 \times \ldots \times A_{n-1} \times (A_n \setminus B_n).$$

Extended types are defined in Figure 6; note that the two definitions are stratified: first types are defined coinductively, then extended types are inductively defined on top of types.

$$\pi ::= \tau \mid \langle f_1{:}\rho_1, \ldots, f_n{:}\rho_n, f_1'?{:}\varrho_1, \ldots, f_k?{:}\varrho_k \rangle \mid \pi_1 \vee \pi_2$$
$$\varsigma ::= \rho \mid \varrho \qquad \rho ::= \tau \mid \rho - \tau \qquad \varrho ::= -\tau \mid \varrho - \tau$$

Fig. 6. Extended types

The meta-variable ρ corresponds to an extended type that can be associated with a non optional field of an extended record type, and has shape $((\tau_0 - \tau_1) - \ldots \tau_k)$, while the meta-variable ϱ corresponds to an extended type that can be associated with an optional field of an extended record type, and has shape $((-\tau_0 - \tau_1) - \ldots \tau_k)$; finally, the meta-variables ς has been introduced just for practical reasons to avoid useless duplication for all cases where the expected type can be either ρ or ϱ.

Interpretation of extended types is defined in Figure 7 by a corresponding extended judgment for membership $v \in_e \pi$ and $v \in_e \varsigma$ (note that values are not

---

[3] The constructor is overloaded since it denotes both unary absolute complement, and binary relative complement.

extended); as happens for extended types, the definitions of $v \in_e \pi$ and $v \in_e \varsigma$ are stratified over the definition of $v \in \tau$: first $v \in \tau$ is defined coinductively, then $v \in_e \pi$ and $v \in_e \varsigma$ are inductively defined on top of $v \in \tau$.

$$(\text{emb } \in_e) \frac{}{v \in_e \tau} \, v \in \tau \qquad (\text{l-or } \in_e) \frac{v \in_e \pi_1}{v \in_e \pi_1 \vee \pi_2} \, ext(\pi_1 \vee \pi_2) \qquad (\text{r-or } \in_e) \frac{v \in_e \pi_2}{v \in_e \pi_1 \vee \pi_2} \, ext(\pi_1 \vee \pi_2)$$

$$(\text{rec } \in_e) \frac{\begin{array}{c} v(f_i) \in_e \rho_i \; \forall i \in \{1, \ldots, n\} \\ f'_j \in dom(v) \Rightarrow v(f'_j) \in_e \varrho_j \; \forall j \in \{1, \ldots, k\} \end{array}}{v \in_e \pi} \quad \begin{array}{l} \pi = \langle f_1 : \rho_1, \ldots, f_n : \rho_n, \\ \quad f'_1 ? : \varrho_1, \ldots, f'_k ? : \varrho_k \rangle \\ ext(\pi) \\ \{f_1, \ldots, f_n\} \subseteq dom(v) \end{array}$$

$$(\text{comp}) \frac{v \in_e \varsigma}{v \in_e \varsigma - \tau} \, v \notin \tau \qquad (\text{a-comp}) \frac{}{v \in_e -\tau} \, v \notin \tau$$

Fig. 7. Value membership for extended types

Rules defining $v \in_e \pi$ are straightforward. We use the auxiliary predicate ext on extended types s.t. $ext(\pi)$ holds if and only if π is a proper extended type, that is, there is no type τ s.t. $\tau = \pi$. Such a predicate is used to avoid rule (emb $\in_e$) to overlap the other rules.

The complement operator is defined in Figure 8.

$$\tau \setminus \tau = \mathbf{0} \qquad \pi \setminus \mathbf{0} = \pi \qquad \mathbf{0} \setminus \tau = \mathbf{0}$$
$$\tau \setminus \tau' = \tau \text{ if } \tau \neq \tau', \tau \in \{int, null\} \text{ and } \tau' \neq \tau_1 \vee \tau_2$$
$$\pi \setminus \tau = \pi \text{ if } \pi = \langle \ldots \rangle \text{ and } \tau \in \{int, null\}$$
$$\pi \setminus \tau = (\bigvee_{f \in dom(\pi) \cap dom(\tau)} \pi -_f \tau) \vee (\bigvee_{f \in dom(\tau) \setminus dom(\pi)} \pi \sim_f \tau) \text{ if } \pi, \tau = \langle \ldots \rangle$$

$$\text{where } \pi -_f \tau = \pi[f : \rho - \tau'] \text{ if } \pi = \langle \ldots f : \rho \ldots \rangle \, \tau = \langle \ldots f : \tau' \ldots \rangle$$
$$\pi -_f \tau = \pi[f? : \varrho - \tau'] \text{ if } \pi = \langle \ldots f? : \varrho \ldots \rangle \, \tau = \langle \ldots f : \tau' \ldots \rangle$$
$$\pi \sim_f \tau = \pi[f? : - \tau'] \text{ if } \tau = \langle \ldots f : \tau' \ldots \rangle$$

Fig. 8. Complement operator

The complement needs to be computed between an extended type π and a type τ; furthermore, both types cannot be union types except for the two corner cases $\tau \setminus \tau$ and $\mathbf{0} \setminus \tau$ (anyway, as we will see, two subtyping rules allow elimination of union types by splitting them, so that the complement operator can eventually be used). All cases are straightforward, except for the last case involving two record types which has been already explained by an example. In this case, the type returned by $\pi \setminus \tau$ is always a union of records, where the number n of records equals the number of fields contained in τ. Note that if $n = 0$, then the returned type is $\mathbf{0}$; for instance, $\langle f : int \rangle \setminus \langle \, \rangle = \mathbf{0}$. If $n = 1$, then a single record is returned: for instance $\langle \, \rangle \setminus \langle f : int \rangle = \langle f? : - int \rangle$, or $\langle f : null \rangle \setminus \langle f : int \rangle = \langle f : null - int \rangle$.

Recall that the notation $\pi[f{:}\rho - \tau']$ (and, equivalently, $\pi[f?{:}\varrho - \tau']$ and $\pi[f?{:} - \tau']$) denotes the record type updated by the association $f{:}\rho - \tau'$ (or $f?{:}\varrho - \tau'$ and $f?{:} - \tau'$, respectively); note that in the sole case of the definition of $\pi \sim_f \tau$, this update is actually an addition since by definition $f \notin dom(\pi)$.

The following lemmas are instrumental to prove the soundness and completeness of the subtyping rules.

Lemma 12. *If* $\pi \setminus \tau = \pi'$, *then* $[\![\pi]\!] \setminus [\![\tau]\!] = [\![\pi']\!]$.

Proof. Routine verification.

Lemma 13. π *is a record type s.t.* $[\![\pi]\!] = \emptyset$ *if and only if there exist* f, ρ, *and* τ *s.t.* π *has shape* $\langle \ldots f{:}\rho - \tau \ldots \rangle$, *and* $[\![\rho - \tau]\!] = \emptyset$.

Proof. It suffices to notice that by definition of the complement operator of Figure 8, all types τ (hence, not extended) occurring in π comes from non-extended record types which have been normalized, hence cannot be empty by Corollary 2; furthermore, a record type π cannot be empty because of an optional field f, since π can always contain all record values that do not have field f.

The subtyping rules are defined in Figure 9.

$$
\text{(empty} \leq) \frac{}{\mathbf{0} \leq \varXi} \qquad \text{(left-or} \leq) \frac{\pi_1 \leq \varXi \quad \pi_2 \leq \varXi}{\pi_1 \vee \pi_2 \leq \varXi} \qquad \text{(r-or} \leq) \frac{\pi \leq \varXi \cup \{\tau_1, \tau_2\}}{\pi \leq \varXi \cup \{\tau_1 \vee \tau_2\}} \, \tau_1 \vee \tau_2 \notin \varXi
$$

$$
\text{(comp} \leq) \frac{\pi' \leq \varXi}{\pi \leq \varXi \cup \{\tau\}} \, \tau \notin \varXi \atop \pi \setminus \tau = \pi' \qquad \text{(rec} \leq) \frac{\tau' \leq \varXi}{\langle \ldots f{:}\rho - \tau \ldots \rangle \leq \emptyset} \, \rho - \tau \rightsquigarrow \tau' - \varXi
$$

Fig. 9. Subtyping rules

The subtyping judgment has shape $\pi \leq \varXi$, where π is an extended type, and $\varXi$ is a finite set of non-extended types $\{\tau_1, \ldots, \tau_n\}$ corresponding to the union $\tau_1 \vee \ldots \vee \tau_n$ (which collapses to $\mathbf{0}$ when $n = 0$, and to τ_1 when $n = 1$). The set $\varXi$ is required for ensuring termination: union types in $\varXi$ are lazily split and reinserted in $\varXi$ to avoid unbounded growth of union types with duplicate types.

Rules (left-or $\leq$) and (r-or $\leq$) are applied for splitting and eliminating union types on both sides (this can always achieved with a finite number of applications of the rules by virtue of contractivity); then rule (comp $\leq$) removes types from the set $\varXi$. When finally the set $\varXi$ is empty we get the judgment $\pi \leq \emptyset$: if $\pi = \mathbf{0}$, then we can conclude by rule (empty $\leq$); if $\pi \in \{null, int\}$, then no rule can be applied and the judgment fails as expected; if π is a record type, then rule (rec $\leq$) tries to find a non optional field of type $\rho - \tau$, and to check whether such a type is empty.

The side condition in rule (rec $\leq$) is needed for normalizing the types of non optional fields having shape $\rho - \tau$: it transforms the type $(\ldots (\tau - \tau_1) \ldots) - \tau_n$

in the pair $\tau - (\{\tau_1\} \cup \ldots \{\tau_n\})$ (see the straightforward inductive definition in Figure 10). This is essential for avoiding unbounded growth of union types (and, consequently of types having shape $\rho - \tau$) which may have duplicate types; for instance, this would happen for the judgment $\tau_1 \leq \{\tau_2\}$, where $\tau_1 = \langle f{:}\tau_1, g{:}int \rangle$ and $\tau_2 = \langle f{:}\tau_2 \vee \tau_2 \rangle$.

Splitting is performed lazily for two reasons: by running our prototype implementation on numerous tests, we have realized that splitting all union types contained in τ_1 and τ_2 before deciding $\tau_1 \leq \tau_2$ (eager strategy) is less efficient than a lazy strategy; anyway, when the eager strategy is followed, splitting has to be performed repeatedly on the types $\pi \setminus \tau$ generated by rule (comp $\leq$).

$$\frac{\rho - \tau \rightsquigarrow \tau'' - \varXi}{(\rho - \tau) - \tau' \rightsquigarrow \tau'' - (\varXi \cup \{\tau'\})} \qquad \tau - \tau' \rightsquigarrow \tau - \{\tau'\}$$

Fig. 10. Normalization of $\rho - \tau$

The following two lemmas are instrumental to the proofs of soundness and completeness of the subtyping rules, and can be easily proved by induction on the types $\rho - \tau$.

Lemma 14. *For all ρ, τ, there exist unique τ', $\varXi$ s.t. $\rho - \tau \rightsquigarrow \tau' - \varXi$ holds.*

Lemma 15. *If $\rho - \tau \rightsquigarrow \tau' - \{\tau_1, \ldots, \tau_n\}$, then $[\![\rho - \tau]\!] = [\![\tau' - (\tau_1 \vee \ldots \vee \tau_n)]\!]$.*

Proofs of Soundness and Completeness of the Subtyping Rules. We adopt the same technique used for proving the soundness of the judgment $\tau \not\cong \emptyset$. Therefore first we have to define the complement judgment (see Figure 11).

As for the case of the negation of the $\tau \not\cong \emptyset$ judgment, the standard interpretation of the rules is inductive (thin lines), but Lemma 16 shows that the use of the set Ψ of extended types forces the inductive (judgment $\Psi \vdash \pi \not\leq \varXi$) and coinductive (judgment $\Psi \Vdash \pi \not\leq \varXi$) interpretation of the rules to coincide (when we restrict judgments $\Psi \vdash \tau \not\leq \varXi$ to finite sets $\varXi$).

Lemma 16. *For all finite sets $\varXi$, $\Psi \Vdash \tau \not\leq \varXi$ implies $\Psi \vdash \tau \not\leq \varXi$.*

Proof. It suffices to prove that any proof tree for $\Psi \Vdash \pi \not\leq \varXi$ must be finite. To do that, we first observe that, given π and $\varXi$, the cardinality of Ψ in the judgments of the proof tree for $\Psi \Vdash \pi \not\leq \varXi$ must be bounded. This can be proved by firstly observing that Ψ contains only the record types that appear in the left-hand-side of $\not\leq$ in the judgments, that such record types have fields ranging over a finite set (since we assume that initially τ and all types in $\varXi$ are regular, and the set $\varXi$ is finite), and that for all types of shape $((\tau_0 - \tau_1) - \ldots \tau_k)$ associated with non optional fields and generated by rule (comp $\not\leq$), τ_0 corresponds to a subterm of the initial type π, whereas $\tau_1, \ldots, \tau_k$ correspond to subterms of types contained in the initial set $\varXi$.

$$(\text{prim } \not\leq)\frac{}{\Psi \vdash \tau \not\leq \emptyset} \; \tau \in \{null, int\} \quad (\text{l-l-or } \not\leq)\frac{\Psi \vdash \pi_1 \not\leq \Xi}{\Psi \vdash \pi_1 \vee \pi_2 \not\leq \Xi} \quad (\text{r-l-or } \not\leq)\frac{\Psi \vdash \pi_2 \not\leq \Xi}{\Psi \vdash \pi_1 \vee \pi_2 \not\leq \Xi}$$

$$(\text{comp } \not\leq)\frac{\Psi \vdash \pi' \not\leq \Xi}{\Psi \vdash \pi \not\leq \Xi \cup \{\tau\}} \; \substack{\tau \notin \Xi \\ \pi \setminus \tau = \pi'} \quad (\text{r-or } \not\leq)\frac{\Psi \vdash \pi \not\leq \Xi \cup \{\tau_1, \tau_2\}}{\Psi \vdash \pi \not\leq \Xi \cup \{\tau_1 \vee \tau_2\}} \; \tau_1 \vee \tau_2 \notin \Xi$$

$$(\text{rec } \not\leq)\frac{\forall f \in dom(\pi) \; \pi(f) = \rho - \tau \rightsquigarrow \tau' - \Xi \Rightarrow \Psi \cup \{\pi\} \vdash \tau' \not\leq \Xi}{\Psi \vdash \pi \not\leq \emptyset} \; \substack{\pi = \langle \ldots \rangle \\ \pi \notin \Psi}$$

Fig. 11. Negation of subtyping

To prove that all proof trees are finite, we introduce the following measure on the judgments of shape $\Psi \Vdash \pi \not\leq \Xi$ defined on a Noetherian order, and show that for every rule of Figure 11 the measure of its premises is always strictly less than the measure of its consequence.

If B denotes an upper bound of the size of Ψ, then the measure of the judgment $\Psi \Vdash \pi \not\leq \Xi$ is defined by the quadruple $(B - |\Psi|, max_\vee(\Xi), |\Xi|, max_\vee(\pi))$, where $|\_|$ denotes cardinality, $max_\vee(\pi)$ returns the length of the maximum path from the root of π containing only union type constructors (this is always well-defined by contractivity), and $max_\vee(\Xi) = \sum_{\tau \in \Xi} max_\vee(\tau)$. If we consider the standard lexicographic order (where the leftmost value is the most significant one) on quadruples, then we obtain a Noetherian order, since trivially $max_\vee(\Xi) \geq 0, |\Xi| \geq 0$, $max_\vee(\pi) \geq 0$ and $B - |\Psi| > 0$ by virtue of the boundedness of Ψ sets.

We now prove that the measure of the premises of every rule is always strictly less than the measure of its consequence.

Rule (comp $\not\leq$): let (n_1, n_2, n_3, n_4) be the measure value for the consequence, then the value for the premise is $(n_1, n_2, n_3 - 1, n_4')$, and $(n_1, n_2, n_3 - 1, n_4') < (n_1, n_2, n_3, n_4)$;

Rules (l-l-or $\not\leq$) and (r-l-or $\not\leq$): let (n_1, n_2, n_3, n_4) be the measure value for the consequence, then the value for the premise is $(n_1, n_2, n_3, n_4 - 1)$, and $(n_1, n_2, n_3, n_4 - 1) < (n_1, n_2, n_3, n_4)$;

Rule (r-or $\not\leq$): let (n_1, n_2, n_3, n_4) be the measure value for the consequence, then the value for the premise is $(n_1, n_2 - 1, n_3', n_4)$, and $(n_1, n_2 - 1, n_3', n_4) < (n_1, n_2, n_3, n_4)$;

Rule (rec $\not\leq$): let (n_1, n_2, n_3, n_4) be the measure value for the consequence, then the value for any premise is $(n_1 - 1, n_2', n_3', n_4')$, and $(n_1 - 1, n_2', n_3', n_4') < (n_1, n_2, n_3, n_4)$.

Soundness is split into two implications, the first proved by coinduction, the second by induction.

Lemma 17. *Let Ψ be a set of extended types s.t. for all $\pi' \in \Psi$, π' is a record type having shape $\langle \ldots f{:}\rho - \tau \ldots \rangle$. Then $\pi \notin \Psi$ and $[\![\pi]\!] \not\subseteq [\![\tau_1 \vee \ldots \vee \tau_n]\!]$ imply $\Psi \Vdash \pi \not\leq \{\tau_1, \ldots, \tau_n\}$.*

Proof. By coinduction on the rules of Figure 11 and case analysis on π.

If $\pi = \mathbf{0}$, then $[\![\pi]\!] \not\subseteq [\![\tau_1 \vee \ldots \vee \tau_n]\!]$ does not hold, therefore the implication vacuously holds.

If $\pi = \pi_1 \vee \pi_2$, then $[\![\pi]\!] = [\![\pi_1]\!] \cup [\![\pi_2]\!]$, therefore if $[\![\pi]\!] \not\subseteq [\![\tau_1 \vee \ldots \vee \tau_n]\!]$, then either $[\![\pi_1]\!] \not\subseteq [\![\tau_1 \vee \ldots \vee \tau_n]\!]$ or $[\![\pi_2]\!] \not\subseteq [\![\tau_1 \vee \ldots \vee \tau_n]\!]$, hence by coinduction we can apply either rule (l-l-or $\not\leq$) or (r-l-or $\not\leq$) and conclude.

For the remaining cases we distinguish two subcases: either $\Xi \neq \emptyset$ or $\Xi = \emptyset$.

If $\Xi \neq \emptyset$ and $\pi \in \{null, int, \langle \ldots \rangle\}$, then, by coinduction, rule (r-or $\not\leq$) can be applied if $\tau_n = \tau' \vee \tau''$, because $[\![\tau_1 \vee \ldots \vee (\tau' \vee \tau'')]\!] = [\![\tau_1 \vee \ldots \vee \tau' \vee \tau'']\!]$; if τ_n is not a union type, then, by coinduction, rule (comp $\not\leq$) can be applied because there exists τ' s.t. $\pi \setminus \tau_n = \tau'$ (π and τ_n are not union), $[\![\tau']\!] = [\![\pi]\!] \setminus [\![\tau_n]\!]$ by Lemma 12, and $[\![\pi]\!] \not\subseteq [\![\tau_1 \vee \ldots \vee \tau_n]\!]$ implies $[\![\pi]\!] \setminus [\![\tau_n]\!] \not\subseteq [\![\tau_1 \vee \ldots \vee \tau_{n-1}]\!]$.

If $\Xi = \emptyset$ and $\pi \in \{null, int\}$, then we can easily conclude by coinduction and rule (prim $\not\leq$).

If $\Xi = \emptyset$ and π is a record type s.t. $[\![\pi]\!] \not\subseteq \emptyset$; if there is no f, ρ, and τ, s.t. π has shape $\langle \ldots f{:}\rho - \tau \ldots \rangle$, then we can conclude by coinduction and by applying rule (rec $\not\leq$) with no premises (note that the side condition $\pi \notin \Psi$ holds by hypothesis). Otherwise, by Lemma 13, for all f, ρ, and τ s.t. π has shape $\langle \ldots f{:}\rho - \tau \ldots \rangle$, we know that $[\![\rho - \tau]\!] \neq \emptyset$. Furthermore, by Lemma 14 there exist unique τ', Ξ s.t. $\rho - \tau \rightsquigarrow \tau' - \Xi$ holds, and by Lemma 15, if $\Xi = \{\tau'_1, \ldots, \tau'_k\}$, then $[\![\rho - \tau]\!] = [\![\tau' - (\tau'_1 \vee \ldots \vee \tau'_k)]\!]$, hence $[\![\tau' - (\tau'_1 \vee \ldots \vee \tau'_k)]\!] \neq \emptyset$ which implies $[\![\tau']\!] \not\subseteq [\![\tau'_1 \vee \ldots \vee \tau'_k]\!]$. Finally, if for all $\pi' \in \Psi$, π' is a record type having shape $\langle \ldots f'{:}\rho' - \tau'' \ldots \rangle$, then the same property holds for $\Psi \cup \{\pi\}$, and $\tau' \notin \Psi \cup \{\pi\}$ holds because τ' is not an extended type. Hence we can conclude by coinduction and rule (rec $\not\leq$).

Lemma 18. *If $\Psi \vdash \pi \not\leq \Xi$, then $\pi \leq \Xi$ does not hold.*

Proof. By induction on the rules defining $\Psi \vdash \pi \not\leq \Xi$. We detail the proof only for the most involved rule (rec $\not\leq$). If π is a record, then the only applicable rule for proving $\pi \leq \emptyset$ is (rec $\leq$). If rule (rec $\not\leq$) has no premises, then there is no field having type of shape $\rho - \tau$, hence rule (rec $\leq$) is not applicable. If rule (rec $\not\leq$) has premises, then for all fields of type $\rho - \tau$ we know that by Lemma 14 there exist exist unique τ', Ξ s.t. $\rho - \tau \rightsquigarrow \tau' - \Xi$, therefore by induction we deduce that $\tau' \leq \Xi$ does not hold, therefore rule (rec $\leq$) can never be applied, and, hence, $\pi \leq \emptyset$ does not hold.

Soundness trivially derives from the three previous lemmas.

Corollary 3 (Soundness). *If $\pi \leq \{\tau_1, \ldots, \tau_n\}$, then $[\![\pi]\!] \subseteq [\![\tau_1 \vee \ldots \vee \tau_n]\!]$.*

Proof. It suffices to show that $[\![\pi]\!] \not\subseteq [\![\tau_1 \vee \ldots \vee \tau_n]\!]$ implies that $\pi \leq \{\tau_1, \ldots, \tau_n\}$ does not hold. This can be proved directly by applying Lemma 17, Lemma 16, and Lemma 18.

Completeness throws no surprise and can be proved with a standard proof by coinduction on the subtyping rules.

Theorem 4 (Completeness). *If $[\![\pi]\!] \subseteq [\![\tau_1 \vee \ldots \vee \tau_n]\!]$, then $\pi \leq \{\tau_1, \ldots, \tau_n\}$ holds.*

Proof. The proof uses Lemma 12, Lemma 13, Lemma 14 and Lemma 15. See the extended version [2].

6   A Sound and Complete Algorithm

We have proved that the subtyping rules in Figure 9 are sound and complete w.r.t. the definition of semantic subtyping; however, such rules do not directly specify an algorithm for deciding semantic subtyping between coinductive types. In this section we show how it is possible to define a sound and complete algorithm implementing such rules.

The algorithm is specified by the following recursive function **subtype**, which is assumed to be invoked over normalized types; we omit the normalization function that can be derived from the Figure 5 (the interested reader can refer to the prototype implementation).

In order to decide whether π_1 is a subtype of π_2, function **subtype** must be called with $\Psi = \emptyset$, $\pi = \pi_1$, and $\Xi = \{\tau_2\}$.

```
// pre-condition: π and all types in Ξ are normalized
boolean subtype(Set<Pair<ExtType,Set<Type>>> Ψ, ExtType π,Set<Type> Ξ) {
    // rule (empty ≤)
    if(π==0)
        return true
    // termination condition
    if(∃(π',Ξ') ∈ Ψ s.t. π'==π && Ξ' ⊆ Ξ)
        return true
    // rule (right-or ≤)
    while(∃τ₁,τ₂ s.t. τ₁ ∨ τ₂ ∈ Ξ)
        Ξ=(Ξ \ τ₁ ∨ τ₂) ∪ {τ₁,τ₂}
    // rule (left-or ≤)
    if(∃π₁,π₂ s.t. π==π₁ ∨ π₂)
        return subtype(Ψ, π₁, Ξ) && subtype(Ψ, π₂, Ξ)
    // rule (comp ≤)
    else if(∃τ ∈ Ξ) {
        π'=π \ τ
        Ξ'=Ξ \ {τ}
        return subtype(Ψ ∪ {(π,{τ})},π',∅) ||
               Ξ'!=∅ && subtype(Ψ ∪ {(π,Ξ)},π',Ξ')
    }
    // rule (rec ≤)
    else if (π==⟨...⟩){
        foreach f ∈ dom(π)
            if(∃ρ,τ s.t. π(f)==ρ − τ) {
                ρ − τ ⤳ τ' − Ξ'
                if(subtype(Ψ,τ',Ξ'))
                    return true
            }
        return false
    }
    else
        // int ≤ 0 and null ≤ 0 do not hold
        return false
}
```

The algorithm is derived from the rules in Figure 9, but also from the proof of soundness; in particular, Lemma 17, and Lemma 16 show that if $\Xi = \{\tau_1, \ldots, \tau_n\}$, $\tau = \tau_1 \vee \ldots \vee \tau_n$, and $[\![\pi]\!] \not\subseteq [\![\tau]\!]$, then failure of $\pi \leq \Xi$ is always finite (indeed, all proofs for $\emptyset \vdash \pi \not\leq \Xi$ are finite), whereas if $[\![\pi]\!] \subseteq [\![\tau]\!]$ holds, then the proof tree for $\pi \leq \Xi$ could be infinite; however, Lemma 16 shows that such a proof tree is always regular, hence we can use the complement of the side-condition $\pi \notin \Psi$ of rule (rec $\not\leq$) to ensure termination for $\pi \leq \Xi$.

However, the presented algorithm differs from the inference system of Figure 9 for several details:

Order of rule application: as expected, the order in which rules can be applied has been made deterministic. Rule (empty $\leq$) overlaps with (right-or $\leq$), and (comp $\leq$), and is tried first, for obvious efficiency reasons. Rule (right-or $\leq$) overlaps (besides (empty $\leq$)) only with (left-or $\leq$) (recall that $\pi \setminus \tau$ is only defined when both π and τ are not union types, hence rule (comp $\leq$) does not overlap with rules (right-or $\leq$) and (left-or $\leq$)), and it is applied first for efficiency reasons: were rule (left-or $\leq$) be applied first, the applications of rule (right-or $\leq$) would be uselessly duplicated for the two premises of (left-or $\leq$). Rules (left-or $\leq$), (comp $\leq$), and (rec $\leq$) do not overlap, therefore the order in which are considered is immaterial.

Termination condition: the termination condition used by the algorithm is an improvement of that used in rule (right-or $\not\leq$) for the definition of the judgment $\Psi \vdash \pi \not\leq \Xi$ (obviously the termination condition has to be complemented). First, such a termination condition is used for all rules defining $\pi \leq \Xi$ (except (empty $\leq$)), and not just for rule (rec $\leq$). When function subtype has to check whether $\pi \leq \Xi$ holds, it first verifies (unless $\pi = \mathbf{0}$) whether the set Ψ already contains a pair (π, Ξ') such that $\Xi' \subseteq \Xi$; this means that the algorithm is already checking whether $\pi \leq \Xi'$ holds (that is, there is a corresponding call to subtype on the stack) and if $\pi \leq \Xi'$ holds, then $\pi \leq \Xi$ holds as well; therefore, **true** can be returned. If $\pi \leq \Xi$ does not hold, then $\pi \leq \Xi'$ does not hold as well, therefore the corresponding call to subtype will eventually find a counter-example and return **false** as expected.

Finally, new pairs are inserted in Ψ when rule (comp $\leq$) is applied; this is the point where new types can be generated through the computation of $\pi \setminus \tau$ that can contain extended record types with fields having types of shape $\rho - \tau'$; only in this case the application of rule (rec $\leq$) can lead to a potentially infinite loop, as shown by the proof of Lemma 16 (recall that if π is a record that does not contain any field having type of shape $\rho - \tau'$, then rule (rec $\leq$) has no premises). In this way, we give the algorithm more chances to prune the proof tree, and, thus, to avoid combinatorial explosion, but we avoid indiscriminate insertion in Ψ of all pairs corresponding to a call to subtype.

Optimization of rule (comp $\leq$): besides all optimizations explained above, we have also implemented a more refined version of rule (comp $\leq$): before checking that $\pi \setminus \tau \leq \Xi \setminus \{\tau\}$ holds, we verify whether $\pi \setminus \tau$ is already empty (thus, $\pi \setminus \tau \leq \emptyset$ holds), to avoid useless applications of rule (comp $\leq$).

7   Conclusion

In this paper we have tackled the problem of defining a practical top-down algorithm for deciding semantic subtyping for coinductively interpreted types in the presence of record and union types.

We have defined a set of coinductive subtyping rules, and proved that such a set is sound and complete w.r.t. semantic subtyping; from such rules an algorithm has been derived and implemented by a prototype written in Prolog.

As a byproduct, we have proposed and used a new proof technique that can be fruitfully used for proving soundness results for coinductively defined judgments (or, dually, for proving completeness results for inductively defined judgments).

We have shown with an example in Python how coinductive types allow more precise type analysis in the presence of cyclic objects; furthermore, a complete procedure for deciding subtyping makes the analysis even more precise. This work can be directly applied to our previous work on abstract compilation for object-oriented languages [4,3,6,7] to perform static global type analysis; the types employed by abstract compilation are essentially the same studied here, with the difference that the previously defined subtyping rules were sound but not complete [5]. Actually, our prototype implementation supports the same types as defined in our first work on coinductive types [4].

There are several directions for further research on this topic. To simplify the technical details, in this paper we have considered non updatable records (that is, record subtyping is covariant in the types of the fields), but for effectively using our result in object-oriented languages, the subtyping algorithm has to be extended to updatable records (that is, record subtyping is invariant in the types of the updatable fields).

Besides updatable records there are other interesting extensions to the type system and to the subtyping algorithm to obtain more precise type analysis; in particular, the addition of polymorphic types would require a non trivial extension of the subtyping algorithm to handle set of subtyping constraints with type variables.

References

1. Amadio, R., Cardelli, L.: Subtyping recursive types. ACM Transactions on Programming Languages and Systems 15(4), 575–631 (1993)
2. Ancona, D., Corradi, A.: Sound and complete subtyping between coinductive types for object-oriented languages. Technical report, DIBRIS - Università di Genova, Italy (2014), ftp://ftp.disi.unige.it/person/AnconaD/CompleteCoinductiveSubtyping.pdf
3. Ancona, D., Corradi, A., Lagorio, G., Damiani, F.: Abstract compilation of object-oriented languages into coinductive CLP(X): can type inference meet verification? In: Beckert, B., Marché, C. (eds.) FoVeOOS 2010. LNCS, vol. 6528, pp. 31–45. Springer, Heidelberg (2011)
4. Ancona, D., Lagorio, G.: Coinductive type systems for object-oriented languages. In: Drossopoulou, S. (ed.) ECOOP 2009. LNCS, vol. 5653, pp. 2–26. Springer, Heidelberg (2009)
5. Ancona, D., Lagorio, G.: Coinductive subtyping for abstract compilation of object-oriented languages into Horn formulas. In: Montanari, A., Napoli, M., Parente, M. (eds.) Proceedings of GandALF 2010. Electronic Proceedings in Theoretical Computer Science, vol. 25, pp. 214–223 (2010)

6. Ancona, D., Lagorio, G.: Idealized coinductive type systems for imperative object-oriented programs. RAIRO - Theor. Inf. and Applic. 45(1), 3–33 (2011)
7. Ancona, D., Lagorio, G.: Static single information form for abstract compilation. In: Baeten, J.C.M., Ball, T., de Boer, F.S. (eds.) TCS 2012. LNCS, vol. 7604, pp. 10–27. Springer, Heidelberg (2012)
8. Barbanera, F., Dezani-Ciancaglini, M., de'Liguoro, U.: Intersection and union types: Syntax and semantics. Information and Computation 119(2), 202–230 (1995)
9. Bonsangue, M., Rot, J., Ancona, D., de Boer, F., Rutten, J.: A coalgebraic foundation for coinductive union types. In: 41st International Colloquium on Automata, Languages and Programming, ICALP 2014 (to appear, 2014)
10. Brandt, M., Henglein, F.: Coinductive axiomatization of recursive type equality and subtyping. Fundam. Inform. 33(4), 309–338 (1998)
11. Courcelle, B.: Fundamental properties of infinite trees. Theoretical Computer Science 25, 95–169 (1983)
12. Frisch, A., Castagna, G., Benzaken, V.: Semantic subtyping: Dealing set-theoretically with function, union, intersection, and negation types. J. ACM 55(4) (2008)
13. Hosoya, H., Pierce, B.C.: XDuce: A statically typed XML processing language. ACM Trans. Internet Techn. 3(2), 117–148 (2003)
14. Hosoya, H., Vouillon, J., Pierce, B.C.: Regular expression types for XML. ACM Trans. Program. Lang. Syst. 27(1), 46–90 (2005)
15. Igarashi, A., Nagira, H.: Union types for object-oriented programming. Journ. of Object Technology 6(2), 47–68 (2007)
16. Leroy, X., Grall, H.: Coinductive big-step operational semantics. Information and Computation 207, 284–304 (2009)

A Artifact Description

Authors of the Artifact. Davide Ancona and Andrea Corradi.

Summary. We have developed a prototype implementation of the presented algorithm in SWI Prolog; besides allowing rapid prototyping and conciseness, Prolog has the advantage of offering native support for regular terms and unification, which is very useful for defining coinductively defined functions which returns regular terms (consider for instance the problem of implementing type normalization as defined in Figure 5).

Although the prototype has been developed as a proof of concept, and more optimizations and an implementation in a more efficient programming language should be considered, the numerous tests show that the algorithm is usable in practice.

As an example of the performed tests, let us consider the following two types τ_L, τ_{EL}, and τ_{OL} defined by the following equations:

$$\tau_L = \langle el{:}int, nx{:}\tau_L \rangle \vee null$$
$$\tau_{EL} = \langle el{:}int, nx{:}\langle el{:}int, nx{:}\tau_{EL} \rangle \rangle \vee null$$
$$\tau_{OL} = \langle el{:}int, nx{:}\langle el{:}int, nx{:}\tau_{OL} \rangle \rangle \vee \langle el{:}int, nx{:}null \rangle$$

Type τ_L corresponds to all integer lists, whereas τ_{EL} and τ_{OL} represent all integer lists whose length (when finite) is even and odd, respectively. As expected, the tests $\tau_{EL} \vee \tau_{OL} \leq \tau_L$ and $\tau_L \leq \tau_{EL} \vee \tau_{OL}$ succeed, whereas $\tau_L \leq \tau_{EL}$ and $\tau_L \leq \tau_{OL}$ fail.

Content. The artifact package includes:

- README.txt: explanation of how the artifact works and how to use it.
- results.pdf: experimental results.
- src/contractive.pl: contractivity check.
- src/normalization.pl: type normalization as defined in the paper.
- src/plunit.pl: unit testing framework.
- src/subtype.pl: implementation of the main predicate subtype/2.
- src/tests.pl: tests for the subtype predicate and code to run the benchmarks.

Getting the Artifact. The artifact endorsed by the Artifact Evaluation Committee is available free of charge as supplementary material of this paper on SpringerLink. The latest version of our code is available on ftp://ftp.disi.unige.it/person/AnconaD/ECOOP14artifact.zip.

Tested Platforms. The artifact is known to work on any platform running SWI Prolog (http://swi-prolog.org/) version 6.6.

License. GPL-2.0
(https://www.gnu.org/licenses/old-licenses/gpl-2.0.txt)

MD5 Sum of the Artifact. fac97ebe56df60b35de45fe7a32ebd6f

Size of the Artifact. 162 KB

Spores: A Type-Based Foundation for Closures in the Age of Concurrency and Distribution

Heather Miller[1], Philipp Haller[2], and Martin Odersky[1]

[1] EPFL
{heather.miller,martin.odersky}@epfl.ch
[2] Typesafe, Inc.
philipp.haller@typesafe.com

Abstract. Functional programming (FP) is regularly touted as the way forward for bringing parallel, concurrent, and distributed programming to the mainstream. The popularity of the rationale behind this viewpoint has even led to a number of object-oriented (OO) programming languages outside the Smalltalk tradition adopting functional features such as lambdas and thereby function closures. However, despite this established viewpoint of FP as an enabler, reliably distributing function closures over a network, or using them in concurrent environments nonetheless remains a challenge across FP and OO languages. This paper takes a step towards more principled distributed and concurrent programming by introducing a new closure-like abstraction and type system, called *spores*, that can guarantee closures to be serializable, thread-safe, or even have custom user-defined properties. Crucially, our system is based on the principle of encoding type information corresponding to captured variables in the type of a spore. We prove our type system sound, implement our approach for Scala, evaluate its practicality through a small empirical study, and show the power of these guarantees through a case analysis of real-world distributed and concurrent frameworks that this safe foundation for closures facilitates.

Keywords: closures, functions, distributed programming, concurrent programming, type systems.

1 Introduction

With the growing trend towards cloud computing, mobile applications, and big data, distributed programming has entered the mainstream. Popular paradigms in software engineering such as software as a service (SaaS), RESTful services, or the rise of a multitude of systems for big data processing and interactive analytics, evidence this trend.

Meanwhile, at the same time, functional programming has been undeniably gaining traction in recent years, as is evidenced by the ongoing trend of traditionally object-oriented or imperative languages being extended with functional features, such as lambdas in Java 8 [7], C++11 [9], and Visual Basic 9 [16], the perceived importance of functional programming in general empirical studies on software developers [17], and the popularity of functional programming massively online open courses (MOOCs) [20].

One reason for the rise in popularity of functional programming languages and features within object-oriented communities is the basic philosophy of transforming immutable data by applying first-class functions, and the observation that this functional style simplifies reasoning about data in parallel, concurrent, and distributed code. A popular and well-understood example of this style of programming for which many popular

R. Jones (Ed.): ECOOP 2014, LNCS 8586, pp. 308–333, 2014.

frameworks have come to fruition is functional data-parallel programming. Examples across functional and object-oriented paradigms include Java 8's monadic-style optionally parallel collections [7], Scala's parallel [25] and concurrent dataflow [26] collections, Data Parallel Haskell [2], CnC [1], Nova [3], and Haskell's Par monad [12] to name a few.

In the context of distributed programming, data-parallel frameworks like MapReduce [4] and Spark [31] are designed around functional patterns where closures are transmitted across cluster nodes to large-scale persistent datasets. As a result of the "big data" revolution, these frameworks have become very popular, in turn further highlighting the need to be able to reliably and safely serialize and transmit closures over the network.

However, there's trouble in paradise. For both object-oriented and functional languages, there still exist numerous hurdles at the language-level for even these most basic functional building blocks, closures, to overcome in order to be reliable and easy to reason about in a concurrent or distributed setting.

In order to distribute closures, one must be able to serialize them – a goal that remains tricky to reliably achieve not only in object-oriented languages but also in pure functional languages like Haskell:

```
1   sendFunc :: SendPort (Int -> Int) -> Int -> ProcessM ()
2   sendFunc p x = sendChan p (\y -> x + y + 1)
```

In this example, in function sendFunc we are sending the lambda (\y -> x + y + 1) on channel p. The lambda captures variable x, a parameter of sendFunc. Serializing the lambda requires serializing also its captured variables. However, when looking up a serializer for the lambda, only the type of the lambda is taken into account; however, it doesn't tell us anything about the types of its captured variables, which makes it impossible in Haskell to look up serializers for them.

In object-oriented languages like Java or C#, serialization is solved differently – the runtime environment is designed to be able to serialize any object, reflectively. While this "universal" serialization might seem to solve the problem of languages like Haskell that cannot rely on such a mechanism, serializing closures nonetheless remains surprisingly error-prone. For example, attempting to serialize a closure with transitive references to objects that are not marked as serializable will crash at runtime, typically with no compile-time checks whatsoever. The kicker is that it is remarkably easy to accidentally and unknowingly create such a problematic transitive reference, especially in an object-oriented language.

For example, consider the following use of a distributed collection in Scala with higher-order functions map and reduce (using Spark):

```
1   class MyCoolRddApp {
2     val log = new Log(...)
3     def shift(p: Int): Int = ...
4     ...
5     def work(rdd: RDD[Int]) {
6       rdd.map(x => x + shift(x)).reduce(...)
7     }
8   }
```

In this example, the closure (x => x + shift(x)) is passed to the map method of the distributed collection rdd which requires serializing the closure (as, in Spark, parts of the data structure reside on different machines). However, calling shift inside the closure invokes a method on the enclosing object this. Thus, the closure is capturing, and must therefore serialize, this. If Log, a field of this, is not serializable, this will fail at runtime.

In fact, closures suffer not only from the problems shown in these two examples; there are numerous more hazards that manifest *across programming paradigms*. To provide a glimpse, closure-related hazards related to concurrency and distribution include:

- accidental capture of non-serializable variables (including `this`);
- language-specific compilation schemes, creating implicit references to objects that are not serializable;
- transitive references that inadvertently hold on to excessively large object graphs, creating memory leaks;
- capturing references to mutable objects, leading to race conditions in a concurrent setting;
- unknowingly accessing object members that are not constant such as methods, which in a distributed setting can have logically different meanings on different machines.

Given all of these issues, exposing functions in public APIs is a source of headaches for authors of concurrent or distributed frameworks. Framework users who stumble across any of these issues are put in a position where it's unclear whether or not the encountered issue is a problem on the side of the user or the framework, thus often adversely hitting the perceived reliability of these frameworks and libraries.

We argue that solving these problems in a principled way could lead to more confidence on behalf of library authors in exposing functions in APIs, thus leading to a potentially wide array of new frameworks.

This paper takes a step towards more principled *function-passing style* by introducing a type-based foundation for closures, called *spores*. Spores are a closure-like abstraction and type system which is designed to avoid typical hazards of closures. By including type information of captured variables in the type of a spore, we enable the expression of type-based constraints for captured variables, making spores safer to use in a concurrent or distributed setting. We show that this approach can be made practical by automatically synthesizing refinement types using macros, and by leveraging local type inference. Using type-based constraints, spores allow expressing a variety of "safe" closures.

To express safe closures with transitive properties such as guaranteed serializability, or closures capturing only deeply immutable types, spores support type constraints based on type classes which enforce transitive properties. In addition, implicit macros in Scala enable integration with type systems that enforce transitive properties using generics or annotated types. Spores also support user-defined type constraints. Finally, we argue that by principle of a type-based approach, spores can potentially benefit from optimization, further safety via type system extensions, and verification opportunities.

The design of spores is guided by the following principles:

- **Type-safety.** Spores should be able to express type-based properties of captured variables in a statically safe way. Including type information of captured variables in the type of a spore creates a number of previously impossible opportunities; it facilitates the verification of closure-heavy code; it opens up the possibility for IDEs to assist in safe closure creation, advanced refactoring, and debugging support; it enables compilers to implement safe transformations that can further simplify the use of safe closures, and it makes it possible for spores to integrate with type class-based frameworks like Scala/pickling [19].

- **Extensibility.** Given types which include information about what a closure captures, libraries and frameworks should be able to restrict the types that are captured by spores. Enforcing these *type constraints* should not be limited to serializability, thread-safety, or other pre-defined properties, however; spores should enable customizing the semantics of variable capture based on user-defined types. It should be possible to use existing type-based mechanisms to express a variety of user-defined properties of captured types.
- **Ease of Use.** Spores should be lightweight to use, and be able to integrate seamlessly with existing practice. It should be possible to capitalize on the benefits of precise types while at the same time ensuring that working with spores is never too verbose, thanks to the help of automatic type synthesis and inference. At the same time, frameworks like Spark, for which the need for controlled capture is central, should be able to use spores, meanwhile requiring only minimal changes in application code.
- **Practicality.** Spores should be practical to use in general, as well as be practical for inclusion in the full-featured Scala language. They should be practical in a variety of real-world scenarios (for use with Spark, Akka, parallel collections, and other closure-heavy code). At the same time, to enable a robust integration with the host language, existing type system features should be reused instead of extended.
- **Reliability for API Designers.** Spores should enable library authors to confidently release libraries that expose functions in user-facing APIs without concern of runtime exceptions or other dubious errors falling on their users.

1.1   Selected Related Work

Cloud Haskell [5] provides statically guaranteed-serializable closures by either rejecting environments outright, or by allowing manual capturing, requiring the user to explicitly specify and pre-serialize the environment in combination with top-level functions (enforced using a new `static` type constructor). That is, in Cloud Haskell, to create a serializable closure, one must explicitly pass the serialized environment as a parameter to the function – this requires users to have to refactor closures they wish to be made serializable. In contrast, spores do not require users to manually factor out, manage, and serialize their environment; spores require only that *what* is captured is specified, not *how*. Furthermore, spores are more general than Cloud Haskell's serializable closures; user-defined type constraints enable spores to express more properties than just serializability, like thread-safety, immutability, or any other user-defined property. In addition, spores allow restricting captured types in a way that is integrated with object-oriented concerns, such as subtyping and open class hierarchies.

C++11 [9] has introduced syntactic rules for explicit capture specifications that indicate which variables are captured and how (by reference or by copy). Since the capturing semantics is purely syntactic, a capture specification is only enforced at closure creation time. Thus, when composing two closures, the capture semantics is not preserved. Spores, on the other hand, capture such specifications at the level of types, enabling composability. Furthermore, spores' type constraints enable more general type-directed control over capturing than capture-by-value or capture-by-reference alone.

A preliminary proposal for closures in the Rust language [13] allows describing the closed-over variables in the environment using closure bounds, requiring captured types to implement certain traits. Closure bounds are limited to a small set of built-in traits to enforce properties like sendability. Spores on the other hand enable user-defined property definition, allowing for greater customizability of closure capturing semantics. Furthermore, unlike spores, the environment of a closure in Rust must always be allocated on the stack (although not necessarily the top-most stack frame).

Java 8 [7] introduces a limited type of closure which is only permitted to capture variables that are effectively-final. Like with Scala's standard closures, variable capture is implicit, which can lead to accidental captures that spores are designed to avoid. Although serializability can be requested at the level of the type system using newly-introduced intersection types in Java 8, there is no guarantee about the absence of runtime exceptions, as there is for spores. Finally, spores additionally allow specifying type-based constraints for captured variables that are more general than serializability alone.

We discuss other related work in Section 7.

1.2 Contributions

This paper makes the following contributions:

- We introduce a closure-like abstraction and type system, called "spores," which avoids typical hazards when using closures in a concurrent or distributed setting through controlled variable capture and customizable user-defined constraints for captured types.
- We introduce an approach for type-based constraints that can be combined with existing type systems to express a variety of properties from the literature, including, but not limited to, serializability and thread-safety/immutability. Transitive properties can be lifted to spore types in a variety of ways, *e.g.,* using type classes.
- We present a formalization of spores with type constraints and prove soundness of the type system.
- We present an implementation of spores in and for the full Scala language.[1]
- We (a) demonstrate the practicality of spores through a small empirical study using a collection of real-world Scala programs, and (b) show the power of the guarantees spores provide through case studies using parallel and distributed frameworks.

2   Spores

Spores are a closure-like abstraction and type system which aims to give users a principled way of controlling the environment which a closure can capture. This is achieved by (a) enforcing a specific syntactic shape which dictates how the environment of a spore is declared, and (b) providing additional type-checking to ensure that types being captured have certain properties. A crucial insight of spores is that, by including type information of captured variables in the type of a spore, type-based constraints for captured variables can be composed and checked, making spores safer to use in a concurrent, distributed, or in an arbitrary settings where closures must be controlled.

Below, we describe the syntactic shape of spores, and in Section 2.2 we describe the Spore type. In Section 2.4 we informally describe the type system, and how to add user-defined constraints to customize what types a spore can capture.

---

[1] https://github.com/scala/spores

```
1   spore {
2     val y1: S1 = <expr1>
3     ...
4     val yn: Sn = <exprn>
5     (x: T) => {
6       // ...
7     }
8   }
```

} spore header

} closure/spore body

Fig. 1. The syntactic shape of a spore

2.1   Spore Syntax

A spore is a closure with a specific shape that dictates how the environment of a spore is declared. The shape of a spore is shown in Figure 1. A spore consists of two parts:

- **the spore header**, composed of a list of value definitions.
- **the spore body** (sometimes referred to as the "spore closure"), a regular closure.

The characteristic property of a spore is that the *spore body* is only allowed to access its parameter, the values in the spore header, as well as top-level singleton objects (public, global state). In particular, the spore closure is not allowed to capture variables in the environment. Only an expression on the right-hand side of a value definition in the spore header is allowed to capture variables.

By enforcing this shape, the environment of a spore is always declared explicitly in the spore header, which avoids accidentally capturing problematic references. Moreover, importantly for object-oriented languages, it's no longer possible to accidentally capture the this reference.

```
1   {
2     val y1: S1 = <expr1>
3     ...
4     val yn: Sn = <exprn>
5     (x: T) => {
6       // ...
7     }
8   }
```

(a) A closure block.

```
1   spore {
2     val y1: S1 = <expr1>
3     ...
4     val yn: Sn = <exprn>
5     (x: T) => {
6       // ...
7     }
8   }
```

(b) A spore.

Fig. 2. The evaluation semantics of a spore is equivalent to that of a closure, obtained by simply leaving out the spore marker

Evaluation Semantics. The evaluation semantics of a spore is equivalent to a closure obtained by leaving out the spore marker, as shown in Figure 2. In Scala, the block shown in Figure 2a first initializes all value definitions in order and then evaluates to a closure that captures the introduced local variables y1, ..., yn. The corresponding spore, shown in Figure 2b has the exact same evaluation semantics. Interestingly, this closure shape is already used in production systems such as Spark in an effort to avoid problems with accidentally captured references, such as this. However, in systems like Spark, the above shape is merely a convention that is not enforced.

2.2   The Spore Type

Figure 3 shows Scala's arity-1 function type and the arity-1 spore type.[2] Functions are

---

[2] For simplicity, we omit Function1's definitions of the andThen and compose methods.

```
1    trait Function1[-A, +B] {
2      def apply(x: A):  B
3    }
```

(a) Scala's arity-1 function type.

```
1    trait Spore[-A, +B]
2    extends Function1[A, B] {
3      type Captured
4      type Excluded
5    }
```

(b) The arity-1 Spore type.

Fig. 3. The Spore type

```
1    val s = spore {
2      val y1: String = expr1;
3      val y2: Int = expr2;
4      (x: Int) => y1 + y2 + x
5    }
```

(a) A spore s which captures a String and an Int in its spore header.

```
1    Spore[Int, String] {
2      type Captured = (String, Int)
3    }
```

(b) s's corresponding type.

Fig. 4. An example of the Captured type member

Note: we omit the Excluded type member for simplicity; we detail it later in Section 2.4.

contravariant in their argument type A (indicated using -) and covariant in their result type B (indicated using +). The apply method of Function1 is abstract; a concrete implementation applies the body of the function that is being defined to the parameter x.

Individual spores have *refinement types* of the base Spore type, which, to be compatible with normal Scala functions, is itself a subtype of Function1. Like functions, spores are contravariant in their argument type A, and covariant in their result type B. Unlike a normal function, however, the Spore type additionally contains information about *captured* and *excluded* types. This information is represented as (potentially abstract) Captured and Excluded type members. In a concrete spore, the Captured type is defined to be a tuple with the types of all captured variables. Section 2.4 introduces the Excluded type member.

2.3   Basic Usage

Definition. A spore can be defined as shown in Figure 4a, with its corresponding type shown in Figure 4b. As can be seen, the types of the environment listed in the spore header are represented by the Captured type member in the spore's type.

Using Spores in APIs. Consider the following method definition:

```
def sendOverWire(s: Spore[Int, Int]): Unit = ...
```

In this example, the Captured (and Excluded) type member is not specified, meaning it is left abstract. In this case, so long as the spore's parameter and result types match, a spore type is always compatible, regardless of which types are captured.

Using spores in this way enables libraries to enforce the use of spores instead of plain closures, thereby reducing the risk for common programming errors (see Section 6 for detailed case studies), even in this very simple form. Later sections show more advanced ways in which library authors can control the capturing semantics of spores.

Composition. Like normal functions, spores can be composed. By representing the environment of spores using refinement types, it is possible to preserve the captured type information (and later, constraints) of spores when they are composed.

For example, assume we are given two spores s1 and s2 with types:

```
s1: Spore[Int, String] { type Captured = (String, Int) }
s2: Spore[String, Int] { type Captured = Nothing }
```

The fact that the Captured type in s2 is defined to be Nothing means that the spore does not capture anything (Nothing is Scala's bottom type). The composition of s1 and s2, written s1 compose s2, would therefore have the following refinement type:

```
Spore[String, String] { type Captured = (String, Int) }
```

Note that the Captured type member of the result spore is equal to the Captured type of s1, since it is guaranteed that the result spore does not capture more than what s1 already captures. Thus, not only are spores composable, but so are their (refinement) types.

Implicitly Converting Functions to Spores. The design of spores was guided in part by a desire to make them easy to use, and easy to integrate in already closure-heavy code. Spores, as so far proposed, introduce considerable verbosity in pursuit of the requirement to explicitly define the spore's environment.

Therefore, it is also possible to use function literals as spores if they satisfy the spore shape constraints. To support this, an implicit conversion[3] macro[4] is provided which converts regular functions to spores, but only if the converted function is a literal: only then is it possible to enforce the spore shape.

For-Comprehensions. Converting functions to spores opens up the use of spores in a number of other situations; most prominently, for-comprehensions (Scala's version of Haskell's do-notation) in Scala are desugared to invocations of the higher-order map, flatMap, and filter methods, each of which take normal functions as arguments.[5]

In situations where for-comprehension closures capture variables, preventing them from being converted implicitly to spores, we introduce an alternative syntax for capturing variables in spores: an object that is referred to using a so-called "stable identifier" id can additionally be captured using the syntax capture(id).[6]

This enables the use of spores in for-comprehensions, since it's possible to write:

```
for (a <- gen1; b <- capture(gen2)) yield capture(a) + b
```

Note that superfluous capture expressions are not harmful. Thus, it is legal to write:

```
for (a <- capture(gen1); b <- capture(gen2)) yield capture(a) + capture(b)
```

This allows the use of capture in a way that does not require users to know how for-comprehensions are desugared. In Section 6 we show how capture and the implicit conversion of functions to spores enables the use of for-comprehensions in the context of distributed programming with spores.

---

[3] In Scala, implicit conversions can be thought of as methods which can be implicitly invoked based upon their type, and whether or not they are present in implicit scope.

[4] In Scala, macros are methods that are transparently loaded by the compiler and executed (or expanded) during compilation. A macro is defined like a normal method, but it is linked using the macro keyword to an additional method that operates on abstract syntax trees.

[5] For-comprehensions are desugared before implicit conversions are inserted; thus, no change to the Scala compiler is necessary.

[6] In Scala, a stable identifier is basically a selection p.x where p is a path and x is an identifier (see Scala Language Specification [23], Section 3.1).

2.4 Advanced Usage and Type Constraints

In this section, we describe two different kinds of "type constraints" which enable more fine-grained control over closure capture semantics; *excluded types* which prevent certain types from being captured, and *context bounds* for captured types which enforce certain type-based properties for all captured variables of a spore. Importantly, all of these different kinds of constraints compose, as we will see in later subsections.

Throughout this paper, we use as a motivating example hazards that arise in concurrent or distributed settings. However, note that the system of type constraints described henceforth is general, and can be applied to very different applications and sets of types.

Excluded Types. Libraries and frameworks for concurrent and distributed programming, such as Akka [29] and Spark, typically have requirements to avoid capturing certain types in closures that are used together with library-provided objects and methods. For example, when using Akka, one should not capture variables of type Actor; in Spark, one should not capture variables of type SparkContext.

Such restrictions can be expressed in our system by excluding types from being captured by spores, using refinements of the Spore type presented in Section 2.2. For example, the following refinement type forbids capturing variables of type Actor:

```
1   type SporeNoActor[-A, +B] = Spore[A, B] {
2     type Excluded <: No[Actor]
3   }
```

Note the use of the auxiliary type constructor No (defined as **trait** No[-T]): it enables the exclusion of multiple types while supporting desired sub-typing relationships.

For example, exclusion of multiple types can be expressed as follows:

```
1   type SafeSpore = Spore[Int, String] {
2     type Excluded = No[Actor] with No[Util]
3   }
```

Given Scala's sub-typing rules for refinement types, a spore refinement excluding a superset of types excluded by an "otherwise type-compatible" spore is a subtype. For example, SafeSpore is a subtype of SporeNoActor[Int, String].

Subtyping. Using some frameworks typically user-defined subclasses are created that extend framework-provided types. However, the extended types are sometimes not safe to be captured. For example, in Akka, user-created closures should not capture variables of type Actor and any subtypes thereof. To express such a constraint in our system we define the No type constructor to be contravariant in its type parameter; this is the meaning of the - annotation in the type declaration trait No[-T].

As a result, the following refinement type is a supertype of type
SporeNoActor[Int, Int] defined above (we assume MyActor is a subclass of Actor):

```
1   type MySpore = Spore[Int, Int] {
2     type Excluded <: No[MyActor]
3   }
```

It is important that MySpore is a supertype and not a subtype of
SporeNoActor[Int, Int], since an instance of MySpore could capture some other subclass of Actor which is not itself a subclass of MyActor. Thus, it would not be safe to use an instance of MySpore where an instance of SporeNoActor[Int, Int] is required. On the other hand, an instance of SporeNoActor[Int, Int] is safe to use in place of an instance of MySpore, since it is guaranteed not to capture Actor or any of its subclasses.

Reducing `Excluded` ***Boilerplate.*** Given that the design of spores was guided in part by a desire to make them easy to use, and easy to integrate in already closure-heavy code with minimal changes, one might observe that the `Spore` type with `Excluded` types introduces considerable verbosity. This is easily solved in practice by the addition of a macro `without[T]` which takes a type parameter `T` and rewrites the spore type to take into consideration the excluded type `T`. Thus, in the case of the `SafeSpore` example, the same spore refinement type can easily be synthesized inline in the definition of a spore value:

```
1  val safeSpore = spore {
2    val a = ...
3    val b = ...
4    (x: T) => { ... }
5  }.without[Actor].without[Util]
```

Context Bounds for Captured Types. The fact that for spores a certain shape is enforced is very useful. However, in some situations this is not enough. For example, a common source of race conditions in data-parallel frameworks manifests itself when users capture mutable objects. Thus, a user might want to enforce that closures only capture immutable objects. However, such constraints cannot be enforced using the spore shape alone (captured objects are stored in constant values in the spore header, but such constants might still refer to mutable objects).

In this section, we introduce a form of type-based constraints called "context bounds" which enforce certain type-based properties for all captured variables of that spore.[7]

Taking another example, it might be necessary for a spore to require the availability of instances of a certain type class for the types of all of its captured variables. A typical example for such a type class is `Pickler`: types with an instance of the `Pickler` type class can be pickled using a new type-based pickling framework for Scala [19]. To be able to pickle a spore, it's necessary that all its captured types have an instance of `Pickler`.[8]

Spores allow expressing such a requirement using a notion of implicit *properties*. The idea is that if there is an implicit value[9] of type `Property[Pickler]` in scope at the point where a spore is created, then it is enforced that all captured types in the spore header have an instance of the `Pickler` type class

```
1  import spores.withPickler
2
3  spore {
4    val name: String = <expr1>
5    val age: Int = <expr2>
6    (x: String) => { ...}
7  }
```

While an imported property does not have an impact on how a spore is constructed (besides the property import), it has an impact on the result type of the spore macro. In the above example, the result type would be a refinement of the `Spore` type:[10]

---

[7] The name "context bound" is used in Scala to refer to a particular kind of implicit parameter that is added automatically if a type parameter has declared such a context bound. Our proposal essentially adds context bounds to type members.

[8] A spore can be pickled by pickling its environment and the fully-qualified class name of its corresponding function class.

[9] An implicit value is a value in *implicit scope* that is statically selected based on its type.

[10] In the code example, `implicitly[T]` returns the uniquely-defined implicit value of `T` which is in scope at the invocation site.

```
1  Spore[String, Int] {
2    type Captured = (String, Int)
3    implicit val ev$0 = implicitly[Pickler[Captured]]
4  }
```

For each property that is imported, the resulting spore refinement type contains an implicit value with the corresponding type class instance for type `Captured`.

Expressing context bounds in APIs. Using the above types and implicits, it's also possible for a method to require argument spores to have certain context bounds. For example, requiring argument spores to have picklers defined for their captured types can be achieved as follows:

```
def m[A, B](s: Spore[A, B])(implicit p: Pickler[s.Captured]) = ...
```

Defining Custom Properties. Properties can be introduced using the `Property` trait (provided by the spores library): `trait Property[C[_]]`

As a running example, we will be defining a custom property for immutable types. A custom property can be introduced using a generic trait, and an implicit "property" object that mixes in the above `Property` trait:

```
1  object safe {
2    trait Immutable[T]
3    implicit object immutableProp extends Property[Immutable]
4    ...
5  }
```

The next step is to mark selected types as immutable by defining an implicit object extending the desired list of types, each type wrapped in the `Immutable` type constructor:

```
1  object safe {
2    ...
3    import scala.collection.immutable.{Map, Set, Seq}
4    implicit object collections extends Immutable[Map[_, _]] with
5      Immutable[Set[_]] with Immutable[Seq[_]] with ...
6  }
```

The above definitions allow us to create spores that are guaranteed to capture only types T for which an implicit of type `Immutable[T]` exists.

It's also possible to define compound properties by mixing in multiple traits into an implicit property object:

```
implicit object myProps extends Property[Pickler] with Property[Immutable]
```

By making this compound property available in a scope within which spores are created (for example, using an `import`), it is enforced that those spores have both the context bound `Pickler` and the context bound `Immutable`.

Composition. Now that we've introduced type constraints in the form of excluded types and context bounds, we present generalized composition rules for the types of spores with such constraints.

To precisely describe the composition rules, we introduce the following notation: the function *Excluded* returns, for a given refinement type, the set of types that are excluded; the function *Captured* returns, for a given refinement type, the list of types that are captured. Using these two mathematical functions, we can precisely specify how the type members of the resulting spore refinement type are computed. (We use the syntax *.type* to refer to the singleton types of the argument spores and the result, respectively.)

1. $Captured(res.type) = Captured(s1.type), Captured(s2.type)$
2. $Excluded(res.type) = \{T \in Excluded(s1.type) \cup Excluded(s2.type) \mid T \notin Captured(s1.type), Captured(s2.type)\}$

The first rule expresses the fact that the sequence of captured types of the resulting refinement type is simply the concatenation of the captured types of the argument spores. The second rule expresses the fact that the set of excluded types of the result refinement type is defined as the set of all types that are excluded by one of the argument spores, but that are not captured by any of the argument spores.

For example, assume two spores s1 and s2 with types:

```
1   Spore[Int, String] {                1   Spore[String, Int] {
2     type Captured = (Int, Util)       2     type Captured = (String, Int)
3     type Excluded = No[Actor]         3     type Excluded = No[Actor] with No[Util]
4   }                                   4   }
```
(a) Type of spore s1.   (b) Type of spore s2.

The result of composing the two spores, s1 compose s2, thus has the following type:

```
1   Spore[String, String] {
2     type Captured = (Int, Util, String, Int)
3     type Excluded = No[Actor]
4   }
```

Loosening constraints. Given that type constraints compose, it's evident that as spores compose, type constraints can monotonically increase in number. Thus, it's important to note that it's also possible to soundly loosen constraints using regular type widening.

Let's say we have a spore with the following (too elaborate) refinement type:

```
1   val s2: Spore[String, Int] {
2     type Captured = (String, Int)
3     type Excluded = No[Actor] with No[Util]
4   }
```

Then we can soundly drop constraints by using a supertype such as MySafeSpore:

```
1   type MySafeSpore = Spore[String, Int] {
2     type Captured
3     type Excluded <: No[Actor]
4   }
```

2.5 Transitive Properties

Transitive properties like picklability or immutability are not enforced through the spores type system. Rather, spores were designed for extensibility; we ensure that deep checking can be applied to spores as follows.

An initial motivation was to be able to require type class instances for captured types, *e.g.*, picklability; spores integrate seamlessly with Scala/pickling [19].

Transitive properties expressed using known techniques, *e.g.*, generics (Zibin etal's OIGJ system [32] for transitive immutability) or annotated types, can be enforced for captured types using custom spore properties. Instead of merely tagging types, implicit macros can generate type class instances for all types satisfying a predicate. For example, using OIGJ we can define an implicit macro

```
implicit def isImmutable[T: TypeTag]: Immutable[T]
```

which returns a type class instance for all types of the shape C[O, Immut] that is deeply immutable (analyzing the TypeTag). Custom spore properties requiring type classes constructed in such a way enable transitive checking for a variety of such (pluggable) extensions, including compositions thereof (*e.g.*, picklability/immutability).

3   Formalization

$$
\begin{aligned}
t ::= \ & x & \text{variable} \\
| \ & (x : T) \Rightarrow t & \text{abstraction} \\
| \ & t\, t & \text{application} \\
| \ & \texttt{let } x = t \texttt{ in } t & \text{let binding} \\
| \ & \{\overline{l = t}\} & \text{record construction} \\
| \ & t.l & \text{selection} \\
| \ & \texttt{spore } \{ \ \overline{x : T = t} \, ; \overline{pn}; (x : T) \Rightarrow t \ \} & \text{spore} \\
| \ & \texttt{import } pn \texttt{ in } t & \text{property import} \\
| \ & t \texttt{ compose } t & \text{spore composition}
\end{aligned}
$$

$$
\begin{aligned}
v ::= \ & (x : T) \Rightarrow t & \text{abstraction} \\
| \ & \{\overline{l = v}\} & \text{record value} \\
| \ & \texttt{spore } \{ \ \overline{x : T = v} \, ; \overline{pn}; (x : T) \Rightarrow t \ \} & \text{spore value}
\end{aligned}
$$

$$
\begin{aligned}
T ::= \ & T \Rightarrow T & \text{function type} \\
| \ & \{\overline{l : T}\} & \text{record type} \\
| \ & \mathcal{S} \\
\mathcal{S} ::= \ & T \Rightarrow T \{ \texttt{ type } \mathcal{C} = \overline{T} \, ; \ \overline{pn} \ \} & \text{spore type} \\
| \ & T \Rightarrow T \{ \texttt{ type } \mathcal{C} \, ; \ \overline{pn} \ \} & \text{abstract spore type} \\
P \in \ & pn \to \mathcal{T} & \text{property map} \\
\mathcal{T} \in \ & \mathcal{P}(T) & \text{type family}
\end{aligned}
$$

$$
\begin{aligned}
\Gamma ::= \ & \overline{x : T} & \text{type environment} \\
\Delta ::= \ & \overline{pn} & \text{property environment}
\end{aligned}
$$

Fig. 5. Core language syntax

We formalize spores in the context of a standard, typed lambda calculus with records. Apart from novel language and type-systematic features, our formal development follows a well-known methodology [24]. Figure 5 shows the syntax of our core language. Terms are standard except for the spore, import, and compose terms. A spore term creates a new spore. It contains a list of variable definitions (the spore header), a list of property names, and the spore's closure. A property name refers to a type family (a set of types) that all captured types must belong to.

An illustrative example of a property and its associated type family is a type class: a spore satisfies such a property if there is a type class instance for all its captured types.

An import term imports a property name into the property environment within a lexical scope (a term); the property environment contains properties that are registered as requirements whenever a spore is created. This is explained in more detail in Section 3.2. A compose term is used to compose two spores. The core language provides spore composition as a built-in feature, because type checking spore composition is markedly different from type checking regular function composition (see Section 3.2).

The grammar of values is standard except for spore values; in a spore value each term on the right-hand side of a definition in the spore header is a value.

The grammar of types is standard except for spore types. Spore types are refinements of function types. They additionally contain a (possibly-empty) sequence of captured types, which can be left abstract, and a sequence of property names.

3.1 Subtyping

Figure 6 shows the subtyping rules; rules S-REC and S-FUN are standard [24].

The subtyping rule for spores (S-SPORE) is analogous to the subtyping rule for functions with respect to the argument and result types. Additionally, for two spore types to be in a subtyping relationship either their captured types have to be the same ($M_1 = M_2$) or the supertype must be an abstract spore type ($M_2 = \text{type}\,C$). The subtype must guarantee at least the properties of its supertype, or a superset thereof. Taken together, this rule expresses the fact that a spore type whose type member C is not abstract is compatible with an abstract spore type as long as it has a superset of the supertype's properties. This is important for spores used as first-class values: functions operating on spores with arbitrary environments can simply demand an abstract spore type. The way both the captured types and the properties are modeled corresponds to (but simplifies) the subtyping rule for refinement types in Scala (see Section 2.4).

Rule S-SPOREFUN expresses the fact that spore types are refinements of their corresponding function types, giving rise to a subtyping relationship.

$$
\frac{\text{S-REC}}{\overline{l'} \subseteq \overline{l} \qquad l_i = l'_i \to T_i <: T'_i \land T'_i <: T_i}{\{\overline{l:T}\} <: \{\overline{l':T'}\}}
\qquad
\frac{\text{S-FUN}}{T_2 <: T_1 \qquad R_1 <: R_2}{T_1 \Rightarrow R_1 <: T_2 \Rightarrow R_2}
$$

$$
\frac{\text{S-SPORE}}{T_2 <: T_1 \qquad R_1 <: R_2 \qquad \overline{pn'} \subseteq \overline{pn} \qquad M_1 = M_2 \lor M_2 = \text{type}\,C}{T_1 \Rightarrow R_1 \{ M_1 ; \overline{pn} \} <: T_2 \Rightarrow R_2 \{ M_2 ; \overline{pn'} \}}
$$

$$
\frac{\text{S-SPOREFUN}}{}{T_1 \Rightarrow R_1 \{ M ; \overline{pn} \} <: T_1 \Rightarrow R_1}
$$

Fig. 6. Subtyping

3.2 Typing rules

Typing derivations use a judgement of the form $\Gamma; \Delta \vdash t : T$. Besides the standard variable environment Γ we use a property environment Δ which is a sequence of property names that have been imported using `import` expressions in enclosing scopes of term t. The property environment is reminiscent of the implicit parameter context used in the original work on implicit parameters [10]; it is an environment for names whose definition sites "just happen to be far removed from their usages."

In the typing rules we assume the existence of a global property mapping P from property names pn to type families $\mathcal{T}$. This technique is reminiscent of the way some object-oriented core languages provide a global class table for type-checking. The main difference is that our core language does not include constructs to extend the global property map; such constructs are left out of the core language for simplicity, since the creation of properties is not essential to our model. We require P to follow behavioral subtyping:

Definition 1. (Behavioral subtyping of property mapping) *If $T <: T'$ and $T' \in P(pn)$, then $T \in P(pn)$*

The typing rules are standard except for rules T-IMP, T-SPORE, and T-COMP, which are new. Only these three type rules inspect or modify the property environment Δ. Note

T-VAR
$$\frac{x : T \in \Gamma}{\Gamma; \Delta \vdash x : T}$$

T-SUB
$$\frac{\Gamma; \Delta \vdash t : T' \quad T' <: T}{\Gamma; \Delta \vdash t : T}$$

T-ABS
$$\frac{\Gamma, x : T_1; \Delta \vdash t : T_2}{\Gamma; \Delta \vdash (x : T_1) \Rightarrow t : T_1 \Rightarrow T_2}$$

T-APP
$$\frac{\Gamma; \Delta \vdash t_1 : T_1 \Rightarrow T_2 \quad \Gamma; \Delta \vdash t_2 : T_1}{\Gamma; \Delta \vdash (t_1\ t_2) : T_2}$$

T-LET
$$\frac{\Gamma; \Delta \vdash t_1 : T_1 \quad \Gamma, x : T_1; \Delta \vdash t_2 : T_2}{\Gamma; \Delta \vdash \mathsf{let}\ x = t_1\ \mathsf{in}\ t_2 : T_2}$$

T-REC
$$\frac{\Gamma; \Delta \vdash \overline{t : T}}{\Gamma; \Delta \vdash \{\overline{l = t}\} : \{\overline{l : T}\}}$$

T-SEL
$$\frac{\Gamma; \Delta \vdash t : \{\overline{l : T}\}}{\Gamma; \Delta \vdash t.l_i : T_i}$$

T-IMP
$$\frac{\Gamma, \Delta, pn \vdash t : T}{\Gamma; \Delta \vdash \mathsf{import}\ pn\ \mathsf{in}\ t : T}$$

T-SPORE
$$\frac{\forall s_i \in \overline{s}.\ \Gamma; \Delta \vdash s_i : S_i \quad \overline{y : S}, x : T_1; \Delta \vdash t_2 : T_2 \quad \forall pn \in \Delta, \Delta'.\overline{S} \subseteq P(pn)}{\Gamma; \Delta \vdash \mathsf{spore}\ \{\ \overline{y : S = s}\ ; \Delta'; (x : T_1) \Rightarrow t_2\ \} :\quad T_1 \Rightarrow T_2\ \{\ \mathsf{type}\ C = \overline{S}\ ;\ \Delta, \Delta'\ \}}$$

T-COMP
$$\frac{\Gamma; \Delta \vdash t_1 : T_1 \Rightarrow T_2\ \{\ \mathsf{type}\ C = \overline{S}\ ;\ \Delta_1\ \} \quad \Gamma; \Delta \vdash t_2 : U_1 \Rightarrow T_1\ \{\ \mathsf{type}\ C = \overline{R}\ ;\ \Delta_2\ \} \quad \Delta' = \{pn \in \Delta_1 \cup \Delta_2\ |\ \overline{S} \subseteq P(pn) \wedge \overline{R} \subseteq P(pn)\}}{\Gamma; \Delta \vdash t_1\ \mathsf{compose}\ t_2 : U_1 \Rightarrow T_2\ \{\ \mathsf{type}\ C = \overline{S}, \overline{R}\ ;\ \Delta'\ \}}$$

Fig. 7. Typing rules

that there is no rule for spore application, since there is a subtyping relationship between spores and functions (see Section 3.1). Using the subsumption rule T-SUB spore application is expressed using the standard rule for function application (T-APP).

Rule T-IMP imports a property pn into the property environment within the scope defined by term t.

Rule T-SPORE derives a type for a spore term. In the spore, all terms on right-hand sides of variable definitions in the spore header must be well-typed in the same environment $\Gamma; \Delta$ according to their declared type. The body of the spore's closure, t_2, must be well-typed in an environment containing only the variables in the spore header and the closure's parameter, one of the central properties of spores. The last premise requires all captured types to satisfy both the properties in the current property environment, Δ, as well as the properties listes in the spore term, Δ'. Finally, the resulting spore type contains the argument and result types of the spore's closure, the sequence of captured types according to the spore header, and the concatenation of properties Δ and Δ'. The intuition here is that properties in the environment have been explicitly imported by the user, thus indicating that all spores in the scope of the corresponding import should satisfy them.

Rule T-COMP derives a result type for the composition of two spores. It inspects the captured types of both spores ($\overline{S}$ and $\overline{R}$) to ensure that the properties of the resulting spore, Δ, are satisfied by the captured variables of both spores. Otherwise, the argument and result types are analogous to regular function composition. Note that it is possible to weaken the properties of a spore through spore subtyping and subsumption (T-SUB).

E-AppSpore

$$\frac{\forall pn \in \overline{pn}.\ \overline{T} \subseteq P(pn)}{\text{spore}\ \{\ \overline{x : T = v}; \overline{pn}; (x' : T') \Rightarrow t\ \}v' \to [\overline{x \mapsto v}][x' \mapsto v']t}$$

E-Spore

$$\frac{t_k \to t_k'}{\begin{array}{l}\text{spore}\ \{\ \overline{x : T = v}, x_k : T_k = t_k, \overline{x' : T' = t'}\ ; (x : T) \Rightarrow t\ \} \to \\ \text{spore}\ \{\ \overline{x : T = v}, x_k : T_k = t_k', \overline{x' : T' = t'}\ ; (x : T) \Rightarrow t\ \}\end{array}}$$

E-Imp

$$\frac{}{\text{import}\ pn\ \text{in}\ t \to insert(pn, t)}$$

E-Comp1

$$\frac{t_1 \to t_1'}{t_1\ \text{compose}\ t_2 \to t_1'\ \text{compose}\ t_2}$$

E-Comp2

$$\frac{t_2 \to t_2'}{v_1\ \text{compose}\ t_2 \to v_1\ \text{compose}\ t_2'}$$

E-Comp3

$$\frac{\Delta = \{p \mid p \in \overline{pn}, \overline{qn}.\ \overline{T} \subseteq P(p) \wedge \overline{S} \subseteq P(p)\}}{\begin{array}{l}\text{spore}\ \{\ \overline{x : T = v}; \overline{pn}; (x' : T') \Rightarrow t\ \}\ \text{compose}\ \text{spore}\ \{\ \overline{y : S = w}; \overline{qn}; (y' : S') \Rightarrow t'\ \} \to \\ \text{spore}\ \{\ \overline{x : T = v}, \overline{y : S = w}; \Delta; (y' : S') \Rightarrow \text{let}\ z' = t'\ \text{in}\ [x' \mapsto z']t\}\end{array}}$$

Fig. 8. Operational Semantics[11]

H-InsSpore1

$$\frac{\forall t_i \in \bar{t}.\ insert(pn, t_i) = t_i' \qquad insert(pn, t) = t'}{\begin{array}{l}insert(pn, \text{spore}\ \{\ \overline{x : T = t}; \overline{pn}; (x' : T) \Rightarrow t\ \}) = \\ \text{spore}\ \{\ \overline{x : T = t'}; \overline{pn}, pn; (x' : T) \Rightarrow t'\ \}\end{array}}$$

H-InsSpore2

$$\frac{insert(pn, t) = t'}{\begin{array}{l}insert(pn, \text{spore}\ \{\ \overline{x : T = v}; \overline{pn}; (x' : T) \Rightarrow t\ \}) = \\ \text{spore}\ \{\ \overline{x : T = v}; \overline{pn}, pn; (x' : T) \Rightarrow t'\ \}\end{array}}$$

H-InsApp

$$insert(pn, t_1\ t_2) = insert(pn, t_1)\ insert(pn, t_2)$$

H-InsSel

$$insert(pn, t.l) = insert(pn, t).l$$

Fig. 9. Helper function $insert$

3.3 Operational semantics

Figure 8 shows the evaluation rules of a small-step operational semantics for our core language. The only non-standard rules are E-AppSpore, E-Spore, E-Imp, and E-Comp3. Rule E-AppSpore applies a spore literal to an argument. The differences to regular function application (E-AppAbs) are (a) that the types in the spore header must satisfy the properties of the spore dynamically, and (b) that the variables in the spore header must be replaced by their values in the body of the spore's closure. Rule E-Spore is a congruence rule. Rule E-Imp is a computation rule that is always enabled. It adds property name pn to all spore terms within the body t. The $insert$ helper function is defined in Figure 9 (we omit rules for compose and let; they are analogous to rules H-InsApp and H-InsSel).

---

[11]For the sake of brevity, here we omit the standard evaluation rules. The complete set of evaluation rules can be found in the accompanying technical report [18]

Rule E-Comp3 is the computation rule for spore composition. Besides computing the composition in a way analogous to regular function composition, it defines the spore header of the result spore, as well as its properties. The properties of the result spore are restricted to those that are satisfied by the captured variables of both argument spores.

3.4   Soundness

This section presents a soundness proof of the spore type system. The proof is based on a pair of progress and preservation theorems [30]. A complete proof of soundness appears in the companion technical report [18]. In addition to standard lemmas, we also prove a lemma specific to our type system, Lemma 1, which ensures types are preserved under property import. Soundness of the type system follows from Theorem 1 and Theorem 2.

Theorem 1. (Progress) *Suppose t is a closed, well-typed term (that is, $\vdash t : T$ for some T). Then either t is a value or else there is some t' with $t \rightarrow t'$.*

Proof. By induction on a derivation of $\vdash t : T$. The only three interesting cases are the ones for spore creation, application, and spore composition.

Lemma 1. (Preservation of types under import) *If $\Gamma; \Delta, pn \vdash t : T$ then $\Gamma; \Delta \vdash insert(pn, t) : T$*

Proof. By induction on a derivation of $\Gamma; \Delta, pn \vdash t : T$.

Lemma 2. (Preservation of types under substitution) *If $\Gamma, x : S; \Delta \vdash t : T$ and $\Gamma; \Delta \vdash s : S$, then $\Gamma; \Delta \vdash [x \mapsto s]t : T$*

Proof. By induction on a derivation of $\Gamma, x : S; \Delta \vdash t : T$.

Lemma 3. (Weakening) *If $\Gamma; \Delta \vdash t : T$ and $x \notin dom(\Gamma)$, then $\Gamma, x : S; \Delta \vdash t : T$.*

Proof. By induction on a derivation of $\Gamma; \Delta \vdash t : T$.

Theorem 2. (Preservation) *If $\Gamma; \Delta \vdash t : T$ and $t \rightarrow t'$, then $\Gamma; \Delta \vdash t' : T$.*

Proof. By induction on a derivation of $\Gamma; \Delta \vdash t : T$.

3.5   Relation to Spores in Scala

The type soundness proof (see Section 3.4) guarantees several important properties for well-typed programs which closely correspond to the pragmatic model in Scala:

1. Application of spores: for each property name pn, it is ensured that the dynamic types of all captured variables are contained in the type family pn maps to ($P(pn)$).
2. Dynamically, a spore only accesses its parameter and the variables in its header.
3. The properties computed for a composition of two spores is a safe approximation of the properties that are dynamically required.

$$t ::= \dots \qquad\qquad\qquad\qquad\qquad\qquad \text{terms}$$
$$| \text{ spore } \{ \, \overline{x : T = t} \, ; \overline{T}; \overline{pn}; (x : T) \Rightarrow t \, \} \quad \text{spore}$$

$$v ::= \dots \qquad\qquad\qquad\qquad\qquad\qquad \text{values}$$
$$| \text{ spore } \{ \, \overline{x : T = v} \, ; \overline{T}; \overline{pn}; (x : T) \Rightarrow t \, \} \quad \text{spore value}$$

$$S ::= T \Rightarrow T \, \{ \, \text{type } \mathcal{C} = \overline{T} \, ; \, \text{type } \mathcal{E} = \overline{T} \, ; \, \overline{pn} \, \} \quad \text{spore type}$$
$$| \, T \Rightarrow T \, \{ \, \text{type } \mathcal{C} \, ; \, \text{type } \mathcal{E} = \overline{T} \, ; \, \overline{pn} \, \} \qquad \text{abstract spore type}$$

Fig. 10. Core language syntax extensions

S-ESPORE

$$\frac{\begin{array}{c} T_2 <: T_1 \qquad R_1 <: R_2 \\ \overline{pn'} \subseteq \overline{pn} \qquad M_1 = M_2 \vee M_2 = \text{type } \mathcal{C} \qquad \forall T' \in \overline{U'}.\, \exists T \in \overline{U}.\, T' <: T \end{array}}{T_1 \Rightarrow R_1 \, \{ \, M_1 \, ; \, \text{type } \mathcal{E} = \overline{U} \, ; \, \overline{pn} \, \} \quad <: T_2 \Rightarrow R_2 \, \{ \, M_2 \, ; \, \text{type } \mathcal{E} = \overline{U'} \, ; \, \overline{pn'} \, \}}$$

S-ESPOREFUN
$$T_1 \Rightarrow R_1 \, \{ \, M \, ; \, E \, ; \, \overline{pn} \, \} <: T_1 \Rightarrow R_1$$

Fig. 11. Subtyping extensions

E-EAPPSPORE

$$\frac{\forall pn \in \overline{pn}.\, \overline{T} \subseteq P(pn) \qquad \forall T_i \in \overline{T}.\, T_i \notin \overline{U}}{\text{spore } \{ \, \overline{x : T = v} \, ; \, \overline{U} \, ; \, \overline{pn} \, ; \, (x' : T) \Rightarrow t \, \} \, v' \to \qquad \overline{[x \mapsto v]}[x' \mapsto v']t}$$

E-ECOMP3

$$\frac{\Delta = \{ p \mid p \in \overline{pn}, \overline{qn}.\, \overline{T} \subseteq P(p) \wedge \overline{S} \subseteq P(p) \} \qquad \overline{V} = (\overline{U} \setminus \overline{S}) \cup (\overline{U'} \setminus \overline{T})}{\begin{array}{c} \text{spore } \{ \, \overline{x : T = v} \, ; \, \overline{U} \, ; \, \overline{pn} \, ; \, (x' : T') \Rightarrow t \, \} \text{ compose} \\ \text{spore } \{ \, \overline{y : S = w} \, ; \, \overline{U'} \, ; \, \overline{qn} \, ; \, (y' : S') \Rightarrow t' \, \} \to \qquad \text{spore } \{ \, \overline{x : T = v}, \overline{y : S = w} \, ; \, \overline{V} \, ; \, \Delta \, ; \\ (y' : S') \Rightarrow \text{let } z' = t' \text{ in } [x' \mapsto z']t \, \} \end{array}}$$

Fig. 12. Operational semantics extensions

3.6 Excluded Types

This section shows how the formal model can be extended with excluded types as described above (see Section 2.4). Figure 10 shows the syntax extensions: first, spore terms and values are augmented with a sequence of excluded types; second, spore types and abstract spore types get another member $\text{type } \mathcal{E} = \overline{T}$ specifying the excluded types.

Figure 11 shows how the subtyping rules for spores have to be extended. Rule S-ESPORE requires that for each excluded type T' in the supertype, there must be an excluded type T in the subtype such that $T' <: T$. This means that by excluding type T, subtypes like T' are also prevented from being captured.

Figure 12 shows the extensions to the operational semantics. Rule E-EAPPSPORE additionally requires that none of the captured types $\overline{T}$ are contained in the excluded types $\overline{U}$. Rule E-ECOMP3 computes the set of excluded types of the result spore in the same way as in the corresponding type rule (T-ECOMP).

Figure 13 shows the extensions to the typing rules. Rule T-ESPORE additionally requires that none of the captured types $\overline{S}$ is a subtype of one of the types contained in the excluded types $\overline{U}$. The excluded types are recorded in the type of the spore.

T-ESPORE

$$\frac{\forall s_i \in \overline{s}.\; \Gamma; \Delta \vdash s_i : S_i \qquad \overline{y : S}, x : T_1; \Delta \vdash t_2 : T_2}{\forall pn \in \Delta, \Delta'.\; \overline{S} \subseteq P(pn) \qquad \forall S_i \in \overline{S}.\; \forall U_j \in \overline{U}.\; \neg(S_i <: U_j)}$$

$$\Gamma; \Delta \vdash \mathsf{spore}\; \{\; \overline{y : S = s}\; ; \overline{U}; \Delta'; (x : T_1) \Rightarrow t_2\; \} :$$
$$T_1 \Rightarrow T_2\; \{\; \mathsf{type}\; \mathcal{C} = \overline{S}\; ;\; \mathsf{type}\; \mathcal{E} = \overline{U}\; ;\; \Delta, \Delta'\; \}$$

T-ECOMP

$$\Gamma; \Delta \vdash t_1 : T_1 \Rightarrow T_2\; \{\; \mathsf{type}\; \mathcal{C} = \overline{S}\; ;\; \mathsf{type}\; \mathcal{E} = \overline{U}\; ;\; \Delta_1\; \}$$
$$\Gamma; \Delta \vdash t_2 : U_1 \Rightarrow T_1\; \{\; \mathsf{type}\; \mathcal{C} = \overline{R}\; ;\; \mathsf{type}\; \mathcal{E} = \overline{U'}\; ;\; \Delta_2\; \}$$
$$\frac{\Delta' = \{pn \in \Delta_1 \cup \Delta_2 \mid \overline{S} \subseteq P(pn) \wedge \overline{R} \subseteq P(pn)\} \qquad \overline{V} = (\overline{U} \setminus \overline{R}) \cup (\overline{U'} \setminus \overline{S})}{\Gamma; \Delta \vdash t_1\; \mathsf{compose}\; t_2 : U_1 \Rightarrow T_2\; \{\; \mathsf{type}\; \mathcal{C} = \overline{S}, \overline{R}\; ;\; \mathsf{type}\; \mathcal{E} = \overline{V}\; ;\; \Delta'\; \}}$$

Fig. 13. Typing extensions

Rule TECOMP computes a new set of excluded types $\overline{V}$ based on both the excluded types and the captured types of t_1 and t_2. Given that it is possible that one of the spores captures a type that is excluded in the other spore, the type of the result spore excludes only those types that are guaranteed not be captured.

4 Implementation

We have implemented spores as a macro library for Scala 2.10 and 2.11. Macros are an experimental feature introduced in Scala 2.10 that enable "macro defs," methods that take expression trees as arguments and that return an expression tree that is inlined at each invocation site. Macros are expanded during type checking in a way which enables macros to synthesize their result type specialized for each expansion site.

The implementation for Scala 2.10 requires in addition a compiler plug-in that provides a backport of the support for Java 8 SAM types ("functional interfaces") of Scala 2.11. SAM type support extends type inference for user-defined subclasses of Scala's standard function types which enables infering the types of spore parameters.

An expression spore { val y: S = s; (x: T) => /* body */ } invokes the spore macro which is passed the block { val y... } as an expression tree. A spore without type constraints simply checks that within the body of the spore's closure, only the parameter x as well as the variables in the spore header are accessed according to the spore type-checking rules. The expression tree returned by the macro creates an instance of a *refinement type* of the abstract Spore class that implements its apply method (inherited from the corresponding standard Scala function trait) by applying the spore's closure. The Captured type member (see Section 2.2) is defined by the generated refinement type to be a tuple type with the types of all captured variables. If there are no type constraints the Excluded type member is defined to be No[Nothing].

Type constraints are implemented as follows. First, invoking the generic without macro passing a type argument T, say, augments the generated Spore refinement type by effectivly adding the clause with No[T] to the definition of its Excluded type member. Second, the existence of additional bounds on the captured types is detected by attempting to infer an implicit value of type Property[_]. If such an implicit value can be inferred, a sequence of types specifying type bounds is obtained as follows. The type of the implicit

Program	LOC	#closures	#converted	LOC changed	#captured vars	
funsets	99	8	8	7	9	} MOOC
forcomp	201	6	4	4	0	
mandelbrot	325	1	1	9	6	} Parallel Collections
barneshut	722	7	7	8	1	
spark pagerank	64	5	5	8	0	} Spark
spark kmeans	92	5	4	9	2	
Total	1503	32	29	45	18	

Fig. 14. Evaluating the practicality of using spores in place of normal closures

value is matched against the pattern Property[t1] with ... with Property[tn]. For each type ti an implicit member of the following shape is added to the Spore type refinement:

```
implicit val evi: ti[Captured] = implicitly[ti[Captured]]
```

The implicit conversion (Section 2.3) from standard Scala functions to spores is implemented as a macro whose expansion fails if the argument function is not a literal, since in this case it is impossible for the macro to check the spore shape/capturing constraints.

5   Evaluation

In this section we evaluate the practicality and the benefits of using spores as an alternative to normal closures in Scala. The evaluation has two parts. In the first part we measure the impact of introducing spores in existing programs. In the second part we evaluate the utility and the syntactic overhead of spores in a large code base of applications based on the Apache Spark framework for big data analytics.

5.1   Using Spores Instead of Closures

In this section we measure the number of changes required to convert existing programs that crucially rely on closures to use spores. We analyze a number of real Scala programs, taken from three categories:

1. General, closure-heavy code, taken from the exercises of the popular MOOC on Functional Programming Principles in Scala; the goal of analyzing this code is to get an approximation of the worst-case effort required when consistently using spores instead of closures, in a mostly-functional code base.
2. Parallel applications based on Scala's parallel collections. These examples evaluate the practicality of using spores in a parallel code base to increase its robustness.
3. Distributed applications based on the Apache Spark cluster computing framework. In this case, we evaluate the practicality of using spores in Spark applications to make sure closures are guaranteed to be serializable.

Methodology. For each program, we obtained (a) the number of closures in the program that are candidates for conversion, (b) the number of closures that could be converted to spores, (c) the changed/added number of LOC, and (d) the number of captured variables. It is important to note that during the conversion it was not possible to rely on an implicit conversion of functions to spores, since the expected types of all library methods that were invoked by the evaluated applications remained normal function types. Thus, the reported numbers are worse than they would be for APIs using spores.

Project	average LOC per closure	average # of captured vars	% closures that don't capture
sameeragarwal/blinkdb ★268 ♟33 LOC 22,022	1.39	1	93.5%
freeman-lab/thunder ★89 ♟2 LOC 2,813	1.03	1.30	23.3%
bigdatagenomics/adam ★86 ♟16 LOC 19,055	1.90	1.44	80.2%
ooyala/spark-jobserver ★79 ♟6 LOC 5,578	1.60	1	80.0%
Sotera/correlation-approximation ★12 ♟2 LOC 775	4.55	1.25	63.6%
aecc/stream-tree-learning ★1 ♟2 LOC 1,199	5.73	2	54.5%
lagerspetz/TimeSeriesSpark ★5 ♟1 LOC 14,882	2.85	1.77	75.0%
Total LOC 66,324	2.25	1.39	67.2%

Fig. 15. Evaluating the impact and overhead of spores on real distributed applications. Each project listed is an active and noteworthy open-source project hosted on GitHub that is based on Apache Spark. ★ represents the number of "stars" (or interest) a repository has on GitHub, and ♟ represents the number of contributors to the project.

Results. The results are shown in Figure 14. Out of 32 closures 29 could be converted to spores with little effort. One closure failed to infer its parameter type when expressed as a spore. Two other closures could not be converted due to implementation restrictions of our prototype. On average, per converted closure 1.4 LOC had to be changed. This number is dominated by two factors: the inability to use the implicit conversion from functions to spores, and one particularly complex closure in "mandelbrot" that required changing 9 LOC. In our programs, the number of captured variables is on average 0.56. These results suggest that programs using closures in non-trivial ways can typically be converted to using spores with little effort, even if the used APIs do not use spore types.

5.2 Spores and Apache Spark

To evaluate both benefit and overhead of using spores in larger, distributed applications, we studied the codebases of 7 noteworthy open-source applications using Apache Spark.

Methodology. We evaluated the applications along two dimensions. In the first dimension we were interested how widespread patterns are that spores could statically enforce. In the context of open-source applications built on top of the Spark framework, we counted the number of closures passed to the higher-order map method of the RDD type (Spark's distributed collection abstraction); all of these closures must be serializable to avoid runtime exceptions. (The RDD type has several more higher-order functions that require serializable closures such as flatMap; map is the most commonly used higher-order function, though, and is thus representative of the use of closures in Spark.) In the second dimension, we analyzed the percentage of spores that could be converted automatically to spores assuming the Spark API would use spore types instead of regular function types, thus not incurring any syntactic overhead. In cases where automatic conversion would be impossible, we analyzed the average number of captured variables, indicating the syntactic overhead of using explicit spores.

Results. Figure 15 summarizes our results. Of all closures passed to RDD's map method, about 67.2% do not capture any variable; these closures could be automatically converted to spores using the implicit macro of Section 2.3. The remaining 32.8% of closures that do capture variables, capture on average 1.39 variables. This indicates that unchecked patterns for serializable closures are widespread in real applications, and that benefiting from static guarantees provided by spores would require only little syntactic overhead.

5.3 Spores and Akka

We have also verified that excluding specific types from closures is important.

The Akka event-driven middleware provides an actor abstraction for concurrency. When using futures together with actors, it is common to provide the result of a future-based computation to the sender of a message sent to an actor.

However, naive implementations of patterns such as this can problematic. To access the sender of a message, Akka's Actor trait provides a method sender that returns a reference to the actor that is the sender of the message currently being processed. There is a potential for a data race where the actor starts processing a message from a different actor than the original sender, but a concurrent future-based computation invokes the sender method (on this), thus obtaining a reference to the wrong actor.

Given the importance of combining actors and futures, Akka provides a library method pipeTo to enable programming patterns using futures that avoid capturing variables of type Actor in closures. However, the correct use of pipeTo is unchecked. Spores provide a new statically-checked approach to address this problem by demanding closures passed to future constructors to be spores with the constraint that type Actor is excluded.

Methodology. To find out how often spores with type constraints could turn an unchecked pattern into a statically-checked guarantee, we analyzed 7 open-source projects using Akka (GitHub projects with 23 stars on average; more than 100 commits; 2.7 contributors on average). For each project we searched for occurrences of "pipeTo" directly following closures passed to future constructors.

Results. The 7 projects contain 19 occurrences of the presented unchecked pattern to avoid capturing Actor instances within closures used concurrently. Spores with a constraint to exclude Actor statically enforce the safety of all those closures.

6   Case Study

Frameworks like MapReduce [4] and Apache Spark [31] are designed for processing large datasets in a cluster, using well-known map/reduce computation patterns.

In Spark, these patterns are expressed using higher-order functions, like map, applied to the "resilient distributed dataset" (RDD) abstraction. However, to avoid unexpected runtime exceptions due to unserializable closures when passing closures to RDDs, programmers must adopt conventions that are subtle and unchecked by the Scala compiler.

The following typical pattern was extracted from a code base used in production:

```
1  class GenericOp(sc: SparkContext, mapping: Map[String, String]) {
2    private var cachedSessions: spark.RDD[Session] = ...
3
```

```
4    def doOp(keyList: List[...], ...): Result = {
5      val localMapping = mapping
6
7      val mapFun: Session => (List[String], GenericOpAggregator) = { s =>
8        (keyList, new GenericOpAggregator(s, localMapping))
9      }
10
11     val reduceFun: (GenericOpAggregator, GenericOpAggregator) =>
12       GenericOpAggregator = { (a, b) => a.merge(b) }
13
14     cachedSessions.map(mapFun).reduceByKey(reduceFun).collectAsMap
15   }
16 }
```

The doOp method performs operations on the RDD cachedSessions. GenericOp has a parameter of type SparkContext, the main entry point for functionality provided by Spark, and a parameter of type Map[String, String]. The main computation is a chain of invocations of map, reduceByKey, and collectAsMap. To ensure that the argument closures of map and reduceByKey are serializable, the code follows two conventions: first, instead of defining mapFun and reduceFun as methods, they are defined using lambdas stored in local variables. Second, instead of using the mapping parameter directly, it is first copied into a local variable localMapping. The reason for the first convention is that in Scala converting a method to a function implicitly captures a reference to the enclosing object. However, GenericOp is not serializable, since it refers to a SparkContext. The reason for the second convention is that using mapping directly would result in mapFun capturing this.

Applying Spores. The above conventions can be enforced by the compiler, avoiding unexpected runtime exceptions, by turning mapFun and reduceFun into spores:

```
1  val mapFun: Spore[Session, (List[String], GenericOpAggregator)] =
2    spore { val localMapping = mapping
3      (s: Session) => (keyList, new GenericOpAggregator(s, localMapping)) }
4  val reduceFun: Spore[(GenericOpAggregator, GenericOpAggregator),
5                       GenericOpAggregator] =
6    spore { (a, b) => a.merge(b) }
```

The spore shape enforces the use of localMapping (moved into mapFun). Furthermore, there is no more possibility of accidentally capturing a reference to the enclosing object.

7   Other Related Work

Parallel closures [14] are a variation of closures that make data in the environment available using read-only references using a type system for reference immutability. This enables parallel execution without the possibility of data races. Spores are not limited to immutable environments, and do not require a type system extension. River Trail [8] provides a concurrency model for JavaScript, similar to parallel closures; however, capturing variables in closures is currently not supported.

ML5 [22] provides mobile closures verified not to use resources not present on machines where they are applied. This property is enforced transitively (for all values reachable from captured values), which is stronger than what plain spores provide. However, type constraints allow spores to require properties not limited to mobility. Transitive properties are supported either using type constraints based on type classes which enforce a transitive property or by integrating with type systems that enforce transitive properties. Unlike ML5, spores do not require a type system extension.

A well-known type-based representation of closures uses existential types where the existentially quantified variable represents the closure's environment, enabling type-preserving compilation of functional languages [21]. A spore type may have an abstract Captured type, effectively encoding an existantial quantification; however, captured types are typically concrete, and the spore type system supports constraints on them.

HdpH [11] generalizes Cloud Haskell's closures in several aspects: first, closures can be transformed without eliminating them. Second, unnecessary serialization is avoided, e.g., when applying a closure immediately after creation. Otherwise, the discussion of Cloud Haskell in Section 1.1 also applies to HdpH. Delimited continuations [27] represent a way to serialize behavior in Scala, but don't resolve any of the problems of normal Scala closures when it comes to accidental capture, as spores do.

Termite Scheme [6] is a Scheme dialect for distributed programming where closures and continuations are always serializable; references to non-serializable objects (like open files) are automatically wrapped in processes that are serialized as their process ID. In contrast, with spores there is no such automatic wrapping. Unlike closures in Termite Scheme, spores are statically-typed, supporting type-based constraints. Serializable closures in a dynamically-typed setting are also the basis for [28]. Python's standard serialization module, pickle, does not support serializing closures. Dill [15] extends Python's pickle module, adding support for functions and closures, but without constraints.

8   Conclusion

We've presented a type-based foundation for closures, called spores, designed to avoid various hazards that arise particularly in concurrent or distributed settings. We have presented a flexible type system for spores which enables composability of differently-constrained spores as well as custom user-defined type constraints. We formalize and present a full soundness proof, as well as an implementation of our approach in Scala.

A key takeaway of our approach is that including type information of captured variables in the type of the spore enables a number of previously impossible opportunities, including but not limited to controlled capture in concurrent, distributed, and other arbitrary scenarios where closures must be controlled.

Finally, we demonstrate the practicality of our approach through an empirical study, and show that converting non-trivial programs to use spores requires relatively little effort.

Acknowledgements. We would like to thank the anonymous ECOOP 2014 referees for their thorough reviews and helpful suggestions which greatly improved the quality of the paper. Heather Miller was supported by a US National Science Foundation Graduate Research Fellowship.

References

1. Budimlić, Z., Burke, M., Cavé, V., Knobe, K., Lowney, G., Newton, R., Palsberg, J., Peixotto, D., Sarkar, V., Schlimbach, F.: et al. Concurrent collections. Scientific Programming 18(3) (2010)
2. Chakravarty, M.M.T., Leshchinskiy, R., Peyton Jones, S., Keller, G., Marlow, S.: Data Parallel Haskell: A status report. In: Proc. DAMP Workshop, pp. 10–18. ACM (2007)
3. Collins, A., Grewe, D., Grover, V., Lee, S., Susnea, A.: NOVA: A functional language for data parallelism. Technical Report NVR-2013-002, NVIDIA Corporation (July 2013)

4. Dean, J., Ghemawat, S.: Mapreduce: Simplified data processing on large clusters. Commun. ACM 51(1), 107–113 (2008)
5. Epstein, J., Black, A.P., Peyton-Jones, S.: Towards Haskell in the cloud. In: Proc. Haskell Symposium, pp. 118–129. ACM (2011)
6. Germain, G.: Concurrency oriented programming in Termite Scheme. In: Erlang Workshop, p. 20. ACM (2006)
7. Goetz, B.: JSR 335: Lambda expressions for the Java programming language (2013), https://jcp.org/en/jsr/detail?id=335
8. Herhut, S., Hudson, R.L., Shpeisman, T., Sreeram, J.: River trail: a path to parallelism in JavaScript. In: OOPSLA, pp. 729–744 (2013)
9. International Standard ISO/IEC 14882:2011. Programming Languages – C++. International Organization for Standards (2011)
10. Lewis, J.R., Launchbury, J., Meijer, E., Shields, M.: Implicit parameters: Dynamic scoping with static types. In: POPL, pp. 108–118 (2000)
11. Maier, P., Trinder, P.: Implementing a high-level distributed-memory parallel Haskell in Haskell. In: Gill, A., Hage, J. (eds.) IFL 2011. LNCS, vol. 7257, pp. 35–50. Springer, Heidelberg (2012)
12. Marlow, S., Newton, R., Peyton Jones, S.: A monad for deterministic parallelism. In: Proc. Haskell Symposium, pp. 71–82. ACM (2011)
13. Matsakis, N.: Fn types in Rust, take 3 (2013), http://smallcultfollowing.com/babysteps/blog/2013/10/10/fn-types-in-rust
14. Matsakis, N.D.: Parallel closures: a new twist on an old idea. In: HotPar. USENIX (2012)
15. McKerns, M.M., Strand, L., Sullivan, T., Fang, A., Aivazis, M.A.: Building a framework for predictive science. In: Proc. of the 10th Python in Science Conf. (2011)
16. Meijer, E.: Confessions of a used programming language salesman. In: OOPSLA (2007)
17. Meyerovich, L.A., Rabkin, A.S.: Empirical analysis of programming language adoption. In: OOPSLA (2013)
18. Miller, H., Haller, P.: Spores, formally. Technical Report EPFL-REPORT-191240, Department of Computer Science, EPFL, Lausanne, Switzerland (December 2013)
19. Miller, H., Haller, P., Burmako, E., Odersky, M.: Instant pickles: Generating object-oriented pickler combinators for fast and extensible serialization. In: OOPSLA, pp. 183–202 (2013)
20. Miller, H., Haller, P., Rytz, L., Odersky, M.: Functional programming for all! Scaling a MOOC for students and professionals alike. In: ICSE, pp. 265–263 (2014)
21. Morrisett, J.G., Walker, D., Crary, K., Glew, N.: From system F to typed assembly language. ACM Trans. Program. Lang. Syst 21(3), 527–568 (1999)
22. Murphy VII, T., Crary, K., Harper, R.: Type-safe distributed programming with ML5. In: Barthe, G., Fournet, C. (eds.) TGC 2007. LNCS, vol. 4912, pp. 108–123. Springer, Heidelberg (2008)
23. Odersky, M.: The Scala language specification (2013)
24. Pierce, B.C.: Types and programming languages. MIT Press (2002)
25. Prokopec, A., Bagwell, P., Rompf, T., Odersky, M.: A generic parallel collection framework. In: Jeannot, E., Namyst, R., Roman, J. (eds.) Euro-Par 2011, Part II. LNCS, vol. 6853, pp. 136–147. Springer, Heidelberg (2011)
26. Prokopec, A., Miller, H., Schlatter, T., Haller, P., Odersky, M.: FlowPools: A lock-free deterministic concurrent dataflow abstraction. In: Kasahara, H., Kimura, K. (eds.) LCPC 2012. LNCS, vol. 7760, pp. 158–173. Springer, Heidelberg (2013)
27. Rompf, T., Maier, I., Odersky, M.: Implementing first-class polymorphic delimited continuations by a type-directed selective CPS-transform. In: ICFP, pp. 317–328. ACM (2009)

28. Schwendner, A.: Distributed functional programming in Scheme. Master's thesis, Massachusetts Institute of Technology (2009)
29. Typesafe. Akka (2009), http://akka.io/
30. Wright, A.K., Felleisen, M.: A syntactic approach to type soundness. Inf. Comput. 115(1), 38–94 (1994)
31. Zaharia, M., Chowdhury, M., Das, T., Dave, A., McCauley, M., Franklin, M., Shenker, S., Stoica, I.: Resilient distributed datasets: A fault-tolerant abstraction for in-memory cluster computing. In: NSDI. USENIX (2012)
32. Zibin, Y., Potanin, A., Li, P., Ali, M., Ernst, M.D.: Ownership and immutability in generic java. In: OOPSLA, pp. 598–617. ACM (2010)

Rely-Guarantee Protocols

Filipe Militão[1,2], Jonathan Aldrich[1], and Luís Caires[2]

[1] Carnegie Mellon University, Pittsburgh, USA
[2] Universidade Nova de Lisboa, Lisboa, Portugal
{filipe.militao,jonathan.aldrich}@cs.cmu.edu, lcaires@fct.unl.pt

Abstract. The use of shared mutable state, commonly seen in object-oriented systems, is often problematic due to the potential conflicting interactions between aliases to the same state. We present a substructural type system outfitted with a novel lightweight interference control mechanism, *rely-guarantee protocols*, that enables controlled aliasing of shared resources. By assigning each alias separate roles, encoded in a novel protocol abstraction in the spirit of rely-guarantee reasoning, our type system ensures that challenging uses of shared state will never interfere in an unsafe fashion. In particular, rely-guarantee protocols ensure that each alias will never observe an unexpected value, or type, when inspecting shared memory regardless of how the changes to that shared state (originating from potentially unknown program contexts) are interleaved at run-time.

1 Introduction

Shared, mutable state can be useful in certain algorithms, in modeling stateful systems, and in structuring programs. However, it can also make reasoning about a program more difficult, potentially resulting in run-time errors. If two pieces of code have references to the same location in memory, and one of them updates the contents of that cell, the update may *destructively interfere* by breaking the other piece of code's assumptions about the properties of the value contained in that cell—which may cause the program to compute the wrong result, or even to abruptly terminate. In order to mitigate this problem, static type systems conservatively associate an invariant type with each location, and ensure that every store to the location preserves this type. While this approach can ensure basic memory safety, it cannot check higher-level *protocol* properties [1, 4, 5, 13, 20] that are vital to the correctness of many programs [3].

For example, consider a `Pipe` abstraction that is used to communicate between two parts of the program. A pipe is *open* while the communication is ongoing, but when the pipe is no longer needed it is *closed*. Pipes include shared, mutable state in the form of an internal buffer, and abstractions such as Java's `PipedInputStream` also dynamically track whether they are in the open or closed state. The state of the pipe determines what operations may be performed, and invoking an inappropriate operation is an error: for example, writing to a closed pipe in Java results in a run-time exception.

Static approaches to reason about such state protocols (of which we follow the *typestate* [7, 22, 28, 29] approach) have two advantages: errors such as writing to a closed pipe can be avoided on the one hand, and defensive run-time tests of the state of an object can become superfluous on the other hand. In typestate systems, abstractions expose a more refined type that models a set of abstract states representing the internal,

R. Jones (Ed.): ECOOP 2014, LNCS 8586, pp. 334–359, 2014.

changing, type of the state (such as the two states above, *open* and *closed*) enabling the static modular manipulation of stateful objects. However, sharing (such as by aliasing) these resources must be carefully controlled to avoid potentially destructive interference that may result from mixing incompatible changes to apparently unrelated objects that, in reality, are connected to the same underlying run-time object. This work aims to provide an intuitive and general-purpose extension to the typestate model by exploiting (coordination) protocols at the shared state level to allow fine-grained and flexible uses of aliased state. Therefore, by modeling the *interactions* of aliases of some shared state in a protocol abstraction, we enable complex uses of sharing to safely occur through *benign interference*, interference that the other aliases expect and/or require to occur.

Consider once more the pipe example. The next two code blocks implement simplified versions of the pipe's put and tryTake functions. Although each function operates independently of the other, internally they share nodes of the same underlying buffer:

```
// protocol: Empty ⇒ Filled; none
put = fun( v : Value ).
    // Empty shared node, oldlast, to be filled with node
    // containing tagged (#) empty record, {}, as 'Empty'
    let last = new Empty#{} in
    let oldlast = !buffer.tail in // is Empty
        // tags pair of 'v' and 'last' as 'Filled'
        oldlast := Filled#{ v , last };
        buffer.tail := last
    end // last cell is now reachable from head&tail
end // oldlast cell unreachable from tail
```

```
// rec X.( Empty ⇒ Empty; X ⊕ Filled ⇒ none )
tryTake = fun().
    let first = !buffer.head in
    case !first of
        Empty#_ → NoResult#{}
      | Filled#[ v , next ] → // does not return
            delete first; // ownership to the protocol
            buffer.head := next;
            Result#v
    end
end
```

By distributing these functions between two aliases, we are able to create independent *producer* and *consumer* components of the pipe that share a common buffer (modeled as a singly-linked list). Observe how the interaction, that occurs through aliases of the buffer's nodes, obeys a well-defined protocol: the *producer* alias (through the put function) inserts an element into the last (empty) node of the buffer and then immediately forfeits that cell (i.e. it is no longer used by that alias); while the *consumer* alias (using tryTake) proceeds by testing the first node and, when it detects it has been Filled (thus, when the other alias is sure to no longer use it), recovers ownership of that node, which enables the alias to safely delete that cell (first) since it is no longer shared.

1.1   Approach in a Nutshell

Interference due to aliasing is analogous to the interference caused by thread interleaving [15,33]. This occurs because mutable state may be shared by aliases in unknown or non-local program contexts. Such boundary effectively negates the use of static mechanisms to track exactly which other variables alias some state. Therefore, we are unable to know precisely if the shared state aliased by a local variable will be used when the execution jumps off (e.g. through a function call) to non-local program contexts. However, if that state is used, then the aliases may change the state in ways that invalidate the local alias' assumptions on the current contents of the shared state. This interference caused by "alias interleaving" occurs even without concurrency, but is analogous to how thread interleaving may affect shared state. Consequently, techniques to reason about thread interference (such as *rely-guarantee reasoning* [17]) can be useful to reason about aliasing even in our sequential setting. The core principle of rely-guarantee reasoning that we adapt is its mechanism to make strong local assumptions in the face of interference. To handle such interference, each alias has its actions constrained to fit within a *guarantee* type and at the same time is free to assume that the changes done by other aliases of that state must fit within a *rely* type. The duality between what aliases can rely on and must guarantee among themselves yields significant flexibility in the use of shared state, when compared for instance to invariant-based sharing.

We employ rely-guarantee in a novel protocol abstraction that captures a partial view of the use of the shared state, as seen from the perspective of an alias. Therefore, each protocol models the constraints on the actions of that alias and is only aware of the resulting effects ("interference") that may appear in the shared state due to the interleaved uses of that shared state as done by other aliases. A rely-guarantee protocol is formed by a sequence of rely-guarantee steps. Each step contains a rely type, stating what an alias currently assumes the shared state contains; and a guarantee type, a promise that the changes done by that alias will fit within this type. Using these small building blocks, our technique allows strong local assumption on how the shared state may change, while not knowing when or if other aliases to that shared state will be used—only how they will interact with the shared state, if used. Since each step in a protocol can have distinct rely and guarantee types, a protocol is not frozen in time and can model different "temporal" uses of the shared state directly. A protocol is, therefore, an abstracted perspective on the actions done by each individual alias to the shared state, and that is only aware of the potential resulting effects of all the other aliases of that shared state. A *protocol conformance* mechanism ensures the sound composition of all protocols to the same shared state, at the moment of their creation. From there on, each protocol is *stable* (i.e. immune to unexpected/destructive interference) since conformance attested that each protocol, in isolation, is aware of all observable effects that may occur from all possible "alias interleaving" originated from the remaining aliases.

Our main contribution is a novel type-based protocol abstraction to reason about shared mutable state, *rely-guarantee protocols*, that captures the following features:

1. Each protocol provides a *local* type so that an alias need not know the actions that other aliases are doing, only their resulting (observable) effect on the shared state;
2. Sharing can be done *asymmetrically* so that the role of each alias in the interaction with the shared state may be distinct from the rest;
3. Our protocol paradigm is able to *scale* by modeling sharing interactions both at the reference level and also at the abstract state level. Therefore, sharing does not need to be embedded in an ADT [18], but can also work at the ADT level without requiring a wrapper reference [15];
4. State can be shared individually or simultaneously in groups of state. By enabling sharing to occur underneath a layer of apparently disjoint state, we naturally support the notion of *fictional disjointness* [9, 16, 18];
5. Our protocol abstraction is able to model complex interactions that occur through the shared state. These include invariant, monotonic and other coordinated uses. Moreover, they enable both *ownership transfer* of state between non-local program contexts and *ownership recovery*. Therefore, shared state can return to be non-shared, even allowing it to be later shared again and in such a way that is completely unrelated to its previous sharing phases;
6. Although protocol conformance is checked in pairs, *arbitrary aliasing* is possible (if safe) by further sharing a protocol in ways that do not conflict with the initial

sharing. Therefore, global conformance in the use of the shared state by multiple aliases is assured by the combination of individual binary protocol splits, with each split sharing the state without breaking what was previously assumed on that state;

7. We allow *temporary inconsistencies*, so that the shared state may undergo intermediate (private) states that cannot be seen by other aliases. Using an idea similar to (static) mutual exclusion, we ensure that the same shared state cannot be inspected while it is inconsistent. Such kind of critical section (that does not incur in any run-time overhead) is sufficiently flexible to support multiple simultaneously inconsistent states, when they are sure to not be aliasing the same shared state.

With this technique we are able to model challenging uses of aliasing in a lightweight substructural type system, where all sharing is centered on a simple and intuitive protocol abstraction. We believe that by specializing our system to typestate and aliasing [1, 27] properties we can offer a useful intermediate point that is simpler than the full functional verification embodied in separation logic [6,25] yet more expressive than conventional type systems. Our proofs of soundness use standard progress and preservation theorems. We show that all allowed interference is benign (i.e. that all changes to the shared state are expected by each alias) by ensuring that a program cannot get stuck, while still allowing the shared state to be legally used in complex ways. Besides expressing the programmer's intent in the types, our technique also enables a program to be free of errors related to destructive interference. For instance, the programmer will not be able to wrongly attempt to use a shared cell as if it were no longer shared, or leave values in that shared cell that are not expected by the other aliases of that cell.

Section 2 introduces the language but leaves its sharing mechanisms to Section 4, after an overview of the type system. Section 5 discusses technical results, and Section 6 additional examples. The paper ends with Sections for related work and conclusions.

2 Pipe Example

Our language is based on the polymorphic λ-calculus with mutable references, immutable records, tagged sums and recursive types. Technically, we build on [22] (a variant of $\mathbf{L}^3$ [1] adapted for usability) by supporting sharing of mutable state through rely-guarantee protocols. As in $\mathbf{L}^3$, a cell is decomposed in two components: a pure *reference* (that can be freely copied), and a linear [14] *capability* used to track the contents of that cell. Unlike $\mathbf{L}^3$, by extending [22] our language implicitly threads capabilities through the code, reducing syntactic overhead. To support this separation of references and capabilities, our language uses location-dependent types to relate a reference to its respective capability. Therefore, a reference has a type "**ref** t" to mean a **ref**erence to a location t, where the information about the contents of that location is stored in the capability for t. Our capabilities follow the format "**rw** t A" meaning a read-write capability to location t which, currently, has contents of type A stored in it. The permission to access, such as by dereference, the contents of a cell requires both the reference and the capability to be available. Capabilities are typing artifacts that do not exist at run-time and are moved implicitly through the code. Locations (such as t) must be managed explicitly, leading to constructs dedicated to abstracting and opening locations.

Pipes are used to support a *consumer-producer* style of interaction (using a shared internal buffer as mediator), often used in a concurrent program but here used in a single-threaded environment. The shared internal buffer is implemented as a shared singly-linked list where the consumer keeps a pointer to the *head* of the list and the producer to its *tail*. By partitioning the pipe's functions (where the consumer alias uses `tryTake`, and the producer both `put` and `close`), clients of the pipe can work independently of one another, provided that the functions' implementation is aware of the potential interference caused by the actions of the other alias. It is on specifying and verifying this interference that our rely-guarantee protocols will be used.

```
1   let newPipe = fun( _ : [] ).                                    Γ = _ : [] | Δ = ·
2       open <n,node> = new Empty#{} in         Γ = _ : [],node : ref n, n : loc | Δ = rw n Empty#[]
3       share (rw n Empty#[]) as H[n] || T[n];                Γ = ... | Δ = T[n], H[n]
4       open <h,head> = new <n, node::H[n]> in
                  Γ = ...,head : ref h, h : loc | Δ = T[n], rw h ∃p.(ref p :: H[p])
5       open <t,tail> = new <n, node::T[n]> in
                  Γ = ...,tail : ref t, t : loc | Δ = rw t ∃p.(ref p :: T[p]), ...
6         < rw h exists p.(ref p :: H[p]),  // packs a type, the capability to location 'h'
7         < rw t exists p.(ref p :: T[p]),  // packs a type, the capability to location 't'
8         { // creates labeled record with 'put', 'close' and 'tryTake' as members
9           put = fun( e : int :: rw t exists p.(ref p :: T[p]) )./*...shown in Section 4...*/,
19          close = fun( _ : [] :: rw t exists p.(ref p :: T[p]) )./*...*/,
26          tryTake = fun( _ : [] :: rw h exists p.(ref p :: H[p]) )./*...*/
47        } :: ( rw h exists p.(ref p :: H[p]) * rw t exists p.(ref p :: T[p]) ) > >
48      end
49    end
50  end
```

The function creates a pipe by allocating an initial **node** for the internal buffer, a cell to be shared by the **head** and **tail** pointers. The newly allocated cell (line 2) contains a tagged (as `Empty`) empty record ({}). In our language, aliasing information is correlated through static names, *locations*, such that multiple references to the same location must imply that these references are aliases of the same cell. Consequently, the **new** construct (line 2) must be assigned a type that abstracts the concrete location that was created, $\exists t.($ **ref** t :: **rw** t Empty#[]), which means that there exists some fresh location t, and the new expression evaluates to a reference to t ("**ref** t"). We associate this reference with a capability to access it, using a *stacking* operator ::. In this case the capability is **rw** t Empty#[], representing a read and write capability to the location t, which currently contains a value of type Empty#[] as initially mentioned. On the same line, we then **open** the existential by giving it a location variable n and a regular variable **node** to refer that reference. From there on, the capability (a typing artifact which has no actual value) is automatically *unstacked* and moved implicitly as needed through the program. For clarity, we will manually stack capabilities (such as on line 4, using the construct e :: A where A is the stacked capability), although the type system does not require it. On line 3, the type system initially carries the following assumptions:

$$\Gamma = \_ : [], \text{node} : \textbf{ref} \, n, \, n : \textbf{loc} \quad | \quad \Delta = \textbf{rw} \, n \, \text{Empty#[]}$$

where Γ is the lexical environment (of persistent/pure resources), and Δ is a linear typing environment that contains all linear resources (such as capabilities). Each linear capability must either be used up or passed on through the program (e.g. by returning it from a function). The contents of the reference **node** are known statically by looking up the capability for the **loc**ation n to which **node** refers (i.e. "**rw** n Empty#[]").

Capabilities are linear (cannot be duplicated), but aliasing in local contexts is still possible by copying references. All copies link back to the same capability using the location contained in the reference. However, when aliases operate in non-local contexts, this location-based link is lost. Thus, if we were to pack node's capability before sharing it, it would become unavailable to other aliases of that location. For instance, by writing $\langle n, \text{node} :: \textbf{rw } n \text{ Empty}\#[]\rangle$ we pack the location n by abstracting it in an existential type for that location. The packed type now refers a fresh location, unrelated to its old version. Instead, we share that capability (line 3) by splitting it in two rely-guarantee protocols, H and T^1. Each protocol is then assigned to the head and tail pointers (lines 4 and 5, respectively), since they encode the specific uses of each of those aliases. The protocols and sharing mechanisms will be introduced in Section 4.

The type of newPipe is a linear function ($\multimap$) that, since it does not capture any enclosing linear resource, can be marked as pure (!) so that the type can be used without the linear restriction. On line 6 we pack the inner state of the pipe (so as to abstract the capability for t as P, and the one for h as C), resulting in newPipe having the type:

$$\text{newPipe} : !([] \multimap \exists C.\exists P.(![...] :: C * P))$$

where the *separate* capabilities for the Consumer and Producer are stacked together in a commutative group ($*$). In this type, C abstracts the capability $\textbf{rw } h \; \exists p.(\textbf{ref } p :: \text{H}[p])$, and P abstracts $\textbf{rw } t \; \exists p.(\textbf{ref } p :: \text{T}[p])$. Finally, although we have not yet shown the implementation, the type of the elided record ([...]) contains function types that should be unsurprising noting that each argument and return type has the respective capabilities for the head/tail cells stacked on top (similarly to pre/post conditions, but directly expressed in the types). Therefore, those functions are closures that use the knowledge about the reference to the head/tail pointers from the surrounding context, but do not capture the capability to those cells and instead require them to be supplied as argument.

```
[ put      :  !( int :: P ⊸ [] :: P ),
  close    :  !( [] :: P ⊸ [] ),
  tryTake  :  !( [] :: C ⊸ NoResult#([] :: C) + Result#(int :: C) + Depleted#[] ) ]
```

Therefore, put preserves the producer's capability, but close destroys it; while the result of tryTake is a sum type of either Result or NoResult depending on whether the still open pipe has or not contents available, or Depleted to signal that the pipe was closed (and therefore that the capability to C vanished). Observe that the state that the functions depend on is, apparently, disjoint although underneath this layer the state is actually shared (but coordinated through a protocol) so that (benign) interference must occur for the pipe to work properly—i.e. it is *fictionally disjoint* [9, 16, 18].

3   Type System Overview

We now present the type system. Non-essential details are relegated to [21, 22]. For consistency, we include all sharing mechanisms but leave their discussion to Section 4.

---

[1] As a brief glimpse, T is "$\textbf{rw } n$ Empty#[] $\Rightarrow$ ($\textbf{rw } n$ Node#R $\oplus$ $\textbf{rw } n$ Closed#[]); **none**" which relies on n containing Empty#[], ensures n then contains either Node#R or Closed#[], and then loses access to n. Both "$\Rightarrow$" and ";" (and R) will be discussed in detail in Section 4.

$\rho \in$ LOCATION CONSTANTS (ADDRESSES) $t \in$ LOCATION VARIABLES $p ::= \rho \mid t$

$1 \in$ LABELS (TAGS) $f \in$ FIELDS $x \in$ VARIABLES $X \in$ TYPE VARIABLES

$v ::= \rho$	(address)		$v.f$	(field)
$\mid x$	(variable)		$\mid v\ v$	(application)
$\mid$ fun$(x : A).e$	(function)		$\mid$ let $x = e$ in e end	(let)
$\mid \langle t \rangle e$	(universal location)		$\mid$ open $\langle t, x \rangle = v$ in e end	(open location)
$\mid \langle X \rangle e$	(universal type)		$\mid$ open $\langle X, x \rangle = v$ in e end	(open type)
$\mid \langle p, v \rangle$	(pack location)		$\mid$ new v	(cell creation)
$\mid \langle A, v \rangle$	(pack type)		$\mid$ delete v	(cell deletion)
$\mid \{\overline{f = v}\}$	(record)		$\mid !v$	(dereference)
$\mid 1\#v$	(tagged value)		$\mid v := v$	(assign)
			$\mid$ case v of $\overline{1\#x \rightarrow e}$ end	(case)
$e ::= v$	(value)		$\mid$ share A_0 as $A_1 \parallel A_2$	(share)
$\mid v[p]$	(location application)		$\mid$ focus $\overline{A}$	(focus)
$\mid v[A]$	(type application)		$\mid$ defocus	(defocus)

Note: ρ is not source-level. $\overline{Z}$ for a possibly empty sequence of Z. Tuples, recursion, etc. are encoded as idioms, see [22].

Fig. 1. Values (v) and expressions (e)

The (let-expanded [26]) grammar is shown in Fig. 1. The main deviations from standard λ-calculus are the inclusion of location-related constructs, and the sharing constructs (**share, focus** and **defocus**).

We use a flat type grammar (Fig. 2) where both capabilities (i.e. typing artifacts without values, which includes our rely-guarantee protocols) and standard types (used to type values) coexist. Our design does not need to make a syntactic distinction between the two kinds since the type system ensures the proper separation in their use. We now overview the basic types, leaving the rely and guarantee types to be presented in the following Section together with the discussion on sharing. Pure types !A enable a linear type to be used multiple times. $A \multimap A'$ describes a linear function of argument A and result A'. The stacking operation $A :: A'$ stacks A' (a capability, or abstracted capability) on top of A. This stacking is not commutative since it stacks a single type on the right of ::. Therefore, $*$ enables multiple types to be grouped together that, when later stacked, allow that type to list a commutative group of capabilities[2]. Both $\forall$ and $\exists$ offer the standard quantification, over location and type kinds, together with the respective location/type variables. $[\overline{f : A}]$ are used to described labeled records of arbitrary length. A **ref** p type is a reference for location p noting that the contents of such a reference are tracked by the capability to that location and not immediately stored in the reference type. **recursive** types, that are automatically folded/unfolded through subtyping rules (see Fig. 4 and (T:SUBSUMPTION) on Fig. 3), are also supported. Sum types use the form tag#A to tag type A with tag. Alternatives ($\oplus$) model imprecision in the knowledge of the type by listing different possible states it may be in. **none** is the empty capability,

---

[2] Note that while $A_0 :: (A_1 :: A_2)$ and $A_0 :: (A_2 :: A_1)$ are not (necessarily) subtypes, capability commutation is always possible with $*$ such that $A_0 :: (A_1 * A_2) <:> A_0 :: (A_2 * A_1)$.

$A ::=$	$!A$	(pure/persistent)		$\mathbf{ref}\ p$	(reference type)
	$A \multimap A$	(linear function)		$\mathbf{rec}\ X.A$	(recursive type)
	$A :: A$	(stacking)		$\sum_i \mathbf{l}_i \# A_i$	(tagged sum)
	$A * A$	(separation)		$A \oplus A$	(alternative)
	$[\overline{\mathtt{f} : A}]$	(record)		$A\ \&\ A$	(intersection)
	X	(type variable)		$\mathbf{rw}\ p\ A$	(read-write capability to p)
	$\forall X.A$	(universal type quantification)		$\mathbf{none}$	(empty capability)
	$\exists X.A$	(existential type quantification)		$A \Rightarrow A$	(rely)
	$\forall t.A$	(universal location quantification)		$A; A$	(guarantee)
	$\exists t.A$	(existential location quantification)			

Note: $\sum_i \mathbf{l}_i \# A_i$ denotes a single tagged type or a sequence of tagged types separated by +, such as "t#A + u#B + v#C".
Separation, sum, alternative and intersection types are assumed commutative, i.e. without respective subtyping rules.

Fig. 2. Types and capabilities

while $\mathbf{rw}\ p\ A$ is the read-write capability to location p (a memory cell currently containing a value of type A). Finally, an $A\&A'$ type means that the client can choose to use either type A or type A' but not both simultaneously.

Our typing rules use typing judgments of the form: $\Gamma \mid \Delta_0 \vdash e : A \dashv \Delta_1$ stating that with lexical environment Γ and linear resources Δ_0 we assign the expression e a type A and produce effects that result in Δ_1. The typing environments are as follows:

$\Gamma ::=$	$\cdot$	(empty)	$\Delta ::=$	$\cdot$	(empty)
	$\Gamma,\ x : A$	(variable binding)		$\Delta,\ x : A$	(linear binding)
	$\Gamma,\ p : \mathbf{loc}$	(location variable assertion)		$\Delta,\ A$	(capability/protocol)
	$\Gamma,\ X : \mathbf{type}$	(type assertion)		$\Delta^G,\ A_0; A_1 \rhd \Delta$	(defocus-guarantee)

where Δ^G syntactically restricts Δ to not include a defocus-guarantee (a sharing feature, see Section 4.3). Suffices to note that this restriction ensures that defocus-guarantees are nested on the right of $\rhd$ and that, at each level, there exists only one pending defocus-guarantee. Δ^G is also used to forbid capture of defocus-guarantees by functions and other constructs that can keep part of the linear typing environment for themselves.

The main typing rules are shown in Fig. 3, but the last four typing rules are only discussed in Section 4. All values (which includes functions, tagged values, etc.) have no resulting effect ($\cdot$) since, operationally, they have no pending computations. Allocating a new cell results in a type, $\exists t.(\ \mathbf{ref}\ t :: \mathbf{rw}\ t\ A\ )$, that abstracts the fresh location that was created (t), and includes both a reference to that location and the capability to that location. To associate a value (such as $\mathbf{ref}\ t$) with some capability (such as the capability to access location t), we use a *stacking* operator ::. Naturally, to be able to use the existential location, we must first open that abstraction by giving it a *location variable* to refer the abstracted location, besides the usual variable to refer the contents of the existential type. Reading the content of a cell can be either destructive or not, depending on whether its content is pure (!). If it is linear, then to preserve linearity we must leave the unit type ([]) behind to avoid duplication. By banging the type of a variable binding, we can move it to the linear context which enables the function's typing rule to initially consider all arguments as linear even if they are pure. Functions can only capture

$$\boxed{\Gamma \mid \Delta_0 \vdash e : A \dashv \Delta_1}$$ **Typing rules, (T:*)**

(T:REF)

$$\overline{\Gamma, \rho : \mathbf{loc} \mid \cdot \vdash \rho : \mathbf{ref}\ \rho \dashv \cdot}$$

(T:UNIT)

$$\overline{\Gamma \mid \cdot \vdash v : [] \dashv \cdot}$$

(T:PURE-READ)

$$\overline{\Gamma, x : A \mid \cdot \vdash x : !A \dashv \cdot}$$

(T:LINEAR-READ)

$$\overline{\Gamma \mid x : A \vdash x : A \dashv \cdot}$$

(T:PURE)

$$\frac{\Gamma \mid \cdot \vdash v : A \dashv \cdot}{\Gamma \mid \cdot \vdash v : !A \dashv \cdot}$$

(T:PURE-ELIM)

$$\frac{\Gamma, x : A_0 \mid \Delta_0 \vdash e : A_1 \dashv \Delta_1}{\Gamma \mid \Delta_0, x : !A_0 \vdash e : A_1 \dashv \Delta_1}$$

(T:TAG)

$$\frac{\Gamma \mid \Delta \vdash v : A \dashv \cdot}{\Gamma \mid \Delta \vdash 1\#v : 1\#A \dashv \cdot}$$

(T:LOC-PACK)

$$\frac{\Gamma \mid \Delta \vdash v : A\{p/t\} \dashv \cdot}{\Gamma \mid \Delta \vdash \langle p, v \rangle : \exists t.A \dashv \cdot}$$

(T:NEW)

$$\frac{\Gamma \mid \Delta_0 \vdash v : A \dashv \Delta_1}{\Gamma \mid \Delta_0 \vdash \mathbf{new}\ v : \exists t.(\mathbf{ref}\ t :: \mathbf{rw}\ t\ A) \dashv \Delta_1}$$

(T:DELETE)

$$\frac{\Gamma \mid \Delta_0 \vdash v : \exists t.(\mathbf{ref}\ t :: \mathbf{rw}\ t\ A) \dashv \Delta_1}{\Gamma \mid \Delta_0 \vdash \mathbf{delete}\ v : \exists t.A \dashv \Delta_1}$$

(T:FUNCTION)

$$\frac{\Gamma \mid \Delta^G, x : A_0 \vdash e : A_1 \dashv \cdot}{\Gamma \mid \Delta^G \vdash \mathbf{fun}(x : A_0).e : A_0 \multimap A_1 \dashv \cdot}$$

(T:APPLICATION)

$$\frac{\Gamma \mid \Delta_0 \vdash v_0 : A_0 \multimap A_1 \dashv \Delta_1 \qquad \Gamma \mid \Delta_1 \vdash v_1 : A_0 \dashv \Delta_2}{\Gamma \mid \Delta_0 \vdash v_0\ v_1 : A_1 \dashv \Delta_2}$$

(T:DEREFERENCE-PURE)

$$\frac{\Gamma \mid \Delta_0 \vdash v : \mathbf{ref}\ p \dashv \Delta_1, \mathbf{rw}\ p\ !A}{\Gamma \mid \Delta_0 \vdash !v : !A \dashv \Delta_1, \mathbf{rw}\ p\ !A}$$

(T:DEREFERENCE-LINEAR)

$$\frac{\Gamma \mid \Delta_0 \vdash v : \mathbf{ref}\ p \dashv \Delta_1, \mathbf{rw}\ p\ A}{\Gamma \mid \Delta_0 \vdash !v : A \dashv \Delta_1, \mathbf{rw}\ p\ []}$$

(T:ASSIGN)

$$\frac{\Gamma \mid \Delta_0 \vdash v_1 : A_0 \dashv \Delta_1 \qquad \Gamma \mid \Delta_1 \vdash v_0 : \mathbf{ref}\ p \dashv \Delta_2, \mathbf{rw}\ p\ A_1}{\Gamma \mid \Delta_0 \vdash v_0 := v_1 : A_1 \dashv \Delta_2, \mathbf{rw}\ p\ A_0}$$

(T:ALTERNATIVE-LEFT)

$$\frac{\Gamma \mid \Delta_0, A_0 \vdash e : A_2 \dashv \Delta_1 \qquad \Gamma \mid \Delta_0, A_1 \vdash e : A_2 \dashv \Delta_1}{\Gamma \mid \Delta_0, A_0 \oplus A_1 \vdash e : A_2 \dashv \Delta_1}$$

(T:INTERSECTION-RIGHT)

$$\frac{\Gamma \mid \Delta_0 \vdash e : A_0 \dashv \Delta_1, A_1 \qquad \Gamma \mid \Delta_0 \vdash e : A_0 \dashv \Delta_1, A_2}{\Gamma \mid \Delta_0 \vdash e : A_0 \dashv \Delta_1, A_1 \& A_2}$$

(T:CASE)

$$\frac{\Gamma \mid \Delta_0 \vdash v : \sum_i 1_i\#A_i \dashv \Delta_1 \qquad \Gamma \mid \Delta_1, x_i : A_i \vdash e_i : A \dashv \Delta_2 \quad i \leq j}{\Gamma \mid \Delta_0 \vdash \mathbf{case}\ v\ \mathbf{of}\ \overline{1_j\#x_j \to e_j}\ \mathbf{end} : A \dashv \Delta_2}$$

(T:LOC-APP)

$$\frac{p : \mathbf{loc} \in \Gamma \qquad \Gamma \mid \Delta_0 \vdash v : \forall t.A \dashv \Delta_1}{\Gamma \mid \Delta_0 \vdash v[p] : A\{p/t\} \dashv \Delta_1}$$

(T:FORALL-LOC)

$$\frac{\Gamma, t : \mathbf{loc} \mid \Delta^G \vdash e : A \dashv \cdot}{\Gamma \mid \Delta^G \vdash \langle t \rangle e : \forall t.A \dashv \cdot}$$

(T:LOC-OPEN)

$$\frac{\Gamma \mid \Delta_0 \vdash v : \exists t.A_0 \dashv \Delta_1 \qquad \Gamma, t : \mathbf{loc} \mid \Delta_1, x : A_0 \vdash e : A_1 \dashv \Delta_2}{\Gamma \mid \Delta_0 \vdash \mathbf{open}\ \langle t, x \rangle = v\ \mathbf{in}\ e\ \mathbf{end} : A_1 \dashv \Delta_2}$$

(T:LET)

$$\frac{\Gamma \mid \Delta_0 \vdash e_0 : A_0 \dashv \Delta_1 \qquad \Gamma \mid \Delta_1, x : A_0 \vdash e_1 : A_1 \dashv \Delta_2}{\Gamma \mid \Delta_0 \vdash \mathbf{let}\ x = e_0\ \mathbf{in}\ e_1\ \mathbf{end} : A_1 \dashv \Delta_2}$$

(T:SUBSUMPTION)

$$\frac{\Delta_0 <: \Delta_1 \qquad \Gamma \mid \Delta_1 \vdash e : A_0 \dashv \Delta_2 \qquad A_0 <: A_1 \qquad \Delta_2 <: \Delta_3}{\Gamma \mid \Delta_0 \vdash e : A_1 \dashv \Delta_3}$$

(T:CAP-ELIM)

$$\frac{\Gamma \mid \Delta_0, x : A_0, A_1 \vdash e : A_2 \dashv \Delta_1}{\Gamma \mid \Delta_0, x : A_0 :: A_1 \vdash e : A_2 \dashv \Delta_1}$$

(T:CAP-STACK)

$$\frac{\Gamma \mid \Delta_0 \vdash e : A_0 \dashv \Delta_1, A_1}{\Gamma \mid \Delta_0 \vdash e : A_0 :: A_1 \dashv \Delta_1}$$

(T:CAP-UNSTACK)

$$\frac{\Gamma \mid \Delta_0 \vdash e : A_0 :: A_1 \dashv \Delta_1}{\Gamma \mid \Delta_0 \vdash e : A_0 \dashv \Delta_1, A_1}$$

(T:FOCUS-RELY)

$$\frac{A_0 \in \overline{A}}{\Gamma \mid A_0 \Rightarrow A_1 \vdash \mathbf{focus}\ \overline{A} : [] \dashv A_0, A_1 \blacktriangleright \cdot}$$

(T:DEFOCUS-GUARANTEE)

$$\overline{\Gamma \mid \Delta_0, A_0, A_0; A_1 \blacktriangleright \Delta_1 \vdash \mathbf{defocus} : [] \dashv \Delta_0, A_1, \Delta_1}$$

(T:FRAME)

$$\frac{\Gamma \mid \Delta_0 \vdash e : A \dashv \Delta_1}{\Gamma \mid \Delta_0 \circledast\!- \Delta_2 \vdash e : A \dashv \Delta_1 \circledast\!- \Delta_2}$$

(T:SHARE)

$$\frac{A_0 \Rightarrow A_1 \parallel A_2}{\Gamma \mid \Delta, A_0 \vdash \mathbf{share}\ A_0\ \mathbf{as}\ A_1 \parallel A_2 : [] \dashv \Delta, A_1, A_2}$$

Note: all bounded variables of a construct must be fresh in the respective rule's conclusion.

Fig. 3. Static semantics (selected typing rules, see [21] for the rest)

$\boxed{A_0 <: A_1}$ **Subtyping on types, (ST:*)**

(ST:ToLINEAR)   (ST:UNFOLD)   (ST:FOLD)

$$\frac{}{!A <: A} \qquad \frac{}{\textbf{rec } X.A <: A\{\textbf{rec } X.A/X\}} \qquad \frac{}{A\{X/\textbf{rec } X.A\} <: \textbf{rec } X.A}$$

(ST:REC)

$$\frac{A_0 <: A_1}{\textbf{rec } X.A_0 <: \textbf{rec } X.A_1} \qquad \text{(ST:SUM)} \atop \frac{}{\sum_i 1_i\#A_i <: 1'\#A' + \sum_i 1_i\#A_i} \qquad \text{(ST:ALTERNATIVE)} \atop \frac{}{A_0 <: A_0 \oplus A_1} \qquad \text{(ST:INTERSECTION)} \atop \frac{}{A_0 \& A_1 <: A_0}$$

$\boxed{\Delta_0 <: \Delta_1}$ **Subtyping on deltas, (SD:*)**

(SD:STAR)   (SD:VAR)   (SD:TYPE)   (SD:NONE)

$$\frac{}{\Delta, A_0, A_1 <:> \Delta, A_0 * A_1} \qquad \frac{\Delta_0 <: \Delta_1 \quad A_0 <: A_1}{\Delta_0, x : A_0 <: \Delta_1, x : A_1} \qquad \frac{\Delta_0 <: \Delta_1 \quad A_0 <: A_1}{\Delta_0, A_0 <: \Delta_1, A_1} \qquad \frac{}{\Delta <:> \Delta, \textbf{none}}$$

Fig. 4. Subtyping rules (selected, see [21] for the rest)

a Δ^G linear environment to ensure that they will not hide a pending defocus-guarantee (and similarly on ∀ abstractions), since our types do not express such pending operation. *Stacking*, done through (T:CAP-ELIM), (T:CAP-STACK) and (T:CAP-UNSTACK) enables the type system to manage capabilities in a non-syntax directed way, since they have no value nor associated identifier. The (T:CASE) rule allows the set of tags of the value that is to be case analyzed (v) to be *smaller* than those listed in the branches of the case ($i \leq j$). This conditions is safe because it amounts to ignoring the effects of those branches, instead of being overly conservative and having to consider them all. These branches are not necessarily useless since, for instance, they may still be relevant on alternative program states ($\oplus$). (T:ALTERNATIVE-LEFT) expresses that if an expression types with both assumptions, A_0 and A_1, then it works with both alternatives. (T:INTERSECTION-RIGHT) is similar but on the resulting effect of that expression.

Finally, (T:SUBSUMPTION) enables expressions to rely on weaker assumptions while ensuring a stronger result than needed. This rule is supported by subtyping rules (a selection is shown in Fig. 4) that follow the form $A_0 <: A_1$ stating that A_0 is a subtype of A_1, meaning that A_0 can be used wherever A_1 is expected. Similar meaning is used for subtyping on linear typing environments, $\Delta_0 <: \Delta_1$. Among other operations, these rules enable automatic fold/unfold of recursive types, as well as grouping ($*$) of resources.

4   Sharing Mutable State

The goal is to enable reads and writes to a cell through multiple aliases, without requiring the type system to precisely track the link between aliased variables. In other words, the type system is aware that a variable is aliased, but does not know exactly which other variables alias that same state. In this scenario, it is no longer possible to implicitly move capabilities between aliases. Instead, we split the original capability into multiple *protocol* capabilities to that same location, and ensure that these multiple protocols cannot interact in ways that destructively interfere with each other. Such *rely-guarantee* protocol accounts for the effects of other protocols (the *rely*), and limits the actions of this protocol to *guarantee* that they do not contradict the assumptions relied on by other aliases. This allows independent, but constrained, actions on the different protocols to the same shared state without destructive interference. However, it also requires us to leverage additional type mechanisms to ensure safety, namely:

(a) Hide Intermediate States. A rely-guarantee protocol restricts how aliases can use the shared state. However, we allow such specification to be temporarily broken provided that all unexpected changes are private, invisible to other aliases. Therefore, the type system ensures a kind of static mutual exclusion, a mechanism that provides a "critical section" with the desired level of isolation from other aliases to that same state. Consequently, other shared state that may overlap with the one being inspected simply becomes unavailable while that cell is undergoing private changes. Although this solution is necessarily conservative, we avoid any run-time overhead while preserving many relevant usages. To achieve this, we build on the concept of focus [11] (in a non-lexically scoped style, so that there is also a defocus) clearly delimiting the boundary in the code of where shared state is being inspected. Thus, on focus, all other types that may directly or indirectly see inconsistencies must be temporarily concealed only to reappear when those inconsistencies have been fixed, on defocus.

(b) Ensure That Each Individual Step of the Protocol Is Obeyed. In our system, sharing properties are encoded in a protocol composed of several rely-guarantee *steps*. As discussed in the previous paragraph, each step must be guarded by focus since private states should not be visible to other aliases. Consequently, the focus construct serves not only to safeguard from interference by other aliases, but also to move the protocol forward through each of its individual steps. At each such step, the code can assume on entry (focus) that the shared state will be in a given well-defined *rely* state, and must ensure on exit (defocus) that the shared state satisfies a given well-defined *guarantee* state. By characterizing the sequence of actions of each alias with an appropriate protocol, one can make strong local assumptions about how the shared state is used without any explicit dependence on how accesses to other aliases of that shared state are interleaved. This feature is crucial since we cannot know precisely if that same shared state was used between two focus-defocus operations.

4.1 Specifying Rely-Guarantee Protocols

We now detail our rely and guarantee types that are the building blocks of our protocols. To clarify the type structure of our protocols, we define the following sub-grammar of our types syntax (Fig. 2) with the types that may appear in a protocol, P.

$$P ::= \mathbf{rec}\, X.P \mid X \mid P \oplus P \mid P \,\&\, P \mid A \Rightarrow P \mid A; P \mid \mathbf{none}$$

A rely-guarantee protocol is a type of capability (i.e. has no value) consisting of potentially many steps, each of the form $A_C \Rightarrow A_P$. Each such step states that it is safe for the current client to assume that the shared state satisfies A_C and is required to obey the guarantee A_P, usually of the form $A_C'; A_P'$ which in turn requires the client to establish (guarantee) that the shared state satisfies A'_C before allowing the protocol to continue to be used as A'_p. Note that our design constrains the syntactical structure of these protocols through *protocol conformance* (Section 4.2), not in the grammar.

Pipe's Protocols. We can now define the protocols for the shared list nodes of the pipe's buffer. Each node follows a rely-guarantee protocol that includes three possible tagged states: Node, which indicates that a list cell contains some useful data; Empty, which indicates that the node will be filled with data by the producer (but does not yet have any data); and finally Closed, which indicates that the producer has sent all data through the pipe and no more data will be added (thus, it is the last node of the list).

Remember that the producer component of the pipe has an alias to the tail node of the internal list. Because it is the producer, it can rely on that shared node still being Empty (as created) since the consumer component will never be allowed to change that state. The rely-guarantee protocol for the tail alias (for some location p) is as follows:

$$\mathbf{rw}\ p\ \text{Empty\#[]} \Rightarrow (\ \mathbf{rw}\ p\ \text{Node\#R}\ \oplus\ \mathbf{rw}\ p\ \text{Closed\#[]}\ );\mathbf{none}$$

This protocol expresses that the client code can safely assume (on focus) a capability stating that location p initially holds type Empty#[]. It then requires the code that uses such state to leave it (on defocus) in one of two possible alternatives ($\oplus$) depending on whether the producer chooses to close the pipe or insert a new element to the buffer. To signal that the node is the last element of the pipe, the producer can just assign it a value of type Closed#[]. Insertions are slightly more complicated because that action implies that the tail element of the list will be changed. Therefore, after creating the new node, the producer component will keep an alias of the new tail for itself while leaving the old tail with a type that is to be used by the consumer. In this case, the node is assigned a value of type Node#R, where R denotes the type [int , $\exists p.($ **ref** p :: H[p])] (a pair of an integer and a reference to the next shared node of the buffer, as seen from the head pointer). Regardless of its action, the producer then forfeits any ownership of that state which is modeled by the empty capability (**none**)[3] to signal protocol termination.

We now present the abbreviations H and T, the rely-guarantee protocols that govern the use of the shared state of the pipe as seen by the head and tail aliases, respectively. Note that since we intend to apply the same protocol over different locations, we use "$Q \triangleq \forall p.A$" as a type definition (Q) where we can apply a location without requiring $\forall$ to be a value, such as location q in $Q[q]$. The T and H types are defined as follows:

$$T \triangleq \forall p.(\ E \Rightarrow (\ N \oplus C\ )\ )$$
$$H \triangleq \forall p.(\ \mathbf{rec}\ X.(\ N \Rightarrow \mathbf{none}\ \oplus\ C \Rightarrow \mathbf{none}\ \oplus\ E \Rightarrow E\ ;\ X\ )\ )$$

where N is an abbreviation for a capability that contains a node "$\mathbf{rw}\ p\ \text{Node\#R}$", C is "$\mathbf{rw}\ p\ \text{Closed\#[]}$" and E is "$\mathbf{rw}\ p\ \text{Empty\#[]}$". The T type was presented in the paragraph above, so we can now look in more detail to H. Such a protocol contains three alternatives, each with a different action on the state. If the state is found with an E type (i.e. still Empty) the consumer is not to modify such state (i.e., just reestablish E), and can retry again later to check if changes occurred. Observe that the remaining two alternatives have a **none** guarantee. This models the recovery of ownership of that

---

[3] We frequently omit the trailing "; **none**" for conciseness.

$$\boxed{\langle A, P \rangle \rightarrow \langle A', P' \rangle} \qquad\qquad\qquad\qquad\qquad \textbf{Step, (\textsc{step}:*)}$$

$$\frac{}{\langle A, \mathbf{none} \rangle \rightarrow \langle A, \mathbf{none} \rangle} \text{ (\textsc{step}:None)} \qquad \frac{}{\langle A_0, A_0 \Rightarrow A_1; P \rangle \rightarrow \langle A_1, P \rangle} \text{ (\textsc{step}:Step)}$$

$$\frac{\langle A_0, P_0 \rangle \rightarrow \langle A_1, P_2 \rangle}{\langle A_0, P_0 \oplus P_1 \rangle \rightarrow \langle A_1, P_2 \rangle} \text{ (\textsc{step}:Alternative-P)}$$

$$\frac{\langle A_0, P_0 \rangle \rightarrow \langle A_2, P_1 \rangle \qquad \langle A_1, P_0 \rangle \rightarrow \langle A_2, P_1 \rangle}{\langle A_0 \oplus A_1, P_0 \rangle \rightarrow \langle A_2, P_1 \rangle} \text{ (\textsc{step}:Alternative-S)}$$

$$\frac{A_0 <: A_1 \qquad P_0 <: P_1 \qquad \langle A_1, P_1 \rangle \rightarrow \langle A_2, P_2 \rangle \qquad A_2 <: A_3 \qquad P_2 <: P_3}{\langle A_0, P_0 \rangle \rightarrow \langle A_3, P_3 \rangle} \text{ (\textsc{step}:Subsumption)}$$

Fig. 5. Protocol stepping rules

particular node. Since the client is not required to reestablish the capability it relied on, that capability can remain available in that context even after defocus.

Each protocol describes a partial view of the complete use of the shared state. Consequently, ensuring their safety cannot be done alone. In our system, protocols are introduced explicitly through the share construct that declares that a type (in practice limited to capabilities, including protocols) is to be split in two new rely-guarantee protocols. Safety is checked by simulating their actions in order to ensure that they preserve the overall consistency in the use of the shared state, no matter how their actions may be interleaved. Since a rely-guarantee protocol can subsequently continue to be split, this technique does not limit the number of aliases provided that the protocols conform.

4.2 Checking Protocol Splitting

The key principle of ensuring a correct protocol split is to verify that both protocols consider all visible states that are reachable by stepping, ensuring a form of progress. Protocols are not required to always terminate and may be used indefinitely, for instance when modeling invariant-based sharing. However, regardless of interleaving or of how many times a shared alias is (consecutively) used, no unexpected state can ever appear in well-formed protocols. Thus, the type information contained in a protocol is valid regardless of all interference that may occur, i.e. it is *stable* [17,32].

Technically, the correctness of protocol splitting is ensured by two key components: 1) a *stepping* relation, that simulates a single use of the shared state through one focus-defocus block; and 2) a *protocol conformance* definition, that ensures full coverage of all reachable states by considering all possible interleaved uses of those steps. Thus, even as the rely and guarantee conditions evolve through the protocol's lifetime, protocol conformance ensures each protocol will never get "stuck" because the protocol must be aware of all possible "alias interleaving" that may occur for that state.

The stepping relation (Fig. 5) uses steps of the form $\langle A, P \rangle \rightarrow \langle A', P' \rangle$ expressing that, assuming shared state A, the protocol P can take a step to shared state A' with residual protocol P'. Due to the use of $\oplus$ and & types in the protocols, there may be *multiple* different steps that may be valid at a given point in that protocol. Therefore, protocol conformance must account for *all* those different transitions that may be picked.

We define protocol conformance as splitting an existing protocol (or capability) in two, although it can also be interpreted as merging two protocols. Regardless of the direction, the actions of the original protocol(s) must be fully contained in the resulting protocol(s). This leads to the three stepping conditions of the definition below.

Definition 1 (Protocol Conformance). Given an initial state A_0 and a protocol γ_0, such protocol can be split in two new protocols α_0 and β_0 if their combined actions conform with those of the original protocol γ_0, noted $\langle A_0, \gamma_0 \iff \alpha_0 \| \beta_0 \rangle$. This means that there is a set S of *configurations* $\langle A, \gamma \iff \alpha \| \beta \rangle$ closed under the conditions:

1. The initial configuration is in S: $\langle A_0, \gamma_0 \iff \alpha_0 \| \beta_0 \rangle \in S$
2. All configurations take a step, and the result is also in S.
   Therefore, if $\langle A, \gamma \iff \alpha \| \beta \rangle \in S$ then:
   (a) exists A', α' such that $\langle A, \alpha \rangle \to \langle A', \alpha' \rangle$, and for all $A', \alpha', \langle A, \alpha \rangle \to \langle A', \alpha' \rangle$
       implies $\langle A, \gamma \rangle \to \langle A', \gamma' \rangle$ and $\langle A', \gamma' \iff \alpha' \| \beta \rangle \in S$.
   (b) exists A', β' such that $\langle A, \beta \rangle \to \langle A', \beta' \rangle$, and for all $A', \beta', \langle A, \beta \rangle \to \langle A', \beta' \rangle$
       implies $\langle A, \gamma \rangle \to \langle A', \gamma' \rangle$ and $\langle A', \gamma' \iff \alpha \| \beta' \rangle \in S$.
   (c) exists A', γ' such that $\langle A, \gamma \rangle \to \langle A', \gamma' \rangle$, and
       for all $A', \gamma', \langle A, \gamma \rangle \to \langle A', \gamma' \rangle$ implies either:
       – $\langle A, \alpha \rangle \to \langle A', \alpha' \rangle$ and $\langle A', \gamma' \iff \alpha' \| \beta \rangle \in S$, or;
       – $\langle A, \beta \rangle \to \langle A', \beta' \rangle$ and $\langle A', \gamma' \iff \alpha \| \beta' \rangle \in S$.

The definition yields that all configurations must step (i.e. never get stuck) and that a step in one of the protocols (α or β) must also step the original protocol (γ) such that the result itself still conforms. Conformance ensures that all interleavings are coherent. This also means that each protocol "view" of the shared state can work independently in a safe way — even when the other aliases to that shared state are never used. Ownership recovery does not require any special treatment since it just expresses that the focused capability is not returned back to the protocol, enabling it to remain in the local context.

We now apply protocol conformance to our running example, as follows:

$A : E$
$\gamma : \mathbf{rec}\, X.(E \Rightarrow E; X \;\&\; (E \Rightarrow N \oplus C \,;\, (N \Rightarrow \mathbf{none} \;\oplus\; C \Rightarrow \mathbf{none}\,)))$
$\alpha : E \Rightarrow N \oplus C$ (Tail protocol)
$\beta : \mathbf{rec}\, X.(E \Rightarrow E; X \;\oplus\; N \Rightarrow \mathbf{none} \;\oplus\; C \Rightarrow \mathbf{none}\,)$ (Head protocol)

Therefore, applying the definition yields the following set of configurations, S:

$\langle E, \mathbf{rec}\, X.(E \Rightarrow E; X \;\&\; (E \Rightarrow N \oplus C; (N \Rightarrow \mathbf{none} \oplus C \Rightarrow \mathbf{none}\,))) \iff$
$\quad E \Rightarrow C \oplus N \;\|\; \mathbf{rec}\, X.(E \Rightarrow E; X \;\oplus\; N \Rightarrow \mathbf{none} \;\oplus\; C \Rightarrow \mathbf{none}\,)\rangle$ (1)

The initial configuration.

by step on γ (subtyping for &) with $E \Rightarrow E; X$ and same with β, using (STEP:ALTERNATIVE-P).
$\langle N \oplus C, N \Rightarrow \mathbf{none} \;\oplus\; C \Rightarrow \mathbf{none} \iff$
$\quad \mathbf{none} \;\|\; \mathbf{rec}\, X.(E \Rightarrow E; X \oplus N \Rightarrow \mathbf{none} \oplus C \Rightarrow \mathbf{none}\,)\rangle$ (2)

by step on (1) with γ (subtyping for &) with $E \Rightarrow N \oplus C$; ... and similarly using α.
$\langle \mathbf{none}, \mathbf{none} \iff \mathbf{none} \;\|\; \mathbf{none} \rangle$ (3)

by step on (2) with γ and β using (STEP:ALTERNATIVE-S).
S is closed (up to subtyping, including unfolding of recursive types).

Regardless of how the use of the state is interleaved at run-time, the shared state cannot reach an unexpected (by the protocols) state. Thus, conformance ensures the stability of the type information contained in a protocol in the face of all possible "alias interleaving". There exists only a finite number of possible (relevant) states, meaning that it suffices for protocol conformance to consider the smallest set of configurations that obeys the conditions above. Since there is also a finite number of possible inter-leavings resulting from mixing the steps of the two protocols, there are also a finite number of distinct (relevant) steps. Effectively, protocol conformance resembles a form of bisimulation or model checking (where each protocol is modeled using a graph) with a finite number of states, ensuring such process remains tractable.

In the following text we use a simplified notation, of the form $A \Rightarrow A' \parallel A''$, as an idiom (defined in [21]) that applies protocol conformance uniformly regardless of whether A is a state (for an initial split) or a rely-guarantee protocol (to be re-split and perhaps extended). The missing type is inferred by this idiom.

Example. We illustrate these concepts by going back to the pipe's protocols. We intro-duced the protocols for the head and tail aliases through the share construct:

```
3    share (rw n Empty#[]) as H[n] || T[n];
```

which is checked by the (T:SHARE) typing rule, using protocol conformance, as follows:

$$\frac{A_0 \Rightarrow A_1 \parallel A_2}{\Gamma \mid \Delta, A_0 \vdash \text{share } A_0 \text{ as } A_1 \parallel A_2 : [] \dashv \Delta, A_1, A_2} \text{(T:SHARE)}$$

With it we share a capability (A_0) by splitting it in two protocols (A_1 and A_2) whose individual roles in the interactions with that state conform ($\Rightarrow$). Consequently, the con-clusion states that, if the splitting is correct, then in some linear typing environment initially consisting of a type A_0 and Δ, the share construct produces effects that replace A_0 with A_1 and A_2 but leave Δ unmodified (i.e. it is just threaded through).

The next examples show conformance in a simplified way, with only the state and the two resulting protocols of a configuration. Remember that E is the abbreviation for **rw** q Empty#[] that, just like the abbreviations C and N, were defined above. Thus, the use of the share construct on line 3 yields the following set of configurations, S:

$$\langle E \Rightarrow \text{rec } X.(N \Rightarrow \text{none} \oplus C \Rightarrow \text{none} \oplus E \Rightarrow E ; X) \parallel E \Rightarrow (N \oplus C)\rangle \qquad (1)$$
$$\langle N \oplus C \Rightarrow \text{rec } X.(N \Rightarrow \text{none} \oplus C \Rightarrow \text{none} \oplus E \Rightarrow E ; X) \parallel \text{none}\rangle \qquad (2)$$
$$\langle \text{none} \Rightarrow \text{none} \parallel \text{none}\rangle \qquad (3)$$

The definition is only respected if E is the state to be shared by the protocols. If instead we had shared, for instance, C we would get the next set of configurations:

$$\langle C \Rightarrow \text{rec } X.(N \Rightarrow \text{none} \oplus C \Rightarrow \text{none} \oplus E \Rightarrow E ; X) \parallel E \Rightarrow (N \oplus C)\rangle \qquad (1)$$
$$\langle \text{none} \Rightarrow \text{none} \parallel E \Rightarrow (N \oplus C)\rangle \qquad (2)$$

The set above does not satisfy our conformance definition. Both the state in config-uration (1) and **none** in (2) are not expected by the right protocol. Thus, those con-figurations are "stuck" and cannot take a step. Although splittings are checked from a high-level and abstracted perspective, their consequences link back to concrete invalid program states that could occur if such invalid splittings were allowed. For instance, in (2), it would imply that the alias that used the right protocol would assume E on focus long after the ownership of that state was recovered by some other alias of that cell. Consequently, such behavior could allow unexpected changes to be observed by that alias, potentially resulting in a program stuck on some unexpected value.

4.3 Using Shared State

Using shared state is centered on two constructs: focus (that exposes the shared state of a protocol) and defocus (that returns the exposed state to the protocol), combined with our version of the *frame rule* (Section 4.4). We now describe how focus is checked:

$$\frac{A_0 \in \overline{A}}{\Gamma \mid A_0 \Rightarrow A_1 \vdash \text{focus } \overline{A} : [] \dashv A_0,\ A_1 \rhd \cdot} \quad \text{(T:Focus-Rely)}$$

In general, focus may be applied over a disjunction ($\oplus$) of program states and expected to work on any of those alternatives. By using $\overline{A}$, the programmer can list the types that may become available after focus, nominating what they expect to gain by focus.

focus results in a typing environment where the step of the protocol that was focused on ($A_0 \Rightarrow A_1$) now has its rely type (A_0) available to use. However, it is not enough to just make that capability available, we must also *hide* all other linear resources that may use that same shared state (directly or indirectly) in order to avoid interference due to the inspection of private states. To express this form of hiding, the linear typing environments may include a *defocus-guarantee*. This element, written as $A \rhd \Delta$, means that we are hiding the typing environment Δ until A is satisfied. Therefore, in our system, the only meaningful type for A is a guarantee type of the form $A'; A''$ that is satisfied when A' is offered and enables the protocol to continue to be use as A''. Although the typing rule shown above only includes a single element in the initial typing environment (and, consequently, the defocus-guarantee contains the empty typing environment, $\cdot$), this is not a limitation. In fact, the full potential of (T:Focus-Rely) is only realized when combined with (T:Frame). Together they allow for the non-lexically scoped framing of potentially shared state, where the addition of resources that may conflict with focused state will be automatically nested inside the defocus-guarantee ($\rhd$). Operationally share, focus, and defocus are no-ops which results in those expressions having type unit ([]).

$$\frac{}{\Gamma \mid \Delta_0,\ A',\ A'; A'' \rhd \Delta_1 \vdash \text{defocus} : [] \dashv \Delta_0,\ A'',\ \Delta_1} \quad \text{(T:Defocus-Guarantee)}$$

The complementary operation, defocus, simply checks that the required guarantee type (A') is present. In that situation, the typing environment (Δ_1) that was hidden on the right of $\rhd$ can now safely be made available once again. At the same time, the step of the protocol is concluded leaving the remainder protocol (A'') in the typing environment. Nesting of defocus-guarantees is possible, but is only allowed to occur on the right of $\rhd$. Note that defocus-guarantees can never be captured (such as by functions, see Fig. 3 of Section 3) and, therefore, pending defocus operations cannot be forgotten or ignored.

Example. We now look at the implementation of the put and close functions to exemplify the use of focus and defocus. Both functions are closures that capture an enclosing Γ where t is a known location such that tail has type **ref** t. T was defined above as: $\forall p.(\textbf{rw } p \text{ Empty\#[]} \Rightarrow \textbf{rw } p \text{ Node\#R} \oplus \textbf{rw } p \text{ Closed\#[]})$ where R is a pair of an integer and a protocol for the head, H (whose definition, given above, is not important here).

```
 9  put = fun( e : int :: rw t exists p.(ref p :: T[p]) ).
                              Γ = ...,tail : ref t,  t : loc,  e : int | Δ = rw t ∃p.(ref p :: T[p])
10      open <1,last> = new Empty#{} in              Γ = ...,last : ref l,  l : loc | Δ = ...,  rw l Empty#[]
11          open <o,oldlast> = !tail in      Γ = ...,  oldlast : ref o | Δ = rw t [],  rw l Empty#[],  T[o]
12              focus (rw o Empty#[]);   Δ = ...,  rw o Empty#[],  (rw o Node#R) ⊕ (rw o Closed#[]); none ▷ ·
13              share (rw l Empty#[]) as H[l] || T[l];                          Δ = ...,T[l], H[l], ...
14              oldlast := Node#{ e, <1,last::H[l]> };                    Δ = ...,rw o Node#R, ...
15          defocus;                                                  Δ = rw t [], T[l], none
16          tail := <l, last::T[l]>                                   Δ = rw t ∃p.(ref p :: T[p])
17      end
18  end,
19  close = fun( _ : [] :: rw t exists p.(ref p :: T[p]) ).
                              Γ = ...,tail : ref t,  t : loc,  _ : [] | Δ = rw t ∃p.(ref p :: T[p])
20      open <1,last> = !tail in               Γ = ...,last : ref l,  l : loc | Δ = rw t [], T[l]
21      delete tail;                                                            Δ = T[l]
22      focus (rw l Empty#[]);     Δ = rw l Empty#[],  (rw l Node#R) ⊕ (rw l Closed#[]); none ▷ ·
23      last := Closed#{};         Δ = rw l Closed#[],  (rw l Node#R) ⊕ (rw l Closed#[]); none ▷ ·
24      defocus                                                                  Δ = ·
25  end,
```

The put function takes an integer stacked with a capability for t. The capability is automatically unstacked to Δ. Since we are inserting a new element at the end of the buffer, we create a new node that will serve as the new last node of that list. On line 11, the oldlast node is read from the tail cell by opening the abstracted location it contains. Such location refers a protocol type, for which we must use focus (line 12) to gain access to the state that it shares. Afterwards, we modify the contents of that cell by assigning it the new node. This node contains the alias for the new tail as will be used by the head alias. The T component of that split (line 13) is stored in the tail. The defocus of line 15 completes the protocol for that cell, meaning that the alias will no longer be usable through there. Carefully note that the share of line 13 takes place *after* focus. If this were reversed, then the type system would conservatively hide the two newly created protocols making it impossible to use them until defocus. By exploiting the fact that such capability is not shared, we can allow it to not be hidden inside ▷ since it cannot interfere with shared state. close should be straightforward to understand.

4.4   Framing State

On its own, (T:Focus-Rely) is very restrictive since it requires a single rely-guarantee protocol to be the exclusive member of the linear typing environment. This happens because more complex applications of focus are meant to be combined with our version of the frame rule. Together they enable a kind of mutual exclusion that also ensures that the addition of any potentially interfering resources will forcefully be on the right of ▷ (thus making them inaccessible until defocus). The typing rule is as follows:

$$\frac{\Gamma \mid \Delta_0 \vdash e : A \dashv \Delta_1}{\Gamma \mid \Delta_0 \circledast\!\!-\, \Delta_2 \vdash e : A \dashv \Delta_1 \circledast\!\!-\, \Delta_2} \text{ (T:FRAME)}$$

Framing serves the purpose of hiding ("frame away") parts of the footprint (Δ_2) that are not relevant to typecheck a given expression (e), or can also be seen as enabling extensions to the current footprint. In our system, such operation is slightly more complex than traditional framing since we must also ensure that any such extension will not enable destructive interference. Therefore, types that may refer (directly or indirectly) values that access shared cells that are currently inconsistent due to pending defocus cannot be accessible and must be placed "inside" (on the right of ▶) the defocus-guarantee. However, statically, we can only make such distinction conservatively by only allowing types that are **non-shared** (and therefore that are known to never conflict with other shared state) to not be placed inside the defocus-guarantee. The formal definition of **non-shared** is in [21], but for this presentation it is sufficient to consider it as pure types, or capabilities (**rw** p A) that are not rely-guarantee protocols and that whose contents are also non-shared. This means that all other linear types (even abstracted capabilities and linear functions) must be assumed to be potential sources of conflicting interference. For instance, these types could be abstracting or capturing a rely-guarantee protocol that could then result in a re-entrant inspection of the shared state.

To build the extended typing environment, we define an *environment extension* ($\circledast\!\!-$) operation that takes into account frame defocus-guarantees up to a certain depth. This means that one can always consider extensions of the current footprint as long as any added shared state is hidden from all focused state. By conservatively hiding it behind a defocus-guarantee, we ensure that such state cannot be touched. This enables locality on focus: if a protocol is available, then it can safely be focused on.

Definition 2 (Environment Extension). Given environments Δ and Δ' we define environment extension, noted $\Delta \circledast\!\!-\, \Delta'$, as follows. Let $\Delta = \Delta_n, \Delta_s$ where n-indexed environments only contains **non-shared** elements and s-indexed environments contain the remaining elements (i.e. all those that may, potentially, include sharing). Identically, assume $\Delta' = \Delta'_n, \Delta'_s$. Extending Δ with Δ' corresponds to $\Delta \circledast\!\!-\, \Delta' = \Delta_n, \Delta'_n, \Delta''_s$ where:

(a) $\Delta''_s = \Delta_{s_0}, A \triangleright (\Delta_{s_1} \circledast\!\!-\, \Delta'_s)$ if $\Delta_s = \Delta_{s_0}, A \triangleright \Delta_{s_1}$

(b) $\Delta''_s = \Delta_s, \Delta'_s$ otherwise.

that either (a) further nests the shared part of Δ' deeper in Δ_{s_1}; or (b) simply composes Δ' if the left typing environment (Δ) does not carry a defocus-guarantee.

Although the definition appears complex, it works just like regular environment composition when Δ' does not contain a defocus-guarantee, i.e. the (b) case. The complexity of the definition arises from the need to nest these structures when they do exist, which results in the inductive definition above. In that situation, we must ensure that any potentially interfering shared state is placed deep inside all previously existing defocus-guarantees, so as to remain inaccessible. This definition is compatible with the basic notion of disjoint separation, but (from a framing perspective) allows us to frame-away defocus-guarantees beyond a certain depth. Such state can be safely hidden if the underlying expression will not reach it (by defocusing).

The definition allows a (limited) form of *multi*-focus. For instance, while a defocus is pending we can create a new cell and share it through two new protocols. Then, by framing the remaining part of the typing environment, we can now focus on one of the new protocols. The old defocus-guarantee is then nested *inside* the new defocus-guarantee that resulted from the last focus. This produces a "list" of pending guarantees in the reverse order on which they were created through focus. Through framing we can hide part of that "list" after a certain depth, while preserving its purpose.

Example. We now look back at the focus of line 12. To better illustrate framing, we consider an extra linear type (that is *not* **non-shared**), S, to show how it will become hidden (on the right of ▷) after focus. We also abbreviate the two non-shared capabilities ("$\mathbf{rw}\ t\ []$" and "$\mathbf{rw}\ l\ \texttt{Empty\#}[]$")[4] as A_0 and A_1, and abbreviate the protocol so that it does not show the type application of location o. With this, we get the following derivation:

$$\frac{\dfrac{\dfrac{E \in E}{\Gamma \mid E \Rightarrow (N \oplus C) \vdash \textsf{focus } E : [] \dashv E, (N \oplus C); \textbf{none} \triangleright \cdot}}{\Gamma \mid (E \Rightarrow (N \oplus C)) \circledast- S, A_0, A_1 \vdash \textsf{focus } E : [] \dashv (E, (N \oplus C); \textbf{none} \triangleright \cdot) \circledast- S, A_0, A_1}}{\Gamma \mid E \Rightarrow (N \oplus C), S, A_0, A_1 \vdash \textsf{focus } E : [] \dashv E, ((N \oplus C); \textbf{none} \triangleright S), A_0, A_1}$$

(3)

(2)

(1)

where (1) - (ENVIRONMENT EXTENSION), (2) - (T:FRAME), and (3) - (T:FOCUS-RELY).

Note that frame may add elements to the typing environment that cannot be instantiated into valid heaps. That is, the conclusion of the frame rule states that an hypothesis with the extended environment typechecks the expression with the same type and resulting effects. Not all such extensions obey store typing just like such typing rule enables adding multiple capabilities to one same location that can never be realized in an actual, correct, heap. However, our preservation theorem ensures that starting from a correct (stored typed) heap and typing environment, we cannot reach an incorrect heap state.

4.5 Consumer Code

We now show the last function of the pipe example, tryTake:

```
26  tryTake = fun( _ [] :: rw h exists p.(ref p :: H[p]) ).              Δ = rw h ∃p.(ref p :: H[p])
27      open <f,first> = !head in      Δ = rw h [] , (N[f] ⇒ none) ⊕ (C[f] ⇒ none) ⊕ (E[f] ⇒ E[f] ; ...)
        [a] Δ = rw h [], N[f] ⇒ none  [b] Δ = rw h [], C[f] ⇒ none  [c] Δ = rw h [], E[f] ⇒ E[f] ; ...
28        focus C[f], E[f], N[f]; // same abbreviations that were defined above
        [a] Δ = ..., N[f], none;none▷  [b] Δ = ..., C[f], none;none▷·  [c] Δ = ..., E[f], E[f] ; ...▷·
29      case !first of
30        Empty#_ →                                    [c] Δ = rw h [] , rw f [] , rw f Empty#[];...▷·
31          first := Empty#{}; // restore linear type
                    [c] Δ = rw h [] , rw f Empty#[] , rw f Empty#[];...▷·
32          defocus; // the next assignment must occur after defocus and just on this branch
                    [c] Δ = rw h [] , H[f]
33          head := <f,first::H[f]>;                      [c] Δ = rw h ∃p.(ref p :: H[p])
34          NoResult#{} : NoResult#([] :: rw h ∃p.(ref p :: H[p])) //assume auto stacked   [c] Δ = ·
35      | Closed#_ →                                 [b] Δ = rw h [] , rw f [] , none;none▷·
```

---

[4] Note that the content of each capability can be made **non-shared** by subtyping rules.

```
36              delete first;                                      [b] Δ = rw h [] , none; none ▹ ·
37              delete head;                                       [b] Δ = none; none ▹ ·
38              defocus;                                                        [b] Δ = ·
39              Depleted#{} : Depleted#[]                                        [b] Δ = ·
40      | Node#[element,n]  →  //opens pair
            [a] Δ = rw h [] , rw f [] , n : ∃p.(ref p :: H[p]) , none; none ▹ ·
41              delete first;            [a] Δ = rw h [] , n : ∃p.(ref p :: H[p]) , none; none ▹ ·
42              head := n;               [a] Δ = rw h ∃p.(ref p :: H[p]) , none; none ▹ ·
43              defocus;                              [a] Δ = rw h ∃p.(ref p :: H[p])
44              Result#element : Result#(int :: rw h ∃p.(ref p :: H[p]))  // assume auto stacked  [a] Δ = ·
45          end
46      end
```

The code should be straightforward up to the use of alternative program states (⊕). This imprecise state means that we have one of several different alternative capabilities and, consequently, the expression must consider all of those cases separately. On line 28, to use each individual alternative of the protocol, we check the expression separately on each alternative (marked as [a], [b], and [c] in the typing environments), cf. (T:ALTERNATIVE-LEFT) in Fig. 3. Our case gains precision by ignoring branches that are statically known to not be used. On line 29, when the type checker is case analyzing the contents of first on alternative [b] it obtains type Closed#[]. Therefore, for that alternative, type checking only examines the Closed tag and the respective case branch. This feature enables the case to obey different alternative program states simultaneously, although the effects/guarantee that each branch fulfills are incompatible.

5   Technical Results

Our soundness results (details in [21]) use the next progress and preservation theorems:

Theorem 1 (Progress). *If e_0 is a closed expression (and where Γ and Δ are also closed) such that $\Gamma \mid \Delta_0 \vdash e_0 : A \dashv \Delta_1$ then either:*

- *e_0 is a value, or;*
- *if exists H_0 such that $\Gamma \mid \Delta_0 \vdash H_0$ then $\langle H_0 \parallel e_0 \rangle \mapsto \langle H_1 \parallel e_1 \rangle$.*

The progress statement ensures that all well-typed expressions are either values or, if there is a heap that obeys the typing assumptions, the expression can step to some other program state — i.e. a well-typed program never gets stuck, although it may diverge.

Theorem 2 (Preservation). *If e_0 is a closed expression such that:*

$$\Gamma_0 \mid \Delta_0 \vdash e_0 : A \dashv \Delta \qquad \Gamma_0 \mid \Delta_0 \circledast\!\!- \Delta_2 \vdash H_0 \qquad \langle H_0 \parallel e_0 \rangle \mapsto \langle H_1 \parallel e_1 \rangle$$

then, for some Δ_1 and Γ_1 we have: $\Gamma_0, \Gamma_1 \mid \Delta_1 \circledast\!\!- \Delta_2 \vdash H_1 \qquad \Gamma_0, \Gamma_1 \mid \Delta_1 \vdash e_1 : A \dashv \Delta$

The theorem above requires the initial expression e_0 to be closed so that it is ready for evaluation. The preservation statement ensures that the resulting effects (Δ) and type (A) of the expression remains the same throughout the execution. Therefore, the initial typing is preserved by the dynamics of the language, regardless of possible environment extensions (⊛- Δ_2). This formulation respects the intuition that the heap used to evaluate an expression may include other parts (Δ_2) that are not relevant to check that expression.

We define *store typing* (see [21]), noted $\Gamma \mid \Delta \vdash H$, in a linear way so that each heap location must be matched by some capability in Δ or potentially many rely-guarantee protocols. Thus, no instrumentation is necessary to show these theorems.

Destructive interference occurs when an alias assumes a type that is incompatible with the real value stored in the shared state, potentially causing the program to become stuck. However, we proved that any well-typed program in our language cannot become stuck. Thus, although our protocols enable a diverse set of uses of shared state, these theorems show that when rely-guarantee protocols are respected those usages are safe.

6   Additional Examples

We now exemplify some sharing idioms captured by our rely-guarantee protocols.

6.1   Sharing a Linear ADT

Our protocols are capable of modeling monotonic [12,24] uses of shared state. To illustrate this, we use the linear stack ADT from [22] where the stack object has two possible typestates: Empty and Non-Empty. The object, with an initial typestate E(mpty), is accessible through closures returned by the following "constructor" function:

$$!(\,\forall T. \; [] \multimap \exists E. \exists NE. \; ![\quad push \; : \; T :: E \oplus NE \multimap [] :: NE,$$
$$pop \; : \; [] :: NE \multimap T :: E \oplus NE,$$
$$isEmpty \; : \; [] :: E \oplus NE \multimap Empty\#([] :: E) + NonEmpty\#([] :: NE),$$
$$del \; : \; [] :: E \multimap [] \,] \; :: \; E \,)$$

Although the capability to that stack is linear, we can use protocols to share it. This enables multiple aliases to that same object to coexist and use it simultaneously from unknown contexts. The following protocol converges the stack to a non-empty typestate, starting from an imprecise alternative that also includes the empty typestate.

$$(\, NE \oplus E \,) \Rightarrow NE \, ; \; \mathbf{rec} \, X.(\, NE \Rightarrow NE \, ; \; X \,)$$

Monotonicity means that the type becomes successively more precise, although each alias does not know when those changes occurred. Note that, due to focus, the object can undergo intermediate states that are not compatible with the required NE guarantee. However, on defocus, clients must provide NE such as by pushing some element to the stack. The protocol itself can be repeatedly shared in equal protocols. Since each copy will produce the same effects as the original protocol, their existence is not observable.

6.2   Capturing Local Knowledge

Although our types cannot express the same amount of detail on local knowledge as prior work [4, 18], they are expressive enough to capture the underlying principle that enables us to keep increased precision on the shared state between steps of a protocol.

For this example, we use a simple two-states counter. In it, N encodes a number that may be zero and P some positive number, with the following relation between states:

$N \triangleq Z\#[] + NZ\#int \qquad P \triangleq NZ\#int$ (note that: $P <: N$, vital to show conformance)

We now share this cell in two asymmetric roles: IncOnly, that limits the actions of the alias to only increment the counter (in a protocol that can be shared repeatedly); and Any, an alias that relies on the restriction imposed by the previous protocol to be able to capture a stronger rely property in a step of its own protocol. Assuming an initial capability of rw p N, this cell can be shared using the following two protocols:

$$\text{IncOnly} \triangleq \mathbf{rec}\ X.(\ \mathsf{rw}\ p\ \mathsf{N} \Rightarrow \mathsf{rw}\ p\ \mathsf{P}\ ;\ X\ )$$
$$\text{Any} \triangleq \mathbf{rec}\ Y.(\ \mathsf{rw}\ p\ \mathsf{N} \Rightarrow \mathsf{rw}\ p\ \mathsf{P}\ ;\ \mathsf{rw}\ p\ \mathsf{P} \Rightarrow \mathsf{rw}\ p\ \mathsf{N}\ ;\ Y\ )$$

Thus, by constraining the actions of IncOnly we can rely on the assumption that Any remains positive on its second step, even when the state is manipulated in some other unknown program context. Therefore, on the second step of Any, the case analysis can be sure that the value of the shared state must have remained with the NZ tag between focuses. Note that the actions of that alias allow for it to change the state back to Z.

6.3   Iteratively Sharing State

Our technique is able to match an arbitrary number of aliases by splitting an existing protocol. Such split can also extend the original uses of the shared state by appending additional steps, if those uses do not destructively interfere with the old assumptions.

This example shows such a feature by encoding a form of delegation through shared state that models a kind of "server-like process". Although single-threaded, such a system could be implemented using co-routines or collaborative multi-tasking. The overall computation is split between three individual workers (for instance by each using a private list containing cells with pending, shared, jobs) each with a specific task. A Receiver uses a Free job cell and stores some Raw element in it. A Compressor processes a Raw element into a Done state. Finally, the Storer removes the cells in order to store them elsewhere. In real implementations, each worker would be used by separate handlers/threads, triggered in unpredictable orders, to handle such jobs.

We also show how we can share multiple locations together, bundled using ∗, by each job being kept in a *c*ontainer cell while the *f*lag (used to communicate the information on the kind of content stored in the container) is in a separate cell. The raw value is typed with A and the processed value has type B. The types and protocols are:

$$F \triangleq \mathbf{rw}\ f\ \text{Free}\#[]\ *\ \mathbf{rw}\ c\ []\qquad R \triangleq \mathbf{rw}\ f\ \text{Raw}\#[]\ *\ \mathbf{rw}\ c\ A\qquad D \triangleq \mathbf{rw}\ f\ \text{Done}\#[]\ *\ \mathbf{rw}\ c\ B$$

$$\begin{aligned}
\text{Receiver} &\triangleq\ F \Rightarrow R\\
\text{Compressor} &\triangleq\ \mathbf{rec}\ X.(\ F \Rightarrow F; X\ \oplus\ R \Rightarrow D)\\
\text{Storer} &\triangleq\ \mathbf{rec}\ X.(\ F \Rightarrow F; X\ \oplus\ \mathbf{rec}\ Y.(\ R \Rightarrow R; Y\ \oplus\ D \Rightarrow \mathbf{none}\ ))
\end{aligned}$$

The protocol for the Receiver is straightforward since it just processes a free cell by assigning it a raw value. Similarly, Compressor and Storer follow analogous ideas by using a kind of "waiting" steps until the cell is placed with the desired type for the actions that they are to take (note how Storer keeps a more precise context when the state is not F, even though it is not allowed to publicly modify the state). To obtain these protocols through binary splits, we need an *intermediate* protocol that will be split to create the Compressor and Storer protocols. The initial split (of F) is as follows:

$$F \implies \text{Receiver} \parallel \text{rec } X.(F \implies F; X \ \oplus \ R \implies \textbf{none})$$

The protocol on the right is then further split, and its ownership recovery step further extended with additional steps, to match the two new desired protocols:

$$\text{rec } X.(F \implies F; X \ \oplus \ \text{rec } Y.(R \implies R; Y \ \& \ R \implies D; D \implies \textbf{none})) \implies \text{Compressor} \parallel \text{Storer}$$

The Receiver alias never needs to see how the other two aliases use the shared state. Although the second split is independent from the initial one, protocol conformance ensures that it cannot cause interference by breaking what Receiver initially relied on.

7   Related Work

We now discuss other works that offer flexible sharing mechanisms. Although there are other interesting works [1, 2, 4, 5, 7, 31] in the area, they limit sharing to an invariant.

In *Chalice* [19], programmer-supplied permissions and predicates are used to show that a program is free of data races and deadlocks. A limited form of rely-guarantee is used to reason about changes to the shared state that may occur between atomic sections. All changes from other threads must be expressed in auxiliary variables and be constrained to a two-state invariant that relates the *current* with the *previous* state, and where all rely and guarantee conditions are the same for all threads.

Several recent approaches that use advanced program logics [9, 10, 23, 30, 32] employ rely-guarantee reasoning to verify inter-thread interference. Although our approach is type-based rather than logic-based, there are several underlying similarities. *Concurrent abstract predicates* [9] extend the concept of *abstract predicates* [23] to express how state is manipulated, supporting internally aliased state through a *fiction of disjointness* (also present in [16, 18]) that is based on rely-guarantee principles and has similarities to our own abstractions. Their use of rely-guarantee also allows intermediate states within a critical section, which are immediately weakened (made stable) to account for possible interference when that critical section is left. Although our use of rely-guarantee is tied to state (be it references or abstracted state), not threads, our protocols capture an identical notion of stability through a simpler constraint that ensures all visible states are considered during protocol conformance. Another modeling distinction is that our interference specification lists the resulting states (from interference), not the actions that can (or cannot [10]) occur from external/unknown sources.

Monotonic [12, 24] based sharing enables unrestricted aliasing that cannot interfere since the changes converge to narrower, more precise, states. Our protocols are able to express monotonicity. However, since the rely and guarantee types of a step in the protocol must describe a finite number of states, we lack the type expressiveness of [24]. We believe this concern is orthogonal to our core sharing concepts, and is left as future work. We are also capable of expressing more than just monotonicity. For instance, due to ownership recovery, a cell can oscillate between shared and non-shared states during its lifetime, and with each sharing phase completely unrelated to previous uses.

Gordon *et al.* [15] propose a type system where references carry three additional type components: a predicate (for local knowledge), a guarantee relation, and a rely relation. They handle an unknown number of aliases by constraining the writes to a cell to fit within the alias' declared guarantee, similarly to how rely-guarantee is used in program logics to handle thread-based interference. Although they support a limited form of protocol (and their technique can generally be considered as a two-state protocol), their system effectively limits the actions allowed by each new alias to be strictly decreasing since their guarantee must fit within the original alias' guarantee. Since we support ownership recovery of shared state, a cell can be shared and return to non-shared without such restriction. Unlike ours, their work does not allow intermediate inconsistent states since all updates are publicly visible. In addition, their work requires proof obligations for, among other things, guarantee satisfaction while we use a more straightforward definition of protocol conformance that is not dependent on theorem-proving. However, their use of dependent refinement types adds expressiveness (e.g. their predicates capture an infinite state space, while our state space is finite) but increases the challenges in automation, as typechecking requires manual assistance in Coq.

Krishnaswami *et al.* [18] define a generic sharing rule based on the use of frame-preserving operations over a commutative monoid (later shown to be able to encode rely-guarantee [8]). The core principle is centered on splitting the internal resources of an ADT such that all aliases obey an invariant that is shared, while also keeping some knowledge about the locally-owned shared state. By applying a frame condition over its specification, their shared resources ensure that any interference between clients is benign since it preserves the fiction of disjointness. Thus, local assumptions can interact with the shared state without being affected by the actions done through other aliases of that shared state. The richness of their specification language means that although it might not always be an obvious, simple or direct encoding, protocols are likely encodable through the use of auxiliary variables. However, our use of a protocol paradigm presents a significant conceptual distinction since we do not need sharing to be anchored to an ADT. Therefore, we can share individual references directly without requiring an intermediary module to indirectly offer access to the shared state, but we also allow such uses to exist. Similarly, although both models allow ownership recovery, our protocols are typing artifacts which means that we do not need an ADT layer to enable this recovery and the state of that protocol can be switched to participate in completely unrelated protocols, later on. Their abstractions are also shared symmetrically, while our protocols can restrict the available operations of each alias asymmetrically. Additionally, after the initial split, our shared state may continue to be split in new ways. Finally, we use focus to statically forbids re-entrant uses of shared state, while they use dynamic checks that diverge the execution when such operation is wrongly attempted.

8 Conclusions

We introduced a new flexible and lightweight interference control mechanism, *rely-guarantee protocols*. By constraining the actions of an alias and expressing the effects of the remaining aliases, our protocols ensure that only benign interference can occur when using shared state. We showed how these protocols capture many challenging and complex aliasing idioms, while still fitting within a relatively simple protocol abstraction. Our model departs from prior work by, instead of splitting shared resources encoded as monoids, offering an alternative paradigm of "temporal" splits that model the coordinated interactions between aliases. A prototype implementation, which uses a few additional annotations to ensure typechecking is decidable, is currently underway[5].

Acknowledgments. This work was partially supported by Fundação para a Ciência e Tecnologia (Portuguese Foundation for Science and Technology) through the Carnegie Mellon Portugal Program under grant SFRH / BD / 33765 / 2009 and the Information and Communication Technology Institute at CMU, CITI PEst-OE / EEI / UI0527 / 2011, the U.S. National Science Foundation under grant #CCF-1116907, "Foundations of Permission-Based Object-Oriented Languages," and the U.S. Air Force Research Laboratory. We thank the Plaid (at CMU) and the PLASTIC (at UNL) research groups, and the anonymous reviewers for their helpful comments.

References

1. Ahmed, A., Fluet, M., Morrisett, G.: L3: A linear language with locations. Fundam. Inf. (2007)
2. Beckman, N.E., Bierhoff, K., Aldrich, J.: Verifying correct usage of atomic blocks and typestate. In: OOPSLA (2008)
3. Beckman, N.E., Kim, D., Aldrich, J.: An empirical study of object protocols in the wild. In: Mezini, M. (ed.) ECOOP 2011. LNCS, vol. 6813, pp. 2–26. Springer, Heidelberg (2011)
4. Bierhoff, K., Aldrich, J.: Modular typestate checking of aliased objects. In: OOPSLA (2007)
5. Caires, L., Seco, J.A.C.: The type discipline of behavioral separation. In: POPL (2013)
6. Calcagno, C., O'Hearn, P.W., Yang, H.: Local action and abstract separation logic. In: Proc. Logic in Computer Science (2007)
7. DeLine, R., Fähndrich, M.: Typestates for objects. In: Odersky, M. (ed.) ECOOP 2004. LNCS, vol. 3086, pp. 465–490. Springer, Heidelberg (2004)
8. Dinsdale-Young, T., Birkedal, L., Gardner, P., Parkinson, M., Yang, H.: Views: compositional reasoning for concurrent programs. In: POPL (2013)
9. Dinsdale-Young, T., Dodds, M., Gardner, P., Parkinson, M.J., Vafeiadis, V.: Concurrent abstract predicates. In: D'Hondt, T. (ed.) ECOOP 2010. LNCS, vol. 6183, pp. 504–528. Springer, Heidelberg (2010)
10. Dodds, M., Feng, X., Parkinson, M., Vafeiadis, V.: Deny-guarantee reasoning. In: Castagna, G. (ed.) ESOP 2009. LNCS, vol. 5502, pp. 363–377. Springer, Heidelberg (2009)
11. Fähndrich, M., DeLine, R.: Adoption and focus: practical linear types for imperative programming. In: PLDI (2002)
12. Fähndrich, M., Leino, K.R.M.: Heap monotonic typestate. In: IWACO (2003)
13. Gay, S.J., Vasconcelos, V.T., Ravara, A., Gesbert, N., Caldeira, A.Z.: Modular session types for distributed object-oriented programming. In: POPL (2010)
14. Girard, J.-Y.: Linear logic. Theor. Comput. Sci. (1987)
15. Gordon, C.S., Ernst, M.D., Grossman, D.: Rely-guarantee references for refinement types over aliased mutable data. In: PLDI (2013)
16. Jensen, J.B., Birkedal, L.: Fictional separation logic. In: Seidl, H. (ed.) Programming Languages and Systems. LNCS, vol. 7211, pp. 377–396. Springer, Heidelberg (2012)

---

[5] Available at: https://code.google.com/p/deaf-parrot/

17. Jones, C.B.: Tentative steps toward a development method for interfering programs. ACM Trans. Program. Lang. Syst. (1983)
18. Krishnaswami, N.R., Turon, A., Dreyer, D., Garg, D.: Superficially substructural types. In: ICFP (2012)
19. Leino, K.R.M., Müller, P.: A basis for verifying multi-threaded programs. In: Castagna, G. (ed.) ESOP 2009. LNCS, vol. 5502, pp. 378–393. Springer, Heidelberg (2009)
20. Mandelbaum, Y., Walker, D., Harper, R.: An effective theory of type refinements. In: ICFP (2003)
21. Militão, F., Aldrich, J., Caires, L.: Rely-guarantee protocols (technical report). CMU-CS-14-107 (2014)
22. Militão, F., Aldrich, J., Caires, L.: Substructural typestates. In: PLPV (2014)
23. Parkinson, M., Bierman, G.: Separation logic and abstraction. In: POPL (2005)
24. Pilkiewicz, A., Pottier, F.: The essence of monotonic state. In: TLDI (2011)
25. Reynolds, J.C.: Separation logic: A logic for shared mutable data structures. In: Proc. Logic in Computer Science (2002)
26. Sabry, A., Felleisen, M.: Reasoning about programs in continuation-passing style. In: Proc. LISP and Functional Programming (1992)
27. Smith, F., Walker, D.W., Morrisett, G.: Alias types. In: Smolka, G. (ed.) ESOP 2000. LNCS, vol. 1782, pp. 366–381. Springer, Heidelberg (2000)
28. Strom, R.E.: Mechanisms for compile-time enforcement of security. In: POPL (1983)
29. Strom, R.E., Yemini, S.: Typestate: A programming language concept for enhancing software reliability. IEEE Trans. Software Eng. (1986)
30. Svendsen, K., Birkedal, L., Parkinson, M.: Modular reasoning about separation of concurrent data structures. In: Felleisen, M., Gardner, P. (eds.) Programming Languages and Systems. LNCS, vol. 7792, pp. 169–188. Springer, Heidelberg (2013)
31. Tov, J.A., Pucella, R.: Practical affine types. In: POPL (2011)
32. Vafeiadis, V., Parkinson, M.: A marriage of rely/Guarantee and separation logic. In: Caires, L., Vasconcelos, V.T. (eds.) CONCUR 2007. LNCS, vol. 4703, pp. 256–271. Springer, Heidelberg (2007)
33. Yorsh, G., Skidanov, A., Reps, T., Sagiv, M.: Automatic assume/guarantee reasoning for heap-manipulating programs. Electron. Notes Theor. Comput. Sci. (2005)

Stream Processing with a Spreadsheet

Mandana Vaziri, Olivier Tardieu, Rodric Rabbah,
Philippe Suter, and Martin Hirzel

IBM T.J. Watson Research Center, Yorktown Height, NY, USA
{mvaziri,tardieu,rabbah,psuter,hirzel}@us.ibm.com

Abstract. Continuous data streams are ubiquitous and represent such
a high volume of data that they cannot be stored to disk, yet it is often crucial for them to be analyzed in real-time. Stream processing is
a programming paradigm that processes these immediately, and enables
continuous analytics. Our objective is to make it easier for analysts, with
little programming experience, to develop continuous analytics applications directly. We propose enhancing a spreadsheet, a pervasive tool, to
obtain a programming platform for stream processing. We present the
design and implementation of an enhanced spreadsheet that enables visualizing live streams, live programming to compute new streams, and
exporting computations to be run on a server where they can be shared
with other users, and persisted beyond the life of the spreadsheet. We
formalize our core language, and present case studies that cover a range
of stream processing applications.

1   Introduction

Continuous data streams are ubiquitous: they arise in telecommunications, fi-
nance, health care, and transportation among other domains. They represent
such a high volume of data that they cannot be stored to disk in raw form,
and it is often crucial for the data to be analyzed right away. Stream processing
is a programming paradigm that processes sequences of data immediately, and
enables what is called continuous analytics.

In organizations that require stream processing, domain experts may have
limited programming experience to directly implement their desired solutions.
As a result, they rely on developers for the actual implementation. Our objective is to make it easier for these end-users to directly prototype and perform
computations on live data. We believe this is an important facilitator for rapid
turnaround and lower development costs that may otherwise hinder streaming
data analysis.

This paper proposes the use of spreadsheets as a stream programming platform. The choice of spreadsheets stems from the fact that they are a pervasive
tool used in many different domains, and are familiar to non-programmers[1].

---

[1] There are 9 million Java developers
(http://oracle.com.edgesuite.net/timeline/java/),
and an order of magnitude more Microsoft Excel users.
(http://blog.ventanaresearch.com/tag/microsoft-excel/)

R. Jones (Ed.): ECOOP 2014, LNCS 8586, pp. 360–384, 2014.
© Springer-Verlag Berlin Heidelberg 2014

Spreadsheets offer a variety of visualization possibilities, and the ability to analyze, process, or augment source data by entering formulas in cells. They provide a unique interface where data is in the foreground and the code that produced it can be viewed in the same place. This is unlike common integrated development environments (IDEs) where code appears in a dedicated editor, and data visualization plays a subordinate and often orthogonal role.

Although spreadsheets are used for many different applications, they do not readily support online stream processing, which we believe requires the following essential features:

- *Live data in cells:* for online processing, one must have the ability to import live data into cells. Further, as the live data changes, the value of the cell must change contemporaneously.
- *Segmenting streams into windows:* some streaming operations are applied over aggregates of values (e.g., reductions). In spreadsheets, aggregates are groups of rows and columns called ranges. For online stream processing, an analogue between spreadsheet ranges and windows over streams is needed.
- *Stateful cells:* spreadsheets are functional by nature and do not readily support state or cyclic cell references. However, many stream processing applications need state to compute summaries or decisions via finite state machines.

This paper presents ACTIVESHEETS, a programming platform for stream processing that is based on Microsoft Excel with enhancements to meet the challenges described above. It provides a language that an end-user can use to easily populate ranges of cells in a spreadsheet with the desired shape of data, a windowing mechanism that allows computations over windows of streaming data, and the ability to perform stateful computations by treating stateful and stateless cells uniformly. ACTIVESHEETS retains and interoperates with familiar Excel features (e.g., built-in functions and macros, or visualizing live data) but also enhances Excel's native capabilities such that they operate correctly on live data. An example is the Excel *pivot* function which classically operates on a snapshot of cells (i.e., if the cells change, the filtered results do not). In ACTIVESHEETS, it is possible to continuously pivot as the input cells change.

ACTIVESHEETS is a client-server architecture in which the server publishes streams and the client, namely the spreadsheet, allows the user to subscribe to streams and operate on the *live* data; operations include visualization of streams and generation of new streams (Fig. 1). The client provides an export feature, making it possible to share the results with other users, as well as persisting the computation on the server, beyond the life of the spreadsheet.

We present formal semantics for the core language captured by our user interface, which we call the *spreadsheet calculus*. This is a reactive programming model that represents the spreadsheet computation as a combinatorial circuit derived from cell dependencies and formulas contained within the cells. As input cells change over time, any dependent cells are automatically recomputed and updated. Cells that must retain state can be viewed as circuits with latches. This model hides many common concerns from the programmer, because it offers a fixed control structure and manages cell updates automatically based on data

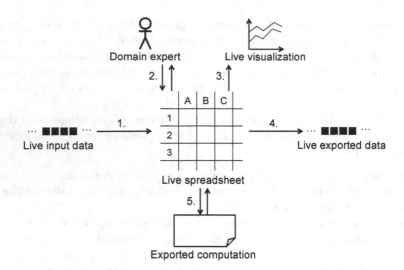

Fig. 1. ACTIVESHEETS Overview: 1. The server publishes lives streams. 2. The domain expert subscribes to these streams and prototypes the computation in a spreadsheet. 3. Spreadsheet functionality is readily available, including visualization. 4. Data computed in the spreadsheet may be exported as its own stream. 5. The entire spreadsheet may be exported to the server, where the computation outlives client shutdown.

dependencies. As a result, the domain expert can focus on the data transformations they wish to compute.

A spreadsheet enables a live programming platform, meaning that code can be modified during the execution of the program. This is an essential feature, because streaming analytics applications cannot be stopped and restarted easily. The user has to be able to quickly modify computations without stopping data sources. This feature creates challenges, especially in the face of stateful computations, and we define its semantics formally in the spreadsheet calculus. Finally, our extensions to the spreadsheet must preserve its highly interactive nature, meaning that on every update to a cell, there can only be a bounded amount of computation and memory usage. We prove this property for our core language, and show that it is also deterministic, meaning that for any given set of inputs, the spreadsheet computation always yields the same result.

This paper makes the following contributions:

- A reactive programming model for stream processing based on spreadsheets and a uniform treatment of stateless and stateful cells.
- Formal semantics for our core language using a new spreadsheet calculus.
- Exporting spreadsheet computation to the server for sharing or persistence.
- A prototype implementation using Microsoft Excel, and case studies covering a range of stream processing applications.

2   Overview

This section presents an overview of how ACTIVESHEETS works, using a streaming stock bargain calculator as a running example. The bargain calculator takes two input streams: Trades and Quotes. A stream is an infinite sequence of tuples, which are sequences of attribute/value pairs. A feed is the infinite sequence of values corresponding to a single attribute of a stream. Thus a stream is comprised of a collection of feeds whose values update synchronously.

The tuples of the Trades stream represent actual trades that have been made, using attributes sym (a stock symbol), ts (a timestamp), price, and vol. Each of these attributes defines a feed of values. The bargain calculator first computes the Volume Weighted Average Price (VWAP). Given a window of prices P_i and volumes V_i, the VWAP is defined as:

$$\text{VWAP} = \frac{\sum_i P_i \times V_i}{\sum_i V_i}$$

After computing the VWAP over the Trades stream, the bargain calculator determines whether or not each price in the Quotes stream is less than the VWAP. If yes, it outputs a bargain. Various streaming languages are well-suited to writing this program, such as CQL [4] or SPL [15]. However, end-users are typically unfamiliar with programming languages, let alone special-purpose languages such as CQL or SPL. Our objective is to bring stream programming to the end-user by enhancing the spreadsheet, a tool that is pervasive and familiar.

ACTIVESHEETS is based on Microsoft Excel enhanced with controls for manipulating live streams as shown in Fig. 2.

Fig. 2. ACTIVESHEETS Controls. Buttons from left to right: connect to and disconnect from the server, add a stream ('+' icon), pause a stream (pause symbol), disconnect from a stream ('−' icon), export data back to the server (flash symbol), stop data export (crossed out flash symbol), export computation (movie symbol), and lastly, debug mode (light bulb), used to debug the implementation of ACTIVESHEETS.

Fig. 3 shows the bargain calculator program in ACTIVESHEETS. We now explain how the user can obtain this program step by step.

Connecting to the server. To start using ACTIVESHEETS, the user first clicks on the connect button. This prompts for the address to the server and connects to it. The server publishes several streams that the client may subscribe to, visualize, and work with. Depending on the server's installation, these streams could come from existing stream processing programs, live feeds, static data that is streamed, or exported streams from other ACTIVESHEETS clients. In the case of this example, the server publishes the two input streams Trades and Quotes.

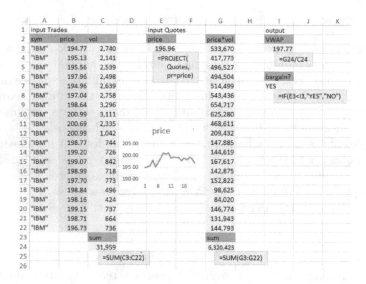

Fig. 3. Bargain Calculator in ACTIVESHEETS

Subscribing to a stream. The next step is to subscribe to a stream. To do this, the user first chooses a window in the spreadsheet, then presses the subscribe button ('+'), and enters the stream name at the prompt. The selected stream is then displayed in the window that the user selected with one column per attribute (feed), and the values scroll from bottom to top. A visual indicator comes on if the user did not select a wide enough range of cells. At any given moment in time, the user sees a window of data that gets updated continuously. In the example, the user first subscribes to the Trades input stream. Fig. 4 shows the Trades input streaming into the spreadsheet in columns A through D over a window of size 20. The data fills the window from bottom to top and continues scrolling. The chosen window size not only specifies how much of the stream is shown at any given moment in time, it also determines the window of data over which the VWAP will be computed. The user may pause a stream by choosing a cell in it, and pressing the pause button. This causes all the feeds in that stream to stop until the user presses pause again to resume, which causes ACTIVESHEETS to display the latest live data.

Adding new feeds. The user can create new data by entering formulas in cells directly, which creates new feeds. Fig. 5 shows how the user enters a standard Excel formula to compute the price times the volume in cell G3. Notice that, in this figure, the timestamp column has been deleted because it is not needed. The user then copies and pastes the formula in the rest of column G with familiar Excel gestures. Even though familiar controls are used to populate column G, the result is live in ACTIVESHEETS: as the values of price and volume are updated, their product is recomputed. Fig. 5 further shows how the user can compute the sum for the volume and price-times-volume columns (cells C24 and G24),

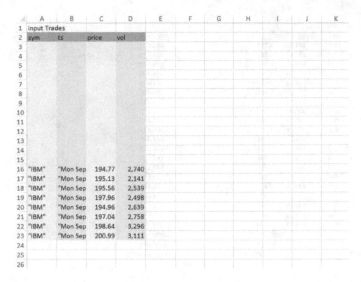

Fig. 4. The `Trades` input streaming in

and enter a formula for the VWAP (cell I3). Each feed in ACTIVESHEETS gets updated at specific points in time, which we call its *tick*. For example, the sum of two cells gets updated whenever either of the cells are updated.

Adding new streams. In addition to entering formulas in cells one at a time, the user can also populate a range of cells with a stream (synchronous feeds) using ACTIVESHEETS' query language. This language is relational in flavor, and includes operators for projection, selection, deduplication, sorting, pivoting, and aggregation. It also supports a simple mechanism for stateful computation. Queries are entered by selecting a window in the spreadsheet and pressing the '+' icon. The simplest query is giving the name of a stream to display all of its attributes. The user may use a selection to filter tuples in `Trades` with a price greater than a certain value

<code>select(Trades, price > 200)</code>

which would populate a range of cells with formulas to produce the desired result: a stream with all the attributes of `Trades` but with tuples having a price greater than 200.

Bargain computation. Notice that the output of a query can still be a single feed: a projection, for example, can be used to view a single attribute of a stream. In cell E3 of Fig. 3, the user has added the `Quotes` input stream, using a query that only shows the price attribute:

<code>project(Quotes, price = Quotes.price)</code>

This query takes the `Quotes` stream and produces a new stream that has a single attribute named `price`. The new stream ticks synchronously with `Quotes`. Finally, the user enters an Excel conditional to determine whether or not the quoted price is a bargain (cell I7 in Fig. 3).

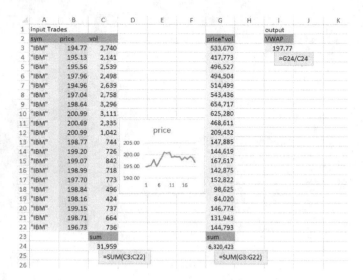

Fig. 5. Computing VWAPs

Exporting data. The user may want to export data back to the server. This can be accomplished by selecting the quoted price and whether or not it is a bargain (cells I3 and I6), and pressing the flash button. ACTIVESHEETS will prompt for a name for this new stream (e.g., `Bargains`), and will start sending this data to the server. The tick of the new stream is the union of the ticks of the feeds that comprise it: i.e., whenever one of the feeds is updated, a new tuple with all the data is sent to the server. Other ACTIVESHEETS users will then be able to subscribe to it. Since the data is computed in the spreadsheet, when the spreadsheet is closed, the stream will no longer be published to the server.

Exporting computation. When the user is ready to deploy the application, he or she can export the computation by pressing the movie button. This feature takes a snapshot of all formulas in the entire spreadsheet and sends it to the server. Each spreadsheet has a single output stream (visible to other users). During export, the user selects the cells that comprise attributes of the output stream. Multiple exports result in separate snapshots on the server. Once computation is exported, it runs at the server side, and exists even after the user closes the spreadsheet. There is a trade-off between data and computation export. In data export, the user may compute new data locally using custom macros and libraries, but the computation disappears when the spreadsheet is closed. In computation export, only a subset of Excel built-in features are supported (at the server), but the computation persists beyond the life of the spreadsheet.

Working with state. In this example, the user wants to keep count of the number of quotes that are bargains. Fig. 6 illustrates how this works. Cell I11 is set to 1 if there is a bargain, and 0 otherwise. Cell I14 is set to the old bargain count

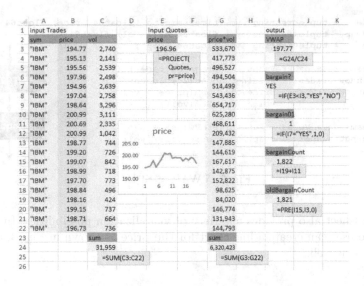

	A	B	C	D	E	F	G	H	I	J	K
1	Input Trades				Input Quotes				output		
2	sym	price	vol		price		price*vol		VWAP		
3	"IBM"	194.77	2,740		196.96		533,670		197.77		
4	"IBM"	195.13	2,141		=PROJECT(		417,773		=G24/C24		
5	"IBM"	195.56	2,539		Quotes,		496,527				
6	"IBM"	197.96	2,498		pr=price)		494,504		bargain?		
7	"IBM"	194.96	2,639				514,499		YES		
8	"IBM"	197.04	2,758				543,436		=IF(E3<I3,"YES","NO")		
9	"IBM"	198.64	3,296				654,717				
10	"IBM"	200.99	3,111				625,280		bargain01		
11	"IBM"	200.69	2,335				468,611		1		
12	"IBM"	200.99	1,042		price		209,432		=IF(I7="YES",1,0)		
13	"IBM"	198.77	744	205.00			147,885				
14	"IBM"	199.20	726	200.00			144,619		bargainCount		
15	"IBM"	199.07	842				167,617		1,822		
16	"IBM"	198.99	718	195.00			142,875		=I19+I11		
17	"IBM"	197.70	773	190.00			152,822				
18	"IBM"	198.84	496		1 6 11 16		98,625		oldBargainCount		
19	"IBM"	198.16	424				84,020		1,821		
20	"IBM"	199.15	737				146,774		=PRE(I15,I3,0)		
21	"IBM"	198.71	664				131,943				
22	"IBM"	196.73	736				144,793				
23			sum				sum				
24			31,959				6,320,423				
25			=SUM(C3:C22)				=SUM(G3:G22)				
26											

Fig. 6. Stateful computation using PRE

plus cell I11, so it increments iff there is a bargain. And Cell I19 obtains the old bargain count by using the PRE function. Function $PRE(v, t, v_0)$ is formalized later in this paper; intuitively, it obtains the previous value of v, using the tick of t, and using value v_0 as the default when v is not yet defined. Note that the bargain count computation is cyclic (the new count depends on the old count and vice versa). As we shall see, this is well defined as long as every cycle contains a call to PRE.

Discussion. Fig. 7 shows the VWAP calculation in IBM's Streams Processing Language (SPL) [15]. The `Aggregate` operator invocation in Lines 6-10 consumes stream `Trades` and produces stream `PreVwaps`. Just like the ACTIVESHEETS version, it uses a window of 20 tuples that slide at granularity 1. It sets attribute `priceVol` to $\sum_i P_i \times V_i$ and attribute `vol` to $\sum_i V_i$. The `Functor` operator invocation in Lines 11-13 consumes stream `PreVwaps` and produces stream `Vwaps`. It sets attribute `vwap` to `priceVol` / `vol`. Whereas ACTIVESHEETS users always have concrete data to look at, developing code in a streaming language like SPL feels more decoupled from the data. Furthermore, writing code in a language like SPL requires familiarity with programming, which is arguably beyond the reach of an end-user.

Compared to the code in Fig. 7, the ACTIVESHEETS experience makes computing with streams accessible to the end-user. It provides a reactive programming model with a fixed control structure: new tuples cause dependent cells to be recomputed and refreshed. The user is freed to focus on the data and its transformations without having to think about unfamiliar programming language syntax. The interface makes it easy to express computations on a window of data from the same stream, and allows computation export for deployment.

```
1.  type
2.     Trade    = tuple<rstring sym, timestamp ts, float64 price, float64 vol>;
3.     PreVwap  = tuple<rstring sym, float64 priceVol, float64 vol>;
4.     Vwap     = tuple<rstring sym, float64 vwap>;
5.  graph
6.     stream<PreVwap> PreVwaps = Aggregate(Trades) {
7.        window Trades:    sliding, count(20), count(1);
8.        output PreVwaps: priceVol = Sum(price * vol),
9.                         vol      = Sum(vol);
10.    }
11.    stream<Vwap> Vwaps = Functor(PreVwaps) {
12.       output Vwaps:     vwap     = priceVol / vol;
13.    }
```

Trades

Aggregate

PreVwaps

Functor

Vwaps

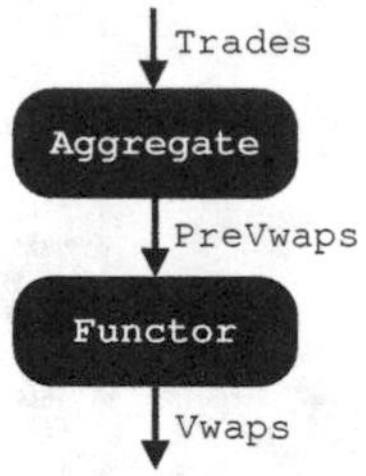

Fig. 7. VWAP in SPL

The spreadsheet also provides a variety of visualization possibilities. In the example, the user can create a line chart for the price as shown in Fig. 3, and the chart is live as well.

3   Spreadsheet Calculus

This section formalizes a core calculus to support our programming model. It first specifies the constructs and semantics of a minimal *client* spreadsheet—a collection of cells and formulas—connected to a *server* providing real-time data feeds. The constructs let us compute over recent feed histories and build stateful spreadsheets. The semantics define when and how cell values are computed. We prove that the resulting executions are well-defined, reactive, and deterministic provided the client spreadsheet is free from immediate cyclic dependencies (Section 3.1).

Clients compute over potentially infinite data feeds. Our programming model is intended to favor real-time analytics and prevent users from engaging into expensive querying of feed histories. A client for example can compute the average of a data feed over time (since the beginning of time), but it must do so incrementally as the live data flows through the client. We formally establish that executions in our model can be computed incrementally over time, using a bounded amount of computation per update (i.e., incoming data packet) and a bounded amount of memory to keep track of the execution state—the "past"—of size proportional to the client itself (Section 3.2).

The end-user can change formulas in the spreadsheet while real-time feeds are being processed. To support this form of live programming, we extend our semantics so that cells no longer contain static formulas, but feeds of formulas that change over time (Section 3.3). Our core calculus is not intended as an actual programming interface for the end-user. To bridge this gap, we specify a stream calculus by reduction to our core calculus. It supports richer notions of data streams—sequences of tuples with named attributes—and formulas (Section 3.4). Finally, we specify a query language that provides familiar relational operators on data streams such as projection and selection (Section 3.5).

3.1   Core Calculus

We start with the definitions, then establish key properties of our core calculus.

Ticks. Let a *tick* T be a possibly empty, at most countable, strictly increasing series of non-negative real numbers $\{t_0, t_1, t_2, \cdots\}$ representing a sequence of arrival times. We require that T is unbounded if infinite.

We write $T \triangleright t$ for the tick T up to time t that is formally the series $T \cap [0, t]$, which is always a finite tick. A non-empty finite tick T always admits a *maximal element* $\max(T)$. Given a finite tick T with at least two elements, we define the *second-to-max element* $\mathrm{prev}(T)$ as $\max(T \setminus \max(T))$. We write $(t_0, t_1) \in T$ if t_0 and t_1 are two *consecutive arrival times* in T, that is, if $t_1 \in T$ and $t_0 = \mathrm{prev}(T \triangleright t_1)$.

Feeds. Let a *feed* ϕ be a map from a tick to values. We write $\mathrm{dom}(\phi)$ for the tick of ϕ. We say that ϕ *ticks* at time t iff $t \in \mathrm{dom}(\phi)$. As a convenience, we overload the notation $\phi(t)$ as follows. If $t \in \mathrm{dom}(\phi)$, then $\phi(t)$ is the usual function application. Otherwise, if $\mathrm{dom}(\phi) \triangleright t \neq \emptyset$, then $\phi(t)$ is defined as $\phi(\max(\mathrm{dom}(\phi) \triangleright t))$. Otherwise, $\phi(t)$ is undefined and we write $\phi(t) = \bot$ using $\bot$ to denote the absence of a value. In short, $\phi(t)$ is always the most recent value of ϕ at time t.

Servers. Let a *server* S be a finite collection of feeds. We define the *server tick* N of S as the tick $\bigcup_{\phi \in S} \mathrm{dom}(\phi)$. Because of the required properties of ticks, it makes sense to think of N as $\mathbb{N}$ or a subset of $\mathbb{N}$ if it helps the reader. While ticks are intended to model real-time arrival times, our semantics really think of arrival times as logical instants. The order matters, but the time difference between two instants does not.

Clients, cells, and formulas. Let a *client* C be a finite collection of *cells*. Each cell has a unique name c and contains a formula f. We write $c \equiv f$ iff c contains formula f. The syntax of formulas is defined as follows, where f denotes a formula, c a cell name, ϕ a server feed, and op a family of operators on values (such as division $/$, greater-than $>$, or Excel's IF function).

$$f ::= \phi \mid op(c_1, \cdots, c_n) \mid c_0 @ c_1 \mid \mathbf{latch}(c_0, c_1)$$

For simplicity, our core calculus does not permit nesting constructs. The stream calculus of Section 3.4 lifts this restriction.

We do not explicitly model constant formulas as these can be obtained by means of constant server feeds. Observe that our semantics will distinguish constant feeds with the same value but distinct ticks.

Our core calculus is untyped. We assume all op operators are total functions. For simplicity, we do not consider "eager" operators capable of producing values even if not all operands are defined, but such operators could be added easily.

The calculus has two constructs to manipulate time: @ and **latch**. The @ construct makes it possible to sample a feed according to a Boolean condition (a feed with Boolean values): $c_0 @ c_1$ ticks when c_1 does and evaluates to *true*, returning the current value of c_0. The **latch** construct provides a general mechanism to delay a feed so that a feed value that is not the most recent can be accessed: **latch**(c_0, c_1) ticks when c_1 does returning the value of c_0 at the previous tick of c_1. We illustrate the two constructs below as we specify their semantics. In Section 3.4, we show how PRE can be defined using **latch**.

Well-formedness. We define the set of *immediate dependencies deps(c) of a cell* c as follows.

$$\text{deps}(c) = \begin{cases} \emptyset & \text{if } c \equiv \phi \\ \{c_1, \cdots, c_n\} & \text{if } c \equiv op(c_1, \cdots, c_n) \\ \{c_0, c_1\} & \text{if } c \equiv c_0 @ c_1 \\ \{c_1\} & \text{if } c \equiv \textbf{latch}(c_0, c_1) \end{cases}$$

In essence, our semantics are such that if $c \equiv \textbf{latch}(c_0, c_1)$ then c only depends on the past of c_0, hence c does not immediately depend on c_0. Reciprocally, if c immediately depends on c_0 then the semantics of c at time t will potentially be derived from the semantics of c_0 at time t. We therefore need immediate dependencies to be acyclic. We say that a client is *well-formed* iff the directed graph $\mathcal{G}$ of immediate dependencies is acyclic, where the vertices of $\mathcal{G}$ are the cell names and there exists an edge (c, c') in $\mathcal{G}$ iff $c' \in \text{deps}(c)$. If a client is not well-formed, we can identify a cycle and notify the user.

Semantics. We now specify the semantics of well-formed clients by recursion. Lemma 1 will establish that this recursion is well-founded.

We define by mutual recursion the tick $\mathcal{T}(c)$ of a cell c of a well-formed client C and the value $\mathcal{E}(c, t)$ of c at time $t \in [0, \infty)$ as follows, starting with $\mathcal{T}(c)$.

$$\mathcal{T}(c) = \begin{cases} \text{dom}(\phi) & \text{if } c \equiv \phi \\ \{t \in \bigcup_{i=1}^{n} \mathcal{T}(c_i) | \forall i \in \{1, \cdots, n\} : \mathcal{T}(c_i) \triangleright t \neq \emptyset\} & \text{if } c \equiv op(c_1, \cdots, c_n) \\ \{t \in \mathcal{T}(c_1) | \mathcal{E}(c_1, t) = true, \mathcal{T}(c_0) \triangleright t \neq \emptyset\} & \text{if } c \equiv c_0 @ c_1 \\ \mathcal{T}(c_1) & \text{if } c \equiv \textbf{latch}(c_0, c_1) \end{cases}$$

In contrast with typical synchronous programming models [8], our core calculus does not require the operands of an operator op to be synchronous (share the same tick). Instead, an operator op ticks each time an operand does (once all operands are defined). Once c_0 is defined, $c_0 @ c_1$ ticks when c_1 does and evaluates to *true*. The tick of **latch**(c_0, c_1) is simply the tick of the second argument c_1.

We now consider the definition of $\mathcal{E}(c,t)$.

$$\mathcal{E}(c,t) = \begin{cases} \phi(t) & \text{if } c \equiv \phi \\ op(\mathcal{E}(c_1,t),\cdot\cdot,\mathcal{E}(c_n,t)) & \text{if } c \equiv op(c_1,\cdot\cdot,c_n) \text{ and } \forall i : \mathcal{E}(c_i,t) \neq \perp \\ \mathcal{E}(c_0, \max(\mathcal{T}(c) \triangleright t)) & \text{if } c \equiv c_0 @ c_1 \text{ and } \mathcal{T}(c) \triangleright t \neq \emptyset \\ \mathcal{E}(c_0, \mathrm{prev}(\mathcal{T}(c_1) \triangleright t)) & \text{if } c \equiv \mathbf{latch}(c_0, c_1) \text{ and } |\mathcal{T}(c_1) \triangleright t| \geq 2 \\ & \text{and } \mathcal{T}(c_0) \triangleright \mathrm{prev}(\mathcal{T}(c_1) \triangleright t) \neq \emptyset \\ \mathcal{E}(c_1,t) & \text{if } c \equiv \mathbf{latch}(c_0, c_1) \text{ and } |\mathcal{T}(c_1) \triangleright t| \geq 2 \\ & \text{and } \mathcal{T}(c_0) \triangleright \mathrm{prev}(\mathcal{T}(c_1) \triangleright t) = \emptyset \\ \mathcal{E}(c_1,t) & \text{if } c \equiv \mathbf{latch}(c_0, c_1) \text{ and } |\mathcal{T}(c_1) \triangleright t| = 1 \\ \perp & \text{otherwise} \end{cases}$$

The semantics of operators lifts an operator from values to feeds by simply invoking the operator on the most recent value of each feed.

The formula $c_0 @ c_1$ samples the value of c_0 when it ticks. For instance, if $a \equiv nat$ and $b \equiv isEven(a)$ and $c = a @ b$ where nat is a server feed producing the natural integers and $isEven$ a unary operator with the obvious semantics, then c only produces even integers. The arrival time of each integer in c is the same as the arrival time of the same integer in nat.

The formula $\mathbf{latch}(c_0, c_1)$ provides for each tick of c_1 the value of c_0 recorded at the previous tick of c_1. But it defaults to the value of c_1 instead, if either this is the first tick of c_1 or c_0 was not yet defined when c_1 last ticked.

The **latch** construct serves a double purpose: it makes stateful clients possible and it enables clients to reason about windows of data. For an example of a stateful computation, suppose $zero$ is the unary constant operator with value 0, add is the binary addition, and 1 is a sever feed with tick $\{0\}$ and value 1. The cell d in client $\{a \equiv feed, b \equiv zero(a), c \equiv 1, d \equiv add(c,e), e \equiv \mathbf{latch}(d,b)\}$ counts the number of ticks in the server feed $feed$. Observe that b hence e and d tick exactly when $feed$ does. Moreover, the initial value of d is 1 and each subsequent value of d is obtained by incrementing the previous value of d by one. For a window example, suppose neq is a binary inequality test operator. The cell c in client $\{a \equiv feed, b \equiv \mathbf{latch}(a,a), c \equiv neq(a,b)\}$ ticks when the server feed $feed$ does and evaluates to $true$ iff the current value of $feed$ is different from the previous value. In general, windows into feed histories can be obtained by chaining latches, e.g., $\{a \equiv feed, b \equiv \mathbf{latch}(a,a), c \equiv \mathbf{latch}(b,b), d \equiv \mathbf{latch}(c,c)\}$. Cell a provides the current value of $feed$, b the previous value, c the value before that, etc.

Observe that in the stateful example, the **latch** is used to form a cycle of cells, whereas in the window examples, there is no such cycle. In the latter, the two arguments to **latch** can be the same. But well-formedness forbids cyclic uses of **latch** (via its second argument) as in the ill-formed client $\{a \equiv \mathbf{latch}(a,a)\}$.

We now prove that the recursive definition of $\mathcal{T}$ and $\mathcal{E}$ is well-founded for well-formed clients. In the sequel, we require all clients to be well-formed.

Lemma 1 (Soundness). *For a cell c of a well-formed client C and a time t, the value $\mathcal{E}(c,t)$ of c at time t and the tick $\mathcal{T}(c) \triangleright t$ of c up to time t are defined via a well-founded recursion.*

Proof. Let depth(c) be the length of the longest path in $\mathcal{G}$ with source c. For a cell $c \in C$ and time $t \in [0, \infty)$ we define $\sigma(c, t) \in N \times \mathbb{N}$ as $(\max(N \triangleright t), \text{depth}(c))$. The lexicographic order $\leq$ of $N \times \mathbb{N}$ is well-founded, since C is well-formed.

We can rewrite the definition of $\mathcal{T}(c)$ as a definition of $\mathcal{T}(c) \triangleright t$ so that every tick instance of the right-hand side is only needed up to time t. In the definition of $\mathcal{E}(c_0 @ c_1, t)$, we can expand $\mathcal{T}(c) \triangleright t$ into its definition. We now establish that the recursive co-definition of $\mathcal{T}(c) \triangleright t$ and $\mathcal{E}(c, t)$ is well-founded using $(\sigma, \leq)$ to order the tuples $(c, t) \in C \times [0, \infty)$.

In all induction cases except for the definition of $\mathcal{E}(\mathbf{latch}(c_0, c_1), t)$, the terms of the right-hand side are only concerned with time up to t and cells of strictly lower depth. Moreover, the tick up to t and value at t of the cell c with formula $c \equiv \mathbf{latch}(c_0, c_1)$ are defined using $\mathcal{T}(c_1) \triangleright t$ and $\mathcal{E}(c_1, t)$ (same time, strictly lower depth) and possibly $\mathcal{T}(c_0) \triangleright t_0$ and $\mathcal{E}(c_0, t_0)$ with $t_0 = \text{prev}(\mathcal{T}(c_1) \triangleright t)$ such that $\max(N \triangleright t_0) < \max(N \triangleright t)$. □

Our calculus is therefore *deterministic*: the tick and values of a cell of a well-formed client are unambiguously defined at all times. Our calculus is also *reactive* in the sense that everything happens in *reaction* to the ticks of the server feeds.

Lemma 2 (Reactivity). *The tick of a cell c of a well-formed client C is a subset of the server tick N. The value of c at a time t is equal to the value of c at the most recent arrival time of c if any or undefined if none.*

Proof. The tick of $c_0 @ c_1$ is a subset of $\mathcal{T}(c_1)$. The tick of $op(c_1, \cdots, c_n)$ is a subset of $\bigcup_{i=1}^{n} \mathcal{T}(c_i)$. By induction over the depth of the cell. □

3.2 Boundedness

Because of **latch**, the values of the cell at time t are defined using past values of cells and feeds. But a careful look at the definitions shows that the dependency on past values is bounded. Concretely, $c \equiv \mathbf{latch}(c_0, c_1)$ only needs to retain one value of c_0 at a time (in addition to the current value of c). Formally, for all $c \in C$ and $t \in N$ we define:

$$\mathcal{H}(c, t) = \begin{cases} \mathcal{E}(c_0, \max(\mathcal{T}(c_1) \triangleright t)) & \text{if } c \equiv \mathbf{latch}(c_0, c_1) \text{ and } |\mathcal{T}(c_1) \triangleright t| > 0 \\ \bot & \text{otherwise} \end{cases}$$

Lemma 3 (Boundedness). *For all $(t_0, t) \in N$, the values of $\mathcal{H}$ and $\mathcal{E}$ at time t for each $c \in C$ can be computed as a function of $\mathcal{H}$ and $\mathcal{E}$ at time t_0 and the ticks and values of the server feeds at time t.*

Proof. We observe that we can rewrite the semantics of the core calculus as follows.

$$t \in \mathcal{T}(c) \Leftrightarrow \begin{cases} t \in \text{dom}(\phi) & \text{if } c \equiv \phi \\ (\exists i : t \in \mathcal{T}(c_i)) \wedge (\forall i : \mathcal{E}(c_i, t) \neq \bot) & \text{if } c \equiv op(c_1, \cdots, c_n) \\ t \in \mathcal{T}(c_1) \wedge \mathcal{E}(c_1, t) = true \wedge \mathcal{E}(c_0, t) \neq \bot & \text{if } c \equiv c_0 @ c_1 \\ t \in \mathcal{T}(c_1) & \text{if } c \equiv \mathbf{latch}(c_0, c_1) \end{cases}$$

If $t \notin \mathcal{T}(c)$ then $\mathcal{H}(c,t) = \mathcal{H}(c,t_0)$ and $\mathcal{E}(c,t) = \mathcal{E}(c,t_0)$ by Lemma 2. Otherwise, $\mathcal{H}(c,t) = \mathcal{E}(c_0,t)$ if $c \equiv \mathbf{latch}(c_0,c_1)$ or $\perp$ if not, and

$$
\mathcal{E}(c,t) = \begin{cases}
\phi(t) & \text{if } c \equiv \phi \\
op(\mathcal{E}(c_1,t), \cdots, \mathcal{E}(c_n,t)) & \text{if } c \equiv op(c_1, \cdots, c_n) \text{ and } \forall i : \mathcal{E}(c_i,t) \neq \perp \\
\mathcal{E}(c_0,t) & \text{if } c \equiv c_0@c_1 \\
\mathcal{H}(c,t_0) & \text{if } c \equiv \mathbf{latch}(c_0,c_1) \text{ and } \mathcal{H}(c,t_0) \neq \perp \\
\mathcal{E}(c_1,t) & \text{if } c \equiv \mathbf{latch}(c_0,c_1) \text{ and } \mathcal{H}(c,t_0) = \perp \\
\perp & \text{otherwise}
\end{cases}
$$

By induction using the well-foundedness argument of Lemma 1, the two semantics define the same tick and values for all cells at all times. $\qquad\square$

In summary, storing one value for each occurrence of **latch** enables the incremental computation of these semantics over time. In particular, the memory required is bounded by the client size. Moreover, the amount of computation per tick is also bounded by the client size (assuming unit cost for the operators op).

3.3 Live Calculus

We now define the semantics of live clients where we permit formulas to evolve over time. We suppose that each cell $c \in C$ has a *feed of formulas* $\hat{c}$ with tick $\mathrm{dom}(\hat{c})$ and formula $\hat{c}(t)$ at time t. While we do not model cell creation or deletion explicitly we permit cells to be initially empty. The formula feeds model external changes to formulas (e.g., user input). We do not consider "higher-order" spreadsheets where formulas could be computed by the spreadsheet itself.

We define the *immediate dependencies of cell c at time t* as follows.

$$
\mathrm{deps}(c,t) = \begin{cases}
\emptyset & \text{if } \hat{c}(t) = \phi \\
\{c_1, \cdots, c_n\} & \text{if } \hat{c}(t) = op(c_1, \cdots, c_n) \\
\{c_0, c_1\} & \text{if } \hat{c}(t) = c_0@c_1 \\
\{c_1\} & \text{if } \hat{c}(t) = \mathbf{latch}(c_0,c_1)
\end{cases}
$$

We say a client is well-formed iff the graph of immediate cell dependencies is acyclic at all times. We define the tick of cell c, $\mathcal{T}(c)$, by concatenating the ticks of its successive formulas over time. We first define the *tick of a cell c around time t* as follows.

$$
\mathcal{T}[t](c) = \begin{cases}
\mathrm{dom}(\phi) & \text{if } \hat{c}(t) = \phi \\
\{t \in \bigcup_{i=1}^n \mathcal{T}(c_i) | \forall i \in \{1, \cdots, n\} : \mathcal{T}(c_i) \triangleright t \neq \emptyset\} & \text{if } \hat{c}(t) = op(c_1, \cdots, c_n) \\
\{t \in \mathcal{T}(c_1) | \mathcal{E}(c_1,t) = true, \mathcal{T}(c_0) \triangleright t \neq \emptyset\} & \text{if } \hat{c}(t) = c_0@c_1 \\
\mathcal{T}(c_1) & \text{if } \hat{c}(t) = \mathbf{latch}(c_0,c_1)
\end{cases}
$$

$$
\mathcal{T}(c) = \mathrm{dom}(\hat{c}) \cup \left(\bigcup_{(t_0,t_1) \in \mathrm{dom}(\hat{c})} \mathcal{T}[t_0](c) \cap [t_0,t_1) \right) \cup \left(\bigcup_{t=\max(\mathrm{dom}(\hat{c}))} \mathcal{T}[t](c) \cap [t,\infty) \right)
$$

By convention, a cell also ticks when its formula feed does. The last term in this union handles the case of a finite formula feed.

We define the value of cell c at time t using the current formula $\hat{c}(t)$ as in the core calculus except for the **latch** construct. Let $t_0 = \max(\mathrm{dom}(\hat{c}) \triangleright t)$ be the most recent arrival of the formula feed $\hat{c}$ if defined. If $\hat{c}(t) = \mathbf{latch}(c_0, c_1)$ then

$$
\mathcal{E}(c,t) = \begin{cases}
\mathcal{E}(c_0, \mathrm{prev}(\mathcal{T}(c) \triangleright t)) & \text{if } \mathcal{T}(c) \triangleright t > t_0 \text{ and } \mathcal{T}(c_0) \triangleright \mathrm{prev}(\mathcal{T}(c) \triangleright t) \neq \emptyset \\
\mathcal{E}(c_1, t) & \text{if } \mathcal{T}(c) \triangleright t > t_0 \text{ and } \mathcal{T}(c_0) \triangleright \mathrm{prev}(\mathcal{T}(c) \triangleright t) = \emptyset \\
\mathcal{E}(c_1, t) & \text{if } \mathcal{T}(c) \triangleright t = t_0 \\
\bot & \text{otherwise}
\end{cases}
$$

Intuitively, a **latch** does not access values that predate the formula that contains the **latch**. This ensures that these semantics are still incrementally computable without the need for an "oracle" to predict future **latch** occurrences.

3.4 Stream Calculus

Our core calculus from Section 3.1 is not intended as an actual programming interface for the end-user. This section introduces a stream calculus that enriches the core calculus with higher-level notions of streams and formulas. A stream is a sequence of tuples with named attributes. The stream calculus permits nesting constructs in formulas, handles constant values, and formalizes PRE.

To simplify the presentation, we return to the fixed formulas of the core calculus, but the techniques for live editing in Section 3.3 remain applicable.

Streams. We say that two feeds are *synchronous* if they have the same tick. We define a *stream* s to be a non-empty, finite collection of synchronous feeds. The feeds in a stream are labeled with *attributes*. Given a stream s, we write $s.a$ to denote the feed of s labeled a. We write $\mathcal{A}(s)$ for the set of attributes of s.

Semantics. We now define a calculus over streams by reduction to the core calculus of Section 3.1. The syntax of formulas is as follows, where v stands for a constant value:

$$f ::= v \mid s.a \mid c \mid op(f_1, \cdots, f_n) \mid f_0 @ f_1 \mid \mathbf{latch}(f_0, f_1) \mid \mathsf{PRE}(f_0, f_1, v) \mid \mathsf{PRE}(f, v)$$

Constructs can be nested. Formulas v and $s.a$ are server feeds ϕ. Formula v denotes a feed with value v and tick $\{0\}$. Formula $\mathsf{PRE}(f_0, f_1, v)$ is a syntactic shortcut for $\mathbf{latch}(f_0, \mathit{first}(v, f_1))$ where the *first* operator maps (x, y) to x. Therefore, $\mathit{first}(v, f_1)$ produces a constant feed of values v with tick $\mathcal{T}(f_1)$. Formula $\mathsf{PRE}(f, v)$ is a shorthand for $\mathsf{PRE}(c, c, v)$ where c is a fresh cell with formula f. The binary form of PRE is the most intuitive one: $\mathsf{PRE}(f, v)$ ticks when f does, evaluates to v initially then to the previous value of f. This form cannot express cyclic computations such as accumulators. The tick of cell c in client $\{c = add(\mathsf{PRE}(c, 0), 1)\}$ cannot be defined by recursion.[2] The ternary form of

---

[2] Least-fixed-point approaches would not work either as our calculus supports substraction by means of the @ construct.

PRE therefore permits the independent specification of the formula f_0 to latch, the tick f_1 of the latch, and the initial value v of the latch. It is less expressive than the core **latch** construct—it restricts its second argument to a constant feed—but easier for the user to reason about.

Let C be a client in the stream calculus. We define the semantics of C by constructing a client C' in the core calculus. In particular, we specify that C is well-formed iff C' is. The semantics of a cell c in C is specified as the semantics of the cell c in C', that is, the cell with the same name in the reduced client.

Intuitively, the reduced client is simply defined by introducing helper cells for every subformula and replacing subformulas with references to these helper cells. Concretely, we specify by induction over the structure of formulas, a reduction $\mathcal{R}$ that maps a cell c with formula f in the stream calculus to a fragment of a client in the core calculus, that is, one or more cells with their respective formulas in the core calculus. All cells but c itself in each map are *fresh*, i.e., have a globally unique name.

The reduced client C' of C is then simply the union of these fragments for each cell c in C.

$$\mathcal{R}(c, f) = \begin{cases} \{c \equiv f\} & \text{if } f \in \{v, s.a, c_0\} \\ \{c \equiv op(c_1, \cdots, c_n)\} \cup \bigcup_{i=1}^{n} \mathcal{R}(c_i, f_i) & \text{if } f = op(f_1, \cdots, f_n) \\ \{c \equiv c_0@c_1\} \cup \mathcal{R}(c_0, f_0) \cup \mathcal{R}(c_1, f_1) & \text{if } f = f_0@f_1 \\ \{c \equiv \mathbf{latch}(c_0, c_1)\} \cup \mathcal{R}(c_0, f_0) \cup \mathcal{R}(c_1, f_1) & \text{if } f = \mathbf{latch}(f_0, f_1) \\ \{c \equiv c_0\} \cup \mathcal{R}(c_0, \mathbf{latch}(f_0, \mathit{first}(v, f_1))) & \text{if } f = \mathsf{PRE}(f_0, f_1, v) \\ \{c \equiv c_0\} \cup \mathcal{R}(c_0, \mathsf{PRE}(c_1, c_1, v)) \cup \mathcal{R}(c_1, f) & \text{if } f = \mathsf{PRE}(f, v) \end{cases}$$

3.5 Query Language

The stream calculus assumes a programming model where the user modifies one cell at a time, defining one value feed at a time. In contrast, ACTIVESHEETS' query language allows the user to enter formulas in a range of cells at once by defining a stream with multiple attributes and a window over this stream history, all in a single step. Moreover, this query language provides higher-level mechanisms to process streams inspired from relational operators—emphasizing relations and deemphasizing arrival times.

In this section, we specify a basic query language over streams, and show how it reduces to the stream calculus. It consists of projection and selection operators. Our implemented query language supports other traditional relational operators such as sort, pivot, aggregate, and deduplicate. Excel has native features that support static version of some of these constructs (sort, pivot), and our query language complements these features with streaming ones.

The query language is tightly integrated with the UI. In particular, the number of rows in the target range of a query defines the length of the stream history to preserve. We do not model this coupling here.

Queries. The syntax of queries is defined as follows where q denotes a query, s a stream, a an attribute, and f a formula in the stream calculus.

$$q_s ::= s'$$
$$| \; \mathsf{PROJECT}(q_s, a_1 = f_1, \cdots, a_n = f_n)$$
$$| \; \mathsf{SELECT}(q_s, f)$$

A query q_s defines a new *client stream* named s. We require that the names of the streams (client and server) are pairwise distinct. The $\mathsf{PROJECT}$ construct defines a new stream with attributes a_1 through a_n, with formulas f_1 through f_n, respectively. In essence, the $\mathsf{PROJECT}$ construct allows the user to synchronize a collection of feeds to produce a stream: the values of f_1 through f_n are sampled according to the tick of the first parameter of $\mathsf{PROJECT}$, and assigned to the attributes of the resulting stream. The SELECT construct defines a new stream with all the attributes of its first parameter, but with tuples that have been filtered according to the Boolean formula f.

Semantics. A client (C, Q) in the query language combines a client C in the stream calculus—a finite collection of cells and formulas—and a finite collection of queries Q. We denote by W (Y) the set of all the client streams (server streams, respectively).

The attributes $\mathcal{A}(s)$ of s in W are defined as follows:

$$\mathcal{A}(s) = \begin{cases} \mathcal{A}(s') & \text{if } q_s = s' \text{ or } q_s = \mathsf{SELECT}(q'_{s'}, f) \\ \{a_1, \cdots, a_n\} & \text{if } q_s = \mathsf{PROJECT}(q'_{s'}, a_1 = f_1, \cdots, a_n = f_n) \end{cases}$$

We map each attribute a of each client stream s to a fresh cell in C' denoted c_s^a. We define by induction on the structure of queries a reduction from a query q_s to a collection of cells $\mathcal{C}(s)$ in the stream calculus as follows.

$$\mathcal{C}(s) = \begin{cases} \bigcup_{a \in \mathcal{A}(s)} \{c_s^a \equiv s'.a\} & \text{if } q_s = s' \text{ and } s' \in Y \\ \bigcup_{a \in \mathcal{A}(s)} \{c_s^a \equiv c_{s'}^a\} & \text{if } q_s = s' \text{ and } s' \in W \\ \mathcal{C}(s') \cup \bigcup_{i=1}^{n} \{c_s^{a_i} \equiv nth(i, f_1, \cdots, f_n)@true(c_{s'}^{a'})\} & \\ \quad \text{if } q_s = \mathsf{PROJECT}(q'_{s'}, a_1 = f_1, \cdots, a_n = f_n) \text{ and } a' \in \mathcal{A}(s') & \\ \mathcal{C}(s') \cup \bigcup_{a \in \mathcal{A}(s)} \{c_s^a \equiv c_{s'}^a@(f@true(c_{s'}^a))\} & \text{if } q_s = \mathsf{SELECT}(q'_{s'}, f) \end{cases}$$

For the $\mathsf{PROJECT}$ construct, we resample each f_i using the tick of $q'_{s'}$, which we can obtain by applying the constant unary *true* operator to one of its attributes a'. But we need to make sure that all f_i are defined before we emit a value for any attribute. We therefore combine all the f_i together using operator $nth : (i, a_1, \cdots, a_n) \mapsto a_i$. Like any operator lifted to feeds, it only starts ticking once all arguments are defined.

For the SELECT construct, we first sample the Boolean condition f according to the tick of the target stream s' using the rightmost @ construct, then apply the resulting filter to the stream s' using a second @ construct. This ensures that the output stream is synchronous with the input stream.

The reduced client C' is obtained as $C \cup \bigcup_{s \in W} \mathcal{C}(s)$. We specify that (C, Q) is well formed iff C' is.

4 Implementation

ACTIVESHEETS is implemented as a client-server architecture. The client is a thin layer that implements minimal functionality by design so that it may be easily repurposed for integration with multiple spreadsheet front-ends. In the current implementation, the client is integrated with Microsoft Excel. It interacts with the server via a RESTful interface [12] that provides an API to discover available streams, subscribe to streams and create feeds, as well as to export data and computation. Fig. 8 sketches the overall system architecture.

4.1 Client Side

The client consists of two components. The first is the client proxy. It encapsulates front-end independent functionality including a session manager and a real-time data service that continuously updates the cells in the spreadsheet when ticks advance. The second is the front-end user interface and integration with the spreadsheet application (e.g., Microsoft Excel). The client UI and some of its features were described earlier in Section 2.

In our current implementation, the client proxy is written in C# and the UI front-end consists of a collection of Visual Basic macros. The client proxy implements the Real-Time Data Server interface (IRtdServer) to communicate with Excel. It makes it possible for the client proxy to notify Excel that new data is available and for Excel to asynchronously pull the data from the client proxy. The client proxy therefore acts as a buffer between the ACTIVESHEETS server and Excel. The client proxy runs as a dynamic-link library (DLL) plugin inside Excel.

4.2 Server Side

The server side consists of the server proxy and a stream processing engine. The former implements the primary functionality while the latter is used to deploy generated stream processors when the client exports computation to the server. The server side proxy is comprised of a (1) name manager, (2) query processor, and (3) spreadsheet compiler.

The name manager maintains a directory of client connections and dispatches client requests to dedicated handlers. When a query is received that subscribes a client to a particular stream, the name manager allocates a dedicated handler to service the request. The handler persists as long as the client connection is maintained. The current implementation is written in Java and based on Akka, an actor-based system for highly concurrent and event-driven applications [1]. It is conceptually a message-driven runtime, where actors execute when messages are received, producing new messages that are consumed by subsequent actors or pushed to the client. Actors in ACTIVESHEETS input tuples from existing streams, parse and reformat the tuples if necessary, and output the resulting tuples as new messages that are dispatched to registered listeners (e.g., clients). Data that is exported from the spreadsheet is handled by the name manager.

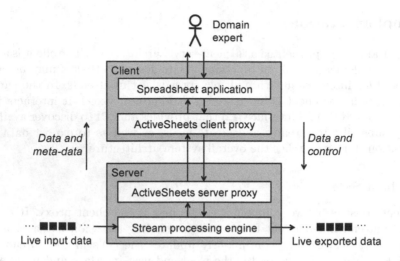

Fig. 8. ACTIVESHEETS System Architectures

The query processor is an actor that applies a given set of transformations to a sequence of input tuples. The query is received from the client as a string, parsed on the server, and interpreted accordingly. All of the query operators described in Section 3.5 are supported. The operators are applied sequentially in the order implied by the programmer, although we believe the order of application is amenable to optimizations since some operators are commutative and may reduce the amount of computation applied to any given tuple.

The spreadsheet compiler is responsible for handling exported computation. It parses the spreadsheets and builds a dependence graph between the cells, which in turn is used to derive a computational circuit for the spreadsheet. Terminal cells which have no incoming edges or outgoing edges in the dependence graph are input and output signals, respectively. Internal cells contain formulas that correspond to gates in the circuit, with input wires flowing from and output wires flowing to other cells as in the dependence graph. One circuit is created for each exported spreadsheet, and it is encapsulated within a single actor that will update the output signals as new ticks arrive. Output signals are visible to other users as new streams. The computation on the server persists even if the spreadsheet is no longer running.

5   Case Studies

The goal of this section is to convey a feeling for what kind of streaming computations are natural to implement in a spreadsheet. The examples are drawn from a variety of domains (commerce, transportation, infrastructure, and security), and illustrate how the features of ACTIVESHEETS play out in practice. Fig. 9 shows an Excel spreadsheet for the examples.

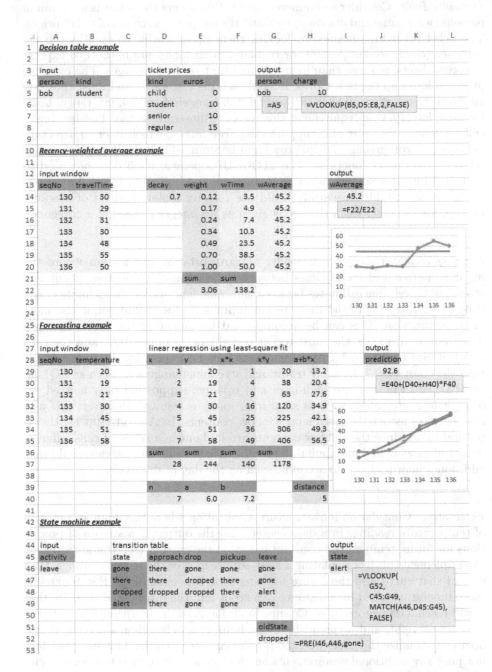

Fig. 9. Case studies. Yellow background indicates live streaming data, blue background indicates constants, and green rectangles show formulas.

Decision Table. Consider a commerce application where the input is a stream of persons (with name and age category), and the output is a stream of ticket prices. The ticket prices are obtained by looking them up in a table indexed by the age category (child, student, senior, or regular). Such tables are natural to express in spreadsheets, more so than in traditional text-based languages. The example in Fig. 9 looks up the ticket price for Bob, who is a student, and must thus pay 10 Euro. Excel offers VLOOKUP(key: ref, tab: rangeRef, valCol: int, range: bool) for table lookup. One requirement this use case illustrates is that besides single-cell references, we must also support range-references, which refer to a rectangular region comprising multiple rows and columns. The calculus models range references via n-ary functions. The VLOOKUP operator itself does not need to be baked into the calculus, since it is stateless and built into Excel. Variations on the decision-table case study could use relative lookup instead of absolute lookup, for instance, when the age is given as an integer instead of a category.

Recency-Weighted Average. Consider a transportation application where the input is a stream of travel times between two landmarks, and the output is a stream of travel time estimates between the same landmarks. To estimate travel time in current traffic, the most recent input samples should count the most in the estimation. This can be accomplished by weighting the window with a decay curve. In Fig. 9, the most recent travel time is in cell B20, and the cells above it use PRE to get earlier readings. Cell D14 specifies the decay factor with the constant 0.7. In many traditional streaming languages, such as CQL [4] or SPL [15], windows are high-level and opaque, supporting only a fixed set of built-in aggregations such as sum, min, max, or average. However, this use-case requires associative access on window contents. In ACTIVESHEETS, this is natural to do, since the window contents are laid out in a range of cells, offering users full viewing and manipulation power. Variations of this use case could take additional information into account, such as the day of the week.

Forecasting. Consider an infrastructure application where the input is a stream of temperature readings in a data center, and the output is a stream of predictions for future temperature readings based on the current trend. A spreadsheet can implement this by calculating a least-square fit over the recent readings, then extend that curve into the future for forecasts. The example in Fig. 9 extends the temperature trend by a distance of 5 steps into the future, and predicts that it will reach a dangerous 92.6° Celsius. Such forecasting algorithms are not that easy to get right, and a spreadsheet can help with debugging, since the developer can visualize the curve and the prediction interactively. This use case does not pose any additional requirements on the calculus; it suffices to offer associative history access as is the case with recency-weighted average. As a variation, instead of predicting the temperature at a fixed distance in the future, the application could predict how long it would take to reach a fixed threshold value (say, 100° Celsius). This could be used for an evacuation count-down.

State Machine. Consider a security application where the input is a stream of activities at a business location, and the output is a stream of suspicious events that ought to be checked out by authorities. An example of a suspicious event would be when a person enters the business location, drops an object and then leaves the premises without taking back the object. This is easy to specify via a deterministic finite automaton (DFA). A spreadsheet can implement a DFA via a transition table indexed by the previous state and the current activity, to yield the next state and an output. Just like a decision table, a DFA transition table can be naturally represented by a block of cells in a spreadsheet. As cell I46 in Fig. 9 illustrates, the lookup in this case is two-dimensional, using VLOOKUP in combination with MATCH. As far as the calculus is concerned, this use case combines the requirement for a decision table with the requirement for history access. But in contrast to windows, which use PRE on input streams only, here, the old state in cell G52 comes from using PRE on the current state in cell I46, which is itself computed. Besides this security application, state machines are also useful in other stream processing domains, such as for detecting M-shape patterns in streams of stock quotes [14].

6   Related Work

This paper covers topics at the intersection of spreadsheet programming and stream processing.

Spreadsheets as a programming platform. The idea to use spreadsheets for coding is not new. In Haxcel, each cell can hold a Haskell definition [16]. Similarly, Wakeling also proposes a Haskell-based spreadsheet [22]. As in our approach, this is motivated by wanting to offer an interactive programming experience, where changes to code have immediate visible effects. Unlike our approach, these approaches assume that the programmer already knows Haskell, and these approaches do not attempt to tackle stream processing.

Woo et al. use spreadsheets as a tool for data analysis over sensor networks [23]. This work comes closer to streaming, since sensors continuously produce data. But the work is custom-tailored for the sensor domain, whereas we address stream processing more generally. Sestoft compiles spreadsheets to a functional implementation [20]. Like our work, this means exporting computation from a spreadsheet. Serafima augments spreadsheets to work with trees, motivated by processing XML data [19]. Neither Sestoft nor Serafima tackle using spreadsheets for stream processing.

McGarry augments spreadsheets with streaming data import and windows, but offers no feature to export data or code [17]. The StreamBase platform offers adapters that import and export data to Excel spreadsheets [21]. Like our work, this addresses programming with spreadsheets for stream processing. Unlike our work, the StreamBase Excel adapters export no code from the spreadsheet. Cloudscale uses Excel spreadsheets to configure streaming analytics [10]. Unlike our work, the user does not describe the analytics directly using the built-in computation features of Excel.

Programming models for streaming. Diverse programming models have been proposed to make it easier to write streaming applications. The programming languages community has developed several dedicated streaming languages, including LUSTRE for programming real-time controllers [8], StreamIt for programming many-cores [13], Lime for programming FPGAs [5], and SPL for programming distributed clusters [15]. These language-centric approaches enable advanced compiler optimizations, but require programmers to learn a new language.

Instead of requiring programmers to learn a new language, another approach is to build a library in an existing language. Spark Streaming, which is based on Scala, is an example for this [25]. However, Scala requires more sophistication, and has a smaller user base, than spreadsheets.

A popular approach for making programming of streaming applications more high-level is to offer not a full-fledged language, but simple patterns. Examples for this include SASE [24], Cayuga [11], and MatchRegex [14]. The patterns match over sequences of events to detect situations worthy of reporting. But while these might be easier to learn than a full language, they still come with a learning curve hindering wide-spread adoption.

The databases community tackles programming models for streaming by observing that many users are already familiar with SQL. Hence, approaches like CQL [4] or the language for Microsoft StreamInsight [2] use SQL as a starting point, and then add extensions such as windowing constructs for streaming. But for non-programmer end-users, spreadsheets are still more familiar than SQL.

At the far end of the spectrum, Mario requires no programming at all [7]. Instead, the user merely enters tags as they might in a web search engine. The system then guesses what might be the right stream program based on these tags. Like spreadsheets, this is immediately usable by end-users. Unlike spreadsheets, it offers far less control over what streaming application comes out in the end.

The formalization of our core calculus—choice of constructs, semantics, and properties—has a lot in common with synchronous programming languages [6]. It adopts the *synchrony hypothesis*: outputs are produced instantly so that inputs and outputs are formally synchronous. It has ticks but not clocks: arrival times are not required to be periodic or regular. It is asynchronous in that its constructs can compose arbitrary feeds irrespective of their relative arrival times. Feeds are implicitly sampled (i.e., re-clocked) when not in sync. As a consequence, we have no need for a clock calculus to ensure proper pairing and boundedness. While the calculus permits cyclic definitions, it guarantees causality. We choose to ensure causality by preventing timing cycles and making sure every value cycle includes a delay (a latch). While some synchronous programming languages such as ESTEREL favor more sophisticated causality analyses [18], we do not think these would be sensible extensions to the execution strategy of a typical spreadsheet. Because filtering is such an essential feature of our system, we choose to break timing cycles by explicitly clocking latches—separating the input tick from the input value—rather than introducing a delay in the @ construct, akin to delaying the reaction to absence in reactive programming models [3].

Our live calculus is not as expressive as higher-order synchronous models [9] but preserves the guarantees (bounded time and memory usage) of the core calculus in the presence of dynamically changing formulas.

7 Conclusion

This paper presents ACTIVESHEETS, a system for visualizing and programming live streams in a spreadsheet. Stream processing has gained importance as many businesses have continuous data feeds, and analyzing these on-the-fly helps find opportunities and avoid risks. Using a spreadsheet makes streaming accessible to the end-user. Furthermore, a spreadsheet offers a very hands-on experience, since the data is manipulated directly where the user can see it, and interactive code changes have immediate visible effects. We formalize the semantics of ACTIVESHEETS, and describe an implementation of ACTIVESHEETS that uses Microsoft Excel as the client front-end. When the user programs a streaming application using ACTIVESHEETS, he or she can elect to export either data or computation. Exported *data* can be further processed by the server, or can be used to initiate actions, such as alerts or sales. Exported *computation* can run directly on the server, and live on even when the client is closed. Since exported computation runs on the server, it saves the cost of communicating with the client; furthermore, it can be optimized and compiled to machine code. Overall, ACTIVESHEETS enables end-users to author powerful and efficient streaming applications using familiar spreadsheet features.

Acknowledgements. We thank James Giles, Louis Mandel, and anonymous reviewers for their feedback and suggestions.

References

1. The Akka project, http://akka.io (retrieved November 2013)
2. Ali, M., Chandramouli, B., Goldstein, J., Schindlauer, R.: The extensibility framework in Microsoft StreamInsight. In: International Conference on Data Engineering (ICDE), pp. 1242–1253 (2011)
3. Amadio, R.M., Boudol, G., Castellani, I., Boussinot, F.: Reactive concurrent programming revisited. CoRR abs/cs/0512058 (2005)
4. Arasu, A., Babu, S., Widom, J.: The CQL continuous query language: semantic foundations and query execution. Journal on Very Large Data Bases (VLDB J.) 15(2), 121–142 (2006)
5. Auerbach, J., Bacon, D.F., Cheng, P., Rabbah, R.: Lime: a Java-compatible and synthesizable language for heterogeneous architectures. In: Object-Oriented Programming, Systems, Languages, and Applications (OOPSLA), pp. 89–108 (2010)
6. Benveniste, A., Caspi, P., Edwards, S.A., Halbwachs, N., Guernic, P.L., de Simone, R.: The synchronous languages 12 years later. Proceedings of the IEEE 91(1), 64–83 (2003)

7. Bouillet, E., Feblowitz, M., Liu, Z., Ranganathan, A., Riabov, A.: A tag-based approach for the design and composition of information processing applications. In: Onward! Track of Object-Oriented Programming, Systems, Languages, and Applications (Onward!), pp. 585–602 (2008)
8. Caspi, P., Pilaud, D., Halbwachs, N., Raymond, P.: Lustre: a declarative language for real-time programming. In: Symposium on Principles of Programming Languages (POPL), pp. 178–188 (1987)
9. Caspi, P., Pouzet, M.: Synchronous Kahn networks. In: International Conference on Functional Programming (ICFP), pp. 226–238 (1996)
10. Cloudscale big data analytics, http://www.hashdoc.com/document/8626/big-data-analytics (retrieved November 2013)
11. Demers, A., Gehrke, J., Panda, B., Riedewald, M., Sharma, V., White, W.: Cayuga: A general purpose event monitoring system. In: Conference on Innovative Data Systems Research (CIDR), pp. 412–422 (2007)
12. Fielding, R.T., Taylor, R.N.: Principled design of the modern web architecture. ACM Trans. Internet Technol. 2(2), 115–150 (2002)
13. Gordon, M.I., Thies, W., Amarasinghe, S.: Exploiting coarse-grained task, data, and pipeline parallelism in stream programs. In: Architectural Support for Programming Languages and Operating Systems (ASPLOS), pp. 151–162 (2006)
14. Hirzel, M.: Partition and compose: Parallel complex event processing. In: Conference on Distributed Event-Based Systems (DEBS), pp. 191–200 (2012)
15. Hirzel, M., Andrade, H., Gedik, B., Jacques-Silva, G., Khandekar, R., Kumar, V., Mendell, M., Nasgaard, H., Schneider, S., Soulé, R., Wu, K.L.: IBM Streams Processing Language: Analyzing big data in motion. IBM Journal of Research & Development 57(3/4), 7:1–7:11 (2013)
16. Lisper, B., Malström, J.: Haxcel: A spreadsheet interface to Haskell. In: Workshop on the Implementation of Functional Languages (IFL), pp. 206–222 (2002)
17. McGarry, J.: Processing continuous data streams in electronic spreadsheets. Patent No. US 6,490,600 B1 (2002)
18. Potop-Butucaru, D., Edwards, S.A., Berry, G.: Compiling Esterel, 1st edn. Springer Publishing Company, Incorporated (2007)
19. Serafimova, I.: Spreadsheet-based template language prototype for tree data structure description and interpretation. In: International Conference on Computer Systems and Technologies (CompSysTech), pp. 148–154 (2012)
20. Sestoft, P.: Implementing function spreadsheets. In: Workshop on End-User Software Engineering (WEUSE), pp. 91–94 (2008)
21. StreamBase Microsoft Excel adapter, http://docs.streambase.com/sb66/index.jsp?topic=/com.streambase.sb.ide.help/data/html/samplesinfo/Excel_sample.html (retrieved November 2013)
22. Wakeling, D.: Spreadsheet functional programming. Journal of Functional Programming (JFP) 17(1), 131–143 (2007)
23. Woo, A., Seth, S., Olson, T., Liu, J., Zhao, F.: A spreadsheet approach to programming and managing sensor networks. In: Conference on Information Processing in Sensor Networks (IPSN), pp. 424–431 (2006)
24. Wu, E., Diao, Y., Rizvi, S.: High-performance complex event processing over streams. In: International Conference on Management of Data (SIGMOD), pp. 407–418 (2006)
25. Zaharia, M., Das, T., Li, H., Hunter, T., Shenker, S., Stoica, I.: Discretized streams: Fault-tolerant streaming computation at scale. In: Symposium on Operating Systems Principles (SOSP), pp. 423–438 (2013)

Implicit Staging of EDSL Expressions: A Bridge between Shallow and Deep Embedding

Maximilian Scherr and Shigeru Chiba

The University of Tokyo, Japan
scherr@csg.ci.i.u-tokyo.ac.jp,
chiba@acm.org

Abstract. Common implementation approaches for embedding DSLs in general-purpose host languages force developers to choose between a *shallow* (single-staged) embedding which offers seamless usage, but limits DSL developers, or a *deep* (multi-staged) embedding which offers freedom to optimize at will, but is less seamless to use and incurs additional runtime overhead. We propose a metaprogrammatic approach for extracting domain-specific programs from user programs for custom processing. This allows for similar optimization options as deep embedding, while still allowing for seamless embedded usage. We have implemented a simplified instance of this approach in a prototype framework for Java-embedded EDSL expressions, which relies on load-time reflection for improved deployability and usability.

Keywords: DSL, metaprogramming, Java, programming languages.

1 Introduction

In recent years, the study of domain-specific languages (DSLs) and the investigation of their usage and implementation methods have attracted increasing interest. These languages, which are limited in scope and tailored to a specific problem domain, are said to be easier to reason about and maintain, and open the door to domain-specific optimizations [1].

One form of DSL implementation of particular interest is the embedding of DSLs by means of the available language constructs of an enclosing general-purpose programming language. These embedded DSLs (EDSLs) bring several advantages to the table. For one, sizable parts of the existing tool and general language support (e.g. syntactic and semantic analysis) can be inherited from the host language [1]. More importantly, they enable the embedded usage of DSL programs side by side with host language code. As they have a look-and-feel similar to the host language code, they can be approached by programmers in a fashion similar to using traditional libraries.

Recent examples of such EDSLs in object-oriented programming are JMock [2], Guava's fluent APIs (e.g. `FluentIterable`, `Splitter`, etc.) [3], SQuOpt [4], and jOOQ [5].

R. Jones (Ed.): ECOOP 2014, LNCS 8586, pp. 385–410, 2014.
© Springer-Verlag Berlin Heidelberg 2014

When using only facilities expressible within the host language, an EDSL developer may commonly approach pure language embedding, i.e. without "preprocessor, macro-expander, or generator" [1], in one of two different fashions:

- Execution of the atomic surface elements of the EDSL is directly governed by the semantics of the host language. Evaluation of DSL programs occurs immediately in small steps, yielding and passing intermediate results. This implementation approach is called *shallow embedding*.
- Execution of the atomic surface elements of the EDSL first produces (or *stages*) an intermediate representation (e.g. AST) of the expressed program or snippet. Evaluation to final result values occurs separately. This approach is called *deep embedding*.

Hybrid forms are also possible, where only selected parts of an EDSL are deeply embedded. Intuitively, it may help to think of depth here as a measure of freedom of EDSL programs from the host language's semantics. This has implications on the degree of expressiveness and ability to optimize domain-specific computation. In section 2 we describe the trade-offs between these two approaches.

The strength of deep embedding lies in the fact that computation is staged, allowing for intermediate, customized processing. However, staging commonly occurs in an explicit fashion with the potential to detract users and cause overhead. In order to approximate this staging without incurring penalties we propose a method called *implicit staging*, which takes the form of a framework to be employed by EDSL developers. Section 3 outlines this approach in general.

The main idea behind implicit staging is to statically extract domain-specific code before it is executed by means of static analysis, in particular abstract interpretation. This yields a representation of the domain-specific code that can be processed by an EDSL's developer in a customized fashion. We make the following contributions:

- Implicit staging is a method to channel the processing of domain-specific computation within its static context by semi-automatically isolating it from general-purpose code.
- We present how increasing the amount of contextual information bears the potential for rich optimizations that take into account the intermixed nature of both shallow as well as deep EDSLs.
- In order to concretely illustrate and evaluate our approach, we implemented a proof-of-concept framework using load-time reflection [6] for the Java language. It enables implicit staging of compound EDSL expressions and is mainly focused on bridging the gap between shallow and deep embedding. We present this implementation in section 4 and its evaluation in section 5.
- The prototype shows that our approach is feasible even without full source code availability and that even basic data-flow analysis suffices to extract worthwhile portions of EDSL subprograms.

2   Implementation of Embedded DSLs

In our treatment of EDSLs, provided as libraries, we distinguish between three main roles (cf. figure 1): The *developer* (alternatively *implementor* or *provider*) of the EDSL defines the interface, implements the language behavior, and writes its documentation. The *user* of the EDSL is any developer who employs the EDSL (directly or indirectly) to support the implementation of programs. The *end user* then is anyone who actually causes the execution of these programs.

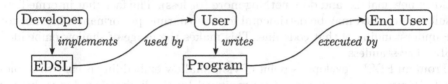

Fig. 1. EDSL implementation and usage roles

Depending on the choice of host language, the choice of basic building bricks of an EDSL varies. For instance, in modern ML variants and Haskell these are commonly data constructor and function applications. In Java they are mainly field accesses and method calls. In our treatment we simply call these atomic surface elements the *tokens* of an EDSL. Furthermore, in statically typed host languages the introduction of EDSL-specific types and the restriction of type signatures in effect allow developers to restrict certain combinations of EDSL tokens, i.e. the EDSL's specific syntax. It is mainly the runtime behavior of these tokens that defines the concrete nature of the embedding.

In the following, we introduce shallow and deep embedding [7] by example of a simple EDSL for matrix operations in Java. A materialized matrix is represented by a `Matrix` data type which wraps a two-dimensional `double` array. We assume the existence of factory methods for creating matrices from given elements. We consider only three tokens: static methods for matrix addition (`add`) and multiplication (`mul`), and a static method to stand for a uniform scaling matrix (`sca`), i.e. a diagonal matrix of a given dimension and a scaling factor on its diagonal.

2.1   Shallow Embedding

When operations of an embedded language are directly mapped to equivalent operations of its host language the embedding is said to be shallow. This means that EDSL tokens both represent a domain-specific operation and their implementation or meaning is to immediately perform it. In a shallow embedding of our matrix EDSL this means that the `add` method is implemented to take in two matrices and return a new one with added elements. The case of matrix multiplication is analogous to addition, and the `sca` method creates an actual scaling matrix. Listing 1 shows a simple usage example.

Listing 1. Shallow EDSL usage example

```
1  Matrix a, b, c;
2  // Omission
3  Matrix d = add(add(a, b), mul(c, sca(5, 3.0)));
4  Matrix e = add(a, d);
```

The advantage from an EDSL user's point of view lies in the fact that the behavior of an EDSL expression is easily predictable right where it appears in the code. The expression `add(add(a, b), mul(c, sca(5, 3.0)))` on line 3 yields a new matrix, and does nothing more (or less). The fact that intermediate results are created may be detrimental for the runtime performance, but not for the understanding of that code line. This makes the usage of shallow embedded DSLs very seamless.

From an EDSL developer's point of view shallow embedding is easy to implement. However, this advantage is outweighed by the limitations due to having to directly adhere to the host language's semantics. In particular, this means that optimizations such as common subexpression elimination or fusion of operations cannot be implemented, execution cannot be chunked and scheduled in sizes worthwhile for parallel execution, and execution is bound to occur on the same machine and architecture that executes the host program.

2.2 Deep Embedding: Staging at Runtime

Instead of directly mapping tokens to equivalent host language operations, it is possible to make them generate an intermediate representation (IR), usually an AST. Here, the sole purpose of token execution is to contribute to building and composing the next stage of computation, i.e. staging. This IR can be processed (e.g. optimized, transformed, compiled, etc.) in a separate step and subsequently executed. This typically yields the end result of the expressed computation. However, it is also possible for the result to be a further stage. A case for this would be a program P_1 whose evaluation generates a program P_2 whose evaluation generates a program P_3, and so on.

For a deep embedding of our matrix EDSL we could use an abstract data type `MatrixExp` with concrete data types for the different AST node types. The token methods are implemented to create corresponding nodes. Instead of taking arguments of type `Matrix`, the `add` and `mul` methods now take arguments of type `MatrixExp`. We add a method `cnst` to create an AST node that will evaluate to a provided (materialized) matrix.

Listing 2 shows a simple usage example. Lines 3–4 show the rough equivalent of listing 1, lines 6–7 show a different usage of the EDSL in which the multi-staged nature of the embedding is more apparent.

Listing 2. Deep EDSL usage example

```
1   Matrix a, b, c;
2   // Omission
3   Matrix d = add(add(cnst(a), cnst(b)), mul(cnst(c), sca(5, 3.0))).evaluate();
4   Matrix e = add(cnst(a), cnst(d)).evaluate();
5   // Omission
6   MatrixExp dExp = add(add(cnst(a), cnst(b)), mul(cnst(c), sca(5, 3.0)));
7   Matrix f = add(cnst(a), dExp).evaluate();
```

When the `evaluate` method is called, the entire EDSL program has already been staged and can be fully inspected. This enables domain-specific optimizations, alternative interpretations, or compilation to a possibly different target language and execution. For instance, nested binary additions can be specialized to a flattened addition which does not produce fully materialized intermediate results.

There are potential downsides to deep embedding. Depending on the host language, it can be hard to hide from the programmer the fact that computation is staged. This may sometimes be desirable, but when not it arguably adds an additional layer of complexity for code understanding, especially if the ability to dynamically create and pass around computation (e.g. ASTs) is abused by users. Furthermore, EDSL developers have to build data structures for their specific IR and make the tokens generate the correct IR nodes.

From a runtime performance point of view, the overhead associated with IR construction, in particular the IR's memory footprint, optimization, and interpretation (or compilation) need to be carefully considered. After all, an EDSL developer has no picture of and no influence on how the EDSL's users place EDSL expressions and trigger their evaluation in their programs.

2.3 No Middle Ground?

It is no surprise that deep embedding allows for much more powerful and expressive EDSLs than shallow embedding. Essentially, it can be seen as "just" providing an elegant way to explicitly perform (domain-specific) code generation and execution at runtime. On the other hand, shallow embedding offers a more immediate and seamless usage than deep embedding. However, this immediate usage relies on the immediate execution by the host language, limiting EDSL performance and expressiveness.

Both have in common the fact that it is reasonable to assume that snippets of EDSL programs do in fact occur as static, compound expressions. However, EDSL developers are unable to exploit this fact with either of the embedding styles. Without the ability to do so, a true alternative between shallow and deep embedding seems unattainable.

3   Implicit Staging

Custom treatment of EDSL programs, the crucial step for optimization, occurs after a representation for them has been constructed. In the case of shallow embedding, this step is never really allowed to happen. Although a sort of representation is in fact implicitly constructed during compile time or interpretation time, commonly there is neither awareness of what constitutes domain-specific code, nor is it possible to customize its processing. As described, deep embedding can be used to circumvent this. However, it means explicit IR construction, explicit processing, and explicit triggering of execution at runtime.[1]

We propose an approach called *implicit staging* that aims to reduce explicitness to a minimum where it is a hindrance, i.e. the IR construction and execution triggering, and retains it where it is desirable, i.e. customized IR processing, while not changing the way EDSL programs are expressed by EDSL users.

Unlike the described pure embedding approaches it is an impure approach. Namely, it requires an outside, static, meta-level view and transformations on user programs. With the exception of languages which allow arbitrary self-modification, implicit staging can typically occur only once before the execution of a program. Figure 2 shows the general overview of an implicit staging system for a given program and EDSL:

1. **Staging:** Domain-specific parts are automatically extracted, reified, and made available for processing to EDSL developers in the form of an IR.
2. **Processing:** The result of this customized processing forms a so-called *residue* of the domain-specific computation.
3. **Unstaging:** The residue is reflected within the original program, yielding a new, transformed program.

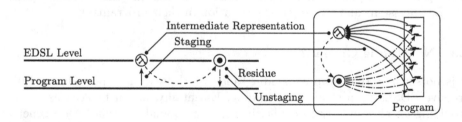

Fig. 2. Implicit staging overview

In principal, the staging step should be able to be performed on the basis of a simple description or enumeration of the EDSL's tokens by its developer. The processing step is to be entirely defined and customized by EDSL developers to form a desired residue suitable for unstaging. Like staging, the unstaging step might also be guided by configuration, which is to be kept simple. Hence, implicit staging lends itself to be provided in the form of a framework to EDSL developers for whom it performs the staging and unstaging tasks.

---

[1] Though in practice some of these steps can be combined, the separation of steps here is helpful for a high-level discussion.

3.1 Staging by Static Token Reinterpretation

The extraction of domain-specific code can be approached by statically simulating runtime staging behavior to varying degrees. Since EDSL tokens are elements of the host language, they commonly have a defined runtime behavior. However, during implicit staging, tokens may be regarded as mere markers and identifiers for domain-specific computation.

If we assume a representation of the input user program that retains token identifiability, even if it does not retain all the original source code structure, the tokens can be reinterpreted as performing the construction of a generic IR. However, unlike runtime interpretation or execution, as is the case with pure embedding approaches, this staging reinterpretation is to be performed statically and abstractly.

The IR can be further augmented with data-flow and control-flow information, providing detailed information on the static context in which domain-specific computation occurs. For instance, this might include type information, uses and definitions, or value ranges. During processing of the IR, developers can use this to improve the residue generation, e.g. perform better optimizations. Some of it might even be necessary for the unstaging step, for instance to perform type conversions for the residue.

3.2 The Approach's Potential

Implicit staging provides the basis for exposing a non-atomic, non-local, or even global view on domain-specific computation. In particular, this means that deep embedding style freedom can be approximated for traditionally shallowly embedded DSLs. For instance, in an expression like add(mul(a, b), mul(a, b)), which yields a materialized matrix, the common subexpression can be eliminated during processing. This is the middle ground we were looking for. However, implicit staging does not necessarily stop there. In fact, it is an extension to both shallow as well as deep embedding.

The fact that implicit staging may provide contextual information about the input program and contained EDSL subprograms opens the door to optimizations that are not possible with the described pure embedding approaches on their own. After all, even with deep embedding, what can be inspected during (runtime) IR processing is only what has been dynamically constructed. For instance, in the deeply embedded expression add(mul(cnst(a), cnst(b)), mul(cnst(a), cnst(b))) the fact that there is a common subexpression may eventually be discovered (during processing steps at runtime), but this is redundantly and possibly repeatedly done. With implicit staging it can be optimized in the residue to help reduce runtime staging overhead.

If we can extend our view even further, assuming an IR that provides information on dependencies between compound EDSL expressions, further optimization opportunities arise. More generally, implicit staging could not only be used to separate domain-specific computation from general purpose one, but help incorporate the relation between the two levels of computation into the EDSL's design and implementation. After all, unlike dedicated DSLs, embedded DSL code snippets live within a general purpose program with its own data flow and control flow. With an appropriate interface for EDSL developers, global optimizations could be applied to EDSL programs which are intermixed and dispersed in user code.

Sometimes, the purpose of dynamically staging an EDSL program at runtime is to gather as big a program as makes sense in order to increase the chance of finding redundant code and other optimization opportunities. Recall our deeply embedded matrix DSL from section 2.2 and consider the user code in listing 3. It might be wise to ever so slightly alter the surrounding user program to maintain as much of the dynamically generated EDSL program as possible until a matrix result needs to be materialized, i.e. when EDSL-external code needs it.

Listing 3. Deep EDSL context example (eager)

```
1   MatrixExp aExp, bExp, cExp, dExp;
2   // Omission
3   Matrix e = add(aExp, bExp).evaluate();
4   System.out.println(mul(cnst(e), add(cExp, dExp)).evaluate());
5   System.out.println(e);
```

Listing 4 shows such a lazier version. However, if we (statically) knew that **evaluate** does not perform optimizations in this situation, it might be worthwhile to stay with the eager version of listing 3 or make different changes.

Listing 4. Deep EDSL context example (lazy)

```
1   MatrixExp aExp, bExp, cExp, dExp;
2   // Omission
3   MatrixExp eExp = add(aExp, bExp);
4   System.out.println(mul(eExp, add(cExp, dExp)).evaluate());
5   System.out.println(eExp.evaluate());
```

It is our vision for implicit staging, with a sufficiently rich IR and powerful unstaging process, to eventually make it possible for EDSL developers to transparently adapt user programs in the described fashion. This would free EDSL users from the burden to consider the implementation details of the EDSL at hand (in our example the **evaluate** method).

3.3 Design Aspects

Designing an actual framework for implicit staging requires careful consideration of the following aspects:

- The choice of host language determines the type of language elements that can be used as EDSL tokens. Furthermore, properties such as dynamic linking and potential self-modification capabilities may limit the extent of implicit staging. This means that not all host languages are equally suited. Generally speaking, any language that makes static code analysis hard is unlikely to be a good candidate.

- The timing of performing IR construction is mainly determined by the type of representation in which user programs can be provided to the framework. While dedicated (pre-)processing of source code is an option, it usually comes with restrictions regarding the deployment of both the EDSL itself as well as end-user applications, e.g. upgrades require recompilation. Additionally, working entirely at compile time restricts data sharing and forces an early code generation phase.
- The scope of the IR, its contained contextual information, and its construction greatly influence implementation difficulty for both the framework developer as well as EDSL developers. This is the main hurdle anticipated for fully realizing the vision outlined in section 3.2.

4   Implicit Staging at Load Time

In order to concretely illustrate and evaluate implicit staging, we developed a simple and limited proof-of-concept framework for DSLs embedded in Java. As indicated in section 3, implicit staging does not necessarily have to occur at compile time. Java serves well to show this, as it is a language environment where compilation, class loading, and runtime are closely related. Compilation results in bytecode [8] which retains sufficient language-level information (e.g. method names) and its loading occurs on demand at runtime.

Java neither has compile-time metaprogramming facilities, nor does it allow for simple compiler customization without relying on a custom compiler. However, it does allow for customized bytecode transformation at load time, i.e. when a class file is loaded by the Java Virtual Machine (JVM). Choosing load time as the time for performing implicit staging has the following advantages:

Seamless Workflow Integration: There exists a dedicated mechanism to perform bytecode transformations at load time on the JVM. Hence, setting up our implicit staging implementation should not be harder than using other bytecode instrumentation tools and should not substantially impair software development and usage workflows.

Runtime System Specialization: User programs and contained EDSL expressions in bytecode remain as is until they are loaded on a specific runtime system. The processing of their IR can be specialized dynamically to that runtime system. For instance, in presence of specific libraries, drivers, or hardware, EDSL expressions could be compiled to exploit these, and in their absence a fallback implementation could be used.

Shared Environment: Loaded user programs share the same runtime environment (including the heap) as the staging, IR processing, and unstaging steps. This establishes *cross-stage persistence* [9–11] which grants EDSL developers certain freedoms and ease of use. For instance, in our implementation it is used to provide a simple interface for returning the results of IR processing as live objects.

EDSL Deployment and Evolution: Any upgrade or patch of an EDSL's implementation as well as of our implicit staging framework itself can be supplied modularly. There is no need to recompile user programs from Java source files with updated library versions. For instance, this is useful in cases where user programs are only deployed as binaries and cease to be maintained. Implicit staging at load time enables the evolution and improvements of an EDSL to still be reflected in such cases.

Working with Java comes with the issues of late binding (i.e. virtual method calls) which restrict whole-program analysis. However, these issues are shared with other OOP language environments. Being able to work at load time is in so far beneficial as it allows us to consider more information on the actual state of the whole program when it is run than at compile time. However, the main technical challenge lies in having to process low-level (i.e. machine language like) bytecode instead of structured source code.

4.1   Prototype Overview

In the following we will describe the components, interfaces, and workflow of our prototype implementation. We designed it with a focus on enabling optimization and semantic customization of (mostly local) compound EDSL expressions in user programs, in order to offer a bridge between shallow and deep embedding for EDSL developers. Compound EDSL expressions are individual Java expressions that are composed of EDSL tokens either in a nested or chained fashion.

Aside from providing skeleton token implementations, an EDSL's developer is required to provide an implementation of the `TokenDeclaration` interface to specify the set of tokens of the embedded language, as well as an implementation of the `ExpressionCompiler` interface to specify how EDSL expressions are to be translated. The former implicitly configures the staging step, the latter corresponds directly with the custom processing step mentioned in section 3.

Figure 3 shows a simplified, combined workflow for the usage as well as the inner workings of our prototype. EDSL users, e.g. application developers, may

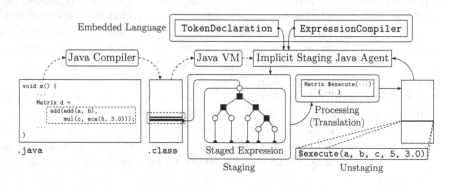

Fig. 3. Java prototype overview

write EDSL expressions as they traditionally could with pure embedding approaches. After all, the tokens (i.e. methods or method calls) may exist independently of our framework. User programs are compiled as usual and deployed with application startup configured to use the implicit staging framework.

At the core of our prototype lies a custom *Java programming language agent* (of java.lang.instrument) which intercepts class loading. When an end user starts the application, the JVM feeds classes to be loaded to the agent and subsequently finalizes the loading of the returned, potentially transformed classes. Staging, processing, and unstaging are all performed within this agent.

During staging, the bytecode in method bodies is analyzed and all contained EDSL expressions are extracted according to the token declaration provided by the EDSL developer. Note that in the interest of simplicity, figure 3 only shows this simplified for a single expression. Then, for the EDSL-specific custom processing all expressions are eventually translated to static methods one by one using the provided expression compiler. Finally, unstaging consists of replacing the original EDSL expressions with calls to the corresponding methods.

4.2   Staging: Expression Extraction

The staging process is configured and guided by the *token declaration* of an EDSL. It specifies which methods[2] belong to the EDSL and is provided as an implementation of the TokenDeclaration interface with the following methods:

- boolean isToken(CtMethod method), a characteristic function for membership of a method in the set of EDSL tokens.
- boolean hasTokens(CtClass clazz), a method to help quickly exclude classes that do not contain EDSL tokens.

Our implementation uses the hasTokens method to skip the analysis of classes which do not refer to classes containing EDSL tokens. It only serves optimization purposes. The classes CtMethod and CtClass are reified method and class types similar to java.lang.reflect.Method and java.lang.Class<T>, provided by the Javassist library [6] used in our implementation. Additionally, our prototype offers a helper class which allows simple registration of tokens and implements the interface by standard semantics for superclass and interface lookup.

Being equipped with the information necessary to distinguish between general and EDSL-specific parts of a program, we can perform staging using a simple abstract interpretation (forward flow) data-flow analysis approach [12]. A trivial parsing of the input bytecode is not sufficient, since compound EDSL expressions are not guaranteed to be neatly clustered after compilation and depend on the flow of data and control.

The idea of implicit staging extends beyond mere syntactic extraction. Instead, we attempt to statically interpret tokens as if they were deeply embedded and thus retrieve a static, anticipated shape of compound EDSL expressions. For

---

[2] This could be extended to fields but in our current implementation we limit ourselves to methods.

the sake of simple API design and implementation complexity, our prototype is still very limited in that it only extracts expressions on a mostly local scale.

Intermediate Representation. The staged IR in terms of section 3 is simply a list of the contained EDSL expressions' ASTs. In the following we will discuss their representation. Every instance of **Expression** holds at least:

- Its *positions*, i.e. the positions of the instructions that caused the original expressions to be placed on the operand stack (before a potential merge).
- Its *type*, i.e. the type of the value this expression would have during actual execution (as specific as this can be determined statically).
- Its *value number*, i.e. a number that can be used to determine whether two expressions would yield the same concrete result during execution.

Type analysis and value numbering analysis are currently performed as part of the same data-flow analysis. The latter is currently very simple and only tracks storing and loading of local variables and some stack operations such as duplication, the former follows a similar pattern as is found in bytecode verification in the JVM. In fact, our data-flow analysis is an extension of such type-analysis component already present in Javassist[3]. Hence, for the sake of brevity, we will omit value numbering and type analysis for the rest of our description.

Local variables, or **StoredLocal** (*loc*) instances, store the same information with the difference that it holds *stored-by positions* instead of positions, i.e. the positions of the instructions that caused the storing of the local variable.

There is currently only one type of expression that is considered EDSL-specific: **InvocationExpression** (*inv*). In addition to the general information, it holds both the EDSL token method and its arguments as a sequence of expressions. A similar expression type is **ConversionExpression** (*cnv*) that wraps a convertee expression. It integrates with the parameters of invocation expressions to bookkeep for potential conversions (casting, boxing, unboxing).

The following expressions constitute the terminal leaves of a resulting expression AST and are considered *parameter expressions* (**ParameterExpression**) as they stand for the parameters to domain-specific computation:

- **LocalAccessExpression** (*lac*) holds the stored local variable that is accessed and its potential indices in the local variable array.
- **StringConstantExpression** (*str*) and **NullExpression** (*nul*) stand for (and hold) constant values. This can be easily extended to other constants.
- **StandaloneExpression** (*sta*) wraps an expression that is to be treated as standalone.
- **UnknownExpression** (⊤) stands for a value resulting from unknown, usually EDSL-external, computation.

Figure 4 shows the AST resulting from staging the expression `add(add(a, b), mul(c, sca(5, 3.0)))` (cf. listing 1). The reason for the two rightmost leaf expressions being ⊤ is that we currently do not handle numeric constants. We would get the same result if the two values came from non-EDSL method calls.

---

[3] `javassist.bytecode.analysis.Analyzer`.

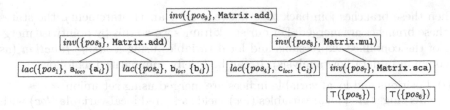

Fig. 4. AST for add(add(a, b), mul(c, sca(5, 3.0)))

The `StandaloneExpression` type requires additional explanation. Consider the following expression: `add(a, d = mul(b, c))`. The `mul(b, c)` part is required to be considered standalone, as it could be shared with EDSL-external code. For the current discussion it can be considered equivalent to $\top$.

Abstract Interpretation (Transferring States). The subject states of our data-flow analysis are JVM stack frames containing the contents of the operand stack (i.e. expressions) as well as local variables. Our abstract interpretation models the effect of bytecode instructions using a *transfer function* (as is common in data-flow analysis) which transfers the state before interpreting an instruction to that after it. We informally describe this function as follows:

(i) If we encounter an invocation instruction for a method m, we first check whether m is a token of the EDSL using `isToken`. If so, we pop the number of parameters for this method from the stack, create a new invocation expression (*inv*) with these parameters and the instruction's position, and add this expression to a (global) list of extracted expressions. If the method returns a value, we also push the expression onto the stack. If m is not a token but one of the auto-boxing and unboxing methods, we pop an expression from the stack, wrap it into a conversion expression (*cnv*) with the instruction's position, and push it onto the stack. Checked cast instructions are handled in a similar fashion.

(ii) If we encounter a store instruction, we pop an expression from the stack and create a stored local variable (*loc*) with the instruction's position and place it at the desired index into the local variable array of the stack frame. We also mark the positions of the popped expression as standalone.

(iii) In case of a load instruction, we retrieve the associated stored local variable (*loc*), then create a new local access expression (*lac*) containing this (with its index) as well as the instruction's position, and push it onto the stack.

(iv) Handling the various constant instructions is trivial.

(v) Any other instruction or case that causes popping of the stack marks the popped expression's positions as standalone. Any push onto the stack that is not part of the aforementioned cases causes an unknown expression ($\top$) with the instruction's position to be pushed onto the stack.

Abstract Interpretation (Merging States). When our abstract interpretation encounters a branching instruction, it needs to explore all the branches.

When these branches join back together (e.g. after an if statement), the states of these branches are merged. For our stack frames we do this by pointwise merging of the contained expressions and local variables using a *merge function* (as is common in data-flow analysis). It can be briefly summarized as follows:

(i) Positions and local variable indices are merged using set union.
(ii) Merging stored local variables (*loc*) yields a stored local variable (*loc*) with merged elements.
(iii) Merging constant expressions yields the same constant if they share the same value and are of same type, otherwise $\top$ with merged positions.
(iv) Merging invocation expressions (*inv*) yields an invocation expression (*inv*) with merged elements (arguments, etc.) if they share the same token, otherwise $\top$ with merged positions.
(v) Merging different types of expressions and merging any expression with $\top$ always yields $\top$ with merged positions.
(vi) Merging expressions of same type and not of the aforementioned cases yields the same expression with merged elements.

Merging with a yet undefined element of the stack frame is realized by simply overwriting. Merging stack frames of different size should not happen and when detected produces an error.

Post-processing. After a fixed point is reached, i.e. transferring and merging of states do not produce new results, the data-flow analysis stops. In a final post-processing step the global list of expressions is then purged of true subexpressions, and expressions whose positions have been marked standalone are turned into standalone expressions.

Having introduced this, we can now illustrate the effects of the abstract interpretation. Consider the expression mul(a, x > 0 ? add(b, c) : mul(b, c)). Java's ternary operator is not reconstructed by our analysis. Instead, the analysis deals with this situation by merging the stack frames at the end of the two branches. For the case that x is greater than zero we have this expression at the top of the abstract operand stack:

$$e_1 = inv(\{pos_4\}, \texttt{Matrix.add}, [lac(\{pos_2\}, \texttt{b}_{loc}, \{\texttt{b}_i\}), lac(\{pos_3\}, \texttt{c}_{loc}, \{\texttt{c}_i\})])$$

For the case that x is at most zero we get the following expression at the top of the stack:

$$e_2 = inv(\{pos_7\}, \texttt{Matrix.mul}, [lac(\{pos_5\}, \texttt{b}_{loc}, \{\texttt{b}_i\}), lac(\{pos_6\}, \texttt{c}_{loc}, \{\texttt{c}_i\})])$$

Our data-flow analysis needs to merge these two expressions when control-flow merges, yielding $\top(\{pos_4, pos_7\})$. Hence, the outer expression will be:

$$e_3 = inv(\{pos_8\}, \texttt{Matrix.mul}, [lac(\{pos_1\}, \texttt{a}_{loc}, \{\texttt{a}_i\}), \top(\{pos_4, pos_7\})])$$

This means that our analysis would yield all three expressions e_1, e_2, and e_3 separately. Note that if both e_1 and e_2 were invocations of the same method this would not be the case, since both would merge into a true subexpression of an expression similar to e_3 but with a known second argument.

4.3   Processing: Expression Translation

The expressions resulting from staging are wrapped into so-called *expression sites* (`ExpressionSite`) one by one and provided to the *expression compiler* provided by the EDSL developer. Expression sites represent the place and context in which an expression was staged and offer methods to support expression translation.

Translation to Source Code. Implementing the `ExpressionCompiler` interface directly allows EDSL developers to provide meaning to staged expressions in the form of Java source code. This interface only requires one method to be implemented: `void compile(ExpressionSite expressionSite)`.

Connecting parameter expressions with runtime values is accomplished indirectly. Namely, the passed `ExpressionSite` instance offers utility methods to generate source code for value access from `ParameterExpression` nodes.

The translated code for the whole expression is passed to the given expression site via an instance method on it, called `setCode`.

Translation to Live Objects. Since compiling from our intermediate representation AST format to source code can be a daunting task, we also offer a high-level alternative: Translation to live objects. To this end, we provide the abstract class `ExpressionToCallableCompiler` which implements the low-level `ExpressionCompiler` interface.

EDSL developers implement the `compileToCallable` method which returns an instance of `Callable<T>`. Eventually, our framework implementation will replace the original EDSL expression (site) with a call to the `call` method of the returned `Callable<T>` instance. Our `Callable<T>` interface is similar to the interface of the same name found in the Java API but its `call` method takes an argument of type `Environment`. During execution time, this environment serves as storage for the actual arguments passed to the staged EDSL expression.

Environment elements can be accessed through instances of the `Variable<T>` class, which trivially implements the `Callable<T>` interface. Internally, these variables are wrapped indices into the environment and provide access methods. The `ExpressionToCallableCompiler` class provides factory methods to create variables from parameter expressions or fresh ones that can be used as intermediate values. Glue code generated by our framework implementation establishes that during execution time, retrieving the value of a variable created from a parameter expression will yield the value of the associated argument.

`ExpressionToCallableCompiler` implements the low-level `compile` method in three steps. First, `compileToCallable` is called. Then, an accessor class is created and the return value from the first step is written to a static field of this accessor class (using runtime reflection). Finally, glue code is generated which creates an `Environment` instance filled with the expression's arguments and calls the `Callable<T>` instance via its accessor class. This code includes boxing, unboxing, and checked casting if required.

As a concrete illustration, consider an expression representation for our matrix EDSL as a tree with node types `Add`, `Mul`, and `Sca` which implement our

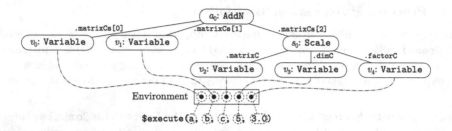

Fig. 5. Optimized `Callable<T>` tree for `add(add(a, b), mul(c, sca(5, 3.0)))`

`Callable<T>` interface with semantics close to the shallow embedded methods of similar names introduced in section 2.1. We also consider two additional types: `AddN`, representing n-ary matrix addition (using a single accumulator), and `Scale`, representing the scaling of a matrix by a given factor.

Take again the expression `add(add(a, b), mul(c, sca(5, 3.0)))` (cf. figure 4). A high-level expression compiler can be defined by the EDSL developer to optimize and translate this expression to the tree presented in figure 5. As described, the compiler keeps a mapping between parameter expressions and variables for generating the correct glue code to fill the environment with values. Listing 5 shows this glue code, assuming the generated accessor class is called `$CallableAccessor`.

Listing 5. Glue code (shortened) in `$execute` method

```
1  static Matrix $execute(Matrix u, Matrix v, Matrix w, int x, double y) {
2      Object[] values =
3          new Object[] { u, v, w, Integer.valueOf(x), Double.valueOf(y) };
4      Environment environment = $CallableAccessor.createEnvironment(values);
5      return (Matrix) $CallableAccessor.callable.call(environment);
6  }
```

Glue code generation happens behind the scenes and can safely be ignored by EDSL developers. All of this allows the definition of an expression's semantics via an essentially static computational object entry point. What this actually looks like internally is in the hands of the EDSL developer.

4.4   Unstaging: Relinking Expression Sites

Having translated all expressions and provided Java method bodies (e.g. as in listing 5) for the expression sites, our framework implementation then needs to establish the appropriate links in the user program.

For every expression site, a (uniquely named) static method (like `$execute` in figure 4 and listing 5) with the expression site's (flattened) type signature is added to the surrounding class, and its body is set to the provided source code. Javassist comes with an inbuilt, custom compiler that makes this possible. Subsequently, every instruction associated with non-parameter subexpressions of an EDSL expression site are removed from the bytecode. Finally, a call to the associated method is inserted at the expression site's position.

For the sake of brevity, we omitted the description of some minor details of the implementation here, like the exact method of bytecode editing and the treatment of issues such as a potential exceeding of the maximum number of method parameters (as imposed by the JVM).

5   Evaluation

The evaluation of our prototype is split into two parts. We first discuss the limitations of our current IR and data-flow analysis and give hints at potential extensions. In the second part we present simple EDSLs and experiments on the runtime performance impact of implicit staging.

5.1   IR and Staging Limitations

We kept our prototype simple both for illustration purposes as well as for the simplification of implementation and API design. This means that the vision outlined in section 3.2 has by no means been fully achieved. The most significant limitations currently stem from the very simple data-flow analysis used for the extraction of EDSL programs. Namely, only domain-specific code originally occurring as compound expressions is extracted. Furthermore, these expressions are treated in a very isolated fashion.

While not discussed in section 4, we have actually experimented with allowing the inspection of variable accesses (*lac*) to offer some level of non-local view. Take for instance the code snippet in listing 6. During expression translation our prototype allows the inspection of the accesses to t in order to optimize all multiplications referring to it, e.g. to perform appropriate scalar scaling instead of matrix multiplication.

Listing 6. Non-local, interleaved EDSL code example

```
1  t = sca(5, 3.0);
2  u = mul(a, t);
3  if (/* Omission */) { v = mul(u, t); } else { v = add(u, t); }
```

However, we found it challenging to devise an easy-to-use API on the current level of processing single expressions that would also allow dealing with the removal of line 1. Whether it can be removed or not depends on the EDSL and whether it is actually inlined by all other expressions and external uses. We believe it is necessary to expose more details (for instance as graphs of shared expression usage) to EDSL developers to handle these non-local aspects.

Note that with deep embedding the aforementioned case is not an issue. Furthermore, at the end of the given code snippet, v would be a dynamically staged program that depends on the actual flow of control. However, in a static setting we cannot predict what path will be taken. One way around this would be to pre-optimize expressions for every possible shape they may take. However, in the general case this is likely to cause intractable code explosion. Another approach currently under consideration is to implicitly switch to runtime staging for these dynamic, interleaved code situations using site-specific type conversions.

Listing 7 provides another example trivially solved by staging at runtime. However, in cases like this, a more powerful data-flow analysis could actually statically determine that this code can be unrolled to stand for `t = add(add(add(a, b), b), b)`. Doing so, we enter the realm of partial evaluation to improve the prediction of the concrete shape of EDSL code, while still allowing its processing to be guided by the EDSL developer.

Listing 7. Constant EDSL expression generation example

```
1  t = a;
2  for (i = 0; i < 3; i++) { t = add(t, b); }
```

To some extent this notion could be extended to staging occurring over several method calls. However, in Java and many other OOP languages it is not always possible to statically determine the exact target of a method call. Such highly dynamic cases are best left to deep embedding, not precluding the aid of implicit staging (cf. 3.2) within method bodies.

5.2   Experiment A: Matrix EDSL

For evaluation purposes we implemented three versions of the matrix EDSL appearing throughout this paper, using shallow embedding, implicit staging per our prototype (with compilation to `Callable<T>`) imitating the look-and-feel of the shallowly embedded version, and deep embedding. The latter two perform optimizations as indicated in section 4.3, i.e. fusing binary additions and turning multiplications with scaling matrices into scaling operations with further fusion when applicable. We made the utmost effort to keep these implementations as comparable as possible to each other.

We set up an experiment to assess not only how effective our optimizations actually are, but also to get a rough idea of how often they might actually be applicable. To this end, we considered randomly generated matrix operation expressions up to a depth of 5 for which we counted `Matrix` variables and `sca` expressions as leaves. For each depth we have 30 such expressions, once occurring in a warm-up loop and once in a loop for which execution time is measured. We generated random 8×8 matrices and scalar values of type `double` to serve as parameters for these expressions and assign them to local variables as we were not interested in the literal generation time. This generated benchmark was also adapted for the deeply embedded language version. Note that all randomness was only part of the benchmark code generation.

Initially we ran the benchmark code ten times for each version with 100000 loop iterations for warm-up and measurement, each on a 3 GHz Intel Core i7 machine with 8 GB of RAM with JRE 7[4]. Due to measurement fluctuations,

---

[4] Java(TM) SE Runtime Environment (build 1.7.0_21-b12)
  Java HotSpot(TM) 64-Bit Server VM (build 23.21-b01, mixed mode).

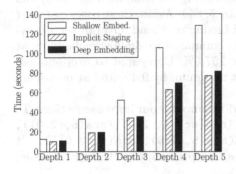
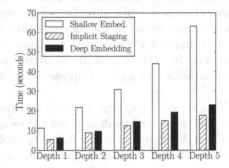

Fig. 6. Random matrix expr. results   **Fig. 7.** Biased matrix expr. results

we opted to increase the number of loop iterations to 10000000 and reran the benchmark code, this time only three times per EDSL implementation version due to the increased running time per benchmark. Apart from the much lower fluctuations between the results, on average these new measurements match very closely with the results of the earlier, shorter experiment. We will mainly discuss the results of the 10000000 iterations experiment here.

Figure 6 shows the results of our experiment with random expressions. Due to space concerns, we summarize the results by averaging over all 30 expression execution times per expression depth. For expressions at depth 1, implicit staging was faster than shallow embedding for 7 of the 30 expressions and faster than deep embedding for 21 of the 30 expressions. This can be explained by the low probability of optimization opportunities for expressions of depth 1 and the added overhead of boxing and `Callable<T>` calling. Still, the maximum slowdown experienced at depth 1 was only by about 6.1% compared to shallow embedding and 4.7% compared to deep embedding. On average, implicit staging was 22.9% faster than shallow embedding and 7.6% faster than deep embedding.

For expressions at depth 2 to 5, implicit staging was faster than shallow embedding for more than 25 of the 30 expressions each. At depth 2, deep embedding was still faster than implicit staging for 17 of the 30 expressions, but for deeper expressions implicit staging was faster than deep embedding for more than 26 of the 30 expressions each. It appears that in the cases where deep embedding was faster, boxing of `double` values is to blame for the slowdown. Overall (depth averages), implicit staging sped up execution compared to shallow embedding at minimum by 22.9% and at maximum by 74.3%. Compared to deep embedding, implicit staging sped up execution at minimum by 2.5% and at maximum by 10.8%.

We also generated the same type of benchmark with a bias towards optimizable expressions. Figure 7 shows the results of our experiment with this benchmark code. It is no surprise that shallow embedding did not fare well in this experiment. Even deep embedding seems to fare worse than it did in the non-biased expressions experiment. Even so, there are cases, i.e. expressions, where implicit staging was slower than shallow embedding (at maximum by 7.6%) and slower than deep embedding (at maximum by 7.9%). Again, these cases can most likely be attributed to the aforementioned boxing overhead. Overall (depth averages), implicit staging sped up execution compared to shallow embedding at minimum by 100.4% and at maximum by 257.5%. Compared to deep embedding, implicit staging sped up execution at minimum by 9.4% and at maximum by 29.7%.

We also wanted to explore worst-case performance for our implementations. To this end, we chose the expression `mul(mul(add(sca(5, 2.0), sca(5, 2.0)))`, `add(sca(5, 2.0), sca(5, 2.0)))`, `add(sca(5, 2.0), sca(5, 2.0)))`. It lends itself as a worst-case specimen, since no optimizations (though possible) were implemented for adding scaling matrices.

Implicit staging was 103.2% slower than shallow embedding. However, deep embedding fared no better with a slowdown by 104.5%. This indicates that the overhead caused by expression tree (or `Callable<T>` tree) evaluation is significant. In order to further test this case, we implemented an expression compiler that generates Java code identical to the original expression instead of a `Callable<T>`. This implementation was only 1.1% slower (for our worst-case expression) than shallow embedding. Hence it seems advisable to move away from the simpler `Callable<T>` compilation for final versions of an implicitly staged EDSL implementation. It may be worthwhile to investigate how we can automate this code generation from a compiled `Callable<T>` instance.

Implicit Staging Overhead. Unfortunately, our implicit staging implementation incurs substantial overhead at class-loading time. In our experiments, expressions at a certain depth were collected in their own class whose static initializers we used for measuring the time class loading took. As a basis for comparison, we took our earliest ten runs experiment and therein the class loaded last, i.e. the one for depth 5, as we can assume the runtime environment to be warmed up at this point. For this case, we measured that our implementation slowed down the class-loading process by 529.4 ms. That was 138.3 times slower than without using implicit staging.

It is important to note that this overhead is incurred only once per class and only if this class actually contains code potentially referring to EDSL expressions. In a large code base, this overhead might indeed become problematic but to a certain degree it is an inevitable side effect of our approach. We will still attempt to further optimize at least the fixed parts of our framework implementation (data-flow analysis, expression site relinking, etc.).

Implementation Complexity. Although only of limited reliability, we use lines of code as a metric to estimate the implementation complexity for each of the approaches. The shallow embedding implementation was accomplished in about 100 lines of code, the implicit staging implementation took up about 360 lines of code, and the deep embedding implementation took up about 300 lines of code. It appears that implicit staging does not incur much more implementation complexity than deep embedding. Of course, this can mainly be attributed to the fact that we tried (and managed) to stay as similar as possible with our implementations.

5.3   Experiment B: Chained Filtering and Mapping EDSL

Our previous example language used static method call nesting for its syntax. Of course, it is also possible to implicitly stage EDSLs which use method chaining.

We implemented an abstract data type `FunSequence<T>` which allows for (immutable) list operations as are common in functional programming, i.e. filtering (`filter` with `Predicate<T>`) and mapping (`map` with `Function<T, R>`). Two concrete classes implement this data type, the list-backed `FunList<T>`, and the array-backed `FunArray<T>`. Again, we started out with a naive shallow embedding.

Consider the code snippet presented in listing 8 and assume that the functions and predicates used as arguments are defined outside. Every mapping or filtering creates a new list and makes this compound expression rather memory demanding and slow.

Listing 8. FunSequence usage example

```
1   FunSequence <Integer> res = inputSeq.map(sqrt).map(square).map(increment)
2                                     .filter(even).filter(greaterThanZero)
3                                     .map(invert).map(invert).map(increment)
4                                     .filter(divisibleByFour);
```

Running this code (warmed up) in a loop with 10 iterations, `inputSeq` initialized to 6000000 random elements with values between -100 and 100, took on average across 10 runs about 14613.4 ms ($\sigma = 1178.2$ ms) with `FunArray<T>` and about 31221 ms ($\sigma = 2192.2$ ms) with `FunList<T>`[5].

With the help of implicit staging, we implemented optimizations for this EDSL, notably the fusion of filtering and mapping operations into a single loop. Its implementation was encapsulated in an non-type-safe method and should thus not be exposed publicly. Though artificial this example may seem, it showcases that implicit staging can be used to expose optimized but unsafe functionality in a type-safe fashion.

Running the aforementioned benchmark with implicit staging took 8786.3 ms on average ($\sigma = 180.2$ ms) with `FunArray<T>` and about 9790.8 ms ($\sigma = 934$ ms) with `FunList<T>`. The former was faster by 66.3% compared with pure shallow embedding, the latter by 218.9%.

5.4   Experiment C: Safe Arithmetic EDSL

Our last example is a language for performing integer arithmetic with overflow detection. It is based on one of the methods described in "The CERT Oracle Secure Coding Standard for Java" [13], which involves conversion to values of `BigInteger` type.

---

[5] In the latter case it was necessary to increase the maximum heap space size.

Listing 9. Safe addition

```
1   public static final int add(int left, int right) {
2       return intRangeCheck(
3           BigInteger.valueOf(left).add(BigInteger.valueOf(right))).intValue();
4   }
```

Listing 9 shows the implementation for addition, where `intRangeCheck` will throw a runtime exception in case of detected overflow. Other operations are implemented in a similar fashion. Warmed up, executing the loop shown in listing 10 takes across 10 runs on average 2490.3 ms ($\sigma = 21.8$ ms).

Listing 10. Safe arithmetic EDSL benchmark

```
1   for (int i = 0; i < 10000000; i++) {
2       int j = i % 100;
3       res = mul(mul(add(a, j), add(a, j)), add(a, b));
4   }
```

We also implemented an implicitly staged version, which does away with the redundant conversion of intermediate values. All parameters are converted to `BigInteger` and only at the end, before converting back to `int`, overflow checking is performed. This simple optimization reduces the running time of the benchmark (with implicit staging) on average to 2372.9 ms ($\sigma = 35.3$ ms). This may not seem much, but consider that our prototypical EDSL implementation causes additional boxing, unboxing, and `Callable<T>` calling overhead. With an additional common subexpression elimination optimization, the benchmark running time is reduced to 2066.7 ms ($\sigma = 17.5$ ms). Of course, this effect is more drastic the more common subexpressions occur.

Note that implicit staging here effectively changes the semantics. Namely, it is fine for intermediate results to exceed the `int` extrema as long as the end result is within them. The expression `sub(add(Integer.MAX_VALUE, 5), 5)` will throw an exception in the shallowly embedded implementation, whereas our implicitly staged implementation would return `Integer.MAX_VALUE`. This is intentional, since we want to consider compound expressions of the EDSL as closed entities. This may seem as an unfair advantage against shallow embedding but the fact that implicit staging allows us to do so is in the first place is exactly what we want to highlight here.

6   Related Work

DSLs and little ad-hoc languages have been advocated for use in domain-specific tasks at least since Bentley's article on "Little Languages" [14]. Syntactic extension allows general-purpose languages to embed such languages. There exist general-purpose languages such as Converge [15] or Lisp with powerful compile-time metaprogramming features that allow this in an integrated fashion.

Converge is a dynamically typed language with a strong focus on allowing custom and rich syntax extensions in combination with splicing annotations for DSL development. Domain-specific code (with custom syntax) is explicitly marked as DSL blocks or shorter DSL snippets. In most Lisp dialects syntactic extension are somewhat limited in the framework of S-expressions, yet powerful macro systems effectively allow for a great deal of linguistic customizations and domain specialization. Template Haskell [16] allows compile-time metaprogramming in a type-safe fashion with explicit notation for compile-time expansion.

It is important to note that these compile-time facilities rely on the availability of source code user programs and consider syntactic entities. Our load-time implicit staging approach for Java is based on data-flow analysis instead, which manages to recover EDSL code snippets while hiding non-EDSL code.

As shown in section 5.2, there is a substantial overhead associated with our current prototype and undeniably with our load-time approach in general. This issue is not shared by traditional compile-time metaprogramming approaches. However, for these approaches it is much harder or impossible to avoid deployability issues and to enable cross-stage persistence in a way that allows generated code to access data available during the staging phase. At load time, the latter becomes a trivial issue. Furthermore, while our current prototype is still limited in scope and might in fact somewhat resemble a load-time hygienic macro system, we believe its abstract EDSL token interpretation approach is more amenable to further extensions, as indicated in section 3.2 and 5.1.

Even without syntactic extension capabilities or macro functionality, embedded DSLs have been shown to be feasible using deep or shallow embedding, or combinations thereof [7]. Hudak [1] and Elliot et al.[17] have shown that Haskell is well suited for this. Yet, even languages with stronger restrictions on syntax and more verbosity, such as Java, have been used to implement EDSLs [2, 3, 5].

To overcome runtime performance issues, Hudak [1] has proposed partial evaluation. Czarnecki et al. [18] have presented an effective approach using staged interpreters which requires a host language with *multi-stage programming* (MSP) support [9, 11]. Bagge et al. [19] have used a source-to-source transformation solution for the C++ language, enabling optimizations via rewrite rules. Guyer et al. [20] have introduced a compiler architecture for the C language which enables domain-specific optimizations not on the syntactic level but on the data-flow level. In fact, Guyer et al. [20] claim not to target the optimization of DSLs, but that of the domain-specific aspects of software libraries. These optimizations are communicated to the compiler by analysis and action annotations (written in their own dedicated language). It is similar to implicit staging in its (external) specification of domain-specific procedures as well as its detachment from the mere source code syntax level.

The aforementioned ideas either rely on non-mainstream host languages or compiler extensions. Rompf et al. [10] have introduced a method called Lightweight Modular Staging (LMS) which is a purely library based approach. LMS brings MSP support to the Scala [21] language as a library, where lifted Rep[T] data-types stand for staged code. Using Scala's traits, it is easy to extend this library and implement EDSLs with it.

When optimizing EDSL programs, it is similar to the deep embedding approach but more elegantly hides its nature by employing Scala's type inference, trait composition, and implicit conversion features. LMS has been used to implement several EDSLs with the Delite [22, 23] back end, such as OptiML [24] and OptiCVX [25], with great results. However, while the usage of EDSLs implemented using LMS is mostly seamless, the unstaging (i.e. the code generation, compilation, and loading) of staged code is triggered explicitly.

JIT macros as described by Rompf et al. in Project Lancet [26], a very ambitious and promising JVM implementation, resemble parts of our load-time staging approach. Combined with LMS, JIT macros are described as allowing domain-specific optimizations at JIT-compile time. However, their expansion or handling necessitates the localized, explicit triggering of JIT compilation in user programs, a feature of Lancet.

7   Conclusion

To address the issue of DSL (expression) embedding, we proposed implicit staging, an impure approach to language embedding. We have further concretely implemented and introduced an instance of implicit staging for the Java language using load-time reflection. Our prototype implementation has shown to be an effective tool for implementing EDSL expression semantics in a customized fashion, while letting EDSLs expose a shallow interface. By moving the process of staging to load time, we gain an advantage in reducing overhead compared to deep embedding.

Our prototype offers an improvement over pure shallow embedding and we believe it can serve as an alternative to deep embedding in many cases. Namely, when true, dynamic runtime staging of EDSL code is not mandatory. However, it remains to be seen how our approach scales beyond the small examples we evaluated. We intend to investigate this in the future.

Despite its current limitations we believe our framework can be used as stepping stone to more elaborate implicit staging (at load time) systems. It is our future work to explore designs, implementations, and use cases for exploiting static and dynamic contextual information both within user programs as well as the runtime system.

References

1. Hudak, P.: Modular domain specific languages and tools. In: Proceedings of the 5th International Conference on Software Reuse, ICSR 1998, pp. 134–142. IEEE Computer Society, Washington, DC (1998)
2. Freeman, S., Pryce, N.: Evolving an embedded domain-specific language in java. In: Companion to the 21st ACM SIGPLAN Symposium on Object-oriented Programming Systems, Languages, and Applications, OOPSLA 2006, pp. 855–865. ACM, New York (2006)
3. https://code.google.com/p/guava-libraries/ (retrieved December 2, 2013)

4. Giarrusso, P.G., Ostermann, K., Eichberg, M., Mitschke, R., Rendel, T., Kästner, C.: Reify your collection queries for modularity and speed? In: Proceedings of the 12th Annual International Conference on Aspect-Oriented Software Development, AOSD 2013, pp. 1–12. ACM, New York (2013)
5. http://www.jooq.org/ (retrieved December 2, 2013)
6. Chiba, S.: Load-time structural reflection in java. In: Bertino, E. (ed.) ECOOP 2000. LNCS, vol. 1850, pp. 313–336. Springer, Heidelberg (2000)
7. Svenningsson, J., Axelsson, E.: Combining deep and shallow embedding for EDSL. In: Loidl, H.-W., Peña, R. (eds.) TFP 2012. LNCS, vol. 7829, pp. 21–36. Springer, Heidelberg (2013)
8. Gosling, J.: Java intermediate bytecodes: Acm sigplan workshop on intermediate representations (ir 1995). In: Papers from the 1995 ACM SIGPLAN Workshop on Intermediate Representations, IR 1995, pp. 111–118. ACM, New York (1995)
9. Westbrook, E., Ricken, M., Inoue, J., Yao, Y., Abdelatif, T., Taha, W.: Mint: Java multi-stage programming using weak separability. In: Proceedings of the 2010 ACM SIGPLAN Conference on Programming Language Design and Implementation, PLDI 2010, pp. 400–411. ACM, New York (2010)
10. Rompf, T., Odersky, M.: Lightweight modular staging: A pragmatic approach to runtime code generation and compiled DSLs. Commun. ACM 55(6), 121–130 (2012)
11. Taha, W., Sheard, T.: MetaML and multi-stage programming with explicit annotations. Theor. Comput. Sci. 248(1-2), 211–242 (2000)
12. Kildall, G.A.: A unified approach to global program optimization. In: Proceedings of the 1st Annual ACM SIGACT-SIGPLAN Symposium on Principles of Programming Languages, POPL 1973, pp. 194–206. ACM, New York (1973)
13. https://www.securecoding.cert.org/confluence/display/java/ NUM00-J.+Detect+or+prevent+integer+overflow (retrieved December 2, 2013)
14. Bentley, J.L.: Programming pearls: Little languages 29(8), 711–721 (1986)
15. Tratt, L.: Domain specific language implementation via compile-time metaprogramming. TOPLAS 30(6), 1–40 (2008)
16. Sheard, T., Jones, S.P.: Template meta-programming for haskell. SIGPLAN Not. 37(12), 60–75 (2002)
17. Elliott, C., Finne, S., De Moor, O.: Compiling embedded languages. J. Funct. Program. 13(3), 455–481 (2003)
18. Czarnecki, K., O'Donnell, J.T., Striegnitz, J., Taha, W.: DSL implementation in MetaOCaml, Template Haskell, and C++. In: Lengauer, C., Batory, D., Blum, A., Odersky, M. (eds.) Domain-Specific Program Generation. LNCS, vol. 3016, pp. 51–72. Springer, Heidelberg (2004)
19. Bagge, O.S., Kalleberg, K.T., Haveraaen, M., Visser, E.: Design of the Code-Boost transformation system for domain-specific optimisation of C++ programs. In: Binkley, D., Tonella, P. (eds.) Third International Workshop on Source Code Analysis and Manipulation (SCAM 2003), pp. 65–75. IEEE Computer Society Press, Amsterdam (2003)
20. Guyer, S., Lin, C.: Broadway: A compiler for exploiting the domain-specific semantics of software libraries. Proceedings of the IEEE 93(2), 342–357 (2005)
21. http://www.scala-lang.org/ (retrieved December 2, 2013)
22. Brown, K.J., Sujeeth, A.K., Lee, H.J., Rompf, T., Chafi, H., Odersky, M., Olukotun, K.: A heterogeneous parallel framework for domain-specific languages. In: Proceedings of the 2011 International Conference on Parallel Architectures and Compilation Techniques, PACT 2011, pp. 89–100. IEEE Computer Society, Washington, DC (2011)

23. Chafi, H., Sujeeth, A.K., Brown, K.J., Lee, H., Atreya, A.R., Olukotun, K.: A domain-specific approach to heterogeneous parallelism. In: Proceedings of the 16th ACM Symposium on Principles and Practice of Parallel Programming, PPoPP 2011, pp. 35–46. ACM, New York (2011)
24. Sujeeth, A.K., Lee, H., Brown, K.J., Chafi, H., Wu, M., Atreya, A.R., Olukotun, K., Rompf, T., Odersky, M.: Optiml: an implicitly parallel domainspecific language for machine learning. In: Proceedings of the 28th International Conference on Machine Learning, ICML (2011)
25. http://stanford-ppl.github.io/Delite/opticvx/index.html (retrieved December 2, 2013)
26. Rompf, T., Sujeethy, A.K., Browny, K.J., Lee, H., Chafizy, H., Olukotuny, K., Odersky, M.: Project lancet: Surgical precision JIT compilers. Technical report (2013)

Babelsberg/JS
A Browser-Based Implementation of an Object Constraint Language

Tim Felgentreff[1], Alan Borning[2,3], Robert Hirschfeld[1], Jens Lincke[1],
Yoshiki Ohshima[3], Bert Freudenberg[3], and Robert Krahn[4]

[1] Hasso Plattner Institute, University of Potsdam, Potsdam, Germany
[2] University of Washington, Seattle, WA, USA
[3] Viewpoints Research Institute, Los Angeles, CA, USA
[4] Communications Design Group, SAP Labs, San Francisco, CA, USA

Abstract. Constraints provide a useful technique for ensuring that desired properties hold in an application. As a result, they have been used in a wide range of applications, including graphical layout, simulation, scheduling, and problem-solving. We describe the design and implementation of an Object Constraint Programming language, an object-oriented language that cleanly integrates constraints with the underlying language in a way that respects encapsulation and standard object-oriented programming techniques, and that runs in browser-based applications. Prior work on Object Constraint Programming languages has relied on modifying the underlying Virtual Machine, but that is not an option for web-based applications, which have become increasingly prominent. In this paper, we present an approach to implementing Object Constraint Programming without Virtual Machine support, along with an implementation as a JavaScript extension. We demonstrate the resulting language, Babelsberg/JS, on a number of applications and provide performance measurements. Programs without constraints in Babelsberg/JS run at the same speed as pure JavaScript versions, while programs that do have constraints can still be run efficiently. Our design and implementation also incorporate incremental re-solving to support interaction, as well as a cooperating solvers architecture that allows multiple solvers to work together to solve more difficult problems.

Keywords: Constraints, Object Constraint Programming.

1   Introduction

Constraints are relations among objects that should hold. This could be that all parts in an electrical circuit simulation obey the laws of physics, that the rows in a Sudoku include each digit from 0 to 9, or that a streamed video plays smoothly in the presence of changing CPU and network load. We also want to support interactive use of constraints, for example, continuously re-satisfying a set of layout constraints on screen widgets as they are moved with

R. Jones (Ed.): ECOOP 2014, LNCS 8586, pp. 411–436, 2014.
© Springer-Verlag Berlin Heidelberg 2014

the mouse. In addition, it is useful to extend the constraint formalism to allow soft constraints as well as required ones, where the system should try to satisfy the soft constraints if possible, but it is not an error if they cannot be satisfied. For example, we might have a soft constraint for video quality that we are willing to relax if necessary, given the current network load, or a desired ideal spacing between two widgets that again can be relaxed if need be. In the work reported here, we want to support constraints in a clean way in an object-oriented language running in a lightweight, web-based programming environment.

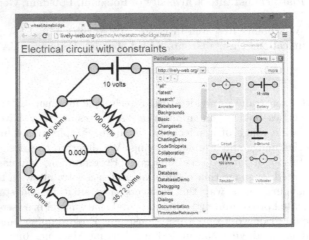

Fig. 1. Constructing a Constraint-based Wheatstone Bridge Simulation

Figures 1 and 2 are screenshots from our prototype system that illustrate the kinds of capabilities we want. Both are constructed in the Lively Kernel environment [1], an entirely web-based programming environment built on JavaScript.

Figure 1 shows a constraint-based simulation of Wheatstone Bridge being constructed. (A Wheatstone Bridge is used to measure an unknown electrical resistance by balancing two pairs of resistors so that the electrical potential between them is 0.) Parts representing batteries, resistors, and meters are copied from the Lively Kernel parts bin [2] on the right, dropped into the circuit on the left, and wired together. These parts carry constraints representing Ohm's Law, Kirchhoff's Current Law, and so forth. The system automatically solves the constraints when the parts are first connected, and re-solves them if the battery's supply voltage or a resistance is edited, updating the voltage displayed by the meter. (See Appendix A for the implementation.)

Figure 2 shows a color chooser from the parts bin that can be used to create a color palette for a website. Users can specify the desired average hue and luminance using the sliders, as well as change each color individually using a color chooser. The system automatically updates the colors and sliders according to user input — for example, the hue slider adjusts when the user changes the luminance slider. The system supports incremental re-solving, so that colors change smoothly when dragging the sliders. Furthermore, the constraints on hue, luminance, and specific color selection have different priorities. The system is allowed to make changes to individually selected colors or cause changes to other colors to keep the average hue and luminance constant, whereas dragging the sliders forces the system to use the new value. The widget has additional constraints that luminance and hue of each individual color must be at least 80% of the average luminance and hue, and that the system cannot set red, green, and blue values outside the range 0–1.

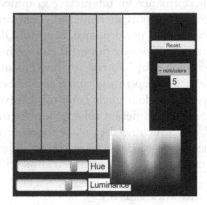

Fig. 2. Color Palette Chooser with Hue and Luminance Goals

While the capability to graphically construct constraint-based simulations dates back to Sketchpad [3] and ThingLab [4], in the current work we want to enable a true integration of constraints with the host object-oriented programming language, and further support this in a web-based environment. To accomplish this, we build on our recent work on Babelsberg [5], a language framework that supports an integration of constraint satisfaction with objects and their methods. Babelsberg in turn builds on earlier work on constraint-imperative programming in Kaleidoscope [6] and Turtle [7]. In Babelsberg, constraints are expressed as predicates using the underlying object-oriented language. The constraint is that the predicate evaluates to true, and the system maintains this constraint automatically whenever objects that participate in the constraint change.

Babelsberg improves on related approaches to constraint satisfaction in object-oriented programs, which use libraries [8,9,10], domain-specific languages [11,12], or (more recently) functional-reactive programming [13,14] to specify and solve constraints. These approaches do not need special runtime support, but require the programmer to call specific application programming interfaces (APIs) or follow certain rules to not accidentally circumvent the constraints.

We first implemented the Babelsberg design as a prototype in Ruby [15], called Babelsberg/R. This implementation depends on extending the Ruby Virtual Machine (VM). However, applications written in e.g. JavaScript typically have to work on a variety of client VMs included in different Web browsers. This makes it infeasible to implement Babelsberg in a JavaScript VM. JavaScript is currently of considerable interest in the industry and research communities. Thus, an implementation as an extension written entirely in JavaScript enables us to apply constraint programming to a variety of existing problems, and to compare it directly with alternative solutions on a variety of platforms. Another goal for our design is good performance. As with the original Babelsberg/R implementation, we want the extension to have at most minimal impact on speed for programs without constraints; and for programs with constraints, we still want to have good performance for interactive graphical applications, which generally implies the need to support incremental constraint solvers [16].

In addition to the goal of good performance, a useful Object Constraint Programming language requires sufficiently powerful constraint solving capabilities. In prior work [5], we identified (but had not yet implemented) an important requirement, namely support for *cooperating constraint solvers*. The motivation is that it is often infeasible to provide a single constraint solver that works well for all aspects of a problem; instead, different solvers may be more appropriate than others for some aspects, and which need to work together to solve the problem. Our design and implementation in Babelsberg/JS provides this capability, in a way that supports incremental re-solving of constraints without requiring access to the VM.

The contributions of this work thus are:

- A design for Object Constraint Programming (OCP) languages that does not require VM support
- An implementation of cooperating constraint solvers, including techniques to do so without VM support and that support incremental constraint satisfaction
- A realization of these in an operational implementation in JavaScript, running in the Lively Kernel environment, including additional support within the language extension for writing constraint programs

The rest of this paper is structured as follows. Section 2 describes related work and the Babelsberg framework on which we build. In Section 3, we describe the features a language must provide to support Babelsberg without VM extensions. This design is realized in Babelsberg/JS (Section 3), which also includes support for cooperating constraint solvers (Section 3.1) and incremental re-solving (Section 3.2). We then describe the implementation of Babelsberg/JS in the Lively Kernel environment (Section 4), and the results of performance evaluation (Section 5). Section 6 describes future work and concludes.

2   Background and Related Work

Programs frequently have some set of constraints that should hold. In a standard imperative language, the usual approach to dealing with such constraints is to leave it entirely up to the programmer to ensure that they are satisfied — the constraints may be implicit in the code and just expressed explicitly in comments and documentation, or perhaps in the form of machine-checkable assertions.

For some constraints, programmers may write assertions to fail early if the constraints are unexpectedly not satisfied [17], while other constraints describe invalid system states that can be automatically corrected. In our color chooser example, when the user selects a specific color that does not meet the luminance constraints, the system is allowed to change it. To deal with these kinds of situations, programmers may write corrective code that is executed at various times (for example, color adjustments may run while the user is dragging the luminance slider). This code uses branches and state changing operations to check and correct invalid state. However, these statements are order dependent, and the branching code expresses the constraints implicitly. Furthermore, it can be unclear whether a solution is complete in that it covers all possible cases or optimal. As argued in our prior work on Babelsberg [5] and elsewhere, it is usually clearer to express and satisfy constraints explicitly, rather than encoding them in control flow.

One approach to making the constraints explicit is to use a library that provides one or more constraint solvers. Numerous solvers, covering a wide range of type domains (including reals, booleans, and finite sets), are available for imperative languages and can be called from imperative code [8,9,10,16]. For more specialized domains such as user interface layout, some libraries provide separate domain specific languages (DSLs) to express, for example, minimal distances between graphical objects. Prominent examples here include the Mac OS X layout specification language [11] or the SQUANDER framework [18]. For our example, these approaches replace the branching and state changing code with declarative constraints. However, these constraints are expressed in the language of the library, using solver-specific types and expressions. To interact with the imperative state of the system, the solver must be called explicitly, and the constrained values must be copied between the solver and runtime data structures whenever either imperative code or the solver update them. This is error-prone, because programmers may accidentally circumvent the solvers if they do not call the solver in all required places. Further, because solvers often operate on a limited number of domain-specific primitive types, object-oriented abstractions cannot be used to express constraints.

An alternative approach is to integrate a means to express and maintain one-way constraints with the language itself. Some languages such as Scratch [19], LivelyKernel [1], and KScript [13] have built-in support for data flow, which allows programmers to express unidirectional constraints among objects. Babelsberg/JS shares with these systems the need to intercept object access and solve constraints when the system is disturbed.

To support a broader set of constraints, other languages directly integrate one or more solvers into their execution model. Again, there is a large body of prior art in this area, including Constraint Logic Programming [20], Constraint Imperative Programming [6,7], and Object Constraint Programming [5].

As illustrated by the color palette chooser example, it can be useful to extend the concept of constraints to include soft constraints with different priorities as well as required ones. There are various ways to formalize multiple priorities for soft constraints, and how to trade off conflicting soft constraints with the same priority; here we use the formalism described in [21]. In addition to hard and soft constraints, it is useful to add support for placing a *read-only annotation* on a variable in a given constraint. Operationally, a read-only annotation tells the system that it may not change the value of that variable to satisfy the given constraint.[1] Another useful extension is the addition of *stay constraints* and *edit constraints* [8], which provide important tools for integrating constraints with a language with state and in supporting interactive constraint systems. Stay constraints specify that a variable should keep its previous value. Soft stay constraints with a very low priority are used to express frame axioms, i.e., the desire that things remain the same unless there are some other constraints that force them to change. For example, suppose we are moving one part of a geometric figure with constraints. Without weak stay constraints to try and keep things where there used to be, the entire figure might collapse to a single point (still satisfying all its required constraints, but to the surprise of the user). Finally, edit constraints provide a concise and efficient way to support incremental updates, for example, moving a constrained object with the mouse. A typical sequence of actions when moving a part of a constrained figure is to first add edit constraints on the x and y values of a point being moved, then repeatedly provide new x and y values given the mouse position (and let these values propagate through the other constraints), and then finally remove the edit constraint when done moving.

2.1   Object Constraint Programming and Babelsberg

Object Constraint Programming differs from Constraint Imperative Programming in that it focuses on object-orientation as the main paradigm. It seeks to integrate declarative constraints in a way that does not compromise the expectations of imperative object-oriented programmers and that provides a declarative semantics that is compatible with these expectations.

Babelsberg is a design for a family of Object Constraint Programming languages. Since the language we present in this paper is an instance of this design, we summarize its goals in this subsection. These include:

- a syntax and semantics that are a strict superset of and fully compatible with the base language
- a unified mechanism for abstraction shared between constraints and object oriented code, so that constraints can re-use object-oriented methods and respect encapsulation

---

[1] For example, if we have a constraint $a + b = c?$, where c has been annotated as read-only, the system may change a or b or both to satisfy the addition constraint, but not c. Other constraints might change c, however, which would of course force changes to a or b. For simplicity, here we have given an intuitive, operational description of read-only annotations; please see [21] for a formal, declarative semantics.

- performance that is competitive with the base language for standard object-oriented code without constraints
- support for both required and soft constraints, constraints on object identity, variables that are read-only to solvers or imperative code, as well as incremental re-solving for use in interactive applications
- an API for constraint solvers that makes it straightforward to add new solvers and does not privilege the solvers provided with the implementation, to make it easy to use different solvers in different programs

2.2 Babelsberg/R

In [5] we describe Babelsberg/R, an implementation of Babelsberg based on a modified Ruby VM. The modifications are almost all semantic extensions, with only one minor syntactic extension, plus libraries for constraint satisfaction. The semantic model is also an extension of Ruby's, and supports all of the existing Ruby constructs such as classes, instances, methods, message sends, blocks (closures), object identity, and the language's control structures.

All these Ruby constructs are also supported in constraints. However, there are two important restrictions:

- The expression that defines a constraint should return a boolean, just like an assertion. The constraint is that the boolean is *true*.
- Constraints can be placed on the results of message sends, as long as the execution of these messages does not have side-effects (or those side-effects are benign, like caching), and repeated execution of the expression produces the same result, as long as no variables participating in the constraint have changed (so system calls for example to a random number generator or a file stream do not qualify)

For example, the constraint in the color chooser that each color should have a luminance at least 80% of the global targeted average can be expressed concisely in Babelsberg/R:

```
1 colors.each do |color|
2    always { palette.target_luminance * 0.8 <= color.luminance() }
3 end
```

What looks like an assertion on each element in the colors collection is actually a constraint. Whenever any color or the target palette luminance changes, the system will automatically adapt to ensure that this constraint is always satisfied. This snippet also shows that constraints can be used within imperative constructs and constrain the values of properties (the target_luminance) as well as the results of object-oriented message sends (the result of the calculated luminance of colors).

Given a set of constraint expressions, Babelsberg can choose among multiple solvers to find a solution to them. The architecture makes it straightforward to add new solvers, and does not privilege the solvers provided with the language (they are merely the ones that come with the standard library). However, the programmer has to indicate which solver is available to the runtime, and there may be constraints that are too difficult for the solvers. Additionally, features such as incremental solving, read-only variables, soft constraints, and stay constraints are only available with some solvers.

Babelsberg/R was implemented by modifying the Ruby VM. It uses two interpretation modes: imperative evaluation mode and constraint construction mode. The interpreter normally operates in imperative evaluation mode. In the absence of constraints, this is the standard Ruby VM. However, if the interpreter encounters a LOAD or STORE instruction for a variable with a constraint on it, rather than directly loading or storing into the variable, it calls the appropriate constraint solver to retrieve the variable's value or to solve an equality constraint between the variable and the new value. When a constraint is being added, the interpreter switches to *constraint construction* mode. It continues to evaluate expressions using message sends, but rather than computing the result, it builds up a network of primitive constraints that represent the constraint being added, keeping track of the dependencies in the process.

To support this, the Ruby VM was extended to support *constrained variables*. These variables refer to different objects depending on the context they are used in. One is the normal object-oriented binding used in the host language execution. The other is a constraint object that can be used by a solver for constraint construction and solving. Variables become constrained variables only when they are used in a constraint, minimizing the performance impact for parts of the program where only normal variables are accessed.

3   Object Constraint Programming without VM Support

In industry, JavaScript has become the de-facto standard for Web programming, and a huge amount of code exists in the language. This fact, along with JavaScript's unique design and its execution environment in a Web browser, also make it of great interest to the research community, motivating work on revising and adapting useful features of other languages to include in it [22,23].

To provide practical support for OCP in JavaScript, we adapt the Babelsberg design to not require support from the underlying VM. This enables us to run Babelsberg/JS in modern browsers and use it in a variety of practical Web applications.

For Babelsberg/JS, since we do not have access to the VM, we cannot redefine the operation of LOAD and STORE instructions to handle variables with constraints on them. Instead, the unmodified JavaScript VM is used only for imperative evaluation mode. To intercept accesses and assignments to constrained variables, we wrap properties with property accessors that interact correctly with the constraint solver. To get the value of a constrained variable, the accessor gets the value for that variable from its solver. For a store, the setter in general calls the appropriate constraint solver to solve an equality constraint between the variable and its new value for a store.

For constraint construction mode, we use a custom JavaScript interpreter, itself written in JavaScript. This custom interpreter is about three orders of magnitude slower than the underlying one. However, since evaluating code in constraint construction mode is a much less common activity, and one that doesn't occur in inner loops, the performance penalty is not a significant issue.

Generalizing our approach, we have thus identified the following requirements for implementing the Babelsberg scheme without VM support:

– The host language must support a means to intercept variable lookup, so names can refer to different objects.
– The VM-based implementation of Babelsberg assumes that the VM provides access to the program state so solvers can ignore encapsulation and modify data structures directly. In contrast, here the extension must enable calling the appropriate API functions to manipulate data structures.
– The host language must provide a means to modify interpretation of a block of code to implement the constraint construction mode.

The first requirement is only partially supported in JavaScript, namely for object fields using property accessors. We therefore limit ourselves to constraining field storage in Babelsberg/JS, but not storage into local variables. (Some compiled OO languages, for example C#, also support property accessors; and other dynamic OO languages, such as Python and Smalltalk, support *method wrappers* to enable intercepting accessors, again within the limitation of only constraining field access.) As with the original Babelsberg/R design, it does not matter whether the fields are constrained directly or whether they are used in the execution of a method that was constrained to produce a certain result. A property that is accessed in the execution of a constraint expression is wrapped with property accessor that intercepts lookup and storage.

Property Accessors for Constrained Objects. When an object has been used in a constraint, its constrained properties have been replaced with property accessors. The *property getter* is a simple wrapper that reads from the solver variable in the most upstream region in which the field is referenced (cf. 3.1). Instead of returning the field value of the object, it returns the value of that variable in the solver data structure. The *property setter* distinguishes two cases. If the variable is writable from a solver, an equality constraint for that solver is created and the updated constraint system is solved, potentially triggering other solvers. On the other hand, if the variable is not writable (either because it is of a type that no available solver supports or because it has been marked as read-only by the programmer), its new value is stored, and all dependent constraints are recalculated. These dependent constraints have treated the variable as a constant (because they cannot modify it). To recalculate them, the constraints are deactivated in the solvers, and the expressions that created them are re-evaluated in constraint construction mode to create new constraints based on the new value. (The implementation of edit constraints (Section 3.2) handles the situation of repeated changes much more efficiently.)

Creating Constraints. As an example of defining constraints, consider an interactive temperature converter, which maintains the relation between sliders representing values on the Fahrenheit, Celsius, Rankine, and Kelvin scales.

```
1  var converter = {},
2      cassowary = new CLSimplexSolver ();
3  always: { solver:   cassowary
4      converter.C * 1.8 == converter.F - 32 &&
5      converter.C + 273.15 == converter.K &&
6      converter.F + 459.67 == converter.R
7  }
```

In Babelsberg/JS, a source-to-source transformation creates a call to a global function — always — from an always: expression of this form (this transformation just provides syntactic sugar – the function can also be called directly with function object.) Once this function has executed, a change to any one of the temperature values in the converter object will trigger changes to the other three values to keep the constraint satisfied through property accessors described above.

The always function passes the predicate expressing the constraint and information about the context into a custom JavaScript interpreter. This interpreter is used to evaluate expressions in constraint construction mode, which is provided as part of the Babelsberg/JS library. The custom interpreter creates property accessors (getters and setters) for the C, F, K, and R fields of the converter object. The appropriate accessor is then called whenever some other part of the program uses one of those fields. However, within the constraint expression, accesses to these fields do not use these accessors, but instead return *Constrained Variable* objects. Messages are then sent to these objects, and instead of calculating values, build up networks of primitive constraints that can then be satisfied by a solver. The always function returns a Constraint object that provides meta-level access to the asserted relations, using the protocol described for Babelsberg/R [5].

In this example, the constraints are on the fields of the object. However, constraints in Babelsberg/JS (as with any instance of the Babelsberg scheme) can also invoke methods that perform computations. For example, imagine the converter uses the getCelsius method to return a cached temperature value that is updated in regular intervals from a Web service:

```
1  var converter = {},
2      cassowary = new CLSimplexSolver ();
3
4  converter.getCelsius = function () {
5      if (!converter.updater) {
6          updateCelsius (converter); // updateCelsius omitted for brevity
7          converter.updater = setInterval (5000, function () {
8              updateCelsius (converter);
9          });
10     }
11     return converter.C;
12 }
13
14 always: { solver:   cassowary
15     converter.getCelsius () * 1.8 == converter.F - 32 &&
16     converter.getCelsius () + 273.15 == converter.K &&
17     converter.F + 459.67 == converter.R
18 }
```

By placing the constraint on the result of sending messages rather than on fields, Babelsberg respects object encapsulation. The value returned from the message send in this example is simply a float, but return values can also be arbitrary objects and computed values. For example, we could constrain the maximum pressure of a volume of dry air with a fixed density and gas constant, which would effectively limit the maximum temperature to around 36° Celsius.

```
1 converter.pressure = function () {
2     var gasConstantDryAir = 287.058, // J/(kg * K)
3         density = 1.293; // kg/m^3
4     return density * gasConstantDryAir * converter.K / 1000;
5 }
6
7 always: { solver: cassowary
8     converter.pressure() <= 115 // kPa
9 }
```

3.1   Cooperating Constraint Solvers

The temperature converter described above has no graphical representation. Cassowary only works on reals, yet in order to display the temperature scales, we need to convert the values into strings and update the Web browser's Document Object Model (DOM) using the appropriate API. This is best done with a local propagation solver, which can invoke arbitrary methods to satisfy the constraints, in this case by calling the API. (The constraints that define the temperature converter are simple enough that we could have used a local propagation solver for all of them, but this is unsatisfactory for many problems, such as the Wheatstone bridge example in Figure 1, since local propagation cannot handle such situations as simultaneous equations or inequalities.)

There is currently no single solver that can efficiently handle all constraints that arise in a typical application (and it seems unlikely that one can be created). To address this, we extend the work presented in [5] to include an architecture for cooperating constraint solvers, allowing a problem to be partitioned among multiple solvers. For this example, we use two solvers: one for linear arithmetic on the reals, and one for local propagation constraints.

Our architecture for cooperating solvers partitions constraints into regions that are connected via read-only variables, implementing the design proposed in [24]. The result is a very loose coupling among the cooperating solvers. This approach is in contrast to the more commonly-used Satisfiability Modulo Theory (SMT) technique for supporting cooperating constraint solvers [25], which uses inferred equality constraints as the means for the cooperating solvers to communicate (including the case when neither of the equated variables has a specific value). Our experience so far indicates that our approach is more suited to integration with imperative constructs, in which variables do always have specific values, and lends itself well to support edit constraints for incremental re-solving. (While we have not yet done so in our implementation, the architecture described in [24] in fact allows hierarchies of cooperating solvers, so that within a single region, there could be multiple solvers that cooperate by sharing inferred equality constraints.)

In the cooperating solvers architecture, each constraint belongs to exactly one solver. All constraints that belong to the same solver are in the same region. While constraints belong to exactly one region, variables may be shared across regions. This happens if variables occur in multiple constraints that belong to different regions. These variables must be read-only in all but one of the regions. Read-only variables are represented in a solver-specific manner, either using stay constraints for solvers that support them, or through required equality constraints. To support this, solver libraries should provide a method that makes a variable read-only for them.

In this architecture, the regions must form an acyclic graph, so that solving can simply proceed from the upstream to the downstream regions, propagating variable values. Figure 3 shows an example configuration. Solving proceeds from the left and each solver propagates values for its variables to downstream solvers that need them. The downstream solvers can only read, not write to those variables. This architecture prohibits loops and a system that oscillates without finding a solution. To create this graph, the system determines an order for the solvers based on the dependencies between the constraints. The programmer can explicitly control the position of a solver in this graph, or the libraries can provide information so the system can create the order without the programmer's support. Applications can use multiple instances of the same solver type that are used one after the other (for example, for a problem that first uses Cassowary to solve simultaneous linear constraints, then DeltaBlue for local propagation constraints, then Cassowary again).

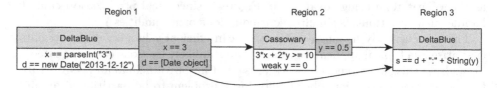

Fig. 3. Regions propagating variable values downstream

Once the solver regions are sorted, solving proceeds from the furthest upstream region. Each region will determine values for the variables it can write to, and the downstream regions will adjust to accommodate the new values propagated to their read-only variables from higher level regions. Soft constraints are solved for just within each region — in keeping with the theory of hard and soft constraints in the presence of read-only variables [21], if a soft constraint in an upstream region restricts a variable to a certain value, then a downstream region must use that value and can in fact not distinguish if this value was determined by a required or a soft constraint. If constraints in a downstream region cannot be satisfied due to an upstream soft constraint, we do not backtrack.

Given these additional capabilities, we can now add a graphical representation to our temperature converter. We want the color of a DIV element to change when the temperature is above 30° C.

```
1  var el = jQuery("#tooHotWarning");
2
3  always: { solver: deltablue
4      el.color.formula([converter.getCelsius()], function(celsius) {
5          var color = celsius > 30 ? "red" : "blue";
6          el.setAttribute("class", color);
7          return color;
8      });
9  }
```

Note that for the DeltaBlue local propagation solver, we do not provide a predicate (although we could — in that case it would be run to test whether re-solving is necessary). Instead, local propagation solvers need formulas for all writable variables that state their dependencies and how to update the variable. In this case, we want the Celsius value to be used as input for the color, but not vice versa, so we only provide one formula. The only dependency here is on the return value of converter.getCelsius(), passed explicitly in line 4. (Note that this could be omitted Babelsberg/R, because its version of DeltaBlue supports deducing the dependencies from the formula function — a feature we have not yet implemented here.) The dependencies are passed as arguments to the formula function, so we can use them directly to update the DOM using the browser's setAttribute API and return the new value. These functions, just like the predicates for Cassowary, are evaluated in constraint construction mode which wraps variables with property accessors — the function formula is simply a function defined by DeltaBlue.

3.2 Incremental Re-solving for Cooperating Constraint Solvers

Some applications involve repeatedly re-satisfying the same set of constraints with differing input values. A common such case is an interactive graphical application with a constrained figure, in which we move some part of the figure with the mouse. For such applications, it is important to re-solve the constraints efficiently, and a number of constraint solvers, including DeltaBlue and Cassowary, support this using edit constraints that allow a new value for a variable to be repeatedly input to the solver.

The original Babelsberg design did not include support for incremental re-solving at the language level — it was up to the solver library to provide access to such functionality. However, to integrate with our cooperating solvers architecture, Babelsberg/JS does include support for incremental re-solving through a solver-independent edit function that takes the variables to be edited and returns a callback function. The process that produces new values can use this callback to input new values into the solvers for the variables to be edited.

The edit function gathers all the constraints in which the passed variables participate. Only variables that occur solely in solver regions that support edit constraints can be edited; otherwise an exception is raised. The read-only annotations for variables in the solvers for downstream regions are converted to edit constraints, reflecting the fact that the upstream regions will be providing new values for these variables. Finally, the edit function creates a callback function and returns it. This callback can then be used to feed new values into the solvers.

As an example, suppose we wanted to connect the Celsius value of our temperature converter to a graphical slider. We wrap the original onDrag (which updates the slider's value) to input the new value into the edit callback as well.

```
1 var callback = edit(converter, ['C']);
2 slider.onDrag = slider.onDrag.wrap(function (originalOnDrag, evt) {
3     originalOnDrag(evt);
4     callback([slider.value]);
5 });
```

Two restrictions apply to the use of incremental re-solving with cooperating solvers: first, all variables that are edited must be only in regions of solvers that support edit constraints; and second, while the edit callback is used, no new constraints can be created. (Edit constraints are just a technique for optimizing the sequence of repeatedly replacing a constraint that a variable equal a constant with a new constraint with a new constant. Thus, if the restrictions aren't met, it is still possible to express and solve the desired constraints, just not as efficiently.)

4   Implementation in Lively Kernel

We have implemented Babelsberg/JS in the Lively Kernel environment [1]. We provide pure JavaScript implementations of DeltaBlue and Cassowary as constraint solvers and extend the Lively Kernel JavaScript interpreter to evaluate constraint expressions. The code is not Lively specific – we use the collection APIs and class system of Lively, but this could be trivially changed. However, when used in the Lively environment, we provide a source transformation that makes writing constraints in the Object Explorer [2] more convenient.

4.1   Assignment

Assignment to objects that are constrained in Babelsberg/JS is the core concept that binds the declarative constraints and imperative code together. Whereas in standard imperative code an assignment writes a value to a memory location, assignments in Babelsberg add equality constraints on constrained objects and trigger re-satisfaction. The new equality constraint may be unsatisfiable, in which case the assignment is not executed and a runtime exception is generated.

As in Babelsberg/R, the Babelsberg/JS runtime informs the developer of a failed assignment by generating a runtime exception. To support the cooperating solvers design, assignment in Babelsberg/JS is a 3-step process:

Set Value. If the new value is the same as the old, we simply return. Otherwise, we convert all read-only constraints on the assigned variable either to required edit constraints (for solvers that support them) or to equality constraints.

If the assigned value has an external variable, i.e., it is constrained by a solver that can handle its type (for example a real in Cassowary), the new value is input into the furthest upstream solver using an equality constraint and this solver is then called. Afterwards, the equality constraint for assignment is removed. However, if the solver cannot satisfy its constraints with the new value, an exception is raised.

Update Downstream Variables. For all external variables except the primary one (the one in the most upstream solver), the new value is input into the solver. If any of the solvers fail to satisfy their constraints with the new value, an exception is generated and all read-only constraints are re-enabled as above.

All remaining constraints are in solvers that cannot handle the type of that variable. Consequently, its value was treated as a constant in their constraint expressions. With the new value, these have to be recalculated. The old variable value is remembered and the new value is stored. These constraints are disabled, their expressions re-evaluated in constraint construction mode, and then the constraints are re-enabled. If any constraint in this set fails to run its expression or cannot be satisfied with the new value, the old value is restored and an exception is generated.

Update Connected Variables. Finally, we have to update the variables connected to the assigned variable. To do so, we create the transitive closure of all variables connected to the assignee through constraints. For all these variables, a new value has already been created for all solvers that already ran, but their downstream read-only constraints still have to be updated. These variables have to go through the first two steps of the assignment process, returning early if their values have not changed.

At this point, assignment can only fail for variables that are in solvers that have not run yet. These are only solvers that the primary assignee is not part of. If any one of these solvers cannot satisfy their constraints with the new value, we restore the old value, re-satisfy the constraints, and raise an exception. While this may leave the system in a different state than it was in before assignment (depending on the implementation of the participating solvers, they may not deterministically find the same solution to the same set of constraints) the system will still be in a state that satisfies all previous constraints.

Deferred Assignment of Connected Variables. Babelsberg/R included an optimization to defer copying the values from a solver to the object-oriented variable location after assignment. Instead of copying the values for all affected variables immediately, the variable's values would be copied when they are next used in imperative code. This optimization cannot be used with our cooperating constraint solver architecture. Consider the following contrived example:

```
1  var obj = {a: 10, b: 10, c: true};
2  always: { solver: cassowary
3      obj.a + obj.b == 20
4  }
5  always: { solver: deltablue
6    obj.c.formula([obj.b], function (b) {
7      if (b == 13) throw "unlucky";
8      return b < 10;
9    })
10 }
11 obj.a = 7;
```

When `obj.a` changes, Cassowary is called to resatisfy the first constraint. However, to trigger DeltaBlue to solve the second constraint, the new value for `obj.b` has to be copied immediately, rather than when obj.b is next read. Otherwise, a failure to satisfy the second constraint is only encountered sometime later in the execution and difficult to trace back to the assignment that caused it.

Assigning Mutable Objects. So far we have described how assignment is handled for atomic objects, such as integers and floats. We have not, in our design, addressed the case of mutable objects with substructure. Consider the following midpoint line:

```
1 var line = {start: pt(0,0), end: pt(1,1), midpoint = pt(0,0)};
2 always: { solver: cassowary
3   var center = line.start.getPosition().
4                  addPt(line.end.getPosition()).scaleBy(0.5);
5   line.midpoint.getPosition().eqPt(center);
6 }
7
8 line.midpoint = pt(1, 1);
```

There are two ways to look at such an assignment: a) the assignment asserts equality between midpoint and pt(1, 1) — both mutable objects — not their x and y parts. So the solver could also modify the parts of the newly assigned point to satisfy the constraint. This seems counter-intuitive, so presumably the right-hand side of an assignment should be read-only to the solver. On the other hand, there are use-cases for constraints for example in input rectification [26], where programmers may expect the system to fix the assigned object, rather than reject the assignment.

For now, we consider the behavior in this case to be implementation defined. Babelsberg/JS marks the assigned objects' parts with strong stay constraints. This means that, as long as other constraints allow, the solver will not change the new position for the midpoint. The design of a general solution is subject of further research.

Changing the Type of Variables. Most solvers only provide support for a limited number of type domains (such as reals or booleans). When variables are used in constraints, their current values determine how they are handled by the solvers. Changing the type of a variable, although possible in a dynamic language, is a relatively uncommon operation, so slow performance is acceptable. When it does occur, the variable is removed from all solvers, all its constraints are disabled, and its constraint expressions are re-executed in constraint construction mode, thus creating new solver-specific representations.

4.2 Constraint Construction

When a programmer writes a function that contains a constraint expression, this expression is evaluated using our JavaScript *ConstraintInterpreter*. Popular JavaScript VMs[2] (Apple Safari's SquirrelFish[3], Google Chrome's V8[4], Mozilla

---

[2] http://www.w3schools.com/browsers/browsers_stats.asp
[3] http://trac.webkit.org/wiki/SquirrelFish
[4] https://code.google.com/p/v8/

Firefox's SpiderMonkey [27], or Microsoft's Chakra[5]) do not provide direct access to the native interpreter or execution context of the caller, so our interpreter cannot look up names used in the constraint expression in the caller's environment. Instead, those names have to be passed explicitly.

Babelsberg/JS provides a source-to-source transformation based on *UglifyJS*[6], which collects names from the context and modifies the source code to pass those names into the constraint expression. This source transformation is enabled automatically when programmers use Babelsberg/JS in the Lively Kernel's Object Editor. For other JavaScript code, they have to provide a context object explicitly.[7]

Given a context, a function, and a solver, the ConstraintInterpreter executes the expressions in the function to create the constraint. The ConstraintInterpreter subclasses a JavaScript interpreter, modifying its behavior in three main aspects:

1. Slot accesses are intercepted. For each slot accessed during the execution of a constraint expression, property accessors are created that delegate access to a *ConstrainedVariable* object. For each slot, only one ConstrainedVariable is created on first access. ConstrainedVariables manage the communication with the various solvers and create solver specific representations of the slot value.

2. Certain unary (! and -) and binary operations (arithmetic, equality, inequalities, conjunction) are not interpreted as usual if an operand is a ConstrainedVariable or an expression involving ConstrainedVariables. Instead, the constraint object is sent a message to construct a solver-specific expression representing the operation and that expression is returned. For example, in Cassowary, the expression a.value <= b.value would return a *LinearInequality* object.

3. Functions invoked in the expression are also interpreted in the ConstraintInterpreter by default. However, the plain JavaScript interpreter is used if the receiver is a ConstrainedVariable. In that case, the call is executed using normal JavaScript execution semantics. This is required to avoid creating constraints on the state of the solvers themselves.

The responsibility of ConstrainedVariables during constraint construction is to pass calls to the appropriate solver. To that end, a ConstrainedVariable lazily builds a mapping from solvers to solver-specific representations of its value. During construction, if the programmer has explicitly selected a solver, this solver is

---

[5] http://en.wikipedia.org/wiki/Chakra(JScriptengine)

[6] http://lisperator.net/uglifyjs/

[7] Note that we cannot use eval to access the outer scope. If we only supported constraints that access fields of objects in the scope and do not call user defined functions, we could have rewritten the code and evaluated the constraint expression using JavaScript's eval function, which has access to the enclosing scope. Using a custom interpreter, however, allows us to easily instrument the execution of most user-defined functions, so we can use normal object-oriented methods in constraint expressions.

asked to provide a value representation by sending the message constraintVariableFor with the value as argument. If no solver was provided, the value is sent the constraintSolver message. Solver libraries may override this message for types that they can operate on. If the value responds with a solver instance, this solver becomes the active solver for the currently constructed constraint and is asked to provide a representation, again by sending constraintVariableFor.

Whenever a new representation is created in this manner, the solvers are sorted to determine which region the variable belongs to. Only the solver responsible for this region may write to the variable; as far as all other solvers are concerned it is read-only.

4.3   Determining Cooperating Solver Regions

The architecture for cooperating constraint solvers requires that each variable must be read-only in all but one of the regions that it occurs in. Furthermore, the regions and associated solvers must form an acyclic graph.

In Babelsberg/JS, when a variable appears in a new solver, we gather the solvers for the variable and sort them into regions. The region information is stored as a property of a solver instance. This allows, for example, the use of multiple instances of the same solver in different regions.

The variable is marked read-only for all solvers except the one in the furthest upstream region, the *defining solver*. This means that new values are assigned by calling suggestValue on the defining solver, and that all other solvers are triggered (in descending order of regions) once the defining solver has resatisfied its constraints, as described in Section 4.1.

4.4   Edit Constraints

Since the original Babelsberg design did not include language-level support for edit constraints, these were supplied by the solver libraries. In Babelsberg/R, the meta-level protocol for inspecting constraints was used to support edit constraints in Cassowary and DeltaBlue. The programmer called the appropriate edit method with the objects to be edited and a stream that would provide new values. The Constraint meta-protocol was used to create edit variables, constrain them to be equal to the supplied variables, and update them from the stream.

To support cooperating incremental re-solving (cf. Section 3.2), in Babelsberg/JS there are two changes to this scheme. First, to support edit constraints within a single thread, the edit method returns a callback to input new values into the solvers, rather than taking a stream of values. Second, since the language design now supports edit constraints explicitly, the solvers have to provide a specific edit constraint API.

Upon calling the edit method, the following methods are called on the solvers and the supplied variables, in order:

prepareEdit is called on each solver variable. In this method, variables can prepare themselves for editing. In Cassowary, for example, this would call the addEditVar method on the solver with the variable as argument. For DeltaBlue, this creates an EditConstraint on the variable and adds it to the list of constraints.

beginEdit is called once for each solver participating in the edit before the callback is returned. In Cassowary, this initializes the edit constants array and prepares the solver for fast re-solving when these constants change. In DeltaBlue, the solver generates an execution plan to solve the constraints starting with the EditConstraints as input.

Now the callback can be used to input new values into the system and trigger re-solving. The callback will call resolveArray on each solver with the new values and update the object's storage (so other observers and hooks around the values still work). Because the solver's execution plan is fixed for the duration of an edit, we disallow creating new edit callbacks before the current edit has finished. When new constraints are created, the execution plan may also become invalid, but we do not enforce invalidating the edit callback in this case.

To finish editing, the callback is simply called without supplying new values.

finishEdit is sent to each solver variable. Cassowary variables do nothing here, DeltaBlue variables remove their EditConstraints from the solver.

endEdit is called once for each solver to reset the solver state.

Compared to Babelsberg/R, this makes the interface for edit constraints uniform across solvers and also allows it to work with cooperating solvers. However, each solver now has to provide some support for this, so more work is required to enable the feature.

5 Performance Evaluation

Our design tries to provide reasonable performance for a variety of applications. To evaluate its performance, we investigated two scenarios: a) how constraint solving performance compares with using imperative code to satisfy the constraints, b) how object-oriented performance is affected by our extension (thus comparing the use of Babelsberg/JS with calling a constraint satisfaction library from standard imperative code).

For the first problem, we used a Kaleidoscope example as a benchmark [28]. (The same benchmark was used for Babelsberg/R.) In this example, we simulate a user interaction in which the user drags a slider to adjust the upper end of the mercury in a thermometer. The constraints are that the mercury should follow the mouse if possible, but must not go outside the thermometer, and that the graphical representation of the thermometer and mercury (using a gray and a white rectangle) as well as a number displaying the current value, should be updated.

We compare the performance of a purely imperative solution using branches and assignments, a constraint version that calls the Cassowary constraint satisfaction library from imperative code, and a version with the same set of constraints in Babelsberg/JS (cf. Appendix B). Both of the constraint versions use edit constraints.

	Imperative	Library	Babelsberg/JS
100x	1.47 ± 0.128	24 ± 0.486	109 ± 2.29
1,000x	1.62 ± 0.0922	143 ± 4.26	214 ± 4.89
10,000x	1.86 ± 0.382	1445 ± 270	1311 ± 304

	Unconstrained Access	Constrained Access
1,000x	3.31 ± 0.289	8.57 ± 1.08
10,000x	20.4 ± 0.694	29.8 ± 1.82
100,000x	189 ± 5.83	241 ± 15.9

All numbers are the average execution time in milliseconds ± the standard deviation. We ran each set of iterations 10 times on Firefox 27 on a 3.2 Ghz Intel Core i5. This micro-benchmark show that, in extreme cases, the object-constraint versions are many hundred times slower than the purely imperative solution. However, Babelsberg/JS is comparable to the library-based approach. Using a library has less overhead for few iterations (where creating the constraints takes a large portion of the time in Babelsberg/JS). However, in both cases, by using edit constraints, we can achieve acceptable performance for repeatedly solving a set of constraints with varying input values. Considering that Babelsberg/JS is intended for imperative programmers who want to express constraints in some parts of their programs, we expect that most of the time the VM will not be solving constraints in tight loops, but running mostly imperative code intermingled with constraint re-satisfaction. Furthermore, we think the benefits for comprehensibility, code size, and robustness justify the performance impact in some system parts. The imperative code is more complex because it has to make all cases explicit using branches, it is hard to tell whether the solution is optimal or complete, and the constraints are hard to derive from the code.

To test how the purely object-oriented parts of a system are affected if we pass objects with constraints to them, we measured the overhead of field access for constrained versus unconstrained fields by repeatedly reading the same 5 properties from an object first without and then with equality constraints on each variable. These results are comparable to those for Babelsberg/R and show that the overhead for reading constrained objects in purely imperative parts of the code is minimal.

In our example applications — the circuit simulation, color palette chooser, and temperature converter presented above, as well as a simple particle simulation, an available-to-promise function, and a layout example — the overhead of constraints was much less pronounced and they provided interactive performance, often even without using edit constraints.

6   Future Work and Conclusion

We have presented a design for implementing an Object Constraint Programming language without VM support, which is realized as a JavaScript extension called Babelsberg/JS. We have also implemented a number of features from the original

OCP design, including unified language constructs for constraint definition and object-oriented code, automatic maintenance of constraints, integration with the existing syntax and semantics, an interface to add new solvers and constraint solver constructs such as read-only variables and incremental re-solving; and also extended the design to support cooperating constraint solvers. There are a number of directions for future work.

Usability of Babelsberg/JS. An important area for future work is the evaluation of the usability of our approach in general applications. We are interested in the comprehensibility of Babelsberg/JS code, especially to the target group for this language, i.e., imperative programmers with little prior experience with constraint programming. This will also provide opportunity to compare performance on more practical examples.

Debugging, Explanation, and Solver Selection. It is currently difficult to tell why a solver may not be able to satisfy a given constraint, why it produced an unexpected result, or why finding a solution is slow. Our ConstraintInterpreter should include support for reasoning about the constraint system it builds. Prolog (or just a direct backtracking algorithm) may be useful as a "meta-solver" to automatically find a solver (or set of solvers) for a particular configuration of constraints.

Other Babelsberg/R features. Babelsberg/R included support for more OCP features that we have omitted for now in this work. Specifically, we want to add support for identity [29], class, and message protocol constraints. Furthermore, to control when solving is invoked, Babelsberg/R provides multi-assignments to update multiple values simultaneously before a solver is invoked. Finally, we plan to add the convenience methods once and assert ... during... to control the duration of constraints, although these could be trivially added using the meta-protocol of Constraint objects.

Babelsberg/JS, compared to the earlier Babelsberg/R implementation, can be applied more directly to existing problems. It runs unmodified in different Web browsers, and integrates with the existing imperative language and libraries. The work reported here is quite recent, and we expect to continue to evolve both the language and its implementation.

References

1. Ingalls, D., Palacz, K., Uhler, S., Taivalsaari, A., Mikkonen, T.: The lively kernel A self-supporting system on a web page. In: Hirschfeld, R., Rose, K. (eds.) S3 2008. LNCS, vol. 5146, pp. 31–50. Springer, Heidelberg (2008)
2. Lincke, J., Krahn, R., Ingalls, D., Roder, M., Hirschfeld, R.: The Lively PartsBin– a cloud-based repository for collaborative development of active web content. In: 2012 45th Hawaii International Conference on System Science (HICSS 2012), pp. 693–701. IEEE (2012)

3. Sutherland, I.: Sketchpad: A man-machine graphical communication system. In: Proceedings of the Spring Joint Computer Conference, IFIPS, pp. 329–346 (1963)
4. Borning, A.: The programming language aspects of ThingLab, a constraint-oriented simulation laboratory. ACM Transactions on Programming Languages and Systems 3(4), 353–387 (1981)
5. Felgentreff, T., Borning, A., Hirschfeld, R.: Babelsberg: Specifying and solving constraints on object behavior. Technical Report 81, Hasso-Plattner-Institut, Potsdam, Germany (May 2014)
6. Lopez, G., Freeman-Benson, B., Borning, A.: Kaleidoscope: A constraint imperative programming language. In: Constraint Programming. NATO Advanced Science Institute Series, Series F: Computer and System Sciences, vol. 131, pp. 313–329. Springer (1994)
7. Grabmüller, M., Hofstedt, P.: Turtle: A constraint imperative programming language. In: Research and Development in Intelligent Systems XX, pp. 185–198. Springer (2004)
8. Badros, G.J., Borning, A., Stuckey, P.J.: The Cassowary linear arithmetic constraint solving algorithm. ACM Transactions on Computer-Human Interaction (TOCHI) 8(4), 267–306 (2001)
9. De Moura, L., Bjørner, N.: Z3: An efficient SMT solver. In: Ramakrishnan, C.R., Rehof, J. (eds.) TACAS 2008. LNCS, vol. 4963, pp. 337–340. Springer, Heidelberg (2008)
10. Torlak, E., Jackson, D.: Kodkod: A relational model finder. In: Grumberg, O., Huth, M. (eds.) TACAS 2007. LNCS, vol. 4424, pp. 632–647. Springer, Heidelberg (2007)
11. Sadun, E.: iOS Auto Layout Demystified. Addison-Wesley (October 2013)
12. Enthought Inc: Enaml 0.6.3 documentation (February 2014)
13. Ohshima, Y., Lunzer, A., Freudenberg, B., Kaehler, T.: KScript and KSWorld: A time-aware and mostly declarative language and interactive GUI framework. In: Proceedings of the 2013 ACM International Symposium on New Ideas, New Paradigms, and Reflections on Programming & Software, Onward! 2013, pp. 117–134. ACM, New York (2013)
14. Meyerovich, L.A., Guha, A., Baskin, J., Cooper, G.H., Greenberg, M., Bromfield, A., Krishnamurthi, S.: Flapjax: A programming language for Ajax applications. ACM SIGPLAN Notices 44(10), 1–20 (2009)
15. Flanagan, D., Matsumoto, Y.: The Ruby Programming Language. O'Reilly (January 2008)
16. Freeman-Benson, B.N., Maloney, J., Borning, A.: An incremental constraint solver. Communications of the ACM 33(1), 54–63 (1990)
17. Rinard, M., Cadar, C., Nguyen, H.H.: Exploring the acceptability envelope. In: Companion to the 20th Annual ACM SIGPLAN Conference on Object-oriented Programming, Systems, Languages, and Applications (OOPSLA 2005), pp. 21–30. ACM (October 2005)
18. Milicevic, A., Rayside, D., Yessenov, K., Jackson, D.: Unifying execution of imperative and declarative code. In: 33rd International Conference on Software Engineering (ICSE), pp. 511–520 (May 2011)
19. Resnick, M., Maloney, J., Monroy-Hernández, A., Rusk, N., Eastmond, E., Brennan, K., Millner, A., Rosenbaum, E., Silver, J., Silverman, B., et al.: Scratch: programming for all. Communications of the ACM 52(11), 60–67 (2009)
20. Jaffar, J., Lassez, J.L.: Constraint logic programming. In: Proceedings of the 14th ACM Principles of Programming Languages Conference (POPL 1987), pp. 111–119. ACM (January 1987)

21. Borning, A., Freeman-Benson, B., Wilson, M.: Constraint hierarchies. LISP and Symbolic Computation 5(3), 223–270 (1992)
22. Van Cutsem, T., Miller, M.S.: Proxies: Design principles for robust object-oriented intercession APIs. ACM Sigplan Notices 45(12), 59–72 (2010)
23. Kang, S., Ryu, S.: Formal specification of a JavaScript module system. In: Proceedings of the ACM International Conference on Object-Oriented Programming Systems Languages and Applications, pp. 621–638. ACM (2012)
24. Borning, A.: Architectures for cooperating constraint solvers. Technical Report VPRI Memo M-2012-003, Viewpoints Research Institute, Glendale, California (May 2012)
25. Nelson, G., Oppen, D.: Simplification by cooperating decision procedures. ACM Transactions on Programming Languages and Systems 1, 245–257 (1979)
26. Long, F., Ganesh, V., Carbin, M., Sidiroglou, S., Rinard, M.: Automatic input rectification. In: 2012 34th International Conference on Software Engineering (ICSE), pp. 80–90. IEEE (2012)
27. Gal, A., Eich, B., Shaver, M., Anderson, D., Mandelin, D., Haghighat, M.R., Kaplan, B., Hoare, G., Zbarsky, B., Orendorff, J., et al.: Trace-based just-in-time type specialization for dynamic languages. ACM Sigplan Notices 44(6), 465–478 (2009)
28. Lopez, G., Freeman-Benson, B., Borning, A.: Kaleidoscope: A constraint imperative programming language. In: Constraint Programming. NATO Advanced Science Institute Series, Series F: Computer and System Sciences, vol. 131, pp. 313–329. Springer (1994)
29. Lopez, G., Freeman-Benson, B., Borning, A.: Constraints and object identity. In: Pareschi, R. (ed.) ECOOP 1994. LNCS, vol. 821, pp. 260–279. Springer, Heidelberg (1994)

A   Examples

Circuits. The circuit parts are represented by classes that create constraints in their initializers. (The context has to be passed because classes are written in plain JavaScript files in Lively without source transformation.) The code to connect leads is omitted (it constrains voltages to be equal and the sum of currents to be 0.0 between leads).

```
1  Object.subclass('TwoLeadedObject', {
2      initialize: function() {
3          this.lead1 = {voltage: 0.0, current: 0.0};
4          this.lead2 = {voltage: 0.0, current: 0.0};
5          always({solver: cassowary, ctx: {self: this}}, function () {
6              return self.lead1.current + self.lead2.current == 0.0;
7          });
8      },
9  });
10 TwoLeadedObject.subclass('Resistor', {
11     initialize: function($super, resistance) {
12         $super();
13         this.resistance = resistance;
14         always({solver: cassowary, ctx: {self: this}}, function () {
15             return self.lead2.voltage - self.lead1.voltage ==
16                     self.lead2.current * resistance
17         })
18     },
19 });
20 TwoLeadedObject.subclass('Battery', {
21     initialize: function($super, supplyVoltage) {
22         $super();
23         this.supplyVoltage = supplyVoltage;
24         always({solver: cassowary,
25                 ctx: {self: this, supply: this.supplyVoltage}},
26         function () {
27             return self.lead2.voltage - self.lead1.voltage == supply
28         })
29     },
30 });
31 Object.subclass('Ground', {
32     initialize: function() {
33         this.lead = {voltage: 0.0, current: 0.0};
34         always({solver: cassowary, ctx: {self: this}}, function () {
35             return self.lead.voltage == 0.0 && self.lead.current == 0.0
36         })
37     },
38 });
39 TwoLeadedObject.subclass('Wire', {
40     initialize: function($super) {
41         $super();
42         always({solver: cassowary, ctx: {self: this}}, function () {
43             return self.lead1.voltage == self.lead2.voltage
44         })
45     },
46 });
47 TwoLeadedObject.subclass('Voltmeter', {
48     initialize: function($super) {
49         $super();
50         this.readingVoltage = 0.0;
51         always({solver: cassowary, ctx: {self: this}}, function () {
52             return self.lead1.current == 0.0 &&
53                 self.lead2.voltage - self.lead1.voltage == self.readingVoltage
54         })
55     },
56 });
```

B   Benchmarks

For comparing purely imperative to purely constraint-oriented performance we started with the following imperative version.

```
 1 for (var i = 0; i < this.Iterations; i++) {
 2     mouse.location_y = i
 3     var old = mercury.top
 4     mercury.top = mouse.location_y
 5     if (mercury.top > thermometer.top)
 6         mercury.top = thermometer.top
 7     if (old < mercury.top) // move gray rect upwards (draws over the white)
 8         gray.top = mercury.top
 9     else // move white rect downwards (draws over the gray)
10         white.bottom = mercury.top
11     display.number = mercury.top
12 }
```

In the constraint library and Babelsberg/JS versions, we specify the same constraints and use an edit constraint in the same manner, once through the Cassowary API and once in the syntax of Babelsberg/JS. Given below is the Babelsberg/JS version. (The solver argument is omitted for brevity.)

```
 1 always(function() { return display.number == mercury.top });
 2 always(function() { return white.top == thermometer.top });
 3 always(function() { return white.bottom == mercury.top });
 4 always(function() { return gray.top == mercury.top });
 5 always(function() { return gray.bottom == mercury.bottom });
 6 always(function() { return mercury.top <= thermometer.top });
 7 always(function() { return mercury.bottom == thermometer.bottom });
 8 always({priority: "strong"}, function() {
 9     return mercury.top == mouse.location_y
10 });
11
12 var cb = edit(ctx.mouse, ["location_y"]);
13 for (var i = 0; i < this.Iterations; i++) {
14     cb(i);
15 }
```

To compare accessor performance with and without constraints, we measured the following two loops individually:

```
 1 var o = {get a() {return 0}, get b() {return 0}, get c() {return 0}},
 2     oc = {a: 0, b: 0, c: 0};
 3 always({solver: cassowary, ctx: {oc: oc}}, function() {
 4     return oc.a==0 && oc.b==0 && oc.c==0
 5 });
 6
 7 for (var i = 0; i < this.Iterations; i++) {
 8     sum = o.a + o.b + o.c;
 9 }
10 for (var i = 0; i < this.Iterations; i++) {
11     sum = oc.a + oc.b + oc.c;
12 }
```

C Artifact Description

Authors of the Artifact. Design and documentation: Tim Felgentreff, Alan Borning, Robert Hirschfeld, Jens Lincke, Yoshiki Ohshima, Bert Freudenberg, Robert Krahn. Core developer: Tim Felgentreff.

Summary. The artifact shows Babelsberg/JS, an implementation of the Babelsberg design for object-constraint programming in the Lively Kernel. It includes an installation of the Lively Kernel environment and a number of example applications, some of which are mentioned in the paper. A screencast shows how the examples can be accessed. The provided package is designed to support repeatability of the experiments of the paper: in particular, it allows users to try and modify the example applications from the paper, as well as to run the benchmarks.

Babelsberg/JS uses a modified JavaScript interpreter to transform constraint expressions into constraints that are handed to the Cassowary and DeltaBlue constraint solver libraries. The full source code is included in the Lively Kernel environment, and instructions for exploring it are included.

Content. The artifact package includes:

- a Babelsberg/JS installation in a local Lively Kernel environment;
- the Chromium browser already open on a Lively Kernel world;
- a screencast that shows how to interact with the examples.

We provide a VirtualBox disk image for testing Babelsberg/JS. The image contains a stripped down installation of Ubuntu 13.10 LTS set up to launch Chromium directly with the screencast and the Lively Kernel page already open. Through port forwarding the environment is also accessible from the host: `http://localhost:9001/users/timfelgentreff/ecoop_artifact.html`.
Note that to access the latter, we recommend a WebKit-based browser (Safari, Chrome, or their derivatives) or a recent version of Firefox (29 at the time of this writing).

Getting the Artifact. The artifact endorsed by the Artifact Evaluation Committee is available free of charge as supplementary material of this paper on SpringerLink.

Tested Platforms. The artifact is known to work on Oracle VirtualBox version 4 (`https://www.virtualbox.org/`) with at least 512 MB RAM.

License. BSD-3-Clause (`http://opensource.org/licenses/BSD-3-Clause`) for Babelsberg/JS, MIT (`http://opensource.org/licenses/MIT`) for the Lively Kernel environment

MD5 Sum of the Artifact. 57324cb58f7a517ab1abd1088bbd9d0f

Size of the Artifact. 810 MB

Automated Multi-Language Artifact Binding and Rename Refactoring between Java and DSLs Used by Java Frameworks

Philip Mayer and Andreas Schroeder

Programming & Software Engineering Group
Ludwig-Maximilians-Universität München, Germany
{mayer,schroeder}@pst.ifi.lmu.de

Abstract. Developing non-trivial software applications involves using multiple programming languages. Although each language is used to describe a particular aspect of the system, artifacts defined inside those languages reference each other across language boundaries; such references are often only resolved at runtime. However, it is important for developers to be aware of these references during development time for programming understanding, bug prevention, and refactoring. In this work, we report on a) an approach and tool for automatically identifying multi-language relevant artifacts, finding references between artifacts in different languages, and (rename-) refactoring them, and b) on an experimental evaluation of the approach on seven open-source case studies which use a total of six languages found in three frameworks. As our main result, we provide insights into the incidence of multi-language bindings in the case studies as well as the feasibility of automated multi-language rename refactorings.

Keywords: multi language software, polyglot programming, Java, domain-specific languages, program comprehension, refactoring, experiment.

1 Introduction

The use of multiple programming languages in the development of a software system is a common occurrence in software creation. In many cases, a multitude of languages is used; this includes the well-known general purpose languages Java, C, C++, JavaScript, or Ruby; but also domain-specific languages (DSLs) which are dedicated to certain areas, such as the database field (SQL, HQL, Entity Mapping Files), user interface design (HTML, JSP, JSF, OpenGL, SVG, CSS) or system setup and configuration (WSDL, Spring IOC, OSGi DS).

There are different reasons for using multiple languages in the development of a software system. A usually cited benefit is increased productivity [3] through the use of specialized languages for a certain domain (language-as-a-tool metaphor). Additional reasons lie in the use of legacy code (system integration) and in the expertise of the developers at hand.

R. Jones (Ed.): ECOOP 2014, LNCS 8586, pp. 437–462, 2014.
© Springer-Verlag Berlin Heidelberg 2014

Applications consisting of parts written in different programming languages have been called Multi-Language Software Applications (MLSAs) [9]. Each part and thus language is used to encode a particular aspect of the system. However, each of the parts usually also contains software artifacts which, due to certain properties such as their name or position, are relevant *across language borders*, being *bound* to artifacts in a different language. Binding of such artifacts usually happens at runtime by a framework or (virtual) machine.

Unfortunately, such multi-language bindings can lead to problems, both in the initial software creation phase and in maintenance, since they must be kept intact for the system to exhibit the proper behavior. Throughout development and maintenance as well as in program understanding, programmers must be aware not only of the semantics of the individual languages, but also of the semantics of the frameworks which handle the multi-language bindings which leads to added mental load. This is a particular problem in refactoring: If an artifact is changed without changing the referenced artifacts in other languages, the overall system semantics changes (and the system might break altogether). Worrying about such problems may lead developers to be hesitant about refactorings, which means the accumulation of technical debt [15].

We believe that a generic and systematic approach to supporting multi-language software systems can help to improve the situation for developers and increase productivity. In this work, we report on an investigation into such an approach within the Java ecosystem, i.e. in software systems which use Java as their main programming language and employ frameworks with domain-specific languages for implementing the non-Java parts of the system.

Our work contributes to the state of the art in three ways:

- we propose an approach for multi-language support in IDEs in which language artifacts and artifact bindings are handled as top-level entities,
- we present an implementation of this approach, including automated discovery and binding of artifacts at design time as well as rename refactoring across six languages from three frameworks,
- we evaluate our approach and tool on seven open-source case studies, giving empirical evidence of a) incidence of multi-language artifacts and bindings and b) accuracy of discovery, binding, and rename refactoring of our tool.

Our evaluation shows that we can indeed automatically discover, bind, and refactor artifacts in 3783 multi-language bindings — with full success in 95.96% of cases and with well-justified warnings to the user in the remaining cases.

2   Exploration Area and Motivating Example

We have selected the Java ecosystem as our area of investigation, that is software which uses Java as the main programming language and domain-specific languages provided by Java frameworks for encoding specific aspects of the system. The three areas, or domains, of *system configuration*, *database querying*, and *user interface design* each feature a number of such frameworks; from each, we have selected one framework for further investigation:

- The *Spring framework*[1] includes an XML dialect for configuring Java objects, in particular using dependency injection through JavaBean-style properties. We refer to this language as the Spring language.
- The *Hibernate OO mapper*[2] allows definition of the mapping between Java classes and database tables in another XML dialect (HBM). Additionally, the Hibernate Query Language (HQL) is used for querying the database (in the form of the defined entities). We refer to the first as the HBM language, the second as the HQL language.
- The *Wicket UI framework*[3] also contains two conceptual languages. The first is an extension to HTML used for defining HTML rendering templates. These templates are inflated and populated using a corresponding UI component tree providing dynamic data, which is defined in Java using the Wicket API, an internal DSL which we call Wicket/API. Bindings between Wicket/HTML and Wicket/API are established through the use of corresponding identifier strings.

Each of the languages in these frameworks offer two to five artifact types which are potentially bound to artifacts in other languages. These artifacts, which are shown in Figure 1, are defined and exemplified in the corresponding framework documentations and implementations.

The diagram shows the Java language in the center with the artifact types Constructor, Type, Parameter, and Method/Field (mostly, one or the other is used; therefore, they are shown together). These artifacts may be bound to three DSLs: Spring, HBM, and Wicket/API. From HBM and Wicket/API, additional multi-language bindings may lead to HQL and Wicket/HTML, respectively.

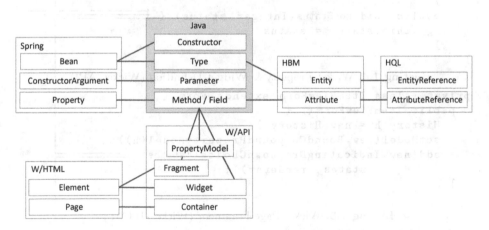

Fig. 1. Artifact Bindings Across Languages

---

[1] www.springsource.com
[2] www.hibernate.org
[3] wicket.apache.org

Listing 1.1. Hibernate Queries (HQL)

```
1 public class HibernateJtracDao {
2   public int bulkUpdateStatusToOpen(Space sp,
3                                     int st) {
4     int c = bulkUpdate("update Item i set i.status=?
          where i.status=? and i.space.id=?",
5       new Object[] { State.OPEN, st, sp.getId()});
6   }
7 }
```

Listing 1.2. Hibernate Mapping (HBM)

```
1 <hibernate-mapping package="info.jtrac.domain">
2   <class name="Item" table="items">
3     <property name="status" column="status"/>
4   </class>
5   <class name="History" table="history">
6     <property name="status" column="status"/>
7   </class>
8 </hibernate-mapping>
```

Listing 1.3. Java

```
1 public abstract class AbstractItem {
2   public Integer getStatus() {
3     return status;
4   }
5   public void setStatus(Integer status) {
6     this.status = status;
7   }
8 }
```

Listing 1.4. Wicket Property & Widget Definition (Wicket/API)

```
1 private class ItemViewForm extends Form {
2   public ItemViewForm() {
3     History h = new History();
4     setModel(new BoundCompoundPropertyModel(h));
5     add(new IndicatingDropDownChoice("status",
6             states, renderer));
7   }
8 }
```

Listing 1.5. Wicket Page Fragment (Wicket/HTML)

```
1 <form wicket:id="form">
2   <select wicket:id="status"/>
3 </form>
```

As a motivation for our work, we give an example from one of our case studies which shows how multi-language bindings look like in real life. The example, which is shown in Listings 1.1 to 1.5, shows bindings between Java, HBM, HQL, Wicket/API, and Wicket/HTML.

We begin with the property `status` in Listing 1.3, which is defined with JavaBean-style getters and setters in the abstract class `AbstractItem`. This class is the common superclass of the classes `Item` and `History` (which are not shown). However, these two classes are also Hibernate entities and defined as such in Listing 1.2 along with a `status` property each, which is bound to the getters and setters for `status` as shown. This Hibernate property is used in HQL queries in Listing 1.1; in this case, on the entity `Item` or rather its alias `i`.

The property `status` of the `History` subclass of `AbstractItem`, as defined in Listing 1.3, is also referenced from Wicket/API (Listing 1.4, line 4) through a `BoundComponentPropertyModel`, where `History` is defined as a data source for the `DropDownChoice` widget in line 5. The `status` string used in line 5 is also used as a widget identifier between Wicket/API and Wicket/HTML; the latter is shown in Listing 1.5.

Thus, the example shows a total of nine multi-language bindings between eight artifacts across five languages (or one general-purpose language and two frameworks). If any of these elements is renamed, all of the others must be renamed as well since the bindings are created (among other things) due to name resolution. It is additionally to be expected that the getters and setters from Java are also referenced elsewhere such that any invocations must be refactored as well. The same applies to any other use of the Hibernate HBM property definition and the ID of the Wicket/API widget.

To evaluate automated discovery and rename refactoring of such bindings, we employed seven open-source case studies with a size between 6k and 110k LOC (see Table 1). Two of the case studies use mainly Spring; two use mainly Hibernate; and two use mainly Wicket. A seventh uses all three frameworks in combination. We discuss how the case studies were used for evaluation in Section 4.

3   Multi-Language Artifact Binding and Rename Refactoring

The use of multiple additional languages in Java software systems is not new. Accordingly, existing Java IDEs already contain some support for finding artifacts bindings and for refactoring across language borders. However, such solutions are usually rather isolated: There is sporadic support in the form of IDE plug-ins for particular frameworks such as Spring or Hibernate, for example for Eclipse. There are three major drawbacks to current implementations.

Firstly, there is no generic support for multi-language artifact binding *per se*; that is, IDEs are generally unaware of such bindings unless a plug-in contributes them, in which case each plug-in must provide its own data structure, navigation menus, and so on.

Secondly, current Java IDEs (Eclipse, IDEA, NetBeans) use a *participant* approach to refactoring non-Java elements: Usually, DSL refactorings are implemented as add-ons to existing Java refactorings instead of refactorings in their own right since there is specific support for such participation. By contrast, implementing completely new DSL refactorings with participant support of their own involves significant additional effort. Also, refactoring changes might need to be propagated back and forth between languages as new bindings are identified which is also difficult to implement using current participant approaches (first, participants need to be enabled and disabled depending on where a refactoring is started; second, changes must be gathered in a sort of feedback loop to ensure that every participant may react to changes by others).

Finally, there is no systematic support for handling more than two languages, in particular if they are not directly bound to Java. As indicated above, the artifacts of some DSLs (HQL) might bind to artifacts of other DSLs instead of Java (namely HBM), thus creating cascades of bindings (and thus refactorings).

We believe that a generic, systematic approach to multi-language artifact binding and refactoring will make it easier to implement MLSA support in IDEs and thus lead to better support for developers. We thus investigate an approach to handling multiple languages in IDEs which

- treats all languages, including DSLs, as equals and offers the infrastructure to make artifacts of each language centrally available,
- defers handling of binding resolution between each of the languages to dedicated binding resolvers,
- and allows per-language refactorings to trigger, and be triggered from, generic refactoring routines which propagate changes based on artifact bindings.

We discuss this approach, and a prototype implementation within Eclipse, in the next three sections. Note that the tool we have implemented is not intended to be a product; rather, its aim is demonstrating feasibility and generating the data about real-life software analysis and refactorings.

Section 3.1 discusses artifact discovery, i.e. reading source code and providing artifacts. Section 3.2 discusses the dedicated binding implementations which resolve multi-language bindings. Finally, Section 3.3 discusses how refactorings across language borders are implemented.

3.1   Artifact Discovery

Our approach is based on automated discovery of artifacts relevant for multi-language bindings. With the term *artifact* we refer to a representation of a concept used in the source code, such as, for Java, `TypeDeclarations` which in turn contain `MethodDeclarations`, `LocalVariableDeclarations`, `Statements`, and so on. These artifacts form a *semantic model* [5] in which references or in-language bindings between them are already resolved; for example, a Java `MethodInvocation` is bound to its `MethodDeclaration`.

The benefit of using semantic models is a simplification of the navigation within the code base as well as uniquely identifying artifacts; it is furthermore useful in code analysis and visualization and, in our case, in separating the difficulties in finding artifacts within a language with other multi-language concerns.

A semantic model must be extracted from the source code — a parser is required as well as resolution mechanisms for in-language bindings. We call this process *model discovery*; for each language, a model discoverer must be written and registered with the platform. In our approach, we use one meta-model per language, not a single language-agnostic model. Analysis is later done by analyzing relationships between pairs of individual language models.

Required Effort. The effort required for model discovery routines depends entirely on the language which is analyzed. Regarding difficulty, we can separate the languages we have investigated into two groups. The first group contains Java (the base language, without data flow), Spring, Hibernate Mapping (HBM), and Wicket/HTML. In these languages, it is relatively easy to extract the structure and all artifacts from the source code; furthermore, in-language bindings between elements may be complex, but are based on straightforward and exact rules. Parsers with in-language binding resolution already exist for Java; Spring and HBM are XML-based files such that existing XML parsers may be used to extract data, with a follow-up of in-language binding resolution implemented by hand.

The second group contains HQL and Wicket/API; in other words, languages whose source fully or partially consist of strings handled by Java statements. In both cases, identifiers or query fragments may be combined using an arbitrary number and combination of loops, decisions, and values passed in from the outside. In case of Wicket/API, data and control flow is furthermore used to (manually) construct a UI tree out of objects in memory. This tree of Java objects is required to correspond to the tree created in HTML out of HTML widgets.

Finding and resolving all HQL and Wicket identifiers and artifacts is generally undecidable in the environment they live in, i.e. in a general purpose programming language. We have gone to great length in the model discovery for these languages; however, some elements could not be extracted which in turn leads to various problems in artifact binding and refactoring.

An example of this from one of the case studies is shown in Listing 1.6, where the variable `field` is used in the construction of the query. The contents of `field`, in this case, cannot be resolved in general since it represents a custom contributed database table column. Thus, it is known that *some* attribute of `Item` is accessed, but not which one. In such cases, a specific *unresolved artifact* is added to the model to make this problem explicit (this information is later used to add refactoring warnings).

Listing 1.6. Dynamic Query in HQL

```
bulkUpdate("update Item item set item." +
            field.getName() + " = null");
```

Besides unresolved elements, there may also be *orphan artifacts*. Contrary to the example above, these are artifacts whose reference *from* other model elements cannot be resolved — that is, for example, a widget creation is found in the code, but it is unknown to which page or parent element it belongs. Like unresolved elements, these are reported explicitly in the model.

Static Analysis. For discovering HQL and Wicket artifacts embedded in API calls, we have created a custom static analysis approach on top of the MoDisco Java semantic model[4]. In terms of data flow analysis, our approach is interprocedural (in that it treats method invocations non-atomic) and flow-sensitive (in that it considers the order of statements).

The domain over which our analysis operates is the domain of method and object environments: we keep track of approximations of valuations of stack and heap variables (i.e. local variables and object fields). The values we approximate are strings for HQL queries as well as custom representations of framework data structures such as UI trees for Wicket and query trees for HQL. The transfer functions we use depend on the source of the code they represent: for application code, we use standard transfer functions that correspond to the semantics of Java. For invocations of framework methods, we use custom transfer functions on the representations of framework data structures. For instance, the transfer function for line 5 in Listing 1.4 creates a new drop down choice component, and adds it as child to the `ItemViewForm` component. Invocations of framework methods that are not analyzed (for example, the Java Collections framework) are treated as atomic and ignored.

Our static analysis only performs a single pass over a sequence of program statements following method invocations, and has therefore two pragmatic limitations: firstly, loops found in program code are handled by performing a single pass of the loop body. Secondly, recursive methods are handled by ignoring back-edges in the call graph, i.e., by skipping recursive method calls. Because of these limitations, our static analysis will miss fabricated identifiers and overapproximates artifacts in looping and recursive program code. In the context of model discovery for multi-language artifact binding, however, this is no severe limitation, as every multi-language binding must point to a corresponding static name in another language, and thus fabrication of names is not encouraged in any of the analyzed frameworks.

The analysis routines we implemented proved sufficient to discover the vast majority of artifacts relevant to multi-language artifact binding, as discussed in the next section. Since artifact discovery in HQL and Wicket/API is only a partial aspect of our work, it was not our goal to provide full coverage. In particular, we did not go as far as creating grammars for string expressions found in Java code as in Christensen et al. [2]. Also, we do not provide support for the Java Collection Framework and do not analyze uses of Java Reflection as in Livshits et al. [10].

---

[4] `www.eclipse.org/MoDisco`

3.2 Multi-Language Artifact Binding Resolution

Multi-language binding resolution is concerned with associating artifacts from two languages with one another, based on the rules of the underlying framework (such as Spring). Considering our example in Section 2, the two HQL `AttributeReference` artifacts with name `status` must each be bound to the HBM `Property` with the same name.

The name of an artifact is, in most cases, an important aspect of binding, but it is nearly never the only one: All languages we have investigated are strongly hierarchical; thus, the position of artifacts within such hierarchies is crucial. In our example, the HQL attribute `status` only refers to the `status` property of class `Item`; not any other class. It is obvious that a purely textual search will fail in most cases given such a structure. Furthermore, frameworks usually give developers quite a lot of freedom, i.e. different ways of achieving the same thing, optional bindings, or double meanings for identifiers. The binding resolution routines must take these into account and thus depend on the positioning of elements, attribute value grouping, different naming conventions, and so on. Multi-language binding resolution fails if an artifact is found in one language but its required complementary artifact — based on all the framework rules and options — in another language is not.

For each interesting language pair, we have created dedicated binding resolvers which each use their own custom resolution algorithm. These algorithms are based on the binding logic of the underlying frameworks (i.e. Spring, Hibernate, and Wicket); we have discussed some of these algorithms in detail in [11]. As an example, the binding resolver for Spring first binds Spring beans (from the Spring artifact model) to Java classes (from the Java artifact model) based on fully qualified class names. Afterwards, it binds nested Spring properties to members in the previously bound Java classes based on simple names.

The binding resolution algorithms in our approach thus always bind artifacts of two languages together. This yields five resolution implementations for the six languages we have investigated: Spring and Java, HBM and Java, and Wicket/API and Java are the ones grouped around Java; while HQL and HBM and Wicket/HTML and Wicket/API deal with DSLs on both sides.

The binding results in the form of individual artifacts and the links between them are reported in a common language-agnostic *linking model*. This model later allows identifying the necessary rename operations for a change; its contents are centrally available on the IDE level; thus, two binding resolvers may bind the same Java artifact into different languages, which is what happens, for example, with the `status` property in the example (Listing 1.2). In this way, the IDE can support navigation from artifact to artifact and is aware of transitively connected artifacts; in the case of binding errors, it can report and annotate the offending artifact.

As in model discovery, writing a binding resolver requires effort. While the code implementing the actual resolving is already part of each framework implementation (e.g., in Spring, Hibernate, and Wicket), it is written with a focus on runtime and thus not easily extracted. In fact, in our case, we have re-implemented all resolution code by hand based on the framework documentation and the available framework code. While a good knowledge of the framework involved is certainly a requirement for writing a binding resolver, in most cases the logic, though complex, is not overly difficult and thus does not require a large investment.

3.3 Multi-Language Rename Refactoring

The last part of our approach is support for multi-language rename refactoring. Many refactoring procedures have been defined in the literature [4]. Of these, the most important ones across language borders are rename refactorings, to which we restrict ourselves in this work. These are also the most commonly used automated refactorings: A study in 2012 has shown 44% of all tracked refactorings to be rename refactorings [22].

Renaming artifacts even in one language can get very complex (especially in Java [18]); thus, we believe it is best to re-use existing refactorings rather than implementing new ones for multi-language refactorings. In our work, we therefore assume that each language comes with its own set of automated rename refactorings. This is certainly true for Java in most IDEs; it is less true for the DSLs we have looked at. For some, plug-ins are available which add this functionality, for some, there are not. In the latter cases, we have implemented single-language rename refactorings by hand to ensure an equal setup for all languages (fortunately, the selected DSLs include only limited amounts of in-language bindings and thus the refactorings are rather simple).

Relating Artifact Names. To support rename refactoring across language borders, we need to know how the names of the artifacts relate. Using the information from the multi-language artifact binding, we already know which artifacts are bound across language borders. The binding resolvers discussed in the last section also have the information which properties of these artifacts carry the names relevant for the binding, and how the names are related; to support the refactoring step, this information needs to be attached to the bindings (on a meta-level).

In some cases, the relationship is very simple: If a Spring property is bound to a Java field, the names must match exactly. In other cases, some transformation takes place: If the property is bound to a setter, for example, the Java method name must be prefixed with set and the first letter of the property name must be uppercased (adhering to the JavaBean convention).

Changing Artifacts. Refactoring usually starts from a single change of an artifact property (such as a Java method name) which is triggered by the user. Once known to the multi-language enabled IDE, this change can now be propagated through the multi-language bindings to all artifacts which are (transitively) bound to the artifact in which the change originated, i.e., to its *transitive binding closure*. This closure can be found generically without involving language-specific routines. Note that we may move back and forth between languages in this process: If, for example, we start with Item.status from Listing 1.2 and move to Java, the fact that status is not defined in Item but in a superclass and is used also in History requires us to move back to HBM (and perhaps even HQL).

The resulting transitive closure may contain artifacts from many different languages, each annotated with the information which properties must be changed to which new value. The actual source code-changing rename can now be performed by language-specific refactoring routines as discussed above, which may lead to additional in-language binding renames. For example, renaming a Java method may involve renaming all of the method invocations, which are not relevant across languages but certainly relevant within Java.

Error Conditions. Multi-language refactorings can only be executed on artifacts with established multi-language bindings (otherwise, the original artifact is annotated as having a binding error during binding resolution). Still, a refactoring may not always be possible.

Firstly, there are conditions in which we must inform the user that we do not have sufficient information to guarantee a successful refactoring execution: Such *warnings* result from problems in artifact discovery. As mentioned in Section 3.1, there may be cases where we know that there is an artifact reference present but not exactly which one, indicated through the presence of an *unresolved artifact*. In this case, a warning is attached to the refactoring (as, e.g., the Java rename refactoring does in the presence of parsing errors).

Secondly, any of the single-language refactorings invoked may veto a change (for example, due to a restricted name in a language). In this case, the overall refactoring is aborted with an *error*.

4   Experimental Evaluation

The underlying rationale for automated multi-language binding and refactoring support is improving developer productivity. However, productivity is hard to measure directly. We have thus instead opted for measuring a surrogate endpoint, which is given by the fitness for the particular purpose of our approach; in particular that our tool is able to *automatically* and *correctly*:

- identify multi-language relevant artifacts in each individual language,
- identify and establish the bindings between said artifacts,
- refactor the previously bound artifacts across multiple languages.

Our assumption is that a developer with such tool support is more productive than without. It is future work to test the surrogate against the actual endpoint with adequate empirical studies. In the following, we discuss the setup, execution, and results of our evaluation.

4.1   Experimental Setup

Case Study Setup. We selected seven open-source applications which make use of Java and at least one of the three frameworks we support. Our sampling process was as follows: After having selected the frameworks to investigate (Spring, Hibernate, and Wicket), we performed a search for applications using these frameworks (two for each) in the ohloh.net repository. Unfortunately, the population size was quite small, i.e. we did not find many applications which were a) not trivially sized, b) not frameworks or framework extensions themselves, and c) in a compilable and unit-testable state. We selected the first seven applications for which a) to c) were satisfied.

Table 1. Case Studies

Case	Domain	Languages	Version	LOC
Plazma	ERP+CRM solution	Spring	1.0.2	78k
Tudu Lists	Todo Lists Management	Spring, Hibernate	2.3	6k
itracker	Issue Tracker	Hibernate, Spring	3.1.5	110k
PicketLink	Identity Management	Hibernate	1.3.1	42k
Brix	Content Managament	Wicket	2013-08-21	31k
gidooCMS	Content Management	Wicket	2013-08-21	10k
JTrac	Issue Tracker	All	2.1.0	14k

The cases are listed in Table 1. If possible, the latest stable version was downloaded either from the repository or from a release website. In the case of gidooCMS and Brix, no such version was available; a snapshot was instead taken from the repository. The cases were prepared for analysis as follows:

- Since our tool is Eclipse-based, all case studies were converted to Eclipse projects such that the code compiles with the JDT and unit tests could be run within the Eclipse environment, and without any other build system (such as Maven).
- Since we use the MoDisco discoverer for Java, all classes relevant for discovery must be available as source code; the relevant library classes were thus extracted and added as source files (and removed from the libraries).
- For refactoring testing, we require a dense test net for all multi-language relevant artifacts. Where such was not available, we have implemented additional tests by hand.

Creating tests for each case study ranged from trivial to demanding. In the case of Spring and HBM, it was sufficient to instantiate the frameworks since they perform start-up tests to ensure integrity of the bound artifacts. However, for HQL as well as for Wicket, no such start-up test mechanisms were available. However, executing the code containing the artifacts leads the framework to fail; thus, tests were implemented to cover all the relevant lines of code.

Tool Setup. Our tool provides three types of results: artifacts, bindings, and refactoring closures. Firstly, the artifact discovery results in a list of all artifacts potentially multi-language relevant which are available in a project. Since it is not possible to test the correct discovery of these artifacts automatically, we have created tool support (in addition to orphan detection) specifically for the task of annotating artifacts and have manually read through the source code to ensure that all relevant artifacts were covered.

Secondly, the binding resolvers discover relationships between artifacts from different languages. As above, these bindings need to be checked by hand. Again, we have created specific tool support for the visualization of such bindings, which allowed us to manually iterate over the bindings, checking both successful bindings and error cases.

The final result are transitive artifact closures and their refactoring. In this case, we have opted for automated verification in the same spirit as in "normal" refactorings: By using unit tests. As mentioned in the previous chapter, refactorings are executed on the transitive closures of refactoring changes, i.e. on a group of artifacts which need to be renamed together. To verify whether the renamings performed are correct, the following process was run for all closures, one after the other:

– All unit tests were first run on the unchanged source code. The tests were expected to pass.
– In the second phase, artifacts were grouped by language. One by one, these artifact groups were renamed individually, i.e. first the Java artifacts, then the Spring artifacts, and so on. After each rename, the tests were run and expected to fail to ensure that renaming the artifacts individually actually introduces problems. After each test, the changes were undone again.
– Finally, all artifacts in the current closure were renamed and the tests were run one more time; in this case, they were expected to succeed. This change was undone as well before proceeding to the next closure.

This process is a very thorough test on many parts of the framework: It requires that the correct artifacts are grouped into closures; that each artifact is correctly resolved and has the right source code location attached; that each individual language refactoring is triggered correctly; and (on the case study side) that there are indeed tests which cover the multi-language bindings of the closure.

4.2 Results

Artifact Discovery. The result of artifact discovery is a list of potentially multi-language relevant artifacts (see again Figure 1). The discovery results are shown in Table 2 (note that the figure starts at 50%, the remainder being Java artifacts).

Since all of the cases are written using Java as the main language, the percentage of Java artifacts is rather high. In Java, potentially relevant artifacts include

Table 2. Discovered Artifacts for each Case Study per Language

Language	Plazma	Tudu	itracker	pLink	Brix	gidoo	JTrac	Total
Java	12 525	1083	4922	2963	5342	1469	3027	31 331
Spring	450	78	236	0	0	0	102	866
HBM	0	21	198	59	0	0	150	428
HQL	0	3	205	244	0	0	182	634
W/API	0	0	0	0	574	224	648	1446
W/HTML	0	0	0	0	368	183	466	1017
Unresolved	0	0	0	0	18	19	19	56
Orphan	0	0	0	0	92	6	0	98
Total	12 975	1185	5561	3266	6394	1901	4594	35 876

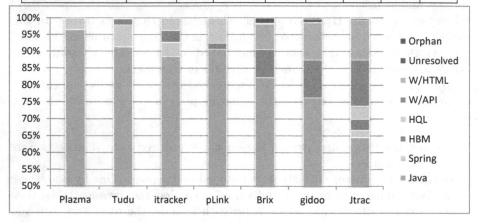

all types, public methods, fields, etc. Considering this, it is quite interesting to see that DSL artifacts amount to as much as they do (from 3.47% to 34.11%, mean 12.67%).

The *unresolved* and *orphan* rows in Table 2 show artifacts which could not be fully discovered. These numbers only occur in the projects which make use of HQL and Wicket/API and are indeed related to these two languages. As discussed in Section 3.1, it is not possible in these two languages to statically discover and properly place each element in the language models.

First, unresolved elements (56) refer to cases where a reference to an artifact was found but its value could not be determined — as in the HQL query example in Section 3.1. These elements are later important in refactoring, where they induce warnings for refactorings; however, due to their incomplete nature (in particular, their lack of name or identifier) they can not be bound.

Second, orphan elements (98) refer to cases where elements were found but their context, contrary to unresolved elements, is unknown such that a reference could not be added to the model. Multi-language binding resolution is not possible with orphans, thus no navigation is available and the orphans cannot take part in refactoring. In all of the cases reported here (as manually verified), the elements would not have been resolved across languages or taken part in refactoring anyway: Most of the orphans lie in Wicket JUnit test case implementations, where their IDs are ignored (54 cases); the remaining occurrences either use passed-in IDs (39) or lie within Wicket library code (5). Thus, there is no further impact of missing these elements here (this may obviously be different in other cases).

Artifact Binding Resolution. In binding resolution, artifact bindings from one language to artifacts from a second language are resolved based on the rules of the underlying framework. The resulting numbers are shown in Table 3.

Table 3. Discovered Multi-Language Bindings for each Case Study per Resolver

Resolver	Plazma	Tudu	itracker	pLink	Brix	gidoo	JTrac	Total
Spring to Java	517	89	241	0	0	0	123	970
HBM to Java	0	25	151	65	0	0	271	512
HQL to HBM	0	3	429	215	0	0	199	846
W/API to Java	0	0	0	0	108	4	216	328
W/API to HTML	0	0	0	0	382	192	553	1127
Total	517	117	821	280	490	196	1362	3783
Binding Error	0	0	0	0	26	11	5	42

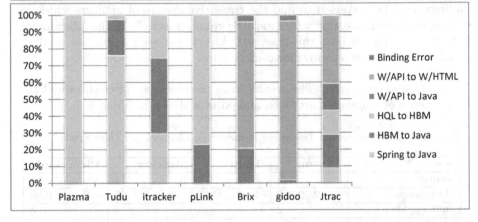

Again, due to the nature of the underlying case studies, we see a progression from Spring-related bindings via Hibernate-related bindings to Wicket-related bindings from left to right, with the exception of JTrac on the far right which uses all frameworks. In total, we have found 3783 bindings between elements in all case studies; the average number of bindings per case is 540. Considering that these bindings must be intact for the software to work correctly and are only partially supported by tools, possibilities for things to go wrong abound. From a purely statistical point of view, in the case with the most bindings (JTrac), this would amount to *one multi-language binding every 11 lines of code*.

In the three projects to the right, we see a total of 42 binding errors; as mentioned in Section 3.2, a binding error is reported if an artifact was found without its expected corresponding artifact in another language. All errors are reported on HQL and Wicket artifacts.

In 14 cases, these errors are actual problems in the observed code (JTrac: 2 / gidooCMS: 5 / Brix: 7), that is, an artifact should indeed have a partner in another language but did not. The other 28 cases are erroneously reported errors and can be separated into three categories. The first category is the originally expected one: Binding errors due to unresolved artifacts, of which there are only two (0/2/0). The second category contains problems due to the if-then-else over-approximation in the HQL and Wicket/API static analysis; i.e. some artifacts are present in more than one position in the model of which some are inaccurate (3/0/15). The third category contains missing bindings which are due to references in Wicket library code (0/4/4) which is due to the use of MoDisco.

Thus, all 28 erroneous reports (0.74%) are due to shortcomings in the static analysis. The two binding errors due to unresolved artifacts will lead, additionally and independently, to refactoring warnings. The others, which are due to over-approximation or use of library code and refer to "missing" artifacts do not carry identifiers and thus have no further impact on refactoring.

Refactoring Change Closures. If an element, or rather a name property of an element is selected for a rename refactoring, all existing multi-language bindings must be traversed to find the transitive closure of artifacts which are affected by the rename, and which must be changed as well. In the following, we first report on results from this traversal. Afterwards, we present the results of actually executing refactorings for each closure.

Closure Discovery Results. The results from the discovery of closures and thus the incidence of languages, artifacts, and edits is shown in Table 4.

Table 4. Discovered Transitive Refactoring Closures per Case Study

Case	Plazma	Tudu	itracker	PicketLink
Closures	122	72	214	55
Ø Languages	2.00 ± 0	2.03 ± 0.17	2.28 ± 0.45	2.56 ± 0.50
Language Max	2	3	3	3
Ø Artifacts	4.69 ± 12.00	2.21 ± 0.47	4.32 ± 5.54	6.09 ± 6.08
Ø Edits	4.28 ± 12.06	4.42 ± 12.41	28.58 ± 68.32	16.93 ± 19.47
Artifacts > 2 (%)	4.92	18.06	69.63	72.73

Case	Brix	gidoo	JTrac	Total
Closures	398	174	674	**1709**
Ø Languages	2.05 ± 0.21	2.00 ± 0	2.14 ± 0.48	$\mathbf{2.15 \pm 0.39}$
Language Max	3	2	5	**5**
Ø Artifacts	2.22 ± 0.79	2.13 ± 0.79	2.90 ± 2.70	$\mathbf{3.51 \pm 4.39}$
Ø Edits	3.49 ± 2.91	3.60 ± 5.08	6.07 ± 17.04	$\mathbf{9.62 \pm 28.25}$
Artifacts > 2 (%)	11.56	4.02	32.34	**28.03**

Overall, the number of transitive closures range from 55 (PicketLink) to 674 (JTrac); the total is 1709 closures with an average of 244 closure per case. The average of artifacts in all closures is 3.51; however, with a standard deviation of 4.39. In Plazma, itracker, PicketLink, and JTrac, the standard deviation is quite high, while in Tudu, Brix, and gidooCMS it is quite low. The maximum number of artifacts in a closure is 61 (in Plazma), where the Spring property dataSource is renamed; this property is injected into 60 beans which share a common setter method (hence 61 artifacts).

An interesting observation is the number of closures in which there are more than 2 artifacts. Here, the case studies seem to fall into three groups: The first group includes itracker and PicketLink with around 70% of closures with more than 2 artifacts; the second group consisting of just JTrac with around 30%, and finally all others with less than 20%. Since itracker and PicketLink mostly use HBM/HQL and JTrac has a HBM/HQL part, we have investigated whether this phenomenon is language-specific. Figure 2 shows closure artifact counts per language (that is, size of closures which have artifacts in the given language), where it becomes clearly visible that we mostly deal with only 2 artifacts in Spring, Wicket/HTML and Wicket/API. In HBM and HQL, however, the majority of closures have 3 or more artifacts.

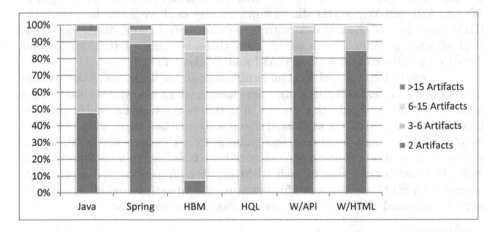

Fig. 2. Artifacts per Closure and Language

Another observation regards the number of languages involved in the closures also shown in Table 4. In four case studies, we mostly or exclusively deal with two languages per closure: In Plazma, only Spring and Java are involved; in gidooCMS, only Wicket/API and Wicket/HTML. There are two closures with HQL and HBM artifacts in Tudu and 19 closures with Java in Brix, which is why the maximum number of languages is three in these cases. The highest number of languages involved in one closure is 5 in JTrac, which nevertheless only has an average number of 2.14 languages per closure. The remaining two case studies lie in the middle with 3 maximum languages and an average of 2.28 (itracker) and 2.56 (PicketLink) artifacts per closure. An example of a closure with 5 languages (from JTrac) has already been shown in Section 2 (Listings 1.1 to 1.5).

An inverse representation of these numbers is shown in Figure 3 which shows the percentage of closures with 2 to 5 languages having at least one element from

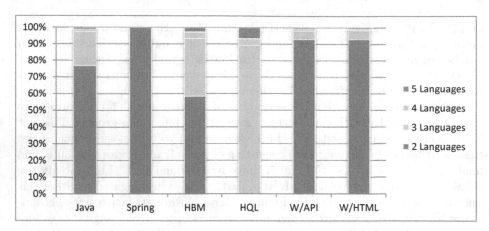

Fig. 3. Languages per Closure

the chosen language. This correlates with the number of artifacts: In Spring, Wicket/API and Wicket/HTML, closures mostly deal with two languages. In HBM, over 40% of closures deal with three and more languages. As expected, HQL-affected closures always use at least three languages (HQL, HBM, and Java), with extensions into Wicket/API and Wicket/HTML.

As an insight into the technical underpinnings, Table 4 also gives the average number of actual text edits performed per closure, which also varies greatly. This number depends not only the number of artifacts relevant for multi-language bindings, but also on all the additional changes the per-language refactorings had to add. The maximum number of text changes for a closure is 620 (in itracker), where an `id` attribute is renamed: This attribute is defined in an abstract entity superclass and is thus used in each HBM entity definition as well as all HQL queries for any of these elements; furthermore, the `id` getters and setters in Java must be renamed which are again heavily used in the code base.

Refactoring Results. The results from executing the refactoring actions on all of the closures found is shown in Table 5. Note that the figure starts from 80%, the remainder being successful tests.

The results show that the tests after refactoring each closure succeeded in 95.96% of cases across all case studies (1640 of 1709 closures). In the remaining 69 cases, a warning was attached to the closure (based on incomplete artifact discovery, as discussed above); in 38 of these cases, the tests still succeeded; thus, the warning was unnecessary; in 31 cases the test failed, thus the warning was accurate. No closure test failed without a warning being attached. In all cases, problems are again down to artifact discovery in HQL and/or Wicket/API; in all of these cases, we can warn the user of potential problems.

The last row in Table 5 shows the number of closures in which at least one single-language tests succeeded. Recalling from the experimental setup, each closure was refactored multiple times: Firstly, each language on its own (which should lead to test failures), and finally all together (which should succeed).

Table 5. Results from Refactoring Transitive Closures

Language	Plazma	Tudu	itracker	pLink	Brix	gidoo	JTrac	Total
OK	122	72	214	55	398	162	617	1640
OK (warned)	0	0	0	0	0	7	31	38
FAIL (warned)	0	0	0	0	0	5	26	31
Total	122	72	214	55	398	174	674	1709
Single Language Success	0	0	0	1	17	3	39	60

Thus, it is interesting to look at why the single-language tests succeeded despite having not renamed all elements.

First, there is one succeeding test in PicketLink on an HQL attribute called `binaryValue`. This attribute is used in an unreachable part of code which thus could not be tested. In Brix, gidooCMS, and JTrac, most (56) of the test successes refer to the Java language and are due to fallback behavior of Wicket: If a Java getter/setter is not found for a certain entity, Wicket looks for a field of the same name. Since we only rename the JavaBean-style getters and setters and all relevant fields have exactly the same property name, the field is still found by Wicket and thus the tests succeed. Manual renaming of the field leads to test failures in every case. In the remaining three cases (two from Brix, one from gidooCMS), the success affects both Wicket/HTML and Wicket/API. In the first two cases, the references are overwritten by generated HTML code (Brix), in the second, we deal with dead code (gidooCMS); thus, they are not testable.

4.3 Discussion

Our experimental evaluation has covered six languages across seven case studies; each language was present in at least three case studies.

The artifact discovery process has reported 35876 multi-language relevant artifacts across all case studies. As discussed, 154 these (56 unresolved elements, 98 orphans) from the languages HQL and Wicket/API could not be extracted due to static analysis limitations in these languages.

In the follow-up multi-language binding resolution, 3783 unique bindings between artifacts across languages have been automatically resolved. Again due to limitations in the static analysis, some bindings have been erroneously reported as missing in 18 cases (0.74%).

Regarding the refactoring step, we were able to automatically refactor all 1709 closures found. The test run results after refactoring the closures show a success rate of 95.96%, i.e. in 1640 of 1709 closures, the tests after a full refactoring succeeded. The remaining 69 cases were attached with warnings due to incomplete artifact discovery; in about half of them, the refactorings and subsequent tests succeeded despite warnings.

The single-language test runs which were supposed to show that single-language changes do not suffice only succeeded in 60 cases, of which most are due Wicket's fallback mechanisms; the remaining four are due to unreachable or dead code. This clearly shows that the system functionality, as far as the tests are concerned, is only kept intact by multi-language refactoring.

Thus, we believe that the fitness for the intended purpose of our tool (i.e., discovery, binding, and refactoring for multi-language software applications) has been established. The automated refactoring and testing approach we have used in this experimental evaluation has been helpful in reaching this goal, in debugging, and in establishing trust in our own system, since all aspects of the system must work together to lead to succeeding tests after refactoring.

The numbers also show that, in particular regarding HQL and HBM applications, more than two artifacts and languages are involved in multi-language transitive refactoring closures. We believe that this shows the need for generic support for languages and language bindings instead of a participant-based two-language approach.

Finally, the implementation and validation of our tool has shown which language features are particularly difficult to support. In fact, all artifact discovery, binding, and refactoring problems ultimately originate in the languages HQL and Wicket/API and the fact that the statements of these languages are embedded in Java and it is allowed to manipulate them using Java control flow constructs, necessitating extensive (and expensive) static analysis. Compared to the length to which one has to go to to support such languages, supporting external languages such as Spring, HBM, or Wicket/HTML is almost trivial.

It is interesting to ask the question if the ability to manipulate the language constructs in HQL and Wicket/API in this manner is really necessary, i.e. if it is crucial to the usability or fitness for purpose of these languages. This is to be investigated in the future. If no reasons can be found, we recommend not allowing such manipulations in future languages, and suggest using external, clearly separated languages instead.

Although our tool showed good results on the languages we investigated, it is unclear how these results translate to other languages. Several frameworks within the Java world deal with similar domains (i.e. system configuration, querying, and UI); these would present a good starting point for further evaluation.

Regarding refactorings, a possible conceptual difficulty of our approach lies in the re-use of existing refactorings, which might change elements in the source code, affecting artifacts that are part of another multi-language binding. Since this change is encapsulated behind the refactoring, it is not possible to react before the change has been committed. Note that this is only a problem if the artifacts changed are not bound in the semantic model as well (otherwise, the propagation algorithm would have found them). We have not encountered this problem in our test cases, but it is conceivable that such situations may occur.

4.4 Threats to Validity

Our claim is the fitness for the intended purpose of our tool, i.e. that artifact discovery, binding, and refactoring works as expected when tested on real-life cases for the languages involved. Obviously, we can only claim this for the seven case studies we have investigated; however, we believe that they represent a good spread of cases; we have also taken care to implement a general solution. Still, other cases may lead to different and possibly more error cases in each of the areas of artifact discovery, binding, and refactoring.

Regarding our evaluation, artifact discovery and binding resolution have been executed manually, i.e. we investigated the source code to determine whether discovery and binding were accurate. We have created and used tool support specifically for this task for artifact annotation and orphan detection and have taken care to find all elements; however, it is still possible that we have missed artifacts and bindings during this process. Refactoring success was tested by JUnit tests; although we have checked coverage regarding the artifacts found, some closures may still be incomplete without us noticing. In the other direction, some closures may also be too extensive, i.e. include elements which would not have needed renaming. Since the renaming and tests of the individual language artifact groups failed as described, there is a strong indication that all bindings in each closure are relevant; however, we did not unit-test each binding individually.

Since our model discovery partially relies on an incomplete static analysis, some artifacts are reported as unresolved or orphans; also, several binding errors are reported which do not in fact exist. However, the number of such problems is rather low; thus we believe that we can still claim usefulness of our tool.

A final issue is how well our approach can be adapted to an interactive mode, since our refactoring tests have been carried out in batch mode. Model discovery and binding is currently a non-incremental process and takes up to a minute, depending on the number of bindings in the code. It is future work to investigate incremental discovery (as, for example, in the JDT compiler) as well as incremental artifact binding routines.

5 Related Work

We discuss adjacent existing work in three parts: Firstly, works which focus on a particular language binding or bindings; secondly, works which focus on multiple, but similar languages, and finally, other related work.

To our knowledge, our work is the first which ranges across six languages and three frameworks, focuses on a generic framework to be placed inside an IDE to treat all languages and language bindings in an equal way, and contains a systematic unit-test based evaluation of multi-language refactorings on seven open-source case studies.

Domain- or Language Specific Approaches. Firstly, there are several works which implement support for individual language pairings which usually go deeper into individual language semantics whereas our approach is focused on a generic integration architecture.

In 2008, the workshop on refactoring tools has drawn two papers on cross-language refactoring. Chen and Johnson [1] present an approach for refactoring references to Java in XML code (examples given are Spring, Struts, and Hibernate). XPath expressions are used to locate references in XML code, and rename refactorings are considered. Kempf et al. [6] have discussed cross-language refactoring between Java and the Groovy programming language, also with a focus on renaming. A follow-up paper in 2009 [7] has shown these refactorings to be completely automatable, and the implementation is now part of the official Groovy Eclipse plugin. In both cases, the implementations presented are specific to the target languages (i.e. XML and Groovy); our own approach could be used to integrate these languages and binding implementations with others.

A similar work which deals with interactions between two particular languages is Tatlock et al. [21] (2008). They use the term deep refactoring for their approach to the refactoring of Java applications using a JPA-based framework. Both class and field renames between Java entities and JPA queries are considered. Their approach uses data flow analysis to also collect partial queries. Furthermore, they include a type checking algorithm for verifying inputs and outputs of queries, i.e. whether the correct Java types are used as parameters and returning elements in JPA. Thus, their approach goes beyond what we offer for JPA, but is in turn restricted to JPA and queries, since the grammar-based approach they use is not easily extensible to other, non-query languages.

Schink et al. [16] have presented, in 2011, an approach to refactor Hibernate applications which include entity definitions (in this case, as annotations) and queries. The refactorings analyzed are *Rename Method, Pull Up Method* and *Introduce Default Value*. An interesting aspect here is the discussion of the data present in the database, and of the impact of refactorings (such as pull up method) on such data. Thus, this approach goes beyond rename and even uses a dedicated database refactoring; again, it would be interesting to integrate these efforts (and investigate different refactorings for additional languages).

In 2012, Nguyen et al. [13] have presented the tool BabelRef which handles cross-language function calls and widget references in the web application languages PHP, JavaScript, and HTML with the goal of renaming elements. Their specific focus is on the partial nature of HTML page parts in PHP, where they use symbolic execution to create a single tree structure called D-model; by contrast, our own approach uses an artifact model with separate bindings.

Refactorings on Similar Languages. Secondly, there is some work on refactoring multiple languages which share similar concepts, such as being object-oriented. Such approaches can take advantage of language similarities, which however makes them specific to this context.

The first two of these are by Strein et al.[19,20] (2006). Here, a generic framework based on a common meta-model is presented with the aim of renaming elements, in particular methods, across languages. They present the tool X-Develop, which implements these refactorings for the languages of the .NET framework (C#, J#, and Visual Basic). A key difference in this approach is the use of a common meta-model, which is beneficial if the target languages are similar, as in .NET — all languages share the same or very similar concepts such as types, methods, and properties. Thus, elements from all languages are represented in the same way on this level, and it is indeed feasible to write refactorings on this level. By contrast, we have investigated very different languages in which there are few common concepts; we therefore use per-language models and re-use existing individual refactoring implementations for each language.

Sobernig and Zdun [17] (2010) discuss multi-language refactoring as an evaluation technique for implementing multi-language method calls in a scenario in which one OO language is embedded into another (in this case, the Frag language into Java). The main goal of this work is a comparison between reflective and generative integration techniques, where the amount of effort required for implementing refactorings can be used for comparison. Besides renaming, they also consider the very interesting refactorings *replace embedded with host object* and *replace embedded with host method*, as well as *remove host method*. Such refactorings are naturally only possible in languages with similar functionality; not between a general-purpose and a domain-specific language as in our case.

Other Related Work. We have investigated patterns of cross-language linking between Java and DSLs before [11] (namely, Spring, Hibernate, and Android), identifying how to describe and implement binding resolution between artifacts in these frameworks. In a follow-up paper [12], we have presented results from the application of such resolution on a single case study. Building on these results, the current paper provides a comprehensive description of an approach and implementation of a generic and systematic multi-language support framework, and includes a thorough empirical investigation on seven case studies.

In 2012, Pfeiffer and Wasowski [14] have executed a user study to show multi-language support mechanisms in general to aid software developers. This experiment with 22 participants has evaluated the tool TexMo, which includes support for links between Java, Hibernate and Wicket, and is based on the JTrac case study which we use as well. The main differences lie in the fact that artifact bindings in TexMo are manually established, and are based on a common, text-based model. In comparison, our tests show the feasibility of automation as well as the usefulness of cross-language renames from the unit testing perspective.

A more general discussion of program comprehension and maintenance of multi-language application can be found in Kontogiannis et al. in 2006 [8]. Open issues relate to gathering data, formalization and modeling of multi-language

systems, extraction, discovery and storage of extracted information, and how to
support exploration, queries, and knowledge management.

6   Conclusion

Multi-language software applications (MLSAs) are a common occurrence for
which systematic tool support is lacking in today's IDEs. We believe that such
support can make a significant difference for developers, and have thus
investigated an approach and tool for multi-language software. Our implementation supports six languages (Java, Spring, HBM, HQL, Wicket/API and
Wicket/HTML) across three frameworks (Spring, Hibernate, and Wicket).

Our approach treats languages and language bindings as first-level entities,
and includes systematic support for multiple (in particular, more than two at a
time) languages without language bias. We provide a generic refactoring algorithm which re-uses existing single-language refactorings and propagates changes
across languages based on artifact bindings.

Using manual inspection for artifact and binding discovery as well as automated refactoring and unit testing, we have evaluated our tool on seven open
source case studies with a total of 3768 bindings between artifacts in different
languages. The automated refactorings succeeded in 95.96% of the 1709 transitive closures of artifacts which must be renamed together. The remaining cases
were annotated with warnings such that the user is aware of potential problems.

Through our experiments, we have shown that the tool is fit for the purpose it
was created, i.e. automatically and correctly finding multi-language relevant artifacts, discovering the bindings between them, and (rename) refactoring element
across language borders.

Acknowledgement. This work has been partially sponsored by the EU project
ASCENS, 257414.

References

1. Chen, N., Johnson, R.: Toward Refactoring in a Polyglot World. In: Proceedings
   of the 2nd Workshop on Refactoring Tools, pp. 1–4. ACM (2008)
2. Christensen, A.S., Møller, A., Schwartzbach, M.I.: Precise Analysis of String Expressions. In: Cousot, R. (ed.) SAS 2003. LNCS, vol. 2694, pp. 1–18. Springer,
   Heidelberg (2003)
3. Fjeldberg, H.C.: Polyglot Programming. A Business Perspective. Master thesis,
   Norwegian University of Science and Technology (2008)
4. Fowler, M., Beck, K., Brant, J., Opdyke, W., Roberts, D.: Refactoring: Improving
   the Design of Existing Code. Pearson Education (2012)
5. Fowler, M.: Domain-Specific Languages. Addison-Wesley Professional (2010)
6. Kempf, M., Kleeb, R., Klenk, M., Sommerlad, P.: Cross language refactoring for
   Eclipse plug-ins. In: Proceedings of the 2nd Workshop on Refactoring Tools, pp.
   1:1–1:4. ACM (2008)

7. Klenk, M., Kleeb, R., Kempf, M., Sommerlad, P.: Refactoring support for the Groovy-Eclipse plug-in. In: Companion to the 23rd ACM SIGPLAN Conference on Object-Oriented Programming Systems Languages and Applications, pp. 727–728. ACM (2008)
8. Kontogiannis, K., Linos, P., Wong, K.: Comprehension and Maintenance of Large-Scale Multi-Language Software Applications. In: Proceedings of the 22nd IEEE International Conference on Software Maintenance, pp. 497–500. IEEE Computer Society (2006)
9. Linos, P.: PolyCare: A Tool for Re-engineering Multi-language Program Integrations. In: Proceeding of the 1st IEEE International Conference on Engineering of Complex Computer Systems, pp. 338–341. IEEE Computer Society Press (1995)
10. Livshits, B., Whaley, J., Lam, M.S.: Reflection Analysis for Java. In: Yi, K. (ed.) APLAS 2005. LNCS, vol. 3780, pp. 139–160. Springer, Heidelberg (2005)
11. Mayer, P., Schroeder, A.: Patterns of Cross-Language Linking in Java Frameworks. In: Proceedings of the 21st IEEE International Conference on Program Comprehension, pp. 113–122 (2013)
12. Mayer, P., Schroeder, A.: Towards Automated Cross-Language Refactorings between Java and DSLs used by Java Frameworks. In: Proceedings of the 6th ACM Workshop on Refactoring Tools, pp. 1–4 (2013)
13. Nguyen, H.V., Nguyen, H.A., Nguyen, T.T., Nguyen, T.N.: BabelRef: detection and renaming tool for cross-language program entities in dynamic web applications. In: Proceedings of the 34th International Conference on Software Engineering, pp. 1391–1394. IEEE Press (2012)
14. Pfeiffer, R.-H., Wąsowski, A.: Cross-Language Support Mechanisms Significantly Aid Software Development. In: France, R.B., Kazmeier, J., Breu, R., Atkinson, C. (eds.) MODELS 2012. LNCS, vol. 7590, pp. 168–184. Springer, Heidelberg (2012)
15. Pfeiffer, R.-H., Wąsowski, A.: TexMo: A Multi-language Development Environment. In: Vallecillo, A., Tolvanen, J.-P., Kindler, E., Störrle, H., Kolovos, D. (eds.) ECMFA 2012. LNCS, vol. 7349, pp. 178–193. Springer, Heidelberg (2012)
16. Schink, H., Kuhlemann, M., Saake, G., Lämmel, R.: Hurdles in Multi-language Refactoring of Hibernate Applications. In: Proceedings of the 6th International Conference on Software and Data Technologies, pp. 129–134. SciTePress (2011)
17. Sobernig, S., Zdun, U.: Evaluating java runtime reflection for implementing cross-language method invocations. In: Proceedings of the 8th International Conference on the Principles and Practice of Programming in Java, pp. 139–147. ACM (2010)
18. Steimann, F., Thies, A.: From Public to Private to Absent: Refactoring Java Programs under Constrained Accessibility. In: Drossopoulou, S. (ed.) ECOOP 2009. LNCS, vol. 5653, pp. 419–443. Springer, Heidelberg (2009)
19. Strein, D., Kratz, H., Lowe, W.: Cross-Language Program Analysis and Refactoring. In: Proceedings of the 6th IEEE International Workshop on Source Code Analysis and Manipulation, pp. 207–216. IEEE Computer Society (2006)
20. Strein, D., Lincke, R., Lundberg, J., Löwe, W.: An Extensible Meta-Model for Program Analysis. IEEE Transactions on Software Engineering 33(9), 592–607 (2007)
21. Tatlock, Z., Tucker, C., Shuffelton, D., Jhala, R., Lerner, S.: Deep typechecking and refactoring. In: Proceedings of the 23rd ACM SIGPLAN Conference on Object-Oriented Programming Systems Languages and Applications, pp. 37–52. ACM (2008)
22. Vakilian, M., Chen, N., Negara, S., Rajkumar, B.A., Bailey, B.P., Johnson, R.E.: Use, disuse, and misuse of automated refactorings. In: Proceedings of the 34th International Conference on Software Engineering, pp. 233–243. IEEE Press (2012)

A   Artifact Description

Authors of the Artifact. Design and Core Implementation: Philip Mayer, Andreas Schroeder. Language Metamodels and Parsers: Thomas Neumeier

Summary. This aim of this artifact is demonstrating feasibility of an implementation for analysis and refactoring of multi-language software systems (MLSAs), and for collecting data from this process. As such, the routines for gathering artifacts, artifact bindings, and for executing refactorings are targeted at batch processing, using (lengthy) tables with CSV export functionality as output. Support is also available for graphically visualizing some aspects of the data, and for navigating to the source code positions of artifacts, bindings, and closures.

The implementation is realized as a set of Eclipse plug-ins. These plug-ins include EMF meta-models, model parsers, language binding implementations, and refactoring add-ons for six languages (Java, Spring, Hibernate/HBM, Hibernate/HQL, Wicket/API, and Wicket/HTML). Additional code (views, editors, actions) provides the user interfaces and glue code required to use the core routines as well as automated regression tests for all case studies.

The artifact package provides a virtual machine image designed to support repeatability of the experiments in the paper and thus regenerating the data we have presented. It also includes the code of the seven case studies we have used in our analysis.

Content. The artifact package consists of a VirtualBox VM image which hosts:

- an Eclipse installation with all required plug-ins and the source code of our tool implementation in the workspace
- a configured runtime Eclipse launch configuration with all seven case studies in the workspace to be used for testing
- detailed instructions for using the artifact to test some interesting language links as well as reproducing the data used in the paper

Getting the Artifact. The artifact endorsed by the Artifact Evaluation Committee is available free of charge as supplementary material of this paper on SpringerLink. Additionally, the source code and instructions for installation are available on our website: http://www.xllsrc.net/.

Tested Platforms. Being Java- and Eclipse-based, the artifact should work on all major platforms. The virtual machine image is known to work on any platform running Oracle VirtualBox (with around 4GB of main memory).

License. EPL-1.0 (http://www.eclipse.org/legal/epl-v10.html)

MD5 Sum of the Artifact. e4be341e2b4a02b9bd118a5488125ba5

Size of the Artifact. 4.03 GB

Retargetting Legacy Browser Extensions to Modern Extension Frameworks

Rezwana Karim[1], Mohan Dhawan[2], and Vinod Ganapathy[1]

[1] Rutgers University, Piscataway NJ, USA
{rkarim,vinodg}@cs.rutgers.edu
[2] IBM Research, New Delhi, India
mohan.dhawan@in.ibm.com

Abstract. Most modern Web browsers export a rich API allowing third-party extensions to access privileged browser objects that can also be misused by attacks directed against vulnerable ones. Web browser vendors have therefore recently developed new extension frameworks aimed at better isolating extensions while still allowing access to privileged browser state. For instance Google Chrome extension architecture and Mozilla's Jetpack extension framework.

We present Morpheus, a tool to port legacy browser extensions to these new frameworks. Specifically, Morpheus targets legacy extensions for the Mozilla Firefox browser, and ports them to the Jetpack framework. We describe the key techniques used by Morpheus to analyze and transform legacy extensions so that they conform to the constraints imposed by Jetpack and simplify runtime policy enforcement. Finally, we present an experimental evaluation of Morpheus by applying it to port 52 legacy Firefox extensions to the Jetpack framework.

Keywords: JavaScript browser extensions. Privilege separation.

1 Introduction

Extensions enhance the core functionality of Web browsers, enabling end users to customize the look and feel of their browsing experience. The ease with which browser extensions can be written, downloaded and installed and the features that they enable have all contributed tremendously to their popularity, as well as to the browsers that they target. Browsers such as Mozilla Firefox and Google Chrome have galleries with thousands of extensions implementing a wide array of features. Popular extensions often have in excess of a million users.

To support extensions, browsers typically expose an API that gives access to privileged browser objects. For example, Mozilla's XPCOM (cross-domain component object model) API [25] allows browser extensions to access the file system, the network, the cookie store, and user preferences, among others. Such a rich API is often necessary to implement extensions with useful features. In sharp contrast, code that executes within a Web page is often tightly sandboxed by the browser, *e.g.*, using the same-origin policy, and does not have access to such privileged browser APIs.

Unfortunately, browser extensions do not undergo the same quality control as the rest of the browser, and are riddled with vulnerabilities. In a recent study of over 2400

R. Jones (Ed.): ECOOP 2014, LNCS 8586, pp. 463–488, 2014.
© Springer-Verlag Berlin Heidelberg 2014

Mozilla Firefox extensions, Bhandakavi *et al.* [8] found several instances of insecure programming practices that can easily be exploited for malicious purposes. Any such exploit would endow the attacker with access to privileged browser APIs, thereby completely undermining the security of the Web browser.

Given such concerns, browser vendors have begun to develop new frameworks that aim to better isolate extensions [9, 2, 6, 5]. These frameworks force extension authors to adhere to core security principles, such as privilege separation and least privilege to some extent. They partition extensions to limit how extensions access privileged browsed objects. An attacker who hijacks one of the partitions of such an extension is unable to access privileged browser objects available to other partitions. Mozilla's Jetpack framework and the Google Chrome extension model are two popular examples of modern extension frameworks that use these techniques to improve extension security.

While the quantitative impact of such frameworks at reducing attacks against extensions is as yet unknown, it is qualitatively clear that by embracing first principles, they improve extension security. However, such frameworks require extensions to be written from ground up, adhering to the programming disciplines that they enforce. To be applicable to legacy extensions, the extensions must be ported to the new frameworks. However, doing so manually would be expensive and time-consuming.

In this paper, we present Morpheus, a static analysis and transformation tool that allows legacy extensions to be systematically ported into modern extension frameworks in a manner that allows enforcement of fine grained security policies without any modification to browser runtime. Our prototype targets legacy Mozilla Firefox extensions, and rewrites them to make them compatible to the Jetpack framework while conforming to the security principles. We chose to focus on Firefox because of the abundance of legacy extensions for this browser. There are currently over 9000 extensions available for Firefox. Morpheus targets an important subset of these extensions, those written fully in JavaScript. Rather than require these extensions to be rewritten for Jetpack from scratch, Morpheus preserves the investment in these extensions and provides a path for automatically refactoring them to work in Jetpack. We have applied Morpheus to port 52 popular Firefox extensions into the Jetpack framework, and are actively applying it to more extensions from the Firefox extension gallery.

This paper makes the following contributions:

• We identify the key challenges in building a reliable and usable toolchain (Morpheus) for systematic conversion of legacy Firefox extensions to the more secure Jetpack framework.

• We present an automated transformation toolchain to partition legacy extension code into Jetpack modules that satisfy the principle of least privilege. Each module encapsulates objects corresponding to sensitive browser APIs and enables accessor methods which provide the required API functionality.

• We present a policy checker framework for Jetpack extensions. The modular and extensible architecture of Jetpack extensions allows developers to seamlessly add or remove security policies without affecting the rest of the code.

• Our evaluation with a suite of 52 popular legacy extensions demonstrates that the design of Morpheus is practical and it is deployable for real world use.

2   Overview

In this section, we describe the architecture of legacy extensions, with a particular focus on issues that motivated browser vendors to develop new extension frameworks. We then discuss the key components of the new Jetpack framework from Mozilla.

2.1   Threats to Extension Security

Browser extensions are written using open technologies such as HTML, CSS and JavaScript, but they often utilize privileged browser APIs to perform useful tasks. For example, Mozilla's XPCOM API gives an extension access to the file system, the network, and sensitive browser state such as cookies and browsing history. The goal of an attacker is to misuse the extension to access the capabilities provided by browser APIs.

A typical browser extension can interact with content on Web pages and any remote server on the Internet. For example, a DisplayWeather extension may access the Web page to search for locations in the text as specified by the user, and its home server to get the corresponding weather data to be shown in the Web page itself. An attacker can hijack an extension by either (1) tricking the user into visiting a malicious Website and then exploiting vulnerabilities in the extension, or (2) compromising the extension's communication with its home server, *i.e.,* the attacker can inject malicious packets in the network stream or compromise the remote server to which the extension communicates.

Browsers attempt to safeguard against the first class of attacks by isolating the execution of JavaScript code on the Web page (unprivileged *content scripts*) from the JavaScript code executing within the extension (privileged *chrome scripts*). This isolation of content scripts from chrome scripts limits the threats posed by a Web attacker by disallowing direct access to sensitive browser APIs. Nevertheless, there are often bugs in this isolation mechanism, leading to exploits. To defend against the second class of network-based attacks, extensions can use SSL to secure their connection with their home server.

2.2   Legacy Extensions on Firefox

Consider Figure 1, which shows a snippet from the DisplayWeather extension that we developed. The extension provides options to overlay weather information on a browser panel for which it reads the zipcode from persistent storage. In lines 1-6, the function getZipCode reads the file 'zip.txt' from the user's profile directory to retrieve the zipcode for the user specified location. In line 2, import attaches the FileUtils object to the extension's global namespace. FileUtils.jsm internally invokes XPCOM APIs to enable all file I/O operations. Lines 9-28 define the Weather object that encapsulates properties and methods to fetch weather data from a remote server. The method requestDataFromServer defined in lines 16-27 uses XMLHttpRequest to fetch weather data for a given zipcode from a remote server. Line 30 registers a click event listener with the extension's icon in the browser's status bar to display weather in a panel. In lines 33-37, the code creates an event listener addWeatherToWebpage to overlay weather information on the Web page, whenever a new Web page is loaded.

```
(1)  function getZipCode(locationStr){
(2)      Components.utils.import('resource://gre/modules/FileUtils.jsm');
(3)      var dir = 'ProfD', filename = 'zip.txt';//get the 'zip.txt' file from profile directory
(4)      var file = FileUtils.getFile(dir, [filename]);
(5)      var locationZipcodeMap = readFile(file);
(6)      return locationZipcodeMap[locationStr]; //retrieve zipcode for the location
(7)  }
(8)  ...
(9)  var Weather = {
(10)     temperature: null,
(11)     ...
(12)     getWeatherData: function(zipcode){
(13)         Weather.requestDataFromServer(zipcode);
(14)         return processWeatherData(Weather.temperature);// format weather data
(15)     },
(16)     requestDataFromServer: function(sendData){
(17)         var httpRequest = new window.XMLHtttpRequest();
(18)         ...
(19)         //set the listener to handle response from Server
(20)         httpRequest.onreadystatechange = function(){
(21)             // extract temperature data from response and set Weather.temperature
(22)             Weather.extractTemperature(httpRequest.response);
(23)             ...
(24)         }
(25)         httpRequest.open('GET', serverUrl, true);
(26)         httpRequest.send(sendData);//contact remote server
(27)     }
(28)  }
(29)  //Add the click listener to the extension's icon to show Weather in panel
(30)  document.getElementById('weatherStatusBar').addEventListener
(31)  ...                      ('click', showWeatherInPanel, false);
(32)  window.addEventListener('DOMContentLoaded', addWeatherToWebpage, false);
(33)  function addWeatherToWebpage(){
(34)      var locationStr = getLocationFromWebpage(gBrowser.contentDocument);
(35)      var temperature = Weather.getWeatherData(getZipCode(locationStr));
(36)      modifyWebpageContent(gBrowser.contentDocument, temperature);
(37)  }
```

Fig. 1. Code snippet from the DisplayWeather extension

Lines 34-36 identify all DOM[1] elements that contain a user-specified location in the active Web page and invoke `getWeatherData` method defined on the `Weather` object to retrieve latest weather updates. The method `modifyWebpageContent` in line 36 actually overlays the weather information on the active Web page.

This example highlights several features used by legacy Firefox extensions:

(1) *Unified JavaScript heap*: Mozilla's legacy extension development environment provides a unified heap for all JavaScript code execution. Both privileged chrome scripts and unprivileged content scripts reside in the same heap, raising the risk of shared references. For example, line 36 invokes the `modifyWebpageContent` method with a reference to the document object of the active Web page. Mozilla uses XrayWrappers (also know as XPCNativeWrappers) to isolate the untrusted references of the content JavaScript from the chrome JavaScript. However, this mechanism has a history of exploitable bugs [9, 29]. If this interface is exploited, and the user navigates to a malicious Web page, the document object would belong to the attacker, who could then influence the execution of the privileged code within the extension [30].

A second consequence of having a unified heap for JavaScript execution results is that top-level objects declared in chrome scripts are attached as properties of the global object. This often results in namespace collisions across different extensions or even

---

[1] Document Object Model (DOM) provides a structural representation of the document, enabling developers to modify its content and appearance using JavaScript.

different chrome scripts within the same extension. Further, since globals defined in one script can be accessed and modified from another script, data races may occur.

(2) *Privileged objects*: All chrome scripts have default access to the global `window` object and its properties. The `Components` object is a special property of the `window` which provides access to the browser's sensitive XPCOM APIs. If an attacker gets a reference to the `Components` object, he effectively has control over the entire browser. The fact that the `Components` object is so powerful and is yet available to all scripts by default is a significant threat to security in a shared heap environment.

(3) *Chrome DOM*: Much as the DOM API available to content scripts on a Web page, chrome scripts also have access to the chrome DOM. The chrome DOM is responsible for the visual representation of the browser's UI including toolbars, menus, statusbar and icons. Since much of Firefox's UI is also written in JavaScript, chrome scripts can programmatically access and modify the browser's entire UI (line 30).

The issues discussed above stem in part due to the architecture of Mozilla's legacy extension framework. Parts of the browser itself are written in JavaScript, as are extensions. With a unified heap and lack of any isolation primitives in the language itself, extension developers must consciously and carefully restrict access to critical functionality. The legacy extension framework makes it easy for developers to commit mistakes, and much prior work has shown the pitfalls of legacy extensions [13, 8, 14, 9].

2.3   The Jetpack Extension Framework

The Jetpack extension framework [2, 20] is an effort by Mozilla to incorporate security principles in the design of the extension architecture, thereby improving the overall security of extensions. Jetpack uses a layered defense architecture to make it harder for an attacker to compromise extensions, and limit the damage done if he succeeds in compromising all or part of the extension. The Jetpack project shares ideological similarities with the Google Chrome extension architecture [9]. It has also been motivated by the goal of easing extension development process with an emphasis on modular development and code sharing, and partly by the new multi-process Firefox architecture [24].

Conceptually, each Jetpack extension has two parts: (1) at least one add-on script (also known as *chrome script*) that interacts with a set of *core modules*, which have access to the sensitive browser APIs, and (2) zero or more *content scripts*. The chrome script(s) execute within the Web browser with restricted but elevated privileges: it must explicitly request access at load time to the browser APIs that it requires access to; any attempt to access other APIs at runtime is blocked. Content scripts interact with the Web page and are unprivileged. In addition, Jetpack incorporates these features:

(1) *Chrome/content heap partitioning*. Chrome and content scripts execute in separate processes. This partitioning guarantees isolation of the JavaScript heap for the chrome and content scripts and prevents inadvertent access by content scripts to privileged references in the chrome code. Communication amongst the chrome and content scripts is made possible through IPC with all messages exchanged in the JSON [3] format.

(2) *Content script integrity*. Content scripts execute in the context of the Web page and a malicious Web page can redefine objects referenced by the content script, thereby

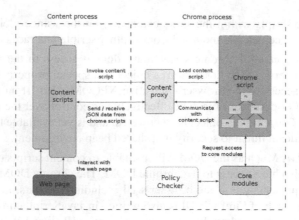

Fig. 2. Architecture of a simple Jetpack extension. Policy Checker is not part of original architecture and is introduced by Morpheus.

affecting its integrity. Jetpack uses *content proxies* to protect the integrity of content scripts. Content proxies allow the content script to access the content on the Web page while still having access to the native objects and APIs (*e.g.,* `document` and `window`), even if the Web page has redefined them.

(3) *Chrome privilege separation.* Jetpack provides developers with a set of core modules that encapsulate the functionality of the privileged browser APIs, thus preventing inadvertent misuse of these APIs by the developer. Further, developers must explicitly request these core modules as required by the extension's chrome scripts. If compromised, this restricts the set of privileges that an attacker can obtain to only those requested by the exploited script.

The Jetpack framework further recommends developers to partition the chrome script and organize an extension as a hierarchy of user modules, each of which may itself request other user modules and zero or more core modules using the `require` interface. The set of privileges thus acquired by each user module is determined statically by analyzing the source code and enforced by the framework at runtime. The Jetpack framework further provides isolation among all modules. Objects declared within a module are local to the module unless exported via the module's `exports` interface.

Figure 2 shows the overall architecture of a Jetpack extension. In summary, Jetpack attempts to improve extension security by separating content scripts from chrome scripts, employing privilege separation for chrome scripts, and restricting the privileges of chrome scripts to those declared at load time. While this architecture does not prevent vulnerabilities in extension scripts, it ensures that the effect of any exploits is contained to the vulnerable components of the extension, and will not give the attacker unbridled access to privileged browser APIs.

However, a compromised chrome script can still trick core modules to access sensitive resources of the attacker's choice. Consider the scenario where the attacker has compromised the chrome script in the DisplayWeather extension, and has changed the parameter value in `FileUtils.getFile()` to read the passwords stored on disk. The core module with privileges to access file-system will then read and return all the saved passwords to the attacker. Similarly, the attacker can redirect stolen data to an attacker-controlled remote server by changing `serverUrl` in `httpRequest.open()`. In both cases, the attacker does not need to extend the script's privileges at runtime. Instead, lack of policy checker to enforce fine-grained access control enables the attacker to exploit benign extensions even in the security enhanced Jetpack framework.

3   Morpheus

While the Jetpack framework provides clear security benefits to extensions, legacy extensions must be rewritten in Jetpack in order to enjoy these benefits. Morpheus is a static dataflow analysis and transformation tool that automates this process. In this section, we identify the key requirements that Morpheus's analysis and transformation must provide and describe its design.

3.1   Design Requirements

The transformations in Morpheus must perform the following tasks:

(1) *Chrome/content partitioning*. Jetpack requires chrome and content scripts to execute in isolated heaps. Morpheus must analyze the code of the legacy extension and identify object references that should be part of either chrome scripts or content scripts. Code that transitively accesses these object references should also correspondingly be marked for execution within the context of chrome or content scripts.

In Jetpack, chrome scripts interact with content scripts via asynchronous message passing protocols using JSON. In contrast, legacy extensions use synchronous calls for content/chrome communication. For example, calls to `getLocationFromWebPagecontent` and `modifyWebPageContent` (lines 34-36, Figure 1) are synchronous invocations in the legacy extension. Thus, to preserve the control flow of the legacy extension, Morpheus must use the asynchronous communication API available in Jetpack and emulate the synchronous nature of content/chrome communication in legacy extensions.

(2) *Module construction*. The Jetpack framework encapsulates a selection of the privileged browser APIs as core modules and requires developers to arrange their code as user modules to limit the extent of the damage in case of a breach. A Jetpack extension is a hierarchical collection of such core and user modules. Morpheus must identify the use of privileged browser APIs in the legacy extension and create core modules for them. Although creation of user modules is not mandatory, it is recommended. Thus, Morpheus must analyze the legacy extension and extract related functionality that can be compiled into a user module.

Modules interact using the `require` and `exports` interfaces. Although modules are allowed to export privileged objects that they access, doing so would undermine the security of the whole extension (by exposing the object to other modules). Morpheus must therefore ensure that the modules it creates never export references to privileged objects. Instead, they should export accessor methods to these privileged objects, which can be invoked by other modules to achieve their desired tasks. One may argue that exporting accessor methods is akin to accessing capabilities to achieve the desired functionality. However, as will be described later in Sections 3.3 and 4, isolating capabilities in separate JavaScript modules makes it harder for an attacker to compromise other modules.

(3) *Scope and global objects.* Legacy extensions make frequent use of global objects as shown in Figure 1. Morpheus must ensure that partitioning the code into chrome/content and user/core modules does not affect visibility of the globals (or other objects in scope) in the Jetpack extension.

(4) *Policy Checker.* Benign software that exposes an API to third-party code is often vulnerable to the confused deputy problem [16]. To safeguard core Jetpack modules from becoming confused deputies themselves, (see Section 2) and also protect benign-but-buggy extensions, Morpheus must allow enforcement of fine-grained access control and other security policies at runtime. A key requirement here is that the extension code should be oblivious to the security policies and the policy checker implementation.

(5) *Preserve extension UI.* The transformed Jetpack extension must retain the look and feel of the legacy extension. Thus, the browser's UI overlays, including any CSS, XUL and icons, must be appropriately mapped.

In our work to date, we have not attempted to optimize the performance of the transformed extension. The goal of Morpheus is to preserve the investment in legacy extensions, while also improving their security by making them amenable for use within Jetpack. In doing so, Morpheus may degrade the performance of the legacy extension, *e.g.*, by using an asynchronous communication API to emulate synchronous communication. We plan to optimize performance in future work.

3.2   Analyses and Transformations

Morpheus invokes TRANSFORM (see algorithm 1) over the legacy extension to transform it into the corresponding Jetpack extension. TRANSFORM takes in (i) the JavaScript code of the legacy extension L, which has been preprocessed to resolve any global-local scope conflict, (ii) an alias relation A as computed by the CFA2 algorithm [32] over the extension's JavaScript code, and (iii) some basic transformation rules $\mathcal{R}$ (see Table 2). Each transformation rule modifies an expression ξ from the program's abstract syntax tree (AST) T. TRANSFORM in turn invokes algorithms 2(a), 2(b) and 3 to complete the transformation. Table 1 lists the common notations used in all algorithms and rules.

We now discuss in detail the analyses and transformations implemented in Morpheus corresponding to each of the design requirements listed above.

Chrome/Content Separation. To identify object references that must appear in chrome or content scripts, Morpheus identifies the context in which object references and their property accesses should be evaluated. The context of an object reference is the context in which it was declared. Thus, any object declared in chrome code must be evaluated in chrome context and similarly all accesses to content objects must be evaluated in the context of the current Web page (content). For the rest of the paper, we refer chrome context as chrome and content context as content.

Morpheus uses static dataflow analysis to identify whether code that accesses an object reference should be evaluated in either chrome or content. Our analysis leverages the dataflow rules given in prior work [32]. The analysis is based on the observation that

Table 1. Common notations used in transformation rules and algorithms

$\mathbb{E}$	Set of all expressions
E_{pa_f}	Fixed property access expression of the form $\texttt{e.x, e['x']}$
E_{pa_d}	Dynamic property access expression of the form $\texttt{e[v]}$
E_{pa}	Property access expression where $E_{pa} := E_{pa_f} \cup E_{pa_d}$ where $E_{pa} \subset \mathbb{E}$
E_{mi}	Method invocation expression $\texttt{e.f(args), e['f'](args), e[vf](args)}$
E_{xpcom}	XPCOM invoke expression, where $E_{xpcom} \subset \mathbb{E}$. It can be one of the two forms, either
	(i) $\texttt{Components.classes[.*].getService(Components.interfaces[.*]])}$, or
	(ii)$\texttt{Components.utils.import("resource://gre/modules/*.jsm");}$
$E_{objInit}$	Object Literal expression of the form { $\texttt{a:1, b:function(){}}$ }, where $E_{objInit} \subset \mathbb{E}$
E_{decl}	Function/ variable declaration expression, where $E_{decl} \subset \mathbb{E}$. Can be any of the following expressions $\texttt{const c; let l; var a; var b=5; function foo( ){}}$
EXPRESSION(η)	Expression for AST node η
OBJECT(ξ)	expression representing object whose property is accessed in expression ξ, where $\xi \in (E_{pa} \cup E_{mi})$
PROPERTY(ξ)	expression representing property being accessed in expression ξ, where $\xi \in E_{pa}$
NODE(η, ξ)	AST node for expression ξ and a descendant of node η
GETALIASSET($\mathcal{A}, n$)	Consults alias relation $\mathcal{A}$ and returns all may-alias for the node n.
INCONTENT(ξ)	Checks if object denoted by expression ξ belongs to content context.
CANMAKEMODULE($n, \mathcal{T}$)	Decides if code corresponding to AST node n can be extracted and put in a separate module. In our implementation, it embodies the criteria that the object, represented by n, must have at least one method defined as its property that is invoked from outside the object.

TRANSFORM($L, \mathcal{A}, \mathcal{R}$)
Input: L : Legacy code, $\mathcal{A}$: alias relation, $\mathcal{R}$: set of rewriting rules
Output: $\mathbb{M}$ a set of Jetpack modules
Initialize:
  $\mathcal{T} := AST(L)$; $\mathbb{O} := \emptyset$ /*Set of AST nodes for object literals*/
  $S := $ COMPUTESENSITIVESET($L, \mathcal{A}$) ; $D := $ COMPUTEDOMSET($L, \mathcal{A}$)

foreach $n \in$ NODES($\mathcal{T}$) **do**
    $\xi_n := $ EXPRESSION(n)
    if $\xi_n \in E_{xpcom}$ **then** REWRITE($\xi_n, \mathcal{T}, \mathcal{R}1$) /*rewrite with require, import core modules*/;
    else if $\xi_n \in E_{mi} \wedge$ (NODE($n,$ OBJECT(ξ_n)) $\in S$ $\vee$ NODE($n,$ OBJECT(ξ_n)) $\in D$) **then** REWRITE($\xi_n, \mathcal{T}, \mathcal{R}3$) ;
    else if $\xi_n \in E_{pa} \wedge$ (NODE($n,$ OBJECT(ξ_n)) $\in S$ $\vee$ NODE($n,$ OBJECT(ξ_n)) $\in D$) **then** REWRITE($\xi_n, \mathcal{T}, \mathcal{R}2$) ;
    else if $\xi_n \in E_{objInit} \wedge$ CANMAKEMODULE($n, \mathcal{T}$) **then** $\mathbb{O} \cup = \{n\}$;
  $\mathbb{M} := $ EXTRACTMODULE($\mathcal{T}, \mathbb{O}$) /*Creates user modules from the relevant code*/
  return $\mathbb{M}$

Algorithm 1. Transforming legacy extension code to Jetpack modules

JavaScript code in legacy extensions is evaluated in chrome unless it specifically makes a transition to access objects in content scripts. There are only a limited number of ways to make a transition from chrome code to content code, *i.e.,* by accessing content, contentWindow and contentDocument properties on selected chrome objects, like window and gBrowser. This observation forms the basis of our static analysis.

All JavaScript in a legacy extension executes in the same heap, and thus objects have global visibility. To precisely identify which objects must reside in the chrome or content, Morpheus does a whole program analysis of the legacy extension. It concatenates all JavaScript code within the extension before performing the static analysis. This concatenation includes scripts defined within JavaScript files, event handlers and globals declared within overlay files and also JavaScript code modules. The result of the static analysis is a table where each entry is an object reference and the context in which it should be evaluated.

Static analysis to determine the chrome/content context of object references can suffer from false positives and negatives when content references are accessed using JavaScript's reflective constructs. This happens, for instance, when object references are used within the eval string, or passed as parameters to functions but are accessed

COMPUTEDOMSET(L, $\mathcal{A}$)

Input: L: Legacy code, $\mathcal{A}$: Alias relation
Output: D : set of AST nodes for DOM objects

Initialize:
$\quad \mathcal{T} := AST(L)$; $D := \emptyset$

foreach $n \in$ NODES($\mathcal{T}$) **do**
$\quad \xi_n :=$ EXPRESSION(n)
$\quad \xi_n^r :=$ RVALUEEXP(ξ_n), $\xi_n^l :=$ LVALUEEXP(ξ_n)
$\quad$ **if** ($\xi_n^r \in D$)
$\quad\quad \vee(\xi_n^r \in E_{mi} \wedge ((\text{NODE}(n, \text{OBJECT}(\xi_n^r)) \in D)$
$\quad\quad\quad\quad \vee \text{INCONTENT}(\text{OBJECT}(\xi_n^r))))$
$\quad\quad \vee(\xi_n^r \in E_{pa} \wedge ((\text{NODE}(n, \text{OBJECT}(\xi_n^r)) \in D)$
$\quad\quad\quad\quad \vee \text{INCONTENT}(\text{OBJECT}(\xi_n^r))))$
$\quad\quad \vee(\xi_n^r \in E_{pa} \wedge ((\text{NODE}(n, \text{OBJECT}(\xi_n^r)) \in D)$
$\quad\quad\quad\quad \vee \text{INCONTENT}(\text{PROPERTY}(\xi_n^r)))))$ **then**
$\quad\quad D \cup = \{\text{NODE}(n, \xi_n^l)\}$
$\quad\quad A_l :=$ GETALIASSET($\mathcal{A}$, NODE(n, ξ_n^l))
$\quad\quad D \cup = A_l$ /*add all alias of ξ_n^l to D*/
return D

(a)

COMPUTESENSITIVESET(L, $\mathcal{A}$)

Input: L: Legacy code, $\mathcal{A}$: Alias relation
Output: S : set of AST nodes for sensitive objects

Initialize:
$\quad \mathcal{T} := AST(L)$; $S := \emptyset$

foreach $n \in$ NODES($\mathcal{T}$) **do**
$\quad \xi_n :=$ EXPRESSION(n)
$\quad$ **if** $\xi_n \in E_{xpcom}$
$\quad\quad \vee(\xi_n \in E_{mi} \wedge (\text{NODE}(n, \text{OBJECT}(\xi_n)) \in S))$
$\quad\quad \vee(\xi_n \in E_{pa} \wedge (\text{NODE}(n, \text{OBJECT}(\xi_n)) \in S))$ **then**
$\quad\quad S \cup = \{n\}$
$\quad\quad A_n :=$ GETALIASSET($\mathcal{A}, n$)
$\quad\quad S \cup = A_n$ /*add all alias of ξ_n
$\quad\quad\quad\quad$ to S*/
return S

(b)

Algorithm 2. Algorithms for computation of set of nodes corresponding to (a) content DOM objects and (b) sensitive objects

Table 2. Rewrite rules for expression. Each rule modifies an expression ξ and updates AST T

Rule: $(\xi \Rightarrow \xi') \rightarrow (T \Rightarrow T')$, where $\xi :=$ expression(n). T is set to T' after applying each rule

Rule $\mathcal{R}1$: Import Module
$m :=$ get-module-name(ξ)
$\xi' :=$ `require('m')`

Rule $\mathcal{R}2$: Rewrite property access with `setProperty`, `getProperty`
$o :=$ object(ξ), prop := property(exp)

$(\mathcal{R}2.a)\ \dfrac{\text{property-read}(T, \xi)}{\xi' := \text{o.getProperty('p')}}$ $(\mathcal{R}2.b)\ \dfrac{\text{property-write}(T, \xi)\quad v := \text{value-to-store}(T, \xi)}{\xi' := \text{o.setProperty('p', v)}}$

Rule $\mathcal{R}3$: Rewrite method invocation with `invoke`
$o :=$ object(ξ), $\mu :=$ method(exp), $\alpha :=$ arguments(exp)
$\xi' :=$ `o.invoke('`μ`', ` α`)`

Rule $\mathcal{R}4$: Rewrite Global Access with `GlobalGET`, `GlobalSET`

$(\mathcal{R}4.a)\ \dfrac{\text{Global-read}(T, \xi)}{\xi' := \text{GlobaGET}('\xi')}$ $(\mathcal{R}4.b)\ \dfrac{\text{Global-write}(T, \xi)\quad v := \text{value-to-store}(T, \xi)}{\xi' := \text{GlobaSET}('\xi', v)}$

Rule $\mathcal{R}5$: Global Write ** This rule creates a new statement
$\sigma :=$ `GlobaSET('`ξ`',`ξ)

as elements of the `arguments` array within the function. Morpheus currently does not handle such cases and instead relies on the developer to rewrite the code to make it more amenable to analysis, or to manually classify the context of the object reference.

By default, a legacy extension executes in `chrome`, so object references that remain in `chrome` in Jetpack can be evaluated as before. To evaluate objects in `content`, Morpheus considers the `content` as a sensitive resource and models it as a core Jetpack module called `contentDOM`. Algorithm 2(a) identifies all program points corresponding to property accesses of content objects and Morpheus then rewrites these accesses by accessor methods to abstract away the design of the content module from the extension code. For example, the code `gBrowser.contentDocument` in a legacy extension would be rewritten as `gBrowser.getProperty('contentDocument')`. Likewise, the property access `gBrowser.contentDocument.location` would be rewritten as `gBrowse.getProperty('contentDocument').getProperty('location')`.

```
var table = require('core_module_table');         switch(property) {
var policyChecker = require('policy_checker');         case '< depends on the core module >':
var _module_ = {                                           var retval = ref[property];
  id: initModule(), /*initializes the module*/             var newref = < new core module instance>
  getProperty: function() {                                 table.setReference(newref.id, retval);
    var property = arguments[0];                            return newref;
    var violated = policyChecker.check                 ... /* more case statements */
        (<core module name>, property);              default:
    if(violated){                                        return null;
      return {};                                      }
    }                                                },
    var ref = table.getReference(this.id);          /*code for setProperty, invoke*/
                                                  }
                                                  exports.module = _module_;
```

Fig. 3. Template for secure core module with policy

Morpheus addresses a key challenge that arises as a result of the design of Jetpack's `contentDOM` module. As shown in line 36 in Figure 1, legacy extensions may contain statements that refer to objects in both `chrome` and `content`, *i.e.*, `modifyWebPageContent` is a method defined in the `chrome` while `gBrowser.contentDocument` is the active window's `document` object and is therefore an object in `content`. Moreover, the call to `modifyWebPageContent` is synchronous in the legacy extension. Since the Jetpack framework executes chrome scripts and content scripts in separate processes, they cannot share object references, but only exchange data in JSON format asynchronously. Thus, in the Jetpack counterpart of this extension, the call in line 36 would be asynchronous because `modifyWebPageContent` should be part of content script as they operate on the `gBrowser.contentDocument` from the active Web page. Morpheus addresses this challenge by creating opaque identifiers for objects in the `content` and transmitting these identifiers across the JSON pipe to the `chrome`. Morpheus's transformation also attempts to retain the control flow of the original extension code as intended by the developer (see Section 5).

Module Construction. Modules in Jetpack must ideally not export references to privileged objects. Any such *leaking references* to other modules can lead to privilege escalation attacks, *i.e.*, a module to which a reference is leaked may be able to access a privileged object without explicitly requesting access to it at load time. Morpheus creates extensions that do not export privileged objects. Instead, Morpheus creates module templates (see Figure 3) that export accessor methods to these privileged objects. These modules export only four properties, namely `id`, `getProperty`, `setProperty` and `invoke` to privileged objects. Each module encapsulates a privileged object, which is assigned an opaque identifier (`id`) on module initialization. Other modules access the object using `getProperty` and `setProperty`, which are getter and setter methods, and `invoke`, which allows invocation of methods defined on the privileged object. The first argument to each of `getProperty`, `setProperty` and `invoke` is the property to be accessed followed by a list of arguments. Each of these methods can either return primitive values or an instance of a module. Accessor methods also embody any security policies associated with access to privileged objects. Section 4 discusses the security implications of creating modules in this way.

Morpheus transforms legacy extensions to use core modules designed as above in the following way. It first analyzes the legacy extension to locate the use of browser's privileged XPCOM APIs and generates a list of program points (as shown in algorithm 2(b)) for the property access and methods invoked on corresponding privileged XPCOM

```
ExtractModule(T, O, A)
Input: T : AST for Legacy, O : Set of nodes for object literals, A : alias relation
Output: M a set of Jetpack modules
Initialize:
    T := ∅ /*Map from node n ∈ O to AST*/;    ι := ∅ /*Map from node n ∈ O to parentAST from
which it is extracted*/
foreach n_i ∈ O do
    T_{n_i} := CopyAstForNode(T, n_i);  T[n_i] := T_{n_i};  ι[n_i] := T
/*update parent AST for nested object Literal expression*/
foreach n_i ∈ O do
    if IsNestedObject(n_i, T) then
        T^p := FindParentAST(n_i, T);  ι[n_i] := T^p /*T^p is the smallest AST T from T[n_i] such that
        n_i ≠ root(T)*/

foreach n_i ∈ O do
    T_{n_i} := T[n_i] /*AST for node n_i*/
    G_{n_i} := GetGlobalIdentifiers(T_{n_i}) /* G_{n_i} is set of identifiers used but not defined in T_{n_i}*/
    H_{n_i} := GetLocalIdentifiersGloballyUsed(T, O, T_{n_i}) /*Identifiers defined in T_{n_i} but also used
    in other T*/
    /*H_{n_i} is set of identifiers defined in T_{n_i} and used in other modules*/
    foreach q ∈ Nodes(T_{n_i}) do
        ξ_q := Expression(q)
        if ξ_q ∈ G_{n_i} then Rewrite(ξ_q, T_{n_i}, R4) /*rewrite with GlobalGET, GlobalSET*/;
        else if ξ_q ∈ E_{decl} then
            σ := CreateNewStatement(lValueExp(ξ_q), R5) /*create a GlobalSET*/
            AddToAst(T_{n_i}, σ)
    m_i := MakeNewModule(T_{n_i}) /*Place the code for AST T_{n_i} in a new module and append
    necessary code*/
    M ∪ = m_i

    /*modify the parent AST*/
    T^p := ι[n_i] /*get parent AST*/
    ξ_{n_i} := Expression(GetNodeFromAst(n_i, T^p));  Rewrite(ξ_{n_i}, T^p, R1) /* rewrite with require*/
    A_{n_i} := GetAliasSet(A, GetNodeFromAst(n_i, T^p))
    foreach λ ∈ Nodes(T^p) do
        ξ_λ := Expression(λ)
        if ξ_λ ∈ E_{mi} ∧ (Object(ξ_λ) = ξ_{n_i}) then Rewrite(ξ_λ, T^p, R3) /*rewrite with invoke*/;
        else if ξ_λ ∈ E_{pa} ∧ (Object(ξ_λ) = ξ_{n_i}) then Rewrite(ξ_λ, T^p, R2) /*rewrite property access*/;
    m := MakeNewModule(T);  M ∪ = m /*construct the main module and add to set M*/
    return M
```

Algorithm 3. Algorithm for extracting user modules

API. Morpheus then rewrites the extension code by replacing all such references as per the rules $R1$, $R2$, $R3$ in Table 2 for the corresponding core module in Jetpack. The Jetpack framework does not provide core modules for all XPCOM APIs, so core modules may have to be supplied separately. We have used our module template to build a suite of core modules for a variety of XPCOM APIs. We developed these core modules by hand, and used an off-the-shelf static analysis tool [17] to verify that these core modules do not export references to privileged objects.

Morpheus also creates user modules by analyzing legacy extension code. The main objective is to partition the chrome script into multiple modules in a way to attenuate the authority of individual modules and limit the effect of a vulnerability exploit. Ideally, user modules should be generated by clustering functions based on access to XPCOM functionality. However objects with privilege to access different XPCOM can be used in a single statement. This makes splitting based on XPCOM access non-trivial, since it would require more precise and sophisticated static analysis and semantic-preserving transformation algorithm. Therefore we adopted a simpler approach of encoding the developer's way of partitioning code.

Morpheus identifies code fragments in the legacy extension that achieve related functionality. The underlying intuition is that these code fragments can then be grouped into a single module. Morpheus uses a simple notion of object ownership to identify related functionality: it identifies a set of functions that are owned by the same object, and groups such functions into a single module. This heuristic is based on the observation that developers often group functionality as object hierarchies that are more likely to access similar, if not the same, XPCOM interfaces within one object. Even though this might provide less meaningful partitions if the developer does not arrange his code using purposeful object hierarchies, our evaluation shows that this approach is practical and we do extract a reasonable number of user modules with most of them accessing only a few core modules. User modules follow the same template as core modules with the difference that the object encapsulated within the module is the one that owns the functions grouped in that module, instead of a sensitive XPCOM object as for core modules. Morpheus rewrites references to the encapsulated objects with a `require` invocation. Algorithm 3 encodes the user modules extraction and rewriting technique.

As shown in line 2 in Figure 1, an extension can load a JavaScript code module (JSM) using an invocation to `Components.utils.import`. The `import` API takes as arguments the URL of the script to be loaded and an optional scope object. On execution of the `import` statement, the array of objects defined in the script (referenced by the URL) is attached to the scope object. In case the scope object is not defined, the imported objects are attached to the global object, *i.e.*, they can be accessed and modified by any script in the extension code. Browser-provided JSMs internally access XPCOM interfaces and therefore are treated as privileged API by Morpheus. Core modules are constructed for them and accesses of such JSMs are rewritten accordingly. In contrast, Morpheus rewrites all JSMs, defined by legacy extension developers, to access only core modules designed as above. However since these JSMs are self contained code fragments with a well defined interface for exporting objects, Morpheus rewrites the entire JSM as a user module, and does not partition it further into smaller modules.

Scope and Global Objects. When Morpheus creates user modules from a legacy extension, it is possible that the resulting user modules may require access to scope or global variables defined in the legacy extension. However, Morpheus creates modules, which are isolated by the Jetpack framework, and therefore cannot share references/updates to scope and global variables. Morpheus therefore creates a new `global` module that (1) stores references to all the scope and global variables, and (2) exports two methods `GlobalGET` and `GlobalSET` to enable access to these variables. It then analyzes all user modules, identifies instances of scope or global variables used (but not defined) and rewrites access to these variables as per rule $\mathcal{R}4$ in Table 2, *i.e.*, using either `GlobalGET` or `GlobalSET`.

Preserving Extension UI. As mentioned in Section 2.2, most of the browser's UI is scriptable, *i.e.*, it can be accessed and modified using JavaScript. Morpheus leverages this ability and generates JavaScript code to dynamically modify the browser's UI on invocation of the Jetpack functionality. To do so, Morpheus analyzes the legacy extension's CSS and XUL overlay files, which represent UI descriptions as XML markups, and dynamically loads the appropriate JavaScript code at runtime to preserve the UI of the legacy extension.

```
(2)  var FileUtils = require('core/FileUtils').module;
(4)  var file = FileUtils.invoke('getFile',dir, [filename]);
(9)  var Weather = require('user/Weather').module;
()   GlobalSET('Weather', Weather); /*new statement added*/
(30) document.invoke('getElementById','weatherStatusBar')
          .addEventListener('click', showWeatherInPanel, false);
(32) window.invoke('addEventListener','DOMContentLoaded', addWeatherToWebpage, false);
(34) var locationStr = getLocationFromWebpage(gBrowser.getProperty('contentDocument'));
(35) var temperature = Weather.invoke('getWeatherData', getZipCode(locationStr));
(36) modifyWebpageContent(gBrowser.getProperty('contentDocument', temperature));
```

Fig. 4. Code snippet from *Main* module of the transformed DisplayWeather Jetpack extension. Only statements from Figure 1 that are rewritten by Morpheus are shown.

```
(9)  var _module_ = {
(12)   getWeatherData: function(zipcode){
(13)     GlobalGET('Weather').invoke('requestDataFromServer', zipcode);
(14)     return processWeatherData(GlobalGET('Weather').getProperty('temperature'));
(15)   },
(16)   requestDataFromServer: function(sendData){
(17)     var httpRequest = require('core/XMLHttpRequest').module;
(20)     httpRequest.setProperty('onreadystatechange', function(){
(22)       GlobalGET('Weather').invoke('extractTemperature', httpRequest.getProperty('response'));
(24)     });
(25)     httpRequest.invoke('open', 'GET', serverUrl, true);
(26)     httpRequest.invoke('send', sendData); /*contact remote server*/
(27)   }
(28) }
()   exports.module = _module_; /*new statement added*/
```

Fig. 5. Code snippet from *Weather* module of the transformed DisplayWeather Jetpack extension. Only the statements from Figure 1 that are rewritten by Morpheus are shown.

Figures 4 and 5 show the rewritten statements and extracted user modules on applying Morpheus to our DisplayWeather extension (see Figure 1).

3.3 Policy Checker

Transformations on legacy extensions as applied by Morpheus greatly simplify enforcement of security policies on a per extension granularity. Morpheus supports both simple access control checks as well as complex stateful policy checks on sensitive browser resources and APIs managed by the core modules.

Security policies for preventing undesired accesses by the core modules are encoded in a separate Jetpack module named `PolicyChecker`, and all accessor methods in core modules must consult the `PolicyChecker` before actually granting access to the sensitive resources requested by a potentially compromised user module. To do so, Morpheus mandates that core modules place a trap in their accessor methods, as shown in Figure 3. `PolicyChecker` exports an API `check` to validate the request for accessing the sensitive resource by the user module. If the request does not conform to the extension's security policy, a violation is raised and the `PolicyChecker` simply blocks the requested access and returns an empty object.[2]

Since policies are encoded within the isolated `PolicyChecker` module and core modules can only invoke the `check` API to validate the access, Morpheus allows policies to be added or removed with no modification of the extension code.

---

[2] The supplementary materials contain an example of a security policy.

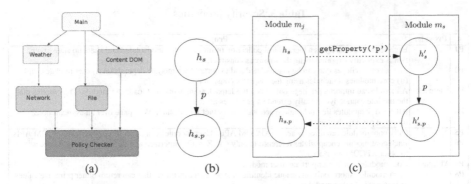

Fig. 6. (a) Module hierarchy in transformed DisplayWeather extension. Difference of heap map of property access of a sensitive object where h_ξ is the heap object for the expression ξ. (b) s.p in legacy extension (c) s.getProperty('p') in Jetpack. m_j is a user module, m_s is a module wrapping sensitive object s.

4   Security Analysis

A Jetpack extension's ability to limit the consequences of a breach depends on the structure of its modules and the security policies. Figures 6(b) and 6(c) show the effect of Morpheus's transformations in accessing property of sensitive object in terms of the heap model.

In a legacy extension when accessing a property p in sensitive object s, the heap object h_s for s and $h_{s.p}$ for s.p lies in the same address space, as shown in Figure 6(b). However when processed by Morpheus, s.p is rewritten as s.getProperty('p') and the heap object h_s for s does not have direct access to $h_{s.p}$, as shown in Figure 6(c). Instead, invoking the getProperty method gives it access to the actual heap object h'_s that has direct access to its property p heap object $h'_{s.p}$. The dotted line between $h'_{s.p}$ and $h_{s.p}$ denotes that (i) the latter is the wrapped version of the former object, and (ii) this relation is further protected by the policy enforcement mechanism. Note that both h'_s and $h'_{s.p}$ lie in a different module m_s, which is isolated from the module m_j corresponding to the transformed legacy code. Thus, if an attacker manages to compromise m_j he will not have direct access to the actual heap object from m_j.

Given the above heap model, we now analyze the security of a legacy extension transformed by Morpheus using several properties (enumerated in Table 3), provided in part by the Jetpack framework, Morpheus's transformation, and Morpheus's PolicyChecker for policy enforcement.

Let $P(m)$ denote the set of privileges that can be accessed by a module m. It is computed as follows:

$P(m) := (\bigcup_{m \to x} P(x)) \bigcup (\bigcup_{m \mapsto m^u} LP(m^u)) \bigcup (\bigcup_{m \to m^c} P(m^c))$, where

    $m \to x$ means module m has direct access to XPCOM interface x,

    $m_i \mapsto m_j$ means module m_i imports module m_j,

    U is the set of user modules m^u in an extension,

    C is the set of core modules m^c in an extension and $U \cap C$ is $\emptyset$, and

    $LP(m^u)$ denotes the set of privileges leaked from user module m^u

Table 3. Security properties

#	Provider	Property
P1		Each Jetpack extension is a hierarchical collection of modules that are isolated and share no state except that is explicitly exported using the `exports` construct.
P2		The set of privileges that can be manipulated and exported by a module depends on (i) user modules, and (ii) core modules it includes using the `require` construct.
P3	Jetpack	A module can import a privilege only when the Jetpack framework first loads the module. This implies that the module cannot dynamically extend its privileges at runtime.
P4		All Jetpack modules lie in chrome space and can contact with content Web page over an asynchronous message passing channel.
P5		Only core module can directly access XPCOM APIs. User modules can never directly access XPCOM APIs.
P6		Each core module encapsulates reference to only one XPCOM interface and does not have direct access to other XPCOM interfaces
P7	Morpheus	Core modules can not import any user module
P8		Each module exports only an opaque identifier and accessor methods, that can return either primitive values or instances of other modules
P9		Each module stores the reference to the sensitive object it encapsulates within another designated module, *i.e.*, all core modules share a common module to store sensitive objects.
P10	Policy Checker	Each core module can access a specific sensitive resource after being verified by security policy mediate the particular sensitive resource that a core module can access.

P3 together with **P2** guarantees that $P(m)$ can be statically determined and cannot be changed during execution, and thus prevents the attacker from creating and dynamically loading instances of other core modules inside the compromised core (or user) module m. **P5**, **P6** and **P7** limit the privileges $P(m)$ for any core module $m \in C$ to $(\bigcup_{m \to x} P(x)) \bigcup (\bigcup_{m \to m^c} P(m^c))$. In case m is compromised, **P9** guarantees that the attacker only has access to the reference to the privileged object encapsulated by it (see Figure 6(b)), and no access to objects managed by other core modules, *e.g.*, m_j^c. This is because `core_module_table`, which stores the sensitive references for other core modules, does not support iteration and its accessor methods need an opaque identifier to return the sensitive reference. Since the opaque identifier itself is a reference, it is not possible for the attacker to manufacture the reference and access all sensitive objects.

For a user module $m \in U$, **P5** and **P8** guarantee that $\bigcup_{m \to x} P(x)$ is $\emptyset$ at all times. This implies that a user module cannot export references to privileged objects, because it has none. Therefore, we need not implement accessor methods for user modules, but Morpheus still keeps the same interface as it allows developers to conveniently enforce security policies on user modules. **P8** also guarantees that $\bigcup_{m \to m^u} LP(m^u)$ is $\emptyset$ that makes $P(m)$ for any user module $m \in U$ equal to $\bigcup_{m \to m^c} P(m^c)$. In other words, the privileges of a user module can be determined by inspecting privileges of the core modules it imports. Thus, the above properties ensure that for any module m, $P(m) \equiv \bigcup_{m \to m^c} P(m^c)$ always holds.

The DisplayWeather extension with access to the user's file system and the network is an attractive target for Web attackers, who may want to steal sensitive user data, such as stored passwords, from the file system and send it over to an attacker controlled remote server. We now illustrate how Morpheus improves the security of the transformed DisplayWeather extension. Figure 6(a) shows the module hierarchy for the transformed Jetpack extension. Using the above formula and the transformed code (Figures 4 and 5), we claim that $P(m_{File}) \equiv \{file\}$, $P(m_{Network}) \equiv \{network\}$, $P(m_{Main}) \equiv \{file\}$, and $P(m_{Weather}) \equiv \{network\}$ holds even if these modules get compromised.

Unlike in the legacy DisplayWeather extension, **P4** guarantees that the modules in the corresponding Jetpack are isolated from the `content`. Assuming that the attacker has

(i) compromised the asynchronous message passing channel between the content and the chrome, and (ii) can infiltrate into the chrome space (that contains all the modules), we consider the case of a security breach in a user module $m_{Weather}$. The only privilege that the attacker gets is access to the network via the $m_{Network}$ module. Although we place no restriction on the nature of code that the attacker can evaluate within the extension, as listed earlier, **P3** restricts the powers of the attacker by disallowing him from loading a new core module $m_{LoginManager}$ (to read all stored passwords), as it was not requested by the compromised $m_{Weather}$ module at load time.

Due to the fixed module hierarchy in Jetpack extensions, the attacker cannot even trick m_{File} module (to read the password file) by only compromising $m_{Weather}$, and must also compromise m_{Main} or m_{File}. If we assume that the attacker has managed to infiltrate a core module m_{File}, then the only privilege he gets is $file$, $i.e.$, access to the file system. Similar scenario applies if the attacker has managed to infiltrate the core module $m_{Network}$. In each of the above cases, the attacker only gets access to the privileges available in the compromised module m computed by $P(m)$ and no more. This is in contrast to the legacy extensions where a breach in any portion of an extension enables the attacker to obtain access to any privileged object managed by the browser.

P10 further attenuates the authority of core modules. Let us assume that the attacker has compromised both the m_{Main} and $m_{Weather}$ modules, and also managed to modify the file path in FileUtils.getFile to the intended password file, and the URL for the remote server to one that is controlled by attacker. In such a scenario, the PolicyChecker will prevent the m_{File} and $m_{Network}$ core modules to read file other than ProfD/zip.txt from the file system and contact a remote server other than the legitimate weather server. Even if the attacker has compromised m_{File} and $m_{Network}$ module, the PolicyChecker will still prevent access to unauthorized resources.

We note that if the $m_{Weather}$ module was not extracted using Morpheus's transformations, $P(m_{Main})$ would have evaluated to $\{file, network\}$. In the absence of any security policy, compromising only m_{Main} module would have sufficed for the attacker. In other words, Morpheus does not worsen the security guarantees given by Jetpack framework. In fact, its module extraction based on the owning object algorithm along with the PolicyChecker make it harder for the attacker to mount a successful attack, by increasing the minimum number of modules that need to be compromised.

5   Implementation

We realized the entire Morpheus toolchain in about 13, 400 lines of JavaScript (node.js [4]), of which about 10, 500 lines were devoted to implement 100 core modules with wide ranging functionality. We used node.js to ease the implementation of the prototype. We leveraged Doctor JS [1], which also uses node.js as its backend, to implement our JavaScript code analyzer. Specifically, we added about 100 lines of code to customize Doctor JS for analysis of legacy extensions. Generation of Jetpack modules and rewriting of the global variables utilized the Narcissus [21] parser and decompiler to (i) rewrite the source ASTs, and (ii) convert the rewritten ASTs back to source code. This required about 4200 lines of JavaScript code. Finally, dynamic generation of the UI and subsequent packaging of the modules into a Jetpack addon required 900 and 100 lines of JavaScript code, respectively. Another 370 lines of shell scripts were required to automate the entire toolchain. Policy checker is implemented as a Jetpack module and requires only 150 lines of JavaScript code to encode all policies listed in Table 6.

The transformation of legacy extension into the corresponding Jetpack, and correct evaluation of chrome and content scripts in the transformed Jetpack posed several issues. We discuss a few of them here:

- *Content proxy.* A content proxy is required for mediating interaction between chrome and content scripts (see Section 2.3). The default content proxy implemented in the Jetpack framework was stateless, *i.e.,* execution of content scripts across different invocations of the proxy did not share any execution context. This stateless execution posed a problem since the transformed Jetpack requires multiple invocations to the proxy depending upon context switches, *i.e.,* from chrome to content and back (see line 36 in Figure 1). We overcame the problem by modifying the default content proxy to retain all execution state after initialization. The content proxy is initialized every time a new document is loaded.

- *Opaque identifiers.* Message exchange between the chrome and content scripts is asynchronous and is limited to transfer of primitive values and opaque identifiers only. Since object creation may also happen in the content, management of opaque identifiers must also be done in the content. We therefore inject the content proxy with scripts to manage opaque identifiers during its initialization.

- *Synchronous execution.* In order to retain the synchronous execution semantics as intended by the extension developer, Morpheus implements a synchronous execution protocol for evaluating object references in the content. Specifically, Morpheus utilizes the processNextEvent API defined on XPCOM's thread interface to implement the synchronous behavior by repeatedly processing the next pending event on the currently executing thread until it receives a response from the content process. This technique along with a stateful content proxy ensures that the transformed extension achieves synchronous execution semantics without blocking the CPU. However, this mechanism may affect the performance of the transformed extension if it makes numerous context switches between the chrome and the content.

- *Custom XPCOM interface.* Firefox allows extension developers to declare their own XPCOM components and register them with the extension architecture by packaging supporting JavaScript files, which implement the component interfaces, with the extension. Morpheus treats such JavaScript files as modules, redefines the components using helper methods provided by Jetpack and rewrites them like other JavaScript code in the legacy extension. All top level objects in extension scripts are also added to global module so that they can be accessed by the modules defining the XPCOM interface.

6   Evaluation

We evaluated Morpheus using four criteria: (i) correctness of the transformation, (ii) conformance to the principle of least authority (POLA), (iii) effectiveness of user module creation and (iv) effectiveness of policy-checker. We performed the evaluation using a suite of 52 legacy extensions (50 popular legacy extensions from Mozilla's addon

Table 4. Legacy extensions transformed using Morpheus and corresponding Jetpack statistics

Legacy Extension	Functionality	# Users
Amazon Search	Search in amazon.com using the right click context menu from any Website.	1,866
BlockSite	Blocks Websites and disables hyperlinks of user's choice.	214,173
Bookmark All	Bookmark all opening tabs quickly without any dialog.	5,304
Clear Cache	Clears the browser cache with one click	10,557
Clear Cache Button	Clears the browser cache.	44,843
Comment Blocker	Blocks or hides all unwanted comments on Websites.	1,415
Context Search	Expands the context menu's "Search for" item for all installed search engines.	67,070
Copy Link Text	Adds an option to the context menu to select the text of a link on right-click.	5,199
Copy Link URL	Copy the URLs of the selected links to clipboard.	13,025
Ebay Quick Search	Search in ebay.com using the right click context menu from any Website.	1000
Email This	Email link, title, and a selected summary of the Web page being viewed.	15,853
Empty Cache Button	Cache clearing made easy. One click.	53,048
Facebook Bookmark	Allow visiting Facebook Bookmarks by adding a special Button to Toolbar.	11,222
Facebook New Tab	Loads Facebook.com quickly when a new tab is opened.	7,439
Facebook Toolbar Button	Loads Facebook.com on clicking toolbar icon.	21,026
Facebook Touch Panel	Allow quick check Facebook Notifications and Messages by a touch Panel.	10,054
FlagFox	Displays a country flag depicting the location of the current Website's server.	1,296,480
FlashBlock	Blocks all Flash content from loading.	1,372,826
Go To Bing	Loads bing.com in a new tab when clicked on status-bar Bing icon.	139
Go To Google	Loads google.com in a new tab when clicked on status-bar Google icon.	15,700
Google Search By Image	Adds Google Search by Image context menu item for images.	45,838
Google Translator	Translates selected text or page into chosen language with a click or hot-key.	453,029
Google Viewer	Prompt to open supported documents with Google Docs Viewer.	1,472
Image Block	Adds a toggle button to conditionally block/allow images on Web pages.	22,147
ImageSearch	Adds a context-menu item for images to search Google for that image.	14,285
LEOs Dictionaries	Translates selected words/phrases with the help of LEOs Online Dictionaries	10,501
Leo Search	Searches selected words at dict.leo.org and opens the result in a new tab.	9,835
LibraryDetector	Detects which JavaScript libraries are being used on the current Web page.	1,590
Live IP address	Retrieves Live IP Address and displays in the status bar.	9,090
My Home Page	Load the homepage in a new Tab.	40,439
My Public IP Address	Show browser IP address.	2,959
New Tab Homepage	Load the homepage in a new tab; load the first in case of multiple homepages.	245,540
Open Bookmark (new tab)	Always opens new tab from bookmarks.	44,683
Open GMail (new tab)	Opens Google Mail Web page on a new tab.	22,107
Open GMail (pinned tab)	Opens Google Mail Web page on a new pinned tab in HTTPS mode.	10,092
Open Image (new tab)	Adds right-click context menu item for opening images in new tabs.	14,285
Place Cleaner	Replace the default "Print" button with Mozilla's "Print Preview" button.	21,878
Plain Text links	Open plain-text urls as links via context menu.	4,738
Print Preview	Replace the default "Print" button with Mozilla's "Print Preview" button.	37,966
Really Simple Sticky	Allow to add notes, reminders directly in the browser.	924
Right Click Link	Opens selected text in a new tab.	6,861
Search IMDB	Search the highlighted text at IMDB.	19,635
Show MyIP	Displays user's current IP address in the status bar.	11,239
Tab History Menu	Enables opening the history menu for a selected tab just by clicking on it.	7,237
TinEye Rev Img Srch	Adds a context menu to search for an image, where it came from, etc.	208,496
Twitter New Tab	Loads twitter.com quickly when a new tab is opened.	830
Twitter Toolbar Button	Loads twitter.com on clicking toolbar icon.	210
Web2Pdf Converter	Web page to PDF conversion tool.	42,185
YouTube Auto Replay	Enables automatic replay of a YouTube video or part of it.	26,478
YouTube IT	Search the selected Text in Youtube.	15,036
DisplayWeather	Displays weather of chosen location	N/A
Steal-login	Steal passwords and send to remote server	N/A

gallery (AMO) and 2 synthetic extensions) and then transformed them using Morpheus. Our dataset contained extensions that use common extension development technologies, such as JavaScript, HTML, XUL, CSS, etc., and did not contain any binary XP-COM component.

Correctness of transformation. We tested the correctness of the transformation by exercising the advertised functionality of each of the 52 extensions transformed with Morpheus. In each case, we enhanced the browser with the Jetpack extension being tested and observed the results of interaction with the extension's UI. Table 4 lists the extensions evaluated along with their functionality. The top 50 entries are for the real-world extensions whereas the bottom 2 correspond to the synthetic ones. For all cases the Jetpack extension was able to provide the advertised functionality of the original (legacy) extension.

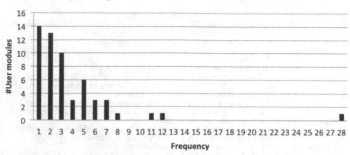

Fig. 7. Frequency of core modules in Jetpack user modules

FlagFox is one of the larger extensions that we transformed. It utilizes 28 core modules, and over 1307 lines of JavaScript (out of 3971 lines of extension code) are used to implement the UI. The remaining 2667 lines implement the core functionality of the legacy extension. We also observed that several extensions from our dataset had just a single user module after being transformed to Jetpack extension. Go To Google, Go To Bing, Steal-login are few instances of such case. This is due to the absence of any object definition or absence of property method invocations from objects defined in the legacy code. We also noticed the same Jetpack extension structure for TinEye Reverse Image Search entry even though the legacy code defines a top-level object. This is because it had all the functionality included in just that one object whose methods were invoked from event handlers.

Conformance to POLA. We used an off-the-shelf tool Beacon [17] to check whether modules in a Jetpack extension adhere to the principle of peast authority (POLA). Beacon detects whether a Jetpack module leaks references to privileged objects that it encapsulates. If so, any other code that `requires` this module will be able to directly access the privileged object without an explicit `require` of this object, thereby violating POLA. None of the 100 core modules leaks any object reference or violates POLA.

Privilege separation in user modules. We estimated the effectiveness of our user module extraction algorithm in approximating the ideal privilege separation by counting the number of core modules imported by each user module. The less the number of core modules accessed by a user module, the more effective is our module extraction algorithm in separating the privileges in extension code, as this corresponds to possible increase in the minimum number of modules that needs to be compromised to misuse multiple privileges.

We analyzed the user modules produced by Morpheus for all 52 Jetpack extensions and observed the frequency of the `require` invocation for various core modules within each user module. The goal is to demonstrate that user modules created using the owning object algorithm do not have access to large number of privileged objects as compared to legacy extensions. Figure 7 reflects the frequency distribution of core modules. We see that out of a total of 100 user modules across all the Jetpack extensions, there are

Table 5. List of Jetpack modules accessing multiple categories of core modules[3]. User modules created using owning object algorithm are named using random strings, except when they are either JavaScript code modules (JSMs) or the entry point of the extension *i.e.,* main module. Extensions not invoking any core module corresponding to XPCOM interfaces are omitted.

Jetpack	Module name	I	II	III	IV	V	VI	Jetpack	Module name	I	II	III	IV	V	VI
Amazon Search	M-1	✓						Google Translator	M-1	✓					
	M-1	✓		✓				Image Block	M-1	✓					
BlockSite	M-2	✓						ImageSearch	M-1	✓			✓	✓	
	main	✓					✓	LEOs Dictionaries	M-1	✓					
Bookmark All	M-1	✓				✓		Leo Search	main				✓		✓
	M-2				✓			Live IP Address	main	✓					
Clear Cache	main	✓						My Home Page	M-1	✓			✓		✓
Clear Cache Button	main	✓	✓					My Public IP	M-1	✓			✓		✓
CommentBlocker	appl (JSM)							New Tab Homepage	main	✓			✓		
	main	✓						Open Bookmark (new tab)	main	✓			✓	✓	
Context Search	M-1	✓						Open Gmail (pinned tab)	M-1	✓					
	main	✓						Open Image (new tab)	M-1	✓					
Copy Link Text	M-1	✓	✓					Plain Text Links	M-1	✓		✓			
Copy Link URL	M-1	✓	✓					Places Cleaner	M-1	✓		✓			✓
Email This	M-1	✓		✓		✓			M-2	✓		✓			
Empty Cache Button	M-1	✓	✓					Really Simple Sticky	M-1	✓		✓	✓		
Facebook Bookmarks	M-1	✓	✓	✓				Search IMDB	M-1	✓		✓	✓		
Facebook New Tab	M-1	✓	✓	✓				Show MyIP	main	✓					
	main							Tab History Menu	main	✓					
Facebook Toolbar Button	M-1	✓	✓	✓				Twitter New Tab	M-1	✓		✓	✓		
	M-2	✓	✓	✓				Twitter Toolbar Button	M-1	✓		✓	✓		
Facebook Touch Panel	M-1	✓	✓	✓				YouTubeIT	M-1	✓					
	M-2	✓	✓	✓				TinEye Rev Img Srch	main	✓			✓		
FlagFox	flagfox (JSM)	✓	✓	✓	✓	✓	✓	Web2Pdf	M-1	✓			✓		
	ipdb (JSM)			✓					main	✓					
	main	✓							M-1						✓
FlashBlock	M-1	✓	✓		✓		✓	Dispaly Weather	main						✓
	M-2	✓						Steal Login	main					✓	✓

56 modules with one or more accesses to distinct core modules. From the distribution, it is seen that around 14 modules use only one core module and as the number of core modules increases, the number of modules requesting multiple core modules decreases. We also note that there is one user module with 28 accesses to core modules. This user module is part of the FlagFox extension and is in fact a JavaScript code module (JSM) that was wrapped as a user module. Recall that JSMs are not partitioned into smaller modules because they are self contained code fragments (see Section 3.2).

Table 5 categorizes the usage of core modules corresponding to XPCOM interfaces across different categories, and we make four observations about it. First, most of the table is relatively sparse which indicates that user modules use related functionality. Second, almost all Jetpack extensions use core modules under the Application category and the reason is because they set user preferences. Third, since user modules created from JavaScript code modules, like flagfox in the FlagFox Jetpack, are just wrappers, they typically use core modules across multiple categories. Fourth, many Jetpack extensions which interact with content on Web pages, like DisplayWeather, do not explicitly invoke the core module `contentDOM` (see Section 3.2) responsible for access to the content objects. Instead they access properties of either chrome `window` or `gBrowser`,

---

[3] Core modules are grouped into 6 categories. Modules that access application or user preferences, create application threads, etc. are categorized under **I**. **II** contains core modules that represent browser neutral functionality such as access to timers and console. Modules facilitating access to content objects like `window` and `document` are grouped under **III**. Modules that handle browser permissions and cookies are grouped under **IV**, while those that access network, file system or storage come under **V**. The remaining modules are grouped under **VI**.

Table 6. List of policies checked for evaluation data set

Policy	Generic	# extensions
Contact only specified remote server	No	3
Access only files in profile directory as advertised	No	1
Cannot access preference branch other than its own	Yes	2
Cannot contact server if the extension has already accessed file system	Yes	1
Cannot contact server if the extension has already accessed LoginManager	Yes	1
Cannot contact server if the extension has access browsing history	Yes	1
Cannot contact server if the extension has access browser cache	Yes	2

which in turn invoke the `contentDOM` to make a transition to the `content`. Because of this implicit invocation, column entires in category **III** are empty for such Jetpack extensions.

Runtime policy checking. We evaluated the effectiveness of `PolicyChecker` at blocking attacks originating from misuse of the core modules. To do so, we encoded seven policies in the `PolicyChecker` module for the transformed extensions in our dataset. Table 6 lists these policies, which are classified as being either generic or extension-specific. The first three policies enforce fine-grained access control over extension resources, and the remaining policies are stateful. Of the extensions in our dataset, only Steal-login exhibits malicious activity, while the others are benign and do not violate the policies in Table 6. Thus, to verify that `PolicyChecker` can actually identify and block violations in core module, we introduced synthetic violations in benign extensions. We did so by appending additional code within the user modules of the benign but transformed extensions to trigger policy violations. The third column in the table lists the number of extensions that were used to check such synthetic violations of the corresponding policy. In each case, we observed that `PolicyChecker` was able to identify the violation and block the undesired operation in the core module. In our experiments, we refrained from checking any policy for an extension if it can potentially block the advertised functionality. For example, we did not apply policy to block network access after file system access for the DisplayWeather extension, as the extension contacts a weather server after reading 'zip.txt' from the file system, which is its advertised functionality. We do envision developer assistance when encoding such policies.

We now list specific observations on applying Morpheus over legacy extensions.

(1) An extension from our dataset CommentBlocker[4] installs event handlers that manipulate objects from both `chrome` and `content` to achieve its advertised functionality. Specifically, it installs two mutation event listeners (for `DOMNodeInserted` and `DOMNodeRemoved` events) in the `content` while their handlers are declared in the `chrome`. Execution of such event handlers invokes frequent invocations to the synchronous execution mechanism due to context switches between the `chrome` and `content`. Since the Jetpack framework disallows direct access of references across the `chrome`/`content` boundary, Morpheus transforms the handler defined in the `chrome` to operate using opaque identifiers for the `event` object (which is passed implicitly to all handler functions). Creating opaque identifiers for `event` attributes like `target` and `originalTarget` allows most functionality, but prevents operations such as `evt.target instanceof HTMLDocument`. This is because the Jetpack framework

---

[4] CommentBlocker:https://addons.mozilla.org/en-US/firefox/addon/commentblocker/

itself does not provide support for all objects available in the legacy Firefox extension architecture. For example, comparison of object instances against HTMLDocument and other HTML elements using the instanceof operator does not succeed in the Jetpack framework. Thus, legacy extension using such comparisons must be rewritten to use alternate comparisons (such as Ci.nsIHTMLDocument and Ci.nsIHTMLElement).

(2) The interface definitions for most XPCOM APIs inherit from other interfaces. For example, the nsILocalFile interface inherits from nsIFile. QueryInterface [22] is a construct that allows JavaScript to perform runtime type discovery and identify the interfaces supported by an object. Thus, on instantiating an object of type nsILocalFile, the object can perform a QueryInterface to access methods and properties defined on the nsIFile interface as well. With the core modules exporting only accessor methods, QueryInterface on module objects would be incorrect. To correctly implement the behavior of QueryInterface, the getter method in core_module_table maintains a linked list of objects which were QueryInterface'd on a module object and on every property access, it traverses the list and returns the object on which the property was defined.

(3) If an XPCOM API returns an instance of a string object, its core module returns a wrapped string object that exports an opaque identifier and the three accessor methods (i.e., getProperty, setProperty and invoke). Since this wrapped string object cannot be directly used for string operations like concatenation, Morpheus appends an additional toString property on the wrapped string object.

In its current form, Morpheus is constrained mainly due to Narcissus and Doctor JS. The Morpheus toolchain uses both these tools during different phases of its operation. Both Narcissus and Doctor JS are under active development and do not support all JavaScript constructs and features. For example, Narcissus does not support various forms of the let block, array comprehension, destructuring, generators, etc. Doctor JS uses the CFA2 algorithm [32] for JavaScript implemented atop Narcissus. Doctor JS also does not support a number of JavaScript statements. For example, it throws exceptions when performing string concatenation via the += shorthand operator, or if the loop variable is not defined explicitly within the for loop itself. We are actively working to remove such limitations by porting Morpheus to a more stable platform, like SpiderMonkey [23], and allow evaluation of more complex extensions.

7   Related Work

There has been much interest recently in the research community to improve defenses against vulnerable and malicious browser extensions. This paper presents an automated approach to port legacy extensions to secure, modern platforms and to our knowledge, Morpheus is the first tool to do so.

Securing browser extensions. The Jetpack framework is similar to the Google Chrome extension architecture [9] which encourages a modular design. Recent work [11, 19] explores the latter to highlight its deficiencies in developing secure Chrome extensions.

VEX [8] implements a flow- and context-sensitive static analysis of JavaScript to study vulnerabilities in legacy Firefox extensions. Beacon [17] performs information-flow for modular JavaScript extensions and is designed to detect poor software engineering practices in modules, *i.e.,* violation of POLA or leaked capabilities across module interface. Sabre [13] and Djeric and Goel [14] both present dynamic information flow tracking system to detect extensions that can leak sensitive browser data. IBEX [15] is a framework for specifying fine-grained access control policies guarding the behavior of monolithic browser extensions, but requires extensions to first be written in a dependently-typed language (to make them amenable to verification), following which they are translated to JavaScript.

Runtime policy enforcement has also been applied to prevent extensions from leaking sensitive data and limiting extension privilege in [27, 31]. Even though the approach presented in [27] is more light-weight than [31], both techniques require modifications to the browser. Similar to Morpheus, [27] wraps all accesses to XPCOM interfaces in legacy extensions to validate the operations with regard to security policies specified on the extension. In contrast, our main goal in wrapping privileged objects in individual modules is to adhere to Jetpack's security principles and limit the damage to only the compromised module. The extension architecture also enables embedding fine-grained security policy enforcement without modifying browser or Jetpack runtime. Morpheus improves security of extensions by both porting to Jetpack and enforcing policies.

Privilege separation. Morpheus is most closely related to Privtrans [10] and Swift [12]. Privtrans automatically integrates privilege separation into legacy source code using context switching between a secure monitor and an untrusted slave. Swift defines a principled approach to build secure web applications by partitioning the source code. Morpheus uses both approaches. It defines an evaluation context for object references, as either `chrome` or `content`, and switches contexts when execution of a JavaScript statement contains references from both contexts. This context switching approach is needed because the Jetpack framework is restrictive and does not allow placement of content code in `chrome` or vice-versa. Morpheus differs from both Privtrans and Swift and several other privilege separation mechanisms [28, 18, 26, 33, 34], because it is entirely automatic and does not require any user annotations to accomplish partitioning. A new architecture is proposed in [7] to achieve privilege separation for HTML5 web applications including browser extensions. Morpheus is orthogonal to [7] and ports legacy code to the Jetpack framework that mandates chrome-content privilege separation.

8   Conclusion

We present Morpheus, a streamlined mechanism to port legacy Firefox extensions to the more secure Jetpack framework. It utilizes module isolation provided in Jetpack framework to overcome challenges in code partitioning and secure module construction. Transformation applied by Morpheus enables fine-grained policy enforcement on ported Jetpack extension. We evaluate Morpheus with a suite of 52 legacy extensions and show that the automatically transformed extensions are secure by construction.

Acknowledgments. This work was funded in part by AFOSR grant FA9550-12-1-0166 via subaward 4628-RU-AFOSR-0166. We thank Santosh Nagarakatte, Chung-chieh Shan, and the anonymous reviewers for comments on early drafts of this paper.

References

1. Doctor, J.S.: http://doctorjs.org/
2. Jetpack, https://wiki.mozilla.org/Jetpack
3. JSON, http://www.json.org/
4. node.js, http://nodejs.org/
5. Opera extensions, http://dev.opera.com/extension-docs/
6. Safari extensions, https://developer.apple.com/library/safari/documentation/Tools/Conceptual/SafariExtensionGuide/Introduction/Introduction.html
7. Akahawe, D., Saxena, P., Song, D.: Privilege separation in HTML5 applications. In: USENIX Security Symp. (2012)
8. Bandhakavi, S., King, S.T., Madhusudan, P., Winslett, M.: Vetting browser extensions for security vulnerabilities with VEX. CACM 54(9) (September 2011)
9. Barth, A., Felt, A.P., Saxena, P., Boodman, A.: Protecting browsers from extension vulnerabilities. In: Network and Distributed Systems Security Symp. (2010)
10. Brumley, D., Song, D.: Privtrans: automatically partitioning programs for privilege separation. In: 13th USENIX Security Symp. (2004)
11. Carlini, N., Felt, A.P., Wagner, D.: An evaluation of the google chrome extension security architecture. In: USENIX Security Symp. (2012)
12. Chong, S., Liu, J., Myers, A.C., Qi, X., Vikram, K., Zheng, L., Zheng, X.: Secure web applications via automatic partitioning. SIGOPS Oper. Syst. Rev. 41(6) (2007)
13. Dhawan, M., Ganapathy, V.: Analyzing information flow in javascript-based browser extensions. In: Annual Computer Security Applications Conference (2009)
14. Djeric, V., Goel, A.: Securing script-based extensibility in web browsers. In: USENIX Security Symp. (2010)
15. Guha, A., Fredrikson, M., Livshits, B., Swamy, N.: Verified security for browser extensions. In: Proc. of IEEE Symp. on Security and Privacy (May 2011)
16. Hardy, N.: The confused deputy (or why capabilities might have been invented). SIGOPS Oper. Syst. Rev. 22(4) (October 1988)
17. Karim, R., Dhawan, M., Ganapathy, V., Shan, C.-c.: An analysis of the Mozilla Jetpack extension framework. In: Noble, J. (ed.) ECOOP 2012. LNCS, vol. 7313, pp. 333–355. Springer, Heidelberg (2012)
18. Kilpatrick, D.: Privman: A Library for Partitioning Applications. In: USENIX Annual Technical Conference, FREENIX Track (2003)
19. Liu, L., Zhang, X., Yan, G., Chen, S.: Chrome Extensions: Threat Analysis and Countermeasures. In: Network and Distributed Systems Security Symp. (2012)
20. Mozilla. Add-on SDK, https://addons.mozilla.org/en-US/developers/docs/sdk/latest/
21. Mozilla. Narcissus, http://mxr.mozilla.org/mozilla/source/js/narcissus/
22. Mozilla. Query Interface, https://developer.mozilla.org/en-US/docs/XPCOM_Interface_Reference/nsISupports#QueryInterface
23. Mozilla. Spidermonkey, https://developer.mozilla.org/en/SpiderMonkey
24. Mozilla Developer Network. Electrolysis, https://wiki.mozilla.org/Electrolysis
25. Mozilla Developer Network. XPCOM, http://developer.mozilla.org/en/XPCOM
26. Myers, A.C.: Jflow: practical mostly-static information flow control. In: ACM Principles of Programming Languages (1999)

27. Onarlioglu, K., Battal, M., Robertson, W., Kirda, E.: Securing legacy firefox extensions with SENTINEL. In: Rieck, K., Stewin, P., Seifert, J.-P. (eds.) DIMVA 2013. LNCS, vol. 7967, pp. 122–138. Springer, Heidelberg (2013)
28. Provos, N., Friedl, M., Honeyman, P.: Preventing privilege escalation. In: 12th USENIX Security Symp. (2003)
29. Addon SDK. Content proxy, https://addons.mozilla.org/en-US/developers/docs/sdk/latest/dev-guide/guides/content-scripts/accessing-the-dom.html
30. Simon Willison. Understanding the Greasemonkey vulnerability, http://simonwillison.net/2005/Jul/20/vulnerability/
31. Ter Louw, M., Lim, J.S., Venkatakrishnan, V.N.: Enhancing web browser security against malware extensions. J. Computer Virology 4 (2008)
32. Vardoulakis, D., Shivers, O.: CFA2: a context-free approach to control-flow analysis. In: Gordon, A.D. (ed.) ESOP 2010. LNCS, vol. 6012, pp. 570–589. Springer, Heidelberg (2010)
33. Zdancewic, S., Zheng, L., Nystrom, N., Myers, A.C.: Secure program partitioning. ACM Trans. Comput. Syst. 20(3) (August 2002)
34. Zheng, L., Chong, S., Myers, A.C., Zdancewic, S.: Using Replication and Partitioning to Build Secure Distributed Systems. In: IEEE Symp. Security & Privacy (2003)

Capture-Avoiding and Hygienic Program Transformations

Sebastian Erdweg[1], Tijs van der Storm[2,3], and Yi Dai[4]

[1] TU Darmstadt, Germany
[2] CWI, Amsterdam, The Netherlands
[3] INRIA Lille, France
[4] University of Marburg, Germany

Abstract. Program transformations in terms of abstract syntax trees compromise referential integrity by introducing variable capture. Variable capture occurs when in the generated program a variable declaration accidentally shadows the intended target of a variable reference. Existing transformation systems either do not guarantee the avoidance of variable capture or impair the implementation of transformations.

We present an algorithm called *name-fix* that automatically eliminates variable capture from a generated program by systematically renaming variables. *name-fix* is guided by a graph representation of the binding structure of a program, and requires name-resolution algorithms for the source language and the target language of a transformation. *name-fix* is generic and works for arbitrary transformations in any transformation system that supports origin tracking for names. We verify the correctness of *name-fix* and identify an interesting class of transformations for which *name-fix* provides hygiene. We demonstrate the applicability of *name-fix* for implementing capture-avoiding substitution, inlining, lambda lifting, and compilers for two domain-specific languages.

1 Introduction

Program transformations find ubiquitous application in compiler construction to realize desugarings, optimizers, and code generators. While traditionally the implementation of compilers was reserved for a selected few experts, the current trend of domain-specific and extensible programming languages exposes developers to the challenges of writing program transformations. In this paper, we address one of these challenges: capture avoidance.

A program transformation translates programs from a source language to a target language. In doing so, many transformations reuse the names that occur in a source program to identify the corresponding artifacts generated in the target program. For example, consider the compilation of a state machine to a simple procedural language as illustrated in Figure 1. The state machine has three states opened, closed, and locked. For each state the compiler generates a constant integer function with the same name. Furthermore, for each state the compiler generates a dispatch function that takes an event and depending on the event returns the subsequent state. For example, the dispatch function for opened

R. Jones (Ed.): ECOOP 2014, LNCS 8586, pp. 489–514, 2014.

state opened
    close => closed
 	
state closed
    lock => locked
    open => opened
 	
state locked
    unlock => closed
	1 **fun** opened() = 0;
	2 **fun** closed() = 1;
	3 **fun** locked() = 2;
	4 **fun** opened-dispatch(event) =
	5 **if** (event == "close") **then** closed() **else** error();
	6 **fun** closed-dispatch(event) =
	7 **if** (event == "open") **then** opened()
	8 **else if** (event == "lock") **then** locked() **else** error();
	9 **fun** locked-dispatch(event) =
	10 **if** (event == "unlock") **then** closed() **else** error();
	11 **fun** main-dispatch-next-event(state, event) =
	12 **if** (state == opened()) **then** opened-dispatch(event)
	13 **else if** (state == closed()) [...];

(a) Door state machine   (b) Program generated for the door state machine

Fig. 1. Many transformations reuse names from the source program in generated code

tests if the given event is close and either yields the integer constant representing the following state closed or a dynamic error. Finally, the compiler generates a main dispatch function that calls the dispatch function of the current state.

A naive implementation of such compiler is easy to implement, but also runs the risk of introducing variable capture. For example, if we consistently rename the state locked to opened-dispatch as shown in Figure 2(a), we expect the compiler to produce code that behaves the same as the code generated for the state machine without renaming. However, a naive compiler blindly copies the state names into the generated program, which leads to the incorrect code shown in Figure 2(b): The function definition on line 4 shadows the constant function on line 3 and thus captures the variable reference opened-dispatch on line 8 (we assume there is no overloading). For the example shown, the problem is easy to fix by renaming the dispatch function on line 4 and its reference on line 12 to a fresh name opened-dispatch-0. However, a general solution is difficult to obtain. Existing approaches either rely on naming conventions and fail to guarantee capture avoidance, or they require a specific transformation engine and affect the implementation of transformations.

We propose a generic solution called *name-fix* that guarantees capture avoidance and does not affect the implementation of transformations. *name-fix* compares the name graph of the source program with the name graph of the generated program to identify variable capture. If there is variable capture, *name-fix* systematically and globally renames variable names to differentiate the captured variables from the capturing variables, while preserving intended variable references among original variables and among synthesized variables, respectively. *name-fix* requires name analyses for the source and target languages, which often exists or are needed anyway (e.g., for editor services, error checking, or refactoring), and hence can be reused. *name-fix* treats transformations as a black box and is independent of the used transformation engine as long as it supports origin tracking for names [27].

<table>
<tr><td>

state opened
   close => closed

state closed
lock=>opened-dispatch
  open => opened

state opened-dispatch
  unlock => closed

</td><td>

```
 1  fun opened() = 0;
 2  fun closed() = 1;
 3  fun opened-dispatch() = 2;
 4  fun opened-dispatch(event) =
 5    if (event == "close") then closed() else error();
 6  fun closed-dispatch(event) =
 7    if (event == "open") then opened()
 8    else if (event == "lock") then opened-dispatch() else ...
 9  fun opened-dispatch-dispatch(event) =
10    if (event == "unlock") then closed() else error();
11  fun main-dispatch-next-event(state, event) =
12    if (state == opened()) then opened-dispatch(event)
13    else if (state == closed()) [...];
```

</td></tr>
</table>

(a) Consistently renaming door state machine   (b) Program generated for the renamed door state machine is incorrect: Variable capture of opened-dispatch

Fig. 2. Variable capture can occur when original and synthesized names are mixed

name-fix enables developers of program transformations to focus on the actual translation logic and to ignore variable capture. In particular, *name-fix* enables developers to use simple naming schemes for synthesized variables in the transformation and to produce intermediate open terms. For example, in Figure 1, we append "-dispatch" to a state's name to derive the name of the corresponding dispatch function. This construction occurs at two independent places in the transformation: When generating a dispatch function for a state, and when generating the main dispatch function. The connection between these is only established when assembling all parts of the generated program in the final step of the transformation. Using *name-fix*, it is safe to apply global naming schemes with intermediate open terms to associate generated variable references and declarations. Transformations of this kind fall into the class of transformations for which *name-fix* guarantees hygiene, that is, α-equivalent source programs are always mapped to α-equivalent target programs.

In summary, we make the following contributions:

- We studied 9 existing DSL implementations that use transformations and found that 8 of them were prone to variable capture.
- We present *name-fix*, an algorithm that automatically eliminates variable capture from the result of a program transformation.
- We state and verify termination and correctness properties for *name-fix* and show that *name-fix* produces α-equivalent programs for programs that are equal up to consistent but possibly capturing renaming.
- We propose a notion of hygienic transformations and identify an interesting class of transformations for which *name-fix* provides hygiene.
- We present an implementation of *name-fix* in the metaprogramming system Rascal. Our implementation supports capture avoidance for transformations that generate code as syntax trees or as strings.

- We demonstrate the applicability of *name-fix* in a wide range of scenarios: for capture-avoiding substitution, for optimization (function inlining), for desugaring of language extensions (lambda lifting), and for code generation (compilation of DSLs for state machines and for digital forensics).

2   Capture-Avoiding Transformations: What and Why

Capture avoidance is best known from capture-avoiding substitution: When substituting an expression e_2 under a binder as in $\lambda x.\ (e_1[y := e_2])$, variable x may not occur free in e_2 otherwise the original binding of x in e_2 would be shadowed by the λ. To implement capture-avoiding substitution, we must rename x to a fresh variable $\alpha \notin \{y\} \cup FV(e_1) \cup FV(e_2)$ to avoid the capture: $\lambda \alpha.\ (e_1[x := \alpha][y := e_2])$. Ensuring capture avoidance is already relatively complicated for substitution in the λ-calculus. For larger languages and more complex program transformations, ensuring capture avoidance is a non-trivial and error-prone task.

2.1   Variable Capture in the Wild

To better understand the relevance of the problem of variable capture, we studied implementations of a DSL for questionnaires in 10 state-of-the-art language workbenches in the context of the Language Workbench Challenge 2013 [10].[1] The questionnaire DSL features named declarations of questions and named definitions of derived values. 9 of the 10 language workbenches translate a questionnaire into a graphical representation using either Java or HTML with CSS and JavaScript as target language. One workbench uses interpretation instead of transformation. In most cases, the implementation of the DSL was conducted by the developers of the workbench themselves.

The result of our study is shocking: The DSL implementations in 8 of the 9 language workbenches that use transformations fail to address capture avoidance and produce incorrect code even for minimal changes to the definition of a questionnaire. For example, some implementations fail when a question name is changed to container, questions, or SWTUtils, because these names are implicitly reserved for synthesized variables. Other implementations of the DSL use naming schemes similar to the one we illustrated in the state-machine example. If there is already a question called Q, these implementations fail when naming another question QBlock, calculated_Q, or grp_Q. Some of the variable captures result in compile-time errors of the generated Java code, others result in misbehaved code that, for example, silently skips some of the questions when storing answers persistently. Debugging such errors typically requires investigation of the generated code and can be very time-consuming.

Of the studied DSL implementations, only the transformation implemented in Más addressed variable capture. It uses global name mappings to generate

---

[1] We studied all workbenches of the previous study [10]: Ensō, Más, MetaEdit+, MPS, Onion, Rascal, Spoofax, SugarJ, the Whole Platform, and Xtext.

unique names from source-language variables for the generated code. The usage of these name mappings and similar approaches is cross-cutting and relies on the discipline of the developer; it is not enforced or supported by the framework. We seek a solution that provides stronger guarantees and has less impact on the implementation of a transformation.

2.2 Problem Statement

The goal of this work is to provide a mechanism that avoids variable capture in code that is generated by program transformations. To this end, we seek a mechanism that satisfies the following design goals:

G1: Preserve reference intent: If a reference from the source program occurs in the target program, then the original declaration must also occur in the target program and the reference is still bound by it. In other words, source-program variables may neither be captured by synthesized declarations nor by other source-program declarations.

G2: Preserve declaration extent: If a declaration from the source program occurs in the target program, then only source-program references may be bound by it. In other words, synthesized variable references may not be captured by source-program declarations.

G3: Noninvasive: Avoidance of variable capture should not impact the readability of generated code. This is important in practice, where the generated code is often manually inspected when debugging a program transformation. In particular, a generated program should be left unchanged if it does *not* contain variable capture.

G4: Language-parametric: It should be possible to eliminate variable capture from virtually all source and target languages that feature static name resolution.

G5: Transformation-parametric: The mechanism should work with different transformation engines and should not impose a specific style of transforming programs. Ideally, the mechanism supports existing transformations unchanged.

In the following sections, we present our solution *name-fix*. It fully achieves the first three goals. In addition, *name-fix* is language-parametric provided the name analysis of source and target language satisfy modest assumptions. Finally, *name-fix* works with any transformation engine that provides origin tracking [27] for variable names, so that names originating from the source program can be distinguished from names synthesized by the transformation.

3   Graph-Guided Elimination of Variable Capture

The core idea of our solution is to provide a generic mechanism for the detection and elimination of variable capture based on name graphs of the source and target program. We use the term *name* for the string-valued entity that occurs in the abstract syntax tree of a program. Naturally, the same name may occur at multiple locations of a program. To distinguish different occurrences of the same name, we assume names are labeled with a variable ID. In source programs, such IDs are unique. However, for target programs generated by some transformation, we do not require that variable IDs are unique, because the transformation may have copied and duplicated names from the input program to the output program.

We write x^v to denote that name x is labeled with variable ID v, and we write $p^{@v}$ to retrieve from program p the name corresponding to variable ID v. Nodes that share the same ID must have the same name so that $p^{@v}$ is uniquely determined. The nodes of a name graph are the variable IDs that occur in a program and the edges connect references to the corresponding declarations.

Definition 1. The *name graph* of a program p is a pair $G = (V, \rho)$ where

V is the set of variable IDs in p (references and declarations),

$\rho \in V \to V$ is a partial function from references to declarations,

and if $\rho(v_r) = v_d$, then reference and declaration have the same name $p^{@v_r} = p^{@v_d}$.

For example, Figure 3 displays the name graph of the state machine in Figure 1(a), where we use line numbers as variable IDs: ID 1 represents the declaration of opened, ID 2 represents the reference to closed in the transition on line 2, ID 4 represents the declaration of closed, and so on.

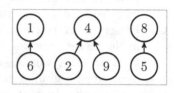

Fig. 3. Name graph of state machine in Figure 1(a)

We require that transformations preserve variable IDs when reusing names from the source program in the generated code. For example, when compiling the state machine of Figure 1(a) to the code in Figure 1(b), the compiler reuses the names of state declarations for the declaration of constant functions and for references to these constant functions in the main dispatch. Accordingly, in the generated code, these names must have the same variable ID as in the source program. Essentially, whenever a transformation copies a name from the source program to the target program, the corresponding ID must be copied as well and thus preserved. In contrast, names that are synthesized by the transformation should have fresh variable IDs.

For example, Figure 4 shows the name graph of the compiled state machine (we left out nodes of function parameters event and state for clarity). We use line numbers from the source program as variable IDs for reused variables, and *ticked* line numbers of the target program as variable IDs for synthesized variables. In addition, we depict nodes of synthesized variables with a darker background color. We have cycles in the name graph for source nodes 1, 4, and 8 because the transformation duplicated the names at these labels to generate constant functions and references to these constant functions.

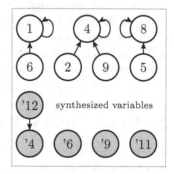

Fig. 4. Names of compiled state machine of Figure 1(b)

One important property of the name graph in Figure 4 is that the source nodes are disconnected from the synthesized nodes, and all references from the original name graph in Figure 3 have been preserved. In contrast, consider the name graph in Figure 5 that displays result of compilation after renaming state locked to opened-dispatch as in Figure 2(b). The graph illustrates that a source variable has been captured (dashed arrow) during compilation: The variable at line 5 of the source program was intended to point to the state declared at line 8, but after compilation it points to the dispatch function at line 4 of the synthesized program.

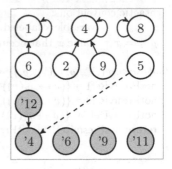

Fig. 5.   Variable   capture (dashed arrow) in the code of Figure 2(b)

Our solution identifies variable capture by comparing the original name graph of the whole program with the name graph of the generated code. Function *find-capture* in Figure 6 computes the set of edges that witness variable capture. In the state-machine example, *find-capture* finds only one edge $(5 \mapsto\ '4)$ as part of notPresrvRef1. We discuss the precise definition of variable capture in the subsequent section.

If there are witnesses of variable capture, our solution computes a variable renaming that has two properties. First, for each witness of variable capture, the renaming renames the capturing variable to eliminate the witness. Second, the renaming ensures that intentional references to the capturing variable are renamed as well. This can be difficult because the name graph of the generated code is inaccurate due to variable capture. Therefore, our solution conservatively approximates the set of potential references by including all synthesized variables of the same name. Function *comp-renaming* in Figure 6 computes the renaming as a function from a variable ID to the variable's fresh name, computed by gensym. For the example, we get $\pi_{src} = \emptyset$ because $'4 \notin V_s$ and $\pi_{syn} = \{'4 \mapsto$ "opened-dispatch-0", $'12 \mapsto$ "opened-dispatch-0"$\}$ because $t^{@'4} = t^{@'12}$. Function *rename* in Figure 6 visits all nodes in a syntax tree (represented as s-expression) and applies the renaming π to variables with the corresponding IDs. For the example, the renaming yields a capture-free program with the same name graph as shown in Figure 4.

Function *name-fix* in Figure 6 brings it all together and is the main entry point of our solution. It takes the name graph of the source program and the generated target program as input. First, it computes the name graph of the target program using the function $resolve^T$ that we assume to provide name resolution for the target language T. *name-fix* then calls *find-capture* to identify variable capture. If *find-capture* finds no capturing edges, *name-fix* returns the generated program unchanged. Otherwise, *name-fix* calls *comp-renaming* and *rename* to compute and apply the renaming that eliminates the witnessed variable capture. Since the name graph G_t of t may be inaccurate due to variable capture, *name-fix* recursively calls itself to repeat the search for and potential repair of variable capture. Note that

Syntactic conventions:

x^v variable x labeled with variable ID v

$p^{@v} = x$ name x that occurs in program p at variable ID v

$find\text{-}capture((V_s, \rho_s), (V_t, \rho_t)) = \{$

    notPresrvRef1 = $\{(v \mapsto \rho_t(v)) \mid v \in dom(\rho_t), v \in V_s, v \in dom(\rho_s), \rho_s(v) \neq \rho_t(v)\};$

    notPresrvRef2 = $\{(v \mapsto \rho_t(v)) \mid v \in dom(\rho_t), v \in V_s, v \notin dom(\rho_s), v \neq \rho_t(v)\};$

    notPresrvDef   = $\{(v \mapsto \rho_t(v)) \mid v \in dom(\rho_t), v \notin V_s, \rho_t(v) \in V_s\};$

    return notPresrvRef1 $\cup$ notPresrvRef2 $\cup$ notPresrvDef;

$\}$

$comp\text{-}renaming((V_s, \rho_s), (V_t, \rho_t), t, capture) = \{$

    $\pi_{src} = \emptyset;$

    $\pi_{syn} = \emptyset;$

    foreach v_d **in** $codom(capture)$ $\{$

       usedNames = $\{t^{@v} \mid v \in V_t\} \cup codom(\pi_{src}) \cup codom(\pi_{syn})$

       fresh = gensym($t^{@v_d}$, usedNames);

       if $(v_d \in V_s \wedge v_d \notin \pi_{src})$

          $\pi_{src} = \pi_{src} \cup \{(v_d \mapsto \text{fresh})\} \cup \{(v_r \mapsto \text{fresh}) \mid v_r \in dom(\rho_s), \rho_s(v_r) = v_d\};$

       if $(v_d \notin V_s \wedge v_d \notin \pi_{syn})$

          $\pi_{syn} = \pi_{syn} \cup \{(v \mapsto \text{fresh}) \mid v \in V_t \setminus V_s, t^{@v} = t^{@v_d}\};$

    $\}$

    return $(\pi_{src}, \pi_{syn});$

$\}$

$rename(t, \pi) = \{$

    return t **match** $\{$

       case x^v **if** $v \in dom(\pi)$ => $\pi(v)^v$

       case x^v => x^v

       case c   => c

       case $(t_1 \ldots t_n)$ => $(rename(t_1, \pi) \ldots rename(t_n, \pi));$

    $\}$

$\}$

$name\text{-}fix(G_s, t) = \{$

   $G_t = resolve^T(t);$

   capture = $find\text{-}capture(G_s, G_t);$

   if (capture == $\emptyset$) **return** t;

   $(\pi_{src}, \pi_{syn}) = comp\text{-}renaming(G_s, G_t, t, capture);$

   t' = $rename(t, \pi_{src} \cup \pi_{syn});$

   return $name\text{-}fix(G_s, t');$

$\}$

Fig. 6. Definition of *name-fix* that guarantees capture-avoidance

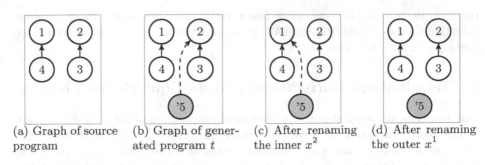

(a) Graph of source program

(b) Graph of generated program t

(c) After renaming the inner x^2

(d) After renaming the outer x^1

Fig. 7. Name graphs during execution of *name-fix* for $t = \lambda x^1.(\lambda x^2. x^3 x'^5) x^4$

name-fix applies a closed-world assumption to infer that all unbound variables are indeed free, and thus can be renamed at will.

In the following, we present examples that illustrate two design choices of *name-fix* that may be somewhat unintuitive: Why are multiple rounds of renaming required, and why do we rename all synthesized variables of the same name. For the former property, consider the lambda expression $t = \lambda x^1.(\lambda x^2. x^3 x'^5) x^4$, where we use superscripts to annotate variable IDs and ticked IDs for synthesized variables. The first graph in Figure 7 shows the original binding structure of the hypothetical source program that t is generated from. The second graph shows the binding structure of t. The synthesized variable x'^5 is captured by the binding of x^2, which is illegal due to notPresrvDef in *find-capture*. Accordingly, *comp-renaming* initiates a renaming of x^2, also renaming x^3 to preserve the source reference. This yields expression $t' = \lambda x^1.(\lambda \alpha^2. \alpha^3 x'^5) x^4$ with binding structure as shown in the third graph. Indeed, x^2 no longer captures x'^5. However, now x^1 captures x'^5. Thus, by renaming x^1 and its reference x^4, we get $t'' = \lambda \beta^1.(\lambda \alpha^2. \alpha^3 x'^5) \beta^4$ with capture-free binding structure as shown in the last graph. The iterative renaming was necessary because the name graph of t did not indicate that x'^5 is eventually captured by x^1. We could have preemptively renamed x^1 together with x^2, but this contradicts our goal for minimal invasiveness.

To illustrate why *name-fix* renames all synthesized variables of the same name, consider the expression $t = \lambda x'^3. x^1(\lambda x^2. x'^4)$ in which x'^3 captures x'^1 and x^2 captures x'^4. Thus, *name-fix* needs to rename x'^3 and x^2. Because x'^3 and x'^4 are both synthesized and have the same name, renaming of x'^3 entails the renaming of x'^4 even though they are unrelated in the name graph of t. Thus, *name-fix* yields the correct result $t' = \lambda \alpha'^3. x^1(\lambda \beta^2. \alpha'^4)$. To see why x'^3 should bind x'^4, consider what happens had the source program consistently used y in place of x: $t_2 = \lambda x'^3. y^1(\lambda y^2. x'^4)$. This program has no variable capture and is returned unchanged by *name-fix*. Since we want the result of *name-fix* to be invariant under consistent renamings of the source variables, x'^3 must bind x'^4 in both t and t_2. By renaming all synthesized variables of the same name, *name-fix* ensures that no potential variable reference is truncated.

Both of the above examples also illustrate another point: *name-fix* does not guarantee valid name binding with respect to the target language. The final result in both examples contains a free variable. Instead, *name-fix* guarantees that there is no variable capture. We state and verify the precise properties of *name-fix* in the next section.

4 Termination, Correctness, and an Equivalence Theory

Our solution *name-fix* iteratively eliminates variable capture in a fixed-point computation. In this section we show three important properties of *name-fix*: *name-fix* terminates, *name-fix* eliminates variable capture, and *name-fix* yields α-equivalent outputs for inputs that are equal up to consistent (but possibly capturing) variable renaming.

We represent programs as s-expressions with constant symbols c, labeled variable names x^v, and compound terms $(t_1 \ldots t_n)$. We shall frequently require two programs to be equal up to unconditional renaming:

Definition 2. Two programs are *label-equivalent* $p_1 \equiv_{\mathcal{L}} p_2$ iff they are equal up to variable names:

$$
\begin{aligned}
c_1 &\equiv_{\mathcal{L}} c_2 & &\text{if } c_1 = c_2 \\
x_1^{v_1} &\equiv_{\mathcal{L}} x_2^{v_2} & &\text{if } v_1 = v_2 \\
(t_1 \ldots t_n) &\equiv_{\mathcal{L}} (t_1' \ldots t_n') & &\text{if } t_i \equiv_{\mathcal{L}} t_i' \ \ \forall 1 \le i \le n
\end{aligned}
$$

To simplify our formalization, we do not consider bijective relabeling functions and assume label-equivalence instead. As first metatheoretical result we state that *name-fix* terminates.[2]

Theorem 1. *For any name graph G_s and any program t, name-fix(G_s, t) terminates in finitely many steps.*

4.1 Assumptions on Name Resolution

We present our framework for capture-avoiding transformations independent of any concrete source and target languages. Since our technique works on top of name graphs, we require functions *resolve^L* that compute the name graph of a program of some language L by name analysis. However, instead of requiring a specific form of name analysis, we specify minimal requirements on the behavior of *resolve^L* that suffice to show our technique is sound. The first assumption states that name analysis must produce a name graph.

Assumption 1. *Given a program p, resolve$^L(p)$ yields the name graph $G = (V, \rho)$ of p according to Definition 1.*

The second assumption requires *resolve^L* to behave deterministically. First, given two programs p_1 and p_2 that are equal up to variable names, names that are references in p_1 must be references in p_2 if the declaration is available (but it can refer to another declaration). Second, given a reference with two potential declarations in p_1 and p_2, *resolve^L* must deterministically choose one of them.

---

[2] Proofs of theorems and additional lemmas appear in a technical report [9].

Assumption 2. *Let* $p_1 \equiv_{\mathcal{L}} p_2$ *be label-equivalent with name graphs* $resolve^L(p_1) = (V, \rho_1)$ *and* $resolve^L(p_2) = (V, \rho_2)$.

(i) *If* $\rho_1(v_r) = v_d$ *and* $p_2^{@v_r} = p_2^{@v_d}$, *then* $v_r \in dom(\rho_2)$.

(ii) *If* $\rho_1(v_r) = v_d$, $\rho_2(v_r) = v_d'$, $p_1^{@v_d} = p_1^{@v_d'}$, *and* $p_2^{@v_d} = p_2^{@v_d'}$, *then* $v_d = v_d'$.

In addition to these assumptions, we require that the name graph (V, ρ) of the original source program satisfies $dom(\rho) \cap codom(\rho) = \emptyset$. We call such graphs *bipartite name graphs*. Note that $resolve^L$ often does not produce bipartite name graphs for generated code due to name copying as in Figure 4. We believe our requirements are modest and readily satisfied by name analyses of most languages.

4.2   *name-fix* Eliminates Variable Capture

We define the notion of capture-avoiding transformations in terms of the name graph of the source and target programs, before we show that *name-fix* can turn any transformation into a capture-avoiding one.

Definition 3. A transformation $f : S \to T$ is *capture-avoiding* if for all $s \in S$ with $resolve^S(s) = (V_s, \rho_s)$ and $t = f(s)$ with $resolve^T(t) = (V_t, \rho_t)$:

1. Preservation of reference intent: For all $v \in dom(\rho_t)$ with $v \in V_s$,
   (i) if $v \in dom(\rho_s)$, then $\rho_s(v) = \rho_t(v)$,
   (ii) if $v \notin dom(\rho_s)$, then $v = \rho_t(v)$.
2. Preservation of declaration extent: For all $v \in dom(\rho_t)$, if $v \notin V_s$, then $\rho_t(v) \notin V_s$.

The first condition states that a capture-avoiding transformation must preserve references of the source program. That is, if a variable v occurs in the target program and this reference was bound in the source program, then the target program must provide the same binding for v. That is, the transformation must preserve the reference intent of the source program's author.

If the source program does not contain v as a bound variable (but maybe as a declaration), v can only refer to itself in the target program. We specifically admit such self-references to allow transformations to duplicate names of source-program declarations in order to introduce additional delegation. For example, our compiler for state machines illustrated in Figure 1(a) uses names of state declarations to generate constant functions and references to these functions. Note that we also admit duplication of reference names, each of which has the same variable ID and thus must refer to the original declaration.

The second condition states that a capture-avoiding transformation must keep synthesized variable references separate from variables declared in the source program. We consider all variables of the source program V_s to be original and all variables of the target program that do not come from the source program $(V_t \backslash V_s)$ to be synthesized. This condition prevents synthesized variable references to be captured by original variable declarations, that is, synthesized variables can only be bound by synthesized declarations.

Function *find-capture* in Figure 6 implements the test for capture avoidance and collects witnesses in case of variable capture. Since *name-fix* only terminates when *find-capture* fails to find variable capture, the correctness of *name-fix* follows from its termination.

Theorem 2 (Capture avoidance). Given a transformation $f : S \rightarrow T$, *name-fix* yields a capture-avoiding transformation $\lambda s. \ name\text{-}fix(resolve^S(s), f(s))$.

4.3   Definitions of α-equivalence and Sub-α-equivalence

It is not enough to ensure that *name-fix* eliminates variable capture, because, for example, a function that returns the empty program would satisfy this property. To ensure the usefulness of *name-fix*, we need to show that, given two programs that are equal up to possibly capturing renaming, it produces α-equivalent programs (and not just any programs). Two programs are α-equivalent if they are equal up to non-capturing renaming, that is, if they have the same syntactic structure and binding structure.

Definition 4. Two programs p_1 and p_2 with name graphs $resolve^L(p_1) = (V_1, \rho_1)$ and $resolve^L(p_2) = (V_2, \rho_2)$ are α-equivalent $p_1 \equiv_\alpha p_2$ iff $p_1 \equiv_{\mathcal{L}} p_2$ and $\rho_1 = \rho_2$.

Note that $p_1 \equiv_{\mathcal{L}} p_2$ entails $V_1 = V_2$. As expected, our definition of α-equivalence is independent of the concrete names that occur in the programs. The following examples illustrate our definition of α-equivalence.

Program	Name graph
$p_1 = \lambda x^1. \, (\lambda y^3. \, y^4 \, y^5) \, x^2$	$G_1 = (\{1,2,3,4,5\}, \{(2 \mapsto 1), (4 \mapsto 3), (5 \mapsto 3)\})$
$p_2 = \lambda x^1. \, (\lambda x^3. \, x^4 \, x^5) \, x^2$	$G_2 = (\{1,2,3,4,5\}, \{(2 \mapsto 1), (4 \mapsto 3), (5 \mapsto 3)\})$
$p_3 = \lambda x^1. \, (\lambda y^3. \, x^4 + y^5) \, x^2$	$G_3 = (\{1,2,3,4,5\}, \{(2 \mapsto 1), (4 \mapsto 1), (5 \mapsto 3)\})$
$p_4 = \lambda x^1. \, (\lambda x^3. \, x^4 + x^5) \, x^2$	$G_4 = (\{1,2,3,4,5\}, \{(2 \mapsto 1), (4 \mapsto 3), (5 \mapsto 3)\})$

Our definition correctly identifies $p_1 \equiv_\alpha p_2$, because they are label-equivalent and have the same name graphs. Indeed, p_2 can be derived from p_1 by consistently renaming all occurrences of the bound variable y to x. In contrast, $p_3 \not\equiv_\alpha p_4$ because the binding structure differs: x^4 is bound to x^1 in p_3, but to x^3 in p_4. All other combinations of above programs (modulo symmetry of $\equiv_\alpha$) are not α-equivalent because they fail the required label-equivalence. In particular, $p_2 \not\equiv_\alpha p_4$ in spite of having the same binding structure.

To relate programs that are equal up to possibly capturing renaming, we propose the following notion of sub-α-equivalence.

Definition 5. Two programs are *sub-α-equivalent* $p_1 \equiv_\alpha^G p_2$ under a name graph $G = (V, \rho)$ iff $p_1 \equiv_{\mathcal{L}} p_2$ and, given V_p is the set of labels in p_1 and p_2,

(i) for all $v_r, v_d \in V_p \cap V$ with $\rho(v_r) = v_d$, $\quad p_1^{@v_r} = p_1^{@v_d} \Leftrightarrow p_2^{@v_r} = p_2^{@v_d}$

(ii) for all $v_r, v_d \in V_p \setminus V$, $\qquad\qquad\qquad\quad p_1^{@v_r} = p_1^{@v_d} \Leftrightarrow p_2^{@v_r} = p_2^{@v_d}$

Sub-α-equivalence compares two programs based on the actual names occurring in them, and not based on the binding structure. The relation is parameterized over a name graph G. The first condition states that for each binding in this graph, p_1 and p_2 need to agree on whether reference and declaration share the same name or not. Even if the reference and declaration have the same name, it does not imply that there is a corresponding binding in either p_1 or p_2, because another declaration can also have this name and capture the reference. The second condition states that for all variables not in G, p_1 and p_2 need to agree on which variable occurrences share names. To illustrate sub-α-equivalence, let us consider $G = (\{1, 2, 3\}, \{(2 \mapsto 1), (3 \mapsto 1)\})$ and the following programs:

$[p_1]_{\equiv_\alpha^G}$	$p_1 = \lambda x^1.\ (\lambda y'^4.\ x^3 + y'^5)\ x^2$	$p_2 = \lambda z^1.\ (\lambda y'^4.\ z^3 + y'^5)\ z^2$
	$p_3 = \lambda x^1.\ (\lambda z'^4.\ x^3 + z'^5)\ x^2$	$p_4 = \lambda z^1.\ (\lambda z'^4.\ z^3 + z'^5)\ z^2$
$\neg[p_1]_{\equiv_\alpha^G}$	$p_5 = \lambda \underline{z}^1.\ (\lambda y'^4.\ x^3 + y'^5)\ x^2$	$p_6 = \lambda x^1.\ (\lambda y'^4.\ \underline{z}^3 + y'^5)\ x^2$
	$p_7 = \lambda x^1.\ (\lambda \underline{z}'^4.\ x^3 + y'^5)\ x^2$	$p_8 = \lambda x^1.\ (\lambda y'^4.\ x^3 + \underline{z}'^5)\ x^2$

The first four programs are sub-α-equivalent to p_1 under G. We have $p_1 \equiv_\alpha^G p_2$ because they agree on the name sharing at variable IDs 1, 2, and 3, which is required because of the bindings in G, and on the name sharing at variable IDs '4 and '5, which is required because these IDs are not in G. Similar analysis shows $p_1 \equiv_\alpha^G p_3$ and $p_1 \equiv_\alpha^G p_4$. Programs p_5 through p_8 are examples that are not sub-α-equivalent to p_1 under G. For p_5 and p_6 the first condition of sub-α-equivalence fails because there is no agreement on the name sharing at 1 and 3. For p_7 and p_8 the second condition fails because there is no agreement on the name sharing at '4 and '5.

Note that $p_1 \equiv_\alpha^G p_4$ illustrates that sub-α-equivalence is weaker than α-equivalence because $p_1 \not\equiv_\alpha p_4$. In the following subsection we use sub-α-equivalence to characterize programs that *name-fix* can repair to α-equivalent programs.

4.4   An Equivalence Theory for *name-fix*

We now turn to one of the main results of our metatheory: Function *name-fix* is noninvasive, preserves sub-α-equivalence, and is invariant under consistent (but possibly capturing) renaming of original and synthesized variables, as specified by sub-α-equivalence.

For capture-free programs, *name-fix* yields the input program unchanged, that is, *name-fix* is noninvasive:

Theorem 3. For any name graph $G_s = (V_s, \rho_s)$ and any program t with $find\text{-}capture(G_s, resolve^T(t)) = \emptyset$, $name\text{-}fix(G_s, t) = t$.

Given a bipartite name graph of the source program, *name-fix* preserves sub-α-equivalence:

Theorem 4. *For any bipartite name graph* $G_s = (V_s, \rho_s)$ *and any program* t, $name\text{-}fix(G_s, t) \equiv_\alpha^{G_s} t$.

Given a bipartite name graph of the source program, *name-fix* maps sub-α-equivalent programs to α-equivalent ones:

Theorem 5. *For any bipartite name graph* $G_s = (V_s, \rho_s)$ *and programs* $t_1 \equiv_\alpha^{G_s}$ t_2, *name-fix*$(G_s, t_1) \equiv_\alpha$ *name-fix*(G_s, t_2).

5   Hygienic Transformations

In the previous section, we demonstrated that for any transformation $f : S \to T$, *name-fix* provides a capture-avoiding transformation $\lambda\, s.name\text{-}fix(G_s, f(s))$. However, for some transformations *name-fix* yields a transformation that adheres to the stronger property of hygienic transformations.

Definition 6. A transformation $f : S \to T$ is *hygienic* if it maps α-equivalent source programs to α-equivalent target programs:

$$s_1 \equiv_\alpha s_2 \implies f(s_1) \equiv_\alpha f(s_2).$$

This definition of hygiene for transformations follows Herman's definition of hygiene for syntax macros [11].

Transformations can inspect the names of variables and can generate structurally different code for α-equivalent inputs. For example, a transformation may decide to produce thread-safe accessors for variables with names prefixed by sync_. Accordingly, a consistent renaming from sync_foo to foo in the source program leads to generated programs that are not structurally equivalent, let alone α-equivalent. However, there is an interesting class of transformations for which *name-fix* provides hygiene:

Definition 7. A transformation $f : S \to T$ is *sub-hygienic* if it maps α-equivalent source programs $s_1 \equiv_\alpha s_2$ to sub-α-equivalent target programs $f(s_1) \equiv_\alpha^{G_s} f(s_2)$ under the name graph G_s of s_1 (or s_2).

The class of sub-hygienic transformations includes some common transformation schemes. First, it includes transformations that transform a source program solely based on the program's structure but independent of the concrete variable names occurring in it. In such transformations, synthesized variable names are constant and the same for any source program. Second, for a source language without name shadowing (such as state machines), sub-hygienic transformations include those that derive synthesized variable names using an injective function $g : string \to string$ over the corresponding source variable names. For example, in Figure 1, we derived the name of a dispatch function by appending -dispatch to the corresponding state name. In both cases *name-fix* eliminates all potential variable capture and yields a fully hygienic transformation:

Theorem 6. *For any sub-hygienic transformation* $f : S \to T$, *transformation* $\lambda\, s.name\text{-}fix(G_s, f(s))$ *is hygienic.*

```
fun zero() = 0;
fun succ(x) = let n = 1 in x + n;
let n = x + 5 in
  succ(succ(n + x + zero()))
```

```
fun zero() = 0;
fun succ(x) = let n = 1 in (x + n);
let n0 = 2*n + 5 in
  succ(succ(n0 + 2*n + zero()))
```

(a) Program with free variable x   (b) Result of substituting 2*n for x

Fig. 8. *name-fix* yields a capture-avoiding substitution that renames local variables

6   Case Studies

To evaluate the applicability of capture-avoiding program transformation in practice, we have successfully applied *name-fix* in three different scenarios:

- Optimization: Function inlining via substitution in a procedural language.
- Desugaring of language extensions: Lambda lifting of local functions.
- Code generation: Compilation of state machines and of Derric, an existing DSL for digital forensics, to Java.

We have implemented all case-studies in Rascal, a programming language and environment for source code analysis and transformation [14]. The source code of our implementation and all case studies are available online: http://github.com/seba--/hygienic-transformations.

6.1   Preservation of Variable IDs with String Origins in Rascal

As described in Section 3, a transformation must preserve variable IDs of the source program when reusing these names in the target program. While it is possible for a developer of a program transformation to manually preserve variable IDs via copying, it is easier and safer if the transformation engine does it automatically. We extended Rascal to preserve variable IDs automatically via a new Rascal feature called *string origins* [25]. Every string value (captured by the **str** data type) carries information about its origin. A string can either originate from a parsed text file, from a string literal in a metaprogram, or from a string computation such as concatenation, slicing, or substitution.

String origins allow us to obtain precise offsets and lengths for known substrings (e.g., names) so that it is possible to replace substrings. We use this feature to support *name-fix* for transformations that produce a target program as a string instead of an abstract syntax tree. Despite the higher fragility of string-based transformations, they are common in practice. In our case studies, we use string-based transformations to generate Java code.

6.2   Capture-Avoiding Substitution and Inlining

Substitution and inlining are program transformations that may introduce variable capture. Using *name-fix*, the definition of capture-avoiding versions of these transformations becomes straight-forward because *name-fix* takes over the responsibility for avoiding variable capture. Figure 8 illustrates the application of capture-avoiding substitution to a program of a simple language with global first-order functions and local *let*-bound variables. In the example, we use substitution to replace free occurrences of variable x by 2*n. To prevent capture, our capture-avoiding substitution function renames the locally bound variable n.

Substitution is a program transformation where the source and the target language coincide. Capture-avoiding substitution must retain the binding structure of the original (source) program. Since this requirement is part of our definition of capture-avoiding transformations, we can use *name-fix* to get a capture-avoiding substitution function from a capturing substitution function. This simplifies the definition of substitution for our procedural language to the following:

```
subst(p, x, e) = name-fix(resolve(p), substP(p, x, e));
substP(p, x, e) = prog([substF(f, x, e) | f ← p.fdefs], [substE(e2, x, e) | e2 ← p.main]);
substF(fdef(f, params, b), x, e) = fdef(f, params, x in params ? b : substE(b, x, e));

substE(var(y), x, e)        = x == y ? e : var(y);
substE(let(y, e1, e2), x, e) = let(y,  substE(e1, x, e),  x == y ? e2 : substE(e2, x, e));
substE(e1, x, e)            = for (Exp e2 ← e1) insert substE(e2, x, e);
```

Function substP takes a program p and substitutes e for x in all function definitions and expressions of the main routine using substF and substE, respectively. Function substF substitutes e for x in the body of a function only if x does not occur as parameter name of the function, that is, only if x is indeed free in the function body. Function substE proceeds similarly for *let*-bound variables. The final case of substE uses Rascal's generic-programming features [14] to provide a default implementation: We substitute e for x in each direct subexpression of e1 and insert the corresponding result in place of the subexpression.

Function subst ensures capture avoidance, but function substP does not: When pushing expression e under a binder, the bound variable may occur free in e, in which case the bound variable should be renamed. By using *name-fix*, we can omit checking and potentially renaming the bound variable both for function definitions and for *let* expressions and still get a capture-avoiding substitution function subst that behaves as illustrated in Figure 8.

Inlining of functions is a common program-optimization technique used by compilers. We illustrate our implementation of capture-avoiding inlining in Figure 9. The left column shows a simple program using two logical functions or and and. The central column shows the program after inlining and. Note that our language uses a single namespace for functions and *let*-bound variables. We avoid capture of the reference to or by renaming the local variable or to or0. The right column shows the result of inlining or in the central program. The local variable tmp in the definition of or is renamed to tmp0 since otherwise it would capture the reference to the variable tmp of the main body.

Based on our implementation of substitution, we can easily implement inlining by calling substE to substitute all arguments of a function call into the body of the function. Like for substitution, it suffices to call *name-fix after* function

```fun or(x, y) =```	```fun or(x, y) = ...;```	```fun or(x, y) = ...;```
```let tmp = x in```	```fun and(x, y) = ...;```	```fun and(x, y) = ...;```
```if tmp == 0```		
```then y```	```let or0 = 1 in```	```let or0 = 1 in```
```else tmp;```	```let tmp = 0 in```	```let tmp = 0 in```
```fun and(x, y) =```	```!or(!or0, !tmp)```	```let tmp0 = !or0 in```
```!or(!x, !y);```		```if tmp0 == 0```
```let or = 1 in```		```then !tmp```
```let tmp = 0 in```		```else tmp0```
```and(or, tmp)```		
(a) Original program	(b) First inline function and	(c) Then inline function or

Fig. 9. Capture-avoiding function inlining is similar to hygienic macro expansion

inlining is complete. Intuitively, this is because *name-fix* only renames bound variables, which are ignored by substE anyway. A detailed investigation of *when* to call *name-fix* is part of our future work.

6.3 Lambda Lifting

Language extensions augment a base language with additional language features. Many compilers first *desugar* a source program to a core language. Extensible languages like SugarJ [8] enable regular programmers to define their own extensions via custom desugaring transformations. Such desugaring transformations should preserve the binding structure of the source program. In fact, the lack of capture-avoiding and hygienic transformations in extensible languages was a major motivation of this work.

Exemplary, to show that *name-fix* supports language extensions, we implemented an extension of our procedural language for local function definitions that we desugar by lifting them into the global toplevel function scope [13]. The left column of Figure 10 shows an example usage of the extension, where we have a global function f that is shadowed by a local function f, which is used in another local function g. When lifting the two local functions, we get two toplevel functions named f, where the originally local f captures a call to the originally global f in the definition of y. Accordingly, *name-fix* renames the lifted function f and its calls, both in the main program and the lifted version of g.

We implement lambda lifting by recursively (i) finding local functions, (ii) adapting calls to the local function to pass along variables that occur free in the function body, and (iii) lifting the function definition to the toplevel. To identify calls of a local function, we use the name graph of the non-lifted program. A single call to *name-fix* after desugaring suffices to eliminate potential name shadowing between functions in the toplevel function scope.

```
fun f(x) = x + 1;
let y = f(10) in
  let fun f(x) = f(x + y) in
    let fun g(x) = f(y + x + 1) in
      f(1) + g(3)
```

```
fun f(x) = x + 1;
fun f0(x, y) = f0(x + y, y);
fun g(x, y) = f0(y + x + 1, y);
let y = f(10) in
  f0(1, y) + g(3, y)
```

(a) Example with local functions f and g   (b) Desugaring of local functions

Fig. 10. Lambda lifting of local functions f and g requires renaming to avoid capture

```
list[FDef] compile(list[State] states) =
  map(state2const, states) + map(state2dispatch, states) + mainDispatch(states)

FDef state2const(State s, int i) =
  fdef(s.name, [], val(nat(i)));
FDef state2dispatch(State s) =
  fdef("<s.name>-dispatch", ["event"], transitions2cond(s.transitions, val(error()))));
Exp transitions2cond([t, *ts], Exp els) =
  cond(equ(var("event"), val(string(t.event)))
      , call(t.state, [])
      , transitions2cond(ts, els));
FDef mainDispatch(states) =
  fdef("main", ["state","event"], mainCond(states, val(error())))
Exp mainCond([s, *ss], Exp els) =
  cond(equ(var("state"), call(s.name, []))
      , call("<s.name>-dispatch", [var("event")])
      , mainCond (ss, els));
```

Fig. 11. Implementation of compiler from state machines to our procedural language

6.4 State Machines

In Section 1, we introduced a language for state machines to illustrate the problem of inadvertent capture in program transformation. The *name-fix* algorithm can be used to repair the result of the transformation without changing the transformation itself. As a result, developers can structure transformations in almost arbitrary ways. In the case of the state-machine compiler, a simple naming convention suffices to link generated references to declarations. In our case study, the conventions are that state names become constants and state names suffixed with -dispatch become dispatch functions.

We believe the increased liberty of using naming conventions simplifies the implementation of program transformations. We illustrate the main part of the compiler of state machines to our procedural language in Figure 11. In contrast to approaches based on explicit binders such as HOAS [19] or FreshML [23], generated references do not have to literally occur below their binders in the

```
state current                public class Door {
  close => closed              final int current = 0, closed = 1, token = 2;
end                            void run(...) {
                                 int current0 = current;  String token0 = null;
state closed                     while ((token0 = input.nextLine()) != null) {
  open => current                  if (current0 == current)
  lock => token                    {if (close(token0)) current0 = closed; else continue;}
end                                if (current0 == closed)
                                   {if (open(token0)) current0 = current;
state token                        else if (lock(token0)) current0 = token; else continue;}
  unlock => closed                 if (current0 == token)
end                                {if (unlock(token0)) current0 = closed; else continue;}
                             }}}
```

(a) Renamed   door (b) Renaming of local variables current and token to preserve
state machine   the references of the state machine (exemplarily highlighted)

Fig. 12. Application of *name-fix* for generated Java code with JDT name resolution

transformation itself. For example, function compile independently generates state
constants, state dispatch functions, and the main dispatch function (by mainCond),
even though the main dispatch function refers to both generated constants and
state dispatch functions via naming conventions.

Compilation to Java. To exercise capture-avoiding transformation in a more realistic setting, we also applied *name-fix* on the result of compiling state machines
to Java. To obtain a name graph for Java, we used Rascal's M^3 source code
model of Java, which provides accurate name and type information extracted
from the Eclipse JDT [12]. The compiler from state machines to Java generates
Java code as structural strings (cf. Section 6.1). It generates a constant for each
state and a single dispatch loop in a run method.

We illustrate the application of the compiler and the use of *name-fix* on the
generated Java code in Figure 12. The left column shows the state machine from
Figure 1(a) where we consistently renamed states opened and locked to current
and token, respectively. The right column shows the compiled Java program.
Since the dispatch loop in run uses current to store the current state and token to
save the last-read token, the compilation introduces variable capture. Note that
even without using *name-fix*, the generated code compiles fine but is ill-behaved
because current==current in the first *if* would always succeed. *name-fix* repairs
the variable capture by renaming the local variables. This case study shows that
name-fix and our implementation are not limited to simple languages, but are
applicable for generating capture-free programs of languages like Java.

6.5   Digital Forensics with DERRIC

DERRIC is a domain-specific language for describing (binary) file formats [26].
Such descriptions are used in digital forensic investigations to recover evidence

```
format Bad

sequence S1 S2

structures
S1 { x: 0x0;  y: S2.x; }
S2 { x; }
```

```
public class Bad {
  private long x;
  private boolean S1() {
    markStart();
    long x0 = ...;  ValueSet vs2 = ...;
    vs2.addEquals(0);
    if (!vs2.equals(x0)) return noMatch();
    long y = ...;  ValueSet vs5 = ...;
    vs5.addEquals(x);
    if (!vs5.equals(y)) return noMatch();
    addSubSequence("S1");
    return true;
}...}
```

(a) A DERRIC format   (b) The local variable shadows the field and must be renamed

Fig. 13. *name-fix* eliminates variable capture for existing DSL compiler of DERRIC

from (possibly damaged) storage devices. DERRIC descriptions consist of two parts. The first part describes the high-level structure of a file format by listing sequence constraints on basic building blocks (called structures) of a file. The second part describes each structure by declaring fields, their type, and inter-structure data dependencies. From these descriptions, the DERRIC compiler generates high-performance validators in Java that check whether a byte sequence matches the declared format.

We show a minimalist, artificial DERRIC format description in the left column of Figure 13. The format declares two structures (S1 and S2), which must occur in sequence. S1 contains two fields: x, which must be 0, and y, which should be equal to field x of S2, which is not further constrained. We show an excerpt of the code generated by the DERRIC compiler in the right column of Figure 13. The main issue is in method S1, which handles format recognition of structure S1. Field x, which DERRIC uses to communicate S2's field x to method S1 is shadowed by the local variable x which corresponds to S1's field x. Without going into too much detail, it is instructive to note that the Java code compiles fine even without any renaming, but it behaves incorrectly: Instead of checking S1.y = S2.x, it checks S1.y = S1.x. Such scenario occurs whenever two structures have a field of the same name and one structure access this field of the other structure in a constraint. *name-fix* restores correctness by consistently renaming the local variable in case of capture.

The DERRIC case study illustrates the flexibility and power of *name-fix*. DERRIC is a real-world DSL compiling to a mainstream programming language (Java). The compiler consists of multiple transformations for desugaring and optimization. The result of these transformations is an intermediate model of a validator, which is then pretty printed to Java. Nevertheless, we did not have to modify the DERRIC compiler in any significant way to be able to repair inadvertent captures, nor was the compiler designed with *name-fix* in mind. This is shows that our approach is readily applicable in realistic settings.

7 Discussion

We reflect on the problem statement of this work, explain how *name-fix* supports breaking hygiene, and point out open issues and future work.

Problem statement. In section 2.2, we postulated five design goals for *name-fix*, all of which it satisfies. In Section 4, we have verified that *name-fix* preserves reference intent (G1) and declaration extent (G2) of the source program. Moreover, we have established an equivalence theory for *name-fix* that at least supports noninvasiveness (G3). In the previous section, we have shown how *name-fix* can be applied in a wide range of scenarios using different languages: state machines, a simple procedural language, DERRIC, and Java. These results support our claim that capture elimination with *name-fix* is language-parametric (G4).

Although the case studies are all implemented in Rascal, any transformation engine that propagates the unique labels of names is suited for *name-fix*. Similar to our encoding, one could easily imagine representing names as tagged strings Name = (String,Int). A structural representation of strings or compound identifiers are not necessary. Moreover, we do not require that transformations are written in any specific style to support capture elimination. In particular, our transformations make use of sophisticated language features such as intermediate open terms or generic programming. We conclude that a mechanism like *name-fix* is transformation-parametric and realizable in other transformation engines (G5).

Breaking hygiene. Some transformations require that source programs refer to names synthesized by a transformation. Such breaking of hygiene often occurs with implicitly declared variables. In other words, intended capture implies that there is a source reference that is not bound by a declaration in the source program. Consider, *anaphoric conditionals* which are like normal *if*-expressions but allow reference to the result of the condition using a special variable it [1]. For instance, in the expression aif c then !it else it, the variable it implicitly refers to a local variable generated by the desugaring of aif. Applying *name-fix*, however, resolves the capture which in this case is intended: let it0 = c in if it0 then !it else it. To break hygiene in such cases, the transformation must mark the source occurrences of it when they are carried over to the result: aif(c, t, e) $\Rightarrow$ let("it", c, cond(var("it"), $mark$("it", t), $mark$("it", e))). In our implementation, $mark(s, t)$ sets a synthesized=true attribute on the ID of any string s in t. Effectively this means that such names are treated as synthesized names instead of source names. As a result, *name-fix* does not rename the binder, and the result of desugaring the above expression will be let it = c in if it then !it else it.

Future work. Theorem 6 shows that *name-fix* turns sub-hygienic transformations into hygienic transformations. However, there is currently no decision procedure for whether a transformation is sub-hygienic or not. For a Turing-complete metalanguage, a static analysis can only approximate this property. Nevertheless, a conservative analysis would be useful as it can *guarantee* that a transformation is sub-hygienic. For example, all transformations of our case studies except substitution are sub-hygienic, but we have not formally ensured that. We expect a type system that checks sub-hygiene to provide guidance to transformation developers similar to FreshML [23], but without reducing the flexibility.

Another open issue is *when* to apply *name-fix*. This is important when building transformations on top of other transformations or composing transformations sequentially into transformation pipelines. After every application of a transformation, there could be inadvertent variable capture that *name-fix* can eliminate. For our case studies we used informal reasoning to decide whether the call to *name-fix* can be delayed, but more principled guidance would be useful. For example, a simple class of transformations that commutes with applications of name-fix is the class of name-insensitive transformations, such as constant propagation. More generally, care has to be taken whenever a transformation compares two names for equality, because intermediate variable capture may yield inaccurate equalities. Since name-fix is the identity on capture-free programs (Theorem 3), applying name-fix more than necessary is at most inefficient, but not unsafe.

name-fix renames not only synthesized names but also names that originate from the source program. This may break the expected interface of the generated code. Accordingly, *name-fix* currently is a whole-program transformation that does not support linking of generated programs against previously generated libraries, because names in these libraries cannot be changed. Therefore, *name-fix* is currently ill-suited for separate compilation. We have experienced this problem in the DERRIC compiler, where a DERRIC field named BIG_ENDIAN will shadow a constant with the same name that occurs in DERRIC's precompiled run-time system. We leave the investigation of a modular *name-fix* for future work.

Finally, the current implementation of *name-fix* requires repeated execution of the name analysis of the target language. As a result, *name-fix* can be expensive in terms of run-time performance. When a compiler is run continuously in an IDE, this penalty can be an impediment to usability. Fortunately, incremental name analysis is a well-studied topic (e.g., [20,28]) that is likely to yield benefits for *name-fix* because (i) we know the delta induced by *name-fix* (renamed variables) and (ii) new variable capture can only occur in references that have changed.

8 Related Work

Various approaches to ensuring capture avoidance have been studied in previous work. Many of them represent a program not as a syntax tree, but use the syntax tree as a spanning tree for a graph-based program representation with additional links from variable references to the corresponding variable declarations. The advantage of graph-based representations is that variable references are unambiguously resolved at all times, which can guide developers of transformations. For example, nameless program representations such as de Bruijn indices [5] encode the graph structure of variable bindings via numeric values; Oliveira and

Löh directly encode recursion and sharing in the abstract syntax of embedded DSLs [17] via structured graphs. The disadvantage of these techniques is that they require explicit handling of graphs (updating indices, redirecting edges) and do not support open terms well.

In higher-order abstract syntax (HOAS) [19] variable references and declarations are encoded using the binding constructs of the metalanguage. Thus, developers of transformations inherit name analysis and capture-avoiding substitution from the metalanguage and work with fully name-resolved terms. It is well-known that HOAS has a number of practical problems [22]. For instance, the use of metalevel functions to encode binders makes them opaque; it is not possible to represent open terms or to pattern match against variable binders inside constructs such as let.

FreshML [23] uses types to describe the binding structure of object-language variable binders. This enables deconstruction of a variable binder via pattern matching, which yields a fresh name and the body as an open term in which the bound variable has been renamed to the fresh one. Due to using fresh variables, accidental variable capture cannot occur but intentional variable capture is possible. FreshML is limited by using types for declaring variable scope, because this is only possible for "declare-before-use" lexical scoping and not, for example, for the scoping of methods in an object-oriented class.

In model-driven engineering it is common to describe abstract syntax using class-based metamodels [18]. Syntactic categories correspond to classes, parent-child relations and cross-references are encoded using associations. Metamodels are expressive enough to model programs with each name resolved to its declaration using direct references (pointers). As a result, a large class of model-transformation formalisms are based on graph rewriting [4]. However, we are unaware of any work in this area that addresses capture avoidance. Especially, in the case of model-to-text (M2T) transformations, names have to be output and all guarantees about capture avoidance (if any) are lost.

Seminal work on hygiene has been performed in the context of syntax macros [15,3]. Like *name-fix*, hygienic macro expansion automatically renames bound variables to avoid variable capture. In related work, a number of approaches to hygienic macro expansion have been proposed [2,3,7,11]. Closest to our work is the expansion algorithm proposed by Dybvig, Hieb, and Bruggeman [7] in that they also associate additional contextual information to identifiers in syntax objects, similar to our string origins. However, in their work renamings appear during macro expansion (modulo lazy evaluation), whereas we perform renamings after transformation. Moreover, since for macros the role of an identifier only becomes apparent after macro expansion, they have to track alternative interpretations for a single identifier. In contrast, we require name analysis for the source language, which enables a completely different approach to hygienic transformations.

Marco [16] is a language-agnostic macro engine that detects variable capture by parsing error messages produced by an off-the-shelve compiler of the base language. Marco checks whether any of the free names introduced by a macro is captured at a call-site of the macro. While Marco does not require name analysis, it has to rely on the quality of error messages of the base compiler, provides no safety guarantees, and can only detect but not fix variable capture.

Generation environments [24] are metalanguage values that allow the scoping of variable names generated by a program transformation. A program transformation can open a generation environment to generate code relative to the encapsulated lexical context. Since generation environments can be passed around as metalanguage values, different transformations can produce code for a shared a lexical context. While generation environments simplify the implementation of transformations, they rely on the discipline of developers and do not provide static guarantees.

Another area where capture avoidance is important is rename refactorings. In particular, previous work on rename refactoring for Java [21] omits checking preconditions and instead tries to fix the result of a renaming through qualified names so that reference intent is preserved. De Jonge et al. generalize this approach to support name-binding preservation in refactorings for other languages [6]. In contrast to our work, rename refactorings are a limited class of transformations that do not introduce any synthesized names.

9   Conclusion

We presented *name-fix*, a generic solution for eliminating variable capture from the result of program transformations by comparing name graphs of the transformation's input and output. This work brings benefits of hygienic macros to the domain of program transformations. In particular, *name-fix* relieves developers of transformations from manually ensuring capture avoidance, and it enables the safe usage of simple naming conventions. We have verified that *name-fix* terminates, is correct, and yields α-equivalent programs for inputs that are equal up to possibly capturing renaming. As we demonstrated with case studies on program optimization, language extension, and DSL compilation, *name-fix* is applicable to a wide range of program transformations and languages.

Acknowledgement. We thank Mitchel Wand, Paolo Giarrusso, Justin Pombrio, Atze van der Ploeg, and the anonymous reviewers for helpful feedback.

References

1. Barzilay, E., Culpepper, R., Flatt, M.: Keeping it clean with syntax parameters. In: Scheme (2011)
2. Bawden, A., Rees, J.: Syntactic closures. In: LFP, pp. 86–95. ACM (1988)
3. Clinger, W., Rees, J.: Macros that work. In: POPL, pp. 155–162. ACM (1991)
4. Czarnecki, K., Helsen, S.: Feature-based survey of model transformation approaches. IBM Systems Journal 45(3), 621–645 (2006)
5. de Bruijn, N.G.: Lambda calculus notation with nameless dummies, a tool for automatic formula manipulation, with application to the Church-Rosser theorem. Indagationes Mathematicae 75(5), 381–392 (1972)

6. de Jonge, M., Visser, E.: A language generic solution for name binding preservation in refactorings. In: LDTA. ACM (2012)
7. Dybvig, R.K., Hieb, R., Bruggeman, C.: Syntactic abstraction in scheme. Lisp and Symbolic Computation 5(4), 295–326 (1992)
8. Erdweg, S.: Extensible Languages for Flexible and Principled Domain Abstraction. PhD thesis, Philipps-Universität Marburg (2013)
9. Erdweg, S., van der Storm, T., Dai, Y.: Capture-avoiding and hygienic program transformations (incl. proofs). CoRR, abs/1404.5770 (2014)
10. Erdweg, S., et al.: The state of the art in language workbenches. In: Erwig, M., Paige, R.F., Van Wyk, E. (eds.) SLE 2013. LNCS, vol. 8225, pp. 197–217. Springer, Heidelberg (2013)
11. Herman, D.: A Theory of Typed Hygienic Macros. PhD thesis, Northeastern University, Boston, Massachusetts (2012)
12. Izmaylova, A., Klint, P., Shahi, A., Vinju, J.: M^3: An open model for measuring source code artifacts. arXiv:1312.1188, BENEVOL 2013 (2013)
13. Johnsson, T.: Lambda lifting: Transforming programs to recursive equations. In: Jouannaud, J.-P. (ed.) FPCA 1985. LNCS, vol. 201, pp. 190–203. Springer, Heidelberg (1985)
14. Klint, P., van der Storm, T., Vinju, J.: Rascal: A domain-specific language for source code analysis and manipulation. In: SCAM, pp. 168–177 (2009)
15. Kohlbecker, E., Friedman, D.P., Felleisen, M., Duba, B.: Hygienic macro expansion. In: LFP, pp. 151–161. ACM (1986)
16. Lee, B., Grimm, R., Hirzel, M., McKinley, K.S.: Marco: Safe, expressive macros for any language. In: Noble, J. (ed.) ECOOP 2012. LNCS, vol. 7313, pp. 589–613. Springer, Heidelberg (2012)
17. B.C.: d. S. Oliveira and A. Löh. Abstract syntax graphs for domain specific languages. In: PEPM, pp. 87–96. ACM (2013)
18. Paige, R.F., Kolovos, D.S., Polack, F.A.C.: Metamodelling for grammarware researchers. In: Czarnecki, K., Hedin, G. (eds.) SLE 2012. LNCS, vol. 7745, pp. 64–82. Springer, Heidelberg (2013)
19. Pfenning, F., Elliott, C.: Higher-order abstract syntax. In: PLDI, pp. 199–208. ACM (1988)
20. Reps, T., Teitelbaum, T., Demers, A.: Incremental context-dependent analysis for language-based editors. TOPLAS 5(3), 449–477 (1983)
21. Schäfer, M., Ekman, T., de Moor, O.: Sound and extensible renaming for Java. In: OOPSLA, pp. 227–294. ACM (2008)
22. Sheard, T.: Accomplishments and research challenges in meta-programming. In: Taha, W. (ed.) SAIG 2001. LNCS, vol. 2196, pp. 2–44. Springer, Heidelberg (2001)
23. Shinwell, M.R., Pitts, A.M., Gabbay, M.J.: FreshML: Programming with binders made simple. In: ICFP, pp. 263–274. ACM (2003)
24. Macko, M., Batory, D.: Scoping constructs for software generators. In: Czarnecki, K. (ed.) GCSE 1999. LNCS, vol. 1799, pp. 65–78. Springer, Heidelberg (2000)
25. Valdera, P.I., van der Storm, T., Erdweg, S.: Tracing model transformations with string origins. In: ICMT. Springer (to appear, 2014)
26. van den Bos, J., van der Storm, T.: Bringing domain-specific languages to digital forensics. In: ICSE, pp. 671–680. ACM (2011)
27. van Deursen, A., Klint, P., Tip, F.: Origin tracking. Symbolic Computation 15, 523–545 (1993)
28. Wachsmuth, G., Konat, G.D.P., Vergu, V.A., Groenewegen, D.M., Visser, E.: A language independent task engine for incremental name and type analysis. In: Erwig, M., Paige, R.F., Van Wyk, E. (eds.) SLE 2013. LNCS, vol. 8225, pp. 260–280. Springer, Heidelberg (2013)

A   Artifact Description

Authors of the Artifact. Design, implementation, and documentation: Sebastian Erdweg, Tijs van der Storm, Yi Dai.

Summary. We provide implementations of the name-fix algorithm and our case studies, all implemented in the Rascal metaprogramming language (rascal-mpl.org). We use Rascal's built-in support for syntax definitions and parsing. Program transformations and the name-fix algorithm itself are standard Rascal functions.

Content. The main code is stored in directory *projects/Rascal-Hygiene*. Below we summarize its contents.

- *src*: Source code of name-fix and case studies
- *src/name*: Implementation of name-fix and required data structures
- *src/name/tests*: Unit tests for all case studies.
- *src/lang/simple*: Implementation of the simple procedural language
- *src/lang/java*: Name analysis for Java using Eclipse JDT
- *src/lang/missgrant*: Implementation of the state-machine language
- *src/lang/derric*: Implementation of the Derric language (copied), see http://derric-lang.org
- *src/org/derric_lang*: runtime classes needed for compiling the Derric language (copied), see http://derric-lang.org
- *input*: Example state machines
- *output*: Generated state machines
- *format*: Example format descriptors for the Derric case study

In addition to the source of name-fix and the case studies, the unzipped artifact contains the Rascal in form of an Eclipse update site. To run the case studies, install Rascal from this update site in a fresh Eclipse installation. The artifact contains detailed documentation on how to install and run the code.

Getting the Artifact. The artifact endorsed by the Artifact Evaluation Committee is available free of charge as supplementary material of this paper on SpringerLink. The latest version of our code is available online and includes installation and usage instructions: https://github.com/seba–/hygienic-transformations.

Tested Platforms. The artifact is known to work on any platform running Oracle's JDK 1.7 and Eclipse Kepler.

License. LGPL-3.0 (https://www.gnu.org/licenses/lgpl-3.0.txt)

MD5 Sum of the Artifact. 64d3406286a99f048c9bc3d754a52e84

Size of the Artifact. 50 MB

Converting Parallel Code from Low-Level Abstractions to Higher-Level Abstractions

Semih Okur[1], Cansu Erdogan[1], and Danny Dig[2]

[1] University of Illinois at Urbana-Champaign, USA
{okur2,cerdoga2}@illinois.edu
[2] Oregon State University, USA
digd@eecs.oregonstate.edu

Abstract. Parallel libraries continuously evolve from low-level to higher-level abstractions. However, developers are not up-to-date with these higher-level abstractions, thus their parallel code might be hard to read, slow, and unscalable. Using a corpus of 880 open-source C# applications, we found that developers still use the old **Thread** and **ThreadPool** abstractions in 62% of the cases when they use parallel abstractions. Converting code to higher-level abstractions is (i) tedious and (ii) error-prone. e.g., it can harm performance and silence the uncaught exceptions.

We present two automated migration tools, TASKIFIER and SIMPLI-FIER that work for C# code. The first tool transforms old style **Thread** and **ThreadPool** abstractions to **Task** abstractions. The second tool transforms code with **Task** abstractions into higher-level design patterns. Using our code corpus, we have applied these tools 3026 and 405 times, respectively. Our empirical evaluation shows that the tools (i) are highly applicable, (ii) reduce the code bloat, (iii) are much safer than manual transformations. We submitted 66 patches generated by our tools, and the open-source developers accepted 53.

1 Introduction

In the quest to support programmers with faster, more scalable, and readable code, parallel libraries continuously evolve from low-level to higher-level abstractions. For example, Java 6 (2006) improved the performance and scalability of its concurrent collections (e.g., `ConcurrentHashMap`), Java 7 (2011) added higher-level abstractions such as lightweight tasks, Java 8 (2014) added lambda expressions that dramatically improve the readability of parallel code. Similarly, in the C# ecosystem, .NET 1.0 (2002) supported a Threading library, .NET 4.0 (2010) added lightweight tasks, declarative parallel queries, and concurrent collections, .NET 4.5 (2012) added reactive asynchronous operations.

Low-level abstractions, such as **Thread**, make parallel code more complex, less scalable, and slower. Because **Thread** represents an actual OS-level thread, developers need to take into account the hardware (e.g., the number of cores) while coding. Threads are *heavyweight*: each OS thread consumes a non-trivial amount of memory, and starting and cleaning up after a retired thread takes hundreds

R. Jones (Ed.): ECOOP 2014, LNCS 8586, pp. 515–540, 2014.

of thousands of CPU cycles. Even though a .NET developer can use `ThreadPool` to amortize the cost of creating and recycling threads, she cannot control the behavior of the computation on `ThreadPool`. Moreover, new platforms such as Microsoft Surface Tablet no longer support `Thread`. .NET also does not allow using the new features (e.g., `async/await` abstractions) with `Thread` and `ThreadPool`. Furthermore, when developers mix old and new parallel abstractions in their code, it makes it hard to reason about the code because all these abstractions have different scheduling rules.

Higher-level abstractions such as .NET `Task`, a unit of parallel work, make the code less complex. `Task` gives advanced control to the developer (e.g., chaining, cancellation, futures, callbacks), and is more scalable than `Thread`. Unlike threads, tasks are *lightweight*: they have a much smaller performance overhead and the runtime system automatically balances the workload. Microsoft now encourages developers to use `Task` in order to write scalable, hardware independent, fast, and readable parallel code [26].

However, most developers are oblivious to the benefits brought by the higher-level parallel abstractions. In recent empirical studies for C# [18] and Java [25], researchers found that `Thread` is still the primary choice for most developers. In this paper we find similar evidence. Our corpus of the most popular and active 880 C# applications on Github [12] that we prepared for this paper, shows that when developers use parallel abstractions they still use the old `Thread` and `ThreadPool` 62% of the time, despite the availability of better options. Therefore, a lot of code needs to be migrated from low-level parallel abstractions to their higher-level equivalents.

The migration has several challenges. First, developers need to be aware of the different nature of the computation. While blocking operations (e.g., I/O operations, `Thread.Sleep`) do not cause a problem in Thread-based code, they can cause a serious performance issue (called thread-starvation) in Task-based code. Because the developers need to search for such operations deep in the call graph of the concurrent abstraction, it is easy to overlook them. For example, in our corpus of 880 C# applications, we found that 32% of tasks have at least one I/O blocking operation and 9% use `Thread.Sleep` that blocks the thread longer than 1 sec. Second, developers need to be aware of differences in handling exceptions, otherwise exceptions become ineffective or can get lost.

In this paper, we present an automated migration tool, TASKIFIER, that transforms old style `Thread` and `ThreadPool` abstractions to higher-level `Task` abstractions in C# code. During the migration, TASKIFIER automatically addresses the non-trivial challenges such as transforming blocking to non-blocking operations, and preserving the exception-handling behavior.

The recent versions of parallel libraries provide even higher-level abstractions on top of Tasks. For example, the `Parallel` abstraction in C# supports parallel programming design patterns: data parallelism in the form of parallel loops, and fork-join task parallelism in the form of parallel tasks co-invoked in parallel. These dramatically improve the readability of the parallel code. Consider the example in Code listing 1.1, taken from ravendb [1] application. Code listing 1.2 represents the same code with a `Parallel` operation, which dramatically reduces the code. According to a study [15] by Microsoft, these patterns may also lead to better performance than when using `Task`, especially when there is a large number of work items (`Parallel` reuses tasks at runtime to eliminate the overhead).

Code 1.1 Forking Task in a loop

```
1 List<Task> tasks = new List<Task>();
2 for (int i = 0; i <= n; i++)
3 {
4     int copy = i;
5     Task taskHandle = new Task(
6                 () => DoInsert(..., copy));
7     taskHandle.Start();
8     tasks.Add(taskHandle);
9 }
10 Task.WaitAll(tasks);
```

Code 1.2 Equivalent Parallel.For

```
1 Parallel.For(0,n,(i)=>DoInsert(...,i));
```

Despite the advantages of the higher-level abstractions in the `Parallel` class, developers rarely use them. In our corpus we found that only 6% of the applications use the `Parallel` operations. We contacted the developers of 10 applications which heavily use `Thread`, `ThreadPool`, and `Task` abstractions, and asked why they are not using the `Parallel` operations. The major reason given by developers was lack of awareness. This indicates there is a need for tools that suggest transformations, thus educating developers about better coding practices.

Transforming the Task-related code into higher-level `Parallel` operations is not trivial: it requires control- and data-flow analysis, as well as loop-carried dependence analysis. For the example in Listing 1.1, the code does not execute the assignment in Line 4 in parallel with itself in other iterations (only the code in the task body – Line 6 – is executed in parallel). However, after converting the original `for` into a `Parallel.For`, the assignment in Line 4 will also execute in parallel with other assignments. Thus, the programmer must reason about the loop-carried dependences.

Inspired from the problems that developers face in practice, we designed and implemented a novel tool, SIMPLIFIER, that extracts and converts Task-related code snippets into higher-level parallel patterns. To overcome the lack of developer awareness, SIMPLIFIER operates in a mode where it suggests transformations as "quick-hints" in the Visual Studio IDE. If the developer agrees with the suggestion, SIMPLIFIER automatically transforms the code.

This paper makes the following contributions:

Problem: To the best of our knowledge, this is the first paper that describes the novel problem of migrating low-level parallel abstractions into their high-level counterparts. We show that this problem appears in real-life applications by bringing evidence of its existence from a corpus of 880 C# open-source applications.

Algorithms: We describe the analysis and transformation algorithms which address the challenges of (i) migrating `Thread`-code into `Task` abstractions and (ii) transforming `Task` code snippets into higher-level `Parallel` design patterns.

Tools: We implemented our algorithms into two tools, TASKIFIER and SIM-PLIFIER. We implemented them as extensions to Visual Studio, the primary development environment for C#.

Evaluation: We empirically evaluated our implementations by using our code corpus of 880 C# applications. We applied TASKIFIER 3026 times and SIM-PLIFIER 405 times. First, the results show that the tools are widely *applicable*: TASKIFIER successfully migrated 87% of `Thread` and `ThreadPool` abstractions to `Task`. SIMPLIFIER successfully transformed 94% of suggested snippets to `Parallel`. Second, these transformations are *valuable*: TASKIFIER reduces the size of the converted code snippets by 2617 SLOC and SIMPLIFIER reduces by 2420 SLOC in total. Third, the tools save the programmer from manually changing 10991 SLOC for the migration to `Task` and 7510 SLOC for the migration to `Parallel`. Fourth, automated transformations are safer. Several of the manually written `Task`-based codes by open-source developers contain problems: 32% are using blocking operations in the body of the `Task`, which can result in thread-starvation. Fifth, open-source developers found our transformations useful. We submitted 66 patches generated by our tools and the open-source developers accepted 53.

2   Background on Parallel Abstractions in .NET

Our tools target the parallelism paradigms in .NET. Here we give a gentle introduction to parallel programming in .NET. There are four main abstractions that allow developers to spawn asynchronous computation.

2.1   Thread

Operating systems use processes to separate the different applications that they are executing. Thread is the basic unit to which an operating system allocates processor time, and more than one thread can be executing code inside one process. Threading library in .NET provides an abstraction of threads, `Thread` class since its first version, 2003.

`Thread` represents an actual OS-level thread, so it is expensive to use; creating a `Thread` needs about 1.5 MB memory space. Windows also creates many additional data structures to work with this thread, such as a Thread Environment Block (TEB), a user mode stack, and a kernel mode stack. Bringing in new `Thread` may also mean more thread context switching, which further hurts performance. It takes about 200,000 CPU cycles to create a new thread, and about 100,000 cycles to retire a thread.

On one hand, `Thread` class allows the highest degree of control; developers can set many thread-level properties like the stack size, priority, background and foreground. However, general-purpose apps do not need most of these low-level features. On that matter, Microsoft discourages developers to use these features because they are usually misused [26]. In modern C# code, developers should rarely need to explicitly start their own thread.

On the other hand, `Thread` has some limitations. For example, a `Thread` constructor can take at most one parameter and this parameter must be of type `Object`. In Code listing 1.3, a `Thread` is first created with its body which is `MailSlotChecker` method. `ParameterizedThreadStart` indicates that this method needs to take a parameter. After priority and background properties are set, the parameter, `info` is created and given to `Start` method that asynchronously executes the `Thread`. When the instance `info` of `MailSlotThreadInfo` type is passed to `Thread` body, it will be forced to upcast to `Object` type. Developers manually need to downcast it to `MailSlotThreadInfo` type in `MailSlotChecker` method. Hence, this introduced verbose code like explicit casting, `ParameterizedThreadStart` objects. To wait for the termination of the `Thread`, the code invokes a blocking method, `Join`.

Code 1.3 Thread usage example from Tiraggo [7] app

```
Thread thread = new Thread(new ParameterizedThreadStart(MailSlotChecker));
thread.Priority = ThreadPriority.Lowest;
thread.IsBackground = true;
MailSlotThreadInfo info = new MailSlotThreadInfo(channelName, thread);
thread.Start(info);
...
thread.Join(info);
```

2.2 ThreadPool

To amortize the cost of creating and destroying threads, a pool of threads can be used to execute work items. There is no need to create or destroy threads for each work item; the threads are recycled in the pool. .NET provides an abstraction, the `ThreadPool` class, since its first version.

Although `ThreadPool` class is efficient to encapsulate concurrent computation, it gives developers no control at all. Developers only submit work which will execute at some point. The only thing they can control about the pool is its size. `ThreadPool` offers no way to find out when a work item has been completed (unlike `Thread.Join()`), neither a way to get the result.

Code listing 1.4 shows two main examples of `ThreadPool` usage. `QueueUserWorkItem` is used to put work items to the thread pool. The first example executes `foo(param)` method call in the thread pool but it is unclear because of the syntax. The second example executes the same thing with a lambda function which is introduced in C# 4.0. Developers can directly pass the parameters to the lambda function. However, `QueueUserWorkItem` only accepts a lambda function that takes one parameter: `(x)=> ....`. Developers always need to provide one parameter, regardless of whether they use it or not, thus many times they call this parameter `unused` or `ignored`.

Code 1.4 ThreadPool example

```
1 ThreadPool.QueueUserWorkItem(new WaitCallback(foo),param);
2 ThreadPool.QueueUserWorkItem((unused)=> foo(param));
```

2.3 Task

The Task abstraction was introduced in the Task Parallel Library [16] with the release of .NET 4.0 in 2010. Task offers the best of both worlds, Thread and ThreadPool. Task is simply a lightweight thread-like entity that encapsulates an asynchronous operation. Like ThreadPool, a Task does not create its own OS thread so it does not have high-overhead of Thread. Instead, it is executed by a TaskScheduler; the default scheduler simply runs on the thread pool. TaskScheduler use work-stealing techniques which are inspired by the Java fork-join framework [14].

Unlike the ThreadPool, Task also allows developers to find out when it finishes, and (via the generic Task<T>) to return a result. A developer can call ContinueWith() on an existing Task to make it run more code once the task finishes; if it's already finished, it will run the callback immediately. A developer can also synchronously wait for a task to finish by calling Wait() (or, for a generic task, by getting the Result property). Like Thread.Join(), this will block the calling thread until the task finishes.

The bottom line is that Task is almost always the best option; it provides a much more powerful API and avoids wasting OS threads. All newer high-level concurrency APIs, including PLINQ, async/await language features, and modern asynchronous methods are all built on Task. It is becoming the foundation for all parallelism, concurrency, and asynchrony in .NET. According to Microsoft, Task is the only preferred way to write multithreaded and parallel code [26].

2.4 Parallel

The Parallel class is a part of the TPL library. It provides three main methods to support parallel programming design patterns: data parallelism (via Parallel.For and Parallel.ForEach), and task parallelism (via Parallel.Invoke).

Parallel.For method accepts three parameters: an inclusive lower-bound, an exclusive upper-bound, and a lambda function to be invoked for each iteration. By default, it uses the work queued to .NET thread pool to execute the loop with as much parallelism as it can muster. Parallel.For(0, n, (i)=> foo(i));

Parallel.ForEach is a very specialized loop. Its purpose is to iterate through a specific kind of data set, a data set made up of numbers that represent a range. Parallel.ForEach(books, (book)=>foo(book))

Parallel.Invoke runs the operations (lambda functions) given as parameters concurrently and waits until they are done. It parallelizes the operations, not the data. Parallel.Invoke(()=> foo(), ()=> boo());

Parallel class works efficiently even if developers pass in an array of one million lambda functions to Parallel.Invoke or one million iterations to Parallel.For. This is because Parallel class does not necessarily use one Task per iteration or operation, as that could add significantly more overhead than is necessary. Instead, it partitions the large number of input elements into batches and then it assigns each batch to a handful of underlying tasks. Under the covers, it tries to use the minimum number of tasks necessary to complete the loop (for `For` and `ForEach`) or operations (for `Invoke`) as fast as possible. Hence, Microsoft shows that `Parallel` class performs faster than equivalent `Task`-based code in some cases [15].

`Parallel` class will run iterations or operations in parallel unless this is more expensive than running them sequentially. The runtime system handles all thread scheduling details, including scaling automatically to the number of cores on the host computer.

3 Motivation

Before explaining TASKIFIER and SIMPLIFIER, we explore the motivations of these tools by answering two research questions:

Q1: What level of parallel abstractions do developers use?
Q2: What do developers think about parallel abstractions?

We first explain how we gather the code corpus to answer these questions. We use the same code corpus to evaluate our tools (Section 6).

3.1 Methodology

We created a code corpus of C# apps by using our tool COLLECTOR. We chose GitHub [12] as the source of the code corpus because Github is now the most popular open-source software repository, having surpassed Google Code and Source-Forge.

COLLECTOR downloaded the most popular 1000 C# apps which have been modified at least once since June 2013. COLLECTOR visited each project file in apps in order to resolve/install dependencies by using nuget [17], the package manager of choice for apps targeting .NET. COLLECTOR also eliminated the apps that do not compile due to missing libraries, incorrect configurations, etc. COLLECTOR made as many projects compilable as possible (i.e., by resolving/installing dependencies).

COLLECTOR also eliminated 72 apps that targeted old platforms (e.g., Windows Phone 7, .NET Framework 3.5, Silverlight 4) because these old platforms do not support new parallel libraries.

After all, COLLECTOR successfully retained 880 apps, comprising 42M SLOC, produced by 1859 developers. This is the corpus that we used in our analysis and evaluation.

In terms of the application domain, the code corpus has (1) 364 libraries or apps for desktops, (2) 185 portable-libraries for cross-platform development, (3) 137 Windows Phone 8 apps, (4) 84 web apps (ASP.NET), (5) 56 tablet applications (Surface WinRT), and (6) 54 Silverlight apps (i.e., client-side runtime environment like Adobe Flash). Hence, the code corpus has apps which (i) span a wide domain and (ii) are developed by different teams with 1859 contributors from a large and varied community.

Roslyn: The Microsoft Visual Studio team has released Roslyn [22] with the goal to expose compiler-as-a-service through APIs to other tools like code generation, analysis, and refactoring. Roslyn has components such as Syntax, Symbol Table, Binding, and Flow Analysis APIs. We used these APIs in our tools for analyzing our code corpus.

Roslyn also provides the Services API allowing to extend Visual Studio. Developers can customize and develop IntelliSense, refactorings, and code formatting features. We used Services API for implementing our tools.

3.2   Q1: What Level of Parallel Abstractions Do Developers Use?

In a previous study [18], we found out that developers prefer to use old style threading code over `Task` in C# apps. We wanted to have a newer code corpus which includes the recently updated most popular apps. We used Roslyn API to get the usage statistics of the abstractions.

As we explained in Section 2, there are 4 main ways to offload a computation to another thread: (1) creating a `Thread`, (2) accessing the `ThreadPool` directly, (3) creating a `Task`, (4) using task or data parallelism patterns with `Parallel.Invoke` and `Parallel.For(Each)`. Table 1 tabulates the usage statistics of all these approaches. Some apps use more than one parallel idiom and some never use any parallel idiom.

Table 1. Usage of parallel idioms. The three columns show the total number of abstraction instances, the total number of apps with instances of the abstraction, and the percentage of apps with instances of the abstraction.

	#	App	App%
Creating a `Thread`	2105	269	31%
Using `ThreadPool`	1244	191	22%
Creating a `Task`	1542	170	19%
Data Parallelism Pattern with `Parallel.For(Each)`	432	51	6%
Task Parallelism Pattern with `Parallel.Invoke`	53	12	1%

As we see from the table, developers use `Thread` and `ThreadPool` more than `Task` and `Parallel` even though our code corpus contains recently updated apps which target the latest versions of various platforms. The usage statistics of `Parallel` are also very low compared to `Task`. These findings definitely show that developers use low-level parallel abstractions.

Surprisingly, we also found that 96 apps use `Thread`, `ThreadPool`, and `Task` at the same time. This can easily confuse the developer about the scheduling behavior.

3.3   Q2: What Do Developers Think about Parallel Abstractions?

In this question, we explore why developers use low-level abstractions and whether they are aware of the newer abstractions.

We first asked the experts on parallel programming in C#. We looked for the experts on StackOverflow [20] which is the pioneering Q&A website for programming. We contacted the top 10 users for the tags "multithreading" and "C#", and got replies from 7 of them. Among them are Joe Albahari who is the author of several books on C# (e.g., "C# in a Nutshell"), and John Skeet who is the author of "C# in Depth" and he is regarded as one of the most influential people on StackOverflow.

All of them agree that Task should be the only way for parallel and concurrent programming in C#. For example, one said *"Tasks should be the only construct for building multithreaded and asynchronous applications"*. According to them, Thread should be used for testing purposes: *"threads are actually useful for debugging"* (e.g., guaranteeing a multithreading environment, giving names to threads). When we asked them whether an automated tool is needed to convert Thread to Task, they concluded that the existence of some challenges makes the automation really hard. For example, one said that *"I wonder whether doing it nicely in an automated fashion is even feasible"* and another said that *"Often there's in-brain baggage about what the thread is really doing which could affect what the target of the refactoring should actually be"*.

Second, we contacted the developers of 10 applications which heavily mix Thread, ThreadPool, and Task. Most of them said that the legacy code uses Thread and ThreadPool and they always prefer Task in the recent code. The developer of the popular ravendb application [1], Oren Eini, said that *"We intend to move most stuff to tasks, but that is on an as needed basis, since the code works"* and another said that his team *"never had time to change them"*. This comment indicates that the changes are tedious.

We also asked the developers whether they are aware of the Parallel class. Developers of 7 of the apps said that they are not aware of the Parallel class and they were surprised seeing how much it decreases the code complexity: *"Is this in .NET framework? It is the most elegant way of a parallel loop"*.

4   Taskifier

We developed TASKIFIER, a tool that migrates Thread and ThreadPool abstractions to Task abstractions. Section 4.1 presents the algorithms for the migration from Thread to Task. Section 4.2 presents the migration from ThreadPool to Task. Section 4.3 presents the special cases to handle some challenges. Section 4.4 presents how developers interact with TASKIFIER.

4.1   Thread to Task

First, TASKIFIER needs to identify the Thread instances that serve as the target of the transformation. In order to do this, TASKIFIER detects all variable declarations of Thread type (this also includes arrays and collections of Thread). For each Thread variable, it iterates over its method calls (e.g., thread.Start()) and member accesses (e.g., thread.IsAlive=...). Then, TASKIFIER replaces each of them with their correspondent from the Task class. However, corresponding operations do not necessarily use the same name. For instance, thread.ThreadState, an instance field of Thread class gets the status of the current thread. The same goal is achieved in Task class by using task.Status.

Some low-level operations in Thread do not have a correspondent in the Task class. For example, (1) Priority, (2) Dedicated Name, (3) Apartment State.

After studying both Thread and Task, we came up with a mapping between them. TASKIFIER uses this map for the conversion. If TASKIFIER finds operations that have no equivalents, it will discard the whole conversion from Thread to Task for that specific Thread variable.

The most important transformations in the uses of Thread variables are for creating, starting, and waiting operations. Code list. 1.5 shows a basic usage of Thread and Code list. 1.6 represents the equivalent code with Task operations. Developers create Thread by using its constructor and providing the asynchronous computation. There are various ways of specifying the computation in the constructor such as delegates, lambdas, and method names. In the example below, a delegate (ThreadStart) is used. TASKIFIER gets the computation from the delegate constructor and transforms it to a lambda function. For starting the Thread and Task, the operation is the same and for waiting, Task uses Wait instead of Join.

Code 1.5 Simple Thread example   **Code 1.6** Equivalent Task code

```
ThreadStart t = new ThreadStart(doWork); Task task = new Task(()=>doWork());
Thread thread = new Thread(t);            task.Start();
thread.Start();                           task.Wait();
thread.Join();
```

While the transformation in Code listings 1.5 and 1.6 shows the most basic case when the asynchronous computation does not take any arguments, the transformation is more involved when the computation needs arguments. Consider the example in Code listing 1.7. The asynchronous computation is the one provided by the Reset method (passed in line 1), but the parameter of the Reset method is passed as an argument to the Thread.Start in line 3. Since the Thread.Start can only take Object arguments, the developer has to downcast from Object to a specific type (in line 7).

Code listing 1.8 shows the refactored version, that uses Task. Unlike in Thread, Task.Start does not take a parameter. In order to pass the state argument e to the asynchronous computation Reset, the code uses a lambda parameter in the Task constructor. In this case, since there is no need to cast parameters in the Reset method body, TASKIFIER also eliminates the casting statement (Line 7 from Code list. 1.7).

Code 1.7 Thread with dependent operators from Dynamo [3] app

```
1 ParameterizedThreadStart threadStart = new ParameterizedThreadStart(Reset);
2 Thread workerThread = new Thread(threadStart);
3 workerThread.Start(e);
4 ...
5 private void Reset(object state)
6 {
7     var args = (MouseButtonEventArgs)state;
8     OnClick(this, args);
9     ...
10 }
```

$$\Downarrow$$

Code 1.8 Code listing 1.7 migrated to Task

```
1 Task workerTask = new Task(()=>Reset(e));
2 workerTask.Start();
3 ...
4 private void Reset(MouseButtonEventArgs args)
5 {
6     OnClick(this, args);
7     ...
8 }
```

TASKIFIER also changes the variable names such as from `workerThread` to `workerTask` by using the built-in Rename refactoring of Visual Studio.

After TASKIFIER migrates the `Thread` variable to `Task`, it makes an overall pass over the code again to find some optimizations. For instance, in Code listing 1.8, there is no statement between `Task` constructor and `Start` method. In `Task`, there is a method combining these two statements: `Task.Run` creates a `Task`, starts running it, and returns a reference to it. TASKIFIER replaces the first two lines of Code listing 1.8 with only one statement: `Task workerTask = Task.Run(()=>Reset(e));`

TASKIFIER successfully detects all variable declarations of `Thread` class type; however, we noticed that developers can use threads through an anonymous instance. The example below from antlrcs app [2] shows such an anonymous usage of `Thread` on the left-hand side, and refactored version with `Task` on the right-hand side. TASKIFIER replaces the `Thread` constructor and the start operation with a static method of `Task`.

```
new Thread(t1.Run).Start(arg);    =>    Task.Run(()=>t1.Run(arg));
```

4.2   ThreadPool to Task

The conversion from `ThreadPool` to `Task` is less complex than the previous transformation. There is only one static method that needs to be replaced, `ThreadPool.QueueUserWorkItem(...)`. TASKIFIER simply replaces this method with the static `Task.Run` method and removes the parameter casting from `Object` to actual type in the beginning of the computation. The example below illustrates the transformation.

```
WaitCallback operation= new WaitCallback(doSendPhoto);
ThreadPool.QueueUserWorkItem(operation, e);
```

```
Task.Run(()=>DoSendPhoto(e));
```

4.3 Special Cases

There are three special cases that make it non-trivial to migrate from `Thread` and `ThreadPool` to `Task` manually:

1 I/O or CPU-Bound Thread: During manual migration, developers need to understand whether the candidate thread for migration is I/O or CPU bound since it can significantly affect performance. If an I/O-bound `Thread` is transformed to a `Task` without special consideration, it can cause starvation for other tasks in the thread pool. Some blocking synchronization abstractions like `Thread.Sleep` can also cause starvation when the delay is long.

Manually determining whether the code in a `Thread` transitively calls some blocking operations is non-trivial. It requires deep inter-procedural analysis. When developers convert `Thread` to `Task` manually, it is easy to miss such blocking operations that appear deep inside the methods called indirectly from the body of the `Thread`. In our code corpus, we found that 32% of tasks have at least one I/O blocking operation and 9% use `Thread.Sleep` that blocks the thread longer than 1 second. It shows that developers are not aware of this issue and their tasks can starve.

Thus, it is crucial for TASKIFIER to determine whether the nature of the computation is I/O or CPU-bound. If it finds blocking calls, it converts them into non-blocking calls, in order to avoid starvation.

To do so, TASKIFIER checks each method call in the call graph of the `Thread` body for a blocking I/O operation by using a blacklist approach. For this check, we have the list of all blocking I/O operations in .NET. If TASKIFIER finds a method call to a blocking I/O operation, it tries to find an asynchronous (non-blocking) version of it. For example, if it comes across a `stream.Read()` method call, TASKIFIER checks the members of the `Stream` class to see if there is a corresponding `ReadAsync` method. Upon finding such an equivalent, it gets the same parameters from the blocking version. `ReadAsync` is now non-blocking and returns a future `Task` to get the result when it is available. After finding the corresponding non-blocking operation, TASKIFIER simply replaces the invocation with the new operation and makes it `await`'ed. When a `Task` is awaited in an `await` expression, the current method is paused and control is returned to the caller. The caller is the thread pool so the thread pool will choose another task instead of busy-waiting. When the `await`'ed `Task`'s background operation is completed, the method is resumed from right after the `await` expression.

```
var string = stream.Read();        =>      var string = await stream.ReadAsync();
```

If TASKIFIER cannot find asynchronous versions for all blocking I/O operations in the `Thread` body, it does not take any risks of blocking the current thread and, instead, it inserts a flag to the `Task` creation statement: `TaskCreationOptions.LongRunning`. This flag forces the creation of a new thread outside the pool. This has the same behavior as the original code, i.e., it explicitly create a new `Thread`. But now the code still enjoys the many other benefits of using Tasks, such as compatibility with the newer libraries and brevity.

In the case of `Thread.Sleep`, TASKIFIER replaces this blocking operation with a timer-based non-blocking version, `await Task.Delay`. Upon seeing this statement, the thread in the thread pool does not continue executing its task and another task from the thread pool is chosen (cooperative-blocking).

2 Foreground and Background Thread: By default, a `Thread` runs in the foreground, whereas threads from `ThreadPool` and `Task` run in the background. Background threads are identical to foreground threads with one exception: a background thread does not keep the managed execution environment running. `Thread` is created on the foreground by default but can be made background by "`thread.IsBackground = true`" statement. If a developer wants to execute `Task` in a foreground thread, she has to add some extra-code in the body of `Task`.

Since the intention is to preserve the original behavior as much as possible, TASKIFIER should do the transformations accordingly. In the example below, the program will not terminate until the method, `LongRunning` reaches the end. However, when this `Thread` is turned into `Task` without any special consideration, the program will not wait for this method and it will immediately terminate. While it is easy to diagnose the problem in this simple example, it can be really hard for a fairly complex app.

```
public static void main(String args[])
{
    ...
    new Thread(LongRunning);
}
```

Although, in some cases, TASKIFIER is able to tell from the context if the thread is foreground or background, it is usually hard to tell if the developer really intended to create a foreground thread. Developers usually do not put much thought into a thread's being a foreground thread when created. We chose to implement our algorithm for TASKIFIER to transform `Thread` to `Task` by default to work in the background. The developer still has the option of telling TASKIFIER to create foreground tasks; however, the reasoning behind going with the background by default is that when we contacted the developers, most of them did not want the `Task` to work in the foreground even though they created foreground threads.

3 Exception Handling: Another difference between `Thread` and `Task` is the mechanism of unhandled exceptions. An unhandled exception in `Thread` and

`ThreadPool` abstractions results in termination of the application. However, unhandled exceptions that are thrown by user code that is running inside `Task` abstractions are propagated back to the joining thread when the static or instance `Task.Wait` methods are used. For a thrown exception to be effective in a `Task`, that `Task` should be waited; otherwise, the exceptions will not cause the termination of the process.

A simple direct migration from `Thread` and `ThreadPool` to `Task` can make the unhanded exceptions silenced so developers will not notice them. This situation may destroy the reliability and error-recovery mechanism that developers put into the original program.

To take care of this, TASKIFIER adds a method call to make sure exception handling is preserved and unhandled exceptions are not ignored when non-waited threads are migrated to tasks. During the transformation of the example below, TASKIFIER adds a new method, `FailFastOnException` to the project just once. Other instances of `Task` in the project can use this method. However, this stage is optional and can be enabled by the user upon request.

```
new Thread(method).Start();
void method()
{
    throw new Exception();
}
```

$$\Downarrow$$

```
Task.Run(()=>method()).FailFastOnException();
void method()
{
    throw new Exception();
}
public static Task FailFastOnException(this Task task)
{
    task.ContinueWith(c => Environment.FailFast("Task faulted", c.Exception),
        TaskContinuationOptions.OnlyOnFaulted |
        TaskContinuationOptions.ExecuteSynchronously |
        TaskContinuationOptions.DetachedFromParent);
    return task;
}
```

4.4 Workflow

We implemented TASKIFIER as a Visual Studio plugin, on top of the Roslyn SDK [22]. Because developers need to run TASKIFIER only once per migration, TASKIFIER operates in a batch mode. The batch option allows the programmer to migrate automatically by selecting any file or project in the IDE. Before starting the migration, TASKIFIER asks the user for two preferences: *Foreground Thread* option and *Exception Handling* option. When it operates at the file levels, TASKIFIER might still modify other files when necessary (e.g., if the method in `Thread` body is located in another file). TASKIFIER migrates `Thread` and `ThreadPool` abstractions to `Task` in about 10 seconds on an average project (100K SLOC).

5   Simplifier

TASKIFIER automatically migrates old-style parallel abstractions (`Thread` and `ThreadPool`) to the modern `Task`. However, there are still some opportunities for higher-level abstractions that can make the code faster and more readable.

`Parallel` class (see Section 2.4) provides parallel programming design patterns as a higher-level abstraction over `Task` class. Implementing these design patterns with tasks requires developers to write code with several instances of Tasks. A much simpler alternative is to use a single instance of the `Parallel` class, which encapsulates the main skeleton of the design patterns. While the direct usage of Tasks affords more flexibility and control, we found out that in many cases, developers do not use the extra flexibility, and their code can be greatly simplified with a higher-level design pattern.

We developed SIMPLIFIER that converts multiple `Task` instances to one of three `Parallel` operations (`Parallel.For`, `Parallel.ForEach`, `Parallel.Invoke`). SIMPLIFIER suggests code snippets that can be transformed to `Parallel` operations and then does the actual transformation on demand. Hence, we divided the explanation of the algorithms into two parts: *Suggestion* and *Transformation*. In the Suggestion part, we explain how SIMPLIFIER chooses the code candidates. In the Transformation part, we explain how SIMPLIFIER transforms these candidates to `Parallel` operations. After explaining the three algorithms, we discuss how developers interact with SIMPLIFIER in Section 5.4.

5.1   Multiple Tasks to Parallel.Invoke

SIMPLIFIER offers the transformation of task parallelism pattern composed of a group of `Task` instances to `Parallel.Invoke`. First we explain the properties of code snippets that can be transformed to this operation.

Suggestion: As we explained in Section 2.4, `Parallel.Invoke` is a succinct way of creating and starting multiples tasks and waiting for them. Consider the example below. `Parallel.Invoke` code on the right-hand side is the equivalent of the code on the left-hand side. For the purpose of simplifying the code with `Parallel.Invoke`, SIMPLIFIER needs to detect such a pattern before suggesting a transformation.

Code 1.9 Multiple Tasks

```
Task t1=new Task(()=>sendMsg(arg1));
Task t2=new Task(()=>sendMsg(arg2));
t1.Start();
t2.Start();
Task.WaitAll(t1,t2);
```

Code 1.10 Equivalent with Invoke

```
Parallel.Invoke(()=>sendMsg(arg1),
                ()=>sendMsg(arg2));
```

Listing 1.9 shows the simplest form of many variations of code snippets. In order to find as many fits as possible, we need to relax and expand this pattern to detect candidates. First step to detect the pattern is that the number of `Task` variables should be at least 2, as `Parallel.Invoke` can take unlimited work items as parameters. Second, SIMPLIFIER has to consider that there are many syntactic variations of task creation and task starting operations. Also, there are some operations that combine both *creation* and *starting* like `Task.Factory.StartNew` and `Task.Run` methods. Third, one should keep in mind that there is no need to separate the creation of Tasks into one phase and starting them into another. Each Task can be created then started immediately. Fourth, there may be other statements executing concurrently in between the start of a `Task` and the barrier instruction that waits for all spawned tasks. In case of such statements, SIMPLIFIER encapsulates them in another `Task` and passes the task to `Parallel.Invoke`. Code listing 1.11 shows a more complex pattern of task parallelism from a real-world app and demonstrates the last point.

After SIMPLIFIER finds out the code snippets that fit into the pattern stated above, it checks if some preconditions hold true to ensure that the transformation is safe. These preconditions are not limitations of SIMPLIFIER; they are caused by how `Parallel.Invoke` encapsulates the task parallelism pattern. Because it is a higher-level abstraction, it waives some advanced features of `Task`. The preconditions are:

P1: None of the `Task` variables in the pattern can be result-bearing computations, i.e., a *future* – `Task<ResultType>` – also called a *promise* in C#. The reason is that after the transformation, there is no way to access the result-bearing from the `Parallel` class.

P2: There should be no reference to the `Task` variables outside of code snippet of the design pattern. Such references will no longer bind to a `Task` after the transformation eliminates the `Task` instances.

P3: None of the `Task` variables in the pattern can use the chaining operation (`ContinueWith`). Since the chaining requires access to the original task, this task will no longer exist after the transformation.

Transformation: If SIMPLIFIER finds a good match of code snippets, its suggestion can be executed and turned into a transformation which yields `Parallel.Invoke` code. Code listing 1.12 shows the code after the transformation of Code listing 1.11.

During transformation, the main operation is to get work items from `Task` variables. In the example below, the work item of first `Task` is `()=> DoClone(...)`. These work items can be in different forms such as method identifiers, delegates, or lambda functions as in the example below. SIMPLIFIER handles this variety of forms by transforming the work items to lambda functions.

After SIMPLIFIER gets the work items for the tasks `t1` and `t2`, it forms another work item to encapsulate the statements between task creation and task waiting statements (line 3 and 4 in Code List. 1.11).

SIMPLIFIER gives all these work items in the form of lambda functions to `Parallel.Invoke` method as parameters. It replaces the original lower-level task parallelism statements with this `Parallel.Invoke` method.

Code 1.11 Candidate from Kudu [5] app

```
1 var t1 = Task.Factory.StartNew(() => DoClone("PClone1", appManager));
2 var t2 = Task.Factory.StartNew(() => DoClone("PClone2", appManager));
3 ParseTheManager();
4 DoClone("PClone3", appManager);
5 Task.WaitAll(t1, t2);
```

$$\Downarrow$$

Code 1.12 Equivalent Parallel.Invoke code

```
1 Parallel.Invoke(() => DoClone("PClone1", appManager),
2                  () => DoClone("PClone2", appManager),
3                  () => {ParseTheManager();
4                         DoClone("PClone3", appManager);})
```

5.2   Tasks in Loop to Parallel.For

SIMPLIFIER can transform a specific data parallelism pattern to `Parallel.For`.
First we explain the properties of code snippets that can be transformed to this
operation.

Suggestion: As we explained in Section 2.4, `Parallel.For` is a more concise
way to express the pattern of forking several tasks and then waiting for them all
to finish at a global barrier.

Considering the example below, the `Parallel.For` code on the right is the
equivalent of the code on the left.

Code 1.13 Forking tasks in a loop

Code 1.14 Equivalent with Parallel.For

```
Task[] tasks = new Task [n];              Parallel.For(0,n,(i)=> Queues[i].Stop());
for(int i=0; i<n; i++)
{
    int temp = i;
    tasks[i]= new Task(
              ()=>Queues[temp].Stop());
    tasks[i].Start();
}
Task.WaitAll(tasks);
```

SIMPLIFIER needs to detect usages of Tasks that form the pattern on the left
example above. The code snippet in Listing 1.13 is one of the basic represen-
tatives of this design pattern; there are other variations who fit the pattern.
First thing the tool looks for in the code to decide if it matches the pattern is
that the increment operation of the loop must be of the form ++ or += 1 (i.e.,
increments should only be by 1). The loop boundaries do not matter as long as
they are integers. Second, as explained in Sec. 5.1, there may be many syntactic
variations for the task creation and starting operations.

Third, the collection of tasks does not have to be of type `Array`, they may
be of another type like `List`. In this case, tasks are added with `tasks.add(...)`
method to the collection in the loop. Fourth, as long as there is no modification

to the collection, there may be other statements between creating the collection of tasks and the for loop. During the transformation, these statements are not discarded and they take place before `Parallel.For`.

Fifth, there might be other statements in the loop besides task creation, starting, and adding to the collection. In the Code List. 1.13 above, there is one such statement: `int temp=i;`. This causes each task to have its own copy of the loop index variable during the iteration of the loop.

Sixth and last, some simple assignment operations may also exist between the loop and the barrier operation that waits for all spawned tasks. Code listing 1.15 shows a more complex pattern of data parallelism from a real-world app and demonstrates the last point with the statements in Line 8-9.

After SIMPLIFIER detects the code snippets that fit into the pattern stated above, it checks some preconditions ensuring that the transformation is safe. These preconditions are the result of how the `Parallel.For` encapsulates the date parallelism pattern.

P1, P2, P3: The first three preconditions are the same as the first three preconditions in Sec. 5.1.

P4: The operations in the loop except the task-related statements should not carry any dependence between iterations. Consider the Code listing 1.15, the statements in Line 4-5 will sequentially execute because they are not included in `Task`. After transforming to `Parallel.For`, the whole body of the loop will be parallelized.

P5: The statements after the loop (e.g., Line 8-9 in Code List. 1.15) but before the `Task.WaitAll` should not access any data from the Task body. At first, Simplifier did not allow any statement between the loop and `Task.WaitAll`. After we manually analyzed the statements between the loop and `WaitAll` in our code corpus, we noticed that many of them are simple variable declarations which do not use any data from the loop and do not contain any method call sites like in the Code List. 1.15. Therefore, we relaxed this precondition and allowed the statements after the loop but before the `Task.WaitAll` unless they do not access any data from the `Task` body in the loop. To detect such cases, SIMPLIFIER used an intra-procedural data-flow analysis to determine that these statements are independent from the loop. Roslyn [22] provides ready-to-use control & data flow analysis APIs that SIMPLIFIER used to understand how variables flow in and out of regions of source.

Transformation: Code listing 1.16 shows the code after the transformation of Code listing 1.15 showing a more complex example.

During transformation, the main operation is to the get loop boundaries and the work item from the task in the loop. In the example below (Line 6), the work item is `()=> MultiSearcherCallableNoSort(...)`. The loop boundaries are 0 and `tasks.Length`. However, the collection of tasks will be deleted after the transformation. Hence, when SIMPLIFIER detects such a dependence on the size of task collections in the loop boundaries, it replaces this boundary with the original size of the task collection, which is `searchables.Length`.

Then, SIMPLIFIER needs to make sure that the statements in the loop (e.g. Line 4-5 in List. 1.15) are not dependent on loop iterations. If they are not, these statements are put in the beginning of the work item; otherwise, the transformation will not occur. If one of these statements is the temporary holder of the iteration value like cur = i in the example below, SIMPLIFIER removes it and replaces the holder (cur) with the iteration variable (i) in the work item as seen in List. 1.16.

Lastly, SIMPLIFIER replaces the original lower-level data parallelism statements with the Parallel.For method.

Code 1.15 Candidate from lucene.net [6] app

```
 1  Task[] tasks = new Task[searchables.Length];
 2  for (int i = 0; i < tasks.Length; i++)
 3  {
 4      int cur = i;
 5      cur = callableIterate(cur);
 6      tasks[i] = Task.Factory.StartNew(() => MultiSearcherCallableNoSort(cur, ...));
 7  }
 8  int totalHits = 0;
 9  float maxScore = float.NegativeInfinity;
10  Task.WaitAll(tasks);
```

⇓

Code 1.16 Equivalent Parallel.For code

```
1  Parallel.For(0, searchables.Length, (i) => {
2                      i = callableIterate(i);
3                      MultiSearcherCallableNoSort(i, ...);} );
4  int totalHits = 0;
5  float maxScore = float.NegativeInfinity;
```

5.3   Tasks in Loop to Parallel.ForEach

While this transformation is very similar to Parallel.For, it transforms foreach loops instead of for loops. foreach loops are a special case of loops that are used to iterate over the elements of a collection.

First we explain the properties of code snippets that can be transformed to this operation.

Suggestion: Considering the example below, the Parallel.ForEach code on the right is the equivalent of the code on the left.

Code 1.17 Equivalent Task example   **Code 1.18** Parallel.ForEach example

```
Task[] tasks = new Task[sables.Length];      Parallel.ForEach(sables,
foreach (var sable in sables)                          (sable)=>sable.DocFreq(term));
{
    tasks[i] = Task.Run(
        () => sable.DocFreq(term));
}
Task.WaitAll(tasks);
```

SIMPLIFIER needs to detect usages of Tasks in a `foreach` loop that form the pattern on the left example above. We will generalize this pattern with the same 5 variations in the `Parallel.For` algorithm, except the first one which represents the custom loop boundaries.

After SIMPLIFIER detects the code snippets that fit into the pattern, it checks for the same preconditions as in the `Parallel.For` transformation.

Transformation: Code listing 1.20 shows the code after the transformation of Code listing 1.19. The transformation is done in a very similar manner with the `Parallel.For` version, except the loop boundaries.

After the work item is extracted from `Task`, SIMPLIFIER needs to get the collection variable and iteration variable from the loop declaration (`functions`, `functionText`). Then, SIMPLIFIER replaces the original lower-level data parallelism statements with the `Parallel.ForEach` method.

Code 1.19 Candidate from Jace [4] app

```
 1  List<Task> tasks = new List<Task>();
 2  foreach (string functionText in functions)
 3  {
 4      Task task = new Task(() =>
 5      {...
 6          function(functionText, ...); ...
 7      });
 8      tasks.Add(task);
 9      task.Start();
10  }
11  Task.WaitAll(tasks.ToArray());
```

⇓

Code 1.20 Equivalent Parallel.ForEach code

```
 1  Parallel.ForEach(functions,(functionText) =>{...
 2                              function(functionText, ...); ...
 3                              });
```

5.4 Workflow

We implemented SIMPLIFIER as a Visual Studio plugin, on top of the Roslyn SDK [22]. SIMPLIFIER's workflow is similar to a "quick hint" option which exists in major IDEs such as Eclipse, Netbeans, IntelliJ. SIMPLIFIER scans the file that is open in the editor in real-time. It tries to find code snippets that fit into the patterns of the three transformations discussed above. Because it executes on the background (triggered by any keystroke), the analysis of finding code snippets should be fast enough to prevent sluggishness. However, the analyses for `Parallel.For(Each)` require some expensive checking of preconditions such as P4 and P5 in Sec. 5.2. Because they require dependence and data-flow analyses, we do not execute them in the suggestion phase, but in the transformation phase.

If SIMPLIFIER finds candidates, it suggests the places where the transformations can be useful by underlining the code snippet and displaying a hint in the sidebar. After the user clicks the hint and confirms, SIMPLIFIER transforms the code for the `Parallel.Invoke`. SIMPLIFIER tests long-running preconditions, such as for the `Parallel.For(Each)`, in the transformation phase. If the candidate passes these preconditions too, the code will be transformed to the `Parallel.For(Each)`. If not, SIMPLIFIER will give an informative warning.

6 Evaluation

We conducted two kinds of empirical evaluation. First, we *quantitatively* evaluate based on case studies of using our tools on open-source software. Second, we *qualitatively* evaluate based on patches that we sent to open-source developers.

6.1 Quantitative

To quantitatively evaluate the usefulness of TASKIFIER and SIMPLIFIER, we answer the following research questions:

RQ1: How **applicable** are the tools?
RQ2: Do the tools reduce the **code bloat**?
RQ3: How much **programmer effort** is saved by the tools?
RQ4: Are the automated transformations **safe**?

Experimental Setup: To answer the questions above, we ran TASKIFIER and SIMPLIFIER on our code corpus that we gathered from Github. The code corpus has 880 C# apps, comprising 42M SLOC, spanning a wide spectrum from web & desktop apps to libraries and mobile apps.

We ran both tools in batch mode over this code corpus. Even though SIMPLIFIER was not designed to run in a batch mode, we implemented a batch mode specifically for the purpose of the evaluation. TASKIFIER visits all `Thread` variable declarations and anonymous instances, and applies the migration algorithm. SIMPLIFIER finds the candidates of code snippets for each source file, then transforms the snippets to the targeted pattern.

Table 2 summarizes the results for the first three research questions.

RQ1: How applicable are the tools?   Out of our corpus of 880 apps, 269 used Threads (see Table 1). Together, they account for 2105 `Thread` instances. Based on our discussion with experts (see Section 3.3), they suggested we discard `Thread` usages in test code because developers may need threads for enforcing a multithreading testing environment. After eliminating the `Thread` usages in test code, we were left with 1782 `Thread` instances in production code, as shown in Table 2.

TASKIFIER migrated 78% of the `Thread` instances. The remaining 22% of `Thread` instances used operations that are not available in the `Task` class, thus are not amenable for migration. For example, one can set up the name of a Thread,

Table 2. Taskifier and Simplifer Conversion Results. The first column shows the total number of instances that the tool applied. The second column shows the total number of instances that the tool successfully converted and the third column shows the percentage of successfully transformed instances. The fourth column shows the total number of reduced SLOC by the transformations and the fifth column shows the percentage of the reduced lines. The last column shows the total number of modified SLOC.

	Applicability			Reduction		Modified
	Applied	Conv.	Conv. %	SLOC	%.	SLOC
Thread to Task	1782	1390	78%	2244	24%	8876
ThreadPool to Task	1244	1244	100%	173	14%	2115
Task to Parallel.Invoke	85	85	100%	502	44%	1870
Task to Parallel.For(Each)	205	188	92%	1918	62%	5640

but not of a Task. Deciding whether the name is important requires domain knowledge, thus Taskifier stays on the safe side and warns the programmer.

Because there are no preconditions for the migration of ThreadPool instances, TASKIFIER migrated all of them to Task.

As for SIMPLIFIER, it successfully transformed 100% of the 85 Task-based fork-join patterns to Parallel.Invoke. Out of the 205 identified Task-based data-parallelism patterns, it transformed 92% to Parallel.For or Parallel.ForEach. The remaining 8% did not pass the preconditions. A major number of them was failed due to P4: loop-carried dependence.

RQ2: Do the tools reduce the code bloat? The second column, *Reduction*, of Table 2 shows by how much each tool eliminates bloated code. As we expect, because SIMPLIFIER transforms *multiple* Task operations and helper operations to *one* equivalent method in the Parallel class (i.e., a *many-to-one* transformation), it has the largest impact. For the transformation to Parallel.Invoke, SIMPLIFIER achieved on average a 44% reduction in SLOC for each code snippet that it transformed. For the transformation to Parallel.For(Each), it achieved on average a 62% reduction for each transformed code snippet.

TASKIFIER migrates *one* Thread operation to *one* equivalent Task operation (i.e., a *one-to-one* transformation), so we expect modest reductions in LOC. These come from optimizations such as combining the creation and start Task operations, removing explicit casting statements which are not needed in Task bodies, etc. However, the advantages brought by TASKIFIER are (i) the modernization of the legacy code so that it can now be used with the newer platforms, and (ii) the transformation of blocking operations to the equivalent non-blocking operations.

RQ3: How much programmer effort is saved by the tools? The last column of Table 2 shows that the transformations are tedious. Had the programmers manually changed the code, they would have had to manually modify 10991 SLOC for the migration to `Task` and 7510 SLOC for the migration to `Parallel`.

Moreover, these changes are non-trivial. TASKIFIER found that 37% of `Thread` instances had at least one I/O blocking operation. To find these I/O blocking operations, TASKIFIER had to check deeper in the call-graphs of `Thread` bodies, which span 3.4 files on average. SIMPLIFIER found that 42% of the loops it tried to transform contained statements that needed an analysis to identify loop-carried dependences.

RQ4: Are the automated transformations safe? We used two means to check the safety of our transformations. First, after our tools applied any transformation, our evaluation script compiled the app in-memory and determined that no compilation errors were introduced. Second, we sampled and manually checked 10% of all transformed instances and determined that they were correct. Also, the original developers of the source code thought that the transformations were correct (see Section 6.2).

In contrast to the code that was transformed with the tools, we found that 32% of the `Task`-code manually written by open-source developers contained at least one I/O blocking operation which can cause serious performance issues (see Section 4.3). However, the code transformed by TASKIFIER into `Task` instances does not have this problem.

6.2 Qualitative Evaluation

To further evaluate the usefulness our of tools in practice, we identified actively developed C# applications, we ran our tools on them, and submitted patches[1] to the developers.

For TASKIFIER, we selected the 10 most recently updated apps that use `Thread` and `ThreadPool` and transformed them with TASKIFIER. We submitted 52 patches via a pull request. Developers of 8 apps out of 10 responded, and accepted 42 patches.

We received very positive feedback on these pull requests. Some developers said that migration to `Task` is on their TODO list but they always postponed it because of working on new features. It is tedious to migrate `Task` and developers can easily miss some important issues such as blocking I/O operations during the migration. TASKIFIER helps them migrate their code in a fast and safe manner.

For SIMPLIFIER, we selected a different set of 10 most recently updated apps that had a high chance of including good matches of code snippets for `Parallel.For(Each)` or `Parallel.Invoke` patterns. We submitted 14 patches. Developers of 7 apps out of 10 responded, and accepted 11 patches. All of them liked the new code after the transformation and asked us whether we can make the tool available now.

---

[1] All patches can be found on our web site: `Taskifier.NET`

6.3   Discussion

As explained in Section 4.3, TASKIFIER analyzed the call graph of `Thread` body to detect I/O blocking operations, using a blacklist approach. Although we have the list of I/O blocking operations in .NET framework, TASKIFIER is not aware of I/O blocking operations implemented by 3rd-party libraries whose source code is not available in the app. However, we don't expect that the number of blocking I/O operations implemented by external libraries to be high.

Most of non-blocking I/O and synchronization operations were released in .NET 4.5 (2012). If an application does not target .NET 4.5, it cannot take advantage of the non-blocking operations. However, applications that are targeting the new platforms (e.g, Windows Phone 8, Surface) are forced to use .NET 4.5.

With respect to releasing TASKIFIER and SIMPLIFIER, we will be able to publish the tools when Microsoft publicly releases the new version of Roslyn (expected by Spring '14). Because we used an internal version of Roslyn, we had to sign an NDA, which prohibits us from releasing tools based on Roslyn.

7   Related Work

Empirical Studies about Parallelism: Pankratius et al. [21] analyzed concurrency related transformations in a few Java applications. Torres et al. [25] conducted a study on the usage of concurrent programming constructs in Java, by analyzing around 2000 applications. In our previous study [10] we cataloged the kinds of changes that Java developers perform when they write parallel code. We have also conducted an empirical study [18] on how developers from thousands of open source projects use C# parallel libraries.

In this paper, we do not only target the usage statistics of parallel abstractions but also provides TASKIFIER and SIMPLIFIER for helping developers migrate from low-level parallel abstractions to higher-level abstractions.

Refactoring Tools for Parallelism: There are a few refactoring tools that specifically target concurrency. Dig et al. [9,11] retrofit parallelism into sequential applications via Java concurrent libraries. In the same spirit, Wloka et al. [27] present a refactoring for replacing global state with thread local state. Schafer et al. [24] present Relocker, a refactoring tool that lets programmers replace usages of Java built-in locks with more flexible locks. Schafer et al. [23] also investigated the problem of whether existing sequential refactorings are concurrency-aware. Gyori et al. [13] present Lambdaficator, that refactors existing Java code to use lambda expressions to enable parallelism. We previously studied asynchronous programming and developed Asyncifier [19], an automated refactoring tool that converts old style asynchronous code to use new language features (i.e., `async/await`). However, none of these previous tools address the problem of migrating between different levels of abstractions in (already) parallel code.

Balaban et al. [8] present a tool for converting between obsolete classes and their modern replacements. The developer specifies a mapping between the old

APIs and the new APIs. Then, the tool uses a type-constraint analysis to determine if it can replace all usages of the obsolete class. Their tool supports a one-to-one transformation whereas SIMPLIFIER supports many-to-one transformations. Even our one-to-one transformations from TASKIFIER require custom program analysis, e.g., detecting I/O blocking operations, and cannot be simply converted by a mapping program.

8 Conclusions

To make existing parallel code readable, faster, and scalable, it is essential to use higher-level parallel abstractions. Their usage is encouraged by the industry leaders as the old, low-level abstractions are subject to deprecation and removal in new platforms.

Our motivational study of a corpus of 880 C# applications revealed that many developers still use the lower-level parallel abstractions and some are not even aware of the better abstractions. This suggests a new workflow for transformation tools, where suggestions can make developers aware of new abstractions.

Converting from low-level to high-level abstractions can not be done by a simple find-and-replace tool, but it requires custom program analysis and transformation. For example, 37% of `Thread` instances use blocking I/O operations, which need special treatment when they are converted to `Task` instances, otherwise it can create severe performance bugs. We found that 32% instances of manually written `Task` indeed contain blocking I/O operations.

In this paper we presented two tools. Our first tool, TASKIFIER, converts `Thread`-based usage to lightweight `Task`. We were surprised that despite some differences between `Thread` and `Task` abstractions, 78% of the code that uses `Thread` can be successfully converted to `Task`. Our second tool, SIMPLIFIER, converts `Task`-based code into higher-level parallel design patterns. Such conversions reduce the code bloat by 57%. The developers of the open-source projects accepted 53 of our patches and are looking forward to using our tools.

Acknowledgements. This research is partly funded through NSFCCF-1439957 and CCF-1442157 grants, a SEIF award from Microsoft, and a gift grant from Intel. The authors would like to thank Cosmin Radoi, Yu Lin, Mihai Codoban, Caius Brindescu, Sergey Shmarkatyuk, Alex Gyori, Michael Hilton, and anonymous reviewers for providing helpful feedback on earlier drafts of this paper.

References

1. RavenDB 2nd generation document database (May 2014), http://ravendb.net
2. Antlrcs (May 2014), http://github.com/antlr/antlrcs
3. Dynamo App. (May 2014), https://github.com/ikeough/Dynamo
4. Jace App. (May 2014), https://github.com/pieterderycke/Jace
5. Kudu App. (May 2014), https://github.com/projectkudu/kudu
6. Lucene.NET App. (May 2014), https://github.com/apache/lucene.net

7. Tiraggo App. (May 2014), https://github.com/BrewDawg/Tiraggo
8. Balaban, I., Tip, F., Fuhrer, R.: Refactoring support for class library migration. In: Proceedings of the OOPSLA 2005, pp. 265–279 (2005)
9. Dig, D., Marrero, J., Ernst, M.D.: Refactoring sequential Java code for concurrency via concurrent libraries. In: Proceedings of the ICSE 2009, pp. 397–407 (2009)
10. Dig, D., Marrero, J., Ernst, M.D.: How do programs become more concurrent: A story of program transformations. In: Proceedings of the IWMSE 2011, pp. 43–50 (2011)
11. Dig, D., Tarce, M., Radoi, C., Minea, M., Johnson, R.: Relooper. In: Proceedings of the OOPSLA 2009, pp. 793–794 (2009)
12. Github (May 2014), https://github.com
13. Gyori, A., Franklin, L., Dig, D., Lahoda, J.: Crossing the gap from imperative to functional programming through refactoring. In: Proceedings of the FSE 2013, pp. 543–553 (2013)
14. Lea, D.: A Java fork/join framework. In: Proceedings of the ACM 2000 Conference on Java Grande, pp. 36–43 (2000)
15. Leijen, D., Hall, J.: Parallel Performance: Optimize Managed Code For Multi-Core Machines. In: MSDN (October 2007)
16. Leijen, D., Schulte, W., Burckhardt, S.: The design of a task parallel library. ACM SIGPLAN Notices 44(10), 227 (2009)
17. Nuget (May 2014), http://www.nuget.org/
18. Okur, S., Dig, D.: How do developers use parallel libraries? In: Proceedings of the FSE 2012, pp. 54–65 (2012)
19. Okur, S., Hartveld, D.L., Dig, D., van Deursen, A.: A study and toolkit for asynchronous programming in C#. In: Proceedings of the ICSE 2014, pp. 1117–1127 (2014)
20. Stack Overflow (May 2014), http://stackoverflow.com
21. Pankratius, V., Schaefer, C., Jannesari, A., Tichy, W.F.: Software engineering for multicore systems. In: Proceedings of the IWMSE 2008, pp. 53–60 (2008)
22. The Roslyn Project (May 2014), http://msdn.microsoft.com/en-us/hh500769
23. Schäfer, M., Dolby, J., Sridharan, M., Torlak, E., Tip, F.: Correct refactoring of concurrent java code. In: D'Hondt, T. (ed.) ECOOP 2010. LNCS, vol. 6183, pp. 225–249. Springer, Heidelberg (2010)
24. Schäfer, M., Sridharan, M., Dolby, J., Tip, F.: Refactoring Java programs for flexible locking. In: Proceedings of the ICSE 2011, pp. 71–80 (2011)
25. Torres, W., Pinto, G., Fernandes, B., Oliveira, J.P., Ximenes, F.A., Castor, F.: Are Java programmers transitioning to multicore?: a large scale study of java FLOSS. In: Proceedings of the SPLASH 2011 Workshops, pp. 123–128 (2011)
26. Toub, S.: Patterns of Parallel Programming. Microsoft Corporation (2010)
27. Wloka, J., Sridharan, M., Tip, F.: Refactoring for reentrancy. In: Proceedings of the FSE 2009, pp. 173–182 (2009)

Portable and Efficient Run-Time Monitoring of JavaScript Applications Using Virtual Machine Layering

Erick Lavoie[1,*], Bruno Dufour[2], and Marc Feeley[2]

[1] McGill University, Montreal, Canada
erick.lavoie@mail.mcgill.ca
[2] Université de Montréal, Montreal, Canada
{dufour,feeley}@iro.umontreal.ca

Abstract. Run-time monitoring of JavaScript applications is typically achieved either by instrumenting a browser's virtual machine, usually degrading performance to the level of a simple interpreter, or through complex *ad hoc* source-to-source transformations. This paper reports on an experiment in layering a portable JS VM on the host VM to expose implementation-level operations that can then be redefined at run-time to monitor an application execution. Our prototype, Photon, exposes object operations and function calls through a meta-object protocol. In order to limit the performance overhead, a dynamic translation of the client program selectively modifies source elements and run-time feedback optimizes monitoring operations. Photon introduces a 4.7× to 191× slowdown when executing benchmarks on popular web browsers. Compared to the Firefox interpreter, it is between 5.5× slower and 7× faster, showing the layering approach is competitive with the instrumentation of a browser VM while being faster and simpler than other source-to-source transformations.

Keywords: JavaScript, Virtual Machine, Runtime Monitoring, Performance Evaluation, Optimization, Metaobject Protocol

1 Introduction

JavaScript (JS), the *de facto* language of the web, has recently gained much popularity among researchers and practitioners alike. In particular, due to the highly dynamic nature of the language, there is a growing interest in observing the behavior of JS programs. For instance, run-time monitoring is being used for widely different purposes, such as gathering empirical data regarding the dynamic behavior of web applications [10], automatically extracting benchmarks from web applications [11], and enforcing access permission contracts [6].

Common profiling tasks in JS, such as intercepting all object operations or function calls, are difficult to achieve in a portable and efficient manner. A popular approach consists of modifying a production virtual machine (VM). While

---

* This work was done at Université de Montréal.

R. Jones (Ed.): ECOOP 2014, LNCS 8586, pp. 541–566, 2014.

this approach guarantees a high level of compliance with the source language, it suffers from some important drawbacks. Most modern JS implementations are production-quality VMs that are optimized for performance and thus difficult to modify. Generally, this approach also binds the profiling system to a single VM, and therefore greatly limits the portability of the approach. Moreover, modifications to the VM codebase must evolve as the VM is being developed upstream, which can happen at a rapid pace. As a result, many attempts to modify a JS VM are punctual efforts that are abandoned shortly thereafter [3,8,10].

The most popular alternative approach for instrumenting JS programs consists of implementing an *ad hoc* source-to-source translator and runtime library tailored to the problem at hand. While this approach is easier to maintain and more portable than instrumenting a VM, implementing a correct source-to-source transformation is deceptively difficult in practice, even for seemingly simple tasks. For instance, instrumenting all object creations also requires instrumenting all function calls because any function call could potentially be a call to `Object.create` through an alias. Other dynamic constructs in JS, such as `eval`, are notoriously difficult to instrument while guaranteeing that the observed behavior of the program will remain unaffected. Also, JS programs can easily redefine core operations from `Object` and `Array`. Such modifications are difficult to handle. A profiler that is unaware of such redefinitions could behave incorrectly, or worse, cause a change in the observed behavior of the profiled program. Finally, the profiler code itself must maintain various invariants. For example, instrumentations that rely on extending existing objects with new properties must take proper care not to leak information that is visible to user code by introspection (e.g., by iterating over all properties of an object[1]).

Both VM instrumentation as well as source-to-source transformations can have unexpected performance costs. VM instrumentation often settles for modifying a simple non-optimizing interpreter to avoid the additional complexity of instrumenting a commercial Just-In-Time (JIT) compiler. The performance hit incurred by disabling the JIT compiler in a modern JS implementation is significant, often an order of magnitude or more. Second, while source-to-source transformations can benefit from the full range of optimizations performed by the JIT, a naive transformation often results in a similar slowdown.

In this paper, we present an alternative technique for run-time monitoring of JS applications based on *virtual machine layering*. Virtual machine layering consists of exposing implementation-level operations performed by the VM through various abstraction layers. Specifically, our approach uses a flexible *object model* as a basis to build the abstraction layers. A JS application is then transformed to make use of these abstractions. Because this transformation is performed during the execution, the resulting framework can be viewed as a metacircular VM written on top of a host VM for the source language. This approach has three main advantages. First, exposing implementation-level operations provides

---

[1] Marking properties as non-iterable is not sufficient in general, since `Object.getOwnPropertyNames` will return all property names, irrespective of their iterable nature.

a good compromise between the portability offered by source-to-source translations and the expressiveness of VM modifications. For instance, profilers can easily extend or redefine the implementation-level operations to accomplish their specific tasks. Second, by exposing implementation-level operations in a separate layer, our approach can prevent interference between VM code and user code. This is achieved by ensuring that user code only manipulates objects through *proxies*[2], which provide a form of sandboxing over the native objects provided by the host VM. Finally, the metacircular VM can leverage fast operations provided by the underlying host VM to reduce the overhead of the transformation. This is achieved by (i) letting the host VM execute operations for which no abstraction is necessary, and (ii) providing abstractions that use or support the operations that are efficiently implemented by the host VM. Reusing complex primitive operations from the host VM also greatly reduces the development effort required to provide a fully compliant VM implementation.

Virtual machine layering is not new and has been previously studied as an implementation technique for metaobject protocols [7]. It can add to JS many of the functions of an intercession API such as the Java Virtual Machine Tools Interface (JVMTI) by reifying implicit operations of the language. In contrast to JVMTI, it does not require the modification of the internals of a VM, only a single intercession point in the browser to maintain the invariants of the layered VM by translating dynamically loaded code before it is executed by the host VM. However, it cannot give access to implementation-specific information such as garbage collection events or exact memory usage. A standard API would supersede it, but until consensus is reached by VM implementors, VM layering can help build on a common instrumentation infrastructure and explore the API design space. One of the authors wrote a small patch to add an intercession point to the Debugger API in Firefox[3]. We believe it should be straightforward to implement and require little maintenance to support on all major browsers.

Photon[4], our prototype implementation of this technique, uses a single primitive operation, message-sending, to reify implementation-level operations such as object operations and function calls. The use of the message-sending primitive provides a simple and dynamic mechanism to instrument and even redefine the behavior of a reified operation. For instance, a profiler could intercept all calls by providing a wrapper function for Photon's `call` primitive operation. In order to offset the cost of the message-sending mechanism, Photon implements a *send cache* optimization. This optimization allows the behavior of a message send (e.g., a property access) to be specialized at a given program point. This caching optimization is crucial to obtain a good performance in practice, making Photon on average 19% faster than a commercial interpreter while providing a much higher degree of flexibility and dynamism.

This paper makes two main contributions: (i) the design of a VM that reifies object operations and function calls around a single message-sending primitive

---

[2] We refer to the implementation concept in general, not the upcoming JS Proxies.
[3] https://bugzilla.mozilla.org/show_bug.cgi?id=884602
[4] https://github.com/elavoie/photon-js/tree/ecoop2014

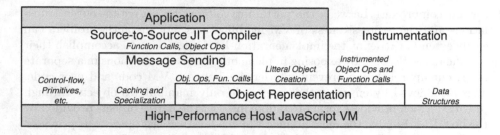

Fig. 1. Components of the Photon virtual machine

so that their behavior can be redefined dynamically, (ii) an object representation exploiting the underlying host VM's inline caches and dynamic object model for performance. Both are shown to provide a significant performance increase over existing approaches and are an important step towards portable and efficient instrumentation frameworks for JavaScript.

We present in turn, an overview of the components of the system, the object representation, the message-sending semantics, a compilation example, a performance evaluation, and related work.

2   Overview

In a conventional JS setting, an application runs over a high-performance host VM. In the case of a *metacircular* VM, an additional VM layer is inserted between the application and the host VM. This layer can be a *full* or a *differential* implementation. In a full implementation, the metacircular VM provides all functionalities of the source language. In a differential setting, however, the metacircular VM only implements parts of the required functionality, and delegates the remaining operations to the underlying host VM. Our approach follows a differential strategy. Object operations are handled by one of the layers introduced by Photon while primitive operations are handled by the host VM.

This section presents Photon's design goals and components.

2.1   Design Goals

Our design aims to achieve the following properties:

- **Isolation**: The application is isolated to avoid any interference with instrumentation code, while still allowing an instrumentation to fully inspect and modify the application state.
- **Abstraction**: Low-level details, mostly related to performance optimizations, are encapsulated to simplify the definition of instrumentations.
- **Performance**: Native features are reused when possible (e.g. control-flow operations). The performance of some host features (e.g., fast global function calls) is leveraged in optimizations that reduce the overhead of abstractions.

In this paper, we focus on the performance aspect to stress the feasibility of virtual machine layering on modern JS VMs.

2.2 Overview of the Components

Figure 1 shows a structural view of the components of Photon.

Source-to-Source Compiler. The source-to-source compiler translates the original JS code to use the runtime environment provided by Photon. Non-reified elements, such as control-flow operations as well as primitive values and operations are preserved. Object operations and function calls are translated to make use of the message sending layer. Literal object creations are translated to use the object representation. The source-to-source compiler is itself written in JS and is therefore available at run-time. By staging it in front of every call to `eval`, it effectively provides a JIT compiler to Photon.

Message Sending. Photon uses a message sending primitive to reify operations internal to the implementation, such as property accesses on objects and function calls. These reified operations can then easily be overridden and redefined when required, for example to profile the application or to specialize the behavior of an operation. Photon itself makes use of this extra level of indirection for performance by providing a caching mechanism at each site that performs a message send, a form of memoization.

Object Representation. In order to isolate the application from the instrumentation and the host VM, Photon provides a virtualized representation of objects (including functions). Each JS object in the original application is represented in Photon by *two* distinct objects: a property container and a proxy[5]. The property container corresponds to the original object, and acts as storage for all properties that are added to an object. For performance reasons, the property container object is a native JS object provided by the host VM. This allows Photon to leverage its efficient property access mechanism.

The native property container can only be accessed through Photon, and never directly from the application. All object operations go through the proxy object, which is the object that is manipulated directly by the transformed application code. Object representation operations can be specialized in certain classes of objects for performance, such as indexed property accesses on arrays. The use of proxy objects also simplifies the task of implementing instrumentations because it abstracts implementation details that are required for performance. It also allows object-specific instrumentation information to be stored on a proxy without risk of interference with the application properties.

Instrumentation. An instrumentation can redefine the behavior of object operations and function calls by replacing the corresponding method on a root object with an instrumented version using the object representation operations. The ability to completely replace a method provides maximum flexibility to instrumentation writers as opposed to being limited to a specific event before and

---

[5] Implemented using a regular object. It would be interesting future work to investigate how the upcoming JS proxies perform.

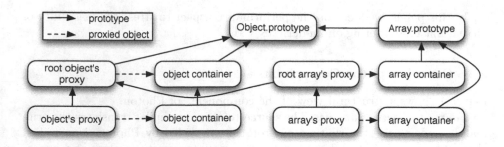

Fig. 2. Representation for objects and arrays

after an operation. However, most instrumentations will choose to simply delegate to the original implementation of an operation and act as wrappers. An instrumentation is executed with the same privileges as the VM, and can therefore directly access the execution environment of the VM. It can also use native objects as data structures.

The next sections expand on the object representation and message sending.

3   Object Representation

Conceptually, all JS objects are associative arrays where the keys represent the *properties* of an object. As with many dynamic languages, properties can be dynamically added, redefined or removed from an object. Each object also has a reference to a *prototype* object from which it inherits properties. The sequence of prototype objects until the root of the object hierarchy forms the *prototype chain* of an object. Functions are also objects, and are first-class citizens in the language. Methods on objects are simply properties with functions as values. JS also treats all global variables and function declarations as properties of a singleton *global object*.

Photon virtualizes the host VM objects exposed to the application in order to provide isolation between the application and the instrumentations, and to reify the object operations supported by JS. While this design provides a high level of flexibility, it also introduces a source of overhead. Proper care must be taken to limit the performance impact of the object representation.

Figure 2 illustrates the object representation used in Photon, with `Object.prototype` as the root of all objects. Photon structures the object representation as proxies to native objects [5]. Each original JS object is therefore represented by two distinct objects in the transformed application. In this representation, the structure of the native (i.e., proxied) object is the same as with the original representation. Using native objects to store properties is motivated by performance. Modern JS VMs aggressively optimize property accesses and method calls on objects, as these operations are key to good performance in

Table 1. Object representation operation interfaces

Operation	Interface	Example
Property read	`get(id)`	`o.get("p")`
Property write	`set(id, val)`	`o.set("p",42)`
Property delete	`del(id)`	`o.del("p")`
Prototype read	`getPrototype()`	`o.getPrototype()`
Object creation	`create()`	`parent.create()`
Call	`call(rcv, ..args)`	`fun.call(global)`

practice. Therefore, preserving the internal structure of the represented objects enables the optimizations performed by the host VM, such as lookup caching.

The application root objects are virtualized for isolation. For example, the application `Object.prototype` is a child of Photon's `Object.prototype`. It is referred to as `root.object` in Photon's implementation. Other JS object model root objects, such as `Array.prototype` are also reified and have `root.object` for prototype.

The proxy object encapsulates the logic implementing the object operations, as well as the invariants that are required for performance (e.g., invalidating caches in response to a redefined operation). Table 1 lists the methods that are provided by proxy objects in order to reify object operations.

Additionally, in order to exploit the fast lookup chain implementations provided by the host VM, the prototype chain of the proxies mirrors the prototype chain of the native objects. This organization of the proxy objects enables specializing and optimizing the operations performed on the object representation at run-time by strategically defining specialized methods along the proxy prototype chain. For example, property accesses performed on array objects can be optimized for the case where the property is numerical rather than using a less efficient, generic mechanism.

However, this strategy does not work well with native types that can be created using a literal syntax, such as arrays, functions and regular expressions. In order to preserve the prototype chain invariant, it would be necessary to change the prototype of these objects after their creation. While technically possible, doing so would invalidate structural invariants assumed by the host VM, at the cost of performance. For such objects, the original native prototype is maintained. When a lookup is needed, it is performed explicitly through the proxy prototype chain. This is illustrated for arrays in the right part of Figure 2.

Although proxies mirror native objects in their prototype chain, they do not mirror their properties. In fact, their properties will be fixed for the whole execution if the object operations are not redefined (e.g., through an instrumentation). Proxies can therefore adapt to dynamic circumstances by adding specialized methods at run-time, which can be used for performance gains. The next subsections demonstrate how this can be exploited to specialize operations for a fixed number of arguments.

3.1 Specialization on a Fixed Number of Arguments

Our object representation does not mandate a specific calling convention for functions. Function calls are reified through a `call` method implemented by function proxies. The naive implementation of `call` uses the equivalent `call` or `apply` method provided by the host VM. However, this generic mechanism is inefficient. It can be avoided by globally rewriting every function to explicitly pass the receiver object. This way, a specialized call operation on a proxy object can simply and efficiently invoke the native function with all arguments passed explicitly. Therefore, function calls can be specialized for the number of arguments found at a given call site. For example, a `call` operation specialized for one argument in addition to its receiver could be implemented as follows:

```
fn_proxy.call1 = function ($this, arg0) {
    return this.proxiedObject($this, arg0);
};
```

Note that all callable proxies must provide an implementation of `call1` (e.g., by defining this operation on the `FunctionProxy` root).

4 Message-Sending Semantics

Source-level instrumentations aim to intercede on common and often opaque operations performed by the host VM. Our object representation provides a mechanism that reifies implementation-level object operations. In order to enable the redefinition of such operations in a flexible, dynamic and efficient way, our approach uses a single message sending primitive. Translating opaque operations to our message-sending primitive makes them available for instrumentation, and provides additional performance benefits.

4.1 Reifying Object Operations

Reifying opaque operations in source-level instrumentations is typically achieved by transforming the original code so that all such operations go through globally accessible functions. For example, in the case of the property read `var v = o.foo`, the program could be instrumented as follows:

```
function __get__(o, p) {
    <before>
    var r = o[p];
    <after>
    return r;
};
...
var v = __get__(o,"foo");
```

This strategy exposes the details of the opaque operation, such as the identity of the object as well as the name of the property being accessed. It allows an instrumentation to perform some work *before*, *after* or even *instead of* the original operation. However, it lacks flexibility. For instance, instrumentations requiring a fine-grained control over which objects need to be monitored would need to introduce tests in the global function, at a cost in performance. Also, this rigid design makes it difficult to disable the instrumentation dynamically without incurring the run-time cost introduced with the instrumentation mechanism. Furthermore, multiple optimizations cannot be combined seamlessly without adapting the intercession mechanism.

To address these limitations, our approach replaces globally accessible functions with methods defined on the objects being monitored. This strategy exploits the object-oriented nature of the underlying implementation, and enables a fine-grained monitoring strategy to be implemented easily. For example, an instrumentation of property reads could be implemented as follows:

```
o.__get__ = function (p) {
    <before 1>
    var r = this[p];
    <after 1>
    return r;
};
Array.prototype.__get__ = function (p) {
    <before 2>
    var r = this[p];
    <after 2>
    return r;
};
Object.prototype.__get__ = function (p) {
    <before 3>
    var r = this[p];
    <after 3>
    return r;
};
...
var v = o.__get__("foo");
```

This example illustrates how an instrumentation can be applied selectively to a set of objects based on their hierarchy. This example performs a different instrumentation for three distinct classes of objects: a given instance o, all arrays, and all other objects. While there is an added cost to this technique, it preserves the ability of the host VM to optimize the calls to __get__ using its regular inline caching mechanism.

Table 2. Object model operations and examples of their equivalent message sends

Object Model Operation	Example	Equivalent Message Send
Property read	o.p	send(o,"__get__","p")
Property write	o.p=42	send(o,"__set__","p",42)
Property delete	delete o.p	send(o,"__del__","p")
Object creation with literal	{p:42}	send({p:42},"__new__")
Object creation with constructor	new C()	send(C,"__ctor__")

Note that to ensure isolation, this instrumentation strategy is combined with the object representation presented in Section 3. All operations are therefore performed on proxies instead of accessing the native object directly:

```
proxy.set("__get__",
    new FunctionProxy(function (p) {
        <before 1>
        var r = this.get(p);

        <after 1>
        return r;
    }));
...
function send(proxy, msg, ..args) {
    return proxy.get(msg).call(obj, ..args);
}
var v = send(proxy, "__get__", "foo");
```

The send function in the previous example encapsulates the message sending logic as implemented by Photon. The semantics of the send operation correspond to a regular method call: the function proxy corresponding to a given message is first looked up, possibly using the prototype chain, and is then invoked with the provided arguments. While this formulation is not strictly necessary to obtain the desired semantics, our current implementation relies on it for performance optimizations, as explained in Section 4.3.

The strategy used to support __get__ can be used to support all other object operations. A summary of the supported operations and their equivalent message sends is listed in Table 2.

4.2 Reifying Function Calls

JS functions can be called directly (e.g., f()) or indirectly through their call method. This mechanism can be seen as a form of built-in reification of the calling protocol. However, there is no causal connection between the state of the call method and the behavior of function calls: redefining the call method on Function.prototype does not affect the behavior of call sites. Therefore, call is not sufficient to expose all function calls for instrumentation purposes.

This causal relationship is established in our approach by providing a call operation on all function proxies. Similarly to other object operations, all function calls in the original program are transformed into a send of the call message to a function proxy. Table 3 lists the transformation strategy for each type of function call provided by JS. Note that global function calls are translated directly into method calls on the global object, thereby exposing their semantics at the compilation stage. In order to implement both method calls and regular function calls using the same mechanism, a modification of the send operation ensures that the reified call operation is used for all calls throughout the system:

Table 3. Call types and their equivalent message sends

Call Type	Description	Equivalent Message Send
Global	Calling a function in the global object. Ex: `foo()`	Sending a message to the global object. Ex: `send(global,"foo")`
Local	Calling a function in a local variable. Ex: `fn()`	Sending the `call` message to the function. Ex: `send(fn,"call")`
Method	Calling an object method. Ex: `obj.foo()`	Sending a message to the object. Ex: `send(obj,"foo")`
apply or call	Calling the `call` or `apply` function method. Ex: `fn.call()`	Sending the `call` or `apply` message. Ex: `send(fn,"call")`

```
function send(rcv, msg, ..args) {
    var m = rcv.get(msg);
    // Use reified "call"
    var callFn = m.get("call");
    return callFn.call(m, rcv, ..args);
}
```

With these mechanisms in place, all function calls can be instrumented simply by redefining the root function's `call` method.

4.3 Efficient Implementation

In order to reduce the indirection introduced by the transformation process, Photon uses a caching mechanism for send operations. *Send caches* use global function calls both as an optimized calling mechanism as well as operations that can be redefined dynamically. They provide the same ability as code patching in assembly. On the state-of-the-art JS VMs, inlining functions becomes possible when their number of expected arguments matches the number of arguments supplied. If the global function is redefined at a later time, the call site will be deoptimized transparently. This is a highly powerful mechanism because much of the complexity of run-time specialization is performed by the underlying host. The caches implemented by Photon piggyback on this approach.

For example, sending the message `msg` to an object `obj` inside a `foo` function can be written as follows:

```
function foo(obj) {
    send(obj, "msg"); // Equivalent to obj.msg();
}
```

The `send` function is a global function. It can be replaced with another global function that is guaranteed to be unique, so that each call site effectively receives its own version of the `send` primitive. In addition to the message to be sent, this global function is also provided with a unique identifier used to access the corresponding global function name, for later specialization of the call site:

```
function initialState(rcv, dc, ..args) {
```

```
    <<<code updating variable "scN" (N=dc[0])>>>
    return send(rcv, dc[1], ..args);
}

var sc0 = initialState;
var dc0 = [0, "msg"];

function foo(obj) {
    sc0(obj, dc0);
}
```

Note that the `initialState` function follows the same calling convention as the `send` function. Furthermore, `dc0` can be used to store additional information according to the state of the cache, if needed.

After an initial execution, the cache will dynamically be redefined to hold an optimized version of the operation. For the example, the default caching mechanism implemented by Photon will specialize the cache as follows:

```
var sc0 = function (rcv, dc) {
    return rcv.get("msg").call(rcv);
};
var dc0 = [0, "msg"];

function foo(obj) {
    sc0(obj, dc0);
}
```

Apart from the indirection of the global function call, this example is optimal with regard to the chosen object representation. If the underlying host VM chooses to inline the global function, the cost of the indirection will be effectively eliminated in practice.

In addition to the inlining of the message sending operation in terms of the object operations, as shown previously, Photon also uses the cache to avoid the cost of message sending altogether for reified operations, by inlining an optimized version of its behaviour. In this case, the reified operation is assumed to be defined only once on the root object. Photon tests it by looking for a __memoize__ property on the method (explained in the next subsection).

That limitation is necessary because, when an instrumentation redefines the reified operation simultaneously on more than one object, Photon's current invariant tracking mechanism cannot detect whether the instrumented method of the current receiver object would resolve to the one inlined. It is assumed, in this case, that an instrumentation writer would not define a __memoize__ property on the instrumented operation in order to prevent the application of that second optimization.

Memoized Methods. Memoization is usually associated with functional programming and entails trading space-efficiency for time-efficiency by remembering past return values of functions with no side-effect. By analogy, we define a memoized method in our approach to be a method that performs the same operation, albeit possibly more efficiently by exploiting run-time information (e.g., argument count). This particular functionality is necessary to efficiently implement the JS object operations in our system because they are reified as methods.

The basic principle behind memoizing methods is to allow a method to inspect its arguments and receiver in order to specialize itself for subsequent calls. The first call is always performed by calling the original function while all subsequent calls will be made to the memoized function. A function call defines its memoization behavior by defining a __memoize__ method.

There is an unfortunate interaction between memoization and the reification of the call protocol. A further refinement specifies that memoization can only occur if the call method of the function has not been redefined. Otherwise, the identity of the function passed to the call method would not be the same. To preserve identity while allowing memoization, the behavior of the cache can be different depending on the state of the Function.prototype's call method. If its value is the default one, the identity of the function is not important and memoization can be performed. Otherwise, memoization will be ignored. This definition has the advantage that there is no penalty for temporarily redefining the calling method after the original method has been restored.

Specializing Instrumentations. Performance-critical instrumentations can use memoization to provide efficient specialized operations. For example, consider a simple instrumentation that counts the number of property accesses:

```
root.object.set("__get__",
                new FunctionProxy(
                    function ($this, prop) {
                        counter++;
                        return $this.get(prop);
                }));
```

The redefinition of the __get__ operation prevents the use of the default inlining mechanism, and therefore reverts the send cache behavior to the following:

```
var counter = 0; // Added by the instrumentation

var sc0 = function (rcv, msg, prop) {
    return rcv.get("__get__").call(rcv, prop);
};

sc0(o, "__get__", "p");
```

To limit the incurred performance overhead, this instrumentation could provide an implementation of __get__ that additionally responds to the __memoize__ message. After the first execution of the property access, the optimized version of the send cache would become specialized as follows, thereby eliminating much of the additional overhead from the naive implementation:

```
var counter = 0; // Added by the instrumentation
```

```
var sc0 = function (rcv, msg, prop) {
    counter++;
    return rcv.get(prop);
};

sc0(o, "__get__", "p");
```

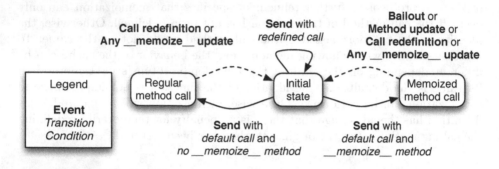

Fig. 3. Cache States and Transitions

Cache States and Transitions. In order to guarantee the correct behavior of an application, caches need to be invalidated when their invariants are violated. This requires tracking the invariants for each cache used in the system. To simplify tracking the invariants, we always perform lookups for method calls (i.e., method calls are always a get followed by a call). This is a reasonable choice if the object representation can piggyback on the host optimizations.

In addition to its *initial state*, each cache can be in one of two states, *regular method call*, in which the method is first looked up and called, and *Memoized method call*, in which a method-specific behavior is executed.

Transitions between states happen on message-sends and object-operation events. We choose to under-approximate the tracking of invariants and conservatively invalidate more caches than minimally required. As long as the operations triggering the invalidation of caches are infrequent, the performance impact should be minimal. We therefore track method values cached in memoized states by name without consideration for the receiver object. If a method with the same name is updated on any object, all caches with a given message name will be invalidated. Also, if the call method on the Function.prototype object or any method with the __memoize__ name is updated, *all* caches will be invalidated. This way, we only need to track caches associated with names. Memory usage is proportional to the number of active cache sites.

There is no state associated with a redefined call method. In that particular case, all caches will stay in the initial state and a full message send will be performed. Figure 3 summarizes those elements in a state diagram. A more detailed explanation of every event and transition conditions is given in Table 4.

Our current tracking strategy was chosen to evaluate the performance of our prototype with a minimal implementation effort. However, it is not granular enough to track instrumentations redefining operations on non-root objects. A more granular strategy should be used for instrumentations requiring different operations for different groups of objects.

Table 4. Cache Events and Transition Conditions

Cache Events	Explanation
Send	A message is sent to a receiver object.
Call redefinition	The `call` method on `Function.prototype` is redefined.
Any memoized redefinition	Any `__memoize__` method is being redefined.
Bailout	A run-time invariant has been violated.
Method redefinition	An object with a method with the same name has its method being updated.

Cache Transition Condition	Explanation
Default call	`Function.prototype call` method is the same as the initial one.
Redefined call	`Function.prototype call` method is different than the initial one.
No `__memoize__` method	No method named `__memoize__` has been found on the method to be called.
`__memoize__` method	A method named `__memoize__` has been found on the method to be called.

5   Compilation and Execution Example

We now show how the components of Photon work together using an example. It illustrates many of the reified operations discussed previously: property reads and writes as well as function and method calls. Consider the following program:

```
var f = function (n, d) {

  for (var i=1; i<=2; i=i+1) {
    n = n + d.getTime();
  }

  return n;
};

f(42, new Date(100));
```

Note that the `getTime` method call will be executed twice during execution.

The source-to-source compiler translates each reified operation to a message send according to Table 2 and Table 3. Each occurrence of a message send has an associated send cache (scn) initialized to the `initialState` function, and a data cache (dcn), containing the cache identifier (n), the message name and compile time information about arguments. Each literal object created is wrapped in a proxy to obey the object representation, a function literal is therefore wrapped with a `FunctionProxy`. Non-reified operations, such as the scope chain accesses, control-flow operations, such as the **for** statement, numbers and arithmetic operations are preserved as-is in their original form.

The commented original code is weaved with the generated code for clarity:

```
sc1 = initialState; // SC for: var f = ...
dc1 = [1,"__set__",["ref","string","scSend"]];

sc2 = initialState; // SC for: function (n,d)...
dc2 = [2,"__new__",[]];

sc3 = initialState; // SC for: d.getTime()
dc3 = [3,"getTime",["get"]];

sc4 = initialState; // SC for: f(42, ...)
dc4 = [4,"f",["ref","number","scSend"]];

sc5 = initialState; // SC for: new Date(100)
dc5 = [5,"__ctor__",["scSend","number"]];

sc6 = initialState; // SC for: Date
dc6 = [6,"__get__",["ref","string"]];

sc1(root_global,          // var f =
    dc1,
    "f",
    sc2(root.func,        // function (n,d) {
        dc2,
        new FunctionProxy(
            function ($this,n,d) {
                var i = undefined;
                for (i=1; i<=2; i=i+1) {
                    // n = n + d.getTime();
                    n = n + sc3(d, dc3);
                }
                return n;
            }))); // };

sc4(root_global,          // f(42,
    dc4,
    42,
    sc5(sc6(root_global,  //    new Date(100));
```

```
        dc6,
        "Date"),
    dc5,
    100));
```

When executed, this code will perform message sends at each of the send caches. The third send cache (`sc3`) will benefit from the caching mechanism. The first time around the loop, the `initialState` function in the Photon runtime will be called. Since `getTime` is a regular method call, Photon's runtime will inline the send semantics and specialize it for the number of arguments at `sc3`'s call site by storing a specialized function in `sc3`, equivalent to:

```
sc3 = function ($this) {
    return $this.get("getTime").call0($this);
};
```

Further calls will be made to this function rather than to `initialState`.

6 Performance

Currently there is no general purpose instrumentation framework that has been shown to work on a wide-array of web applications, across browsers, and at a reasonable performance cost. The task of porting to multiple browsers and supporting the fast evolution of web standards is beyond the capacity of a small research team, and we did not attempt it. The rest of this performance evaluation should be read in that light.

Nonetheless, our work on Photon has produced interesting performance results. When compared to the slowdowns observed on other systems, they suggest the approach helps reduce the perceivable latency on instrumented applications.

We identified interpreter-level performance as the target because from private communications with other researchers and anecdotal evidence from published work [11,10], this is what typically ends up being instrumented in practice, without any portability across browsers or browser versions. That level of performance is reported to be "barely noticeable on most sites" [11]. Our approach provides a similar performance while being portable.

Our evaluation shows that Photon is portable across many popular browser VMs and that it is faster than other published systems.

6.1 Setting

We chose CPU-bound benchmarks, which although not representative of typical web applications [10], represent the worst-case in terms of instrumentation overhead. For this reason we have mainly used the V8 benchmark suite version 7 in our performance evaluation. These benchmarks are self-checking to detect execution errors. We ran the benchmarks five times and took the average.

To investigate portability, we have used four different JS VMs in our experiments: three VMs based on JIT compilers and one VM based on an interpreter. The following web browsers were used:

- **Safari** version 6.0.2 (8536.26.17), which is based on the Nitro JS VM.
- **Chrome** version 25.0.1364.172, which is based on the V8 JS VM.
- **Firefox** version 20.0, which is based on the SpiderMonkey JS VM. Firefox
  was run with the JIT enabled, and also with the JIT disabled (which causes
  the SpiderMonkey interpreter to be used). To disable the JIT we have set the
  following Firefox javascript options to false, as suggested by the SpiderMonkey development team: `ion.content`, `methodjit.chrome`, `methodjit.content`,
  `typeinference`. Note that disabling SpiderMonkey's type inference actually
  accelerates the execution of all programs because the interpreter does not
  take advantage of the type information.

Chrome does not have an interpreter and recently, the Safari interpreter was
rewritten in an assembly language dialect for performance, making its modification for instrumentation more complicated. We therefore think that the only
remaining interpreter that is both simple and fast enough for instrumentation is
the Firefox interpreter.

To simplify the description of the results, we will conflate the name of the
web browser with that of its JS VM.

A computer with a 2.6 GHz Intel Core i7 processor and 16 GB 1600 MHz
DDR3 RAM and running OS X 10.8.2 is used in all the experiments.

The experiments can be run by visiting the corresponding links from the
project web page[6]. Individual results are reported as well as average value,
standard-deviation, and ratios between configurations.

6.2   Related systems

To put the performance results we obtained in context, we compared against
alternatives. Either they ran fewer of the V8 benchmarks than Photon, they
had a higher slowdown or both. The related work section compares them with
Photon in more details.

Js.js [13] is a JS port of the Firefox interpreter compiled using the Emscripten
C++ to JS compiler. This is a heavy-weight approach with a significant performance overhead and, presumably, would require a similar amount of effort to
instrument as if the Firefox interpreter was instrumented. The EarleyBoyer and
Splay benchmarks ran out of memory, RayTrace crashed the version of Chrome
we were using and RegExp would trigger a malloc error in Js.js. NavierStokes
would take more than 10 minutes to complete and the other benchmarks would
show slowdowns between 5243× and greater than 18515×.

Jalangi [12] is a record-replay and dynamic analysis framework for JavaScript.
We independently tested their system using V8 benchmarks using the precon-
figured virtual machine[7] they provide on their website and found their system

---

[6] http://elavoie.github.io/photon-js/

[7] On OS X 10.8.5, on an 1.8GHz Intel Core i7 with 4 GB of RAM, with the virtual
image running LUbuntu 13.04 with 2GB of RAM and Jalangi commit 5f6d538d9e....
The virtualization was found to introduce a 15% slowdown compared to running the
V8 benchmarks on the host.

to introduce slowdowns between 384× and 2520× during recording, except for RegExp (15×) and Splay (29×). We also verified that on some of the interactive application they used for testing, the slowdown was noticeable but not to the point of completely hindering the interaction. The main take away is that although some of the slowdowns on CPU-bound benchmarks may seem impressive, the additional latency is acceptable in practice.

AspectScript [14] is similar to Photon but uses the aspect formalism as an interface for designing dynamic analyses. We executed the latest version of AspectScript against the V8 benchmarks, and found it to be between 10× and 454× slower than Photon on Safari. Additionally, only four of the benchmarks ran without errors.

JSProbes [3] and work by Lerner et al. [8] modified the host VM but both are now incompatible with current browser VMs.

Narcissus could run none of the V8 benchmarks and was two orders of magnitude slower than Photon on a micro-benchmark stressing the function calls.

In the next sections, we investigate the performance behaviour of Photon.

6.3   Comparison with Interpreter Instrumentation

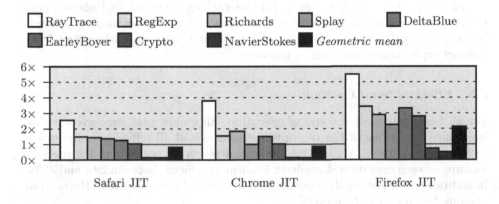

Fig. 4. Relative performance of Photon on various VMs compared to the Firefox interpreter

Figure 4 gives for each benchmark and JIT VM the execution speed ratio between Photon with no instrumentation and the Firefox interpreter. Therefore, on average, Photon without instrumentation runs the benchmarks faster on Safari JIT (by 19%) and Chrome JIT (by 14%) than when they are run directly on the Firefox interpreter. The execution speed with Photon is consistently faster over all JIT VMs for Crypto and NavierStokes which run about 7× faster with Photon on Safari JIT and Chrome JIT. The major increase in performance can be attributed to a substantial proportion of the time spent in features that are not instrumented by Photon, either native libraries or language features other than object operations and function calls. The worst case for all JIT VMs occurs for RayTrace, which is 2.5× to 5.5× slower when executed with Photon. This shows that the performance of Photon running on a JIT VM is roughly in the same ballpark as an interpreter.

6.4   Inherent Overhead Compared to JIT Compilation

Figure 5 shows the slowdown caused by Photon on each VM relative to executing the program without Photon on the same VM. These results mostly show that (1) selective program transformation can benefit from the native performance of features that are not instrumented, that (2) performance is not portable across browsers, given the significant variability in performance results observed on the same benchmarks between browsers, and (3) the interpreter is much less affected by program transformation than JITs are, which suggests that the peformance of JITs is highly dependent on the nature of the code.

Newer experiments[8] show the maximum memory usage ratios to be between 1.25× and 4.0× with EarleyBoyer(27.7/7.2MB) and Splay(164/92.5MB) being the relative and absolute worst. The absolute memory usage suggests Photon is practical on current desktop and laptop machines.

They also show that the host VM inline caching is crucial for Photon's performance and execution. Disabling inline caches on Chrome[9] slows down Photon by an additional factor between 9× and 156× and prevents EarleyBoyer from completing because it runs out of memory.

6.5   Effect of Send Caching

For all benchmarks, at the end of execution, all caches that were executed at least once are in one of the two optimized cases and all reified operations are in a memoized state. Deactivating the optimization by performing the method lookups on each operation slows down Photon by a factor between 29× and 320× in addition to the previously reported slowdowns, and prevents EarleyBoyer from running because of a stack overflow.

6.6   Performance with Instrumentation

We have evaluated the performance of Photon with an instrumentation that counts the number of run-time occurrences of the following object representation operations: property read, write and deletion. We chose this particular instrumentation because it is simple, it covers frequently used object model operations and it was actually used to gather information about JS (it can be used to reproduce the object read, write and deletion proportion figure from [10]).

---

[8] On OS X 10.8.5, on an 1.8GHz Intel Core i7 with 4 GB of RAM running Chrome version (33.0.1750.117), because the old setup was not available anymore.

[9] By starting it with the –js-flags="–nouse_ic" option.

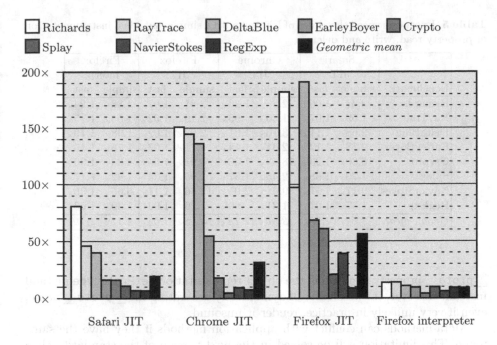

Fig. 5. Inherent overhead (factor slowdown) of Photon on various VMs

Two implementations of this instrumentation were used; a simple (~16 lines of code) and a fast version (~100 lines of code)[10]. The simple version does not exploit memoization and corresponds to the straightforward implementation: incrementing a counter and calling the corresponding object representation operation. The fast version uses the memoization protocol to inline the counter incrementations inside the optimized version of the object operations.

The execution speed slowdown of Photon with each version of the instrumentation for each JS VM is given in Table 5. This means that on Safari JIT and Chrome JIT, on average, the benchmarks run with the fast version of the instrumentation on Photon essentially at the same speed as the uninstrumented original benchmarks directly on the Firefox interpreter, while in many cases the simple version is sufficient to obtain a reasonable performance.

7   Limitations

Due to our implementation of the prototype chain, accessing the __proto__ property leaks the internal representation. This can be solved at a substantial performance cost by testing every property access. Alternatively, it can be mitigated with no run-time penalty by detecting, at compile-time, accesses to the

---

[10] https://github.com/elavoie/photon-js/tree/ecoop2014/
    instrumentations

Table 5. Execution speed slowdown of Photon with a simple and a fast instrumentation of property read, write and delete

Benchmark	Safari JIT simple	fast	Chrome JIT simple	fast	Firefox JIT simple	fast	Firefox interp. simple	fast
Richards	2.31×	1.06×	2.38×	1.26×	2.81×	1.07×	1.88×	1.24×
RayTrace	1.59×	1.07×	1.30×	.93×	2.19×	1.02×	1.55×	1.15×
DeltaBlue	2.68×	1.11×	3.16×	1.01×	2.03×	1.02×	1.98×	1.19×
EarleyBoyer	2.18×	1.12×	2.31×	1.14×	2.71×	1.07×	1.78×	1.15×
Crypto	16.80×	1.23×	18.53×	1.00×	6.91×	1.00×	4.33×	1.30×
Splay	1.70×	1.68×	2.45×	1.37×	1.96×	1.05×	1.42×	1.17×
NavierStokes	29.17×	1.07×	39.41×	2.05×	11.86×	1.11×	5.65×	1.36×
RegExp	1.37×	1.01×	1.31×	.99×	1.29×	1.02×	1.30×	1.03×
Geom. mean	*3.54×*	*1.15×*	*3.90×*	*1.18×*	*3.03×*	*1.04×*	*2.15×*	*1.19×*

__proto__ property and calling the object representation getPrototype method instead. However, the possibility of dynamically generating the __proto__ name, even if very unlikely in practice, render it unsound.

Meta-methods can conflict with application methods if they have the same name. This limitation will be solved in the next version of the standard, when unforgeable names will be available in user space. Until then, we can rely on unlikely names to minimize possible conflicts with existing code.

Setting the __proto__ property throws an exception. This might be fixed by invalidating all caches should the prototype of an object change. A more sophisticated mechanism could be devised if the operation is frequent.

Operations on *null* or *undefined* might throw a different exception because they might be used as base objects for an object representation method. The exception will say that the object representation is missing instead of the property. This problem only happens for incorrect programs because otherwise an exception would still interrupt it. We don't think it is worth handling.

Functions passed to the standard library are wrapped to remove the extra arguments introduced by our compilation strategy. However, the wrappers do not perform message sends, therefore these calls are invisible to an instrumentation.

Photon objects cannot be manipulated outside of Photon, the execution environment (e.g. DOM) needs to be virtualized. For the DOM, Andreas Gal's implementation in JavaScript seems a good starting point[11].

8   Related Work

The layering of a metacircular implementation implementing reflection techniques with an object-oriented approach was beautifully explained in "The Art of the Metaobject Protocol" [7]. This paper revisited those ideas while considering the performance behavior of modern JS VMs.

---

[11] https://github.com/andreasgal/dom.js

Sandboxing frameworks for JS, such as Google Caja [1], BrowserShield [9] and ADSafe [2] guarantee that guest JS code cannot modify the host JS environment outside of a permitted policy. We focus here on Google Caja as a representative candidate. The Caja sandbox provides a different global object to the guest code and performs a source-to-source translation to ensure that all operations on host objects are mediated by proxies enforcing a user-defined security policy. Photon also provide a different global object for the purpose of simplifying reasoning about instrumentations while providing an acceptable level of performance. Our sandboxing strategy does not need to be as stringent, therefore we deem acceptable the possibility of leaking the native objects by accessing the `__proto__` property.

JSBench [11] performs instrumentation of object operations and function calls for recording execution traces of web applications that can be replayed as stand-alone benchmarks. JSBench instrumentation is specially tailored to the task of recording benchmarks while Photon aims to be a general framework.

The idea of using aspect-oriented programming for profiling tasks has been explored in the past, although some limitations of the model have been identified (e.g., [4]). AspectScript [14] has similar aims as Photon, namely providing for JS a general interface for dynamic instrumentation of object operations and function calls. It uses a source-to-source translation scheme with a single *reifier* primitive which is analogous to our *message-sending* primitive. Compared to our instrumentation interface, they use the dynamic weaving of aspect formalism instead of our "operations as methods" approach. Because of the use of the aspects formalism, their approach provides better encapsulation of the instrumentation strategy at the expense of flexibility and performance.

Js.js [13] is a JS port of the Firefox interpreter compiled using the Emscriptem C++ to JS compiler. It is intended for sandboxing web applications. The resulting JS interpreter then runs in the browser on top of an existing VM. Photon avoids reimplementing features other than object operations and function calls. The resulting implementation is both faster and simpler to instrument.

Other approaches target the host VM for efficiency reasons. JSProbes [3] is a series of patches to the Firefox interpreter that allow instrumentations to be written in JS and target pre-defined probe points, such as object creation, function calls and implementation events such as garbage collector start and stop events. JSProbes provides much of the same properties as Photon at a much lower execution overhead and with additional information about implementation events that are inaccessible to Photon. At the time of writing, maintenance of JSProbes has stopped, making the approach unavailable in practice. In a different setting, Lerner et al. explored the requirement for implementing aspect support in an experimental JIT-compiler [8]. They reported a simpler and more efficient implementation than other aspect-oriented approaches. Their work was intended to inform possible ways to open native implementations to instrumentation with an aspect formalism. So far, no production VM implements aspects, which makes this approach unavailable in practice. Photon does not require modifications to the host VM. It therefore does not add to the maintenance cost of production VMs to be usable in practice.

Jalangi [12] is a record-replay and dynamic analysis framework for JavaScript. It performs an ahead-of-time (static) source-to-source translation of the program to replace instrumented operations with function calls. The instrumented program is executed to record a trace of execution, which is then used to perform dynamic analyses. Being static, their translation strategy cannot handle the dynamic aliasing of `eval` or `Object.create`. Photon however, by virtualizing the execution environment, provides wrapper around these methods, which supports dynamic aliasing.

Narcissus JS in JS interpreter implementation by Mozilla that reifies all the language operations of the language. However, compared to Photon, Narcissus is much slower and none of the V8 benchmarks could be executed.

9   Conclusion and Future Work

Run-time monitoring of JS applications is crucial to obtain empirical data about current web applications, to improve their efficiency and improve VM technologies. Unfortunately, there is no general purpose instrumentation framework that has been shown to work on a wide-array of web applications, across browsers, and at a reasonable performance cost. Existing approaches have either modified browser VMs at the expense of portability, or relied on source-to-source transformations that are complex to develop and still incur a significant overhead.

In this paper, we explored the performance aspects of *virtual machine layering*, in which a portable implementation of a JS implementation exposes implementation-level operations that can be redefined at run time to monitor the application execution. We have shown that by a selective dynamic translation of source elements, combined with run-time feedback to optimize the reified operations, we could obtain significantly better performance than existing approaches when exposing object operations and function calls to the point where the approach can be competitive with the instrumentation of a browser interpreter while being portable across VM implementations.

The major challenge remaining, which prevents the application of the approach in practice, is the full and efficient virtualization of the execution environment, whether it is the browser libraries such as the Document Object Model (DOM) or the extensions of the NodeJS framework. One requirement is the possibility of full intercession of all the code loaded. Work is under way to extend Debugger API in Firefox based on the work done at Mozilla by one of the authors to support it. The other requirement is the proper wrapping of all the environment libraries, which is a significant engineering effort but could be reusable for different implementation strategies of virtual machine layering and instrumentation APIs. This could be tackled as a community effort.

Acknowledgement. This work was supported in part by the Natural Sciences and Engineering Research Council of Canada (NSERC), the Fonds Québécois de la Recherche surla Nature et les Technologies (FQRNT) and Mozilla Corporation.

References

1. Google Caja (December 2012), http://code.google.com/p/google-caja/
2. ADSafe (March 2013), http://www.adsafe.org/
3. JSProbes (March 2013), http://brrian.tumblr.com/search/jsprobes
4. Binder, W., Ansaloni, D., Villazón, A., Moret, P.: Flexible and efficient profiling with aspect-oriented programming. Concurrency and Computation: Practice and Experience 23(15), 1749–1773 (2011)
5. Bracha, G., Ungar, D.: Mirrors: design principles for meta-level facilities of object-oriented programming languages. In: Proceedings of the 2004 ACM SIGPLAN Conference on Object-Oriented Programming, Systems, Languages, and Applications, pp. 331–344. ACM, New York (2004)
6. Heidegger, P., Bieniusa, A., Thiemann, P.: Access permission contracts for scripting languages. In: Proceedings of the 39th Annual ACM SIGPLAN-SIGACT Symposium on Principles of Programming Languages, POPL 2012, pp. 111–122. ACM, New York (2012)
7. Kiczales, G., Rivieres, J.D.: The Art of the Metaobject Protocol. MIT Press, Cambridge (1991)
8. Lerner, B.S., Venter, H., Grossman, D.: Supporting dynamic, third-party code customizations in JavaScript using aspects. In: Proceedings of the ACM International Conference on Object Oriented Programming Systems Languages and Applications, OOPSLA 2010, pp. 361–376. ACM, New York (2010)
9. Reis, C., Dunagan, J., Wang, H.J., Dubrovsky, O., Esmeir, S.: BrowserShield: Vulnerability-driven filtering of dynamic HTML. ACM Trans. Web 1(3) (September 2007)
10. Richards, G., Lebresne, S., Burg, B., Vitek, J.: An analysis of the dynamic behavior of JavaScript programs. In: Proceedings of the 2010 ACM SIGPLAN Conference on Programming Language Design and Implementation, pp. 1–12. ACM (2010)
11. Richards, G., Gal, A., Eich, B., Vitek, J.: Automated construction of JavaScript benchmarks. In: Proceedings of the 2011 ACM International Conference on Object Oriented Programming Systems Languages and Applications, OOPSLA 2011, pp. 677–694. ACM, New York (2011)
12. Sen, K., Kalasapur, S., Brutch, T., Gibbs, S.: Jalangi: A selective record-replay and dynamic analysis framework for javascript. In: Proceedings of the 2013 9th Joint Meeting on Foundations of Software Engineering, ESEC/FSE 2013, pp. 488–498. ACM, New York (2013),
    http://doi.acm.org/http://dx.doi.org/10.1145/2491411.2491447
13. Terrace, J., Beard, S.R., Katta, N.P.K.: JavaScript in JavaScript (js.js): sandboxing third-party scripts. In: Proceedings of the 3rd USENIX Conference on Web Application Development, WebApps 2012, p. 9. USENIX Association, Berkeley (2012)
14. Toledo, R., Leger, P., Tanter, E.: AspectScript: expressive aspects for the web. In: Proceedings of the 9th International Conference on Aspect-Oriented Software Development, AOSD 2010, pp. 13–24. ACM, New York (2010)

A   Artifact Description

Authors of the artifact. Erick Lavoie

Summary. The artifact comprises both Photon, the layered virtual machine used for dynamic program analysis described in the previous paper, and the performance experiments used to obtain the performance figures. The current implementation of Photon initially performs a source-to-source translation of JavaScript code, while running over NodeJS. The resulting code then runs in the browser in a virtualized environment that abstracts the standard libraries and also includes Photon, for correct translation of dynamically generated code. The experiments come packaged as ready-to-run web pages for easy comparison of performance results with newer configurations of browser and machines.

Content. The artifact package includes:

– a set of experiments packaged as ready-to-run web pages;
– the Photon system;
– detailed instructions for using the artifact and running the experiments, provided as an `index.html` file.

To simplify repeatability of our experiments, we provide a VirtualBox disk image containing a Ubuntu Linux image fully configured for testing Photon.

Getting the artifact. The artifact endorsed by the Artifact Evaluation Committee is available free of charge as supplementary material of this paper on SpringerLink. The latest version of Photon code is available on GitHub at https://github.com/elavoie/photon-js and a copy of the `index.html` page, including all the performance experiments, is available at the corresponding GitHub page http://elavoie.github.io/photon-js/.

Tested platforms. The artifact is known to work on any platform running Oracle VirtualBox version 4 (https://www.virtualbox.org/) with at least 5 GB or free space on disk and at least 1 GB of free space in RAM.

License. MIT Licence

MD5 sum of the artifact. 7d38dddb53c801fff254123f45074144

Size of the artifact. 1.03 GB

An Executable Formal Semantics of PHP

Daniele Filaretti and Sergio Maffeis

Department of Computing, Imperial College London, London, United Kingdom (UK)
{d.filaretti11,sergio.maffeis}@imperial.ac.uk

Abstract. PHP is among the most used languages for server-side scripting. Although substantial effort has been spent on the problem of automatically analysing PHP code, vulnerabilities remain pervasive in web applications, and analysis tools do not provide any formal guarantees of soundness or coverage. This is partly due to the lack of a precise specification of the language, which is highly dynamic and often exhibits subtle behaviour.

We present the first formal semantics for a substantial core of PHP, based on the official documentation and experiments with the Zend reference implementation. Our semantics is executable, and is validated by testing it against the Zend test suite. We define the semantics of PHP in a term-rewriting framework which supports LTL model checking and symbolic execution. As a demonstration, we extend LTL with predicates for the verification of PHP programs, and analyse two common PHP functions.

1 Introduction

PHP is one of the most popular languages for server-side scripting, used by amateur web developers as well as billion-dollar companies such as Google, Facebook and Yahoo!. It is used for developing complex programs, enabling all sort of sensitive activities such as online banking, social networking, and cloud computing. Despite the flexibility and ease of use of PHP, its dynamic features (shared by similar scripting languages) make it easy to introduce errors in programs, potentially opening security holes leading to the leakage of sensitive data and other forms of compromise.

Many web applications have reached a level of complexity for which testing, code reviews and human inspection are no longer sufficient quality-assurance guarantees. Tools that employ static analysis techniques [9,34,20] are needed in order explore all possible execution paths through an application, and guarantee the absence of undesirable behaviours. However, due to classic computability results, this goal can be accomplished only by applying a certain degree of abstraction, with consequent loss of precision (i.e. introducing false positives). To make sure that an analysis captures the properties of interest, and to navigate the trade-offs between efficiency and precision, it is necessary to base the design and, we add, the development, of static analysis tools on a firm understanding of the language to be analysed.

R. Jones (Ed.): ECOOP 2014, LNCS 8586, pp. 567–592, 2014.
© Springer-Verlag Berlin Heidelberg 2014

The main contribution of this paper is to present KPHP, the first formal (and executable) semantics of PHP, which can serve as a basis to define program analyses and semantics-based verification tools (Section 3).

Some programming languages, such as Standard ML [30], already come with a formal specification. Others, such as C [19] and JavaScript [18] are specified in English prose with varying degrees of rigour and precision, and have recently been formalised [32,25,3,15,11,4]. PHP is only implicitly defined by its *de facto* reference implementation (the Zend Engine [14]), and the (informal) PHP reference manual [13]. Due to the lack of a document providing a precise specification of PHP, defining its formal semantics is particularly challenging. We have to rely on the approximate information available online, and a substantial amount of testing against the reference language implementation. We do not to base our semantics on the source code of the Zend Engine in order to avoid bias towards inessential implementation choices. In defining our semantics, we identify several cases where the behaviour of PHP is complicated and unexpected. Some of these examples are known to PHP programmers, and have contributed to driving our design. Other examples are new, and were discovered by us as a consequence of semantic modelling (Section 2). Although useful to get introduced to each language construct, the online PHP language reference [13] is not precise enough to serve as a basis for a formal semantics. Quite the opposite, we hope that our formal semantics may serve as a basis to create a precise, English prose specification of PHP in the style of the ECMA specification of JavaScript [18].

We write our semantics in K [39,37], a framework for defining programming languages on top of the Maude [8] term-rewriting tool. A language semantics as expressed in K has a rigorous meaning as a term rewriting system, and is suitable for formal reasoning and automated proofs. Moreover, it is directly executable, enabling a tight design-test loop which is crucial for the test-driven semantics development needed in the case of PHP. Extensive testing using official test suites is becoming "best practice" to validate executable semantics of programming languages [15,11,4]. We validate KPHP by automated testing against the Zend PHP test suite [40] (Section 4), and we design additional PHP tests in order to cover all of the semantic rules, including those not exercised by [40].

The main goal of our semantics is to provide a formal model of PHP upon which semantics-based verification tools (such as abstract interpreters, type systems and taint-checkers) can be built. Developing such tools goes beyond the scope of this paper. However, we are able to begin demonstrating the practical relevance of KPHP by using it for program verification. In particular, the K framework exposes Maude's explicit-state Linear Temporal Logic (LTL) model checking to the semantics [11], and supports symbolic execution for any language definition [1]. We define an extension of LTL with predicates to express interesting temporal properties of PHP programs, and verify two representative PHP functions from phpMyAdmin [33] and the PHP documentation [10] (Section 5).

An extended version of this paper, together with the latest version of the semantics, and all the KPHP development (including KPHP interpreter, tests and verification examples) is available on http://phpsemantics.org.

2 A PHP Primer

In this Section, we give a brief introduction to the PHP language and its usage, and present examples of some challenging and surprising features of the language. [1] Some of these examples are known to PHP programmers, and have contributed to driving the design of our semantics. Others are new, and were discovered by us, as a consequence of semantic modelling.

Hello World Wide Web. PHP scripts are typically run by web servers. Typing a URL such as `http://example.com/hello.php?name=xyz` in a browser may cause the responding server to invoke PHP on the file `hello.php` listed below:

```
<? echo "<HTML><Body>Hello_".$_GET["name"]."!</Body></HTML>"; ?>
```

This minimal example illustrates the typical behaviour of a PHP script. It receives inputs from the web and it responds by generating an HTML page depending on such inputs. The predefined `$_GET` array is in fact populated from the parameters of the HTTP request, and `echo` is a simple output command that in shell mode prints to standard output but that in server mode generates the body of the HTTP response message. In this paper, we focus on PHP as a programming language, and leave the important topic of formalisation of the server execution model to future work.

2.1 PHP: A Closer Look

We now describe some features of the core PHP language which may be unfamiliar to programmers used to different languages, challenging to represent in an operational semantics, or both.

Aliasing and References. PHP supports variable aliasing via the *assignment by reference* construct. This mechanism provides a means of accessing the same variable content by different names.

```
$x = 0;
$y = &$x;    // $x and $y are now aliased
$y = "Hello!";
echo $x;     // prints "Hello!"
```

Aliasing can be useful for example to write functions that operate on parameters containing large data structures, avoiding the overhead of copying the data structure inside the local scope of the function. On the other hand, aliasing is notoriously difficult to analyse statically. PHP references are different from pointers (as in C) in that neither address-arithmetic nor access to arbitrary memory is allowed. For example, the following code would be rejected:

```
$x = (&$x + 1); // causes a parse error
```

---

[1] All the examples are reproducible by pasting the code in the PHP Zend Interpreter (version 5.3.26 or similar) available in most OSX or Linux distributions. The symbol > precedes the shell output. For readability, here we re-format the output of `var_dump`.

Braced and Variable Variables. The official PHP documentation gives the following description for *variable variables*: "A variable variable takes the value of a variable and treats that as the name of a variable". Here is an example:

```
$x = "y";
$y = "Hello!";
echo $$x;          // prints "Hello!"
```

Hence, in a PHP semantics, variable names should be modelled as a set of string-indexed constructors, rather than as a set of unforgeable identifiers.

Variable variables are useful for example to simulate higher-order behaviour by passing functions *by name*. On the other hand, they hinder static analyses, because it is not possible in general to determine statically the set of variables used by a PHP script. A similar argument applies to braced variables, a syntax to turn the result of an arbitrary expression into an identifier, as for example in

```
${"x"} = "y";        // defines variable $x
$z -> {"x".$x};      // access field xy of object $z
```

Type Juggling. Each PHP value has a type (boolean, integer,...). Automatic type conversions are performed when operators are passed operands of the incorrect type. For example, non-empty strings are translated to the boolean true, and booleans true and false are converted respectively to the integers 1 and 0.

```
if ("false") echo true + false;  else echo "false"; // prints "1"
```

Some type conversions need to be defined explicitly. For example, an object can be converted to a string by defining the *magic method* __toString. If such method is undefined, the attempted conversion triggers an exception.

Type juggling makes it easier to write code that does not get stuck, but also increases the probability that such code will not behave as expected. For example, although the conversion of objects to numbers is undefined according to the online documentation, the Zend engine converts objects to the integer 1 (our semantics mimics this behaviour, and issues an additional warning).

Arrays. Arrays in PHP are essentially *ordered* maps from integer or string *keys* to language values. If a value of a different type is given as a key, type juggling will try to convert it to an integer.

```
$x = array("foo" => "bar",4.5 => "baz");
```

The array $x above maps "foo" to "bar" and 4 to "baz". Note how the float value 4.5 was automatically converted to the integer value 4.[2] Array elements can be accessed via standard square-bracket notation, and it is also possible to assign an element to an array without specifying a key.

```
$x[] = "default"      // use default key 5
$echo x[5]        // prints "default"
```

---

[2] Although we model array key conversions in our semantics, we do not give full details about them here. The interested reader can try evaluating this: `$x = array( 1=>"foo", "2"=>"wow", 3.5=>"doh", "4.5"=>"omg", NULL=>"lol");`.

In this case, a default key (the greatest integer key already defined, plus one) is used. Arrays contain an internal pointer to the *current* element (the first by default), which can be manipulated using functions current next, each and reset:

```
echo current($x);    // prints "bar"
next($x);            // advances the pointer
echo current($x);    // prints "baz"
```

Objects. From a semantic standpoint, PHP objects can be seen as string-indexed arrays with additional visibility attributes (public, protected or static), and with methods inherited by their defining class. Just like arrays, (stdClass) objects can be initialised "on the fly":

```
$obj -> x = 0;
var_dump($obj);
> object(stdClass)#1 (1) { ["x"]=> int(0) }
```

Access to an array element is always granted, whereas access to an object property is regulated by the visibility attribute, and depends on the context whence the property is being accessed. Inheritance is class-based. Consider the following example from the Zend test suite [40]:

```
class par {                        class chld extends par {
  private $id = "foo";               public $id = "bar";
  function displayMe() {             public function displayHim() {
    echo $this -> id; }}               parent::displayMe(); }}

$obj = new chld();
$obj -> displayHim();    // prints "foo"
```

Crucially, this code returns "foo" because $id is declared private in the superclass par. If instead par defined $id as public, the code would return "bar". In Section 3.2, we shall see how we capture this subtlety in our semantics by indexing the arrays of object fields by *key-visibility* pairs. A notable difference between objects and arrays is that objects are copied by reference whereas arrays are copied by value. Most existing analysis tools for PHP do not support objects, because their semantics is not easy to analyze.

2.2 PHP: Digging Deeper

We now look more in depth, to uncover difficult "corners" of PHP. While the first example below on array copy is a well-known PHP issue [41], the others are our original observations, discovered while developing the relevant semantics rules. Although some PHP experts may be aware of these cases, they are not part of the mainstream knowledge about PHP, and are hence worth discussing.

Array Copy Semantics. In PHP arrays are copied by value. For example, the code below copies each element of the array stored in $x into a fresh array to be stored in $y, and then updates the first element of $x, without affecting $y:

```php
$x = array(1, 2, 3);
$y = $x;
$x[0] = "updated";
echo $y[0];            // prints 1
```

Yet, in PHP it is possible to alias a variable to a particular array element. If such sharing happens *before* the array copy, its semantics become quit subtle. Consider the following code:

```php
$x = array(1, 2, 3);
$temp = &$x[1];        // we introduce sharing
$y = $x;               // and assign normally
$x[0] = "regular";     // update a regular element
$x[1] = "shared";      // update the shared element
```

```
var_dump($x);                      var_dump($y);
> array(3) {                       > array(3) {
   [0]=> string(7) "regular"          [0]=> int(1)
   [1]=> &string(6) "shared"          [1]=> &string(6) "shared"
   [2]=> int(3) }                     [2]=> int(3) }
```

These results show that array $x is copied element by element in $y, so that the assignment to $x[0] affects only $x, *except* for the aliased element $x[1], which is now shared with $y, which therefore also sees the side effects of the second assignment. Accordingly, our semantics copies the shared elements of the array by reference, and the non-shared elements by value. If a non-shared element is an array itself, the process continues recursively. Matters get even more complicated when taking into account the *copy-on-write* semantics of PHP arrays, as shown by Tozawa *et al.* [41], who first identified this problem and pointed out inconsistencies in the Zend implementation.

Global Variables as Array Properties. In PHP, *global* variables are visible at the top level, and can be imported in functions explicitly using the `global $x;` command. *Superglobals* are special variables directly accessible inside any scope that does not shadow them. Shadowing occurs for example when a function defines a parameter or a local variable with the same name as the superglobal. The superglobal variable `$GLOBALS` points to an array whose properties are the global variables, so that effectively these can be manipulated with the dual syntax of variables or object properties. For example,

```php
$GLOBALS["x"] = 42;
echo $x;               // prints 42
```

Because of this ambivalence of global variables, in the semantics it is natural to model scopes as heap-allocated arrays, rather than as frames of a stack independent from the heap. This is analogous to what happens in JavaScript semantics [25,4], where global variables are the properties of the global object, and scopes are heap-allocated objects. Maffeis *et al.* [27,26] show that confusing variables (which can usually be identified statically) with object properties (which can be computed at run-time) complicates security analyses for JavaScript. The case for PHP is even more desperate, as "thanks" to variable variables even variables on their own cannot be determined statically.

Evaluation Order. In C, the evaluation order of expressions is undefined. In most languages, it follows a left-to-right order. Let us see what happens in PHP.

```
$a = array("one");                  $a = array("one");
$c = $a[0].($a[0] = "two");         $c = ($a[0] = "two").$a[0];
echo $c; // prints "onetwo"         echo $c; // prints "twotwo"
```

This example suggests that the operands of the string concatenation operator "." are indeed evaluated left-to-right. That it should be so easy! Let us see what happens if the operands are simple variables instead of array elements:

```
$a = "one";                         $a = "one";
$c = $a.($a = "two");               $c = ($a = "two").$a;
echo $c; // prints "twotwo"         echo $c; // prints "twotwo"
```

Both print "twotwo", contradicting our hypothesis: the example on the left suggests that expressions are evaluated right-to-left. Through the lenses of our formal semantics, we can explain this behaviour: the arguments to binary operators are indeed evaluated left-to-right, but while evaluating array elements (or object properties) yields the corresponding value, evaluating simple variables yields a pointer that is dereferenced only when the value is effectively needed. In this case, the value of $a to the left of the string concatenation is read only after the assignment to the right has taken place.

Object and Array Iteration. Scripting languages such as JavaScript and PHP provide constructs to iterate over all the properties of an object. Such constructs can be tricky to implement, and hard to model in a formal semantics. For example, the JavaScript formalisation of [4] does not model the for-in loop, as the corresponding ECMA5 standard is inconsistent when it comes to describe object updates within the loop. We discovered that the corresponding foreach statement in PHP is also very challenging, due to the presence of aliasing and the behaviour of the explicit current pointer.

Consider this example, where we iterate twice through the fields of array $a:

```
$a = array('a', 'b', 'c');
foreach ($a as &$v) {};        // aliasing on $v
foreach ($a as $v) {};
```

Since there is no code inside the bodies of the two loops, we could expect the array to remain unchanged. However, a call to var_dump($a) shows that that is not the case:

```
array(3) { [0]=> string(1)  "a"
           [1]=> string(1)  "b"
           [2]=> string(1)  "b" }
```

This is what happens: variable $v, introduced by the first foreach, has global visibility; at the end of the first foreach, $v and $a[2] are aliased; at every

iteration of the second foreach, a simple assignment $v = $a[...] is made, storing
the current array element in $v, and hence in $a[2].

There is even worse. Consider the code below: it initialises two objects, creates
an aliasing to $obj1 and iterates on its fields. When the current element is 1 (at
the first loop iteration), it replaces the object being iterated upon.

```
$obj1 -> a = 1; $obj1 -> b = 2;
$obj2 -> a = 3; $obj2 -> b = 4;
$ref = &$obj1;        // aliasing on $obj1
foreach ($obj1 as $v){ echo "$v,"; if ($v === 1) $obj1=$obj2; };
if ($obj1 === $obj2) echo "true";
```

This code outputs 1,3,4,true: the iterator is swapped, and iteration continues
on the second object. But if we remove the aliasing on $obj1 by commenting out
the 3rd line, then the output surprisingly becomes 1,2,true, where the update
to $obj1 is visible only at the end of the loop.

In absence of aliasing, the foreach on arrays is analogous. In presence of aliasing instead foreach behaves differently. Consider the code below:

```
$a1 = array(1,2); $a2 = array(3,4);
$ref = &$a1;          // aliasing on $a1
foreach ($a1 as $v){ echo "$v,"; if ($v === $a1[0]) $a1=$a2; };
```

This code enters an infinite loop outputting 1,3,3,3,3.... Since PHP arrays
are copied by value (as opposed to objects which are copied by reference), the
assignment $a1 = $a2 copies the whole data structure associated to $a2, including
its current pointer, which is used to perform the iteration, causing the infinite
loop (see Section 3.3 for more details on array assignment).

To be precise, during array copy, the original current pointer is copied to the
new array only if it points to a valid element. If instead the original current is
overflown, the current pointer of the new copy is reset:

```
$x = array(0,1);      // initialise $x
next($x); $y = $x;    // increment current & copy array
echo current($y);     // prints 1 (current was copied)
next($x); $z = $x;    // overflow current & copy array
echo current($z);     // (1) prints 0 (current was reset)
echo current($x);     // (2) prints "" (current is overflown)
```

Once again, we find some erratic behaviour of PHP: if we comment out the
output line marked with (1) above, the current of $x is reset instead, and line
(2) prints 0. We consider this to be a bug in the current version of PHP,[3] and
our semantics prints "" for line (2) in both cases (see Section 3.3).

3   𝕂PHP

In this Section, we describe our formalisation of the operational semantics of
PHP. Our semantics is vast (more that 800 rules), so we can only provide a

---

[3] This behaviour is related to PHP Bug 16227, which was resolved in PHP 4.4.1 and
was reintroduced since PHP 5.2.4.

roadmap through it, selectively explaining some of the crucial features, and referring the reader to http://phpsemantics.org for the gory details.

3.1   Preliminaries: The $\mathbb{K}$ Framework

We write our semantics in $\mathbb{K}$ [39,37], a framework for defining programming language semantics on top of the Maude [8] term-rewriting tool. We chose $\mathbb{K}$ for three main reasons: (i) a semantics in $\mathbb{K}$ has a rigorous meaning as a term rewriting system, supporting fully formal proofs; (ii) a semantics in $\mathbb{K}$ is directly executable, enabling a tight design/test loop; (iii) once a semantics is defined, the $\mathbb{K}$-Maude toolchain provides automatic support for model checking and symbolic execution of programs.

In order to model a language in $\mathbb{K}$, the first thing to be defined is a *configuration*. Intuitively, configurations specify the structure of the *abstract machine* on which programs written in the language will be run, and are represented as labeled, possibly nested multisets, called *cells*. Cells contain pieces of the program state, such as the program to be evaluated, the heap, and function and class definitions. A $\mathbb{K}$ semantic rule for assigning a value to a variable in a simple imperative language looks like this:

$$\left\langle \frac{X = V}{\cdot} \ ... \right\rangle_k \ \left\langle ... \ X \mapsto N \ ... \right\rangle_{env} \ \left\langle ... \ N \mapsto \frac{\_}{V} \ ... \right\rangle_{store}$$

In this simple case, the configuration has three cells, k, env and store. The k cell, by convention, always represents a list of computations waiting to be performed, where the left-most element is a local rewriting rule stating that, after execution, command X=V should be removed from the stack ("." is the empty list or set). The rest of the program is denoted by the *don't care* notation "..." for lists. The env cell maps variables to locations, and it is used to find the address of X via pattern matching. Finally, the store cell maps locations to values. The rule above says that if location N can be found, its content is overwritten by V ("_" matches any term). $\mathbb{K}$ rules can be quite compact and modular, as they only need to mention the cells relevant to the rule at hand. If the only cell needed by a rule is k, it can be omitted. For example we can write directly $\frac{X = V}{\cdot}$ instead of $\langle \frac{X = V}{\cdot} \ ... \rangle_k$.

To control the evaluation order of sub-expressions, rules can be annotated with *strictness* and *context* information. For example, one can write

```
syntax Stmt ::= Id "=" Exp [strict(2)]
```

meaning that Exp (meta-variable 2 of the production) is meant to be evaluated before the assignment takes place. Hence, Exp is placed at the front of the execution list in the k cell, as in $\langle Exp \curvearrowright Id = \square \ \cdots \rangle_k$, where $\curvearrowright$ denotes the sequential composition of tasks to be performed, and $\square$ is a place holder that will be replaced by the result of evaluating Exp. Further details of the $\mathbb{K}$ framework will become apparent as we describe our semantics.

3.2 KPHP Overview

Parsing. For parsing, we use the PHP grammar from PHP-front, a package for generating, analysing and transforming PHP code used by the PHP-sat [7] project. The grammar is in the *SDF* [17] format, which can be passed to the sdf-2-kast tool [6], which generates an abstract syntax tree for K.

Values. PHP supports three categories of data types: *scalar*, *compound* and *special*. Scalar types are the boolean, integer, float and string types, compound types are the array and object types, and special types are the NULL and resource types. The resource type is used for files and other external resources, and is left for future work. For simplicity, we model scalar types by the corresponding built-in types of K, although there may be some subtle differences for example in the approximations made by floating-point computations.

Arrays and Objects. We model arrays as pairs array(C,EL) where EL is a list of array elements and C is an optional *current element*. Array elements are represented as triples [k, v, l] where k is an integer or string *key*, l is the memory location where the actual value is stored, and v a *visibility* attribute (discussed below). Objects are triples OID(L,CL,ID) where L is the location of an array containing the fields of the object, CL is the name of the object's class and ID is a unique numeric object identifier. Classes are 4-tuples Class(SC,IV,MT,SV) where SC is the name of the superclass, IV is the list of instance and static variables, MT is the method table, and SV is a pointer to the scope holding static variables (those shared across all objects from the given class).

The visibility attribute is always public for *proper* array elements, whereas it can be also protected or private for objects fields. As implied by the object inheritance example of Section 2.1, the correct handling of visibility of object properties is subtle. In particular, array elements are identified by a combination of the key and the visibility attribute. In that example, the field array of $obj will contain two separate entries ["id",public,11] and ["id",private(par),12], necessary to resolve the right element depending on the context. The modelling of arrays, especially when considering the interaction with other features such as aliasing, was one of the main challenges of this and related efforts (e.g. [21,43]).

Finally, the NULL value is the value returned when attempting to read any non previously initialised variable, array or object elements.

Values in Memory. Following the online documentation, in the memory we wrap values into four-tuples zval(Value, Type, RefCount, Is_ref). Each zval contains the value, its type, a reference counter keeping track of the number of locations currently pointing to the value, and a boolean flag indicating whether or not the value is aliased.[4] We define a number of internal low-level operations which manipulates zvals (zvalRead, incRefCount, etc.), and use them as building blocks for defining higher level functions (read, write, etc.) providing the illusion of operating directly on simple values, increasing the modularity of the semantics.

---

[4] The flag is_ref is used for implementing the array *copy-on-write* optimisation. We include it just for completeness, since in our semantics, is_ref is true iff refcount>1.

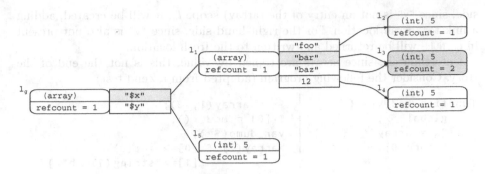

Fig. 1. Example heap, where the reserved location l_g contains the global scope

Memory. The heap, which is contained in the heap cell, is a map $\mathbb{H} : loc \to zval$, where loc is a countable set of locations $l_1, \ldots, l_n$. Fig. 1 shows the heap after executing the program

```
$x = array("foo" => 5, "bar" => 5);
$y = 5;
next($x);
$x["baz"] = &$x["bar"];
$x[12] = 5;
```

where the elements pointed to by the array *current* pointers are shaded (in yellow), and shared zvals are shaded (in red), and l_g is the location containing the global scope, which is a special array where both $x and $y are defined. We have shown in Section 2.2 how the global scope can be accessed directly via the variable $GLOBALS. In fact, just like in JavaScript, it is convenient to represent all PHP scopes as heap-allocated arrays.

References. Several programming languages internally use references, and so does PHP, but with its own original twist. Consider running a simple program unset($y) on the state shown in Fig. 1. If the argument $y were to be evaluated to a value we would reach unset(5) which is nonsensical. Even evaluating $y to the location l_5 would not be the right choice, since in that case we could successfully free the location, but not remove the link from $y to l_5 (which is stored in the array at l_g). This is just an example of a general class of cases, which imply that variables need to be evaluated to references of the form ref(L, K) where L is the address of the array or object containing the variable, and K is the variable name. When the actual value stored in the variable is needed, further steps of reduction can be taken to resolve the reference. This is not a trivial process, as the lookup depends on whether the reference appears on the left or right hand side of an assignment. Consider the code

```
$x = $y;
```

where neither $x nor $y have been initialised. The first step is to evaluate the variables obtaining the references $\text{ref}(l_g, \text{"x"})$ and $\text{ref}(l_g, \text{"y"})$. On the left-hand side, since "x" is not an entry of the (array) scope l_g, it will be created, adding a link to a fresh location. For the right-hand side, since "y" is also not present in l_g, NULL will be returned and written to the fresh location.

Unfortunately, since arrays are copied by value, this is not the end of the story. Consider the following program (adapted from a Zend test):

```
function mod_x() {            $x = array(1, 2);
    global $x;               $x[0] = mod_x();
    $x = array('a','b');     var_dump($x);
    return 0;                >array(2) { [0]=> int(0)
}                                      [1]=> string(1) "b" }
```

If $x[0] was evaluated to a reference before calling mod_x (as in JavaScript), it would become ref(L1,0), where L1 is obtained by resolving the reference ref(L,"x") in the current scope L. Hence, the assignment would affect the original array and the output would still show "a" (instead of 0) at position 0. In order to model the observed PHP behaviour, we introduce a more general type of reference (lref) which can be thought as a "path". In the example above, the expression $x[0] effectively evaluates to lref(ref(L,"x"),0), a value which represent a path starting at the current scope L and ending at the desired location.

The lref mechanism is also fundamental to handle assignments to arrays and objects created on-the-fly. Assume that variable $y is undefined. Consider:

```
$y[] -> x = 42;
```

This is indeed valid PHP code, that creates an array and an object on the fly, adds the object as element 0 to the array, and adds 42 as field x to the object.

Exceptions. The treatment of exceptions is based on an exceptionStack cell where we push the catch branch and the program continuation. If an exception is thrown, the catch is executed, otherwise the continuation is executed.

HTML. In general, a PHP script can be an HTML document that contains several PHP tags <? ... ?> (or <?PHP ... ?>) delimiting regions of PHP code that are executed as part of the same script. The HTML is treated as part of the program output, in the order it is encountered. Our semantics implements this behaviour. Hence, the hello.php example of Section 2 is equivalent to

```
<HTML><Body><? echo "Hello_".$_GET["name"]."!"; ?></Body></HTML>
```

Configuration. The global configuration of PHP, which represents the global state of the abstract machine, consists of 42 cells, and is shown in Figure 2 (we hide some of the nested cells to improve readability). The script cell contains details of the script being executed, and in particular a cell k with the actual program in the meta-variable PGM. The tables cell contains function, class and constant definitions. The scopes cell contains pointers to the various (global, super-global, current) scopes in the heap. The control cell contains the function stack, and information about the current object and class. The IO cell contains the input and output buffers, which $\mathbb{K}$ automatically connects to stdin and stdout. The instrumentation cell gathers meta-information for analysis purpose,

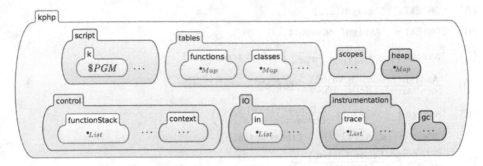

Fig. 2. Overview of the global configuration for KPHP

such as the trace of semantic rules used during an execution. Finally, the gc cell is used for bookkeeping by our implementation of garbage collection.

Semantic Rules. Each non-trivial language construct is described by several rewrite rules, each performing a step towards the full evaluation of the construct. Conceptually, the evaluation process happens in three steps. First, *structural* and *context* rules are applied. Their role is to rearrange the current program so that other rules can be applied. These include for example *heating* and *cooling* rules, which move the arguments of an expression to the top of the computation stack (cell k) and plug the results back once evaluated, and *desugaring* rules. Next, *intermediate* rules apply. Their role is mostly to pre-process arguments. For example, they convert types, resolve references, or read from memory. Finally, *step* rules apply. They give semantics to the actual language constructs, and cause the term being evaluated to be consumed, returning a value where necessary, so that the computation may progress.

Besides rewrite rules, K definitions also include *functions*, which do not have side effects on the configuration. In our semantics, we mostly use these functions to define logical predicates for the side-conditions of other rewrite rules.

3.3   KPHP: Selected Semantic Rules

Overall, the semantics comprises over 1,200 definitions: more than 700 are proper transition rules, the others are auxiliary definitions. As representative examples, we describe below the rules for assignment and functions.

Assignment. The rules for assignment are reported in Figure 3. Assignment is a binary expression whose arguments are evaluated left-to-right. We model this by two CONTEXT rules that enforce that evaluation order: rule (A) does not prescribe a type for the wildcard _ variable, that can match any term, including an unevaluated expression, whereas rule (B) can apply only after the first argument is evaluated to a KResult. In an assignment, the LHS will evaluate to a reference. Rule (C) resolves the reference to a location. If the RHS is a value, rule (D) puts the internal operation copyValueToLoc at the front of the k cell, and puts the value V to be returned as a continuation. copyValueToLoc takes care of writing

(A)   CONTEXT   'Assign($\Box$,_)

(B)   CONTEXT   'Assign(_:KResult,$\Box$)

(C)   'Assign $\left(\dfrac{\text{R:Ref}}{\text{convertToLoc(R)}}, -\right)$ [intermediate]

(D) $\dfrac{\text{'Assign(L:Loc, V:Value)}}{\text{copyValueToLoc(V, L)}\frown\text{V}}$ [step]

(E)   'Assign $\left(\_ : \text{KResult}, \dfrac{\text{V:ConvertibleToLoc}}{\text{convertToLoc(V,r)}}\right)$

      when $\neg$ isLiteral(V)   [intermediate]

(F) $\dfrac{\text{'Assign(L:Loc,L1:Loc)}}{\text{reset(L)} \frown \text{'Assign(L, L1)}}$

      when currentOverflow(L1)   [intermediate]

(G) $\dfrac{\text{'Assign(L,L1)}}{\text{'Assign(L, convertToLanguageValue(L1))}}$

      when $\neg$ currentOverflow(L1)   [intermediate]

Fig. 3. Semantic rules for assignment

V in L, operating recursively if V is an array. If the RHS is not a value, then rule (E) forces it to be converted to a location. If the location L1 thus obtained contains an array whose current pointer is overflown, the current pointer of the assignment target L is reset by rule (F). In the remaining cases, rule (G) converts the location L1 to a value, enabling rule (D).

Functions. When a function definition is executed, we create a new entry in the functions cell mapping the function name to a 4-tuple f(FP,FB,RT,LS) containing the function parameter list FP, its body FB, its return type RT (by value/by reference) and a pointer LS to a scope holding the static variables (which persist across function invocations).

A function call is parsed in the AST as 'FunctionCall(E,Args). Expression E is evaluated to a string FN (the function name), used to retrieve from the functions cell the various parameters described above. Execution continues by placing at the front of the k cell the internal runFunction term shown in the rule below, which replaces the contents of the cell k with a new list of internal commands (the current program continuation K will be saved on the stack).

$$\left\langle \dfrac{\text{runFunction(FN:String, f(FP:K, FB:K, RT:RetType, LS:Loc), Args:K)}\frown\text{K}}{\begin{pmatrix} \text{processFunArgs(FP, Args)} \frown \\ \text{pushStackFrame(FN, K, L, CurrentClass, CurrentObj, RT, D)} \frown \\ \text{ArrayCreateEmpty(L1)} \frown \text{setCrntScope(L1)} \frown \text{incRefCount(L1)} \frown \\ \text{copyFunArgs} \frown \text{FB} \frown \text{'Return(NULL)} \end{pmatrix}} \right\rangle_k$$

$\langle \text{L:Loc}\rangle_{\text{currentScope}}$ $\langle \text{CurrentClass:Id}\rangle_{\text{class}}$ $\langle \text{CurrentObj:Loc}\rangle_{\text{object}}$

$\langle \dfrac{\text{D:K}}{\cdot}\rangle_{\text{functionArgumentDeclaration}}$

when fresh(L1)   [internal]

The first command evaluates the function arguments Args in the current scope. This depends on the declaration of the formal parameters FP: if a parameter is declared by reference, the evaluation must stop at a location, and not fetch the value from memory. The next command pushes the current state on the stack, including the current scope L and continuation K. The next three commands create the function local scope L1 (the side condition fresh(L1:Loc) means that location L1 is newly allocated), set it as the current execution scope, and increment its reference counter. The next command assigns the evaluated arguments to the formal parameters allocated on L1. Finally, the function code FB is run, followed by a default return instruction.

3.4 The KPHP Interpreter

Our semantics is defined in 29 ".k" files, and consists of approximately 8500 lines of code. Compiling the semantics with the kompile utility of the K distribution creates a directory of files for the Maude tool. We provide a Unix shell script called kphp that, given the name of a PHP file, invokes the krun utility with appropriate parameters (for the external parser, options, etc.). This runs our semantics as if it was the standard PHP interpreter.

4 Testing and Validation

In this Section we discuss the testing and validation of our (executable) semantics of PHP. Since KPHP is actively developed, the numbers below refer to the release current at the time of publication of this paper.

Test-Driven Semantics Development. As discussed in Section 1, there is no official document providing a specification of PHP. Hence, the development of our semantics was largely test-driven. The choice of specifying the semantics in K meant that at each stage of this work we had a working interpreter corresponding to the fragment of PHP we specified up to that point. This made it possible to test critical semantics rules as they were being developed. For this ongoing testing we wrote snippets of PHP, and compared the results from our interpreter with the ones from the Zend Engine, which is the *de facto* reference interpreter.

Validation. As common in other PHP projects (e.g. Facebook's HHVM), we validated our semantics/interpreter by testing it against the official test suite distributed with the Zend engine. Although our semantics covers most of the core PHP language (including its challenging features, such as arrays, objects, references, aliasing, exceptions, etc.), the test suite includes many tests that refer to constructs or library functions that we do not yet support. The Zend test suite is already split into folders containing different categories of tests. We tested the semantics against all the tests in the folders lang (core language) and functions: we did not pick tests manually to avoid introducing bias.

The lang folder contains 216 tests and we pass 97 of them, the functions folder contains 14 and we pass 4. If a test fails, it is for one of four reasons: (i) our semantics models a feature incorrectly; (ii) a language construct is not

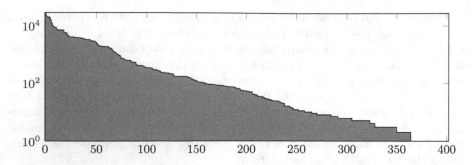

Fig. 4. Coverage of KPHP rules by the Zend test suite (logarithmic scale)

supported by our semantics; (iii) the external parser has a bug, and returns the wrong AST; (iv) the external parser does not support some features added to PHP after version 5.0. For each failed test, our test harness shows one of these four categories. Successful tests are partitioned in 2 sets: 71 are automatically recognised as success, 26 are considered successful after manual review of the output (for example, our warning and error messages do not contain source code line numbers, because they are not recorded by the external parser).

The only test that fails in category (i) is 031.phpt, which tests for the erratic behaviour of current described in Section 2.2. This fail is intentional, as we consider such behaviour to be a bug in the Zend Engine. All the other failed tests belong to categories (ii)-(iv), hence are either not supported by the semantics or by the parser. The total number of passed tests may not seem very high (JSCert passes almost 2,000 tests), but this is due to the size of the Zend test suite, and is outside our control. Moreover, many tests are non trivial, focussing on complex evaluation strategies, classes, constructors, interaction between global variables, functions, objects and aliasing. We are satisfied by this validation experiment - so far, our semantics behaves as the official PHP implementation.

Coverage. In order to assess the level of coverage of our semantics achieved by the Zend test suite, we added a trace cell to the KPHP configuration, where we add the name of each rule as it is executed. Out of 721 semantics rules, 403 are executed at least once, and 318 are never executed. In Figure 4 we show the histogram, ordered by frequency, of the executed rules. There is a big difference in the number of times different rules are exercised by the test suite. This is partly explained by our design. The small group of rules which is called more than 25,000 times by the test suite corresponds to the low-level, internal rules which are used as building blocks by other, higher level rules. Internal rules that perform type conversions, such as *toInt, are also intensively exercised, as expected. 158 of 403 rules are called at least 100 times, and 264 are called more than 10 times. Using the Zend tests alone, coverage amounts to 56% of the semantic rules. In order to achieve full-coverage, we have written targeted additional tests that cover the rules not exercised by the Zend suite.

5   Applications

One of the main goals of our semantics is to provide a formal model of PHP on which semantics-based verification tools (such as abstract interpreters, type systems and taint-checkers) can be built. Developing such tools goes beyond the scope of this paper. However, we are able to begin demonstrating the practical relevance of our semantics by showing potential applications based on the $\mathbb{K}$-Maude tool chain. In particular, the $\mathbb{K}$ framework exposes Maude's explicit-state LTL model checking to the semantics [11], and supports symbolic execution for any language definition [1]

In this Section, we show how we used LTL model checking in conjunction with symbolic execution to obtain a PHP code analyser, and we analyse properties of two 3rd-party PHP functions of practical relevance.

5.1   Temporal Verification of PHP Programs

Model Checking and Symbolic Execution in $\mathbb{K}$. A $\mathbb{K}$ definition is eventually translated to a Maude rewrite theory, which can be model checked against LTL formulas using Maude's built-in model checker. In order to use the model checker in a meaningful way with respect to PHP, we need to instrument the semantics in two ways. First, we must decide what semantics rules should be considered as *state transitions* by the model checker, tag such rules, and pass the tags to the `--transition` compilation option. Second, we need to extend LTL with a set of atomic propositions that can be used to express interesting properties of PHP programs.

Symbolic execution has been recently introduced in $\mathbb{K}$ [1] and is enabled by using the option `--backend symbolic` when compiling the $\mathbb{K}$ definition. When symbolic mode is enabled, programs can be (optionally) given symbolic inputs of any of the types natively supported by the $\mathbb{K}$ tool (`int,float,string,bool`).

We now describe the $\mathbb{K}$PHP extensions needed for model checking and symbolic execution.

State Transitions. Our semantics comprises many internal and intermediate rules, and it is not obvious *what* exactly should represent a change in the program state and what should instead be considered non-observable. Instead of fixing this notion once and for all, we allow ourselves maximum flexibility by defining several sets of semantic rules, and assigning a tag to each set:

- `step`: rules which correspond to the execution of language constructs.
- `internal`: rules used for operations which are not part of the user language, such as incrementing the reference counter.
- `intermediate`: rules which perform auxiliary work, such as performing a type conversion on an argument before a `step` or `internal` rule can be applied.
- `mem`: low-level rules which directly write the memory.
- `error`: orthogonal set of rules which cause a transition to an error state.

Using these tags, we are able to reason about programs at different degrees of abstraction. In the rest of this section, we consider only the state transitions generated by selecting the step rules. An alternative would be for example to consider only the mem rules, if the observations of interest are just the memory updates.

A Temporal Logic for PHP. We now define an extension of LTL with predicates over $\mathbb{K}$PHP configurations (i.e. PHP program states). Given a PHP program, we would like to be able to express conditions such as: "variable $usr never contains 'admin'", or "the local variable $y of function foo will at some point be aliased to the global variable $y". Moreover, we also want to be able to reason about *correspondence assertions* [42], by labelling program points and stating properties such as "after reaching label 'login' variable $sec always contains 1". To this end, we introduce predicates such as eqTo (equals to), gv (global variable), fv (function variable). The LTL formulas corresponding to the informal specifications above are, respectively:

$\square\neg$eqTo(gv(var('usr')),val('admin'))

$\lozenge$alias(fv('foo',var('y')),gv(var('y')))

label('login')$\Rightarrow \square$eqTo(gv(var(sec)),val(1))

Moreover, we also found useful to be able to reason about types. For example, the following formula says that variable $y always has type integer during the execution of function foo:

$\square($inFun('foo')$\Rightarrow$has_type(fv('foo',var('y')),integer))

Each new predicate should be given a precise meaning in the context of the $\mathbb{K}$PHP configuration. We illustrate how we do that through the example of predicate eqTo(e1,e2). Given a configuration B, we need to define when it satisfies the predicate:

B $\models$ eqTo(e1,e2) $\Leftrightarrow$ eval(B,e1) = eval(B,e2)

meaning, that formula eqTo(e1,e2) is true for B if and only if e1 and e2 evaluate to the same value. The definition of functions such as eval is crucial, as it connects the semantics to the model checker. These functions should be written in purely functional style and avoid side effects. In practice they are pretty simple, as they only need to inspect a configuration using pattern matching. As another example, consider predicate alias(e1,e2):

B $\models$ alias(e1,e2) $\Leftrightarrow$ lvalue(B,e1) = lvalue(B,e2)

Function lvalue returns the location of the heap where its argument is stored, so the predicate is true when the arguments are aliased or identical. We use similar techniques to give semantics to all of our predicates, which can be used to form extended LTL formulas together with standard LTL connectives.

Limitations. The approach described here suffers from the known limitations of the underlying verification techniques. In particular, explicit state LTL model checking will struggle to handle programs that generate large state spaces that depend heavily on the program inputs. The support for symbolic execution mitigates this problem, but as common to this approach it does not handle higher order data structures, such as objects, and struggles with loops depending on symbolic values. Despite these limitations, in the rest of this section we show that we can indeed verify some non-trivial properties of real PHP code.

5.2   Case Study: Input Validation

In our first example of model checking, we consider the function PMA_isValid taken from the source code of phpMyAdmin [33], one of the most common open source web applications, which provides a web interface to administer an SQL server.

PMA_isValid takes three arguments (&$var, $type, and $compare) and returns a boolean. Its purpose is to "validate" the argument $var according to different criteria that depend on the other two arguments. We analyse the full source code of PMA_isValid, which is shown in Appendix 1 of the extended version of this paper, available on http://phpsemantics.org.

In the simplest case, PMA_isValid simply checks that $var is of the same type (or meta type) specified by $type, ignoring the remaining argument $compare:

```
PMA_isValid(0, "int");              // true
PMA_isValid("hello", "scalar");        // true
PMA_isValid("hello", "numeric");       // false
PMA_isValid("123", "numeric");         // true
PMA_isValid("anything", false);        // always true
```

A more interesting case is when the argument $type is instantiated with one of "identical", "equal" or "similar". In such case, the validation of $var is performed against $comparison, according to the criterion specified by $type:

```
PMA_isValid(0, "identical", 1);       // false
PMA_isValid(0, "equal", 1);        // true
PMA_isValid("hello", "similar", 1); // false
```

If $type is an array, validation succeeds if $var is an element of that array. If $type is "length", validation succeeds if $var is a scalar with a string length greater that zero, If $type = false, validation always succeeds.

```
PMA_isValid(0, array(0,1,2));       // true
PMA_isValid(true, "length");        // true, as (string) true = "1"
PMA_isValid(false, "length");       // false, as (string) false = ""
```

The developer had an informal specification of this function in mind, which he wrote in a comment at the beginning of the function. However, it is not obvious wether such specification is met by the actual implementation. Leveraging model checking and symbolic execution we are able to prove that the function behaves as expected, by verifying each sub-case.

We first write some code accepting (possibly) symbolic inputs, and calling the function:

```
$var = user_input();         // symbolic
$type = user_input();        // symbolic
$compare = user_input();     // symbolic
$result = PMA_isValid($var, $type, $compare);
```

then we attempt to verify multiple times the LTL formula

$$\Diamond \mathtt{eqTo(gv(var('result'),val(true)))}$$

each time providing different combinations of symbolic and concrete inputs, until all of the cases discussed above are covered. Indeed, these verifications succeed, proving the correctness of the function.

As a concrete example, in order to prove that the result of calling `PMA_isValid` with `$type="numeric"` is true when `$var` is an integer, we provide the symbolic input `#symInt(x)` to `$var`, and the concrete input `"numeric"` to `$type`. We proved analogous results for the case of `float` variables, and for the other similar cases. We proved that `PMA_is_Valid($var, "similar", $compare)` returns true for any integer `$var` and string `$compare`, by providing symbolic values `#symInt(x)` and `#symString(y)` to `$var` and `$compare`.

5.3 Case Study: Cryptographic Key Generation

In our second example, we consider the Password-Based Key Derivation Function `pbkdf2` from the PHP distribution [10]. `pbkdf2` takes five parameters: the name of the algorithm to be used for hashing (`$algo`), a `$password`, a `$salt`, an iteration `$count` and the desired `$key_length`. It returns a key derived from `$password` and `$salt` whose length is `$key_length`. We wish to prove that the function always returns a `string`, and that its length is equal to the requested `$key_length`.

Using the same approach as for the previous example, we write some initial code accepting (possibly) symbolic inputs, and calling the function:

```
$algo = "sha224";
$pass = user_input();        // symbolic input
$salt = user_input();        // symbolic input
$count = 1;
$key_len = 16;
$result = pbkdf2($algo, $pass, $salt, $count, $key_len);
```

Next, we run the model checker on our query formulae:

1. The result is a string: $\Diamond \mathtt{has\_type(gv(var('result')),string)}$
2. The length of the output is as requested:

$$\Diamond \mathtt{eqTo(gv(var('key\_len')),len(gv(var('result'))))}$$

3. The length of the string stored in local variable `$output` grows, and eventually becomes greater than the required output length:

$$\Box(\ (\mathtt{inFun('pbkdf2')} \land \neg\mathtt{inFun('top')} \land \Diamond\mathtt{inFun('top')}) \implies$$
$$(\Diamond(\mathtt{geq(len(fv('pbkdf2',var('output')))),\ fv('pbkdf2',\ var('key\_len')))})$$
$$\mathcal{U}\ \mathtt{inFun('top')})\ )$$

Property (3) shows that property (2) is non-trivial. Moreover, it illustrates a technically more intriguing LTL formula. Using the model checker, we are able to verify that all three properties in less than a minute. Unlike the previous example, which we were able to run and analyse out-of-the-box, in this case we had to provide implementations for an number of functions (such as hash), which belong to libraries outside of the core language. For the sake of verification, we only provide simple stubs for these functions, making sure to preserve the type and output length properties of their original versions. The complete source code of pbkdf2 and related functions can be found in Appendix 2 of the extended version of this paper, available on http://phpsemantics.org.

6   Limitations and Future Work

A formal, executable semantics of a real programming language is too large a task to be completed in one single effort. This paper models the core of PHP, which includes the features we considered more important and instructive, leaving out some non-core features and the numerous language extensions. In this Section, we summarise what we left out of the current formalisation, and indicate what we think are the next priorities to take this work further.

Parsing Limitations. As discussed in Section 4, the external parser we currently use does not understand some language constructs introduced after version 5.0, such as for example the literal array syntax with square brackets ([1,2,3] instead of array(1,2,3)). It also does not parse correctly some constructs such as $this->a[] which gets parsed as $this->(a[]) instead of ($this->a)[]. In future development, we plan to adopt a fully-compliant external parser.

Missing Language Features. We have not (yet) implemented a number of non-core language features, and in particular: bit-wise operators, most escape characters, regular expressions, namespaces, interfaces, abstract classes, iterators, magic methods and closures. We do not foresee significant obstacles in integrating these into KPHP. For example, magic methods are special object methods (__toString, __get, __call, etc.) with reflective behaviour that are called automatically by PHP. JavaScript has similar reflective methods, and techniques to formalise them are well documented [25,4]. As a taster, we included in the core language the __construct magic method, which is used by the new command when creating a fresh object. Since version 5.3, PHP includes anonymous functions, implemented as objects of a special Closure class. These are not supported by our parser, but can be easily modelled in our semantics by adding to the object OID constructor an optional argument pointing to the entry of the functions cell where the anonymous function definition would be stored (using the same mechanism of regular functions).

Internal Functions. As in related projects, a challenge when dealing with a real language is the sheer number of built-in library functions that operate on numbers, strings, arrays and objects. At the moment we model just a small, representative subset of them (e.g. strlen, substr, count, is_int, is_float, var_dump, etc.). Where possible, we define such functions in PHP directly; we define them in $\mathbb{K}$ in the remaining cases (this corresponds to PHP native functions implemented in C).

Language Extensions. Language extensions, such as the functions that provide access to an SQL database, or that connect a PHP script with a server (and hence with the network) are of fundamental importance for developing web applications, but are squarely beyond the scope of our current work. Our goal is to provide a sound semantic foundation to the core language that glues all such functions together. Until (semi-)automated techniques that help giving semantics to language extensions are developed, our view is that such extensions need to be investigated on a case-by-case basis. Often, they can be abstracted in terms of approximate information such as for example their types, taint behaviour, or side effects, as exemplified by our case study of Section 5.3.

7   Related Work

In this Section, we discuss related work on the mechanised formalisation of programming languages, and on the analysis of PHP.

Mechanised Formalisation of Programming Languages. Proof assistants such as Coq [2], Isabelle/HOL [31], are a popular choice for the mechanised specification of programming languages. For example, HOL was used by Norrish [32] to specify a small-step operational semantics of C, and to prove meta-properties of the language. Blazy and Leroy, as part of the CompCert project [3], have built a verified compiler for a significant fragment of C, formalised in Coq. They have proved that the semantics of source programs is preserved by the compilation process. In the JSCert project [4], Bodin *et al.* have built a mechanised formalisation of JavaScript (ECMAScript 5) and tested it again the ECMA262 test suite. In Coq, they have developed an inductive definition of the semantics and a separate fixpoint definition of a JavaScript interpreter, and proved that the interpreter is sound with respect to the semantics. From the Coq fixpoint definition they have automatically extracted OCAML code to execute the interpreter.

In the $\mathbb{K}$ framework instead a semanticist may directly focus on writing and analysing language definitions: execution is taken care of by the tool. Ellison and Rosu [11] have defined an executable formal semantics of C in $\mathbb{K}$ [37]. Their formalisation has been extensively tested against the GCC torture suite [12], and they demonstrate examples of the debugging and model checking C code using the built-in capabilities of $\mathbb{K}$. On a smaller scale, $\mathbb{K}$, has also been used to formalise, Python [16], Scheme [28], Verilog [29], Haskell [23] and Java [5]. A number of program analysis techniques such as *symbolic execution* [1], *program logics* [36] and *program equivalence* [24] are being developed and incorporated into the $\mathbb{K}$, extending the potential benefits of defining a programming language semantics in this framework.

For PHP, we followed the approach of [11]. In the absence of a specification document, it was crucial to be able to immediately execute operational semantics rules as they were being developed, in order to compare with the reference implementation of the language. Moreover, we were intrigued by the possibility to leverage existing model checking and symbolic execution capabilities to demonstrate our semantics at work.

The approach to define an executable semantics of a *real* programming language and validating it by testing against official test suites was trail-blazed by Guha *et al.* [15], who give semantics to JavaScript via a translation to a simpler intermediate language called λ_{JS}, formalised in the PLT Redex tool [22] (which also takes care of execution). More recently, the same approach was adopted by Politz *et al.* [35] to Python.

PHP Analysis. Analysis of PHP and other web languages is an important topic, given the prevalence of security flaws such as XSS, CSRF and SQL injection. There are many research and commercial tools that statically analyse PHP code, including Pixy [21], WebSSARI [43], PHP-Sat [7] and HP Fortify [38]. According to the respective papers, all of these tools have specific weaknesses related to language features that are hard to understand and analyse. For example, Pixy and WebSSARI do not follow taint flows across objects. We believe that the next generation of static analysis tools can benefit from a precise, formal semantics of the language.

We are the first to present such a semantics for PHP. The only previous work we are aware of that looks in depth as some aspect of PHP semantics is an analysis of the array-copying mechanism of PHP by Tozawa *et al.* [41]. They formalise a tiny fragment of the language that suffices to describe the array copy mechanism, and show a flaw in a runtime optimisation used by the Zend engine. Their work sheds light on how complex the array semantics in PHP is, and was an inspiration for us to dig deeper into the PHP semantics.

8   Conclusions

In this paper we described the first formal semantics of PHP. We focussed on the core language, leaving language extensions and library functions for future work. Our semantics is executable, meaning that from the formal definition we automatically obtained a trusted interpreter of PHP, which we used for testing and debugging the semantics.

We validated the semantics by showing that is passes all the Zend tests applicable to the PHP fragment we modelled, and we achieved full coverage of our semantic rules by defining new ad-hoc tests. Given a mechanised semantics, it is still an open research problem how to automatically generate a comprehensive regression test suite for a language. If such a systematic approach to test generation was available, our semantics could be the basis for a regression test suite for PHP implementations.

Leveraging built-in features of $\mathbb{K}$ and Maude, we also provided a proof-of-concept infrastructure for the verification of PHP programs, which we demonstrated on two realistic examples. Our work is a first step towards defining semantics-based, static-analysis tools that provide formal guarantees for PHP web applications.

Acknowledgments. We are indebted to Antoine Delignat-Lavaud for many insightful discussions on the arcana of PHP. We would also like to thank the $\mathbb{K}$ team for their technical support on using the $\mathbb{K}$ framework, and Shijiao Yuwen for useful comments on an earlier version of the $\mathbb{K}$PHP semantics. Filaretti and Maffeis are supported by EPSRC grant EP/I004246/1.

References

1. Arusoaie, A., Lucanu, D., Rusu, V.: A Generic Framework for Symbolic Execution. In: Erwig, M., Paige, R.F., Van Wyk, E. (eds.) SLE 2013. LNCS, vol. 8225, pp. 281–301. Springer, Heidelberg (2013)
2. Bertot, Y., Castéran, P., Huet, G., Paulin-Mohring, C.: Interactive Theorem Proving and Program Development - Coq'Art - the Calculus of Inductive Constructions. Texts in theoretical computer science. Springer (2004)
3. Blazy, S., Leroy, X.: Mechanized Semantics for the Clight Subset of the C Language. Journal of Automated Reasoning 43, 263–288 (2009)
4. Bodin, M., Charguéraud, A., Filaretti, D., Gardner, P., Maffeis, S., Schmitt, A., Smith, G.: A Trusted Mechanised JavaScript Specification. In: POPL 2014 (2014)
5. Bogdanas, D.: Formal Semantics of Java in the K Framework, https://github.com/kframework/java-semantics
6. Bogdanas, D.: Label-Based Programming Language Semantics in the K Framework with SDF. In: SYNASC 2012, pp. 170–177 (2012)
7. Bouwers, E.: PHP-Sat, http://www.program-transformation.org/PHP/PhpSat
8. Clavel, M., Durán, F., Eker, S., Lincoln, P., Martí-Oliet, N., Meseguer, J., Quesada, J.F.: Maude: Specification and Programming in Rewriting Logic. Theoretical Computer Science 285(2), 187–243 (2002)
9. Cousot, P., Cousot, R.: Abstract Interpretation: a Unified Lattice Model for Static Analysis of Programs by Construction or Approximation of Fixpoints. In: POPL 1977, pp. 238–252 (1977)
10. PHP Documentation. Cryptographic Function pbkdf2, http://php.net/manual/en/function.hash-hmac.php
11. Ellison, C., Roşu, G.: An Executable Formal Semantics of C with Applications. In: POPL 2012, pp. 533–544 (2012)
12. Free Software Foundation. GCC Torture Suite, http://gcc.gnu.org/onlinedocs/gccint/C-Tests.html
13. The PHP Group. PHP Official Documentation, http://www.php.net/manual/en/
14. The PHP Group. PHP Zend Engine, http://php.net
15. Guha, A., Saftoiu, C., Krishnamurthi, S.: The Essence of Javascript. In: D'Hondt, T. (ed.) ECOOP 2010. LNCS, vol. 6183, pp. 126–150. Springer, Heidelberg (2010)
16. Guth, D.: Python Semantics in K, http://code.google.com/p/k-python-semantics/
17. Heering, J., Hendriks, P.R.H., Klint, P., Rekers, J.: The Syntax Definition Formalism SDF - Reference Manual. SIGPLAN Not. 24(11), 43–75 (1989)
18. ECMA International. ECMA-262 ECMAScript Language Specification (2009), http://www.ecma-international.org/publications/standards/Ecma-262.htm
19. International Organization for Standardization. C Language Specification - C11. ISO/IEC 9899:2011 (2011), http://www.iso.org/iso/iso_catalogue/catalogue_tc/catalogue_detail.htm?%csnumber=57853

20. Jhala, R., Majumdar, R.: Software Model Checking. ACM Compututing Surveys 41(4) (2009)
21. Jovanovic, N., Kruegel, C., Kirda, E.: Static Analysis for Detecting Taint-Style Vulnerabilities in Web Applications. Journal of Computer Security 18(5), 861–907 (2010)
22. Klein, C., Clements, J., Dimoulas, C., Eastlund, C., Felleisen, M., Flatt, M., McCarthy, A., Rafkind, J., Tobin-Hochstadt, S., Findler, R.B.: Run Your Research: On the Effectiveness of Lightweight Mechanization. In: POPL 2012, pp. 285–296 (2012)
23. Lazar, D.: Haskell Semantics in K, https://github.com/davidlazar/haskell-semantics
24. Lucanu, D., Rusu, V.: Program Equivalence by Circular Reasoning. In: Johnsen, E.B., Petre, L. (eds.) IFM 2013. LNCS, vol. 7940, pp. 362–377. Springer, Heidelberg (2013)
25. Maffeis, S., Mitchell, J.C., Taly, A.: An Operational Semantics for JavaScript. In: Ramalingam, G. (ed.) APLAS 2008. LNCS, vol. 5356, pp. 307–325. Springer, Heidelberg (2008)
26. Maffeis, S., Mitchell, J.C., Taly, A.: Isolating JavaScript with Filters, Rewriting, and Wrappers. In: Backes, M., Ning, P. (eds.) ESORICS 2009. LNCS, vol. 5789, pp. 505–522. Springer, Heidelberg (2009)
27. Maffeis, S., Taly, A.: Language-Based Isolation of Untrusted JavaScript. In: CSF 2009, pp. 77–91 (2009)
28. Meredith, P., Hills, M., Roşu, G.: A K Definition of Scheme. Technical Report Department of Computer Science UIUCDCS-R-2007-2907, University of Illinois at Urbana-Champaign (2007)
29. Meredith, P., Katelman, M., Meseguer, J., Roşu, G.: A Formal Executable Semantics of Verilog. In: MEMOCODE 2010, pp. 179–188 (2010)
30. pR. Milner, M. Tofte, and D. Macqueen. The Definition of Standard ML. MIT Press (1997)
31. Nipkow, T., Paulson, L.C., Wenzel, M.T.: Isabelle/HOL. LNCS, vol. 2283. Springer, Heidelberg (2002)
32. Norrish, M.: C Formalised in HOL. University of Cambridge Technical Report UCAM-CL-TR-453 (1998)
33. phpMyAdmin Team. phpMyAdmin, http://www.phpmyadmin.net/home_page/index.php
34. Pierce, B.C.: Types and Programming Languages. MIT Press, Cambridge (2002)
35. Politz, J.G., Martinez, A., Milano, M., Warren, S., Patterson, D., Li, J., Chitipothu, A., Krishnamurthi, S.: Python: the Full Monty. In: OOPSLA 2013 (2013)
36. Roşu, G., Ştefănescu, A.: Checking Reachability using Matching Logic. In: OOPSLA 2012, pp. 555–574 (2012)
37. Roşu, G., Şerbănuţă, T.F.: An Overview of the K Semantic Framework. Journal of Logic and Algebraic Programming 79(6), 397–434 (2010)
38. Fortify Team. Fortify Code Secure, http://www.armorize.com/codesecure/
39. K Team. The K Framework, http://k-framework.org/index.php/Main_Page
40. PHP Quality Assurance Team. Zend Test Suite, https://qa.php.net/write-test.php
41. Tozawa, A., Tatsubori, M., Onodera, T., Minamide, Y.: Copy-On-Write in the PHP Language. In: POPL 2009, pp. 200–212 (2009)
42. Woo, T.Y.C., Lam, M.: A Semantic Model for Authentication Protocols. In: Security and Privacy (SP), pp. 178–194 (1993)
43. Xie, Y., Aiken, A.: Static Detection of Security Vulnerabilities in Scripting Languages. In: USENIX 2006 (2006)

A   Artifact Description

Authors of the Artifact. Daniele Filaretti and Sergio Maffeis.

Summary. The provided package is designed to support repeatability of the experiments of the paper: in particular, it allows users to test the KPHP interpreter and symbolic model checker on a variety of examples, including the ones discussed in the paper. We provide details on how to install and build KPHP, together with step-by-step instructions for running the examples and getting users started with their own experiments.

Content. The artifact package includes:

- the complete source files;
- a build of the K Framework (which is needed for running KPHP);
- all the examples discussed in the paper;
- a self-contained Linux-based virtual machine which can be used to run the artifact, if a user does not want to install KPHP and K directly;
- detailed instructions on how to build and use the artifact in index.html.

Getting the Artifact. The artifact, endorsed by the Artifact Evaluation Committee of ECOOP'14, is available free of charge as supplementary material of this paper on SpringerLink. KPHP is still under development. The latest version of KPHP, together with a user-friendly web interface, is available online at http://www.phpsemantics.org.

Tested Platforms. The K tool binaries (needed for running KPHP) run best on Linux and OS X. On Windows, Cygwin emulation must be used, which may slow down execution. The self-contained Linux-based VMware virtual machine we provide (included in the package) can be used in case of installation problems on non-standard system configurations.

License. EPL-1.0 (http://www.eclipse.org/legal/epl-v10.html).

MD5 Sum of the Artifact. 711cf733df354605ac2f32db942b9a49.

Size of the Artifact. 280.4 MB.

Identifying Mandatory Code for Framework Use via a Single Application Trace

Naoya Nitta[1], Izuru Kume[2], and Yasuhiro Takemura[3]

[1] Graduate School of Natural Science, Konan University, Japan
n-nitta@konan-u.ac.jp
[2] Graduate School of Information Science,
Nara Institute of Science and Technology, Japan
kume@acm.org
[3] Department of Character Creative Arts, Osaka University of Arts, Japan
yasuhi-t@osaka-geidai.ac.jp

Abstract. Application frameworks allow application developers to effectively reuse both designs and implementations which frequently appear in their intended domains. However, when using a framework with large scale APIs, its usage to implement an application-specific behavior tends to be complicated. Thus, in practice, application developers use existing sample application code as references for their development, but the task to locate the parts which are related to their application usually becomes a burden. To address this problem, in this paper, we characterize the problem as a kind of dynamic flow analysis problem, and based on the characterization, we present a method to automatically identify the mandatory code for the framework use using only a single sample application's trace. We have conducted case studies with several real-world frameworks to validate our method and the results indicate that the method is suitable to extract the mandatory framework usage.

1 Introduction

Recently, object-oriented application frameworks (in the following, frameworks for short) are widely used to facilitate application development in various domains. By reusing an appropriate framework, application developers can reduce the costs for their design and implementation processes effectively. They can fulfill their requirements typically by subclassing framework-provided classes and overriding their methods so that their written application-specific code is able to be executed in a run of an instance of the framework.

However, when using a framework with large scale APIs, its usage to correctly attach application code tends to be complicated [1, 2]. For example in [2], it is mentioned that application programmers are often required to attach their code to a framework at multiple and scattered predefined points in the correct manner. The main reason why such predefined points are scattered is that to call an overriding method declared in an application-specific class, the framework instance requires some dependencies to be previously injected by another application-specific code. The pattern in which such dependencies are injected is

R. Jones (Ed.): ECOOP 2014, LNCS 8586, pp. 593–617, 2014.

known as *dependency injection* [3]. Actual implementation steps to attach application code may consist of multiple instances of dependency injection and may include subclassing framework-provided classes, overriding their methods, implementing framework interfaces, instantiating appropriate objects and calling methods defined in the framework classes with correct parameters in the correct order. The same kind of difficulty to use frameworks is also discussed in [4, 5]. In practice, application developers often refer to the code of an existing sample application of a framework as an executable example of framework usage. In this strategy, they are usually required to locate the parts strictly related to their own application to develop in the sample application code, and such a task of locating often becomes a burden since the application-related and the application-unrelated parts are generally tangled within a single component of the code and also both of them are scattered across its multiple components.

To address the problem, several techniques and tools have been proposed. Some of them are based on static approaches and the others are on dynamic approaches. By static analysis, Strathcona [4] and DMMC [6] can automatically extract relevant code or important method calls from the source code of sample applications. Such tools are helpful for application programmers who are faced with difficulties using an unfamiliar framework's APIs. However, such tools tend to require a number of instances of framework usage which appear in the code of many sample applications or source code repositories to obtain one reliable result. In contrast, FUDA [5] uses a lightweight dynamic analysis to automatically extract framework usage from few execution traces of few sample applications. The method can extract not only mandatory but also optional application code to use a framework. However, to refine its output into pure mandatory part, the method requires more execution traces of sample applications as its input.

In this paper, we characterize the problem as a kind of dynamic flow analysis problem, and based on the characterization we can develop an algorithm to extract framework usage which can work with only one execution trace of a single sample application. In the following, we focus on Java as an object oriented programming language. Since generally, employing conventional dynamic flow analysis, such as data or control flow analysis induces a high computing load and may yield oversized results, we define a refined dynamic dependency, *expression level dynamic dependency*, and based on the dependency, we further define a slicing technique, named *asymmetric slicing*. By asymmetric slicing, the flow analysis can be appropriately controlled and unrelated results to the application under consideration will be reduced. We have implemented our method as an Eclipse plug-in, named *AsymmetricTracker* using Java and AspectJ. Similarly to FUDA, AsymmetricTracker can output the extraction results as template code for framework use. To validate our characterization of the problem, we have conducted similar case studies to [5] and check the outputs of AsymmetricTracker against the reference templates presented in [7]. The results show that AsymmetricTracker can output close results to the mandatory parts of the reference templates, despite using only one trace of a single sample application.

The main contributions of this paper are as follows.

- We characterize the problem of framework usage extraction as a kind of dynamic flow analysis problem.
- Based on the characterization, we have developed a method to automatically identify the mandatory code for a framework use through only a single sample application's trace.
- We have evaluated the recall and precision of outputs of the method through case studies.

The remainder of this paper is organized as follows. First, we introduce a motivating and running example in Sect. 2 and explain our characterization of the problem in Sect. 3. Next, several basic concepts to be used in our method are defined in Sect. 4. Then, we explain the whole process of our method in Sect. 5 and its implementation in Sect. 6. The evaluation of our method through case studies is shown in Sect. 7, and we will discuss the validity of the characterization and that of case studies in Sect. 8. Finally, the related work is discussed in Sect. 9, and we will conclude the paper in Sect. 10.

2   Running Example

In this section, we consider implementing a context menu using JFace as a motivating and running example throughout the paper. For the implementation task, we assume that `SampleView` class (shown in Fig. 1, borrowed from [5], 267 LOC) is used as sample code of a context menu. The code provides a visual component in Eclipse platform and displays a tree (represented by `TreeViewer` class) within the component. A context menu can be popped up over the tree. The lines related to the context menu are marked by '*' or '**' in Fig. 1. Among them, the mandatory lines, without any of which the context menu does not work, are marked by '**'. Differently from the sample in [5], in this paper we consider that some parts related to the tree viewer (i.e., line 36 and line 193, in the following, line numbers are abbreviated like l. 36 and l. 193) are also related to the context menu because the menu cannot be popped up without these parts. The tree and the context menu are created within the execution of `createPartControl()` (l. 190~). When the right mouse button is clicked on the tree, `menuAboutToShow()` (l. 205~) is called back from the instance of JFace and the content of the context menu is constructed and showed. If a menu item in the context menu is selected, `run()` (l. 221 or l. 226) is called back from it. Note that with each event, some application-specific code is called back from the framework-provided code. This inverse nature of control flow is called *inversion of control* (often abbreviated as *IoC*). Inversion of control is a main feature of frameworks.

As we can see from the figure, the usage of JFace to implement the context menu is very complicated, that is, instantiating tree viewer, menu manager, menu listener and action, obtaining menu and control objects from the objects, and passing one object to another object in the correct order are all needed. Even for programmers who are given the above sample application code, the task to locate the part related to the context menu is a burden since the part is tangled with the unrelated parts and is scattered across multiple methods in the code.

```
        :
 35:    public class SampleView extends ViewPart {
*36:        private TreeViewer viewer;
 37:        private DrillDownAdapter drillDownAdapter;
*38:        private Action action1;
*39:        private Action action2;
 40:        private WelcomeWindow welcomeWindow;
            :
 98:        class ViewContentProvider
 99:            implements IStructuredContentProvider, ITreeContentProvider {
                :
162:        }
163:        class ViewLabelProvider extends LabelProvider {
                :
189:        }
190:        public void createPartControl(Composite parent) {
191:            welcomeWindow = new WelcomeWindow();
192:            welcomeWindow.open();
**193:          viewer = new TreeViewer(parent, SWT.MULTI | SWT.H_SCROLL | SWT.V_SCROLL);
194:            drillDownAdapter = new DrillDownAdapter(viewer);
195:            viewer.setContentProvider(new ViewContentProvider());
196:            viewer.setLabelProvider(new ViewLabelProvider());
197:            viewer.setInput(getViewSite());
*198:           makeActions();
*199:           hookContextMenu();
200:        }
*201:       private void hookContextMenu() {
**202:          MenuManager menuMgr = new MenuManager("#PopupMenu");
*203:           menuMgr.setRemoveAllWhenShown(true);
**204:          menuMgr.addMenuListener(new IMenuListener() {
**205:              public void menuAboutToShow(IMenuManager mgr) {
*206:                   fillContextMenu(mgr);
**207:              }});
**208:          Menu menu = menuMgr.createContextMenu(viewer.getControl());
**209:          viewer.getControl().setMenu(menu);
*210:           getSite().registerContextMenu(menuMgr, viewer);
*211:       }
*212:       private void fillContextMenu(IMenuManager manager) {
**213:          manager.add(action1);
*214:           manager.add(action2);
*215:           drillDownAdapter.addNavigationActions(manager);
*216:           manager.add(new Separator());
*217:           manager.add(new Separator(IWorkbenchActionConstants.MB_ADDITIONS));
*218:       }
*219:       private void makeActions() {
**220:          action1 = new Action() {
221:                public void run() { showMessage("Action 1 executed"); }
**222:          };
*223:           action1.setText("Action 1");
*224:           action1.setToolTipText("Action 1 tooltip");
*225:           action2 = new Action() {
226:                public void run() { showMessage("Action 2 executed"); }
*227:           };
*228:           action2.setText("Action 2");
*229:           action2.setToolTipText("Action 2 tooltip");
*230:       }
            :
267:    }
```

**: mandatory
*: optional

Fig. 1. A sample application code of context menu

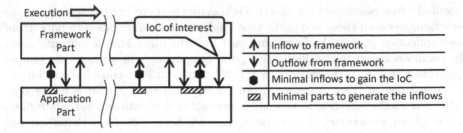

Fig. 2. Our characterization of the problem

3 Our Approach

In this paper, we focus on identifying the mandatory parts in given sample application code which enable a particular application-specific behavior. The reason why we focus on the mandatory parts is that if one is given the mandatory parts, then he/she can have at least one 'executable' code which can be used in his/her own application under consideration.

Before explaining our characterization of the problem, recall the running example explained in the previous section. First, we consider why each line is needed to make the context menu work. For example, if l. 209 is removed, then menuAboutToShow() (l. 205) is not called back from the instance of JFace and the menu cannot be shown. Also if l. 213 is removed, then run() (l. 221) is not called back from it and the menu item cannot be selected. These observations suggest that the mandatory parts of the sample application code can be characterized as a minimal part of the code which leads to the behavior-related occurrences of IoC. Indeed, by our analysis, all of the mandatory lines marked by '**' are related to either of the above two occurrences (calls to l. 205 and l. 221) of IoC. The reason why some additional application code is needed to make the IoC occur is that before the IoC occurs, the framework instance requires some dependencies to be injected by the additional application code. For example, when l. 221 is called back, a runtime dependency previously injected by the invocation of MenuManager.add() at l. 213 is used. The pattern in which such dependencies are injected is known as *dependency injection* [3]. In this paper, we call the framework usage to inject such dependencies *injection points*. A minimal part of the sample application code which leads to the behavior-related occurrences of IoC is considered as an implementation of the corresponding injection points. Therefore, first, we characterize the problem as identifying a minimal part of the sample application code which leads to the behavior-related occurrences of IoC. This is our primary characterization of the problem.

To solve the problem, dynamic analysis approaches will be effective. Thus, next, we refine the above characterization of the problem from a dynamic analysis point of view. Consider the overall structure of traces of framework applications. Each execution trace of a framework application can be divided into two parts; one is a part where the application-specific code is executed (*application part* for short) and the other is one where the framework-provided code is executed (*framework part* for short). Furthermore, there exist two kinds of interactions between these two parts. One kind of the interactions is 'inputs' from the application part to the framework part and the other kind is 'outputs' from the framework part to the application part. For example in a run of the sample application in Fig. 1, the executions of l. 209 and l. 213 are considered as inputs to the instance of JFace, and the calls to l. 205, l. 221 and l.226 are considered as outputs from the instance. In this paper, we call such inputs and outputs *inflows* and *outflows*, respectively (more specifically, see Sect. 4.2). Note that there are several types of inflows to the framework part; 1) a method call to the framework part with several parameters, 2) returning a value in reply to a callback from the framework part and 3) an assignment to a field declared in a framework-provided class. On the other hand, each occurrence of IoC is considered as a kind of outflow from the framework part. Here, we should notice that the whole behavior of the framework part is determined only by the sequence of inflows from the application part if inputs across other boundaries are fixed[1]. Thus, we can refine the primary characterization of the problem into the following two parts. First, identify a minimal subsequence of inflows to the framework part to gain the behavior-related occurrences of IoC (cf. Fig. 2). Next, extract a minimal part of the application code which can generate such a sequence of inflows. The extracted code can be considered as the mandatory part which enables the intended behavior. This is our characterization of the problem.

Note that under the characterization, a user is required to explicitly or implicitly specify behavior-related occurrences of IoC in the trace. This can be done by a similar way to the trace marking step presented in [8] and [5]. Recall the running example explained in the previous section. In an execution of the sample application, a call to `menuAboutToShow()` (l. 205) and calls to `run()` (l. 221 and l. 226) are behavior-related occurrences of IoC because the former is called by the instance of JFace when the right mouse button is clicked on the tree, and each of the latter is called by it when a menu item in the context menu is selected. Thus, if the user could specify from when to when the behavior of interest is active while collecting the trace, then the set of the behavior-related occurrences of IoC can be identified within the collected trace. For this reason, our approach assumes that when the behavior is activated and when deactivated are observable from the user.

At first glance, a minimal subsequence of inflows to the framework part to gain a certain outflow seems to be straightforwardly identified within a trace by a canonical tracking technique of dynamic flows such as data and control flows backward from the outflow. However, in this case such a tracking does not correctly work since full tracking of dynamic flows may lead to many unrelated inflows for the following reasons. First, tracking control flows generated by conditional branches may lead to unrelated code (it will be discussed in Sect. 4.3). Second, the control and data flows come and go across the framework-application boundary many times, but the minimal subsequence to be identified within the

---

[1] In this section, we assume that the user operations of the framework instance are fixed since we focus on one specific execution scenario to obtain a trace to analyze.

Method call:

p1: $\cdots\ r\mathtt{.m}(a_1,\ldots,a_n)\ \cdots$

p2: $T_0\ \mathtt{m}(T_1\ f_1,\ldots,T_n\ f_n)$ {

p3: $\cdots$ this $\cdots$

p4: $\cdots\ e\ \cdots$

p2 is called from p1, and this operator is evaluated at p3 in the method execution started from p2. An expression e is evaluated at p4, and whether p4 is executed or not is directly determined by the method invocation of p2.

$$f_i(\mathrm{p2}) \overset{\mathrm{DD}}{\to} a_i(\mathrm{p1}) \quad (1 \le i \le n) \qquad (1)^*$$

$$\mathtt{this}(\mathrm{p3}) \overset{\mathrm{DD}}{\to} r(\mathrm{p1}) \qquad\qquad (2)^*$$

$$e(\mathrm{p4}) \overset{\mathrm{CD}}{\to} \mathtt{m}(T_1\ f_1,\ldots,T_n\ f_n\ )(\mathrm{p2})\ (3)$$

$$\mathtt{m}(T_1\ f_1,\ldots,T_n\ f_n\ )(\mathrm{p2})$$
$$\overset{\mathrm{CD}}{\to} r\mathtt{.m}(a_1,\ldots,a_n\ )(\mathrm{p1}) \qquad (4)$$

Return:

p1:   return e;

p2: $\cdots\ r\mathtt{.m}(a_1,\ldots,a_n)\ \cdots$

The value of $r\mathtt{.m}(a_1,\ldots,a_n)$ is returned from p1.

$$r\mathtt{.m}(a_1,\ldots,a_n)(\mathrm{p2}) \overset{\mathrm{DD}}{\to} e(\mathrm{p1}) \qquad (5)^*$$

Conditional Branch:

p1: if (e) {

    / while (e) {

    / for $(s_1;\ e;\ s_2)$ {

p2: $\cdots\ e_2\ \cdots$

An expression e_2 is evaluated at p2, and whether p2 is executed or not is directly determined by the evaluation of e.

$$e_2(\mathrm{p2}) \overset{\mathrm{CD}}{\to} e(\mathrm{p1}) \qquad (6)$$

Expressions:

p1: $\cdots\ o\mathtt{.f}\ \cdots$

A field f of a container o is evaluated at p1.

$$o\mathtt{.f}(\mathrm{p1}) \overset{\mathrm{DD}}{\to} o(\mathrm{p1}) \qquad (7)$$

p1: $\cdots\ a[x]\ \cdots$

An array element $a[x]$ of an array a is evaluated at p1.

$$a[x](\mathrm{p1}) \overset{\mathrm{DD}}{\to} a(\mathrm{p1}) \qquad (8)$$

$$a[x](\mathrm{p1}) \overset{\mathrm{DD}}{\to} x(\mathrm{p1}) \qquad (9)$$

p1: $\cdots\ e_1\ \cdots$

p2: $\cdots\ e_2\ \cdots$

An expression e_2 is evaluated at p2, and e_1 is a subexpression of e_2 and evaluated at p1.

$$e_2(\mathrm{p2}) \overset{\mathrm{DD}}{\to} e_1(\mathrm{p1}) \qquad (10)^*$$

Assignment:

p1: $e_2\ \mathtt{=}\ e_1$

The value of an expression e_1 is assigned to e_2 at p1.

$$e_2(\mathrm{p1}) \overset{\mathrm{DD}}{\to} e_1(\mathrm{p1}) \qquad (11)^*$$

DEF-USE:

p1: $v\ \mathtt{=}\ \cdots$

p2: $\cdots v \cdots$

A value is assigned to a variable v at p1, v is used at p2, and there is no assignment to v from p1 to p2.

$$v(\mathrm{p2}) \overset{\mathrm{DD}}{\to} v(\mathrm{p1}) \qquad (12)^*$$

p1: $o_1\mathtt{.f}\ \mathtt{=}\ \cdots$

p2: $\cdots o_2\mathtt{.f}\ \cdots$

A value is assigned to a field $o_1\mathtt{.f}$ at p1, $o_2\mathtt{.f}$ is used at p2, o_1 and o_2 refer to the same object, and there is no assignment to the field f of the same object from p1 to p2.

$$o_2\mathtt{.f}(\mathrm{p2}) \overset{\mathrm{DD}}{\to} o_1\mathtt{.f}(\mathrm{p1}) \qquad (13)^*$$

*: source dependency which will be explained in Sect. 4.3

Fig. 3. Definition of expression level dynamic dependencies

```
35:     public class SampleView extends ViewPart {
                           e34
36:        private TreeViewer viewer;
38:        private Action action1;
190:       public void createPartControl(Composite parent) {
                         e33
193:         viewer = new TreeViewer(parent, SWT.MULTI | SWT.H_SCROLL | SWT.V_SCROLL);
             e31                                      e32
198:         makeActions();
             e30
199:         hookContextMenu();
             e26
200:       }
201:       private void hookContextMenu() {
                         e25
202:         MenuManager menuMgr = new MenuManager("#PopupMenu");
                         e23              e24
                                e22
204:         menuMgr.addMenuListener(new IMenuListener() {
             e20                      e21
                                      e10
205:           public void menuAboutToShow(IMenuManager mgr ) {
                                                        e9
                         e8
206:             fillContextMenu( mgr );
                                 e7
207:         }});
                                                   e19
                                             e18
208:         Menu menu = menuMgr.createContextMenu(viewer.getControl());
             e15      e16                                  e17
                     e14
                 e13
209:         viewer.getControl().setMenu(menu);
                 e11                    e12
211:       }
                                        e6
212:       private void fillContextMenu(IMenuManager manager ) {
                                                     e5
                 e4
213:         manager.add(action1);
             e3          e2
218:       }
                     e29
219:       private void makeActions() {
220:         action1 = new Action() {
                 e27       e28
221:           public void run() { showMessage("Action 1 executed"); }
                                                            e1
222:         };
```

Fig. 4. Expressions in the sample code

inflows should not be affected by any application-specific structure while it will be affected by the internal structures of the framework part. Therefore in the next section, we define a refined dynamic dependency, *expression level dynamic dependency* which may reduce unrelated results to the framework use, and based on expression level dynamic dependency, we further define *asymmetric slicing*, by which dynamic flow tracking can be appropriately controlled.

4   Basic Definitions

As explained in the previous section, we use a dynamic analysis to obtain a minimal sequence of inflows which leads to the specified occurrences of IoC. For this purpose, we define a fine-grained dynamic dependency, which we call *expression level dynamic dependency* in Sect. 4.1. Based on this dependency, we formally define inflow and outflow in Sect. 4.2. Finally, we define *asymmetric slicing* in Sect. 4.3 to appropriately control dynamic dependency tracking.

4.1   Expression Level Dynamic Dependency

Most of static/dynamic slicing techniques use statement level control and data dependencies. A statement level dependency is a dependency between two distinct statements. For ordinary use, statement level dependencies are sufficient and efficient. However, in this paper, we use more fine-grained dependencies, *expression level dependencies*, so that dependency tracking can be appropriately controlled as discussed in Sect. 3. By using expression level dependencies, more detailed flows of the target program can be obtained. Consider the following sample program.

```
        :
1:      A a = new A();
2:      B b = new B();
3:      C c = new C();
4:      a.set(b, c);
5:      C c2 = a.getC();
        :
7:   public class A {
8:      B b;
9:      C c;
10:     public void set(B b, C c) {
11:        this.b = b;
12:        this.c = c;
13:     }
14:     public B getB() {
15:        return b;
16:     }
17:     public C getC() {
18:        return c;
19:     }
20:  }
```

Assume that the control reaches l. 5, and backward track the part of the code related to c2. With respect to statement level dependencies, l. 5 depends on l. 18, and l. 18 depends on l. 12. Further, l. 12 depends on l. 10, l. 10 depends on l. 4, and finally l. 4 depends on l. 3, l. 2 and l. 1. Here, note that the value of b at l. 2 does not actually affect the value of c2 at l. 5. On the other hand, with respect to expression level dependencies, c at l. 4 can be tracked from c2 at l. 5, but b at l. 4 never be tracked from the same seed. This is because each dependency between two expressions is separately tracked. Thus, also b at l. 2 never be tracked from the seed.

Below, we formally define expression level dependencies. Let T be an execution trace of a program. An evaluation of an expression e at an execution point p in T is denoted by $e(p)$. If $e(p)$ directly dynamically data-depends on $e'(p')$, then we denote $e(p) \overset{DD}{\to} e'(p')$. Also if $e(p)$ directly dynamically control-depends on $e'(p')$, then we denote $e(p) \overset{CD}{\to} e'(p)$. *Expression level dynamic data dependency relation* $\overset{DD}{\to}$ and *expression level dynamic control dependency relation* $\overset{CD}{\to}$ are defined in Fig. 3. Indirect dynamic data and control dependencies are the transitive closures of direct dynamic data and control dependencies and denoted by $\overset{DD}{\to}^{*}$ and $\overset{CD}{\to}^{*}$, respectively. For expressions in Fig. 4, which are extracted from the sample application code in Fig. 1 and numbered in order of the reverse direction of the program execution, we can derive $e_2 \overset{DD}{\to} e_{27} \overset{DD}{\to} e_{28}$ and $e_{28} \overset{CD}{\to} e_{29} \overset{CD}{\to} e_{30} \overset{CD}{\to} e_{33}$, for example. We should notice that there are data dependencies $e_2 \overset{DD}{\to} e_{34}$ and $e_{27} \overset{DD}{\to} e_{34}$ where e_{34} represents implicit this operator. These dependencies are obtained by the rule (7) in Fig. 3 since accesses to fields of this object (i.e., e_2 and e_{27}) implicitly use this operator.

Table 1. Reference point of expression

expression	reference point
variable	declaration location of the variable
field access	declaration location of the field
array element access	declaration location of the array
formal parameter	declaration location of the parameter
this operator	the location where the method declared
any expression which appears at other than the lhs of an assignment[†]	the location where it appears

[†] If one of the above expression (i.e., a variable, a field access, and so on) appears at other than the lhs of an assignment, then it matches at least two rules in this table. In such case, to avoid a collision on its location, we assume that it contains an additional virtual subexpression of the same form whose location corresponds to its declaration location.

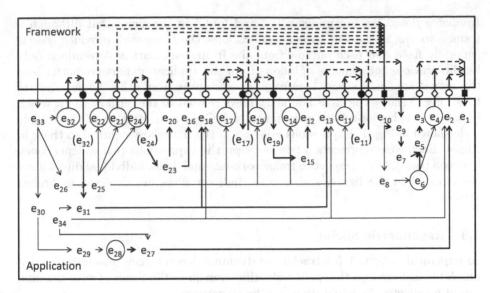

	inputs to framework	outputs from framework
call	◇ (type 1), ○ (type 2)	● (type 3)
IoC	□ (type 4)	■ (type 5)
assignment	△ (type 6)	

Fig. 5. Cross-boundary flows related to e_1 and their types (explained in Sect. 5.3)

4.2 Cross-Boundary Flow

In this subsection, we formally define *inflow* and *outflow* of information flow to model interactions between the application part and the framework part in a trace. First, we define the *reference point* of each expression in a program so that it can be used to determine which part the expression belongs to, the application part or the framework part. The reference point of an expression is defined depending on the type of the expression as shown in Table 1. Since we use expression level dependencies, for each direct dynamic dependency, we can define the parts which the source and the target of the dependency belong to.

We define inflow and outflow based on the direction of each information flow (not on the direction of each direct dependency). Note that a flow is always in the reverse direction of the corresponding dependency. Assume that there exists a direct dynamic dependency d, and let s and t be the source and the target of d, respectively. If the reference points of s and t belong to the application-specific code and the framework-provided code respectively, then we say that there exists an *outflow* from t to s. On the other hand, if the reference points of s and t belong to the framework-provided code and the opposite side code respectively, then we say that there exists an *inflow* from t to s. Also, if both the reference points of s and t belong to the framework-provided code, then the correspnding flow is called *framework-internal*, and both of them belong to the application-specific code then called *application-internal*. Inflow and outflow are called *cross boundary flows*. We use prefixes 'in-' and 'out-' in the sense that although a framework can be used by various applications, the framework-provided code is generally fixed and each outflow from the framework part is determined only by the previous subsequence of inflows from the application part no matter how the actual application part is written where inputs from other boundaries are fixed. Fig. 5 shows the cross boundary flows related to the outflow to e_1, which indicates a behavior-related occurrence of IoC, in an execution of the sample code shown in Fig. 1. Expressions $e_1 \sim e_{33}$ in the figure are identical to those in Fig. 4. Each edge represents a flow between the expressions (not a dependency between them). With respect to framework-internal flows, individual direct flows are omitted in the figure, and instead, indirect flows are depicted as broken arrows.

4.3   Asymmetric Slicing

As explained in Sect. 3, full tracking of dynamic dependencies may lead to much unrelated code to injection points identification since the result of such tracking would be affected by application-specific structures.

For example, consider the dynamic flows shown in Fig. 5 and corresponding code shown in Fig. 4. As shown in Fig. 5, the inflow from e_4 is needed to obtain the outflow to e_1. To generate the inflow, at least an execution of e_4 is needed in any execution of any application. Since e_4 is executed in a method execution started from e_6, e_4 directly control-depends on e_6. However, the invocation of e_6 is not necessary to generate the inflow from e_4 because only the result that the control reaches e_4 is necessary and it does not matter where the control has passed through to e_4. This suggests that dynamic control dependencies within an application part do not need to be tracked.

Similarly, the inflow from e_2 is also necessary to obtain the outflow to e_1. To generate the inflow, at least e_2 should be passed as the parameter of invocation e_4. Since e_2 is a field access of `SampleView`, it directly depends on `this` operator e_{34} in `SampleView`. However, e_{34} is not necessary to generate the inflow because only the fact that the returned value from invocation e_{28} (i.e., created object) is delivered to e_2 is necessary and it does not matter where field e_2 is actually declared. This suggests that dynamic data dependencies on containers of fields within application part do not need to be tracked. For the same reason, dynamic data dependencies of array elements on arrays and indices also do not need to be tracked within any application part. As a result, only expression level dynamic dependencies marked by * in Fig. 3 need to be tracked. We call these dependencies *source dependencies*. Intuitively, source dependency represents the dependency which is needed to generate or deliver a specified value, and roughly corresponds to the dependency to obtain thin slicing [21] and origin relationship of object flow [9].

With respect to framework-internal flows, basically, all of the dependencies should be tracked because the framework-provided code are generally fixed in framework reuse, and the framework-internal flows to obtain the outflow to e_1 are hardly affected by any application-specific structure. However, we will omit only dynamic control dependencies by conditional branches (i.e., (6) in Fig. 3). The reason is as follows. Consider the following simple framework application. In the application, we assume that `Application`, `FeatureA` and `FeatureB` are application-specific, and `Feature` and `FeatureManager` are framework-provided. Further assume that we want to know how to inject the runtime dependency for IoC from l. 18 to l. 23.

```
 1: class Application {
 2:     public void init() {
 3:         FeatureManager featureManager = new FeatureManager();
 4:         FeatureA a = new FeatureA();
 5:         FeatureB b = new FeatureB();
 6:         featureManager.addFeature(a);
 7:         featureManager.addFeature(b);
                :
 8:     }
 9: }
10: public class FeatureManager {
11:     ArrayList<Feature> features = new ArrayList<Feature>();
            :
12:     public void addFeature(Feature f) {
13:         features.add(f);
14:     }
15:     public void activateAll() {
16:         for (int i = 0; i < features.size(); i++) {
17:             Feature f = fratures.get(i);
18:             f.activate();
19:         }
20:     }
21: }
22: public class FeatureB extends Feature {
23:     public void activate() {
24:             :
25:     }
26: }
```

Obviously, the injection point is only the execution of l. 7. However, if we track all of the dependencies within the framework part from the occurrence of the IoC, then also the execution of l. 6 will be extracted since `FeatureB.activate()` indirectly depends on `features.size()` at l. 16, and it indirectly depends on both `featureManager.addFeature(a)` at l. 6 and `featureManager.addFeature(b)` at l. 7. The unrelated code is essentially introduced by the control dependency of `f.activate()` at l. 18 on 'i < `features.size()`' at l. 16. This suggests that dynamic control dependencies by conditional branches should not be tracked. Note that such a case is not specific to this toy example, and a similar case is identified in a subject of the case study presented in Sect. 7.1. Needlessness of tracking control dependencies by conditional branches is also discussed in [21].

Based on the above observations, an *asymmetric slice* for a given seed s is defined as the part of the framework application code which can be obtained by

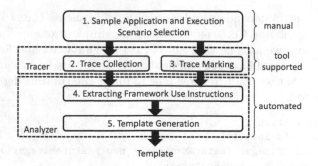

Fig. 6. Method overview

tracking from s, 1) all cross boundary dependencies, 2) all source dependencies within the application part and 3) all expression level dynamic dependencies other than control dependencies by conditional branches within the framework part. In Fig. 5, thick arrows represent the flows backward tracked by asymmetric slicing for seed e_1 and the expressions surrounded by circles are the end points of the tracking.

5 Framework Usage Extraction Method

In this section, we present the entire process of our method to extract framework usage. An overview of the method is shown in Fig. 6. Its process consists of five steps. The first step is performed manually, the second and third steps are performed concurrently and supported by a tool, and the remainder is fully automated. We have implemented the automated parts of the process as an Eclipse plug-in, named *AsymmetricTracker*.

5.1 Sample Application Selection

Our method requires only a single sample application to collect a trace. The sample application is required to show the behavior which the user intends to implement in his/her own application. In general, also unrelated behaviors may be implemented in the same application, but our method can work if the behavior of interest can be observed separately from the other behaviors at runtime.

5.2 Trace Collection and Marking

An execution trace of the sample application can be collected by *tracer* of AsymmetricTracker, which is implemented in AspectJ. It can be woven into either the source code of the application at compile-time or its bytecode at load-time. For load-time weaving, we use Equinox Weaving. Trace data can be collected by running the sample application into which the tracer has been woven. As explained in Sect. 3, the user is also required to mark from when to when the behavior of interest is activated during the trace collecting execution so that the occurrences of IoC which activates the behavior can be specified in the collected data.

```
204: public class menuexampleapplication.views.SampleView.1 extends SomeFWClass {
205:     public void menuAboutToShow(obj411392407) {
213:         obj411392407.add(obj1439519072);
207:     }
207: }
220: public class menuexampleapplication.views.SampleView.3 extends SomeFWClass {
221:     public void run() {
221:     }
222: }
 35: public class menuexampleapplication.views.SampleView extends SomeFWClass {
190:     public void createPartControl(obj1048781428) {
193:         TreeViewer obj326074899 = new TreeViewer(obj1048781428);
202:         MenuManager obj411392407 = new MenuManager();
204:         1 obj995514860 = new 1();
204:         obj411392407.addMenuListener(obj995514860);
208:         org.eclipse.swt.widgets.Control obj1861376421 = obj326074899.getControl();
208:         org.eclipse.swt.widgets.Menu obj336910740
                 = obj411392407.createContextMenu(obj1861376421);
209:         obj1861376421.setMenu(obj336910740);
220:         3 obj1439519072 = new 3();
200:     }
267: }
```

Fig. 7. The generated template

5.3   Extracting Framework Use Instructions

This step is the core of our method. We have implemented this step and the
successive step as *analyzer* of AsymmetricTracker using Java. As discussed in
Sect. 3, we intend to extract a minimal subsequence of inflows to the framework
part to gain the behavior-related occurrences of IoC in a given trace data. The
inputs to this step are the collected trace data, specified occurrences of IoC,
and the boundary between the framework part and the application part. Note
that our method allows a user to specify each of the parts by multiple packages'
names. The extraction is done by asymmetric slicing. In the following, we explain
how the slicing proceeds.

Controlled Tracking. First, consider how behavior-related IoC occurs. As
explained in Sect. 4.2, an occurrence of IoC corresponds to an outflow from the
framework part. Thus, the controlled tracking starts with such an outflow and
proceeds backward. For example, in the running example, the outflow to e_1 in
Fig. 4 and 5 is the last occurrence of behavior-related IoC, and the tracking starts
with e_1. As discussed in Sect. 4.3, to avoid being affected by any application-
specific structure, the backward tracking is controlled by asymmetric slicing.
Fig. 5 shows the controlled backward tracking from e_1 (the arrows in the figure
are in the reverse direction).

Extraction of Instructions. Cross boundary flows within the asymmetric slice
for a specific outflow constitute a minimal set of inflows and outflows to obtain
the outflow. In this paper, we call application-side expressions of minimal inflows
and outflows to obtain the behavior-related occurrences of IoC *framework use
instructions*. For example in Fig. 5, $e_2 \sim e_4$, e_9, e_{10}, $e_{11} \sim e_{14}$, $e_{16} \sim e_{22}$, e_{24}, e_{32}

are framework use instructions. Note that all of these expressions are included in the mandatory lines in the sample code (see Fig. 1 and 4). Each framework use instruction is classified into one of the following types;

type 1: a call to a method declared in a framework's type,

type 2: a call to a method declared in a framework's type with passing appropriate parameters,

type 3: a call to a method declared in a framework's type with receiving its return value,

type 4: an override of a method declared in a framework's type with returning an appropriate return value.

type 5: an override of a method declared in a framework's type with or without receiving its parameters, and

type 6: an assignment to a field declared in a framework's type.

As shown in Fig. 5, type 1, 2, 4 and 6 correspond to inflows to the framework part. The other ones correspond to outflows from the part, which will be needed to generate appropriate inflows to the part. For example, the calls marked by '•' in Fig. 5 are all type 3, and the returned values from them are to be passed as parameters or receivers of the calls of type 2 which are marked by '○'. In the figure, type 1, 2, 3, 4, 5 and 6 instructions are marked by '◇', '○', '•', '□', '■', and '△', respectively. In addition to the type of the instruction, each instruction has the information about the object's ID which should be passed to, received from or returned to the framework part in the trace. Also, each one of type 1 to 5 instructions is related to one call which is located across the framework-application boundary, and it can have zero or more child instructions. A child instruction of an instruction i_2 is an instruction i_1 such that i_1-related call is located at a descendant of i_2-related call in the runtime call hierarchy and there is no instruction between i_1 and i_2. The whole information of instructions is used in the next step.

5.4   Template Generation

Based on the framework use instructions extracted in the previous step, this step generates a template code which leads to the intended occurrences of IoC. The generated template code of the running example and corresponding line numbers in Fig. 1 are shown in Fig. 7. Recall the cross boundary flows in Fig. 5. In the figure, for example, e_{12} is type 2 instruction and e_{11}, e_{19} and e_{24} are type 3 instructions. From these instructions, we can generate the statements corresponding to l. 202, l. 208 and l. 209 in Fig. 7. Note that in the template, l. 208 is divided into two statements since it includes two instructions. The template may include a call to a method declared in a framework's type with passing appropriate parameters and receiving its return value, creation of an instance of an appropriate framework's class, an assignment to a field declared in a framework's type, subtyping an appropriate supertype declared in the framework, and implementation of an appropriate supertype's method. We designed this step so that source dependencies within the application part can be preserved in the template. The template is generated according to the types of instructions. We omit the details of the algorithm from the paper due to limitations of space.

6   Implementation

We have implemented tracer of AsymmetricTracker using AspectJ and analyzer of AsymmetricTracker using Java. The analyzer is also implemented as an Eclipse plug-in. The target Java program into which the tracer has been woven can be launched by the plug-in and its trace is collected and written into a text file.

In expression level dynamic dependencies, a primitive value can be tracked only through the rule (6) or (9) in Fig. 3, or when the seed is of a primitive type. However, the rule (6) is never used in asymmetric slicing since no dynamic control dependency by a conditional branch is tracked by it (as discussed in Sect. 4.3). In addition, a seed of asymmetric slicing in our tool is always a method signature invoked through IoC and it is not of a primitive type (as explained in Sect. 5). Thus, tracking dynamic dependencies among primitive type expressions can be avoided if the rule (9) can be ignored. By designing the tool not to track any dynamic dependency among primitive type expressions,

- the size of the trace data to analyze can be significantly reduced,
- the impacts of the tracer on the performance of the target program's execution can be reduced with the following slight approximation, and
- AspectJ can be used to implement the tracer with the same slight approximation.

The approximation of slices is done as follows. First, we focus on the fact that a reference value is unique to each referred object and it is never recreated by any calculation. Thus, if a reference value is found in a method execution, then it should have originated from one of the following.

case 1: It has been created in the previous part of the method execution.
case 2: It has been returned from a method invocation in the previous part of the method execution.
case 3: It has been passed as a parameter of the method invocation ('this' object is considered as a kind of parameter).
case 4: It has been got from a field in the previous part of the method execution.
case 5: It has been got from an array element in the previous part of the method execution.
case 6: It has been stored in a final local variable in an enclosing method when the method is invoked.

By searching the above origin of a target reference value, expression level dynamic data and control dependencies can be efficiently tracked since the points in the method execution to search the origin are limited as the above and no assignment to a local variable nor an argument within the method execution should be tracked. The search would fail only when more than two origins are found in the same method execution but such a case is almost negligible. If case 5 and 6 of the above origins can be ignored, then we can use AspectJ for the implementation of the tracer to collect the trace data (since AspectJ can not intercept these cases). The details of the algorithm are omitted from the paper due to limitations of space. For the details, the reader can refer to [10].

7   Evaluation

For the evaluation of AsymmetricTracker, we have conducted several case studies (Sect. 7.1). Also, we have evaluated the impacts of AsymmetricTracker's tracer on the performance of the sample application's execution (Sect. 7.2).

7.1   Template Extraction Quality

Subjects of Case Studies. To evaluate the quality of the extracted templates, we compare AsymmetricTracker's extraction results with FUDA's ones given in [5]. Furthermore, to evaluate the effects of asymmetric slicing, we have also implemented an extraction tool, named FullTracker, which works with the same tracer as AsymmetricTracker but uses canonical uncontrolled slicing excepting control dependencies by conditional branches, and compare it with the other tools. In [5], experimental data of 14 subjects from four real-world frameworks are presented. However among them, 6 subjects are out of the AsymmetricTracker's scope since they are unrelated to dependency injection and do not require the slicing technique of FUDA. Moreover, two of the subjects are from Java 2D, and the tracer of AsymmetricTracker cannot be woven into Java 2D class libraries since Equinox Weaving requires that the target system has been put into OSGi bundles. Therefore, we have conducted case studies on the remaining 6 subjects from three frameworks; JFace[2], UI in Eclipse[3] and GEF[4].

Reference Templates. To measure the precision and recall of the extraction results, some appropriate reference templates are needed. In order to keep the comparison fair, we have intended to borrow the mandatory parts of the reference templates at [7] in their original forms. However, slight revisions of the reference templates were needed for the following reasons.

- Several mandatory return statements are missing in the original templates.
- Mandatory but indirect use of the framework (e.g., use of `TreeViewer` at l. 193 in Fig. 1, whose ancestor class is defined in JFace) is often missing in the original templates.
- Several optional but not mandatory statements (e.g., l. 203 in Fig. 1, without which the context menu can work) are included in the original templates.
- The reference templates for two subjects from GEF are somewhat erroneous.
- We think that automatically generated method stubs by IDE such as abstract method overriding are not needed in the mandatory parts. Thus, we have removed such method stubs from the templates, but taken care so that the revisions of the templates do not have harmful effects on the FUDA's results.
- If more than one set of mandatory statements is definable for one subject, then the closest one to the extracted template is selected.

---

[2] http://wiki.eclipse.org/index.php/JFace
[3] http://www.eclipse.org/
[4] http://www.eclipse.org/gef/

Sample Applications. The experimental data in [5] are obtained by using two traces of two sample applications per one subject. Since AsymmetricTracker and FullTracker require only one trace of one sample application, we chose one from the two samples used by FUDA. Some applications are non-small (e.g., Flow in GEF contains 4889 LOC).

Experimental Results. The precision and recall of each generated template is calculated against the corresponding mandatory reference template as follows. Let M be the set of statements in the mandatory reference template and G be those in the generated template. Then the precision is calculated by $|G \cap M|/|G|$ and the recall is calculated by $|G \cap M|/|M|$. Also the numbers of false positives and false negatives are calculated by $|G| - |G \cap M|$ and $|M| - |G \cap M|$, respectively. The comparison among AsymmetricTracker's results, FullTracker's ones and FUDA's ones is shown in Table 2. The detailed results of the case studies are available at online [10]. For all subjects, AsymmetricTracker outputs templates with significantly higher precision than FUDA and also higher precision than FullTracker. Note that to obtain the results, FUDA used two sample applications per one subject, and to improve the precision results, it will require more sample applications. With respect to the recall, there cannot be found any significant difference among them (the averages of AsymmetricTracker and FullTracker are higher than FUDA). In fact, the sets of false negatives in AsymmetricTracker's results and FUDA's ones are incomparable for several subjects. For example, only two false negatives are common to both results about content assist. AsymmetricTracker could not identify two statements due to not tracking control dependencies by conditional branches, and the others due to appearing at the marked region of the trace, within which AsymmetricTracker extracts only callbacks from the framework part. FUDA could not identify six statements (three return statements, two of which are common to AsymmetricTracker's ones, and three indirect uses of framework-provided class). Most of the AsymmetricTracker's false negatives for GEF are caused by only one conditional branch not tracked by asymmetric slicing, but some of them are tracked by FullTracker through a bypass on dependency chains.

7.2 Computing Performance

We have evaluated the impact of the tracer of AsymmetricTracker and FullTracker on the performance of a sample application's execution when collecting a trace. Among the tool-supported steps, the impact on the trace collection step is considered most crucial because only this step needs user operations. Unfortunately, we could not find any implementation of FUDA, and thus could not evaluate its tracer's performance. We have woven the tracer of AsymmetricTracker and FullTracker into UI, JFace and SWT parts of Eclipse platform and measured the time required to launch Eclipse platform with and without the tracer. The reason why we focused on the launching is that its execution is not affected by any user operation. According to our measurements, the sample

Table 2. Comparison among AsymmetricTracker's results, FullTracker's ones and FUDA's ones regarding 6 subjects from JFace, UI, GEF

framework	subject	method	$|M|$	$|G|$	$|M \cap G|$	false positives	false negatives	precision	recall
JFace	context menu	AsymmetricTracker	13	13	12	1	1	92.3%	92.3%
		FullTracker	13	19	12	7	1	63.2%	92.3%
		FUDA	13	16	11	5	2	68.8%	84.6%
	content assist	AsymmetricTracker	20	25	16	9	4	64.0%	80.0%
		FullTracker	20	29	16	13	4	55.2%	80.0%
		FUDA	17	22	11	11	6	50.0%	64.7%
	toolbar button	AsymmetricTracker	9	10	9	1	0	90.0%	100%
		FullTracker	9	12	9	3	0	75.0%	100%
		FUDA	9	13	4	9	5	30.8%	44.4%
UI	navigate	AsymmetricTracker	14	13	13	0	1	100%	92.9%
		FullTracker	14	13	13	0	1	100%	92.9%
		FUDA	14	33	14	19	0	42.4%	100%
GEF	figure	AsymmetricTracker	26	18	16	2	10	88.9%	61.5%
		FullTracker	26	53	19	34	7	35.8%	73.1%
		FUDA	26	67	17	50	9	25.4%	65.4%
	connection	AsymmetricTracker	36	21	19	2	17	90.5%	52.8%
		FullTracker	36	68	23	45	13	33.8%	63.9%
		FUDA	34	75	18	57	16	24.0%	52.9%
	average	AsymmetricTracker	–	–	–	–	–	87.6%	79.9%
		FullTracker	–	–	–	–	–	60.5%	83.7%
		FUDA	–	–	–	–	–	40.2%	68.7%

application ran about 2.8 times slower when collecting its trace on a desktop PC with a Core i7-2600 at 3.40GHz, 16.0GB of RAM and Windows 7. The impact to the execution is considered relatively small.

8   Discussion

The validity of our method strongly relies on that of our characterization of the problem discussed in Sect. 3. Owing to the characterization, we develop a dynamic flow analysis method to identify the parts strictly related to the application-specific behavior of interest using one sample application's trace. In this section, we will discuss 1) the validity of our characterization of the problem, 2) the validity of our dynamic approach, and 3) the feasibility of our method.

Validity of Our Characterization of the Problem. In Sect. 3, we have characterized the problem of framework usage extraction as a kind of strict dynamic flow analysis problem. In the characterization, we focus only on the intended behavior's activations which are caused by some occurrences of inversion of control in a sample application's trace and consider extracting a minimal part of the code which strictly affects the occurrences of inversion of control in the trace. Therefore, if such a part of the code is extracted, then there should be a strict dependency between the behavior's activation and each part of the extracted code. This means that the extracted code reflects a kind of lowerbound of the mandatory framework usage. Thus, we can expect that our method has less potential for false positive results as its nature.

On the other hand, there is no guarantee of less potential for false negative results in the natures of the method. Such a potential may be introduced by our characterization of omitting behavior's aspects other than its activations and/or our approach to tracking i.e., asymmetric slicing. Thus, the validity of our characterization of the problem mainly depends on how little false negatives our method generally causes. We will confirm it through the following discussion.

Validity of Our Dynamic Analysis Approach. As we can see from the results of the case studies shown in Table 2, AsymmetricTracker almost succeeded in extracting the mandatory parts of the reference templates through only a single sample application trace. Almost all false negatives (except for three statements) are caused by not tracking control dependencies by conditional branches. Instead, if such control dependencies are tracked, more false positives (e.g., l. 210 in Fig. 1 for context menu) would be caused. On the other hand, FUDA causes false negatives due to several different reasons. The most essential reason is that FUDA does not track dynamic flows within the framework parts of traces. As a whole, the recall of AsymmetricTracker's results is almost at the same level as FUDA, while the average is higher than FUDA. With respect to the precision, AsymmetricTracker is expected to have less potential for false positive results as its nature (as discussed in the previous subsection). The results of the case studies well support the prediction. In addition, based on the comparison with FullTracker, we can confirm the effectiveness of asymmetric slicing.

Feasibility of Our Method. FUDA requires a user for marking on the trace from when to when the behavior of interest is activated during an execution scenario to refine the results. The task is quite straightforward since no knowledge about the framework's APIs is needed for the task. AsymmetricTracker employs a very similar approach to specifying the origin of dynamic flow tracking, and the marking task is also straightforward. Dynamic analysis approaches such as AsymmetricTracker and FUDA cannot work without any executable sample application. However, a user can hardly find an appropriate sample application especially for rare framework usage. Even if the user can find it, the setup of its runtime environment might not be easy. Since AsymmetricTracker requires only one trace of a single sample application, such difficulties can be mitigated. As explained in 7.2, the impact of the tracer on the trace collection step is considered most crucial, but the tracer still be feasible for a large scale application such as Eclipse platform. With respect to the full-automated steps, each template in the case studies could be obtained within 15 minutes. These steps will significantly reduce manual effort for mandatory part extraction.

Strengths and Weaknesses. As a whole, AsymmetricTracker has almost succeeded in extracting the mandatory code for framework use through only a single application's trace with relatively low false positives and negatives. In comparison with FUDA, AsymmetricTracker fails to extract a mandatory statement when there exists a control dependency by a conditional branch between the statement and the occurrences of inversion of control. On the other hand, FUDA fails to extract a mandatory statement if it is a return statement or indirect use of the framework. AsymmetricTracker is suitable to extract the mandatory part of the application code especially in case of using dependency injection, but FUDA requires two or more applications to obtain such a part. Instead, FUDA can extract optional parts which are excluded by AsymmetricTracker. Since AsymmetricTracker well preserves the traceability links between the template and the sample application, as suggested in [5], they would be helpful to manually locate optional parts. For example in Fig. 1, optional statements (e.g., l. 216 and l. 223) are placed close to mandatory statements. Thus, locating them and determining whether they are optional or not are rather straightforward.

9   Related Work

9.1   Framework Usage Support

Many research efforts have been paid to support complicated framework use. We categorize the researches into the following three groups by their usage context.

Example Recommender Tools. Many tools have been presented to support a programmer who is faced with difficulties using unfamiliar framework's APIs by recommending example component, usage or code snippet. Such approaches are categorized by their underlying techniques. Several tools have been proposed [4, 11–15] which recommend examples by mining source code repositories or an existing application. CodeWeb [11] uses software structure to obtain usage patterns, CodeBroker [12] uses comments and method signatures to locate task-relevant components, and Strathcona [4] uses structural context to generate a source code snippet. MAPO [13] clusters code snippets which are obtained from a repository and mines API usage patterns. In [14], path sensitive static dataflow analysis, clustering and pattern abstraction are used to human-readable usage examples. In [15], a client change history is used to detect temporal usage patterns. These approaches does not assume the programmer's knowledge about the framework's APIs, but they require source code repositories. Prospector [16], XSnippet [17] and PARSEWeb [18] use source and destination types to recommend examples to obtain an object of the destination type from that of the source type. These approaches are quite helpful in specific usage contexts. However, they require the knowledge of these types and their usage contexts.

Defect Detection Tools. Programmers who use unfamiliar framework's APIs are often required to follow some implicit rules. If they do not use the API's without following the rules, then potential defects can be introduced. To detect such potential defects, several tools [6, 19, 20] have been proposed. For example, PR-Miner [19] and JADET [20] can detect such potential defects using API usage patterns which frequently appear in a repository. DMMC [6] detects missing method calls based on usage pattern mining with relatively low false positives. From the aspect of framework usage extraction, these tools can be considered as kinds of code completion tools. If a partial usage of the framework's APIs has been written by a programmer, then the tools can help him/her complete his/her code by detecting missing code. In this paper, we focus on writing such a partial usage rather than completing its implementation.

Framework Usage Extraction Tools. Most of the above tools use static approaches to retrieve source code repositories. The main advantage of static approaches is that they do not require any executable application and any run-time environment. However, such tools tend to require a number of instances of framework usage which appear in the code of many sample applications or source code repositories to obtain one reliable result. In contrast to them, dynamic approaches may allow a user to work with a smaller number of applications. FUDA [5] is a pioneering work to use dynamic approach for framework usage extraction, and it is one of the closest researches to ours. It can extract mandatory and optional code for framework use as a template from few traces of few sample applications. They also demonstrated the quality of the generated templates by showing high precision and recall of the templates through case studies of several real-world frameworks. Employing a stricter dynamic flow analysis, we improve their results in terms of the number of sample applications to use. Our method requires only a single sample application's trace to obtain mandatory code. As is the case with FUDA, our method generates mandatory code as a template for certain framework use. The validity of our results is confirmed by comparing the results with FUDA's reference templates. The main difference from FUDA in terms of technical aspects is that FUDA uses a lightweight slicing technique, which only tracks object IDs of parameters, return values and receivers which appear at the framework-application boundary, to reduce false positives but our method uses a stricter dynamic flow analysis. This feature will work in the direction to reduce false positives and to possibly increase false negatives. We have confirmed that our method causes significantly low numbers of false positives in the case studies. With respect to false negatives, the results of our method and those of FUDA are generally incomparable. Since our method has less potential for false positive results as its nature, it will be suitable to extract mandatory framework usage. In contrast, if one wishes to obtain some optional framework usage in addition to mandatory one, then FUDA will be more helpful than ours.

9.2   Program Analysis

From a technical point of view, object flow [9] is a closest one to our dynamic analysis technique, namely asymmetric slicing. The dependency used by asymmetric slicing within the application specific part correspond to origin relationship of object flow, and the dependency within the framework part are a strict extension of that part of object flow. Although a static analysis technique, thin slicing [21] uses a similar data dependency to object flow. As is the case with object flow, the dependency within the framework part cannot be completely tracked by thin slicing with no expansion. The paper also presents a method for hierarchically expanding thin slices, but it cannot be used in automated framework usage extraction since the expansion is controlled manually. Among trace analysis methods, we should pick up Scenariographer [22]. It extracts sequences of method invocations to the objects of a target class from a trace, and generates class usage scenarios from the method invocation sequences. FUDA and our method also extract sequences of method invocations from a trace, but they are not restricted to invocations to the objects of one class but focus on the invocations between the framework and the application parts.

10   Conclusion

We have characterized the framework usage extraction problem as a kind of strict dynamic flow analysis problem and presented a method to automatically solve the problem which can work with only a single execution trace of a single sample application. By this method, a user can understand why each statement of the extracted usage is needed. The results of the case studies indicate that our characterization of the problem is valid and our method is suitable to extract mandatory framework usage from application code. As future work, we wish to improve the recall of AsymmetricTracker's outputs by distinguishing types of control dependency to track from those not to track. To extract optional parts, we expect that calls to the framework part in the marked region are useful.

Acknowledgment. The authors would like to thank Yusuke Tezuka for his initial contribution to this work, and also thank Keishi Yamane for his efforts to implement AsymmetricTracker. This work was partly supported by Grants-in-Aid for Scientific Research (C) No.25350306 from the Japan Society for the Promotion of Science and Grant-in-Aid for Challenging Exploratory Research No.23650016 from the Japan Ministry of Education.

References

1. Ko, A., Myers, B., Aung, H.: Six learning barriers in end-user programming systems. In: Proceedings of the 2004 IEEE Symposium on Visual Languages Human Centric Computing (VLHCC 2004), pp. 199–206 (2004)
2. Fairbanks, G.: Software engineering environment support for frameworks A position paper. In: Proceedings of the ICSE 2004 Workshop on Directions in Software Engineering Environments (WoDiSEE 2004), pp. 70–73 (2004)
3. Fowler, M.: Inversion of control containers and the dependency injection pattern (2004), http://www.martinfowler.com/articles/injection.html#FormsOfDependencyInjection

4. Holmes, R., Murphy, G.C.: Using structural context to recommend source code examples. In: Proceedings of ICSE, pp. 117–125 (2005)
5. Heydarnoori, A., Czarnecki, K., Bartolomei, T.T.: Supporting framework use via automatically extracted concept-implementation templates. In: Drossopoulou, S. (ed.) ECOOP 2009. LNCS, vol. 5653, pp. 344–368. Springer, Heidelberg (2009)
6. Monperrus, M., Bruch, M., Mezini, M.: Detecting missing method calls in object-oriented software. In: D'Hondt, T. (ed.) ECOOP 2010. LNCS, vol. 6183, pp. 2–25. Springer, Heidelberg (2010)
7. Generative Software Development Lab.: FUDA supporting material, http://gsd.uwaterloo.ca/tse-fuda
8. Salah, M.: An environment for comprehending the behavior of software systems, Ph.D. dissertation, Drexel University (2005)
9. Lienhard, A., Gîrba, T., Wang, J.: Practical object-oriented back-in-time debugging. In: Vitek, J. (ed.) ECOOP 2008. LNCS, vol. 5142, pp. 592–615. Springer, Heidelberg (2008)
10. Software Design and Verification Lab.: ECOOP 2014 artifacts page, http://nitta-lab-www.is.konan-u.ac.jp/ECOOP2014
11. Michail, A.: Data mining library reuse patterns using generalized association rules. In: Proceedings of ICSE, pp. 167–176 (2000)
12. Ye, Y., Fischer, G.: Supporting reuse by delivering task-relevant and personalized information. In: Proceedings of ICSE, pp. 513–523 (2002)
13. Zhong, H., Xie, T., Zhang, L., Pei, J., Mei, H.: MAPO: Mining and recommending API usage patterns. In: Drossopoulou, S. (ed.) ECOOP 2009. LNCS, vol. 5653, pp. 318–343. Springer, Heidelberg (2009)
14. Buse, R.P.L., Weimer, W.: Synthesizing API usage examples. In: Proceedings of ICSE, pp. 782–792 (2012)
15. Uddin, G., Dagenais, B., Robillard, M.P.: Temporal analysis of API usage concepts. In: Proceedings of ICSE, pp. 804–814 (2012)
16. Mandelin, D., Xu, L., Bodík, R., Kimelman, D.: Jungloid mining: helping to navigate the API jungle. In: Proceedings of PLDI, pp. 48–61 (2005)
17. Sahavechaphan, N., Claypool, K.: XSnippet: mining for sample code. In: Proceedings of OOPSLA, pp. 413–430 (2006)
18. Thummalapenta, A., Xie, T.: PARSEWeb: A programmer assistant for reusing open source code on the web. In: Proceedings of ASE, pp. 204–213 (2007)
19. Li, Z., Zhou, Y.: PR-Miner: automatically extracting implicit programming rules and detecting violations in large software code. In: Proceedings of ESEC/FSE, pp. 306–315 (2005)
20. Wasylkowski, A., Zeller, A., Lindig, C.: Detecting object usage anomalies. In: Proceedings of ESEC/FSE, pp. 35–44 (2007)
21. Sridharan, M., Fink, S.J., Bodík, R.: Thin slicing. In: Proceedings of PLDI, pp. 112–122 (2007)
22. Salah, M., Denton, T., Mancoridis, S., Shokoufandeh, A., Vokolos, F.I.: Scenariographer: A tool for reverse engineering class usage scenarios from method invocation sequences. In: Proceedings of ICSM, pp. 155–164 (2005)

Cooperative Scheduling of Parallel Tasks with General Synchronization Patterns

Shams Imam and Vivek Sarkar

Department of Computer Science, Rice University
{shams,vsarkar}@rice.edu

Abstract. In this paper, we address the problem of scheduling parallel tasks with general synchronization patterns using a cooperative runtime. Current implementations for task-parallel programming models provide efficient support for fork-join parallelism, but are unable to efficiently support more general synchronization patterns such as locks, futures, barriers and phasers. We propose a novel approach to addressing this challenge based on *cooperative scheduling* with *one-shot delimited continuations* (OSDeConts) and *event-driven controls* (EDCs). The use of OSDeConts enables the runtime to suspend a task at any point (thereby enabling the task's worker to switch to another task) whereas other runtimes may have forced the task's worker to be blocked. The use of EDCs ensures that identification of suspended tasks that are ready to be resumed can be performed efficiently. Furthermore, our approach is more efficient than schedulers that spawn additional worker threads to compensate for blocked worker threads.

We have implemented our cooperative runtime in Habanero-Java (HJ), an explicitly parallel language with a large variety of synchronization patterns. The OSDeCont and EDC primitives are used to implement a wide range of synchronization constructs, including those where a task may trigger the enablement of multiple suspended tasks (as in futures, barriers and phasers). In contrast, current task-parallel runtimes and schedulers for the fork-join model (including schedulers for the Cilk language) focus on the case where only one continuation is enabled by an event (typically, the termination of the last child/descendant task in a join scope). Our experimental results show that the HJ cooperative runtime delivers significant improvements in performance and memory utilization on various benchmarks using *future* and *phaser* constructs, relative to a thread-blocking runtime system while using the same underlying work-stealing task scheduler.

Keywords: Task Parallelism, Cooperative Scheduling, Delimited Continuations, Async-Finish Parallelism, Habanero-Java.

1 Introduction

With the advent of the multicore era, it is clear that future improvements in application performance will primarily come from increased parallelism in software.

R. Jones (Ed.): ECOOP 2014, LNCS 8586, pp. 618–643, 2014.

A dominant programming model for multicore processors is the Task Parallel Model (TPM), as exemplified by programming models such as Cilk [2], TBB [25], OpenMP 3.0 [24], Java's ForkJoinPool [22], Chapel [4], X10 [5], Habanero-C [31], and Habanero Java (HJ) [3]. Current implementations for the TPM provide efficient support for fork-join parallelism, but are unable to efficiently support more general synchronization patterns that are important for a wide range of applications. In the presence of patterns such as futures [17], barriers, and phasers [26], current TPM implementations revert to thread-blocking scheduling of tasks. Barriers and futures are two common synchronization patterns advocated by many industry multicore programming models that go beyond the fork-join model. But, there is as yet no demonstration of an effective solution to schedule programs with futures and barriers in a scalable fashion when the number of blocked tasks exceeds the number of worker threads.

In this paper, we address the problem of efficient cooperative scheduling of parallel tasks with general synchronization patterns. Our solution is founded on the use of *one-shot delimited continuations* (OSDeConts, Section 4.1) and *single-assignment event-driven controls* (EDCs, Section 4.2) to schedule tasks cooperatively in the presence of different synchronization patterns. The OSDe-Cont and EDC primitives can be used to support a wide range of *synchronization constructs* (SyncCons) including those where a task/event may trigger the enablement of multiple suspended tasks. This general case is not supported by work-stealing schedulers for Cilk and other fork-join models for task parallelism. While efficient continuation-based scheduling is well established for fork-join parallelism in well structured *tree-like* computations in projects such as Cilk and Manticore [10], we are unaware of any past work that supports more general (and a wide variety of) synchronization patterns in a scalable manner with support for large numbers of suspended tasks. To the best of our knowledge, our paper is the first to support synchronization patterns that represent arbitrary computation graphs through the use of one-shot continuations.

Our cooperative approach of using OSDeConts and EDCs is more performant than schedulers that spawn additional worker threads to compensate for blocked worker threads (as well as approaches that leave worker threads blocked without spawning new worker threads). Transparent use of OSDeConts allows us to leverage the benefits of event-driven programming while the user code remains in standard thread-based structure, thereby avoiding the need to write fragmented difficult to understand event-driven programs where logical units are broken down into multiple callbacks [9]. Section 2 uses simple example programs to illustrate the performance issues with scheduling programs that use blocking SyncCons and the productivity issues with event-driven programming. The contributions of this paper are:

- Use of OSDeConts and EDCs to create a new generic cooperative runtime for task-parallel programs (Section 4). We believe that any task-parallel Sync-Con can be supported by this cooperative runtime. To the best of our knowledge, this is the first effort to systematically use OSDeConts to support a task-parallel runtime. A key challenge we address in our runtime is that

the resolution of a synchronization can, in general, trigger the enablement of multiple suspended tasks, a scenario that does not occur in traditional fork-join operations.
- We include recipes for implementing different SyncCons using the API exposed by our cooperative runtime (Section 5). These (and other) SyncCons are all treated uniformly by the runtime and can all be used together without issues in the same program.
- An implementation of our cooperative runtime for the HJ language which supports a large variety of SyncCons.
- Empirical evaluation of the performance of our cooperative runtime relative to a runtime that uses thread-blocking operations (Section 6). Our experiments on various benchmarks show that the cooperative runtime can achieve over 10× speed-up over a runtime that uses thread-blocking operations while implementing SyncCons such as *futures* and *phasers*.

The rest of this paper includes Section 3 which discusses related work and Section 7 which contains our conclusions. For the interested reader, [21] contains additional details on our implementation, including the use of an extended version of the open source Kilim bytecode weaver [28] to support OSDeConts. Our implementation conforms to all the constraints imposed by a standard Java Virtual Machine (JVM).

2   Motivating Examples

In popular task parallel runtimes such as those for HJ, X10, and Chapel, the runtime is usually able to handle synchronization points associated with fork and join operations without blocking the worker. However, other potential synchronization points (such as resolution of future results, point-to-point synchronization points, lock-based implementation of atomic regions) are blocking operations in the runtime. This may result in the worker threads being blocked, effectively resulting in fewer parallel threads that are executing. The runtime can compensate by creating additional worker threads, but this adds to overhead in the runtime as each thread needs its own system resources. In addition, context switching overhead is incurred when the blocked threads become unblocked.

On Intel processors it takes about 1100 ns per thread context switch (without cache effects) [27]. In contrast, object allocation, method call, and setting fields takes around 30 ns, 5 ns and 1 ns respectively [14] on the CLR (timings on the JVM should be similar). Our continuation creation scheme includes one object allocation, setting fields per live variable to be saved, and returning from method calls. Using continuations should cost less than 50 ns per method in the call chain. Besides, the compensation strategy of creating additional threads is contradictory to the goal of the TPM which relies on using comparatively few heavyweight threads to run many lightweight tasks. Finally, these current solutions do not scale as increasing the number of worker threads can eventually cause the runtime to crash due to exhaustion of memory or other system resources.

In addition to the problems mentioned above, presence of synchronization constraints can also lead to starvation situations when all available worker threads become blocked. In such scenarios, the program behavior can change when the parallel program is run with different numbers of worker threads with the starvation scenario not occurring when enough worker threads are provided to compensate for the number of tasks involved in the synchronization constraint.

```
1  public class CyclicProducers {
2    public static void main(final String[] args) {
3      // number of tasks to create
4      final int numTasks = 64;
5      finish {
6        final ItemHolder itemHolder = new ItemHolder(numTasks);
7        for (int i = 0; i < numTasks; i++) {
8          final int myId = i;
9          async {
10           // first produce an item
11           final int myProducedItem = produceItem(...);
12           itemHolder.put(myId, myProducedItem);
13           ...
14           // now consume item produced by neighbor
15           final int neighId = (myId + 1) % numTasks;
16           // wait until neighbor produces item
17           final Object itemToConsume = itemHolder.get(neighId);
18           consumeItem(myId, itemToConsume);
19  } } } }
```

Fig. 1. An example that can lead to starvation when a thread-blocking runtime runs this program with too few worker threads

Consider an example program, in Fig. 1, which spawns a number of tasks which form a *ring*. Each task is involved in a two stage computation: in the first stage the task produces a value (in lines 11-12) and in the second stage the task consumes the value produced by its immediate right neighbor in the ring (in line 17-18). The synchronization constraint of having to wait for the neighbor to produce the item handled in the get() method of the ItemHolder data structure is not shown in the example, but one can imagine it being implemented by traditional locks in any of the languages mentioned above (HJ, Cilk, X10, etc.). Locks in these languages have blocking implementations and cause the tasks to block worker threads. Consider this program, which spawns 64 tasks, being run with 64 worker threads. In such a scenario, each of the spawned tasks would potentially be assigned to individual worker threads and each task will have an opportunity to run and produce a value. As a result, all of the blocking calls to get() would eventually be satisfied and the computation would complete. Instead, consider the program being run on a runtime with 32 worker threads. If the task scheduler schedules alternate tasks (i.e. tasks with id 0, 2, 4, ..., 62), each of them will produce their value and block in the call to get() since their neighbor has not been scheduled to run and never produces the value that these tasks want to consume. Since all available worker threads become blocked, no computational progress can be made and we have a starvation! If a cooperative

```
1  public class CyclicProducers {
2    public static void main(final String[] args) {
3      // number of tasks to create
4      final int numTasks = 8;
5      finish {
6        final promise<int>[] items = new promise<>[numTasks]...;
7        for (int i = 0; i < numTasks; i++) {
8          final int myId = i;
9          async {
10           // first produce an item
11           final int myProducedItem = produceItem(...);
12           items[myId].put(myProducedItem);
13           ...
14           // now consume item produced by neighbor
15           final int neighId = (myId + 1) % numTasks;
16           // trigger callback when neighbor produces item
17           asyncAwait(items[neighId]) {
18             final Object itemToConsume = items[neighId].nbGet();
19             consumeItem(myId, itemToConsume);
20  } } } } } }
```

Fig. 2. An event-driven version of Fig. 1 where callbacks are used to avoid thread-blocking operations. A `promise` can be viewed as a container with a full/empty state that obeys a dynamic single-assignment rule. The `nbGet()` methods represents a non-blocking `get()` operation. The `nbGet()` can only be performed inside an `asyncAwait` block on any promise registered in its await clause (e.g. `items[neighId]` on line 17).

runtime were used instead, no starvation would occur in this program irrespective of the number of worker threads used.

To avoid blocking, programmers can choose to write their code in an event-driven style with callback registrations. Fig. 2 shows an event-driven version of Fig. 1 where callbacks are used to avoid thread-blocking operations. In this version, the possible blocking calls to `get()` are replaced by a callback registration (at line 17-19) on the rest of the computation to run when the value from the neighbor is eventually produced. This version requires additional support from the language or runtime to allow callback registrations on the underlying primitive (e.g. `promise`) being used to implement the data structure. Though this version of the program is cumbersome to write, it will never display starvation irrespective of the task scheduler used since there are no blocking operations and worker threads can always be used to make computation progress.

As another example, Fig. 3 shows the classic (and inefficient) parallel version of the Fibonacci function written in an event-driven style. This style of programming makes writing and maintaining code somewhat onerous and error-prone. A key difficulty is that the logical unit of work is broken across callbacks and methods are passed extra parameters to help registering on the callbacks. There is no direct return of a value from the callee to the caller. These make the code harder to read and maintain, especially as the method size grows and multiple parameters need to be passed along the call chain.

Fig. 4 shows an example program to compute Fibonacci numbers using futures to asynchronously compute values of the subproblems. The code for this version follows a more standard program structure and is easier to read and

```
1  public class FibCallback {
2    public static void fib (int n, promise<int> f) {
3      if ( n < 2) { f.put(n); return; }
4      promise<int> x = newPromise<>();
5      promise<int> y = newPromise<>();
6      async { fib(n-1, x); };
7      async { fib(n-2, y); };
8      asyncAwait(x, y) { f.put(x.nbGet() + y.nbGet()); }
9    }
10   public static void main (String[] args) {
11     int n = Integer.parseInt(args[0]);
12     promise<int> res = newPromise<>();
13     async { fib(n, res); };
14     asyncAwait(res) {
15       println(res.nbGet());
16 } } }
```

Fig. 3. Version of the Fibonacci numbers program that uses event-driven style with callbacks and asynchronous tasks. Asynchronous tasks are created with **async**; asynchronous callbacks are registered on promises using **asyncAwait**. The **fib()** method needs an extra parameter to store the promise and allow callback registrations. Calling **fib** does not return a result directly, rather an additional callback needs to be registered on line 14 to receive and display the result.

```
1  public class FibFuture {
2    public static int fib (int n) {
3      if ( n < 2) { return n; }
4      future<int> x = async<int>{ fib(n-1); };
5      future<int> y = async<int>{ fib(n-2); };
6      return x.get() + y.get();
7    }
8    public static void main (String[] args) {
9      int n = Integer.parseInt(args[0]);
10     future<int> res = async<int>{ fib(n); };
11     println(res.get());
12 } }
```

Fig. 4. Version of the Fibonacci numbers program that uses futures for synchronization with asynchronous tasks. Calls to future **get()** wait until the value in the future becomes available. This example is aligned with thread-based code where no extra parameters are required to register callbacks and the function calls return values directly.

maintain compared to Fig. 3. The **get()** operations are potential synchronization points where the task may suspend itself if the value of the future has not already been resolved. In many current runtimes, these potential synchronization points could result in thread blocking operations. In our runtime, we handle the synchronization points cooperatively using OSDeConts without blocking the worker thread. This allows us to leverage the benefits of event-driven programming while the user code remains in standard thread-based structure (i.e. the user writes programs similar to Fig. 1 and Fig. 4). As we see in Section 6.2, the non-blocking version of Fibonacci with futures clearly outperforms a blocking version by a factor that exceeds $100\times$. Similar performance gains can also be achieved by cooperatively scheduling tasks with other SyncCons, such as phasers (see Section 6.3).

3   Related Work

The general idea of using event-based programming in thread-based code has also been explored by others in the past. In Tasks [9], explicit method annotations provide yield points. These annotations are used to translate the code into event-based style using a form of continuation passing style (CPS) translation. Unlike what its name might suggest, Tasks has nothing to do with task parallelism, instead it is a programming model for writing event-driven programs. Our implementation requires no explicit method annotations, uses OSDeConts, and runs safely on a parallel scheduler (i.e. the operations are thread-safe).

Use of continuations for task parallelism was popularized by Cilk [2], an extension to C that provides an abstraction of threads in explicit CPS. Our approach uses OSDeConts to achieve the same goal as Cilk where there are no thread blocking operations in the generated code. We support additional SyncCons where a task may trigger the enablement of multiple suspended tasks (as in futures, barriers and phasers) in contrast to Cilk where only one continuation is enabled by an event (the termination of the last child/descendant task in a join scope). Since Cilk relies on serial elision to be equivalent to a sequential program, such programs are not supported in Cilk as there may be no equivalent sequential program which use these SyncCons. Having nonblocking operations allows us to provide proper time guarantees, since some progress is continually made towards the computation. In Cilk, such time guarantees are lost when locks, which are typically blocking, are used. However, supporting the time bound guarantee comes at a cost of space bound with all the additional space for temporary local variables in the heap.

The Intel Threading Building Blocks (TBB) [25] task scheduler is inspired by the early Cilk work-stealing scheduler. TBB deals with possible blocking operations by running other tasks on the same stack, effectively stitching the call stack of the new tasks on top of the blocked task's stack. TBB also allows the parent tasks to specify another "continuation" task that will continue its work when such blocking scenarios arise. This minimizes the load on the scheduler and the uncontrolled overflow of the stack. However, this places the burden on the programmer to detect and schedule tasks to avoid blocking. In our approach, the user does not have to deal with the blocking constructs manually, the runtime implicitly handles the creation of continuations and the scheduler picks the next tasks to execute. Also, since each task has its own stack, we do not have to worry about the stack overflowing due to stitching of frames from multiple tasks. Overall, we go a step further than Cilk and TBB by showing how additional SyncCons such as futures, phasers and isolated blocks can be supported in a nonblocking manner.

Qthreads [30] is a lightweight threading library for C/C++ applications that also uses call stack stitching, it allows spawning and controlling tasks with small (4k) stacks. Our runtime is based on OSDeConts and poses no limits on the stack size of tasks created by the runtime, the stack size for worker threads in our implementation is limited by the JVM thread stack size (default around 1M for 64-bit JVMs) and the limits for OSDeConts is defined by the size of the heap. The qthreads API provides access to full/empty-bit (FEB) semantics (producer-consumer pattern with mutable buffer) and the threads need to be able to interact with the FEB for synchronization. In our runtime, tasks synchronize among themselves using the EDC primitive which is based on the observer pattern.

Li et al. present an alternative approach to implement concurrency in Glasgow Haskell Compiler (GHC) [23]. The runtime offers continuations as a mechanism from which concurrency can be built and also supports preemptive concurrency of very lightweight threads. In their implementation of GHC, the list of suspended continuations is periodically polled by the scheduler to see if the cause for blocking has been resolved. We differ in that we use OSDeConts and avoid any polling while deciding to resume suspended tasks by allowing EDCs to add resumed tasks into the scheduler's work queue. Also, we run inside the JVM where we cannot create continuations directly and have to rely on CPS-like transforms to support OSDeConts.

Fluet et al. [10] use full continuations to support fine-grained parallelism in their Manticore project. Manticore, like the GHC, is based on a functional language. It relies on a tree of futures that allows stacking continuations and a comparatively limited set of synchronization patterns (mainly futures). In contrast, our abstractions support a wide variety of synchronization patterns (e.g. futures, phasers, atomic) and arbitrary computation DAGs where continuations may be placed in the work queue without restrictions.

The use of continuations in task parallel programs has also been proposed by the C++ implementation of X10 [29]. The work-stealing scheduler in their implementation supports the work-first policy inspired from Cilk. Their implementation supports distributed `async-finish` programs along with conditional atomic blocks but does not support clocks (a precursor to HJ phasers). In our approach we rely on the help-first policy to have independent stack frames for tasks to enable use of OSDeConts and can use either a work-sharing or work-stealing scheduler. Our cooperative runtime is general enough to support a wide variety of SyncCons as we prove in our implementation.

Continuations are also used in the Continuators construct for an implicitly parallel implementation of Scheme [19]. There continuations are used to invoke the body of a function application (without blocking the interpreter) after the arguments have been evaluated in parallel. We employ delimited continuations with the same goal of avoiding thread blocking operations, additionally, our proposal provides an API to implement SyncCons which subsumes the parallel argument evaluation case. Also, our implementation dynamically discovers suspension points and minimizes overhead by avoiding continuation creations when EDCs have already been resolved.

4   Cooperative Runtime for Task Scheduling

The general TPM allows programmers to represent their computations as directed acyclic graphs with dependences between inter-dependent tasks. As a result, there has been a lot of work done in developing structured synchronization constructs (SyncCons) on the TPM by the community. These constructs include the well structured `async-finish` variant of fork-join style tasks, point-to-point synchronization with futures, localized and group synchronization using phasers, and weak atomicity in critical sections [2,17,26,3]. Such constructs introduce new challenges for the runtime while scheduling and executing tasks.

Synchronization constraints can prevent a currently executing task from making further progress as it *waits* to synchronize with other ready but not executing task(s). Many task parallel runtimes implement such waits by either busy-waiting until the constraint is resolved or by blocking the worker thread. An alternative approach is to use cooperative scheduling of tasks where an executing task, via runtime support, decides to actively suspend itself and yield control back to the runtime. The runtime can then perform book-keeping on the suspended task and use the worker thread to execute other ready tasks. The suspended task can be resumed and scheduled for execution when the synchronization constraint that caused it to suspend is resolved. This approach allows the runtime to continue making progress in the computation and to constantly exploit available parallelism during application execution without spawning additional threads. This nonblocking approach enables us to provide proper time guarantees since each worker is actively making some progress towards the computation. Supporting the time bound guarantee comes at a cost of space bound since many tasks may be *in flight* (either suspended, ready, or executing) with all the additional space for temporary local variables in the heap.

In the rest of the section, we present some background on one-shot OSDeConts and EDCs. Then we describe the API we expose in our runtime to allow language/library developers implement a variety of SyncCons. Finally, we explain how OSDeConts and EDCs are used to build a cooperative task-parallel runtime.

4.1 One-Shot Delimited Continuations

Delimited continuations (DeConts) were introduced by Felleisen in 1988 [8] where he referred to them as *prompts*. Continuations represent the rest of a computation from any given point. They refer to the ability to *capture* the state of a computation at that point, the computation can later be *resumed* from that point by resuming the continuation. In contrast, DeConts represent the rest of the computation from a well-defined outer boundary, i.e. a subcomputation. This allows DeConts to return to their caller allowing the program to proceed at the call site. DeConts are hence a good choice when a limited part of the computation needs to be saved/restored [6]. In general, a continuation can be resumed multiple times from the same captured state; however one-shot continuations refer to continuations that are resumed at most once. This guarantee makes them cheaper to implement because they don't require making additional copies of the state.

4.2   Event-Driven Controls

Event-Driven Controls (EDCs) are an extension to Data-Driven Controls (DDCs) which were presented in [20] and used to support event-driven actors in a task parallel runtime. A DDC lazily binds a value and a closure called the execution body (EB), both the value and the EB follow the dynamic single-assignment property ensuring data-race freedom. When the value becomes available, the EB is executed using the provided value. We generalize DDCs to EDCs in this work to allow multiple EBs to be attached to the EDC as callbacks. We treat the availability of a value in the EDC as an *event* and use the event to trigger the execution of EBs. Due to the single-assignment property, the registered EBs are executed at most once. We also allow multiple values to be added into the EDC as long as the values are *logically equivalent*, this does not violate the dynamic single assignment property and it does not trigger re-executions of the EBs. Attempting to add unequal values into the EDC is reported as a runtime error. Fig. 5 shows a simplified implementation of a DDC excluding SyncCons. The EB of the EDC may be executed either asynchronously or synchronously. For example, in a task parallel runtime the EB could store book-keeping data and act as a synchronous callback into the runtime. The EB could trigger possible asynchronous actions, such as scheduling and execution of a task, by interacting with the runtime.

```
 1 class EventDrivenControl {
 2   ValueType value = ...;
 3   List<ExecBody> ebList = ...;
 4   /** triggers callback execution **/
 5   void setValue(ValueType theValue) {
 6     if (!valueAvailable()) {
 7       value = theValue;
 8       // execute the callbacks/EBs
 9       ebList.each().scheduleWith(value);
10     } } else {
11       // check for error
12   } }
13   /** enables callback registration **/
14   void addExecutionBody(ExecBody theBody) {
15     if (valueAvailable()) {
16       // value available, execute immediately
17       theBody.scheduleWith(value);
18     } else {
19       // need to wait for the value
20       ebList.add(theBody);
21 } } }
```

Fig. 5. Simplified representation of an EDC not displaying synchronizations or validations. Both the value and the execution body can be lazily attached. The execution body determines whether it is scheduled asynchronously or synchronously in the `scheduleWith()` method.

4.3   Cooperative Runtime - Design

To allow library/language developers to create their own SyncCons, we expose
EDCs as an API in our runtime. The OSDeConts created to manage the book-
keeping are not exposed to the developer; this is especially desirable since continuations are notorious for being hard to use and to understand by developers
(as opposed to compilers and runtime systems). The API contains the following
operations:

- The static newEDC() factory method is used to instantiate a new EDC. EDCs
  are initialized without a resolved value and with an empty EB list. The EDC
  can be used like a regular object, e.g. stored as a field, passed around as
  parameters, invoked as receivers for methods, etc.
- The static suspend(anEdcInstance) method signals possible creation of a
  suspension point. If the EDC passed as an argument has not been resolved,
  the current task is suspended and the runtime handles the book-keeping to
  register an EB to resume the task when the EDC is resolved.
- The setValue(someValue) method resolves the EDC, i.e. it binds a value
  with the EDC and triggers the execution of any EB registered with the EDC.
  Suspended tasks registered with the EDC will be resumed and scheduled for
  execution by the runtime.
- The isValueAvailable() can be used to check whether the value in the
  EDC has been resolved.
- The getValue() method retrieves the value associated with the EDC. It
  is only safe to call this method if the value in the EDC has already been
  resolved. If execution proceeds past a call to suspend(), it is guaranteed
  that a value is available in the EDC.

With these operations in place, language/library developers can implement
their custom SyncCons and synchronization patterns. The same API is used
in our implementation of Habanero-Java to support the constructs such as end
of finish, futures, phasers, etc. For example, Fig. 6 shows how simple it is to
implement futures using the exposed API. A single EDC is used to suspend all
consumers who try to read the value of the future before it has been resolved.
When the value of the future is available, the EDC is resolved with a call to
setValue() and any suspended consumer tasks are resumed by the runtime.

4.4   The Cooperative Runtime

In our cooperative runtime, when a potential synchronization point is discovered
dynamically, thread blocking operations are avoided by suspending the currently
executing task and cooperatively scheduling other ready tasks from the work
queue. When the EDC is resolved, the suspended task (and its continuation) is
put back into the work queue to eventually be resumed by a worker thread. Task
suspensions are implemented by using standard OSDeConts and this guarantees
that the runtime never spawns more worker threads than it was initially started
with. The trade-off is that the compiler and the runtime now need to support

```
 1 class Future<T> {
 2   EventDrivenControl<T> edc = EventDrivenControl.newEDC<T>();
 3   public void put(T item) {
 4     edc.setValue(item); // resumes consumer(s)
 5   }
 6   public T get() {
 7     // suspend consumer task till value produced
 8     EventDrivenControl.suspend(edc);
 9     // return value after it is resolved
10     return edc.getValue();
11 } }
```

Fig. 6. Futures implemented using the EDC API provided by the cooperative runtime. All consumer tasks suspend until the item is produced. Once the item is available, multiple suspended consumers are resumed by the runtime.

the overhead of creating the OSDeConts and handling the management of the EDCs in addition to the management of threads and tasks.

A pictorial summary of our runtime is provided in Fig. 7. The runtime co-operatively schedules tasks using OSDeConts and EDCs in the presence of ar-bitrary dependences or synchronization constraints. The runtime places tasks into queues while the pool of worker threads continuously attempt to execute tasks dequeued from these queues. Execution of tasks may result in more tasks being spawned and enqueued into the queues. An application starts with a sin-gle *main* task in the work queue which promptly gets executed by one of the worker threads. The application terminates when *a*) the work queues are empty; and *b*) all synchronization constraints in the program have been satisfied (i.e. no deadlocks).

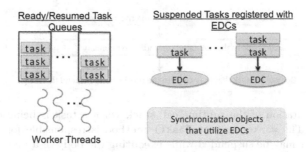

Fig. 7. The cooperative runtime includes worker threads and ready task queues like most other task parallel runtimes. In addition, there are EDCs which maintain a list of suspended tasks to implement higher-level synchronization constructs. Resolving an EDC moves a suspended task into the ready queue.

Our runtime uses a *help-first* policy [15] while scheduling tasks. Under this policy, spawning a child task enqueues it is in the task queue and allows the parent task to continue execution past the spawn operation. The child task hence has a stack of its own and can be executed by any of the worker threads. The independent stack allows us to treat the task as a subcomputation and to have a well-defined outer boundary while forming the OSDeCont. In contrast, using a *work-first* policy [15] does not provide an independent call-stack for a spawned task and requires maintaining fragmented call-stacks to allow helper threads to resume computations. This precludes the use of OSDeConts in a work-first policy (though the work-first policy can be more efficient than help-first for recursive divide-and-conquer parallelism when steals are infrequent, the work-first policy cannot be used to support general SyncCon). In addition, constructs such as phasers are not amenable to work-first scheduling since these constructs do not satisfy the "serial elision" property.

With the help-first policy in effect, we wrap the stack of each task around an OSDeCont which defines an `execute()` method as the continuation boundary. When a worker thread executes a task, it resumes the computation of the OS-DeCont which in turn invokes the `execute()` method, as shown in Fig. 8. At synchronization points where a task is not allowed to make progress semantically, an OSDeCont is captured and only the state until the `execute()` method needs to be saved. On returning from a call to `execute()`, the runtime verifies the cause for the return and performs book-keeping if the task was suspended. The worker thread then goes ahead and tries to dequeue other scheduled tasks to execute and continue making progress towards the overall computation.

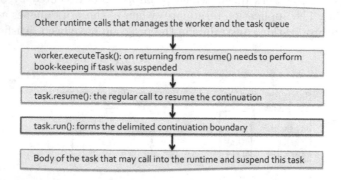

Fig. 8. Representation of the runtime call stack when a task is being executed by a worker thread. The `worker.executeTask()` method is responsible for managing the OSDeConts that may be suspended while executing the body of a task.

In our runtime, the static `suspend` method of the API (Section 4.3) restricts the cause of OSDeCont suspensions to instances of EDCs. On returning to the `worker.executeTask()`, the runtime checks whether an EDC was returned as a cause (i.e. the task was suspended) and registers an EB with that EDC. There is no limit to the number of tasks that can be registered to an EDC (in the form of an EB). When the EDC is resolved, the EBs are executed and the suspended tasks are rescheduled. Note that this approach does not need to use polling to keep track of when suspended tasks can be resumed. After being scheduled, the queued task is picked up by a worker thread and execution is resumed from the previous suspension point. When the execution of the task completes normally, without suspending, the runtime performs any cleanup operations associated with the task and looks for more work from the queue.

The remaining pieces in the runtime are the steps to undertake where synchronization points: a) capture continuations, b) create EDCs, and c) resolve EDCs. The use of OSDeConts and EDCs are abstracted by the implementer of the SyncCons and transparent to an end user of these constructs. We discuss how various SyncCons can be developed in our runtime in Section 5.

Work-Stealing Scheduler. The exact policy to retrieve tasks from work queues is unspecified in our cooperative runtime. Recent work has shown that work-stealing policies work very well on multicore architectures. A scheduler using a work-stealing policy maintains a queue of pending tasks per worker thread. When a worker completes a task, it pops a pending task from its own queue. If the queue is empty, it attempts to steal a task from another worker's queue. Our runtime uses the help-first policy and maintains an independent stack for each task, the OSDeCont created is thread independent and can be run by any thread. Hence, any worker thread may execute a task and we are able to use both the work-stealing or work-sharing scheduling policies in our runtime.

Serializability of Computations. Serializability of a group of parallel or concurrent statements refers to the ability to provide a serial ordering of the statements. In our runtime, since a single worker thread can execute the entire computation, that schedule provides a serializable order for the statements. The caveat is that the granularity of the statement blocks is around suspension points rather than user-written tasks. These new statement blocks can be used to form structures to represent the program dependence graph of the computation and reason about parallel portions and simplify, for example, data race analysis. With additional support from a scheduler, the statement blocks from the dependence graph can be scheduled in a deterministic order if so desired or can be used to generate different schedules, both of which can be very useful for debugging programs.

5   Support for Synchronization Constructs

Synchronization constructs (SyncCons) are used to coordinate the parallel execution of tasks. In this section, we describe how various SyncCons can be supported by our cooperative runtime. The key idea is to translate the coordination constraints into producer-consumer constraints on EDCs and to use OSDeConts to suspend consumers when waiting on item(s) from producer(s). We claim that any task-parallel SyncCon can be translated in such a manner and hence be supported by our runtime. The constructs we present include: a) termination detection of child tasks, b) producer-consumer synchronization, c) collective barrier synchronization, d) single blocks executed by only one task in a group, and *e)* weak isolation while accessing a shared resource. While constructs a) through d) are typically used for deterministic parallelism, construct e) can be used to support nondeterminism as well.

5.1   Fork-Join Synchronization

In structured fork-join parallelism, a *parent* task can spawn one or more *child* tasks that can logically run in parallel with the parent task. The parent task can then wait, by joining, until all of its transitively spawned children complete execution. An EDC, which wraps a counter[1], is created for each parent task. The counter is atomically incremented each time a child task is forked and atomically decremented as each child task completes execution, either normally or abnormally. When the count reaches zero, the value of the EDC is resolved. The join operation serves as a possible suspension point in our runtime and uses the EDC as its cause for suspending if it is invoked before the count reaches zero. If the count is zero when the join operation is called, execution of the parent task continues without the need for suspension. This model can be easily extended to also support nested fork-join parallelism.

5.2   Producer-Consumer Synchronization

In producer-consumer patterns, producer tasks are responsible for resolving the values inside EDCs while consumer tasks suspend until the value inside an EDC has been resolved. A common case is the single-producer multiple-consumer case, also known as *futures* [17]. A future represents an immutable value, an EDC in our runtime, which will become available at a later point by a producer task. When the producer task completes execution it resolves the value inside the EDC thus resuming any previously suspended consumers. Consumers who read the value of the future after it has already been resolved can continue execution without being suspended. The single-producer single-consumer case can be supported by further wrapping an EDC and ensuring that only one consumer is able to read the value of the EDC, read requests from other consumers report an error.

The general producer-consumer problem with a mutable buffer location can also be modeled using our API. An example of such a construct is the synchronization variable construct available in Chapel [4]. In effect, the buffer location is either empty or full and producers/consumers need to wait when the location is full/empty, respectively. This can be modeled in our runtime by maintaining a doubly-linked list of a pair of EDCs and a pointer to the active pair. The first element in the pair represents whether a producer has produced the item making the location full, while the second element represents whether a consumer has consumed the item making the location empty. A producer suspends until the previous consumer-EDC has been resolved, while a consumer suspends until the producer-EDC in the currently active pair has been resolved. Separate producer

---

[1] Distributed counters can be used for increased scalability.

```
 1 class EdcPair<T> {
 2   EventDrivenControl<T> p = EventDrivenControl.newEDC<>();
 3   EventDrivenControl<Boolean> c = EventDrivenControl.newEDC<>();
 4 }
 5 class SynchronizationVariable<T> {
 6   Node<EdcPair<T>> pNode; // producer chain
 7   Node<EdcPair<T>> cNode; // consumer chain
 8   Node<EdcPair<T>> nextNode(Node<EdcPair<T>> n) {
 9     if (n.nextNode == null)
10       n.nextNode = new Node<>(n, ...);
11     return n.nextNode;
12   }
13   public SynchronizationVariable() {
14     Node<...> item = new Node<>(null, ...);
15     item.c.setValue(true);
16     cNode = pNode = nextNode(item);
17   }
18   public void write(T item) { /*suspendable method*/
19     Node<EdcPair<T>> n;
20     isolated { n = pNode; pNode = nextNode(n); }
21     EventDrivenControl.suspend(n.prevNode.c);
22     n.p.setValue(item);
23   }
24   public T read() { /*suspendable method*/
25     Node<EdcPair<T>> n;
26     isolated { n = cNode; cNode = nextNode(n); }
27     EventDrivenControl.suspend(n.p);
28     n.c.setValue(true);
29     return n.p.getValue();
30 } }
```

Fig. 9. Synchronization variables implemented using operations provided in the cooperative runtime. Producers suspend until the previous item is consumed, consumers suspend until the current item is produced.

and consumer pointers are maintained and they are advanced to the next node in the list when write and read operations are invoked, respectively.

An example implementation of synchronization variables recipe using the cooperative API is provided in Fig. 9. There are two pointers being maintained to track progresses made by producers and consumers. A pair of EDCs are maintained to ensure there is the strict alternation of writes and reads by producers and consumers, respectively, while accessing the synchronization variable. If a producer arrives before the previous value has been read by a consumer it is suspended and vice versa.

5.3 Collective Barrier Synchronization

A barrier synchronization provides a means to ensure a group of tasks have all arrived at a particular point before advancing. This is especially useful in phased computations by ensuring each task in the group of tasks has completed one phase before starting the next phase of the computation. It is possible that the group of tasks involved in the barrier remain static or change dynamically over time, either form of barriers can be supported by our API/runtime. Implementing barriers in a runtime that uses thread-blocking operations is not scalable if the number of tasks registered on the barrier exceeds the number of available worker threads. This can lead to deadlocks if the runtime is not allowed to create additional worker threads to allow all tasks to reach the barrier and release the blocked threads. In the case where the runtime can compensate by creating additional worker threads, scalability and efficiency are affected due to the overhead of having to manage additional worker threads. In our cooperative runtime, since there are no thread blocking operations, the tasks can suspend themselves if they arrive too early at a barrier allowing the worker threads to execute other ready tasks and reach the barrier point. Eventually all tasks will arrive at the barrier and the suspended tasks will be resumed.

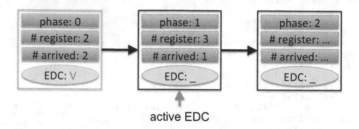

active EDC

Fig. 10. The barrier represents each phase with two counters to keep track of registered and arrived tasks and an EDC which is used to track *early* arrivers. As each phase completes, the EDC in the current phase is resolved resuming suspended tasks and the active phase pointer is moved to the next item in the linked list.

To support barriers with dynamic task registration (the static task version is a special case), we maintain a count of registered tasks, a count of arrived tasks, and an EDC for each phase in the barrier computation as shown in Fig. 10. When a task dynamically registers on the barrier, it registers on the *next* phase and increments the count of registered tasks for that phase. However, a task always deregisters in the current phase of the barrier and increments the arrived task count. As each task arrives at the barrier it increments the count for arrived tasks in the current phase and the count for registered tasks in the next phase. Additionally, if the task is not the last to arrive at the barrier point it suspends itself using the EDC for the current phase as the cause. The last task to arrive at the current phase of the barrier resolves the EDC of the current phase, advances the phase of the barrier, and continues without suspending. Resolving the EDC resumes all the tasks suspended on the barrier and the tasks now participate in the next phase of the computation when executed.

5.4 Phaser Synchronization

An extension to barrier synchronization is provided by phasers [26]. They unify collective and point-to-point synchronization for phased computations. Unlike traditional barriers where tasks register in *signal-and-wait* mode, tasks can also be registered on a phaser in *signal-only* or *wait-only* modes. Tasks registered on a wait mode (wait-only or signal-and-wait) need to wait for all tasks registered on a signal mode to arrive at the barrier point. The implementation for barriers (Section 5.3) needs to be extended by allowing only signalers to increment the counts of their local phase. Since signaler tasks can be in different phases, care is required to ensure that the correct counters are incremented. Tasks registered in signal-only mode never suspend and continue to make progress. Tasks registered in wait mode need to suspend themselves and wait for the EDC for a given phase to be resolved when all signaler tasks for a given phase arrive at the barrier point. As the EDC for the *oldest* phase is resolved by the last signaler task, it also advances the current phase for use by the waiter tasks.

5.5   Single Blocks

The OpenMP `single` construct specifies that a statement block is executed by only one task among a group of registered tasks [24]. The *wait* version requires that all registered tasks wait until some task has executed the `single` block. This is similar to supporting barriers with a single phase. All tasks, except the last task, that arrive at the `single` suspend themselves. The last task that resolves the EDC executes the statement block before resolving the EDC and causing the tasks registered on the `single` to be resumed. The *nowait* version does not require to suspend tasks, it requires some bookkeeping to ensure that exactly one task to arrive at the `single` executes the statement block.

Phasers also support a variant of `single` blocks when tasks are registered using the *signal-wait-single* mode. The semantics defines that the single block is executed only after all the signalers and waiters have arrived at the `single` block. Both the signalers and the waiters need to ensure they proceed only after all signalers have arrived and at least one task has executed the `single` block. Supporting such blocks in our runtime requires the use of two EDCs for each phase of the phaser. The first EDC keeps track of whether all signalers have arrived while the second EDC is used to track whether the statements inside the `single` block has been executed by some task. Thus tasks can possibly be suspended twice while executing a single block.

5.6   Weak Isolation

Habanero-Java provides the isolated SyncCon, which can be used to implement critical sections and coordinate the mutation of shared data. The weak isolation guarantee states that the statements inside the critical sections will be executed mutually exclusively with respect to other demarcated critical sections (DCS). In general, weak isolation enforces a serializability bottleneck as only one critical section may be executed by the runtime in the absence of a more sophisticated analysis. Often this serializability is implemented using locks where worker threads block while waiting to attain the lock. Use of locks can limit performance in scenarios where there is moderate or high contention for the lock by the interfering DCS. In the cooperative runtime, blocking of threads while using locks is avoided by maintaining a dynamic linked-list of EDCs. Each task executing the DCS registers itself to an EDC in the list and suspends itself if it does not link to a resolved EDC. The first EDC in the list already resolved by default to allow the first requestor of the lock to make progress in its DCS without suspending. Any task linked to a resolved EDC gets to execute its DCS and resolves the next EDC in the list.

6   Experimental Results

The benchmarks were run on individual nodes in a IBM POWER7 compute cluster. Each node contains 256GB of RAM and four eight-core IBM POWER7 processors running at 3.8GHz each. There is a 32 kB L1 cache and a 256 KB L2 cache per core. The software stack includes IBM Java SDK Version 7 Release 1 and Habanero-Java (HJ) version 1.3.1 (r33926). Each benchmark used the same JVM configuration flags[2] and was run for ten iterations in ten separate JVM invocations, the arithmetic mean of thirty execution times (last three from each invocation) are reported. This method is inspired from [13] and the last three execution times are used to approximate the steady state behavior. In the bar charts, the error bars represent one standard deviation.

We implemented our cooperative runtime in the Habanero-Java (HJ) language supporting all its available constructs without requiring any changes to the syntax of HJ programs, i.e. users are unaware of the use of EDCs and one-shot OSDeConts by the runtime. Our implementation is briefly described in [21]. The implementation of our cooperative runtime for HJ conforms to the constraints imposed by a standard Java Virtual Machine (JVM). In particular, such JVMs do not provide support for continuations or for storing and restoring the stack. We use an extended version of the open source bytecode weaver provided by the Kilim framework [28] to support one-shot OSDeConts that are thread independent and can be restored on threads managed by the HJ runtime.

We focus on benchmarks for the different SyncCons to compare the performance of our implementation of the cooperative runtime with *a*) the existing work-sharing runtime available in HJ which has *blocking* implementations for most of the SyncCons, and *b*) the `ForkJoinPool` and helper classes from the `java.util.concurrent` package in Java like `AtomicInteger`, `CyclicPhaser`, `CountDownLatch`, etc.[3] Both these blocking runtimes have been shown to deliver performance competitive with other runtimes (e.g., OpenMP, X10), for general SyncCons. Both HJ runtimes were configured to use the same work-stealing scheduler (`ForkJoinPool` from the standard JDK) as previous experience has shown the scheduling policy to be more effective than a work-sharing policy. All the benchmarks were run using **thirty-two** worker threads as the starting seed.

---

[2] Flags: `-Xms6344m`   `-Xmx65536m`   `-XX:MaxPermSize=256m`   `-XX:+UseParallelGC` `-XX:+UseParallelOldGC` `-XX:-UseGCOverheadLimit`.

[3] Not all benchmarks have a corresponding Java implementation / data for execution times of the benchmarks. In such cases the performance numbers are not shown in the charts.

In the blocking runtimes, additional threads are created around blocking suspension points, while the cooperative runtime never creates more worker threads. All benchmarks use the same algorithm in their implementation. For the HJ file(s) as input, only the runtime is switched from the blocking version to the cooperative version during compilation.

6.1 Fork/Join Benchmarks

Fig. 11 shows the result of fork-join benchmarks using the `async-finish` constructs from HJ. The first benchmark is the Java Grande Forum (JGF) Fork-Join (FJ) microbenchmark [7], it measures the time taken to spawn and join asynchronous tasks inside a single `finish` scope. Each task does a minimal amount of work before it terminates. Since there is only a single `finish`, this benchmark effectively measures the relative overhead in the two runtimes to spawn and manage tasks. The cooperative runtime is slower by about 40% as it has the overhead of wrapping the task in a OSDeCont and checking whether the task suspended when it is executed (even though the tasks themselves never suspend in this benchmark). One optimization technique to reduce the overhead is to avoid transforms of tasks that are statically known to be nonblocking. The next benchmark, N-body (Computer Language Benchmarks Game [12]), shows a similar slowdown while using the cooperative runtime as there are few `finish`

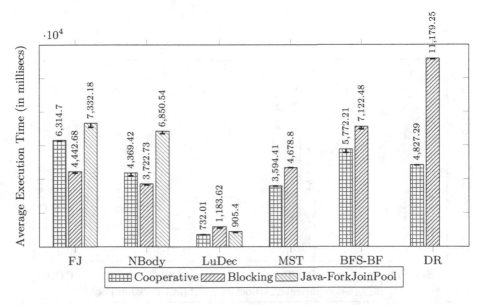

Fig. 11. Results for `async-finish` benchmarks. JGF Fork Join (FJ) with 4 million tasks. NBody with 300K steps. LU-Decomposition (LuDec) with an array size of 2K and block size of 128. MST, BFS-BF and DR with an input graph of size 512 nodes and artificial load values of 500K, 20M, and 8M respectively.

blocks created compared to `async` blocks (a ratio of 1:7). The effects of blocking are shadowed to some extent since there are fewer join points resulting in fewer blocked threads. The LU Decomposition (LuDec) benchmark, from the Cilk Benchmark [1], is the first to show speed-up of around 60% as there are relatively more `finish` blocks created compared to `async` blocks. The next set of benchmarks, Minimum Spanning Tree (MST), Breadth First Search using Bellman Ford algorithm (BFS-BF), and Dijkstra Routing (DR), come from the IMSuite benchmark suite [16] for various graph algorithms written in task parallel languages. The relatively larger number of finish blocks allow the cooperative runtime to show speedups of around 20% for MST and BFS-BF, while the DR benchmark executes over 2× faster. The Java versions of the benchmarks have their `finish` implemented using atomic integers and latches which have blocking semantics. The Java versions are slower than the cooperative runtime implementation in all the fork-join benchmarks, for which data is available, due to blocking at the end of `finish` using countdown latches.

6.2 Future Benchmarks

The Fibonacci microbenchmark does almost no computation inside the task thus allowing us to measure the overheads of the future SyncCon in the two runtimes. Two versions of the Fibonacci program were mentioned in Fig. 3 and Fig. 4. With the cooperative runtime we achieve performance close to the program written in event-driven style while still using the easier to read thread-based style. The

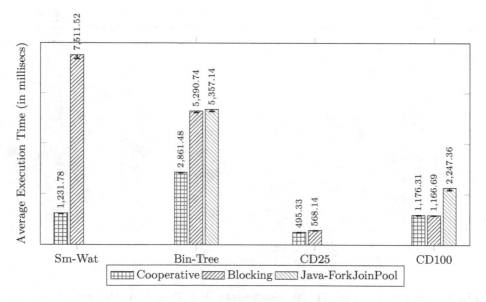

Fig. 12. Smith Waterman on strings of length 960 and 928. Binary Tree operating on a tree with depth of 14. Cholesky Decomposition on an input matrix of size 2000×2000 with tile sizes of 25 and 100.

cooperative version using futures comfortably outperforms the blocking version, e.g. computing the 20th term of fib resulted over $100\times$ speed-up. In fact, the blocking version runs out of memory for values of n larger than 20 as the runtime attempts to create extra threads to compensate for the blocked threads while the cooperative version completes in around 100 milliseconds. The Java future implementation is similar to the HJ blocking runtime's implementation of futures. Hence, the running times for the future benchmarks on these two variants are similar.

In the Smith-Waterman benchmark, futures are used to represent the value at each cell of the dynamic programming *table* and backtracking starts at the highest corner cell. Each cell depends on values from three neighboring cells and thus each cell has exactly three suspension points, once for each attempt to resolve the future of a neighboring cell, while computing its own value. Due to the comparative lack of delay while trying to resolve a future after its creation many blocking operations are performed in the blocking runtime. This degrades performance, as seen in Fig. 12, and the cooperative version outperforms the blocking version by a factor of $6\times$.

The Binary Trees benchmark, from the Computer Language Benchmarks Game [11], involves allocating binary trees, walking the trees bottom-up, and deallocating many nodes after the walk. In this benchmark, there is a relatively larger delay between the creation of the future and the attempt to resolve its value. This nature of the benchmark allows the blocking scheduler to make some progress in executing the futures and thus helps minimize blocking operations due to calls on unresolved futures. Even with this property, the cooperative runtime still outperforms the blocking version by a factor close to $2\times$.

The next benchmark is Cholesky Decomposition, a dense linear algebra application. We use futures to enforce the data dependences and exploit loop and pipeline parallelism. With smaller tile sizes, more tasks/futures are created and there is a higher probability of blocking on a future. Hence, the cooperative runtime performs better by about 13% at the smaller tile size of 25. As the tile size increases there are fewer blocked threads on unresolved futures and the blocking runtime performs as well as the cooperative runtime.

6.3   Phaser Benchmarks

To compare the performance of phasers we implemented two microbenchmarks: Barrier (BAR) (tasks registered on phasers in *sig-wait* mode) and Reduction (RED) (tasks registered on phasers in *sig-wait-single* mode using sum accumulators). We also implemented two additional benchmarks from the JGF benchmark suite: Moldyn (MOL) and LU-Factorization (LUF). Since our hardware had thirty-two cores, we registered more than forty tasks (i.e. more than thirty-two) on the phasers to stress test the runtimes. This ensures that most of the registered tasks encounter a *forced* suspension point at the *next* operation as only a maximum of thirty-two tasks can be running at any given time. In the blocking runtime, each such suspension point causes the worker thread to block and additional threads are created to run the other tasks. As such the runtime

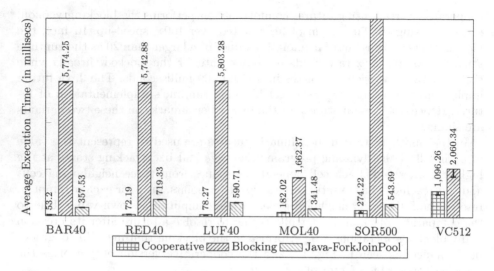

Fig. 13. Phaser benchmark results. BAR, RED, LUF, and MOL with 40 tasks registered on the phaser. SOR benchmark with an input array size of 500. VC coloring with an input graph of 512 nodes and artificial load of 10M.

has to deal with the overhead of these additional thread context switches. In contrast, the cooperative runtime avoids such thread context switches and relies on the continuations to perform the relatively lightweight task context switches. We can see that we can achieve more than 100× for BAR, RED, and LUF and close to 10× speed-up for MOL in the cooperative runtime. These speed-ups are even greater when more than forty tasks are registered on the phasers. We also include results from two other phaser benchmarks: JGF's Successive Over-Relaxation (SOR) with an input size of 500 and IMSuite's Vertex Coloring with an input graph of 512 nodes. In these benchmarks, where more computation is done between phases and overheads from context switching can be amortized to some degree, we get over 50× speed-up for SOR and 2× speed-up for VC.

Java's implementation of `CyclicPhaser` is noticeably more performant than the HJ blocking runtime version. However, `CyclicPhaser`s are still slower than our cooperative implementation which does not block worker threads. On the various phaser benchmarks, the HJ cooperative version ranges from being 2× to 10× faster than the pure Java version.

7   Conclusions and Future Work

In this paper, we address the problem of scheduling parallel tasks with general synchronization patterns using a cooperative runtime for scalability and performance. Our solution is founded on a novel use of one-shot delimited continuations and event-driven controls. We describe recipes for implementing various

SyncCons using our cooperative API and provide an implementation of our cooperative runtime for the Habanero-Java language. Experimental results for our implementation for Habanero-Java, on various future and phaser benchmarks, show that the cooperative runtime delivers significant improvements in performance and memory utilization relative to a thread-blocking runtime system while using the same underlying work-stealing task scheduler.

We are working on further extending our cooperative runtime to support preemptive scheduling using the notion of Engines [18] to ensure fairness in the scheduling of tasks. Such a scheme also requires support for runtime generated priorities while scheduling tasks. Engines will enable us to support speculative parallelization, e.g. in the form of Cilk's [2] abort statement, more efficiently. Exploiting the dynamic dependence graph around suspension points to detect dataraces and to help in debugging is also an interesting area of future research which we are looking forward to pursue.

Acknowledgments. This work was supported in part by NSF award CCF-0964520. Any opinions, findings and conclusions or recommendations expressed in this material are those of the authors and do not necessarily reflect those of the National Science Foundation. The results in this paper were obtained on a system that was supported in part by NIH award NCRR S10RR02950 and an IBM Shared University Research (SUR) Award in partnership with CISCO, Qlogic and Adaptive Computing. We are grateful to Vincent Cavé and Jun Shirako for discussions on the Habanero Java runtime system and phasers, respectively. We also thank Akihiro Hayashi, Sağnak Taşırlar, and Jisheng Zhao for sharing their benchmarks with us. We are grateful to Deepak Majeti, Rishi Surendran, Nick Vrvilo, and the anonymous reviewers whose feedback on earlier drafts helped improve the presentation of this paper.

References

1. Blumofe, R.: LU decomposition - Cilk,
   http://courses.cs.tau.ac.il/368-4064/cilk-5.3.1/examples/lu.cilk
2. Blumofe, R.D., Joerg, C.F., Kuszmaul, B.C., Leiserson, C.E., Randall, K.H., Zhou, Y.: Cilk: An Efficient Multithreaded Runtime System. In: Proceedings of the Fifth ACM SIGPLAN Symposium on Principles and Practice of Parallel Programming, PPOPP 1995, pp. 207–216. ACM, New York (1995)
3. Cavé, V., Zhao, J., Guo, Y., Sarkar, V.: Habanero-Java: the New Adventures of Old X10. In: PPPJ, pp. 51–61 (2011)
4. Chamberlain, B.L., Callahan, D., Zima, H.P.: Parallel Programmability and the Chapel Language. International Journal of High Performance Computing Applications 21(3), 291–312 (2007)
5. Charles, P., Grothoff, C., Saraswat, V., Donawa, C., Kielstra, A., Ebcioglu, K., von Praun, C., Sarkar, V.: X10: An Object-Oriented Approach to Non-uniform Cluster Computing. SIGPLAN Not. 40, 519–538 (2005)
6. Drago, I., Cunei, A., Vitek, J.: Continuations in the Java Virtual Machine. In: International Workshop on Implementation, Compilation, Optimization of Object-Oriented Languages, Programs and Systems (2007)

7. EPCC: The Java Grande Forum Multi-threaded Benchmarks,
   http://www2.epcc.ed.ac.uk/computing/research_activities/
   java_grande/threads/s1contents.html
8. Felleisen, M.: The Theory and Practice of First-Class Prompts. In: Proceedings
   of the 15th ACM SIGPLAN-SIGACT Symposium on Principles of Programming
   Languages, POPL 1988, pp. 180–190. ACM, New York (1988)
9. Fischer, J., Majumdar, R., Millstein, T.: Tasks: Language Support for Event-driven
   Programming. In: Proceedings of the 2007 ACM SIGPLAN Symposium on Partial
   Evaluation and Semantics-Based Program Manipulation, PEPM 2007, ACM, New
   York (2007)
10. Fluet, M., Rainey, M., Reppy, J., Shaw, A.: Implicitly Threaded Parallelism in
    Manticore. J. Funct. Program. 20(5-6) (November 2010)
11. Fulgham, B.: binary-trees benchmark,
    http://benchmarksgame.alioth.debian.org/u32/
    performance.php?test=binarytrees
12. Fulgham, B.: n-body benchmark,
    http://benchmarksgame.alioth.debian.org/u32/performance.php?test=nbody
13. Georges, A., Buytaert, D., Eeckhout, L.: Statistically Rigorous Java Performance
    Evaluation. In: Proceedings of the 22nd Annual ACM SIGPLAN Conference on
    Object-Oriented Programming Systems and Applications, OOPSLA 2007, pp. 57–
    76. ACM, New York (2007)
14. Gray, J.: Writing Faster Managed Code: Know What Things Cost,
    http://msdn.microsoft.com/en-us/library/ms973852.aspx
15. Guo, Y., Barik, R., Raman, R., Sarkar, V.: Work-First and Help-First Schedul-
    ing Policies for Async-Finish Task Parallelism. In: Proceedings of the 2009 IEEE
    International Symposium on Parallel & Distributed Processing, IPDPS 2009, pp.
    1–12. IEEE Computer Society, Washington, DC (2009)
16. Gupta, S., Nandivada, V.K.: IMSuite: A Benchmark Suite for Simulating Dis-
    tributed Algorithms. CoRR abs/1310.2814 (2013)
17. Halstead, R.H.: Multilisp: A Language for Concurrent Symbolic Computation.
    ACM Transactions on Programming Languages and Systems 7, 501–538 (1985)
18. Haynes, C.T., Friedman, D.P.: Engines Build Process Abstractions. In: Proceedings
    of the 1984 ACM Symposium on LISP and Functional Programming, LFP 1984,
    pp. 18–24. ACM, New York (1984)
19. Herzeel, C., Costanza, P.: Dynamic Parallelization of Recursive Code Part I: Man-
    aging Control Flow Interactions with the Continuator. In: Proceedings of the ACM
    International Conference on Object Oriented Programming Systems Languages
    and Applications, OOPSLA 2010, pp. 377–396. ACM, New York (2010)
20. Imam, S., Sarkar, V.: Integrating Task Parallelism with Actors. In: Proceedings
    of the ACM International Conference on Object Oriented Programming Systems
    Languages and Applications, OOPSLA 2012, pp. 753–772. ACM, New York (2012),
    http://doi.acm.org/10.1145/2384616.2384671
21. Imam, S., Sarkar, V.: A Case for Cooperative Scheduling in X10's Managed Run-
    time. In: The 2014 X10 Workshop (X10 2014) (June 2014)
22. Lea, D.: A Java Fork/Join Framework. In: Java Grande, pp. 36–43 (2000)
23. Li, P., Marlow, S., Peyton Jones, S., Tolmach, A.: Lightweight Concurrency Prim-
    itives for GHC. In: Proceedings of the ACM SIGPLAN Haskell Workshop, Haskell
    2007, pp. 107–118. ACM, New York (2007)
24. OpenMP Application Program Interface, Version 3.0 (May 2008),
    http://www.openmp.org/mp-documents/spec30.pdf

25. Reinders, J.: Intel Threading Building Blocks, 1st edn. O'Reilly & Associates, Inc., Sebastopol (2007)
26. Shirako, J., Peixotto, D.M., Sarkar, V., Scherer, W.N.: Phasers: a Unified Deadlock-Free Construct for Collective and Point-to-Point Synchronization. In: Proceedings of the 22nd Annual International Conference on Supercomputing, ICS 2008, pp. 277–288. ACM, New York (2008)
27. Sigoure, B.: How long does it take to make a context switch, http://blog.tsunanet.net/2010/11/how-long-does-it-take-to-make-context.html
28. Srinivasan, S., Mycroft, A.: Kilim: Isolation-Typed Actors for Java. In: Vitek, J. (ed.) ECOOP 2008. LNCS, vol. 5142, pp. 104–128. Springer, Heidelberg (2008)
29. Tardieu, O., Wang, H., Lin, H.: A Work-Stealing Scheduler for X10s Task Parallelism with Suspension. In: Proceedings of the 17th ACM SIGPLAN Symposium on Principles and Practice of Parallel Programming, PPoPP 2012, pp. 267–276. ACM, New York (2012)
30. Wheeler, K., Murphy, R., Thain, D.: Qthreads: An API for programming with millions of lightweight threads. In: IEEE International Symposium on Parallel and Distributed Processing, IPDPS 2008, pp. 1–8 (2008)
31. Yan, Y., Chatterjee, S., Budimlic, Z., Sarkar, V.: Integrating MPI with Asynchronous Task Parallelism. In: Cotronis, Y., Danalis, A., Nikolopoulos, D.S., Dongarra, J. (eds.) EuroMPI 2011. LNCS, vol. 6960, pp. 333–336. Springer, Heidelberg (2011), http://dx.doi.org/10.1007/978-3-642-24449-0_41

MiCA: A Compositional Architecture for Gossip Protocols

Lonnie Princehouse[1], Rakesh Chenchu[1], Zhefu Jiang[1],
Kenneth P. Birman[1], Nate Foster[1], and Robert Soulé[2]

[1] Cornell University, USA
{lonnie,rr548,zj46,ken,jnfoster}@cs.cornell.edu
[2] University of Lugano, Switzerland
robert.soule@usi.ch

Abstract. The developers of today's cloud computing systems are expected to not only create applications that will work well at scale, but also to create management services that will monitor run-time conditions and intervene to address problems as conditions evolve. Management tasks are generally not performance intensive, but robustness is critical: when a large system becomes unstable, the management infrastructure must remain reliable, predictable, and fault-tolerant.

A wide range of management tasks can be expressed as *gossip protocols* where nodes in the system periodically interact with random peers and exchange information about their respective states. Although individual gossip protocols are typically very simple, by composing multiple protocols one can create a wide variety of interesting, complex functionality with strong (albeit probabilistic) robustness and convergence guarantees. For example, in a system with a sufficiently dense topology, all nodes will learn the information being disseminated in expected logarithmic time. Unfortunately, programmers today must typically build gossip protocols by hand—an approach that makes their programs more complicated and error-prone, and hinders attempts to optimize gossip implementations to achieve better performance.

MiCA is a new system for building gossip-based management tools that are highly resistant to disruptions and make efficient use of system resources. MiCA provides abstractions that enable expressing gossip protocols in terms of functions on pairs of node states, along with a rich collection of composition operators that facilitates constructing sophisticated protocols in a modular style. The MiCA prototype realizes these abstractions on top of the Java Virtual Machine, and implements optimizations that greatly reduce the number and size of messages used.

Keywords: Gossip protocols, fault tolerance, composition, distributed systems, program partitioning, Java.

1 Introduction

Monitoring and management infrastructure is critical for ensuring the reliability of modern cloud computing applications. In practice, each application typically

R. Jones (Ed.): ECOOP 2014, LNCS 8586, pp. 644–669, 2014.

has a distinct notion of what constitutes a healthy system state. For example, a scientific computing application might be especially sensitive to CPU utilization, while a database application might depend on the size of buffer queues, and the throughput of a streaming video service might be determined by available network capacity. Other examples include distributed hash tables, which must build and maintain structured overlay networks, and data mining applications, which must ensure the convergence of results produced by iterative computation.

Unfortunately, programmers today typically develop monitoring and management infrastructure by hand—a rudimentary approach that leads to a number of practical problems. First, because they lack tools that provide high-level abstractions, programmers must deal with a host of low-level details such as setting up and maintaining network connections, serializing and deserializing application data, and dealing with exceptions and failures. Second, because standard infrastructure is not available, they must reimplement conventional algorithms, such as computing the minimum value in the system, from scratch in each new tool. Third, when several different tools are deployed on the same platform, the aggregate behavior can be unpredictable and can produce unexpected errors—nullifying the very properties the tools were designed to ensure!

Clearly, there is a growing need for higher-level frameworks that would enable programmers to rapidly build robust monitoring and management tools. To address this need, this paper presents MiCA (Microprotocol Composition Architecture). Unlike frameworks based on pub-sub [13,6] or any-cast [15,3] communication models, MiCA is based on gossip. In a gossip protocol, each node exchanges information with a randomly selected peer at periodic intervals. Because it is based on periodic peer-to-peer communication, gossip's network load tends to be well-behaved, scaling linearly with system size and not prone to reactive feedback. Moreover, because peers are selected randomly, no single node is indispensable, so tools built on gossip are extremely tolerant to disruptions and able to rapidly recover from failures. Accordingly, gossip is an attractive choice for system monitoring tools [26,22,27], network overlay management [14], and even distributed storage systems [26,8,20,5].

MiCA enables programmers to describe gossip protocols in terms of three functions: a function view that is used to determine peers to gossip with; a function update that takes states of gossiping nodes and computes the new states following an exchange; and a function rate that determines how frequently exchanges should occur. This abstraction exposes the essential characteristics of gossip protocols, but hides low-level implementation details such as how random numbers are picked, how network connections are managed, and how protocol messages are constructed. Because the MiCA run-time system handles all these details, programmers are free to focus on higher-level issues.

To facilitate building more sophisticated protocols, MiCA also provides a collection of composition operators that combine several smaller protocols into a single larger one. These operators are made possible by MiCA's abstractions, which provide a clean interface for merging protocols while preserving their essential behavior. As examples of protocol composition, a MiCA programmer might develop a layered protocol that first creates a tree overlay on top of an otherwise unstructured network and then aggregates data values up the tree. Or, they might implement a transformation that takes an unreliable protocol and makes it fault-tolerant by running multiple copies of the protocol concurrently in a pipeline [2]. Protocol transformations of these kinds would be extremely tedious to implement by hand but are easy to express in MiCA.

Describing gossip protocols using higher-level abstractions provides the MiCA system with opportunities for optimizing implementations of protocols automatically. For example, although the `update` function is defined on pairs of node states, the compiler can often determine that only a portion of the state of each node actually needs to be serialized and sent over the network using program analysis. In composite protocols, the run-time system can often bundle messages from different sub-protocols together, thereby reducing the communication cost of running those protocols simultaneously. Consequently, MiCA programs can provide correct behavior and predictable performance, while substantially reducing overhead compared to hand-written code.

We have built a prototype implementation of MiCA and used it to implement a wide range of standard protocols. To evaluate the performance of our system, we have performed experiments using MiCA on a collection of micro-benchmarks and simulations. Overall, these experiments demonstrate the effectiveness and robustness of our approach—in particular, that MiCA effectively bounds the costs of monitoring applications with hundreds of distinct components.

In summary, the main contributions of this paper are as follows:

1. We design a novel framework for building gossip protocols that captures their essential features while eliding tedious low-level implementation details.
2. We develop a collection of primitive gossip protocols and well-behaved protocol composition operators that satisfy natural correctness criteria.
3. We present our implementation and results from experiments illustrating the expressiveness and robustness of our framework.

The rest of the paper is structured as follows: § 2 and § 3 motivate MiCA's design using intuitive examples and experimental results from a simple simulation; § 4 describes operators for composing protocols and discusses correctness; § 5 discusses state management and an optimization; § 6 describes the MiCA prototype; § 7 presents an evaluation; § 8 discusses related work; and § 9 concludes.

2   Overview

This section introduces MiCA, using an epidemic protocol as a running example.

Assumptions. MiCA is based on a model of gossip in which the behavior of the system emerges from frequent pairwise interactions between nodes in the system. We call each interaction an *exchange*, and the nodes participating in an exchange a *gossip pair*. The state of the system evolves as the result of repeated, concurrent exchanges.

This model reflects several assumptions that hold in real-world cloud computing and data center environments: messages may be reordered or lost by the network, and the local clocks on each node all run at the same rate (though the clocks need not be synchronized). The evolution of the system state proceeds in loose rounds, with each correctly functioning node initiating a gossip exchange once every unit of time. Although the probabilistic nature of this model means that gossip protocols do not provide firm guarantees at fine-grained time scales, the expected behavior of the system over time can be reasoned about accurately.

Failures are inevitable in any real-world system, and systems based on gossip protocols are no exception. MiCA uses a failure model that includes both fail-stop and Byzantine nodes: nodes may crash and messages may be forged or lost, either due to network faults or malicious code executing on some of the nodes in the system. We do assume, however, that all messages are well formed and that malfunctioning nodes do not overwhelm the system by sending messages at arbitrary rates (an assumption that could be enforced by the network itself).

These assumptions mean that failures can prevent an otherwise correct node from gossiping in any particular round, but over time, such failures are likely to be vastly outnumbered by successful exchanges. Primitive gossip protocols are expected to tolerate transient failures—*e.g.*, selecting sufficiently long rounds to prevent endemic timeouts—and programmers are expected to avoid pathological topologies and communication patterns that could lead to partitions or bottlenecks. In practice, most gossip protocols are designed to overcome transient faults and achieve convergence under less than ideal network conditions.

Programming model. The programming abstraction provided in MiCA closely follows the informal model of gossip protocols just described. With MiCA, programmers write gossip protocols by specifying the implementation for one participant node. Each participant in a protocol is a Java object implementing the following interface:

```
interface GossipParticipant {
  ProbMassFunc<Address> view();
  double rate();
  void update(GossipParticipant other);
}
```

The first method, view, controls peer selection during gossip exchanges. Unlike other gossip systems, which assume uniform random selection from a set of neighboring nodes or the global set of nodes, MiCA allows the programmer to specify the view as a discrete probability distribution on the set of network addresses. The MiCA run-time samples this distribution to select a gossip peer. The view method returns a probability mass function object (i.e., ProbMassFunc), which supports a sample method. As we will discuss in § 4, MiCA composition operators ensure that the probability mass function is scaled to provide a proper distribution over gossip nodes.

This approach has several advantages. First, working with probability distributions allows greater flexibility than uniform random selection. For example, probabilities can be used to encode notions of locality ("gossip more frequently with nearby neighbors") and capacity ("gossip more frequently with super-peers"), and even to encode overlay topologies [14]. Second, it allows developers to implement their protocols as if they were deterministic. Sources of non-determinism (e.g., peer-selection) are abstracted away and handled by the MiCA runtime. This makes programs simpler and eliminates a potential source of bugs. Third, it retains precise information about distributions and makes them available for analysis and manipulation by other operators. In particular, these distributions are used heavily by MiCA's composition operators—*e.g.*, composing two protocols with uniform random peer selection over different sets of nodes yields a non-uniform distribution over the union of those sets—unlike other systems, where views are sampled and discarded prior to composition, losing opportunities for optimization.

The `view` function also serves as a way to delegate overlay topology maintenance to another software component. When populating the view, developers often need to pay attention to the structure of the selected nodes: correctness and convergence are usually tied to particular topological properties, which may not hold for ad-hoc topologies. The MiCA programmer can use Java's type system to declare these requirements; for example, a protocol that outsources its view to an overlay maintenance layer might accept this layer as an instance of the interface `ExpanderGraphOverlay`.

The second method, `rate`, specifies the local node's gossip rate relative to the basic unit of time. A constant rate such as 1.0 is usually sufficient for non-composite protocols, but variable rates are used by composition to multiplex sub-protocols without slowing down their overall convergence rates against wall-clock time. Per-node variable rates are also used by some gossip protocols, for example, as a mechanism to compensate for dropped packets [24].

The third method, `update`, takes the state of the gossip peer as input and performs an exchange, potentially modifying the states of the initiating node and the peer. Due to failures, one or both of the nodes may not actually be updated—modifications are not guaranteed to be atomic. However, the widespread success of gossip protocols testifies to the utility of this abstraction, and its simplicity: programmers are able to work with pairs of node states rather than having to explicitly send and receive messages, and the tedious logic needed to manually deal with timeouts and failures is subsumed by the model.

2.1 Example

As an example, consider the MiCA program in Figure 1. `MinFinder` nodes implement a simple epidemic protocol that, given a system in which nodes initially contain arbitrary integer values, eventually converges to a global system state where every (correctly functioning) node contains the minimum value in the system. The `view` method returns a probability distribution on network addresses. For the purpose of this example, we assume the view is known in advance and is supplied as a parameter to the constructor. The `rate` method returns a constant indicating that 1.0 gossip exchanges should occur every round. The `update`

```
class MinFinder implements GossipParticipant {
  int value;
  ProbMassFunc<Address> view;
  MinFinder(int value, ProbMassFunc<Address> view) {
    this.value = value;
    this.view = view;
  }
  ProbMassFunc<Address> view() { return view; }
  double rate() { return 1.0 }
  void update(GossipParticipant other) {
    MinFinder that = (MinFinder) other;
    this.value = min(this.value, that.value);
    that.value = this.value;
  }
}
```

Fig. 1. Anti-entropy protocol in MiCA

method implements a push-pull anti-entropy protocol: it compares the values
stored on the initiating node and the receiving node, and updates both values
to the minimum. It is worth pointing out that while the update method allows
developers to transmit data between nodes, it is ultimately the MiCA runtime
that determines which data is sent. As a result, the runtime can optimize the
exchange. For example, if it can determine that some data will not be used by an
update, it will only send the relevant subset of the data. It is straightforward to
show that MinFinder participants converge to the minimum value in expected
logarithmic time (in the absence of failures) on a complete graph [9].

3   Naïve Composition

Cloud computing platforms such as Amazon EC2, Microsoft Azure, IBM Websphere, Google Compute Engine, and Facebook consist of tens or even hundreds of thousands of individual components that must be monitored to ensure
the health of the platform. Gossip protocols provide a simple way to ensure
that monitoring tools will behave predictably and have bounded communication costs. However, while it is not difficult to monitor multiple components
of a system simultaneously—one can fork a new process for each component—
combining tasks naïvely leads to increasing demands on system resources such
as CPU, memory, and network bandwidth. In large systems, these demands can
cause the cost of monitoring to rapidly dominate the very system being monitored. Addressing this issue is one of the primary motivations for MiCA.

To quantify the cost of naïve composition (and the potential for optimization)
we conducted an experiment in which we executed several monitoring tasks simultaneously. We executed an increasing number of copies of an anti-entropy

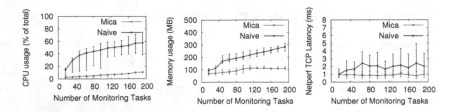

Fig. 2. The average CPU, memory, and network utilization when running an increasing number of monitoring tasks with both naïve composition and MiCA

protocol and measured CPU utilization, memory utilization, and network latency. Intuitively, this experiment can be thought of as modeling the situation where an administrator must monitor an aggregate value for each of a large number of components. We ran the experiment on a testbed consisting of 32 virtual machines on a Eucalyptus cluster. Each VM was configured with an emulated 2.9GHz CPU, 4GB memory, 10GB ATA disk, and 1Gb/s NIC. The physical nodes hosting the VMs were 15 Dell-R720 servers with two 8-core 2.9GHz E5-2690 CPUs, 96GB RAM, 2×900GB disks, and two 10Gb/s Ethernet NICs each.

The results of the experiment are given in Figure 2. They show that CPU, memory, and network utilization rapidly increased under naïve composition, whereas MiCA was able to scale out to hundreds of monitoring tasks with only a little additional cost compared to running a single copy of the epidemic protocol. For example, with 200 monitoring components, CPU utilization on each instance exceeded 50% and required 250MB of memory, and network latency for other traffic was increased by a factor of two. Overall, this experiment demonstrates how interactions between monitoring components can incur substantial costs, and highlights the benefits that can be gained using optimized implementations of higher-level abstractions provided in systems such as MiCA.

4   Protocol Combinators

MiCA not only helps developers build complex monitoring tools out of simpler reusable components—it also provides operators that combine protocols while preserving semantics and guaranteeing predictable performance. As motivation for these operators, suppose that we want to execute two copies of the `MinFinder` protocol: one copy to compute the minimum address in the system, and a second copy to compute the smallest amount of free memory of any node in the system. Why might we want to do this? Perhaps the first copy implements leader election and the second implements a monitoring application. Using the abstractions described in the last section, it would not be difficult to construct a new `MinFinderTwo` protocol that implements both tasks. This protocol would maintain a pair of values, and would update both components of the pair on each

Table 1. Forms of gossip protocol composition

		Communication	
		Isolated	Combined
State	Isolated	With this naïve implementation strategy, each application is completely independent.	Subsystems cannot share state, but can multiplex messages (e.g., MQ[30], TIBCO[23]).
	Combined	An application can have many shared subsystems, but each communicates independently (e.g, JXTA[15], Bast[13]).	Composition reduces the overhead of executing multiple monitoring applications simultaneously (e.g., MiCA).

exchange. Of course, it would be even better if we could simply reuse our existing implementation of MinFinder instead of building a whole new protocol from scratch. This section presents composition operators that do just this—merging one or more gossip protocols into a single protocol that implements the behaviors of each sub-protocol.

There are many different ways of combining protocols. MiCA compositional operators can be categorized along two axes: whether the *state* and *communication* of the composed protocols are *isolated* or *shared*. Table 1 presents an overview of various approaches for protocol composition:

− *Isolated state, isolated communication*: This is the naïve multiplexing approach discussed in § 3, in which each protocol executes completely independently. As demonstrated by our simulations, this approach does not scale.
− *Isolated state, shared communication*: This approach provides communication primitives that can combine messages with the goal of reducing network congestion. This approach is used in pub-sub message buses, like TIBCO [23], and message-storage middleware, such as IBM WebSphere MQ [30]. POSIX streams also provide a similar style of message multiplexing.
− *Shared state, isolated communication*: This approach enables a single application to have many subsystems, each of which is monitored independently. For example, each job in MapReduce [7] runs in its own thread and communicates independently, but the overall system state is shared. Examples of this kind of system include JXTA [15] and Bast [13].
− *Shared state, shared communication*: This new approach combines the advantages of the previous two, allowing a single application to be expressed in terms of several sub-protocols whose state depends on each other, while reducing communication overhead by bundling messages together.

Note that although Table 1 locates MiCA in the quadrant for shared-state and shared-communication, MiCA actually provides a comprehensive suite of composition operators that capture each of these forms of composition. The rest of this section discusses correctness criteria for protocol composition operators, and then presents the operators that we find most useful in applications in detail.

4.1   Correctness Properties

To reason effectively about a composite protocol, programmers need assurance that the semantics of the combined protocol faithfully encodes the behavior of each sub-protocol. This section identifies essential properties for gossip composition:

- *View preservation:* A *view-preserving* operator ensures that the ratio of the frequencies with which it initiates gossip exchanges that update sub-protocols are identical to the ratio (calculated pointwise) of the distributions generated by each sub-protocol's `view` method. In other words, the rate of events where the composite chooses to execute P_i.update may be reduced or increased, but must be done so uniformly for all nodes in P_i's view.
- *Rate preservation:* A *rate-preserving* operator ensures that each sub-protocol continues to run at the same wall-clock rate as it would if run in isolation. Of course, there is a tension between view preservation and rate preservation: to ensure the former, a composite protocol must only execute each sub-protocol on certain exchanges, while to ensure the latter, it must not delay the rate at which the sub-protocol gossips.
- *State preservation:* A *state-preserving* operator ensures that the effect on the state of each sub-protocol is either the outcome of executing the `update` method of that sub-protocol or a no-op. In other words, composition does not introduce any co-mingling of sub-protocol states. Note that deliberate state sharing is still allowed—indeed, it is vital for building layered protocols where a lower-level protocol computes some form of state (such as a mesh-overlay), which is imported as a read-only input by one or more higher-level protocols layered over it. In the context of MiCA, state corresponds to an instance of a `GossipParticipant`, and everything reachable from it.

Together, these properties facilitate reasoning about composite protocols in a modular way: the programmer can write, reason about, and deploy a smaller protocol within a larger composite, and understand the way that it will behave without having to consider the entire program. They serve as guides while designing and debugging the operators presented in the rest of this section.

4.2   Operators

We now define a few useful MiCA composition operators. We begin with an obvious operator, round-robin merging, whose behavior is intuitive but restrictive and inefficient, before moving on to more sophisticated probabilistic operators.

```
class RoundRobinMerger implements GossipParticipant {
  GossipParticipant g1, g2;
  boolean g1Next; // if true, g1 gossips next
  ...
  ProbMassFunc<Address> view() {
    if(g1Next) return g1.view();
    else return g2.view();
  }
  double rate() { return g1.rate() + g2.rate(); }
  void update(GossipParticipant other) {
    RoundRobinMerger that = (RoundRobinMerger) other;
    if(g1Next) g1.update(that.g1);
    else g2.update(that.g2);
    g1Next = !g1Next;
  }
}
```

Fig. 3. Round-robin merging. Note: assumes g1 and g2 to gossip at the same rate.

Round-robin merging. Arguably the most obvious way to merge multiple protocols into a single protocol is to interleave their operations in round-robin fashion. Figure 3 defines a simple composition operator that does exactly this: given sub-protocols g1 and g2, it alternates between g1 exchanges and g2 exchanges, using a boolean g1Next to keep track of the next sub-protocol to execute. For reasons discussed below, this operator assumes that the rate methods of g1 and g2 are equivalent. The view method branches on g1Next and dispatches the view method from g1 or g2. The update method is similar, but also updates g1Next so that the other protocol will execute on the next exchange. The rate method is slightly different: it returns the *sum* of the rates for g1 and g2. This is correct since doubling the rate of the combined protocol compensates for the fact that each sub-protocol is only able to initiate an exchange every other round. Hence, the rate at which each sub-protocol converges will be preserved in the composite protocol. Note that if g1 and g2 have different rates, then it would be incorrect to combine them using round-robin merging—a more sophisticated strategy would be needed to account for the rate disparity. The next operator provides a possible approach.

Correlated merging. Another way to combine several protocols into one is to do so probabilistically. That is, instead of alternating between the sub-protocols in sequence, we can invoke the view methods to compute the probability distributions for each sub-protocol and construct a composite distribution that represents the peer selection preferences of both. This approach takes advantage of the fact that both sub-protocols may sometimes be willing to gossip with the same peer, allowing execution of both update methods to be *bundled* into a single exchange and reducing the overall number of messages sent without degrading performance. The correlated merge operator (Figure 4) is aggressive in trying to exploit this form of overlap—it bundles messages as often as possible while still

```
class CorrelatedMerger implements GossipParticipant
  GossipParticipant g1, g2;
  ...
  ProbMassFunc<Address> view() {
    double r1 = g1.rate();
    double r2 = g2.rate();
    double w = r1 / (r1 + r2);
    ProbMassFunc<Address> d1 = g1.view().scale(w);
    ProbMassFunc<Address> d2 = g2.view().scale(1-w);
    return ProbMassFunc.max(d1, d2).normalize();
  }
  double rate() {
    double r1 = g1.rate();
    double r2 = g2.rate();
    ProbMassFunc<Address> d1 = g1.view().scale(r1);
    ProbMassFunc<Address> d2 = g2.view().scale(r2);
    return ProbMassFunc.max(d1, d2).magnitude();
  }
  void update(CorrelatedMerger other) {
    CorrelatedMerger that = (CorrelatedMerger) other;
    double r1 = g1.rate();
    double r2 = g2.rate();
    double w = r1 / (r1 + r2);
    double pr1 = g1.view().get(that) * w;
    double pr2 = g2.view().get(that) * (1-w);
    double pmin = Math.min(pr1,pr2);
    double pmax = Math.max(pr1,pr2);
    double alpha = (pr1 - pmin) / pmax;
    double beta = (pr2 - pmin) / pmax;
    double gamma = pmin / pmax;
    switch (weightedChoice({ alpha, beta, gamma })) {
    case 0: // only g1 gossips
      g1.update(that.g1); break;
    case 1: // only g2 gossips
      g2.update(that.g2); break;
    case 2: // both g1 and g2 gossip
      g1.update(that.g1);
      g2.update(that.g2);
    }
  }
}
```

Fig. 4. Correlated merging.

satisfying the view-preservation and rate-preservation properties. Because this operator is somewhat involved, we step through each of its methods in detail.

The view method works more or less in the way just described: it computes the views for g1 and g2 and scales them by w and (1-w) respectively, where w is the relative weight of g1's rate with respect to g2. It then computes the pointwise max of the scaled distributions and normalizes the result. This produces a distribution that reflects the peer selection preferences of g1 and g2 with respect to their relative rates. This is equivalent to summing the two rate-scaled views and then subtracting their intersection, where the area of the intersection represents the fraction of correlation between views that can be exploited by bundling— two sub-protocols with identical views intersect completely, whereas two disjoint views have none. The `rate` method calculates the views for g1 and g2, scales them by r1 and r2, and then takes the area under the pointwise maximum of the resulting distributions. This calculation determines the rate needed to correctly execute both sub-protocols while preserving their rates, and anticipating opportunistic bundling of messages. The `update` method must decide whether to gossip g1, g2, or both. To do this, it uses the sub-protocol views to compute three probabilities: given that a particular peer was sampled from the composite view, let `alpha` be the probability that only g1 chose to gossip with that peer, `beta` be the same for g2, and `gamma` be the probability that both nodes choose to gossip—i.e., the view intersection for the selected peer's address. A pseudo-random choice selects one of these three possibilities and executes the respective `update` methods.

Correlated merge has two significant advantages over simple round-robin. First, it is completely general, in that it does not make any assumptions about the protocols being combined. This is unlike round-robin merge, which assumes that the two sub-protocols gossip at the same rate. Second, it can greatly reduce the number of messages needed to implement the composite protocol; this is advantageous because it amortizes overheads over the messages in the bundle. The degree to which the operator is able to bundle messages depends on the amount of overlap in the peer selection preferences of g1 and g2—the greater the overlap of their distributions, the greater the benefit.

To illustrate correlated merging, consider the following abstract examples.

- Suppose that g1 gossips by selecting randomly from nodes with odd addresses, and g2 by selecting randomly from nodes with even addresses. That is, if there are n nodes in total, g1's `view` method returns a distribution where odd nodes have probability mass $2/n$ and even nodes have probability mass 0, and symmetrically for g2. Because these distributions are disjoint, the `view` method for the merged protocol returns the uniform distribution on all n addresses. For a given gossip partner b, the distribution computed by g1 assigns probability mass 0 to b if b's address is even, and the distribution computed by g2 assigns probability mass 0 to b if b's address is odd. The combined `update` method invokes g1's `update` method when called with a partner b whose address is odd and otherwise invokes g2's `update` method. Importantly, it never invokes both `update` functions as the peer selection preferences are disjoint. In a sense, probabilistic merge operator subsumes round-robin merging when the sub-protocol distributions are disjoint.
- Suppose instead that both g1 and g2 gossip by selecting randomly from all nodes—i.e., the `view` method for both sub-protocols returns a uniform

```
class IndependentMerger implements GossipParticipant
  GossipParticipant g1, g2;
  ...
  ProbMassFunc<Address> view() {
    double r1 = g1.rate();
    double r2 = g2.rate();
    double w = r1 / (r1 + r2);
    ProbMassFunc<Address> d1 = g1.view().scale(w);
    ProbMassFunc<Address> d2 = g2.view().scale(1-w);
    return d1.add(d2).normalize();
  }
  double rate() { return g1.rate() + g2.rate(); }
  void update(IndependentMerger other) {
    IndependentMerger that = (IndependentMerger) other;
    double r1 = this.g1.rate();
    double r2 = this.g2.rate();
    double w = r1 / (r1 + r2);
    double pr1 = g1.view().get(that) * w;
    double pr2 = g2.view().get(that) * (1-w);
    double alpha = pr1 / (pr1 + pr2);
    double beta = pr2 / (pr1 + pr2);
    switch (weightedChoice({ alpha, beta })) {
    case 0: // Only g1 gossips
      g1.update(that.g1); break;
    case 1: // Only g2 gossips
      g2.update(that.g2); break;
    }
  }
}
```

Fig. 5. Independent merging

distribution where every node has probability mass $1/n$. The combined `view` method returns the same uniform distribution and the `update` method evaluates g1 and g2 every round, where round length is a system-wide constant. This example shows how probabilistic merge allows protocols with equivalent `view` methods to be combined without additional messages or rate increases.

– Finally, suppose that g1 gossips randomly with odd nodes, and g2 gossips randomly with all nodes. The combined `view` method returns a distribution in which nodes with odd addresses are assigned probability mass $4/(3 \cdot n)$ and nodes with even addresses are assigned probability mass $2/(3 \cdot n)$. Hence, the run-time chooses peers with odd addresses twice as often as it chooses peers with even addresses. The combined `update` method has two cases: if the node has an odd address, it always invokes g1's `update` method and additionally invokes g2's `update` method with probability $1/2$. Or, if the node has an even address, then it only invokes g2's `update` method. Hence, the merged protocol distributes exchanges evenly between g1 and g2, allowing many exchanges with odd peers to execute both sub-protocols.

```
class EpochPipeliner<G extends GossipParticipant> extends
   CorrelatedMerger {
 GossipParticipantFactory<G> factory = null;
 int epochLength = 0;
 int currentEpochStart = 0;
 EpochPipeliner(GossipParticipantFactory<G> factory, int epochLength) {
   super(factory.create(), factory.create());
   ...
 }
 void update(EpochPipeliner<G> other) {
   int now = getRuntimeState().getSystemClockRounds();
   if(now - currentEpochStart >= epochLength) {
     g1 = g2; // promote backup to primary
     g2 = factory.create();
     currentEpochStart = now;
   }
   super.update(other);
 }
}
```

Fig. 6. Epoch-based "pipelining" operator

Independent merging. Although it is often advantageous to bundle messages from multiple sub-protocols together, there is also a downside to the correlated merge operator: the peer selection preferences of the sub-protocols are no longer independent. This could violate assumptions in a program that depends on independence. For example, the correctness of the random walk protocol developed by Massoulié et al. [17] depends on randomly sampling locations in the system. If we mistakenly composed two copies of this protocol using the correlated merging operator just defined, believing that this would yield samples from two distinct random walks, both instances would actually generate the same walks. Such problems could have dire consequences in systems whose robustness assumes independent peer selection. Another example involving random walks comes from Broder et al. [4], who solve the problem of generating independent paths between pairs of nodes with a random walk approach. More generally, any system relying on the independence of concurrent gossip protocols could be inadvertently sabotaged by the correlated merge operator. To address this concern, we present an independent probabilistic merge operator (Figure 5). Like correlated merge, independent merge makes probabilistic gossip choices, and combines sub-protocol `view` and `rate` methods. However, the independent merge ensures that the probabilistic decisions made by each sub-protocol are independent.

Epoch pipelining. The final operator presented in this section implements a completely different kind of composition. Rather than composing multiple sub-protocols in parallel, it composes a single protocol with itself, running two instances in a primary-backup configuration for enhanced fault tolerance.

As a motivating example, recall the `MinFinder` example from the previous section, which gossips the minimum value in the system using a simple anti-entropy protocol. This protocol converges rapidly to a stable state and is extremely robust—a small number of lost messages or transient failures have little affect on overall convergence. However, it is susceptible to a particular failure that can easily lead to unintuitive behavior. To illustrate, consider a system in which each node executes `MinFinder`. Next, suppose that after running the protocol for a while, the node that originally contained the minimum value crashes. What should happen? We might want the system to converge to the next smallest value in the system. But, assuming the crashed node successfully communicated with at least one other node, this is not what will happen. Instead, the system will continue gossiping the old minimum value even though none of the nodes in the system still have that value.

To address this problem, we can execute two copies of `MinFinder` side by side. The primary protocol, by convention `g1`, contains the definitive copy of the protocol while the backup protocol, `g2`, executes a second copy of the protocol from a fresh state. The composite protocol executes the two copies in parallel until a certain number of rounds have elapsed—sufficiently many to ensure that the backup copy has converged to a stable value. At that point, the composite protocol replaces the primary with the backup and resets the backup to a fresh copy of the protocol. It is easy to see that this "pipelined" protocol does not suffer from the anomaly described above, since the minimum value is recomputed from scratch in each epoch. Note that this implementation of pipeline parallelism requires system-wide clock drift to be less than one half of a round, to prevent possible contamination from the primary layer to the backup layer. This is a reasonable constraint in a data center, where round-trip communication times between nodes are no more than a few milliseconds.

We can define pipelining on top of any of the merging operators just defined. Figure 6 gives a definition using correlated merge operator. Note that the `view` and `rate` functions are inherited from the super class. The definition of a pipelining operator based on independent merge is similar, and preferable in many scenarios since it makes completely independent choices when selecting a peer. On the downside, however, it requires extra messages and an increased rate, whereas the operator based on correlated merge only requires larger messages since it can always bundle messages from each pipeline stage. A more general `EpochPipeliner` implementation might admit other implementations of epoch-switching, for example, triggered by a consensus threshold instead of a clock [10]. Finally, although we do not develop it here, one can define pipelining of k protocol copies at a time for higher levels of fault tolerance.

5   State Management and Data Movement

MiCA is designed to abstract away the details of handling distributed state. In particular, developers write the `update` function with the illusion that each participating node is able to access the other's state as if it were local. In actuality,

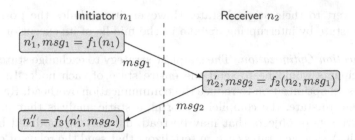

Fig. 7. Execution of a gossip exchange with the explicit messages used by the low-level target of the MiCA compiler. Provided the synthesized functions f_1, f_2, f_3 are correct, the final states of both nodes are guaranteed to be the same as if update had executed locally: $(n_1'', n_2') = \text{update}(n_1, n_2)$.

the update function is a distributed program that exchanges messages using the communication pattern illustrated in Figure 7. The MiCA compiler transforms the update function into the distributed implementation, and the MiCA runtime manages the exchange of state between the nodes.

To transform update into the distributed equivalent, MiCA partitions the function into three fragments, f_1, f_2, and f_3, that cooperate to execute the gossip exchange. First, the initiator of the exchange updates its own state by applying f_1, and sends its updated state to the receiver node in message msg_1. Next, the receiver executes its fragment, f_2, using the initiator state and its own state, and then returns its new state in msg_2. Finally, the initiator updates its state, using f_3, with the data from the receiver. Note that when partitioning the function into fragments, the compiler must ensure that the fragments obey the constraints imposed by the program dependence graph (PDG). So, f_1 cannot execute code that may read state from n_2, and f_3 cannot execute code that may modify the state of n_2. This can be expressed as two cuts in the PDG, breaking update into three regions corresponding to f_1, f_2, and f_3.

Consistency Model. A key challenge for maintaining MiCA's local state abstraction is handling failures during the execution of update. Ideally, MiCA would provide guarantees about an exchange, even if failures occur. Unfortunately, it is impossible to guarantee the obvious property—transactional atomicity—because when a network fault is detected on a given node, that node has no way of determining whether the remote node has successfully completed its last phase. This means that the node cannot decide whether or not to roll back its local state or not (this is an instance of the classic Two Generals' problem).

To avoid these issues, MiCA employs a relaxed consistency model. MiCA saves node state before executing calls to update. If a network error is detected (including timeouts, which do not necessarily mean the message failed to reach its destination), the state is rolled back. All state changes that occurred during the unsuccessful update are erased by the rollback. This leaves four possible outcomes for each gossip exchange: each node completes successfully, or one or both revert to their original state. However, it precludes the possibility of corrupting state by interrupting `update` in the middle of its execution.

Communication Optimization. The simplest strategy to exchange state between the participants would be to send the entire state of each node. In contrast, MiCA uses an optimization to reduce the communication overhead. Rather than send the entire state, the compiler performs a static analysis that determines conservative sets of objects that may be read and may be modified by f_1, f_2, and f_3. MiCA then generates custom serializers that send the relevant objects in messages msg_1 and msg_2. This analysis is currently performed at the granularity of fields of the root protocol objects. While coarse, this is a significant improvement over the naïve strategy, in that fields that will definitely not be used are not exchanged. It would be natural to duplicate the execution of side-effect-free code to further reduce the amount of state that needs to be transmitted, but MiCA does not currently implement this extension.

6 Implementation

We have built a full working prototype of MiCA, implemented as an extension to Java, and made it available under an open-source license. Our implementation can be obtained at: `https://github.com/mica-gossip/mica`. It includes the compiler and runtime, as well as a library of primitive protocols and implementations of the composition operators presented in this paper.

The MiCA compiler is implemented as a bytecode post-processor. Post-processing allows MiCA to partition the `update` function into methods for each node participating in the gossip exchange, and perform the static analysis for the communication optimization.

The current implementation uses TCP/IP for network communication. One connection is kept alive for the duration of the gossip exchange. However, the communication layer of MiCA does not depend on this particular implementation choice. In ongoing work, we are exploring an alternative implementation that uses UDP. Because gossip protocols are tolerant of failures, the unreliable communication mechanism seems like a natural choice if some performance benefit can be gained due to smaller packet headers, reduced connection state, etc.

MiCA uses the Soot analysis framework [25] for analysis and transformation, and relies on Soot for computing the program dependence graph, points-to sets, and call graph. For functions f_1, f_2, and f_3, the remote node (either n_1 or n_2) is replaced with a custom-generated proxy class, inspired by the Uniform Proxies of Eugster [12]. An instance of this proxy class may represent a local or remote GossipParticipant object; in the case of a remote object, the proxy acts as a container for the subset of fields that may be necessary for remote execution.

7 Experience and Case Studies

To evaluate our design and implementation of MiCA, we asked volunteers in an undergraduate course to use MiCA for developing distributed applications.

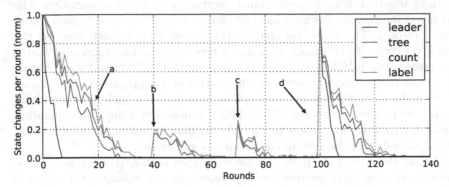

Fig. 8. Convergence of all four layers. Arrows indicate (a) Convergence from arbitrary starting state; (b) a transient fault: 10% of nodes crash; (c) failed nodes recover; (d) a large artificial disruption of the bottom layer's state. Note that the leader election layer was not affected by the transient fault because the leader did not crash.

To explore how MiCA performs in real-world scenarios, we performed two case studies in a simulated environment.

In the undergrad course, a number of students who had no connection to our research efforts used MiCA to develop their projects. Using MiCA, they developed a data replication protocol for use in coherent distributed caching, a probabilistic consensus protocol, scalable distributed denial-of-service (DDoS) detection application, and a storage backend for a peer-to-peer social network.

The case studies were performed in a simulated runtime. This runtime simulates a gossip network of many logical nodes with a discrete event simulation passing messages via message queues on a single machine. All of the MiCA logic and state serialization is the same as in the TCP/IP runtime. The simulated runtime allowed us to perform experiments faster than realtime. For the first case study, we implemented a four-layer composite protocol that builds a tree over an otherwise unstructured topology and then labels the nodes of the tree according to a depth-first traversal. During execution, we introduced several disruptions, and measured the time needed for each layer to converge back to a stable state. This experiment demonstrates how MiCA facilitates building sophisticated protocols out of simple components, as well as the resilience of such composite protocols to various kinds of failures. For the second case study, we studied the effect on convergence times for protocols built using probabilistic merge. Because this operator changes the gossip rate for each sub-protocol from a deterministic to an probabilistic value, the expected convergence time is increased in certain topologies. This experiment illustrates this effect, which we call dilation, using another simulation.

7.1   Layered Protocol

The first case study is based on a four-layer composite protocol originally proposed by Dolev [11]. The layers represent several standard varieties of gossip, all working together: overlay maintenance, aggregation, and dissemination. The lowest layer, **leader**, gossips on a fixed topology and executes a standard leader election protocol. The leader selected by the lowest layer is then used by the second layer, **tree**, to construct a spanning tree overlay. The third and fourth layers, **count** and **label**, gossip over the tree overlay. The **count** layer recursively counts the number of nodes in each sub-tree and aggregates the results up the tree to the root, while **label** assigns a numeric label to each node, resulting in a depth-first traversal ordering. The labeling is achieved using a dissemination protocol: a parent assigns labels to its children based on its own label plus an offset calculated from the sizes of the children's sub-trees.

Unlike all the composite protocols we have seen so far, this layered protocol requires sharing state between the sub-protocols. For example, the protocol for the **tree** layer depends on the state maintained by the **leader** layer. It is straightforward to encode this behavior in MiCA—the programmer simply creates references between the sub-protocols using ordinary Java references. For example the following code creates the layers needed for the case study:

```
LeaderElection leader = new LeaderElection(topology);
Tree tree = new Tree(leader, topology);
Count count = new Count(tree);
Label label = new Label(tree, count);
GossipParticipant g = new IndependentMerger(leader,
                        new IndependentMerger(label,
                            new IndependentMerger (tree, count)));
```

Note that sharing state between sub-protocols using references obviously breaks the state preservation property, albeit in a fairly innocuous way.

After implementing the layered protocol, we then executed it on a random topology in a simulated environment and measured the amount of time needed for each layer to converge under various disruptions. Figure 8 present the convergence results for all four layers on a 100-node random graph of degree four, starting from arbitrary initial states. To model failures, we introduced a transient disruption by crashing 10% of the nodes at $t = 40$ and restarting them at $t = 70$. At $t = 100$, we introduced a major disruption by clobbering the state of the **leader** layer with arbitrary values. We measured convergence as the normalized per-round rate of change: a value of 1.0 indicates that 100% of the nodes were changing in a given round while a value of 0.0 indicates the protocol has converged. As these graphs show, MiCA can be used to implement protocols that will recover rapidly from transient failures, even major ones, and even when several protocols are combined together.

We also ran the experiment using correlated merge instead of independent merge. This resulted in similar convergence times, but each gossip exchange bundled together the messages for 2.3 layers on average, dramatically reducing the total number of gossip exchanges by 56%. Note, however, that this is not a general result: this particular layered protocol is amenable to correlation because **count** and **label** always gossip together, as do **leader** and **tree**.

7.2   Dilation

The second case study illustrates an effect that we call *dilation*, and that can arise when protocols running at different rates are merged probabilistically. Recall that the rate of a gossip protocol controls the frequency at which the node initiates exchanges with another node. When a protocol runs in isolation, rate is completely deterministic: the node sleeps until the appropriate time, initiates an exchange with that node, and then sleeps again. However, in a composite protocol implemented using the probabilistic merge operator, a given sub-protocol will only be able to initiate gossip at an *expected* rate. In particular, although the average rate will faithfully track the value specified by the `rate` method for that sub-protocol, the variance of the distribution of the interval between gossip exchanges increases as sub-protocols are added to the composite.

To demonstrate this effect, we simulated the anti-entropy protocol from Figure 1, obtaining the results seen in Figure 9. The graph in the upper left corner gives the baseline: the protocol executes deterministically, and the distribution of intervals between exchanges is tightly clustered around 1.0 (because no packet loss occurs in this experiment, it would be exactly 1.0 were it not for measurement artifacts). The next graph, on the upper right, shows the effect when the protocol is composed with another protocol using probabilistic merge. Now the distribution contains values ranging from less than 1.0 all the way up to 5.0. That is, some exchanges occur faster than the stated rate, and some occur slower, even though the average exactly matches the target rate. As additional sub-protocols are added to the composite, shown by the graphs on the bottom row, the dilation becomes increasingly evident.

A natural question to ask is whether this phenomenon affects important properties of a protocol, such as convergence. The answer is that it can, depending on the protocol and topology, but significant consequences are seen only in somewhat artificial situations. Figure 10 depicts the convergence rate for the anti-entropy protocol with various degrees of dilation on a system whose topology is a complete graph. The x-axis contains the number of gossip rounds and the y-axis contains the number of changes induced on that round. A protocol converges when the number of changes reaches 0. In a complete graph topology, the effect of dilation is minimal: because we are executing an anti-entropy protocol and every node is connected to every other node, overall convergence does not hinge on specific nodes being able to gossip at particular moments. We believe that this would be the most common case in real uses of MiCA.

Note that dilation does not mean that probabilistic merge is incorrect—on the contrary, all our operations correctly produce protocols that faithfully implement the sub-protocol, and faithfully run them at the correct average rate. The point is somewhat more subtle: what we see here is that turning a deterministic behavior into a probabilistic one can sometimes slow convergence if the underlying topology has a slow information-dissemination time, but would not have this impact when running on a topology with the properties of an *expander graph*, of which the complete graph is an extreme example. We plan to continue studying dilation in the future, with the goal of fully characterizing the

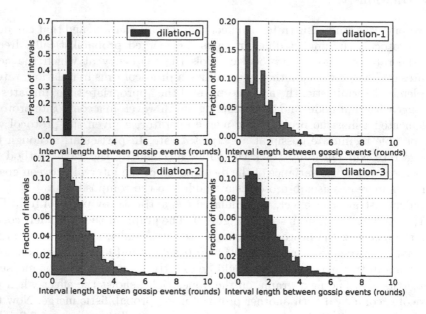

Fig. 9. Effect of dilation for an anti-entry protocol on intervals between gossip exchanges. The labels indicate the degree of dilation: d0 is no dilation, d2 is two nested operators, etc.

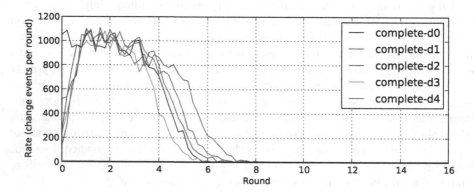

Fig. 10. Effect of dilation for an anti-entropy protocol in a complete topology. The labels indicate the degree of dilation: d0 is no dilation, d2 is two nested operators, etc.

classes of protocols and topologies that are guaranteed to be immune to this effect. We are also exploring other ways to implement the composition operators that incorporate mechanisms for limiting or otherwise bounding the effects of dilation.

8   Related Work

Work related to MiCA falls into several general categories: gossip-specific frameworks (Opis [6], Gossip Objects [28]); object-oriented distributed system libraries (Bast [13], Jini [29]); compositional network transport protocol systems (Appia [18], Cactus [31]); and languages and abstractions for distributed programming (P2 [16], MACEDON [21], BLOOM [1]). In this section, we discuss each of these in turn. It should also be noted that MiCA's core abstraction—the pairwise representation of gossip protocols—was originally presented in a short workshop paper [19]. This earlier work did not define gossip protocols precisely and did not include an implementation or experiments.

The first of these categories contains systems closest to MiCA, namely, those concerned specifically with gossip. *Opis* [6] is an OCaml-based framework for gossip. It offers a formal definition of gossip similar to that used in MiCA. In Opis, gossip protocols are event-driven programs that react to user-defined external network events and internal timer events. This is an interesting contrast to MiCA's protocol representation, which could also be regarded as using events to drive state changes, but has only a small, fixed number of state transitions exposed to the programmer. Like MiCA, Opis leverages object-oriented composition for protocols, but with added benefit from OCaml's rich type system. However, Opis offers no analog to MiCA's compositions, which consider not only the object-oriented composition of classes, but also explore strategies for semantic-preserving combination of protocol views.

The *Gossip Objects* framework [28] offers a compositional infrastructure for publish-subscribe gossip protocols. Unlike MiCA, Gossip Objects is an implementation specifically for publish-subscribe gossip, and not a general framework. Like MiCA, Gossip Objects has optimizations for running many concurrent systems. Composition takes the form of speculative message delivery, bundling messages to non-subscribers in an effort to have them delivered indirectly and accelerate the overall gossip rate. Gossip Objects does not preserve the relative rates of protocols being combined. This is a design decision, not a bug: Gossip Objects' purpose is to improve the efficiency of message delivery.

The next category of related work consists of general-purpose, object-oriented approaches to building distributed systems. These frameworks do not provide MiCA's gossip-centric world view, but do share a common philosophy for protocol composition. *Bast* [13] is an object-oriented library of distributed system components, whose main goals were modular composition and code reuse. The platform introduced a primitive group type and allowed developers to define subtypes supporting additional properties. The primary focus in Bast was on atomic broadcast with various levels of ordering and durability. For example, a database built using Bast might obtain ACID guarantees by exploiting ordering and other atomicity properties of the underlying groups (e.g., in implementations of locking or propagation of updates to replicas). However, while Bast's Java implementation is similar to MiCA's in that both represent protocols as classes and use object-oriented composition mechanisms such as inheritance, MiCA focuses on gossip protocols, and on optimizations that reduce communication while preserving semantics. To the best of our knowledge, Bast never explored gossip protocols, and generally avoided transformations where knowledge of protocol semantics would be needed.

Apache River [29] (originally Jini) is a Java framework for client-server distributed services, originally created by Sun Microsystems. It provides extensible components for service registration and discovery for distributed systems, and other utilities to facilitate distributed systems programming such as remote method invocation and mobile code. Less broad than Bast, it is a good example of an off-the-shelf component available to Java developers building distributed systems. River's services are good examples of the protocol layers that could be implemented in a MiCA stack.

Cactus [31] and Appia [18] both undertake the challenge of transport protocol composition. Recognizing that transports like TCP and UDP are not ideal for all situations, these two systems provide ways to modularly compose a transport protocol that has desired properties; for example, Cactus could be used to satisfy the statement "I need a transport protocol with congestion control, but I don't need reliable ordering". Cactus includes a library of "micro-protocols", each of which implements a particular functionality; the philosophy of composition is similar to MiCA's. Although MiCA gossip protocols run at a layer above the transport, some functionality, such as quality-of-service, could be implemented either in transport or as a MiCA gossip layer.

Finally, there are languages designed for directly programming an entire distributed system. Although MiCA is not a language, its distribution of the update function onto a pair of nodes is similar to what these whole-system languages accomplish. P2 [16] and Bloom [1] are declarative languages that approach distributed systems programming from a databases perspective. P2 allows programmers to specify properties of distributed system state and compiles to a dataflow-oriented runtime system. Bloom is a Ruby-like language, designed for efficient and concise query execution on distributed data tables. MACEDON [21] is a language for building P2P-style overlay networks. Like MiCA, it uses a domain-specific language extension to describe its systems; unlike MiCA, its domain is not gossip, but overlay networks. The programmer writes from a single-node perspective, but MACEDON includes tools for analyzing whole-system behavior.

9   Future Work

Today's data center operators lack tools for creating new services to manage networks and applications, both within enterprise networks and even in the new class of wide-area enterprise VLANs that span between today's massive cloud-computing data center systems. This paper presents MiCA, a new compositional architecture and system for building network management protocols. The system assists developers in creating applications from micro-protocols implemented using gossip or self-stabilization mechanisms, which can then be composed in a property-preserving manner to build sophisticated functionalities. Unlike protocols built in a more classical manner, which have been known to misbehave in unexpected and disruptive ways when deployed on a very large scale, MiCA yields scalable solutions with absolutely predictable, operator-controlled, worst-case message rates and sizes. Using the techniques of the gossip and self-stabilization communities, the developer creates components that are provably convergent under the MiCA run-time model. Moreover, the framework provides abstractions for composing protocols in a manner that preserves their semantics while optimizing across components to make the best possible use of available communication resources. In this manner, MiCA makes it easy to build the massively scalable applications needed to efficiently operate today's data centers.

Acknowledgements. This work was supported by grants from the National Science Foundation, DARPA, and ARPA-e, and a Sloan Research Fellowship.

References

1. Alvaro, P., Condie, T., Conway, N., Elmeleegy, K., Hellerstein, J.M., Sears, R.: Boom analytics: exploring data-centric, declarative programming for the cloud. In: European Conference on Computer Systems, pp. 223–236 (2010)
2. Ben-Or, M., Dolev, D., Hoch, E.N.: Fast self-stabilizing byzantine tolerant digital clock synchronization. In: Symposium on Principles of Distributed Computing, pp. 385–394 (August 2008)
3. Bonjour, http://www.apple.com/support/bonjour/
4. Broder, A.Z., Frieze, A.M., Upfal, E.: Static and dynamic path selection on expander graphs: A random walk approach. Random Structures and Algorithms 14(1), 87–109 (1999)
5. Apache Cassandra, http://cassandra.apache.org
6. Dagand, P.-E., Kostić, D., Kuncak, V.: Opis: Reliable distributed systems in OCaml. In: International Workshop on Types in Language Design and Implementation, pp. 65–78 (January 2009)
7. Dean, J., Ghemawat, S.: MapReduce: Simplified data processing on large clusters. In: Symposium on Operating Systems Design and Implementation, pp. 137–150 (December 2004)
8. DeCandia, G., Hastorun, D., Jampani, M., Kakulapati, G., Lakshman, A., Pilchin, A., Sivasubramanian, S., Vosshall, P., Vogels, W.: Dynamo: Amazon's highly available key-value store. In: Symposium on Operating Systems Principles, pp. 205–220 (October 2007)
9. Demers, A., Greene, D., Hauser, C., Irish, W., Larson, J., Shenker, S., Sturgis, H., Swinehart, D., Terry, D.: Epidemic algorithms for replicated database maintenance. In: Symposium on Principles of Distributed Computing, pp. 1–12 (August 1987)
10. Dolev, D., Hoch, E.N.: Byzantine self-stabilizing pulse in a bounded-delay model. In: Masuzawa, T., Tixeuil, S. (eds.) SSS 2007. LNCS, vol. 4838, pp. 234–252. Springer, Heidelberg (2007)
11. Dolev, S.: Self-Stabilization. MIT Press (2000)
12. Eugster, P.: Uniform proxies for java. In: Conference on Object-Oriented Programming Systems, Languages, and Applications, pp. 139–152 (October 2006)

13. Garbinato, B., Guerraoui, R.: Flexible protocol composition in Bast. In: International Conference on Distributed Computing Systems, pp. 22–29 (May 1998)
14. Jelasity, M., Montresor, A., Babaoglu, Ö.: T-Man: Gossip-based fast overlay topology construction. Computer Networks 53(13), 2321–2339 (2009)
15. JXTA The Language and Platform Independent Protocol for P2P Networking, https://jxta.kenai.com
16. Loo, B.T., Condie, T., Hellerstein, J.M., Maniatis, P., Roscoe, T., Stoica, I.: Implementing declarative overlays. In: Symposium on Operating Systems Principles, pp. 75–90 (October 2005)
17. Massoulié, L., Le Merrer, E., Kermarrec, A.-M., Ganesh, A.: Peer counting and sampling in overlay networks: random walk methods. In: Symposium on Principles of Distributed Computing, pp. 123–132 (August 2006)
18. Miranda, H., Pinto, A., Rodrigues, L.: Appia, a flexible protocol kernel supporting multiple coordinated channels. In: International Conference on Distributed Computing Systems, pp. 707–710 (April 2001)
19. Princehouse, L., Birman, K.: Code-partitioning gossip. Operating Systems Review 43, 40–44 (2010)
20. Riak, http://basho.com/riak/
21. Rodriguez, A., Killian, C.E., Bhat, S., Kostic, D., Vahdat, A.: MACEDON: Methodology for automatically creating, evaluating, and designing overlay networks. In: Symposium on Networked Systems Design and Implementation, pp. 267–280 (March 2004)
22. Subramaniyan, R., Raman, P., George, A.D., Radlinski, M.A., Radlinski, M.A.: GEMS: Gossip-enabled monitoring service for scalable heterogeneous distributed systems. Cluster Computing 9(1), 101–120 (2006)
23. Tibco message bus, http://www.tibco.com/products/automation/messaging/default.jsp
24. Tölgyesi, N., Jelasity, M.: Adaptive peer sampling with newscast. In: Sips, H., Epema, D., Lin, H.-X. (eds.) Euro-Par 2009. LNCS, vol. 5704, pp. 523–534. Springer, Heidelberg (2009)
25. Vallée-Rai, R., Hendren, L., Sundaresan, V., Lam, P., Gagnon, E., Co, P.: Soot – a Java optimization framework. In: Conference of the Centre for Advanced Studies on Collaborative Research, pp. 125–135 (November 1999)
26. Van Renesse, R., Birman, K.P., Vogels, W.: Astrolabe: A robust and scalable technology for distributed system monitoring, management, and data mining. Transactions on Computing Systems 21(2), 164–206 (2003)
27. van Renesse, R., Minsky, Y., Hayden, M.: A gossip-based failure detection service. In: International Middleware Conference, pp. 55–70 (September 1998)
28. Vigfusson, Y., Birman, K., Huang, Q., Nataraj, D.P.: Optimizing information flow in the gossip objects platform. Operating Systems Review 44(2), 71–76 (2010)
29. Waldo, J.: The Jini architecture for network-centric computing. Communications of the ACM 42(7), 76–82 (1999)
30. WebSphere MQ, http://www-03.ibm.com/software/products/en/wmq/
31. Wong, G.T., Hiltunen, M.A., Schlichting, R.D.: A configurable and extensible transport protocol. In: International Conference on Computer Communications, pp. 319–328 (April 2001)

A Artifact Description

Authors of the Artifact. Lonnie Princehouse

Summary. The artifact is a prototype implementation of the MiCA gossip framework. It includes the runtime and libraries used to develop and experiment with MiCA. It also includes implementations of the protocol composition operators and examples given in the paper. The implementation is able to run MiCA protocols on a real network or on a simulated network with a variety of network topologies.

Content. The artifact package includes:

- A runnable jar with bundled dependencies
- Source code
- Documentation and examples

Start with index.html

Getting the Artifact. The artifact endorsed by the Artifact Evaluation Committee is available free of charge as supplementary material of this paper on SpringerLink. The latest version of our code is available at: https://github.com/mica-gossip/mica.

Tested Platforms. The artifact requires Java 6 or greater to run the compiled jar, or a recent version of Eclipse to use the pre-built Eclipse workspace.

License. BSD 3-Clause License (http://opensource.org/licenses/BSD-3-Clause)

MD5 Sum of the Artifact. 68988b8c4623a529366a01d89113ec66

Size of the Artifact. 26521350

Semantics of (Resilient) X10

Silvia Crafa[1], David Cunningham[2], Vijay Saraswat[3],
Avraham Shinnar[3], and Olivier Tardieu[3]

[1] University of Padova, Italy
crafa@math.unipd.it
[2] Google Inc., USA
sparkprime@gmail.com
[3] IBM TJ Watson Research Center, USA
{vsaraswa,shinnar,tardieu}@us.ibm.com

Abstract. We present a formal small-step structural operational semantics for a large fragment of X10, unifying past work. The fragment covers multiple places, mutable objects on the heap, sequencing, try/catch, async, finish, and at constructs. This model accurately captures the behavior of a large class of concurrent, multi-place X10 programs. Further, we introduce a formal model of resilience in X10. During execution of an X10 program, a place may fail for many reasons. Resilient X10 permits the program to continue executing, losing the data at the failed place, and most of the control state, and repairing the global control state in such a way that key semantic principles hold, the Happens Before Invariance Principle, and the Exception Masking Principle. These principles permit an X10 programmer to write clean code that continues to work in the presence of place failure. The given semantics have additionally been mechanized in Coq.

1 Introduction

The need for scale-out programming languages is now well-established, because of high performance computing applications on supercomputers, and analytic computations on big data. Such languages – based for example on a partitioned global address space ([21,9], [10]) – permit programmers to write a single program that runs on a collection of places on a cluster of computers, can create global data-structures spanning multiple places, can spawn tasks at remote places, detect termination of an arbitrary tree of spawned tasks etc. The power of such languages is shown by programs such as M3R, which implement a high-performance, main-memory version of Hadoop Map Reduce [22] in a few thousand lines of code. Other high performance multi-place libraries have been developed for graph computations [12] and sparse matrix computations [23].

At the same time, the practical realities of running large-scale computations on clusters of commodity computers in commercial data centers are that nodes may fail (or may be brought down, e.g. for maintenance) during program executions. This is why multi-place application frameworks such as Hadoop [13], Resilient Data Sets [25], Pregel [18] and MillWheel [2] support resilient computations out of the box. In case of node failure, relevant portions of the user computation are restarted.

A new direction has been proposed recently in [11]: extending a general purpose object-oriented, scale-out programming language (X10) to support resilience. The hypothesis is that application frameworks such as the ones discussed above can in fact be

R. Jones (Ed.): ECOOP 2014, LNCS 8586, pp. 670–696, 2014.
© Springer-Verlag Berlin Heidelberg 2014

programmed in a much simpler and more direct fashion in an object-oriented language (powerful enough to build parallel, distributed libraries) that already supports resilience. It is feasible to extend X10 in this way since is based on a few, orthogonal constructs organized around the idea of *places* and *asynchrony*. A place (typically realized as a process) is simply a collection of objects together with the threads that operate on them. A single computation may have tens of thousands of places. The statement async S supports asynchronous execution of S in a separate task. finish S executes S, and waits for all tasks spawned by S to terminate. Memory locations in one place can contain references (*global refs*) to locations at other places. To use a global ref, the at (p) S statement must be used. It permits the current task to change its place of execution to p, execute S at p and return, leaving behind tasks that may have been spawned during the execution of S. The termination of these tasks is detected by the finish within which the at statement is executing. The values of variables used in S but defined outside S are serialized, transmitted to p, de-serialized to reconstruct a binding environment in which S is executed. Constructs are provided for unconditional (atomic S) and conditional (when (c) S) atomic execution. Finally, Java-style non-resumptive exceptions (throw, try/catch) are supported. If an exception is not caught in an async, it is propagated to the enclosing finish statement. Since there may be many such exceptions, they appear wrapped in a MultipleExceptions exception.

[11] shows that this programming model may be extended to support resilience in a surprisingly straightforward way. A place p may fail at any time with the loss of its heap and tasks. Any executing (or subsequent) tasks on that place throw a DeadPlaceException (DPE). Global refs pointing to locations hosted at p now "dangle"; however they can only be dereferenced via an at (p) S, and this will throw a DPE exception. If a task at a failed place has started a task T at another place, this task is not aborted. Instead Resilient X10 posits a high-level principle, the Happens Before Invariance (HBI) principle: failure of a place should not alter the happens before relationship between statement instances at remaining places. [11] shows that many interesting styles of resilient programming can be expressed in Resilient X10. The language is implemented at a fairly modest cost.

In this paper we formalize the semantics of Resilient X10. Our fundamental motivation is to provide a mechanized, formal semantics for a core fragment of Resilient X10 that is separate from the implementation and can be used as a basis for reasoning about properties of programs and for establishing that principles such as HBI actually hold.

We proceed as follows. Our first task is to formalize a large portion of X10, called TX10. We build on the small-step, transition system for X10 presented in [24] which deals with finish, async and for loops. We extend it to handle multiple places and at, exceptions and try/catch statements, necessary to express place failure. (In the spirit of [24] we omit formalization of any of the object-oriented features of X10 since it is fairly routine). Configurations are just pairs $\langle s, g \rangle$ representing a statement s (the program to be executed) and a global heap g, a partial map from the set of places to heaps. Transitions are (potentially) labeled with exceptions, tagged with whether they were generated from a synchronous or asynchronous context. We establish desirable properties of the transition system (absence of stuck states, invariance of place-local heaps). We establish a bisimulation based semantics that is consistent with the intuitions underlying the "gap based" trace set semantics of Brookes [8]. We establish a set of equational laws for this semantics.

On this foundation we show that the semantics of Resilient X10 can be formalized with just three kinds of changes. (1) A place failure transition models the failure of a place p by simply removing p from the domain of g. This cleanly models loss of all data at p. Next, the transition rules for various language constructs are modified to reflect what happens when those constructs are "executed" at a failed place. (2) An attempt to activate any statement at a failed place results in a DeadPlaceException. (3) Consistent with the design of Resilient X10, any synchronous exception thrown by (the dynamic version of) an at(q) s at a failed place q are masked by a DPE. These are the only changes needed.

We show that the main properties of TX10 carry over to Resilient TX10. We also show important resilience-related properties: our main theorem establishes that in fact Resilient TX10 satisfies Happens Before Invariance. We also present a set of equational laws and discuss differences with the laws for TX10.

We have encoded a mechanized version of the syntax and semantics of both TX10 and Resilient TX10 in Coq, an interactive theorem prover [4]. In doing so we addressed the challenge of formalizing the copy operation on heaps and establishing termination (even in the presence of cycles in the object graph). We mechanize the proof that there are no stuck configurations, and furthermore prove that the relation is computable, yielding a verified interpreter for TX10 and Resilient TX10.

Related work. Our work is related to three broad streams of work. The first is formalization of X10 and Java with RMI. The first formalization of X10 was in [21]. This paper adapts the framework of Middleweight Java [5] to represent a configuration as a collection of stacks and heaps. This choice led to a rather complex formalization. [17] presents an operational semantics for the X10 finish/async fragment, but again with a complex representation of control. We build on the work of [24] which for the first time represents the control state as a statement, and presents a very simple definition of the Happens Before relation. We extend that work to handle exceptions (necessary for the formalization of resilience), and place-shifting at, and formally treat resilience. [1] presents a semantics for Java with remote method invocation; hence they also deal with multiple places and communication across places. In particular they formalize a relational definition of copying an object graph, although they do not formalize or mechanize an implementation of this specification. Their formalization does not deal with place failure, since Java RMI does not deal with it.

The second stream is the work on formalization of the semantics of concurrent imperative languages [7,6,8]. Our work can be seen as adding block-structured concurrency constructs (finish, async), exceptions, and, of course, dealing with multiple places, and place failure.

The third stream is the work on distributed process algebras that deal with failure [14,16,15,3,19]. [3] introduces an extension of the π-calculus with located actions, in the context of a higher-order, distributed programming language, Facile. [14] introduces locations in the distributed join calculus, mobility and the possibility of location failure, similar to our place failure. The failure of a location can be detected, allowing failure recovery. In the context of Dπ [16], an extension of the π-calculus with multiple places and mobility, [15] gives a treatment of node- and link-failure. In relationship with all these works, this work differs in dealing with resilience in the context of distributed state, global references, mobile tasks with distributed termination detection (finish), and exceptions, and formalizing the HBI principle. Our work is motivated by formalizing a real resilient programming language, rather than working with abstract calculi.

Summary of Contributions. The contributions of this paper are:

- We present a formal operational semantics for TX10, a significant fragment of X10, including multiple places, mutable heap, `try`/`catch` statements, `throws`, `async`, `finish` and `at` statements. The semantics is defined in terms of a labeled transition relation over configurations in which the control state is represented merely as a statement, and the data state as a mapping from places to heaps.
- We present a set of equational laws for operational congruence.
- We extend the formal operational semantics to Resilient TX10, showing that it enjoys Happens Before Invariance and Exception Masking Principles.
- We present equational laws for Resilient X10.
- We mechanize proofs of various propositions in Coq. More precisely, all the the proofs in the paper have been mechanized but for Theorem 4.8, Theorem 4.10, Theorem 3.3 and the equational laws, which have been proved manually. In particular, the mechanization of the proof that no configurations are stuck yields a verified executable version of the semantics.

Rest of this paper. Section 2 introduces TX10, informally describing the basic constructs and a small-step operational semantics of TX10. Section 3 presents laws for equality for a semantics built on congruence over bisimulation. The second half of the paper presents a semantic treatment of resilience. Section 4 discusses the design of Resilient TX10. formalizes this semantics using the idea of rewriting the control state to represent place failure. Finally, presents equational laws for congruence, and Section 5 concludes.

2   TX10

We describe in this section the syntax and the semantics of TX10, the formal subset of the X10 language [20] we consider in this work. We have also encoded a mechanized version in Coq, which will be discussed in Section 2.2.

The syntax of TX10 is defined in Table 1. We assume an infinite set of values Val, ranged over by v, w, an infinite set of variables ranged over by x, y, and an infinite set of field names ranged over by f. We also let p, q range over a finite set of integers Pl= $0...(n-1)$, which represent available computation *places*. A source program is defined as a static statement s activated at place 0 under a governing `finish` construct. The syntax then includes dynamic statements and dynamic values that can only appear at runtime. Programs operate over objects, either local or global, that are handled through object identifiers (object ids). We assume an infinite set of object ids, Objld (with a given bijection with the natural numbers, the "enumeration order"); objects are in a one to one correspondence with object ids. Given the distributed nature of the language and

Table 1. Syntax of TX10

(Values) v, w ::=		(Expressions) d, e ::=	
o	*(Runtime only.) Object ids*	v	*Values*
$o\$p$	*(Runtime only.) Global Object ids*	x	*Variable access*
E, BF, BG, DP	*Exceptions*	$e.f$	*Field selection*
		$\{f{:}e, \ldots, f{:}e\}$	*Object construction*
(Programs) pr ::=		$\texttt{globalref}\ e$	*GlobalRef construction*
$\texttt{finish at}\ (0)\ s\ activation$		$\texttt{valof}\ e$	*Global ref deconstruction*

(Statements) s, t ::=	
$\texttt{skip;}$	*Skip – do nothing*
$\texttt{throw}\ v;$	*Throw an exception*
$\texttt{val}\ x = e\ s$	*Let bind e to x in s*
$e.f = e;$	*Assign to field*
$\{s\ t\}$	*Run s then t*
$\texttt{at}(p)(\texttt{val}\ x = e)\ s$	*Run s at p with x bound to e*
$\texttt{async}\ s$	*Spawn s in a different task*
$\texttt{finish}\ s$	*Run s and wait for termination*
$\texttt{try}\ s\ \texttt{catch}\ t$	*Try s, on failure execute t*
z	*Runtime versions*

(Dynamic Stmts) z ::=	
$\overline{\texttt{at}}\ (p)\ s$	*Runtime only*
$\overline{\texttt{async}}\ s$	*Runtime only*
$\texttt{finish}_\mu\ s$	*Run s, recording exceptions in μ*

to model X10's global references, we assume that each object lives in a specific (home) place, and we distinguish between local and global references, denoted by o and $o\$q$. More precisely, we use the following notation:

- $\mathsf{p} : \mathsf{ObjId} \to \mathsf{Pl}$ maps each object id to the place where it lives;
- $\mathsf{ObjId}_q = \{o \in \mathsf{ObjId} \mid \mathsf{p}(o) = q\}$ and $\mathsf{grObjId} = \{o\$p \mid o \in \mathsf{ObjId}_p \land p \in \mathsf{Pl}\}$

Then given $o \in \mathsf{ObjId}_q$, we say that o is a local reference (to a local object) while $o\$q$ is a global reference (to an object located at q).

The expression $\{f_1 : e_1, \ldots, f_n : e_n\}$ (for $n \geq 0$) creates a new local object and returns its fresh id. The object is initialized by setting, in turn, the fields f_i to the value obtained by evaluating e_i. Local objects support field selection: the expression $e.f$ evaluates to the value of the field with name f in the object whose id is obtained by evaluating e. Similarly, the syntax of statements allows field update. X10 relies on a type system to ensure that any selection/update operation occurring at runtime is performed on an object that actually contains the selected/updated field. Since TX10 has no corresponding static semantic rules, we shall specify that $o.f$ throws a *BadFieldSelection* BF exception when the object o does not have field f.

The expression $\texttt{globalref}$ e creates a new global reference for the reference returned by the evaluation of e. Whenever e evaluates to a global reference, the expression $\texttt{valof}$ e returns the local object pointed by e. Errors in dealing with global references are modelled by throwing a *BadGlobalRef* exception BG. (see Section 2.1 for a detailed explanation of the semantics of global references).

TX10 deals with exception handling in a standard way: the statement $\text{throw}\,v$ throws an exception value v that can be caught with a $\text{try}\,s\,\text{catch}\,t$ statement. For simplicity, exception values are constants: besides BF and BG described above, we add E to represent a generic exception. The exception DP stands for *DeadPlaceException*, and will only appear in the semantics of the resilient calculus in Section 4. Variable declaration $\text{val}\,x = e\,s$ declares a new local variable x, binds it to the value of the expression e and continues as s. The value assigned to x cannot be changed during the computation. We shall assume that the only free variable of s is x and that s does not contain a sub-statement that declares the same variable x.This statement is a variant of the variable declaration available in X10. In X10 the scope s is not marked explicitly; rather all statements in the rest of the current block are in scope of the declaration. We have chosen this "let" variant to simplify the formal presentation.

The construct $\text{async}\,s$ spawns an independent lightweight thread, called *activity*, to execute s. The new activity running in parallel is represented by the dynamic statement $\overline{\text{async}}\,s$. The statement $\text{finish}\,s$ executes s and waits for the termination of all the activities (recursively) spawned during this execution. Activities may terminate either normally or abruptly, *i.e.* by throwing an exception. If one or more activities terminated abruptly, $\text{finish}\,s$ will itself throw an exception that encapsulates all exceptions. In TX10, we use the parameter μ in $\text{finish}_\mu\,s$ to record the exception values thrown by activities in s. μ is a possibly empty set of values; we simply write $\text{finish}\,s$ instead of $\text{finish}_\emptyset\,s$.

The sequence statement $\{s\,t\}$ executes t after executing s. Note that if s is an async, its execution will simply spawn an activity $\overline{\text{async}}\,s$, and then activates t. Therefore, $\{\overline{\text{async}}\,s\ t\}$ will actually represent s and t executing in parallel. We say that sequencing in X10 has *shallow* finish *semantics*.

Finally, $\text{at}(p)(\text{val}\,x = e)\,s$ is the place-shifting statement. We assume that the only free variable in s is x. This statement first evaluates e to a value v, then copies the object graph rooted at v to place p to obtain a value v', and finally executes s synchronously at p with x bound to v'. Running s at p synchronously means that in $\{\text{at}(p)(\text{val}\,x = e)\,s\ t\}$, t will be enabled precisely when the at statement has only asynchronous sub-statements left (if any). Thus at also has shallow finish semantics, just like sequential composition. In the cases when the programmer does not need to transmit values from the calling environment to s, the variant $\text{at}\,(p)\,s$ may be used instead. As an example, the program $\text{finish}\,\text{at}(0)\,\{\text{at}(1)\,\text{async}\,s\ \text{at}(2)\,\text{async}\,s\}$ evolves to a state where two copies of s run in parallel at places 1 and 2. The entire program terminates whenever both remote computations end.

Currently, X10 supports a variant of these at constructs. The programmer writes $\text{at}\,(p)\,s$ and the compiler figures out the set of variables used in s and declared outside s. A copy is made of the object reference graph with the values of these variables as roots, and s is executed with these roots bound to this copied graph. Moreover X10, of course, permits mutually recursive procedure (method) definitions. We leave the treatment of recursion as future work.

2.1   Operational Semantics

We build on the semantics for X10 presented in [24]. In this semantics, the data state is maintained in a shared global heap (one heap per place), but the control state is represented in a block structured manner – it is simply a statement.

$$Heap \ h ::= \emptyset \mid h \cdot [o \mapsto r] \qquad Global \ heap \ g ::= \emptyset \mid g \cdot [p \mapsto h]$$

The local heap at a place p is a partial map that associates object ids to objects represented by partial maps r from field names to object ids. The global heap g is a partial map form the set of places Pl to local heaps. Heaps are inductively defined with the operator $\cdot$ used to append a new entry. We let $\emptyset$ denote the unique partial map with empty domain, and for any partial map f by $f[p \to v]$ we mean the map f' that is the same as f except that it takes on the value v at p. Moreover, in the following we write $s[^v/_x]$ for variable substitution.

X10 is designed so that at run-time heaps satisfy the *place-locality invariant* formalized below. Intuitively, the domain of any local heap only contains local object references, moreover any object graph (rooted at a local object) only contains references to either (well defined) local objects or global references.

Let h be a local heap and $o \in dom(h)$ an object identifier. We let $h\downarrow_o$ denote *the object graph rooted at o*, that is the graph with vertexes the values reachable from o via the fields of o or of one or more intermediaries. In other terms, it is the graph where an f-labelled edge (v, f, v') connects the vertices v and v' whenever v is an object with a field f whose value is v'. We also denote by h_o the set of all object values that are reachable from o, that is the set of all vertices in the object graph $h\downarrow_o$.

Definition 2.1 (Place-local heap). *A global heap g is* place-local *whenever for every* $q \in dom(g)$, *and* $h = g(q)$

– $dom(h) \subseteq \mathsf{ObjId}_q$ *and* $\forall o \in dom(h). \ h_o \subseteq (\mathsf{ObjId}_q \cap dom(h)) \cup \mathsf{grObjId}$

The semantics is given in terms of a transition relation between *configurations*, which are either a pair $\langle s, g \rangle$ (representing the statement s to be executed in global heap g) or a singleton g, representing a computation that has terminated in g. Let k range over configurations. The transition relation $k \xrightarrow{\lambda}_p k'$ is defined as a labeled binary relation on configurations, where $\lambda \in \Lambda = \{\epsilon, v\times, v\otimes\}$, and p ranges over the set of places. The transition $k \xrightarrow{\lambda}_p k'$ is to be understood as: the configuration k executing at p can in one step evolve to k', with $\lambda = \epsilon$ indicating a normal transition, and $\lambda = v\otimes$, resp. $v\times$, indicating that an exception has thrown a value v in a synchronous, resp. asynchronous, subcontext. Note that failure is not fatal; a failed transition may be followed by any number of failed or normal transitions. We shall write $\xrightarrow{\epsilon}_p$ as $\longrightarrow_p$, and we let $\xrightarrow{*}$ represent the reflexive, transitive closure of $\xrightarrow{\lambda}_0$.

Definition 2.2 (Semantics). *The operational semantics* $\mathcal{O}[\![s]\!]$ *of a statement s is the relation* $\mathcal{O}[\![s]\!] \stackrel{def}{=} \{(g, g') \mid \langle \mathtt{finish} \ \overline{\mathtt{at}} \ (0) \ s, g \rangle \xrightarrow{*} g'\}$.

Table 2. Synchronous and Asynchronous Statements

$$\vdash \text{isAsync } \overline{\text{async}}\, s \qquad \frac{\vdash \text{isAsync } s}{\vdash \text{isAsync } \overline{\text{at}}\,(p)\, s} \qquad \frac{\vdash \text{isAsync } s \quad \vdash \text{isAsync } t}{\vdash \text{isAsync } \{s\, t\}}$$
$$\vdash \text{isAsync try } s \text{ catch } t$$

$$\vdash \text{isSync } s^* \qquad \qquad \frac{\vdash \text{isSync } s}{\vdash \text{isSync } \{s\, t\}}$$

$$\text{with } s^* \in \left\{ \begin{array}{l} \texttt{skip, val x=e } s,\ e.f = e, \\ \texttt{at}(p)(\texttt{val } x = e)\, s,\ \texttt{async } s, \\ \texttt{finish}_\mu\ s, \texttt{throw}\, v \end{array} \right\} \qquad \begin{array}{l} \vdash \text{isSync } \{t\, s\} \\ \vdash \text{isSync } \overline{\text{at}}\,(p)\, s \\ \vdash \text{isSync try } s \text{ catch } t \end{array}$$

In order to present rules compactly, we use the "matrix" convention exemplified below, where we write the left-most rule to compactly denote the four rules obtained from the right-most rule with $i = 0, 1, j = 0, 1$.

$$\frac{\gamma \xrightarrow{\lambda} \gamma_0 \mid \gamma_1}{\begin{array}{l} cond_0 \ \ \delta^0 \xrightarrow{\lambda_0} \delta_0^0 \mid \delta_1^0 \\ cond_1 \ \ \delta^1 \xrightarrow{\lambda_1} \delta_0^1 \mid \delta_1^1 \end{array}} \qquad\qquad \frac{\gamma \xrightarrow{\lambda} \gamma_i \quad cond_j}{\delta^j \xrightarrow{\lambda_j} \delta_i^j} \quad i = 0, 1\ j = 0, 1$$

We also introduce in Table 2 two auxiliary predicates to distinguish between *asynchronous* and *synchronous* statements. A statement is asynchronous if it is an $\overline{\text{async}}\, s$, or a sequential composition of asynchronous statements (possibly running at other places). The following proposition is easily established by structural induction.

Proposition 2.3. *For any statement s, either $\vdash$ isAsync s xor $\vdash$ isSync s.*

In order to define the transition between configurations, we first define the evaluation relation for expressions by the rules in Table 3. Transitions of the form $\langle e, h \rangle \longrightarrow_p \langle e', h' \rangle$ state that the expression e at place p with local heap h correctly evaluates to e' with heap h'. On the other hand an error in the evaluation of e is modeled by the transition $\langle e, h \rangle \xrightarrow{v\otimes}_p h$. An object creation expression is evaluated from left to right, according to rule (EXP CTX). When all expressions are evaluated, rule (NEW OBJ) states that a new local object id is created and its fields set appropriately. Rule (NEW GLOBAL REF) shows that a new global reference is built from an object id o by means of the expression $\texttt{globalref}\ o$. A global reference $o\$p$ can be dereferenced by means of the $\texttt{valof}$ expression. Notice that rule (VALOF), according to X10's semantics, shows that the actual object can only be accessed from its home place, i.e. $\mathsf{p}(o) = p$. Any attempt to select a non-existing field from an object results in the BF exception by rule (SELECT BAD), while any attempt to access a global object that is not locally defined results in a BG error by rule (VALOF BAD). In X10, the static semantics guarantees that objects and global references are correctly created and that any attempt to select a field is type safe, hence well typed X10 programs do not occur in BF and BG exceptions, however we introduce rules (SELECT BAD), (VALOF BAD) and (BAD FIELD UPDATE) so that the operational semantics of TX10 enjoys the property that there are no stuck states, i.e. Proposition 2.10 in Section 2.3.

Table 3. Expression Evaluation

(NEW OBJ)

$$\dfrac{o \in \mathsf{ObjId}_p \backslash dom(h) \qquad n \geq 0}{\langle \{f_1{:}v_1, ..., f_n{:}v_n\}, h \rangle \longrightarrow_p \langle o, h \cdot [o \mapsto \emptyset[f_1 \mapsto v_1] ... [f_n \mapsto v_n]] \rangle}$$

(SELECT)   (SELECT BAD)

$$\dfrac{h(o)=r[f \mapsto v]}{\langle o.f, h \rangle \longrightarrow_p \langle v, h \rangle} \qquad \dfrac{v{\neq}o \vee (v{=}o \wedge f{\notin}dom(h(o)))}{\langle v.f, h \rangle \overset{\mathsf{BF}\otimes}{\longrightarrow}_p h}$$

(NEW GLOBAL REF)

$$\dfrac{}{\langle \texttt{globalref}\, o, h \rangle \longrightarrow_p \langle o\$p, h \rangle}$$

(VALOF)

$$\dfrac{}{\langle \texttt{valof}\, o\$p, h \rangle \longrightarrow_p \langle o, h \rangle}$$

(BAD GLOBALREF)

$$\dfrac{}{\begin{array}{l} v \neq o\$p \ \langle \texttt{valof}\, v, h \rangle \overset{\mathsf{BG}\otimes}{\longrightarrow}_p h \\ v \neq o \quad \langle \texttt{globalref}\, v, h \rangle \overset{\mathsf{BG}\otimes}{\longrightarrow}_p h \end{array}}$$

(EXP CTX)

$$\dfrac{\langle e, h \rangle \overset{\lambda}{\longrightarrow}_p \langle e', h' \rangle \mid h}{\begin{array}{c} \langle e.f, h \rangle \overset{\lambda}{\longrightarrow}_p \langle e'.f, h' \rangle \mid h \\ \langle \texttt{globalref}\, e, h \rangle \overset{\lambda}{\longrightarrow}_p \langle \texttt{globalref}\, e', h' \rangle \mid h \\ \langle \texttt{valof}\, e, h \rangle \overset{\lambda}{\longrightarrow}_p \langle \texttt{valof}\, e', h' \rangle \mid h \\ \langle \{f_1{:}v_1, ..., f_i{:}v_i, f_{i+1}{:}e, ...\}, h \rangle \overset{\lambda}{\longrightarrow}_p \langle \{f_1{:}v_1, ..., f_i{:}v_i, f_{i+1}{:}e', ...\}, h' \rangle \mid h \end{array}}$$

The following proposition shows that the heap modifications performed by rules (NEW OBJ) and (NEW GLOBAL REF) respect the place-locality invariant.

Proposition 2.4. *Let g be a place-local heap, $p \in dom(g)$ and $h = g(p)$. We say that $\langle e, h \rangle$ is place-local whenever for any local object id o occurring in e it holds $o \in dom(h)$. If $\langle e, h \rangle$ is place-local and $\langle e, h \rangle \longrightarrow_p \langle e', h' \rangle$, then $g \cdot [p \mapsto h']$ is place-local, and $\langle e', h' \rangle$ is place-local.*

Now we turn to the axiomatization of the transition relation between configurations. Table 4 collects a first set of rules dealing with basic statements. These rules use the condition $p \in dom(g)$, which is always true in TX10 since places do not fail. We include this condition to let Table 4 to be reused when we consider place failure in Section 4. Most of these rules are straightforward. Rule (EXCEPTION) shows that throwing an exception is recorded as a synchronous failure. Moreover, rule (BAD FIELD UPDATE) throws a BF exception whenever f is not one of its fields.

The rest of operational rules are collected in Table 5. These rules, besides defining the behavior of the major X10 constructs, also illustrate how the exceptions are propagated through the system and possibly caught. In words, *synchronous failures* arise from synchronous statements, and lead to the failure of any synchronous continuation, while leaving (possibly remote) asynchronous activities that are running in parallel free to correctly terminate (cf. Proposition 2.11). On the other hand, *asynchronous failures*

Table 4. Basic Statements

(SKIP)

$$\frac{p \in dom(g)}{\langle \mathtt{skip}, g \rangle \longrightarrow_p g}$$

(EXCEPTION)

$$\frac{p \in dom(g)}{\langle \mathtt{throw}\, v, g \rangle \xrightarrow{v \otimes}_p g}$$

(FIELD UPDATE)

$$\frac{p \in dom(g) \quad f \in dom(g(p)(o))}{\langle o.f{=}v, g \rangle \longrightarrow_p g[p \to g(p)[o \to g(p)(o)[f{\mapsto}v]]]}$$

(DECLARE VAL)

$$\frac{p \in dom(g) \quad \langle s[^v/_x], g \rangle \xrightarrow{\lambda}_p \langle s', g' \rangle \mid g'}{\langle \mathtt{val}\, x = v\, s, g \rangle \xrightarrow{\lambda}_p \langle s', g' \rangle \mid g'}$$

(BAD FIELD UPDATE)

$$\frac{p{\in}dom(g) \quad (v{\neq}o \lor (v{=}o \land f{\notin}dom(g(p)(o))))}{\langle v.f = v', g \rangle \xrightarrow{\mathit{BF}\otimes}_p g}$$

(CTX)

$$\frac{p \in dom(g) \quad \langle e, g(p) \rangle \xrightarrow{\lambda}_p \langle e', h' \rangle \mid h' \quad g' = g[p \mapsto h']}{}$$

$$\langle \mathtt{val}\, x = e\, s, g \rangle \xrightarrow{\lambda}_p \langle \mathtt{val}\, x = e'\, s,\, g' \rangle \mid g'$$
$$\langle e.f = e_1, g \rangle \xrightarrow{\lambda}_p \langle e'.f = e_1,\, g' \rangle \mid g'$$
$$\langle o.f = e, g \rangle \xrightarrow{\lambda}_p \langle o.f = e',\, g' \rangle \mid g'$$
$$\langle \mathtt{at}(p)(\mathtt{val}\, x = e)\, s, g \rangle \xrightarrow{\lambda}_p \langle \mathtt{at}(p)(\mathtt{val}\, x = e')\, s,\, g' \rangle \mid g'$$

arise when an exception is raised in a parallel thread. In this case the exception is confined within that thread, and it is caught by the closest finish construct that is waiting for the termination of this thread. On termination of all spawned activities, since one (or more) asynchronous exception were caught, the finish constructs re-throws a synchronous failure (cf. Proposition 2.12).

Let us precisely discuss the rules in Table 5. The async construct takes one step to spawn the new activity by means of the rule (SPAWN). Moreover, according to rule (ASYNC), an exception (either synchronous or asynchronous) in the execution of s is *masked* by an asynchronous exception in $\overline{\mathtt{async}}\, s$. We let $\mathsf{MskAs}(\lambda)$ be the label λ where we highlight the fact that an exception masking has occurred. The finish s statement waits for the termination of any (possibly remote) asynchronous (and synchronous as well) activities spawned by s. Any exception thrown during the evaluation of s is absorbed and recorded into the state of the governing finish. Indeed, consider rule (FINISH) where we let be $\mu \cup \lambda{=}\mu$ if $\lambda{=}\epsilon$ and $\mu \cup \lambda{=}\{v\} \cup \mu$ if $\lambda{=}v\times$ or $\lambda{=}v\otimes$. Then this rule shows that the consequence has a correct transition $\longrightarrow_p$ even when $\lambda \neq \epsilon$: i.e., the exception in s has been absorbed and recorded into the state of finish. Moreover, the rule (END OF FINISH) shows that finish terminates with a generic synchronous exception whenever at least one of the activities its governs threw an exception (in X10 it throws a MutipleExceptions containing the list of exceptions collected by finish).Two rules describe the semantics of sequential composition. When executing $\{s\, t\}$, rule (SEQ) shows that the continuation t is activated whenever s terminates normally or with an asynchronous exception. On the other hand, when the execution of s throws a synchronous exception (possibly leaving behind residual statements s') the continuation t is discarded. Rule (PAR) captures the essence of asynchronous execution allowing reductions to occur in parallel components.

Table 5. Statements Semantics

(ASYNC)

(SPAWN)

$$\langle s,g\rangle \xrightarrow{\lambda}_p \langle s',g'\rangle \mid g'$$

$$\frac{}{\langle \texttt{async}\,s,g\rangle \longrightarrow_p \langle \overline{\texttt{async}}\,s,g\rangle} \qquad \frac{\lambda=\epsilon \qquad \langle \overline{\texttt{async}}\,s,g\rangle \longrightarrow_p \langle \overline{\texttt{async}}\,s',g'\rangle \mid g'}{\lambda=v\times,v\otimes \quad \langle \overline{\texttt{async}}\,s,g\rangle \xrightarrow{\mathsf{MskAs}(v\times)}_p \langle \overline{\texttt{async}}\,s',g'\rangle \mid g'}$$

(FINISH)

(END OF FINISH)

$$\frac{\langle s,g\rangle \xrightarrow{\lambda}_p \langle s',g'\rangle}{\langle \texttt{finish}_\mu\,s,g\rangle \longrightarrow_p \langle \texttt{finish}_{\mu\cup\lambda}\,s',g'\rangle}$$

$$\frac{\langle s,g\rangle \xrightarrow{\lambda}_p g' \qquad \lambda'=\begin{cases}\epsilon & \text{if } \lambda\cup\mu=\emptyset \\ \mathsf{MskAs}(E\otimes) & \text{if } \lambda\cup\mu\neq\emptyset\end{cases}}{\langle \texttt{finish}_\mu\,s,g\rangle \xrightarrow{\lambda'}_p g'}$$

(SEQ)

(PAR)

$$\frac{\langle s,g\rangle \xrightarrow{\lambda}_p \langle s',g'\rangle \mid g'}{\begin{array}{l}\lambda=\epsilon,v\times \;\; (\{s\,t\},g\rangle \xrightarrow{\lambda}_p \langle\{s'\,t\},g'\rangle \mid \langle t,g'\rangle \\ \lambda=v\otimes \;\;\; \langle\{s\,t\},g\rangle \xrightarrow{\lambda}_p \langle s',g'\rangle \mid g'\end{array}}$$

$$\frac{\vdash \texttt{isAsync}\,t \quad \langle s,g\rangle \xrightarrow{\lambda}_p \langle s',g'\rangle \mid g'}{\langle\{t\,s\},g\rangle \xrightarrow{\lambda}_p \langle\{t\,s'\},g'\rangle \mid \langle t,g'\rangle}$$

(PLACE SHIFT)

(AT)

$$\frac{(v',g')=\mathsf{copy}(v,q,g)}{\langle \texttt{at}(q)(\texttt{val}\,x{=}v)\,s,g\rangle \longrightarrow_p \langle \overline{\texttt{at}}\,(q)\,\{s[^{v'}/_x]\,\texttt{skip}\},g'\rangle}$$

$$\frac{\langle s,g\rangle \xrightarrow{\lambda}_q \langle s',g'\rangle \mid g'}{\langle \overline{\texttt{at}}\,(q)\,s,g\rangle \xrightarrow{\lambda}_p \langle \overline{\texttt{at}}\,(q)\,s',g'\rangle \mid g'}$$

(TRY)

$$\frac{\langle s,g\rangle \xrightarrow{\lambda}_p \langle s',g'\rangle \mid g'}{\begin{array}{l}\lambda=\epsilon,v\times \;\; \langle \texttt{try}\,s\,\texttt{catch}\,t,g\rangle \xrightarrow{\lambda}_p \langle \texttt{try}\,s'\,\texttt{catch}\,t,g'\rangle \mid g' \\ \lambda=v\otimes \;\;\; \langle \texttt{try}\,s\,\texttt{catch}\,t,g\rangle \longrightarrow_p \langle\{s'\,t\},g'\rangle \mid \langle t,g'\rangle\end{array}}$$

The rule (PLACE SHIFT) activates a remote computation; it uses a *copy* operation on object graphs, $\mathsf{copy}(o,q,g)$, that creates at place q a copy of the object graph rooted at o, respecting global references. In X10 place shift is implemented by recursively serializing the object reference graph G rooted at o into a byte array. In this process, when it is encountered a global object reference $o\$p$, the fields of this object are not followed; instead the unique identifier $o\$p$ is serialized. The byte array is then transported to q, and de-serialized at q to create a copy G' of G with root object a fresh identifier $o' \in \mathsf{ObjId}_q$. All the objects in G' are new. G' is isomorphic to G and has the additional property that if z is a global ref that is reachable from o then it is also reachable (through the same path) from o'.

Definition 2.5 (The copy operation). *Let g be a global heap, q a place with $h = g(q)$. Let be $o \in \mathsf{ObjId}$ such that $\mathsf{p}(o) \in dom(g)$, then $\mathsf{copy}(o,q,g)$ stands for the (unique) tuple $\langle o', g[q \to h']\rangle$ satisfying the following properties, where $N = dom(h')\backslash dom(h)$.*

- *N is the next $|N|$ elements of ObjId_q.*
- *$o' \in N$*

- *There is an isomorphism ι between the object graph $g(\mathsf{p}(o))\!\downarrow_o$ rooted at o and the object graph $h'\!\downarrow_{o'}$ rooted at o'. Further, $\iota(v) = v$ for $v \in \mathsf{grObjId}$*
- $h'_{o'} \subseteq N \cup \mathsf{grObjId}$.
- $h' = h \cdot [o' \mapsto r]$ *where r is the root object of the graph $h'\!\downarrow_{o'}$*

We extend this definition to arbitrary values, that is $\mathsf{copy}(v, q, g)$ is defined to be v unless v is an object id, in which case it is defined as above.

Proposition 2.6. *Let g be a place-local heap. Let $p, q \in dom(g)$ be two (not necessarily distinct) places, and let $o \in \mathsf{ObjId}_p$. Let $\mathsf{copy}(o, q, g) = \langle o', g' \rangle$. Then g' is place-local.*

Place-shift takes a step to activate. Moreover, in the conclusion of the rule (PLACE SHIFT) the target statement contains a final skip in order to model the fact that the remote control has to come back at the local place after executing the remote code $s[^{v'}/_{x'}]$. As an example, consider $\{\overline{\mathtt{at}}\,(p)\,\{\overline{\mathtt{async}}\,s\ \mathtt{skip}\}\ \ t\}$ and $\{\overline{\mathtt{at}}\,(p)\,\{\overline{\mathtt{async}}\,s\}\ \ t\}$. The local code t is already active only in the second statement while in the first one it is waiting for the termination of the synchronous remote statement. Accordingly, the second program models the situation where the control has come back locally after installing the remote asynchronous computation. Modeling this additional step is actually relevant just in the resilient calculus, where we need to model the case where the remote place precisely fails after executing s but before the control has come back. Indeed, consider $\{\overline{\mathtt{at}}\,(p)\,\{\overline{\mathtt{async}}\,s\ \mathtt{skip}\}\ \ t\}$ and $\{\overline{\mathtt{at}}\,(p)\,\{\overline{\mathtt{async}}\,s\}\ \ t\}$. The local code t is already active only in the second statement while in the first one it is waiting for the termination of the synchronous remote statement. Accordingly, the second statement models the situation where the control has come back locally after installing the remote asynchronous computation.

As for error propagation, by rule (AT) we have that any exception, either synchronous or asynchronous, that occurred remotely at place p is homomorphically reported locally at place r. As an example, consider $\overline{\mathtt{at}}\,(r)\,\{\overline{\mathtt{at}}\,(p)\,\mathtt{throw}\,\mathtt{E}\ \ t\}$, then the exception at p terminates the remote computation and is reported at r as a synchronous error so that to also discard the local continuation t, whose execution depends on the completion of the remote code. In order to recover from remote exceptions, we can use the try-catch mechanism and write $\overline{\mathtt{at}}\,(r)\,\{\mathtt{try}\,(\overline{\mathtt{at}}\,(p)\,\mathtt{throw}\,\mathtt{E})\,\mathtt{catch}\,t'\ \ t\}$ so that the synchronous exception is caught at r according to the rule (TRY). More precisely, the $\mathtt{try}\,s\,\mathtt{catch}\,t$ statement immediately activates s. Moreover, the rule (TRY) shows that asynchronous exceptions are passed through, since they are only caught by finish. On the other hand, synchronous exceptions are absorbed into a correct transition and the catch-clause is activated, together with the (asynchronous) statements s' left behind by the failed s.

Example 2.7. Consider the two programs $s_1 = \overline{\mathtt{at}}\,(p)\,\mathtt{finish}\,\overline{\mathtt{at}}\,(q)\,\overline{\mathtt{async}}\,s$ and $s_2 = \mathtt{finish}\,\overline{\mathtt{at}}\,(p)\,\{\overline{\mathtt{at}}\,(q)\,\overline{\mathtt{async}}\,s\}$. In both programs the termination of s is detected by the finish construct, that is, at place p in s_1 and at place 0 in s_2. Moreover, if the execution of s at q throws an exception, we have that the asynchronous exception is also caught by the finish construct, that is it is caught at place p for s_1 and at place 0 for s_2. Such a difference is not observable in TX10, indeed we will provide in Section 3 an equational law (cf. law (24)) showing that s_1 and s_2 are observationally equivalent. On the other hand, we will see that in Resilient TX10 the two statements behave differently when places p and q are subject to failure. As a further example consider the programs $s_1' = \{s_1 \, s'\}$ and $s_2' = \texttt{finish} \, \{\overline{\texttt{at}} \, (p) \, \{\overline{\texttt{at}} \, (q) \, \overline{\texttt{async}} \, s\} \, s'\}$. In s_1' we have that s' is executed at place 0 after the termination of s, while in s_2' we have that s' is executed at place 0 in parallel with s running at q. Moreover, let s throw an exception, then in s_1' we have that the $\texttt{finish}$ at p re-throws a (masked) synchronous exception that discards the continuation s', while in s_2' we have that s' correctly terminates since the asynchronous exception is captured by the outer $\texttt{finish}$.

2.2   Mechanization in Coq

We have encoded the syntax and semantics of TX10 in Coq, an interactive theorem prover. Encoding the syntax and semantics are mostly straightforward, and closely follows the paper presentation. However, the mechanized formalism has a richer notion of exception propagation, which was omitted from the paper for compactness. Labels can carry a list of exceptions, allowing multiple exceptions to be propagated by $\texttt{finish}$ (instead of using a single generic exception). Additionally, labels / exceptions can be any value type. This complicates the rules, since the (AT) rule needs to copy any values stored in the labels from the target heap to the caller's heap. This is done by the actual X10 language, and correctly modeled by our mechanized semantics.

The most challenging part of encoding the semantics is encoding the copy operation given in Definition 2.5, which copies an object graph from one heap to another.

Mechanizing the Copy Operation.   Definition 2.5 provides a declarative specification of the copy operation, asserting the existence of a satisfying function. The mechanization explicitly constructs this function. In particular, it provides a pure (provably terminating and side-effect free) function with the given specification.

We first encode definitions of (local) reachability and graph isomorphism, proving key theorems relating them. We also define what it means for a value to be *well-formed* in a given heap: all objects (locally) reachable from that value must be in the heap. In other words, the object graph rooted at the value may not contain dangling pointers.

The tricky part of implementing this algorithm in Coq is proving termination. This is not obvious, since there can be cycles in the object graph that we are copying. To prevent looping on such cycles, the implementation carefully maintains and uses the set of existing mappings from the source to the destination heap. To prove termination for a non-structurally recursive function, we define a well-founded measure that provably decreases on every recursive call. We omit details for lack of space.

As well as proving that the implementation is total, we also prove that it has the required specification. Moreover, if copy fails, there must exist some object id reachable from the root that is not contained in the heap. This last part of the specification in turn enables us to prove that copy will always succeed if the initial value is well formed.

2.3   Properties of the Transition Relation

TX10 satisfies a number of useful properties, given below. We have mechanized all these proofs in Coq, using our encoding of TX10. This provides a high level of assurance in these proofs, and fills in the details of the various well-formedness conditions, such as place-locality, needed to ensure that the properties hold.

Definition 2.8 (Place-local Configuration). *Given a place-local heap g, we say that a configuration $\langle s, g \rangle$ is place-local if*

- *for any local object id o occurring in s under $\mathtt{at}(p)$ or $\overline{\mathtt{at}}\,(p)$, we have that $o \in dom(g(p))$ (hence $o \in \mathsf{Objld}_p$ by place-locality of g), and*
- *for any global reference $o\$q$ occurring in s, we have that $o \in dom(g(q))$.*

Proposition 2.9 (Place-locality). *If $\langle s, g \rangle$ is a place-local configuration and $\langle s, g \rangle \xrightarrow{\lambda}_p \langle s', g' \rangle \mid g'$, then $\langle s', g' \rangle$ is a place-local configuration, resp. g' is a place-local heap.*

Proposition 2.10 (Absence of stuck states). *If a configuration k is terminal then k is of the form g.*

The mechanized proof of Proposition 2.10 additionally proves that the evaluation relation is computable: if the configuration is not terminal, we can always compute a next step. This is of course not the only step, since the relation is non-deterministic. Similarly, we prove that the transitive closure of the evaluation relation does not get stuck and is computable. This proof can be "run", yielding a simple interpreter for TX10.

The following propositions deal with error propagation. Proposition 2.11 shows that *synchronous failures* arise from synchronous statements; they entail the discard of any synchronous continuation, while leaving (possibly remote) asynchronous activities running in parallel free to correctly terminate. On the other hand, Proposition 2.12 shows that *asynchronous failures* are caught by the closest $\mathtt{finish}$ construct that is waiting for the termination of the thread where the failure arose. We rely on the following definition of *Evaluation Contexts*, that is contexts under which a reduction step is possible:

$$E ::= [\,] \mid \{E\ t\} \mid \{t\ E\}\ \text{with}\ \vdash \mathsf{isAsync}\ t \mid \overline{\mathtt{at}}\,(p)\ E$$
$$\mid\ \overline{\mathtt{async}}\ E \mid \mathtt{finish}_\mu\ E \mid \mathtt{try}\ E\ \mathtt{catch}\ t$$

Proposition 2.11 (Synchronous Failures). *If $\langle s, g \rangle \xrightarrow{v\otimes}_p k$ then $\vdash \mathsf{isSync}\ s$. Moreover, if $k \equiv \langle s', g' \rangle$, then $\vdash \mathsf{isAsync}\ s'$.*

Proposition 2.12 (Asynchronous Failures)

- *If $\langle s, g \rangle \xrightarrow{v\times}_p k$ then there exists an evaluation context $E[\,]$ such that $s = E[s_1]$ with $\langle s_1, g \rangle \xrightarrow{v\times}_p k'$ and $\vdash \mathsf{isAsync}\ s_1$.*
- *If $\langle \mathtt{finish}_\mu\ s, g \rangle \xrightarrow{\lambda_1}_p \ldots \xrightarrow{\lambda_n}_p g$ because of $\langle s, g \rangle \xrightarrow{\lambda'_1}_p \ldots \xrightarrow{\lambda'_n}_p g$, then*
  1. *$\lambda_i = \epsilon$ for $i = 1, \ldots, n-1$, and*
  2. *either $\lambda_n = \mathsf{E}\otimes$ or $\lambda_n = \epsilon$ and $\forall j = 1, \ldots, n\ \lambda'_j = \epsilon$.*

The proofs of the propositions above easily follow by induction on the derivation of $\langle s, g \rangle \xrightarrow{v\otimes}_p k$, resp. $\langle s, g \rangle \xrightarrow{v\times}_p k$, and an inspection of the rules for finish.

Proposition 2.13. *Let be* $\langle s, g \rangle \xrightarrow{\lambda}_p \langle s', g' \rangle$, *then if* $\vdash$ isAsync s *then* $\vdash$ isAsync s', *or equivalently, if* $\vdash$ isSync s' *then* $\vdash$ isSync s.

3   Equivalence and Equational Laws

In this section we define a notion of equivalence for TX10 programs along the lines of [21]. We consider weak bisimulation defined on both normal transitions and transitions that throw an exception. Moreover, the bisimulation encodes the observation power of the concurrent context in two ways: (i) it preserves the isSync/isAsync predicate and (ii) takes into account concurrent modification of shared memory. As a result, the equivalence turns out to be a congruence (cf. Theorem 3.3).

We use a notion of *environment move* to model the update of a shared heap by a concurrent activity. The store can be updated by updating a field of an existing object, by creating a new (local) object, or by means of a serialization triggered by a place shift.

Definition 3.1 (Environment move). *An environment move Φ is a map on global heaps satisfying:*

1. *if g is place-local, then $\Phi(g)$ is place-local,*
2. $dom(\Phi(g)) = dom(g)$, *and* $\forall p \in dom(g)\ dom(g(p)) \subseteq dom(\Phi(g)(p))$.

Let $(\longrightarrow_p)^*$ denote the reflexive and transitive closure of $\xrightarrow{\epsilon}_p$, that is any number (possibly zero) of ϵ-steps. Then we let $\Longrightarrow_p$ stand for $(\longrightarrow_p)^* \xrightarrow{\lambda}_p (\longrightarrow_p)^*$ when $\lambda \neq \epsilon$, and $(\longrightarrow_p)^*$ if $\lambda = \epsilon$.

Definition 3.2 (Weak Bisimulation). *A binary relation $\mathcal{R}$ on closed configurations is a* weak bisimulation *if whenever*

1. *$g\ \mathcal{R}\ k$ then $k = g$,*
2. *$\langle s, g \rangle\ \mathcal{R}\ k$ then $k = \langle t, g \rangle$ for some t, and*
   - $\vdash$ isSync s *if and only if* $\vdash$ isSync t *and*
   - *for every environment move Φ, and for every place p it is the case that*
     (a) *if $\langle s, \Phi(g) \rangle \xrightarrow{\lambda}_p \langle s', g' \rangle$ then for some t', $\langle t, \Phi(g) \rangle \Longrightarrow_p \langle t', g' \rangle$ and $\langle s', g' \rangle\ \mathcal{R}\ \langle t', g' \rangle$, and vice versa.*
     (b) *if $\langle s, \Phi(g) \rangle \xrightarrow{\lambda}_p g'$ then $\langle t, \Phi(g) \rangle \Longrightarrow_p g'$ and vice versa.*

Two configurations are weak bisimilar, written $\langle s, g \rangle \equiv \langle t, g' \rangle$, whenever there exists a weak bisimulation relating them. The weak bisimilarity is the largest weak bisimulation between configurations.

Theorem 3.3. *Weak bisimilarity is a congruence.*

The theorem comes by a standard argument showing that the smallest congruence containing weak bisimilarity is a weak bisimulation. We illustrate the equivalence by means of a number of equational laws dealing with the main constructs of TX10. To ease the notation we write laws between statements rather than configurations. We start with laws for sequencing and asynchronus actvities:

$$\vdash \text{isSync } s \qquad \{\text{skip}; s\} \equiv s \qquad \{s \text{ skip};\} \equiv s \tag{1}$$

$$\{\text{throw } v \ s\} \equiv \text{throw } v \tag{2}$$

$$\{\{s\,t\}\,u\} \equiv \{s\,\{t\,u\}\} \tag{3}$$

$$\vdash \text{isAsync } s, \vdash \text{isAsync } t \qquad \{s\,t\} \equiv \{t\,s\} \tag{4}$$

$$\text{async async } s \equiv \text{async } s \tag{5}$$

$$\overline{\text{async}} \text{ skip} \not\equiv \text{skip} \qquad \overline{\text{async}} \text{ throw } v \not\equiv \text{throw } v \tag{6}$$

$$\{\overline{\text{async}} \text{ throw } v \ \overline{\text{async}} \text{ throw } v\} \not\equiv \overline{\text{async}} \text{ throw } v \tag{7}$$

Observe that (1) only hold for synchronous statements since both $\{\text{skip } s\}$ and $\{s \text{ skip}\}$ are synchronous statements irrespective of s, hence the equivalence only holds when also the r.h.s. is synchronous. Laws (6) do not hold since only the l.h.s. are asynchronous. Law (7) does not hold since weak bisimilarity counts the number of (asynchronous) exceptions, and the l.h.s. throws two asynchronous $\text{E}\times$ while the r.h.s. just one. Notice that by law (2) we have instead $\{\text{throw } v \text{ throw } v\} \equiv \text{throw } v$, which is correct because the l.h.s. throws a single $\text{E}\otimes$ since synchronous errors discard the continuation. The following set of laws deals with the try/catch construct:

$$\text{try skip catch } t \equiv \text{skip} \tag{8}$$

$$\vdash \text{isSync } s \qquad \text{try throw } v \text{ catch } s \equiv s \tag{9}$$

$$\text{try } s \text{ catch throw } v \equiv s \tag{10}$$

$$\vdash \text{isAsync } s \qquad \text{try } s \text{ catch } u \equiv s \tag{11}$$

$$\vdash \text{isAsync } s \qquad \text{try } \{s\,t\} \text{ catch } u \equiv \{\text{try } s \text{ catch } u \text{ try } t \text{ catch } u\} \tag{12}$$

$$\text{try } (\text{try } s \text{ catch } t) \text{ catch } u \equiv \text{try } s \text{ catch } (\text{try } t \text{ catch } u) \tag{13}$$

Notice that law (12) does not hold if s is a synchronous statement. Indeed, a synchronous error in s implies that in the l.h.s. the continuation t is discarded, while the execution of the r.h.s. might activate two copies of u when both s and t fail in sequence.

$$\mathtt{at}\,(p)\,\mathtt{skip} \equiv \mathtt{skip} \tag{14}$$

$$\mathtt{at}\,(p)\,\mathtt{throw}\,v \equiv \mathtt{throw}\,v \tag{15}$$

$$\mathtt{at}\,(p)\,\{s\,t\} \equiv \{\mathtt{at}\,(p)\,s\ \mathtt{at}\,(p)\,t\} \tag{16}$$

$$\mathtt{at}\,(p)\,\mathtt{at}\,(q)\,s \equiv \mathtt{at}\,(q)\,s \tag{17}$$

$$\mathtt{async}\,\mathtt{at}\,(p)\,s \equiv \mathtt{at}\,(p)\,\mathtt{async}\,s \tag{18}$$

$$\mathtt{at}\,(p)\,(\mathtt{try}\,s\,\mathtt{catch}\,t) \equiv \mathtt{try}\,(\mathtt{at}\,(p)\,s)\,\mathtt{catch}\,(\mathtt{at}\,(p)\,t) \tag{19}$$

All the laws above for place shift also hold for the dynamic version of $\mathtt{at}$. Finally, the following set of laws deal with the finish construct:

$$\mathtt{finish}\,\mathtt{skip} \equiv \mathtt{skip} \tag{20}$$

$$\mathtt{finish}\,\{s\,t\} \equiv \mathtt{finish}\,s\ \mathtt{finish}\,t \tag{21}$$

$$\mathtt{finish}\,\mathtt{async}\,s \equiv \mathtt{finish}\,s \tag{22}$$

$$\mathtt{finish}\,\{s\,\mathtt{async}\,t\} \equiv \mathtt{finish}\,\{s\,t\} \tag{23}$$

$$\mathtt{finish}\,\mathtt{at}\,(p)\,s \equiv \mathtt{at}\,(p)\,\mathtt{finish}\,s \tag{24}$$

$$\mathtt{finish}\,\mathtt{finish}\,s \equiv \mathtt{finish}\,s \tag{25}$$

Notice that law (23) comes form (21) and (22). We conclude with a set of inequalities, where we write $\vdash \mathsf{noAsync}\,s$ if s has no sub-term of the form $\mathtt{async}\,s'$ for some s', i.e., if s cannot evolve to an asynchronous statement.

$$\mathtt{finish}\,\mathtt{throw}\,v \not\equiv \mathtt{throw}\,v \tag{26}$$

$$\mathtt{finish}\,\{s\,\mathtt{throw}\,v\} \not\equiv \{\mathtt{finish}\,s\,\mathtt{throw}\,v\} \tag{27}$$

$$(\vdash \mathsf{noAsync}\,s)\,\mathtt{finish}\,s \not\equiv s \tag{28}$$

$$(\vdash \mathsf{noAsync}\,s)\,\mathtt{finish}\,\mathtt{try}\,s\,\mathtt{catch}\,t \not\equiv \mathtt{try}\,s\,\mathtt{catch}\,\mathtt{finish}\,t \tag{29}$$

All these laws do not hold because of the exception masking mechanism performed by the finish construct. For instance, in law (26) the exception $v\otimes$ thrown by $\mathtt{throw}\,v$ is masked in the l.h.s. by $\mathsf{E}\otimes$ by the finish construct.

4 Resilient TX10

The resilient calculus has the same syntax of TX10. We now assume that any place $p \in \mathsf{Pl}\backslash\{0\}$ can fail at any moment during the program computation. Place 0 has a special role: programs start at place zero, then this place is used to communicate the result to the user, so we assume it can never fail (if it does fail, the whole execution is torn down). In order to define the semantics, we now let global heaps g to be partial (rather than total) maps from places to local heaps. Intuitively, $dom(g)$ is the set of

Table 6. Resilient Semantics I

(PLACE FAILURE)

$$\frac{p \in dom(g)}{\langle s, g \rangle \longrightarrow_p \langle s, g \setminus \{(p, g(p))\}\rangle}$$

(SPAWN)

$$\frac{}{p \in dom(g) \; \langle \texttt{async } s, g \rangle \longrightarrow_p \langle \overline{\texttt{async }} s, g \rangle}$$
$$p \notin dom(g) \; \langle \texttt{async } s, g \rangle \xrightarrow{\mathsf{DP} \otimes}_p g$$

(LOCAL FAILURE)

$$\frac{p \notin dom(g)}{\begin{array}{l} \langle \texttt{skip}, g \rangle \xrightarrow{\mathsf{DP} \otimes}_p g \\ \langle \texttt{throw } v, g \rangle \xrightarrow{\mathsf{DP} \otimes}_p g \\ \langle \texttt{val } x = e \; s, g \rangle \xrightarrow{\mathsf{DP} \otimes}_p g \\ \langle e_1.f = e_2, g \rangle \xrightarrow{\mathsf{DP} \otimes}_p g \end{array}}$$

(ASYNC)

$$\frac{\langle s, g \rangle \xrightarrow{\lambda}_p \langle s', g' \rangle \mid g'}{\begin{array}{ll} \lambda = \epsilon & \langle \overline{\texttt{async }} s, g \rangle \longrightarrow_p \langle \overline{\texttt{async }} s', g' \rangle \mid g' \\ \lambda = v \times, v \otimes & \langle \overline{\texttt{async }} s, g \rangle \xrightarrow{\mathsf{MskAs}(v \times)}_p \langle \overline{\texttt{async }} s', g' \rangle \mid g' \end{array}}$$

(FINISH)

$$\frac{\langle s, g \rangle \xrightarrow{\lambda}_p \langle s', g' \rangle}{\langle \texttt{finish}_\mu \, s, g \rangle \longrightarrow_p \langle \texttt{finish}_{\mu \cup \lambda} \, s', g' \rangle}$$

(END OF FINISH)

$$\frac{\langle s, g \rangle \xrightarrow{\lambda}_p g' \quad \lambda' = \begin{cases} \epsilon & \text{if } \lambda \cup \mu = \emptyset \\ \mathsf{E} \otimes & \text{if } \lambda \cup \mu \neq \emptyset, p \in dom(g) \\ \mathsf{DP} \otimes & \text{if } \lambda \cup \mu \neq \emptyset, p \notin dom(g) \end{cases}}{\langle \texttt{finish}_\mu \, s, g \rangle \xrightarrow{\mathsf{MskAs}(\lambda')}_p g'}$$

non-failed places. The semantics of Resilient TX10 is given by the rules in Table 3 and Table 4 from Section 2 plus the rules in Tables 6, 7 and 8 given in this section. More precisely, the resilient calculus inherits from TX10 the rules for expression evaluation (i.e., Table 3) and those in Table 4 which correspond to basic statement executed at non-failed place p, i.e. $p \in dom(g)$. The rules for TX10's main constructs, i.e. those in Table 5, hold also in the resilient calculus when $p \in dom(g)$, but they must be integrated with additional rules dealing with the case where the local place p has failed. Therefore, in order to improve the presentation, rather than inheriting Table 5, we collect here all the operational rules for the main constructs, compacting them in Tables 6, 7 and 8.

The place failure may occur at anytime, and it is modelled by the rule (PLACE FAILURE), which removes the failed place from the global heap. The semantics of TX10 is then extended according to the behaviour of Resilient X10 ([11]), that is so to ensure that after the failure of a place p:

1. any attempt to execute a statement at p results in a DP exception (Theorem 4.8);
2. place shifts cannot be initiated form p nor launched to the failed p (rule (PLACE SHIFT));
3. any remote code that has been launched from p before its failure is not affected and it is free to correctly terminate its remote computation. If a synchronous exception escapes from this remote code and flows back to the failed place, then this exception is masked by a DP (Proposition 4.7) which is thrown back to a parent finish construct waiting at a non-failed place.

More precisely, we will show that the operational semantics of Resilient TX10 enforces the following three design principles:

Table 7. Resilient Semantics II

(SEQ)

$$\frac{\langle s,g\rangle \xrightarrow{\lambda}_p \langle s',g'\rangle}{\begin{array}{l} \lambda = \epsilon, v\times \ \langle \{s\,t\},g\rangle \xrightarrow{\lambda}_p \langle \{s'\,t\},g'\rangle \\ \lambda = v\otimes \quad \langle \{s\,t\},g\rangle \xrightarrow{\lambda}_p \langle s',g'\rangle \end{array}}$$

(PAR)

$$\frac{\vdash \mathsf{isAsync}\ t \quad \langle s,g\rangle \xrightarrow{\lambda}_p \langle s',g'\rangle \mid g'}{\langle \{t\,s\},g\rangle \xrightarrow{\lambda}_p \langle \{t\,s'\},g'\rangle \mid \langle t,g'\rangle}$$

(SEQ TERM)

$$\frac{p \in dom(g) \quad \langle s,g\rangle \xrightarrow{\lambda}_p g'}{\begin{array}{l} \lambda = \epsilon, v\times \ \langle \{s\,t\},g\rangle \xrightarrow{\lambda}_p \langle t,g'\rangle \\ \lambda = v\otimes \quad \langle \{s\,t\},g\rangle \xrightarrow{\lambda}_p g' \end{array}}$$

(SEQ FAILED TERM)

$$\frac{p \notin dom(g) \quad \langle s,g\rangle \xrightarrow{\lambda}_p g'}{\begin{array}{l} \vdash \mathsf{isSync}\ s \ \ \langle \{s\,t\},g\rangle \xrightarrow{\mathsf{DP}\otimes}_p g' \\ \vdash \mathsf{isAsync}\ s \ \langle \{s\,t\},g\rangle \xrightarrow{\mathsf{DP}\times}_p \langle t,g'\rangle \end{array}}$$

1. ***Happens Before Invariance Principle:*** failure of a place q should not alter the happens before relationship between statement instances at places other than q.
2. ***Exception Masking Principle:*** failure of a place q will cause synchronous exceptions thrown by $\overline{\mathtt{at}}\,(q)\ s$ statements to be masked by DP exceptions.
3. ***Failed Place Principle:*** at a failed place, activating any statement or evaluating any expression should result in a DP exception.

We now precisely describe the rules for the main constructs. The rule (LOCAL FAILURE) shows that no expression is evaluated at a failed place; any attempt to execute a basic statement at the failed place results in a synchronous DP exception. Similarly, rule (SPAWN) shows that new activities can only be spawned at non-failed places. On the other hand, rule (ASYNC) is independent form the failure of p, so that any remote computation contained in s proceeds not affected by the local failure. The semantics of $\mathtt{finish}$ is the same as in Section 2, but for the rule (END OF FINISH), which now ensures that when $p \notin dom(g)$ a DP$\otimes$ (rather than E$\otimes$) exception is thrown whenever one of the governing activities (either local or remote) threw an exception.

The rules for sequences are collected in Table 7. Rules (SEQ) and (PAR) are the same as in the basic calculus, allowing remote computation under sequential or parallel composition to evolve irrespective of local place failure. The failure of p plays a role only in rule (SEQ FAILED TERM): in this case the termination of the first component s in the sequence $\{s\,t\}$ always results in a DP exception. Moreover, the continuation t is discarded when s is a synchronous statement. On the other hand, when s is an asynchronous statement, t might be an already active remote statement, hence the rule gives to t the chance to terminate correctly.

Rule (PLACE SHIFT) allows the activation of a place-shift only when both the source and the target of the migration are non-failed places. Rule (AT) behaves like in TX10 except that it masks any remote synchronous exception with a DP exception. As an example consider $\overline{\mathtt{at}}\,(p)\,\{\overline{\mathtt{at}}\,(q)\,s\,\overline{\mathtt{at}}\,(r)\,t\}$; if p fails while s and t are (remotely) executing, it is important not to terminate the program upon completion of just s (or just t). Then with rule (AT) we have that a remote computation silently ends even if the control

Table 8. Resilient Semantics III

(PLACE SHIFT)

$$(v', g') = \text{copy}(v, q, g)$$

$$p, q \in dom(g) \quad \langle \text{at}(q)(\text{val } x = v) \, s, g \rangle \longrightarrow_p \langle \overline{\text{at}}(q) \, \{s[{}^{v'}/_x] \text{ skip}\}, g' \rangle$$

$$q \notin dom(g) \quad \langle \text{at}(q)(\text{val } x = v) \, s, g \rangle \xrightarrow{\text{DP}\otimes}_p g$$

$$p \notin dom(g) \quad \langle \text{at}(q)(\text{val } x = e) \, s, g \rangle \xrightarrow{\text{DP}\otimes}_p g$$

(AT)

$$\dfrac{\langle s, g \rangle \xrightarrow{\lambda}_q \langle s', g' \rangle \mid g' \quad \lambda' = \begin{cases} \text{MskAs}(\text{DP}\otimes) & \text{if } \lambda = v\otimes, p \notin dom(g) \\ \lambda & \text{otherwise} \end{cases}}{\langle \overline{\text{at}}(q) \, s, g \rangle \xrightarrow{\lambda'}_p \langle \overline{\text{at}}(q) \, s', g' \rangle \mid g'}$$

(TRY)

$$\langle s, g \rangle \xrightarrow{\lambda}_p \langle s', g' \rangle \mid g'$$

$$\lambda = \epsilon, v\times \qquad \langle \text{try } s \text{ catch } t, g \rangle \xrightarrow{\lambda}_p \langle \text{try } s' \text{ catch } t, g' \rangle \mid g'$$

$$p \in dom(g), \lambda = v\otimes \quad \langle \text{try } s \text{ catch } t, g \rangle \longrightarrow_p \langle \{s' \, t\}, g' \rangle \mid \langle t, g' \rangle$$

$$p \notin dom(g), \lambda = v\otimes \quad \langle \text{try } s \text{ catch } t, g \rangle \xrightarrow{\lambda}_p \langle s', g' \rangle \mid g'$$

comes back at a failed home. As another example, consider $\overline{\text{at}}(r) \, \{\overline{\text{at}}(p) \text{ skip } t\}$ with $p \notin dom(g)$, then the failure of skip at p must be reported at r as a synchronous error so that the continuation t is discarded.

Example 4.1. Consider the following program, where the code s_q is expected to be executed at q after the termination of any remote activities recursively spawned at p:

$$\overline{\text{at}}(q) \, \{\text{finish } \overline{\text{async}} \, \overline{\text{at}}(p) \, \{\text{finish } s \ s_p\} \ \ s_q\}$$

Let us also assume that s spawns new remote activities running in a third place r. Now, assume that both p and r fail while s is (remotely) executing. We have that s throws an exception that should be detected by the inner finish, however since p is a failed place, termination and error detection in s must be delegated to the outer finish waiting at non failed place q: that is indeed performed by rule (END OF FINISH). Hence we have that the finish at q throws a synchronous error and the continuation s_q is discarded. Notice that enclosing the inner finish within a try-catch construct is only useful when p is a non failed place. Indeed, consider the program

$$\overline{\text{at}}(q) \, \{\text{finish } \overline{\text{async}} \, \overline{\text{at}}(p) \, \{\text{try } (\text{finish } s) \text{ catch } t \ s_p\} \ \ s_q\}$$

then by the rule (TRY) for exception handling we have that when p is a failed place the clause is never executed, hence the two programs above have the same semantics. On the other hand, we can recover from an exception in s by installing a try/catch at the non failed place q: $\overline{\text{at}}(q) \, \{\text{try } (\text{finish } \overline{\text{async}} \, \overline{\text{at}}(p) \, \{\text{finish } s \ s_p\}) \text{ catch } t \ \ s_q\}$.

Example 4.2. Let review Example 2.7 in the context of Resilient TX10. Let be $s_1' =$ $\{\overline{\text{at}}\,(p)\,\texttt{finish}\,\overline{\text{at}}\,(q)\,\overline{\text{async}}\,s\;s'\}$ and $s_2' = \texttt{finish}\,\{\overline{\text{at}}\,(p)\,\{\overline{\text{at}}\,(q)\,\overline{\text{async}}\,s\}\;s'\}$. Assume that place p fails during the remote execution of s at q. Despite such a failure, the behaviour of the two programs is the same as in Example 2.7, according to the Happens Before Invariant Principle That is s' is executed at place 0 after the completion of s in the case of program s_1' while in s_2' we have that s' runs in parallel with s. Moreover, let s throw an exception; since the asynchronous remote exception is caught by the closest finish construct, in s_2' we have that the asynchronous exception flows at place 0 while s' correctly continues its execution. On the other hand, the rule (END OF FINISH) ensures that in s_1' a DP$\otimes$ exception is thrown and the continuation s' is discarded, according to the Exception Masking Principle.

4.1 Properties of the Transition Relation

The main properties of the operational semantics of TX10 scale to Resilient TX10. We have encoded the syntax and semantics of Resilient X10 in Coq, as we did for TX10 (see Section 2.2). Using this encoding, we have mechanized the analogous proofs for Resilient X10. First of all, the definition of place-locality must be generalized to the case of partially defined heaps. More precisely, given a configuration $\langle s, g \rangle$, any local object id o in s must be locally defined, while a global reference $o\$p$ might now be a dangling reference since the global object's home place p might have failed.

Definition 4.3 (Place-local Resilient Configuration). *Given a place-local heap g, we say that a configuration $\langle s, g \rangle$ is place-local if $\forall p \in dom(g)$*

– *for any local object id o occurring in s under $\text{at}(p)$ or $\overline{\text{at}}\,(p)$, we have that $o \in dom(g(p))$ (hence $o \in \text{Objld}_p$ by place-locality of g).*

Given the definition above, we can prove that resilient semantics preserves place-locality of resilient configurations and that the semantics has no stuck states.

Proposition 4.4 (Place-locality). *If $\langle s, g \rangle$ is a place-local resilient configuration and $\langle s, g \rangle \xrightarrow{\lambda}_p \langle s', g' \rangle \mid g'$, then $\langle s', g' \rangle$ is a place-local resilient configuration, resp. g' is a place-local heap.*

Proposition 4.5 (Absence of stuck states). *If a configuration k is terminal then k is of the form g.*

Proposition 2.11 and 2.12 dealing with error propagation hold also in Resilient TX10, with a minor modification: in the second clause of Proposition 2.12 the final error thrown by a finish construct might be either E$\otimes$ or DP$\otimes$.

The main results of this section are the three principles stated above. We start with the Exception Masking Principle, formalized by Theorem 4.6, showing that no synchronous exception other than DP can arise form a failed place.

Theorem 4.6 (Exception Masking Principle). *Let be $p \notin dom(g)$ and $\langle s, g \rangle \xrightarrow{\lambda}_p k$. If $\lambda = v\otimes$, then $v = \text{DP}$.*

The following proposition states that remote computation at a non-failed place proceeds irrespective of local place failure, but for the exception masking effect. Then Theorem 4.8 formalizes the Failed Place Principle, showing that if s performs a correct step at a failed place p, then either (i) s contains a substatement that remotely computed a correct step at a non failed place, or (ii) a local activity ended at p with a DP that has been absorbed by a governing finish. We introduce the following notation: we write $\vdash$ isLocal s whenever s does not contain active remote computation, that is s has no substatements of the form $\overline{at}\,(q)\,s'$. We write $\vdash$ isRemote$_p$ s when any basic statement in s occurs under a $\overline{at}\,(q)$ construct for some place q with $q \neq p$.

Proposition 4.7 (Remote computation). *Let be* $\vdash$ isRemote$_p$ s. *If* $\langle s, g \rangle \xrightarrow{\lambda}_p$ $\langle s', g' \rangle \mid g'$ *with* $p \in dom(g)$, *then* $\langle s, g \rangle \longrightarrow_p \langle s, g \setminus \{(p, g(p))\} \rangle \xrightarrow{\lambda'}_p \langle s', g'_* \rangle \mid g'_*$ *where* $g'_* = g' \setminus \{(p, g'(p))\}$ *and* $\lambda' = \lambda$ *if* $\lambda = \epsilon, v\times$ *while* $\lambda' = \mathsf{DP}\otimes$, *if* $\lambda = v\otimes$. *Moreover* $\vdash$ isRemote$_p$ s'.

Theorem 4.8 (Failed Place Principle). *If* $\langle s, g \rangle \longrightarrow_p \langle s', g' \rangle \mid g'$ *with* $p \notin dom(g)$, *then either*

- $s = E[s_1]$ *with* $\vdash$ isRemote$_p$ s_1, $\langle s_1, g \rangle \longrightarrow_p \langle s'_1, g' \rangle \mid g'$ *and* $s' = E[s'_1]$, *or*
- $s = E[\mathtt{finish}_\mu\, t]$, $s' = E[\mathtt{finish}_{\mathsf{DP}}\, t']$ *and* $\langle t, g \rangle \xrightarrow{\mathsf{DP}\otimes \text{ or } \mathsf{DP}\times}_p \langle t', g' \rangle$.

We refer to [24] for a precise definition of the happens before relation in terms of paths that identify occurrences of static statements. We rely here on a much simpler definition in terms of the operational semantics. Intuitively, given a program s with two substatements s_1, s_2, we say that s_1 happens before s_2 whenever in any program execution s_1 is activated, i.e. it appears under an evaluation context, before s_2. This definition is weaker than that in [24] since it captures the idea of "is enabled before" rather than "happens before". However, we think that the core of the Happens Before Invariance is already carried over by Theorem 4.10, and we think that its proof scales to a standard "happens-before" relation at the price of labelling substatements and transitions along the lines of [24].

We denote by $\vec{k}$ a trace $\langle s_0, g_0 \rangle \xrightarrow{\lambda_1}_0 \langle s_1, g_1 \rangle \xrightarrow{\lambda_2}_0 \cdots \xrightarrow{\lambda_n}_0 \langle s_n, g_n \rangle$. Moreover we write $|\vec{k}|$ for the length n of such a trace, and k_i to indicate the i-th configuration $\langle s_i, g_i \rangle$, $i = 0, ..., n$.

Definition 4.9 (Happens Before). *Let s_0 be a program and let s_1, s_2 be two substatements of s_0, i.e. $s_0 = E_1[s_1]$ and $s_0 = E_2[s_2]$ for some evaluation contexts E_1, E_2. Then we say that s_1 happens before s_2, written $s_1 < s_2$, whenever for any trace $\vec{k}$ such that $k_0 = \langle s_0, g_0 \rangle$ and $k_{|\vec{k}|} = \langle E[s_2\rho], g \rangle$ for some g, some evaluation context E and some variable substitution ρ, there exists $i \in 0, ..., |\vec{k}|$ such that $k_i = \langle E'[s_1\rho'], g' \rangle$ for some g', E', ρ'.*

Notice that the definition of the Happens Before relation is parametric on a transition relation. Let write $s_1 < s_2$ when we restrict to (traces in) TX10 semantics, and $s_1 <_R s_2$ when considering (traces in) the resilient semantics.

Theorem 4.10 (Happens Before Invariance). *Let s_0 be a program and let s_1, s_2 be two substatements of s_0. Then $s_1 < s_2$ if and only if $s_1 <_R s_2$.*

4.2   Equational laws

The equational theory of TX10 can be smoothly generalized to the resilient calculus. In order to scale the notion of weak bisimilarity to Resilient TX10 we have to consider generalized environment moves that take into account the failure of a number of places.

Definition 4.11 (Resilient Environment move). *An environment move Φ is a map on global heaps satisfying:*

1. *if g is place-local, then $\Phi(g)$ is place-local,*
2. *$dom(\Phi(g)) \subseteq dom(g)$, and $\forall p \in dom(\Phi(g))\ dom(g(p)) \subseteq dom(\Phi(g)(p))$.*

The weak bisimilarity for Resilient TX10 is then defined as in Definition 3.2, where we rely on resilient environment moves and the operational steps used in the bisimulation game are those defined in this section. In particular, this means that also place failures occurring at any time must be simulated by equivalent configurations. We discuss in the following which of the equational laws of Section 3 are still valid in the resilient calculus.

$$\vdash \mathsf{noAsync}\, s \quad \vdash \mathsf{isLocal}\, s \quad \{\mathtt{skip};\, s\} \equiv s \qquad (1\mathrm{a\,R})$$

$$\vdash \mathsf{isSync}\, s \quad \{s\, \mathtt{skip};\} \not\equiv s \qquad (1\mathrm{b\,R})$$

$$\vdash \mathsf{noAsync}\, s \vdash \mathsf{isLocal}\, s \quad \mathtt{try}\,\mathtt{throw}\, v\, \mathtt{catch}\, s \equiv s \qquad (9\,\mathrm{R})$$

The law (1) of Section 2 is not valid anymore, as illustrated by (1a R) and (1b R) above. The problem is that now the place where the commands are executed may fail at any time. Hence, in order for the law to be valid also at a failed place, law (1a R) requires a stronger constraint for s so to ensure that also the r.h.s throws a DP$\otimes$. On the other hand law (1b R) never holds since the failure of the local place can happen after the completion of s but before the execution of $\mathtt{skip}$, thus only the l.h.s. would throw a DP$\otimes$. Similarly, law (9) of Section 2 is replace here by the stricter law (9 R) to ensure that s throws a synchronous DP$\otimes$ error whenever the local place is failed. All the other laws of TX10 are still valid in Resilient TX10, but for those involving place shifting, summarized below:

$$\mathtt{at}\,(p)\,\mathtt{skip} \not\equiv \mathtt{skip} \qquad (14\,\mathrm{R})$$

$$\mathtt{at}\,(p)\,\mathtt{throw}\, v \not\equiv \mathtt{throw}\, v \qquad (15\,\mathrm{R})$$

$$\mathtt{at}\,(p)\,\{s\,t\} \not\equiv \{\mathtt{at}\,(p)\, s\ \mathtt{at}\,(p)\, t\} \qquad (16\,\mathrm{R})$$

$$\overline{\mathtt{at}}\,(p)\,\{s\,t\} \equiv \{\overline{\mathtt{at}}\,(p)\, s\ \overline{\mathtt{at}}\,(p)\, t\} \qquad (16\,\mathrm{dyn\,R})$$

$$\mathtt{at}\,(p)\,\mathtt{at}\,(q)\, s \not\equiv \mathtt{at}\,(q)\, s \qquad (17\,\mathrm{R})$$

$$\mathtt{async}\,\mathtt{at}\,(p)\, s \not\equiv \mathtt{at}\,(p)\,\mathtt{async}\, s \qquad (18\,\mathrm{R})$$

$$\mathtt{at}\,(p)\,(\mathtt{try}\, s\, \mathtt{catch}\, t) \not\equiv \mathtt{try}\,(\mathtt{at}\,(p)\, s)\,\mathtt{catch}\,(\mathtt{at}\,(p)\, t) \qquad (19\,\mathrm{R})$$

$$\mathtt{finish}\,\mathtt{at}\,(p)\, s \not\equiv \mathtt{at}\,(p)\,\mathtt{finish}\, s \qquad (24\,\mathrm{R})$$

The laws (14) and (15) for place shift does not hold in the resilient calculus since they involve two terms that run in different places that might fail at different moments. Rule (16) does not hold anymore since the local place can fail after the completion of s but before the place shift of t. On the other hand its dynamic version, i.e., law (16 dyn R) is still valid since both terms already run at the same place p and the failure of local place does not affect remote computation. The law (17) does not hold since p may fail before the place-shift at q. Note that also the dynamic version of rule (17) does not hold, i.e. $\overline{at}\,(p)\,\overline{at}\,(q)\,s \not\equiv \overline{at}\,(q)\,s$ since the failure of p would mask any exception thrown at q. Law (18 R) (as well as its dynamic version) does not hold anymore because of the exception masking effect. Indeed, if s remotely throws a synchronous exception $v\otimes$ and the home place is failed, we have that the r.h.s. throws a $v\times$ exception while the l.h.s. throws $DP\times$ by means of masking. Law (19) does not hold anymore since p may fail after s has thrown an exception but before the activation of the handling t. Finally, in law (24 R) a difference appears between the two terms when the remote place p fails after the remote code has been activated. In this case s throws a DP exception at the failed place, but in the l.h.s. the local (non failed) `finish` masks this exception as a generic E, while in the r.h.s. the exception reported locally is still DP.

5   Conclusions and Future work

We have studied a formal small-step structural operational semantics for TX10, that is a large fragment of the X10 language covering multiple places, shared mutable objects, sequences, `async`, `finish`, `at` and `try/catch` constructs. We have then shown that this framework smoothly extends to the case where places dynamically fail. Failure is exposed through exceptions thrown by any attempt to execute a statement at the failed place. The error propagation mechanism in Resilient TX10 extends that of TX10 (i) by discarding exception handling at failed places, i.e. no `catch` clause is ever executed at failed places, and (ii) by masking with a *DeadPlaceException* any remote exception flowing back at the failed place. Moreover, we established a Happens Before Invariance Principle showing that the failure of a place p does not alter the happens before relationship between statements at places other than p.

 As an example of formal methods that can be developed on top of the given operational semantics, we studied a bisimulation based observation equivalence. We showed that it correctly encodes the observation power of the concurrent context by proving that it is a congruence. We illustrated this equivalence by means of a number of laws dealing with the main constructs of the language, discussing which of these equivalences are invariant under place failures. The axiomatization of the given equivalence is left for future work. We think that the resilient equational theory opens the way to the development of laws that can be used in the X10 compiler to optimize programs, e.g. using polyhedral analysis [24]. We also plan for future work the extension of the framework we presented to cover the `atomic` and `when` constructs from X10. We also plan to develop a denotational semantics for TX10 based on a pomset model that naturally allows the definition of the happens before relation. Another promising approach seems to be the study of full abstraction by extending to this setting the trace set model of S. Brookes [7].

References

1. Ahern, A., Yoshida, N.: Formalising java rmi with explicit code mobility. In: OOPSLA 2005, pp. 403–422. ACM, New York (2005)
2. Akidau, T., Balikov, A., Bekiroglu, K., Chernyak, S., Haberman, J., Lax, R., McVeety, S., Mills, D., Nordstrom, P., Whittle, S.: MillWheel: Fault-Tolerant Stream Processing at Internet Scale. In: Very Large Data Bases, pp. 734–746 (2013)
3. Amadio, R.M.: An asynchronous model of locality, failure, and process mobility. In: Garlan, D., Le Métayer, D. (eds.) COORDINATION 1997. LNCS, vol. 1282, pp. 374–391. Springer, Heidelberg (1997)
4. Bertot, Y., Castéran, P.: Interactive Theorem Proving and Program Development: Coq'Art: The Calculus of Inductive Constructions. Texts in Theoretical Comp. Sci. Springer (2004)
5. Bierman, G.M., Parkinson, M.J., Pitts, A.M.: Mj: An imperative core calculus for java and java with effects. Technical report, University of Cambridge Computer Laboratory (2003)
6. de Boer, F.S., Kok, J.N., Palamidessi, C., Rutten, J.J.M.M.: The failure of failures in a paradigm for asynchronous communication. In: Groote, J.F., Baeten, J.C.M. (eds.) CONCUR 1991. LNCS, vol. 527, pp. 111–126. Springer, Heidelberg (1991)
7. Brookes, S.: Full abstraction for a shared variable parallel language. In: Proceedings of the 8th Annual IEEE Symposium on Logic in Computer Science, pp. 98–109. IEEE Computer Society Press (1993)
8. Brookes, S.: A semantics for concurrent separation logic. Theor. Comput. Sci. 375(1-3), 227–270 (2007)
9. Charles, P., Grothoff, C., Saraswat, V., Donawa, C., Kielstra, A., Ebcioglu, K., von Praun, C., Sarkar, V.: X10: an object-oriented approach to non-uniform cluster computing. In: OOPSLA 2005, pp. 519–538. ACM, New York (2005)
10. UPC Consortium, et al.: UPC language specifications. Lawrence Berkeley National Lab Tech Report LBNL–59208 (2005)
11. Cunningham, D., Grove, D., Herta, B., Iyengar, A., Saraswat, V., Tardieu, O., Kawachiya, K., Murata, H., Takeuchi, M.: Resilien X10: Efficient failure-aware programming. In: PPoPP 2014, pp. 67–80. ACM, New York (2014)
12. Dayarathna, M., Houngkaew, C., Suzumura, T.: Introducing Scalegraph: an X10 library for billion scale graph analytics. In: X10 2012, pp. 6:1–6:9. ACM, New York (2012)
13. Dean, J., Ghemawat, S.: Mapreduce: Simplified data processing on large clusters. In: OSDI 2004, p. 10. USENIX Association, Berkeley (2004)
14. Fournet, C., Gonthier, G., Lévy, J.-J., Maranget, L., Rémy, D.: A calculus of mobile agents. In: Sassone, V., Montanari, U. (eds.) CONCUR 1996. LNCS, vol. 1119, pp. 406–421. Springer, Heidelberg (1996)
15. Francalanza, A., Hennessy, M.: A theory of system behaviour in the presence of node and link failure. Inf. Comput. 206(6), 711–759 (2008)
16. Hennessy, M.: A Distributed Pi-Calculus. Cambridge University Press, New York (2007)
17. Lee, J.K., Palsberg, J.: Featherweight X10: a core calculus for async-finish parallelism. In: PPoPP 2010, pp. 25–36. ACM, New York (2010)
18. Malewicz, G., Austern, M.H., Bik, A.J.C., Dehnert, J.C., Horn, I., Leiser, N., Czajkowski, G.: Pregel: A system for large-scale graph processing. In: Proceedings of the 2010 ACM SIGMOD International Conference on Management of Data, SIGMOD 2010, pp. 135–146. ACM, New York (2010)
19. Riely, J., Hennessy, M.: Distributed processes and location failures. Theor. Comput. Sci. 266(1-2), 693–735 (2001)
20. Saraswat, V., Bloom, B., Peshansky, I., Tardieu, O., Grove, D.: X10 language specification version 2.2 (March 2012),
    x10.sourceforge.net/documentation/languagespec/x10-latest.pdf

21. Saraswat, V.A., Jagadeesan, R.: Concurrent clustered programming. In: Abadi, M., de Alfaro, L. (eds.) CONCUR 2005. LNCS, vol. 3653, pp. 353–367. Springer, Heidelberg (2005)
22. Shinnar, A., Cunningham, D., Saraswat, V., Herta, B.: M3R: increased performance for in-memory Hadoop jobs. Proc. VLDB Endow. 5(12), 1736–1747 (2012)
23. X10 Global Matrix Library (October 2011), https://x10.svn.sourceforge.net/svnroot/x10/trunk/x10.gml
24. Yuki, T., Feautrier, P., Rajopadhye, S., Saraswat, V.: Array dataflow analysis for polyhedral x10 programs. In: PPoPP 2013, pp. 23–34. ACM, New York (2013)
25. Zaharia, M., Chowdhury, M., Franklin, M.J., Shenker, S., Stoica, I.: Spark: cluster computing with working sets. In: HotCloud 2010, p. 10 (2010)

A   Artifact Description

Authors of the Artifact. Avraham Shinnar.

Summary. The artifact is a mechanization of the semantics for TX10 and Resilient X10 in Coq. The mechanization verifies key properties of both language(s), bringing an additional level of assurance to the paper versions. These properties include the totality and computability of both languages. The latter proofs additionally serve as interpreters for the languages. An important part of the mechanization effort is the implementation of a total heap copy algorithm. This algorithm is shown to have the properties states in the accompanying paper. In particular, the result is a heap isomorphism of the original.

Content. The artifact package includes:

- An html page (index.html) describing the structure of the development, and an overview of the content of each file.
- The actual mechanization, presented as a series of Coq source (*.v) files.
- A Makefile that can be used to automate building (verifying) the development.

Getting the Artifact. The artifact endorsed by the Artifact Evaluation Committee is available free of charge as supplementary material of this paper on SpringerLink.

Tested Platforms. This artifact should compile on any platform that supports Coq 8.4pl3 (http://coq.inria.fr/download). A few Gigabytes of RAM are required for the compilation process. Compiling the artifact (in particular CopyObj) takes multiple hours.

License. EPL-1.0 (http://www.eclipse.org/legal/epl-v10.html)

MD5 Sum of the Artifact. 52acdbfd95ad5a7f48b959a253a286a9

Size of the Artifact. 90K

Author Index